THE REFERENDUM PAPERS:
ESSAYS ON SECESSION AND NATIONAL UNITY

The close outcome of the October 1995 referendum on Quebec separation was a jarring wake-up call for English Canada, forcing Canadians outside Quebec to confront the unthinkable. This collection of papers by leading academics and analysts offers the most thorough examination yet of the main issues arising out of the October referendum. It considers not only what might be done to help the country survive, but what should be done if it doesn't.

The book is divided into two parts, the first focusing on ways to improve the social, political, and economic union of Canada. The second confronts head-on the possibility of Quebec separation, and discusses the terms and processes of Quebec's possible departure.

As the recent Supreme Court decision made clear, the time for reasoned negotiation with a soon-to-be-independent Quebec may come. Although committed to keeping the country together, all the contributors to this volume share a commitment to democracy and the peaceful resolution of conflict. The individual papers go beyond analysis to provide a clear set of proposals for action and change. Originally commissioned by the C.D. Howe Institute, the papers provide the first real blueprint for 'thinking about the unthinkable.' As such, this collection will be of great interest to anyone concerned about the future of Canada, and the future of Quebec.

DAVID CAMERON is a Professor in the Department of Political Science, University of Toronto.

The Referendum Papers: Essays on Secession and National Unity

edited by
David Cameron

Published in Association with C.D. Howe Institute

UNIVERSITY OF TORONTO PRESS
Toronto Buffalo London

University of Toronto Press Incorporated
Toronto Buffalo London
Printed in Canada

ISBN 0-8020-4449-2 (cloth)
ISBN 0-8020-8238-6 (paper)

Printed on acid-free paper

Canadian Cataloguing in Publication Data

Cameron, David
    The referendum papers: essays on secession and national unity

    'Published in Association with C.D. Howe Institute.'
    ISBN 0-8020-4449-2 (bound).
    ISBN 0-8020-8238-6 (pbk.)

    1. Federal government – Canada.   2. Federal-provincial relations –
    Canada.   3. Quebec (Province) – History – Autonomy and
    independence movements.   I. Cameron, David, 1941–
    II. C.D. Howe Institute.

    JL65.1999.R44 1999   320.471   C99-901092-1

University of Toronto Press acknowledges the support of the Canada Council for the
Arts and the Ontario Arts Council for our publishing program.

University of Toronto Press acknowledges the financial support for its publishing
activities of the Government of Canada through the Book Publishing Industry
Development Program (BPIDP).

Canadä

Contents

Introduction

DAVID CAMERON

What is This Book About?

The ten essays contained in this volume are the children of the 1995 Quebec referendum. But for that fateful October evening, and the knife-edge result it yielded, this book would not exist.

Each of these papers originally appeared as a part of the C.D. Howe Institute's series on Canada in the post-referendum period. Because of the referendum, the unity question once again joined the C.D. Howe Institute's core agenda of research on fiscal, monetary, trade, and social policy. Although Quebecers voted down the sovereignty option, the tiny margin of the victory demonstrated several things: that the federal government's lack of forethought about the possible consequences of a Yes vote had placed the interests of all Canadians seriously at risk; that the unpreparedness of the English-speaking Canadian public was a luxury we could no longer afford; and that strategies for reinforcing the Canadian union were urgently needed.

So the C.D. Howe Institute commissioned a series of policy papers on issues that could no longer be ignored. Half are engaged in what might be termed contingency planning – that is to say, hard-headed thinking about the issues that will have to be addressed if there is a Yes vote on sovereignty in a future referendum. The 1995 result makes planning and analysis of this kind an unavoidable, if melancholy, necessity. The other half of the papers examine, or make proposals to improve, the way the country works, with the aim of helping to head off another referendum vote.

As a collection, the essays address the following themes:

- keeping Quebec in Confederation;
- renewing the federation;

- preparing for a possible future referendum;
- thinking about secession; and
- thinking about a new Canada without Quebec.

Underlying all the papers is the conviction that the *process* by which Quebec's relationship with the rest of Canada is worked out matters, and that it should respect certain operating principles. The first of these principles is that democratic norms should be fully respected at all stages and by all participants. The second is that the manner in which the collective choices are made should be fair, transparent, and open to the participation of citizens. The third is that Canadians should be seeking an authoritative settlement of this matter so that the profound uncertainty that has plagued our national life can be dissipated. The fourth and last is that – whatever the outcome of the debate about the future of the country – the real interests of citizens should be protected as much as possible. While recognizing that some imaginable scenarios would inevitably impose costs and burdens on many Canadians, this last principle calls for reducing the sphere of uncertainty as much as possible so that the transition costs can be minimized for all concerned.

Clearly, it is difficult to determine what these principles mean in practice, particularly in times of acute stress. What constitutes democratic practice in the midst of breaking up a country? Are the decision-making arrangements fair and unbiased? Is a simple majority sufficient to unleash the secession process? Do citizens outside of Quebec have a voice? If so, what weight do their views have and how do they get expressed? Is it enough to say that the majority rules, and that, in the case of a Yes vote, the minority must agree to the redefinition of their nationality, particularly if the minority is geographically concentrated and linguistically differentiated? What does democracy have to say about the position of Aboriginal people in such circumstances? Complex questions such as these arise from all of the operating principles identified above, and can be readily multiplied in number. The authors of the essays forming this collection recognize the difficulty of applying these principles, while acknowledging their authority as guides to analysis and conduct, and as a means of giving shape to the work the authors have done.

All the papers share the same two-fold approach. They analyze a given issue, policy, or problem relating to Canada's future; and they offer proposals for action based on that analysis. The fact that there is both an analytical and a policy dimension to each contribution, sets them apart from many of the other offerings Canadians have received over the years.

Most of the political discussion and a fair amount of the press and intellectual commentary on our unity travails has been rhetorical in intent; its aim has been to persuade rather than to explain. In a highly charged political atmosphere, in which passionate convictions on both sides are strong and feelings run high, this predominance of rhetoric is to be expected. There is a place, however, for explanation. A matter as weighty as political secession needs to be understood, analyzed, and reflected upon – not just espoused or opposed. This volume is a step toward fulfilling this need for reflection.

Nevertheless, there is no doubt which side of the national question the authors of these articles find themselves on: all desire the continuation of the Canadian union with Quebec included. But all share an unshakable commitment to democracy, due process, and the peaceful resolution of conflict, and all can imagine circumstances in which the departure of Quebec from the Canadian union could be defended and supported on democratic grounds, as well as on the basis of protecting the interests of the people living in the two emergent communities.

The last of C.D. Howe's ten post-referendum papers was released in March 1998. As it happened, the release of the tenth paper coincided with Jean Charest's entry into Quebec provincial politics, and with the resultant surge of confidence among federalist forces in Quebec. This event, combined with the evidence of recent Quebec opinion polls suggesting a steady decline in support for sovereignty and a pronounced popular hostility to the prospect of yet another referendum, has, at least temporarily, reduced anxiety among Canadians about national unity. The August 1998 release of the Supreme Court's opinion on the secession reference, while potentially controversial, was in fact greeted calmly by all concerned. Since that time, however, the re-election of Lucien Bouchard and the Parti Québécois in the provincial election of November 30, 1998 – albeit with a reduced majority and a lower popular vote – has ensured that the possibility of another referendum on sovereignty remains on the country's agenda. Despite that fact, the difficulty Premier Bouchard appears to be having in establishing the 'winning conditions' necessary for a successful referendum vote has encouraged the belief among many that Canada may yet weather the storm.

Why Now?

Thus the long-suffering reader might very well question the timing of this publication. Why should a collection of essays on the future of Canada with or without Quebec be published at a moment when the sovereignty impulse appears to be in decline, and when there are grounds for believing we may at last be moving beyond this debilitating preoccupation?

In reply, I can offer four reasons and a rumination. The rumination first.

The web of relations between French and English has been at the centre of our existence for as long as we have had the makings of a national community in this part of North America. Often a source of anxiety and vexation, occasionally a factor in civil conflict, this existential duality has deeply shaped who we are and what we have been able to become. It has held out the promise of a distinctive, pluralistic Canadian way, saving us from a traditionalistic, British North American monoculturalism ill equipped to withstand expansionary American liberalism in the modern age. It has in this sense helped to provide space for cultural pluralism writ larger, a kind of cultural openness to the Aboriginal reality and to the national diversity that has resulted from substantial, continous immigration. It has offered us an authentic understanding of ourselves and our place on the continent.

While every plausible representation of the nature of the Canadian community includes the French-English reality as a central force, it is nevertheless true that this reality – as understood from the perspective of Canada as a whole – can be experienced in healthy, life-affirming ways, as well as in diseased, pathological forms. A triumphalist desire for anglo-domination that denies the significance of the French fact and refuses it space for expression is one such pathology. A separatist aspiration to conquer dualism by escaping from it altogether is another. Neither is consistent with the duality that is a central, invigorating feature of Canadian life.

Canada, since Quebec's Quiet Revolution of the early 1960s, has displayed both signs of health and indicators of disease. Indeed, it is not an easy matter to represent accurately just what has been going on here in the past four decades. On the one hand, it is possible to present Canada's experience as the story of a country radically redefining itself, successfully withstanding challenges to its identity and to its very existence, and preparing itself deftly for the circumstances it is likely to face in the twenty-first century. This account of reconstruction and transformation relates not only to Quebec, but to Canada as a whole; both have gone through quite remarkable processes of change in the last several decades. On the other hand, one could argue that during the last forty years Canada has lost its way, that it is standing powerless, watching, as a nation within a nation is struggling to be born. This view focuses on the country's inability to reach a fully consensual constitutional settlement, and on the apparent rise in support for sovereignty evident in the fifteen years between the 1980 and 1995 referendums. You can make a plausible case for either view, and many people have.

Those who have spent years working on 'the national unity file' might therefore be forgiven for admitting that the country's ultimate fate, quite simply, defies their understanding. It probably defies everyone's understanding. We all do our analysis, adopt our positions, launch our arguments, make our predictions, and reconstruct the past to fit our present requirements – but the full picture consistently escapes us. We are unfailingly surprised; consider, for example:

- Who, in the 1960s – with the separatists nothing more than a disreputable fringe movement – would have thought that a sovereignist party would form the Government of Quebec in 1976 and become an enduring political force?
- Who could have foreseen the rapid, though temporary, demobilization of the sovereignist movement following the patriation of the Constitution without Quebec's consent in 1982?
- Who, in 1987, could have anticipated the demise of the Meech Lake Accord three years later?
- Who would have predicted that the 'yes' side would come within a hair's breadth of winning the 1995 referendum on sovereignty?

It is as if the country is a giant, complex organism, moving according to rhythms and cadences all its own. Each generation struggles to understand, aspires to direct or control, but the creature moves how and when and where it wants, observant of its own sovereign imperatives, and faithful to a life cycle it keeps to itself. Hence our sense of wonder as the next station in this unfathomable creature's procession through life is duly revealed to us.

Hence, too, the most basic justification for publishing this collection. It points us to an enduring reality at the core of our national being. It reminds us of where we have been, not long ago. It examines public issues of high importance. But most important, perhaps, it helps us prepare our minds for several of the plausible futures with which we may be confronted.

So much for the rumination. Now, the four reasons.

The first reason for collecting these papers together and releasing them now is that they depict English-speaking Canada seeking to come to terms with the new situation that the 1995 referendum created. Prior to the vote, which almost everyone thought the No side would win, the general feeling in many parts of the country was that secession couldn't and wouldn't happen here. After the vote, we realized it could and it might. Large, difficult questions with no easy answers grew like mushrooms overnight. These essays represent a sampling of considered reactions to the 1995 referendum from thoughtful, informed analysts in English-speaking Canada.

The second reason is that serious contingency planning for secession is long overdue. In the light of the referendum outcome, it is no less than a pressing necessity. The contention that discussing an unwanted possibility is more likely to bring it about is threadbare and unconvincing in present circumstances. Pre-

paring for the unhappy possibility of Quebec's separation may seem less necessary now, as this introduction is being written, given that the prospects for the
country have apparently improved. But bear in mind that such preparations
looked to be completely unnecessary prior to October 1995, even to our
national government. Had the scales tipped over to the Yes side, as so very
nearly happened, English-speaking Canada would have been completely at a
loss, since no-one had planned for the unthinkable.

The re-election of the Parti Québécois as the government of Quebec could
very easily lead to secession being put back at the top of the public agenda.
Those who seek sovereignty have spent two decades acclimatizing their supporters and the population at large to their conception of an alternative state of
affairs and the process by which they will achieve it. Those who oppose
secession have done virtually no serious thinking about the circumstances the
rest of the country would face if Quebec were to leave, nor have they systematically examined how their interests could be protected during the secession
process. This book makes a start at filling that void. Five of the contributions
tackle difficult issues contingent on the secession of Quebec; in many cases,
for the first time.

A third reason is that we need to be sure that all feasible avenues of reform
have been canvassed. Where it is possible to make the country work better, or to
strengthen French-English relations, we should do so; several papers in this volume suggest ways of accomplishing these aims. Where there are serious concerns with the direction in which the country is currently moving, these should
be expressed; the papers do this as well.

It is noteworthy that none of the authors recommends comprehensive constitutional change as a response to our current situation. Indeed, apart from John
Richards's proposal to amend the constitution to accommodate Quebec's Bill
101, this volume does not include a single recommendation for constitutional
reform, narrow or broad.

This insistence on reform outside of the constitutional arena echoes the mood
of the country, certainly in English-speaking Canada, and possibly in Quebec as
well. There appears to be a widely shared view that we are not likely to succeed
in addressing the concerns of Quebec and others through constitutional amendments. Constitutional reform may sound like a fine idea in theory, but our
national experience since 1982, with Meech Lake and Charlottetown, has
shown that it is amazingly difficult to manage in practice – and that, moreover,
each time we try and fail, we end up angry and embittered, with the country
weaker than before. Prudence suggests, therefore, that we should give what
Peter Russell calls 'mega-constitutional change' a wide berth.[1]

The fourth and final reason for publishing this collection now has to do with access and communication. The C.D. Howe studies were released one at a time over a period of eighteen months. Putting them between the covers of a single volume will extend their shelf life making them more readily accessible and will enable them, we hope, to reach a wider public. If we are right in believing that the country may not be out of the woods yet, then the broadest possible dissemination of these ideas is all to the good.

Let us turn now to a brief review of the two groups of papers themselves.

The Canadian Union Papers

The essays in this first group examine, as the heading suggests, how the Canadian federal system might be reformed, or its operation strengthened.

There are five essays in this category. The first two – written respectively by Robert Howse, a law professor at the University of Toronto, and Daniel Schwanen, a senior policy analyst at C.D. Howe – consider how Canada's economic union can be strengthened. Each examines the Agreement on Internal Trade (AIT), signed by all provinces and territories, as well as the federal government, in 1994; it is a nonbinding political accord designed to eliminate discrimination on the basis of province of residence in various provincial and federal practices, and to harmonize standards where differences cannot be justified using objective criteria.

Both authors propose further steps that the federal government, or all governments, might take to proceed further down the path of economic integration. Schwanen argues that the role of the Internal Trade Secretariat set up under the AIT should be strengthened. It should be empowered to analyze obstacles to the implementation of the agreement and to recommend solutions and deadlines to remove them. Canadian governments should then be required to vote on these recommendations using a qualified majority system rather than the consensus rule now in place.

Howse contends that the federal government has a special role to play in giving the AIT greater political legitimacy and weight: it should broaden access to dispute settlement mechanisms by private parties, educate the public as to the AIT's importance, and undertake a comprehensive study of trade barriers in Canada. The Government of Canada should also consider the use of the mobility rights provisions of the Charter of Rights and Freedoms to remove barriers to internal trade, and should reflect on whether the Supreme Court's broader view of Ottawa's powers to enable 'trade and commerce' and ensure 'peace, order, and good government' gives the federal government wider scope to pursue economic integration through harmonizing legislation.

The third paper, by Rogèr Gibbins, a University of Calgary political scientist, offers a critical assessment of the current province-led effort to address some of Quebec's needs, along with the needs of the rest of the country, by engaging in wholesale decentralization, using the mechanism of intergovernmental negotiations to achieve this end. Gibbins argues that this combination of decentralization and 'intergovernmentalism' raises concerns about the nature of federal and democratic Canada. It foreshadows a future in which ties between individual Canadians and the federal government are weakened, government becomes more rather than less complex, democratic accountability is undermined, and many of the alleged advantages of decentralization are lost. He argues that Canada should declare a 'time out' to reassess this incremental strategy before it takes the country too far down a path that may not serve Canadians well, with or without Quebec.

The fourth paper, by C.D. Howe adjunct scholar John Richards of Simon Fraser University in British Columbia, argues that the status and security of the French language is the key issue in the unity debate for francophones, and that Quebec's *Charte de la langue française* (Bill 101) has been controversial but necessary. Unilingual French signs were an unnecessary affront to linguistic minorities, but, in general, Bill 101's restrictions on the use of English are reasonable if Quebec as a whole, and Montreal in particular, are to remain majority francophone regions. Richards proposes an explicit federal-provincial division of powers over language, which, among other things, would accord a robust general authority to Quebec to legislate in this domain. Specifically, he recommends that Section 92 of the Constitution Act be amended to grant Quebec explicit jurisdiction over the public use of language, subject to the existing set of minority language services specified in the Charter of Rights and Freedoms and the maintenance of bilingualism within federal institutions.

The fifth and final paper in this category, prepared by Janice Stein, David Cameron, and Richard Simeon, all political scientists at the University of Toronto, asserts that Canadians are engaged in a conflict of identities that, if unsettled, will have enormously adverse consequences for the well-being of all. The authors suggest that it is time to draw on the experience of other countries that have faced similar divisions, and to consider their experience in engaging citizens in the resolution of conflicts as a source of guidance to resolving Canada's problems. In particular, this paper explores the prospective benefits of deeper, more sustained citizen engagement in interactive conflict resolution at two levels. The first level entails the involvement of influential leading citizens outside formal politics who have close links to the political leadership and the wider society in their respective communities. The second level involves the engagement of 'ordinary citizens,' as individuals and as members of voluntary associations, in processes designed to foster mutual understanding, encourage citizenship 'ownership' of the issues, and increase awareness of the compromises and tradeoffs that must be made if we are to move beyond our current debilitating, conflicted state. In both cases, the goal is not any particular outcome, but rather a process that will maximize the likelihood of peaceful resolution.

The Secession Papers

The five papers in this series tackle some of the difficult issues that would need to be addressed, should Quebec seek to secede from the Canadian union after a Yes vote in a sovereignty referendum. Together, these essays constitute an extended effort at contingency planning. Taking as a starting point the unpleasant but possible hypothesis that Quebecers have voted to secede from Canada, the authors of these pieces scrutinize various issues, some of which have been very little examined thus far, that we Canadians would then have to face.

Alan Cairns, a political scientist currently at the University of Saskatchewan, contends that Canadians outside of Quebec are utterly unprepared for the task of constructing a new country of their own – yet this is the daunting challenge they would face following Quebec's departure. He argues for a 'Plan C,' an operating agreement that would deal first with the removal of Quebec from the federation, and only after that, as a separate issue, with the fundamental decisions about what kind of country (or countries) and what set of constitutional arrangements should be constructed for English-speaking Canadians.

The second paper, by Patrick Monahan of Osgoode Hall Law School and Michael Bryant, a lawyer in private practice, fashions a set of guidelines for governing an orderly secession process. The authors argue that the current absence of agreement about the manner in which Quebec would secede in the event of a Yes vote serves nobody's interest, and in fact carries great risks. Far better that there be a clear set of established rules, even if (or perhaps precisely because) they impose constraints on the freedom of the actors in a period of acute pressure and uncertainty. The authors propose ten principles that should underlie any practical plan to regulate Quebec's departure from Canada.

In the next essay, Peter Russell, an emeritus professor of political science at the University of Toronto, and Bruce Ryder, a professor at Osgoode Hall Law School, consider how and to what extent the existing amending formulas of the 1982 Constitution could be used to give effect to Quebec's secession. Their analysis demonstrates both the desirability and the feasibility of Quebec committing itself to due constitutional process, even in the act of secession, – despite the objections of some sovereignists that Quebec need not abide by the terms of the Constitution Act, 1982, which it has never ratified. Any other process, the authors contend, is likely to lead to chaos and disruption above and beyond that which would necessarily accompany secession. Considerations of moral and political legitimacy would then require that such changes be ratified through a national referendum, and that the separate consent of Aboriginal peoples in Quebec be sought.

The fourth paper, by David Laidler, an economist at the University of Western Ontario, and William Robson, a senior policy analyst at C.D. Howe, looks carefully at the little-known working institutions that make it possible for monetary unions to function. They reflect on the likely behaviour of the principal players in Canada's financial system, faced with the prospect of Quebec's secession, and contend that by far the heaviest burden of responsibility for maintaining a monetary union between a seceding Quebec and the rest of Canada would fall on the shoulders of Quebec. The authors argue that, if the Quebec government wants to avoid a financial crisis and have some assurance of being able to continue to use the Canadian dollar after secession, it will have to amass a huge war-chest of funds prior to the next referendum to support its banking system.

The final paper in the book, by Richard Simeon of the University of Toronto, seeks to answer the question of whether partnership is possible between a sovereign Quebec and what remains of Canada. Noting the long-standing desire on the part of sovereignists to maintain an economic partnership with the rest of Canada, and positing assumptions favourable to the sovereignty-association model, Simeon nevertheless concludes that, for a variety of structural reasons, the relationships between a sovereign Quebec and Canada would likely not differ much from those that currently exist between Canada and the United States.

Conclusion

Taken together, these ten papers are an eloquent representative sampling of current English-Canadian views of the country and the important issues it faces. They contain virtually no talk of constitutional change as a response to Canada's situation, and none whatsoever of comprehensive, mega-constitutional reform; they consider earnestly several improvements to the federation outside the constitutional process that might serve both the needs of Quebec and the interests of the rest of the country; and they provide thoughtful, level-headed analysis of the secession of Quebec and its likely consequences: they speak to a widespread judgment about what is possible and what is, in present circumstances, beyond practical consideration.

This approach to the national question appears to reflect the mood of Canadians today. There is no public taste, within or outside Quebec, for another round of constitutional talks. The Calgary Framework is a cautious, non-constitutional attempt by political leaders, in the wake of the too-close referendum, to encourage English-speaking Canadians to speak softly and nicely to Quebecers about their position in the country. The effort initiated by provincial premiers to 'rebalance' the federation – that is, to clarify federal and provincial roles and to effect some further decentralization – was conceived in part to address practical problems experienced by a number of premiers, and in part to appeal to Quebec opinion. Negotiations with the Government of Canada on this initiative produced agreement on the Social Union Framework on 4 February 1999, regrettably, but not surprisingly, without the Quebec Government's signature. Plan B, a policy of head-to-head opposition to the PQ and its arguments, including the Supreme Court reference on secession, is grounded in both the need to provide Quebecers with a reality check on sovereignty and the imperative of preparing the terrain in English-speaking Canada for a possible Yes vote. The papers in this volume arose from this context; they share a low-key, unsentimental, practical approach to the issues they are tackling.

These essays offer analysis not found elsewhere. They are written from the point of view of Canadians living outside of Quebec, with two audiences in mind.

First of all, they are addressed to the puzzled, concerned, fed-up or inattentive Canadians from nine provinces and two territories whose interests and aspirations are far more tied up with the fortunes of Quebec than many realize. For such people as these, we hope that the papers in this collection will illuminate, explain, and provoke. The stakes are high: thus the papers invite readers in English-speaking Canada to consider the initiatives they might take, or the reforms they might accept, to foster reconciliation and head off secession – or, failing reconciliation, consider the steps they would need to take to preserve what they value and minimize the damage of the separation process as much as possible.

The second audience is the people of Quebec. Quebec is far from being an independent actor in the national-unity drama. Even if the Government of Quebec were to attempt a unilateral declaration of independence after a 'yes' vote, it would not by that simple declaration cease to have relations with other interested actors. These actors include the entire population of English-speaking Canada, represented by both federal and provincial governments. Their preferences and behaviour would have a signal impact on the fortunes of a sovereign Quebec. It is important, then, that Quebecers have a realistic appreciation of what people in the rest of the country think: what they are prepared to support or resist; under what conditions; and why. The papers in this collection offer to Quebecers a good sampling of informed opinion from English-speaking Canada about a number of key issues relating to the repair or dismantling of the country.

Canada has followed a lot of twists and turns in its road over the last forty years. Both Quebec and Canada have been transformed, as has the world around us. While we all like to groan about our failures and misfortunes, there is in fact a great deal to celebrate in the Canadian story. Canadians have learned to live with multiple identities, and to accept the right of their compatriots to live with identity patterns different from their own. Increasingly, this pluralistic understanding of citizenship and political community is one that people in the rest of the world are called upon to share.

Balancing the competing needs and preferences of a diverse population such as ours is no easy task, but, so far, Canadians both inside and outside Quebec have managed it. But what if – despite our collective best efforts – we lose our balance? What if the country goes off the rails, and a radical reconfiguration of political arrangements becomes necessary? The ideas and proposals contained in these pages offer assistance to Canadians in the light of both possible outcomes of the unity question – they offer reform proposals on the assumption that the country will remain a going concern, and they suggest ways of thinking through the situation in the event that it doesn't.

Whatever the future holds – and only a foolhardy person would declare confidently what our country's ultimate fate will be – the shared conviction of the Canadians represented within the covers of this book is that the process by which we fashion our future is as important as the outcome itself, for it is in their reaction to the day-to-day unfolding of events, big and small, that citizens display their deep-seated beliefs and demonstrate the values by which they are prepared to live and be judged. Helping Canadians in Quebec and in the country as a whole to clarify their views on the national question, and to assess the practical implications of these views, is the central ambition of this book.

NOTE

1 Ironically, during this supposed period of avoiding constitutional issues, there *has* been a significant amendment of the Constitution of Canada, relating to a highly sensitive matter, yet it has not aroused public opinion outside of Quebec. In 1997, the Quebec National Assembly and the Parliament of Canada passed a resolution amending the Constitution bilaterally. The effect of the amendment is to replace the constitutionally mandated denominational school system of Quebec with a linguistically defined system of public education. The provision of denominational schools would have been regarded as one of the structural elements of the British North America Act at the time of Confederation in 1867. Perhaps, in the success of this venture and the failure of Meech and Charlottetown, there is a message – namely, that bilateral amendments, and amendments dealing with specific, practical problems, are achievable, even in the present environment, whereas multilateral, complex packages of amendments are not.

THE CANADIAN UNION PAPERS

Drawing on Our Inner Strength: Canada's Economic Citizenship in an Era of Evolving Federalism

DANIEL SCHWANEN

This *Commentary* focuses on the means available to preserve and enhance the Canadian economic union in the context of evolving federalism. In particular, it looks at the extent to which the underpinnings of this citizenship are being modified by the globalization of trade and the trend toward the decentralization of power and the disentanglement of responsibilities between Ottawa and the provinces. It explores how policies and institutions affecting the Canadian economic union can respond effectively to these changes.

These trends, which are beneficial in themselves, do not obviate the advantages of a well-functioning internal economic union. Instead, they point to the need for better management of the common economic union – one which combines added flexibility and representativeness in decision-making institutions with improved policy coordination between levels of government and a greater commitment to build on the guarantees already underpinning Canada's common economic citizenship.

In the first section, I summarize the importance for Canadians of citizenship in a common economic union and review some key institutions underpinning the functioning of this union. In the second section, I address the challenges that current external and internal trends pose to the way Canadians manage their economic union. In the third section, I propose some basic operational principles to deal with these challenges. Specific policy recommendations follow in the final section.

The Underpinnings of Canada's Economic Union

The Role of Economic Citizenship in the Lives of Canadians

All Canadians possess rights of citizenship which, by definition, they can only

---

Box 1   Economic Opportunities and Citizenship Rights

The economic dimension of Canadian citizenship means that a student from Quebec can be employed for the summer in a national park in Alberta, a banker from Alberta can gain experience in the Toronto head office of a financial institution of global size, or an Ontario retiree can move to British Columbia and pursue other interests while receiving his pension, all without having to obtain permission from a government or give up other rights attached to citizenship. Indeed, every year, hundreds of thousands of Canadians exercise their right to pursue their livelihood or new interests in a different part of the country.

For firms, common economic citizenship means relatively unhindered access to Canada's diverse human, physical, and financial resources, and the ability to build on success from a home base without having to set up separate subsidiaries. The Canadian economic union is especially important for small and medium-sized enterprises, since it allows them to grow within a relatively large market without having to worry about the intricacies of a foreign legal system, possible protectionist actions under 'trade remedy' laws, the need to document the origin of their products, or the difficulties of enforcing judgments against foreign debtors.

---

exercise in Canada. The existing degree of political association among the provinces makes these multidimensional rights quite extensive.

One dimension of these rights is economic, so that we can speak of all Canadians' holding common *economic* citizenship. This aspect of citizenship is an important source of economic well-being and social mobility, because it affords individuals greater possibilities for earning a livelihood and firms more opportunities to become competitive than would be the case if each region of Canada were a separate economic entity (see Box 1).

The potential benefits of common economic citizenship for Canadians living in various regions include the following:

• Access to a sizable market and to factors of production (for example, specialized skills) over and above those provided by markets outside the union. This enhances the competitiveness of firms within the union and increases incomes for individuals.
• Economies of scale – hence savings for taxpayers – in performing certain

administrative functions, such as representation abroad, policing, or monitoring activities of common interest.

- Insurance against instability. In a regionally diversified economy, when one region benefits from, say, higher resource prices but another is hurt, the blow to the losing region may be cushioned by transfers to it. The reverse is true in the event of a decline in resource prices or demand. The advantages of this are akin to those of holding a diversified investment portfolio.[1] For the same reason, separate currencies for Canada's regions would likely be more volatile than a common currency. The mobility of labor can also be seen as partial insurance for both people and firms against the adverse effects of structural changes in the economy.
- Better protection of interests and increased leverage on international issues – for example, in trade or environmental negotiations. This naturally occurs when different regions have a common interest, but economic union means that the weight of the union as a whole is sometimes brought to bear in the interest of one of its parts in international forums.

The Nature of Economic Citizenship

The benefits of Canadian economic citizenship flow from the ability of individuals and businesses to interact across the country in a relatively unhindered fashion, rather than being forced to confine their horizons to any particular region or rely on more uncertain external markets for growth. These benefits also depend on the willingness of different levels of government to cooperate in facilitating these interactions. This fact has a number of implications with respect to how Canadians should assess their economic union.

First, because many of the advantages of the union for individual Canadians and regions stem from the mobility of people, investments, and ideas and from the ability to spread costs or insure against risk, they can be understood only incompletely if one looks only at the actual *amount* of trade conducted among the provinces. The volume of interprovincial trade is important, as we will see in the next section, but a better indicator of the benefits of economic union is the relative *ease* with which trade can be conducted among the provinces, compared with the often much closer and bigger markets to the south.[2]

Second, for the same reasons, the benefits flowing from economic citizenship cannot be measured by whether a particular province registers a fiscal 'surplus' or 'deficit' within the federation over a particular period. However, fiscal transfers that permanently redistribute income from one region to the next ought to be justifiable as improving the functioning of the economic union as a whole, and identified as such.

Third, to be able to generate these gains, an effective economic union requires some common authority and/or effective agreements regarding the behavior of governments to ensure that beneficial exchanges can take place and that they apply across the union. This requirement is fundamentally different from the rationale for, say, common social standards. This is because common economic citizenship cannot exist unless firms and individuals are able to transact business or operate across the country, whereas the gains from social policy do not, by and large, involve such interprovincial transactions. Common rules and standards across the country, therefore, are not essential to the conduct of effective social policy in each province in the way they are a necessary underpinning of common economic citizenship.

Fourth, notwithstanding the above, social standards and the benefits of economic citizenship interact. Close economic interaction, particularly if it permits the mobility of people, may affect the ability of each province to set its own social standards. Conversely, large differences in social standards can hinder useful interprovincial mobility; it can also generate mobility that is not justified on the basis of available economic opportunities.

These basic implications of common economic citizenship will inform the rest of this analysis of the challenges faced by the Canadian economic union and the basic operational principles that must be put into practice to meet these challenges.

Canadian Regions and Common Economic Citizenship

Despite the need for common rules for trade within the economic union, common economic citizenship should not mean forced uniformity of standards and policies. This is especially true in Canada, where each province faces societal and economic conditions and challenges that are sometimes vastly different from its neighbors'. In this context, creating uniform standards for the sake of easier mobility could just as easily be detrimental to the welfare of Canadians as beneficial. As Trebilcock and Behboodi put it, forced harmonization in areas where the 'virtues of more decentralized political arrangements ... such as ... fuller accomplishment of citizen preferences, ... greater accountability of political representation, ... and greater room for policy experimentation and innovation' are being denied can in fact lead to a reduction in well-being.[3] This is because the terms of such an economic union would not allow public services tailored to the needs of its members and adequately subject to taxpayers' control. Nor would services be delivered in a way that was flexible enough to be modified to take account of evolving regional or provincial supply and demand realities.

In fact, optimal economic gains from an economic union can occur only if such differences are allowed to attain their full expression and if the gains from free exchange are then allowed to take place as a result. The challenge for Canada is to meet the obligations of common citizenship without stifling differences based on needs and circumstances.

To achieve this balance, the common institutions of the economic union, while effectively securing the removal of barriers to productive exchanges, must also refrain from imposing uniformity where this would actually run counter to identifiable regional or provincial needs. I aim later to turn this general rule into more specific recommendations. For now, it is useful to review very briefly the institutions currently underpinning Canadian economic citizenship, with added emphasis on the newest and probably least well-known of these – the Agreement on Internal Trade.

Institutions of the Canadian Economic Union

The Constitution and Federal Powers
Two sections of the Constitution Act, 1867 attempt to reduce trade barriers. Section 121 states:

All Articles of the Growth, Produce, or Manufacture of any one of the Provinces shall, from and after the Union, be admitted free into each of the other Provinces.

Despite its sweeping tone, this section has proven of limited use, partly because it does not deal effectively with restrictions other than tariffs and similar barriers.

Section 91 extends the exclusive legislative authority of Parliament to the regulation of trade and commerce and the currency, two key sectors among other federal powers related to the Canadian economic union. The fact that these powers are vested in a common authority is crucial to understanding why the degree of access to opportunities Canadians currently enjoy within their own country is, in most cases, superior to the access that separate countries, even within the European Union, grant each other's citizens. Canada's common currency and clearing system, competition policy, and standards in federally regulated industries – all tools which facilitate exchanges among Canadians – flow from these powers.

The courts, however, have not interpreted section 91 as extending federal jurisdiction to the regulation of trade within a province, even when a province's internal policies have a deleterious effect on out-of-province firms or on individuals who wish to conduct business in the province.

Article 6 of the Charter of Rights and Freedoms, entrenched as a constitutional amendment in 1982, guarantees mobility rights for individuals. While this has allowed the courts to strike down egregious limitations on individuals employed in one province from practicing their trade in another,[4] it does not preclude obstacles arising from differences in required qualifications *per se*.

Thus, the Constitution, while ensuring basic mobility rights among provinces, leaves a number of unnecessary obstacles to economic mobility within Canada. These include discriminatory practices in awarding public sector procurement contracts and different standards for professionals or qualified labor not justified by local circumstances. Several factors, however – including the work of the Macdonald Commission in the early 1980s, an increase in scholarly and business interest in the issue of internal trade barriers, and a number of agreements in the late 1980s and early 1990s to remove barriers in certain regions or sectors – led Canadian governments to embark on comprehensive negotiations in 1993, which culminated in the 1994 Agreement on Internal Trade (AIT).

The Agreement on Internal Trade
The AIT was signed by the federal, provincial, and territorial governments in July 1994 and began to be implemented a year later.

It is important to note that the AIT does not supersede any of the constitutional guarantees or federal powers respecting the economic union. Rather, it is an attempt to address undue barriers to trade and mobility resulting from both provincial and federal practices in a wide range of sectors (see Box 2). The agreement's general rules require that governments not discriminate against people, goods, services, or investments on the basis of their origin within Canada, nor hinder rights of entry into or exit from individual provincial markets. A government measure can deviate from these general rules if its purpose is to achieve one of a limited number of permissible 'legitimate objectives,' but in so doing it must be no more trade restrictive than necessary and must not create a disguised restriction on trade. As well, the general rules commit governments to reconcile regulatory and standards-related measures and to sustain transparency with respect to their policies and practices affecting other Canadians.

The AIT in its general rules provides a good balance between acknowledging the full rights of governments to take measures to achieve legitimate objectives in their spheres of authority and ensuring that these measures do not constitute unnecessary obstacles to trade across internal Canadian borders.

It also contains some interesting institutional innovations, such as a dispute settlement mechanism to which – unlike most such mechanisms in international trade agreements – firms and individuals have some access, albeit through a

Box 2   Examples of Commitments by Canadian Governments under the AIT

Public sector procurement: Governments have pledged not to engage in discriminatory practices among Canadian suppliers, such as imposing conditions based on a supplier's place of business, biasing technical specifications in favor of local firms, or using preferential margins to favor particular suppliers. Specific procedures are to be followed to increase transparency in the awarding of contracts, and there are provisions for a bid protest procedure. These rules will apply to goods, most services, and construction contracts over a threshold amount, but not to certain publicly owned entities that are not accountable to the executive branches listed in the AIT. However, the provisions will eventually be extended to municipalities, academic institutions, and hospitals.

Labor mobility: The AIT eliminates residency and other discriminatory requirements for working in a province. The agreement spells out a detailed plan, but without a firm deadline, for the mutual recognition of occupational qualifications and the reconciliation of differences in occupational standards.

Alcoholic beverages: Governments have undertaken to eliminate discriminatory and other administrative obstacles with respect to the listing, pricing, sale, and distribution of alcoholic beverages, although change will be slow because provinces can maintain a number of nonconforming measures (listed in the agreement) for at least a few years.

Road transportation: Governments have agreed to maintain uniform rules regarding the size and weight of commercial motor vehicles, fully implement the National Safety Code, establish a uniform national bill of lading, create a harmonized mechanism for the collection of taxes and fees, and harmonize or mutually recognize a number of other measures related to road transportation by January 1, 1998.

Regional development programs: The AIT restricts governments' ability to use regional development programs as an excuse for denying access to their markets to other Canadians, and institutes reporting requirements regarding the operation of these programs. It contains a code of conduct on incentives, aimed at limiting the use of subsidies in one region that are clearly harmful to another.

Investment: Governments have agreed not to use local content, sourcing, or purchasing requirements in their decisions to permit investment, except for regional development purposes in exceptional cases. They have also agreed to reconcile their corporate reporting and registration requirements.

convoluted process involving the complainant's provincial government and/ or an independent screener.

Although the AIT made some headway toward removing existing barriers in a number of sectors, in virtually all cases favorable judgments about the liberalizing effects of the agreement must be qualified. This is not because the principles on which the agreement is based are unsound. Rather, too many details of its implementation are left to future negotiations to be conducted by government officials responsible for the particular sectors to be liberalized – some without specific deadlines – and to a rule of unanimity among participating governments on all decisions. As well, the AIT leaves out certain sectors, such as financial services, altogether.

Given their limitations, it is proper to ask whether, in their current form, these institutions can best ensure the economic citizenship rights of Canadians, especially in light of the challenges changing external and internal circumstances pose to the economic union. The next section examines these challenges in greater detail.

Challenges to the Canadian Economic Union

The latest pressures for change on a virtually universal range of policies and arrangements within the Canadian federation fall into two major categories, as described by Courchene.[5] The first is globalization, the most immediately visible impact of which has been a large increase in Canada's external trade relative to the size of its economy. The second consists of fiscal pressures, which are compelling a re-examination of the degree and manner of government intervention in the economy.

Partly as a result of these two relatively new trends, some long-standing issues – in particular, pressures on the federal government to retreat from provincial spheres of jurisdiction and pressures for political reforms – have taken on a new impetus, and their impact on the economic union must also be analyzed in this new light.

A particular policy or institutional configuration that makes sense under one set of circumstances may not be reasonable under another. Flexibility, therefore, is of prime importance in the long-term arrangements of the economic union. I do not explore this dimension here, however; suffice it to say that Courchene has shown overwhelming evidence that such flexibility can be found within the Canadian federal system. Rather, I prefer to explore how this flexibility can be used to enhance Canadian economic citizenship so as to achieve the best outcome for all Canadians.

In order to do this, I attempt to define below the extent to which changes in trade flows between Canada and the outside world and pressures to disentangle and decentralize various policy areas should inform Canadians' view of what constitutes a well-functioning economic union.

International Integration

Over the past 15 years, total trade between the provinces and the rest of the world has increased much faster than trade within Canada. Exports of goods and services to foreigners rose from the equivalent of 27 percent of gross domestic product (GDP) in 1981 to 33 percent of GDP in 1994. Much of this increase is accounted for by increased north-south trade, particularly following the 1989 implementation of the Canada-US Free Trade Agreement (FTA) and the recent sharp increase in Canadian cost competitiveness *vis-à-vis* the United States. Meanwhile, internal trade fell, in relative terms, from the equivalent of 28 percent of GDP in 1981 to 21 percent in 1994.

What does this trend mean in terms of the importance of maintaining a common economic union? Is the economic future of Canadian provinces now so dependent on their links with corresponding economic regions in the United States that this future does not depend on – and may even be hindered by – the fostering of strong east-west economic links, as some analysts have suggested?[6]

Instead, I believe the evidence shows that strong internal economic links remain vital to Canadian industry and to Canadians' own personal economic prospects, and that these links should be strengthened. Consider, for example, that, even though the importance of Canada's external trade has increased lately relative to internal trade, internal trade *as a percent of GDP* remains more important in Canada than it is in the European Union (see Table 1), despite the considerably greater distances between the provincial markets here than between the national markets there.

The results of this comparison are clearly due to the fact that most European economies are considerably larger than most Canadian provincial ones and hence more self-contained; that is, most European exchanges occur within the borders of the respective EU countries. While perhaps obvious, this observation is not trivial: if the relatively larger EU countries felt that strengthening their economic links through the institution of common economic citizenship was vital to their interests, this should apply all the more to trade among relatively smaller units such as Canadian provinces.

The difference is, of course, that Canadian provinces are also much more open to foreign trade than are European countries. To the extent that their openness to and reliance on foreign markets is greater, they have a correspondingly greater need for policy to take into account their competitive position *vis-à-vis*

Table 1
Exports within and outside the European and Canadian Economic Unions, 1994

	EU Members	Canadian Provinces
	(percent of GDP)	
Exports within the Union		
Goods	13.5	12.2
Services[a]	3.8	8.6
Total	17.3	20.8
Exports outside the Union		
Goods	8.3	29.3
Services[a]	2.3	4.0
Total	10.6	33.3

aTotal services exports of 15 EU member countries represent 6.1 percent of GDP. The breakdown of intra-EU and outside EU exports is the author's estimate, but probably overstates intra-EU trade.
Sources: Statistics Canada, *Provincial Economic Accounts* CANSIM on CD-ROM, 1996–1; International Monetary Fund, *Direction of Trade Statistics Year-book* (Washington, DC: IMF, 1995); idem, *Balance of Payments Statistics Year-book* (Washington, DC: IMF, 1995); Organisation for Economic Cooperation and Development, *Main Economic Indicators* (Paris: OECD, Statistics Directorate, March 1996); United States, Department of Commerce, Bureau of Economic Analysis, *Survey of Current Business*, various issues.

foreign markets. This may require some policy differentiation on a provincial or regional basis regarding, for example, sales taxes or labor market training in particular trade-related industries. But there is no reason this kind of differentiation should be incompatible with a more open internal Canadian market.

If foreign markets were completely open, the economic benefits of reinforcing the Canadian economic union would be diminished. In reality, however, foreign and Canadian markets are not perfectly substitutable. Canadian exporters continue to face far more constraints in the US market than they do at home, particularly in the areas of services and government procurement, and continue to face harassment from protectionist lobbies in some important manufacturing sectors such as steel. The need for proof of origin in order to ship goods duty free to other members of the North American Free Trade Agreement and the pitfalls of the US legal system[7] are further examples of external trade hassles that make the much smoother east-west links vital for Canadian firms, particularly small and medium-sized ones, and for the self-employed.

Furthermore, the relative export figures must be interpreted with caution, because two-way trade figures between Canada and the United States can inflate the value-added implications of this trade for Canadian employment and income. Thus, $10 million in automobile exports to the United States might represent far less value added in Canada – hence fewer jobs and less income – than the equivalent amount of interprovincial trade in financial services because there is a significant import component to auto exports.[8]

Finally, the movement of certain factors of production, notably qualified labor and capital, is greatly facilitated by opportunities for mobility between Canadian provinces.[9] For example, between 1985 and 1995, 520,000 Canadians left British Columbia for other provinces, while 400,000 went to Quebec from other provinces. These gross population movement figures – on a net basis, British Columbia actually gained 280,000 people from other provinces and Quebec lost 95,000 over the period – show the extent to which individual Canadians and businesses alike rely on a high degree of personal mobility across the country. To a certain extent, this movement of people substitutes for trade between the provinces.

All in all, while the trend points to a greater integration of provincial economies into north-south regions, in many sectors Canadian firms still depend to a large extent on a domestic base for markets and factors of production, which, in turn, depend on the continued maintenance of a strong internal economic union – indeed, on the strengthening of this union where this is not incompatible with regional interests.

Disentanglement and Decentralization of Policies

The benefits of disentangling and decentralizing economic and social responsibilities between the central government and the provinces have been well explored.[10] They include bringing control closer to the citizen, accommodating diversity, increasing political correspondence between beneficiaries and payees, eliminating overlap and duplication, increasing sources of innovation for the union as a whole in terms of policies or delivery techniques, and generally dealing with problems through the most appropriate and cost-efficient means. An important theme in the literature on this topic is that certain things are better left to the market – that is, that they do not require public intervention, or require less public intervention than they currently receive.

Certainly, various principles and criteria have been proposed by which the disentanglement of policy instruments – the choice of which level of government does what – could be effected, the most prominent being that of 'subsidiarity.' As implemented in Europe, this means, in essence, that the European Union should do only those things that cannot be done as effectively at the national or regional level.[11] Yet one principle alone cannot determine the 'appropriate' degree of economic integration within an economic union or indeed among any number of regions or countries. The appropriate degree is inevitably a product of external circumstances and of the extent to which members share political, social, legal, and other traditions and objectives. After all, if access to a sizable market and economies of scale were the only consideration, a logical starting point for Canadian provinces might be to seek to join the United States.

The question is whether association with other provinces rather than with US states provides superior representation for a province's interests. The answer lies in the degree to which noneconomic characteristics and objectives are shared or are complementary, which then makes sensible the removal of internal barriers to greater integration.

Indeed, in practice, the existence of an economic union need not imply that different regions of the union will all trade heavily with each other. This has prompted Krugman to observe that, in economic terms, 'countries are defined by their restrictions'[12] – those that apply *vis-à-vis* the outside world and are not applied within the country itself or vice-versa (as in the case of taxes) – rather than by the size of their internal trade.

Thus, at the limit, applying the ultimate level of disentanglement – *chacun chez soi* – could be very counterproductive in terms of lost opportunities, and one must not confuse greater north-south orientation and decentralization with a diminished need to coordinate policies within the economic union.

Meeting the Challenges: Operational Principles

The economic union is, then, still an important source of economic well-being and competitiveness for Canadians. This means that, in the current context, just as too much 'entanglement' of responsibilities reduces the benefits of the association, a badly handled 'disentanglement' could have serious costs. The 'deep integration' of policies, which is becoming increasingly evident internationally as a by-product of more open markets for products and factors of production, applies *a fortiori* in a closely integrated economic union, and must be taken into account. The effectiveness of a central government's trade and monetary policies, for example, cannot be dissociated from the training policies, purchasing policies, or overall fiscal stance of other levels of government. Thus, decentralization must mean increased efforts at 'vertical' cooperation on policies, so that each level of government can more effectively discharge its responsibilities *vis-à-vis* not only its constituents but the union as a whole.

Obligations of Economic Citizenship

As well, in a union from which members expect a combination of economic and social benefits, each member should behave in a way that does not negate these benefits for other members or their citizens. Thus, just as the autonomy of one level of government may be limited in a 'vertical' sense by the need to secure cooperation in certain areas with another level, in practice the exercise of state or provincial powers ought, in some areas, to be subject to 'horizontal' obligations of economic citizenship *vis-à-vis* other members of the association. These obligations can be divided into four types.

Mobility, Nondiscrimination, and Transparent Treatment
The first type of obligation refers to rights to mobility, nondiscrimination, and transparent treatment. These rights protect the ability of citizens, firms, services, products, and investments originating in one area to do business in or move to another area and be treated there in a transparent way and on par with their local counterparts. These rights do not affect the ability of governments to legislate specific standards within their jurisdiction, but only require that citizens of the union be treated equally with respect to local policies and standards wherever they go. Thus, they are a basic right of economic citizenship, and not an infringement on the ability of jurisdictions to be responsive to local needs. As such, they should be generally applicable. Most economic unions – indeed, in certain specific areas, free trade agreements as well – require that persons and firms within the union have these rights of 'national treatment.'

Harmonization of Standards and Policies, Where Possible
Another obligation of economic citizenship is to harmonize standards and economic policies throughout the union. Obstacles to mobility – due, for example, to differences in standards on food labeling, certification, or emission standards – should be effectively limited to those that are demonstrably necessary to satisfy local demands for different levels of protection or different competitive circumstances. In the absence of any such demonstrated need, obstacles should be regarded as merely protectionist and thus contrary to the spirit and obligations of the economic union.

Dealing with Externalities
A third type of obligation of economic citizenship is to put in place effective mechanisms to prevent or compensate for externalities. These externalities can be negative, as when policies in one region are implemented without regard for

the costs they impose on another, or positive, as when expenditures end up benefiting a province other than the one incurring the expenditure. As I have indicated, these effects are potentially important in a union that is economically well integrated, yet in which public standards or expenditure levels with respect to, say, social policy or education can differ considerably from one part of the union to another.

For example, a reduction in public services in one province may impose costs on another if people move to the other province simply to continue receiving a government service. It is also possible that one province will, out of its own resources, provide a public service that benefits other provinces. Examples include the movement of an educated workforce from one province to another or the provision of health care for visitors from another province. If the province is not compensated in some form, it may stop providing a valuable service.

These issues can be dealt with in various ways. One is to use federal law to obligate each province to deliver a certain level of public services. Another way is to use the federal spending power. But these federal instruments can be too blunt – ultimately reducing public welfare by infringing on the right of provinces to deliver services tailored to the specific needs of their residents – and risk introducing regionally differentiated expenditures which actually prevent economically and socially useful mobility.

Another, more targeted way would be to 'internalize' these costs through the use of interprovincial compensating mechanisms. If a province bears the cost of the negative spillovers it creates but reaps the benefits of the positive ones, then the externality problem – sometimes thought of as a 'race to the bottom' or the 'underprovision' of public services in certain regions – would be reduced without the need to resort to federal standards or spending.

Redistribution

The fourth type of obligation of economic citizenship generally involves some central redistributive mechanisms. Most often, these are meant to insure against the risk of economic downturns, or when temporary or permanent structural transfers are required to help maintain services or population in areas that might otherwise experience severe poverty or outmigration or even leave the union, to the detriment of the well-being of all.

In Canada, this obligation is recognized in the equalization program. To maintain a workable economic union, one in which all members subscribe to certain reciprocal obligations, it is necessary to correct for the fact that some provinces' tax bases allow them to mount social programs which others cannot afford, a capacity they would share if these programs (and the revenues to pay for them) were national in scope.[13] It makes sense to share some of this capacity to finance basic public programs (in the same way, for example, that police in rural Ontario and schools in rural Alberta are financed by economic activity in these provinces' metropolitan areas).

In other respects, Canadians may care more about whether a particular province reforms its health care or education system or cuts its welfare rates than about how a US state would deal with similar issues. But these pure 'caring' aspects can lead to counter-productive intervention on the presumption that the interests of some are the interests of all. For example, some national programs, such as unemployment insurance and the Canada Health and Social Transfer, contain regionally redistributive elements as well, in that different rules for the receipt of these transfers apply to different regions, but the redistributive components of these programs may actually undermine their purpose.[14]

Institutional Considerations

These four principles suggest that, as government responsibility for policies affecting Canadians' economic well-being become more diffuse, there needs to be greater cooperation and a stronger subscription to a range of reciprocal obligations on the part of all members of the economic union. What kinds of institutional mechanisms could bring this about?

In principle, there is a wide range of such tools, including the courts, if governments are prepared to bind themselves legally to an arrangement; tools under the control of either Ottawa or the provinces; or perhaps 'federalized' institutions comprising the two levels of government or even the provinces alone. Such federalized institutions would be most useful in areas that call for common decision-making or for policy coordination and consultation between the constituent parties, but that are not necessarily required to be under the authority of a central government. (One example of such an institution is the Council of the European Union, which, for all intents and purposes, is made up of member states' governments, and is not effectively controlled by the European Parliament.)

In turn, these tools can exhibit various degrees of coerciveness, according to whether they are constitutional obligations binding on all governments, legislative or regulatory instruments, binding or nonbinding intergovernmental agreements to harmonize, compensate, cooperate, or consult. Some obligations might also apply only to some of the members – for example, in cases where some might want to institute common administrative practices in certain areas, while others pursue a different route (the asymmetry implied in the concept of a 'two-speed' Europe).

All economic unions exhibit a mixture of such mechanisms, and the international differences in the mix are instructive.[15] Inevitably, however, some degree of effective decision-making, followed by the ability to enforce these decisions, is required. In no economic union is consensus required under all circumstances, and in none can governments, organizations, or individuals disregard the obligations of common economic citizenship without other members' being able to seek a correction of the situation.

In some countries, notably the United States, the central government is the ultimate arbiter of what constitutes a policy not in accordance with the terms of common economic citizenship. This may not be realistic in Canada's case, however. First, there are objective reasons related to the sometimes disparate economic interests across the country. Second, to the extent that some regions perceive that common decision-making institutions do not adequately represent their interests, they tend to view centralizing initiatives – even those that could, in principle, be better conducted from the center – with suspicion. The danger is that this perception could lead to less effective federal economic policies. If current discussions on the shape of Canada's political institutions resulted in a sense that regional interests were better represented in the economic union, the union would work more effectively.

The overall conclusion to this section of the paper, then, is that, if the reduced costs that would come from disentangling federal and provincial responsibilities for economic and social policy could be combined with the maintenance or increase of benefits provided by better management of vertical and horizontal policy interactions, Canadians will have made the best of the tradeoffs inherent in an economic union among decentralized parts.

Choosing the Right Policies and Tools

Canadian governments should commit themselves to building a common economic citizenship that complements the advantages of both increased international trade and the decentralization of policymaking – that is, that helps Canadians benefit from these trends. Following from the analysis above, I suggest that this goal can be achieved through:

- enhanced 'vertical' policy cooperation among levels of government as a response to more diffuse decision-making;
- clarifying and strengthening the 'horizontal' rules of economic citizenship, including nondiscrimination on the basis of provincial origin and the elimination of unnecessary obstacles to trade and mobility;
- greater attention to the potential effects of negative and positive policy spillovers in an era of lessening federal involvement, particularly with respect to social policy; and

• strengthening the common institutions that manage the economic union.

In my view, the recommendations that follow, which are listed by these objectives but meant to be taken as a whole, would foster such an outcome.

Enhance Vertical Policy Cooperation

A number of welcome disentanglement and decentralization initiatives are currently at work in the Canadian federation. In 1993, the federal government and nine premiers launched an 'Efficiency of the Federation' initiative aimed at eliminating overlap and duplication in the provision of certain services between the two levels of government. The recent Environmental Management Framework Agreement, also involving the federal government and nine provinces, adopted the same principles.[16]

These initiatives are hampered somewhat by their relative obscurity, which deprives them of potential public support, and by the refusal of the Quebec government to participate in them, even though they eliminate overlap and duplication and limit federal involvement to areas of common interest to all Canadians. Nevertheless, such initiatives should be explored systematically in other broad portfolios – particularly natural resources, culture, tourism, sports and recreation, housing, and labor market policies – which have long been candidates for decentralization.

As a rule, however, broad areas should not be devolved wholesale without ensuring that decision-making in areas of common interest remain with the federal government, where there are no *a priori* expectations of benefits from greater regional flexibility or where significant economies of scale would be lost. In forestry, for example, greater provincial control over most aspects of the timber industry should not preclude nationally mandated standards for paper and wood products to make them easier to sell internationally. With respect to culture, the federal government would naturally be entrusted with the promotion of 'Canada,' but other cultural involvement should be left to the provinces. And while the provinces may be the most efficient overseers of programs related to, say, sports and recreation, few Canadians would wish this to mean the end of a national Olympic program. And in the area of labor policy, the overall needs of the union must be reflected in providing information on pan-Canadian employment opportunities or maintaining the existing national industry sector councils.

Furthermore, while disentanglement and decentralization along these lines should result in savings for the public purse and better targeted policies, there is a risk that potential synergies favorable to the development of coherent national policies will be lost. As a case in point, if most aspects of labor training were devolved to the provinces, while immigration policy required an improved focus on skills requirements, then just maintaining the current degree of coherence in Canada's immigration policy would require greater provincial involvement in its formulation even as the federal government retains ultimate responsibility.

Indeed, issues of greater federal-provincial policy coordination can probably be dealt with in the same way external trade policy is now being conducted – with increasing provincial input through fairly formal mechanisms, but with the federal government firmly at the helm in steering national policy.[17]

This proposal is a two-way street. With the provinces taking or regaining greater control over a wide range of previously shared policy areas, it will be important that they interact with the federal government and each other to increase these policies' compatibility with national goals (for example, with respect to taxation issues).

To give the various disentanglement initiatives a higher profile and a steadier impetus and to explore the need for coordination mechanisms, I recommend that – in addition to existing federal, provincial, or joint initiatives – a cabinet committee on decentralization composed of the federal ministers of Intergovernmental Affairs, Industry, Finance, and Human Resources be formed with a mandate to launch a more complete program than has so far been the case. As well, a blue-ribbon commission made up of business, consumer, and labor representatives and unaffiliated citizens should be set up to report on whether decentralizing and disentangling initiatives are proceeding in a comprehensive, well-thought-out fashion, and to identify areas where these initiatives will generate a need for greater coordination of policies.[18]

Clarify and Strengthen 'Horizontal' Economic Citizenship Rules

In addition to existing constitutional guarantees respecting the economic union, there is, as we have seen, another tool with which to entrench the rights of economic citizenship – namely, the 1994 Agreement on Internal Trade.

The AIT embodies the essential concepts of and key commitments to a stronger economic union, while fully preserving flexibility of action in areas of provincial jurisdiction where this is not inconsistent with a common economic citizenship.

Thus, at a minimum, the federal government should insist that these basic principles be followed – including implementation of the decisions of dispute settlement panels. Failing this, Ottawa should use the constitutional means at its disposal to implement them.[19]

Over the longer run, the basic principles of economic citizenship contained in the AIT should be entrenched in the Constitution.

As well, the harmonization of policies and standards should be fostered wherever possible. Thus, the provinces should be held to their basic commitment to recognize each other's product, services, and labor standards where these are compatible, to develop common standards in other areas, and to justify their failure to do so in terms of objective criteria contained in the AIT. In this area as well, the federal government should explore its options to intervene as a last resort if the provinces do not implement the agreement.

Pay Greater Attention to Policy Spillovers

If Canadians want to maintain and improve the labor mobility underpinning the economic union *and* the provinces' ability to adopt policies and standards best suited to their own circumstances, then the issue of compensation for positive and negative spillovers should be looked at. Given Ottawa's reduced role as purveyor of monetary transfers and standards setter in the social policy arena, the potential spillovers may become more pronounced and may induce provinces to take steps to reduce reciprocal access to occupational markets in order to preserve their ability to provide locally tailored programs. In the two key areas of education and welfare, at least, there are possible antidotes to this situation:

Education: If graduates of publicly funded institutions consistently must look outside their province to find jobs (as is the case for many graduates of Newfoundland and some Quebec universities), a reduction in federal involvement may, over time, result in the provinces' reducing their funding for these institutions to a level that would reduce their contribution to the economic union as a whole. However, if, through the federally run personal income tax, these provinces had first call on the provincial income taxes of these graduates, even if they moved, up to the point where the province's investment in their education is recouped, then there would be no incentive to underfund education from a national welfare perspective.

Welfare: A province that cuts back welfare rates may create negative spillovers in another province, which might then feel justified in imposing residency requirements that would impede the efficiency of the economic and social union. One way to deal with this issue would be to have the 'sending' province continue to be responsible for these cases, at least for a set period of time. The same concept could apply if a province were to enrich its welfare program and attract recipients from another province.

Finally, a national body focused on social policy could, as my colleague Bill

Robson has suggested,[21] play a useful role in gathering and disseminating information on the effectiveness of social policies across the provinces, so that 'from the bottom up' comparisons can be made and rendered public, which would maximize political incentives for voluntary harmonization and reduce problems associated with policy spillovers.

Strengthen Common Institutions

In order to achieve these goals, I recommend that the following steps be taken to strengthen the AIT:

- Governments should take advantage of the terms of the AIT and expand the role of the Internal Trade Secretariat as much as possible to help implement the agreement. Its role could be akin to that of the European Commission – though on a much more modest scale, since the Canadian economic union is already significantly more integrated than that in Europe – and consist of monitoring and reporting on obstacles to implementation of the agreement, and proposing solutions. The Committee on Internal Trade – that is, the representatives of the federal and provincial governments – must formally vote on these proposals.
- With respect to AIT undertakings that do not yet have a deadline, the Secretariat should be empowered to suggest such time limits as it sees fit, on which the Committee on Internal Trade should also be required to pronounce.
- The Secretariat should issue an annual report on the implementation of the AIT's various chapters, including an evaluation of the reasons for missed deadlines and an assessment of outstanding issues. This report should subsume or summarize all other reports which governments are committed to provide under the terms of the AIT, including those on progress toward harmonizing labor standards and on the operation of their regional development programs.
- The current consensus rule on measures to implement the AIT should be replaced by a qualified majority voting rule, as is the case in the European Union.[20] After all, the federal and provincial governments have already agreed to the principles contained in the agreement, so no one government should be able to block its implementation at this stage.
- The Secretariat should report on whether and how the principles of the AIT can be extended to sectors (such as financial services) and policies not currently covered. In other words, can a 'second round' AIT be launched?
- The AIT's dispute settlement mechanism should be streamlined and strengthened, principally by making access to it easier for individual citizens and businesses.

In addition, if provinces or regions feel their interests are underrepresented at the center, they will naturally want to constrain the role of the federal government more than is necessary. In particular, they may be reluctant to accept that, in some areas of the economic union (for example, in ensuring accords such as the AIT are implemented), Ottawa's role may have to be strengthened, rather than weakened.

Therefore, reform of federal institutions to allow greater representation of regional views in national policymaking should be of great interest to those who wish for a better-functioning economic union. Proposals for reform are numerous and range from provinces' naming directors of the Bank of Canada[22] to more ambitious ones such as an elected and effective Senate. All such proposals are likely to improve the functioning of the economic union and should be encouraged.

Conclusion

Canadians benefit greatly from their economic union. In part, this is because the terms of the union, with respect to ease of access to markets and mobility of people, are far superior to those Canadians are offered in other markets. But it is also because, to the extent that Canadians have distinct social and political standards, common economic citizenship allows us to benefit economically from access to a fairly sizable and diversified market without having to compromise those standards.

Many analysts have suggested that, in some respects, the Canadian federation still operates in an unnecessarily centralized fashion given the different needs and constraints of its regions. Although this needs to be corrected, *how* the correction occurs is bound to affect significantly whether Canadians can maintain – and enhance – the benefits of their economic union. The good news is that, in principle, further decentralization and disentanglement of responsibilities can actually enhance the benefits of the union, by allowing a better translation of regional preferences into specific policies. The bad news is that decentralization and disentanglement could cause a disengagement from the vertical and horizontal integration necessary for the success of the economic union and jeopardize the economic health of the country.

Canadians therefore should demand that the decentralization and disentanglement of responsibilities currently under way among the different levels of government improve their access to economic opportunities and that governments strengthen their commitment to common economic citizenship.

NOTES

1 For some of the implications of this approach, see Michael A. Goldberg and Maurice
   D. Levi, 'A Portfolio View of Canada,' *Canadian Public Policy 20* (December
   1994): 341–352.
2 See John F. Helliwell and John McCallum, 'National Borders Still Matter for Trade,'
   Policy Options, July–August 1995, pp. 44–48.
3 Michael J. Trebilcock and Rambod Behboodi, 'The Canadian Agreement on Internal
   Trade: Retrospect and Prospects,' in Michael J. Trebilcock and Daniel Schwanen,
   eds., *Getting There: An Assessment of the Agreement on Internal Trade*, Policy
   Study 26 (Toronto: C.D. Howe Institute, 1995).
4 See Mollie Dunsmuir, 'Mobility Rights, the Economic Union and the Constitution'
   (Ottawa: Library of Parliament, Research Branch, January 1990), mimeographed.
5 See Thomas J. Courchene, *Celebrating Flexibility: An Interpretive Essay on the Evolution of Canadian Federalism*, Benefactors Lecture, 1995 (Toronto: C.D. Howe
   Institute, 1995).
6 The possibility has been suggested by some sovereigntist economists in Quebec. See,
   for example, Pierre-Paul Proulx et al., *Intégration économique et modèles d'associations économiques Québec-Canada* (Montréal: INRS-Urbanisation, 1995).
7 See Brian Milner, 'Canadian firms fear U.S. justice: legal horror stories abound as
   Tilden awaits day in court,' *Globe and Mail* (Toronto), May 9, 1996, p. B1.
8 See James McCormack, 'The Impact of Exports: An Input-Output Analysis of Canadian Trade,' Staff Paper (Ottawa: Department of Foreign Affairs and International
   Trade, December 1994).
9 On the mobility of capital, see David M. Brown, 'Efficiency, Capital Mobility, and
   the Economic Union,' in David M. Brown, Fred Lazar, and Daniel Schwanen, *Free
   to Move: Strengthening the Canadian Economic Union*, The Canada Round 14
   (Toronto: C.D. Howe Institute, 1992).
10 See, for example, William B.P. Robson, *Dynamic Tensions: Markets, Federalism,
   and Canada's Economic Future*, Policy Review and Outlook, 1992 (Toronto:
   C.D. Howe Institute, 1992); and Michael J. Trebilcock, *The Prospects for Reinvent-
   ing Government*, Observation 38 (Toronto: C.D. Howe Institute, 1994).
11 See G. Bruce Doern, *Europe Uniting: The EC Model and Canada's Constitutional
   Debate*, The Canada Round 7 (Toronto: C.D. Howe Institute, 1991).
12 Paul Krugman, *Geography and Trade* (Leuven, Belgium; Cambridge, Mass.: Leuven
   University Press and MIT Press, 1991).
13 See Dan Usher, *The Uneasy Case for Equalization Payments* (Vancouver: Fraser
   Institute, 1995).
14 See, for example, Thomas J. Courchene, 'Chaste and Chastened: Canada's New
   Social Contract' (Paper prepared for 'The Welfare State in Canada: Past, Present and

Future' Conference, Mount Allison University, Sackville, New Brunswick, April 1996); and Kenneth J. Boessenkool, *The Illusion of Equality: Provincial Distribution of the Canada Health and Social Transfer*, C.D. Howe Institute Commentary 80 (Toronto: C.D. Howe Institute, June 1996).

15 On this question, see the brief review of the main tools used to manage the economic unions of the European Community, Australia, the United States, and Germany (the last three being federal states) in Daniel Schwanen, 'Open Exchange: Freeing the Trade of Goods and Services within the Canadian Economic Union,' in Brown, Lazar, and Schwanen, *Free to Move.*

16 Under this agreement, Ottawa's authority would be recognized in national and trans-boundary measures, the conduct of international environmental relations, environmental matters related to federal lands, relationships with aboriginal peoples, and, in cooperation with the provinces, the protection of nationally significant ecosystems. The provinces would assume primary jurisdiction in most other areas. See Robert Matas, 'Sweeping environment pact transfers powers to provinces,' *Globe and Mail* (Toronto), January 20, 1996, p. A9.

17 For an excellent exposition of these mechanisms, see Douglas M. Brown, 'The Evolving Role of the Provinces in Canadian Trade Policy,' in Douglas M. Brown and Murray G. Smith, eds., *Canadian Federalism: Meeting Global Economic Challenges?* (Kingston, Ont.: Queen's University, Institute of Intergovernmental Relations, 1991).

18 I am particularly indebted to my colleague Ken Boessenkool for his reflections on this section of the paper.

19 For a review of the legal force of the obligations contained in the AIT, and of the federal government's options for securing a stronger economic union, see Robert Howse, *Securing the Canadian Economic Union: Legal and Constitutional Options for the Federal Government* , C.D. Howe Institute Commentary 81 (Toronto: C.D. Howe Institute, June 1996).

20 In an earlier paper, I suggested that such a 'qualified majority' could comprise 19 of 29 provincial votes distributed as follows: Quebec and Ontario, four each; Alberta and British Columbia, three each; Prince Edward Island and the territories, one each, and all other provinces, two votes. See Schwanen, 'Open Exchange.'

21 William B.P. Robson, 'Getting Radical: Federalism's Only Hope,' *Gravitas* 3 (spring 1996): 9–12.

22 As proposed by David Laidler in *How Shall We Govern the Governor? A Critique of the Governance of the Bank of Canada*, The Canada Round 1 (Toronto: C.D. Howe Institute, 1991).

Securing the Canadian Economic Union: Legal and Constitutional Options for the Federal Government

ROBERT HOWSE

In the wake of failed attempts to strengthen the economic union provisions of the Constitution, the federal government proceeded in 1993 to initiate multilateral negotiations for reducing interprovincial trade barriers. The resulting Agreement on Internal Trade (AIT), signed by the First Ministers in 1994 and in force since July 1995, concluded a year-long period of intense federal-provincial dialogue which, for the first time, addressed concurrently a comprehensive range of internal barriers to the mobility of goods, capital, and services across Canada.

The AIT, though a nonbinding political understanding among the federal government, the provinces, and the territories, tracks closely the kinds of obligations or commitments that one finds in international trade treaties with respect to trade between sovereign countries. Thus, in many areas such as services, investment, and government procurement, provincial measures that discriminate against out-of-province economic actors are prohibited or disciplined, subject to various exceptions or saving clauses. At the same time, the AIT sets out a large number of commitments to harmonization or regulatory rapprochement which are meant to address situations where nondiscriminatory measures have the effect of creating barriers to trade.

As various commentators, including Katherine Swinton and Armand de Mestral, have noted, the AIT states nonlegal obligations or commitments in legal language. It also contains a formal dispute settlement mechanism, to which private parties have limited access and governments have broader access. However, the formal rulings of these dispute panels have no legal effect.

The AIT deals with matters that are the subject of legal rights and obligations in other trade agreements, such as the General Agreement on Tariffs and Trade/ World Trade Organization (GATT/WTO) and the North American Free Trade Agreement (NAFTA). It also seeks to constrain or guide law and regulation by governments in a wide range of areas. One would think, therefore, that the non-legal status of the AIT would be a major liability in achieving its goals. Not all commentators, however, see the political character of the AIT as a drawback. Swinton, for instance, has argued that, despite its political status, the AIT

is likely to have an important impact on Canadian law and government policy. Most of its effects will come because governments feel an obligation to comply, whether or not they have the legal ability to do otherwise.[1]

Nevertheless, almost a year after coming into effect, the AIT has more or less sunk into obscurity. Admittedly, there is quiet, behind-the-scenes work on a number of the regulatory harmonization initiatives proposed in the AIT, along with implementation more generally.[2] But one hardly has the impression of significant momentum toward deeper economic integration within Canada. Of course, for those who have maintained that the economic impact of provincial barriers to trade is rather modest,[3] this outcome may be both predictable and desirable. For others who have hoped for a much more liberal economic union, this must be a major disappointment.

This *Commentary* is concerned with the question of how, given the apparent limited potential of the AIT as it now stands to remove barriers to economic mobility in Canada, we should best proceed to strengthen the Canadian economic union. My own perspective is that, regardless of the actual magnitude of economic welfare losses from barriers to trade within Canada, these barriers are in many instances at odds with the idea of a common Canadian citizenship, and undermine equality of economic opportunity within the federation, a principle I believe is implicit in the Charter of Rights and Freedoms as well as other parts of the Constitution, such as section 36.[4]

The *Commentary* is divided into five parts. The first considers options for giving legal force to the AIT itself, or at least to some of its provisions. Here, I note that the courts have given some legal instruments, such as human rights codes, priority over normal legislation, despite the absence of constitutional entrenchment.

The second part reviews the options for giving greater political legitimacy and weight to the AIT, so that it influences governments in the nonlegal manner Swinton suggests. These options include undertaking new research on barriers to trade within Canada and their impact on particular economic interests; providing financial and other support for private parties who wish to challenge barriers through the dispute settlement mechanism; and mobilizing stakeholders (such as industry and consumer groups) in support of the various harmonization initiatives proposed in the AIT.

The third part considers the alternative of constitutional litigation as a means of removing barriers to internal trade, and briefly examines recent jurisprudence of the Supreme Court of Canada with respect to Charter mobility rights, as well as the limits of provincial jurisdiction implicit in general constitutional requirements of order and fairness in the Canadian union.

The fourth part reviews the federal government's constitutional powers to pursue economic integration through harmonizing legislation that may impinge on areas of provincial jurisdiction. Here, I argue that recent jurisprudence concerning both the federal 'trade and commerce' power and the 'peace, order, and good government' power provides Ottawa with rather wide scope to act, particularly where cooperative federalism has failed to produce a solution that adequately addresses the interprovincial effects of provincial regulation. In both parts three and four, I address the issue of whether the existence of the AIT, as an alternative mechanism for integration, should make the courts more or less willing to entertain constitutional claims related to strengthening the economic union.

In the final part of this *Commentary*, I address what is an often-cited but infrequently analyzed dimension of the challenge of strengthening the Canadian economic union – the impact of globalization and international trade obligations on barriers to interprovincial trade. To the extent that barriers to trade from other provinces also affect international trade, they will continue to come under challenge on the basis of international trade agreements, which in large measure apply to provincial laws and regulations as well as to federal ones. Once impugned in international forums, the sustainability, not to mention legitimacy, of these barriers as barriers to *interprovincial* trade becomes highly questionable. Moreover, whether in the area of product standards, food safety, or environmental regulation, international trade liberalization increasingly is being linked to harmonization at the global level or through plurilateral institutions such as the Organisation for Economic Co-operation and Development. It is the federal government that is at the table in these processes and is responsible for advancing a conception of the national interest that takes into account the interests of all provinces. At the current juncture, it is perhaps the federal government's role as the interface between provincial regulation and the process of globalization that provides it with the most scope to shape the future of the Canadian economic union.

Options for Legalizing the AIT

In the framework of Canadian public law, the only manner in which governments can enter into binding arrangements with each other that genuinely constrict the will of future legislatures is through constitutional amendment.[5] Swinton, who has written the authoritative discussion of this doctrine in the context of the AIT, perhaps underestimates the importance of translating the AIT's obligations into law, even if this law can always be repealed or amended by an individual legislature in the future.

The strongest form of legalization along these lines would be to make the obligations of the AIT directly applicable. This would require, as is the case for some human rights codes, stipulating (for instance in the provincial *Interpretation Act*) that, unless specifically provided for, the obligations of the AIT take precedence over any conflicting statutes and regulations. Normally, courts and other bodies would defer to such a provision. This kind of legalization would probably also entail, as a matter of form, embodying the obligations of the AIT itself in a statute.[6] Thus, as a technical matter, courts and other bodies would apply the statute containing these obligations as a kind of superior law. It should be noted that, in the European Union, direct interpretation and application of the norms of the Treaty of Rome by domestic courts of the member states was an important integrating influence. In the Canadian case, the unity of the Canadian court system would ensure consistent judicial interpretation of the AIT across Canada (a function served in the EU case by references to the European Court of Justice).

This kind of legalization would, it should be emphasized, do little or nothing to prevent a legislature from simply rescinding, with a subsequent ordinary vote, any legal effect that the AIT may have within its jurisdiction. There are, however, important legitimacy dimensions to legalization that do not depend on the ability to bind future legislatures. Aside from the advantage of the AIT's becoming part of the normal functioning of the legal and regulatory processes within the jurisdiction, Canadians take the rule of law very seriously, and it is my impression (although I am no pollster) that they take legal rules much more seriously than political promises or commitments that have no legal impact. While repeal of the legal status of the AIT might not attract the same degree of scrutiny as the invocation of the override to suspend Charter rights, it would almost certainly provoke public debate both within the jurisdiction as well as nationally.

The steps that several provinces and the federal government have taken to date toward legalization reflect a quite different and much more modest approach. Instead of establishing a framework that would empower the courts and other bodies to determine the consistency of existing law with the AIT, most of the four provinces that have passed or are about to pass implementing legislation have attempted to make quite minor changes to provincial laws, deeming these to be sufficient to bring their laws into compliance with the

AIT.[7] Three other provinces – New Brunswick, Prince Edward Island, and Manitoba – and the Northwest Territories have made a number of minor adjustments to existing statutes and regulations in order to bring the existing provincial legislative and regulatory framework into compliance with the AIT.

Only Nova Scotia's implementing legislation (section 2) makes any mention of the principles or objectives of the AIT itself. Inasmuch as they do not simply purport to consolidate minor changes to other statutes, the implementing acts (or draft legislation in the case of Quebec) mostly embody housekeeping provisions, such as providing ministerial authority for appointments under the AIT. One notable exception is that the implementing legislation in Alberta and Nova Scotia, as well as the draft legislation in Quebec, allows for cost awards to individuals with respect to dispute settlement actions to be legally binding and enforceable in court.

The federal government's implementing legislation (Bill C-19, *An Act to Implement the Agreement on Internal Trade*), which is currently in the final stages of passage in the Senate,[8] is disappointing in that it fails to make the AIT directly applicable in federal law or to give it a legal status that would normally be superior to other statutes. Given such a failure, it hardly stands up as a model for the provinces to follow. Section 7 of the draft implementing legislation merely states that '[t]he Agreement is hereby approved.'

Moreover, in section 5, there is an attempt to limit the ability of an individual to bring administrative law or civil law proceedings to enforce the AIT. Thus, para. 5(2) states:

There is no cause of action and no proceedings of any kind shall be taken, without the consent of the Attorney General of Canada, to enforce or determine any right or obligation that is claimed or arises solely under or by virtue of the Agreement.

This provision does, however, offer some hope for legalization through the judicial process, since it suggests that the AIT *could* be invoked in a proceeding without the consent of the attorney general as long as there is some other independent ground for the action – for example, a Charter mobility rights claim or even an administrative law claim of error of law based on a tribunal interpretation of a statute. At a minimum, it could be argued, on the basis of the language of the statement 'the Agreement is hereby approved,' that, where two interpretations of a statute or regulation are possible, the court or tribunal should adopt the interpretation most consistent with the AIT. (This, of course, would fall considerably short of the kind of direct applicability discussed above, where, in the event of a *direct conflict* between one statute and another incorporating AIT obligations, the AIT obligations would prevail.)

Nonlegal Options for Enhancing the AIT's Legitimacy and Effectiveness

Quite apart from the possibilities of legalization, a number of concrete measures can be taken to enhance the AIT's contribution to securing the Canadian economic union.

One measure would be to facilitate access of private parties to dispute settlement mechanisms. So far, the provinces – perhaps set in the ways of old-style, 'behind closed doors,' Meech/Charlottetown executive federalism – have shown little enthusiasm for resolving their trade disputes through a rules-based, transparent, public dispute settlement mechanism. Indeed, as I have suggested elsewhere,[9] the dispute settlement chapter itself may in some ways reinforce these tendencies, since it requires or at least provides the possibility of all kinds of consultation and mediation arrangements before formal dispute settlement starts. The key, therefore, to a meaningful activation of the norms in the AIT could well be person-to-government dispute settlement.

There are two ways a person (including a corporation) may have access to dispute settlement. One way is for a government to pursue the complaint on the person's behalf. Unfortunately, under the AIT, Ottawa has little scope, despite its overall constitutional responsibility for the Canadian economic union, to take up complaints on behalf of private parties. It can do so only where the 'person' who has suffered an economic injury or denial of benefit is a federally constituted entity, a federal work or undertaking, or otherwise under federal authority (1704(8)).

Another way for a person to gain access to dispute settlement is through direct person-to-government means. Here, however, the complaint must pass a cumbersome vetting mechanism whereby a government-appointed screener decides if the complaint has sufficient merit to proceed. The limits of person-to-government dispute settlement are further evident when one considers that, while a person bears the risk of having to pay considerable legal costs to bring a dispute before a panel, he or she cannot obtain any kind of award for damages that is directly enforceable. A year ago, I predicted that

it seems highly improbable that an individual or corporation would have much interest in pursuing dispute settlement where, in effect, publicity or moral suasion are the only instruments available to address noncompliance with a successful dispute settlement outcome.[10]

This prediction shows every sign of being fulfilled. Thus, I reiterate my proposal that the federal government initiate a challenges program that would assist persons bringing actions before the dispute settlement mechanism with legal costs or advice. Moreover, the federal government could provide a legal aid hotline to individuals and firms that believe they have suffered from violations of the AIT's norms. In fact, much of the best legal expertise on trade rules of the kind found in the AIT is located in federal government offices, so this service could be highly effective without entailing significant expenditure outlays.[11]

While major industry and trade associations have the resources to identify barriers to trade that have a negative effect on their members, significant difficulties arise when some members are being disadvantaged by particular barriers to trade while others are gaining economic rents from those barriers. Nevertheless, some such associations (such as the Construction Association) have already lobbied effectively to dismantle barriers. A different problem is that many provinces are 'small worlds' where business and governmental elites are closely entwined, and a firm that has major economic interests in a particular province may feel uncomfortable challenging the provincial government head-on in public dispute settlement.

As subsidies and regulatory rents decrease with the restructuring of government, this may start to change. But I predict that it is small and medium-sized businesses' simply wanting to get their services and products into a province on equal competitive terms that are the most likely to press disputes and to seek the removal of regulatory barriers through positive integration, including harmonization. Yet these businesses may be unwilling to risk the costs of a dispute resolution whose concrete impact is so uncertain. Moreover, these businesses are, individually, unlikely to have the resources to undertake the kind of studies that would identify subtler regulatory barriers and attempt to estimate their impacts. And, as diffuse and sometimes competing actors, small and medium-sized businesses face considerable challenges in working together to lobby governments effectively to fulfill their commitments under the AIT (harmonization or rapprochement of divergent regulations).

Here, as well, there is arguably a case for federal leadership to address the problem. Indeed, it is my understanding that Industry Canada is considering, or may actually be close to, commissioning a comprehensive independent study of barriers to economic mobility within Canada, which will entail extensive surveys of the private sector. This would be an important initiative, if the resources necessary for first-rate empirical work are put into it. A model for this type of initiative is the Cecchini Report,[12] which, despite some methodological shortcomings, played an important role in the debate over harmonization in Europe. In some instances, rigorous empirical work on barriers to trade within Canada could also help persons advance their dispute settlement complaints, including providing them with proof that trade barriers are causing them economic harm.

Indeed, an important barrier to dispute settlement may well be that smaller actors face prohibitive costs in generating the sophisticated economic evidence required in some cases to pursue a complaint effectively.

Finally, the federal government should raise the consciousness of individual Canadians about the AIT. It should consider producing something like a Citizen's Charter of Economic Opportunity within Canada, which states and explains the provisions of the AIT in terms of Charter values of personal mobility, equality of opportunity, and individual freedom, and which emphasizes the real and symbolic importance of access to dispute settlement for nongovernmental actors. It is important that Canadians understand that the AIT affects them and (if somewhat indirectly) that it purports to confer on them, at least as a matter of political commitment, rights to trade – that is, that the AIT is not just another arcane federal-provincial talkshop.

Negative Integration through Constitutional Litigation: Alternative or Supplement to the AIT?

It is worth recalling that the AIT did not emerge out of intergovernmental anarchy, as do international trade treaties, but in the context of a single nation, with a constitution that, as Justice LaForest has suggested in a number of Supreme Court decisions,[13] can be interpreted as already implying or requiring an economic union within Canada. Armand de Mestral has suggested that the norms of the AIT should have been directly grounded in Canadian constitutional law and has commented, 'Canada has been a federation with an intense economic union since 1867, a fact of which the Agreement's negotiators appear to have been unaware.'[14]

Mobility Rights

Various provisions of the AIT may overlap with the mobility rights entrenched in section 6 of the Charter of Rights and Freedoms. Under that section, Canadians are guaranteed the right to take up residence and to gain a livelihood in any province. These rights are subject to the general 'reasonable limits' provision of the Charter (section 1) and to a special limitation clause that exempts general nondiscriminatory provincial laws, reasonable residency requirements for the receipt of public services within a province, and programs aimed at countering the social and economic disadvantage of individuals in high-unemployment provinces. Mobility rights are a fundamental part of the Charter and are not subject to the 'notwithstanding' clause (section 33) or 'legislative override,' as this section is often called.

In the early Charter case of *Law Society of Upper Canada v. Skapinker*,[15] the Supreme Court held that section 6(2)(b) did not confer a right to earn a livelihood independent of some element of mobility. The Court suggested, however, that this element need not always be the taking up of residence in the province concerned by the individual who is asserting a right to earn a livelihood. The notion that one does not have to 'move to and take up residence' in a province implies that mobility rights in section 6 could be extended to economic activity by out-of-province actors who nevertheless do not have an ongoing personal presence in the province where the economic activity in question is conducted. On this reading, the concept of economic mobility is already embedded in section 6.

In the case of *Black*, the Supreme Court of Canada went quite far toward adopting such a view of section 6. This case concerned an attempt by the Toronto-based law firm of McCarthy and McCarthy (now McCarthy Tétrault) to create an interprovincial law firm by setting up an office in Calgary in association with lawyers who were resident in Alberta. The challenged provisions prevented Alberta lawyers from entering into partnerships, associations, or 'other arrangements' for the joint practice of law in that province with a non-resident member of the Alberta bar.

In striking down these provisions, Justice LaForest suggested the following as a basis for interpreting section 6(2)(b):

The concept of Canada as a single country comprising what we would now call a common market was basic to the confederation arrangements and the draft resolution of the *British North America Act* attempted to pull down the existing control barriers that restricted movement within the country.[16]

There are two main limits, however, to the potential of rights in section 6 to secure the Canadian economic union. First, the section does not apply to corporations, the most obvious litigants with respect to many barriers to economic mobility. (Nevertheless, the Supreme Court has not explicitly foreclosed the possibility that a person, such as an employee or shareholder, who has a direct economic interest in a corporation's capacity to trade freely can make a mobility rights claim, even if the effects of the barrier are, in the first instance, felt by the corporation as an economic actor.) Second, in *Devine v. Quebec (P.G.)*,[17] the Supreme Court suggested that provincial measures that are not purposely discriminatory but are 'simply conditions of doing business in the province with which anyone must comply' are not violations of mobility rights, an interpretation recently, if laconically, reaffirmed by the Court in *Walker v. Prince Edward Island*.[18]

Since the *Black* decision, there has been little high-profile section 6 litigation. Two recent Court of Appeal cases merit particular attention, however, as they show the promise of section 6 in helping to secure the Canadian economic union.

In *Canadian Egg Marketing Agency v. Richardson*,[19] the Northwest Territories Court of Appeal held that the federal interprovincial egg marketing scheme violated section 6 to the extent that it prohibited Northwest Territories' egg producers from selling their eggs elsewhere in Canada, thus preventing the applicant from the pursuit of a livelihood in another province. The court stressed that the scheme did not merely regulate exports of eggs from the Northwest Territories into the rest of Canada, but that it rendered such exports illegal in all cases.[20] The court also emphasized that personal mobility across provincial borders need not always be an important component of the applicant's section 6 claim.

In *Canadian Egg Marketing Agency*, the court relied in part on an earlier decision of the Prince Edward Island Court of Appeal, *Island Equine Clinic Ltd. v. Prince Edward Island*.[21] In that case, a provincial regulation granting subsidies to a closed list of veterinary clinics was found to violate section 6 since, in creating a 'preferred class' of veterinary clinics, it excluded the applicant who had moved to Prince Edward Island from Ontario. What is interesting here is that the court found a violation of section 6 even though one could have argued that the recently arrived applicant was being treated no worse than long-standing PEI veterinarians who were not on the particular list in question. Nevertheless, the regulation clearly had a disparate impact on newcomers by creating a competitive advantage for some PEI residents.

As these cases illustrate, the potential for mobility rights litigation to strike down barriers to trade within Canada is not insignificant. The federal government could exploit this potential through referring to the courts lists of barriers to mobility in Canada (particularly in areas such as occupational qualifications, certification, and licensing) in a series of omnibus reference actions. The kind of state-of-the art empirical study advocated above would provide a concrete context for the Supreme Court to consider the effects of such measures on mobility rights. Perhaps less aggressively, the federal government could at least provide financial assistance for court challenges on mobility rights that might have significant implications for the Canadian economic union. This could hardly be seen as unfair to the provinces since, as *Canadian Egg Marketing Agency* illustrates, federal laws and regulations that impede mobility are equally as susceptible to challenge under section 6 as are provincial ones.

The existence of the AIT should lead to a less deferential standard of review in section 6 cases, for several reasons. First, many of the measures challenged in such litigation may well be those that also violate norms to which all governments have agreed in the AIT – thus, the Supreme Court may have to worry less that it is imposing its own interpretation of the foundations of the economic union on the political branches.

Second, the limitations clauses in the AIT itself can help guide and narrow the Court's analysis of whether measures found to violate section 6 are 'reasonable limits' to rights within the meaning of section 1 of the Charter.

Third, in setting out a process for positive integration through harmonization or regulatory rapprochement, the AIT provides assurance that judicially imposed constraints on policy measures need not lead to an overall retreat of democratic regulation.[22] In the AIT, Ottawa and the provinces have committed themselves to various processes of regulatory cooperation, which may allow a political avenue for addressing the Supreme Court's concerns about mobility while respecting the democratic will of governments to protect their citizens through economic and social regulation.[23] (Unfortunately, however, the processes contemplated in the AIT seem heavily based on the 'closed door,' Meech/Charlottetown model of executive federalism.)

Morguard *and* Hunt: *Toward a Canadian Version of* Cassis de Dijon?

As cases such as *Devine* and *Walker* make clear, section 6 mobility rights do not as such imply that a province must recognize or accept another province's regulations (for example, with respect to licensing of professionals) as a basis for a resident of that other province doing business intraprovincially – that is, a province can impose its own regulatory scheme on out-of-province providers of goods and services as long as it does not discriminate against them in favor of its own providers. As students of the European Union are well aware, however, it was precisely such a court-imposed requirement of recognition that – beginning with the famous *Cassis de Dijon* case – was of crucial importance to deeper and, ultimately, positive integration in Europe through mutual recognition arrangements combined with minimum regulatory criteria as a basis for recognition.[24] In two cases that concern interprovincial aspects of civil justice, the Supreme Court of Canada has gone a long way toward constitutionalizing the concept of mutual recognition.

In *Morguard*, the Court held that the idea of the Canadian economic union – as embodied in various constitutional provisions (including the ban on interprovincial tariffs [section 121]), the federal 'trade and commerce' power, and the mobility rights under section 6 – implies that the court of one province must recognize and enforce the judgment of the court of another province, provided the other province's court has taken jurisdiction on the basis of a real and substantial connection with the defendant (that is, not arbitrarily or unreasonably).

In *Hunt*, the Court held that the constitutional principles of order and fairness implicit in the conception of Canada as a common market or economic union also bind legislatures, not just courts. In that case, the Court found that a Quebec statute that purported to block the removal from the province of litigation-related documents was unconstitutional inasmuch as it might be applied to other Canadian provinces rather than foreign powers. A crucial dimension of the Court's reasoning was that the frustration of interprovincial civil litigation in this fashion would unduly increase the 'transaction costs' of doing business across provincial boundaries. Justice LaForest noted:

The resultant higher transaction costs for interprovincial transactions constitute an infringement on the unity and efficiency of the Canadian market-place.

If the Court further develops the approach it took in both *Morguard* and *Hunt*, it will have to craft some reasonable limits to the requirement of recognition, or at least find a means of balancing the effects on the economic union of provincial barriers against the legitimate policy goals that those measures purportedly serve.[25] In *Hunt*, however, the Court clearly saw that some limits were needed on judges' having the final say on such a balance, emphasizing in *obiter dicta* that it was constitutional for the federal government to legislate on the recognition and enforcement of judgments and related matters, pursuant to its 'trade and commerce' and 'peace, order, and good government' powers. It is to these powers that we now turn, in part because they offer considerable potential for positive integration, which advances the economic union by harmonizing, rather than simply constraining, government action.

Federal Harmonizing Regulation in Areas of Provincial Jurisdiction

In a number of regulatory fields, such as telecommunications, banking, and intellectual property rights, the federal government has exclusive jurisdiction under the Constitution as interpreted by the courts. However, the legacy of the Privy Council era of jurisprudence was to establish most areas of economic and social regulation as matters of provincial jurisdiction, including the regulation of any single industry or trade, the intraprovincial environment, labor relations, and so forth. Generally speaking, the courts have interpreted the federal 'peace, order, and good government' and 'trade and commerce' powers extremely narrowly, with the former increasingly limited to situations of national emergency and the latter limited to the regulation of flows of goods across international and interprovincial borders. Thus, the federal government was seen as having very little scope to enact national legislation where divergent provincial regulatory approaches undermined the Canadian economic union. Over the past few years, however, decisions of the Supreme Court have indicated the emergence of a very different, broader view of the federal general powers, as well as an explicit recognition of the importance of federal legislative activity to the securing of the Canadian economic union through harmonization.[26]

In *Crown Zellerbach*,[27] the Supreme Court revived the notion that Ottawa could invoke its 'peace, order, and good government' power to deal with a matter of national concern. According to Justice LeDain for the majority,

[f]or a matter to qualify as a matter of national concern ... it must have a singleness, distinctiveness and indivisibility that clearly distinguishes it from matters of provincial concern and a scale of impact on provincial jurisdiction that is reconcilable with the fundamental distribution of legislative power under the Constitution.[28]

In clarifying the concept of 'singleness, distinctiveness and indivisibility,' Justice LeDain emphasized the consequences of 'a provincial failure to deal effectively with the control or regulation of the inter-provincial aspect of the matter.' In addition, he stipulated that 'a national dimension justifies no more federal intervention than is necessary to fill the gap in provincial powers.'[29] Thus, as the Court would emphasize in the subsequent case of *Oldman*,[30] the national dimensions branch of the 'peace, order, and good government' power does not provide a basis for plenary federal jurisdiction over a very broad regulatory field, such as the environment in general.

In *Crown Zellerbach*, the issue was the constitutionality of federal legislation regulating marine pollution in *intraprovincial* waters. While existing constitutional doctrine permitted the federal government to regulate pollution within the province to the extent necessary to prevent the flow of pollution between provinces[31] or into the seas and oceans, the legislation in question was much broader than that, extending as it did to all intraprovincial marine waters.

What, then, would be the 'extraprovincial effects' of a provincial failure to regulate *all* intraprovincial marine pollution even if the federal government possessed sufficient authority (apart from the 'peace, order, and good government' power) to regulate actual spillovers or externalities across provincial boundaries? Justice LeDain's response hinged on the fact that marine pollution is treated as a single, indivisible subject in an international convention (*The Convention on the Prevention of Marine Pollution by Dumping of Wastes and Other Matters*) to which Canada is a signatory. This reasoning would seem to imply that the failure of any province to regulate intraprovincial pollution of marine waters could compromise Canada's adherence to the obligations of this international agreement, which benefits the entire country.

In a vigorous dissenting judgment, Justice LaForest, writing for himself and three other members of the Court, placed in question not so much the general approach in the majority judgment as whether it had been accurately applied. In particular, he raised concerns about whether the test with respect to intensity had really been applied at all: the federal legislation was so broad that it extended well beyond pollution as such to the dumping of *any* substance in marine waters. Thus, it was far from clear that the federal intervention was limited to the minimum necessary to fill a gap or to obviate the extraprovincial effects of a provincial failure to regulate. Nevertheless, there was empirical evidence (cited in the majority judgment) that the statute was drawn in such broad terms due to the monitoring and enforcement advantages of not having to identify the specific substance dumped in order to identify an infringement of the regulations. Permitted dumping of waste would be confined to license holders, and regulators could focus their intention on the content and quantity of the waste being dumped.

The General Motors *Case and the 'Trade and Commerce' Power*

In *General Motors*,[32] the Supreme Court moved beyond the restrictive approach to the 'trade and commerce' power taken by the Judicial Committee of the Privy Council and activated the long dormant 'general regulation of trade' dimension of this power. At issue in *General Motors* was the constitutionality of federal competition law, which, in the past, had been justified as an exercise of the federal criminal law power. The impugned provisions in *General Motors*, however, purported to create a civil right of action for violations of the *Competition Act*, thus arguably constituting an interference in provincial jurisdiction over property and civil rights.

Chief Justice Dickson, writing on behalf of a unanimous Court, elaborated the following criteria for determining whether a federal regulatory scheme that infringes provincial jurisdiction can be sustained as 'a general regulation of trade affecting the whole dominion':

- the legislation must be part of a general regulatory scheme;
- the scheme must be monitored by a regulatory agency;
- the scheme must not constitute the regulation of a single industry or trade;
- the matter of the legislation must be such that joint action by the provinces would be constitutionally impossible; and
- the refusal of one or more provinces to participate in a joint federal-provincial regulatory effort would put the whole scheme in jeopardy.

While the first three criteria primarily reconcile the Court's decision in *General Motors* with previous constitutional jurisprudence, the fourth and fifth are clearly closely analogous to the provincial inability test established in *Crown Zellerbach*.

The Court went on to distinguish between minor and major intrusions into exclusive provincial jurisdiction. In the case of a minor intrusion, it would be necessary to show only a functional or rational relationship between the interference with provincial jurisdiction and the national purposes reflected in the regulatory scheme as a whole. By contrast, for an intrusion to be considered 'major,' a close fit would be required between the particular intrusive feature of the scheme being impugned and the national purposes of the whole scheme.

Both *Crown Zellerbach* and *General Motors* clearly afford the federal government some scope to sustain constitutionally harmonizing regulation that impinges on areas of provincial jurisdiction, whether in consumer protection, environment, or financial services. Subsequently, even in cases such as *Hunt*, where no federal statute has been at issue, the Supreme Court has emphasized the importance of federal jurisdiction to securing the economic union. In *Hunt*, the Court even went so far as to suggest that the federal government could set rules for the recognition and enforcement of private law judgments by provincial courts where necessary to ensure order and fairness within the Canadian economic union.[33] I do not think one could ever expect a clearer statement by the Court on the link between the expanded scope of the federal government's general powers and the need for harmonization of provincial laws to secure the Canadian economic union.

Given Ottawa's legal scope to act in a range of areas where harmonization would support the economic union, a unilateral alternative exists where the intergovernmental processes contemplated in the AIT do not succeed in producing a satisfactory result.

An important limitation, however, is that a national regulatory scheme enacted pursuant to the general trade power or the national concern branch of the 'peace, order, and good government' power will not simply pre-empt provincial laws but normally will operate concurrently with them – except in cases of explicit conflict, where the paramountcy doctrine would operate to trump the provincial law in question. Thus, there is the risk that, without cooperation from the provinces, any such national scheme would actually create more, not less, regulatory diversity and possibly higher transaction costs for internal trade.[34]

This risk may be somewhat lower if one assumes a broad judicial interpretation of the paramountcy doctrine (toward which the Supreme Court seems to be inching).[35] Such a risk could also be addressed by carefully drafting federal laws to provide, for example, that goods and services shall enter freely every province and territory as long as they comply with federal regulatory requirements. However, the political rhetoric of federalism adopted by Ottawa is at odds with the assertion of its legal powers. This rhetoric tends to suggest that, if anything is to be done about the economic union, it must be done with the consent of the provinces. Indeed, David Cohen, Dean of the University of Victoria, attributes the 'overall weakness' of the AIT itself to 'the practical and political inability of the federal government to use its legal authority to act unilaterally to create a common market in Canada.'[36]

It is understandable and appropriate that the federal government should seek a consensus-based approach to eliminating obstacles to trade within Canada. The AIT is often touted as an example of the success of such an approach but, as we have seen, in many respects it is merely an agreement to agree, and is far from producing concrete results. It is sometimes argued that the GATT/WTO agreements are examples of the deep economic integration that can be achieved by consensus among a large number of parties without the need for a supranational government to herd uncooperative ones into line. In fact, however, the supposed consensus-based achievements of the GATT/WTO owe a great deal to the leadership – some would say bullying – of a few major powers that have unilateral options should consensus fail. Indeed, the entire Uruguay Round of multilateral trade negotiations depended for its success on an eleventh-hour deal between two such powers, the United States and the European Union.

At a minimum, the federal government should consider actively using the jurisprudence of the Supreme Court as a basis for enhancing the legitimacy of its leadership and weight in intergovernmental negotiations on harmonization or national approaches in areas such as food safety or consumer protection. It is perhaps the central insight of law and economics that the ultimate effect of legal rules is seen in the bargains that people strike in light of those rules under circumstances where transaction costs are above zero (the Coase theorem). It is quite conceivable that, at a crucial juncture in an intergovernmental negotiation, the prospect of unilateral federal action in the event of failure could persuade a recalcitrant province to come onside. In this respect, the leverage that Ottawa has as a result of its constitutional powers may actually help to produce a consensus-based outcome by overcoming holdouts.

Thus, the federal government should not view unilateral and consensus based alternatives as mutually exclusive, in the belief that to advance the latter it must delegitimize the former. At the same time, the fact that a consensus-based approach has been tried and found wanting may be an important support to Ottawa's case should it ultimately have to defend unilateral action in court. Here, it should be recalled that, in *Crown Zellerbach*, a key requirement for justifying the federal government's exercising its 'peace, order, and good government' power nationally was if the provinces appeared to be incapable of addressing, singly or jointly, the interprovincial dimensions of the matter. As well, the more specific commitments to harmonization in the AIT constitute an admission by the provinces that there is a legitimate need for a national approach in many regulatory areas in order to remove or reduce barriers to trade.

A contrary argument, of course, would be that, by entering into the AIT, the federal government has given the provinces some legitimate expectation that it is renouncing a unilateral approach to securing the Canadian economic union, or at least that it is demonstrating the view that consensus-based political approaches are adequate to the task. This is at odds, however, with the very explicit affirmation of existing constitutional powers in Article 300 of the AIT. In any case, such an argument would also imply the legitimacy of exercising federal powers should other governments fail to uphold their commitments in the AIT with respect to harmonization. To rely on the AIT as a kind of political estoppel of unilateral federal action, one must surely have to honor one's own commitments under the Agreement.

Globalization, International Trade Law, and the
Canadian Economic Union

Article 105 of the NAFTA states:

The Parties shall ensure that all necessary measures are taken in order to give effect to the provisions of this Agreement, including their observance, except as otherwise provided in this Agreement, by state and provincial governments.

On its face, this provision is stronger than the comparable GATT obligation, which refers to the requirement to take 'such measures as may be available' to ensure compliance of subnational governments.[37]

With respect to the vast majority of NAFTA and GATT/WTO obligations that affect the provinces, the federal government rightly does not intend to pursue a strategy of pre-empting provincial jurisdiction. Instead, it could wait until provincial measures are found by a dispute panel to be in violation of the NAFTA, then seek the provinces' agreement to a solution that is satisfactory from the perspective of the complaining party – which is what has already happened with respect to violation by the provinces of GATT and Canada-US Free Trade Agreement provisions on alcoholic beverages. Ultimately, should a province fail to agree, the complaining party may, under some circumstances, be permitted to retaliate against Canada by withdrawing trade concessions to Canada under the NAFTA. It will usually be in the complaining party's interest to withdraw concessions so as to have a maximum impact on the economy of the offending province.

In the *Labour Conventions* case,[38] it was held that the federal government has no general constitutional authority to implement treaties by legislating in areas of exclusive provincial jurisdiction. Therefore, any federal legislative or regulatory action to ensure provincial conformity with the GATT or the NAFTA must be consistent with the distribution of legislative powers in sections 91 and 92 of the *Constitution Act* (1867 and 1982). In contemporary circumstances, Ottawa's power to regulate with respect to international trade and commerce (section 91 (2)) extends to measures that would otherwise be within exclusive provincial jurisdiction, where necessary and incidental to the regulation of international trade and commerce. Elsewhere,[39] I have suggested that recent Supreme Court interpretations of the general 'trade and commerce' power (*General Motors*) and the 'peace, order, and good government' power (*Crown Zellerbach*)[40] might provide, in some circumstances, additional avenues for the federal government to legislate in otherwise exclusively provincial fields in order to assure compliance with Canada's international obligations.

Ultimately, however, no matter how much importance one attaches to *Labour Conventions* today, the federal government may not even have to attempt to flex its constitutional muscles since, as the beer saga illustrates, the threat of retaliation from trading partners can be an extremely powerful incentive to bring a province to the table and work with Ottawa toward a solution that ensures compliance with international trade law.[41]

Once a province is put into a position where, under international trade law, it must eliminate discrimination against imports from abroad, then continuing to discriminate against imports from other Canadian provinces may well be futile. In this connection, it should be stressed that, given the interpretation of 'national treatment' adopted by GATT panels in the beer cases, the provinces cannot use the defense that they are treating foreign imports just as badly as products from other provinces. In effect, Canadians have US beer makers and GATT dispute panels largely to thank for opening up the internal beer market in this country!

A second international trade dispute – between Canada and the United States over the entry of UHT milk from Quebec into Puerto Rico – illustrates a different but equally important way in which globalization may be overtaking the AIT initiative as a force for securing the Canadian economic union.[42] In this case, Puerto Rican and US authorities insisted that, for such imports to continue, Quebec or Canada would have to join a US regulatory regime for milk safety or undertake costly and time-consuming measures to persuade US authorities of the equivalence of the Quebec-Canada system. Key to the US claim that it could not simply recognize the Canadian regime as equivalent was the notion that 'the Quebec/Canada system does not include the federal oversight and verification elements that are essential components of the US system.'[43] Although the panel ruled in favor of Canada on one of the legal issues, the ultimate resolution of the dispute involved Ottawa's assurances that Quebec milk exporters were meeting the equivalent of US standards.

More generally, inconsistencies in federal and provincial approaches to standards and inspection will make it increasingly difficult to justify controls on imported food based on scientific risk-assessment criteria (as required by the GATT Agreement on Sanitary and Phytosanitary Measures) or to justify measures otherwise inconsistent with GATT provisions (for example, national treatment as 'necessary' for the protection of human or animal health under Article XX(b) of the GATT). Thus, this is one area where, despite virtually nothing having been agreed to in the AIT, progress is being made toward harmonizing divergent provincial standards and procedures. Indeed, there is the possibility that the First Ministers will agree to a National Dairy Code when they meet in late June 1996.

A final example is trade in electricity. Discussions have gone on for many years about facilitating interutility trade in electricity across Canada through the creation of a national grid, or at least significant interprovincial wheeling capability, but with no concrete result. However, as provinces begin to open up their electricity markets to intraprovincial competition, the national treatment and related obligations of international trade agreements apply to those markets as well.[44] In fact, some Canadian utilities may already have joined regional groupings of US utilities intended to manage interface and access issues that are crucial to interjurisdictional trade in electricity, on the basis of ground rules set by regulators in Washington. The ultimate result of Ottawa's unwillingness to take the lead and the usual provincial intransigence and bickering may be the bypassing of the Canadian economic union and the eventual wheeling of power across Canada largely according to a regulatory design made in the United States.

These three examples relate to an even more broadly based trend of globalized regulation and standards setting, as reflected in the Codex Alimentarius in the case of food safety, the ISO with respect to product standards, and various global environmental regimes. International trade agreements now link up to these globalized regulatory processes by requiring that a country strictly justify the adoption of regulations not based on international norms, at least where such regulations are likely to have a trade-restricting impact.

As has often been the case in the past, the provinces may call on the federal government to shelter them from such trends. But this is no longer possible: the simple result of not complying with international standards or internationally recognized national standards is that one's products and services will have an ever more difficult time entering foreign markets. Moreover, even in the absence of formal barriers, the products and services of an offending country may not enjoy the confidence of increasingly wary and informed consumers in markets such as the European Union.

Of course, globalized regulation and standards setting is made in forums where national governments have a major role – although, in the case of the ISO, one cannot underestimate the extent to which the process is private sector driven. And such regulation does not often simply pre-empt domestic regulatory regimes. Thus, the federal government now has a window of opportunity to lead in developing or consolidating distinctly Canadian approaches to interactions with global regulatory processes. If the provinces choose not to co-operate in the development of a national approach, they will find themselves subject, willy-nilly, to whatever is negotiated at these forums. The question the provinces now face is: Would they prefer to be seen as contributors to a distinctive Canadian approach to globalization through the concentration of Canadian will and imagination, or are their concerns about pride and power within the federation so important that they would prefer simply being buffeted by the winds of global change?

NOTES

I am grateful to Sven Milelli for excellent research assistance, including many useful insights on the constitutional jurisprudence of economic union. I have also learned much from comments by David Schneiderman and Kathy Swinton on my earlier work on the economic union, and by the latter on an earlier draft of this *Commentary*. Responses to the earlier draft when it was presented at the C.D. Howe Institute, especially from Armand de Mestral and Daniel Schwanen, were also most helpful.

1 K. Swinton, 'Law, Politics, and the Enforcement of the Agreement on Internal Trade,' in M.J. Trebilcock and D. Schwanen, eds., *Getting There: An Assessment of the Agreement on Internal Trade*, Policy Study 26 (Toronto: C.D. Howe Institute, 1995), p. 209.

2 The developments are summarized in A. Dimitrijevic, 'The Agreement on Internal Trade: Overview and Progress,' Internal Trade Secretariat, Ottawa, undated.

3 See, for example, M.J. Trebilcock and R. Behboodi, 'The Canadian Agreement on Internal Trade: Retrospect and Prospects,' in Trebilcock and Schwanen, eds., *Getting There*, pp. 21–22.

4 I develop this liberal philosophical perspective on economic union at length in R. Howse, *Economic Union, Social Justice, and Constitutional Reform: Towards a High but Level Playing Field* (North York: York University, Centre for Public Law and Public Policy, 1992).

5 *Reference Re Canada Assistance Plan*, (1991) 83 D.L.R. (4th) 297 (S.C.C.). For excellent discussions of this issue, see Swinton, 'Law, Politics, and the Enforcement of the Agreement on Internal Trade'; and L. Friedlander, 'Constitutionalizing Inter-governmental Agreements,' *National Journal of Constitutional Law* 4 (1994): 153.

6 Some of the obligations in the AIT may be difficult to translate into statutory require-ments, particularly those which entail governments' collectively committing them-selves to various processes with respect to harmonization, for example. Thus, only some subset of the AIT provisions could be appropriately incorporated into statutes in this way. These, however, would certainly include basic nondiscrimination norms as they apply to the various measures and sectors covered by the AIT. I am grateful to Kathy Swinton for this point.

7 Alberta, *Agreement on Internal Trade Statutes Amendment Act* (1995), Bill 36 (passed May 17, 1995); *Agreement on Internal Trade Amendment Act* S.N. 1995, c. A-5.1; *Internal Trade Agreement Implementation Act*, S.N.S. 1996, c. 8; Quebec, *An Act Respecting the Implementation of the Agreement on Internal Trade*, 1996 (Bill 15).

8 This information is based on an interview of a federal government official by Sven Milelli in mid-May 1996.

9 R. Howse, 'Between Anarchy and the Rule of Law: Dispute Settlement and Related Implementation Issues in the Agreement on Internal Trade,' in Trebilcock and Schwanen, eds., *Getting There*.

10 Ibid., pp. 185–186.

11 Another avenue for raising the profile of dispute settlement and making it more effective would be to strengthen the Internal Trade Secretariat, which at present has few resources at its disposal to support dispute settlement or to advocate for the implementation of the AIT. This useful suggestion is developed in D. Schwanen, *Drawing on Our Inner Strength: Canada's Economic Citizenship in an Era of Evolv-ing Federalism*, C.D. Howe Institute Commentary 82 (Toronto: C.D. Howe Institute, June 1996), which should be viewed as a companion piece to this paper.

12 P. Cecchini, *The European Challenge, 1992: The Benefits of a Single Market* (Brussels: European Community, 1988).

13 *Black v. Alberta Law Society*, [1989] 1 S.C.R. 591; *Morguard Investments Ltd. v. De Savoye*, [1990] 3 S.C.R. 1077; *Hunt v. T & N plc*, [1993].

14 A. de Mestral, 'A Comment,' in Trebilcock and Schwanen, eds., *Getting There*, p. 96.

15 *Law Society of Upper Canada v. Skapinker*, [1984] 1 S.C.R. 357.

16 *Black v. Alberta Law Society*, [1989] 1 S.C.R. 591.

17 *Devine v. Quebec (P.G.)*, [1988] 2 S.C.R. 790, 55 D.L.R. (4th) 641, at 657–658. Note, however, that this case dealt with mobility rights only in passing. It was primarily concerned with determining the consistency of Quebec's Bill 101 with the guarantees of freedom of expression in the Charter.

18 *Walker v. Prince Edward Island*, [1995] 2 S.C.R. 407.

19 *Canadian Egg Marketing Agency v. Richardson*, [1996] 132 D.L.R. (4th) 274 (N.W.T.C.A.).

20 Ibid., at 303.

21 *Island Equine Clinic Ltd. v. Prince Edward Island*, [1991] 81 D.L.R. (4th) 350 (P.E.I.C.A).

22 This is a concern about court-based economic integration that has been expressed by Kathy Swinton and David Schneiderman, both of whom have criticized my earlier work for being too open or favorable to judicial constraint of barriers to economic mobility. See K. Swinton, 'Courting Our Way to Economic Integration: Judicial Review and the Canadian Economic Union,' *Canadian Business Law Journal* 25 (1995): 280; and D. Schneiderman, 'Economic Citizenship and Deliverative Democracy: An Inquiry into Constitutional Limitations on Economic Regulation,' *Queen's Law Journal* 21 (1995): 125.

23 This does *not* imply that section 6 creates a positive obligation to harmonization or regulatory rapprochement. The point is that these instruments of positive integration provide a democratic safety valve, where the Court has struck down legislation under section 6.

24 See, for example, D. Vogel, *Trading Up: Consumer and Environmental Regulation in a Global Economy* (Cambridge, Mass.: Harvard University Press, 1995), ch. 2.

25 Robert Wisner has argued for a minimum impairment approach, which seems consistent with European Union jurisprudence flowing from *Cassis de Dijon* and with the concept of 'reasonable limits' employed in the most doctrinally solid Supreme Court interpretations of section 1 limits on Charter rights. Under this test, the Court would ask whether the provincial measures in question impair the economic union to the minimum extent necessary to advance legitimate provincial policy objectives. See R. Wisner, 'Uniformity, Diversity and Provincial Extraterritoriality: *Hunt v. T&N plc*,' *McGill Law Journal* 40 (1995): 759.

26 For a view that suggests that these cases, taken together, indicate a much more modest scope for securing the Canadian economic union than I suggest below, see Swinton, 'Courting Our Way to Economic Integration.'

27 *R v. Crown Zellerbach Canada Ltd.*, [1988] 1 S.C.R. 401.

28 Ibid., at 432.

29 Ibid., at 433.

30 *Friends of the Oldman River Society v. Canada (Minister of Transport)*, [1992] 1 S.C.R. 3.

31 See *Interprovincial Co-Operatives Ltd. v. The Queen*, [1976] 1 S.C.R. 477.

32 *General Motors of Canada v. City National Leasing*, [1989] 1 S.C.R. 641.

33 *Hunt v. T&N plc*, at 42.

34 See Swinton, 'Courting Our Way to Economic Integration,' p. 300.

35 See *Bank of Montreal v. Hall*, [1990] 2 S.C.R. 121. In this case, the Court suggested that the provincial law would be pre-empted not only where the citizen is incapable of obeying both laws, as had been suggested by earlier jurisprudence, but also where there is a significant policy inconsistency, so that the provincial law undermines the policy that underlies the federal law. See also the notion of operational conflict between federal and provincial laws that informs the majority judgment in *Husky Oil Operations Ltd. v. Minister of National Revenue*, [1995] 3 S.C.R. 453.

36 D. Cohen, 'The Internal Trade Agreement: Furthering the Canadian Economic Disunion?' *Canadian Business Law Journal* 25 (1995): 279.

37 In recent GATT panel jurisprudence, however, the provision in question has been interpreted as imposing a rather stringent obligation on the federal government.

38 *A.-G. Can. v. A.-G. Ont.*, [1937] A.C. 326, 1 D.L.R. 673 (P.C.) [hereafter referred to as *Labour Conventions*].

39 R. Howse, 'The *Labour Conventions* Doctrine in an Era of Global Interdependence: Rethinking the Constitutional Dimensions of Canada's External Economic Relations,' *Canadian Business Law Journal* 16 (1990): 160; and idem, 'NAFTA and the Constitution: Does *Labour Conventions* Really Matter Any More,' *Constitutional Forum* 3 (1994): 54.

40 As was noted earlier, in sustaining federal legislation that impinged on exclusive provincial jurisdiction over intraprovincial waters, the majority Supreme Court judgment emphasized the fact that the federal legislation corresponded to the subject matter of a single international convention on marine waters.

41 Here, I have benefited from remarks by my colleague Michael Trebilcock.

42 The following draws on a study on reforming the Canadian food inspection system undertaken for the federal government task force on alternative delivery mechanisms.

43 Letter of Acting US Trade Representative Katz to the Canadian Minister of International Trade, August 24, 1992, as quoted in *In the Matter of Puerto Rico Regulations on the Import, Distribution, and Sale of U.H.T. Milk from Quebec*, Final Report of the Panel, June 3, 1993.

44 See R. Howse and G. Heckman, 'The Regulation of Trade in Electricity: A Canadian Perspective,' in R.J. Daniels, ed., Ontario Hydro at the Millennium (Montreal; Kingston: McGill-Queen's University Press, 1996), pp. 105–155.

Time Out: Assessing Incremental Strategies for Enhancing the Canadian Political Union

ROGER GIBBINS and
KATHERINE HARMSWORTH

Canadians face a perplexing dilemma in coming to grips with the results of the 1995 sovereignty referendum in Quebec. Given the closeness of the result and the absence in subsequent polls of any signal of a significant decline in support for sovereignty,[1] there is a growing national consensus that the federal status quo must change. Bluntly put, the federalists will lose the next referendum unless they put something on the table other than the status quo and threats about the dire economic consequences of a 'yes' vote.

Yet belief in the need for change is coupled with pessimism about the possibility of achieving change, or at least constitutional change. This pessimism springs in part from the failure of past efforts at what Peter Russell has called 'mega-constitutional change.'[2] Here, the Meech Lake and Charlottetown Accords loom large, although the *Constitution Act, 1982* counts among the failures for Quebec nationalists and Charter-skeptics in English Canada. These failures – particularly the referendum rejection of the Charlottetown Accord – cast serious doubts on Canadians' ability to find common ground. They have also undermined public confidence in executive federalism as a vehicle for constitutional renewal, and thereby appear to have left Canada without a viable constitutional process.[3]

There is, then, a sense that Canada 'can't get there from here' because the constitutional process has broken down and nothing has been put in its place. As a consequence, the belief in the need for change, combined with pessimism about the possibility of change, has given birth to a renewal strategy based on cautious incrementalism. If mega-constitutional change is impossible and the status quo is unacceptable, the only option appears to be incrementalism pursued through conventional political processes. As a recent editorial in the *Calgary Herald* concluded, '[Canadians] need to seek smaller, more realistic compromises rather than attempting to take giant steps forward together into the unknown.'[4]

Within this incremental strategy are nestled two different, albeit complementary, options. The first option rests on the belief that, while substantive constitutional changes might be impossible if they are approached as a single package, they might be achievable through first taking a series of small incremental steps that, at least at the outset, would not entail formal amendment.[5] These steps would attempt to improve the country's mood, perhaps by creating a pause for citizen initiatives.[6] As the Group of 22 has expressed it,

[w]e hope that progress along this path will recreate a climate of mutual trust and good will, in which constitutional issues can once more be approached with greater hope of agreement.[7]

Only then might it be possible to formalize incremental changes through constitutional amendment.

The second option rests on the belief that nonconstitutional changes may preclude the need for constitutional change. The assumption here is that nonconstitutional change by itself (that is, in the absence of any other changes) can forge a dramatically different Canada within which Quebec sovereigntists, alienated western Canadians, and others can find meaningful political space.

The two options share the assumption that incremental nonconstitutional change will suffice in the runup to the next Quebec referendum; they differ as to whether incrementalism is a *precondition* or a *substitute* for constitutional change. The short-term intention is to ensure that, should another sovereignty referendum be held, the 'no' side will win by a comfortable majority. Success, then, means shifting a small portion of the soft nationalist vote in Quebec from 'yes' to 'no.' As a recent *Globe and Mail* editorial observed,

Full and due respect for provincial jurisdiction will not convert true separatists to the Canadian cause, but it will undermine the separatist argument with a good portion of 'soft nationalists' in Quebec who are looking for a response to their demands for more autonomy within Canada.[8]

Not incidentally, public opinion outside Quebec is irrelevant in this scenario. Other Canadians, although not necessarily their governments, are cast into a passive, bystander role. It is Quebec opinion, not Canadian opinion, that counts.

Given recent failures at mega-constitutional change and national anxiety in the wake of the Quebec referendum, the appeal of incrementalism is not surprising. It promises something for federalist forces in Quebec while not violating the English-Canadian taboo against asymmetrical responses to the national unity crisis. Many components of the incremental agenda can be packaged to appeal to all regions, not just to Quebec. Most important, incrementalism avoids hopeless causes such as trying to generate western Canadian support for a distinct society clause.[9]

Incrementalism, however, is more than a process for the renewal of the Canadian federal state. The dominant *strategy* of the day also privileges a particular *outcome*, one characterized by decentralization and intergovernmentalism. It is this vision of Canada, the vision embedded within incrementalism, that provides the focus for this *Commentary*.

Before turning to the core of our analysis, it is important to stress that the goal is not to produce another set of reform proposals. Rather, it is to provide a framework through which the incremental strategy for addressing the national unity crisis can be assessed. And, it should be clear, crisis is the appropriate word. Though Canadians are not rushing to the barricades, the Quebec referendum has brought into bold relief a fundamental schism within the Canadian political community – a schism that places the survival of that community in doubt. Thus, our focus on incrementalism should not suggest that we endorse a 'business as usual' approach. Instead, we ask whether incrementalism and its concomitant federal vision will provide a durable solution to the nationalist challenge from Quebec – and if so, at what cost to the Canadian federal state as the country prepares to enter the next century.

Principal Components of the Incremental Strategy

The results of the Quebec referendum have sparked another round in the ongoing debate on redesigning the Canadian federal state; from this round, a rough-and-ready consensus is emerging on the components of an incremental strategy. This consensus is anchored by a commitment to greater decentralization, including a respect for provincial legis- lative autonomy and the rollback of federal intrusions stemming from the spending power. The consensus is also anchored by a reliance on intergovernmentalism, by the faith that executive provincialism can replace many of the integrative functions performed in the past by the central government. While decentralization and intergovernmentalism are not always linked in the renewal debate, it is the thesis of this *Commentary* that they are yoked in the incremental strategy.

Rebalancing the Federation

Decentralization is generally addressed under the rubric of rebalancing, which is seen as the means to create a new partnership between the provincial and federal governments. For example, taking an approach that is typical among proponents of decentralization, the participants at the Confederation 2000 conference observed that the purpose of rebalancing would be to provide greater clarity in the functions of the two orders of government and to reduce overlap and duplication, thereby allowing governments to focus more effectively on their respective roles and responsibilities.[10] The participants recommended that rebalancing be achieved through devolving powers to the provinces, curtailing the federal spending power, and increasing provincial input with regard to national standards, new national programs, and national economic management. In these respects, the Confederation 2000 participants were also typical of decentralization's proponents: with very few exceptions (discussed below), rebalancing is sought through a uni- directional shift in responsibility from Ottawa to the provinces. Overlap and duplication are to be pruned by cutting back on the activities of the federal government, not on those of the provinces.

Proponents of this approach usually call for greater decentralization in at least the following areas: labor market training; natural resources (such as forestry and mining); recreation; tourism; housing; and municipal and urban affairs. There is also moderate support among participants in the informal renewal debate for some measure of decentralization in other jurisdictional domains. Jean Chevrier, for instance, draws on 30 years of constitutional analysis to recommend that language, culture, and communications be managed concurrently, with federal or provincial paramountcy being stipulated.[11] Others support the expanded use of concurrent powers in a renewed federation, but with the specific intent of extending provincial influence.[12] A default legislative role for the federal government would be retained, albeit one tied to a more restricted spending power. In a similar vein are suggestions to curb the federal spending power by replacing transfer payments with tax points. For example, the Reform Party recommends that federal block grants to the provinces be replaced with tax points, established as a fixed percentage of federal tax revenue.[13] Thomas Courchene sees tax point replacements as an indispensable element of a reformed federal state.[14]

The rebalancing initiative was pulled into sharp focus by the August 1996 Premiers' Conference in Jasper. Though the premiers eventually drew back from the radical positions initially advanced by Ontario Premier Mike Harris and Alberta Premier Ralph Klein, nine of the ten expressed their determination to work with the federal government to strengthen provincial input into the determination of national standards (or guidelines, as Premier Klein prefers) for social programs, environmental protection, and interprovincial trade.[15] It is the premiers' quest for a reduced federal role in social programs that captures the core of decentralization.

The proponents of rebalancing, such as Courchene, see greater decentralization as an inevitable reflection of fiscal realities in Ottawa, global economic changes, and the nationalist threat in Quebec. However, greater decentralization is also portrayed as a state of affairs toward which Canada *should* move.

The normative case for decentralization is advanced along two fronts. First is the recommendation that the federal government withdraw from provincial areas of responsibility, a recommendation reflected in the August 1996 Premiers' Conference and, more emphatically, in Courchene's working paper for the Ontario government that was released to coincide with that conference.[16] Here, the intention is to change federal practice rather than the formal constitutional division of powers. The call is for greater fidelity to the existing Constitution. In the words of Premier Klein:

It's not a matter of wrestling away powers [from Ottawa]. It's a matter of restoration of constitution[al] authority, authority that was ours in the first place. I mean, this country is not a union. This country is a confederation. Right?[17]

Second is the recommendation that the exercise of federal powers be constrained by provincial consultation and consent: joint management of the economic and social union should replace unilateral federal management. Constraint, it is argued, should be exercised not only with respect to the spending power and areas of concurrent jurisdiction (such as environmental protection), but also within the federal government's constitutional domain as set forth in section 91 of the *Constitution Act*. Ottawa, in effect, would work in partnership with the provincial governments and eschew unilateral action in such fields as international trade agreements. Melvin H. Smith, for example, calls for a multilateral policy forum in which a new federal-provincial partnership would use intergovernmental agreements as an alternative to constitutional amendments.[18] Here again, the intention is to change federal practice rather than the division of powers; constitutional amendment could be avoided by Ottawa's legislated commitment not to act without provincial consent.[19]

Recommendations for the formal transfer of legislative responsibilities from the federal government to the provinces would entail a constitutional amendment, and would therefore have to overcome the new five-region parliamentary veto. Not surprisingly, proposals requiring constitutional amendment do not figure prominently in the incremental strategy; John Richards' suggestion that the division of powers with respect to language be rewritten to provide a more robust general authority for Quebec is an exception.[20] More informal arrangements, including intergovernmental agreements and delegated authority, are preferred. But in all cases, the end is clear: provincial governments would have greater flexibility in the design and administration of public policy, greater protection from federal intrusions, and a greater say in the federal government's residual legislative domain.

The case for rebalancing often draws on the concept of subsidiarity, which the Group of 22 defines as a process in which 'decision-making should be as close as possible to citizens' and in which '[g]overnment powers should be assigned to the lowest level [at which] they can be effectively exercised.'[21] As the European experience shows, subsidiarity does not automatically entail decentralization. In some cases, powers can be exercised more effectively by the senior level of government; thus, some upward migration in powers has been seen as the European Union has been constructed within the pre-existing European state system. Yet in the Canadian debate, subsidiarity means decentralization. Any upward shift of powers or responsibilities is entertained only when the destination is an intergovernmental authority, not the federal government alone.

Exceptions can be found, but they truly are exceptions. For example, the Reform Party recommends that the powers of the federal government be increased to enable it to effectively represent Canadian interests in negotiations with the other parties to the North American Free Trade Agreement, with the European Union, with the countries of Asia Pacific Economic Cooperation, and with the World Trade Organization.[22] There has also been some support for the creation of a Canadian Securities Commission that would 'reduce jurisdictional overlap, lower legal costs and eliminate gaps in enforcement.'[23] However, it is difficult to avoid the conclusion that this idea has been advanced primarily as a foil to fend off critics of decentralization. Premier Klein, for example, has cited negotiations to create the Commission as evidence that the provinces are willing to have Ottawa take on additional responsibilities,[24] but British Columbia and Quebec were quick to dissociate themselves from the proposal, and the Alberta Stock Exchange has recommended that Alberta do the same.[25] A Canadian Securities Commission that did not include Quebec, British Columbia, or Alberta would be little more than the existing Ontario Securities Commission writ large.

Past proposals for mega-constitutional change have often begun by recommending that decentralization with respect to social programs be counterbalanced by a strengthened federal role in managing the economic union. For example, Ottawa's September 1991 constitutional reform initiative included a variety of measures aimed at strengthening the economic union.[26] Recent reform proposals, including Courchene's ACCESS model, begin in the same fashion. The Group of 22, for instance, notes that,

[t]o meet the global challenges of today, we need a strong economic union in which

Canadians and their skills can move freely across the country in response to new opportunities in other provinces or to difficulties at home.[27]

In the past, however, provincial governments have been quick to endorse decentralization with respect to social programs while condemning any strengthened federal powers with respect to the economic union. Ottawa's 1991 proposals were rejected out of hand by provincial governments, and there is no reason to expect this pattern to change. The transfer of such responsibilities as labor market training to the exclusive control of the provinces makes provincial management of the economy even more important, and it is unlikely that the provinces would endorse federal government or constitutional constraints on that management. The primary test case, as always, is Quebec. If federalist forces in Quebec are unwilling to endorse strengthened federal powers with respect to national economic management, this change cannot be incorporated into an incremental national unity strategy. Since there is no indication that endorsement will be forthcoming from that group, any lack of enthusiasm by other provincial governments is beside the point.

The only proposals likely to remain in play are those that enhance the role of provincial governments in the management of the economic union. Strengthening the economic union could be achieved, for example, by building on the recent Agreement on Internal Trade (AIT). And indeed, there is considerable support for extending the AIT. Daniel Schwanen sees the AIT as a prototype for more general forms of intergovernmental collaboration, a success story to be emulated even as its economic application is strengthened.[28] Thus, joint management, not a strengthened federal role, is the primary feature of the incremental strategy.

It should be noted, however, that the AIT is not universally seen as a prototype to be emulated. A recent *Globe and Mail* editorial about the dispute between British Columbia and New Brunswick regarding location incentives for United Parcel Service was caustic in its assessment of the AIT:

[The dispute] illustrates again the weakness of the interprovincial trade agreement and the suspicion, indeed resentment, with which the provinces regard it. It remains vague in definition, narrow in scope and unenforceable in application ... Our failure to make progress on an issue this fundamental devalues our citizenship, diminishes our nationhood and darkens our future ... .

The premiers have consistently fought every attempt to establish a full economic union, achieving notable success in resisting it at Charlottetown in 1992. That they cobbled together a clutch of flaccid half-measures last year and called it a victory was sadly predictable.[29]

The concern is that removal of interprovincial trade barriers is to be entrusted to the same governments that erected those barriers in the first place, but are now presumably driven by a different political logic. Thus, the entrails of the AIT can be read in different ways, only some of which support the AIT as a positive model for joint economic management.

Discussions of the economic union inevitably bring human capital into play. The Group of 22, for instance, stresses that the development of human capital will be essential in the twenty-first century, and therefore recommends better public schools, retraining for workers, training programs for employable Canadians on welfare, and vigorous programs aimed at enhancing employment opportunities for aboriginal peoples. Virtually all of these matters fall within the provincial field of jurisdiction, where a strong argument can be made for coordinating labor market training with provincial education and welfare services. At the same time, the Group recognizes that,

because of spillover effects, provincial governments might provide less training or education than is appropriate from the standpoint of the country as a whole.[30]

Here, the concern is not with precipitous reduction in provincial support, which is unlikely, but with the gradual erosion of support in those areas where spillover effects are most pronounced.

This is a classic example of a situation in which the logic of subsidiarity might call for a stronger role for the federal government in addressing spillover effects. Yet Canadians, locked in by Quebec's insistence on exclusive control over labor market training, have little alternative but to march resolutely in the opposite direction. Ensuring that Canada's position in the global economy remains competitive is increasingly entrusted to provincial governments, whose primary concern must be the health of their respective provincial economies, and not individual mobility across provincial boundaries.

National Standards

All of the above feeds into the inevitable debate on national standards. As earlier constitutional debates were opened up to a wider range of participants, the protection of national standards and the role of the federal government in so doing provoked major controversy. However, in the more constrained intergovernmental environment that shapes the current debate, incremental reform proposals are pursuing a different theme: *national standards need not be federal government standards.* Indeed, in the more radical of the recent Courchene recommendations, the federal government would not even be involved in setting or enforcing national standards. Jim Gray, in line with the less radical of Cour-chene's proposals, has commented on the need to create minimum standards that would be mutually agreed on by Ottawa and the provinces. National standards unilaterally imposed by Ottawa, he argues, contribute to national disunity.[31]

The heart of the matter rests with who should set national standards, how restrictive they should be, and how such standards should be enforced. It is clear that Ottawa's ability to impose financial penalties is rapidly evaporating, particularly with respect to the wealthier provinces. What, then, if anything, might be substituted for such penalties? Will provincial governments willingly exchange federal government enforcement for intergovernmental enforcement? For example, would it be any less of an encroachment on Quebec sovereignty if enforcement passed from the federal government (where Quebec politicians play a dominant role) to provincial governments in Ontario and the West (where the Quebec electorate has no leverage)?

Here, some useful insight is provided by the discussions surrounding the August 1996 Premiers' Conference. In a Calgary speech delivered shortly before the Conference began, Premier Harris stressed that 'national standards do not have to be federal government standards.' He went on to say:

We are talking about leaving areas of provincial jurisdiction in the hands of provinces to set the standards. I think we can do a lot better than the federal government. The federal government is bankrupt. It has no dollars ... It's time for provinces to step forward.[32]

Premier Klein also attacked federal enforcement, calling it (in politically cor-rect fashion) 'big brotherism or big sisterism at its worst.'[33] However, the pre-mier recoiled even from the idea of interprovincial enforcement:

I hate to use the word enforce. I don't think enforcement is a word we like to hear in Canada unless it applies to criminals. And none of us are criminals.[34]

Enforcement, he insisted, is simply a matter of governments' behaving them-selves and playing by the rules they set. In this view, national standards or guidelines would be very loose indeed. As Robert Mason Lee concludes,

[t]here is no reason to believe the premiers are too criminal, too unpatriotic or even too dull to represent the national interest. It's just that they have no imperative to do so, being answerable only to their provinces. The whole idea is so destructive that even Lucien Bouchard liked it.[35]

An even softer approach to national standards is found in discussions of the

Canadian political culture. Participants at the Confederation 2000 conference stated that Canadians need to foster mutual understanding and to know their own country, its history, and other Canadians better.[36] Participants in the March 1996 CBC television initiative *72 Hours to Remake Canada* expressed a set of principles aimed at defining Canada's identity and providing the basis for the continued association between Quebec and the rest of Canada. David V.J. Bell writes that Canadians from the grass roots up should develop a sense of mission for their country,[37] and Ronald L. Watts wrote after the failure of the Charlottetown Accord that Canadians must develop a wider sense of shared values and common destiny.[38] The hope, then, is that the potentially disintegrative effect of decentralization will be offset by a stronger and more explicitly articulated collective vision. Common values, not the federal government, will hold interprovincial variance in social programs in check, or at least will do so for those provinces that are not culturally distinct.

Equalization

Participants in the renewal debate generally assume that shared values will include a commitment to equalization and that decentralization is compatible with continued support for fiscal equalization. However, this latter assumption may reflect wishful thinking rather than hard-headed political analysis. Citizens' commitments to the national community may weaken as the federal government's influence on individuals' lives comes to be filtered more and more through intergovernmental agreements and forums. Political support for equalization may also weaken as a greater proportion of political space is filled by provincial programs and priorities. Increasing governmental and electoral unease are already being seen in Alberta, British Columbia, and Ontario with federal redistribution beyond the equalization formula itself. It is in this context that Saskatchewan Premier Roy Romanow described the emerging Alberta-Ontario alliance on decentralization as 'elephants dancing among the chickens.'[39]

It must be stressed that greater provincial asymmetry with respect to social programs and standards is not only the inevitable result of greater decentralization; it is the very goal of such a shift. As Courchene points out, 'any notion of identical standards across all provinces is a non-starter.'[40] Decentralization makes sense if one recognizes that provinces *are* and *should be* significantly different with respect to social programs and economic management. Only then is federalism's potential for policy innovation and experimentation fully unleashed. Formal constitutional symmetry might be maintained in a more decentralized federation, but symmetry of result is incompatible with the logic of decentralization.

At some level, therefore, the logic of decentralization works against the logic of equalization: the former celebrates the interprovincial variation for which the latter tries to correct. While the provincial governments themselves cannot dismantle federal equalization programs, political support for those programs could erode among the federal electorates of the wealthier provinces (Alberta, British Columbia, and Ontario combined contain 59 percent of Canada's population). As 'one top provincial official' quoted by Giles Gherson notes, '[t]he whole subtext of [the August 1996] premiers' conference was the rich provinces saying, "We want to keep more of what we have; we want to keep our money at home."'[41] Thus, while lip service to equalization may continue, the long-term tension between equalization and decentralization must be recognized.

Intergovernmentalism

If Canada is to move beyond its current crisis to a renewed federation, some mechanism must aid the transition. In this respect, considerable support exists for the creation of a constituent assembly to initiate discussion on changes to the federation. Chevrier, for example, states that governments should not bear total responsibility for creating policies of renewal and that constituent assemblies would allow Canadians to express their ideas on reform.[42] The Canada West Foundation agrees, and supports constituent assemblies as a vehicle for directly involving Canadians in the reform process.[43] (The Foundation also proposes a Reconfederation Council that would operate at arm's length from the federal and provincial governments in drawing up proposals for consideration by both.) In a similar vein, David Kilgour promotes a constitutional convention, made up of 100 representatives from across the country, to propose a new constitution capable of winning general approval.[44] Allan Tupper acknowledges a new 'constitutional culture' that demands citizen participation and refuses to entrust constitutional discussions to elites.[45]

There is, however, a basic problem with the constituent assembly route: there is no guarantee that such assemblies would be constrained by the modest objectives of incremental change. Constituent assemblies are more likely than conventional bodies such as First Ministers' Conferences to promote fundamental or radical reform, if only because they are less dominated by incumbents. Indeed, constituent assemblies are by their very nature incompatible with, even hostile to, incremental reform. It is not surprising, therefore, to encounter proposals that seek to contain the reform process within more conventional channels. The public may have rejected intergovernmentalism in the wake of the Meech Lake and Charlottetown Accords, but faith in intergovernmentalism remains the guiding light for the incremental strategy.

This shift to intergovernmentalism is startling when one considers that 'only four years ago people were saying they did not want the fate of the country left in the hands of "the elites".'[46] Evidence of the withering of the populist impulse is provided in a recent column by Gordon Gibson, long one of the most articulate populist voices in Western Canada. On the occasion of the August 1996 Premiers' Conference, Gibson advanced a theme that would have warmed the hearts of the architects of the Meech Lake Accord:

If Canada should be reinvented, and the forces for change say the time is now, why should the premiers be our agents? Because they are our last, best hope in this great game....

There is always another tide, and in the long run Canada will do well, be it one country or five. But there is pain in the shallows, so why not seize this tide? Say a quiet prayer for our provincial captains.[47]

What is particularly important to note about the stress on intergovernmentalism is the emphasis on a strengthened *permanent* role for intergovernmental bodies in the management of the federal state. The general direction of reform proposals is to move the control of public policy from legislative bodies to new intergovernmental institutions and their bureaucratic extensions. This approach would give provincial governments enhanced leverage over the management of national affairs, but it would also further remove that management from legislative and electoral accountability. Thus, despite the public's distaste for the Meech Lake and Charlottetown experiences, the integrating thread of the incremental reform strategy is to be found in the (growing) reliance on intergovernmentalism.

For example, the recommendations of the Confederation 2000 conference propose using the First Ministers' Conference to make and enforce decisions reached between federal and provincial governments. They propose cochairing these conferences and giving the prime minister or provincial co-chair the right to call a meeting at any time.[48] The Group of 22 would use a Council of First Ministers to establish guidelines for the federal spending power, create a clearer definition of powers and responsibilities, and manage government interdependence.[49] Smith proposes a permanent Council of the Federation, comprising ministerial representatives from the federal and provincial governments, that would act as a ratifying body with respect to federal legislation that might impinge on the provincial domain.[50] Courchene proposes a new federal-provincial agency or group of ministers who would report to the first ministers.[51]

This move to increased intergovernmentalism is widely portrayed as both inevitable and positive. Canada, it is sometimes suggested, lags behind other federal states in the creation of institutional mechanisms to handle mutual interdependence. Chevrier therefore suggests that a Council of First Ministers would 'spearhead a renewed sense of purpose and direction, make the system more accountable and give Canadians a better understanding of the inner workings of their federation.'[52] We would argue, however, that a greater reliance on intergovernmental mechanisms would erode the role of legislative assemblies and weaken democratic accountability. The result – if not necessarily the intention – of intergovernmentalism is to remove government from public forums rather than to increase democratic participation. We would also argue, although Chevrier disagrees, that intergovernmentalism will increase the complexity of government by imposing a new layer of government forums and their attendant bureaucracies between the federal and provincial governments.

Despite such concerns, there is no question that a greater reliance on intergovernmentalism forms one of the two principal anchors for the incremental strategy. Decentralization forms the other. What is interesting to note, however, is that some tension exists between the two. If intergovernmentalism is taken too far, if it includes decision rules that can force compliance on dissenting provinces, then intergovernmentalism may constitute a new variant of centralism that could negate the policy flexibility associated with decentralization. Thus, the gains accruing to the provinces through decentralization could be lost to new intergovernmental agreements and councils. It is not surprising, therefore, that strong proponents of decentralization like Premier Klein are uneasy about having compliance mechanisms attached to intergovernmental councils or agreements. But without compliance mechanisms, intergovernmentalism may prove to be a hollow shell rather than an effective means of governance for the next century.

Public Support

As experience has shown, a consensus among political elites and constitutional aficionados should not be confused with one that would withstand popular ratification. It is useful, therefore, to check briefly the fit between the emergent elite consensus outlined above and the disposition of public opinion. Though the incremental strategy relies on intergovernmental mechanisms and is designed to avoid popular ratification, public opinion may still exercise some degree of constraint through conventional electoral processes.

Survey findings support the incremental strategy in a number of ways. First, they show relatively high levels of public discontent with the state of the federation, thereby demonstrating, at least implicitly, an appetite for change.[53] Second, they show support for the principle of decentralization, provided that decentralization is symmetrical.[54] Third, they show a great deal of opposition outside Quebec to the big-ticket constitutional issues – the recognition of Quebec as a distinct society, the more general recognition of duality, and a constitutional veto for Quebec.[55] Given this opposition, the prospects for progress beyond modest incremental change appear slight; thus, the appeal of an incremental response to the national unity crisis is increased.

The disposition of public opinion takes us back to one of the most compelling attractions of the incremental strategy: the illusion that the reform agenda is not simply Quebec's agenda, or the agenda of Quebec federalists in that province's protracted family dispute. As Lysiane Gagnon explains,

[a]bove all, this massive decentralization... would not be Quebec-driven. Each province would have an equal chance of acquiring more powers. There would be no cries of 'Me too!', no hostility, no Quebec-bashing.[56]

Thus, the current federalist agenda in Quebec, like the initial Meech Lake agenda before it, has been universalized to all provinces. Perhaps the only difference this time around is that the provincial governments, and particularly their *electorates*, are in a more receptive mood.

Path Dependency on Prior Constitutional Negotiations

It should not be surprising that the incremental strategy builds on what has been accomplished in the past; this is, after all, the essence of incrementalism. However, current incrementalism builds on the *failures* of the past. Although the Meech Lake and Charlottetown Accords were unsuccessful, their content continues to shape the agenda for incremental reform. The 'substance of Meech' lies at the core of many reform proposals,[57] and the specifics of decentralization reflect the Charlottetown Accord. In this critical respect, the incremental strategy is path dependent on past failures. Yet, while many components of past failures are faithfully carried forward, the reform strategy has changed. Mega-packages have been broken up into more bite-sized pieces, and priority is given to those changes, such as decentralization, that can be accomplished without formal constitutional change. Of perhaps greatest importance, the intrastate reform of parliamentary institutions has been largely discarded in the incremental strategy.

Quebec's status as a distinct society with respect to federal legislation and program administration has now won parliamentary recognition, and the federal government is actively pursuing constitutional recognition. Thus, a key component of the Meech Lake and Charlottetown Accords remains in play, complicating the incremental strategy. Many supporters of incrementalism hope that extensive decentralization will suffice to preserve Canadian unity, that within a sufficiently decentralized federal state, the Quebec National Assembly will have all the powers it needs to preserve a distinct society. This view is certainly the one advanced by the western premiers. However, the federal government, the Quebec Liberal Party, and the federal Progressive Conservatives have opted for asymmetrical symbolic recognition. Success with this latter option requires that public opinion outside Quebec be finessed: only if the popular ratification of constitutional amendments can be circumvented does it stand a chance. While it is not apparent how this circumvention can be achieved, the amending process is more malleable than the framers of the *Constitution Act, 1982* could ever have imagined. The Liberal government may argue that its inevitable win in the next federal election will be a proxy endorsement of distinct society, and therefore that the western premiers should set aside their provincial requirements for democratic participation in constitutional amendment. Western premiers are already under strong federal pressure to disengage their support for constitutional change from legislative commitments to democratic participation.

Other elements of the Meech Lake Accord also live on, albeit in somewhat different forms. Perhaps because parliamentary modification of the amending formula has already secured a Quebec veto on future constitutional change, there are few advocates of a more rigorously entrenched constitutional veto. The more immediate problem is that the new amending procedures make it difficult to secure *any* further constitutional amendments, including the constitutional recognition of Quebec as a distinct society. As Thomas Flanagan points out, the five-region veto effectively freezes the constitutional status quo.[58] As a consequence, the federal government may have locked itself into a nonconstitutional strategy. In modifying the amending formula by parliamentary decree, Ottawa has left itself only the incremental card to play.

There is broad support for constraints on the federal spending power such as those embedded in the two accords. Indeed, contemporary proposals for constraints on the federal spending power go well beyond Meech. For example, the Group of 22 advocates that shared-cost programs in areas of provincial jurisdiction should be implemented only with the consent of seven provinces representing 50 percent of the population. Further, provinces should be able to opt out with fair compensation.[59] Participants in the Confederation 2000 conference stated that, in any new national program in areas of provincial jurisdiction, nonparticipating provinces should be entitled to unconditional compensation that 'should not be contingent on the establishment of any comparable initiatives.'[60] The decentralizing thrust of the contemporary reform agenda carries with it the understanding that the federal spending power will be constrained and will not be the source of financial penalties for nonparticipating provinces.

The Meech proposal that Quebec be given greater control over immigration policy has been carried forward to the contemporary reform agenda and generalized to all provinces. A communiqué from the 1996 Western Premiers' Conference, for instance, stated that the western provinces would be willing to enter into negotiations with the federal government for greater provincial control over immigration.[61] Given that most proposals for decentralization entail increased provincial responsibility for training and for labor market adjustment, and given that immigration policy is an essential component of labor market adjustment, it is perhaps inevitable that immigration will shift more and more into provincial hands. Moreover, if decentralization shifts the center of gravity of citizen loyalties to provincial communities, it will only be appropriate that new Canadians are assimilated through those communities.

The Meech proposal for provincial government input into the nomination of Quebec judges to the Supreme Court of Canada opened up a much broader discussion of national political institutions, the treatment of which was expanded in the Charlottetown Accord to include Senate reform, representation in the House of Commons, and aboriginal self-government. This debate continues today; thus, for example, the Group of 22 advocates that the centerpiece of institutional reform should be the method of selection for Supreme Court justices, senators, and directors of the Bank of Canada. The prime minister, the Group suggests, should make appointments from lists of nominees prepared by the provincial governments, with the current rules on regional and provincial compositions remaining the same.[62] The Reform Party still proposes modernizing central institutions to allow for greater democracy in the Senate and the House of Commons, although it has backed away from full-blown Triple-E Senate reform. Informal changes to the Senate, it suggests, should be modeled on the 1989 Alberta Senate selection process, and members of Parliament should be given greater freedom of action.[63] Smith proposes the popular election of senators, the constitutionalization of the Supreme Court, and the ratification of appointments to the board of the Bank of Canada by a Council of the Federation.[64]

However, it is hard to escape the conclusion that most of the proposals for intrastate reform have been brought forward only to prop up the central pillars of decentralization and intergovernmentalism. They are peripheral and disposable elements of the incremental strategy; moreover, they tend to generate implacable opposition in Quebec. It is inconceivable, for instance, that Quebec will buy into the West's Senate reform agenda unless decentralization proceeds so far that the federal government comes to lack any relevance to Quebec. Thus, while the institutional reform debate lingers on, the new political reality is that substantive reform apart from decentralization and its accompanying institutional apparatus is not in the cards. Even aboriginal concerns have largely fallen from the agenda as the federal government pursues an incremental approach to the implementation of aboriginal self-government and as the political leadership of the aboriginal community continues to fragment.

Following its expansion between Meech Lake and Charlottetown, the reform agenda is now in a period of contraction. While in many ways the renewal debate is path dependent on the previous (and unsuccessful) accords, much of what has been carried forward is either window dressing (rhetorical appeals to strengthen the economic union) or unattainable (the constitutional recognition of Quebec as a distinct society). The hard core of the current reform agenda is extensive symmetrical decentralization.

Tipping the Playing Field

It would be foolish to presume that the outcomes of any renewal process will be independent of the process adopted. How Canada gets from here to there determines where 'there' will be, if for no other reason than that the choice of process determines what actors and interests will be brought to the table.

For example, the reform agenda expanded considerably as the constitutional process changed between the Meech Lake Accord and the October 1992 constitutional referendum. Aboriginal peoples were not at the Meech Lake table; not surprisingly, the resulting accord did not mention their concerns and aspirations. However, aboriginal peoples were centrally involved in the negotiations leading up to the Charlottetown Accord; again not surprisingly, their concerns and aspirations were woven into virtually every section of that accord. Thus, as Canada moved from the initial first-ministerial endorsement of the Meech Lake Accord to the national referendum on the Charlottetown Accord, the number of constitutional players expanded progressively and dramatically. The mythical '11 white men in suits' gave way to the almost 15 million Canadians who voted in the 1992 referendum. And the expansion was not just in numbers. As the concerns of first ministers began to be supplemented by those of aboriginal leaders, interest groups, and public forums, the constitutional agenda grew and became increasingly complex.

Incrementalism is designed to roll back the 1987–92 expansion and to limit the range of interests and players engaged in the renewal process. An incremental renewal strategy is first and foremost an intergovernmental strategy that removes debate from public forums and lodges it within intergovernmental forums such as premiers' conferences. Such a strategy maximizes the influence of governments and minimizes the influence of nongovernmental players and interests. It also maximizes the influence of provincial and territorial governments, given their numerical dominance within the intergovernmental process. Thus incrementalism tips the playing field in favor of solutions based on decentralization and 'rebalancing.' A process in which provincial governments debate how best to counter the nationalist movement in Quebec could have no other outcome. To argue for incremental change is to argue for decentralization; to choose this process is also to choose its inevitable outcome.

Now, this conclusion may appear to give the provinces too much weight in the intergovernmental process and to assume that all provinces share an interest in greater decentralization. In the past, the federal government has been the major player in the intergovernmental process, and the *Constitution Act, 1982* offers ample proof that neither the provinces nor decentralization will necessarily carry the day. In the current environment, however, the federal government is not prepared to defend the center. Driven by fiscal constraints and by the need to provide a credible alternative to the nationalist vision in Quebec, and egged on by the business community (which assumes that decentralized government is necessarily smaller government), Ottawa is unlikely to apply the brakes to decentralization. It may do so further down the road if deficit-elimination targets are met and the sovereigntist threat recedes; but in the near term, the imperatives of a Quebec-driven national unity strategy offer little room in which to maneuver.

But will provincial governments that question the need for greater decentralization be able to provide an effective brake? If the federal government, Quebec, Ontario, Alberta, and British Columbia now support decentralization, will Manitoba, Saskatchewan, and the Atlantic provinces be able to argue effectively in intergovernmental forums for some restraint? While this possibility should not be dismissed out of hand, its prospects are remote.

Much of the past resistance to decentralization came from those provinces (with the notable exception of Quebec) that have been beneficiaries of equalization, and particularly of equalization that is indirectly derived from federal fiscal support for social programs. It was feared that decentralization would undercut the commitment of taxpayers in wealthier provinces to sustaining an equivalent level of public services in less well-to-do provinces. As noted above, this fear has not been laid to rest by the proponents of decentralization. The logic of decentralization requires weakening the constraints of national programs and emphasizing the importance of provincial communities at the expense of the national community. To suggest, then, that political support for equalization would not be threatened by decentralization is Pollyannish. If Canada becomes less relevant to the economic and social lives of taxpayers in

Alberta, British Columbia, and Ontario, if the locus of political life shifts more to the provinces, political support will be eroded. Though the spirit of decentralization will not redefine equalization as foreign aid, and equalization will not disappear as a feature of the Canadian federal state, current levels of equalization will be difficult to maintain. The issue, then, is whether an intergovernmental reform strategy will provide an effective opportunity for the supporters of equalization to make their case. While the outcome of the August 1996 Premiers' Conference shows that the decentralization juggernaut can be slowed, it is not at all clear that it can be stopped.

Of course, it is still an open question whether a governmental strategy yoked to decentralization and intergovernmentalism will be successful. Success requires that the public be supportive of decentralization and deferential with respect to intergovernmentalism. While support for decentralization appears to be in place, deference toward intergovernmentalism cannot be assumed.[65] Success also depends on a limited reform agenda: the more limited the agenda, the less likely governments are to encounter demands for public input. Finally, it is essential to avoid the need for formal constitutional change; any move in that direction would be met, at least in the western provinces, with the demand for public hearings and popular ratification. If public participation cannot be shut down, then the incremental strategy itself may fail. All these requirements suggest real limits on incremental change, for curtailing public involvement will be difficult if major institutional or constitutional change is envisioned.

A potential wild card in the incremental deck is the upcoming federal election, in which the national unity issue may play a significant role. Even if that proves to be the case, however, alternatives to government-driven decentralization are unlikely to be brought into play. The Liberals, the Bloc Québécois, and the Progressive Conservatives will be battling for the soft nationalist vote in Quebec; therefore, the competing partisan visions will be sovereignty on the one hand and a combination of decentralization and constitutional recognition on the other. Outside Quebec, the three primary contenders all share a core commitment to decentralization. Only the New Democratic Party provides a potential alternative for Canadians who are wary of decentralization, but there is little indication at this time that the NDP will be a significant factor. If the current incremental strategy tips the playing field to the advantage of decentralization and intergovernmentalism, the upcoming federal election is unlikely to provide any adjustment.

Limits on Incremental Reform

An assessment of the incremental strategy must determine what the strategy's limits might be. Are there reforms that cannot be achieved incrementally? And are there *normative* limits that should be imposed on the incremental strategy? Should popular ratification be brought into play at some point in the renewal of the Canadian federal state?

The Empirical Question

As noted above, proposals for fundamental change are still to be found in the contemporary renewal debate. But can fundamental change be realized incrementally? The answer to that question is to be found in the avoidance of formal constitutional change – an avoidance that lies at the heart of the incremental strategy. If constitutional change is to be avoided, the symbolic recognition of duality cannot be woven into Canada's Constitution. If constitutional change is to be avoided, the types of institutional reform western Canadians traditionally advocate cannot be realized. Neither can the constitutional recognition of the right to aboriginal self-government be achieved. Put somewhat differently, incrementalism assumes that all parties will be satisfied in the short run with changes to the *practice* of Canadian federalism and that changes to the institutions, the Constitution, and symbolic projections are of secondary concern.

The limitations of an incremental strategy can be illustrated by the issue of Senate reform. If Canadians reject the possibility of fundamental institutional reform – reform that would necessitate formal constitutional amendment – can the Senate still be reformed through incremental measures? In part, Alberta's *Senatorial Selection Act*, which called for the public approval of any senatorial nominations, was an attempt to do so. Under the act, senators would still be appointed by the federal government, for to do otherwise would require formal constitutional change and was therefore beyond the reach of the Alberta legislature, but the act sought to ensure that future appointees would first have to be successful in a province-wide election.

The Alberta initiative tried to set Senate reform in motion, but it raised a host of problems. The elected or 'selected' senators would be in office until age 75 and would not, under the terms of the Alberta legislation, be subject to re-election or recall. Of greater importance, the Alberta legislation was designed to put into place an elected Senate without changing either the regional allocation of seats or the Senate's formal powers. Whether Albertans or Canadians at large would be well served by having elected senators who operate within the existing institutional environment was not clear.

This illustration shows how difficult it can be to reform institutions one step at a time. If senators are to be elected, the powers of the Senate and its relationship with the House of Commons become very important. If the power of senators and the role of the Senate are to change, as they inevitably would if senators were elected, the regional distribution of seats would also have to be reassessed. In short, incremental change to the Senate is difficult if not impossible to achieve; the various aspects of Senate reform must be considered as a package. While the Group of 22 suggests that incremental change, such as appointing senators from provincial lists, might destabilize the Senate over the long run and thus foster more fundamental change,[66] there is no evidence that anyone is prepared to start this particular ball rolling. The prime minister, for example, has ignored the existing Alberta legislation in recent appointments, and it is unlikely that any Quebec-based prime minister would initiate Senate reform in the face of inevitable nationalist opposition from his or her own province.

Adopting an incremental approach to the renewal of the federation effectively precludes Senate reform. It is, therefore, a strategic choice with significant implications. In this case it means that the long-standing, if not always intensely expressed, western Canadian desire for institutional reform is a nonstarter. The incremental approach is inherently hostile to traditional western Canadian aspirations unless those aspirations can be folded into decentralization.

But here is the nub of the issue: extensive decentralization may well preclude the need for institutional reforms such as Senate reform. The quest for more effective regional representation within parliamentary institutions is important only so long as those institutions themselves are important. However, if they become less important as a consequence of decentralization, the quality of regional representation also becomes less important. Moreover, if the federal government eschews unilateral action in such areas as social policy, environmental protection, and national economic management, and instead opts for joint federal-provincial management, then MPs and senators become less relevant. The important forms of regional representation will be intergovernmental. In a federal system designed to reflect a decentralized intergovernmental partnership, regional representation at the center fades as an issue. The critical issues of institutional design become, first, the decision rules that govern intergovernmental agreements and, second, the extent to which those rules reflect the competing principles of duality, provincial equality, and representation by population.

The incremental strategy, then, does not fail to meet long-standing western Canadian aspirations; instead, it rechannels those aspirations through decentralization. The traditional western vision of effective regional representation within a strong national government is displaced by a vision of strong provincial governments competing effectively with other provincial governments in loosely structured intergovernmental alliances. The key players are the western premiers and their executives. As MPs and senators drift even more toward the margins of regional political life, how well or how poorly they perform will become less and less of an issue. This new western vision certainly enjoys governmental support, and public support may also be in place.

The same logic can be applied to nationalist aspirations in Quebec, for at some point decentralization shades into the *de facto* recognition of Quebec sovereignty. The less Ottawa does and the more it acts with provincial consent, the more sovereignty passes to the provinces. Though this approach does not provide the symbolic recognition of duality that the distinct society clause would provide, it does provide instrumental recognition. The practical issues, then, are: How far must decentralization be pushed in order to draw Quebec nationalists back into the Canadian fold? And what will remain of the Canadian fold when decentralization has been pushed to that point? Also at issue is the willingness of Quebec nationalists, particularly those within the provincial Liberal Party, to trade off symbolic recognition for decentralized powers.

There is an interesting irony here. To the extent that decentralization and intergovernmentalism dominate the new federal state, Quebec may drop its traditional opposition to Senate reform. However, for the same reasons that would cause Quebec to drop its opposition, Senate reform would be irrelevant to the West. Quebec has nothing to fear, and the West nothing to gain, from a reformed Senate in a federal state characterized by extensive decentralization and intergovernmentalism.

The basic point is that decentralization is an alternative to, not a facilitator of, institutional and constitutional reform. Such issues as Quebec's constitutional recognition as a distinct society or Senate reform will remain in play only if the country's embrace of decentralization is halfhearted. Those who oppose decentralization are thus trapped in their own box: they will have to tackle both the recognition of duality, which cannot be sold in the West, and the reform of central institutions, for which a significant Quebec audience cannot be found. It is little wonder, then, that the incremental strategy exerts such strong appeal.

Many Canadians would argue that they have been well served either by the status quo or by slow evolutionary change. The fact that incrementalism constrains change may thus be seen as a plus rather than as a minus. Not surprisingly, incrementalism is the preferred strategy of incumbent governments, sitting politicians, and the business community that has played an influential role in national political life. In the context of Alan Cairns's distinction between constitutional insiders and outsiders,[67] incrementalism is emphatically an insider strategy.

The Normative Question

The normative question relates to the degree to which the nature of the Canadian federal state *should* be changed without public consultation, debate, and ratification. Here we return to an earlier point: an important feature of the incremental strategy is that it precludes public consultation, debate, and ratification. The incrementalists' goal is to use conventional political means to bridge divisions in the federation, to allow Canada to move forward while still accommodating Canadians' diverse views about their federation. Proponents of this approach argue that subjecting incremental changes to a national referendum, or insisting on immediate formal constitutional change, may further divide rather than renew Canada. In this context, Peter Russell subtitled his recent book (*Constitutional Odyssey*) 'Can Canadians Become a Sovereign People?'[68] The answer, it seems, is no, or at least not so long as Canada relies on incremental change lodged within intergovernmental forums and processes.

If the incremental strategy does privilege particular outcomes, it may be appropriate to allow Canadians to express their views about such outcomes. If incrementalism is a process that leads to an identifiable end point, Canadians should be able to pass judgment on that end point. But the incremental nature of reform may be used as an excuse to avoid public debate or ratification. Any one reform will seem too minor to submit to a national referendum. Yet the accumulated changes favored by the incremental strategy will transform Canada into a very different political community. Perhaps, then, this new community should be identified and held up for public debate, not simply imposed one small step at a time.

Here we suspect that western Canadian governments and their electorates will play a critical role. There is little appetite in Ottawa for national referendums, and in any event the recent changes to the amending formula delegate parliamentary approval to provincial legislatures.[69] Quebec has been emphatically democratic in its approach to constitutional decisionmaking, but only with respect to the provincial community. Nowhere but in the West does one find a legislative commitment to popular ratification of constitutional amendment. This commitment may bring the public back into play, although only in the West – and only if formal changes to the Constitution are proposed. Incremental change brought about through intergovernmental negotiation and agreement is still possible without public involvement. There is, then, no guarantee that the public will be brought back into an increasingly intergovernmental renewal process.

The Sequence of Reform

The queuing of steps has long been an important issue in Canadian constitutional politics, and it remains so within the context of the incremental strategy. The sequence of steps envisioned by the proponents of incrementalism may turn out to be much shorter than is often suggested. As each step is taken, the incentives for taking additional steps are reduced for those whose interests have been addressed. Western Canadians, for example, recognize that a strategy for addressing Quebec's concerns first and their concerns second is a strategy for addressing Quebec's concerns alone. Once Quebec's concerns had been addressed, Quebecers would have no incentive to address western aspirations; indeed, the first stage of reform might give the Quebec government additional means by which to block those aspirations. (This has already happened with the recent creation of regional vetoes; the only intrastate reforms that can be pursued are those that can pass muster with the Quebec National Assembly.) Therefore, a strategy involving incremental steps may turn out to produce a very short dance. For western Canadians or aboriginal peoples to accept an incremental strategy would be a fool's game unless it were conceded from the outset that only those reforms consistent with political opinion in Quebec would be pursued.

In short, the incremental strategy provides an effective veto to the party whose interests are addressed first. Incrementalism is a means of redistributing political power so that those at the start of the sequence have the most power, while those at the end have the least. It is not surprising, therefore, that everyone wants to be first. Incrementalism is not a neutral strategy with respect to the distribution of spoils – to pretend otherwise is to misread the political dynamics of renewal. In a similar vein, it would be a mistake to assume, when assessing the first steps, that later steps will follow. The more realistic question to ask is whether Canadians will be better off if just the first step – in this case, extensive decentralization cast within a framework of intergovernmentalism – is taken. To assume that subsequent steps will necessarily follow would be risky indeed.

The pace of incremental reform will ultimately depend on the federal government; the provinces can urge, but only Ottawa can act. Under most circumstances, one would not expect the federal government to be in any rush to hand over program responsibility to the provinces and to accept provincial constraints on its own authority. However, there is nothing normal about Canada's current circumstances. The electoral strength of the Parti Québécois and continuing public support for the sovereignty option provide great leverage for proponents of decentralization inside and outside Quebec. The alliance of soft nationalists in Quebec with the Ontario and Alberta governments will be difficult for the federal government to resist, even if it were inclined to do so. Unfortunately, there is little evidence that the federal government either wants to resist or has arguments in place on which resistance might be based. Apart from a rhetorical and largely empty (at least financially) commitment to medicare, the federal government has left itself no principled ground on which to stand.

Incremental Change and the New Canadian Vision

The incremental strategy is more than a series of small, disjointed steps. Embedded within the strategy lies a new vision of Canada that has been pulled into focus by the Ontario government and the report prepared for that government by Courchene. The report recommends that the provinces assume sole responsibility for designing and delivering health, welfare, and education services, including the enforcement of national standards in those spheres. It also calls for a new intergovernmental partnership, one that would give provincial governments greater leverage on those responsibilities left in Ottawa's hands. In this vision, Ottawa's powers would be substantially curtailed and the federal government would be placed under the watchful eyes of its provincial counterparts. Finally, the new vision is symmetrical in design, recognizing the constitutional equality of the provinces, but asymmetrical in result. Differences among provinces will increase and, incrementalists hope, Quebec will find enough flexibility and political space to defuse the quest for full sovereignty.

The combination of decentralization and intergovernmental partnership that is so central to this vision has interesting implications for democratic government. On the one hand, it would bring government 'closer to the people.' (Provincial and federal governments may in fact differ less in how close they are to the people and more in which people they are close to.) It would also simplify the complex financial arrangements of Canadian federalism, which at present weaken democratic accountability. However, being 'close to the people' can be a mixed blessing. As democratic experience from the founding of the United States onward has shown, governments that are close to the people are sometimes (but not always) less attentive to human rights and more attentive to localized economic interests than are governments that remain more remote from the people. For this reason, Canada has opted for a judicial system that is remote from the people; judges are not elected but are instead appointed without definite term.

On the other hand, the combination of decentralization and intergovernmentalism would shrink the range of accountable, democratic government at the federal level. Decentralization would mean not only that Ottawa would do less, but also that what it would do would be accomplished through intergovernmental forums placed largely beyond the reach of electoral accountability. How, for example, could federal MPs be held accountable for programs and policies that were the product of intergovernmental agreements and that were policed through intergovernmental forums? And for the same reasons, how could provincial governments be held responsible or accountable? National programs or standards entrusted to intergovernmental management would be beyond the control of any one provincial government – unless, as Premier Klein envisions, such management had no powers of enforcement beyond moral suasion.

Extensive decentralization divorced from intergovernmentalism, decentralization that vests program control solely in individual provincial governments, has the virtue of retaining accountability. Indeed, the strict division of powers that accompanies extensive decentralization reinforces accountability by disentangling the two orders of government and by limiting the intrusion of the national government into provincial affairs.[70] Responsibility may shift from Parliament to provincial legislatures, but it need be neither lost nor diluted in the process. However, the marriage of decentralization and intergovernmentalism is a retreat from open democratic government. It moves political power behind the closed doors of intergovernmental forums: elected assemblies do less, and the executive arm of government does more. In this case, the promise of 'bringing government closer to the people' is illusory, for the conduct of government comes to reside in those forums most removed from democratic participation and accountability. Thus, the most striking feature of the new vision of Canada embedded within the incremental strategy is its promotion of intergovernmentalism and its aversion to open legislative government. The new vision is a direct refutation of the populist impulse in Canadian politics.

But is this really a *new* vision? Certainly the call for greater decentralization is not new, and a heavy reliance on executive federalism has been characteristic of the Canadian federal state for at least a generation. Nor, for that matter, is the retreat from democratic responsibility new; one could argue that support for executive federalism and suspicion toward legislative politics are deeply embedded within Canadian political culture, or at least within the elite culture. The vision is new, however, in a number of respects.

First, the groups that opposed decentralization in the past have drifted to the wings of the political stage. The New Democrats lack a significant federal presence; the Reform Party has picked up the torch of decentralization just as it has all but abandoned the quest for institutional reform; and both the federal Liberals and the federal Progressive Conservatives are committed to a Quebec platform premised on decentralization. As Jeffrey Simpson observes, 'the perceived need to buy off secession with a transfer of power animates all federal political parties to varying degrees.'[71] As a consequence, there is no partisan voice left to speak for the center, and thus the center may not hold. The healthy tension Canada experienced in the past between centrifugal and centripetal forces has been lost in the battle for soft nationalist support in Quebec. Ironically, the most powerful voices one hears for the center today are those of the proponents of intergovernmentalism, who, in their own fashion, seek to strengthen the role played by central institutions, albeit intergovernmental institutions, in designing and implementing public policy.

Second, this vision reduces the role of the federal government to the point where it represents a qualitative change. Clearly, in the recommendations examined so far, the proponents of decentralization are not arguing that the federal government should become merely a headwaiter overseeing the work of the provincial premiers. But equally clearly, they *are* arguing that the federal government should have a reduced capacity for autonomous action. Ottawa, they maintain, should act in partnership with, or with the consent of, provincial governments. Few, unfortunately, offer clear suggestions on how to set up a workable process for determining whether or not provincial consent exists. If Canadians move to address this question, the issues of duality, provincial equality, and distinct society will undoubtedly rear their (not necessarily ugly) heads again. Nonetheless, a federal government capable of only limited autonomous action is clearly an essential part of the new vision. In the blunt words of the Group of 22 report, 'partnership means an end to unilateralism.'[72]

These new federal arrangements would make Canadian government more, rather than less, cumbersome and complex. The federal and provincial governments would remain in place, albeit weakened in the former case and strengthened in the latter. However, a new layer of intergovernmental institutions and agreements would be added, along with the extensive bureaucracies that these additions would spawn. Councils of ministers would be wedged between the federal and provincial governments, accountable to neither but charged with designing public policy. If decentralization is combined with intergovernmentalism to police national standards and constrain the federal government, the size and complexity of government will increase in lockstep.

This chain of reasoning takes us back to the incrementalists' emphasis on intergovernmentalism. While this approach is by no means a new feature of the Canadian federal state, it is being taken to new extremes by the proponents of incremental change and of the federal vision embedded within that strategy. They maintain that the consent needed by the federal government to act is not consent from the people, expressed through elected MPs, but rather merely the consent of provincial governments. If their strategy were to succeed, the operation of the federal government in Ottawa would boil down to a series of intergovernmental agreements. Elected federal politicians would still provide a negotiating mandate for representatives of the federal government, but the design and implementation of public policy would be the product of intergovernmental processes that were beyond the control of Parliament alone – and, for that matter, beyond the control of any single government. The insightful term used by Robert Mason Lee to describe this new approach is 'executive provincialism.'[73] Not incidentally, this model of government is compatible with the partnership model being advanced by nationalists in Quebec.

Third, the vision is also new in, or at least is given a new gloss by, being linked to globalization. Incrementalists argue – indeed, they assume – that the federal state *must* be decentralized if Canadians are to be competitive in the new global economy.[74] Curiously, however, Canada's major economic competitors have not embarked on extensive decentralization. In fact, economic success seems to be coupled with relatively strong national governments (albeit governments that themselves are constrained by new global realities) and with relatively centralized federations. Decentralization may be better designed to improve the provinces' position, rather than that of Canada, on the global stage. Thus, the new vision of Canada is one in which provinces increasingly go head to head in economic competition with international trading blocs or the massive economies of the United States, Japan, and China. As Simpson notes, however, there is an irony in this drive to decentralization:

It responds to a growing sense that people are losing control of their lives in the face of far-away government and impersonal corporations, and it demands more control for weaker provincial and state governments that in most cases are less capable of influencing the very outside forces people dislike.[75]

In some respects the new vision would result in Quebec's becoming increasingly uncoupled from the rest of Canada; the province's remaining links would run not through Parliament but through intergovernmental agreements with other provincial governments and perhaps, although not necessarily, with the federal government. In the latest Courchene model, for instance, the federal government would fade from the scene, and Quebec's intergovernmental ties with other provinces – and indeed the ties among those other provinces – would not differ in character from agreements among and between sovereign states. Simply put, the new vision would transfer effective sovereignty from Parliament, or from Parliament and the provincial legislatures combined, to the provinces alone. Thus, the incrementalists' solution to Canada's unity crisis is similar to that advanced by the nationalist movement in Quebec: both seek to remove any independent role for Parliament in the lives of Canadians. Ironically, the same strategy that is advanced by the former to save Canada is advanced by the latter to create an independent Quebec.

The catch for the nationalists, however, comes from the potential impact of the new provincialism on provincial sovereignty. If provincial sovereignty were recaptured from the federal government and then surrendered again to intergovernmental councils, Quebec nationalists would not necessarily be any further ahead. They might in fact lose ground unless intergovernmentalism were to provide for a distinct decisionmaking status for Quebec, something that does not seem to be in the cards. Hence the irony: the decentralization designed to keep Quebec in Canada could produce an intergovernmental morass within which Quebec sovereignty would be more fully compromised than ever.

Conclusions

The heavy reliance on intergovernmentalism found in the federal vision that is embedded within the incremental strategy is not alien to Canadian political practice. Furthermore, the incremental strategy's symmetrical approach and its avoidance of formal constitutional change will appeal to many Canadians and to their governments. It must also be kept in mind, as the proponents of decentralization are quick to point out, that national standards and the internal common market might be sustained through interprovincial cooperation: intergovernmentalism might replace the heavy hand of Ottawa. While this latter scenario must be seen not as a conclusion well anchored in Canadian political experience but as an article of faith, it is not an unreasonable one.

For the reasons outlined in this *Commentary*, the incremental strategy may be the only game in town – particularly so long as

- the reform debate remains a relatively muted concern of governments that is not subjected to wide-ranging public scrutiny; and
- the debate remains directed toward the next referendum in Quebec and is therefore tightly constrained by the options palatable to federalist forces in Quebec.

Nonetheless, or perhaps as a consequence, a number of important questions should be addressed before Canadians fully embrace the incremental strategy and its twin pillars, decentralization and intergovernmentalism.

First, does the incremental strategy offer a *stable* solution with respect to Quebec, one that takes Canada past the upcoming federal election and even past the next sovereignty referendum? Can symmetrical decentralization go far enough to derail the sovereignty movement? More important, can intergovernmentalism be structured in a way that provides effective political space for Quebec sovereignty? If the answer to any of these questions is no, Canada may not be heading for a stable situation. If the incremental strategy does not offer some reasonable assurance of keeping Quebec in Canada, its outcomes must be assessed on another criterion: as an appropriate blueprint for a Canada without Quebec. Failure to assess decentralization and intergovernmentalism against this criterion would leave the rest of Canada ill-prepared should Quebec nationalists decide that they are not prepared to submerge their province in new intergovernmental forums within which they might exercise less influence than they do in Parliament today.

Second, can the combination of decentralization and intergovernmentalism sustain citizenship ties between individual Canadians and their federal government? If such ties are increasingly mediated through intergovernmental forums and agreements, with federal representatives exercising less autonomous and accountable political authority, will Canadians come to see the federal government *and the national community for which it speaks* as less relevant for their lives? In that case, will there also be a weakening of citizen support for the principle of equalization, for the protection of mobility rights, or for the reduction of interprovincial trade barriers?

Third, does the *combination* of decentralization and intergovernmentalism produce a significant democratic deficit? Does it move decisionmaking to those forums least open to public participation, thereby diluting electoral accountability with forums that answer to no single electorate? If the answer to each of these question is yes, it might be wise to consider the advantages of decentralization without the encumbrances of intergovernmentalism. Maybe Premier Klein is right in arguing that decentralization should mean provincial control without the imposition of national standards. While this option would inevitably produce greater regional diversity, it would also maintain electoral accountability. If the destination of decentralization is government that is closer to the people, intergovernmentalism may be the wrong route to follow. A large dose of intergovernmentalism may be inevitable and essential in complex federal states, but intergovernmentalism must also be recognized as a new form of centralism that could potentially reduce democratic control while negating many of the advantages of decentralization.

Fourth, will the incremental strategy preclude rather than establish the preconditions for significant constitutional and institutional reform? If so, will the Canadian federal state be well equipped to handle the political challenges of the next century? The incremental strategy is likely to be an alternative to rather than a step toward intrastate reform. However, to assume that parliamentary institutions should remain untouched, that all Canada needs to do is impose an additional layer of intergovernmental institutions between the federal and provincial governments, seems unimaginative and premature.

Fifth, can a way be found to bring Canadians back into a renewal debate that is cast in incrementalist terms? If the renewal debate withdraws once again behind closed doors, if it becomes the fodder for intergovernmental discussions rather than public debate, there is some risk that the final product will face public repudiation should Canadians find the opportunity to express themselves.

Finally, will the incremental strategy enhance the political union? The answer to this last question depends on how one positions oneself on the contemporary political landscape. In many respects, incrementalism will reinforce more than threaten the status quo. It builds on constitutional principles rejected by the Canadian public but embraced as dogma by political elites; it enhances the influence of governments at the expense of citizens; and it retains federalist support in Quebec as the criterion against which the health of the Canadian political community is to be assessed. Some will equate these effects with enhancing the political union. However, those whose primary political identity is not to be found in provincial communities, who seek greater citizen leverage on Canada's constitutional evolution, and who desire to transcend rather than consolidate duality may be excused a good measure of skepticism. As in most situations, where one stands on incrementalism depends on where, and how comfortably, one sits.

None of this is to say that the products of the incremental strategy – decentralization and intergovernmentalism – are ill conceived or necessarily pernicious in their effects. Indeed, they may simply be inevitable. Nonetheless, the questions posed above should be addressed before Canada moves too far and too quickly down the incremental path. Incrementalism is more than a process. It is also a destination that must be held up to careful *public* debate before Canada has gone too far down the path to change direction.

NOTES

1 In a poll of 1,001 Quebec voters conducted by Groupe Léger & Léger between September 20 and 29, 1996, 49.4 percent of decided voters said they would vote 'yes' in a referendum on sovereignty, while 50.6 percent would vote 'no' (Richard Mackie, 'Quebecers want votes delayed,' *Globe and Mail* [Toronto], October 4, 1996, p. A1).

2 Peter H. Russell, *Constitutional Odyssey: Can Canadians Become a Sovereign People?* 2nd ed. (Toronto: University of Toronto Press, 1993).

3 This lack of confidence was symbolized at the June 1996 First Ministers' Conference

by Alberta Premier Ralph Klein's refusal to address constitutional matters behind closed doors. Klein's resolve on this point was not severely tested, but there is little doubt that his refusal captured the public mood.

4 'Disunity train,' *Calgary Herald*, August 23, 1996, p. A16.

5 Peter Leslie has aptly called this constitutional change 'by stealth.'

6 John Halstead, 'A Vision for Canada,' *Opinion* (Council for Canadian Unity) 4 (April 1996): 5.

7 Group of 22, *Making Canada Work Better* ([Toronto], May 1, 1996), p. 19.

8 'A case for the Constitution Act, 1867,' *Globe and Mail* (Toronto), August 20, 1996, p. A16.

9 The combination of provincial legislation and parliamentary modifications to the amending formula means that any attempt to constitutionally recognize Quebec as a distinct society must pass a provincial referendum in both Alberta and British Columbia; the 7/50 formula no longer applies. Referendums in the two western provinces are not in the cards.

10 Confederation 2000, *Today and Tomorrow: An Agenda for Action* (May 3–4, 1996), p. 6.

11 Jean Chevrier, 'What Commissions and Task Forces Have Said about Renewing Canada,' *The New Federation* 5 (July/August 1996): 13.

12 Thomas Courchene, for example, has proposed that concurrent powers be associated with provincial paramountcy (*In Praise of Renewed Federalism*, The Canada Round 2 [Toronto: C.D. Howe Institute, 1991], p. 89).

13 Reform Party of Canada, *Twenty Proposals for a New Confederation* (Calgary: Reform Party of Canada, 1996), p. 10.

14 Thomas J. Courchene, *ACCESS: A Convention on the Canadian Economic and Social Systems* (working paper prepared for the Ontario Ministry of Intergovernmental Affairs, August 1996), p. 18.

15 Quebec Premier Lucien Bouchard refused to participate in any such federal-provincial discussions, arguing that to do so 'would be a formal recognition by Quebec that the federal government is entitled to step in our jurisdiction on social programs' (Larry Johnsrude, 'Premiers will work with feds,' *Calgary Herald*, August 23, 1996, p. A1).

16 Courchene, *ACCESS*.

17 Edward Greenspon, 'Take charge, provinces urged,' *Globe and Mail* (Toronto), August 21, 1996, p. A3.

18 Melvin H. Smith, *The Renewal of the Federation: A British Columbia Perspective* (Victoria, May 1991), p. 93.

19 There is a close parallel here with recent changes in the amending formula; there is no need for formal constitutional amendment so long as Parliament commits itself not to act without specified forms of provincial consent.

20 John Richards, *Language Matters: Ensuring That the Sugar Not Dissolve in the Coffee*, C.D. Howe Institute Commentary 84 (Toronto: C.D. Howe Institute, October 1996).

21 Group of 22, *Making Canada Work Better*, p. 5.

22 Reform Party, *Twenty Proposals*, p. 6.

23 Barrie McKenna and Alan Freeman, 'Eight premiers endorse national securities commission,' *Globe and Mail* (Toronto), June 22, 1996, p. B4.

24 Ashley Geddes, 'ASE opposes national watchdog,' *Calgary Herald*, August 21, 1996, p. C1. The same article quotes Alberta Treasurer Jim Dinning as having said that a national commission that was not 'very, very responsive' to the needs of the Alberta market would be a 'non-starter.'

25 Geddes, 'ASE opposes national watchdog,' p. C8.

26 Canada, *Shaping Canada's Future Together: Proposals* (Ottawa: Supply and Services Canada, 1991), pp. 43–44.

27 Group of 22, *Making Canada Work Better*, p. 4. Internal barriers to trade continue to be identified as a problem.

28 Daniel Schwanen, *Drawing on Our Inner Strength: Canada's Economic Citizenship in an Era of Evolving Federalism*, C.D. Howe Commentary 82 (Toronto: C.D. Howe Institute, June 1996).

29 'Toward a true economic union,' *Globe and Mail* (Toronto), September 21, 1996, p. D6. Recent journalistic commentary on the AIT has been even less flattering. Andrew Coyne refers to it as a 'collective passing of wind in the direction of economic union that depends first, last and always on the goodwill of the selfsame governments that got us into this mess' ('Provincial barriers destroy Canadian nationhood,' *Calgary Herald*, September 19, 1996, p. A15). Giles Gherson observes that 'a ridiculously tortuous set of federally supervised interprovincial negotiations' produced an agreement 'riddled with loopholes, exemptions and exclusions' ('It's harder to sell goods to Manitoba than Montana,' Calgary Herald, September 13, 1996, p. A15).

30 Group of 22, *Making Canada Work Better*, p. 18.

31 Canada West Foundation, *Realizing Change '96–'97* (Calgary: Canada West Foundation, 1996), p. 4.

32 Claire Hoy, 'Hand social programs to provinces,' *Calgary Herald*, August 26, 1996, p. A8.

33 Edward Greenspon and Brian Laghi, 'Harris, Klein shake up federation,' *Globe and Mail* (Toronto), August 24, 1996, p. A4.

34 Robert Mason Lee, 'The plan to replace Momma Ottawa with executive provincialism,' *Globe and Mail* (Toronto), August 24, 1996, p. D2.

35 Ibid.

36 Confederation 2000, *Today and Tomorrow*, p. 16.

37 David V.J. Bell, 'Remaking Canada: The Role of the People,' *Canada Watch* 4 (April/May 1996): 82–83.

38 Ronald L. Watts, 'Canada in Question, Again,' *Queen's Quarterly* 99 (Winter 1992): 804.

39 Don Martin, 'Ontario report derails unity hopes,' *Calgary Herald*, August 11, 1996, p. A12.

40 Courchene, *ACCESS*, p. 5.

41 Giles Gherson, 'Canada drifts toward balkanization,' *Calgary Herald*, September 25, 1996, p. A14.

42 Chevrier, 'What Commissions and Task Forces Have Said,' p. 14.

43 Canada West Foundation, *Realizing Change*, p. 3.

44 David Kilgour, *Quebec Nationalism, Western Alienation and National Reconciliation*, Occasional Paper 7 (Plattsburgh, NY: State University of New York, Center for the Study of Canada, March 1996), p. 6.

45 Allan Tupper, 'Reflections on the 1995 Quebec Referendum: Problems and Possibilities,' *Constitutional Forum* 7 (Winter-Spring 1996): 30–32.

46 Mark Lisac, 'Nation heads for decentralization,' *Calgary Herald*, June 21, 1996, p. A18.

47 Gordon Gibson, 'Memo to the premiers: seize the day,' *Globe and Mail* (Toronto), August 20, 1996, p. A17.

48 Confederation 2000, *Today and Tomorrow*, pp. 12–13.

49 Group of 22, *Making Canada Work Better*, p. 15.

50 Smith, *Renewal*, pp. 88–89.

51 Courchene, *ACCESS*, p. 13.

52 Chevrier, 'What Commissions and Task Forces Have Said,' p. 13.

53 R. Gary Edwards and Jon Hughes, 'Increased Dissatisfaction with Direction of Country,' *The Gallup Poll* 56 (April 11, 1996): 1. Results based on 1,005 telephone interviews.

54 R. Gary Edwards and Jon Hughes, 'Citizens Queried on the Fundamental Nature of Canadian Union,' *The Gallup Poll* 55 (November 30, 1995): 1.

55 R. Gary Edwards and Jon Hughes, 'Canadians Weigh Constitutional Options,' *The Gallup Poll* 55 (November 27, 1995): 1.

56 Lysiane Gagnon, 'Courchene plan crumbled before the unity train arrived in Jasper,' *Globe and Mail* (Toronto), August 24, 1996, p. D3.

57 For example, see Group of 22, *Making Canada Work Better*; and André Burelle, 'A Renewed Canada to Which Quebec Could Say `Yes',' *Canada Opinion* 4 (February 1996).

58 Thomas Flanagan, 'Amending the Canadian Constitution: A Mathematical Analysis,' *Constitutional Forum* (Winter-Spring 1996): 101.

59 Group of 22, *Making Canada Work Better*, p. iv.

60 Confederation 2000, *Today and Tomorrow*, pp. 8–9.
61 Western Premiers' Conference, 'Rebalancing Roles and Responsibilities,' *Communiqué*, 1996, p. 1.
62 Group of 22, *Making Canada Work Better*, p. 12.
63 Reform Party, *Twenty Proposals*, p. 11.
64 Smith, *Renewal*, p. 92.
65 In many respects, the reform proposals advanced by the premiers in August 1996 were more radical than those embedded in the Meech Lake Accord, yet there was no public outcry about the closed nature of the premiers' meeting.
66 Group of 22, *Making Canada Work Better*, p. 13.
67 Alan C. Cairns, 'Citizens (Outsiders) and Governments (Insiders) in Constitution-Making: The Case of Meech Lake,' *Canadian Public Policy* 14 Supplement (September 1988): 139–140.
68 Russell, *Constitutional Odyssey*.
69 Although the new amending formula forbids Parliament to act without the consent of the five regions/ provinces specified in the formula, it does not require Parliament to act in the event of regional consent. However, Parliament would have difficulty refusing to do so, given that the intent of the recent parliamentary amendment was to place the moral weight of constitutional amendment in the hands of provincial legislatures.
70 Currently, if Parliament intrudes into the legislative domain of, say, Saskatchewan's Legislative Assembly, the federal government can be held accountable for its action only to the extent that the Saskatchewan electorate can determine the outcome of the federal election.
71 Jeffrey Simpson, 'Decentralization is the rage everywhere, despite its ironies,' *Globe and Mail* (Toronto), August 21, 1996, p. A18.
72 Group of 22, *Making Canada Work Better*, p. 4. The Group refers here to unilateralism by either the federal government or a provincial government. If the capacity of provincial governments to act in a unilateral fashion is also to be constrained, the benefits of decentralization will be lost to a new form of intergovernmental centralism.
73 Lee, 'The plan.'
74 For example, see Courchene, *ACCESS*, p. 4.
75 Simpson, 'Decentralization.'

Language Matters: Ensuring that the Sugar Not Dissolve in the Coffee

JOHN RICHARDS

Canada poses a conundrum. It is a prosperous peaceful country that by and large respects human rights and has a good (if far from perfect) set of social programs. Relative to those of most countries on the globe, its political and economic problems are trivial. Yet Canada ranks high among countries likely to fall apart. That probability is higher now than at any time in its history since Joseph Howe was elected premier of Nova Scotia in 1868 with a mandate to pull his province out of the young and fragile Dominion.

How to explain this riddle? At the core of any satisfactory answer, I argue, is the perfectly reasonable anxiety of the Québécois[1] over survival of French as the lingua franca within their province (see Box 1). Given the powerful processes leading to intergenerational assimilation of non-English speakers in North America – including francophones outside Quebec – the Québécois want provincial legislation to promote French and, to some extent, to limit the use of English.

Their *Charte de la langue française* (Charter of the French Language), most often still called Bill 101 although it was enacted in 1977, has done the job. It has strengthened the status of French as the working language in the province, preserved Montreal as a predominantly francophone metropolis, and confirmed that French remain the dominant language in the school system. Bill 101 has been controversial but necessary.

Unfortunately, the Canadian political elite has not found a way to provide for the political legitimacy of Bill 101. In debating this matter, the principal protagonists over the past quarter-century have been the provincial Parti Québé-cois and the Ottawa Liberals. On occasion one or the other has endorsed a cooperative *beau risque*, but in general both have pursued noncooperative strategies. The former have argued that nothing short of Quebec sovereignty is adequate to protect language and culture; the latter have insisted on

Box 1   Like Sugar in the Coffee

The title of this *Commentary* comes from an image used by Greg Marchildon, Saskatchewan deputy minister of intergovernmental affairs, in the preface to an important compromise proposal (discussed further below). Marchildon briefly describes the fate of his *pure laine* family, which migrated from Quebec to Ontario following the *Patriotes* rebellion of 1837. In the early twentieth century, his branch came west to Saskatchewan. 'Those members of my paternal family who stayed within the protective womb of their community or moved back to Quebec have remained resolutely francophone, but those who moved to other parts of Canada assimilated within one generation.' Central to any cooperative outcome, Marchildon suggests, is the simple idea that English-speaking Canadians pursue a strategy offering a credible guarantee to Québécois that they 'not dissolve like the proverbial lump of sugar in an English cup of coffee.'*

* Greg Marchildon, 'An Attempt to Reconcile the Irreconcilable,' *Inroads* 5 (1996): 99, 101.

pan-Canadian bilingualism as a feasible substitute for language protection legislated by Quebec City.

The policy conclusion of this *Commentary* is straightforward: if the federation is to survive intact, a necessary reform is an explicit compromise on the language dossier that, among other provisions, accords a robust general authority to Quebec to legislate in this domain.

Despite the importance of language laws in Canada, the authority of either Ottawa or the provinces to legislate on this matter presently rests on constitutional quicksand. As one historian summarizes, '[t]here is no general authority to enact legislation with respect to language.'[2] The preferable option is, I suggest, an amendment to the Constitution to grant Quebec explicit jurisdiction over the public use of language, subject to the existing set of minority language services in both Quebec and the rest of Canada (ROC) and to the maintenance of bilingualism within federal institutions.

In outline, I proceed as follows. In the first section, I survey data on language use in Canada and the basic idea of language as a form of human capital with major external effects. Then I introduce three alternative principles upon which to base language policy and review the stark conflict between Ottawa's preference for individual choice between the two official languages and Quebec

City's insistence on a formal federal-provincial division of powers. I also provide some history. The third section deals briefly with the controversial matter of commercial signs, which illustrates the conflicts between Bill 101 and the Canadian Charter of Rights and Freedoms. In the fourth section, I introduce three tactical options and make the case for explicit provincial jurisdiction over language. I conclude by speculating on the practical implications such a reform would have for Canada.

Why Language Matters

A large portion of the human brain is given over to acquiring and using language, which is perhaps the most important characteristic distinguishing human beings from all other species. Despite its immense importance, people generally think about their own language, like their health, only when it is threatened. English-speaking Canadians have few occasions to feel their language threatened. Hence, they tend to ignore language policy and to suspect that those who insist on the subject harbor an illiberal desire to suppress freedom of speech. Most do not understand what is required to preserve a small linguistic community in an industrial society with mass communication and significant migration.

Linguistically, Quebec is like Denmark, Finland, Hungary, Singapore, the cantons of Switzerland, and other small jurisdictions whose respective languages differ from the languages spoken by their large adjacent neighbor(s). Not coincidentally, linguistic boundaries in these cases roughly correspond to the relevant political boundaries. The languages of small linguistic communities do not remain as lingua francas unless buttressed by law.

Although not unusual internationally, Quebec is unique within the Western Hemisphere. The Québécois are the only linguistic community on this side of the globe to have simultaneously built a prosperous industrial society and avoided linguistic assimilation to one of the three dominant languages (English, Spanish, and Portuguese).[3] Marcel Côté, a prominent political consultant and a leading francophone federalist, nicely captures the linguistic reality lived by the Québécois:

Quebec is different, not only because a majority happen to speak a different language but because this language, being a minority language on the continent, provides a collective bonding. There is more to Quebec's distinctiveness than language and culture. There are all the other attributes of a people, resulting in a clear 'us and them.' The 'us' speak French, live in Quebec, share a common culture and, more importantly, have developed among themselves a high degree of social trust. Because of their language, Québécois are bound together like the Swedes, the Danes or the French.

The consequence, Côté explains,

is a 'social trust divide' along linguistic lines, between 'us' who speak French and 'them,' other Canadians who do not. At the end of the day, when everything else is accounted for, Québécois will trust each other for any collective decision more than they will trust non-Quebec Canadians.

The glue underlying social trust is the distinct common language. It determines whom we know, where we go to school, where we live, what we read, the news we listen to on TV, the particular college buddies we reunite with later in life. It provides the raw material for the comedians who ridicule our collective flaws, and for opinion makers who form the conventional wisdom of the day.

Language is a very powerful social definer.[4]

One of the sources of 'us-versus-them' divisions in Canadian public life is the country's vast size, which limits social exchange among Canadians living in different areas. A major role for our politicians is therefore to adjudicate the inevitable interregional conflicts. Similarly, Canadian politicians must adjudicate the inevitable conflicts that arise from diverging identities defined by language.

Not surprisingly, states that are both geographically large and multilingual are inherently hard to govern; unforeseen shocks can generate divisive social dynamics. In Canada's case, the linguistic division is exacerbated because the anglophone group is large and linguistically secure while the francophone group is relatively small and linguistically insecure. Approximately 6 million Québécois live in a continent of 300 million anglophones or immigrants whose children will become anglophones.

Below some population threshold, small linguistic communities cannot support the cultural industries (newspapers, publishers, theater, film, and television) that generate new 'linguistic goods.' They survive, if at all, in a truncated form, and over time they quite literally die off. A century ago, Yiddish was the vehicle for a vibrant North American culture of some 2.5 million European immigrants. But the relative attraction of English proved overwhelming for their children. Despite Jewish culture's emphasis on learning, the number of people speaking Yiddish has declined to the point at which its survival depends on small ultraorthodox communities. (Ruth Wisse compares the fate of Yiddish to that of French in Quebec.[5])

Above a threshold of, say, 4 million, linguistic communities can realize the scale economies required to support a lively cultural sector.[6] But small communities must bear a cost for linguistic distinctiveness. Parents individually and the state collectively must devote considerable resources to foreign-language

---

Box 2   Cultural Protectionism: An Analogue

An analogue to Quebec's linguistic protectionism that many Canadians in the ROC can appreciate is the promotion of autonomous Canadian culture in the context of a North American cultural mainstream dominated by the United States. The language barrier provides some protection to francophones against imported US cultural products. No such barrier protects English-Canadian cultural industries, and fear of US domination is common to many Canadians, particularly those with a strong involvement in Canadian culture.

---

instruction and to protection of the lingua franca. Most professionals must become proficiently bi- or multilingual in order to be as productive as their unilingual colleagues who live in large linguistic communities. And inevitably, a high proportion of the community's linguistic goods is consumed in translation (consider the Finns) or borrowed from larger communities with the same language (Geneva from France, Singapore from Hong Kong and China).

From the perspective of a large, secure community, linguistic protection may appear a Canute-like exercise in resisting the inevitable. From the perspective of a small, more precarious community, however, cultural/linguistic survival is something worth paying for. One of the most robust of political propositions is that, wherever small linguistic communities are territorially compact and can exercise political power, they rank cultural/linguistic survival above most other collective goals.

Take two examples. Over the past decade, it has been uncertain whether or not the Georgians would remain within the Russian empire and whether or not the Danes would join the European Union. In neither case has the debate included any discussion of abandoning protection for their respective languages. These communities may engage in economic free trade and even political union; they do not engage in linguistic free trade.

French in Canada Today

It is useful at this point to summarize the recent trends of language use in Canada and to briefly address the economics of language as a form of human capital.

Linguistic Trends
Such is the political importance of language in Canada that the Canadian cen-

sus, the Quebec government, and academics exhaustively analyze the distribution of language communities, French-English bilingualism, and rates of language retention. There is general agreement on four basic points.

1. *Within Quebec, French has retained its status as the overwhelmingly dominant language.* The census uses two concepts to measure the linguistic distribution of Canadians: *mother tongue* and *home language* (see Box 3 for definitions). If the latter is the same as the former, language is being retained; if not, linguistic transfer has taken place.

By both measures, the proportion of Quebec francophones has fluctuated little since 1931 (see Table 1). In 1991, it was roughly five out of six, both in terms of mother tongue and of home language. Because of the high birth rate among the Québécois before World War II, the province's population share increased between 1931 and 1951; because of a subsequent, precipitate decline in the birth rate and rising net outmigration, its share has declined since 1951.

The distribution of nonfrancophones with-in Quebec has not been stable. The proportion of anglophones has declined, especially since 1971; many anglophones have left the province, and relatively few moved there. Simultaneously, the number of *allophones* (see Box 3) has increased. In 1951, Quebec was much more homogeneously French-English than the ROC. The proportion of allophones in that year's census was only a quarter of the corresponding ROC statistic. By 1991, Quebec was becoming more like the rest of the country in this respect; the proportion of allophones had more than doubled to nearly half the corresponding ROC statistic.

2. *Outside Quebec, French is declining as a language of use.* With the exception of the bilingual belts of eastern Ontario and Acadia, regions adjacent to Quebec, French is not intergenerationally surviving as a home language. In terms of mother tongue, the proportion of francophones in the ROC was down to less than 5 percent in 1991, and in terms of home language, it was only 3 percent. Table 2 flips the point of view, documenting the geographic distribution of language communities, rather than the linguistic distribution of those within geographic regions. Measured by mother tongue, six out of seven French-speaking Canadians were living in Quebec by 1991. Measured by home language, the geographic concentration of francophones in 1991 was even greater: nine out of ten lived in Quebec.

The tables here do not disaggregate the geographic distribution of language communities beyond Quebec and the ROC. It is worth noting, however, the importance of physical proximity to Quebec among non-Quebec francophones. As of 1991, 77 percent of mother-tongue francophones outside Quebec lived in

---

Box 3   Some Canadian Language Terms Defined

Canadian analysts of language employ the following terms with quite exact definitions.

- A person's *home language* is the language spoken most often at home by that person at the time of the census. In 1991, Statistics Canada aggregated responses into eight mutually exclusive categories: (1) English; (2) French; (3) nonofficial language; (4) English and French; (5) English and nonofficial language; (6) French and nonofficial language; (7) English, French, and nonofficial language; (8) nonofficial languages. Note that definitions and data presentation have changed slightly between censuses. The 1971 census did not record use of multiple languages, and the earliest data on home language date from that census. Earlier censuses collected data only on mother tongue.
- A person's *mother tongue* is the first language learned at home in childhood and still understood by that person at the time of the census. Statistics Canada aggregates responses into the same eight categories as for home language.
- *Knowledge of a language* refers to the ability to conduct a conversation in it. It does not imply full written and oral fluency, or that it is a home language.
- *Rate of French-language retention* is defined for 1991 as the proportion of those whose mother tongue is French and who use French *or* French plus other languages (one of which is almost always English) as their home language(s). The results from 1971 and 1991 are not exactly comparable; multiple language responses were not recorded in the 1971 census, so the retention rate for that year refers solely to the ratio of those whose mother tongue is French and who use French only as their home language.
- Canada's *official languages* are French and English.
- *Nonofficial languages* are all languages other than French and English.
- An *allophone* is an individual whose mother tongue is not an official language.

---

either New Brunswick or Ontario, and fully 85 percent of home-language francophones outside Quebec lived there.[7]

Another way to assess the intergenerational survival of a linguistic community is to measure the proportion of those who, having learned a language as infants, still use it at home as adults. Table 3 reports the rate of French-language

Table 1
Distribution of Population in Regions of Canada, by Mother Tongue and Home Language, 1931–91

	French	English	Other	Share of Canadian Population
	(percent)			
By Mother Tongue				
Quebec				
1931	79.7	15.0	5.3	27.7
1951	82.5	13.8	3.7	29.0
1971	80.7	13.1	6.2	27.9
1991	82.2	9.7	8.1	25.2
Rest of Canada				
1931	7.2	73.1	19.7	72.3
1951	7.2	77.6	15.2	71.0
1971	6.0	78.4	15.6	72.1
1991	4.8	77.7	17.5	74.8
Canada				
1931	27.3	57.0	15.7	
1951	29.0	59.1	11.9	
1971	26.9	60.1	13.0	
1991	24.3	60.4	15.3	
By Home Language, 1991				
Quebec	83.0	11.2	5.8	
Rest of Canada	3.2	87.6	9.3	
Canada	23.3	68.3	8.4	

Notes: For definitions, see Box 3. Some rows may not add to 100 percent because of rounding.
Sources: For 1931 to 1971: Marc Termote, 'L'évolution démolinguistique du Québec et du Canada,' in Quebec, Commission on the Political and Constitutional Future of Quebec [Bélanger-Campeau Commission], *Éléments d'analyse institutionnelle, juridique et démolinguistique pertinents à la révision du statut politique et constitutionnel du Québec* [Background papers]. vol. 2 (Quebec 1991). For 1991: Canada, Statistics Canada, *Language Retention and Transfer, 1991*, Cat. 94-319 (Ottawa, 1993); Quebec, *Le français langue commune: enjeu de la société québécoise*, Report of the Interministerial Committee on the Situation of the French Language (Quebec: Ministère de la Culture et des Communications, 1996), p. 272.

Table 2
Distribution of Population in Language Communities, by Regions of Canada, 1931–91

	Quebec	Rest of Canada
	(percent)	
By Mother Tongue		
French		
1931	80.9	19.1
1971	84.0	16.0
1991	85.1	14.9
English		
1931	7.3	92.7
1971	6.1	93.9
1991	3.8	96.2
By Home Language, 1991		
French	89.9	10.1
English	4.1	95.9
Other	17.5	82.5

Note: For definitions, see Box 3.
Sources: For 1931 to 1971: Marc Termote, 'L'évolution démolinguistique du Québec et du Canada,' in Quebec, Commission on the Political and Constitutional Future of Quebec [Bélanger-Campeau Commission], Éléments d'analyse institutionnelle, juridique et démolinguistique pertinents à la révision du statut politique et constitutionnel du Québec [Background papers]. vol. 2 (Quebec 1991). For 1991: Canada, Statistics Canada, *Language Retention and Transfer, 1991*, Cat. 94-319 (Ottawa, 1993).

retention among Canadians for whom French is the mother tongue. (The home-language data for this calculation were not available for years before 1971; hence, that is the first year of the table.) Within Quebec, retention is nearly 100 percent, and it rose marginally between 1971 and 1991. Among New Brunswick francophones, retention is also high, but notice that roughly one in ten Acadians have abandoned their mother tongue.

Elsewhere in the ROC, the evidence is grim. In Ontario, French-language retention declined between 1971 and 1991 from 70 percent to 59 percent. (The retention rates reported here are, of course, averages for entire provinces. The rate for the bilingual belt of eastern Ontario is higher than elsewhere in the province.)

For the nine jurisdictions (seven provinces and two territories) beyond

Table 3
Rate of French-Language Retention, by Region and Province, 1971 and 1991

	1971	1991
	(percent)	
Newfoundland	56.5	45.0
Prince Edward Island	56.8	53.1
Nova Scotia	65.9	58.3
New Brunswick	91.2	90.3
Quebec	98.4	98.8
Ontario	69.7	59.1
Manitoba	62.8	49.7
Saskatchewan	47.6	32.4
Alberta	45.9	35.2
British Columbia	26.4	26.7
Yukon	25.6	45.7
Northwest Territories	46.6	45.7
Rest of Canada	70.2	64.7
Rest of Canada, less Ontario and New Brunswick	51.3	40.8
Canada	93.8	93.8

Note: For a definition of French-language retention, see Box 3.
Sources: Author's calculations from census data in Canada, Statistics Canada, *Population: Statistics on Language Retention and Transfer*, Cat. 92-776 (SP-6) (Ottawa, 1975), and idem, Language Retention and Transfer, 1991, Cat. 94-319 (Ottawa, 1993).

Quebec and the provinces adjacent to it, the retention rate fell over these two decades from 51 percent to 41 percent. Despite the support provided to official language minorities, in these nine jurisdictions only two out of five mother-tongue francophones speak French at home.

3. *French has a weak attraction for allophones, even within Quebec.* Outside Quebec, a trivially small percentage of allophone immigrants transfer their linguistic loyalties from their native tongue to French.[8] Even within Quebec, English has a stronger attraction than French (and one can guess it would be even stronger in the absence of restrictive provincial legislation). In Table 4, which is restricted to Quebec, English as measured by home use consistently exceeds English as measured by mother tongue. Most of the explanation for the gap must be allophones transferring to English.

Table 4
Distribution of Population in Regions of Quebec, by Mother Tongue
and Home Language, 1971–91

	French	English	Other
	(percent)		
By Mother Tongue			
Island of Montreal			
1971	61.2	23.7	15.1
1991	56.8	20.6	22.6
Montreal metropolitan area			
1951	64.9	26.5	8.6
1971	66.3	21.7	12.0
1991	68.5	15.7	15.8
All Quebec			
1951	82.5	13.8	3.7
1971	80.7	13.1	6.2
1991	82.2	9.7	8.1
By Home Language			
Island of Montreal			
1971	61.2	27.4	11.4
1991	58.5	25.7	15.9
Montreal metropolitan area			
1971	66.3	24.9	8.8
1991	69.4	19.3	11.3
All Quebec			
1971	82.5	12.7	4.8
1991	83.0	11.2	5.8

Notes: Some rows may not add to 100 percent because of rounding.
For definitions, see Box 3.
Source: Quebec, *Le français langue commune: enjeu de la société québécoise*, Report of the Interministerial Committee on the Situation of the French Language (Quebec: Ministère de la Culture et des Communications, 1996), pp. 271–272.

Table 5 concerns the less stringent, but useful, linguistic measure known as *knowledge of a language* (see Box 3 for a definition). By this measure, the relative position of French among allophones has improved since 1971. In that year, the proportion of allophones who knew only French was less than half the proportion of those who knew only English. By 1991, the position of French among allophones had improved; the proportion knowing only French had risen and the proportion knowing only English had fallen such that the former was in fact slightly higher than the latter. The proportion that had become French-English bilingual had also risen, from a third to nearly a half.

Montreal has been Canada's principal linguistic battleground during the past half-century. As can be inferred from Table 4, the great majority of allophone immigrants to Quebec have chosen Montreal, which is also home to most Quebec anglophones. The world's second most important francophone city straddles the boundary between a small, unilingual French-speaking hinterland and an immensely larger, English-speaking one.

The linguistic composition of Montreal has fluctuated dramatically over the past 300 years. The city began as a francophone settlement in the seventeenth century; at times in the nineteenth century, it had an anglophone majority. In the second half of this century, the francophone share, defined in terms of mother tongue or home language, has been roughly two-thirds, rising slightly over time in metropolitan Montreal and falling slightly on the Island of Montreal (which includes the core city).

Although the shifts in the city's francophone share have been small, those among anglophones and allophones have been much larger. If we consider metropolitan Montreal in terms of residents' mother tongues, the proportion of anglophones declined by two-fifths, while the allophone share nearly doubled. The allophones' share now slightly exceeds the anglophone one.

4. *French-English bilingualism has risen in both Quebec and the ROC.* The proportion of Canadians with a knowledge of both official languages rose from 13 percent in 1971 to 16 per- cent in 1991. In Quebec, the increase was from 28 to 35 percent; in the ROC, from 7 to 10 percent (see Tables 5 and 6 for details).

In explaining this increase, federal bilingualism policy and Quebec's Bill 101 both play a part.

Ottawa's support for instruction in minority official languages played a central role in increasing French-English bilingualism in the ROC. But the most dramatic increase in French-English bilingualism occurred among Quebec anglophones. In 1971 only 37 percent of them could speak French; by 1991 a clear majority, 59 percent, could do so (see Table 5).

Two factors are important in explaining this jump in Quebec. First, the outmigration of unilingual anglophones increased the ratio. Second, by increasing the importance of French at work and in education, Quebec government policies raised the utility of a knowledge of French to those remaining in the province.

French-English bilingualism also rose in Quebec among francophones over the past two decades, thought not as dramatically as among anglophones.

Table 5
Knowledge of Official Languages in Quebec, 1971–91

Mother Tongue	French Only	French and English	English Only	Neither English nor French
		(percent)		
French				
1971	74.3	25.7	–	–
1981	71.2	28.7	–	–
1991	68.4	31.5	–	–
English				
1971	–	36.7	63.3	–
1981	–	53.4	44.8	–
1991	–	59.4	39.2	–
Other				
1971	14.0	33.1	35.8	17.0
1981	17.7	44.6	26.1	11.6
1991	22.0	46.6	20.9	10.4

Notes: Some rows may not add to 100 percent because of rounding. For definitions, see Box 3.
Source: Quebec, *Le français langue commune: enjeu de la société québécoise*, Report of the Interministerial Committee on the Situation of the French Language (Quebec: Minis-tère de la Culture et des Communications, 1996), p. 274.

Language as Human Capital

The most important generalization to be drawn from this survey data is the rele-vance of the economics of language. Language is a kind of human capital. Like any kind of capital, language skills are costly to acquire – in terms of time and effort – but generate important benefits.

The first benefit is simply the ability to read cultural artifacts. Consider that a small number of people today continue to learn dead languages such as ancient Greek, Old English, and Sanskrit in order to access literary and/or religious works in the original.

The second and most important benefit is the ability to communicate with others who also speak and write the language. This second benefit entails a major external effect (an impact on other people). When an allophone immi-grant to Montreal invests in learning French, for example, she generates a bene-fit for herself (ease of communication with her francophone neighbors); she also bestows a benefit on her neighbors (who can now communicate with her).

Table 6
French-English Bilingualism, 1971–91

	1971	1981	1991
		(percent)	
Quebec	27.6	32.4	35.4
Rest of Canada	6.9	9.2	9.9
Canada	13.4	15.3	16.3

Source: Canada, Statistics Canada, *The Daily*, Cat. 11-001E (Ottawa, January 12, 1993).

Conversely, if allophone immigrants transfer their linguistic loyalties to English, they lower the value of the human capital of francophones.

The third benefit is the ability to participate in the production and consumption of *new* cultural goods. Since many of these activities display scale economies – the unit cost of a newspaper, a literary novel, or a rock concert falls with a rise in the size of the potential market – this third benefit also generates external effects. When an immigrant transfers his linguistic loyalty to French, he increases the market for francophone cultural activities. Were the majority of Montrealers ever to cease being francophone, the Québécois would lose the one metropolitan center in North America large enough to generate a consistent supply of high-quality journalism, television, fiction, drama, popular music, and film in French.

Humans begin acquiring their first – and usually sole – language at an age when the primary struggle is learning to walk. Babies do not choose their language on the basis of a cost-benefit analysis. On the other hand, immigrants to a country whose lingua franca is other than their mother tongue do make such an analysis. The elderly may decide the costs of acquiring a new language are too high and choose to live out their lives in their mother tongue. Younger immigrants must consciously decide whether to learn a new language and, if the new country is multilingual, which new language (or languages) to learn.

For an allophone immigrant to Montreal, who may well choose to relocate within Canada, the net benefits of learning the language of 300 million North American anglophones usually outweigh the benefits of learning the language of the 6 million Québécois. In the absence of Quebec's language laws, the distribution of linguistic choices among allophone immigrants to Quebec would probably not have differed much in 1991 from what it was in 1971.

Allophone immigrants are not the only ones who make an implicit cost-benefit assessment concerning linguistic investment. So too do francophones who migrate beyond Quebec and the adjacent bilingual belts. The language-retention results of Table 3 indicate that, despite improvement in the French-language services associated with official bilingualism, the proportion of francophones using English at home increased between 1971 and 1991. Outside Quebec and the adjacent bilingual belts, the only province with stable retention rates over the past two decades was British Columbia, a province in which French has always been a minor immigrant language, less important in terms of home use than Cantonese or Punjabi.

Language Policy and Its Results

If multilingual states are to be politically stable over the long term, they must reach a social contract with respect to the public use of language. The experiences of India and Pakistan, two other multilingual countries to have emerged from the British Empire, offer a good contrast.

Following independence in 1947, regional movements demanding redefinition of internal boundaries and powers arose in both countries. Frequently, promotion of a regional language was the most prominent feature of these movements. In summary, the center in India accepted a formal division of jurisdiction over language policy; in Pakistan, it did not.[9] In other words, although Pakistan abjectly failed to realize linguistic accommodation, the Indian experience illustrates that reasonably peaceful accommodation is possible, even under conditions of extreme poverty.

Specifically, following mass protests, Prime Minister Jawaharlal Nehru reluctantly created a new state (Andhra Pradesh) in 1953 to accommodate Telegu speakers. Subsequently, a government committee recommended wholesale redefinition of internal borders based essentially on linguistic criteria, and by 1960 the reorganization was more or less accomplished.

At the level of national institutions, a compromise emerged in the 1960s. Hindi, the most important of the Indo-Aryan languages of the north, became the country's sole official language. But the elites of non-Hindi regions opposed expansion of the use of Hindi, preferring English for purposes of national and interregional communication. Accordingly, English survives as an associate official language, and 14 other languages have been designated as official regional languages.

In contrast to this reasonably peaceful accommodation is the breakup of Pakistan, a spectacular illustration of what can happen when a multilingual country fails to reach a social contract on language. The word *Bangladesh* means simply 'land of people who speak Bengali,' a language used by roughly 200 million people living around the delta of the Ganges. East and West Pakistan fractured for many reasons, including lack of physical contiguity, but the most important was the failure of the Urdu-speaking majority in the west to recognize that language was as important as religion in defining loyalties. Restriction of the use of Bengali was the catalyst for the formation in the 1950s of a nationalist movement in the area that became, in 1971, a sovereign country. (Incidentally, independence did not bring prosperity for Bangladesh. In the economic and political chaos following independence, this very poor region grew poorer yet.)

Different Principles for Language Policy

In broad strokes, multilingual states base their language policy on some combination of the three principles described below.

- *Assimilation to the dominant language(s)*. Government policy may explicitly favor the country's dominant language(s) and discourage all others. Canada seeks to assimilate allophone immigrants to one or other of the official languages – hence school instruction is almost exclusively in English or French. Allophone immigrants expect to make a linguistic investment and, in general, consider linguistic assimilation legitimate. Where they comprise a significant community, however, they often seek public resources to fund programs intended to preserve their linguistic heritage (for example, instruction in Ukrainian in the prairies, in Cantonese and Punjabi in Vancouver). And, as discussed more fully below, they have objected to Quebec language policy, which restricts their access to English.
- *Linguistic free trade*. Language policy may be the equivalent of a free trade agreement among a group of countries. The federal government has sought to establish a bilingual infrastructure such that there is no supply side impediment to individual choice between the two official languages. That is the principle underlying both the *Official Languages Act* and the Charter of Rights and Freedoms. Over the past generation, Ottawa has dramatically improved the language services available to official language minorities, extending more generous support to them and imposing more stringent bilingual requirements on the federal government. Ottawa has thereby attempted to make French-English bilingualism more attractive across the country.
- *A formal division of powers over use of language*. Many multilingual states, from India to Switzerland, explicitly allocate jurisdiction over the public use of language to regional governments with the full expectation that they will adopt divergent policies reflecting the interests of their majority language

communities. This principle enables local majorities to determine most aspects of language policy, but it still requires linguistic communities to effect a compromise applicable to national institutions, such as the central civil service and state-run media, and to define some set of minority language services. In designing language laws that promote French and, to some extent, limit English, the Quebec government has *de facto* insisted that this principle apply to Canada.

No country consistently bases policy on any one principle. As the summary of Indian language policy illustrates, life entails messy compromises. In Canada, however, the past generation has seen stark disagreement between Ottawa's preference for free trade between the two official languages and Quebec City's insistence on a division of power over language.

Quebec and Bill 101

Bill 101, the *Charte de la langue française*, was one of the first pieces of legislation enacted by the newly elected Parti Québécois (PQ) government in 1977 and has assumed great symbolic importance in Quebec. The preamble contains the following statement:

[T]he National Assembly of Quebec recognizes that Quebecers wish to see the quality and influence of the French language assured, and is resolved therefore to make of French the language of Government and the Law, as well as the normal and everyday language of work, instruction, communication, commerce and business; ...

[T]he National Assembly intends to pursue this objective in a spirit of fairness and open-mindedness, respectful of the institutions of the English-speaking community of Quebec, and respectful of the ethnic minorities, whose valuable contribution to the development of Quebec it readily acknowledges; ...

[T]he National Assembly of Quebec recognizes the right of the Amerinds and the Inuit of Quebec, the first inhabitants of this land, to perserve and develop their original language and culture.[10]

Bill 101 has been amended many times since 1977. Its major provisions can be summarized as follows:[11]

* French is the official language of Quebec. The Quebec government seeks to promote French as the *langue commune* (common language) understood and used in public by all Quebecers. This goal is deemed incompatible with institutional bilingualism, which accords equal individual rights to use of English and French within Quebec public institutions.[12]

- Major workplaces must be *francisé*. Quebec citizens should be able to work in French, and major enterprises (those with more than 50 employees) must ensure that it is feasible to do so throughout their establishments.
- Provincially licensed professionals must, as a condition of licensure, demonstrate a working knowledge of French.
- Immigrants coming to Quebec must send their children to French-language schools. Before the enactment of the Charter, Bill 101 restricted access to English-language schools to children of Canadian citizens who had themselves received their education *in Quebec* in English.
- As a symbol that French is the official language of the province, Bill 101 originally required that all commercial signs be unilingual French. This provision has been the subject of much controversy over the past two decades. As amended in 1993, current Quebec law permits, in most instances, bilingual commercial signs provided that French predominates.
- Provided the use of other languages does not adversely affect the integration of cultural minorities into a French-speaking society, the Quebec government respects the use of other languages. In particular, it recognizes 'that Quebec anglophones must preserve their language, their style of life and their culture.'[13] Furthermore, learning of additional languages is important. This applies to the promotion of English as a second language among francophones, as well as the learning of aboriginal languages.

Ottawa and the Charter

The federal Liberals interpreted the 'no' victory in Quebec's 1980 referendum as a mandate to introduce constitutional changes consistent with the classic liberal ideals of then-Prime Minister Pierre Trudeau.

As a politically engaged intellectual before his entry into politics, Trudeau had been as eloquent as any Québécois nationalist in his criticisms of the fate accorded francophones in Manitoba in the nineteenth century and the restrictions placed on the use of French in Ontario schools before World War I. Yet he aggressively opposed the nationalist Quebec response, which he characterized as ethnic nationalism.[14] Canada could not survive, he argued, if each linguistic community retreated into its respective solitude. The country required more people who were effectively French-English bilingual. His solution was official bilingualism: policies to enhance dramatically the services provided to official language minorities across the country.

Since the sovereignists decisively lost their 1980 referendum, it was not surprising that the victors chose the opportunity to redefine the political game in a manner corresponding to their vision of the country. The most important aspect of the 1982 constitutional reforms was the adoption of the Charter of Rights and Freedoms, whose linguistic provisions can be summarized as follows:

- 'English and French are the official languages of Canada and have equality of status ... in all institutions of the ... government of Canada' (section 16(1)).
- New Brunswick having opted in 1981 to become an officially bilingual province, its government is given the same linguistic obligations as Ottawa (sections 16–22). At various times, Ottawa has proposed that other provinces, in particular Ontario, follow New Brunswick's precedent.
- A set of primary and secondary education services in the minority language are defined as justiciable rights (section 23).[15] As it stands, the Charter defines somewhat asymmetric minority education rights in Quebec and the ROC. In Quebec, it allows anglophone Canadians who received their primary education in English in Canada to educate their children in English. In the ROC, francophone Canadians whose first language is French *and who learned it anywhere in the world* have the right to educate their children in French. If Quebec agrees at some future time, the more generous minority language right would extend to that province as well. The right is qualified by addition of a clause stipulating that it can only be exercised 'wherever in the province the number of children of citizens who have such a right is sufficient to warrant the provision to them out of public funds of minority language instruction' (section 23(3)(a)).

Notice that the Charter made no attempt to accommodate the historic compromise, dating from the days of New France (as discussed below), whereby Quebec could exercise local control over linguistic/cultural institutions. Ottawa's single important concession in constructing the Charter was to accept the demand of the four western premiers for a limited legislative override of Charter-based court decisions – section 33, the 'notwithstanding' clause.

Consider too that, in several cases (most significantly *Ford v. A.G. Quebec*, discussed below), the courts have given a broad interpretation to the Charter's section 2, which defines 'fundamental freedoms.' Their interpretation of the legal protection for 'freedom of thought, belief, opinion and expression' (section 2(b)) has become an important potential constraint on the ability of the Quebec government to define language policy.

Opposing Principles
The conflict between the principles underlying the Charter and Bill 101 is like a chronic disease. Much of the time it is in remission, but occasionally it erupts. It is potentially fatal. In summer 1996, conflict broke out, once again, over the use

of English on commercial signs. Aggressive English-rights groups demanded more use of English in anglophone regions of the province and condemned Bill 101 as an unwarranted constraint on their choice of language. The *purs et durs* militants within the PQ insisted on strengthening Bill 101 to restrict further the use of English.

It is well known in game theory that a prisoners' dilemma game of this sort can never end with *both* parties' gaining everything they want. Cooperate strategies can, however, lead to less-than-disastrous outcomes all around. In Canada's language game, however, both the federal and the Quebec governments have been obdurate about not cooperating.

It is always dangerous to speculate on motivations of individuals, but, with that caveat, I must say that it appears that the principals in this scenario – the senior members of the governments in Ottawa and Quebec City – are playing games with this current conflict. Each side remains committed to its noncooperative strategy and is adamantly uninterested in political compromise.

PQ cabinet members fully understand that linguistic anxiety among Québécois is an important source of their political support and have consistently stressed that the principle underlying federal language policy is incompatible with Bill 101. They interpret the failure of constitutional compromise over the past generation as proof that only in a sovereign Quebec will the French language and culture be secure.[16]

The PQ cabinet has a second tactical concern. Before any further referendum, it intends to eliminate the provincial deficit and hopes to increase the attraction of sovereignty among allophone and anglophone Quebecers. Accordingly, through time of writing (September 1996) it has resisted the demands of its militants to strengthen Bill 101 and further antagonize the linguistic minority.

Ottawa Liberals have also played games. In the current conflict, the prime minister has spoken in defense of linguistic minorities; he has made no parallel acknowledgment of the value of Bill 101 in preserving the francophone character of the province. Federally, Liberal electoral support lies disproportionately with official language minority and allophone communities across the country, groups that have benefited from the linguistic provisions of the Charter. Nonetheless, Ottawa is reluctant to see Quebec English-rights groups pursue their challenge to Bill 101, for fear that such activities will augment support for sovereignty among the Québécois.

The Historical Context

That matters have come to this standoff is not surprising given the record of British North America since 1760. This is not the place for a thorough survey of the role of language in Canadian history but a little history is unavoidable. My conclusion from what follows is that Québécois have been remarkably consistent ever since Wolfe defeated Montcalm on the Plains of Abraham. The majority have opted to cohabit with English-speaking Canadians provided – a major proviso – they could control institutions crucial to their cultural/linguistic survival.

Pre-Confederation
In a successful attempt to secure the neutrality of its French-speaking Roman Catholic colonists in the escalating conflict with its English-speaking Protestant colonists to the south, Britain enacted in 1774 the *Quebec Act*. This law gave legislative security to the seigneurial system of property rights and to the institutions of the Roman Catholic church.

Until the middle of the twentieth century, Quebec society inextricably mixed faith, culture, and language – a situation well summarized by the maxim *celui qui perd la langue perd la foi* (he who loses his language loses his faith). Attempts at cultural assimilation, most notably the 1840 *Act of Union*, were failures: in order to function, the legislature that act created required joint majorities from Upper Canada (Ontario) and Lower Canada (Quebec).

Confederation
Expectations for industrial growth and fear of the US army's turning north were central factors in persuading politicians in London and in the colonial capitals to envision Confederation in the 1860s. (Were they conducting their debates today, they would have called it 'rebalancing the empire.')

Nonetheless, cultural and linguistic differences mattered. Indeed, they were central to explaining why the Dominion became a federation rather than a unitary state, the latter being the preference of John A. Macdonald.[17] George-Étienne Cartier prevailed and, in addition to the list of exclusive provincial powers enumerated in section 92 of the *British North America Act* (BNA Act), Quebec and the other provinces obtained jurisdiction over education (section 93). On the basis of this compromise, the Quebec elite agreed that, since they had to enter into a marriage of convenience with someone, better to do so with the *Anglais* next door than the *Anglais* in London.

Some French Canadians hoped that Confederation would allow the expansion of francophone culture across Canada. They were quickly disabused of this ambition.

The one significant attempt to establish a French-speaking, Catholic presence beyond Quebec and the adjacent bilingual regions was in Manitoba under the leadership of Louis Riel. Perhaps it would have failed under the most auspicious of government policies. But the Protestant, English-speaking, white majority pursued the most inauspicious of policies with respect to the French-speaking, Roman Catholic Métis. There was no local equivalent to the *Quebec Act* to accommodate Métis landholding traditions and cultural institutions. The geometric grid homestead survey prevailed.

The situation culminated tragically with Riel's execution in 1885, but the ripple effect went on and on. In 1890, despite the terms of Confederation specified in the 1870 *Manitoba Act* (the imperial legislation whereby Manitoba become a province), anglophone Manitobans, now in the majority, enacted the *Official Languages Act*, stating that henceforth English would be the province's sole official language. These events in Manitoba poisoned official French-English relations in Canada for the next half century.

The episode had a late-twentieth-century postscript. Inspired by federal policies of official bilingualism across Canada, franco-Manitobans challenged the 1890 Manitoba legislation. In 1979, the Supreme Court ruled that the provincial statute was indeed unconstitutional because it violated the bilingual provisions of the 1870 *Manitoba Act*.

The challenge was quixotic, however. Beyond creating employment for bilingual lawyers and legal translators, who quickly brought many Manitoba statutes into French, the Supreme Court could do little. It had acted a century too late to have any real effect on the language spoken in the streets of Winnipeg.

The Quiet Revolution

Following the Quiet Revolution of the 1960s, the Québécois abandoned *la foi* but not *la langue*. Almost immediately, they demanded improved educational services and entered, en masse, into technical and business occupations formerly dominated by anglophones. Meanwhile, allophone immigrants became a much more significant component of Quebec society.

Two questions arose: How to assure the ability of the Québécois to work in French? How to induce the majority of immigrants to assimilate to French? The Quebec government having replaced the Roman Catholic church as the primary institution protecting and promoting francophone language and culture within the province, the answer lay in the National Assembly. Synthesizing a series of less-comprehensive laws, the Parti Québécois in 1977 enacted Bill 101, the *Charte de la langue française*.

Bill 101 proved extremely popular among the Québécois – and for good reason. It is the twentieth-century equivalent to the eighteenth-century *Quebec Act* and to sections 92 and 93 of the nineteenth-century BNA Act. All three acts limited to some extent individual freedom of access to anglophone institutions, in particular to English-language schools. The first two accorded special powers to the Roman Catholic church, the key collective institution of the Québécois before 1960; the third accorded analogous powers to the Quebec government. They were essentially pragmatic responses to the local franco-phone majority's demand for control over matters pertaining to cultural/linguistic survival.

The Next Step

By now it is obviouss that I favor a formal division of powers over language jurisdiction. So it is time to get to the heart of this *Commentary*, the pragmatic and moral arguments for accepting that path.

The Pragmatic Argument

The strictly pragmatic argument is that the Québécois' anxiety over linguistic survival is fundamental to explaining their support for sovereignty. If federal-ists, both inside and outside Quebec, want to maintain Canada intact, they must accord the Québécois a more credible guarantee than presently exists about the legitimacy of Bill 101.

Setting aside for the moment the moral question of whether a linguistic com-munity should exercise such powers, I maintain that Bill 101 or its equivalent was essential if Quebec was simultaneously to be a secular industrial society open to immigration and to remain francophone. In an environment of linguistic free trade, the great majority of allophones would have assimilated to English, and firms – especially those controlled by Anglo-Canadians – would probably have been slower to accommodate the much-enlarged cohorts of well-trained francophones.

The election of the PQ in 1976 prompted creation of the federal Task Force on Canadian Unity, jointly chaired by Jean-Luc Pepin (subsequently a federal Liberal cabinet minister) and John Robarts (a Conservative former Ontario pre-mier). On the subject of language policy, the Pepin-Robarts report accepted the pragmatic argument on behalf of a federal division of powers:

We support the efforts of the Quebec provincial government and of the people of Quebec to ensure the predominance of the French language and culture in that province. We believe that the people of Quebec must feel as confident and secure in the present and future potential of their language and culture as do the people of Ontario and the other English-speaking provinces. There can be nothing more damaging, in our view, to the cause of Canadian unity than the rejection of these aspirations of francophone Québécois by English-speaking Canadians. We believe that present constitutional arrangements which allow the provinces to adopt those laws and regulations which they deem suitable are appropriate to the present and emerging Canadian social context.[18]

(See the Appendix for the report's explicit language recommendation.)

Ironically, Bill 101 was probably a principal reason for the PQ's defeat in the 1980 referendum. Many moderate Québécois nationalists, reassured over linguistic matters, voted 'no.' Why incur the uncertainties of sovereignty if the prospects for a French Quebec were reasonably secure?

By the time of the 1995 referendum, however, Bill 101 was nearly two decades old. By and large, it had realized the goals of its authors, improving the status of French as the working language of the province and confirming Montreal as a primarily francophone metropolis. And so language figured less prominently in the 1995 public debate than it had in 1980.

Some analysts have concluded, therefore, that the Québécois' anxieties on this subject are no longer central in explaining why a majority of them voted 'yes.'[19] (Given the overwhelming support for the 'no' side among allophones and anglophones, the 49.4 percent overall 'yes' support implies that roughly 60 percent of the Québécois voted 'yes.')

Polling evidence suggests, however, that linguistic matters continue to explain a good deal – though not all – of Québécois attitudes.

Table 7 reports results from a mid-1995 province-wide survey of Québécois. In summary, more than half thought that the situation of French in Quebec would, to some extent, be better if the province were a sovereign country; about a third thought it would be the same; only 9 percent thought it would be worse. And a third thought the disappearance of French in Quebec was 'somewhat likely' or 'very likely' if the province remained in Canada.

The sponsors of this survey were a group of academics at the Université de Montréal, who used the results to conduct a statistical analysis of variables that materially affected the probability of voting 'yes' in the forthcoming referendum.[20] The three most significant variables in explaining the probability of a 'yes' vote were the extent to which a respondent (1) believed that Quebec would perform economically better if sovereign; (2) identified primarily as a Quebecer (rather than a Canadian); and (3) believed that the situation of French would improve were Quebec sovereign.[21] The Québécois may be mistaken in their beliefs about the effect of sovereignty on both economic prosperity and the fate of their language, but the undeniable conclusion is that language matters in explaining their choice between federalism and sovereignty.

Another way to judge the importance of language is to ask whether the Québécois are now prepared to relax provisions of Bill 101. Polling evidence reveals they are not.

Table 7
Québécois Assessments of Alternate Constitutional Outcomes

In your opinion, if Quebec became a sovereign country, would the situation of French in Quebec be ...

	(percent)
worse/much worse	3
worse/little worse	3
same/little worse	3
same/exactly the same	35
same/little better	12
better/little better	20
better/much better	24

If Quebec remains in Canada, do you think that the French language could one day disappear in Quebec?

	(percent)
very likely	13
somewhat likely	23
not very likely	30
not at all likely	34

Note: These are two questions from a survey conducted by the polling firm Léger & Léger in June 1995 on behalf of Martin, Nadeau and Blais, professors at the Université de Montréal. The reported results refer only to respondents whose first language of use at home is French. The total in this subset of respondents was 666.
Source: P. Martin, R. Nadeau, and A. Blais, 'Choosing a Nation: Risk, Uncertainty, and Political Choice in the Quebec Referendum on Sovereignty' (Paper presented at the annual meeting of the American Political Science Association, 1995).

The results reported in Table 8 are typical. A plurality (almost two out of five) of francophones support strengthening it; roughly a quarter favor leaving it as is; and fewer than a third want to relax the law. Conversely, among non-francophone Quebecers, only about one in ten accept Bill 101 as is; the great majority (almost three-quarters) favor relaxing it; and an inconsequential minority (4 percent) want to strengthen it.

The pragmatic argument is straightforward: Québécois want the anglophone majority in Canada to provide a credible guarantee that they, the Québécois, can legislate over their cultural/linguistic fate within Quebec.

Table 8
Attitudes toward Bill 101

For several years, different groups within Quebec society representing primarily anglophones and allophones have questioned certain aspects of Bill 101, while several groups
representing primarily francophones want to preserve Bill 101. According to you, should
we ...

	Leave It as Is	Relax It	Strengthen It	No Answer
		(percent)		
Total (n = 1,002)	20	40	33	7
Region				
Metropolitan Quebec (n = 300)	26	35	29	10
Metropolitan Montreal (n = 452)	20	44	27	9
Rest of province (n = 250)	20	34	41	5
Mother Tongue				
French only (n = 837)	23	32	39	6
English/other (n = 158)	11	72	4	13

Note: This survey was conducted by the Montreal polling firm SOM for *La Presse* and the
Société Radio Québec in February 1996, with a sample size of 1,002. The heading above
is a translation by the author of the actual French question posed, which read: '*Depuis plusieurs années, certains aspects de la Loi 101 sont remis en question par différents
groupes de la société québécoise regroupant surtout des anglophones et des allophones
alors que plusieurs groupes regroupant surtout des francophones veulent conserver la loi
101, selon vous devrait-on. ...*' The column headings are translations of the following
responses offered to respondents: '*garder telle quelle,*' '*l'assouplir,*' and '*la renforcer.*'
Source: D. Lessard, 'Les Québécois partagés en deux blocs sur tous changements à la
Loi 101,' *La Presse* (Montreal), March 2, 1996, p. A8.

The Moral Arguments

A formal division of powers over language jurisdiction does, however, lead to
more losses for linguistic minorities than a policy based on linguistic free trade.
This calculus poses some difficult questions. Why should our moral conclusion
about Bill 101 differ from that about the 1890 Manitoba *Official Languages
Act*? The English majority trampled on the long-established interests of the
Métis. Why should the Québécois be able to restrict the linguistic choices of the
long-established anglophone minority within Quebec? Why should allophone
immigrants be restricted in their choice between the two official languages if
they settle in Montreal but not if they settle in Toronto?

Setting aside the injustices perpetrated against aboriginals and African
slaves, Canada and the United States are democratic societies to which many

linguistic minorities have voluntarily migrated, and these immigrants have made their way intergenerationally without linguistic protection. Why should the Québécois have a unique ability to dictate the linguistic evolution of a region where they happen to be the majority?

These questions have three fundamental answers based respectively on ending discrimination, on the economics of language, and on the distinction between rights and interests.

Overcoming Past Discrimination

Knowledge of a society's elite language affords an individual an economic advantage independent of his or her qualifications. This advantage is both unjust and inefficient. Productive people fail to secure promotion, and aggregate economic performance suffers. (An extreme example was the disadvantage suffered by Russian speakers within their own country during the eighteenth and nineteenth centuries, when French was the preferred language of the nobility.)

Until the Quiet Revolution, English was the language of business within the province of Quebec. The current policy of *francisation* of the workplace has probably generated inefficiencies by, for example, accelerating the emigration of anglophone professionals. But it has also probably contributed positively to the partial economic catchup since 1960 by assuring appropriate private sector employment for the much-enlarged cohort of well-trained Québécois. By the simple measure of per capita gross domestic product (GDP),[22] Quebec has closed roughly 30 percent of the gap between its productivity and that of Ontario, the other heavily industrialized province in Canada.[23]

In considering any policy justified as affirmative action, one must weigh the benefit of advancing a disadvantaged group against the costs imposed on the advantaged. Using 1970 data, Daniel Shapiro and Morton Stelcner find evidence of discrimination in earnings: bilingual francophone males earned 9 percent less than comparably qualified bilingual anglophones. By 1980, that gap had fallen to 3 percent.[24] Some portion of this collapse in the earnings differential was the result of the lowering of linguistic barriers for the Québécois and some the result of the exodus of high-earning anglophones.

In addition to the costs imposed on anglophones, Quebec policymakers face the reality that English is the pre-eminent language of international business and of information technology. Although the Quebec government can subsidize translations and encourage the use of French in computer software,[25] if Quebec business is to be productive, the Québécois must accommodate English or suffer serious economic costs.

Like other small jurisdictions whose respective languages differ from those of large adjacent neighbors, Quebec faces tradeoffs between the value of protecting the local 'minor' language and the need to use 'major' languages in order to remain productive and to respect the interests of linguistic minorities. Workable compromises are feasible, as demonstrated by the combination of stable linguistic patterns with high per capita incomes in countries such as Switzerland and Denmark. Bill 101 has not imposed a language regime on Montreal that is more restrictive than that of Geneva, Zurich, or Copenhagen.

Two 'sins' are worth mention. One is the matter of commercial signs, which is discussed in detail below. The second is the composition of the Quebec civil service, which, over the past generation, has made inadequate attempts to hire among linguistic minorities. According to one study, the proportion of anglophones shrank from 7 percent in 1941 to 1 percent in 1991.[26] Over the past generation, Ottawa encouraged francophones to enter the federal civil service; as they should, linguistic minorities are now insisting that Quebec City do likewise.

The Economics of Language

One implication of the economics of language is the importance of external effects of any one group's language choices. Whenever effects on third parties are significant – whether in transactions generating pollution or in choice of language – free market transactions are potentially inefficient and unjust.

If language policy differs across jurisdictions, inevitably some linguistic communities find themselves on the wrong side of the linguistic border. This is particularly true when that border runs near a major metropolitan center, as is the case with Brussels, Mumbai (Bombay), and Montreal. To see the problem, imagine that, over the past generation, Quebec had embraced federal policies on official bilingualism and placed no barriers on allophone assimilation to English. In that case, Montreal might have preserved its status as the principal financial center of the country, and allophone immigrants might have settled there in as large numbers as in Toronto. But Montreal would by now be a majority anglophone city, and many young Québécois in Montreal would probably be transferring their linguistic loyalties to English. As happened to Yiddish culture in New York, Montreal francophone culture would be in sharp decline. Although that outcome might be acceptable to many Canadians, it would be a traumatic loss to most of the Québécois.

When faced with the economics of language, moral arguments about language policy cannot retreat into liberal discussions about free choice. Quebec – and Canada – faces a stark choice: which linguistic community has the better moral claim to pursue language policy conducive to its survival – the Québécois or Quebec anglophones?

Unambiguously, the answer must come down on the side of the Québécois. The first reason is utilitarian. The Québécois are the majority within Quebec, and fewer face linguistic losses with a policy that favors French than under an alternative, such as linguistic free trade, that favors English. (The implicit assumptions here are that this generation can legitimately decide the linguistic environment not only for themselves but also for their children and future generations, and that we should ignore the linguistic preferences of people living outside Quebec.)

The second reason is that, for better or worse, ever since the enactment of the *Quebec Act* in 1774, the basic rules of the Canadian political game have been that the francophone majority controls the institutions governing language and culture within New France. As already discussed, Bill 101 is a secular age's logical extension of section 93 of the BNA Act. Both the ROC and, to a lesser extent, Quebec are now multicultural societies, but, unlike the United States and France, we Canadians did not set up our political game on the basis of a revolutionary break with the past and an assertion of liberal individual rights. We formed an ambiguous entity, a dominion, on the basis of a pragmatic social compact among the contemporary elites of British North America.

Ironically, on matters constitutional, the Québécois have remained more British than other Canadians. They continue to adhere to ideas of classic federalism espoused by Victorian legal scholars such as A.V. Dicey and to Burkean concepts of parliamentary authority. The majority of Canadians in the ROC have fully embraced the Charter and, like Americans, are now prone to frame political problems in terms of justiciable rights (those to be determined by the courts). In Quebec, however, political dialogue continues to turn more on negotiations among encompassing interest groups; the Charter figures less prominently.[27]

To advocate linguistic free trade as a substitute for territorial allocation of jurisdiction over language is a form of moral evasion. Although elaboration of a set of minority language services is important, there simply is no escape from making explicit choices about winners and losers in linguistically contested regions. To insist on linguistic free trade as an adequate principle is itself a choice: it condemns minor linguistic communities to intergenerational extinction.

Legitimate Interests, Not Fundamental Rights
The rationale for entrenched legal rights is a negative theory of human liberty. The exercise of liberty requires protection of individuals from coercion by others, particularly when those others are using the power of the state. Entrenching rights renders them more visible and enhances the legitimacy of the courts in the ongoing task of preventing such coercion.

This argument is strongest when applied to *fundamental* rights, such as freedom of religion, of peaceful assembly, and of expression, and the common law tradition of *habeas corpus*. The argument for entrenching rights is much weaker when extended to embrace the positive role of the state. The danger then arises of judges' assuming powers that should remain in the hands of democratically elected legislators.

The state's positive role includes activities such as redistribution of income, the provision of primary/secondary education and social insurance, and the determination of the language(s) to use and promote in legislatures, in schools, and via the regulation of commercial activity. In very general terms, the rationale here is that individuals pursuing their own self-interest are prone to produce a result that the community collectively finds unacceptable. The government's involvement in these activities inevitably entails exercising discretion and making tradeoffs. Overall, government can advance the public interest, but it also creates losers. The appropriate mechanism for scrutinizing and correcting bad public decisions in this domain is via representation to legislators or via elections, not via the courts.

Where public use of language is a matter of contention, most nations do not treat the claims of linguistic communities as justiciable rights. When German speaking Swiss citizens migrate from Zurich to francophone Geneva, they enjoy much less generous public support for their mother tongue than do Genevans; migrating in the reverse direction, citizens of Geneva lose out. In the United States, Spanish speakers enjoy more services in their language in Miami than they do in Seattle. In both countries, language policy is at times a matter of political debate and language-based interest groups contend. In neither do citizens expect to resolve the matter via judicial decisions.

The Charter recognizes something of this argument by, for example, qualifying the exercise of minority language education rights to places where numbers warrant the provision of publicly funded instruction. Imagine the outcry if the Charter introduced analogous qualifiers to truly fundamental rights. For example, section 3 stipulates that every citizen has the right to vote in elections for Parliament and his or her legislative assembly; section 11 states that 'any person charged with an offence has the right ... to be tried within a reasonable time.' Quite rightly, the Charter does not qualify either of these sections by reference to the cost of government compliance.

In summary, it is entirely legitimate for linguistic minorities within Quebec to protest provisions of Bill 101 and to seek to expand minority English-language services available. An analogy is the ongoing debate in all societies over the extent to which government should use the tax-transfer mechanism to redistribute income away from the wealthy. But these political debates should be resolved democratically within the appropriate jurisdiction; they should not – with rare exceptions – be matters for the courts.

Bill 101 and the Charter: An Unstable Mixture

The simultaneous existence of Bill 101 and the Charter – manifestations of two divergent language policy principles – has proved an unstable mixture, one that threatens to explode the federation.

Commercial Signs and Rights

Most people (fortunately) do not spend their time perusing the implications of constitutional law. Thus, implications of the Charter for language policy were not widely appreciated until 1988, when the Supreme Court invoked it in a case that dealt with Bill 101's requirement for unilingual French commercial signs.

The PQ had defended the provision as a symbol of Montreal as a francophone city, arguing that it did not impose an undue burden. Montreal anglophones and allophones intensely disliked the provision; they were very public in saying so, and they regularly flouted the law. The advent of the Charter gave nonfrancophones an occasion to translate their opposition from the political to the legal arena.

The Supreme Court decision in this case, *Ford v. A.G. Quebec*, was complex.[28] It allowed, for example, that there were legitimate grounds for the Quebec government to legislate over language. But it ruled that Bill 101's requirement for unilingual French commercial signs was in violation of the Charter right to 'freedom of thought, belief, opinion and expression' (section 2(b)).

This very broad interpretation of fundamental rights raised the prospect for justiciation of minority language interests far beyond the matter of minority education services explicitly specified in the Charter, extended the concept of freedom of expression firmly into the domain of commercial language, and established a major precedent for future Charter-based challenges intended to limit the Quebec government's ability to regulate *francisation* at the workplace.

At the time, the Parti Québécois seemed a spent force. It had been soundly defeated in the 1985 provincial election, and the Meech Lake Accord appeared a done deal. But the *Ford* decision was a catalyst that immediately brought language concerns to the fore and resurrected the PQ's fortunes. With near unanimity Québécois opinion opposed the decision; anglophones both in Quebec and elsewhere supported it.

Then-Premier Robert Bourassa attempted a legislative compromise. He used the notwithstanding clause to enact Bill 178, which provided that outside signs remain unilingually French but inside signs could be bilingual. Québécois opinion was divided; some were willing to accept the compromise, while others wanted simply to reinstate the original unilingual sign provisions of Bill 101. Anglophone opinion, both inside and outside Quebec, was adamantly hostile to Bourassa's resort to the notwithstanding clause.

More than any other event, this controversy turned the country's opinion against the Meech Lake Accord and made it impossible to sustain sufficient public support in the ROC for its entrenchment.[29]

The View from Quebec

It is hard to exaggerate the destructive effect on French-English relations of the Supreme Court's broad interpretation of Charter rights with respect to language. Probably most Canadians in the ROC believe that the Court's decisions with respect to Bill 101 have been minor, largely justified limitations on the excesses of Quebec linguistic protectionism. But for most of the Québécois, the Charter now appears as an ill-defined threat to their language laws.

Even as convinced a federalist as Stéphane Dion has articulated this fear.

Since the [Supreme Court] judgments have been issued, one may think that the survival of [Quebec language] policies is secured. In fact, nothing is less certain. A Supreme Court might decide someday that denying the right of a new immigrant or of a francophone to go to an English school, when English speakers have such a right, is contrary to the *Charter of Rights*; the Court could invoke ... Article 15 prescribing legal equality of all citizens. Such a judgment may seem unlikely today, but who knows for the next generation? The French presence will decrease as a demographic reality outside Quebec, and Quebec's weight will decline in Canada. Therefore, it is necessary to solidify language protections now.[30]

To Dion,

[t]he key issue is and always will be language. The government of Quebec would better serve its citizens if it focused the negotiations on such a critical issue, instead of bringing on the table vague notions (distinct society) as it did during Meech Lake, or instead of demanding almost everything as it did after Meech Lake (the Allaire report).[31]

Dion has subsequently modified his position. At times, he has argued that entrenchment of a distinct society clause is sufficient to assure Quebec's cultural/linguistic interests; at other times, he has called for some as-yet-unspecified constitutional guarantee for the French language in Quebec.[32] The precise nature of Dion's position is irrelevant to the argument at hand. What is important is to recognize that, for many thoughtful Québécois, *a fortiori* for sovereignists, the Charter poses a significant threat to the historic compromise whereby they could effectively legislate over cultural/linguistic matters within their own province.[33]

Federalists want Québécois sovereignists to ask themselves, is independence worth the disruptions to social and economic relations that it would entail? Simultaneously, federalists must ask themselves hard questions about the non-cooperative strategy on language policy implicit in the Charter. Admittedly, the commercial sign provisions of Bill 101 are a blunt means to make a point, but surely they come under the category of bureaucratic annoyances. Are the costs imposed on Quebec allophones and anglophones by Bill 101 of such gravity that they should be elevated to the status of violations of fundamental, justiciable human rights? Does the ROC so mistrust the current generation of Québécois political leaders that the Supreme Court must assume wide responsibility for language policy within Quebec? At present, Quebec has no firm constitutional basis on which to legislate over the public use of language in the province. Is that reasonable, given the importance to most Québécois of language legislation?

What Is to Be Done?

On both sides of the Ottawa River pessimism prevails. Any constitutional compromise is now destined for failure, say many: constitutional reform is the equivalent of Sisyphus's futilely rolling his stone uphill.

In part, this pessimism merely reflects the depressing fact that *both* the PQ and the federal Liberals have pursued noncooperative strategies since 1976. It seems to me only realistic that Canadians in the ROC should at this stage explore options for dealing with possible Quebec secession. But if Canadians – anglophones and francophones – invest all their political energy in analyzing a future in separate beds, they should not be surprised if divorce is what comes to pass. (Indeed, if Gordon Gibson is correct in his predictions of a subsequent breakup of the ROC,[34] the children may also fall out among themselves.) Given that caveat, I see three tactical options:

• Ignore the language problem and rebalance the federation.
• Try, for a third time, to entrench a distinct society clause in the Constitution.
• Negotiate a more explicit federal/provincial division of jurisdiction over the public use of language.

Box 4   It's Not Only Language

In my emphasis on the centrality of language, I do not mean to imply that the unity problem is solely a function of language conflicts. Clarifying federal and provincial responsibilities for social and economic policy is equally important. The key reform needed here is probably for Ottawa to agree to vacate the field of worker training in favor of any province that wants to take it on, and for the provinces to pursue more aggressively active labor market policies designed to return the unemployed to work. The manifesto recently published by the Group of 22* provides a good synthesis of ingredients for a cooperative strategy pertaining to social and economic policy. Furthermore, these reforms can, as Gilles Paquet has eloquently put it, use the 'downtrodden administrative road' and thereby minimize traffic on the 'constitutional high road.'†

* Group of 22, *Making Canada Work Better* ([Toronto?], 1996).
† Gilles Paquet, 'The Downtrodden Administrative Route,' *Inroads* 5 (1996): 121.

As I have already said, I believe the preferable option is the third, explicit provincial language jurisdiction, but each is worth considering briefly.

Ignore the Language Problem

Some federalists, while sensitive to the importance of language matters, argue that the failure of the Meech Lake and Charlottetown Accords is proof of the impossibility of realizing any constitutional compromise on cultural/ linguistic matters. However important is language, ignore it, they say. Attempts to improve the probability of the federation's survival should pursue other directions, in particular administrative devolution of responsibilities from Ottawa to all provinces. Along this route lies a convergence of interests between the majority of the Québécois and many Canadians in the ROC.[35]

This first tactic falls under the category of letting sleeping dogs lie. It might succeed, and some decentralization is worth pursuing (see Box 4). But decentralization should be defended on its own grounds (in general, it allows for a more efficient provision of public goods and services). I doubt it can serve as an adequate substitute to explicitly tackling the problem of language. To the extent Stéphane Dion is correct in saying 'the key issue is and always will be language,'[36] the unresolved conflict between the principles underlying Bill 101 and the Charter will sooner or later frustrate the expectations of those who advocate decentralization as a sufficient solution to the unity problem.

Pragmatic federalists should not let this dog sleep. The refusal of most federalist politicians – in the ROC especially, but also in Quebec – to discuss jurisdiction over language amounts to what Michael Mandel calls the legalization of politics, an abdication by politicians in favor of judges.[37] The government in London achieved a workable social compact for New France in the 1770s; John A. Macdonald and George-Étienne Cartier worked one out for the new Dominion in the 1860s. Surely, Canadian politicians can do likewise in the 1990s.

Entrench a Distinct Society Clause

The essence of the second tactic is to insert a clause in the Constitution calling on the courts to interpret constitutional cases from the perspective that Quebec is distinct relative to the rest of Canada.

It was the tactic chosen by the Quebec Liberals and federal Conservatives as they attempted, between 1985 and 1992, to define a cooperative strategy, and many people have conducted a great deal of analysis in attempting to explain why it failed. Suffice it to say that, among the leading opponents of adding any distinct society clause to the Constitution were many leaders of the PQ and the federal Liberals. While out of power, both remained committed to their respective noncooperative strategies.

The two versions of a distinct society clause – from the Meech Lake and Charlottetown Accords – can be summarized as follows. (See the Appendix for the precise texts of both versions.) Both 'affirmed' the role of the Quebec government to 'preserve and promote the distinct society of Quebec.' The Meech Lake version called on the courts to interpret the constitution in a manner consistent with the idea that 'Quebec constitutes within Canada a distinct society.' It did not define distinct society; the Charlottetown version, however, defined it in terms of 'a French-speaking majority, a unique culture and a civil law tradition.'

The Meech Lake version noted 'the existence of French-speaking Canadians, centred in Quebec but also present elsewhere in Canada, and English-speaking Canadians, concentrated outside Quebec but also present in Quebec.' Furthermore, this version 'affirmed' the role of Ottawa, Quebec, and the other provinces to 'preserve' this 'fundamental characteristic of Canada.' The Charlottetown version imposed a more ambitious obligation on all Canadian governments: that they be 'committed to the vitality and development of official language minority communities throughout Canada.' Both versions insisted that the amendment entailed no transfer of powers between Ottawa and any province.

This tactic with regard to distinct society, which specified very little and relied on the good will of the principals, can be summarized as creative ambiguity. Ambiguity plays a useful role in diplomacy where the parties agree that the political process is likely to allow future mutually satisfactory negotiation of unspecified matters. In the mid-1980s, that was the prevailing sentiment among most Canadians. Even a superficial reading of the speeches and analyses of Meech Lake supporters reveals the conciliatory intent: the desire to put an end to the noncooperative strategies that had been pursued by the PQ and the federal Liberals.

Many federalists, in particular the leadership of the Quebec Liberal Party, remain committed to this tactic.[38] But, to import a baseball metaphor, the distinct society tactic has struck out twice, and in what has become a close game, the federalist coaches should send it to the benches. Its virtues have now become its vices. Because its meaning is so imprecise, both its supporters and its opponents have interpreted it to mean wildly divergent things.

Donald Savoie nicely summarizes the prevailing confusion:

Canadians simply do not understand what the term 'distinct society' actually means nor, were it enshrined in the constitution, what difference it would make to the running of our country. Furthermore, I doubt that anyone really knows for sure what it means. Some constitutional experts insist that the phrase is two symbolic words with negligible substantive meaning, while others argue that, once in the constitution, 'distinct society' would take on a life of its own and there is no telling where it would take us.[39]

Private polling evidence suggests that a distinct society clause means very different things to different people. Furthermore, these differences are not regionally random. For example, the evidence suggests that the majority in the ROC think that a distinct society clause would encourage Quebec to reduce further the use of English and presumably promote further the use of French; the majority in Quebec disagree that it would have this result.

The prevailing confusion and divergent regional interpretations have led to a marked regional variance in support for and opposition to this tactic (see Table 9). A large majority in Quebec want their province to be recognized as a distinct society; in the ROC, a majority do not want Quebec to receive that status. While all ROC regions oppose the distinct society designation, opposition is stronger in the four western provinces than in the Atlantic region or in Ontario.

In summary, the phrase distinct society now has too may contradictory meanings and is too adamantly opposed in western Canada to be of much use in defining a cooperative strategy. A minor role remains, and is discussed below in the context of establishing an effective provincial language jurisdiction.

Table 9
Public Support for Constitutional Recognition of Quebec as a Distinct Society

	Agree	Disagree
	(percent)	
Atlantic	42	53
Quebec	80	13
Ontario	47	50
Prairies	38	60
British Columbia	36	61
Rest of Canada	43	55
Rest of Canada, 1995–96 average	43.5	53

Source: These statistics are from polls conducted by Environics Research Group Ltd. All results – except the four-poll average – are from a national poll conducted in March 1996, with a sample of 2,249 adult Canadians. The average ROC statistics are calculated from four polls conducted between February 1995 and March 1996.

Negotiate a Division of Language Jurisdiction

This third tactic is based on the idea that it is better to be hanged for a wolf than a sheep. Language is so inherently controversial a matter that it is better to be frank about our differences and attempt to negotiate an explicit compromise over the division of powers.

How could such an outcome be accomplished? Logically, any constitutional amendment dealing with language belongs in section 92, the section specifying provincial powers. Perhaps luckily, section 92A – the specification of federal and provincial jurisdiction over the management and taxation of nonrenewable natural resources, which was entrenched in 1982 (see Box 5) – provides precedent for adding a complex clause to clarify a matter of serious interregional conflict. If we can open the constitution to relieve Westerners' anxiety over the Supreme Court's interpretation of provincial resource jurisdiction, we can surely do the same to accommodate Québécois anxieties over the status of Bill 101.

A Constitutional Amendment

If we attempted to solve the language problem with an addition to the Constitution – call it section 92B – what would it say? Three significant attempts to grapple with the complexities of the problem have appeared over the past two decades: the report the Pepin-Robarts Task Force in 1979; the Beige Paper pub-

---

Box 5   Section 92A of the Constitution

The 1970s saw considerable federal/provincial conflict over natural resource industries, with both levels of government legislating and attempting to regulate and capture windfall revenues. Tempers ran high.

Many of the provinces, especially in the west, had set in place complex regimes to regulate natural resource production and extract royalty revenues. Their constitutional basis for doing so was ambiguous, however, and two contentious Supreme Court decisions brought the matter to a head.

In *CIGOL v. Government of Saskatchewan* and *Central Canada Potash v. Government of Saskatchewan*, the Court ruled that Saskatchewan legislation went beyond provincial jurisdiction, infringing on federal jurisdiction over taxation and interprovincial trade and commerce.*

These decisions eroded what the provinces had thought to be their jurisdiction over natural resources and prompted appeals from western Canada for constitutional redress. The result was section 92A, a complex clarification of respective provincial and federal powers to regulate and tax resource industries. It was entrenched in the Constitution (along with the Charter and the amending formula) in 1982.

* For a survey of the complex legal and political debates of the 1970s about resource jurisdiction, see J. Richards and L. Pratt, *Prairie Capitalism: Power and Influence in the New West* (Toronto: McClelland & Stewart, 1979), chap. 11.

---

lished by the constitutional committee of the Quebec Liberal Party before the 1980 referendum; and the PQ proposals released in the waning months of its first government. Excerpts from these documents bearing on language are reproduced in the Appendix.

All are useful in considering the content of a section 92B, where the necessary ingredients are threefold:

• Specification of the bilingual nature of federal institutions.
• Definition of a suitably robust general provincial power to legislate over the public use of language.
• Specification of a set of language services to be enjoyed by official language minorities.

The Charter does a good job in defining the bilingual nature of federal institutions. The tough problems all reside in getting the right mix of the second and third ingredients. Box 6 contains my own suggestions for a section 92B and an accompanying revision to the Charter. (My reasons for the latter are explained below.)

Some Outstanding Questions

The previous subsection certainly does not answer all the questions about what we need by way of constitutional amendment. Two of the most obvious are:

- Should all provinces or Quebec alone receive specific language powers?
- Should minority language services be defined in terms of existing justiciable rights or in statutes (or constitutional language) outside the Charter?

I shall discuss each in turn.

Language Powers to Quebec Alone?
Should all provinces receive language powers? My personal preference is for an asymmetric answer – for Quebec alone to enjoy constitutional power over language. But one can raise good tactical arguments on behalf of provincial symmetry.

The Pepin-Robarts report and the Beige Paper both advocated symmetry. Moreover, preserving equality of constitutional treatment among provinces has become a central position of many in constitutional debates over the last decade. Reform Party leaders, for example, have simultaneously championed provincial equality and, usually *sotto voce*, supported provincial language jurisdiction. They have also called *fortissimo* for less bilingualism within the federal jurisdiction, raising once again the tradeoff between majority and minority linguistic interests.

Given the need to garner western support for any constitutional change, the Reform position must not be treated lightly.

On the other hand, the provinces are obviously distinct in terms of their respective language preferences. Most Québécois want a credible guarantee of their government's power to protect French. New Brunswick is the only genuinely bilingual province in the country; its governments have been content with the self-imposed requirements of official bilingualism entrenched in the Charter in 1982. Elsewhere in the country, provincial governments have shown little interest in changing their constitutional status on this matter.

An amendment that defined a language power for Quebec alone would have several advantages. It would not raise the threat that militant English-rights groups in New Brunswick would seek to use the new provincial language juris-diction to undo that province's special linguistic provisions. (Indeed, the special treatment already accorded to New Brunswick is a precedent for the idea that, on this matter, Quebec could be treated differently from other provinces.)

Also, such a constitutional amendment would not require approval under sec-tion 38's standard 7-50 rule (support by the House of Commons and by legisla-tures of two-thirds of the provinces representing more than half the Canadian population). An amendment that affected only Quebec could be entrenched with approval of the House of Commons and the legislature of that province under section 43.

Minority Language Services as Charter Rights?
To what extent should individuals be able to use the courts to define what they perceive to be appropriate minority language services? The question looks back to the earlier discussion about whether language communities have interests or fundamental rights. Aggrieved individuals can initiate Charter-based court cases; they can also challenge the constitutionality of a statute, arguing that it exceeds the jurisdiction of the province or of Ottawa. If a government loses a conventional court challenge of a statute, it may be able to realize its goal by rewriting the law or by negotiating with the other level of government. If a gov-ernment seeks to overturn a Charter-based decision, on the other hand, the not-withstanding clause may or may not be applicable, and even if it is, invoking it will involve political cost.

This question poses yet another tradeoff for policymakers: using the Charter would give greater assurance to linguistic minorities but conversely weaken the credibility of whatever political compact was struck among linguistic majori-ties. The Pepin-Robarts report advocated that minority language services be expressed in provincial statutes and be entrenched only in the case of unani-mous provincial agreement. I agree in principle. But given the sensitivity of minority language issues and given that some minority language services are already entrenched in the Charter, the only feasible policy is to leave what is there intact.

We cannot, however, let the genie of litigation over minority language rights completely out of the bottle; we must be able to dispatch it when necessary. In a valuable trial balloon recently launched on behalf of the Saskatchewan govern-ment, Greg Marchildon, the province's deputy minister of intergovernmental affairs, addressed this problem:

We need creative thinking to address both Quebec's need for some greater degree of leg-islative jurisdiction than it has at present to protect and promote its language and culture

Box 6   Proposed Constitutional Amendments

Section 92B: Powers to Legislate over Public Use of Language

My proposal features two constitutional changes: a new section 92B that specifies the federal/provincial division of jurisdiction over languages, and the introduction of a very limited distinct society clause.

As discussed in the main text, this amendment could be symmetric and accord a language power to all provinces. Alternatively, it could apply to Quebec alone.

Section 92B(1)
This section would open with a blunt statement to the effect that each province (or Quebec alone) can determine an official language or languages for itself and can legislate over matters pertaining to the public use of language within the province.

Tactically, it would make sense to resurrect the wording of the Pepin-Robarts report* (with suitable modifications in the event of a Quebec-only clause): 'Each provincial legislature should have the right to determine an official language or official languages for that province, within its sphere of jurisdiction.'

Section 92B(2)
This subsection should state that the power specified in subsection 92B(1) is to be interpreted in a manner consistent with the minority language services specified in the Charter. In particular, it should not curtail official language minority education services and, if the clause is drafted symmetrically, it does not modify the official bilingual status of New Brunswick.

The Pepin-Robarts Task Force proposed that official language minorities should have access to essential health and social services in their language and be able to plead before any court in their language, but qualified the provision with reference to 'wherever feasible'; the PQ in 1985 made somewhat similar proposals.† Subsection 92B(2) could specify these minority language services as desirable but note that, being outside the Charter, there would be no intent that they become justiciable rights.

Section 92B(3)
Following the precedent of subsection 92A(3), the section should contain a statement to the effect that 'nothing in this section derogates from the authority of Parliament' to legislate for the equal treatment of French and English within the federal jurisdiction.

The thorny matter of the federal spending power with respect to official bilingualism must be considered. This section could specify that Ottawa be able to spend in this domain, but if undertaken in an area of provincial jurisdiction, such spending would be subject to the approval of the relevant province. This specification would allow Ottawa to continue funding, without constraint, minority language associations across Canada, but it would also assure the provinces that this spending power would not become a means of infringing on provincial jurisdiction in areas such as education.

The Canadian Charter of Rights and Freedoms: Revised Section 27

As discussed in the text, the courts should be instructed to interpret the Charter from the perspective that Quebec is distinct with respect to its language, culture, and civil law tradition. The purpose of a Charter amendment is pragmatic. Expressed bluntly, it is to lower the probability that the courts repeat the mistake of the *Ford* decision.

A distinct society clause could usefully draw on the precedent of the existing interpretive clause in section 27. (It reads: 'This Charter shall be interpreted in a manner consistent with the preservation and enhancement of the multicultural heritage of Canadians.') An appropriate means to introduce a severely qualified distinct society clause is an amendment to section 27:

This Charter shall be interpreted in a manner consistent with the preservation and enhancement of the following fundamental characteristics of Canada:
a) Quebec as a distinct society, which includes a French-speaking majority, a unique culture and a civil law tradition; and
b) the multicultural heritage of Canadians.

The placement of any distinct society amendment poses a tradeoff. Placing it up front would appeal to those Québécois wanting symbolic recognition of their distinctness; placing it at the back would minimize its symbolic import and somewhat placate those concerned with the inherent ambiguities of 'distinct society.' Relegating it to the back is preferable, I think. The appropriate symbolism implicit in section 92B and this Charter amendment is not that Quebec enjoys an ambiguous special status within Canada. To the extent that symbols can be separated from specific powers and rights, the intended symbolism is that *all* Canadians accept the legitimacy of the Québécois' deciding collectively their linguistic destiny.

* Canada, Task Force on Canadian Unity, *A Future Together*, chaired by Jean-Luc Pepin and John Robarts (Ottawa: Supply and Services, Canada 1979), p. 121.
† Ibid; and Quebec, *Draft Agreement on the Constitution: Proposals by the Government of Quebec* (Quebec City, 1985). The relevant sections of both documents appear in the Appendix.

and for a *Charter of Rights* that is more sensitive to the challenges faced by Quebecers in ensuring that they do not dissolve like the proverbial lump of sugar in an English cup of coffee. We also need to reassure the rest of Canada that we are not giving an open-ended ill-defined set of special powers to Quebec.[40]

To avoid the dilemma, he suggests:

- We could grant provinces exclusive jurisdiction over public use of language ... with that power subject to limits imposed by the *Charter*.
- To assure Quebecers that the *Charter* does not take away with one hand the jurisdiction afforded by the other, the *Charter* itself could be amended by addition of a qualified distinct society – or equivalent – clause. The clause would specify that Quebec is distinct with respect to its language, culture and civil law tradition, and provide an interpretive 'lens' through which *Charter* cases should be viewed. Application of the clause would be limited to the Charter alone. This would at least partially reassure those concerned about an open-ended distinct society clause as contained in the Meech Lake Accord.[41]

The introduction of a limited distinct society clause, applicable solely to interpretation of the Charter, seems a nice compromise. (See Box 6 for further elaboration.)

Conclusion

What substantive difference would it make to entrench a section 92B in the Constitution? No answer to such a question can be definitive, so in conclusion, I indulge in some speculation with respect to the implications for another referendum, to bilingualism in federal institutions, and finally to official language minorities.

The Sovereignty Question

A depressing parallel exists between the failure of the Meech Lake Accord and, a century earlier, the defeat of British Prime Minister William Gladstone's Irish home rule bill. Both were attempts at accommodation. In 1886, the Unionists triumphed over Gladstone and in the short run prevented devolution of power to an Irish assembly. In the long run, positions hardened; those leaders who shared some elements of Victorian liberalism were replaced by others who did not. The Unionists' refusal to compromise has now become part of a festering wound in British society.

Fortunately, the major protagonists in Canada's unity conflicts remain genuine democrats. Positions have hardened in recent decades, however, and the window for compromise may be slowly closing. Many Québécois of this generation are convinced sovereignists; nothing short of a sovereign Quebec state can satisfy their expectations. Conversely, many Canadians in the ROC identify adamantly with the rights-based approach to the Constitution entailed by the Charter and believe that all provinces must be constitutionally equal regardless of manifest differences among them.

Fortunately, polls show that the majority of Québécois still prefer some variant of 'renewed federalism.' This term has as imprecise a meaning as 'distinct society,' but a common thread among its advocates is that all Canadians accept the legitimacy of the Québécois' deciding collectively their linguistic destiny.

An optimistic but nonetheless reasonable prognosis is that, if something like my section 92B were entrenched, if Ottawa engaged in a credible exercise of devolving jurisdiction over matters such as manpower training, and if all ten provinces behaved as statesmen in assuming enhanced social policy responsibilities (see Box 4), support for sovereignty would decline substantially among 'soft nationalists.' Overall, support for sovereignty might quickly decline from its present 50 percent range to, say, 35 percent, and the PQ would be obliged to repeat René Lévesque's *beau risque* (when he accepted Brian Mulroney's call for reconciliation within a federal context).

Two swallows do not a summer make. But the Reform Party's *sotto voce* support for provincial language jurisdiction and the Saskatchewan government's trial balloon indicate some political willingness in the ROC to accommodate Québécois linguistic concerns. Negotiation of an explicit provincial language jurisdiction is for many in the ROC a more attractive option than establishing Quebec as a 'distinct society,' which has come to imply that it would obtain a nebulous set of special powers, powers not available to the 'indistinct' ROC provinces.

Admittedly, my proposal contains a Charter amendment that introduces a distinct society clause. However, it is so circumscribed I doubt it could excite passionate opposition. The core of this proposal is section 92B (see Box 6), the negotiation of which would undoubtedly entail controversy.

The Status of Official Languages

How might explicit Quebec language jurisdiction for Quebec affect the status of English in that province and the status of French in central institutions, such as the federal civil service and the Canadian Broadcasting Corporation? Again, no answer can be definitive.

Already – and probably inevitably – Québécois insistence on preservation of the francophone character of Montreal has shifted both the financial center of English-speaking business and the preferred destination for most allophone immigrants outside Quebec. That shift has dramatically eroded the power and influence of the Quebec anglophone community over the past half-century.

The proposed section 92B would extend this erosion inasmuch as it restricted the ability to use Charter-based court challenges in bargaining over English language services. Anglophones' status would unambiguously be that of a minority contending within the arena of Quebec provincial politics. Perhaps, the francophone majority would prove ungenerous. It is far more likely, I predict, that the Québécois would demonstrate their commitment to pluralist democratic traditions and respond flexibly. Indeed, they might well respond more generously than in the past. At present, Quebec governments fear the potential for the courts to exploit flexible language provisions as precedents for restricting future legislative initiatives. With a firm constitutional basis for legislating over language, that fear would be attenuated.

If linguistic jurisdiction was resolved in Quebec's favor, Canadians in the ROC might be less willing to promote bilingualism in central institutions. But even Reform Party leaders have recognized the need for extensive bilingualism within these institutions. The primary Reform complaint lies elsewhere: frustration at the ability of Quebec-based MPs of all stripes – from Trudeau Liberals through Mulroney Tories and Bouchard Bloquistes – to act as a large unified bloc in Parliament and thereby obtain policies that transfer excessive income from Canadians west of the Ottawa River to Canadians east of it.

French in the ROC

A standard objection to my kind of proposal is the need to protect the language of francophones in the ROC. Following such a reform, ROC Canadians might be less willing to subsidize ROC francophones outside Quebec. A far greater threat to their survival than reduced federal funding, however, is Quebec secession, which would reduce the extent of their informal exchange with a major francophone community. The great majority of ROC francophones, recall, live in the two provinces adjacent to Quebec, and their fate depends crucially on the continuation of Quebec as a francophone province within Canada. More even than Montreal anglophones – who live in an anglophone continent and, at worst, can always migrate to Toronto – ROC francophones have a stake in the federation's survival.

For a moment, view the conflict as a game of chess in which ROC francophones have been pawns. Ottawa claims official bilingualism is a means to prevent their assimilation, but simultaneously Ottawa has promoted official bilingualism as an alternative within Quebec to Bill 101 and, more generally, as evidence that federalism is superior to secession. Its potential has been oversold. The evidence on language retention (recall Table 3) is that, beyond Acadia and eastern Ontario, official bilingualism has at best slowed the rate of linguistic assimilation and that French-language retention nonetheless declined between 1971 and 1991.

Were there a more satisfactory social contract among the major linguistic communities – francophone in Quebec and anglophone in the ROC – Ottawa and the provinces could examine minority communities' fate more realistically. ROC francophones would no longer be pawns. Quebec City would not fear federal support to them as a tactic to undermine Bill 101's restrictions on use of English within Quebec, and the ROC provinces would be less inclined to view official bilingualism as an extension of the 'Quebec problem.'

A Closing Warning

In closing, I can only paraphrase Georges Clemenceau: language is too important to the survival of the Canadian federation to leave to the Quebec academics, politicians, and journalists who have exhaustively debated the matter over the past generation, or to Supreme Court justices. If Canadians want to preserve the federation, a necessary (if far from sufficient) condition is that Canadians in the ROC engage the debate. Without a modern equivalent of the deal between John A. Macdonald and George-Étienne Cartier, the probable long-term outcome is Quebec secession.

Appendix: Some Important Language Policy Documents

This appendix reproduces the section(s) most relevant to language policy of several important documents from the past 15 years or so of the constitutional debate. They are presented uncommented and unedited, in chronological order.

The Task Force on Canadian Unity (Pepin-Robarts), 1979

(from Canada, Task Force on Canadian Unity, *A Future Together*, chaired by Jean-Luc Pepin and John Robarts (Ottawa: Supply and Services Canada, 1979)

1 The principle of the equality of status, rights and privileges of the English and French languages for all purposes declared by the Parliament of Canada, within its sphere of jurisdiction, should be entrenched in the constitution.

These purposes should include:

(i)   The equality of both official languages in the Parliament of Canada;

(ii) the right of members of the public to obtain services from and communicate with the head offices of every department, agency or Crown corporation of the Government of Canada, the central administration in the National Capital Region, and all federal courts in Canada in either of the official languages. Elsewhere, members of the public should be able to obtain services from and communicate with the central administration in both official languages where there is significant demand, and to the extent that it is feasible to provide such services;

(iii) the equality of both official languages as languages of work in the central administration in the National Capital Region, in all federal courts, and in the head offices of every department, agency or Crown corporation of the Government of Canada. Elsewhere, the usual language or languages of work in central institutions should be the language or languages of work normally used in the province in which the central institution is operating. This recommendation is subject to the previous recommendation concerning the languages of service;

(iv) the right of any person to give evidence in the official language of his or her choice in any criminal matter;

(v)   the right of every person to have access to radio and television services in both the French and English languages;

(vi) the availability in both official languages of all printed material intended for general public use.

2 Each provincial legislature should have the right to determine an official language or official languages for that province, within its sphere of jurisdiction.

3 Linguistic rights should be expressed in provincial statutes, which could include:

(i)   the entitlement recognized in the statement of the provincial first ministers at Montreal in February 1978: 'Each child of a French-speaking or English-speaking minority is entitled to an education in his or her language in the primary or secondary schools in each province, wherever numbers warrant.' This right should also be accorded to children of either minority who change their province of residence.

(ii) the right of every person to receive essential health and social services in his or her principal language, be it French or English, wherever numbers warrant.

(iii) the right of an accused in a criminal trial to be tried in his or her principal language, be it French or English, wherever it is feasible.

4 Should all provinces agree on these or any other linguistic rights, these rights should then be entrenched in the constitution.

5 The provinces should review existing methods and procedures for the teaching and learning of both French and English and make greater efforts to improve the availability and quality of instruction in these languages at all levels of education.

The Beige Paper, 1980

(from Quebec Liberal Party, Constitutional Committee, *A New Canadian Federation* (Quebec, 1980)

1 A Charter of Rights and Liberties should be enshrined in the constitution.

2 The Charter should protect the fundamental rights to life, freedom, physical integrity and privacy; it will also guarantee freedom of thought, of religion, of opinion, of speech, of association and freedom of the press, as well as the basic principles of non-discrimination;

3 The Charter would also enshrine legal rights including:

(a) the right of equality before the law and to the protection of the law;

(b) the right of every person to a public and impartial hearing by an independent tribunal;

(c) the right of every person who is arrested or detained to be promptly informed of the reasons for his arrest or detention and to be promptly brought before a competent tribunal;

(d) the right of protection from unreasonable seizures and searches.

4 The Charter should ensure the right of each Canadian to settle anywhere in Canada and to enjoy rights identical to those of the citizens of the province where he settles.

5 The constitution should recognize that French and English are the official languages of federal political institutions as well as of those bodies which fall within their jurisdiction.

6 The provinces should be empowered to legislate with respect to language, subject however to certain inviolate rights safeguarded by the constitutionally enshrined Charter of Rights and Liberties.

7 The constitution should extend to Ontario and New Brunswick those obligations already incumbent upon Quebec and Manitoba by virtue of sections 133 of the B.N.A. Act and 23 of the Manitoba Act.

8 The Charter should recognize the following language rights:

(a) the right of any French or English-speaking person as well as of any native person to be served by the federal government in their language, wherever the number of people seeking such services justifies it.

(b) the right of every French or English-speaking person and every native person to request primary and secondary level education for their children the province in which they reside in their mother tongue;

(c) the right of French-speaking, English-speaking and native communities whenever they constitute sufficiently large groups, to administer their own public educational institutions;

(d) the right of every person to have access to health and social services in their own language, be it French or English, where the number warrants it;

(e) the right of every French or English-speaking person as well as every native person to demand that a criminal or penal trial which exposes them to possible imprisonment be held in their mother tongue;

(f) the right of every French or English-speaking person to demand access in every region of the country to radio and television services in their mother tongue where the number of people seeking such services justifies it.

The Charter of Rights and Freedoms, 1982

(from Canada, *The Charter of Rights and Freedoms*, 1982)

Official Languages of Canada

Official languages of Canada

16. (1) English and French are the official languages of Canada and have equality of status and equal rights and privileges as to their use in all institutions of the Parliament and government of Canada.

Official languages of New Brunswick

(2) English and French are the official languages of New Brunswick and have equality of status and equal rights and privileges as to their use in all institutions of the legislature and government of New Brunswick.

Advancement of status and use

(3) Nothing in this Charter limits the authority of Parliament or a legislature to advance the equality of status or use of English and French.

Proceedings of Parliament

17. (1) Everyone has the right to use English or French in any debates and other proceedings of Parliament.

Proceedings of
New Brunswick
legislature

(2) Everyone has the right to use English or French in any debates or other proceedings of the legislature of New Brunswick.

Parliamentary
statutes and
records

18. (1) The statutes, records and journals of Parliament shall be printed and published in English and French and both language versions are equally authoritative.

New Brunswick
statutes and
records

(2) The statutes, records and journals of the legislature of New Brunswick shall be printed and published in English and French and both language versions are equally authoritative.

Proceedings in
courts established
by Parliament

19. (1) Either English or French may be used by any person in, or in any pleading in or process issuing from, any court established by Parliament. (2) Either English or French may be used by any person in, or in any pleading in or process issuing from, any court of New Brunswick.

Communications
by public with
federal
institutions

20. (1) Any member of the public in Canada has the right to communicate with, and to receive available services from, any head or central office of an institution of the Parliament or government of Canada in English or French, and has the same right with respect to any other office of any such institution where
(a) there is a significant demand for communications with and services from that office in such language; or
(b) due to the nature of the office, it is reasonable that communications with and services from that office be available in both English and French.

Communications
by public wth
New Brunswick
institutions

(2) Any member of the public in New Brunswick has the right to communicate with, and to receive available services from, any office of an institution of the legislature or government of New Brunswick in English or French.

Communications
by public wth
New Brunswick
institutions

(2) Any member of the public in New Brunswick has the right to communicate with, and to receive available services from, any office of an institution of the legislature or government of New Brunswick in English or French.

Continuation
of existing
constitutional
provisions

21. Nothing in sections 16 to 20 abrogates or derogates from any right, privilege or obligation with respect to the English and French languages, or either of them, that exists or is continued by virtue of any other provision of the Constitution of Canada.

Rights and privileges preserved

22. Nothing in sections 16 to 20 abrogates or derogates from any legal or customary right or privilege acquired or enjoyed either before or after the coming into force of this Charter with respect to any language that is not English or French.

Minority Language Educational Rights

Official languages of Canada

23. (1) Citizens of Canada [section 23(1)(a) currently applies in the ROC only, not in Quebec.]

(a) whose first language learned and still understood is that of the English or French linguistic minority population of the province in which they reside, or (b) who have received their primary school instruction in Canada in English or French and reside in a province where the language in which they received that instruction is the language of the English or French linguistic minority population of the province,

have the right to have their children receive primary and secondary school instruction in that language in that province.

Continuity of language instruction

(2) Citizens of Canada of whom any child has received or is receiving primary or secondary school instruction in English or French in Canada, have the right to have all their children receive primary and secondary school instruction in the same language.

Application where numbers warrant

(3) The right of citizens of Canada under subsections (1) and (2) to have their children receive primary and secondary school instruction in the language of the English or French linguistic minority population of a province

(a) applies wherever in the province the number of children of citizens who have such a right is sufficient to warrant the provision to them out of public funds of minority language instruction; and

(b) includes, where the number of those children so warrants, the right to have them receive that instruction in minority language educational facilities provided out of public funds.

Government of Quebec Proposals, 1985

(from Quebec, *Draft Agreement on the Constitution: Proposals by the Government of Quebec*, Quebec, May 1985)

*Recognition of the Primary Authority of Quebec in the
Matter of Rights and Freedoms*

Quebec can take pride in being the guarantor of individual rights and freedoms through its institutions. The Government of Quebec intends to protect the integrity of its jurisdiction in this matter. This applies to language rights which are so intimately linked to the personality of the people of Quebec: it is Quebec that must assume primary responsibility for these rights. this is also true in the domain of civil, political, economic and social rights codified by the Quebec Charter of Human Rights and Freedoms, which should alone take precedence over Quebec statutes.

1. Quebec's Responsibility for Language Rights
The distinctiveness of the people of Quebec goes far beyond the question of language, but language is at the origin and the heart of that distinctiveness.

   For nearly four centuries, there has existed along the shores of the St. Lawrence a people of French origin which, under two colonial regimes and many constitutional systems, has progressively affirmed itself through its institutions and, with the contribution of other communities, has developed to the point where it has acquired all the characteristics of a distinct society.

   This people spread into the greater part of the continent and contributed to its development, but, in the course of time, the English language gained ascendency everywhere except in Quebec. This is how the Canadian duality came about.

   The advent of mass communications, the spectacular expansion in the dissemination of sound and pictures, books and ideas, and increasingly, the movement of commercial goods and services, both along the north-south and east-west axes, lead us to consider North America as the point of reference of the linguistic, cultural and economic reality in which we are evolving. French-speaking persons today constitute scarcely 2 percent of the North American population. At a ratio of fifty to one, specific measures are required to protect French as the everyday language. This fact is self-evident if we consider the case of the French-speaking communities outside Quebec and it also holds true in Quebec, even though more than 80% of its people are French-speaking.

The interests of French-speaking Quebeckers are akin to those of French-speaking communities outside Quebec. For Quebeckers, the assimilation of French-speaking communities outside Quebec is a loss to, and a dangerous weakening of, the French-speaking cultural mainstream. For their part, the French-speaking minorities in the other provinces recognize the importance of the vitality of the Quebec French fact for the maintenance of their cultural and linguistic identity.

Although there are interests common to both, the means required to promote them differ according to the context. The Quebec context is quite different from that of the other provinces with regard to language. Recognition of this reality is a prerequisite to the development of solutions which penalize neither group.

Thus, in the opinion of French-speaking communities outside Quebec, section 23 of the Canada Act 1982 offers a means, insufficient in itself though it be, for protecting their rights. That section was designed to ensure protection of the linguistic rights of a minority and is, therefore, suited to their reality. On the other hand, the effect of section 23 in Quebec is to neutralize certain measures adopted by the National Assembly of Quebec to ensure the survival, affirmation and development of the French identity in the face of the enormous linguistic pressure placed upon it by the North American environment, and to which these measures were designed to act as a counterweight.

Quebec is the only North American territory where the linguistic, cultural and economic concerns of the French-speaking population are predominant. Therefore, Quebec legitimately claims confirmation of its powers in linguistic matters.

We take into account, however, that the people of Quebec is not entirely composed of French-speaking citizens. The English-language community, the ethnic communities and the native peoples have rights and, over and above their individual and particular rights, they have a more general right of access to all the resources society makes available to everyone.

In the past, Quebec experienced certain periods of tension with regard to language matters. That tension bespoke the concern of the French-speaking population over its future, particularly in regard to the means of ensuring the survival of French over the long term which appeared to be clearly insufficient. In spite of these periods, a climate of tolerance and respect in the treatment of minorities has generally prevailed in the search for affirmation of the French character of Quebec. In that respect we quote from the Pepin-Robarts Commission Report:

We also expect that the rights of the English-speaking minority in the areas of education and social services would continue to be respected. These rights, and this should be stressed, are not now guaranteed by the Canadian constitution. Yet they are recognized under Bill 101, the charter of the French language, a law passed by a Parti Québécois government. Thus, we already have proof that the rights of the English-speaking community in Quebec can be protected, without any constitutional obligation, and that the governments of Quebec are quite capable of reconciling the interest of the majority with the concerns of the minority. (The Task Force on Canadian Unity, *A Future Together*, Observations and Recommendations, January 1979, pp. 52–53)

Quebec intends to fulfill its responsibilities to its minorities: to continue to actively promote their rights and to give them the means necessary to exercise them.

With regard to the English-speaking community, the Government of Quebec is ready to undertake, within this new framework, to enshrine in its laws the right of the English-speaking community to receive health care and social services in its own language, as well as its right to its own cultural and educational institutions.

The Government of Quebec is also ready to amend the Charter of the French Language to secure access to the English school system for the children of those who have received their primary instruction in Canada in English; it expects in return that *throughout Canada* [emphasis in original] those who benefit from section 23 will be able in actual fact to avail themselves of access to the French school system.

Quebec also intends to fully support the French-speaking communities outside Quebec. The Government of Quebec is prepared to cooperate actively with any provincial government that wished to improve the services it provides to its French-speaking minority. It is rather by way of intergovernmental cooperation than by the sole authority of the Constitution that progress can be achieved.

To sum up, the Government of Quebec proposes:

- That the Constitution recognize that Quebec has the exclusive right to determine its official language and to legislate on any linguistic matter within its jurisdiction.
- That Quebec secure the right of the English-speaking minority to its cultural and educational institutions, as well as the right to receive health care and social services in its own language.
- That the Quebec Charter of the French Language be so amended that the children of those who have received their primary instruction in Canada in English be guaranteed access to the English school system, regardless of their number.
- That throughout Canada, those who are eligible for instruction in French may

in fact avail themselves of the rights guaranteed by section 23 of the Canadian Charter of Rights and Freedoms.
- That to support the development of the French-speaking minorities outside Quebec, agreements of mutual assistance be signed between the governments concerned.

The Meech Lake Accord 'Distinct Society' Clause, 1987

(from '1987 Constitutional Accord,' a proposed amendment to the *Constitution Act, 1982*)

1. The *Constitution Act, 1867* is amended by adding thereto, immediately after section 1 thereof, the following section:

Interpretation   2. (1) The Constitution of Canada shall be interpreted in a manner consistent with

(a) the recognition that the existence of French-speaking Canadians, centred in Quebec but also present elsewhere in Canada, and English-speaking Canadians, concentrated outside Quebec but also present in Quebec, constitutes a fundamental characteristic of Canada; and
(b) the recognition that Quebec constitutes within Canada a distinct society.

Role of Parliament and legislatures   (2) The role of the Parliament of Canada and the provincial legislatures to preserve the fundamental characteristics of Canada referred to in paragraph (1)(a) is affirmed.

Role of legislature and Government of Quebec   (3) The role of the legislature and Government of Quebec to preserve and promote the distinct identity of Quebec referred to in paragraph (1)(b) is affirmed.

Rights of legislatures and governments   (4) Nothing in this section derogates from the powers, rights or privileges of Parliament or the Government of Canada, or of the legislatures or governments of the provinces, including any powers, rights or privileges relating to language.

The Charlottetown Accord, 1992

(from the Charlottetown Accord, Draft legal text)

Constitution Act, 1867

1. The *Constitution Act, 1867* is amended by adding thereto, immediately after section 1 thereof, the following section:

Canada Clause

2. (1) The Constitution of Canada, including the *Canadian Charter of Rights and Freedoms*, shall be interpreted in a manner consistent with the following fundamental characteristics:

(a) Canada is a democracy committed to a parliamentary and federal system of government and to the rule of law;

(b) the Aboriginal peoples of Canada, being the first peoples to govern this land, have the right to promote their languages, cultures and traditions and to ensure the integrity of their societies, and their governments constitute one of three orders of government in Canada;

(c) Quebec constitutes within Canada a distinct society, which includes a French-speaking majority, a unique culture and a civil law tradition;

(d) Canadians and their governments are committed to the vitality and development of official language minority communities throughout Canada;

(e) Canadians are committed to racial and ethnic equality in a society that includes citizens from many lands who have contributed, and continue to contribute, to the building of a strong Canada that reflects its cultural and racial diversity;

(f) Canadian are committed to a respect for individual and collective human rights and freedoms of all people;

(g) Canadians are committed to the equality of female and male persons; and

(h) Canadians confirm the principle of the equality of the provinces at the same time as recognizing their diverse characteristics.

Role of legislature and Government of Quebec

(2) The role of the legislature and Government of Quebec to preserve and promote the distinct society of Quebec is affirmed.

Powers, rights and privileges preserved

(3) Nothing in this section derogates from the powers, rights or privileges of the Parliament or the Government of Canada, or of

the legislatures or governments of the provinces, or of the legislative bodies or governments of the Aboriginal peoples of Canada, including any powers, rights or privileges relating to language.

Aboriginal and treaty rights   (4) For greater certainty, nothing in this section abrogates or derogates from the aboriginal and treaty rights of the Aboriginal peoples of Canada.

NOTES

Portions of this *Commentary* appeared in J. Richards, 'The Case for Provincial Jurisdiction over Language,' in J. Richards et al., *Survival: Official Language Rights in Canada*, The Canada Round 10 (Toronto: C.D. Howe Institute, 1992). In the earlier work, I make the same policy argument: that any cooperative solution to the unity game requires more explicit Quebec jurisdiction over the public use of language.

This essay has benefited from animated critiques of earlier drafts by many people. I thank Ken Boessenkool, Michael Bryant, David Cameron, Tom Courchene, Angela Ferrante, Greg Marchildon, John McCallum, Henry Milner, Patrick Monahan, Bill Robson, and Daniel Schwanen. Some strongly agree and others strongly disagree with the basic policy recommendation; none should be blamed for the remaining inadequacies in the argument. Lee and Elizabeth d'Anjou conducted a superb edit of the text, for which I am truly appreciative.

1 Throughout this essay, I use *Québécois* as shorthand for francophone Quebec citizens. In no way should this be interpreted as implying that nonfrancophone Quebecers are less legitimate citizens of the province.

2 B. Reesor, *The Canadian Constitution in Historical Perspective* (Scarborough, Ont.: Prentice-Hall Canada, 1992), p. 303.

3 Were Quebec a sovereign country with its present per capita GNP, it would rank third among countries of the Western Hemisphere, behind the United States and the ROC. In 1993, the United States' per capita GNP was US$24,700; Canada's was US$20,000. Quebec's per capita GNP is approximately nine-tenths of the Canadian average and its population is one-quarter of the total. Based on these approximations, the 1993 per capita GNP for the ROC was US$20,600, and for Quebec US$18,000. (Incidentally, this calculation places Quebec's per capita GNP exactly equal to that for the United Kingdom.) The Quebec figure is two and a half times that of Argentina, currently the third-ranking country in the Western Hemisphere, with a 1993 per capita GNP of US$7,200. World Bank. *Workers in an Integrating World*, World Development Report 1995 (New York: Oxford University Press, 1995), table 1.

4 Marcel Côté, 'What Does Quebec Want?' *Inroads* 5 (1996): 106–107.

5 Ruth Wisse, 'Reaping the benefits of English,' *Globe and Mail* (Toronto), June 15,

1996. Reprinted from *The New Republic*. Like many other nonofficial languages in Europe, Yiddish would probably have declined over the present century, even without the tragedy of the Holocaust. The Holocaust put an abrupt end to European Yiddish culture.

6 Four million is a somewhat arbitrary lower bound. The population of Singapore is roughly 3 million; that of Norway is 4 million; that of Denmark, Finland, and Georgia, about 5 million each.

7 Canada, Statistics Canada, *Language Retention and Transfer*, Cat. 94-319 (Ottawa, 1993).

8 In Ontario, for example, the Canadian census counted nearly 2 million allophones in 1991. In terms of home language, slightly over 1 million retained their mother tongue; 817,000 spoke English, and only 3,200 spoke French. Of the 130,000 who reported multiple home languages, only 2,400 cited French as one of them. Ibid.

9 F. Robinson, ed., *The Cambridge Encyclopedia of India* (Cambridge: Cambridge University Press, 1989) is an excellent introduction to the complex subject of language in South Asia. See also S. Wolpert, *A New History of India*, 4th ed. (Oxford: Oxford University Press, 1993).

10 Quebec, *Charter of the French Language*, R.S.Q. chapter C-11, updated to August 16, 1994, p. 1.

11 This summary is derived from Quebec, *Le français langue commune: enjeu de la société québécoise*, Report of the Interministerial Committee on the Situation of the French Language (Quebec: Ministère de la Culture et des Communications, 1996), pp. 13–16.

12 The courts have limited the ability of Quebec to establish French as the official language within the province. For example, in *A.G. Quebec v. Blaikie*, the Supreme Court struck down certain provisions of Bill 101 as being contrary to the intent of section 133 of the *Constitution Act*, which provides that both French and English enjoy equal status in the records of the Quebec Assembly. Since Quebec had continued to publish unofficial English versions of statutes and many official documents after the passage of Bill 101, the practical import of *Blaikie* has been minor.

13 Quebec, *Le français langue commune*, p. 15.

14 Pierre Elliott Trudeau, *Federalism and the French Canadians* (Toronto: Macmillan, 1968).

15 The Charter obliged the Quebec government to relax restrictions on access to English primary and secondary schools. Simultaneously, it required the ROC provinces to provide more extensive schooling in French for their respective francophone minorities.

16 For a succinct statement of this argument, see, for example, Quebec, Commission nationale sur l'avenir du Québec, *Report* (Quebec, May 1995), pp. 52–54.

17 See D. Creighton, *Canada's First Century* (Toronto: Macmillan, 1970), p. 9.

18 Canada, Task Force on Canadian Unity, *A Future Together*, chaired by Jean-Luc
    Pepin and John Robarts (Ottawa: Supply and Services Canada, 1979), p. 51.
19 A critique of the position being advanced here is contained in two articles written by
    Lysiane Gagnon: 'Language is no longer the issue; control over immigration is,'
    Globe and Mail (Toronto), January 7, 1995, p. D3; and 'Why sovereigntists don't
    attack the Official Languages Act,' *Globe and Mail* (Toronto), January 14, 1995,
    p. D3. These were vigorous rebuttals to an article of mine, 'The case for a simple
    deal with Quebec,' *Globe and Mail* (Toronto), January 3, 1995, p. A17.
20 P. Martin, R. Nadeau, and A. Blais, 'Choosing a Nation: Risk, Uncertainty, and
    Political Choice in the Quebec Referendum on Sovereignty' (Paper presented at the
    annual meeting of the American Political Science Association, 1995).
21 This paragraph summarizes a complex statistical analysis. As constructed, the
    authors' model assumes identity is independent of other variables. Arguably, it is
    not. If the model were specified such that identity depended on expectations about
    linguistic survival and economic performance, then the relative importance of those
    expectations would loom even larger.
22 For the years 1961–65, Quebec's per capita GDP averaged 75.9 percent of Ontario's;
    for the most recent five-year period, 1990–94, the analogous ratio was 82.8 percent.
    Calculated from Canada, Department of Finance, *Economic Reference Tables*
    (Ottawa, 1995), table 8.2.
23 Thomas J. Courchene makes this argument in interpreting Quebec language
    laws:

    Bill 101 was not so much a cultural and linguistic measure as it was an economic
    one – French as the language of work. With the civil service no longer able to absorb
    the new wave of graduating Québécois, Bill 101 ensured that they now had easier
    access to the upper echelons and to the board rooms of Canadian and multinational
    enterprises operating in Quebec.

    T.J. Courchene, 'What Does Ontario Want?' *Rearrangements: The Courchene
    Papers* (Oakville, Ont.: Mosaic Press, 1992), p. 7.
24 D.M. Shapiro and M. Stelcner, 'Earnings Disparities among Linguistic Groups in
    Quebec, 1970–1980,' *Canadian Public Policy* 13 (March 1987): 97–104.
25 According to a recent Quebec government report, in 1986 the language of computer
    programs used by francophone employees in Montreal was 33 percent French, 13
    percent bilingual, and 54 percent English. By 1989, French had made modest gains.
    The analogous statistics were 38 percent French, 21 percent bilingual, and 41 percent
    English. Quebec, *Le français langue commune*, p. 88.
26 J. Gow, 'La gestion des ressources humaines dans une période de compressions
    budgétaires: la fonction publique du Québec de 1981 à 1991,' in R. Bernier and

J. Gow, eds., *Un état réduit? A Down-Sized State?* (Montreal: Presses de l'Université du Québec, 1994), p. 96.

27 On the theme that Quebec remains committed to a British tradition of parliamentary supremacy, whereas ROC constitutional dialogue is increasingly conducted in terms of justiciable rights, see G. Caldwell and J. Legault, 'Demise of the Living Constitution in the Land of the Culturally Deprived,' *Inroads* 1 (1992).

28 Reesor, *The Canadian Constitution*, pp. 303–305.

29 A. Cohen, *A Deal Undone: The Making and Breaking of the Meech Lake Accord* (Vancouver: Douglas & McIntyre, 1990), pp. 195–203.

30 S. Dion, 'Explaining Quebec Nationalism,' in K. Weaver, ed., *The Collapse of Canada?* (Washington, DC: Brookings Institution, 1992), pp. 119–120.

31 Ibid., p. 118.

32 B. Yaffe, '"Distinct Society" is dead, but guarantee is being sought,' *Vancouver Sun*, August 31, 1996.

33 For a survey of what the Quebec government considers unwarranted legal encroachments on its language laws, see Quebec, *Le français langue commune*, chap. 1.

34 G. Gibson, *Thirty Million Musketeers: One Canada for All Canadians* (Vancouver: Fraser Institute, 1995).

35 An important spokesman subscribing to this position has been Alain Dubuc, writing in the editorial pages of *La Presse*.

36 Dion, *The Collapse of Canada?* p. 118.

37 M. Mandel, *The Charter of Rights and the Legalization of Politics in Canada* (Toronto: Wall & Thompson, 1989).

38 In a recent collection of essays, a number of prominent federalists have also come to its defense: Côté, 'What Does Quebec Want?'; G. Robertson, 'Avoiding a Third Referendum,' *Inroads* 5 (1996); and J. Whyte, 'The Language of Accommodation,' *Inroads* 5 (1996). The majority of signatories to the Group of 22 manifesto, *Making Canada Work Better* [Toronto?], 1996) continue to support entrenchment of a distinct society clause.

39 D. Savoie, 'From Six Degrees of Separation to Three Degrees of Reality,' *Inroads* 5 (1996): 126.

40 G. Marchildon, 'An Attempt to Reconcile the Irreconcilable,' *Inroads* 5 (1996): 101.

41 Ibid.

Citizen Engagement in Conflict Resolution: Lessons for Canada in International Experience

JANICE GROSS STEIN, DAVID R. CAMERON, and RICHARD SIMEON, with ALAN ALEXANDROFF

A century and a half ago, Lord Durham wrote of British North America, 'I expected to find a contest between a government and a people; I found two nations warring in the bosom of a single state.' What he was reporting was, to use a modern phrase, an identity conflict between French-speaking and English-speaking Canadians.

This conflict, an enduring feature of Canadian history, has become particularly acute in the constitutional debates and referendums of the past two decades. Fundamental issues of identity are at the heart of the conflict. The hard-fought 1995 referendum campaign highlighted the deeply embedded conflict over identity, which now expresses itself in several ways.

Francophone and anglophone Canadians are at loggerheads over the status of their respective communities and whether a fuller representation of one will compromise the recognition of the other. Among themselves, Quebecers are deeply divided between those who seek a sovereign future in some form of partnership *with* Canada and those who want new federal arrangements *within* Canada. In the rest of the country, many Canadians are alarmed at the possible division of their federation, uncertain about the consequences of that prospect, and frustrated that they seem to have no direct voice on an issue of such overwhelming importance. They feel powerless to determine their own future.

The Canadian dilemma is distinctive but not unique. Serious ethnic and national conflicts threaten the fabric of many pluralistic societies and their peaceful relations with other states. In this *Commentary,* we examine attempts internationally to resolve some of these situations and ask what Canadians may learn from them.

Canada's identity crisis is clearly of a lesser order of intensity than many that currently capture global attention. Canadians have generally conducted the debate within the framework of respect for democratic norms and due process;

they have known only very limited violence. Yet Canada has some important features in common with societies that have suffered bitterly from conflict over identity. In many of these states, citizens have participated in unofficial processes of conflict resolution, processes in which different identities and competing interests have been accommodated and the conflict then routinized through political institutions.

This international experience can speak to Canadians across the country if it is adapted to and rooted properly in the Canadian context. In particular, we have identified two important Canadian issues where the international experiences we discuss seem particularly applicable. The first is the future of Montreal, whose residents have become increasingly polarized since the 1995 referendum. That polarization obscures their shared interests. We suggest a way in which Montrealers – 'ordinary' citizens, civic leaders, and politicians – might build stronger links across the language divide.

The second pressing issue concerns the rules that will govern any future Quebec referendum. We suggest a way in which leading nongovernmental actors, sovereignists and federalists, might develop a process to reach an agreement on those rules, which would be accepted as fair by all sides, and a set of principles to guide postreferendum conduct, faithful to the commitment of all Canadians to democratic values. Such an agreement could prove of real significance in helping to reduce the conflict and uncertainty that will otherwise prevail.

We do not argue that citizens can become decisionmakers and directly fashion solutions. We do argue that official processes are often not the best place to begin to address issues of identity. A more productive approach is to start with unofficial processes of interactive conflict resolution in which citizens can explore their identities and values, learn about the identities and values of others, and assume responsibility for opening common political space in which leaders can craft solutions that are responsive to better informed public judgment. In a polarized political context, where discussion across the fault lines of conflict can be politically risky, citizen engagement can help to create that political space.

The situation is urgent. We believe the process of unofficial but structured citizen engagement must begin *now*, starting with Montreal and with discussion of the rules for future referendums.

Outline of the *Commentary*

This *Commentary* is not for impatient readers. We are drawing on experiences and recommending processes that may be unfamiliar to many. We start therefore with a discussion of identity conflict: what it is, why it is generically so difficult to resolve, and why it has deepened in Canada. We also assess the value of complementing official negotiations with citizen engagement and distinguish among different types of citizen engagement in interactive conflict resolution.

In the next section, we examine and evaluate Canada's experience in citizen consultation. Despite some excellent attempts, none has truly been engagement in interactive conflict resolution.

The third and fourth sections outline the processes of interactive conflict resolution, with examples drawn from international experience. We first examine the role of groups of people political scientists call *influential citizens* – individuals who hold no official positions but are well connected within their own communities and to political leaders. We then turn to the engagement of *'ordinary' citizens* through community-based groups or functional associations.

In the last two sections, we examine ways in which an interactive process could be used to address the Canadian crisis, focusing particularly on Montreal and on a process that could help to create agreed-on rules for a future referendum.

Identity Conflict

Our argument rests on the thesis that fundamental issues of identity are at the heart of the Canadian crisis. Thus, we begin by exploring the nature of identity conflict, the difficulty of resolving it, and some of the reasons it has become so intense in present-day Canada. Only then can we consider the roles citizen engagement might play in resolution.

Identity is the concept that individuals have of themselves and of the way in which they are (or wish to be) known by others; it is a conception both of oneself and of one's relationship to others. Individuals usually hold multiple identities and activate one or another in different situations.

Some of these identities are connected to larger collective identities. Social psychologists suggest that people satisfy their need for positive self-identity, status, or reduction of uncertainty by identifying with a group or collectivity.[1]

Traditionally, collective identities have been regarded as the product of primordial attachments to language, ethnicity, common histories, and shared practices and myths.[2] Increasingly, however, analysts recognize that collective identities are not given. They can be chosen freely, imposed by others who have authority and resources, or socially constructed through interaction with others.[3]

Attachment to collective identities also varies in intensity over time and circumstance. Conflicts of identity escalate when group members consider that recognition of another group's identity can compromise their own, or when they perceive the granting of rights to the other as a challenge to their own identity.

The Israeli-Palestinian conflict, for example, has been an acute identity conflict. Because both identities are tied to the same territory, leaders on both sides have long felt that acknowledgment of the other's identity would fundamentally compromise their own.[4] Similarly, many Canadians outside Quebec fear that recognition of that province as a 'distinct society' would compromise their identity; they equate distinctiveness with superiority and special treatment.

In many identity conflicts, divisions *within* communities exacerbate divisions between communities. Even when leaders begin to grow interested in negotiation, groups that fear the consequences of an agreement may constrain the process in at least two important ways.

First, negotiators may shape their proposals to satisfy the demands of the most vocal and militant within their own societies, the people who are most deeply skeptical of the agreement but are nevertheless essential to ratification.[5] Second, leaders' awareness of these divisions may inhibit anything but an uneasy coalition among those members of each society who are willing to join in a collaborative process of problem solving.[6]

The Difficulty of Resolution

Conflict that focuses primarily on identity, rather than on the distribution or redistribution of material goods, appears to be especially difficult to manage and resolve. Why?

Identity conflicts engage deeply felt images of the self within a community and in the larger political world. They often embody issues of recognition and respect, along with the fear of denial and exclusion. The sense of threat from competing identities may be especially acute. Often, it may seem that there is little room for differences to co-exist within the same political space, and the parties may find it difficult to understand that acknowledging the identity of others need be no threat to one's own. For all these reasons, identity conflicts tend to be expressed in zero-sum language and in the emotive discourse of powerful symbols. Such debates are not nearly as amenable to tradeoffs, compromises, and the kinds of splitting the difference that are characteristic of the resolution of conflicts over the distribution of material goods.[7]

Political conflict over identity can become particularly acute during periods of social, economic, or political transition, when leaders create or reinterpret histories and traditions for partisan political purposes and people seek refuge from the threat and insecurity of change in the affirmation of traditional identities and values.[8]

Finally, conflicts over identity translate quickly into conflicts over representation and hence engage fundamental political institutions and processes in ways quite different from conflicts over material issues. Domestic conflicts over representation frequently lead to constitutional questions. This can make them particularly difficult to resolve because adoption of a constitutional amendment is technically complex and requires a higher-than-usual level of public approval.

In brief, the acute sense of threat people feel when they fear their identities are in jeopardy, the inadequacy of the usual distributive practices to meet these concerns, and the added overlay of complex processes of constitutional change all make identity conflicts particularly intractable.

The Current Dilemma

The Canadian identity conflict has deepened over the past two or three decades, during which, paradoxically, Quebec and the rest of the country have grown more alike in attitudes, values, social preferences, and economic aspirations. Where the two have grown apart is in their individual and collective sense of self.

Francophone Quebecers have always had a strong sense of their collective identity as a distinctive people in Canada and North America, an identity they once expressed largely in religious and cultural terms. With modernization and secularization, they have increasingly expressed that identity in political terms, reflecting their desire to become *maîtres chez nous*. Hence the demand for *constitutional* recognition as a distinct society.

This construction of identity has diverged more and more from that of other Canadians. Indeed, the fuel that fires the current identity conflict is the perception on the part of growing numbers of Quebecers that their identity is ignored or denied by other Canadians.

Fanning the flames in the rest of Canada are two senses of identity that also flow from processes of modernization and secularization. The first, expressed in the Charter of Rights and Freedoms, is that all individuals, wherever they live in Canada, are equal. Therefore, some people perceive constitutional acknowledgment of the distinctiveness of any particular community as dangerous and illegitimate.

Second (and partly in response to the convergence of Quebecers' identity with their provincial government) is the growing sense that what matters for political purposes is not individuals acting on their own or within language collectivities, but provinces, all of which are distinct in their special ways.[9] It follows that all provinces, like individuals, must be equal in the Constitution. This provincialization of identity has moved in tandem with the shrinking federal state of the past several years.

In short, all across Canada, modernization and secularization have changed and sharpened the long-standing identity conflict. They have placed new emphasis on political and legal expressions of identity, elevated the importance of provincial governments as focal points of attachment, and shifted the contest to constitutional debate.

Citizen Engagement

Particularly in deeply embedded ethnic and national conflicts where issues of identity are at the core, constitutional compacts and political agreements are at risk, and their legitimacy challenged.

Until very recently, constitutionmaking and reform in Canada have been the preserve of political elites, but these rules no longer hold. Two broad trends shape the current political context, in Canada as in many other developed democracies. First is the decline of deference and a distrust of politicians, politics, and the political process.[10] Second and closely related is the demand for greater citizen participation in the making of decisions that have important consequences.

In Canada, the rebellion against elites was sharply demonstrated by the mobilization of many citizens against the Meech Lake Accord and by the rejection of the Charlottetown Agreement in 1992. With this change in culture has come change in the institutional rules. The experience of two referendums in Quebec and the national referendum on the Charlottetown Agreement, as well as legislation now in place in several provinces requiring formal citizen approval of constitutional change, all demonstrate unambiguously that no major constitutional change will occur in the future without public ratification. The imperative of engaging civil society is abundantly clear.

Two Perspectives

Analysts have two competing views of the appropriate relationship between citizens and elites in deeply divided societies. The first is that conflict in segmented societies can be managed only by elites who are committed to the system and understand the kind of compromises that must be made.[11] When citizens are directly involved in working out intercommunal relations, this argument suggests, they make conflict resolution more difficult because they work from a narrow and parochial perspective. Their engagement is neither neutral nor beneficial; it can be noxious in its effects as it overloads the agenda for political change or reveals and confirms the deep fissures that divide the country. It is only elites who can accommodate.

The second argument advances the reverse proposition. Conflict is exacerbated, if not created, by elites who seek to manipulate identity in order to advance their own interests and institutional positions. This approach suggests that, if citizens were given primary responsibility, they could find a solution. Particularly in the aftermath of the referendum in Quebec, many citizens in the rest of the country are angry at how badly their leaders underestimated the crisis. 'Part of our problem,' argues Marian Laberge of People to People Search for Canada, 'is we've expected our politicians to save the country. We need to take back our responsibility as citizens.'[12] (It is this kind of reasoning that has led to calls for a constituent assembly that would supplant elected political leaders in any process of constitutional renewal.)

We do not accept either argument. The kinds of consociational bargains the first model requires are possible only in hierarchically organized societies where elites from different communities control their own constituencies and where those communities have few cross-cutting ties. Yet we argue that citizen engagement cannot replace official processes and political leaders. Accommodation among elites is inevitably an essential part of the resolution and routinization of the conflict, but it is not enough.

Yet, international experience in conflict resolution challenges the proposition that public involvement in identity conflict makes it more difficult to manage by overloading the system. Rather, it suggests that the right kind of citizen engagement, at the individual and community levels, and through associational networks, can make important contributions.

Focus

Citizen engagement has a wide focus and a broad agenda. It examines the fundamental issues of identity, values, and needs, which are often outside the scope of formal negotiations.[13]

Fears of threats to identity, values, and needs go to the heart of ethnic and national conflict. In Canada, the repeated failure in constitutional negotiations to find the proper language to describe the uniqueness of Quebecers' identity within the larger whole and the emotional quality of the debate testify to the limits of official processes.

Functions

Citizen engagement in conflict resolution, when conceived as a complement to official processes, can serve a variety of useful functions.[14]

It can help to build social trust by leading people to become better informed about identities and values – their own and others' – and about the common space in which they can coexist. Thus, the context of negotiation changes.

Citizen engagement can also help to develop solutions when official negotiations are recessed or stalemated, and a new phase requires novel ideas and innovative formulations.

Finally, it can increase the chances of public acceptance by creating a sense of citizen ownership of official agreements, building support for new relationships, and mobilizing the public resources necessary to ratify and implement the officially sanctioned solutions.

Citizen engagement in a process of conflict resolution is especially important when

- the conflict is protracted, and long-standing stalemate has hardened positions at the official table;
- communication is difficult or distorted across political boundaries;
- the costs of the stalemate are growing and apparent to the parties;
- frustration with official processes is high; and
- the parties feel that a problem is too dangerous to ignore but formal approaches may not succeed.[15]

At first glance, Canada may not seem an appropriate case for citizen engagement. It has not experienced the kind of violence and civil disorder that focus citizens' attention on the costs of conflict. It has rich and deep democratic traditions and processes, communication among political elites and publics is regular and open, and an active media help to inform public debate.

In brief, the kinds of obstacles to communication that exist in many societies experiencing intense identity conflict do not exist in Canada. Yet a deeper look suggests that many of the conditions we have identified are currently present.

Official positions have hardened, intermediate or compromise options are less and less frequently discussed in public debate, and leaders at many levels of government shy away from the negotiating table because of the political costs of failure. Although established channels of communication exist, contact across the fault lines of conflict is limited, and messages at variance with prevailing political symbolism often have difficulty penetrating political screens.

It is not clear whether Canadians across the country appreciate that the ongoing conflict is already inflicting real and unacceptable costs. Expert analyses underline the economic and political consequences of the ongoing conflict, but these costs are not visible and therefore difficult to appreciate. The shock of the narrow federalist victory in the referendum vote in Quebec brought home to many Canadians the precariousness of the future of their country, but its impact has quickly dissipated. Yet they are frustrated with official processes and exhibit little confidence that one more round of official negotiation will succeed in resolving the conflict.

The stalemate among governments, the absence of any promising new approaches that might break the impasse, and the frustration and anxiety of many Canadians create a favorable climate for citizen engagement. The decline of deference to elites and the new rules for popular ratification of change make it essential.

Forms of Citizen Engagement

Citizen engagement can operate at two levels. The first is the participation of citizens, either as individuals or as members of groups, in the political process linking the populace and its political leaders. In developed democracies, there are many ways in which citizens can become involved in public debate and inject their preferences and values into the political process.

The second level is the engagement of citizens with each other, in the multiple associations that constitute *civil society* – the relatively autonomous domains of social, economic, and religious life that exist in the space between citizens as individuals and mediate between them and their governing institutions.[16]

The two levels are related, and citizen involvement in both are important to an effective process of conflict resolution.

In addition, we can think of different kinds of citizens, playing different roles: citizens as leading members of the community; citizens as members of associations and networks; and citizens as voters. Our focus is on the first two, deeper, forms of engaging citizens beyond the ballot box.

Leaders
Leadership approaches center on the people political scientists call *influential citizens*, a phrase we have already defined as referring to individuals who enjoy the confidence of the political leadership but themselves hold no official position. They are free, therefore, to engage in relatively unconstrained open-ended discussion and exploration of ideas and to communicate these ideas to the political leadership.

Since they are not constrained by partisan commitments and the need to seek election, such leaders are likely to be much freer than office holders to explore new ideas and alternatives, and to think 'outside the envelope.' But at the same time, their stature in the community means that political leaders will, at the very least, pay attention to their views. Thus, influential citizens, from both sides of the divide, may be able to develop accommodations that are beyond the reach of politicians. Once such ideas are articulated, however, politicians may find it expedient to embrace them.

Such citizens are also opinion leaders. They can, therefore, help to shape attitudes and preferences in the wider public. Often, they may be more trusted in this role than political leaders.

Communities, Associations, and Networks

The involvement of citizens through communities and associations differs somewhat from leadership-based processes. At the community level, members participate in public dialogues and confront the conflict between their preferences and those of others. This will help to create the space political leaders need to seek solutions to conflict.

A particularly important dimension of associational life focuses on groups and networks that bridge linguistic, cultural, or ethnic divides and permit face-to-face engagement. In Canada, language and distance unfortunately make such linkages rare and difficult to sustain. Facilitating networks that do cross the fault lines is therefore of critical importance if there is to be an effective process of conflict management.

We believe that associations sharing common functional interests – whether social, religious, professional, business, or cultural – are particularly fruitful arenas for dialogue. The shared interests create a common base of trust, from which members may build understanding on the deeper questions of identity.

This kind of citizen engagement is especially important when pessimism about official processes is high and deference to established leaders is declining, as it is in Canada.

Stages of Conflict Resolution

These different types of citizen engagement are not alternatives to each other (or, we repeat, to an official negotiation process). It is therefore useful to ask at what stages in the policy process different kinds of citizen engagement are likely to be most effective.

At the first broad stage of deliberation, the prenegotiation stage, dialogue among citizens and with government is essential because it sets the context, the parameters, and constraints within which the negotiators will operate. Indeed, this stage is the most important, the one when it is easiest to engage in a wide-ranging exploration of a range of identities and values, since positions have not yet ossified.

Voluntary associations and communities that engage with each other before negotiations begin can multiply their effectiveness by informing one another's processes and shaping the broader context of public preferences that create space for official activity. Influential citizens also are most effective if they begin their work before official processes are under way, when they are freest to explore ideas, to reformulate problems, and to consider a wide set of options. Their work can benefit from that of voluntary associations and communities.

The second stage is the negotiation itself. Negotiators usually work behind closed doors, but it is still possible and desirable for influential citizens to assist and support official processes, especially should they become deadlocked.

Citizens, too, can be engaged. The new South African constitution, for example, went through five drafts, each of which was presented to citizens in several languages, replete with the omissions, contradictions, unresolved questions, alternative formulations, and text in square brackets. At each iteration, a widely distributed and easy-to-read tabloid newspaper, *Constitutional Talk*, summarized the areas of agreement and disagreement, sketched the alternative viewpoints in each area, and invited citizens to suggest which option should be chosen. In effect, citizens were brought into the negotiating forum, even though the politicians led the process.

Finally, at the ratification stage, citizen participation is paramount: the negotiators must present their results for democratic approval and implementation. Communities and associations that have been involved early in the process are more likely to build support for ratification and implementation. Influential citizens can assist by informing the public debate. If the first two stages have been well done, citizens will be ratifying 'their' decisions.

Citizen Consultation in Canada

Canadian citizens have a long history of involvement in efforts to address the country's protracted identity conflict. Yet none seems to have worked. In this section, we consider the problems (as well as the achievements) of some of the most recent experience and begin to suggest another approach that might yield better results.

The Record

As a mature democracy and long-established federation, Canada offers its citizens multiple opportunities and a range of established democratic processes for public participation (see Box 1).

The lengthy list of experiments in consulting citizens about the future of their country bears witness to the commitment and concern Canadians share. Yet the crisis has worsened. Why?

As already suggested, deference has declined in Canada, elites can no longer 'deliver' their constituencies, and evolving constitutional practices and public expectations now require direct citizen approval of constitutional change, certainly for large packages of changes that affect citizenship and identity. Clearly, although political leaders retain a crucial role, a secret accommodation among political elites, without public participation, is no longer politically acceptable. Today, Canadians across the country are determined to have a voice in shaping their political future.

The critical task is the linking of the right kind of citizen processes to official processes under appropriate conditions and with appropriate goals. The efficacy of public participation depends on the purposes it seeks to achieve, the kinds of processes that are used, and the sequencing in a broader process of political discussion and negotiation. When citizens participate principally as advocates for their own interests and do not search for common political space, their participation can indeed overload the agenda.[17]

In other words, what matters is not *whether* citizens are engaged but *how.* Canadians have done a lot of 'citizen work' in recent years, but much of it has not been of the right kind. Better conceived processes and sharply defined goals would yield significant benefits.

Many of the processes of citizen consultation identified in Box 1 were sporadic, partial, and, at times, confrontational. Participants had little opportunity to engage over time, to draw on what they had learned from others, and to reconsider their preferences. The processes were largely static, rather than dynamic. Most did not invite, still less require, citizens to take responsibility for their views, to explain their importance, or to adjust them in the light of evidence and information offered by the other participants. Participants were not given the opportunity to consider systematically the consequences of failing to agree. There were many opportunities to *advocate* preferred options, but there were remarkably few occasions to *deliberate.* There were few inhibitions against the expression of self-interest and very few incentives to seek common interest and accommodation.

Most of these processes were organized by one or more levels of government. Few resulted from citizen initiatives, rooted in a concomitant sense of responsibility and ownership of the issue. Most involved discussion of substantive policy alternatives and reaction to an already-formed menu of proposals; there was much less emphasis on the prior issues of the identities, values, and needs that supported or challenged these policy alternatives and proposals.

Box 1   Three Decades of Citizen Consultation

During the past three decades, there have been countless forums in Canada in which members of the public were invited to participate in a process of public discussion. A highly selective list includes:

- *Commissions of Inquiry.* The federal government has established a rich variety of commissions of inquiry: the Royal Commission on Bilingualism and Biculturalism, 1965; the Task Force on Canadian Unity (Pepin-Robarts), 1979; and the Citizens' Forum on Canada's Future (Spicer Commission), 1991.
- *Parliamentary Hearings.* Parliament has mandated various special committees, many of them from both houses: the Molgat-MacGuigan Special Joint Committee, 1972; the Lamontagne-MacGuigan Special Joint Committee, 1978; the Stanbury Special Committee of the Senate on the Constitution, 1978; the Special Joint Committee on the Constitution, 1981–82; the Special Joint Committee on a Renewed Canada (Beaudoin-Dobbie), 1992.
- *Forums and Processes in Quebec.* Quebec has involved its population widely through referendums and the release of government position papers and through the development of positions by its political parties. For example, the Quebec Liberal Party over the years has released such documents as *A New Canadian Federation* (the beige paper), 1980; *Maîtriser l'avenir*, 1985; *A Quebec Free to Choose* (the Allaire Report), 1991; and, most recently, *Quebec's Identity and Canadian Federalism: Recognition and Interdependence*, 1996. The Parti Québécois has published a number of statements of policy, from *Prochain étape: quand nous serons vraiment chez nous*, 1972, to *Le Québec dans un monde nouveau*, 1993. And the National Assembly has led public discussion through such bodies as the *Commission on the Political and Constitutional Future of Quebec* (Bélanger-Campeau), 1991.
- *Other Provinces.* Every province outside Quebec has at some point held legislative hearings, created advisory bodies, and issued white papers and reports. Examples from as far back as the 1970s include the reports of Ontario's Advisory Committee on Confederation; British Columbia's *Constitutional Proposals*; and Alberta's *Position Paper on Constitutional Change*. More recently, every province in the federation held public hearings of some kind during the course of the Charlottetown constitutional round.
- *Government-Sponsored Initiatives.* Federal, provincial, and territorial gov-

ernments have organized various forums to provide opportunities for the public expression of views. The federal government, for example, organized a series of five conferences before the Charlottetown constitutional negotiations. Held across the country, these conferences brought together an unusually broad mix of experts, officials, and 'ordinary' citizens to identify and discuss central constitutional priorities.

- *Native Peoples.* Since 1980 and the Quebec referendum of that year, organizations representing aboriginal communities have actively participated in the debate about constitutional change by commissioning extensive research, releasing position papers, and participating in public forums. In addition to the five national conferences mentioned above, the aboriginal peoples of Canada conducted four consultations with their constituents and held a national conference.

- *Think Tanks and Expert Analysis.* Private research and public policy organizations, such as the C.D. Howe Institute, the Canada West Foundation, the Institute for Research on Public Policy, and the Fraser Institute, have issued a stream of publications and policy discussions to support the evolving political process. Universities have organized public conferences to ensure broad public discussion of the issues, and academics have published extensively on all aspects of constitutional change. Some of Canada's chartered banks have released reports on the economic impact of political change.

- *Professional Associations and Organized Interest Groups.* Organizations such as the Canadian Bar Association, the Business Council on National Issues, and the Conseil du Patronat, the Canadian and Quebec chambers of commerce, the National Action Committee on the Status of Women, and the Toronto Junior Board of Trade have all contributed to the ongoing discussion.

- *Community Groups.* Church organizations, multicultural associations, and citizens' organizations have organized discussions and held information sessions.

In brief, Canadians had little opportunity to engage in a cumulative process of working through their conflicts and disagreements together, learning from one another, adjusting their preliminary beliefs and preferences, and arriving at strong, stable judgments about matters of common concern. Existing forms of public participation are far more effective at defining difference than exploring accommodation.

Three Examples

From the long list of citizen consultations in Box 1, only three meet some of the criteria of effective citizen engagement that we consider critical: a discussion of identities, values, and needs; an inclusive, fair, and respectful process; an open agenda; and the opportunity to reconsider preferences in the light of learning about others.

The Spicer Commission

Four months after the failure of the Meech Lake Accord, the federal government established the Citizens' Forum on Canada's Future, popularly known by the name of its chairman, Keith Spicer.

Because of time pressures and personality conflicts, as well as a poorly designed process, the commission was riven with dissension and never won the respect and affection of most Canadians. Indeed, it is probably better remembered for the separate remarks the chairman made at the beginning of its final report – 'There is fury in the land against the prime minister'[18] – and the dissenting comments of two commissioners than for the body of the report itself or for the public discussion it fostered.

Yet the commission's mandate is worth recalling. The forum was called on to foster a dialogue among Canadians that would permit them to consider the values and characteristics fundamental to the well-being of the country. It was to obtain views from Canadians from all regions, ethnic, linguistic, and cultural backgrounds, and walks of life; and to ensure that groups of Canadians from different regions met and discussed common and divergent concerns.

To meet these requirements, the forum established a toll-free line to gather suggestions from telephone callers; it fostered group discussions, supported by information kits and moderators; it created a students' forum, to encourage young people to participate; and it held televised discussion groups linking people from a variety of regions.

From the point of view of citizen engagement and informed public judgment, its achievement, was modest. Despite the significant investment of funds, both dissenting commissioners complained about the process's superficiality and the forum's inability to 'deepen the dialogue.'[19]

These complaints are hardly surprising, given that the commission's work lasted just eight months. The process did not foster informed deliberation, nor did it encourage participants to work collectively through the critical tradeoffs and consider the consequences of their choices.

Even though the process was limited and flawed, one can argue that the forum's mandate was targeted correctly. It attempted to engage Canadians within and across language, cultural, and regional divides in a dialogue about values. And it sought to identify a public space in which both citizens and their political leaders could find common ground on which subsequent negotiations could be undertaken. But its processes did not match its purposes.

Conferences on the Renewal of Canada

A different, more restricted, process occurred over six weeks in early 1992. Five conferences were held across the country, involving Canadians from coast to coast. They discussed possible changes in the way the country is governed, examining in particular the set of 28 proposals for constitutional change developed by the federal government and published as *Shaping Canada's Future Together*.[20]

The government conceived the conference process when it appeared that the Beaudoin-Dobbie Committee (see Box 1), which was reviewing the same set of proposals, was close to collapse. During the six weeks, the process developed a significant momentum and degree of autonomy as the organizations mandated by the federal government shaped the process and the delegates asserted control. For example, the conferences flatly rejected some of the federal proposals, and significantly altered many others. The views expressed by participants had some impact on the recommendations of the Beaudoin-Dobbie committee and subsequently on the shape of the Charlottetown constitutional negotiations.

The conferences were designed to discuss broad alternative policy directions. Only a minority of conference participants, however, could be called 'ordinary' Canadians; politicians, officials, experts, interest group representatives, and media far outnumbered people chosen at random.

The sessions did, however, create an opportunity for interested groups and individuals to engage in extended discussions and for negotiators to inform themselves before embarking on the negotiating process itself. Prior to formal negotiations, the participating governments could thus position themselves more intelligently in terms of both the constraints and preferences of an engaged group of Canadians and the aspirations of the other parties.

Nevertheless, the process was far removed from one in which citizens would take responsibility for their choices or could discuss the divergent values and identities that informed their preferences. Nor did they have the opportunity to revisit their preferences in light of what they had learned from others or to consult with their own communities and associations. Participants, in other words, had little opportunity to interact over time in a dynamic process of conflict resolution and to create informed public judgment.

The Bélanger-Campeau Commission

Quebecers have made parliamentary government, with the Quebec National Assembly as its core, the central institution for working through the issues their society confronts.[21] At critical moments in the life of their society, Quebecers turn naturally to the National Assembly, whose televised proceedings are, at such times, the most heavily watched television in the province.

The Commission on the Political and Constitutional Future of Quebec was a body exemplifying the distinctive and often creative fashion in which the predominantly francophone political community of Quebec has adapted the parliamentary system to its needs.

Established in September 1990 in the wake of the demise of the Meech Lake Accord, the commission's mandate was to examine the political and constitutional future of Quebec. Its composition was remarkable. The co-chairs were prominent Quebec businessmen Michel Bélanger and Jean Campeau. Only half of the 36 members appointed by the National Assembly were MNAs. There were representatives from the municipalities, from the business and trade union sectors, and from the cooperative, educational, and cultural sectors. In addition, there were three federal members of Parliament.

In the five months of its life, the commission received more than 600 briefs, heard 235 submissions, and invited 55 specialists in various fields to contribute information. It organized a forum on youth and the future of Quebec, visited 11 administrative regions of the province, and held hearings in 11 cities. It released a series of working papers on critical issues related to its mandate. And the attentive public in Quebec followed its work with intense interest.

The commission was an intriguing example of the way in which political leaders, in conjunction with influential citizens, can lead a broadly based process of public discussion engaging significant sectors of the larger political community. Its virtues were doubtless related to the circumstances of its creation and the society it served. Quebecers had just suffered the shock of the collapse of the highly popular Meech Lake Accord, a collapse widely believed within the province to have been the result of a broad rejection of Quebec by English-speaking Canada. Both leaders and 'ordinary' citizens within the francophone community agreed that this body blow to their national community required a rethinking of Quebec's position.

The problem was that sovereignists and federalists were unable to agree, even in these extraordinary circumstances, on a common policy. While asserting francophone solidarity in reaction to the failure of Meech, the commission could do no more than paper over fundamentally different positions on the national question. The group could agree on: the validity of a two-nations view of Canada; the positive character of Quebec's development since the Quiet Revolution; the fact that Quebec had been ill treated by the rest of Canada; and the importance of maintaining economic ties with the rest of Canada, no matter what happened. Confronted at that point with internal dissension, it then agreed to set out the two options facing Quebecers: to make a further effort to redefine Quebec's status within Confederation, or to seek sovereignty.[22]

The commission's legislative recommendations reflected this fragile consensus. But when the government of Robert Bourassa brought the legislation to the National Assembly, it significantly strengthened the federalist emphasis. The consensus, such as it was, dissolved.

The commission made no headway in bridging the cleavage within Quebec society between those who sought a new relationship with the rest of Canada and those who sought sovereignty. Still less did it explore ways in which the breach between Quebec and the rest of the country could be repaired. That was not its function. Indeed, its proposals encouraged Quebec to draw in on itself (as it had after the 1982 patriation setback). The report called for the establishment of two National assembly commissions: one to examine matters relating to the sovereignty of Quebec, and the other to await and assess any constitutional offer from the federal government and the other provinces. The Bourassa government agreed, serving notice that Quebec would no longer participate actively in the affairs of the federation. One result was its absence from the Charlottetown process until the final stages.

Time for a New Approach

With few exceptions, Canadians have had little opportunity for sustained, facilitated, interactive engagement in conflict resolution. They have been extensively consulted by their governments, but it is governments, rather than citizens, that have taken the principal responsibility to organize these processes. (It is no coincidence that the three experiments we have reviewed were all mandated and financed by governments, working within fairly short time lines.)

Surely it is time for a new approach.

The approach we recommend is a continuing dialogue of citizens – influential and 'ordinary' – with one another and with their political representatives. The specifics of that dialogue will vary with the situation. So will the processes, which we describe in the next two sections. But effective processes will always include:

• discussion of identities, values, and needs;
• procedures that are inclusive, fair, and respectful;

- an open agenda, with everything on the table; and
- opportunities to reconsider preferences in the light of learning about others, so that the dialogue is dynamic and occurs over time.

Engaging Influential Citizens: Some Experience

Interactive conflict resolution works on premises and through processes quite different from those used in traditional bargaining. The processes span a broad range of activities, but all share a commitment to facilitated, face-to-face activities that promote collaborative analysis of the sources of conflict and joint problem solving among the parties engaged in a protracted conflict.[23]

This section examines the processes by which influential citizens can be engaged in resolving identity conflicts. The next section will discuss processes that reach out to 'ordinary' citizens.

Workshops and Dialogues

The problem-solving workshop, one of the earliest forms of interactive conflict resolution, was pioneered more than two decades ago to assist in addressing deep-rooted identity conflict.[24] In the classical workshop, a small group of individuals from all the parties to the conflict, people who hold no official position but are closely connected to senior political leaders, are brought together in a neutral environment for an informal, private, and intensive session, which usually lasts several days.

The workshop is organized by a small facilitating panel of outside experts in conflict resolution, who choose the participants and the neutral site. The process is most frequently underwritten by private, nonprofit foundations, sometimes working directly with independent facilitators, at other times through facilitators in academic or research institutions.

Public dialogues are similar in concept, if not in design. They differ largely in their emphasis on reaching out to the wider community once sufficient progress has been made. Largely funded by private foundations, they engage representative citizens from the conflicting parties in designing steps to be taken in the political arena in order to change perceptions and stereotypes, to create a sense that a resolution of the conflict may be possible, and to broaden political engagement to promote a process of conflict resolution.[25]

Pioneers of public dialogue, who benefited from the experience of problem-solving workshops, have paid particular attention to the process of transferring ideas developed within the dialogue to civil society and the larger body politic, not only to the political leadership.

Problem-solving workshops and dialogues have been used in a wide variety of community, national, and international disputes.[26] They have been held in racially divided communities, in urban communities deeply divided over policy issues, in societies riven by ethnic and identity conflicts, and with participants from countries engaged in long-standing international conflict.

Although the issues differ, the purpose is the same: to facilitate full and open communication among parties to the conflict in a protected environment that is far less risky than public official negotiations. Participants in workshops and dialogues are encouraged to

- work with facilitators;
- analyze jointly the sources of the conflict and the obstacles to its resolution;
- work together collaboratively to build confidence and trust;
- devise mutually acceptable options to reduce tensions and, if possible, generate solutions that reflect a shared vision of a desirable future; and
- transmit new ideas, approaches, and understandings to political leaders at the official level and to civil society.

Facilitating the Process

Facilitators are essential to accomplishing any of the group's tasks. Before the parties to a deeply embedded conflict can begin to work collaboratively, they must develop confidence in their shared interest in finding ways out of deadlock.

Facilitators help to create a respectful environment among parties who usually bring considerable grievances to the table. To insure that all parties have adequate time to address grievances and needs in a fair process, good facilitators manage the agenda, limit disruptive and insulting behavior, and help to keep the discussions focused on the task. They are the guardians of the fairness and integrity of the process.

Diagnosing the Conflict

Facilitators assist the parties in diagnosing the sources of the conflict by clarifying concepts and providing feedback to the parties. An important part of the process is helping the parties to recognize that they perceive and fear a threat to their identities, that each side systematically tends to underestimate the importance of identity to the other, that they remember history differently, and that perceptions are frequently distorted by long periods of conflict and poor communications across political boundaries.[27]

Palestinians and Israelis, for example, have met for almost two decades in more than 20 problem-solving workshops. Many of the early sessions were spent examining the sources of the conflict and acknowledging each other's identities, needs, and fears. While participants from each group continued to assert their own identities and needs, they gradually came to understand the legitimacy of the other's identity and needs and the depth of their fears. This understanding did not weaken participants' commitment to their own identity. It did change the context against which actions to resolve the conflict were considered. At the same time, some of the distortion across political boundaries was reduced.

Other creative techniques have also been used to facilitate joint diagnoses of the conflict and promote long-term change. In any enduring conflict, participants understand its history very differently. For example, Canadians frequently observe that Quebec high schools use history textbooks that differ dramatically from those used in other provinces. A team of historians from Quebec and other provinces is currently writing collectively, with the help of a facilitator, a common textbook.[28] A similar project was successfully completed by black and white historians working together in a large urban area in the southern United States. This kind of collaborative project is likely to have much more positive consequences than unilateral attempts to challenge the other side's 'big lie.'

Building Confidence

Before participants can begin any joint activity, they must overcome the deep distrust that has been built up by years of conflict. Thus, an important early task is testing the intentions of the others. Participants try to establish whether the members of the other party recognize their identity, basic rights, and needs, whether they are genuine in their commitment to a political solution, and whether they represent significant tendencies within their own communities.

This testing process is an essential component in the creation of confidence in a working relationship. The process is never complete and is always hostage to the changing political context outside the workshop process.[29] Once participants have reached an acceptable level of working trust, however, they can begin to focus collaboratively on the measures necessary to build broader confidence.

One of the valuable outcomes of problem-solving workshops at this stage is often sensitizing participants to the different meanings of particular words and to the insults to identity (at times unintended) inherent in a particular vocabulary. For example, by the second day of a recent Turkish-Kurdish workshop, teams of participants began to develop a list of measures that political leaders on both sides could take to begin to build confidence in a political process of conflict resolution.[30] Many of these suggestions focused on changing the language each side used to describe the other.

Similarly, in Israeli-Palestinian workshops over the years, language has been an important part of the process of building confidence. Participants on both sides tend to explain their commitment to peaceful resolution in words that are authentic in their own communities but offensive to the identity of others. For example, Palestinians may call their acceptance of a two-state solution 'unjust' but dictated by their situation; Israelis find this language a challenge to their legitimacy. Israelis explain their acceptance of two states by referring to the 'demographic time bomb' of the Palestinian birthrate that will threaten the Jewish character of the state; Palestinian participants find this phrase insulting and demeaning.

In brief, an important part of the facilitator's role is to sensitize the participants to the multiple meanings and connotations of language.

Creating Options

Once the participants have built confidence in each other, they are better prepared for collaborative problem solving. Facilitators help the parties to develop options by emphasizing the context against which the conflict has unfolded and by calling attention to the costs of the ongoing stalemate, the likelihood of escalating costs in the future, and the benefits (as well as the obvious costs) of any solution.

As participants in the workshop begin to re-evaluate the costs of stalemate and the likelihood of even further deterioration, new space for political solutions begins to open. The costs of concessions, although real in the broader political context, loom less large when considered against the costs of continuing the conflict.

Attitude change is enhanced by participating in the development of a new idea. If a proposal is jointly produced or a new idea emerges as the result of group discussion, members are more likely to take ownership of the idea and then to promote it in their own communities.[31]

Thus, Israeli-Palestinian workshops created a critical mass of informed participants who recognized the others' needs, acknowledged the others' identity, and worked together on confidence-building measures. By autumn 1992, for example, Israeli and Palestinian security experts from the academic community had met repeatedly for nine months under the auspices of the American Academy of Sciences. None were officials, but all were highly placed and well connected to their leaderships.[32] Among the many ideas discussed had been a proposal for Israeli withdrawal from Gaza first. An amended version of 'Gaza first' became an important component of the settlement subsequently reached by Israeli and Palestinian officials.[33]

Transmitting Ideas

A fundamental component of interactive conflict resolution is the expectation that participants will take the ideas they have developed jointly back home. Participants are selected because they are considered representative of the political mainstream within their own communities and respected within their own societies. They are politically influential but not politically accountable, credible, well-liked individuals in their own community.[34] When the workshop finishes, they return to their own political constituencies and transmit the new ideas and proposals to leaders and members.

Re-entry is, however, a complex process. When participants leave the workshop or dialogue, they must engage with people from their own communities who have not participated in the collaborative process and continue to hold stereotypical views of the other parties and rigid definitions of the problem.

When participants transmit new ideas for breaking stalemates, they can be greeted with skepticism and find themselves criticized, if not marginalized, in the political arena and in the broader community.

For example, on the eve of formal negotiations, participants from both sides of the Tajikistan Dialogue (see Box 2) were uncomfortable about how their colleagues would react to their 'talking to the enemy' at that critical moment.[35]

As time passes, participants who find little support in their local communities can find it difficult to sustain their new way of thinking. Over time, their commitment to a process of confidence building and a collaborative solution may erode, and their attitudes may regress.

Many participants from problem-solving workshops and dialogues have, however, managed to transmit proposals to their respective political leaders. Members of the Tajikistan Dialogue, for example, jointly developed a memorandum establishing the guidelines for negotiation between the government and opposition forces. Three drafters subsequently participated in the official negotiation, and opposition members acknowledge that the memorandum served as a guide for the opposition's approach.[36] Re-entry was effective in both the personal and political aspects: participants continued to participate in dialogue sessions and were able to transmit ideas to political leaders.

Similarly, during the Israeli-Palestinian dialogue under the auspices of the American Academy of Arts and Sciences, participants encouraged leaders on both sides to begin thinking about security arrangements within the framework of an interim agreement.[37] Israeli participants distributed reports of the meetings to 30 of their senior military and political leaders. Some participants in the continuing workshop became involved directly in the official negotiating process and inserted ideas developed jointly in the workshop into the negotiation.

Evaluation

The effectiveness of problem-solving workshops and dialogues of influential citizens is often difficult to assess.[38] Long time lags and the array of other factors that contribute to a process of conflict resolution can make it impossible to trace the genesis of ideas.[39]

For example, a set of problem-solving workshops produced a set of agreed principles for a long-term solution to the internal conflict in Lebanon. Several *years* later, some of these principles were incorporated, into the Taif Agreement of 1989.[40] Although it is impossible to judge the extent to which the agreement was directly based on the results of the workshops, it is clear that they had provided suitable language and agreed-on principles that could be – and, in some cases, were – adopted at the official level when the time was opportune.

Another difficulty is the complete confidentiality of the proceedings at problem-solving workshops and dialogues. This confidentiality is necessary to create a safe space for participants to explore ideas and to experiment with strategies. Especially in the earlier stages of a workshop, participants are often reluctant to make statements that differ from the official public positions of their own communities. Indeed, some participants say directly that they cannot become involved in a workshop unless confidentiality is guaranteed.[41]

Some effects of engagement of influential citizens are, however, obvious. Workshops have created or renewed channels of communication and produced agreements on confidence-building measures and templates for resolution of conflict. In many cases, participants have transmitted ideas to officials before and during an official negotiating process.

In Tajikistan, for example, a broad coalition of the middle has increasingly been able to isolate those at the extreme. In the Israeli-Palestinian case, some of the participants moved into official processes and produced the first formal agreement (see Box 3). Although many factors contributed to these outcomes, the engagement of unofficial influential citizens before and during the negotiations facilitated the result. Some analysts make the very strong claim that, without that engagement, agreements would not have been concluded.[42]

Less visible and more difficult to document and evaluate are the important consequences that flow from the process's attention to identities, needs, and fears. In many protracted identity conflicts, repeated official attempts fail because the official negotiating process proves inadequate or inappropriate to deal with the fundamental questions of identity, values, and needs that fuel the conflict. In an official negotiation, representatives often feel it risky to discuss identity and reveal needs and vulnerabilities.[43]

Generally, resolution is least likely when negotiating parties are pessimistic

Box 2   The Tajikistan Dialogue: Engaging Influential Citizens in a Problem-Solving Dialogue

In the wake of the collapse of the Soviet Union in 1991, Tajikistan, with a population of about 5.5 million, became an independent state. A struggle over identity erupted, and successive governments banned opposition parties, both secular and Islamicist, from participating in elections and in the political process. A brutal civil war soon killed thousands and created more than half a million refugees. No official process of negotiation existed between the government under attack and the fragmented opposition.

In March 1993, an interactive problem-solving dialogue began. Participants were closely connected to officials in the government and in the opposition forces but not responsible in any way to official bodies.* The participants required a protracted stage of diagnosis and confidence building. Then, at their sixth meeting, in March 1994, they began detailed discussion of two of the most important problems that would have to be dealt with in constitutional negotiation: defining its purposes and organizing and ordering the work of the negotiating teams. The participants explicitly addressed the identity issues involved: the government's fear that the opposition would use negotiations to delegitimate the government, and the opposition's need to overcome exclusion from the political process.

As the participants talked, the facilitators recorded what seemed to be areas of common approach. The first draft was quickly translated into Russian and Tajik and returned to the participants for oral and written comments after overnight study. Drawing on these comments, facilitators produced a second draft while the group continued to meet. A third draft became an agreed-on Memorandum on a Negotiating Process in Tajikistan.

It was given to the governments of Tajikistan, the United States, and Russia, as well as to the Opposition Coordinating Center, the United Nations envoy, and the Vienna and Warsaw offices of the Conference on Security and Co-operation in Europe.

The group continued to meet even after official negotiations began. When those negotiations deadlocked a year later, the group produced a working paper that outlined possible options to break the stalemate. When political leaders accepted one of the options, the group publicized a second report, which developed the option and suggested detailed procedures for its implementation.

For workshop participants, one of the facilitators comments, the experience of working together to produce a collaborative and mutually agreed-on document allowed them to move forward with confidence. Even when they subsequently disagreed on new subjects, they were capable of dealing with the issues in a collaborative process.†

* Convened under the auspices of the Dartmouth Conference Regional Task Force and chaired by Gennady I. Chufrin and Harold H. Saunders, the Tajikistan Dialogue had met 14 times by the end of 1995. See G.I. Chufrin and H.H. Saunders, 'A Public Peace Process,' *Negotiation Journal* 2 (April 1993): 155–177; H.H. Saunders, 'Sustained Dialogue on Tajikistan,' *Mind and Human Interaction* 6 (August 1995): 123–136; and idem, 'Prenegotiation, Circum-negotiation, and the Peace Process,' in Chester Crocker and Fen Hampson, eds., *Managing Global Chaos: Sources of and Responses to International Conflict* (Washington, DC: United States Institute of Peace, 1996).

† See Saunders, 'Sustained Dialogue on Tajikistan,' p. 129.

about success and accept the likelihood of failure.[44] Interactive problem solving can induce positive attitude change toward the other side and decrease divisive, pessimistic conceptions that the parties are fundamentally incompatible.[45]

In summary, in a protracted identity conflict, interactive conflict resolution is most likely to induce the changes in attitudes and in expectations of others that are essential to move forward a process of conflict resolution. Evidence is cumulating that a two-track approach – citizen engagement in problem solving interacting with a process of official negotiation – is more likely to promote an effective process of conflict resolution than an official process used alone.[46] When engagement of influential citizens in problem solving precedes negotiation, places new ideas and new proposals on the public agenda, and feeds and reinforces the official process when it stumbles, the official process takes place against a background where substantive issues become significantly easier to mediate or negotiate.

Engaging Citizens

If conflict resolution is to progress and endure, it is essential to fully engage a broader array of citizens and the institutions of civil society. The primary reason is normative: a democratic society must be founded on consent.

Other reasons are more immediate and practical. Failure to engage citizens at early stages of the process can be fatal if their formal approval of agreements is necessary. Moreover, citizens who feel excluded are likely to rebel against deals they believe have been imposed on them by unresponsive, manipulative, and secretive elites. These are the lessons of the Canadian experience with the

Box 3   The Israeli-Palestinian Dialogue in Oslo

Although the Oslo dialogue between Israel and the Palestine Liberation Organization (PLO) in 1993 was not an unqualified process of citizen engagement (it involved Palestinian officials from the outset), it offers an interesting example of evolution from a partially private dialogue to official involvement.

The background was stalemate in the official bilateral negotiations being held in Washington between Israelis and Palestinians. Terje Larsen, a Norwegian sociologist, suggested to Yossi Beilin, then a member of the opposition Labor party in Israel's parliament, that direct talks with the PLO could be useful in breaking the deadlock. Israeli law at the time banned contact with PLO officials. Beilin suggested Larsen contact Yair Hirschfeld, an academic who had no official responsibilities.

Hirschfeld met secretly with Abu Alaa, a senior PLO official who was coordinating Palestinian representation in the official negotiations and agreed to secret talks in Oslo. The Labor government had now taken office, and Hirschfeld received approval from Beilin, who was attracted by discussions that would be 'academic,' rather than political, and permit the testing of intentions without requiring an official commitment.*

This dialogue functioned very differently from a traditional problem-solving workshop in the connection between participants and political leaders, the ground rules, and the role of the facilitator. Hirschfeld confronted deep skepticism from Israeli political leaders. Indeed, it was partly because they were so skeptical of the outcome that they approved the meetings and gave him only minimal instructions.

Hirschfeld, Abu Alaa, and their colleagues met in five exploratory rounds over five months. Discussion of identity and history played no part. Instead, the group concentrated on a blueprint for the future. The emphasis was not on collaborative problem solving, but on negotiated agreement.

The two facilitators stayed outside the meeting room, receiving separate briefings from each side before and after sessions. Nevertheless, they were critically important to the dialogue's success, creating a relaxed social atmosphere, encouraging the participants to eat together, passing messages to Jerusalem and Tunis when the group was not in session,† and encouraging both parties even when they faced serious disagreements.

Agreement on general principles came quickly. In the first round of talks, Hirschfeld and Abu Alaa agreed on withdrawal from Gaza, gradual devolution of economic power to Palestinians, and international economic assistance to the nascent Palestinian entity. (These were fundamental elements in the final

Oslo accord.) By the second round, Beilin concluded that the best way to test PLO thinking was to draft a declaration of principles. Abu Alaa quickly agreed.

The draft declaration was completed in only two rounds of meetings. Some provisions went beyond what officials in Jerusalem were prepared to accept. Yet they still saw the dialogue as a useful channel for discussing ideas. They asked Hirschfeld to inform Palestinian participants that continuation was contingent on resumption of the stalemated official talks.

The lines between the official negotiations and the unofficial dialogue were beginning to blur. After the Palestinians made additional concessions, Abu Alaa told Larsen that the dialogue would end unless Israel agreed to upgrade the talks to an official level. Within two weeks, the Israeli foreign minister named his director-general as envoy.‡ The dialogue had become official, and from it came the Declaration of Principles, the first Israeli-PLO agreement and the first important step in resolving their bitter identity conflict.

The Oslo dialogue allowed participants to experiment freely with ideas and construct jointly a framework for moving the relationship forward. It provided distance and space for Israel to explore the *bona fides* of the PLO and accept it as a negotiating partner.

Yet, largely because the facilitator's role was so circumscribed, participants did not reach the usual level of understanding of the others' needs and fears. Nor did they plan for the broader political strategies in civil society that they needed to support the process they hoped to put in place.

* David Makovsky, *Making Peace with the PLO: The Rabin Government's Road to the Oslo Accord* (Boulder, Col.: Westview Press, 1996), p. 19.
† The Norwegians also briefed the United States on a regular basis, a function not normally performed by facilitators (ibid., p. 27).
‡ Ibid., pp. 18–43.

Meech Lake Accord and the Charlottetown Round, as well as of recent referendums on the expansion of the European Union in Norway, France, Denmark, and Sweden.[47]

Engagement is equally necessary in the longer term: the legitimacy of any resolution depends heavily on the extent to which citizens feel a sense of ownership, responsibility for, and pride in the result. When they have such feelings, an agreement becomes not just words on a page but a reflection of deeply held commitments.

Finally, engagement of citizens is valuable because they may see options, possibilities, and alternatives that do not occur to leaders, who may be preoccupied with their own institutional interests or locked into the constraints of past experience.

A good example of wide citizen engagement is the process created by the South African Constitutional Assembly. It made enormous efforts to build citizens' sense of ownership of their new democratic constitution. In major cities, buses were emblazoned not with advertisements but with the slogan 'We are writing South Africa's new constitution.' The tabloid *Constitutional Talk* (published in 11 languages!) explained alternatives in easily understood words and even used cartoon strips to explain concepts such as individual rights. And, as already noted, successive drafts of the constitution were made public and comments invited.

Engagement with Citizens

Although it is easy to argue that citizen engagement is vital, it is difficult to know how to promote *effective* engagement. Not every attempt produces positive results. Consultation of citizens in Canadian constitutional debates during recent decades seems to have fostered – or at least coincided with – greater polarization. We conclude that Canada needs better processes to ensure genuine dialogue, both between citizens and leaders and between members of the major identity groups.

Traditional Techniques
Processes such as public opinion polling, election and referendum campaigns, and public hearings are the primary ways of engaging citizens in the political process.

Their limitations are well known. Polling, even though increasingly sophisticated, presents citizens with alternatives that they have not chosen and about which they may have no information. Polls are also very poor at measuring the intensity of feeling people have about an issue. In election and referendum campaigns, the debate is often thin, uninformed, and adversarial. Referendums to legitimate decisions also occur far too late in the process; without engagement at an earlier period, proposals, however well crafted, are unlikely to win support. Consultations, such as parliamentary hearings, also have important weaknesses. They tend to be sporadic and to involve different individuals each time. More important, proponents of various alternatives usually parade to the microphone one by one, each pressing his or her preference with scant need to consider the views of others, much less make compromises and tradeoffs. That is left to the politicians while citizens escape responsibility for contributing to solutions.

Deliberative Techniques

Most existing processes of citizen engagement are, in other words, opportunities for the simple expression of opinion or the exercise of pressure. They are not *deliberative*. Yet deliberative democracy is what is required to come to public judgment on the profound issues of identity conflict in Canada as elsewhere.[48]

Deliberation involves a number of elements. Participants must have a clear sense of their own interests and preferences and the best available information about the implications, costs, and consequences of those preferences. They must be informed about the interests and preferences of others and be able to delineate areas of agreement and disagreement. They must have ownership of the problem, such that they sense an obligation to search for solutions and accommodation. Above all, they must have an opportunity for dialogue and exchange, especially across the major dividing lines. Engagement must be a learning process, one in which exposure to other groups and new alternatives can lead to a modification of preferences or to the discovery of mutually beneficial outcomes not originally on the table.

These standards would be difficult to meet in any large mass democracy. They are perhaps especially difficult to meet in Canada, where the divisions are so deeply rooted in identity and where vast distances and language differences make it virtually impossible for all but a few to engage in face-to-face dialogue across regional and linguistic lines.

Nevertheless, some interesting experiments are being developed. In one, called *deliberative polling*, representative citizens are invited to spend several days debating issues. Only after facilitators provide high levels of information are participants invited to express their views. These results are communicated to policymakers. (The Kettering Institute in the United States devotes its work largely to fostering such public dialogues.)

In an approximation of such a process in 1995, the Canadian Broadcasting Corporation brought together a small group of Canadians for three days of discussion about the remaking of Canada. Chaired by Thomas Berger, these men and women, who represented a wide range of views and experience, discussed their perceptions of the country and the dilemma it was facing. In the course of their work, they were advised by three experts and met almost a dozen former or active politicians of various political persuasions. At the end of the three days, the group was able to fashion a joint statement about the nature of Canada and a number of the values they had discovered they shared and to block out a general direction for reform. The televised version of the proceedings permitted viewers to participate vicariously in the process. Unfortunately, the participants did not have adequate time to consider identities and values, to engage in facilitated discussion, or to meet on an ongoing basis to reconsider their choices.

In other such experiments, the Canadian Policy Research Network has sponsored sessions in which interested citizens debate 'the society we want' in preparation for making choices about social policy,[49] and the Canada West Foundation, in conjunction with the Council for Canadian Unity and the Atlantic Provinces Economic Council, organized Reconfederation Assembly 96 to provide an opportunity for representative 18-to-29-year-olds, to discuss, assess, and propose solutions to Canada's problems.[50]

Deliberative polling presents major challenges, of course. It is costly and time consuming. It can be employed with only small numbers of people. It is difficult to sustain on a long-term basis, even though ongoing relationships are critical to building trust and understanding. Participants have little ability to communicate their newly achieved insights to members of their communities who were unable to share in the dynamics of the process. Nevertheless, deliberative polling can be a critical supplement to regular polling.

Other interesting experiments focus on building a stronger consultative process in which the participants themselves are led to take responsibility for the results. British Columbia, faced with profound conflict between environmentalists and timber interests, found a broad set of solutions through a process in which the contending groups were mandated to produce agreed solutions among themselves, (with the help of a trained facilitator). A similar process was used in developing the Ontario Environmental Bill of Rights.

Canada and other democracies have much room for further experimentation with such techniques without removing from elected leaders the responsibility for final decisions.

Engagement within Civil Society

A growing literature exploring civic engagement and social capital argues that the health and vitality of democratic regimes are to be found not so much in constitutional documents and institutional structures but in civil society. Indeed, the strength of community norms, networks, and associational life has been linked to phenomena as diverse as educational success, rates of poverty and crime, economic performance, and the quality of governance.[51] It is within strong associations that citizens learn to trust and cooperate with each other and to develop feelings of mutuality, reciprocity, and understanding.

Much less has been written about the role of civil society in reaching accommodations among groups deeply divided over questions of identity. In Canada, the capacity of civil society's associational networks to build bridges across language and regional groups may be declining.

Increasingly, the anecdotal evidence suggests, the civil societies of Quebec and the rest of Canada have been disengaging to form two (or more) distinct civil societies, each turned in on itself, with fewer and fewer ties of mutual benefit. Quebec has been pursuing its own *projet de société*, strengthening networks within the province; the rest of Canada is increasingly preoccupied with alternative bases of identity (gender, ethnic affiliations, environmental concerns) and, therefore, has less time and concern for cross-country linkages.

If this thesis is correct – and the evidence for it is still only impressionistic – its implications are worrying. Unless sustained by strong support within communities, any governmental resolution of a protracted identity conflict is likely to fail.

Among the international examples we considered earlier, the participants in the Tajikistan Dialogue explicitly recognized this need to engage local communities and to build institutions to facilitate communication and ownership of the process of conflict resolution. By contrast, the elite-driven Israeli-Palestinian workshops paid little attention to the need for such institutions – perhaps one reason why large segments of Israeli and Palestinian societies remain deeply fearful of the accommodations their leaders have reached.

Thus, the dynamics of civil society itself are important in the policymaking process. Civil society is not easily manipulated by governments; the impetus for strengthening its potential for accommodation must come from the bottom up.[52] Governments could, however, play a facilitative role – through travel and translation grants, for example, or by insisting that the groups that come before it demonstrate a commitment to working with both language groups.[53]

The organizations of civil society that share common functional interests – professional associations, environmental advocates, humanitarian groups, and so on – are a potentially valuable resource. Private bodies could promote the development of opportunities for the members of such groups to discuss among themselves ways to manage the identity conflict. Shared functional interests would provide a common platform and greater potential for sympathetic engagement than would be present in groups brought together at random. Moreover, functional groups would facilitate the building and maintenance of relationships of ongoing trust and an easy opportunity for participants to report back to the constituencies from which they came.

Overall, functional groups are less likely than governments to be constrained by the increasingly sterile terms and categories that have come to dominate political debate in Canada. They might identify innovative patterns of accommodation that could then be injected into debate at the political level.

Conclusion

The engagement of governments and influential citizens in the resolution of deep-seated identity conflicts is vital but clearly not enough. In addition, the engagement of citizens and groups – in their interaction with the political process and in the dynamics of civil society itself – is critical if agreements are to be reached, and if they are to be sustainable. Citizens must invest in civil society.[54]

The Lessons for Canada

The analysis of Canada's previous attempts at citizen consultation, as well as the premises and processes of interactive conflict resolution that we have examined, suggest the following guidelines for a new process. In contrast to what has been done in the past, the process should involve:

- *An open agenda that deals with fundamental issues.* The emphasis should be on identities, values, and needs, rather than constitutional proposals.
- *Continuing deliberation.* The process should be continuous and recurrent so participants can engage in informed deliberation over time.
- *Facilitation.* What is needed is neutral, outside assistance from individuals who have no interest in any particular substantive outcome but are committed to assisting the participants to keep the process fair, focused, and on task. Facilitators are guardians of the fairness of the process.
- *High-quality, balanced information.* This should include the most complete available evidence about the options, summaries of consensus about their meaning and consequences where it exists, and clear specification of disagreement among experts about the meaning and consequences of the identified choices.
- *Intercommunal discussion.* That is, encounters across communities as well as within them.
- *No predetermined outcome.* The only explicit preference should be a civil resolution of conflict, without violence, in which differing identities and competing interests can be accommodated.
- *The creation of a space safe for negotiation.* This should occur even in a political context in which entering discussion can be politically risky.

Engaging Influential Citizens

Canadian experts have a long history of involvement in discussion of constitutional issues. Their analysis of alternative futures will continue to play a vital role in informing public debate and in helping people understand the different directions in which the country might move. It is, however, different from a process of interactive conflict resolution in which influential citizens, well connected to political leaders and from across the fault lines of conflict, come together, in confidence, over a sustained period of time to diagnose the conflict, consider new options, and, most important, face the difficult tradeoffs.

Such an engagement of influential citizens could make many of the contributions in Canada that it has made internationally. Under the aegis of institutions from the nonprofit sector (such as think tanks, universities, research institutions, and foundations), a small group of unofficial but highly placed individuals well connected to the government and opposition parties in Ottawa, the provinces, and the First Nations could begin a continuing problem-solving workshop with the assistance of a panel of facilitators. No such process has ever taken place in Canada.

Such a workshop could explore the sources of conflict and the obstacles to its resolution; the range of alternative futures and how these might meet important identities, values, and needs; the template for a negotiation; the rules governing another referendum in Quebec; and the framework for a process that might follow a referendum. (The last subject, while understandably taboo publicly in Ottawa and Quebec City under present circumstances, would have large consequences for postreferendum negotiations.)

A workshop need not and should not duplicate official processes. Rather, it should concentrate on deeper questions of identity, values, norms, and rules. The discussion should be wide ranging as participants across the fault lines speak in a private capacity, in confidence, exploring the kinds of frameworks that could accommodate the multiple identities Canadians hold. It could also identify some of the tradeoffs Canadians face.

Should sufficient progress allow the participants to make the results of their work public, they could help to set the context for renewed negotiations and create additional space for political leaders to engage in an official process of conflict resolution.

A workshop could also reinforce and support a process of formal negotiation as it developed, provide ideas and proposals, and assist in legitimating experimentation with a broader menu of options than is currently on a rapidly shrinking table. Finally, members of the workshop could actively assist in informing the public debate and in helping to inform and sustain the process of public dialogue at the community level and within associations.

The funding requirements for such a workshop would not be unmanageable. The costs would essentially be restricted to travel, subsistence, translation, and facilitation. Canadian experts and facilitators are plentiful. Collaboration among institutions in the private sector could easily make such an ongoing workshop possible.

Any of these subjects is a worthy focus for a problem-solving workshop. Our priority, as we explain later in this *Commentary*, is a workshop that concentrates on the rules that would govern another referendum in Quebec. Such a continuing problem-solving workshop could make an important contribution *now*, while official negotiations are largely frozen and public dialogue is increasingly sterile, endlessly repeating old shibboleths.

Engaging Communities and Associations

We also recommend that Canadian citizens in their communities and associations be engaged in public dialogue – but of the right kind, with the right focus.

It seems fair to say that much of the public participation of Canadians in the past has focused too narrowly on the specifics of constitutional change, rather than on the underlying issues of identity, values, and needs that have fueled the conflict. Consequently, the country faces the widely acknowledged and growing phenomenon of 'national unity fatigue' – the increasing resistance of a broad band of the public to engage in serious discussion of alternative political futures or to permit their political leaders to do so.

On the other hand, in the wake of the 1995 Quebec referendum, more than a hundred new grassroots groups organized very quickly. Not surprisingly, most of the larger groups are concentrated in and around Montreal, the epicenter of the conflict, but citizens' groups range right across the country. Rough estimates suggest that approximately 15,000 Canadians remain engaged in groups that are concerned in some way with issues of national unity.[55] Public opinion polling suggests that concern about the political future remains ongoing, although its salience varies from month to month and with events.

The Locus of Connection
The reluctance of many Canadians to engage is not grounded in disinterest or a lack of patriotism. Rather, it seems related to a rational judgment on the part of many citizens about the limits of their political efficacy. If the problem is so intractable and if they fear that they can have little impact on the outcome, they have little incentive to become involved. Citizen participation in public affairs

can be sustained only by a widespread sense that it *matters*, that it will have an impact on the future of the community.

Another challenge to active citizen engagement is the size and diversity of the country. Linguistic and cultural differences make it especially difficult to communicate across the fault lines of conflict.

Both these obstacles – the lack of a sense of efficacy and the size and diversity of the country – paradoxically point to communities and associations as the foundation of citizen engagement. Through them, individual Canadians share geographic proximity and interests respectively. The process must build up and out.

Within communities, local foundations, volunteer groups, school and hospital boards, and citizens' groups could all serve as hosts for a process of public dialogue. With the assistance of facilitators, they could invite participants, organize continuing workshops, and share information about identities, values, and needs within and across groups in their communities.

Similarly, established functional associations, such as religious networks, professional associations, educational associations, chambers of commerce, manufacturers' associations, environmental associations, and labor unions, have the resources and the support in place to organize a series of facilitated workshops for interested members.

The Process

The process used internationally in problem-solving workshops of influential citizens is now 'coming home' to address conflicts within society.[56] Its application to the Canadian context is easy to imagine; indeed, encouraging prototypes of public dialogue are already ongoing in the country.

The process should:

- *Begin with discussion of identities and values.* Discussion could then move to alternative futures and their relative advantages. Particularly in those associations whose members cross the fault lines of identity conflict in Canada, discussion could focus on the capacity of these identities to coexist and overlap, rather than compete. Members of associations would also tend to be sensitive to the costs of ongoing stalemate for their professional and occupational interests. Thus, the discussion would focus naturally on the costs of the status quo and the benefits of the obvious alternatives.

  The Canadian Bar Association, for example, is currently exploring the creation of such a process with an explicit dispute-resolution mechanism whereby members can acknowledge competing values and interests and attempt to address the tradeoffs with respect to Canada's future.[57]

This kind of national association and many others should open dialogue among their members who cross divisions and who are prepared to engage systematically in the kind of deliberation that creates informed public judgment.

- *Provide access to balanced information.* The discussion should rest on the highest quality information about the range of futures participants face. Although the alternatives are generally known, communities and associations generally do not have access to balanced evidence about relative advantages and disadvantages. Yet if information is to break through political screens of deeply entrenched beliefs, the analysis must be balanced and be seen to be balanced, and differences in the assessment of likely costs and benefits need to be addressed explicitly, not glossed over.

  One or more groups could commission a cross-section of experts, from across the fault lines of conflict, to prepare user-friendly kits, which could then be made available to other communities and national associations. (The Canadian Policy Research Network has used such kits effectively in cross-country dialogues with citizens who met to discuss options for social policy.)

- *Be facilitated.* Without facilitators and credible information, group discussion frequently reinforces strongly held beliefs and prejudices and further polarizes opinion. The process of discussion must be designed to encourage all participants to express their views and so should be tolerant of differences. To assure inclusion, fairness, and respect, a facilitator must be guardian of the process, encouraging the participation of those who otherwise might be reserved, ensuring that the discussion is civil, and helping participants to identify the choices they confront and measure these against their identities and values. Ideally, facilitators should be members of the local community or association.

- *Keep the agenda open.* Participants need to be free to discuss the range of identities across the country and the possible futures Canada and their community or association face. A deliberative dialogue helps to create safe space for free experimentation with ideas, with new approaches, and with the politically taboo. This kind of foundational discussion about identities, values, and alternative futures is substantially different from the interest-based and positional consultations around the Charlottetown Agreement that ultimately overloaded the agenda.

- *Allow for continuing deliberation.* Participants should have the opportunity to revisit choices they made earlier. Problem-solving workshops and dialogues have evolved from a single meeting to, for example, a structured series of three or four meetings for the same participants. So, too, communities and associations should have the opportunity to deliberate over time. They could be informed of the identities, values, and choices other groups have made and be invited to reconsider their earlier discussion with that new information.

A process that has been under way in Canada for some months and that draws on many of the approaches outlined in this *Commentary* is a project called Scenarios for the Future. It is modeled on both The Meridian International Institute's long-running Changing Maps roundtable of senior Canadian government officials and private sector executives, which considers the implications of the information society on governance, and the South African Mont Fleur project of the early 1990s, which brought together leaders from all sectors of that society to develop a set of scenarios of the future to assist in the transition to democracy.

The central objective of the Scenarios for the Future project is to encourage a strategic conversation among all Canadians about the future. If Canadians are to be successful in this changed world, the convenors argue, they need to frame the issues and the possibilities in a new way, to construct a different basis on which to work together to thrive in today's world.

To encourage what was defined as a need for reframing among Canadians to get out of the trap they are in, the project has two phases. An extensive public engagement process will be announced and launched this fall. One of the starting points for this broad dialogue will be a set of scenarios about the future that are now being finalized, in the first phase of the project, by a group of 30 or so representative individuals – leaders in their own communities – who have been meeting since August 1996 in a series of professionally facilitated roundtables designed to promote learning and dialogue. The shared understandings, the common maps they have developed, will be reflected in the scenarios they are constructing.

The project was initiated by Michael Adams, head of the polling firm, Environics, who brought together a board of directors or convenors of 36 Canadian leaders from all sectors in the country. The project has been financed entirely by the private sector and managed by the principals of The Meridian International Institute. The convenors of the Scenarios for the Future project are concerned citizens who reflect a wide range of views and interests. They have joined together for one purpose alone: to create a new opportunity to further dialogue among Canadians about the future. They have different views. But they do share the conviction that such a serious conversation, and the development of shared understandings, is essential and urgent.

Organization

Many of the citizens' groups that formed across Canada after the October 1995 referendum in Quebec have since petered out.[58] One might speculate that this is in part owing to a feeling among many of the members that their efforts are not efficacious in affecting the course of events, that their work does not fit in anywhere and therefore does not seem to matter. Many of these groups suffer as well from a lack of resources and an absence of supportive skills to assist them in sustaining their activities. This suggests that the practical requirements of creating a network of communities and associations engaged in conflict resolution are substantial. we do believe, however, that they are attainable.

The Canadian nonprofit sector – private foundations, educational institutions, independent research institutes, and think tanks – could take an essential first step by offering to supply interested communities and associations with the essential 'public goods' of facilitators and information kits. Some government funding would be helpful, but only if it were supplied at arm's length and devoid of any attempt to structure or control the process. Government could, for example, offer matching funds to citizens' groups and associations to jump start the process. Local educational institutions could assist in creating electronic networks for the sharing and exchange of information.

The process need not be massive. It could begin, for example, with a few national associations or community groups that, with help from local institutions and facilitators, shared information and broadened the process of deliberation to other groups within their communities. A network could thus be created to link together groups first within and then across communities.

As the process grows, educational institutions and think tanks could join together to create a network that recorded, organized, and shared the growing data about Canadians' identities, values, and preferences for the future of their country. Technologies of electronic information could be used to create a rolling data base and an interactive network.

The institutions that organized the collection and analysis of the data could share the results with dialogue participants across the country and, at regular intervals, directly with political leaders and officials at all levels and indirectly through the media. Groups and associations would then have the opportunity to revisit their discussion with an expanding knowledge base. At the same time, they would be broadening the political space in which leaders could attempt to renew official processes of negotiation.

Two Immediate Proposals

The engagement of influential citizens, community groups, and voluntary associations in the kinds of processes we have described can be used in a wide variety of contexts. In our view, however, two projects require special and immediate attention: the first is the future of Montreal, and the second is agreement on basic rules should another referendum be held in Quebec.

The Special Case of Montreal

Montreal has been the crucible within which French-English relations in Canada have been played out in their most intense form. Today, divisions are widening within the metropolis. To a much greater extent than elsewhere in Quebec or the rest of Canada, the costs of the continuing conflict are palpable and inescapable. While residents of Halifax, Quebec City, Chicoutimi, Toronto, Winnipeg, Calgary, or Vancouver can easily go for days without thinking about the conflict that is fracturing the country, Montrealers simply cannot do so. Every significant issue, whether it has to do with health, education, social services, business, culture, or community life, is filtered through the lens of French-English relations.

There is, in short, nothing abstract or distant about Canada's identity conflict as it manifests itself on the streets of Montreal, a city to which residents have a legendary attachment. To protect themselves economically and emotionally, people on all sides of the issue in the city – and, indeed, in the country at large – have a common interest in reversing the downward spiral.

Thus, the Montreal community seems an ideal candidate for citizen engagement in a process of interactive conflict resolution that focuses on alternative futures for the city.

Background

Despite the acute linguistic, ethnic, and national tensions in Montreal following the Quiet Revolution, intercommunal relations remained generally good for about 35 years. Deterioration has been marked, however, since October 1995.

The razor-thin outcome of Quebec's second referendum on sovereignty appears to have profoundly affected Montrealers – francophone, anglophone, and allophone alike. The sharp increase in militancy within parts of the English-language community has met a reciprocal hardening within segments of the francophone population.

In other societies under similar circumstances, communal violence has erupted. But, in Montreal, large portions of the population surely wish, as they always have, to reach mutually acceptable compromises that will allow the city they all love to work. As the decibel level of conflict rises, however, it becomes more and more difficult to hear the voices seeking understanding and accommodation.

Most Montrealers, if asked, would acknowledge that acute intercommunal conflict diminishes the city's quality of life, limits its economic prospects, and weakens its capacity to take charge of its future. Most would also agree that sovereignists and federalists have a common interest in preserving the civility of metropolitan life, whatever the outcome of the debate about Quebec's relationship with the rest of Canada. This unarticulated consensus needs to be given active and powerful voice.

The Recommended Process

In this situation, community-based initiatives, supported by the leadership of influential citizens, could make a difference. All of the elements we have identified in this *Commentary* could play a role.

To begin, an informal group of concerned influential citizens from across the fault lines of the conflict, individuals well connected to the political leaderships of the several communities, could join in a problem-solving workshop with several objectives.

The first and most pressing goal would be to halt, then reverse, the deepening polarization that is taking such a toll – psychologically, economically, and politically. Consistent with international experience, participants would start by recognizing and confronting the causes of division and developing a sympathetic understanding of the fears – and hopes – on all sides. There would also need to be a clear-eyed recognition of the already-high costs of polarization and of the potentially explosive relationships that might follow another referendum. The discussions would also reveal to the participants the depth of their shared interests in the well-being of Montreal as a vibrant and dynamic urban community. Most important, if the workshop is well managed, participants would begin to rebuild some of the shattered trust across the fault lines of the conflict.

With this trust and shared understanding, further steps would be possible. These might include a collaboratively developed project – a *projet de cité* – of Montreal's strengths. This concept could include proposals for economic renewal, for invigorating the city's cultural life, and for improving its infrastructure and enhancing its public spaces.

Any of these projects, if successfully initiated, would markedly improve Montrealers' quality of life and expand the base from which workshop participants could continue to build in the future. Ideally, the group would move from 'what divides us' to 'what we can do together.' Aside from the clear and tangible benefits that could flow to Montrealers from any of these projects, shared planning for the betterment of a common urban environment would help to put in place the level of trust that may be required to manage any future crisis.

Ideally, funding for this initiative would come from Montreal's private sector, whose future is so closely tied to the quality of life in the city, as well as to the larger outcome of the debate about political futures. The meetings could be held under the auspices of an independent, Montreal-based institution.

After these leaders have accomplished enough to be able to delineate a set of options for Montreal's future, deliberative polling among a representative sample of the city's citizens could help to frame issues and questions and to define community leaders' informed sense of residents' preferences. The poll could be televised locally, in both English and French, and thus become a shared experience not only for the participants but also for the larger communities.

Community organizations and functional associations in the city could then engage in detailed discussion of the poll results, attempting to extend their reach to those who do not normally participate in this kind of process and to promote broadly based dialogue at the level of the communities themselves. Functional groups with shared interests across conflict lines – nurses, social workers, lawyers, the Chamber of Commerce, artists and other workers in the cultural industries – could come together in their associational context to deliberate among the options identified by the influential citizens and supported in the deliberative poll. The sponsoring institution would coordinate the exchange of information from one association or community organization to another, and participants would be free to add to the agenda as they seek to develop the best possible thinking about the future of their city.

If the process works properly, it should reveal the identities, values, interests, and aspirations Montrealers hold in common *as citizens of the city*, whatever their other differences in political identity. Once firmly established, this common ground might provide the community as a whole with a basis for credible policy directions that would earn the support of the broad majority of the urban population, who would feel ownership of the process.

Advantages
The advantages of success in such a process would extend far beyond the city. If Canadian political leaders are unable to resolve their differences through a civil process, Montreal is widely recognized as the likely flashpoint of conflict. The demonstration effect of successful citizen engagement in Montreal would encourage and sustain people in the rest of Canada who currently feel little sense of political efficacy. Such a process would indeed build up and out.

Rules for Another Referendum

The processes of interactive conflict resolution might also play a constructive and valuable role on a second critical and pressing issue: agreement on the rules that should govern any future referendum on sovereignty. Few issues are more contested; few will be more important in determining whether the outcome will avoid economic and social disruption and perhaps even violence. Federalists and sovereignists share an overwhelming interest in ensuring that, in the event of another referendum, the rules are clear so that the result will be as unequivocal as possible, for two reasons.

First, clear rules that reflect the deep commitment of all Canadians to democratic values have the greatest likelihood of gaining acceptance. The second reason is more pragmatic: clear rules offer the best possible protection to citizens from the harm that could result from a bitterly contested outcome.

Background
In the period preceding the 1980 Quebec referendum, there was remarkably little debate about the legitimacy of the question or the rules governing the referendum process. These issues took on immense significance, however, after the razor-thin result of October 30, 1995. Outside Quebec, the sudden realization that the 'yes' side could well win the next time around sparked consideration of what has come to be called Plan B. It is based on some or all of the following views:

- The decision to dismantle a country cannot be made by one group alone; others across the country must be given the appropriate opportunity to express their views.
- Minorities within Quebec – anglophones, allophones, aboriginal peoples – should not have the majority view imposed upon them.
- The question put before voters should be clear and unambiguous. It should not include promises of partnership that no Quebec government can deliver unilaterally.
- In a decision as momentous as the one to secede, a simple majority (50 percent plus one) is an inadequate measure of democratic legitimacy.
- Whatever the outcome of the vote in any future referendum in Quebec, subsequent changes in the Canadian federation must be accomplished under the existing rules of constitutional amendments.

The overall implication of Plan B is that never again should a sovereignist government in Quebec be permitted to set unilaterally the terms of the referendum or the interpretation of its result. These views have been expressed strongly by nongovernmental analysts[59] and advanced with varying degrees of precision by Prime Minister Jean Chrétien and senior ministers such as

Stéphane Dion and Alan Rock, whose government has referred to the Supreme Court of Canada three questions relating to the secession of Quebec.

The Parti Québécois and many sovereignists, on the other hand, are clear in their insistence:

- that Quebecers themselves have the right to determine their future;
- that the Quebec government has the sole right to determine the question and establish the rules governing a referendum campaign;
- that the rules of international law, not the Canadian Constitution, govern any eventual secession; and
- that a simple majority of 50 percent plus one is decisive.

These two sets of arguments challenge each other at almost every point. Should another referendum be held in Quebec, Quebecers and citizens in the rest of the country will be deeply divided not only about the substance of the issue but also about the rules that govern the making of the decision. One can imagine a situation in which Quebec holds a referendum under its own rules, which conflict with rules that the federal government has established, perhaps in legislation.

The implications of this kind of impasse are extremely worrying. Quebec could proclaim victory and move immediately to the next steps, while the federal government denied any legitimacy to the result and refused to engage with Quebec on the matter. The very meaning of the vote – did Quebecers understand what they were voting for? was it really an endorsement of sovereignty? – would be contested.

The consequences of contestation would be to magnify enormously the potential for serious social unrest and economic chaos. Significant groups within Quebec would assert that the result did not apply to them and seek federal aid. The Quebec government, in the face of opposition, would be tempted to make a unilateral declaration of independence. The stability of Canadian currency, the status of federal and provincial laws, and the continuity of an orderly society would be in jeopardy. It is not difficult to imagine the way in which international financial markets would react to this level of uncertainty.

The crucial point is that the consequences of proceeding to another referendum in the absence of agreed rules of the game would be damaging to both the federal and Quebec governments and to other provincial governments as well. *All* have an overwhelming interest in avoiding these negative consequences. On the other hand, sovereignists and federalists each have a huge investment in rules that maximize the chances of their own success and minimize the chances of the other.

Thus, the question is: How might it be possible to reach prior agreement on the rules? Beginning an open conversation about these rules would be extremely difficult, if not impossible, in the current political environment. For Prime Minister Chrétien and Premier Lucien Bouchard (or their ministers) to discuss the issue with each other would be political suicide; both would be labeled *vendus* or *sellouts*.

Furthermore, any statement about Plan B emanating from Ottawa has little credibility in Quebec, where it is seen as a bargaining tactic or a self-serving threat. Federalists regard Quebec's assertions with equal skepticism. Even analyses of the rules of the game emanating from nongovernmental observers are likely tarred with the same brush. They are seen as *parti pris* and read as lawyers' briefs for one side or the other, rather than as disinterested attempts to seek mutually agreed procedures.

Our analysis suggests, then, that everyone has an interest in agreeing on rules that are as fair and neutral as possible, yet no mechanism is currently available to discuss such a set of rules. The impasse is similar to that in the Israeli-Palestinian conflict: leaders on each side recognized that they had a vital stake in a peaceful settlement, yet neither could take the political risk of negotiating with the other side. It took an informal process to break the impasse and create the common political space for leaders from both sides. *Such a process, we suggest, is necessary, indeed vital, for Canada.*

Process

If governments, with all the constraints operating on them, cannot talk, maybe private citizens can. A group of influential citizens – individuals who are well connected and trusted by governments – should be able to work confidentially to build at least the broad outlines of a consensus.

This consensus on the framework could remain confidential unless and until the Quebec government decides in principle to proceed with another referendum. At that time, the group of influential citizens could present to the Canadian people, Quebecers and non-Quebecers, a set of rules and procedures that citizens and governments would perceive as fair and legitimate. Each government would find it far easier politically to accept the recommendations of such a group, especially if its members were seen to be people of integrity, than they would to accept the proposals of another government.

Critical to the success of such an enterprise would be the convening of a group of people who shared just the one premise: that consensus on the rules of the game is essential if Quebec and the rest of Canada are to avoid unacceptable economic, political, and human costs. Beyond this single premise, the group could – indeed should – represent preferences across the range of political outcomes. Members of the group should have a stature and legitimacy that would ensure that, if they were able to agree on an approach, it would command a respectful hearing across the country.

The group should be sponsored and convened by private interests, preferably leading foundations with deep roots both inside and outside Quebec. Its work should be underpinned by a multi-authored resource document that reviews the lessons to be learned from democratic theory and from international experience respecting major constitutional change, restructuring, and secession. Facilitators – citizens of other countries or Canadians who have played no previous role and bring no political history with them – would be essential.

We believe it is urgent and in the interests of sovereignists and federalists alike that such a group begin work as soon as possible.

Governments need not endorse nor even acknowledge its work, much less commit themselves in advance to follow its advice. But if that advice is the product of an agreement among thoughtful people who are closely connected to one or the other government, it could well have an enormous impact on the conduct of the next referendum and, more important, on what follows.

In short, a properly established group of influential citizens working in a facilitated process to produce recommendations on the single issue of the rules of the game could well have a decisive impact on the well-being not only of Quebecers but also of all Canadians.

Conclusion

In this *Commentary*, we have argued in favor of engaging citizens with their governments and with each other in a sustained process of discussion about their political futures.

We do not underestimate the difficulties, nor do we overestimate the availability of refined social tools to accomplish the task. Neither do we anticipate that Canada will become a town hall of 30 million. Yet we see no alternative, at this stage, to citizen engagement.

Both the Meech Lake Accord and the Charlottetown Agreement, in very different ways, foundered on the rock of resistant public opinion. British Columbia and Alberta are legally required to hold referendums before approving any constitutional change. Quebec, Newfoundland, and the federal government provide for optional referendums, and Ontario is currently considering referendum legislation. Others will certainly hold public hearings. The engagement of citizens in forums where they discuss their political futures is a fundamental part of any process of political change.

Around the world, people are thinking about and experimenting with new forms of governance that give citizens greater voice early on in the political decisionmaking process. There is growing recognition internationally that a simple ratification vote comes too late to give citizens effective voice; they must play a role in defining the agenda and in facing the tradeoffs that go to the heart of any political process. Citizens will no longer accept the role of passive receptors. With deference declining, they insist increasingly on becoming active agents.

And as citizens' involvement grows, so must their assumption of responsibility for difficult and, at times, painful choices. This kind of involvement can happen only if the right processes of engagement are in place.

If Canadians are to reconcile their differences in a civil process, an accommodation among governing elites will be essential, but it will certainly not be enough. We urge that the two processes we have recommended – in Montreal and on rules for the next referendum – begin as quickly as possible. Canadians have only a limited time to learn from others and design processes that encourage informed public dialogue among both elites and 'ordinary' citizens. In a country as large and diverse as Canada, the challenge is real, but the capacity to meet that challenge will shape Canadians' politics – and their future – in the next millennium.

NOTES

None of us assumes a predetermined substantive outcome from the processes of citizen engagement that we recommend. Of course, as citizens we have individual preferences. What drew us together, however, is our shared commitment to an open and civil process that engages citizens with each other and with their leaders, accommodates different identities, and peacefully resolves this conflict.

1 Michael Hogg and Dominic Abrams, 'Toward a Single-Process Uncertainty-Reduction Model of Social Motivation in Groups,' in Michael Hogg and Dominic Abrams, eds., *Group Motivation: Social Psychological Perspectives* (London: Harvester Wheatsheaf, 1993), p. 173.

2 Clifford Geertz, 'The Integrative Revolution: Primordial Sentiments and Civil Politics in New States,' in Clifford Geertz, ed., *Old Societies and New States* (New York: Free Press, 1963).

3 Benedict Anderson, *Imagined Communities*, 2nd ed. (London: Verso, 1991); Ted Hopf, 'Russian Identity and Foreign Policy in Estonia and Uzbekistan,' Ann Arbor, Mich., 1966.

4 Herbert C. Kelman, 'Creating the Conditions for Israeli-Palestinian Negotiations,' *Journal of Conflict Resolution* 26 (March 1982): 61.

5 Peter Evans, Harold Jacobsen, and Robert Putnam, eds., *Double-Edged Diplomacy:*

International Bargaining and Domestic Politics (Berkeley, Cal.: University of California Press, 1993).

6 Herbert Kelman, 'Coalitions across Conflict Lines: The Interplay of Conflicts within and between the Israeli and Palestinian Communities,' in Stephen Worchel and Jeffrey A. Simpson, eds., *Conflict between People and Groups* (Chicago: Nelson-Hall, 1993), pp. 243–244.

7 J. Stephan Dupré, 'Reflections on the Workability of Executive Federalism,' in R.D. Olling and M.W. Westmacott, eds., *Perspectives on Canadian Federalism* (Scarborough, Ont.: Prentice-Hall Canada, 1988), p. 247.

8 T. Ranger, *The Invention of Tradition* (Cambridge: Cambridge University Press, 1983).

9 David Elkins and Richard Simeon, eds., *Small Worlds: Provinces and Parties in Canadian Political Life* (Toronto: Methuen, 1980).

10 Neil Nevitte, *The Decline of Deference* (Peterborough, Ont.: Broadview Press, 1996). See also Peter C. Newman, *The Canadian Revolution, 1985–1995: From Deference to Defiance* (Toronto: Viking, 1995).

11 This view is closely associated with the work of Arend Lijphart. See his *Democracy in Plural Societies* (New Haven, Conn.: Yale University Press, 1977); and *Democracies* (New Haven, Conn.: Yale University Press, 1984).

12 Cited in Ken MacQueen, 'Fasten your seatbelts,' *Ottawa Citizen*, March 8, 1996, p. B1.

13 *Identity* means the collective self and its relationship to others. *Values* refers to the ideas, norms, and processes the collectivity holds to be most important, and *needs* to what the collectivity defines as necessary to fulfill the basic purposes that stem from its identity and values.

14 Harold H. Saunders, 'Prenegotiation, Circum-negotiation, and the Peace Process,' in Chester Crocker and Fen Hampson, eds., *Managing Global Chaos: Sources of and Responses to International Conflict* (Washington, DC: United States Institute of Peace, 1996).

15 For a similar analysis of conditions that facilitate negotiated solutions, see I. William Zartman, *Ripe for Resolution: Conflict and Intervention in Africa* (New York: Oxford University Press, 1989); and Saunders, 'Prenegotiation, Circum-negotiation, and the Peace Process.'

16 Benjamin Barber, *Strong Democracy* (Berkeley, Cal.: University of California Press, 1984).

17 Michael B. Stein, 'Tensions in the Canadian Constitutional Process: Elite Negotiations, Referendums, and Interest Group Consultations, 1980–1992,' in Ronald L. Watts and Douglas M. Brown, eds., *Canada: The State of the Federation, 1993* (Kingston, Ont.: Queen's University, Institute of Intergovernmental Relations, 1993), pp. 97ff.

18 Canada, Citizen's Forum on Canada's Future, *Report to the People and Government of Canada* (Ottawa: Supply and Services Canada, 1991), pp. 6–7.

19 Richard Cashin, 'Comment,' in ibid., p. 141. For Robert Normand's echoing of these remarks, see ibid., p. 144.

20 Canada, *Shaping Canada's Future Together: Proposals* (Ottawa: Supply and Services Canada, 1991).

21 Quebec was, for example, the only province to review and approve in its legislature the draft of the Meech Lake Accord before the agreement was accepted by all governments in its final form at the Langevin meeting in spring 1987.

22 The commission report and a number of the submissions may be found in Richard Fidler, ed., *Canada, Adieu? Quebec Debates Its Future* (Halifax, NS: Institute for Research on Public Policy/Oolichan Books, 1991).

23 R.J. Fisher and L. Keashly, 'Third Party Interventions in Intergroup Conflict: Consultation Is Not Mediation,' *Negotiation Journal* 4 (1988): 381–393.

24 John Burton, *Conflict and Communication* (London: Macmillan, 1969); Herbert C. Kelman, 'The Problem-Solving Workshop in Conflict Resolution,' in R.L. Merritt, ed., Communication in International Politics (Urbana, Ill.: University of Illinois Press, 1972); and C.R. Mitchell, *Peacemaking and the Consultant's Role* (Aldershot, UK: Gower Press, 1981).

25 Saunders, 'Prenegotiation, Circum-Negotiation, and the Peace Process.'

26 R.J. Fisher, 'A Third-Party Consultation Workshop on the India-Pakistan Conflict,' *Journal of Social Psychology* 112 (1980): 191–206; idem, *Interactive Conflict Resolution* (Syracuse, NY: Syracuse University Press, 1997); and R.J. Fisher and J.H. White, 'Reducing Tensions between Neighborhood Housing Groups: A Pilot Study in Third Party Consultation,' *International Journal of Group Tensions* 6 (1976): 41–52.

27 Cynthia J. Chataway and Herbert C. Kelman, 'Researching the Interactive Problem Solving Workshop: Convergent Insights from Action Research, an Evaluative Model, and Direct Research,' in Nadim Rouhana, ed., *Innovations in Unofficial Third Party Intervention in International Conflict* (Syracuse, NY: Syracuse University Press, forthcoming).

28 Interview with Joseph Montville, Washington, DC, June 14, 1996.

29 Kelman, 'Coalitions across Conflict Lines.'

30 J.V. Montville, 'Highlights and Dynamics of a Turkish-Kurdish Workshop, March 22–24, 1996,' Center for Strategic and International Studies, Preventive Diplomacy Program, Washington, DC.

31 R. Petty, J. Priester, and D. Wegener, 'Cognitive Processes in Attitude Change,' in R. Wyer and T. Srull, eds, *Handbook of Social Cognition*, vol. 2 (Mahwah, NJ: Lawrence Erlbaum Associates, 1994).

32 Participating in these meetings were Nizar Amar, at one time a senior member of

Force 17 Commando Group of the Palestine Liberation Organization (PLO); Ahmed Khalidi and Yazid Sayegh, two Palestinian academics in the United Kingdom with close affiliations to the PLO; Shlomo Gazit, former head of Israeli military intelligence; Joseph Alper, deputy head of the Jaffee Center for Strategic Studies at Tel Aviv University; Aryeh Shalev, a senior research associate at the Jaffee Center; and the senior military correspondent for *Ze'ev Schiff*, one of Israel's largest newspapers.

33 David Makovsky, *Making Peace with the PLO: The Rabin Government's Road to the Oslo Accord* (Boulder, Col.: Westview Press, 1996), p. 17.

34 Individuals will be more successful in influencing opinion in their own community if they have previously developed a reputation as competent and contributing members of the group and present their message consistently while at the same time demonstrating flexibility. M. Bray, D. Johnson, and J. Chilstrom, 'Social Influence by Group Members with Minority Opinions: A Comparison of Hollander and Moscovici,' *Journal of Personality and Social Psychology* 43 (1, 1982): 78–88.

35 H.H. Saunders, 'Sustained Dialogue on Tajikistan,' *Mind and Human Infraction* 6 (August 1995): 130.

36 In analyzing the Tajikistan Dialogue, Saunders is very careful not to claim that the memorandum was the most important influence on the shape of the negotiations. 'But exactly what influence it had on the approaches taken in the negotiations by the two teams cannot be determined because of the many different people and factors at play in a complex interaction' (ibid., p. 129).

37 Makovsky, *Making Peace with the PLO*, p. 18.

38 See Fisher, *Interactive Conflict Resolution*, chap. 9, for an evaluation of the 70 problem-solving workshops that he has identified.

39 See ibid., chap. 9, for an assessment.

40 E.A. Azar, *The Management of Protracted Social Conflict* (Aldershot, UK: Dartmouth Publishing, 1990), pp. 55–56.

41 Chataway and Kelman, 'Researching the Interactive Problem-Solving Workshop,' p. 13.

42 Telhami argues strongly that, even when structural conditions changed and created an opportunity for conflict resolution, without the active intervention of international nongovernmental organizations, with both influential citizens and experts, the process of conflict resolution between Israelis and Palestinians would not have moved forward. The minimal trust that was required to assess that an agreement had a better chance of success than the alternative was 'largely' due to informal contacts over the years. Shibley Telhami, 'Israeli Foreign Policy: A Realist Ideal Type or a Breed of Its Own?' in Michael N. Barnett, ed., *Israel and Comparative Perspectives: Challenging the Conventional Wisdom* (Syracuse, NY: Syracuse University Press, 1996), p. 73.

43 Interviews with officials confirm that less formal settings are required for the kind of

open communication that leads to a deeper understanding. See Cynthia J. Chataway, 'How Policy Specialists Perceive Interactive Conflict Resolution' (paper prepared for the National Research Council, Committee on International Conflict Resolution, Washington, DC, June 14, 1996).

44 J. Rubin, S. Kim, and N. Peretz, 'Expectancy Effects and Negotiation,' *Journal of Social Issues* 46 (1990): 125–139.

45 The most systematic analysis of the impact of problem-solving workshops on participants' attitudes compared the process with processes of distributive and integrative bargaining. The study paired Israeli and Jewish-Americans with Arabs and Arab-Americans to discuss the highly contentious issue of Jerusalem. Participants were randomly assigned to work in one of three modes of conflict resolution: distributive bargaining, integrative bargaining, and interactive problem solving. Those in the group of distributive bargainers were told to clarify their positions and reach an agreement through negotiation. Those in the group of integrative bargainers were instructed to develop a definition of the problem, clarify their interests, try to expand the alternatives, and negotiate an agreement that would meet the interests of both sides. Those in the interactive problem-solving group were told to develop a definition of the problem, clarify their own needs and fears as well as those of the other side, and jointly generate ways to meet the needs and fears of both sides and to overcome the barriers to implementing solutions. For a summary and analysis, see Chataway and Kelman, 'Researching the Interactive Problem-Solving Workshop,' pp. 46–47.

46 Loraleigh Keashly and Ronald J. Fisher, 'A Contingency Perspective on Conflict Interventions: Theoretical and Practical Considerations,' in Jacob Bercovitch, ed., *Resolving International Conflicts: The Theory and Practice of Mediation* (Boulder, Col.: Lynne Reiner Publishers, 1996), p. 257.

47 Peter H. Russell, *Constitutional Odyssey: Can Canadians Become a Sovereign People?* 2nd ed. (Toronto: University of Toronto Press, 1993).

48 James F. Fishkin, *Democracy and Deliberation: New Directions for Democratic Reform* (New Haven, Conn.: Yale University Press, 1991); idem, *The Voice of the People (New Haven, Conn.: Yale University Press, 1995); Daniel Yankelovich and I.M. Destler, Beyond the Beltway: Engaging the Public in U.S. Foreign Policy* (New York: W.W. Norton, 1994).

49 *The Society We Want: A Public Dialogue* (Ottawa: Canadian Policy Research Network, 1996).

50 *Reconfederation Assembly 96: A Report* (Calgary: Canada West Foundation, 1996).

51 The converging evidence across disciplines and in multi-policy areas is striking. See Robert Putnam, *Making Democracy Work: Civic Traditions in Modern Italy* (Princeton, NJ: Princeton University Press, 1993); idem, 'Bowling Alone: America's Declining Social Capital,' *Journal of Democracy* (January 1995): 65–78; idem,

'Tuning In, Tuning Out: The Strange Disappearance of Social Capital in America,' *PS: Political Science and Politics* (December 1995): 664–683; Francis Fukuyama, *Trust: The Social Virtues and the Creation of Prosperity* (New York: Free Press, 1995); James C. Coleman, 'Social Capital in the Creation of Human Capital,' *American Journal of Sociology* 94 (Supplement, (1988): S95–S120; and idem, *The Foundations of Social Theory* (Cambridge, Mass.: Harvard University Press, 1990).

52 Although Alan Cairns, among others, argues that states and institutions can have powerful effects on civil society. See his 'The Governments and Societies of Canadian Federalism,' *Canadian Journal of Political Science* 10 (4, 1977); and idem, *Disruptions: Constitutional Struggle from the Charter to Meech Lake* (Toronto: McClelland and Stewart, 1991).

53 Jack Snyder makes the argument strongly that conditional funding can have important consequences when he examines the unintended externalities that the activities of nongovernmental organizations can have on conflict resolution. See Jack Snyder and Karen Ballentine, 'Nationalism and the Marketplace of Ideas,' *International Security* 21 (Fall 1996): 5–40. See also Janice Gross Stein, 'The Resolution of Identity Conflict: The Role of Non-Governmental Organizations,' in Jack Snyder and Shibley Telhami, eds., *Non-Governmental Organizations and Conflict Resolution* (Ithaca, NY: Cornell University Press, forthcoming).

54 Private foundations have been experimenting with programs to promote civic engagement. 'Civil investing' (investment in communities) pays attention to the connective structures and informal groups below the official level and to processes that are not explicitly programmatic. The optic shifts from people as clients to citizens solving problems and the capacity of the community to act together. See *Foundation News & Commentary* (May/June 1996): 21–27.

55 John E. Trent, 'Post-Referendum Citizen Group Activity,' in Douglas M. Brown and Patrick Fafard, eds., *Canada: The State of the Federation, 1996* (Kingston, Ont.: Queen's University, Institute of Intergovernmental Relations, 1996).

56 In 1995, the Greater Baton Rouge Federation of Churches and Synagogues initiated a process of sustained dialogue within its community. Participants across the racial divide committed themselves to meeting every five to six weeks throughout the year. See H. Saunders, 'Sustained Dialogue Comes Home,' *Connections* 6 (December 1995): 5–6.

57 The Canada-for-Tomorrow Committee, 'Proposal for a National Dispute Resolution Initiative' (Vancouver: Canadian Bar Association, 1996). See also Trent, 'Post-Referendum Citizen Group Activity.'

58 Trent ('Post-Referendum Citizen Group Activity,' p. 46) notes 'the seemingly transitory nature of this group activity and its shift from accommodation to opposition.'

59 See Patrick J. Monahan and Michael J. Bryant with Nancy C. Coté, *Coming to Terms with Plan B: Ten Principles Governing Secession*, C.D. Howe Institute Commentary 83 (Toronto: C.D. Howe Institute, June 1996).

THE SECESSION PAPERS

Looking into the Abyss:
The Need for a Plan C

ALAN C. CAIRNS

In his book *Impossible Nation*, Ray Conlogue writes: 'The qualities that make our country so attractive to others and to ourselves – a century-and-a-half of domestic peace, a comfortable standard of living, an idealized notion of ourselves as a kind and gentle people – are the worst possible qualities for dealing with a crisis of this kind.'[1] He is, of course, referring to the fact that, sometime in the next decade, Canadians may face the breakup of one of the oldest continuously functioning constitutional democracies on Earth – their own. The outcome of the October 1995 Quebec referendum confirms, irrefutably, that the breakup of Canada is no longer the implausible, hypothetical future crisis that should not concern practical people.

Canada's history ill prepares us for this challenge. In modern times, Canadians have not experienced invasion, foreign occupation, or revolution. Instead, the lessons of the past have, nineteenth-century rebellions aside, induced us to view certainty, stability, and continuity as natural. This stable history might, of course, suggest that Canadians are more skilled in averting the threats to their survival to which other, less adroit peoples have succumbed. To some extent, this is true. Canadians have enjoyed a living, adaptable Constitution, expanded peacefully from four provinces to ten, and incrementally extricated themselves from the embrace of their imperial mother across the Atlantic. Canadians have weathered depressions and contributed significantly to victory in two world wars. Their federal system has gone through cycles of centralization and decentralization – in most cases without any formal changes to the Constitution. Canadians have democratized the constitutional order and accommodated new categories of voters, and they have developed their own versions of the welfare state and of social rights.

These accomplishments are, without question, major tributes to Canadians' resourcefulness in managing their affairs, but in relative terms the challenges

Canadians have confronted have been minor. In the past, the self-congratulatory assertions of some Canadians that theirs was a difficult country to govern must have been heard with incredulity by most members of the United Nations or of the earlier League of Nations. In fact, by the standards of most of the world, Canada has been an unusually easy country to govern. This historical truth, however, may no longer apply. Federalists may not be able to keep Quebec within Canada; if Quebec goes, Canadians and their governments in the rest of Canada (ROC) may mismanage the terms of secession, making more difficult a subsequent harmonious coexistence with an independent Quebec; and the ROC may bungle the fashioning of a new constitution for those left in the truncated Canada that nobody sought.

This *Commentary* focuses on the initial steps toward meeting the third of these challenges – fashioning Canada's future without Quebec. My purpose is not to argue that Canada without Quebec must survive as a single entity, although that is my strong preference, or that the survivors should continue into the distant future with constitutional arrangements that mirror the current ones. Nor is my task to try to dictate the precise constitutional arrangements appropriate for Canada without Quebec. Rather, I want to suggest ways to increase the likelihood that those arrangements, whatever they might be, emerge out of a reasoned process of constitutionmaking, and to minimize the instability, panic, and chaos inherent in a breakup. The first requirement, therefore, is to reduce the turbulence that would likely follow a 'yes' vote in Quebec. The second, related, requirement is to gain time so that Canadians outside Quebec do not face having to reconstitute themselves while simultaneously removing Quebec as a province in their formerly shared country, as well as working out a limited coexistence with the now foreign neighbor that would then separate Ontario from Atlantic Canada.

Canadians have not faced challenges of this magnitude since before Confederation. Yet, we are almost completely unprepared for the major task of reconstructing Canada without Quebec; indeed, our lack of preparation is essentially inherent in our situation. Thus, the question to which this paper provides one answer, is: How can Canadians outside Quebec prepare to respond intelligently to the reconstitution of the ROC should Quebecers vote convincingly 'yes' in the next referendum?

I begin by providing some background to current responses to the Quebec sovereignty issue and by suggesting why they are insufficient. In the following brief, but crucial, section, I discuss how and why Canadians are in a state of almost total ignorance about the fate of the ROC in the event of Quebec's secession. In the section after that, I discuss how difficult the situation would be for Canadians in such an event, not just in practical terms but in psychological ones as well.

I then come to the heart of the *Commentary*: a proposal to take the first simple, but necessary, step toward reconstituting Canada without Quebec by establishing an interim arrangement that would be as much like the status quo as possible, to provide Canadians with the breathing room to plan for the longer term. I follow this proposal with a brief discussion of what such a transition period might be like, and offer a few hints as to the kinds of steps Canadians might take from there. I conclude the *Commentary* with a plea for governments and key actors to accept the need for 'Plan C,' so that Canadians are not completely unprepared to face an increasingly possible future without Quebec.

Plan B: Not Enough

The secession of Quebec and the resultant breakup of Canada have been serious possibilities for at least 30 years.[2] Until recently, the response to that threat to Canada's survival focused on renewing the federal system by constitutional and nonconstitutional changes designed to increase the attractiveness to Quebecers of remaining in Canada.

In the wake of the October 1995 referendum result, however, the federal government and many Canadians came to realize that *something* more was needed in response to the Quebec sovereignty movement. So renewed federalism was dubbed 'Plan A,' and a supplementary strategy, 'Plan B,' haltingly emerged as both an addition to federalist arguments against secession and a contingency policy in case all arguments, in the end, fail.

The exact scope and meaning of Plan B varies with the commentator who uses the term. For the purposes of this *Commentary*, I use Plan B to refer basically to:

- an elaboration of the ground rules governing a secession attempt; and
- an indication that the costs of secession, especially in the case of a unilateral declaration of independence (UDI), would be very high.[3]

These steps are important and, regrettably, necessary. But they do not address the most important problem that the ROC would confront if Quebec were to secede: the survival and reconstitution of Canada without Quebec. The obvious rubric for policy directed toward this crucial issue is Plan C, a term I use in this way throughout the paper.[4] At the level of official public policy, however, this fundamental concern is not part of any government's plan under any label. This deficiency, as I discuss later, is not merely a regrettable, easily rectifiable oversight, but an inescapable consequence of constraints on the maneuverability of federal and provincial governments outside Quebec.

To understand why a Plan C does not now exist and why it is necessary to have one, a tour of Plans A and B – and of their inadequacies – is a necessary preliminary. Such a tour shows the immense difficulty governments have in responding to the challenge of accommodating Quebec within Canada, or of the ROC's survival without Quebec.

Plan A

Plan A, the attempt to renew federalism, has a long history punctuated by major inquiries, such as the Laurendeau-Dunton Commission, the Pepin-Robarts Task Force, and the Spicer Commission, and by major efforts to amend the Constitution, including the Victoria Charter, Bill C-60, the *Constitution Act, 1982*, and the Meech Lake and Charlottetown Accords. Only the complex process following the 1980 Quebec referendum led to formal change: the *Constitution Act, 1982*, which, however, the Quebec National Assembly has never approved.

While Plan A is driven primarily by the special need to accommodate Quebec, it cannot, in the 1990s, ignore the other provinces or such stakeholders as women, aboriginal peoples, or Charter Canadians, who can frustrate any process that appears to slight their concerns. Consequently, the scant package of constitutional changes directed to federalism in the 1971 Victoria Charter had expanded by the 1992 Charlottetown Accord into a comprehensive smorgasbord that went far beyond federalism in its scope and that spoke directly to all Canadians.

The federal government's latest version of Plan A is a combination of decentralization – devolving responsibilities for tourism, recreation, mining, social housing, forestry, and labor market training to the provinces – a symbolic recognition of Quebec as a distinct society by Parliament,[5] and an amending-formula veto for Quebec as part of the federal government's 'loan' of its amending veto to the five regions of Canada.[6]

This very veto, coupled with the developing convention of requiring a referendum on major constitutional changes, weakens the feasibility and attractiveness of formal constitutional change as a route to solving the problems of federalism. Another reason to avoid the constitutional route is the belief that the Parti Québécois (PQ) government is not open to any effort to renew the federation. The only feasible strategy, therefore, is to work with the opposition Quebec Liberal Party and be prepared to move quickly on constitutional issues with the Quebec provincial government if and when the Liberals are returned to power. Not surprisingly, the federal minister of intergovernmental affairs recently indicated that no formal constitutional changes were planned.[7] Therefore, compared with previous versions, the current official Plan A is relatively unambitious, constrained as it is by memories of how major attempts at formal change have failed in the past. (As Roger Gibbins shrewdly notes, however, Plan A's provincialist thrust – linked to a massive increase in intergovernmental machinery – might result in extensive, if incremental, *de facto* change.[8])

The 1997 version of Plan A may not be enough to win the next referendum for the federalists, but it may not be possible to do more. The emergence of Plan B outside Quebec is a belated recognition of the fact that two different constitutional games are under way simultaneously: one to renew federalism, the other leading to the more drastic outcome of Quebec sovereignty (and by necessary inference the sovereignty of a residual Canada outside Quebec). Quebec politicians have played both games concurrently for 30 years. Until the October 1995 referendum, Canada/ROC had officially played only the renewed federalism game.

Until recently, political actors outside Quebec have avoided outlining a Plan B on the grounds that to prepare for a breakup was to admit publicly that a breakup was possible – and thus to give legitimacy to an unwanted result. Plan B – preparations for the possible failure of Plan A – was, in effect, a taboo subject, surrounded by 'keep out' signs.[9] The fear of a self-fulfilling prophecy has not gone away, but it has been overwhelmed by the closeness of the October 1995 referendum result, which graphically underlined how totally unprepared governments outside Quebec were for a 'yes' victory.[10]

According to Charles Taylor, something 'snapped' in Quebec after the defeat of the Meech Lake constitutional proposals, as Quebecers realized that a modest constitutional package could not make its way through the formalities of the amending process.[11] After the October 1995 referendum, something snapped outside Quebec. Complacency was no longer a defensible stance. In addition to the elementary recognition that an almost total unpreparedness for an increasingly plausible 'yes' victory could be disastrous at the bargaining table, many in the ROC experienced a degree of humiliation at the thought that they and their governments had been so naive, even Panglossian, in their optimism. Those who were politically involved felt a certain shame and anger that they had believed the soothing utterances of their leaders that everything was under control.

Hence, today, there is widespread recognition outside Quebec by opinion leaders and ordinary people alike that Plan A is not enough.[12] If no other options are explored, all constitutional and other efforts will be directed to a project that may fail, leaving Canadians and their governments in the ROC unprepared to respond to the outcome they had hoped to forestall. In a recent article, Douglas Brown notes how academics and other analysts are now remarkably willing to discuss the formerly taboo subjects of responding to a 'yes' victory and thinking about the future of Canada without Quebec.[13] Accordingly, Plan B now attracts significant attention.

Plan B

Plan B signals that one can no longer assume that Canada will acquiesce quietly in its destruction in a constitutional game determined by its opponents. The plan's two essential purposes reinforce each other: by laying out a plan to protect Canada's interests should Quebecers vote 'yes,' it also helps to reduce the chances of such a result. The Reform Party has been in the vanguard of advocates of Plan B, stressing that it

would show the separatists what they would be up against in a real secession negotiation ... and make it crystal clear to every Quebecer ... exactly what the negative implications of secession are.[14]

Gordon Robertson sums up the prevailing mood in his justification for federal contingency legislation for a Quebec referendum: such legislation would reduce the risk and make

very clear to the 'yes' side that it will be up against a well-prepared federal government before there is any agreement to secession by Quebec.[15]

Plan B, as Robertson's statement suggests, elaborates a crucial distinction that hitherto had been obfuscated by the focus on whether or not the federal government would respect a 'yes' vote. Plan B distinguishes between the acceptance of a 'yes' and the agreement on the terms of implementing it, including constitutional amendments. It makes clear that a fair question and a convincing 'yes' only get the two parties to the bargaining table, where the terms of separation would then have to be worked out – that the terms cannot be determined unilaterally by one party on the basis of a 'yes' vote.[16] In the event of such a vote, then, the goal of Plan B would be to effect an orderly separation process, one that is subject to the rule of law.

Such, at any rate, is the theory. At the official level, at least, Plan B today is less a plan than an inchoate set of assumptions that in many cases are still tentative. The term 'plan' in fact suggests a degree of specificity, comprehensiveness, and coherence for an official response that does not exist.

The federal government's version of Plan B is an orientation, not a program. It is not summarized in any document. It is an aggregation of specifics, such as the recent reference to the Supreme Court of Canada[17] and statements by the prime minister and his cabinet colleagues. Some of these statements, often phrased as warnings or questions, are simply trial balloons designed to test opinion and rattle the other side. In fact, part of Plan B may be a scattergun approach of warnings and threats, the very randomness, incompleteness, and possibly even incoherence of which may be deliberate attempts to destabilize the sovereignty movement.[18] Alternatively, the hesitancy that attends Plan B may reflect the fact that it occupies new policy territory. Unlike Plan A, which has a library of material to build on, Plan B has no predecessor, no inherited intellectual capital to exploit. Its creators are necessarily feeling their way in a policy area they have only reluctantly entered. They have a long way to go.

More than a year and a half after a referendum in which the 'yes' forces almost triumphed, there are no legislative committees or task forces examining alternative futures, and not a single major position paper dealing with either Plan A or Plan B has come from any government outside Quebec. The silence is startling and deeply disturbing. The future of Canada without Quebec is not a public concern of any government in the country.[19]

Fortunately, Plan B thinking is not confined to governments. In fact, one of the striking characteristics of the post–1995 Quebec referendum situation is the unwillingness of individuals and organizations to leave the responsibility of either renewing federalism or preparing a response to a future 'yes' victory to governments.[20] Yet it is deeply disturbing that so much of the asking and tentative answering of the fundamental questions of Canada's present and future constitutional existence – with or without Quebec – comes from nongovernmental sources: journalists and academics, with a leading role played by think tanks.[21] Laments over the somnolence outside Quebec on the constitutional abyss that Canadians face are common in English-language newspapers and elsewhere.[22]

Plan B territory, some of it occupied and some of it only gingerly explored, has been mapped out. Drawing on the contributions of several commentators, I consider that it encompasses the following:

- *A requirement that the process for determining the will of Quebecers be fair and transparent – for example, through the use of a fair question.*[23] This means that the rules of the secession game should not leave the unilateral power to determine the wording of the referendum question to a self-interested actor, the Quebec government, which may again, as in the past, be irresistibly tempted to ask a mobilizing question. If a referendum were held on an unacceptably biased question, federalist forces outside Quebec might declare the referendum result invalid. result invalid.
- *An agreement as to what constitutes an acceptable majority.* Both Chrétien

and Dion have stated explicitly that 50 percent plus one would not be enough.[24] Relevant considerations include: (i) the fact that an issue of such surpassing importance might necessitate a supermajority; (ii) the fact that, internally, Quebec is a pluralistic society, with anglophones, allophones, and aboriginal peoples as well as francophones; is a majority in which they do not participate adequate to deprive them of their connection to Canada?; and (iii) the extent to which the failure of the federal government to specify more than a simple majority in the referendums of 1980 and 1995 constitutes a precedent that cannot be overturned.[25]

- *A decision as to whether one referendum would be enough or a second would be required to deal with the results of the negotiations on the terms of separation.* According to José Woehrling, a leading Quebec nationalist law professor, to implement separation on the basis of an initial referendum before the voters can know the consequences of their action would not only offend

  Canadian law, but it [would] also be undemocratic and hence indefensible before international public opinion or on the basis of international law.[26]

- *Consideration of the special position of aboriginal peoples within Quebec.* Would they be expected simply to go along with a majority 'yes' if their own wishes were overwhelmingly 'no,' as they were in October 1995? The answer must take account of the distinct position of aboriginal peoples in domestic and international law.[27]

- *The issue of the territorial integrity of a seceding Quebec, and the linked question of the right of aboriginal peoples to determine the larger community to which they wish to belong.*[28] The general and volatile issue of partition as it relates to other dissenting 'no' minorities is also relevant here.[29]

- *Contingency legislation that would subject Quebec's secession to the rule of law and minimize disruption.* Gordon Robertson's proposals for such legislation include: (i) the illegality and nonrecognition of a UDI; (ii) the continuing applicability of federal law in Quebec regardless of the wishes of the Quebec government; (iii) the retention of all Canadian institutions until Parliament or the Governor-in-Council declares otherwise; and (iv) advance agreement on the procedures to finalize the agreed terms of secession.[30]

- *Substantive issues of immediate, practical concern that would attend the breakup of the country, the responses to which could not be delayed.* These include division of federal debt and assets, the creation of a land corridor between Ontario and the Mari- times, control over the St. Lawrence Seaway, division of the armed forces and the civil service, the position and future of aboriginal nations, the territorial integrity of Quebec, and a few others. Many partnership and some other issues would have to await the reconstitution of Canada after Quebec had departed and hence would not be part of Plan B in this bargaining transition stage.

The View from Quebec

Although Quebec sovereigntists have had counterparts to both Plan A and Plan B since the 1960s, the emergence of the federal government's own shaky Plan B has evoked outraged responses from both the PQ and the Bloc Québécois, presumably because their Plan B presupposed, or hoped for, a defenseless, cooperative partner on the other side.[31] A more cynical view, suggested by one reviewer of this paper, holds that the PQ and the Bloc knew the bargaining would be brutal, but thought their success in a referendum required keeping that information from Quebec voters.

The contemporary sovereigntist alternative to federalism is well developed. The PQ and the Bloc claim that Quebec has an unfettered right to secede unilaterally. They assert that the Canadian Constitution is irrelevant to such a unilateral act, and they justify using their own referendum legislation, which gives the Quebec government control of the timing and wording of the referendum question. They assume that a 50 percent plus one majority would be adequate. They assert that the territorial integrity of Quebec is inviolable, and they claim that, politically, Quebecers are a single people – despite the massive ethnic divisions revealed by the October 1995 referendum, in which anglophones, allophones, and aboriginal nations overwhelmingly voted 'no.'

Prior to the 1995 referendum, the PQ had prepared itself for a 'yes' victory. The Quebec government was ready to move expeditiously and vigorously to implement the mandate it would claim from the electorate. Visits to foreign capitals were to be orchestrated and foreign embassies contacted. There was an understanding – or at least a hope – that France would move quickly to recognize Quebec's independence and then pressure the United States to follow suit. Further, the Quebec government had amassed a $19 billion fund to prop up the Canadian dollar, much of it taken from pension funds. Premier Jacques Parizeau had his victory speech ready. A one-year timetable had been established for negotiation of an economic partnership with Canada, a task to which then-Bloc leader Lucien Bouchard had been appointed and for which organized proposals to Ottawa had been prepared.

A victorious PQ was ready to launch what a press report described as a massive assault on an unprepared Ottawa 'to bring the federal government to its knees.'[32] Further, the PQ government had indicated its willingness to resort to a UDI if negotiations had not proceeded satisfactorily. Hence, the PQ did not see an agreement on the multitude of issues to be resolved with Canada/ROC to have been a prerequisite to independence. More pointedly, the PQ treated the Canadian Constitution as having negligible relevance for the secession process. In brief, Canada outside Quebec was assigned the role of spectator in the referendum while Quebecers – as Quebecers, not as Canadians – decided their (and Canada's) future. Nationalist rhetoric also suggested the ROC would play the role of a complaisant, cooperative partner of an independent Quebec following the hoped-for 'yes' vote.

The PQ justified this readiness for rapid action by rhetoric that assumed Quebecers had a remarkable degree of discretion in determining the route to sovereignty. What made this strategy believable was the relative silence and lack of preparation outside Quebec, on the part of governments and ordinary citizens, concerning a sovereigntist outcome for which many Quebecers had been preparing for three decades.

The Juggling Game

Although both Quebec and Ottawa are now engaged in Plan A and Plan B activities, it is much easier for Quebec than for Ottawa to juggle the two games. In Quebec, diametrically opposed futures have been explored and pursued with vigor since the late 1960s, mostly through competing political parties (the federalist Liberals and the sovereigntist PQ). Occasionally, one party has moved in the direction of the other, as when PQ premier René Lévesque, after the *Constitution Act, 1982*, decided to accept the *beau risque* of renewed federalism, or when Liberal premier Robert Bourassa, after the failure of the Meech Lake Accord, flirted with more drastic options and commissioned what became the Allaire Report, which recommended a renewed federalism with an emasculated Ottawa. Whichever party was in power, the two possibilities were part of official debate: in addition to the Allaire Report, the Bélanger-Campeau Commission and two National Assembly committees explored Quebec's options after Meech Lake.

Outside Quebec, however, it has been much more difficult to play the two games simultaneously. One reason for this is psychological. Not only are the two plans directed to different futures, but the scenario behind each plan portrays the other party in a different light depending on the goal that is sought. Thus, Plan A presupposes a friendly counterpart who can be conciliated, who is now and will remain a member of the same political community. Plan B portrays the other party as the breaker of the nation, as a hostile actor preparing to exit the Canadian community and thus not deserving of the empathy that is reserved for fellow citizens – in other words, it treats Quebecers as the foreigners they might become. By generating contradictory images of the 'other party,' the two plans transmit contradictory messages to those who draft policy and prepare its implementation. Within a single government, sometimes within a single individual, these contradictory cues evoke tensions that are not easily managed. Also, of course, for a single government publicly to play both A and B games simultaneously easily leads to charges of insincerity from its opponents.

Plan B also generates tension between the federalist forces inside and outside Quebec. Naturally, the Daniel Johnson-led provincial Liberals find any focus on Plan B disturbing, as it deflects attention away from Plan A, in which they have placed their faith, and looks to a future in which that plan has failed. Their concern is not irrational, for if Ottawa came to believe that it had boxed Quebec in with court cases and threats of using the stick, it might be less inclined to use the carrot of renewed federalism to induce Quebec to stay.[33] Plan B is opposed by both the sovereigntist PQ government and the official Liberal opposition, although for different reasons. It also probably divides federalist forces within Quebec, getting its strongest support from those anglophones and allophones sympathetic to partition.[34]

The Limitations of Plan B

The leading role with respect to Plan B should come from the federal government, the only government capable of straddling the diversity of interests outside Quebec. For Ottawa to take a leadership role now would position it to continue in that role in the event of a 'yes' vote in Quebec, when its leadership might well be challenged.

But the federal government's Plan B is not intended to be a comprehensive response to the major issues that would emerge should Quebecers vote 'yes.' Its reach is selective: Ottawa is more interested in those aspects of Plan B that seek to influence the rules governing secession, and some of the hard bargaining issues, than in the all-important question of how to reconstitute Canada without Quebec.

Ottawa's dilemma, however, is that, until a 'yes' victory has been accepted, it is obliged to speak for *all* Canadians, including all Quebecers, which effectively prevents it from assuming the leadership role in devising a plan to carry on should those millions of Quebecers decide to leave.[35] Further, in keeping Plan B focused on the rules of secession and on hard bargaining, Ottawa hopes to maximize the plan's effect as a deterrent to secession, as a stick to reinforce the carrot of Plan A. By contrast, the ROC's reconstitution would not be a threat to sovereigntists, so focusing on it would not add to the federalist arsenal. On the contrary, sovereigntists would interpret Ottawa's planning for the ROC's reconstitution in advance of a 'yes' vote as an indication the ROC was preparing to become the kind of partner that Bouchard has so often said it would.

Provincial governments will not do what Ottawa cannot do. Preparations by the provinces for Quebec's secession, if they exist at all, will be secret, and focused on the future of the province, not the country, on economic issues (the gains and losses to be expected from Quebec's departure), not on longer-term constitutional concerns. Even if some provincial governments overcome these biases, they are unlikely to want to begin preparing their publics for a constitutional future without Quebec. People in particular provinces may derive some solace from the knowledge that their provincial governments are quietly looking to a future that cannot be publicly discussed, and that they can look to their provincial governments for leadership if Quebec goes. But while such backroom preparations and the knowledge that they are taking place should not be discounted, neither should their significance be exaggerated.

For the PQ and the Bloc, the sovereignty project is their *raison d'être*. For them, Quebec's sovereignty would be a triumph. By contrast, the current federal government has no similar stake in the future of a Canada without Quebec – indeed, for it, such an outcome would be a humiliating defeat, and is yet another reason it cannot play a leadership role in prereferendum thinking about the reconstitution of Canada without Quebec. In sum, the federal government cannot prepare the ROC for a future without Quebec and, since it is not a politically organized entity in its own right, the ROC cannot prepare itself.

This lack of leadership on such a key issue is a serious matter. In a sense, of course, the Reform Party is positioned to become the voice of the ROC, but even Reform's focus so far has been more on the terms of secession and on Plan A changes to the existing system than on the constitutional future of the ROC should Quebec leave.

For the most part, then, the possible future of a smaller, reconstituted Canada is not Ottawa's concern. Plan B inside Quebec and Plan B outside Quebec are not mirror images of each other. The future of Canada after Quebec leaves – its identity, its constitutional structure, its unity – are likely to remain relatively unexamined by governments in the period preceding a possible 'yes' vote. Such examination as does take place will be secret, infused with a provincial rather than a federal perspective, and inadequate because it will not have been informed and moderated by discussion with other governments or by a dialogue with the public.

The Next Step: Plan C

Outside Quebec, therefore, Plan B is not enough, and neither governments nor private commentators, with a few exceptions, have addressed the issue of the longer-term fate of the ROC after a Quebec secession – that is, Plan C.[36]

While the rudimentary development of an official Plan B to supplement Plan A is a positive one, for Canadians outside Quebec it still does not answer several fundamental questions: How prepared would they be for that future they do not seek? The inevitable answer is: Very little. How, and how successfully, would the ROC reconstitute itself? The question has scarcely been asked, let alone been answered. The immediate aftermath of the referendum would be a remarkably inauspicious time in which to undertake this task. In the absence of preparation, there would be widespread panic, and the task of arranging terms on certain inescapable issues with a seceding Quebec would have priority.

Canadians have overcome the taboo that once kept them from publicly discussing Plan B. Their governments, however, continue to maintain a taboo on discussing Plan C; it is policy territory they will not enter. This lack of preparation would matter little if the shape of Canada's future without Quebec were highly predictable. But it is not.

Ignorance

The most fundamental point about the possible breakup of Canada is the depth of Canadians' ignorance of what would follow. As the following brief survey makes clear, to read the literature that seeks to describe Canadians' future on both sides of a possible divide is to realize our limited capacity – inside and outside Quebec – to discern our destination.

The Literature: No Consensus

Predictions of Canada's future without Quebec display stark disagreement on all the major issues.

Quebec sovereigntists in the partnership camp portray future Quebec-Canada relations in rosy hues, based on the premise that Canadians and their governments outside Quebec would adopt an accounting mentality of narrow self-interest and, after a brief hangover, strike the kind of cooperative partnership arrangements the sovereigntists seek. That, at least, has been their public posture.[37]

Commentators outside Quebec usually characterize this scenario as a fairy tale. On the contrary, they say, the bargaining would be hard, the will to compromise weak, and the ROC's response driven by a visceral anger – the expression of a wounded and cornered nationalism.[38]

Alternatively, commentators outside Quebec sometimes suggest that there would be no 'other side' for Quebec to bargain with following a 'yes' vote. Remarkably, even Prime Minister Chrétien raised this possibility in the closing days of the 1995 referendum campaign.[39] The argument is that either the federal government would virtually collapse as its legitimacy crumbled in the face of its humiliating failure to live up to its *raison d'être* – keeping the country in one piece – or primary attention would be focused on the more pressing task of reconstituting the ROC. Thus, Gordon Gibson argues that a humiliated federal government, its moral authority in tatters, and a triumvirate of the three 'have' provinces (Ontario. Alberta, and British Columbia) would impose a tough deal on Quebec, cooperating only on the bare essentials. Canada would then turn its back on Quebec and attend to the overriding task of deciding its own constitutional future.[40]

Other analysts dispute such a scenario, however, and predict a rush to the center as shocked Canadians invest their security wishes in a federal government that they hope would minimize the financial crisis and strike the best deal possible with Quebec. According to Robert A. Young, once it became clear that the secession process was irreversible, there would be a 'tremendous premium on solidarity' on both sides, which would strengthen Ottawa's leadership role in the post-'yes' bargaining with Quebec.[41]

Views on the chances for the ROC's survival, constitutional structure, and cohesion share little except their tendency to contradict each other. Former Progressive Conservative cabinet minister John Crosbie, for example, has taken the apocalyptic view of a battered Canada breaking up after Quebec's exit.[42] Others who doubt either the will or the capacity of the ROC to survive without Quebec include the late Robert Bourassa, Peter Leslie, and US scholar Charles Doran, writing in the influential journal, *Foreign Affairs*.[43] Joseph Jockel, testifying before a US House of Representatives committee in 1996, said he did not believe that 'English Canada' would fragment in the short run, but that, in the long run, he considered its surviving as one country or dividing into several fragments as 'equally likely.'[44]

Those who advocate the contrary view, that Canada without Quebec would survive as a united polity, tend to stress as unifying factors cultural homogeneity, positive identification with the idea of Canada, the nationalism of Canadians outside Quebec, allegiance to the Charter of Rights and Freedoms, and Canadians' strong feeling of their distinctiveness on the North American continent.

In short, pessimists see Canada structurally in terms of its provincial divisions; optimists stress the citizen base of the constitutional order. These themes run through the writings of several prominent academic commentators.[45] On the other hand, the hopes of even the optimists are guarded. Keith Banting, for example, casts a vote for a continuing Canada, but qualifies it by saying that 'collapse ... seems unlikely, at least in the short and medium term.'[46]

Those who do see Canada as surviving without Quebec nevertheless disagree on the kind of country it would be. Dan Usher sees a virtual unitary state emerging with the eroding of the federalist rationale by Quebec's departure; the largely homogeneous remainder, he says, responding to its own cultural coherence, would quickly assume a unitary posture.[47] Robert Young, in the most exhaustive available analysis of the post-'yes' scenario, predicts the emergence of a Canada with a strong central government following Quebec's departure. His prediction appears to be based partly on the assumption that bargaining the terms of secession and reconstituting the ROC would occur simultaneously. He sees the requirement for solidarity dictated by the former as providing momentum for expanding the role of a strong central government in a reconstituted ROC.[48] Gordon Gibson, by contrast, possibly influenced by his location in British Columbia, sees a future Canada without Quebec as profoundly decentralized, with a weakened, caretaker central government reduced to limited responsibilities. He does not discount additional fragmentation leading to the possible breakup of the country.[49]

An additional area of uncertainty deserves a brief comment. The assumption that Canadians are a peaceable people, immune to incitements to violence, is now held with diminishing conviction. The possibility of violence, although almost universally discouraged, is now almost routinely mentioned. Such talk was almost completely absent at the time of the 1980 referendum.[50] The now-admitted possibility of violence and its unpredictable consequences, coupled with a continuing constraint against serious analysis of the possibility of civil disorder, add to the difficulty of predicting what would happen following a 'yes' vote. It also reinforces the desirability of a negotiated departure by Quebec, to minimize the possibility of violence.'

The preceding discussion was meant to be illustrative, not exhaustive. Nevertheless, the conclusion that dissensus reigns supreme among the analysts and commentators is shared by others who have surveyed the predictions of the Quebec-Canada future following a 'yes' vote,[51] and it confirms that the post-breakup future is a huge question mark.

An Inevitable Uncertainty

This uncertainty is a recurring theme of Robert Young's *The Secession of Quebec and the Future of Canada*, the most serious analysis of the consequences of secession yet undertaken. His point is simple: '[N]o one knows what will happen if Quebec secedes.'[52] Political debate and leadership, he argues, have unpredictable outcomes, yet they are especially important in secession crises, which weaken the impact of socioeconomic factors; the past provides limited guidance for such unique events.[53]

Young addresses several crucial questions: How would a Quebec UDI be received in the international community? There is no consensus about the relevant legal principles or about their application to Quebec.[54] Is it possible to predict the outcome of negotiations between Quebec and the ROC, and how the latter would be reconstituted? No, Young says, one can choose only between 'profound uncertainty ... [and] disagreement about several basic issues.'[55] Would a surviving Canada be more centralized or more decentralized? There are pressures in both directions.[56] How would Canadians in the ROC respond to a smaller, fractured country once Quebec had gone? Would their loyalties be pulled toward the center or to the provinces? One can know only after Quebec goes.[57]

The uncertainty that Young reiterates in area after area is inherent in the situation. There are so many actors, domestic and international, whose behavior would be modified by the breakup of Canada, that no one can predict how the aggregate of this behavior – in which each actor influences the others – would turn out. Further, the odds on particular outcomes would change as the leading actors modify their behavior in the period leading up to secession to increase the likelihood of achieving their goals. Thus, the emergence of Plan B now means that the outcome and consequences of a future 'yes' vote will be very different from what would have occurred had Quebecers voted 'yes' in the 1995 referendum, when no Plan B existed.

The uncertainty of the situation is compounded by the politicized nature of much of the scholarship that self-interestedly seeks to analyze it. Young writes:

Partisans of both federalism and sovereignty construct and deploy alternative futures, aiming to influence the expectations and behaviour of citizens ... [which] makes many extant analyses more suspect than is usual in the social sciences.[58]

Maureen Covell agrees, noting that discussions of the future of

a Canada without Quebec are of necessity an exercise in political science fiction that is only partly grounded in verifiable data and that gives a large role to the assumptions and preferences of the author.[59]

One must, therefore, assume that some of the literature that purports to shed light on the issue is actually an exercise in disinformation.

The particular uncertainty that is the focus of this *Commentary* – the shape of the ROC after Quebec's secession – is unlikely to be reduced in the period leading up to the next referendum. As I have already discussed, governments will engage in neither public discussion of, nor public preparation for, the future of Canada without Quebec. Ottawa is clearly incapable of planning for a future predicated on its own repudiation. Provincial governments, despite the (probably minimal) in-house research they may undertake, can do no more than prepare covert, partial, self-interested visions of what one out of many actors would prefer.

Yet democratic constitutionmaking requires more than the aggregation of separate visions formed in private by governments and in isolation from other players. It involves the testing and shaping of views and proposals that are not initially complementary, in a process of debate and bargaining with other participants. In the contemporary era, Plan C, constitutionmaking for a Canada without Quebec, has to be a shared responsibility of citizens and governments. That such a process could be mounted prior to the next Quebec referendum is inconceivable. That Canadian governments would even discuss with their citizens options for a Canada without Quebec prior to another referendum is highly implausible. That their in-house preparedness would be limited, fragmented, self-interested, and uncoordinated is certain. That, as a people, Canadians would be unprepared is unavoidable. This lack of preparation, therefore, for what would happen to the ROC should Quebecers vote 'yes' is inherent in the circumstances.

In my view, therefore, the situation on the morning after a 'yes' vote would be as follows:

- The scholarly and other literature to which one normally looks for guidance would be in disarray.
- Governments would have prepared Canadians in the rest of Canada only minimally, if at all, for the task of deciding on *their* constitutional future.
- Canadians in the ROC would be ignorant about the future, not just in the sense of their normal inability to predict tomorrow's events in detail, but about the very shape of their society. The old order would be in the process of breaking up, habit and routine shattered, and everyday constraints on behavior slackened. This is the kind of

unpredictability that attends situations when historic civic identities come undone, historic ongoingness has departed, and the future becomes frighteningly open to both exciting and threatening possibilities.[60]

This fundamental, unavoidable ignorance, therefore, is the overwhelming fact Canadians must keep in mind as they confront a possible postbreakup future. We are truly looking into a dark, unknowable abyss.[61]

Panic, Fear, and Insecurity after a 'Yes' Vote

In the absence of preparation, the period after a 'yes' vote in another Quebec referendum that is sufficiently impressive to suggest that two or more new states are in the making north of the US border would be one of panic, fear, and uncertainty in the ROC. Who we are as Canadians and what country we would belong to in a few years would be question marks. Media headlines and the questions on the minds of citizens would be scary: How far will the unraveling go? Will my savings, my pension, my property, my children's future, and my job be safe? Most important for non-Quebecers, will I still be a Canadian citizen and, if so, what will that mean in the new circumstances? Or will I become a citizen of the newly independent states of, say, British Columbia, Newfoundland, a union of the former Maritime provinces, or even the United States?

A lamentably unprepared public would be fearful about its future and angry with those it held responsible. According to Banting, sovereigntist Quebecers naively underestimate 'the political turmoil' that secession would precipitate in the ROC, which would be 'thrown into crisis.'[62] He contrasts the psychological climate inside and outside Quebec that would follow a 'yes' vote. Quebec, he argues, would start with three advantages that the ROC would lack. First, independence would be 'a national affirmation for the Québécois ... [and] in many ways the central psychological framework of that historic society would remain intact.' Second, independence would build on the prior thought and planning that had been devoted to its achievement. Third, Quebec would 'start with a coherent set of political institutions,' with the province of Quebec simply being redefined as a state.[63]

Outside Quebec, there would be little celebration. Instead, Canadians would undergo a 'collective psychological disorientation,' supplemented by anger and resentment. The ROC would be intellectually and emotionally unprepared, as it would not have 'engaged in a collective reflection about how to proceed without Quebec.' Third, and 'most critically, Canada would lack stable political institutions through which to develop a conception of its future.'[64]

In spite of the advantages Quebec would enjoy, however, its domestic situation would also be grave and beset with massive uncertainty. Would aboriginal peoples resist their incorporation in an independent Quebec? Would the partitionist movement now stirring remain small and ineffectual, or grow in scope and support into a dynamic force? How would the 40 percent or so who would have voted 'no' accept the sundering of their civic ties with Canada? 'No' voters would include virtually all of Quebec's anglophones, allophones, and aboriginal peoples, and the ethnic divisions would be wide, deep, and bitter. Banting argues that, within Quebec, instability triggered by the resistance of aboriginal peoples, by the anger of minorities, and by the problem of borders 'hold[s] considerable potential for violence.'[65] Even Premier Bouchard does not disagree. He spoke simple truth when he stated in June 1994 that a narrow sovereigntist referendum victory could put 'the political solidarity of Quebecers in question' and challenge Quebec's 'political cohesion.'[66] But even a more decisive victory would not placate the losers, who would include an overwhelming majority of the nonfrancophone population. Logically, a more decisive victory would be based on an even more divisive ethnic split than the 1995 result, with a smaller percentage of francophone voters on the 'no' side.

Both inside and outside Quebec, public opinion would be unanchored, and volatile. Demagogues skilled at inflaming ethnic or nationalistic passions would find this environment to their liking.

The breakup of a mature, capitalist democracy in which state and society are deeply intertwined can only be traumatic, especially when the catalyst is a politicized nationalism. Both Quebec and the ROC, despite the greater preparedness of the former, would be buffeted by domestic and international forces beyond their control. Their interactions with each other, following a polarizing referendum that would have stimulated ethnic nationalism in Quebec and resentment and shock outside Quebec, likely would be acrimonious. The governments of both Quebec and the now-truncated Canada would be struggling to maintain their authority. The exhilaration of the winners would be accompanied by the same fears and insecurities that would be rife among the losers. In these circumstances, ripe for anomic behavior, policies to minimize disorder and impose some certainty and predictability would be essential.

Plan C and a Plea for Time

Who Will We Be?

If Quebec were to vote to secede, Canadians outside Quebec would have to begin to decide who they are and what they wish to be – something francophone Quebecers have spent the past few decades doing. Even the labels one now uses to describe this entity – 'the rest of Canada' or 'Canada without Quebec' – graphically reveal how far Canadians have to go in this traumatic journey of self-discovery. No self-respecting people describes itself as a rest of anything, or in terms of what it is without. As soon as Quebec's departure became definite, these transitional labels probably would be replaced by a redefined use of 'Canada,' unless the country disintegrated rapidly into smaller entities.

If Quebec's departure were to happen, according to Covell, it

will be too late to begin the process of imagining the future of what remains of Canada in conditions allowing for rational thought and the exercise of originality.[67]

On the other hand, as I have already argued, governments will not undertake this anticipatory thinking and planning *before* a 'yes' vote, and in the immediate postreferendum bargaining context, they would be too busy to focus simultaneously on reconstitution issues. The limited intellectual capital on this issue on Canada's bookshelves would make only a marginal contribution to the fundamental political task of educating a distraught people on alternative futures.

Fortunately, as they peer into the abyss, Canadians would have a few certain 'givens,' which would be challenged only at the margins: an independent judiciary and the rule of law, the Charter of Rights and Freedoms, responsible parliamentary government, and a head of state who would be above the fray. Canadians can hope for quick agreement on these anchors, even while realizing that many big questions about their future would remain untouched.

The major issue would be whether we can refashion federalism – both the division of powers and the composition of a revised Senate – that would keep us together. Would Canadians be able to find a workable balance between their federal and provincial selves in new circumstances? A closely linked issue would be the accommodation of aboriginal peoples with significant powers of self-government; with one component of Canada's multinational existence gone, the historically neglected aboriginal dimension would come to the fore and require sensitive constitutional consideration.

In reality, then, the overarching question would be: Could Canadians outside Quebec overcome their divisions and survive as a single people albeit with divided civic identities? While institutional ingenuity would play a big part in success or failure, the outcome would depend more on will, desire, and community identification. These attributes, however, are neither simple inheritances nor automatic. They would need to be uncovered, worked on, and refashioned – a task that cannot be completed through hasty action.

Avoiding Hasty Decisions

If Canadians had to reconstitute the ROC quickly in an atmosphere of panic, their decisions would reflect their lack of preparation. The uncertainty, the erosion of confidence as we adapt to a world we formerly viewed as friendly, and the ambiguity of who we are and who we might become would leave us prey to unpredictable passions. Two antithetical scenarios, focusing on our people-hood, reveal how short-run considerations can generate long-run constitutional consequences.

The Centrifugal Bias
Quebec's departure could destabilize the surviving ROC for two reasons. First, the federal government might be viewed as a humiliated and defeated Goliath. Second, powerful centrifugal forces might be released, forces that pulled the provinces away from Ottawa's influence in the wake of a traumatic self-examina-tion. In either case, the resultant panic would trigger a frantic search for security.

Such a decentralizing scenario would be most likely if the shock of a 'yes' vote were compounded by the second shock of a Quebec UDI. In this outcome, the federal government would be seen as having failed in its most fundamental task – that of preserving the unity and territorial integrity of the country entrusted to it. Further, it would be the federal Parliament, bureaucracy, and land mass – its population diminished by a quarter, its territory by 15 percent – not those of the remaining nine provinces, that would have shrunk. It follows that it would be the federal, not the provincial, dimension of the citizenry that would be wounded.

In such circumstances, the search for the ROC's' reconstitution after Que-bec's departure would, other things being equal, likely privilege provincial gov-ernments, especially those of the wealthier provinces, and thus lead to a more fragmented, provincialized successor state than would be probable if haste could be avoided. It might even result in two or more separate polities.

A province's capacity and willingness to pursue its own self-interest devoid of empathy for the other provinces should not, however, be exaggerated. Pro-vincial governments would also be unprepared, and their citizens troubled, fear-ful, and unready for bold leaps. All the provinces would be restrained by a surviving sense of Canadianism that would be reinforced by ties of family and kinship that cross provincial boundaries. Further, the 'have-not' provinces would come to the aid of the center.

The fact remains, however, that, in this scenario, provincial governments would emerge from a 'yes' vote in Quebec with much less damage to their integrity and continuity than would the federal government. They might be unprepared to pursue their own aggrandizement, especially to the point of leav-ing, but they would not have to carry, during the reconstitution process, the opprobrium of having lost a country.

This exaggerated provincialism, if it came about, would owe its victory not to having survived a democratic process of constitutional deliberation, but simply because it happened to dominate the stage when a decision had to be made. This fractionated future would be less likely to shape the reconstituted ROC if a relative state of normality were allowed to return before any constitutional decisions were made.

The Centripetal Bias

An alternative scenario suggests the opposite of the preceding scenario. It is plausible that hasty decisions on the reconstitutional front could lead to a more centralized future for a smaller, more homogeneous Canada than would emerge if reconstitution were delayed. The likelihood of this outcome would be strengthened if the federal government – perhaps following some version of Robertson's proposal for adopting contingency legislation in advance of the next referendum[68] – were to take charge of the post–'yes' situation, increase the cost to Quebec of a UDI, negotiate a package of agreements with Quebec that is well received outside Quebec, and orchestrate Quebec's exit via the formal amending process, thus preserving the rule of law. Successfully playing the leading role in Quebec's negotiated exit would re-establish the federal government's legitimacy.

If this were to happen, it would reduce the perception of rupture, increase the perception of continuity, and enhance support for the central government. Further, the support engendered for the central government in a successful bargaining process with Quebec almost certainly would lead the provinces to maintain a low profile, their appeals to self-interest having been muted by the crisis. The relevant analogy here is Canada's wartime experience. In this scenario, a hasty reconstitution would doubtless lead to a strong center backed by a positive public response to the temporary nourishment of decisive federal government leadership. The exercise of such leadership in the closing months of the old Canada by what still nominally remained the government of all of Canada would encourage the federal government to transfer its leading role to the new, smaller Canada waiting in the wings for its constitutional redefinition.

One can conjecture many more post-'yes' scenarios – each of which might tilt the balance between centralization and decentralization in one way or another and lead to different long-range constitutional futures for the ROC. But would it be wise to allow the ROC's constitutional future to be heavily influenced by the accident of events immediately flowing from a 'yes' vote, when Canadians' preparedness would be close to nil, or is it possible to find a better, less frantic context for the ROC's reconstitution?

The Crux of Plan C: Take Time

Thus, it is too soon for governments to prepare in advance for a 'yes' vote in another Quebec referendum, and it would be too late, according to some analysts, to think about the ROC's future immediately following such a result. But there is a way out of this dilemma. The solution, which should be the first step of Plan C, would be to buy time, to delay the reconstitution process. There is no need for Canadians to feel trapped and obliged to act on the ROC's reconstitution immediately following Quebec's exit. Why not delay the process and so increase the role of reasoned discussion and debate in making constitutional choices?

In the event of Quebec's secession, therefore, the ROC should continue the existing constitutional arrangements, with Quebec excised, for a transitional period of, say, three to five years (I have a strong preference for the shorter period).

Advantages of Interim Continuity

Stability
One advantage of interim continuity is that it would be the easiest course of action. The machinery would already be in place and, most important, Canadians and their governments in the ROC would be unprepared for anything else. This stabilizing response would reassure not only Canadians outside Quebec but also the international financial community that governments and legitimate authority were still functioning. Disruption of the known, the familiar, and the trusted would be minimized. Federalism, parliamentary government, the constitutional monarchy, the Charter, the existing electoral system, and the administrative structure that applies ongoing policies would remain. The party system, while having to adapt to the new situation, would at least be familiar.

An Aid to Bargaining
Interim continuity would also make it easier for the ROC to bargain with Quebec on a limited set of unavoidable issues prior to a negotiated independence respectful of the Canadian Constitution. Staggering the tasks of bargaining with Quebec and reconstituting the ROC would prevent the agenda from becoming unmanageable. (Such questions as precisely how the bargaining would take place (presuming no Quebec UDI), who the bargainers would be, what the Canadian side would be prepared to discuss, and what would have to be put off

until after the ROC's reconstitution remain immensely complicated and controversial issues beyond the scope of this *Commentary*.)

Until Quebec's departure was finalized, however, bargaining between the
two sides probably would take place under the aegis of a small commission
consisting of the existing federal government, with a drastically diminished role
for its Quebec members (whose legitimacy would be gravely eroded), some
representation from the provinces, territories, and aboriginal peoples, and possibly from the opposition parties.[69]

Many of the issues on Quebec's agenda would be sidelined – those that
were not urgent, and those that could not be addressed until the shape of the
reconstituted ROC had crystallized. Instead, the negotiators would focus on
disentanglement, not on partnership or interstate agreements that lacked
urgency for the ROC side. In any case, the ROC could not enter into partnership arrangements on commercial, economic, political, or other matters that
presupposed its stability, identity, and continuity until the reconstitution process was completed.

Getting to Know the New Quebec State

Delay would also allow the ROC to learn more about its new neighbor. As the
heady days of the referendum triumph receded, Quebec would be settling into
its new status and the answers to a number of important postsecession questions
would become clearer: How significant would be the exodus of population from
Quebec following its secession? Would 'no' voters who chose to remain in
Quebec seem to be adjusting to the new reality, or would a sovereign Quebec
remain a bitterly divided society? What would be the state of relations between
Quebec and its aboriginal peoples? What would be its fiscal situation? How
would the initial limited agreements between Quebec and the ROC be working?
Answers to these questions would be relevant to the ROC's reconstitution. The
foreign environment of the ROC's existence would have changed; for the first
time, as Denis Stairs reminds us, Canada would have two foreign, next-door
neighbors.[70] Finally, the ROC could learn from mistakes made by its newly
independent neighbor.

An Unfair Advantage to the Status Quo?

Some people might oppose a multiyear transition period on the grounds that it
would favor the development of a shrunken version of the old constitutional
order but with a stronger central government. In other words, such a plan would
disadvantage those actors whose influence would be greatest in the period of
maximum uncertainty following a 'yes' vote, when Canadians would be anx-

ious for security but the federal government on which they normally would have relied might have crumbled. In general, then, delay might have less appeal for those who see decentralization as the wave of the future, and even less for those who support secessionist movements in other provinces.

It is true that the transitional stability of the status quo would work against any actor who would profit, politically or otherwise, from the uncertainty my proposal is designed to reduce. That indeed is its purpose. Further, and positively, delay would increase the likelihood of the ROC's survival as one country. Assuming that survival, however, it is still unclear whether a rapid reconstitution following Quebec's departure would serve centralizing or decentralizing forces.

Those who fear that a transitional regime would give extra leverage to the central government in the ROC's reconstitution forget that it would, after all, only be a caretaker government. Provincial governments, by contrast, would be less constrained. Their party systems would suffer a lesser shock. Unlike the federal government, they would still govern the same society as they did before Quebec's departure, and they would not be subject to the same hesitations about their roles as their federal counterpart. Further, if the old system were as inapplicable to the new circumstances as its opponents argue, the transition period experiment would surely confirm their beliefs.

The Constitution and Quebec

Much of the difficulty of reconstituting a smallerCanada reflects the deeply embedded presence of Quebec in the theory and practice of the country's constitutional evolution. The constitutional arrangements of the old Canada have been shaped profoundly by Quebec's presence. Many of the crucial developments in Canada's history – the Riel rebellion, the conscription crises in both world wars, the role of Quebec in shaping the party system, the role of francophone prime ministers, and the halting evolution of the welfare state – underline Quebec's impact on the political life of Canada in the first century after Confederation. In the past three decades, that impact has increased.

Pressure from Quebec has driven the country along a centrifugal path. The constitutional principle – some would say dogma – of the equality of provinces has allowed other provinces to acquire more autonomy on the coattails of Quebec's demands. Although the linkage is indirect, Quebec nationalism has stimulated aboriginal nationalism, by example and by widening the constitutional agenda and providing a stage on which aboriginal peoples have been able to press their claims. Even those who resent Quebec's prominence in Canada's decades-long constitutional introspection nevertheless have become acclimatized to a political world in which Quebec is part of 'us.' To break out of this manner of thinking would take time.

Quebec's departure would not end the constitutional introspection of the surviving Canada. From the 1970s onward, constitutional pressures for change have emanated from other parts of the country as well. Quebec's absence would precipitate difficult new rounds of constitutional self-examination, and require Canadians to develop a new language of constitutional self-understanding. Senate reform, a third order of government (for aboriginal nations), the amending formula, the Charter's place in constitutional arrangements, the issue of popular sovereignty, and the relative roles of the federal and provincial governments would all be revisited in the context of Canada without Quebec. And behind all the others would lurk one crucial question: Can Canadians, without Quebec, survive as one people?

A Herculean Task

It is easier to underestimate than to overestimate the difficulties of the ROC's reconstitution. The task would be nothing less than the creation of a new nation, a new people. Canadians have been schooled by their history, education, lived experiences, and the symbols of their nationhood to think of themselves as including Quebec. Quebec has been central to Canada's self-definition, geographically, culturally, linguistically, and in other ways. The 'rest of Canada' is headless, voiceless, and without definition as long as Quebec remains in Canada. Citizens outside Quebec think of themselves as Canadians. Their leaders have believed that to stimulate a separate identity for the ROC, or for 'English Canada,' would undermine Canadian unity. Abraham Rotstein argues that Canadians view themselves in terms of 'mappism' – an inability to 'conceptualize the country except as a geographical unity.'[71] The ROC's post–'yes' task would necessitate a psychological and intellectual shift to a new identity that would take time to fashion. It would not be possible to extrapolate from Meech Lake (the Quebec round) or Charlottetown (the Canada round) to the kinds of constitutional changes that would be sought if Quebec seceded. In both of those rounds, Quebec's demanding presence influenced the behavior of all the other actors, particularly the federal government.

Unquestionably, three decades of constitutional introspection have contributed to an emerging anticipatory sense of self for the ROC that excludes Quebec. This self, however, is clearly underdeveloped, does not yet think of itself as a people ready for a state of its own, and has not willingly and fully extricated itself from the traditional Canadian self that includes Quebec. It can do so only if and when the old Canada dies.

In the event of Quebec's secession, Canada would not be in the relatively fortunate position of the former Czechoslovakia, where a 'velvet divorce' was possible because the central authority could simply fade away while power naturally devolved to the two successor states. The Czechoslovak case is more accurately characterized as a split than as a secession of one part. Canada's case would be different. Canada is a federal state – a system of competing governments ruling a citizen body with the distinct civic identities appropriate to federalism. If Canada's center simply faded Czechoslovak-style, the recipients of jurisdictional powers outside Quebec would be nine provinces and two territories – an unacceptable outcome. On the other hand, the excision of Quebec from an otherwise unchanged constitutional structure would leave the ROC with constitutional arrangements that might be inappropriate to the new circumstances.

The departure of Quebec and the resultant shaking of established arrangements might stimulate formerly forbidden thoughts in other provincial capitals and among the citizenry, jeopardizing our ability to stay together as one people. If Quebec were to leave by a UDI, the psychological destabilization that might follow could precipitate such a loss of confidence that imitators might surface in other provincial capitals. Even if Quebec were to depart by a negotiated process, to deny the same option to the citizens and governments of other provinces would be difficult. Delay would not prevent such a possibility.

Continuity With or Without a UDI

A transitional constitutional continuity would provide a secure context within which the ROC could concentrate attention on its future after Quebec had gone. That continuity would be desirable whether Quebec departed by a UDI or through a negotiated procedure that employed the existing constitutional amending formula – although the latter would be infinitely preferable.[72] In either case, however, Canadians would have to rethink their constitutional existence. If Quebec's departure were negotiated, the lead role the federal government presumably would play in guiding that process would provide a certain naturalness to keeping the old constitutional structure, minus Quebec, for an interim period. If constitutional thinking about the ROC's future were to follow on a Quebec UDI, however, the necessity for a federal role in such perilous circumstances would still remain, even though Ottawa's legitimacy would be severely weakened. As I discussed earlier, the possibility of a vacuum at the federal level would stimulate centrifugal pressures, encourage the 'have' provinces to take charge, and enhance the likelihood of erratic, panic behavior throughout the system. In such a case, the need for the continuity and security provided by a stable federal framework would be enhanced. Thus, under either a UDI or a negotiated exit by Quebec, it would be wise to continue the existing system while the new Canada sorted itself out.

After the Interim

The process by which the peoples and governments of the ROC should pursue their constitutional redefinition is not the subject of this *Commentary*. To address that question here would distract attention from my basic message: that, in the event of Quebec's secession, precipitous action should be avoided, and that a Plan C is needed, the first step of which should be to create time to canvass alternative futures. Once we have agreed on this first step, we can then turn to the second component of Plan C: how to proceed to decide on the ROC's future. In doing so, Canadians need to remember that their task would be to fashion a new people, not just new governing arrangements. Room should be left for constitutional imagination, meaning that governments must not be allowed to dominate the constitutionmaking process. The ratification process should include a country-wide referendum that would not be subject to the stranglehold of unanimity. Finally, the approval of electorates should be an alternative to the approval of governments – not, as in the Charlottetown Accord, an additional requirement. The most serious mistake Canadians could make would be to forget that the constitutional order has been democratized, that the founding of a new people is not a task for elite manipulation.

A Difficult Transition

If it came to pass, Quebec's sovereignty would usher in a new world for both Quebecers and their new Canadian neighbors. The new Canada would enter that world and adapt to the changed circumstances it presented in three stages:

• first, the immediate, short-term transition period between a 'yes' vote and Quebec's exit, whether by the constitutional rules or by a successful UDI;
• second, the longer, medium-term transition period after Quebec's departure, during which the reconstitution of a smaller Canada would be worked out; and
• third, the long-term implementation of the constitutional arrangements worked out in stage two.

In stage one, the federal government, still the government of all of Canada, would be involved in negotiations with Quebec, or in responding to the early stages of a Quebec UDI. Ottawa's legitimacy and efficacy and the extent to which its various roles would have to incorporate provincial and other input cannot be predicted in advance. In the second stage, assuming the strategy suggested in this Commentary were followed, the inherited constitutional structure, minus Quebec, would provide institutional continuity while Canadians outside Quebec decided on their future.

This three-to-five-year transition period would be stressful. The sooner a considered reconstitution was achieved, the better. Even if Quebec's departure were peaceful and negotiated, many issues would remain to be resolved between the two sides, and while I have argued that many of them should be put on hold while the new Canada decided on its future, irritations and tensions would inevitably arise, not all of which could be shelved. The unsettled state of co-existence between Quebec and Canada would overlap with the question mark of the future of the smaller Canada being worked out by whatever reconstitutionmaking process was chosen.

In the transitional regime following Quebec's excision from the Canadian Constitution, there would be no Quebecers in Parliament, the Supreme Court of Canada, or the numerous federal boards and commissions that now have Quebec representation. These changes and many others would necessarily and immediately follow either from Quebec's negotiated departure or from an effective UDI. They may seem straightforward – as Young notes, 'it is surprising how little excision is required to eliminate Quebec from the constitution.'[73] In reality, however, such changes would be immensely difficult, time consuming, and psychologically debilitating. Rules, operating procedures, decision-making practices, and informal understandings would have to be modified in hundreds of offices and in the major institutions of government.

With respect to legislation and policies, Quebec's presence could be deleted easily in some cases, but where Quebec's presence has been significant, such as in marketing boards and equalization, modifications would be necessary. Logically, for example, language policy would be a candidate for quick modification, as much of its rationale would disappear with Quebec's departure. This would not be accomplished easily, however, because crucial components of the policy are constitutionally enshrined, and to amend those aspects of the Constitution under what would clearly be a transitional regime might encourage similar attempts in other areas, thus defeating the purpose of such a regime – to buy time to sort out where Canadians would like to go.

The removal of Quebec's three members from the Supreme Court of Canada would leave a total of six, increasing the likelihood of judicial stalemates. The francophone-anglophone composition of the House of Commons, which has influenced its social and intellectual climate and many of its practices, would be gone, and the self-definition of the remaining members would be transformed. The society they represented would be more homogeneous, geographically discontinuous, and agitated and un- certain about its future.

These changes are only the tip of the iceberg. Canadian governments and societies are deeply entangled through both law and policy. Their selective disentanglement would require shrewd political leadership.

The transitional period in which the old constitutional structure, minus Quebec, temporarily prevailed would be ambiguous. To the extent that the emerging constitutional arrangements for the new Canada appeared likely to depart from the old structure, the latter's legitimacy and efficacy would be weakened. Canadians would be working with one constitutional structure devised for a vision of Canada that was no longer relevant, while preparing a new set of constitutional arrangements for the Canada that was emerging. The authority of the transitional arrangements would be weakened by competing visions of what the new identity and governing structures should be. The transitional structure would be seen as a holding operation, possibly one leading not to a new, united Canada but to a fragmented group of successor states.

One major problem the transitional regime would confront would be the greatly increased relative clout of Ontario in the new Canada. With its share of MPs in the new House of Commons increased to 45 percent, not only would Ontario's bloc of political power in the transitional regime be viewed with suspicion in the other provinces; it would also be unlikely to survive the remaking of a smaller Canada without some modification. The transitional regime's legitimacy, therefore, would depend on Ontario's forbearance in translating its numbers into self-interested policy; the price of a heavy Ontario hand would be very high. Ideally, the transitional regime would develop understandings and conventions that underlined its caretaker status.

In the transitional regime, MPs and their senior bureaucratic advisors would have little capacity to undertake new initiatives. Even with good fortune, the postbreakup period would almost certainly be one of budgetary stringency and program cutbacks. Major new initiatives would be construed as unfair attempts to tie the future's hands – as attempts to reduce Canadians' maneuvering room in their quest for a new identity. Thus, the transitional period would restrict agreements with Quebec to those that were minimally necessary. Progress toward any kind of association or partnership, especially of a political nature, would be put on hold until the identity, composition, and unity of the new Canada became known.

The issue of the position of aboriginal peoples in a new Canada would not be easily shelved – indeed, the report of the recent Royal Commission on Aboriginal Peoples has given new salience to their concerns. On the other hand, it would be inappropriate to address such concerns during the transitional period. It follows, then, that aboriginal peoples would have to be accorded a prominent place in the remaking of Canada without Quebec, and with the Royal Commission's recommendations in hand, they would have the advantage of a ready-made package to bring to the constitutional process.

Presiding over the process of applying the transitional constitutional order to a shrunken Canada would be a new party system, likely ushered in by new elections following Quebec's leave taking. The revamped system, responding to the new reality of a Canada geographically bifurcated by Quebec's departure, would itself be volatile. The Liberals and Progressive Conservatives, with their historic pan-Canadian roles and party histories deeply influenced by the presence of Quebec, would be affected the most. Reform and, to a lesser extent, the New Democrats, would have much less baggage to shed. All parties would have to respond to the changed configuration of social forces in the new Canada, and to the new issues of identity, alternative constitutional futures, and relations with an independent Quebec that would come to dominate the agenda. Further, as noted above, the inherent ambiguity of the transitional regime would require the parties to live in two worlds at the same time: the known, but perhaps ephemeral, transitional regime, and its emerging, perhaps permanent, but unknown successor.

Politicians and parties would limit their investment in the transitional regime as they looked to the successor regime on the horizon. Some members of the transitional Parliament would advocate either a stronger or a weaker role for an institution that, in more normal times, would routinely capture their loyalty. Politicians' contributions to the creation of a successor regime would be influenced by their natural tendency to see as desirable the kind of future constitutional arrangements in which their party would flourish.

In the three-to-five-year period following Quebec's departure, there might be as many as a dozen provincial elections, three or more territorial (if Nunavut were under way), and one or two federal. These would be important means through which the new Canada would find its voice and debate its future. Although, remarkably, given the constitutional odyssey of recent decades, past elections have paid scant attention to constitutional issues, that aversion to playing constitutional politics through the party system would be unlikely to repeat itself. The elections that took place in the years immediately after Quebec's departure would both high- light the ambiguity of the situation, as alternative futures are vigorously debated, and clarify the choices Canadians would confront. They would be important supplements to whatever on-going constitution-making process had been put in place.

Some constitutional change would surely be necessary to accommodate the new cultural, linguistic, geographic, and economic circumstances and to signal the birth of a new country. The relative influence of the remaining regions and provinces would be altered. Central Canada as such would lose numerical power, while the relative weight of the other provinces would, by definition, be enhanced. But the most visible and problematic change would be the stronger relative presence of Ontario.

In general, all the constitutional clauses based on the existing regional and provincial divisions of Canada, including the amending formula, would have to be revisited. As I mentioned, explicit constitutional provisions dealing with official-language minorities would have to be reassessed, as the primary linguistic division of Canadian history would lose salience. Equalization would almost certainly be re-examined, particularly if constitutional revision were to move the new Canada in a decentralist direction. All constitutional provisions and high state policy that deal with Canada's ethnic demography would have a different context in the absence of Quebec. The constitutional recognition of aboriginal peoples would take on new meaning without the stimulus, model, and rivalry of Quebec nationalism. Finally, the Charter, which has brought new players into constitutional politics and created a tension between the roles of governments and citizens in formal constitutional change, leaves Canadians with a contradiction at the heart of Canada's constitutional life that, inevitably, would find a place on the ROC's constitutional reform agenda. All the proposals of recent decades, from Senate reform to aboriginal self-government to a defining preamble, would resurface alongside the new issues that Quebec's departure would raise.

The difficulties, ambiguities, and uncertainties of the proposed transitional arrangement are not arguments for proceeding immediately to a quick reconstitution of Canada without Quebec. To do so would be a recipe for even greater instability and future dismay as Canadians find themselves having to cope with the consequences of hurried changes made in a crisis atmosphere. The task, after all, would not only be to make institutional choices, but to define a new people, one that would provide a positive answer to Peter Russell's question: Can Canadians become a sovereign people?

Even given the three-to-five-year transition time I suggest, the ROC's reconstitution would not be easy, unless the crisis generated irresistible pressures for a rapid compromise. The proliferation of actors and the various demands for change in recent constitutional discussions indicate the kinds of pent-up pressures Canada would experience as it reconstituted itself. These pressures would, in fact, become even more extreme, since Canadians would be aware that they were creating a new country, and that they could no longer assume constitutional continuity or that they had a living constitution. But this surely is an argument for developing a secure transitional framework, a shelter behind which

Canadians, if necessary, could examine the alternative futures from which they would have to choose.

What Next?

The transitional arrangement is, however, a means to an end. The provision of time and stability, the essential contexts of the reconstitution process, is the necessary first stage of Plan C. The second stage – how, precisely, to go about it – requires careful analysis and constitutional thinking that are far beyond the scope of this paper. Nevertheless, it seems germane at this point to offer a few hints – mostly general principles – toward forming the rest of Plan C.

The first of these is that, while the attempt to create a new Canada might involve the emergence of more than one democratic, well-ordered successor state if the will to continue together could not be sustained, the working assumption of the ROC's constitutional search should be that Canadians would wish to continue as a united people, albeit with possibly major changes in some of their institutions of government.

The second principle is that the task of founding a new people should start from the premise that the people are sovereign. There is no escaping the democratic imperative, given the ethic of citizen participation in constitutional matters that has mushroomed since the 1980 Quebec referendum and the stimulus of the 1982 Charter. The existence next door of an independent Quebec that had repeatedly sought, and finally gained, majority support for sovereignty would greatly reinforce this democratic message. It simply would not be possible for the ROC's political elites to fashion new constitutional arrangements in closed-door sessions and then spring them, Meech-style, on an unprepared public. The new country's citizens would not allow themselves to be treated as subjects, made to stand on the sidelines as their political masters worked out their future. The process of founding a new people would have to be a collaboration between governments and citizens.

Canada without Quebec would have to develop a new sense of self. Canadians would have to adjust to the wounding reality of a gaping hole in their middle. Although some psychological withdrawal from common citizenship has been under way on both sides for some time, Quebec's departure would nevertheless be traumatic. Canada's ethnic demography would take on new meaning as immigrants and their descendants from nontraditional source countries constituted a larger percentage of the population. There would also likely be some language-driven population shifts as some anglophones in Quebec and some francophones in the ROC moved to areas where their linguistic community would be in the majority. More generally, the sense of beginning afresh might weaken the 'Mayflower syndrome' that distributes status based on time of arrival. On the other hand, aboriginal peoples likely would seize the opportunity of the opening up of the post-'yes' constitutional agenda to push their historical claims as First Nations with renewed vigor.

Canada without Quebec would confront a vast array of fundamental questions as 23 million people contemplated a future for which they would be ill-prepared. Such a crisis, however, would also be an opportunity for the surviving Canadian community to reconstitute itself in a very different world from that of the mid-nineteenth century Confederation. That world explains the British cast of the 1867 Constitution, 'similar in principle to that of the United Kingdom,' formed when Britain was a world power, when Canada's trade and immigration patterns linked it to the mother country. The choice the governing elites of the British North American colonies made then was to differentiate themselves from the colossus to the south that was just emerging from civil war. If Quebec were to leave, Canadians would have to confront the removal of one of the key elements that distinguishes their identity from that of Americans, at a time when their economic and cultural embrace with the United States is tightening.

In part, the ROC's reconstitution should be a response to globalization, to a world in which boundaries matter less and less, in which democratic peoples are increasingly multi- ethnic, and in which a widely diffused language of rights is common currency. One possible consolation is that, as Mancur Olson points out, societies with long, stable histories can become sclerotic as the interdependence of state and society constrains growth and fosters inefficiencies. He disputes the thesis that simply because 'social institutions have survived for a long time, they must necessarily be useful to the society.' He argues that,

other things being equal, the most rapid growth will occur in societies that have lately experienced upheaval but are expected nonetheless to be stable for the foreseeable future.[74]

Of course, Canadians may well find, once they have settled down to their new existence, that they have neither fragmented further nor fundamentally changed the old constitutional framework. My assumption that significant changes would be both necessary and attainable would then become simply one more failed attempt to perceive the future. What Canadians would then inherit would have the advantage of inertia and incumbency. It might pass the performance test in the transition period with flying colors, and gain the support of those who wish to minimize the instability of massive constitutional change. Or perhaps the old framework would be seen as a compromise between competing visions of the ROC's future. If that were the outcome, Canadians would still have reconstituted themselves, if only by deciding to remain as they are.

Conclusion

Despite the postreferendum emergence of Plan B, there is minimal likelihood that, before the next referendum, governments outside Quebec will have prepared themselves or their citizens for the reconstitution of the rest of Canada if the sovereigntists win. The work of think tanks, individual academics, and various public-minded organizations will no doubt have filled a small bookcase with their predictions and analyses. While the intellectual capital thus generated will be helpful, it should not be confused with the political process of constitutionmaking, a process that involves the whole society. Moreover, proposals such as a recent one by Keith Spicer – to take the leadership role away from governments now and have both pre- and postreferendum proposals formulated and then voted on in a national referendum sanctioned by Ottawa – have thus far languished.[75]

Not only would Canadians be unprepared for a future they did not seek, there would be no consensus as to whether Canada without Quebec would be more centralized or decentralized, united or fragmented, whether relations with a sovereign Quebec would be peaceful or hostile, or whether Quebec itself would be tranquil and socially cohesive or torn by violence stemming from the bitterness of secession. In brief, Canadians would not just be unprepared, they would be inescapably ignorant – and this would not be the normal ignorance that attends all futures, which is reduced by routine and inertia, but a more profound lack of even the most basic knowledge, when routine and inertia cannot be counted on. A 'yes' victory in Quebec, especially if followed by a UDI, would have the impact of a political earthquake in the rest of Canada. In my view, Canadians would react with fear, panic, anger, and a sense of profound crisis almost certainly dwarfing any hope or relief that might enjoy a furtive existence.

The uncertainty would be triggered both by the immediate need to strike a deal on certain inescapable issues with Quebec, when it would not even be clear as to who should bargain on our behalf, and by the longer-term question of whether a Canada without Quebec could survive. A well-conceived Plan B, outlining the terms of Quebec's secession, if it were in place in time, could ready us for the first issue, but the issue of the ROC's' survival could not be resolved in advance. It would, however, be possible to improve the odds by establishing a stable, transitional constitutional arrangement.

We can neither predict nor control the future. All we can do is to try to so position ourselves that uncontrollable events do not leave us unable to respond if they occur. If Quebec were to leave, therefore, the appropriate response in the ROC would be to delay its reconstitution, to continue with the existing structure, to make a friend of time while a reduced Canada overcame the shock of break-up and undertook the introspection and public education that would be essential to the creation of a new political order north of the United States. Canadians know their current arrangements and how to work the system. They are comfortable with it. As an interim constitution, it would provide stability while Canadians forge a new identity, an existential question that it would be folly to try to answer in panicky haste following Quebec's exit.

The final section of this *Commentary* anticipates the subject of another – the completion of Plan C, taking advantage of the benefits the rest of Canada might extract from a reconstitution process into which it might be pushed unwillingly. My objective, however, has been more limited: to argue for the transitional use of the existing constitutional machinery as the first step of Plan C, to buy the time and security Canadians would need to decide their constitutional future. I make no claim that current arrangements would be appropriate for Canada without Quebec – the fact is that no one knows or can know, since there are just too many unknown variables. Nor do I insist that the new Canada should survive as a single people with a common government, although that is my strong preference. I argue only that, given the magnitude of the demands and the lack of preparation that the smaller Canada would confront, it would make sense to play for time – to give thought the chance to crystallize, and to give Canadians outside Quebec a chance to come to terms with a post-'yes' world.

To be successful, my proposal clearly requires the approval of governments. Its benefits would be maximized if enough relevant actors – governments, political parties, influential elites – were to agree on its desirability before the next Quebec referendum. While a formal, across-the-board agreement of governing authorities is implausible, a widely diffused understanding and sympathy for the idea that the constitutional status quo could be a viable interim arrangement would be an immense improvement over the unpredictability of Canada's immediate future following Quebec's possible separation that now prevails. Public support from private associations and from at least some governments and political parties would qualify as a great leap forward.

NOTES

I wish to thank Christopher Adams for excellent research assistance, and Ken Boessenkool, David Cameron, Patrick Monahan, Daniel Schwanen, and Richard Simeon for helpful critical comments on an earlier draft. My indebtedness to the published work of Gordon Gibson, Patrick Monahan, and Robert Young may not be as evident in the text and notes as it should be. If so, that is a testimony to the extent their groundbreaking work has become part of the basic stock of knowledge on which we build.

An earlier version of some of the arguments in this *Commentary* was presented in Alan C. Cairns, 'Suppose the "Yes" Side Wins: Are We Ready?' *Western Perspectives* (Calgary: Canada West Foundation, February 1995).

1 Ray Conlogue, *Impossible Nation: The Longing for Homeland in Canada and Quebec* (Stratford, Ont.: Mercury Press, 1996), p. 19.

2 The first 'official' warning came in 1965:

> Canada, without being fully conscious of the fact, is passing through the greatest crisis in its history ... the state of affairs established in 1867, and never since seriously challenged, is now for the first time being rejected by the French Canadians of Quebec.

Canada, Royal Commission on Bilingualism and Biculturalism, *Preliminary Report* (Ottawa: Queen's Printer, 1965), p. 13.

3 Plan B, according to Terrance Wills, 'is really a way to prevent separation by portraying its excruciating effects for all to see.' It is intended to undermine the strategy of 'the separatist leadership [which] has spent years, without inhibition or contradiction, developing the myth of a cake-walk to separation.' Terrance Wills, 'Federal cabinet's Quebec strategy beginning to take shape,' *Montreal Gazette*, October 5, 1996. See also Jane Jenson and Antonia Maioni, 'The Political Price of Plan B,' *Canada Watch* 4 (August 1996, nos. 5 and 6): 98–101.

4 The term 'Plan C' has occasionally been put to other uses in the course of the Canadian constitutional debate. The Reform Party, for example, has used it to refer to its proposal for 'new federalizing.' In this *Commentary*, however, I use it to mean the process of reconstituting the rest of Canada in the event of Quebec's secession, a process that can only begin once any bargaining over the actual secession process (Plan B) is completed.

5 The House of Commons resolution introduced by the prime minister on November 29, 1995, reads as follows:

> Whereas the People of Quebec have expressed the desire for recognition of Quebec's distinct society; 1) the House recognize that Quebec is a distinct society within Canada; 2) the House recognize that Quebec's distinct society includes its French-speaking majority, unique culture and civil law tradition; 3) the House undertake to be guided by this reality; 4) the House encourage all components of the legislative and executive branches of government to take note of this recognition and be guided accordingly.

See Canada, Parliament, House of Commons, *Debates*, November 29, 1995,

p. 16971. The resolution was passed on division 148–91; see idem, *Debates*, December 11, 1995, pp. 17536–17537.

6 Other versions of Plan A proliferate outside of government. See, for example, Y. Fortier, P. Lougheed, and J. Maxwell, *Today and Tomorrow: An Agenda for Action*, Report of the Confederation 2000 Conference, May 4, 1996 (Ottawa); and Group of 22, 'Making Canada Work Better' (Toronto, May 1996). See also John McCallum, 'Making Canada Work Better,' *Canada Watch* 4 (August 1996, nos. 5 and 6) for a short version of the Group of 22 proposals.

7 Graham Fraser, 'No major reforms planned to keep Quebec, Dion says,' *Globe and Mail* (Toronto), October 16, 1996; and Joan Bryden, 'Distinct status rests in hands of Canadians, minister says,' *Ottawa Citizen*, October 30, 1996.

8 See Roger Gibbins (with the assistance of Katherine Harmsworth), *Time Out: Assessing Incremental Strategies for Enhancing the Political Union*, C.D. Howe Institute Commentary 88 (Toronto: C.D. Howe Institute, February 1997). Given the minimum public input characteristic of this kind of incrementalism, *de facto* constitutional changes occur by stealth.

9 For a discussion of this phenomenon, see Alan C. Cairns, 'Ritual, Taboo, and Bias in Constitutional Controversies in Canada, or Constitutional Talk Canadian Style,' in Douglas E. Williams, ed., *Disruptions: Constitutional Struggles from the Charter to Meech Lake, selected essays by Alan C. Cairns* (Toronto: McClelland and Stewart, 1991).

10 See, for example, Jeff Rose, 'Beginning to Think about the Next Referendum,' Occasional Paper (University of Toronto, Faculty of Law, November 21, 1995), mimeographed; Thomas R. Berger, 'What about Quebec's next referendum?' *Globe and Mail* (Toronto), November 9, 1995; Keith Spicer, 'A clean start or a clean break: English Canada should prepare two options: A renewed federalism or a Canada without Quebec,' *Montreal Gazette*, January 24, 1996; and Jeffrey Simpson, 'The Liberals wobble with non-answers to Reform's clear questions,' *Globe and Mail* (Toronto), December 14, 1995. For additional references, see Alan C. Cairns, 'The Legacy of the Referendum: Who Are We Now?' *Constitutional Forum* 7 (Winter/Spring 1996, nos. 2 and 3): 39, n. 12.

11 Charles Taylor, 'Shared and Divergent Values,' in Ronald L. Watts and Douglas M. Brown, eds., *Options for a New Canada* (Toronto: University of Toronto Press, 1991), p. 65.

12 For example, Brian Dickson, retired chief justice of the Supreme Court of Canada, asserts the importance of 'discuss[ing] now, in an open and democratic fashion, the ground rules that ought to apply in any future referendum campaign and its aftermath.' He adds that the rule of law must apply 'to the secession of a province.' 'Brian Dickson: 'Two modest observations' on Quebec,' *Globe and Mail* (Toronto), July 5, 1996. See also Richard Gwyn, 'The old Canada is gone forever,' *Toronto*

Star, October 31, 1995; Michael Bliss, 'Canada needs to define the limits of appease-ment,' *Toronto Star*, November 17, 1995; and Jeffrey Simpson, 'With no clear think-ing, Canada was ill prepared for its dismemberment,' *Globe and Mail* (Toronto), November 8, 1995.

13 Douglas M. Brown, 'Thinking the 'Unthinkable',' in Patrick C. Fafard and Douglas M. Brown, eds., *Canada: The State of the Federation 1996* (Kingston, Ont.: Queen's University, Institute of Intergovernmental Relations, 1997).

14 Preston Manning, 'Awakening the Sleeping Giant' (address to the Canadian Club, London, Ontario, November 2, 1995), p. 2. In June 1994, Manning further addressed to the prime minister 20 'hard questions being asked by rank and file Canadians regarding Quebec's potential separation from Canada' (Draft of Open Letter of Preston Manning to Prime Minister Jean Chrétien, June 8, 1994.) The Reform Party subsequently published its own hard-line answers ('Reform Response to the Twenty Questions Posed to the Prime Minister on June 8, 1994,' draft, n.d.)

15 Gordon Robertson, 'Contingency Legislation for a Quebec Referendum,' *Canada Watch* 4 (August 1996, nos. 5 and 6): 95.

16 See the excellent discussion by Peter W. Hogg, 'The Effect of a Referendum on Que-bec Sovereignty,' *Canada Watch* 4 (August 1996, nos. 5 and 6). See also Patrick J. Monahan and Michael J. Bryant (with Nancy C. Coté), *Coming to Terms with Plan B: Ten Principles Governing Secession*, C.D. Howe Institute Commentary 83 (Toronto: C.D. Howe Institute, June 1996), pp. 23, 30.

Then-justice minister Allan Rock's speech to the House of Commons, September 26, 1996, announcing the federal government's reference to the Supreme Court of Canada on whether domestic or international law gives Quebec the right to a unilat-eral declaration of independence, is a eulogy to the rule of law, the framework of order, and refers to his own role as 'custodian of the Constitution of our country' ('Why Ottawa is seeking court ruling,' *Toronto Star*, September 27, 1996).

José Woehrling, however, argues that the complexities of the amending formula could justify a Quebec UDI, based on agreed bargained terms, should an amendment not get over all the hurdles, on the grounds 'that ROC had been reduced to incoher-ence and paralysis by the unwieldy amending formula of the Canadian Constitution' ('Some Ground Rules for the Next Referendum on Quebec's Sovereignty,' *Canada Watch* 4 [August 1996, nos. 5 and 6]: 96).

17 *Reference Re Secession of Quebec from Canada* [1996] C.S.C.R. No. 421 (Q.L.).

18 Robert A. Young (*The Secession of Quebec and the Future of Canada* [Montreal; Kingston, Ont.: McGill-Queen's University Press, 1995], pp. 181–182) discusses the federalist strategy to increase uncertainty by refusing to specify Ottawa's position on contentious issues, such as the necessary size of an acceptable majority. See also p. 292.

19 The government of British Columbia is a possible exception. Andrew Petter,

Minister Responsible for Intergovernmental Relations, has established a group headed by MLA Gordon F.D. Wilson, leader of the Progressive Democratic Alliance, to advise the government, and British Columbians generally, on national unity issues from a BC perspective. Apparently, the group's mandate includes British Columbia's options if Quebec were to secede.

20 See *Canada Watch* 4 (August 1996, nos. 5 and 6), a special double issue focusing on Plan B.

21 For example, the discussion of Plan B has been immeasurably advanced by Monahan and Bryant, *Coming to Terms with Plan B*.

22 See, for example, Jeffrey Simpson, 'With Quebec, Ottawa needs a second plan quickly,' *Globe and Mail* (Toronto), October 10, 1996, reporting former Alberta premier Peter Lougheed's distress over the inactivity.

23 Young, *Secession of Quebec*, pp. 113–114, citing Richard Simeon. The need for a fair, clear question has been reiterated by Prime Minister Chrétien, by Intergovernmental Affairs Minister Stéphane Dion, and by Allan Rock while justice minister. For Chrétien, see Hugh Winsor and Tu Thanh Ha, 'Chrétien signals new resolve on Quebec,' *Globe and Mail* (Toronto), December 12, 1995; and Barry Came, 'A War of Words and Shadows,' *Maclean's*, May 27, 1996. For Dion, see 'Next referendum question must be clear, Dion says,' *Globe and Mail* (Toronto), October 1, 1996. For Rock, see Susan Delacourt, 'Ottawa to seek secession ruling,' *Globe and Mail* (Toronto), September 26, 1996; and idem, 'Rock wants clear choice in referendum question,' *Globe and Mail* (Toronto), September 28, 1996.

24 See Shawn McCarthy, 'PM demands 'clear majority',' *Toronto Star*, October 11, 1996; Ross Howard, 'Slim vote can't split Canada, PM says,' *Globe and Mail* (Toronto), January 31, 1996, attributes similar views to Dion.

25 See Monahan and Bryant, *Coming to Terms with Plan B*, pp. 13–14.

26 Woehrling, 'Some Ground Rules,' p. 95. Hogg ('Effect of a Referendum,' p. 98) agrees that there is 'a moral duty' to hold a second referendum before setting the amending procedures in motion. Monahan and Bryant (*Coming to Terms with Plan B*, pp. 33–34) concur.

27 See Grand Council of Crees, *Sovereign Injustice: Forcible Inclusion of the James Bay Cree and Cree Territory into a Sovereign Quebec* (Nemaska, Que., 1995); and Carol Hilling, 'Autodétermination et sécession confundues,' *Le Devoir* (Montreal), January 13, 1995.

28 See the various statements by then-Indian affairs minister Ron Irwin supporting the rights of aboriginal peoples to remain with Canada should Quebec secede, reported in Jack Aubry, 'Vote could spark violence, Irwin says,' *Toronto Star*, February 10, 1996; and 'Irwin hits a nerve,' *Montreal Gazette*, editorial, February 16, 1996. The PQ government's reply is summed up in Robert McKenzie, 'Bouchard calls Irwin a

'moron',' *Toronto Star* February 15, 1996; and Rhéal Séguin, 'Bouchard says Irwin 'an idiot',' *Globe and Mail* (Toronto), February 15, 1996.

29 For federalist statements on the divisibility of Quebec, see 'Quebec probably is divisible: Charest,' *Ottawa Citizen*, January 29, 1996; B. Cox, 'If Canada is divisible, so is Quebec, Dion says,' *Ottawa Citizen*, January 27, 1996; Ross Howard, 'Quebec divisible, Chrétien says,' *Globe and Mail* (Toronto), January 30, 1996; 'Is Quebec divisible?' *Globe and Mail* (Toronto), editorial, January 30, 1996.

30 Robertson, 'Contingency Legislation,' pp. 93–95.

31 See, for example, Philip Authier, 'Bouchard 'furious': aide,' *Montreal Gazette*, May 13, 1996; Elizabeth Thompson, 'Early vote threatened,' *Montreal Gazette*, April 29, 1996; Robert McKenzie, 'PQ talks tough on rights to vote,' *Toronto Star*, April 29, 1996; Terrance Wills and Paul Wells, 'Canadians 'will have say',' *Montreal Gazette*, February 28, 1996; and Philip Authier, 'Policy a threat to democracy – Quebec,' *Montreal Gazette*, February 28, 1996.

32 Rhéal Séguin, 'Separatists were poised to humble Ottawa,' *Globe and Mail* (Toronto), November 9, 1995.

33 Jenson and Maioni ('The Political Price of Plan B,' p. 101) note the negative effect of tough Plan B talk, especially partition talk, on Quebec federalists, 'in silencing ... those who will have to conduct the next referendum on the ground.' For discussion of the split between federalists inside and outside Quebec over Plan B, see Anne McIlroy, 'Separation possible with 'clear mandate': Provinces would decide, PM says,' *Globe and Mail* (Toronto), May 16, 1996; Rhéal Séguin and Susan Delacourt, 'Bouchard dismisses bid for ruling on sovereignty,' *Globe and Mail* (Toronto), September 27, 1996; Rhéal Séguin, 'Federalists split over call for court ruling,' *Globe and Mail* (Toronto), September 28, 1996; idem, 'Ottawa has no authority to intrude, Johnson says,' *Globe and Mail* (Toronto), September 30, 1996; Elizabeth Thompson, 'Split within Liberals on 'no more referendums',' *Montreal Gazette*, October 2, 1996; and Rhéal Séguin, 'Quebec's Liberals want changes to Constitution,' *Globe and Mail* (Toronto), October 11, 1996.

34 See 'Galganov flops, but the debate carries on,' *Globe and Mail* (Toronto), September 19, 1996.

35 Denis Stairs notes: 'Starkly put, the government of a united Canada *cannot* act for the people of a partitioned Canada' (*Canada and Quebec after Québécois Secession: 'Realist' Reflections on an International Relationship* [Halifax, NS: Dalhousie University, Centre for Foreign Policy Studies, 1996], p. 36; italics in original). Young (*Secession of Quebec*, p. 160) states that, 'as the central government and legislature contain representatives from the potentially seceding state, they cannot readily acknowledge the possibility of fragmentation before it occurs, even to the point of commissioning reports and contemplating scenarios.' See also Tom Kent, 'An Emergency Operation for the Constitution,' in J.L. Granatstein and Kenneth

McNaught, eds., *'English Canada' Speaks Out* (Toronto: Doubleday Canada, 1991), p. 323.

36 Admittedly, Monahan and Bryant do not ignore the issue completely. They recommend that the existing Constitution remain in place throughout the negotiating period, until Quebec has formally seceded, and that, after the necessary amendments to excise Quebec have been enacted, the Constitution continue in place until 'time and careful study' have informed Canadians of the fundamental changes to it that will probably be necessary. In fact, Monahan and Bryant succinctly present the gist of the arguments that I elaborate on in subsequent sections of this *Commentary*, but they do so only as a postscript. See Monahan and Bryant, *Coming to Terms with Plan B*, pp. 38–39.

One honorable and significant exception to the relative lack of thinking about this issue is Gordon Gibson, who originally coined the term 'Plan B' but specifically to refer to the survival of the ROC, a problem he addresses head on in *Plan B: The Future of the Rest of Canada* (Vancouver: Fraser Institute, 1994). As noted above, however, the term has come to have a different focus.

37 See Hogg, 'Effect of a Referendum,' p. 98, on the unrealistic picture portrayed by the 'yes' forces during the 1995 referendum campaign.

38 See, for example, Stairs, *Canada and Quebec*, pp. 5–7; Maureen Covell, *Thinking about the Rest of Canada: Options for Canada without Quebec*, Background Studies of the York University Constitutional Reform Project, Study 6 (North York, Ont.: York University, Centre for Public Law and Public Policy, 1991), p. 27; Reg Whitaker, 'Thinking about the Unthinkable: Planning for a Possible Secession,' *Constitutional Forum* 7 (1996, nos. 2 and 3): 60–61; Philip Resnick, 'Dividing in Two: A Test for Reason and Emotion,' in Daniel Drache and Roberto Perin, eds., *Negotiating with a Sovereign Quebec* (Toronto: Lorimer, 1992), pp. 83–84; and Keith G. Banting, 'If Quebec Separates: Restructuring Northern North America,' in R. Kent Weaver, ed., *The Collapse of Canada?* (Washington, DC: Brookings Institution, 1992), p. 167.

39 See Tu Thanh Ha, 'Yes vote no picnic, Chrétien warns,' *Globe and Mail* (Toronto), October 19, 1995; and Edison Stewart, 'Quebecers given blunt warning,' *Toronto Star*, October 19, 1995. See also Cairns, 'Suppose the 'Yes' Side wins'; and Patrick J. Monahan, *Cooler Heads Shall Prevail: Assessing the Costs and Consequences of Quebec Separation*, C.D. Howe Institute Commentary 65 (Toronto: C.D. Howe Institute, January 1995), pp. 18–20.

40 Gordon Gibson, 'In Cold or Hot Blood? A Response to the C.D. Howe Forecast of the Post-Referendum World,' *Fraser Forum*, February 1995, pp. 8–17; and Gibson, *Plan B*, chap. 7.

41 Robert A. Young, 'Steady as She Went: The Constitutional Modalities of Quebec Secession' (paper presented to the annual conference of the Canadian Law and Eco-

nomics Association, Toronto, September 29, 1995), p. 4. See also William Watson, 'Home Game: Comments on 'The Interests of English Canada',' *Canadian Public Policy* 21 (March 1995): 90–92; and Alan Freeman and Patrick Grady, *Dividing the House: Planning for a Canada without Quebec* (Toronto: HarperCollins, 1995), pp. 27, 33, 34, and 44.

42 See Kent Walker, 'Atlantic Canada to be hardest hit should Quebec separate: Crosbie,' *The Guardian* (Charlottetown), July 20, 1996.

43 See Richard Mackie, 'Bourassa tears into partnership proposal,' *Globe and Mail* (Toronto), August 31, 1995; there is, however, some ambiguity in Bourassa's position, as he appears to waver between saying that Canada *would* break up and that it *could* break up. See also Peter M. Leslie, 'Options for the Future of Canada: The Good, the Bad, and the Fantastic,' in Watts and Brown, eds., *Options for a New Canada*, pp. 132–134; and Charles F. Doran, 'Will Canada Unravel?' *Foreign Affairs* 75 (September/October 1996): 97–109.

44 Joseph T. Jockel, 'If Quebec Becomes Independent,' *Canada Watch* 5 (September/ October 1996): 13.

45 See the discussion in Brown, 'Thinking the 'Unthinkable',' p. 34.

46 Banting, 'If Quebec Separates,' p. 178.

47 Dan Usher, 'The Design of a Government for an English Canadian Country,' in Robin W. Boadway, Thomas J. Courchene, and Douglas D. Purvis, eds., *Economic Dimension of Constitutional Change*, vol. 1 (Kingston, Ont.: Queen's University, John Deutsch Institute for the Study of Economic Policy, 1991).

48 Young, *Secession of Quebec*, pp. 191–198; and idem, 'Steady as She Went,' pp. 7, 13, 17, and 18.

49 Gibson, 'In Cold or Hot Blood?' p. 17; and idem, *Plan B*, chaps. 4, 6, and 8.

50 See, for example, Monahan, 'Cooler Heads Shall Prevail,' p. 28; Stairs, *Canada and Quebec*, p. 7; Jenson and Maioni, 'The Political Price of Plan B,' p. 100; Robertson, 'Contingency Legislation,' p. 93; Banting, 'If Quebec Separates,' pp. 164–165; Gibson, *Plan B*, pp. 28–29; and Alan C. Cairns, 'Dreams versus Reality in 'Our' Constitutional Future: How Many Communities?,' in Douglas E. Williams, ed., *Reconfigurations: Canadian Citizenship and Constitutional Change, selected essays by Alan C. Cairns* (Toronto: McClelland and Stewart, 1995), pp. 329–330, 336–339.

For a general discussion of the issue, see Alex Morrison, ed., *Divided We Fall: The National Security Implications of Canadian Constitutional Issues* (Toronto: Canadian Institute of Strategic Studies, 1991). See also the disturbing argument and data on the very high incidence of violence by host states on the seceding state when a UDI was attempted – in 96 out of 111 cases from 1810 to 1994, often with very heavy loss of life – in John C. Thompson, 'The Price of Independence,' *Canada Watch* 5 (September/October 1996): 21–24.

51 See Brown, 'Thinking the 'Unthinkable'.'

52 Young, *Secession of Quebec*, p. 89.

53 Ibid., pp. 90–91.

54 Ibid., p. 101.

55 Ibid., p. 125.

56 Ibid., pp. 76, 289.

57 Ibid., p. 82.

58 Ibid., p. 3.

59 Covell, *Thinking about the Rest of Canada*, p. 2.

60 Cairns, 'Suppose the 'Yes' Side Wins,' p. 11.

61 Several readers of an earlier version of this paper suggested that I should do my bit to dispel the prevailing ignorance and adjudicate between the conflicting predictions in area after area of this section, such as 'Will the ROC stay together or not?' To do so, however, would have been counterproductive. One more speculation added to the competing ones that already exist would not advance our knowledge. Were I to privilege my own views, I would divert attention from the fundamental fact that one cannot know what Quebec's secession would bring. What I know, and what I wish to signal, is that we are ignorant.

62 Banting, 'If Quebec Separates,' p. 167.

63 Ibid., pp. 162–163.

64 Ibid., pp. 167–168.

65 Ibid., pp. 164–165.

66 'PQ loss won't end debate: Bouchard,' *Montreal Gazette*, June 15, 1994.

67 Covell, *Thinking about the Rest of Canada*, p. 3.

68 Robertson, 'Contingency Legislation for a Quebec Referendum.'

69 The composition of the team would depend on whether the bargaining presupposed Quebec's independence or was a last-ditch effort for renewed federalism. The more the latter, the greater would be the legitimacy of the federal government's role. If the former, then the federal government's leadership role would be weakened and the claims of spokespersons for the reconstituted Canada ambiguously waiting in the wings would be strengthened. The possibility that either or both the PQ and the ROC would be playing the renewed federalism game and the breakup game at the same time – a plausible scenario – would require a role-playing dexterity far too complex to explore in a note. These concerns are not, however, central to my argument, which focuses on the future of Canada without Quebec.

70 Stairs, *Canada and Quebec after Québécois Secession*, p. 26.

71 Rotstein, quoted in Reg Whitaker, 'Life after Separation,' in Drache and Perin, eds., *Negotiating with a Sovereign Quebec*, p. 75.

72 For a powerful argument against a UDI and for the use of the existing constitutional machinery if Quebec were to leave, see Peter Russell and Bruce Ryder, *Ratifying a*

Postreferendum Agreement on Quebec Sovereignty, C.D. Howe Institute Commentary (Toronto, C.D. Howe Institute, forthcoming).

73 Young, 'Steady as She Went,' p. 20.

74 Mancur Olson, *The Rise and Decline of Nations* (New Haven, Conn.: Yale University Press, 1982), pp. 141, 165.

75 Keith Spicer, 'A clean start or a clean break?' *Montreal Star*, January 24, 1996.

Coming to Terms with Plan B:
Ten Principles Governing Secession

PATRICK J. MONAHAN and MICHAEL J. BRYANT with NANCY C. COTÉ

The debate over Quebec's place in Canada assumed a new urgency on the evening of October 30, 1995. Before that date, it was plausible for the prime minister to refuse to answer 'hypothetical' questions about how Ottawa would respond if a majority of Quebecers voted to secede from Canada. According to Jean Chrétien, no matter how many referendums[1] the Quebec government held on the issue, Quebecers would always choose to remain in Canada.

The events of October 30 shattered that strategy of studied indifference, at least for the foreseeable future. The razor thin majority secured by the 'no' forces and subsequent opinion polls indicating that a majority of decided Quebec voters support sovereignty have made it impossible for the prime minister to continue to claim that a 'yes' vote is purely hypothetical and therefore unworthy of his consideration. Canadians recognize that their country survived a near-death experience on October 30 thanks more to happenstance than to a coherent strategy. Increasingly, voices in all parts of the country are calling for the federal government to begin planning now for the next referendum.[2] Part of that strategy must be a contingency plan to use if the referendum is lost and a majority of Quebecers vote to secede from the federation.

This *Commentary* is an attempt to set out the main elements of such a contingency plan – sometimes referred to as Plan B (see Box 1). The key assumption underlying our analysis is that it is imperative that Canada attempt to set down the ground rules governing secession of a province well in advance of the next referendum. We describe what these ground rules might contain and suggest how the federal government might go about implementing them.

Why Ground Rules?

The existing Constitution says nothing about how – or whether – a province can

---

Box 1   *Plan A and Plan B*

The terms *Plan A* and *Plan B* are fairly new to the Canadian constitutional debate. An early appearance seems to have been in February 1996, when the *Globe and Mail* reported:

'There is no Plan A or Plan B,' Mr. Chrétien said ... 'You formulate the plan as being Plan A and Plan B,' he said, less than 24 hours after ... Stéphane Dion identified Plan A as reconciliation terms and Plan B as the terms of secession.*

Somewhat earlier usage had been *Track 1* for a conciliatory approach to Quebec and *Track 2* for a hard line.

* Susan Delacourt, 'Chrétien steps back from unity issue,' *Globe and Mail* (Toronto), February 3, 1996, p. A1.

---

secede from the federation. This silence should be no comfort to federalists (who might mistakenly imagine that the absence of a constitutional procedure for secession makes such an outcome 'impossible'). Rather, it is a cause for deep concern. Canada is a democracy whose ultimate legal and political foundation is the consent of Canadians to be governed under the Canadian Constitution and Canadian law. If a sufficiently large and determined majority of Canadians in a particular province withdraw that consent, then the absence of appropriate legal wording to achieve secession will not prevent them from realizing their goal.

Thus, the absence of an agreed procedure to govern secession will lead to confusion and conflict over the legitimacy of any proposed secession. This confusion will, at a minimum, produce political and economic uncertainty. Accordingly, this *Commentary* proceeds on the premise that it is in the interest of all Canadians, including Quebecers, that such an outcome be avoided to the extent possible.

Many thoughtful and responsible Canadians recognize the dangers inherent in a situation in which there is no consensus over the ground rules that would apply in the event of an attempt by a province to secede. Yet they continue to resist any initiative designed to bring clarity to the situation, thinking that any attempt by the government of Canada to define the rules of the game would be seen in Quebec as unduly provocative; such provocation could boost support for sovereignty and thus, paradoxically, serve to reinforce the very outcome that federalists wish to avoid. Others argue that federalists should avoid venturing onto this terrain since to do so would be unduly defeatist, amounting to giving sovereigntists a blueprint for achieving the dismemberment of Canada. Needless to say, federalists should be wary of Trojan horses of their own making.

Doubtless, any open discussion of the process governing secession could backfire easily. Yet the question is not whether such a discussion is risky but, rather, whether any alternative strategy appears more attractive. The main alternative – a continuing refusal to contemplate the possibility of secession – was the centerpiece of the referendum campaigns in 1980 and 1995. The results on October 30 conclusively demonstrated that this strategy no longer makes sense. Its main byproducts have been confusion and disorder in the federalist camp. while giving sovereigntists a free hand in defining the rules of the game to their advantage.

The danger in further waffling is obvious. The longer the federal government waits before beginning to systematically contradict misleading sovereigntist claims the more it appears to be giving tacit approval to them. To take but one example: the fact that the federal government has participated in two campaigns conducted on the premise that there were no special requirements, such as a qualified majority, to achieve an affirmative answer to the referendum questions makes it much more difficult to claim that a different rule should apply in any future referendum.

Some media commentators have dubbed any attempt to set down ground rules for secession as taking a 'tough love' approach, casting the federal government in the role of a stern but loving parent and Quebec as a spoiled adolescent who must be brought back in line through the belated and reluctant application of strict disciplinary measures. In our view, however, this scenario totally misconceives the purpose and nature of the exercise we propose. The federal government must attempt to deal with the consequences of secession for the simple reason that failing to do so would be morally and politically irresponsible. Governments may wish for the best, but they have an obligation to prepare themselves and their citizens for the worst. The results of the October 30 referendum make it crystal clear that support for sovereignty in Quebec is sufficiently strong that Canadians elsewhere can continue to ignore it only at their peril.

In short, these unpleasant realities must be confronted for their own sake. This realization is distinctly liberating. If Canadians begin to discuss these issues for the simple reason that not doing so would be irresponsible (rather than as a strategy to win the next referendum), they can break the long-standing taboos that have stifled and sterilized this debate. It should finally be possible to initiate a frank and open dialogue on issues that have always remained just below the surface but have never been broached for fear of offending listeners in various parts of the country.

A Role for All Canadians

Some, no doubt, will denounce any attempt by Canada to participate in the process that will determine its own territorial integrity. In fact, it is entirely normal and appropriate in a democratic society for all citizens to have a say in the future of their country.

This point becomes obvious when one contemplates how the government of an independent Quebec would react if, following accession to sovereignty, it were faced with secessionist demands from minorities within its own population. Quebec would undoubtedly reject any claim that only the members of the dissentient minorities had a right to determine whether their secessionist claims should be recognized and assert, instead, that it and the entire Quebec population had a right to participate in decisions that affected Quebec's territorial integrity.

Aside from these considerations of democracy and fairness is a more pragmatic reason for recognizing the right of all Canadians to participate in this debate. Quebec sovereigntists have always argued that the costs of achieving sovereignty are minimal and have labeled suggestions that sovereignty will impose economic costs on Quebecers as economic terrorism. Yet the only possible way to minimize the transition costs is to permit Canadians from all parts of the country to discuss the issues openly. Out of this dialogue may come some measure of consensus on the ground rules that ought to govern any future secession referendum and the process leading out of a majority 'yes' vote. It is therefore in the interest of everyone – even the sovereigntists themselves – to recognize the right of Canadians from across the country to participate in a process designed to establish ground rules for secession.

Of course, some Quebecers may not see it that way. But it is probably impossible to predict with any certainty precisely how Quebecers will react to an open and honest debate of the secession issue. For every voter who takes offense there may be another whose perspective and understanding are broadened. And surely the results of the last referendum have exposed the folly of trying to keep Canada together on the basis of timidity about the capacity of adult citizens in a democracy to debate their own futures maturely and intelligently. In short, Canada should enter the debate directly, rather than through hushed diplomacy and confusing innuendo.

Outline of the *Commentary*

Even if readers accept our initial premise – that the federal government and all Canadians have a role to play in this process – the question that immediately arises is what is the nature of that role? Moreover, on what should the federal government ground its Plan B – what principles should govern the secession process?

We believe that the answers to these questions can be found, at least in part, in the international experience with secession in the recent past. A comparative analysis is useful since it illuminates the practical advantages and disadvantages of different sets of decision rules. By examining the international experience with secession movements and identifying commonly accepted approaches that have produced peaceful and democratic outcomes, Canadians can move past rhetoric and begin to focus on approaches that will be in everyone's best interest.

We turn to this task in the first section of this *Commentary*, reviewing the extent to which the constitutions of various nation-states provide for the possibility of referendums on secession. One obvious point that emerges from this review is that such provisions are extremely rare; given the primordial character of the principle of territorial integrity in international relations, the vast majority of states do not explicitly contemplate their own dismemberment. Nevertheless, a number have made provision for secession, usually because of the existence of significant secessionist movements within their borders.

The second section builds on this comparative analysis, setting out ten principles that we believe ought to govern the secession of a province from the Canadian federation. The key principle, which underlies our entire analysis in this section, is that any secession should respect the principle of the rule of law – that is, it should be achieved through a duly authorized amendment to the Canadian Constitution, rather than through a unilateral declaration of independence (UDI) by the Quebec government. We also propose rules to deal with issues such as the majority that must be obtained in the referendum, the manner in which border questions should be resolved, and whether a referendum should be held nationally or only in the province of Quebec.

In the third section, we consider how the federal government might implement the principles we propose. After examining a number of possible options, we recommend combining elements of several, rather than pursuing one or another in isolation from the others.

The key principle, we suggest, is the need to build consensus and find common ground, rather than dictate outcomes. Indeed, we believe that any attempt to impose conditions unilaterally would be certain to end in failure. The federal government's role must be to supply leadership and direction, and ultimately to facilitate a process whereby Canadians choose for themselves whether they wish to continue to live within a single state and on what terms.

Our analysis is limited to questions of process and does not deal with substantive issues such as debt division, citizenship, trade links, and so on. We have deliberately restricted our focus to process issues since we believe that agreement on a common set of ground rules is a precondition to any successful resolution of the substantive terms of secession.

Nor should the reader assume that we have concluded that secession is somehow inevitable. Canada has obviously seen better times, and its future unity remains uncertain. But Quebecers have flourished within the Canadian federation over the past 129 years, and there is every reason to hope that they will perceive remaining a part of Canada as in their continuing best interest. Thus, we offer the following analysis not because we regard secession as a foregone conclusion. Rather, like homeowners who purchase fire insurance even though they believe the risk of fire may be remote, prudent Canadians should contemplate the possibility of the dismemberment of their country in the hope of containing the calamity and rebuilding a new country if the worst should come to pass.

The International Experience

Before attempting to design a set of ground rules to govern secession in Canada, we believe it essential to review the manner in which other states have approached the issue (and in which Canada and some other states have approached other kinds of referendums).

A comparative analysis will indicate, for example, whether certain ground rules have tended to be accepted elsewhere. Of course, the fact that a particular set of principles has been widely accepted internationally does not mean that Canada should automatically import the same approach; the country's particular circumstances may well justify adopting a different approach. But in devising their own secession ground rules, Canadians should at least be aware of the comparative experience and be ready to justify any differences.

Our first task was to examine all constitutions that contain provisions dealing directly or indirectly with the issue of secession. We then studied the referendums of other nations and subnational groups considering secession or a similar infringement on a nation's sovereignty.

On the basis of this review, we offer the following generalizations about the international approach to secession and similar issues:

1 Secession is usually prohibited.
2 Unilateral secession is always prohibited.
3 The wording of the referendum question is the subject of negotiation and agreement between secessionist and national forces.
4 There is no uniform practice regarding the relevant population entitled to vote in a referendum on secession.

5 Referendums on sovereignty tend to be supervised by national and/or international institutions.
6 There is no uniformity in the majority required to support a successful sovereignty referendum.
7 The effect of the referendum depends on the existing constitutional system.
8 The boundaries of the seceding unit are not guaranteed to remain unchanged following independence.
9 The Swiss experience in creating the canton of Jura provides some model principles for resolving border disputes.
10 The Commonwealth experience suggests that referendums are consultative rather than binding.

Constitutional Provisions

Although a number of analysts have looked at referendums of all types,[3] the paucity of raw data often made it difficult to study the secession process itself. Nevertheless, we made efforts to discover the relevant details for several secession referendums.

Finding constitutions that contemplate succession was also a challenge. A 1992 study by Markku Suksi identifies 85 constitutions that include some form of referendum mechanism.[4] On the assumption that any modern constitution with a procedure for secession would involve a referendum or plebiscite, we reviewed each of the constitutions Suksi identified. We also updated his list by including constitutions that have incorporated some form of referendum procedure since 1992. In all, we reviewed the constitutions of 89 states. (See Box 2.)

From this data we drew the first eight points in the list above. Each demands some explanation.

Prohibition of Secession
The most obvious point that emerges from our review is that states are generally hostile to secession movements. Of the 89 constitutions we examined, 82 do not permit secession of a part of the state's territory under any circumstances. In most cases, the constitution is simply silent on the matter. A total of 22 of the constitutions examined, however, contain explicit affirmation of the primacy of the state's territorial integrity – it is not to be called into question under any circumstances. For example, the preamble to Australia's constitution speaks of its states having agreed to unite in one 'indissoluble' federal commonwealth. Other constitutions refer to the territory of the state being 'inalienable and irreducible' (Equatorial Guinea, article 3), 'indivisible' (Cameroon, article 1(2); Guyana, article 1; Ivory Coast, article 2; France, article 2; Madagascar, article 1; and Romania, article 1(1)), or 'inviolable' (Bulgaria, article

---

Box 2   Two Exceptional Situations

Of the countries whose constitutional arrangements for secession we studied (and report in Table 1), two no longer exist. They are the USSR, where the process of disintegration started in the 1990–91 period, and the Czech and Slovak Federative Republic, which replaced the former Czechoslovakia after the end of the Cold War and was itself replaced by two separate republics in 1992.

We included these countries in our study because both had constitutions that contemplated separation, both actually experienced separations (the Czechs and Slovaks successfully, the USSR far less peacefully), and both are often cited as modern examples of secession.

2(2); Mongolia, article 4(1)). Still others prohibit any amendment to the constitution that would impair the nation's territorial integrity (Cameroon, article 37; Cape Verde, article 313(1)(a); Comoros, article 82; Congo, article 8; Equatorial Guinea, article 104; Iran, article 78; Ivory Coast, article 73; Mali, article 76; Niger, article 124; Panama, article 3; Romania, article 148; and Rwanda, article 96), or prohibit the state from transferring rights to territory or sovereign rights that it exercises over that territory (Suriname, article 2(2)). In all, the overwhelming majority of the constitutions surveyed either implicitly or explicitly prohibit secession.

Referendums on secession were the rare exception to the presumed inviolability of a nation's sovereignty. In most cases in which a sovereign nation contemplated secession by a part of itself, the terms of the process placed onerous hurdles on the road to secession: the state controlled the registration, administration, drafting of the question, decision-rule, balloting, and scrutiny of the vote (as discussed below).

This general hostility toward secession is hardly surprising. Nothing is more fundamental to a state than its territorial integrity. The Charter of the United Nations and the principles of customary international law provide that no state shall interfere with another's territorial integrity.[5] Moreover, it is lawful for a state to use force to protect its territorial integrity from both domestic and foreign interference.

Although international law has also come to recognize the principle of self-determination of peoples, this right applies only in limited circumstances involving colonialization or discrimination against identifiable minorities. The general rule in international law is that minorities or peoples within states have no right to secede, absent evidence of discrimination or colonialization.[6]

Accordingly, the idea of a state's voluntarily forgoing part of its jurisdictional, economic, and territorial domain must be viewed as extraordinary, making any secession process a round peg in the square hole of the past and present statist system.[7]

We emphasize this generalized international hostility toward secessionist claims not because we believe that Canada should adopt a similar prohibitory attitude. (In fact, we later suggest that Canada explicitly recognize that secession is possible in certain circumstances.) Rather, the point is twofold. First, that Canada would be willing to recognize the legitimacy of secession under any circumstances is itself an extraordinary concession, one that only a few states are prepared to make.

Second, it is important to distinguish between a recognition that secession is possible only if certain conditions are met and a willingness to accept secession regardless of the circumstances in which it is attempted. Although a small minority of states adopt the former attitude, none adopts the latter. Even those states that recognize the possibility of secession are willing to do so only if the seceding unit meets certain key conditions or requirements. This principle ought to govern any future secession process in Canada.

Unilateral Secession

Quebec sovereigntists argue repeatedly that Quebec has a right under international law to unilaterally proclaim its sovereignty, regardless of whether Canada has agreed. This, indeed, is the position taken in Quebec's Bill 1, which authorizes its National Assembly to proclaim sovereignty after making Canada a formal offer of a political and economic partnership. The fact that Canada might reject the offer is relevant only in the sense that such a rejection would make it possible for Quebec to declare sovereignty more quickly. Bill 1 provides that, if an independent review committee concludes that negotiations with Canada are fruitless, the National Assembly may declare sovereignty immediately. In any event, Quebec need not obtain Canada's agreement before declaring sovereignty under Bill 1.

Of the 89 constitutions we surveyed, not one approaches secession in this fashion. Table 1 summarizes the relevant provisions in the seven constitutions that regard secession as permissible in certain circumstances. As the column headed 'Legal Authority' indicates, the secession process is never governed by a statute or law passed by the seceding unit alone. Rather, secession is subject to requirements set at the national level, either in the national constitution or in national legislation. Failure to satisfy these requirements would lead the courts to declare that the secession was unlawful.

In short, Quebec's claim – that the terms and conditions governing secession are a matter for its National Assembly alone to decide – is simply unknown in the constitution of any other country.

Ignoring Legal Rules

Of course, the fact that a country's constitution sets certain terms and conditions for lawful secession does not necessarily mean that these requirements will always be followed in practice. For example, the Soviet law on secession required a series of referendums, with the first drawing two-thirds majority support for secession before the process could continue. Many Soviet republics made a UDI in the 1990–91 period, so their subsequent referendums amounted to formal rubber stamping of what was essentially a *fait accompli*. (In Georgia, Lithuania, and Ukraine, for example, a referendum was merely the final symbolic act of secession that had been preceded by more fundamental expressions of dissent by ballot and bullet alike.[8]) Conversely, the USSR-wide referendum of March 17, 1991, sponsored by President Mikhail Gorbachev, did not even leave open the possibility of secession for voters within the Soviet republics.[9]

In brief, that a state's constitution clearly spells out a procedure to govern secession is no guarantee that these requirements will always be honored. Secessionist politicians or governments may choose to act in an illegal fashion and attempt to declare their independence unilaterally, without regard to the requirements of their state's constitution or law. The point is simply that the Quebec government's claim that the seceding unit alone should determine the terms and conditions that govern secession is unknown in the constitutions of the world today.

A related point is that secessionist movements that choose to defy the requirements of the existing constitution and declare independence unilaterally usually provoke the host state to resist in a variety of forms, ranging from military intervention and the use of force (consider, for example, the attempts by the Soviet Union in early 1991 to prevent the secession of the Baltic republics, as well as the resistance of the Federal Republic of Yugoslavia to the secession of a number of republics in 1991[10]), to merely declaring the acts of the secessionist regime illegal and carrying on as if the secession had not occurred. (When the whites-only government of Rhodesia unilaterally declared its independence in 1965, the UK government passed legislation asserting the continued sovereignty of parliament. Even though this legislation was not accompanied by any military intervention, the British courts held that the Rhodesian declaration of independence was legally ineffective on the basis that it was not certain that Britain would be unable to reestablish effective control over Rhodesian territory[11].)

Thus, any secessionist movement that attempts to jump outside the rules of the existing constitutional order and declare sovereignty illegally should expect a challenge from the host government. The result is two rival governments, each contesting the legitimacy of the other's jurisdiction over the territory of the seceding unit.

Plainly, the costs that this kind of conflict would impose on the citizens of a modern state could be very significant. No responsible politician could contemplate asking the citizenry to shoulder this kind of risk without clearly acknowledging the magnitude of the sacrifices involved and providing the population with an opportunity to clearly demonstrate their willingness to bear them. Yet the leaders of Quebec sovereigntists have behaved in precisely the opposite fashion, alleging that the Quebec government could issue a UDI without any significant costs or consequences. Indeed, former premier Jacques Parizeau went so far as to label any attempt to identify the costs associated with a UDI as a form of economic terrorism.

This failure to explain clearly the consequences of a UDI raises questions as to the legitimacy and the wisdom of any attempt by the Quebec government to declare sovereignty other than in accordance with the requirements of the existing Canadian Constitution.

The Referendum Question

In both 1980 and 1995, the Quebec government asserted that the wording of the referendum question was the exclusive responsibility of the pro-sovereigntist forces. Under the *Quebec Referendum Act*, the question is determined by the premier and endorsed by the National Assembly. Assuming the government has a majority, neither the opposition parties in the National Assembly nor the federal government has a way to participate in setting the question.

No constitution anywhere in the world today provides for the referendum question to be formulated in this fashion. As Table 1 indicates, in five of the seven countries whose constitutions contemplate secession, the national authorities, not the secessionist forces, determine the question. In the remaining two instances, the national government or pro-nationalist forces have an opportunity to participate effectively in the wording.

For example, the *Soviet Secession Law* provided for a commission formed by the seceding republic's supreme soviet with representation from all interested parties, including peoples of autonomous republics, autonomous regions, or autonomous national areas within the republic (article 4). The *Constitutional Law of 18 July 1991* of the Czech and Slovak Federative Republic contemplated a cooperative process whereby the president could reject a proposal calling for a referendum on the separation of the two republics if 'the proposed questions, which are to be asked in the referendum, are not unequivocal or understandable' (article 3). The president could return the proposed questions with comments to the legislative body that proposed them. (If that body insisted on the original questions, the president had to call the referendum within 15 days of second receipt of the question proposal (article 3(3)). Also significant was that both the former Soviet Union and the former Czech and Slovak Federative Republic limited the frequency with which secession referendums could be held. The USSR imposed a ten-year period between secession referendums (article 10), while the Czech and Slovak law required a five-year waiting period (article 5(5)).

That the question is a matter of negotiation, not unilateral edict, is also reflected in the wording of referendum questions on secession, which tend to be straightforward and widely understood.[12] As the Helsinki Commission noted in its compendium of reports on independence referendums, all of the Soviet republics choosing to secede from the USSR posed simple questions along the lines of 'Do you agree that _____ should be an independent, sovereign state?'[13] For the Western Australian referendum on secession of 1933, a lack of agreement over the wording of a question resulted in the electorate's facing two questions, one written by the nationalists and one by opponents of separation.[14] Even in the Newfoundland Confederation referendums of 1948, where the wording generated some controversy,[15] the ballot offered straightforward alternatives (see Box 3). By the second referendum, Newfoundland voters faced two unmistakable choices: 'Confederation with Canada' or 'Responsible Government as it existed in 1933.'

Thus, the international experience suggests that, at minimum, the referendum question should not be determined unilaterally by the government of the seceding unit. Political leaders from parties or groups opposed to secession should have some opportunity to participate in wording the question.

The Population Entitled to Vote

If a referendum on secession is to be held, is the vote conducted only among the population of the territory that is proposing to secede or among the entire national population? As Table 1 indicates, this question has no uniform answer. In Austria, Ethiopia, and Singapore, the entire national population is entitled to participate in any secession referendum; the same was true in the Czech and Slovak Federative Republic. In contrast, in St. Christopher and Nevis, the former Soviet Union, and France, the referendum is held only in the territory that is proposing to secede.

We conclude that either approach is consistent with existing international practice.

Table 1
Constitutional Provisions Governing Secession

Country[a]	Legal Authority to Conduct and Supervise Secession Referendum	Referendum Question Formulated by	Relevant Population to Vote in Referendum	Decision Rule (Vote Required for Process to Continue)	Boundaries
Austria	national legislation	national authorities[b]	national population	majority of valid votes cast	changes must be approved by national and subnational governments
Ethiopia	national legislation[c]	national authorities	local population	majority of votes cast	absent agreement, federal council to decide borders based on settlement patterns of peoples and the wishes of the people or peoples concerned[d]
France	national legislation[e]	national and local government[f]	local population	majority of votes cast	assumption that former colonial borders would become borders of the independent state
Singapore	national legislation	national authorities	national population	two-thirds of total votes cast	changes require approval of two-thirds of all voters in national referendum
St. Christopher and Nevis	national legislation[g]	national constitution[h]	local population	two-thirds of total votes cast[i]	Nevis would automatically retain its current borders[j]
Soviet Union	national legislation or law of autonomous republic if the latter is not inconsistent with national law[k]	commission formed by supreme soviet of the seceding republic, including representatives of 'all interested parties' within the republic	local population	two-thirds of eligible voters	specific provision for "autonomous regions" within a seceding republic to remain part of the Soviet Union[l]
Czech and Slovak Federative Republic	national legislation	national president and Czech and Slovak national councils; proposed questions are to be 'unequivocal and understandable'; in and absence of agreement and after a waiting period, each republic can insist that its wording be posed[m]	national population	absolute majority of voters in each republic[n]	assumption that borders of existing republics would remain unchanged following secession

a Most of the constitutions referred to here are the texts found in A.P. Blaustein and G.H. Flanz, eds., *Constitutions of the Countries of the World*, loose-leaf edition (New York: Oceana Publications): For Austria, *The Federal Constitutional Law*, issued December 1985 (hereafter cited as *Austria*); for Ethiopia, *The Constitution of the Federal Democratic Republic of Ethiopia*, issued December 1994 (hereafter cited as *Ethiopia*); for France, *The French Constitution*, issued June 1988 (hereafter cited as *France*); for Singapore, *The Constitution of the Republic of Singapore*, issued September 1995 (hereafter cited as *Singapore*); for St. Christopher and Nevis, *St. Christopher and Nevis Constitution Order*, issued April 1984 (hereafter cited as *St. Christopher and Nevis*); for the Czech and Slovak Federative Republic, *Constitutional Law of 18 July 1991*, issued September 1992 (hereafter cited as *Czech and Slovak*). The exception is the USSR, for which we used *Constitution (Basic Law) of the Union of Soviet Socialist Republics* and *On the Procedure for Deciding Questions Connected with the Secession of a Union Republic from the USSR* (law of the Soviet Union adopted April 3, 1990 (hereafter cited as *Soviet Secession Law*) reproduced in W.E. Butler, *Basic Documents of the Soviet Legal System*, 2nd ed. (New York: Oceana Publications, 1994).

b *Austria*, article 44(1), states that any constitutional change must be approved by a two-thirds vote of the house of representatives.

c Secession must first be approved by a two-thirds majority of the members of the legislative council of any 'nation, nationality or people' (*Ethiopia*, article 39(4)): the federal government must organize a referendum on secession within three years of the request from the legislative council.

d *Ethiopia*, article 39(5), defines a 'nation, nationality or people' as 'a group of people who have or share a large measure of a common culture, or similar customs, mutual intelligibility of language, belief in a common or related identities, and who predominantly inhabit an identifiable, contiguous territory.'

e But secession is possible only in respect of the overseas territories under *France*, article 86. Article 2 provides that the territory of the republic itself is 'indivisible.'

f 'The procedures governing this change [in status] shall be determined by an agreement approved by the Parliament of the Republic and the legislative assembly concerned' (*France*, article 86).

g The referendum is conducted and supervised by the 'supervisor of elections,' appointed by the governor-general after consultations with the prime minister, the premier, and the leader of the opposition.

h *St. Christopher and Nevis*, article 113(2)(c), provides that 'full and detailed proposals for the future constitution of the island of Nevis (whether as a separate state or as part of or in association with some other country) [shall] have been laid before the Assembly at least six months before the holding of the referendum.' Moreover, the constitution sets out a number of changes that will automatically occur in the event of Nevis' secession, including that Nevis will not be entitled to representation in parliament and that parliament will have specific authority to deprive Nevis citizens of their citizenship in St. Christopher.

i The bill authorizing secession must also be approved by a two-thirds majority of the elected members of the Nevis Island assembly.

j *St. Christopher and Nevis*, schedule 3, section 1, sets out the territory of the new state of St. Christopher that would automatically come into existence following the secession of Nevis.

k Under *Soviet Secession Law*, articles 1, 2, and 4, the referendum is to be conducted and supervised by a commission formed by the supreme soviet of the seceding republic, and the commission is to include representatives of 'all interested parties,' including representatives of any autonomous regions or national areas within the seceding republic. Further, article 5 provides for the participation of outside observers, including authorized representatives of the USSR, of autonomous regions within the republic, and of the United Nations, in order to monitor the vote; the exact role is to be agreed on by the supreme soviets of the USSR and the seceding republic.

l Under *Soviet Secession Law*, article 3, 'The right to autonomously decide the question of whether to stay in the USSR or the seceding union republic, as well as the question of its State-law status, shall be retained for the peoples of autonomous republics and autonomous formations.' Border issues will ultimately be determined by the USSR congress of peoples' deputies, after preparation of proposals by the USSR council of ministers, with the participation of the government of the seceding republic (article 12).

m *Czech and Slovak*, article 3(3). It appears that, in the absence of an agreement, either of the republics may propose questions.

n However, if the proposal passes in only one republic, the federation ceases to exist within a year (article 6(2)), and a federal law must be passed dealing with division of assets and liabilities (*Czech and Slovak*, article 6(3)).

Box 3   The Newfoundland Confederation Referendums

Newfoundland had achieved responsible government and full status as a self-governing British colony in the 1850s, but when the bottom fell out of its economy during the 1830s, bankruptcy forced it to turn to the United Kingdom and accept dependant status under a UK-appointed commission of government.

After World War II, an elected constituent assembly considered the future, and recommended putting two choices to the people in a referendum. It tried to keep the option of confederation with Canada off the ballot, but was overruled by London. London also insisted the course taken must receive a majority of the votes cast.

In a first referendum, held June 3, 1948, the ballot asked voters to choose among the following three options:

1 Commission of Government for a period of five years.
2 Confederation with Canada.
3 Responsible government as it existed in 1933.

Responsible government was the most favored choice, but it had drawn only about 45 percent of the vote. So the electorate returned to the polls on July 23, 1948, for a second referendum that dropped the first option, which had received only 14 percent support in the first referendum. Confederation won about 52 percent of the vote, enough to trigger the opening of negotiations.*

* Canada, Canadian Unity Information Office, *Understanding Referenda: Six Histories* (Ottawa: Supply and Services Canada, 1978), ch. 1; and Frank Cramm and Garfield Fizzard. *Our Province: Newfoundland and Labrador* (Markham, Ont.): Breakwater Books/ Fitzhenry & Whiteside, 1983), pp. 124–127.

Supervision by National and/or International Institutions

The need for supervision obviously is connected with whether the population that is to vote is the subnational group or the national electorate. Where the referendum process is carried out by the potentially seceding unit, the national unit and/or international observers tend to supply some form of supervision or scrutiny. This view is supported by the eminent publicist Yves Beigbeder in his work on monitoring votes.[16] Another scholar bluntly states the rationale for outside supervision:

Those who are responsible for the operation of a plebiscite can influence its outcome by setting rules in relation to the registration of voters, campaigning, symbols, location of polling stations, and by setting the timing of the plebiscite. Most importantly, the supervisory authority has an opportunity to rig the ballot. Therefore, the supervising authority should not have any interest in the outcome of the plebiscite in order to ensure the plebiscite's fairness.[17]

Presumably, legitimacy can be obtained by permitting supervision by a combination of interests, including local, national, and international observers.

We conclude that some checks and balances over the registration and scrutiny of ballots are normally instituted in circumstances involving a secession referendum.

The Majority Required

The majority required to attain a mandate for sovereignty emerged as a significant issue in the campaign before the last Quebec referendum. The Quebec government has consistently said that all that should be required is 50 percent plus one of the total valid ballots cast. But federalists (including Prime Minister Chrétien and Intergovernmental Affairs Minister Stéphane Dion) have suggested that a greater threshold should be required.[18]

As Table 1 indicates, existing international practice provides support for both approaches. Three of the constitutions reviewed require that a supermajority of two-thirds of the ballots cast favor independence. Note, moreover, that, in these three cases, the referendum is to be held among the entire national population, making this threshold extremely difficult to achieve. The remaining five constitutions require only a majority of 50 percent of valid votes cast (although the Czech and Slovak Federative Republic required a majority favoring independence in each republic, if the separation proposal passed in only one of them the federation would cease to exist a year after the referendum results were announced [article 6(2)]).

We conclude that either of the approaches suggested is consistent with international practice.

If we look beyond the terms of the constitutions we studied and examine actual secession referendums that have taken place in the recent past, a similar conclusion emerges. In the breakup of the former Soviet Union, for example, some independence votes were not preceded by any statement as to the majority required.[19] In at least a number of those instances, this silence may have been a product of the fact that the outcome was a foregone conclusion: that Latvia or Ukraine made no reference to the majority required may be explained by the fact that less than 10 percent of Latvians and Ukrainians had any intention of remaining in the USSR.[20] On the other hand, Armenia, where support for independence made a referendum essentially a *fait accompli*, the Armenian Central Commission on the Referendum announced that it would comply with the 66 percent threshold required under Soviet law.[21]

Outside the context of a rubber-stamp referendum, experts take various approaches to the decision rule. For those advocating a requirement of *more* than a bare majority of unspoiled ballots, the rationale appears to rest primarily on experience and international legitimacy. As one commentator puts it:

Creating a new state, with all the complexities and sensitivities of redrawing boundaries, is an extremely significant change. It would be unduly disruptive of the international order to legitimize independence where only a bare majority supports it.[22]

And another recalls

A technical majority may not be enough. The Belgians voted in 1949 on whether Leopold III should resume his throne. On the strength of a 58 percent yes he came back to Brussels and then found it was not possible to function as king in a democratic society when 42 percent of the people had declared their opposition.[23]

On the other hand, it would be misleading to suggest that a qualified majority is the norm for secession referendums. The Commonwealth experience (discussed below) may have required a certain percentage of eligible voters to have supported a particular option in order for it to proceed, but there is little precedent for a supermajority requirement of more than 50 percent plus one. The Soviet republican referendums generally operated in the absence of any explicit majority requirement, and most of them did not align themselves with Gorbachev's requirement of 66 percent. Nor did past Canadian referendums or the Newfoundland Confederation referendums of 1948 require a supermajority.

Although it is important to keep in mind all the distinctions between a future Quebec referendum on secession and the comparative examples discussed, the international and national experience with referendums does not provide overwhelming evidence, one way or another, in regard to the majority required.

The Effect of the Referendum

Another important aspect of a referendum's decision rule is the legal effect of the vote. If the answer to a secession vote is in the affirmative and a UDI is illegal, what then is the effect of the referendum?

The short answer is that the effect of a referendum depends on the constitutional system in operation. Some nations, such as Denmark, have a qualified majority requirement to bring about constitutional change, but the corollary is that a referendum is binding. The United Kingdom also has some experience with qualified majorities, yet a binding referendum is an impossibility there since parliament cannot bind itself. Thus, as one commentator concludes about Western European nations, although popular sovereignty is their *raison d'etre*, the practice is different.[24]

Indeed, it is impossible to generalize about the effect of a secession referendum without resort to a nation's constitution. Basically, if it is silent on the subject, a referendum is consultative, if only because there is no legal basis for making it binding. Thus, most referendums are consultative in the sense that the legal status quo remains until a resulting negotiation and eventual legislative measure addresses the referendum result. As one study concludes, '[b]inding referendums are rare in parliamentary democracies, and are best suited to countries with a tradition of direct democracy, such as Switzerland.'[25]

For example, following the 'yes' vote for independence by the people of Western Australia, the prime minister of Australia proposed a secession convention to all states of the federation. The premier of Western Australia eventually petitioned the imperial parliament in Westminster, pursuant to the *Secession Act* of 1934. When Westminster refused to act on the petition, no further actions were taken to achieve secession directly.[26] Similarly, when Newfoundland voted in favor of joining Canada, the result triggered only the initiation of formal negotiations between Newfoundland and a Canadian delegation (which ended, of course, in the terms of union later approved by the Parliament of Canada, the government of Newfoundland, and finally the UK parliament[27]).

In both these circumstances, like those in the former Soviet Union, the referendum result was only consultative, representing an expression of democratic input, not the output itself. Moreover, it is unclear whether a binding referendum, particularly one involving the amendment of a constitution, would be constitutional in a parliamentary system.

In sum, the international experience suggests that parliamentary systems do not permit binding referendums.[28]

The Boundaries of the Seceding Unit

Whether the borders of an independent Quebec would be identical to the borders of the existing province has also emerged as significant, particularly in the period since the October 1995 referendum.

The Quebec government has always maintained that the borders of an independent Quebec would remain unchanged following sovereignty and would not be the subject of negotiations between the Canadian and Quebec governments. It claims that international law supports this conclusion, pointing in particular to a 1992 legal opinion rendered by five international law experts to a Quebec

National Assembly committee studying this question.[29] Some federalists say, however, that the borders of an independent Quebec would necessarily be subject to negotiation and agreement between the Canadian and Quebec governments. According to them, no rule of international law would preclude Canada from raising this issue, nor does international law guarantee or even support Quebec's claim to all of its existing territory in the absence of agreement with the government of Canada.[30]

Legal disputes aside, existing international practice, as reflected in the constitutions that we surveyed, directly contradicts Quebec's claim that existing provincial borders would be guaranteed upon independence. Simply put, there is no uniform or general rule supporting the claim that the borders of the seceding unit cannot be changed upon independence.

For example, the *Soviet Secession Law* (article 12) provided a transition period during which the USSR council of ministers was to prepare, along with the government of the seceding republic, 'proposals' regarding questions affecting the state boundary of the USSR. The proposals were to be considered ultimately by the USSR congress of people's deputies; although it might confirm the existing republican borders as the borders of the new state, there was no requirement or even presumption favoring this result.

Similarly, the Ethiopian constitution (article 48) provides that border disputes between or among states be settled by agreement of the concerned states; if they are unable to agree, the federal council, which is composed of representatives of Ethiopia's nations, nationalities, and peoples, is instructed to decide the issue on the basis of the settlement patterns of peoples and the wishes of the people or peoples concerned. Again, there is no presumption that existing borders will remain unchanged.

A similar result obtains in both Singapore and Austria, although no explicit provisions are directed to the resolution of border questions. In Singapore, the terms of secession must be approved in a national referendum; in Austria, they are a matter of agreement to be reached between the federal authority and the local authority. Thus, the seceding unit would have to resolve any border disputes in a satisfactory manner.

Of course, borders are sometimes not an issue. In St. Christopher and Nevis, for example, the state's existing territory comprises two islands; the secession of Nevis, were it to occur, would naturally include all the territory of that island. In France, the constitution contemplates the secession of colonial territories that are not contiguous to the French mainland; in the case of the Czech and Slovak republics, neither side questioned the existing borders. (Note, however, that the borders of these two states were altered slightly in early 1996.)

The point is simply that no generalized practice favors guaranteeing or protecting existing local or provincial borders at the time of secession. Indeed, it is commonplace to contemplate border adjustments as part of the negotiations between the host state and the seceding unit.

The Jura Precedent

The constitutions described in Table 1 offer no detailed mechanisms for resolving any border disputes that might arise. It is worthwhile, therefore, describing the constitutional provisions that were used to draw the borders of the Swiss canton of Jura when it was created out of the existing canton of Berne in the 1970s. Although this change involved internal reorganization of Switzerland as opposed to outright secession of a part of its territory, the issues that arose were similar to those that would arise in a secession scenario in which boundaries were at issue.

In 1970, the canton of Berne amended its constitution to provide for a referendum among French-speaking districts that had historically expressed a desire to establish a new canton.[31] On June 23, 1974, a majority of the voters in these districts voted 'yes' to the question, 'Do you want to form a new canton?'.[32]

Although 52 percent of the voters voted 'yes,' particular regions or districts within the area voted against the creation of the new canton. The distinctive feature of the Berne constitutional provisions was the possibility for these dissenting districts to require a second referendum in which they could elect to remain within Berne (article 3(1)).[33] Similarly, districts or communes within Berne that had not participated in the first referendum but directly abutted districts that had earlier voted to form the new canton could petition to hold a referendum in which citizens would be asked whether they wished to join Jura (article 4(2)). In effect, local populations determined the borders of the new canton through a series of cascading referendums.

Finally, Switzerland held a national referendum on amending the national constitution to form the new canton according to the borders determined by the results of the earlier local referendums results. The amendment was approved by 82.3 percent of Swiss voters on September 24, 1978.

This process was noteworthy for two reasons. First, the operative principle for resolving border disputes was democracy: rather than officials' drawing lines on a map, the matter was put directly to the people themselves. Second, although existing borders were not automatically guaranteed, neither were they completely up for grabs.

Two limiting principles together enabled the resolution of border issues in an democratic, orderly, and transparent fashion. First, a referendum could be held only within certain geographic units – districts or communes – that had some recognized or pre-existing legal status. It was not possible for simply any group of citizens living in a particular territory to petition to hold a referendum. Second, the cascading referendums were structured so as to ensure that the two cantons would be territorially contiguous. What was desired – and achieved – was a single boundary dividing Berne from Jura, not parts of Berne completely surrounded by Jurassien territory or vice versa.

We have described the Berne-Jura example in some detail because we regard it as having established a model set of principles for resolving border disputes. Such a process furthers democracy by ensuring that border disputes are resolved by reference to the wishes of the people directly concerned. At the same time, the limits mean that the process will not collapse in on itself as smaller and smaller units within a state demand a never-ending series of referendums.

The fact that the procedure has been used successfully is an indication that it is a practical as well as a principled way to resolve border disputes. As we will suggest later, we believe that it represents a useful set of principles for resolving border disputes that could arise between Canada and Quebec.

The Commonwealth Experience

Also worth examining in this survey of recent history are referendums closer to home. We looked at the Canadian experience with referendums in general and also at referendums in the United Kingdom on possible devolutions of parliamentary sovereignty.

The UK Experience
The UK experience is especially important to Canada with its like conventions and institutions. Of course, today British influence over Canadian affairs is primarily nostalgic; whatever constitutional ties that remained after the Statute of Westminster were formally severed by the patriation of Canada's Constitution in 1982. Nevertheless, the preamble to the *Constitution Act, 1867* states that the Canadian Constitution is 'similar in Principle to that of the United Kingdom,' which is true at least in regard to the retention of the parliamentary system and common law.

The UK referendums pertinent here are:

- The 1973 'border poll' in which parliament asked the people of Northern Ireland whether or not they wished to remain part of the United Kingdom. It drew a 98 percent affirmative vote (although the results were tainted by the refusal of many Catholics to participate).[34]

- The 1979 devolution referendums in which the people of Scotland and Wales participated in advisory referendums on proposed regional assemblies. Of the Scots who voted, 51.6 percent said 'yes,' but the participation rate was so low that only 32.9 percent of the total electorate had chosen the affirmative. In Wales, devolution was rejected by a decisive 80 percent of voters (representing 47 percent of the total eligible electorate).[35]
- The 1975 UK referendum on membership in the European Economic Community (EEC) in which all citizens were asked about ceding to the EEC parliament UK sovereignty over certain jurisdictional matters.[36]

In all these referendums, the central government controlled the process. Granted, the UK parliamentary system provides little choice in the matter, but it is noteworthy that, during the devolution referendums, Westminster firmly rejected efforts by Scottish and Welsh elected representatives to alter the process.

The decision rule in these referendums varied, although one expert on referendums categorizes UK referendums as requiring a qualified majority without any binding effect.[37] The referendum on EEC membership relied on a decision rule of a simple majority.

No decision rule was announced for Northern Ireland in 1973, though that referendum contained no suspense as to the outcome. As one commentator puts it:

It was hardly needed to discover the opinion of the majority in Northern Ireland; as long as the majority was Protestant, it was inconceivable that the province would opt to join the [Irish] Republic and the result of the plebiscite was predetermined by the way in which the boundary was drawn between the North and the South in 1920.[38]

The Scottish and Welsh devolution votes used a more sophisticated decision rule to ensure that such a significant alteration of the UK parliamentary system would result only if approval of devolution was truly representative. Particularly, Labour MP George Cunningham introduced an amendment in 1978 (which became known as the Cunningham amendment) providing that devolution would result only if a simple majority of those voting in the referendum voted 'yes' *and* if no fewer than 40 percent of those entitled to vote in fact voted 'yes.'

In the event, although the 'yes' side in Scotland garnered a majority of the votes cast, the 40 percent threshold was not met: 32.9 percent of the total electorate voted 'yes' and 30.8 percent 'no.' The 40 percent minimum may seem low to Canadians, since secession referendums in Quebec have drawn incredibly high voter turnouts of 80 to 90 percent. The rule was, however, hotly contested by Scottish and Welsh separatists; given the expected low turnout in those regions, they realized that 40 percent would be difficult to achieve.[39]

The important lesson from the devolution votes may lie in the parliamentary approach reflected in the 40 percent rule. It indicated to the electorate 'how Parliament intended to use its discretion,' says one commentator, 'and gave a warning that a bare majority of votes cast would not be sufficient to ensure the setting up of the Scottish Assembly.'[40] At the same time, the Cunningham amendment, by its very nature, emphasized the consultative nature of the referendum and the fact that decisions on sovereignty in the end rested with the legislature. It

gave to Parliament the discretion to decide whether a 'Yes' majority which failed to meet the 40 per cent requirement was sufficient to allow devolution to be implemented. Parliament would decide for itself whether the Act should be repealed; and no doubt such a decision would be based to a large extent on the balance between the 'Yes' and 'No' votes. The advisory nature of the referendum made it a flexible instrument enabling Parliament to make the final decision if the 40 per cent requirement was not met.[41]

Moreover, by virtue of the doctrine of parliamentary sovereignty, UK referendums cannot be binding: '[T]hey did not commit the government in any formal sense to act on the results, nor could they have bound Parliament to do so.'[42]

The Canadian Experience

The Canadian experience with referendums confirms our observations about the UK experience. Canadian history has seen only three nationwide referendums: on prohibition of alcoholic beverages in 1898, on conscription in 1942, and on the Charlottetown Accord in 1992.

The prohibition vote saw a 44 percent turnout and a simple majority of 51.3 percent voting 'yes' to prohibition, but a majority of Quebec voters rejected the proposal. Given the divisions on the issue, the Laurier government decided not to proceed with prohibition, despite the slim majority in favor. The military conscription plebiscite also split the nation, with a huge majority in Quebec rejecting conscription while 63.7 percent of the total ballots cast were in the affirmative.

Both these referendums were governed by federal statutes that included the precise wording of the question and form of the ballot. Again, the referendums were not legally binding but consultative only.[43]

The 1992 referendum on the Charlottetown Accord had a number of innovations, including an arrangement for any province to hold its own referendum rather than participate in the federal one. British Columbia and Alberta delayed their decisions as to whether they would participate in the federal referendum, both eventually opted to do so; only Quebec chose to conduct its own event under provincial legislation.[46] It follows, arguably, that Quebec's holding of its own referendum was thus at the discretion of Parliament.

Regardless, the question to be put to the electorate was approved by the House of Commons and by the Senate, with the same question being used on the same date in Quebec. The voter turnout was 72 percent for the federal referendum: 54.3 percent voted 'no' and 45.7 percent 'yes.' Quebecers also voted in the negative.

In considering Canadian experience with sovereignty referendums, people are sometimes tempted to refer to the Newfoundland Confederation referendums. Yet they were not a national Canadian process but one conducted by the Dominion of Newfoundland. Moreover, although René Lévesque cited them as a precedent for a series of referendums on Quebec secession,[45] the question in Newfoundland did not involve infringement of a nation's sovereignty. Rather, the process was one of decolonization – both the imperial parliament (Westminster) and the local colony (Newfoundland) agreed that the status quo was not an alternative. Thus, to lump future Quebec referendums with Newfoundland's Confederation process is misleading in that the cessation of sovereign rights was not at issue in the latter. After all, the similarities between marriage and divorce end at the altar.

Ten Principles Governing Secession

Guided and informed by international experience, we believe it is possible to identify a set of workable and fair principles to govern any future sovereignty referendum and its aftermath. They are as follows:

1 Clear ground rules governing secession should be set down in advance of any future referendum.
2 Secession of part or all of a province is legally possible under Canadian law.
3 Secession of a province must respect the principle of the rule of law.
4 Secession of part or all of a province can occur only if it is supported in a consultative, province-wide referendum on a clear question conducted according to a transparent and fair procedure.
5 A majority of 50 percent plus one in favor of sovereignty in a referendum conducted in accordance with Principle 4 should be sufficient to trigger secession negotiations.
6 Certainty and the rule of law require advance clarification of the fundamental ground rules governing secession negotiations.

7 Any negotiated secession agreement must be ratified by a definitive Quebec referendum but need not be ratified by the national electorate.

8 Democracy requires that partition is legally and logically compatible with secession.

9 The fiduciary obligation of the Crown in relation to the aboriginal peoples of Canada must be respected.

10 Upon secession of a province, the existing Canadian Constitution would remain intact with only those changes necessary to accommodate the fact of secession being implemented immediately.

Notice that, in the following discussion of these principles, we do not recommend that Canada follow the most frequent international approach in all respects. Indeed, we believe that it should openly accept the possibility that secession can occur under Canadian law, a policy that departs from overwhelming international sentiment on this issue. Our objective is to identify a set of transparent and balanced ground rules that would be in the long-term interest of all citizens and governments in Canada, regardless of whether they are pro-federalist or sovereigntist in political orientation.

Principle 1: Clear Ground Rules in Advance

Principle 1 was, to a large extent, anticipated in the first pages of this *Commentary*, where we argue that it is essential for the federal government to attempt to establish ground rules for secession in advance of the next referendum.

The international experience with secession confirms the validity and importance of this first principle, When secession or territorial reorganization has occurred peacefully, democratically, and with a minimum of economic disruption and dislocation, it has generally been preceded by a consensus over the rules governing the process. Conversely, instances in which the process was marred by violence, infringements of fundamental rights, and severe economic, political, and social dislocation have tended to be those in which such a consensus was lacking.

Two examples of the former scenario are the Czech-Slovak secession in 1992 and the creation of the canton of Jura in Switzerland in the 1970s. In both cases, the ground rules were agreed on in advance and clearly understood by the political elites and the population at large. This prior consensus on process meant that the secession or territorial reorganization could occur in an orderly, fair, and democratic manner.

Examples of the alternative include the breakup of the former Federal Republic of Yugoslavia and the secession of various republics from the former Soviet

Union. In neither instance could the relevant political elites agree on the ground rules governing the process. The absence of such a consensus meant that none of the governments involved was willing to accept the legitimacy of the tactics or decisions of its political competitors. The result was violence, civil disorder, and, in the case of Yugoslavia, a protracted and bloody civil war.

We do not suggest that prior agreement on the process of secession would necessarily have avoided these consequences. We do believe, however, that the absence of such a consensus made some form of impasse virtually unavoidable. In short, we believe that prior agreement on the ground rules increases the likelihood of achieving a peaceful and democratic secession process.

Principle 2: Secession Is Legally Possible

We believe that the Canadian government should recognize that secession of part or all of a province is legally possible. Such a recognition could take the form of a resolution passed by the House of Commons or a statement to this effect by the prime minister.[46] It could also define the secession process, including the level of consent required, whether a referendum ratifying the terms of secession would be necessary in part or all of the country, and how negotiations on secession would be conducted.

Possible Objections

A possible objection to Principle 2 is that it is inconsistent with the policy of the vast majority of countries around the world. Few of them recognize the possibility of secession. Most explicitly or implicitly place the issue of territorial integrity outside the realm of permissible political debate and deny the legitimacy of secessionist claims under any circumstances.

Nevertheless, we believe that Canada should formally recognize that secession is legally possible under Canadian law. Three considerations lead us to this conclusion. First, without such recognition, the whole exercise of attempting to achieve consensus on ground rules governing secession becomes futile. Any such consensus must begin from the premise that secession is an option under some conceivable set of circumstances. Anyone who refuses to accept this premise need not bother trying to go further than the advice locals sometimes offer lost visitors: 'You can't get there from here.' Since we believe that it is essential to attempt to define a set of ground rules to govern the process, we obviously reject the suggestion that secession is impossible under any circumstances.

In other words, the first step in the process must be the open acknowledgment that secession is a legal and political possibility. Once this premise is accepted, the issue becomes a matter of attempting to define in a more precise fashion the exact circumstances in which secession should be permitted and recognized.

A related consideration is the fact that the international experience with secession confirms that the host or predecessor state's recognition of the legal possibility of secession is a precondition to peaceful and democratic resolution of the secession process. This insight is one of the keys offered by Robert Young in his admirable study of the politics of secession. Peaceful secessions, he argues, have all been characterized by an acceptance on the part of the political leadership of the predecessor state that secession could occur. This 'bitter and very difficult decision ... marks the fundamental difference between peaceful secessions and those that are violent.'[47]

Moreover, the only alternative to Principle 2 is to argue that the national government will resist secession under any and all circumstances, even to the point of using military force. In effect, Canada would be taking the position that it would not agree to secession, no matter how strongly Quebecers favored this option.

Yet there is no evidence that Canadians as a whole would support the use of force to keep Quebec in Confederation under any circumstances. Rather, the consensus appears to support the proposition that, assuming a significant majority of Quebecers clearly wish to secede and assuming Canada and Quebec can reach agreement on the appropriate terms, secession should be permitted.[48] Nor is there any evidence that Canada would have the resources to suppress Quebec secession that enjoyed the support of a significant majority of the Quebec population.

Although the Canadian Constitution is silent on the ability of a province to secede from the federation, legal commentators agree that secession is possible under the terms of the existing amending formula because all parts of the Constitution are subject to amendment (assuming the appropriate formula is used), including those provisions that refer to the province of Quebec. The relevant legal question, therefore, is not whether Quebec can legally secede but how secession can be accomplished.[49]

Another Objection

If the secession of a province is already permitted, is it not unnecessary to recognize explicitly that secession is legally possible?

We believe, however, that recognizing the right of part or all of a province to secede would be far from superfluous. First, although the Constitution may implicitly permit secession, this fact is not widely understood or appreciated outside legal circles; even Prime Minister Chrétien has, on occasion, suggested that secession is impossible since the Constitution makes no express provision for it.[50] Thus, it is important to recognize the possibility of secession explicitly so as to remove any confusion on the point.

Second, recognizing this principle would force Canada to go one step further and clarify the precise manner in which secession could be achieved. Since we believe that this kind of debate is essential, we advance Principle 2 as a means of ensuring that it will occur in advance of the next sovereignty referendum.

Principle 3: The Rule of Law

Acceptance of the principle that secession is legally possible leads directly to the question of the requirements that would have to be satisfied before it could proceed. In very general terms, a part or all of a province could secede from Canada by means of a constitutional amendment or by a UDI.

The first method would involve an amendment authorized by the amending formula in part V of the *Constitution Act, 1982,* a scenario consistent with the maintenance of the principle of the rule of law. Such a secession would bring no break in legal continuity. The new legal reality, involving the creation of a separate Quebec state, would be based on and draw its authority from the existing Canadian Constitution.

The alternative scenario is secession achieved through a UDI issued by Quebec, with or without the agreement of Parliament or the provincial legislatures. The existing Canadian Constitution makes no provision for a province to secede on the basis of a unilateral issuance of a declaration to that effect (see Box 4). Thus, this scenario would involve a legal revolution, a break in legal continuity, and the establishment of a new constitutional order based on a new legal foundation. If successful, the seceding province would have jumped outside the rules of the existing Canadian Constitution and come into existence in accordance with international legal principles, under which a state is said to exist when it has achieved, 'the maintenance of a stable and effective government over a reasonably well defined territory, to the exclusion of the metropolitan State, in such circumstances that independence is either in fact undisputed, or manifestly indisputable.'[51]

We believe that provincial secession should be permissible under the first scenario, but not the second. Although Canadian law should explicitly recognize that secession is possible, it should also affirm that it can occur only in accordance with the requirements of the existing Canadian legal order. Moreover, we believe that the federal government should clearly and unequivocally state that it stands behind this rule-of-law principle and is prepared to defend it.

Box 4   The Bertrand *Cases*

One private Canadian has already turned to the courts for judicial review of the constitutionality of the Quebec referendum process of October 1995. In August 1995, Guy Bertrand petitioned the Quebec Superior Court to rule on whether a unilateral declaration of independence by the government of Quebec would be unconstitutional if enacted. Mr. Justice Lesage confirmed the manifest illegality of such a declaration* (although he refused to issue an injunction blocking the vote, as Bertrand had requested).

This year, Bertrand has returned to the courts, applying for a permanent injunction prohibiting any future referendum. The argument commenced in Quebec Superior Court on May 13, 1996, and continues at the time of writing.

The Canadian government refused to participate in the first *Bertrand* case, failing to unequivocally condemn the legitimacy of a UDI prior to the October 1995 referendum. It has, however, intervened in the second case on the narrow question of whether domestic law governs and whether a future referendum would be binding, or merely consultative. It also disputes the Quebec government's claim that the province has a right to secede under the principles of international law.

* *Bertrand v. Quebec* (1995) 127 DLR (4th) 408.

Consequences

Acceptance of the principle that secession is permissible only if undertaken in accordance with the requirements of the Canadian constitution has a number of significant practical consequences. Most important of these is the fact that secession would require the consent of the House of Commons and Senate and at least seven provinces representing more than 50 percent of the combined populations of the provinces. (Although legal commentators are divided on the precise amending formula that would govern a provincial secession, there is general agreement that either section 38 – the 'seven-fifty' formula – or section 41 – unanimous consent – would apply.[52] A little later, we deal with the implications of that uncertainty.)

The practical significance of this requirement is highlighted by considering the provisions of Bill 1, *An Act Respecting the Future of Quebec,* introduced in the Quebec National Assembly by Premier Jacques Parizeau on September 7, 1995.[53] The legislation authorizes the National Assembly to proclaim the sovereignty of Quebec, the only precondition being that such a proclamation be preceded by a 'formal offer of economic and political partnership with Canada' (section 1). The National Assembly is authorized to proclaim sovereignty as soon as it has approved a 'partnership treaty' with Canada or as soon as it has concluded, on the advice of an independent 'orientation and supervision committee,' that the negotiations with Canada have proven fruitless (section 26).

The declaration of sovereignty authorized by Bill 1 would claim to sweep away the entire Canadian Constitution and abolish the jurisdiction of all Canadian institutions over Quebec territory, including that of the Parliament and government of Canada, the Queen, the governor general, and the Supreme Court of Canada (see Box 5). In effect, the act tries to confer on the Quebec National Assembly power to issue a UDI in direct contravention of the requirements of the Canadian Constitution.

In our view, it is in the interests of the government of Canada *and* the government of Quebec to agree in advance that secession can be achieved only through a duly authorized constitutional amendment, and not through a UDI such as was contemplated by Bill 1. The Canadian government would obviously favor acceptance of this rule-of-law principle, given its legal obligation to act in accordance with the terms of the Canadian Constitution.

Because the Quebec government has always maintained that sovereignty can be achieved with a minimal degree of economic and political disruption, we believe that it is equally in its interest to accept the validity of Principle 3.

The Problem with a UDI

The problem with a UDI is precisely that it would make a smooth transition to sovereignty virtually impossible. A UDI would be an attempt to secede from Canada without coming to an agreement on any of the important issues that would require resolution, including the sharing of the Canadian debt, borders, trade relations, and currency. We believe that Canada would have no choice but to challenge the validity of a Quebec UDI, if only to protect its interests on these fundamental questions. In making that challenge, Canada would not be claiming that secession was legally or politically impossible. It would merely be insisting that Quebec come to an agreement on the terms and conditions of secession prior to its being implemented.

So the UDI scenario is a recipe for confrontation and conflict between the governments of Quebec and Canada. Each would maintain that it alone possessed sovereign authority over Quebec territory. The outcome of this contest for supremacy would depend on which proved able to exercise effective control over that territory. The outcome is difficult to forecast, but it is doubtful that Quebec would be able to effectively exclude Canadian authority from its terri-

---

Box 5   Quebec's Bill 1

Section 2 of Quebec's Bill 1 states that, on the date fixed in the proclamation of the National Assembly, Quebec shall become a sovereign country and 'shall acquire the exclusive power to pass all its law, levy all its taxes and conclude all its treaties.' This claim of absolute constituent power is reinforced by later sections of the bill, which provide that, on the declaration of sovereignty, federal laws will continue to apply in Quebec only so long as they are not repealed by the National Assembly (section 18), that the National Assembly has the power to adopt an interim constitution in place of the Canadian Constitution (section 24), and that the jurisdiction of the Supreme Court of Canada over Quebec territory will be extinguished and the new Quebec constitution will provide for a supreme court (section 22).

---

tory. Canada controls the airports, seaports, key federal buildings, and all the international entry points into Quebec; absent voluntary agreement from Canada to depart, it is not clear how the Quebec government could oust Canadian officials and Canadian control of these strategic locations.

Whether or not Quebec would be able to achieve effective control over its own territory is really beside the point. The mere hint that such a contest for supremacy could occur would unleash a political and economic whirlwind that would engulf both Canada and Quebec. Quebec's ability to borrow on international markets would be severely constrained, if not eliminated entirely. Private investors – including citizens of Quebec itself – would immediately attempt to remove all of their liquid assets from the province. The Quebec state would be faced with an immediate political and economic crisis of unprecedented proportions. Of course, it goes without saying that a UDI would provoke bitterness and acrimony in other parts of Canada, making it highly likely that Canada would refuse to enter into any kind of economic or political partnership such as Bill 1 implicitly promised.

No Quebec government – particularly a sovereigntist one – has any interest in imposing these kinds of enormous and unprecedented risks on itself or its population. This is not to deny the international examples of countries whose citizens have demonstrated a willingness to endure enormous hardships in order to achieve independence. But Quebecers have been assured that they will face no such hardships on the road to independence. By issuing a UDI, the Quebec government would guarantee that its rosy assurances of a calm transition to sovereignty would be proven wrong.

It is in everyone's clear interest, therefore, to agree in advance that the rule of law would continue to apply throughout any secession process.

A Possible Objection

A possible objection to Principle 3 is that Quebec cannot afford to agree to such a limitation in advance because doing so would mean holding the achievement of sovereignty hostage to the whims of recalcitrant premiers and to the anti-Quebec sentiments of some Canadians in the rest of Canada (ROC). According to this reasoning, Quebec must retain the threat of a UDI (even if it never intends to use it) in order to induce reasonable behavior on the part of the rest of the country.

Yet surely the answer to this objection is for the Quebec government to settle in advance a series of fair and reasonable ground rules that would govern any secession process. It is manifestly in its interest to agree to be bound by such rules (assuming that they are fair and balanced) since by doing so it would obtain the binding agreement of the Canadian government and of the other provinces to the same rules. Such a set of ground rules would mandate a reasoned response from the ROC, rather than one driven by spite or vengeance.

To secure the binding commitment of other governments to such rules, the Quebec government itself would have to agree to be bound in like fashion, precluding the possibility of declaring sovereignty through a UDI. But if, we have argued, a UDI is not a viable option in any event, then the Quebec government would merely have acknowledged reality by accepting the primacy of the rule of law. Moreover, it would have demonstrated its desire to take into account Canadian interests in reaching a negotiated solution. This show of good faith would legitimize the moderate voices within the ROC and increase the possibility that the rest of the country would respond in a similarly reasoned and balanced fashion.

Another Objection

Another possible objection to Principle 3 is that it is somehow undemocratic since it requires the Canadian government to declare in advance that it would not recognize the legitimacy of a UDI issued by the Quebec government. A related objection is that, if Quebec proceeded to issue a UDI despite Canada's stated position, Canada might have to resort to the use of force to ensure the continuity of the rule of law.

These objections, in our view, are unpersuasive. The Quebec government has never sought a mandate from the Quebec people to declare sovereignty in a manner designed to undermine the rule of law. Rather, it has insisted that sovereignty would be achieved on an orderly and consensual basis, even claiming that it would seek a negotiated partnership with Canada before declaring sovereignty. What would be antidemocratic would be the Quebec government's issuance of a UDI without an adequate democratic mandate, not the attempt by the Canadian government to protect the rule of law.

As for the possibility that Canada might be required to employ force in order to preserve the integrity of the rule of law, it would merely be responding to the illegal use of force by those seeking to overthrow the authority of Canadian law through unlawful means. The *Criminal Code of Canada* currently makes it an offense to 'use force or violence for the purpose of overthrowing the government of Canada' (section 46(2)). We suggested earlier that Canadians would accept secession if a clear majority of Quebecers favored this option and if an agreement on terms had been negotiated with Canada. It is quite another matter to suggest that the federal government should stand idly by if the Quebec government resorted to the illegal use of force and violence in defiance of the principle of the rule of law. For Canada to fail to respond to what would amount to an unconstitutional *coup d'état* would be an abdication of its own responsibilities as a sovereign nation. Of course, it would not be denying the possibility that Quebec could secede in appropriate circumstances. It would simply be refusing to recognize the validity of any attempt to subvert Canadian law through violent and illegal means and insisting that it would continue to enforce Canadian law in Quebec until such time as an appropriate constitutional amendment had been agreed to.

Amending the Constitution

If this rule-of-law principle is accepted, two subsidiary questions immediately arise. The first is the precise legal requirements that would have to be met for secession to occur. Legal scholars are divided as to whether sovereignty would require the unanimous consent of the provinces and both of the federal Houses or whether the general amending formula in section 38 of the *Constitution Act, 1982* would be applicable.[54] The only way that this uncertainty could be resolved in an authoritative manner is for the Supreme Court of Canada to pronounce on the issue. As we argue in a later section of this paper, the best way to obtain a ruling is for the federal government to refer this issue (along with other legal issues potentially in dispute) directly to the Court.

The second subsidiary question is how to ensure that the applicable constitutional amending formula does not become a straitjacket preventing the implementation of a fairly bargained agreement between Canada and Quebec over the terms of secession. As experience over the past decade has indicated, the amending formula in the 1982 Constitution is extremely cumbersome and unwieldy. The inability of Canadian governments to implement the Meech

Lake Accord over the 1987–90 period is a clear illustration of the difficulty. Despite the fact that all governments had agreed on the terms of a constitutional amendment on two separate occasions (in 1987 and again in 1990), it proved impossible to obtain legislative ratification. Moreover, the two provinces that refused to ratify the accord represented less than 10 percent of the total Canadian population.

Thus, if the existing amending formula is to govern the secession of Quebec, it will obviously be necessary to devise some mechanism to ensure that this kind of paralysis is avoided. The approach we suggest is to develop a negotiating body to represent the collective 'Canadian' interest in any negotiations, thus ensuring that Canada speaks with a single voice. All governments and legislatures should commit themselves in advance to voting on any agreement recommended by this negotiating body as a single package, without any amendments.

As we explain in more detail below, we believe that this kind of mechanism would ensure that any agreement reached between the parties could be successfully implemented. It would also avoid the possibility of small minorities in certain provinces attempting to exercise a veto over the process without regard to the large costs that such a veto would have on other Canadians.

Principle 4: The Referendum

The existing amending formula does not require a referendum as a precondition to a constitutional amendment. Nevertheless, we believe that it is now clearly established, as a matter of political practice, that secession is appropriate and legitimate only if it has been endorsed in a referendum. In fact, given the criteria for identifying a constitutional convention articulated by the Supreme Court of Canada in the *Patriation Reference* case,[55] we believe that a constitutional convention has likely now crystallized in favor of this proposition (see Box 6).

A Consultative Referendum

The fact that there may well be a constitutional convention mandating a referendum should not be taken to mean that a majority 'yes' vote would automatically trigger secession. As we made clear in discussing Principle 3, secession requires a constitutional amendment in accordance with either section 38 or 41 of the *Constitution Act, 1982*. The fact that a majority of voters in a particular province vote in favor of secession does not obviate the requirement of obtaining an appropriate constitutional amendment. In other words, any referendum should be regarded as consultative only; a majority 'yes' vote would not, in itself, alter the legal status quo or provide a basis for the government of the province wishing to secede to do so unilaterally through a UDI. This conclusion

---

Box 6   A Constitutional Convention Requiring a Referendum for Secession?

A *constitutional convention* is a constitutional rule that is not in the formal constitution but that has come to be accepted by the relevant political actors. In order to establish the existence of a constitutional convention, three factors must be present: (a) the political practice or precedents must be consistent with the rule; (b) the relevant political actors must regard the rule as binding in a political sense; and (c) there must be a reason for the rule.

A constitutional convention may now exist in Canada requiring the government of a province that wants to secede to use a referendum to obtain a mandate from its electors. All three prerequisites of such a convention are satisfied. The 1980 and 1995 referendum campaigns in Quebec represent political precedents in favor of this rule. There is a consensus amongst political leaders to the effect that a referendum is required prior to the commencement of the process leading to secession. And the reason underlying the rule is simply that secession is such a fundamental and momentous political event as to require a popular mandate.

Although conventions are not legally binding, constitutional scholars have an ongoing argument as to their status. At most, they are obligatory in the political (rather than legally enforceable) sense.*

* Geoffrey Marshall, Constitutional Conventions: The Rules and Forms of Political Accountability (Oxford: Clarendon, 1993).

---

is consistent with parliamentary traditions and international experience, as already discussed.

The practical importance of this principle can be seen by contrasting it with the terms of the draft version of Quebec's Bill 1, which was tabled in the National Assembly on December 6, 1994. This early version of Bill 1 declared that Quebec was a sovereign country and that legislation to that effect would come into force within a year of a positive vote in a referendum. Thus, the referendum result would directly trigger the legal achievement of sovereignty. In contrast, we are suggesting that any referendum be regarded as consultative only and that changes in legal status require a duly authorized constitutional amendment.

The issue that arises is why the Quebec government would agree to this principle, given that it contradicts the terms of Bill 1. We have already explained why we believe it is in Quebec's interest to agree that secession can be accomplished only through a duly authorized constitutional amendment.

An additional observation worth mentioning here relates to the threshold of support that should be required in a sovereignty referendum. We argue below for a majority of 50 percent plus one. One of the main factors leading us to support this minimal threshold is the fact that a referendum in a parliamentary democracy is consultative only. If a referendum could provide a legal basis for a declaration of sovereignty, we would argue for a much higher threshold. Thus, an indirect benefit for Quebec of agreeing that a referendum is merely consultative may be Canada's acceptance of a threshold of 50 percent plus one as a trigger for secession negotiations.

Moreover, if the referendum were to have a binding legal effect, we would argue that the entire referendum procedure would have to be entrenched in the Constitution. (That is, if Canada were to make an exception to the principle of parliamentary sovereignty, as it does with the Charter of Rights and Freedoms, it would have to be constitutionally entrenched.) Such a constitutional amendment would clarify the manner in which the referendum was to be conducted, provide for the legal effect of a referendum vote, and determine the threshold of support required. Since such an amendment would be a change to the amending formula, it would clearly require the unanimous consent of the federal government and all provinces. These additional complications would be avoided if all parties agreed that any secession referendum would be consultative and that a majority 'yes' vote would not have any determining legal consequences.

Transparency

The other condition suggested in Principle 4 is transparency: that the referendum be on a clear question and that the voting procedures be transparent and fair. Arguably, the most recent referendum in Quebec failed to satisfy these criteria. The question referred to a political and economic partnership with Canada, which was actually an extremely remote possibility, so the wording was misleading in that it gave a false view of the conditions that were likely to prevail following the achievement of sovereignty. And in the voting itself, large numbers of ballots were rejected as spoiled in certain ridings with a large pro-federalist vote.

In our view, it is demonstrably in the interests of all Canadians that voters in any secession referendum be asked a clear and unambiguous question and that the votes be tabulated in a fair and transparent manner. The entire legitimacy of the referendum process depends on its accurately reflecting the will of the residents of the province. If the question is ambiguous or if the votes are tabulated improperly, this legitimacy is eroded, making the entire process suspect.

The difficulty is in determining how best to ensure that pitfalls are avoided. As noted earlier, some countries' constitutions provide for the participation of the national government or of international observers in the conduct of a sovereignty referendum, including the formulation of the question and the tabulation of the ballots. It would clearly be both appropriate and desirable for the Quebec government to permit the Canadian government to take this role. It is highly unlikely, however, that the Quebec government would accept this kind of federal participation, given its generalized hostility to federal 'intrusions' in areas that it regards as falling under exclusive provincial jurisdiction.

An alternative that might avoid this problem would be the participation of a representative group of Quebecers in setting any future referendum question. Under existing Quebec law, a premier who leads a majority government has exclusive control over the wording of the referendum question and has the opportunity to exert influence over those responsible for tabulating the ballots.

This unilateral and undemocratic method of setting the referendum question is quite extraordinary in comparison to the manner in which other constitutions deal with this matter. We believe that it is inappropriate for the Quebec premier, who represents only one side in the debate, to have exclusive authority to set the referendum question. Far more appropriate, in our view, would be the Quebec government's permitting the federalist forces within the province some meaningful opportunity to participate in the process of determining the referendum question. Give such an approach, all parties within Quebec would be more likely to regard the question-setting process as legitimate, increasing the likelihood that the result would be accepted. Moreover, such an approach is consistent with the parliamentary traditions of accountability – both to the legislature directly and to the populace at large.

What the Federal Government Can Do

Whether the Quebec government under Premier Lucien Bouchard will accept these democratic prerequisites is unclear. Further, there appears to be very little that the Canadian government can do in practice to prevent the government of Quebec from holding a referendum on any question and in any manner it desires. Granted that the prime minister suggested immediately after the October 30 referendum that the federal government could and would ensure that any future referendums in Quebec were conducted on a clear question:

Mr. Chrétien told a CBC town-hall program ... that he is prepared to use a sweeping but seldom-used power to maintain peace, order and good government to disallow a future Quebec referendum if the question is not clear. ... 'I'm saying we have powers and we have to use the powers to make sure that the question will be fair to Quebecers and will be fair to the rest of the country,' Chrétien said.[56]

It is unclear to us, however, how the federal government could prevent Quebec from proceeding with a referendum on a question that Ottawa regarded as ambiguous. Even if Parliament were to pass legislation to prohibit the holding of such a referendum or seek judicial review of Quebec's jurisdiction in this regard, the Quebec government would likely proceed anyway. Moreover, the political confrontation that would ensue would itself become an issue that would be used against federalists in any referendum campaign.

Rather than attempt to prohibit the holding of a referendum that was ambiguous or unfair, the preferable approach, we believe, is for the federal government to state clearly in advance the circumstances under which it would recognize the legitimacy of a majority 'yes' vote.

As the international experience with secession referendums indicates, there is no precise formula or form of words that must be employed. What is required is a question that gives the voters of the area involved an opportunity to clearly express their opinion of the intention of forming a separate and independent country. (For example, the wording of the question in the December 1994 draft of Bill 1, 'Are you in favor of the Act passed by the National Assembly declaring the sovereignty of Quebec,' would likely be regarded as sufficiently clear.)

Once the question has been set and well in advance of the referendum date, the federal government should state whether it would regard a majority 'yes' on that particular question as a sufficient mandate to commence sovereignty negotiations. If it regards the question as ambiguous, it should indicate the nature of the modifications that might make the wording more acceptable. Further, it should make plain that the votes would have to be tabulated in accordance with a transparent and fair procedure for the outcome to be regarded as legitimate.

Possible Objections

Objections can, of course, be raised against the approach we recommend. One is that the wording of the question is irrelevant since, sovereigntists claim, Quebecers clearly understood in both campaigns what was really at stake. Yet, if the wording is truly irrelevant, then the Quebec government should have no objection to any question that might be proposed by the government of Canada or by Quebec federalists. Sovereigntists cannot have it both ways – insisting that the wording of the question is irrelevant but then refusing to permit federalists to participate in setting it.

In any event, it is now evident that large numbers of Quebecers failed to appreciate the real consequences of a vote for sovereignty. (For example, significant numbers believed that Quebec would remain a province of Canada and would continue to send MPs to the federal House of Commons after sovereignty.[57]) In the face of this kind of confusion, it is essential that any referendum question clearly set out the political options being presented.

Another potential objection is that the Canadian government would be acting undemocratically in challenging the validity of a referendum outcome, even if the question was vaguely worded. In fact, precisely the opposite is the case. There is nothing democratic about granting the Quebec premier absolute and unreviewable power to set the wording of the question without regard to whether it is fair and clear. Canada would be abandoning democratic principles if it were prepared to accept a 'yes' vote on a misleading or vague question as a legitimate mandate for secession.

Principle 5: A Majority of 50 Percent plus One

Some constitutions that contemplate secession require a qualified majority (a vote other than 50 percent plus one) for secession to occur. Moreover, the prime minister of Canada hinted in the days before the October 1995 referendum that he might not recognize the legitimacy of a bare majority in favor of secession.[58] Polls taken in Quebec and in Canada generally indicate that most voters favor a higher threshold for secession to occur (see Box 7).

Despite these considerations, we conclude, on balance, that a simple majority of 50 percent plus one is appropriate for triggering negotiations on the terms and conditions of secession. Two kinds of arguments lead us to this conclusion.

Experience
International experience does not necessarily favor requiring a supermajority for a lawful secession. Although the constitutions of the vast majority of states do not contemplate secession under any circumstances, some permit it on the basis of a 50-percent-plus-one vote in the territory proposing to secede.[59]

Also to be considered is the Canadian government's equivocal response in the 1980 and 1995 referendum campaigns as to the majority required to trigger the secession process. In both campaigns, the Quebec government took the position that a simple majority in favor of sovereignty would constitute a mandate to begin secession negotiations. The federal government never clearly contradicted this claim, nor did it suggest any alternative majority it would find

---

Box 7   Can a Referendum Authorize Quebec to Secede?

The *CBC The National/SRC Le Point* poll released March 25, 1996 (conducted between March 11 and 17, 1996, by CROP in Quebec) indicates that approximately 90 percent of Canadians recognize that, with an appropriate majority in a referendum, the Quebec government should be authorized to secede from Canada.

What is that majority? In response to the question, 'In the event of a referendum on Quebec sovereignty, what is the percentage of votes required, in your opinion, for the government of Quebec to obtain the mandate to proclaim Quebec's sovereignty?', the poll obtained the following answers:

	Total Canada	Quebec	Rest of Canada
50%	5	4	5
50% + 1	11	27	6
50% + 1 to 55%	12	11	12
56% to 60%	13	12	13
More than 60%	49	40	53
Any percentage acceptable	1	1	1
Don't know / no response	9	6	10

Note: Totals may not add to 100 because of rounding.

---

more appropriate. In fact, statements made by the prime minister in the final week of the 1995 campaign to the effect that Quebecers were voting decisively on whether to remain Canadians might reasonably have been interpreted as an acceptance of the 50-percent-plus-one threshold advocated by the Quebec government.

Given that the federal government has never clearly contradicted the claim that a 50-percent-plus-one vote would represent a mandate to achieve secession, it would now have difficulty arguing that a higher threshold must be met. Moreover, if it did so argue, what principled way could it use to select which of the various possible thresholds was to be achieved? The choice of any number larger than 50 percent would appear to be entirely arbitrary. The Canadian government would seem to be raising the bar after having implicitly accepted the legitimacy of a 50-percent-plus-one vote because it now realized that it was possible that it would lose the next campaign.

Practical Considerations

A strong argument in favor of accepting the 50-percent-plus-one standard is the fact that any attempt to impose a higher threshold would undoubtedly provoke an intractable and highly risky confrontation with the Quebec government. Of course, the mere fact that the Quebec government favors something should not, in itself, force Canada to accept the same standard. On the other hand, in formulating its own position on these issues, it would be irresponsible for the Canadian government to ignore the Quebec government's likely reaction.

If Canada refused to entertain negotiations with Quebec despite a majority vote in favor of sovereignty on a clear question, the Quebec government would be faced with two options: it could back down and abandon its plans for sovereignty, or it could proceed to issue a UDI. Even contemplating the first option would be politically unimaginable for the Quebec government. Having fought a referendum campaign promising sovereignty on the basis of a 50-percent-plus-one vote, it could not back away from that commitment simply because Canada refused to go along. Thus, Canada's refusal to commence secession negotiations following a majority 'yes' vote would greatly increase the likelihood that Quebec would resort to the only other alternative – issuing a UDI in defiance of the requirements of Canadian law.

For the federal government to play such a scenario of Russian roulette would leave it exposed to charges of hypocrisy. As we have already indicated, it is absolutely fundamental that all parties accept the principle that secession should occur only through a duly authorized constitutional amendment, rather than a UDI. Attempting to impose a threshold higher than 50-percent-plus-one would indirectly but unnecessarily undermine that principle by significantly increasing the possibility of unilateral action by Quebec.

Another practical consideration is that, assuming any referendum is to be consultative (Principle 4), its only effect would be to trigger negotiations with Canada on the terms of secession. The actual *achievement* of sovereignty would still require a negotiated agreement with Canada. Further, as we argue below, we believe that any such agreement should be submitted to the voters of the seceding province for ratification in a second referendum. If Quebec agrees to these additional safeguards, the Canadian government would find it difficult to refuse to even entertain negotiations on sovereignty following a majority 'yes' vote in a referendum.

A final consideration is still more practical. Even if the federal government determined that a threshold greater than 50-percent-plus-one were desirable, how would it enforce this requirement? Merely issuing a statement favoring a supermajority would not necessarily mean that it would become widely accepted. In our view, the federal government would have to seek some form of popular ratification of its position, either through a referendum or an election. There is obviously no guarantee that the federal government's view as to the appropriate majority would prevail.

Even worse, Canadians inside and outside Quebec might take different views as to the majority that ought to be required, and the federal government would be in the invidious position of having to choose between the views of Quebecers and those of other Canadians on this fundamental issue. This would be a lose-lose proposition. No matter what Ottawa decided, its choice would be denounced in at least part of the country, deepening the conflict and making the likelihood of a consensual resolution of the issues even more remote.

Principle 6: Fundamental Rules for Secession Negotiations

We have argued that it is of fundamental importance that all governments in Canada accept the primacy of the rule of law in any secession scenario. That is, it should be generally agreed that secession can occur only in accordance with a duly authorized constitutional amendment. But achieving this objective would require some agreement as to the terms and conditions of any secession, which, in turn, would require an agreed-on process for negotiating the terms of such a settlement. The difficulty is that there is absolutely no consensus as to who should be the parties to these negotiations or how they should be conducted.

Negotiations: Parties and Conduct

As to the appropriate parties to the negotiations, many commentators assume that an entity they call the ROC – existing Canadian territory minus Quebec – would negotiate the terms and conditions of Quebec's departure from Canada. This suggestion presents two obvious difficulties. First, the ROC does not exist as an organized political entity. (The Canadian government, of course, is the representative of Canada as a whole, not of certain parts of the country.) Thus, there is, by definition, no one who could represent the ROC in any secession negotiations.

Second and more fundamentally, even if the ROC could be treated as an organized entity and political representatives appointed on its behalf, it is not at all clear that it would be the appropriate non-Quebec participant in the negotiations. The ROC includes only the part of Canada that is outside of the province of Quebec, so its representatives could not speak on behalf of the interests of Canadians living in the province of Quebec. Yet Quebecers would remain citizens of Canada throughout any secession negotiations. The government of Quebec might well be able to represent those who favored secession, but what of

---

Box 8   Representation and Aggregation

Effective participation in negotiations requires a structure in which each party can perform two functions simultaneously. The first is *representation* – giving expression to all of the various interests and constituencies that are at stake in the negotiations. The second is *aggregation* – ensuring that there is a mechanism for achieving tradeoffs between the various interests at stake. Ultimately, each party must be able to speak with a single voice on the key issues in dispute.

For a party as diverse as Canada, achieving both roles is difficult, but it is absolutely necessary for success in negotiations.

---

those who wished to remain within Canada? Given that the Quebec government has declared firmly that it will not agree to the partition of its territory, Canadians within Quebec who favored this option would be entirely unrepresented in any negotiations conducted between a sovereigntist Quebec government and representatives of the ROC.

If the ROC is not the appropriate party to negotiate with Quebec, what of the possibility that the federal government would be given a mandate to negotiate the terms of secession? This approach would certainly provide representation of the interests of federalist Canadians living in Quebec, but in solving that problem, it would create another. The prime minister and a significant proportion of the federal cabinet are Quebec residents, so both sides of the secession negotiations would be subject to the control and direction of Quebec-based politicians. Any outcome generated by this process – one necessarily involving tradeoffs and compromises that would at least in part favor Quebec – would be difficult to justify in other parts of the country.[60]

What is left is a third alternative – the creation of a hybrid, special-purpose Canadian negotiating authority (CNA) jointly appointed by the federal government and the nine provinces outside Quebec plus representatives of the aboriginal peoples. Such a body could be created through federal legislation, which would define its mandate and authority. The CNA would be designed to represent and to aggregate all of the various 'Canadian' interests (including the interests of Canadians resident in the province of Quebec) that would be at stake in the secession negotiations (see Box 8).

A Proposal for a CNA
A CNA could take a variety of forms. We propose the following structure as an

example of the kind of organization that would be both workable and representative.

The decisionmaking body would be a governing board of 21 representatives, nine appointed by the federal government, nine by the nine provinces outside Quebec, and three by the aboriginal peoples of Canada. (The enabling legislation would require the appointing governments to consult among themselves and with their respective opposition parties to ensure that the overall membership of the governing board was representative in terms of political affiliation, gender, regional balance, and so on.)

The chief Canadian negotiator, who would chair the governing board and be the CNA's chief executive officer, would be nominated by the federal government and confirmed by a two-thirds vote of the board's membership. The governing board would be authorized to retain such experts and professional staff as it deemed appropriate for the efficient conduct of the negotiations.

The CNA's mandate would be to negotiate an agreement with Quebec on the terms and conditions of its secession from Canada. Any such agreement would require the approval of a special majority – perhaps two-thirds – of the members of the governing board. This special majority requirement is appropriate, in our view, given the fundamental nature of the interests involved in any secession negotiations. It would ensure that any agreement reflected a broad-based consensus and took into account the interests of all the different regions and communities in the country, but not make achievement of agreement impossible or unworkable.

A CNA would thus enable Canada to speak with a single voice on the important issues.

Constitutional Amendment

The CNA would not circumvent the existing constitutional amending formula. Even if the body negotiated and approved an agreement on the terms of secession, Parliament and the provincial legislatures would still need to provide the appropriate approvals for a constitutional amendment. Federal law could and should, however, provide that no amendment proposing the secession of a province could be introduced into the House of Commons by a member of the government in the absence of the agreement of the CNA.[61]

Conferring this kind of gatekeeper role on the CNA would ensure that the province of Quebec was not tempted to try to bypass the agreed procedure and attempt to cut separate deals with individual provinces or with the government of Canada.

One or more provinces with a relatively small proportion of the Canadian population might, however, fail to ratify an agreement (the situation that arose in relation to the Meech Lake Accord), leading to stalemate and even confrontation. To deal with this problem, we contemplated a proposal whereby all provinces would agree in advance to ratify automatically any agreement that the CNA reached. Such a commitment would not be legally binding (absent a constitutional amendment), but it could be reflected in a political accord signed by all governments and endorsed by legislatures.

We are doubtful, however, that governments or legislatures in the nine provinces outside Quebec would be prepared to commit themselves in advance to acting as a mere rubber stamp for the work of the CNA. It is also arguable that legislatures, which are the only bodies directly accountable to the electorate, should exercise some critical review of an agreement dealing with a matter as fundamental as the secession of a province. Moreover, at least three provinces are required by law to hold a referendum before ratifying any constitutional amendment,[62] and we doubt that they would be prepared to repeal this legislation.

A middle position – one that we believe might prove acceptable to governments and legislatures – is for the federal government and all the provinces to commit themselves to voting on any agreement reached by the CNA as a single package, without any amendments. The process would be similar to the fast-track procedure the US Congress employs in the ratification of some trade agreements, agreeing in advance that any treaty negotiated by the administration will be voted on 'straight up,' without amendments. This approach reflects the reality that any trade treaty is likely to be the product of a complex series of interconnected compromises and tradeoffs. Once they have been bargained for and agreed to by the administration, the only real question is whether the entire package is acceptable. If the answer is no, then the solution is to send the parties back to the negotiating table – not to permit one of the parties to cherry pick through the agreement by proposing one-sided amendments that fail to take account of the interests of the other party to the negotiations.

We believe that the same dynamic could and should obtain in the context of an agreement negotiated between the CNA and Quebec. Since any agreement would be a complicated series of tradeoffs, it would not make sense to allow individual provinces to reopen portions and make amendments that favor their particular interests or concerns. Thus, we propose that all provinces and the federal government sign a political accord committing themselves to placing any agreement approved by the CNA board before their legislatures for ratification without amendment.

We believe it is highly unlikely that any agreement that must be approved in this straight-up fashion would fail to achieve the necessary legislative ratification. The provinces would feel overwhelming pressure to proceed expeditiously to ratify an agreement that the CNA recommended because the only real alternative to legislative ratification would be unilateral action by the Quebec government, which, as we have explained at length, would impose significant costs on all parts of the country.

The only provinces with the ability to refuse to ratify an agreement in the face of these kinds of consequences would be Ontario, British Columbia, and Alberta, which together would dominate the new Canada that would emerge in the wake of Quebec's departure. Conversely, assuming these 'big three' provinces all favored an agreement, the remaining provinces would have no option other than to go along and ratify.

We assume that the concerns of the 'big three' would have been adequately taken into account in the deliberations of the CNA itself. In effect, therefore, it is likely that they would also ratify any agreement it endorsed.

We conclude that, assuming some sort of mechanism along the lines proposed were adopted, the existing amending formula would not pose a significant obstacle to ratification of an agreement permitting Quebec to secede. (Of course, an amendment could fail to achieve the necessary ratification. The result would be a major political crisis for Canada itself, calling into question whether the country would even continue to exist following secession or whether it would break up into a number of successor states.)

Principle 7: Ratification by Quebecers

In the 1980 referendum, the Quebec government committed itself to holding a second referendum in which Quebec residents would be asked to ratify the precise terms of any secession agreement. This approach is consistent with democratic principles and with Canadian and international practice on these questions. For example, in the October 1992 referendum on the Charlottetown Accord, the terms of the accord were publicly available approximately two months before the vote and a draft legal text, reflecting the precise constitutional amendments that would be enacted if the accord were approved, was published in early October. Some of the countries whose constitutions contemplate secession through referendum require that the electorate be provided with details on the terms before the ratification vote.[63]

In contrast, the 1995 Quebec referendum had no provision for popular ratification of the terms of secession through a second referendum. The National Assembly was authorized to proclaim sovereignty following a single referendum, the only precondition being that Quebec must have made a formal offer of a political and economic partnership with Canada. Thus, voters were asked to authorize a true blank cheque – to grant the government the right to proclaim

secession without having any obligation to reveal the actual terms of the declaration, which could well have differed radically from those described in Bill 1.
The legislation suggested that Quebec and Canada would negotiate a political
and economic partnership before secession, that Quebecers would retain their
Canadian citizenship, that Quebec would continue using the Canadian dollar,
that Quebec would automatically accede to the North American Free Trade
Agreement, and that the borders of the new state would be identical to those of
the province of Quebec. It is possible that none of these fundamental terms
would have been reflected in the actual declaration of sovereignty.

In our view, democracy requires that voters know in advance at least the
broad outlines of the terms of any secession. Further, if the actual terms of
secession differ materially from what was approved in an initial referendum,
then it is appropriate that the people be given a second opportunity to approve
those changes. Otherwise the entire process is rendered illegitimate.

We hope that the Quebec government under Premier Bouchard would recognize that democratic principles require that Quebecers approve the terms of
secession prior to its implementation. But regardless of the position of the Quebec government, the government of Canada should signal its clear support for
this principle. If the Quebec government refused to hold a second referendum
ratifying the actual terms of secession, then the Canadian government should
commit itself to doing so on the petition of a specified percentage of Quebec
electors.

Given the foregoing discussion, some may think that a principled approach to
the secession process would require a ratification referendum in other parts of
the country. The constitutions of some countries permit secession only after a
referendum of the electors of the entire state, rather than a referendum held only
in the region proposing to secede. But other constitutions provide for a referendum in the seceding region only.[64] In our view, democratic and practical considerations suggest that the latter approach is preferable.

To uphold democracy, all Canadians should indeed have a voice in the future
of the Confederation. That principle is, however, effectively addressed by Principle 6: the CNA-Quebec negotiation process would ensure the representation
of all Canadians. The corollary of this principle is that if a majority of residents
in a defined region or province wish to form an independent state and have
come to an agreement with duly authorized representatives of the predecessor
state as to the terms and conditions of secession, it is difficult to see how a negative vote in another region of the predecessor state could justly prevent them
from seceding.

Pragmatically, such a blocking referendum would likely prove ineffective
since the seceding unit would probably not be deterred from its objective just

because voters in another part of the country opposed the secession. What seems most likely is that the seceding unit would simply proceed to declare sovereignty unilaterally, based on the terms and conditions that had been agreed to with the duly authorized representatives of the predecessor state. Thus, a blocking strategy would not only be futile; it would also undermine the principle of the rule of law and increase legal and political uncertainty.

Certainly, no one could object to the Canadian government's or the government of other provinces' holding ratification votes of their own. Indeed, as already noted, some provinces must hold a referendum prior to legislative approval of any constitutional amendment. We believe, on balance, however, that no such ratification referendums should be required and that any that are held should be consultative only, not legally binding. In our view, it is appropriate that a ratification referendum be required only in the region or province that proposes to secede, rather than in the country as a whole.

Principle 8: Partition

The issue of whether the borders of an independent Quebec would be identical with those of the existing province has been an increasing focus of debate since the October 30 referendum. The government of Quebec takes the position that its borders are nonnegotiable, both politically and legally.

Sovereigntists consistently argue that Canadian constitutional law and principles of international law guarantee that the administrative or local borders of a seceding unit cannot be altered without its consent. We take a different view. The Canadian Constitution does not explicitly provide for any terms and conditions for secession, making the issue of borders a matter for negotiation and agreement. In the absence of an agreement and a constitutional amendment, the territorial status quo remains unchanged; that is, the province remains a part of Canada (not an independent state with its borders intact).

The arguments from international law are rather more complicated but ultimately lead to the conclusion that the borders of the seceding unit are a matter for negotiation. There is no basis for saying that, in the absence of agreement, the previous administrative or internal borders of the seceding unit become its international borders.

This conclusion was confirmed in our examination of secession provisions in other constitutions; as we noted, there is no general or uniform practice whereby the previous internal borders of a seceding unit would automatically become the borders of the new state.

Moreover, a compelling normative argument supports the principle that Canadians living in identifiable regions of Quebec who wish to remain within

Canada should be permitted to do so. This argument is simply that Quebec must accord to minorities within the province the same rights and privileges that it asserts on its own behalf against Canada. Quebec claims the right to secede from Canada on the basis of a majority vote of Quebecers. Consistency requires that Quebec be willing to accord the same right to identifiable regions within its boundaries that do not wish to become part of a sovereign Quebec. In short, if Canada is divisible, then Quebec must also be divisible.

Indeed, the case for minority groups wishing to remain Canadian is arguably even stronger than that of Quebec in relation to the rest of Canada. Quebec is seeking to alter the territorial status quo through secession. Minority groups within Quebec, on the other hand, do not seek any change in their existing status; they simply want the right to continue living within Canada. Quebec must argue, in other words, that those voting for secession have a right not only to secede but also to require other identifiable groups to secede against their will. We know of no principled argument that would justify this result.

Arguments against Permitting Partition

A number of arguments have been raised against the partition thesis, but, in our view, none of them is particularly plausible or convincing. One is that partition would lead to a division of Quebec territory along racial, ethnic, or linguistic lines. This argument mistakes the nature of the partition thesis, which suggests only that residents within a particular province should be given an opportunity to determine whether they wish to remain within Canada or to become a part of the new state that would result from the secession. In other words, residents of Quebec, regardless of their ethnic, racial, or linguistic background, should have a voice in determining for themselves whether their region is to remain within Canada.

It is entirely possible that some regions with a significant francophone majority would vote to remain a part of Canada if given the option.[65] But even if only regions with a nonfrancophone majority voted to remain in Canada, there is no moral or principled basis for denying them this right based on their linguistic or racial background. It would be immoral and discriminatory to override the rights of racial or linguistic minorities, including their right to the protection of the Canadian Constitution and the Charter of Rights, in order to satisfy the desires of the majority. A democratic society is founded on precisely the opposite premise – that all citizens are entitled to equal respect and dignity, and that fundamental rights are not subject to this kind of crude numbers game.

An additional argument sometimes raised against the partition thesis is that it would lead to bloodshed and violence. For example, Julius Grey argues that attempts to divide states along religious or ethnic lines have almost inevitably led to violent conflict and that any attempt to partition Quebec would mean that hard-line Quebec nationalists would come to the fore.[66]

The problem with this argument against partition is that it legitimizes violence and the use of force. What Professor Grey is essentially saying is that, even if the partition argument is morally and legally valid, it must be rejected because it would provoke hard-line Quebec nationalists to take up arms to defend Quebec's territorial integrity. But how could the valid moral claims of Canadian citizens to remain a part of Canada be defeated by the barrel of a gun? In effect, Professor Grey's argument amounts to accepting the legitimacy of threats of force and violence on the part of Quebec nationalists.

In any event, the consequence of this argument may well be to hasten the very bloodshed it seeks to avoid. The assumption seems to be that, whereas Quebec nationalists would take up arms to defend Quebec's territorial integrity, minorities within Quebec would accept their fate quietly and peacefully. Yet if those minorities were themselves willing to take up arms to defend their rights, this would somehow improve their claims to remain part of Canada, since it could no longer be said that preserving the territorial integrity of Quebec would avoid bloodshed and conflict. This logic only confirms the conclusion that the resolution of territorial issues should not depend on different groups' relative willingness to resort to violence to further their objectives.

A Practical Proposal

A final more practical argument against the advisability of partition does possess a certain plausibility. This argument is simply that any attempt to partition Quebec would be totally impractical since there is no straightforward way to redraw its borders effectively without creating Canadian enclaves within Quebec that would be geographically isolated from the rest of Canada. The creation of such enclaves would raise a host of practical and administrative complications that make this result appear quite undesirable.

We regard these practical considerations as relevant and important but not insuperable. In general terms, we propose an approach along the lines of that used in drawing the borders of the new Swiss canton of Jura following its separation from the canton of Berne in the 1970s. As described earlier, voters in the canton of Berne were provided with opportunities to indicate whether they wished to remain within Berne or to be part of the new canton. The exercise of this choice was not open ended. Rather, it was subject to two limiting principles. First, the opportunity to hold a second referendum was available only to communes or districts (distinct geographic entities with an existing legal status), not individuals, neighborhoods, or other groups without a recognized geographic significance in law.

Second, communes or districts were permitted to choose a particular territorial status only if that same status had been selected by an immediately adjacent district or commune. This second limitation ruled out the possibility of creating enclaves within either canton and meant that the entire territory of each would be territorially contiguous. (This limitation also required a willingness to hold a cascading series of referendums, as already described, since the ability of any particular commune to attach itself to one or the other of the cantons depended on an adjacent district's or commune's having made a similar choice.)

We believe that both these limiting principles would be appropriate and desirable in resolving territorial disputes between Quebec and Canada. Regions within Quebec that wished to remain within Canada would have to have a distinct legal status and an identifiable territory. (In other words, the geographic entity would have to be a legal 'person,' such as a municipal corporation.) Second, such regions would have to be territorially contiguous with Canada – that is, directly linked to its territory by either land or water. (Some regions in northern Quebec or on the island of Montreal could choose to remain part of Canada since they can be directly accessed by Canadian or international water routes.)

We believe these two limiting principles would resolve the practical objections that have been raised against the possibility of partitioning the territory of a sovereign Quebec. Moreover, it should be kept in mind that any impracticalities arising from partition would hardly be the *cause* of federalists within Quebec but rather would represent another complicated *effect* of Quebec secession.

Principle 9: The Aboriginal Peoples

The Crown has a fiduciary obligation in relation to aboriginal peoples.[67] That legal statement means the relationship between the Crown and aboriginals is trust-like, rather than adversarial, and the Crown must exercise its discretionary powers so as to ensure that their interests are protected. The fiduciary relationship is constitutionally entrenched through section 35(1) of the *Constitution Act, 1982*, so legislative powers must be exercised in a manner consistent with the Crown's fiduciary relationship.[68] In other words, any law or regulation affecting aboriginal rights must be justified as a legitimate regulation of a constitutional right.[69]

Arguably, the fiduciary obligation of the Crown requires it to obtain the consent of aboriginal peoples for any amendment affecting rights under section 35.[70] The point for the present discussion is that the secession of a province would involve a very particular and exceptional derogation from section 35 rights. Since the seceding province would no longer be a part of Canada, the fiduciary relationship between the Crown and the aboriginal peoples concerned

would be permanently terminated. To permit the termination of a fiduciary relationship without the consent of the beneficiary is inconsistent with the very
existence of such a relationship. It is well established that trust-like or fiduciary
obligations that arise from the operation of law cannot be unilaterally terminated by the fiduciary.[71]

Thus, regardless of whether aboriginal consent is required for a constitutional
amendment affecting section 35 rights generally, such a requirement probably
exists for an amendment that would terminate altogether the fiduciary relationship between the Crown and the aboriginal peoples. The aboriginal peoples in
the seceding province would find themselves in a foreign country, their links
with the Crown in right of Canada irrevocably severed. (They could, of course,
maintain their connection with the federal Crown by migrating into another part
of Canada, but such forced migration would itself be a denial of section-35
rights.) Before the federal government could agree to a constitutional amendment terminating the fiduciary relationship, it is arguable that it must obtain the
consent of the aboriginal peoples who would be affected.

This requirement of aboriginal consent is indirect in the sense that it must be
expressed through and by the government of Canada. But being indirect does
not make the requirement any less meaningful or legally enforceable. In the
absence of appropriate aboriginal consent, the members of the Canadian government would be required to oppose any amendment presented for parliamentary approval.

Two consequences flow from this analysis of the Crown's fiduciary obligations to aboriginal peoples. The first is a strong argument in favor of permitting
representatives of aboriginal peoples to participate directly in any negotiations
aimed at establishing the conditions for Quebec's departure from Canada. We
have accommodated this concept in the design of the CNA by providing for
three such representatives on the governing board. Together they would not
have a veto over the negotiations (since any agreement could be concluded with
the approval of two-thirds of the entire 21-member board), but they would have
a significant voice in setting the terms of any agreement with Quebec.

Second, the federal government's fiduciary obligation toward aboriginal peoples reinforces our earlier conclusions about Quebec's territorial integrity. In
both 1980 and 1995, the aboriginal peoples in Quebec held separate referendums of their own in which more than 90 percent of the ballots cast rejected
sovereignty. Assuming that a similar majority expressed a desire to remain
within Canada at the time of any secession, the Crown would be obligated to
attempt to accommodate that desire. Even some sovereigntist commentators
concede that Quebec would have no right to force aboriginal peoples to be part
of an independent state against their wishes.[72]

Once an exception to Quebec's territorial integrity is acknowledged for the benefit of aboriginal peoples, it becomes more difficult to deny the same rights to other identifiable groups within Quebec that wish to remain part of Canada.

Principle 10: The Existing Canadian Constitution

Some commentators argue that, if Quebec seceded, resolving the resulting issues within the rest of Canada would be far more difficult than reaching agreement on the terms and conditions of Quebec's departure.[73] The political balance within the ROC – between centralists and decentralists and between east and west – would be changed. Trade links would be broken. Canada would be territorially divided. A single province – Ontario – would have close to half the entire population of the country. These observations have led some commentators to conclude that major constitutional changes would be required for the remainder of Canada to continue to exist as a single entity.

This conclusion may well be correct. It is also possible that discussion of these various 'domestic' Canadian issues would commence even during the period when negotiations were continuing with Quebec on the terms of secession. We believe, however, that the existing Canadian Constitution should remain in place until amendments are enacted in accordance with the constitutional amending formula. Moreover, we do not believe that agreement on the terms of Quebec's departure should be contingent on resolution of issues relating to the restructuring of Canadian institutions. If there is general agreement on the terms of exit, they should be implemented immediately, regardless of whether there is a simultaneous agreement on the restructuring of Canadian insti- tutions to take account of Quebec's departure.

Of course, if part or all of the former province of Quebec seceded, the Canadian constitution would have to be modified in certain respects to take account of the departure. For example, all references to the province of Quebec would automatically be removed; Quebec would no longer be represented in federal institutions such as the House of Commons, the Senate, or the Supreme Court of Canada; provisions that apply only in Quebec (such as a portion of section 133 of the *Constitution Act, 1867* and section 59 of the *Constitution Act, 1982*) would lapse. But apart from the modifications that are necessary to reflect the departure of Quebec, the remainder of the Canadian constitution should continue in place until such time as it is modified in accordance with the amending formula.

The rule of law requires such an outcome. We further advocate this approach because any other strategy would overload the agenda and lead to paralysis. Canadian institutions would likely have to be fundamentally changed over the medium to long term, but this kind of restructuring takes time and careful study. It should not be undertaken in the hothouse atmosphere likely to prevail in the negotiations over the terms of Quebec's secession from Canada. Otherwise Canadians risk making fundamental mistakes that might be very difficult to remedy later.

One of the greatest risks, of course, would be the remainder of Canada's fracturing into two or more successor states because of an inability to agree on the kind of restructuring required. We believe this risk of further fragmentation would be increased dramatically if Canada attempted to reshape national institutions in a hasty manner. Such ill-considered changes could well render Canadian institutions wholly unworkable and at the same time leave the country unable to achieve the agreement necessary to remedy the difficulties that had emerged. The preferable approach is to proceed in a careful and considered manner, separating issues related to the restructuring of Canadian institutions from those related to the terms and conditions of Quebec's exit.

From Theory to Practice: Implementing Plan B

Stating general principles that ought, in an ideal world, to apply to any future sovereignty referendum is one thing. Attempting to ensure that governments – particularly the Quebec government – recognize and apply these principles is another matter entirely.

One of the biggest obstacles to be overcome is the fact that Canadians have already lived through two referendum campaigns without the federal government's even attempting to state a position on many issues discussed here. This silence has left the Parti Québécois free to describe how and on what terms secession would be negotiated.

So it will be far from easy for the federal government to begin at this late hour to attempt to persuade Canadians in Quebec and elsewhere that some of the Quebec government's preferred ground rules are unacceptable or unwise. Nevertheless, we believe it would be irresponsible for Canada to maintain its silence. Moreover, the principles that we have outlined are fair and balanced. We do not believe that we have set unrealistic hurdles in the path of sovereigntists; we merely propose that secession occur in accordance with an orderly, fair, and transparent procedure. It is manifestly in the interests of all Canadians that all political leaders agree to principles along the lines of those we have suggested.

How might the government of Canada go about implementing these principles? We consider the following options:

1 Attempt to persuade the Quebec government to accept the ground rules we have suggested, or some variation thereof.
2 Hold a federally sponsored sovereignty referendum in Quebec that is based on the ground rules we have suggested.
3 Refer the issue of secession to the Supreme Court of Canada for a ruling as to its constitutionality.
4 Ask Parliament to enact contingency legislation setting out the ground rules we have described.
5 Establish a panel of internationally recognized experts to recommend a model set of secession rules.
6 Call a national election, referendum, or some other form of public consultation to seek a mandate on the process governing secession.

Keeping in mind that these options are not necessarily mutually exclusive, we turn now to a consideration of their relative advantages and disadvantages.

Negotiate Terms with Quebec

The first possible course of action is to attempt to obtain the voluntary agreement of the government of Quebec to the principles we propose. The federal government could announce its willingness to negotiate with the government of Quebec the ground rules that would apply to any future referendum and invite it to begin negotiations based on the ten principles (or some variant thereof) we have described.

The advantage of this alternative is its simplicity. The prime minister would assert his leadership, finding common ground that would produce a process agreeable to both the Quebec National Assembly and the Parliament of Canada. However, the simplicity and legitimacy are circular. This alternative would be an obvious choice if it were plausible both that such common ground could be reached *and* that the federal government could legitimately speak on behalf of all Canadians.

Neither precondition is present today. The government of Quebec has not accepted a single constitutional proposal of the federal government since the Charlottetown Accord in 1992, which was voted down by both the province of Quebec and the entire nation. To think that the prime minister could find common ground with the present Quebec government ignores the history of this crisis and the dynamic of federal-provincial leadership today. Quebec Premier Lucien Bouchard and his predecessor have rejected any suggestion that anyone outside the National Assembly has any say regarding a Quebec secession referendum. There is no reason to think that this impasse will change any time this century.

Moreover, the present government of Quebec has little or no incentive to cooperate with such a process. If the two alternatives were to hold a referendum on either its terms or the federal government's terms, there is every reason to think that the Parti Québécois government would refuse to bow to Ottawa. The federal government would then face the danger of being boxed into a process in which it held no democratic or legal leverage; Ottawa would either have to agree to Quebec's terms, no matter how unfair or inappropriate, or fail to reach an agreement and face an impasse.

Thus, if there were to be an agreement, it would most likely be on Quebec's terms, not Ottawa's. Moreover, it would likely be achieved only through some form of closed-door (and possibly secret) negotiations involving Prime Minister Chrétien and Premier Bouchard.[74] Such a compromise would therefore be open to attack on process as well as substantive grounds. In other words, simply because Quebec-based politicians in Quebec City and Ottawa agreed on a fair referendum process does not mean that either the other provincial legislatures or the population at large would agree. Regardless of any overtures about public consultation, a tale of two cities does not a referendum process make.

We conclude, therefore, that there is little prospect that the current governments in Ottawa and Quebec could reach agreement on the contentious issues that would be in dispute. Moreover, even if an agreement were possible, it would likely be regarded as suspect or illegitimate, on both process and substantive grounds, in many parts of Canada.

A Federal Referendum on Quebec Sovereignty

A variation of the first option is for the federal government to hold its own sovereignty referendum in Quebec, either at a time of its own choosing or concurrently with a Quebec-run referendum. The federal referendum would have a question drafted by Ottawa; federal electoral authorities could administer the vote, ensuring the impartial tabulation of ballots; and Ottawa could specify that the referendum was purely consultative and that secession would require a formal constitutional amendment.

The difficulty with such a federally sponsored referendum is that it is likely to be widely condemned within Quebec as an illegitimate attempt to interfere with the province's right to self-determination. The Quebec government would likely call for a boycott of the federal vote. It would almost certainly counter any federal referendum with a referendum of its own, probably on a different question, and argue that Ottawa's meddling in Quebec affairs was a justification for a 'yes' vote.

As an illustration of the kinds of difficulties that could arise, consider the competing referendums that were held in various parts of the former Soviet Union during the dying days of that regime. In Ukraine, for example, voters went to the polls twice in 1991 for separate referendums on independence. The first, held on March 17, was originally controlled by President Gorbachev, who determined that eligible voters across the USSR would consider the following question:

Do you consider necessary the preservation of the Union of Soviet Socialist Republics as a renewed federation of equal sovereign republics, in which the rights and freedoms of an individual of any nationality will be fully guaranteed?

Not surprisingly, most voters found this question unsatisfactory, as a 'yes' vote could be interpreted as support for either democratic reform or the status quo. Accordingly, some republics added a question. The Ukrainian Parliament, for example, added:

Do you agree that Ukraine should be part of a Union of Soviet Sovereign Republics on the basis of the declaration on the state of sovereignty of Ukraine?

And three western oblasts added a further question:

Do you agree that Ukraine should be an independent state, which independently decides its domestic and foreign policies, which guarantees the equal rights of all citizens, regardless of nationality and religion?[75]

In short, the central government's imposition of a question did not deter the local legislatures from forming questions more representative of the choices facing them within the USSR.

Nevertheless, the result of the referendum was conflicting; a large majority of Ukrainians voted 'yes' to both Gorbachev's question and their parliament's question, and 85 percent of western Ukrainians voted 'yes' to the independence question.

In the end, however, the people made their wishes clear. Earlier, in July 1990, the Ukrainian supreme soviet had voted overwhelmingly in favor of the Declaration on Sovereignty of Ukraine, asserting primacy over USSR legislation and establishing Ukraine's own currency, bank, army, and relations with foreign countries. In a second referendum, on December 1, 1991, Ukrainians provided final confirmation of that independence; more than 90 percent voted 'yes' to the question:

Do you support the declaration of Ukrainian independence?

The Ukrainian secession story suggests that, in the absence of a single question offered by both the local and central legislatures, the local question may gain more legitimacy. Thus, in the likelihood that Ottawa and Quebec can reach no agreement on a referendum question, the federal government would be taking an enormous risk if it hoped to have its referendum process prevail over that of the Quebec government. Should it go the Gorbachev route, it would probably do so at the Confederation's peril, since Quebec voters would be unlikely to prefer Parliament's process over their own legislature's.

The risk then would lie in whether the national and international community accepted Quebec's ballot or the federal one. For Ukraine, the emerging international consensus was to recognize the republic's secessionist claims amid the disintegration of the USSR. As this result suggests, Gorbachev's approach would be an unnecessary gamble on the part of the Canadian federal government, one that might well fail.

A Reference to the Supreme Court of Canada

The truism that courts are a safety valve, without which no democratic society can survive, is tested in times of national crisis. In the past, the Supreme Court of Canada has proven up to the challenge. To what extent should it be called on to address discrete legal questions on the constitutional validity of a secession process?

In answering this question, it is useful to recall that the Supreme Court of Canada has previously been consulted on legal aspects of the process of constitutional reform. In the *Patriation Reference* (1981),[76] the Court was asked whether the Parliament of Canada could patriate the Constitution without provincial consent. The answer was that, legally, the federal government was unconstrained, but such unilateral federal action would be contrary to the constitutional convention requiring a 'substantial degree' of provincial consent (see Box 6).

The Court has also been asked to outline the operation of the rule of law in circumstances involving a legal vacuum, a prospect of considerable relevance to those contemplating the aftermath of an affirmative secession vote in Québec. In *Re: Manitoba Language Rights* (1985), the Court was asked to rule on the validity of Manitoba's laws, all of which were unilingual and thus contrary to the language guarantees under the Charter of Rights and Freedoms. Did it follow, therefore, that all unilingual laws passed by the Manitoba legislature from 1890 to 1982 were 'of no force or effect' pursuant to section 52 of the *Constitution Act, 1982*?

The Court did not opt for nullifying all Manitoba laws, giving rise to legal 'chaos,' because, it held, that such a course would

undermine the principle of the rule of law, a fundamental principle of our Constitution [which requires] that the law is supreme over officials of the government as well as private individuals, and thereby preclusive of the influence of arbitrary power [and] the creation and maintenance of an actual order of positive laws which preserves and embodies the more general principle of normative order. Law and order are indispensable elements of civilized life.[77]

Accordingly, the Court refused to abdicate 'its responsibility as protector and preserver of the Constitution.'[78] In so holding, it relied on a number of legal doctrines that will be of considerable relevance in the event of a referendum on the outstanding legal issues facing a Quebec secession process.[79]

The relevance of these cases is twofold. First, the Supreme Court of Canada has a history of undertaking judicial references that, in its words, combine 'legal and constitutional questions of the utmost subtlety and complexity with political questions of great sensitivity.'[80] In fact, we find that labeling a question 'political' or 'legal' is of less import than the need for the Court to address certain rudimentary questions better suited for the judiciary than the necessarily partisan and tempestuous legislative branch. Regardless, the Court has expressed a guarded willingness to fulfill its role as safety valve for the state.

Second, the Court had been able to complete its balancing act with prudent reliance on the rule of law, thereby retaining its legitimacy. Some issues truly are best left to a court of law, provided that the scope of the remedy and the questions are limited. Thus, as long as the Court relies on the rule of law as its mantra, its holding is entitled to appropriate respect and weight.[81]

We believe some form of judicial reference to the Supreme Court of Canada is appropriate now because there is total confusion about the legal framework that would apply in the event of an affirmative vote in a sovereignty referendum. The Quebec government maintains that Canadian domestic law would no longer apply, claiming that principles of international law would recognize its right to secede unilaterally. The federal government, after considerable equivocation on the issue,[82] has finally asserted that Canadian law would continue to apply until such time as a formal constitutional amendment approving secession were proclaimed.[83]

As we have argued throughout this *Commentary*, it is in no one's interest to allow such legal confusion to persist. The only way to resolve the issue authoritatively is through a declaration by Canada's highest court as to the relevant legal principles that would apply.

The Content of a Court Reference

What the country needs is a judicial reference that suitably addresses some of the principles we have discussed, particularly those underscoring the rule of law and the need for clear ground rules. Nevertheless, consistent with the principles of democratic accountability, a judicial reference ought to address only the narrow legal issues involving an interpretation of existing constitutional provisions. Nothing more would or could be asserted by the Supreme Court of Canada.

With the scope of this alternative of a constitutional reference thus limited, what questions should be referred to the Court? We suggest the following:[84]

1 Does the secession of part or all of a province from Canada require a constitutional amendment, in accordance with the amending formula in the *Constitution Act, 1982*?

2 If the answer to question 1 is 'yes,' what constitutional amending formula would apply to permit secession?

3 In the absence of a constitutional amendment proclaimed in accordance with the amending formula, what would be the legal effect of a UDI by the Quebec National Assembly? Would Canadian laws continue to apply and be enforced in Quebec after such an event?

4 Would a majority vote in favor of secession in a Quebec referendum entitle the province, under either domestic or international law, to secede from Canada?

5 Would either the government of Canada or the government of Quebec be required to obtain the consent of the aboriginal peoples of Canada presently residing in Quebec prior to consenting to the secession of the province?

6 If the answer to question 5 is 'no,' would meaningful consultation be required before the Crown could give consent?

7 Does any principle of Canadian or international law guarantee that the existing borders of the province of Quebec would be the borders of an independent Quebec state?

The first five questions focus on different aspects of the rule-of-law principle that we have emphasized throughout this *Commentary*. Question 1 seeks to ascertain whether a constitutional amendment is required in order to effect secession, and Question 2 seeks to determine which of the two amending formulas in the *Constitution Act, 1982* would apply to the secession of a province: the seven-fifty procedure of section 38 or the unanimity procedure of section 41. Question 3 explores a related aspect of the same issue, focusing specifically

304 The Referendum Papers

on the legality of a UDI by the Quebec National Assembly. This question also seeks to introduce the concept of the continuing application of Canadian law within Quebec territory, even in the face of a UDI.

Question 4 speaks not to the political effect of a referendum but to its effect on the rule of law; we seek here to confirm that Canadian law remains the legal status quo, notwithstanding the results of a referendum. As well, we introduce the issue of whether any principle of international law would entitle the Quebec government to issue a declaration of independence following a referendum result favoring that option.

Questions 5 and 6 seek clarification of the federal and Quebec governments' constitutional obligations to aboriginal peoples under section 35 of the *Constitution Act, 1982*. These questions are relevant not only in determining the limits on Parliament's authority to negotiate but also in ascertaining any fiduciary obligation and potential liability of Quebec as Crown to the aboriginal peoples living in that territory.[85] Whether aboriginal peoples have a constitutional right to consultation or consent as to the terms of a provincial secession is a question suitable for judicial reference.[86] After all, it was the Supreme Court of Canada that fashioned the Crown-aboriginal relationship as being fiduciary or fiduciary-like.[87] The issue should be clarified by a constitutional reference *before* any potential abdication of the Crown's fiduciary duty.

Finally, question 7 raises the legal issue of partition. Whether the legal viability of partition ought to be put to the Court is not self-evident. One can argue that whether partition is legally possible is too important a determination to be left solely to political negotiations. On the other hand, since the issue of partitioning a sovereign Quebec is currently among the most sensitive issues in the political arena,[88] this question might be best left out of a constitutional reference.

On balance, however, we believe that it would be appropriate to seek the Supreme Court's views on Question 7. The question as framed focuses on the narrow issue of whether any legal principle prohibits the partition of an independent Quebec. In short, it asks whether partition would be legally possible, not whether it would be politically wise or likely.

Of course, the Court's answer would have an important political impact because, as noted elsewhere, the Quebec government has consistently maintained that partition would be contrary to principles of both domestic and international law. But it is precisely because the Quebec government has elected to frame this issue in legal terms, arguing that partition is legally prohibited, that we regard it as appropriate for a court reference. That partition is controversial is not reason enough to seclude the matter from the Supreme Court of Canada, which has proved more than capable of addressing matters of great sensitivity.

Possible Objections

Analysts can (and will) raise numerous objections to the desirability or effi-cacy of a court reference of the questions we have identified. One is that a court reference is inappropriate since the issues are political rather than legal. (The attorney general of Canada took this approach in explaining his govern-ment's initial refusal to intervene in the *Bertrand* case.[89]) Yet the issues involved are *both* political and legal. This fact has been recognized by the Quebec government, which has maintained that Canadian law would not apply in Quebec following a UDI. Far from denying that law is relevant, Quebec is seeking to have its preferred legal argument accepted without having to per-suade a court of its validity. (This strategy is understandable if, as we believe, the legal underpinnings of Quebec's position are suspect and almost certain to be rejected by a court.)

Recognizing that the legal framework is relevant and important differs from claiming that law will determine political outcomes. The law merely provides the context within with political actors will bargain and seek to advance their preferred outcomes. The legal framework will certainly have a significant impact on political outcomes, since it will determine the initial position of the parties, but it will not itself dictate what those outcomes must be.

This observation reinforces the importance of clarifying the relevant legal principles *before* any secession vote. Confusion over the extent of legal rights always makes it more difficult for parties to arrive at a negotiated solution. Clarity over legal rights, on the other hand, promotes consensual outcomes since it provides each party with reliable information about its own rights and the rights of others. The existence of this kind of reliable legal information per-mits the parties to bargain and compromise over their legal rights, rather than engaging in counterproductive posturing about the nature of the rights that each alleges it possesses.

A second possible objection to a court reference is that the government of Quebec would ignore any judgment the courts issued, claiming, as it did follow-ing the judgment of the Quebec Superior Court in the September 1995 *Bertrand* case, that the judgment of a Canadian court is irrelevant since the province is not bound by the *Constitution Act, 1982.*

In fact, however, the Quebec government would have great difficulty main-taining this stance in the face of an authoritative judgment of the Supreme Court of Canada to the contrary, particularly given the presence of three Quebec judges on the Court. The Quebec government would essentially be thumbing its nose at the judges of the Supreme Court of Canada, openly declaring itself a renegade regime, claiming that it stands above the law as declared by the high-est court in the land. We expect that this news would hardly be seen as positive by Quebecers, who expect their governments to abide by the law and who have been assured that sovereignty will be achieved with a minimum of disruption.

Moreover, a Quebec declaration of refusal to recognize the legitimacy of judgments of the Supreme Court of Canada might well influence the international community's reaction to any future declaration of independence by Quebec. It seems unlikely that the international community would accord legitimacy to the actions or declarations of a regime that refused, without any justification, to accept the reasoned judgments of the impartial and independent legal tribunal that is the nation's highest appellate court.

All of which illustrates why federal intervention in the *Bertrand* case (look back at Box 4) is no substitute for a reference to the Supreme Court of Canada. A judgment of a single judge of the Quebec Superior Court simply does not have anything like the weight of the opinion of nine judges of the Supreme Court of Canada. Moreover, the *Bertrand* litigation does not address all of the issues on which we believe it would be desirable to obtain a legal ruling. (It does not, for example, deal with our questions 5, 6, or 7.) In short, the *Bertrand* litigation may not provide the best opportunity for the courts to consider the many implications of the particular issue before the Quebec Superior Court.

In sum, a reference to the Supreme Court of Canada of the questions we have identified would further acceptance of our recommended principles. Resolving the legal framework applicable to any political negotiation would avoid the dangerous uncertainty inherent in a unity crisis and assist in the framing of the agenda of a possible negotiation on secession.

Perhaps more important, such a constitutional reference would lend order to a hitherto inconceivable process. If the Court is not consulted, any federal or provincial party seeking to hijack the process, through unilateral or otherwise unrepresentative action, would confront only a legal vacuum.[90] In contrast, if the federal government brings a constitutional reference, any subsequent attempts to avoid the rule of law would be at the peril of international reaction to actions potentially contrary to the holding of the highest appellate court of a nation-state. In short, a constitutional reference would provide a useful exercise additional to the alternatives recommended below, thereby aiding all Canadians in determining the legitimacy of a secession referendum process.

Contingency Legislation

A judicial reference can go only partway toward providing the certainty and due process necessary for a secession process consistent with the principles we have articulated. The advance setting of ground rules is the major premise of this *Commentary*, so it is paramount that the legislative branch go beyond the limited agenda of a judicial reference and provide the ground rules for a secession process in their entirety. The most effective means for the national government to establish such ground rules is through legislation enacted by Parliament. Federal contingency legislation would attempt to define, by statute, the legal framework that would apply in the context of an affirmative vote in a secession referendum.

Indeed, given the present political climate demanding that the federal government take some action to exercise leadership in a time of national crisis, federal contingency legislation is perhaps inevitable. By its very nature, it would alleviate the inevitable economic and social turbulence resulting from an affirmative secession vote.[91]

In this sense, this option need not be accepted or rejected outright but rather be considered as an approach in parallel with the remaining alternatives. In fact, the enactment of contingency legislation could be seen as a logical consequence of the court reference we have recommended. Such legislation could be introduced into Parliament following the judgment of the Supreme Court of Canada, incorporating and building on the legal framework laid down by the Court.

Scope and Objectives

An initial question is the scope and objectives of such legislation. At one end of the spectrum is affirmation of the operation of the rule of law throughout any secession negotiations. Such minimalist legislation would merely confirm any holding by the Supreme Court of Canada on the legal terms governing secession. At the other end of the spectrum lies some facsimile of the legislation contemplated by the Reform Party of Canada; it would enact practically all terms of secession, from the procedural rules governing a referendum to the specific terms of an agreement to be negotiated in the event of an affirmative vote.[92]

The minimalist legislation would likely provide little in the way of achieving many of our principles. For example, the negotiating structure we envisage, including establishment and appointment of a CNA, would require detailed legislation far beyond concerns associated with maintaining the rule of law. On the other hand, if contingency legislation is overinclusive, creeping into areas for which the legislators lack a popular mandate, this alternative loses its appeal. We thus believe that the main focus of contingency legislation should be on the *process* for negotiating secession, rather than the *outcomes* that would result from that process.

Objections

Even if contingency legislation was restricted to process, people would still question the federal government's right to impose its views on these controversial matters through using its majority in Parliament. We believe that, although the Canadian government and Parliament would have the legal mandate to enact contingency legislation (under the 'peace, order, and good government' clause of the Constitution[93]), the political mandate for such a statute would be another matter entirely. What is essential is that the government be seen to be acting in order to protect the long-term interests of all Canadians, not for partisan or political advantage.

One way to clear the ground for the enactment of contingency legislation is for the government of Canada to appoint a panel of widely respected and representative individuals, including non-Canadians of recognized international stature, to advise on the desirability and content of contingency legislation. (We explore this option in more detail below.) The blue-ribbon panel could be asked to provide a draft statute embodying its recommendations.

If the panel was appointed in the fall of 1996, it could be asked to report by mid-1997, by which time a judgment of the Supreme Court of Canada on the various legal issues in dispute would likely be available.

Proposed Content

What might such contingency legislation contain? We suggest that it ought to include provisions as to the following:

1 The secession of part of the territory of Canada is legally possible. No part of that territory shall be permitted to secede, however, except by a constitutional amendment enacted in accordance with the procedure set out in part V of the *Constitution Act, 1982.*

2 Any laws, orders, or declarations of any person, including the government or legislature of a province, that are inconsistent with paragraph 1 are hereby declared absolutely void and of no force and effect.

3 No secession of any part of a province of Canada shall be permitted unless a majority of the population residing in that province has indicated its desire to secede through a referendum.

4 If at least 5 percent of the persons eligible to vote in a referendum referred to in paragraph 3 object to the wording of the referendum question or to the manner in which the referendum is to be administered or supervised, they may submit a petition to the governor-in-council stating the nature of their objections. The governor-in-council shall appoint a commissioner to investigate and report on the objections and to make recommendations within 30 days of his or her appointment. (We make this suggestion in an attempt to give effect to Principle 4. Although we believe it essential that a referendum be on a clear question and that the process be fairly administered, we do not

believe it is possible or desirable for the federal government to attempt to intervene directly to regulate the process. Rather, it should indicate in advance whether it regards the question and the process as legitimate. Requiring the government to report to Parliament on any significant objections is one way to give effect to this analysis.)

5 The governor-in-council shall table in the House of Commons, within 30 days of the receipt of the report referred to in paragraph 4, a response indicating how the government has acted or proposes to act on the recommendations of the commissioner.

6 No resolution authorizing the secession of any part of the territory of Canada may be introduced into the House of Commons by a member of the governor-in-council unless the response referred to in paragraph 5 has been tabled in the House of Commons.

7 In the event that (a) a referendum referred to in paragraph 3 is held in which a majority of the votes cast favor secession and (b) any report required pursuant to paragraph 5 has been duly tabled in the House of Commons, a Canadian negotiating authority (CNA) shall be established within 30 days of the publication of the final results of the referendum.

8 The affairs of the CNA shall be directed by a governing board consisting of 21 members: nine appointed by the governor-in-council, nine by the governments of the provinces (notice that we leave open the question of whether each province would appoint a single representative or whether provincial representation would be weighted according to relative populations), and three by and on behalf of the aboriginal peoples of Canada. The chief executive officer of the CNA, who shall also chair its governing board, shall be nominated by the governor-in-council and shall be confirmed by a two-thirds vote of the entire governing board.

9 The CNA shall negotiate in good faith with the government of the province in which the referendum referred to in paragraph 3 has taken place, with a view to concluding an agreement on the terms of a constitutional amendment authorizing the province or a portion thereof to secede from Canada.

10 No resolution authorizing the secession of part of the territory of Canada shall be introduced into the House of Commons by a member of the governor-in-council unless (a) it has been approved by a resolution of the governing board of the CNA, supported by a two-thirds vote of the members of the board; (b) a second referendum has been held in the province that proposes to secede in which the terms of the proposed secession have been approved by a majority of votes cast; and (c) in that second referendum, persons residing in the province that proposes to secede are permitted to express their views as to whether they wish to remain within Canada, and the bor-

ders of any new entity are drawn in such a manner as to take account of those views to the greatest extent practical. (The phrase 'to the greatest extent practical' is intended to refer to the two limiting principles we discussed in relation to Principle 8, that the right to dissent can be exercised only by a geographic entity that has a recognized legal existence, such as a municipal corporation, and that the area is territorially contiguous with Canada.)

11 The secession of any part of the territory of Canada must be consistent with the fiduciary obligations of the government of Canada toward the aboriginal peoples of Canada.

12 In the event that the secession of part of the territory of Canada occurs in accordance with the aforementioned procedure, the Constitution of Canada remains in force in the territory of Canada that is not affected by the amendment, with such changes as are necessary to take account of the amendment.

These provisions reflect the analysis outlined in the previous section of this *Commentary*. Thus, although we recognize their controversial nature, we simply state them here without further explanation. (Anyone who desires elaboration or justification, should refer back to the discussion in the section on principles.)

A Panel of Internationally Recognized Experts

One of the greatest challenges facing the federal government in implementing any form of Plan B would be dealing with the charge that it is attempting to undermine the right of Quebecers to self-determination. The overwhelmingly negative reaction in Quebec to the federal government's decision to intervene in the *Bertrand* case illustrate the difficulties quite clearly. It is possible that any good-faith attempt to propose fair and impartial ground rules would be denounced in a similar fashion.

One way to respond to this challenge is to create a body of internationally recognized experts who might be seen in Quebec *and* in the rest of Canada as being impartial and whose opinions would be taken seriously. These experts could be asked to recommend a model set of rules to govern the secession of a province from Canada. Their report should be debated in Parliament and could form the basis for contingency legislation.

Membership

The two questions that immediately arise about such a body are its membership and its terms of reference. Clearly, the panel would have to have Canadian representatives. In light of our desire to establish a body that would be seen as impartial and credible in all parts of the country, we believe, however, that a majority of members should be non-Canadians.

Ordinarily, domestic matters are the exclusive jurisdiction of the sovereign, so non-Canadian membership on this panel would be somewhat exceptional. But extraordinary times often call for extraordinary measures. A possible model would be two Canadians, one from Quebec and the second from another part of the country, plus three non-Canadians, one of whom would chair the panel.

The appointees should all be individuals who have occupied high office in Canada or elsewhere (persons of recognized high standing such as former prime ministers, premiers, governors-general, or supreme court justices) and whose judgment on these delicate political matters would be seen as credible.

Terms of Reference

We propose that the panel be asked to make recommendations as to the principles that ought to govern the secession of a province from Canada, keeping in mind the following objectives:

- Secession should occur in a democratic fashion.
- Secession should occur in a manner that respects the principle of the rule of law as well as the right of peoples to self-determination, as that right has been defined in customary international law.
- Secession should occur in a manner that does not derogate from the individual and collective rights of Canadians, including the rights entrenched in the Charter of Rights and Freedoms and in section 35 of the *Constitution Act, 1982*.
- The principles governing secession should be designed to achieve a peaceful and consensual result, one that minimizes, to the greatest extent possible, the economic, political, and social costs associated with such a change in political status.
- The principles governing secession should, as deemed appropriate by the panel, take account of the international experience with secession and the provisions in other constitutions that contemplate secession.

The panel would be empowered to retain such experts and advisors as it deems necessary to carry out its work. It could hold public hearings but would not be required to do so. It would be asked to report to Parliament within six months of appointment.

Consulting the Voters on Process Issues

Regardless of whether any of the other options outlined above are adopted, at some point it will be necessary for the government of Canada to obtain a popular mandate for its actions. Yet, as Prime Minister Chrétien has said, 'There are many ways to consult the public.'[94] They range from a national referendum on process issues, through a constituent assembly similar to that used by Newfoundland when it was considering Confederation, to a federal election on the issue of Quebec secession and the referendum process.

Each alternative and combination thereof would have costs and benefits. A nationwide referendum might be highly representative, but, some argue, referendums are poor snapshots of public opinion – not to mention being contrary to the parliamentary tradition and risking the rights of minorities to a single majority result.[95] A constituent assembly has both a provincial precedent in Newfoundland and the advantage of being a fresh, novel idea, but it could be viewed as gimmicky or redundant in light of a national election. And although the ability to translate an election into a precise mandate seems questionable, such is the nature of the parliamentary tradition, for which Canada has no substitutes.

Meanwhile, the means of achieving a nationally informed secession process and its timing are questions presently being debated in the national media. To some, it appears that the government of Canada ought not to rush to reopen the tinder box of the referendum process. After all, the argument goes, the premier of Quebec has assured voters that no secession referendum will be held until after a provincial election.[96] To others, it seems that a federal election should not be delayed a moment longer.[97]

We do wish not to take a position on the wisdom of either course except to say that consulting the voters on the secession process ought not be viewed merely through the incompatible lenses of federalism and separatism. Rather, obtaining the democratic mandate of Canadians should represent an end in itself. Surely neither federalist nor separatist proponents could claim the views of the electorate stifle the principles on which Canadian and Quebec nationalists agree: democracy, the rule of law, certainty, due process, and the protection of minorities.

Moreover, the worst scenario unfolding from the present national unity debate would be the chaos that enveloped the laudable *perestroika* process that was to be a pathway to democratic reform in the Soviet Union. To delay matters best put to the people sooner rather than later risks unraveling the legal and social order that all Canadians take for granted.

Therefore, pursuant to the principles of certainty discussed at length in this *Commentary* (Principles 1 and 6), we think that the federal government ought not to wait for events in Quebec to dictate the future of the Confederation. Nor should Parliament proceed without consulting Canadians at the appropriate juncture. Whether that consultation precedes or follows the tabling of contingency legislation raises one question; another is how Parliament should so consult.

These questions could carry us well outside the bounds of this *Commentary*'s subject matter. We do wish not to provide a treatise on the efficacy of particular democratic processes. Rather, we point out only that a mechanism for achieving representation and accountability other than by election would entail many risks. A national referendum on process, in particular, might find itself hoist on its own petard, failing to achieve a coherent consensus over a matter originally undertaken to lend national order to an otherwise provincial process. That is, in the absence of a national majority, if not a supermajority, on various process issues, it would be difficult to demand the same from a Quebec secession referendum.

Moreover, the danger looms that, even if a national referendum achieved the immediate goal of a mandate over the secession process, what of the future? Would a referendum on Canada's secession process crystallize this device into a constitutional convention, thereby requiring any future constitutional amendments to achieve majority (or supermajority) support of Canadians by referendum?

We cannot answer these questions, but we raise them by way of warning: straying too far from Canada's constitutional traditions may entail consequences unforeseen and unwanted. The point of consulting the voters is to further the principles of democracy and order, not to render Canadian Confederation into a veritable Humpty Dumpty.

Conclusion

Many readers, particularly those within the province of Quebec, probably find the analysis and conclusions offered here provocative. That reaction is perfectly understandable and may even be inevitable, given the nature of the task we have set for ourselves. Our objective is to elaborate a set of ground rules that is consistent with the rule of law and that would lead to a transparent and fair secession process. By definition, therefore, we are assuming that the rules governing secession cannot and should not be defined by Quebecers alone. This premise is likely to receive a frosty reception within Quebec, among federalists and sovereigntists alike.

The conventional wisdom in Quebec – as evidenced by the hostile reaction to the federal government's intervention in the *Bertrand* case – is that the decision whether to leave Canada, and on what terms, is a matter for Quebecers to determine without interference from the rest of Canada. The federal government intervened in the *Bertrand* case to make the minimalist argument that Quebec's secession would require the consent of the federal government.

We describe this argument as minimalist because Ottawa did not attempt to state any of the specific terms that it would demand as a condition of obtaining its consent. Yet, despite the narrowness of the claim being advanced by Canada, even Quebec Liberal leader Daniel Johnson has criticized the federal government's intervention and implicitly endorsed Premier Bouchard's claim that Ottawa was seeking to thwart Quebecers' right to self-determination. This suggests to us that any attempt by Canada to define terms and conditions governing secession – regardless of the content of those bottom-line conditions – is likely to provoke a negative reaction in Quebec circles. It will, therefore, hardly be a surprise to us if our own analysis receives a comparably negative review.

This realization reinforces for us the daunting and high-risk nature of the Plan B exercise. It should come as no surprise that there are no easy exits or obvious solutions to the problems and challenges that we have identified. Decisions made in such a harried context often yield little opportunity for compromise; the great Canadian canons of temperance and tolerance will be tested to their limits. Once we embark on Plan B, the terrain in all directions is riddled with land mines and booby traps.

Yet, the alternative – simply ignoring Plan B and focusing entirely on Plan A – appears even more risky. It would mean that Quebecers would have no clear idea of the consequences of a 'yes' vote when they are asked to cast their ballots in the next referendum. Moreover, the Canadian government would lack a strategy and a mandate to respond to a majority 'yes' vote. The result would be that both the Canadian and Quebec governments would be making up policy on the run, and it would be much more difficult for them to resolve the political crisis in an orderly and nonconfrontational manner.

We offer no predictions as to the course of events either before or after the next referendum. Our purpose is simply to sketch for political leaders and for ordinary Canadians a set of ground rules that would lead to a transparent and fair referendum process, along with a method for implementing those rules. We acknowledge that implementation of our proposals would require a delicate and nuanced political strategy, a great deal of political will, and a good measure of luck. Despite the promising intervention by the federal government in the *Bertrand* case, this is merely the first of many difficult decisions for the federal government should it decide to embark seriously on the road to Plan B.

Our paper is an attempt to describe the full range of political possibilities, along with the risks associated with each, so that all Canadians will be aware of the roads that are taken – as well as those not taken – in the months and years ahead.

NOTES

The authors wish to thank, without implication, Ken Boessenkool, Alan Cairns, David Cameron, Angela Ferrante, Roger Gibbins, Peter Hogg, Gordon Robertson, William Robson, Daniel Schwanen, and Richard Simeon for their detailed and constructive comments on an earlier draft of this paper. We also wish to thank Daniel Kumer, a member of the 1998 graduating class at Osgoode Hall Law School, for his timely and efficient research assistance.

1 We speak of *referendums*, not *referenda* in deference to the authority of the *Oxford English Dictionary*. See D. Butler and A. Ranney, eds., *Referendums around the World* (Washington, DC: AEI Press, 1994), n.1.

2 See, for example, Keith Spicer, 'A New Country or No Country? A Strategy for Canada' (unpublished, December 1995); Group of 22, 'Making Canada Work Better' (unpublished, [Toronto], May 1996); and Y. Fortier, P. Lougheed, and J. Maxwell, *Today and Tomorrow: An Agenda for Action*, Report of the Confederation 2000 Conference, May 4, 1996 (Ottawa).

3 D. Butler and A. Ranney, eds., *Referendums: A Comparative Study of Practice and Theory* (Washington, DC: American Enterprise Institute for Public Policy Research, 1978); idem, *Referendums around the World*; M. Suksi, *Bringing in the People: A Comparison of Constitutional Forms and Practices of the Referendum* (London: Martinus Nijhoff, 1993).

4 See M. Suksi, 'Referendum and National Decision-Making: A Study of Constitutional Form and Practice' (SJD thesis, University of Michigan, 1992), p. 293.

5 United Nations, *Charter of the United Nations and Statute of the International Court of Justice* (San Francisco, 1945), article 2(4), recognizes and protects a state's territorial integrity from interference by other states by providing that '[a]ll members shall refrain in their international relations from the threat or use of force against the territorial integrity or political independence of any state.'

6 For a discussion of the relevant principles of customary international law, see N. Finkelstein, G. Vegh, and C. Joly, 'Does Quebec Have a Right to Secede at International Law?' *Canadian Bar Review* 72 (1995): 234–237.

7 For example, the Commission on Global Governance says: 'Despite the use of the words "we the peoples" in the opening line of the UN Charter, the post-war order was designed primarily to serve a world of states.' *Our Global Neighbourhood: The Report of the Commission on Global Governance* (Oxford: Oxford University Press, 1995), pp. 67–68.

8 Commission on Security and Co-operation in Europe (the Helsinki Commission), *Presidential Elections and Independent Referendums in the Baltic States, the Soviet Union and Successor States: A Compendium of Reports 1991–1992* (Washington, DC: CSCE, 1992) (hereafter cited as CSCE 1992).

9 See 'Reports on the Referendum on the Future of the Soviet Union: March 17, 1991,' in CSCE 1992.

10 See H.E. Brady and C.S. Kaplan, 'Eastern Europe and the Former Soviet Union,' in Butler and Ranney, eds., *Referendums around the World*, ch. 6.

11 See *Madzimbamuto v. Lardner-Burke* [1969] AC 645 (PC, So. Rhodesia).

12 The notable exception was the confusing question put by President Mikhail Gorbachev in the March 17, 1990, USSR-wide referendum (discussed below); the thrust of the question pointed neither toward unity nor away from secession. See 'Reports on the Referendum on the Future of the Soviet Union,' in CSCE 1992.

13 CSCE 1992, p. 1.

14 Canada, Canadian Unity Information Office, *Understanding Referenda: Six Histories* (Ottawa: Supply and Services Canada, 1978), ch. 2.

15 Canadians thought the question favored the result of commission government; anti-Confederationists objected to the presence of Canadian Confederation as an alternative, while others thought that union with the United States ought to have been added. See M. Dunsmuir, *Referendums: The Canadian Experience in an International Context* (Ottawa: Library of Parliament, 1992), p. 20.

16 Yves Beigbeder, *International Monitoring of Plebiscites, Referendums, and National Elections* (London: Martinus Nijhoff, 1994).

17 V. Rudrakumaran, 'The 'Requirement' of Plebiscite in Territorial Rapprochement,' *Houston Journal of International Law* 12 (1989): 52.

18 See Ross Howard, 'Slim vote can't split Canada, PM says,' *Globe and Mail* (Toronto), January 31, 1996, p. A1.

19 See CSCE 1992.

20 'Report on the Estonian Referendum and Latvian Public Opinion Poll on Independence: March 3, 1991,' in CSCE 1992.

21 'Report on the Armenian Referendum on Independence: September 21, 1991,' in CSCE 1992.

22 M. Eisner, 'A Procedural Model for the Resolution of Secessionist Disputes,' *Harvard International Law Journal* 33 (1992): 423.

23 Butler and Ranney, eds., *Referendums*, p. 17.

24 V. Bogdanor, 'Western Europe,' in Butler and Ranney, eds., *Referendums around the World*, ch. 3.

25 Dunsmuir, *Referendums*, p. 27.

26 See Canada, *Understanding Referenda*.

27 Ibid.

28 See authorities cited in Dunsmuir, *Referendums*.

29 Thomas Franck et al., 'L'intégrité térritoriale du Québec dans l'hypothèse de l'accession à la souveraineté,' in *Commission d'étude des questions afférentes à l'accession du Québec à la souveraineté: projet de Rapport* (annexe) (Québec, 1992).

30 The relevant legal principles are discussed in Patrick Monahan, 'The Law and Poli-
    tics of Quebec Secession,' *Osgoode Hall Law Journal* 33 (1995); and Grand Council
    of the Crees, *Sovereign Injustice: Forcible Inclusion of the James Bay Crees and
    Cree Territory into a Sovereign Quebec* (Nemaska, Que.: Grand Council of the
    Crees, 1995).

31 The constitutional amendment was approved in a referendum held among all the
    electors of the canton of Berne on March 1, 1970. See *Constitution du canton de
    Berne*, Commentaire à la Constitution (Berne: Chancellerie d'État), p. 10.

32 *Constitution du canton de Berne: nouvelles dispositions constitutionnelles rélatives
    à Jura* (article 2) provided this wording of the question.

33 Conversely, if the overall result in the March 1974 referendum had been against the
    creation of a new canton but certain districts within Jura had voted in favor, they
    could have required a second referendum in which their citizens would have again
    been permitted to indicate whether they wished to form a new canton, albeit one
    smaller than originally envisaged (article 3(2)).

34 See Butler and Ranney, eds., *Referendums around the World*, pp. 36–38.

35 See J.T. Rourke, R.P. Hiskes, and C.E. Zirakzadeh, *Direct Democracy and Interna-
    tional Politics* (Boulder, Col.: Lynne Reinner, 1992), ch. 4.

36 See Canada, *Understanding Referenda*.

37 V. Bogdanor, *The People and the Party System: The Referendum and Electoral
    Reform in British Politics* (Cambridge: Cambridge University Press, 1994), table
    3-1.

38 Ibid., p. 63.

39 Ibid., p. 58.

40 Ibid., p. 56.

41 Ibid.

42 Rodney Brazier, *Constitutional Reform* (Oxford: Clarendon, 1991), p. 36.

43 See J. Patrick Boyer, *Lawmaking by the People: Referendums and Plebiscites in
    Canada* (Toronto: Butterworths, 1982).

44 Canada, *The 1992 Federal Referendum: A Challenge Met* (Ottawa: Elections Can-
    ada), p. xiii.

45 René Lévesque, *My Quebec* (Agincourt, Ont.: Methuen, 1979), pp. 101, 109.

46 Arguably, the prime minister has already acted on this principle. In his May 1996
    interview with the US television program *Good Morning America*, he declared that, if
    a clear majority of Quebecers wish to secede, the rest of the country will not try to
    keep them in by force. See Anne McIlroy, 'Separation possible with "clear mandate":
    provinces would decide, PM says,' *Globe and Mail* (Toronto), May 16, 1996, p. A1.

47 Robert Young, *The Secession of Quebec and the Future of Canada* (Kingston, Ont.:
    McGill-Queen's University Press, 1995), p. 134.

48 See Box 7.

49 Legal commentators who have examined the question are unanimous on this point. See, for example, P.W. Hogg, Constitutional Law of Canada, 3d ed. (Toronto: Carswell, 1992), p. 126; José Woehrling, 'Les aspects juridiques d'une éventuelle accession du Québec à la souveraineté,' Choix: série Québec-Canada, June 1995, p. 25; Monahan, 'The Law and Politics of Quebec Secession'; and N. Finkelstein and G. Vegh, The Separation of Quebec and the Constitution of Canada (North York, Ont.: York University, Centre for Public Law and Public Policy, 1992), p. 2.

50 For example, 'Prime Minister Jean Chrétien says he cannot constitutionally negotiate terms of separation if Quebecers vote in a referendum to leave Canada. Quebec separation is "completely illegal and non-constitutional," he says. "No. It's not in the constitution," Mr. Chrétien replied when asked whether he could negotiate independence if Quebec separatists win in a planned referendum.' Jeff Sallot, 'Quebec separation illegal, non-constitutional, PM says,' Globe and Mail (Toronto), December 20, 1994, p. A6.

51 J. Crawford, The Creation of States in International Law (New York: Oxford University Press, 1979), p. 266.

52 For arguments that section 38 is the applicable formula, see Hogg, Constitutional Law of Canada, p. 126; and Woehrling, 'Les aspects juridiques,' pp. 27–28. For arguments favoring the applicability of section 41, see Monahan, 'The Law and Politics of Quebec Secession,' pp. 5–15; and Finkelstein and Vegh, The Separation of Quebec, pp. 6–8.

53 Bill 1, 35th Legislature of Quebec, first session.

54 See the sources cited in note 49.

55 See Re Resolution to Amend the Constitution [1981] 1 SCR 753.

56 Hugh Winsor and Tu Thanh Ha, 'Chrétien signals new resolve on Quebec,' Globe and Mail (Toronto), December 12, 1995, p. A1.

57 In the CBC Prime Time News/SRC Le Point poll reported on February 16, 1995, question 32(A) reveals that 26 percent of Quebec voters believe that a sovereign Quebec would continue to be a province of Canada, and question 32(B) shows that 27 percent of them believe that a sovereign Quebec would be represented by members of Parliament in the federal House of Commons.

58 One newspaper reported: '"We're not going to split up Canada through a judicial recount," Prime Minister Jean Chrétien told the Commons. "I will not break up the country with one vote. It is not real democracy."' Tu Thanh Ha and Rhéal Séguin, 'Slim yes win won't do, federalists say,' Globe and Mail (Toronto), September 20, 1995, p. A4.

59 See, for example, the provisions in the constitutions of the Czech and Slovak Federative Republic, Ethiopia, and France. Although the referendums on Newfoundland Confederation (July 22, 1946) and the United Kingdom's continued membership in the European Economic Community (June 5, 1975) did not involve secession, they

are also worth considering in that each affected the structure of a country but required only a simple majority vote.

60 In the *CBC Prime Time News/SRC Le Point* poll reported on February 16, 1995, question 16(E) reveals that 47 percent of voters outside Quebec believe that political leaders from Quebec (such as Jean Chrétien) should not represent the ROC in post-referendum negotiations with a sovereign Quebec.

61 A similar provision was included in Bill C-110, *An Act Respecting Constitutional Amendments*, 1st sess., 35th parl., 1995. Section 1 of that act outlines conditions on the introduction of certain amendments into the House of Commons by members of the government. Specifically, any motion for a resolution to authorize an amendment to the Constitution, other than an amendment under sections 41, 43, or 38(3) of the *Constitution Act, 1982*, must have the consent of a majority of the provinces that include Ontario, Quebec, British Columbia, a majority of the Atlantic provinces, and a majority of the Prairie provinces.

62 British Columbia, Alberta, and Saskatchewan. See, respectively, *Constitutional Amendment Approval Act*, SBC 1991, c. 2, s. 1; *Constitutional Referendum Act*, SA 1992, c. 22, s. 1, 2(1); and *An Act respecting Referendums and Plebiscites*, SS 1990–91, c. R-8.01, s. 3(1).

63 See the constitution of St. Christopher and Nevis, for example, which requires that 'full and detailed proposals' for the future constitution of the island of Nevis be published, along with 'adequate explanations' at least 90 days prior to any referendum on secession. (See Table 1, note h.)

64 The constitution of Singapore requires a national referendum. So did the 1991 constitution of the Czech and Slovak Federative Republic, although it also provided that, if a separation proposal was ratified in only one republic, the federation would cease to exist within one year. On the other hand, all Soviet republics that seceded from the USSR did so on the basis of a local referendum only. See CSCE 1992.

65 For example, the *CBC The National/SRC Le Point* poll conducted in March 1996 found that Quebecers as a whole were almost evenly divided when asked, 'If Quebec becomes sovereign, would you want your region to remain part of Canada?' Of the respondents, 46 percent said 'yes,' 47 said 'no,' 7 percent did not know or had no response.

66 J. Grey, 'The folly of severing Montreal from a sovereign Quebec,' *Globe and Mail* (Toronto), January 19, 1996, p. A13.

67 See *Guerin v. The Queen*, [1984] 2 SCR 335.

68 See *R. v. Sparrow*, [1990] 1 SCR 1075.

69 The Supreme Court of Canada recently expanded on the requirements of such justification, in the context of consultation. See *R. v. Nikal*, [1996] SCJ No. 47, unreported, April 25, 1996 (SCC).

70 Finkelstein and Vegh argue that there may be a constitutional convention requiring

the consent of aboriginal peoples to amendments affecting their rights under section 35 (*The Separation of Quebec*, pp. 25–31).

Finkelstein and Vegh were writing prior to the multilateral meetings on the Constitution (MMC), held between March and August 1992, which reinforced their conclusion. Representatives of the aboriginal peoples participated fully in the MMC, and the Charlottetown Accord would have added to the Constitution a provision requiring their consent for any constitutional amendments affecting their rights. Although the accord was defeated in a nationwide referendum, there has never been any suggestion that any Canadian government questions the principle underlying the proposed section. Thus, even if Canada still lacks a specific legal requirement regarding aboriginal consent for amendments affecting section 35 rights, the existence of a constitutional convention requiring such consent seems likely.

71 See the discussion of a trustee's duties and powers in D.W.M. Waters, *Law of Trusts in Canada,* 2d ed. (Toronto: Carswell, 1984), pp. 689–693.

72 See Daniel Turp, 'Quebec's Democratic Right to Self-Determination: A Critical and Legal Reflection,' in Stanley H. Hartt et. al., *Tangled Web: Legal Aspects of Deconfederation*, The Canada Round 15 (Toronto: C.D. Howe Institute, 1992), p.115–121.

73 See, for example, Gordon Gibson, *Plan B: The Future of the Rest of Canada* (Vancouver: Fraser Institute, 1994), pp. 131–178.

74 In *closed door negotiations*, the public is at least aware of the fact of the negotiations taking place, even if it is not informed as to the details of what is being negotiated, whereas in *secret negotiations*, the public is not even told of the existence of the negotiations.

75 'Report on Ukraine's Referendum on Independence and Presidential Election: December 1, 1991,' in CSCE 1992.

76 *Re Resolution to Amend the Constitution,* [1981] 1 SCR 753.

77 (1985), 19 DLR (4th) 1, 22.

78 Ibid., p. 25

79 For example, the de facto doctrine (protecting the legality of that done in reliance of unilingual legislation) and the doctrine of state necessity (permitting laws otherwise unconstitutional to be 'temporarily ... effective and beyond challenge'). The rationale for both doctrines, the Court asserted, rests with the principle of the rule of law: 'The Constitution will not suffer a province without laws.' Ibid., p. 36.

80 Ibid., p. 7.

81 Although even the Court's narrow holdings in the foregoing cases have been criticized as an unjustified political gesture for Canada's highest court. See P.W. Hogg, 'Comment,' *Canadian Bar Review* 60 (1982): 307.

82 Attorney General Allan Rock was quoted in late 1994: "To my mind, it's not constitutional for one province to decide unilaterally it can leave confederation," Rock said. "But that's a technical question. The real question is for Quebecers in a referen-

dum."' Paul Wells and Philip Authier, 'Sovereignty law illegal, Rock says,' *Montreal Gazette*, December 16, 1994, p. A1.

83 In May 1996, the government intervened in the *Bertrand* litigation (see Box 4), arguing that a unilateral declaration of independence would be unlawful. See Rhéal Séguin and Hugh Winsor, 'Quebec, Ottawa head for showdown: PQ hints at snap election after federal government vows to intervene in court case aimed at invalidating secession aims,' *Globe and Mail* (Toronto), May 11, 1996, pp. A1, A14.

84 See also P.W. Hogg, 'Rules for a Referendum on Quebec Sovereignty' (unpublished, Osgoode Hall Law School, North York, Ont., March 1996). We have benefited greatly from Professor Hogg's paper, and our own analysis in this section follows the line of argument he has developed.

85 See M.J. Bryant, 'Crown-Aboriginal Relationships in Canada: The Phantom of Fiduciary Law,' *University of British Columbia Law Review* 27 (1993).

86 See R. Dupuis and K. McNeil, *Canada's Fiduciary Obligation to Aboriginal Peoples in the Context of Accession to Sovereignty by Quebec*, Royal Commission on Aboriginal Peoples (Ottawa: Supply and Services, 1995); and Finkelstein and Vegh, *The Separation of Quebec*, pp. 25–31. Note that the Supreme Court of Canada recently commented on the requirement of effective consultation where the Crown infringed on aboriginal rights (*K v. Nikal*, unreported, April 26, 1996, SCC).

87 *R. v. Sparrow*, [1990] 1 SCR 1075.

88 'The talk about partition last week sent a shiver through Montreal, with French-speaking Quebeckers and non-francophones typically reacting in opposite ways' (Tu Thanh Ha, 'Partition talk gives Quebec a jolt,' *Globe and Mail* [Toronto], February 5, 1996, p. A1).

89 Wells and Authier, 'Sovereignty law is illegal.'

90 Note that it was under such circumstances that MP Jean-Marc Jacob, the Bloc Québécois's national defense critic, invited members of the Canadian Armed Forces stationed in Quebec to transfer their loyalty to 'the new country,' a sovereign Quebec, in the event of a separatist victory in the referendum. 'Referendum: Collenette probes Bloc plans for army,' *Globe and Mail* (Toronto), November 8, 1995, p. A4.

91 The most thorough treatment of contingency legislation to date is provided by the former clerk of the Privy Council: G. Robertson, 'Contingency Legislation for a Quebec Referendum' (unpublished paper distributed at the Confederation 2000 Conference, March 8, 1996). The primary rationale for contingency legislation, Robertson points out, is that after the referendum it will be too late for Parliament to exercise its authority with any legitimacy.

92 See Susan Delacourt, 'Reform drafts secession terms,' *Globe and Mail* (Toronto), January 18, 1996, p. A3.

93 Section 91 of the *Constitution Act, 1867,* and as recognized by the Supreme Court of

Canada in *Re: Anti-Inflation Act,* [1976] 2 SCR 373. See Robertson, 'Contingency Legislation.'
94 See Susan Delacourt, 'PM floats election balloon,' *Globe and Mail* (Toronto), March 1, 1996, p. A1.
95 See Dunsmuir, *Referendums,* pp. 1–13.
96 Rhéal Séguin, 'Plan for referendum firmly on agenda, Bouchard says,' *Globe and Mail* (Toronto), March 19, 1996, p. A6.
97 See Delacourt, 'PM floats election balloon.'

Ratifying a Postreferendum Agreement on Quebec Sovereignty

PETER RUSSELL and BRUCE RYDER

If there is another sovereignty referendum in Quebec and the sovereigntists win, negotiations undoubtedly would follow between the government of Quebec and authorities representing other components of the Canadian federation regarding the terms of Quebec's change in constitutional status. Assuming such negotiations take place and are brought to a successful conclusion, the question of ratification then arises: How could the outcome of these negotiations be approved by the bodies to which the negotiators are responsible, and be given legal effect? The purpose of this *Commentary* is to outline a ratification process for a potential agreement on the terms of Quebec's accession to sovereignty that would be consistent with the requirements of Canadian law.[1]

In the first section, we present our case for choosing to implement sovereignty for Quebec through the instrument of the Canadian Constitution, despite the objections many sover-eigntists have expressed and would no doubt continue to express to such a course. We also stress the importance of a 'good faith' attitude for all participants, and consider the alternatives to a constitutionally sanctioned process – the very undesirability of which, ironically, may help our case.

Next, we briefly outline some issues related to ratification that would need to be covered in the agreement negotiations themselves for the process to work; the more all sides agree on process from the beginning, the better.

The third section outlines the components that would likely be included in a sovereignty agreement with Quebec and the constitutional and other changes that would be required to implement them. Although we advocate (and expect) that these changes would be kept to the minimum necessary in the short term, they are nevertheless extensive – not surprisingly, since the removal of a founding province from the federation would affect almost every aspect of Canadian government, law, and the justice system, as well as relations with Aboriginal peoples.

This exercise allows us, in the next section, to categorize these amendments in terms of what process would be necessary to ratify them. The Canadian Constitution offers five different amending formulas – which one applies in which case depends on the content of the amendment.

Once this 'unpacking' has made clear which legislatures' approval would be *constitutionally* necessary to ratify various parts of a sovereignty agreement, we look at the ratification process in the context of Canadian political realities, which would have to include not just legislative sanction but popular consultation by referendum and treaty arrangements with the Aboriginal peoples of Quebec.

Finally, we briefly discuss an extreme situation in which the limits of constitutionalism might be reached and strict adherence to the rule of law might be unreasonable.

The Constitutional Route to Sovereignty

The Case for a Constitutional Process

We hold the view that, if there is to be a radical change in Quebec's constitutional status – including its becoming an independent state – such a change should be effected through a process that is consensual and retains legal continuity. Thus, we favor a process of ratification that is carried out under the existing rules for amending the Canadian Constitution. This is not the only way Quebec could achieve sovereignty, but it is the way that involves the least chaos and disruption.

Many Canadians may regard this effort to spell out how Quebec's sovereignty could be achieved under the Constitution as a contradictory, dangerous, or even treasonous exercise. In the words of one colleague, 'it is like telling the burglar who is about to break into your house how to unlock the door so that he won't smash any windows.'

On the other hand, Quebec sovereigntists are apt to argue that requiring that the transition to sovereignty be achieved through the rules of the Canadian Constitution places them in a legal straitjacket. 'It is like telling us,' they might say, 'how to unlock the door but giving us a key that just will not work.'

We hope this *Commentary* helps persuade both of these groups that, in the event of a sovereigntist win in a Quebec referendum, it would be in the interest of all parties involved to try to reach a settlement through the existing constitutional machinery.

As for Canadians who oppose thinking about the unthinkable, we join other recent *C.D. Howe Institute Commentary* authors in believing that the narrowness of the federalists' win in the 1995 Quebec referendum demonstrates that we can no longer afford to take an ostrich-like approach to the possibility of Quebec sovereignty.[2] While we would like to see Quebec's constitutional aspirations accommodated through federal restructuring, this may not happen; a Plan B is clearly needed. Only those who are unwilling to support Canada's recognition of Quebec sovereignty *under any circumstances* can oppose efforts to find a process that would reduce the economic and societal disruption that would follow a clear indication by Quebecers of their will to secede. On this point, we support the position taken by then-federal justice minister Allan Rock on announcing his government's decision to refer questions on Quebec secession to the Supreme Court of Canada: 'This country will not be held together against the will of Quebecers clearly expressed.'[3] Like Mr. Rock and most Canadians, we hope that independence from Canada will not become the clear preference of most Quebecers. But if it does, we believe it would be best for everyone that this choice not be blocked by force, and that a serious effort be made to give effect to that choice through a process that observes the rule of law. Such a process entails the least threat of economic dislocation, legal uncertainty, and communal violence.

Sovereigntist Objections

Quebec sovereigntists tend to resist even more than Canadian patriots the idea of achieving Quebec's independence through the instrument of the Canadian Constitution. They advance at least three arguments to support this view:

- that secession following a sovereigntist referendum victory could be accomplished unilaterally, and would be sanctioned by international law despite its violation of Canadian constitutional law;
- that, since the government of Quebec did not ratify the *Constitution Act, 1982*, it should not be bound by the rules for amending the Constitution set out in part V of that act; and
- that any attempt to implement a sovereignty agreement in accordance with the amending procedures would prove futile – the rigidity of the amending formulas means they would simply serve to keep Quebecers in a constitutional straitjacket.

Let us consider each of these objections in turn.

The Right of Self-Determination
The first point, that Quebecers as a people have, under international law, a right

---

Box 1   The Supreme Court of Canada Questions

On September 26, 1996, the federal government announced that it would refer to the Supreme Court of Canada three questions on whether Canadian constitutional law or international law supported the Quebec government's assertion that the province has the right to secede unilaterally from Canada. These questions, set out in Order-in-Council 1996-1497, are as follows:

Whereas the Government of Quebec has expressed its view that the National Assembly or government of that province has the right to cause Quebec to secede from Canada unilaterally;

Whereas the Government of Quebec has expressed its view that this right to cause Quebec to secede unilaterally may be acquired in a referendum;

Whereas many Quebecers and other Canadians are uncertain about the constitutional and international situation in the event of a unilateral declaration of independence by the government of Quebec;

Whereas principles of self-determination, popular will, democratic rights and fundamental freedoms, and the rule of law, have been raised in many contexts in relation to the secession of Quebec from Canada;

And whereas the Government of Canada sees fit to refer the matter to the Supreme Court of Canada;

Therefore, His Excellency the Governor General in Council, on the recommendation of the Minister of Justice, pursuant to section 53 of the *Supreme Court Act*, hereby submits to the Supreme Court of Canada for hearing and consideration the following questions:

1 Under the Constitution of Canada, can the National Assembly, legislature or government of Quebec effect the secession of Quebec from Canada unilaterally?
2 Does international law give the National Assembly, legislature or government of Quebec the right to effect the secession of Quebec from Canada unilaterally? In this regard, is there a right to self-determination under international law that would give the National Assembly, legislature or government of Quebec the right to effect the secession of Quebec from Canada unilaterally?
3 In the event of a conflict between domestic and international law on the right of the National Assembly, legislature or government of Quebec to effect the secession of Quebec from Canada unilaterally, which would take precedence in Canada?

---

of self-determination that takes precedence over the Canadian Constitution, is the nub of two of the questions the federal government has referred to the Supreme Court of Canada (see Box 1).

We believe the Supreme Court will reject the view that international law gives Quebec the right to secede unilaterally. One reason for this conclusion is that the inhabitants of the province of Quebec as a whole are not a single people, and therefore the province does not constitute a self-determination unit for the purposes of international law. Even for a single people, the broadest interpretation of the international right of self-determination gives rise to a right of secession only in situations where the people in question suffer under an alien or colonial regime or endure analogous forms of oppression, such as the widespread deprivation of civil rights. Since, clearly, the Québécois people do not suffer political oppression, there is nearly complete consensus among legal commentators that neither the province of Quebec nor the Québécois people can claim a right to unilateral secession as an element of the right of self-determination as it is currently understood in international jurisprudence.[4]

In the face of this consensus, which the Supreme Court in all likelihood will confirm, sovereigntist commentators no longer rely, in their public statements, on the international right of self-determination as the legal basis for their political project. For example, the text and preamble of Quebec's Bill 1 – introduced just prior to the 1995 referendum to set out the rationale for seeking sovereignty and the procedures by which it would be obtained – contained no reference to the international right of self-determination.[5] Thus, when sovereigntists say that international law will provide the basis for their accession to sovereignty, what they must mean is that, ultimately, the new state would be recognized by other states if it can establish effective political control of its territory.[6] This political control could be accomplished either by constitutional negotiations and agreement or by winning a high-risk contest of political wills with the rest of Canada and dissident minorities within Quebec; our point is simply that the former route is to be preferred.

It must also be recognized that there are a number of Aboriginal peoples within the province of Quebec whose right to self-determination – in both moral and legal terms – is as strong, if not stronger, as any that the Québécois people can claim.[7] Therefore, a majority vote of Quebecers cannot be regarded as having the legal or moral authority to seal the constitutional destiny of Aboriginal peoples whose homeland is partly or entirely in Quebec.[8] On the other hand, because Quebec is also the principal homeland of French Canadians, one of the founding peoples of the federation, a clear expression by Quebecers of their desire for a fundamental change in Quebec's constitutional status would provide a moral imperative on the part of all the constituent parts of the Canadian federation to enter into constitutional negotiations with Quebec.

If we are wrong, and Canada's highest court finds that Canada must recognize the right of the Quebec National Assembly or the Quebec government to effect the secession of Quebec unilaterally, then there would be no need to consider how the terms of secession might be ratified under the Constitution of

Canada. A secession agreement would take the form of an international agreement, and be subject to procedures in the two separate countries for giving legal effect to international treaties. But because such a result is unlikely, we think it is important for sovereigntists to be more amenable to the possibility of achieving sovereignty pursuant to the Constitution.

The 'Illegitimacy' of the *Constitution Act, 1982*

The second sovereigntist argument against requiring that the terms of sovereignty be ratified pursuant to the Constitution is a moral one, alleging the illegitimacy of the changes made to the Constitution in 1982 – which include the rules governing its amendment – because they were not approved by Quebec's National Assembly.[9] Although the *Constitution Act, 1982* is the only instance since Confederation where constitutional changes affecting Quebec's powers have been made without Quebec's consent, the Supreme Court of Canada in its 1982 opinion in the *Quebec Veto Reference* found that there was, in fact, no constitutional convention requiring Quebec's consent for such changes.[10]

The reasons advanced by the Court in support of this finding were not, however, very convincing. As the Court itself acknowledged, in the final analysis constitutional conventions are determined not in the legal but in the political arena. The risk of proceeding with constitutional changes affecting Quebec but not approved by its elected provincial government has been widely acknowledged since 1982; removing this risk to national unity has been the principal rationale for attempting to make further constitutional changes that would restore the legitimacy of the Constitution in Quebec.

Still, while all of this lends support to the illegitimacy charge, the fact remains that the *Constitution Act, 1982* provides the only legally authorized way of formally amending the Constitution. Quebec governments, despite their position on the illegitimacy of the 1982 process, have nonetheless been willing to make use of provisions of the act when they deemed it in their interest to do so – for example, Quebec's use of the notwithstanding clause in the Charter of Rights and Freedoms, and its willingness to explore the possibility of a bilateral agreement with Ottawa regarding denominational school rights. We submit that it would be in the interests of the Quebec government, if it wins a sovereignty referendum, to endeavor to achieve its constitutional objectives through the lawful procedures for effecting constitutional change in Canada.

A Constitutional Straitjacket

This brings us to the third, and most practical, of the objections the Quebec government might have to complying with the Canadian constitutional amending rules: the danger of being subjected to a constitutional straitjacket. Most of the popular and scholarly discussion on this subject – on both the federalist and sovereigntist sides – has emphasized how difficult it would be to settle the terms of Quebec sovereignty through the demanding Canadian constitutional amendment process. Indeed, there has been a tendency on the part of those federalists who insist that Quebec comply with the rule of law almost to flaunt the stringency of the constitutional requirements. This is the epitome of 'tough love' constitutionalism, which has little hope of persuading Quebec sovereigntists that it would be in their interest to make a sincere effort to achieve their goals through established constitutional procedures.

Our approach is not to deny the difficulty of the constitutional process, but to explore carefully how it might apply to a Quebec sovereignty agreement – to see how it could work with maximum flexibility. Recognizing the large number of obstacles to a legally ratified agreement, we also consider the circumstances under which it might be reasonable, for both sides, not to insist on full compliance with the rule of law.

The Need for Good Faith

The workability of constitutional amendment procedures depends on much more than the rules themselves. The likelihood of actually forging an agreement depends just as much on the moods and attitudes of the constitutional negotiators and on the political context in which their efforts take place. There would be virtually no hope of persuading sovereigntist victors in a Quebec referendum to enter into negotiations governed by the existing Constitution if the Canadian government adopted a posture that, in effect, said to Quebec: 'You can only have independence through Canada's constitutional process. You had better understand how long and difficult that process is bound to be, and you can't count on our doing anything to make it any easier. And bear in mind that, if we cannot reach agreement with you through this process, you will just have to forget about your sovereigntist plans.'

Nor would there be any point in the federal government and the other partners in Confederation agreeing to negotiate with a Quebec government that adopted a take-it-or-leave-it approach – that said, in effect: 'Negotiate the terms of the Quebec-Canada partnership we desire or we will simply go ahead and unilaterally declare Quebec's independence from Canada.' Without a commitment on both sides to bargain in good faith – to making an honest effort to come to mutually acceptable terms – there is really no point to constitutional bargaining, no matter how flexible or rigid the formal amending rules may be.

For bargaining in good faith to take place under the existing Constitution, both sides must have strong reasons to want the process to succeed. The incentive cannot be based on shared constitutional objectives. Quite to the contrary, as Alan Cairns so lucidly argues, the constitutional objectives of the Quebec and Canadian governments are likely to be as far apart as they have ever been after yet another acrimonious referendum debate.[11] But both governments – and all Canadians – would have one strong motive for bargaining in good faith under the Constitution: a desire to avoid the unattractive consequences of the alternatives to that process.

Alternatives to the Constitutional Process

What are the alternatives to a negotiated settlement under the Constitution? Essentially, they come down to a unilateral declaration of independence (UDI) by Quebec, followed by two possible responses.

One response – indeed, the one Quebec sovereigntists have been counting on – is for Canada to recognize an independent Quebec before there is any agreement on such vital issues as the rights of Aboriginal peoples and other minorities within Quebec, land transportation connections between the Atlantic provinces and the rest of Canada, apportionment of the debt, currency, citizenship, borders, and trade relations. According to this scenario, Canada would raise these and other matters with Quebec *after* recognizing it as an independent country. Negotiations would then be conducted not within the framework of the Canadian Constitution but on a nation-to- nation basis within the framework of international law.[12]

We can well understand why Quebec sov-ereigntists would welcome this outcome. Except for a political partnership with Canada, it would give them nearly everything they seek, on a silver platter. But we cannot see how it could be right or prudent for the government of Canada to concede so much to Quebec. Among other things, such a course of action would mean abandoning Canada's fiduciary obligation to Aboriginal peoples in Quebec, leaving in limbo the Canadian citizenship rights of Quebecers, and exposing taxpayers in the rest of Canada to a significantly increased burden of public debt. The government of Canada has neither the legal power nor the political mandate to make such concessions.

Ottawa's silence during the 1995 referendum on what it might do if the sovereigntists won may have encouraged sovereigntists to believe that it would accede to a Quebec UDI without any negotiations. Ottawa has since made it clear that it rejects the possibility of unilateral secession, however, and it will likely use the outcome of the reference to the Supreme Court of Canada to underline its newfound resolve on this issue. Thus, for Canada to recognize a sovereign Quebec based on a UDI without any real effort to negotiate the terms of secession is neither a desirable nor a realistic possibility.[13]

The remaining alternative is a unilateral declaration by Quebec that is not accepted by Canada. A challenge by the Canadian government to a Quebec UDI would plunge us all into a situation in which two regimes, the one legal and constitutional, the other illegal and unconstitutional, confront each other, both claiming authority over the same territory and people, both with armed security forces at their disposal, both with passionate supporters. This surely is a recipe for disaster with the gravest consequences for economic stability and social peace. But we might very well end up in just such a mess if a negotiated agreement on the terms of Quebec sovereignty were not reached and ratified. Unless we are convinced that is the only choice, it would be the height of imprudence to plan to be in such a situation from the outset, or to fall into such a situation simply through the lack of any other plan. Our paper aims to show the viability of another plan.

Past rejection of more modest attempts to reach a constitutional accommodation with Quebec may well give rise to skepticism about the possibility of reaching agreement on the terms of Quebec's accession to sovereignty. We acknowledge the possibility that anger and hostility generated by an affirmative referendum vote might prompt some groups to seek to block the move to sovereignty, or to punish Quebec by inflating the costs it would have to bear. We believe, however, that the pressures toward achieving a reasonable and rapid agreement would be more powerful. A postreferendum scenario likely would give rise to a more promising context for agreement than we have seen in previous rounds of constitutional negotiations precisely because of the sense of urgency and crisis it would engender.

The Limits of Constitutionalism

Concerned though we are that, if Quebec were to secede from Canada, it do so in a manner that does not lead to a disruptive break in legal continuity, we recognize that there are very real political limits to maintaining constitutionalism. Even a constitutional process that is entered into in good faith by all concerned, operated with the maximum degree of flexibility, and carried out over a reasonable period of time might still fail to reach the degree of consensus required by the Constitution to achieve Quebec's sovereignty. In such a situation, there would be very little likelihood that a Quebec government that had won a referendum on sovereignty would accept defeat in the Canadian constitutional process and simply abandon the sovereignty project.

At that point, Canada would be at a very dangerous impasse. There would be a strong possibility that the government of Quebec might proceed unilaterally – and, in our view, unconstitutionally – to declare Quebec a sovereign country no longer bound by the Constitution of Canada. We do not think that such a dangerous situation could be avoided by such means as insisting that Quebec agree never to attempt a UDI as a precondition to beginning sovereignty negotiations; such a demand would require Quebec to discard a great deal of its bargaining strength. However much Canadians outside Quebec may detest Quebec's 'knife to the throat' tactics, no Quebec government elected with a sovereignty mandate and accountable to a majority of 'yes' voters following a sovereignty referendum would agree to abandon completely the possibility of a UDI. Insisting on the abandonment of the possibility of unilateralism would simply invite a UDI sooner rather than later.

By the same token, Quebec sovereigntists could not expect the federal government to agree to accept a Quebec UDI unconditionally if the effort to negotiate and effect secession in a constitutional manner were to fail. Ottawa must retain its freedom to withhold recognition of Quebec sovereignty if that sovereignty has been achieved unconstitutionally. It would be unconscionable for the federal government or other negotiating bodies to agree in advance that, no matter what issues have led to a breakdown in negotiations or in what circumstances there has been a failure to ratify a negotiated agreement, it would recognize Quebec as an independent country. Such an agreement would require the government of Canada to abandon its legal and political responsibilities and to concede far too much of its bargaining power.

Participants in sovereignty negotiations might be expected to agree in advance on what they would do if negotiations succeeded, not on what they might do if negotiations or ratification failed. Neither side would forswear, as a precondition of entering into such a process, acting directly to secure its own vital interests if the process failed.

Yet the dire nature of what might happen if a constitutional sovereignty process failed, though fearful to contemplate, may provide the very discipline needed to induce accommodation and compromise.

There is a scenario in which it would be reasonable to recognize Quebec's sovereignty outside of a constitutional process: If a negotiated agreement had been reached and popularly supported by majorities in all parts of Canada but still lacked formal ratification by all of Canada's legislative assemblies, it might, in some circumstances, make sense for the federal government to go ahead and recognize Quebec's sovereignty – on terms that had a wide basis of support across the country – rather than let strict adherence to the letter of the law trump all other principles. We discuss this possibility toward the end of this *Commentary*, in the section on the ratification process.

Ratification Issues in the Negotiations

In the past, efforts at major constitutional change in Canada have failed to take into account how proposals agreed to by the negotiators would be ratified. This lack of sufficient attention to the ratification process was evident in both the Meech Lake and Charlottetown rounds. In both cases, the negotiation stage was a success; the negotiators reached unanimous agreement. Yet both efforts at constitutional renewal failed because the agreements did not survive the ratification process. Any future negotiations contemplating major changes to Canada's Constitution should avoid this mistake.

The negotiating stage of the constitutional amendment process is not governed by rules set out in the Constitution. The only constitutional provision pertaining to the process of negotiating amendments is a requirement that the prime minister invite 'representatives of the aboriginal peoples of Canada to participate in the discussions' of a first ministers' conference before any amendment is made to sections of the Constitution that expressly refer to Aboriginal peoples.[14] Aside from this important legal commitment, all other features of the negotiating process are matters of political judgment.

Canada has a strong tradition of using 'executive federalism' – meetings of first ministers and other senior ministers and officials from both levels of government – as the basic means of negotiating and drafting proposals for constitutional change. In the 'multilateral process' that led to the Charlottetown Accord, territorial ministers and representatives of Aboriginal organizations participated along with federal and provincial ministers. For negotiations on a matter as fundamental as removing a province from the federation or significantly altering its status, the negotiating process is bound to be at least as broad and complex as the Charlottetown process.

In an earlier *Commentary*, Patrick Monahan and Michael Bryant set out a multilateral structure and process for negotiating a post-referendum agreement.[15] Although we do not, in this paper, address the negotiating process *per se*, we consider it crucial to decide on some ratification issues at the negotiating stage. We have identified three such issues for consideration below.

The Referendum Process
First and foremost, negotiators should agree in advance as to whether or not ratifying referendums are to be held in some or all of the jurisdictions. If they are,

further important questions are: What would the question be? What would constitute a 'yes' result, committing the parties to proceed with formal legislative ratification? Some analysts of the Char- lottetown process have argued that the negotiators might have arrived at a somewhat different accord had they agreed from the start that the product of their negotiations was going to be subjected to a referendum process.

A Single Package?

The second issue relates to the package of proposals on which the negotiators have agreed. As we will show, some elements of a sovereignty agreement would not require any kind of constitutional amendment, while others would be subject to constitutional amendment rules more flexible than the unanimity rule, and a few items might require ratification by all the provincial legislatures and the federal Parliament. Therefore, the possibility of breaking the package up for the ratification stage, rather than treating the agreement as a seamless whole, is a vital issue that must be considered in the negotiation phase. The position and expectations of the negotiators regarding this point might well affect bargaining on various parts of the package. Our analysis in the next section of the likely ingredients of a sovereignty agreement will probe the possibility of a multitrack ratification process.

The Timetable

The third ratification process issue that needs to be addressed in the negotiation phase is the timetable. A fatal mistake in the Meech Lake round was the negotiators' failure to commit to a timely ratification schedule. If a referendum is to be part of the process, all parties would need to reach agreement on the timing of both the referendum and the subsequent legislative process. Given that some legislatures require committee hearings on any constitutional proposals brought before them, the timetable would have to accommodate these. Aboriginal participants might well have their own ratification processes, which would also have to be fitted into the ratification timetable.

Likely Components of a Sovereignty Agreement

The Canadian Constitution does not contain an explicit clause setting out the rules for removing a province from the federation. This is not unusual for a constitution; most states – federal or unitary – make no provision in their founding documents for the secession of a part of the state.

The absence of an explicit secession clause does not mean, however, that the general rules governing constitutional amendments cannot be applied to the secession of a province or to any other change in a province's constitutional status. Part V of the *Constitution Act, 1982* sets out amending procedures for different categories of amendment, which together cover all conceivable changes to the Constitution. Thus, we take the view, shared by other constitutional scholars, that the existing procedures for amending the Constitution could be used to effect the secession of a province.[16] Where we depart from others who have written on this subject is in viewing a sovereignty agreement as having a number of components, as well as in questioning the assumption that every part of the agreement would necessarily be subject to a single ratification rule and process.

The Minimum Changes Necessary

To make our case, we must try to predict what the components of a sovereignty agreement with Quebec would be. One key assumption is that the changes to the Constitution at this stage would be the minimum necessary to remove Quebec from, or alter its relationship with, Canada. We know that there would be great pressure to rework the Constitution for a Canada without Quebec. The dominance of Ontario, which would have nearly half the seats in the House of Commons, and the need to replace or abolish the Senate are just two of the issues that would give rise to calls for an immediate revamping of the Constitution should Quebec become sovereign.

These rebalancing issues would not, however, be of direct relevance to the government of Quebec; they are matters for negotiation among the governments that would remain subject to the Constitution. Keeping these rebalancing issues separate from the sovereignty issues in the process of negotiation would be a difficult task, but an essential one. Otherwise, as Monahan and Bryant have argued, the period of uncertainty following the referendum could be far lengthier and costlier than it need be.[17] In the end, we believe Cairns' arguments for a temporary structure as close as possible to the status quo would carry the day, and that the Constitution of a Canada without Quebec would be reconstructed, without Quebec's participation, after the sovereignty process was complete.[18] Thus, our analysis describes only those changes necessary to facilitate an orderly transition to Quebec sovereignty.

Five Categories of Change

These amendments would fall into five categories, as follows:

1 constitutional amendments terminating the authority of existing federal and provincial institutions over the territory and people of Quebec;

2 constitutional and statutory amendments to make remaining federal institutions workable in the short term;

3 provisions, constitutional or otherwise, for any new links established between Quebec and Canada;

4 new treaties, or a commitment to negotiate them, among Aboriginal peoples, Quebec, and Canada; and

5 nonconstitutional items to be implemented by legislation, executive orders, or treaties.

Removing Quebec from Existing Constitutional Arrangements

The first step would be the simple but major one of removing Quebec from the application of the current Canadian Constitution and terminating the authority of existing federal and provincial institutions over the territory and people of Quebec. Amendments would be needed to define the territory of Quebec and to declare it no longer subject to the Canadian Constitution. Existing constitutional provisions referring to the executive, legislative, and judicial branches of the government of Quebec – that is, the lieutenant governor, the National Assembly, and the courts of Quebec – would have to be repealed.

It might seem at first that this step could be accomplished with a long list of amendments removing every reference to Quebec from the Canadian Constitution. However, such an approach would be merely cosmetic, unnecessary, and in some instances would amount to a meddlesome attempt to rewrite history. Consider, for example, section 5 of the *Constitution Act, 1867*, which provides that 'Canada shall be divided into four provinces, named Ontario, Quebec, Nova Scotia, and New Brunswick.' Simply deleting Quebec from this provision would leave the text describing a Canada of three provinces that never existed. Of course, references to the other six provinces and the three territories created since 1867 could be added at the same time as Quebec is deleted, but it is hard to see what the point of such an exercise in modernization might be. The Constitution is composed of many historical layers; those who have drafted its constitutional documents over the past 130 years have generally chosen to add new layers of text rather than to rewrite earlier historical realities. If the *Constitution Act, 1867* has survived this long with its image of a Canada of four provinces nestled snugly under Britain's colonial wing, we see no reason some of its provisions could not be left intact to remind us that a sovereign Quebec was once a province, too.

Redefining Federal Institutions

With Quebec excised from the constitutional definition of Canada, we would need a package of amendments ensuring that the remaining constitutional provisions and federal institutions were legitimate and workable in the short term. Thus, for example, the constitutional provisions setting out Quebec's representation in the House of Commons and the Senate would need amending, and legislation would have to be passed removing the current guarantee that three Quebec judges sit on the Supreme Court of Canada.

Establishing New Links

It is possible that a third group of amendments of a more positive nature would also form part of the sovereignty package – namely, new provisions in the Constitution dealing with relationships between a sovereign Quebec and Canada. These links could include matters ranging from special citizenship or mobility provisions, to a trade dispute mechanism pending Quebec's admission to the North American Free Trade Agreement, to the full political association desired by the present leadership of the Parti Québécois.

We take no position on which, if any, of these links should be agreed to and given constitutional expression. We are concerned only with considering how any such constitutional changes agreed to in negotiations would be ratified.

Concluding Treaties

One kind of constitutional change that would be necessary in the event of Quebec's accession to sovereignty does not involve amendments in the ordinary sense: the conclusion of treaties with Aboriginal peoples. Section 35(1) of the *Constitution Act, 1982* recognizes and affirms the treaty rights of Canada's Aboriginal peoples. Section 35(3) specifically provides that these treaty rights include 'rights that now exist by way of land claims agreements or may be so acquired.'

Much of northern Quebec is covered by the *James Bay and Northern Quebec Agreement* (1975) and the *Northeastern Quebec Agreement* (1978), comprehensive agreements entered into by Quebec, Canada, and the Cree, Inuit, and Naskapi peoples. These agreements include terms stating that they cannot be changed without the agreement of the signatories. Since the provisions of these treaties are constitutionally protected by section 35(1), it follows that, as long as section 35 remains in force in its present form, changes necessitated by Quebec sovereignty would have to be negotiated and agreed to by all parties, and provision would have to be made to entrench the contents of the new treaties in the constitutions of Quebec and Canada. The same would be true of any new comprehensive agreements with Aboriginal peoples in Quebec included in the sovereignty settlement.

The northern Quebec treaties could be legally altered without the consent of the Aboriginal signatories only if section 35 itself were amended to remove the treaties from their existing constitutional protection. This may be legally possible, since the amending formulas in the *Constitution Act, 1982* give no formal role to Aboriginal peoples. But the notion that Aboriginal peoples ought to have a veto over amendments that would affect their rights has become a basic political principle, and perhaps even a constitutional convention.[19] Amending section 35 without Aboriginal consent, to enable the abrogation of treaty rights without Aboriginal consent, would constitute an obvious and flagrant violation of fundamental moral and political principles. It would violate both the Crown's fiduciary obligations embodied in Canadian domestic law, as well as emerging international norms. Indeed, in the face of such an oppressive exercise of state power, the courts might superimpose the Crown's fiduciary obligations on the operation of the amending formulas, thus making it impossible to alter fundamentally the constitutional status of Aboriginal peoples without their consent.

We therefore conclude that, while there is room to debate whether or not it is legally possible to remove by constitutional amendment the current legal requirement of Aboriginal consent to any changes to the northern Quebec treaties, Canadian governments would not consider pursuing such a morally objectionable course. Thus, we assume that changes to existing treaties and new treaties with Aboriginal peoples in Quebec would have to be negotiated and their terms agreed to by all signatories. As we discuss further below, arrangements would have to be made to complete this lengthy negotiation process after Quebec had acceded to sovereignty over much of its territory.

Nonconstitutional Items
Finally, some elements of a sovereignty agreement would not require any form of constitutional expression. These include some of the most important and contentious issues likely to emerge in the negotiations. Consider, for instance, matters such as the apportionment of Canada's national debt; arrangements regarding the potential use of the Canadian dollar as the currency of a sovereign Quebec; the right of Quebecers to maintain Canadian citizenship and Canadian passports; or the status of Hydro-Québec's contract for hydro-electric power from Churchill Falls. These crucial components of a sovereignty agreement might be given legal effect through acts of Parliament, or executive orders, or international treaties between the new Canada and a sovereign Quebec. A large number of these nonconstitutional items would be included in any negotiated agreement on the terms of Quebec's sovereignty.

Summary
We anticipate that a negotiated settlement with Quebec following a sovereign-

tist referendum win could include elements that, from a constitutional perspective, fall into some or all of the five categories discussed above. With these categories in mind, we proceed in the next section to consider the degree of legislative approval necessary to enact into law the constitutional elements of the package (potentially, the first four categories above). We will then be in a position to consider the appropriate process for ratifying a sovereignty agreement under the Constitution of Canada.

The Applicable Constitutional Amending Procedures

The *Constitution Act, 1982* includes five amending formulas; which of them applies in any given situation depends on the part of the Constitution to be amended. The transformation of Quebec's status from province to sovereign nation would have an impact on a wide range of constitutional matters falling under the rubric of several different amending formulas; indeed, all five formulas potentially would be implicated. In this section, we endeavor to further 'unpack' the likely components of a sovereignty agreement, outlined above, in terms of the specific changes that would be needed to various sections of the Constitution, and then group them according to the amending formulas that would need to be applied to implement them.

Seeking Flexibility in Ratification

Given a sovereignty package of proposed constitutional amendments that fall under several different amending formulas, two possible paths to ratification present themselves. The first would be to put the entire package of constitutional amendments forward for ratification together, in which case the cumulative requirements of the applicable amending formulas would have to be followed. Since Quebec's accession to sovereignty would affect several matters subject to the unanimity procedure, the entire package would have to be ratified by both houses of Parliament and all of the provincial legislatures. This was the procedure that governments attempted to follow with respect to the Meech Lake Accord and that they appeared prepared to follow had the Charlottetown Accord been approved in the national referendum.

The second approach would be to break up the package of constitutional amendments according to the applicable amending formulas and to pursue their ratification on separate tracks. This approach would offer the obvious advantage of greater flexibility, since those matters requiring unanimity could be dealt with separately, while the rest of the package could be subjected to the more forgiving requirements of the other amending formulas. Even though – as we conclude in the next section – there would be great pressure to subject all substantial or controversial amendments to a single ratification process, if the possibility of pursuing a multitrack ratification process is to be considered at all, which we believe it should, the 'unpacking' exercise we pursue below is a necessary one.

One could argue that flexibility would be enhanced by drafting amendments that would remove Quebec from Canada with a few broad legal strokes. The unanimity amending formula could then be circumvented, some might argue, by avoiding explicit reference to any of the matters listed in section 41 of the *Constitution Act, 1982* that require unanimity to be amended.

Yet, whatever the wording of the amendments, there is no doubt that Quebec sovereignty would have a dramatic impact on these section 41 matters. For example, the office of the lieutenant governor of Quebec would cease to exist in its current form in an independent Quebec; all 75 Quebec seats in the House of Commons would have to be removed; and constitutional protection of language rights might be modified or eliminated.

José Woehrling has argued that, as long as an amendment says nothing on its face about these subjects, it would not be 'in relation to' section 41 matters, and therefore unanimous approval would not be required to implement it.[20] Woehrling's position appears to be that an amendment is 'in relation to' a matter such as the office of the lieutenant governor of Quebec only if its *purpose* or *object* is to alter that matter. In his view, indirect effects on section 41 matters do not trigger the unanimity requirement; thus, since the abolition of the office of the lieutenant governor would be an indirect consequence, rather than the object, of secession amendments, the unanimity rule would not apply.

We share the spirit of Woehrling's attempt to interpret section 41 narrowly and thus introduce greater flexibility into the amending procedures. However, we cannot agree that even amendments with drastic effects on section 41 matters are not 'in relation to' those matters. In our view, not just the purposes but the *effects* of a proposed amendment must determine which amending formula applies to it. Otherwise, as Monahan has argued, the form in which an amendment is pursued would triumph over its substance.[21] The strong degree of constitutional protection afforded to section 41 matters should not be so easily circumvented. In our view, the unanimity procedure should be applicable whenever a proposed amendment would have a substantial or material impact on a matter listed in section 41.[22] Several of the amendments that would be necessary to implement a sovereignty agreement with Quebec certainly qualify. Thus, we are of the view that the strictures of the unanimity rule cannot be avoided with respect to at least some aspects of such an agreement.

The '7/50' Procedure

Most amendments necessary to accomplish Quebec's orderly secession would fall within the section 38 general ('7/50') amending formula, which applies to all amendments in relation to matters not specifically allocated to one of the other four formulas. Secession is such a matter. Amendments under the section 38 formula require the passage of resolutions by both houses of Parliament and the legislatures of at least seven of the provinces constituting together at least 50 percent of Canada's population.

The *Constitutional Amendments Act*, which came into force in February 1996, superimposed five regional vetoes on the operation of the '7/50' amending formula.[23] The combined effect of the Constitution and the legislation is that a proposed '7/50' amendment must have the support of the federal Parliament, British Columbia, Ontario, Quebec, at least two of the prairie provinces comprising 50 percent of their combined population – that is, at current population levels, Alberta and at least one of Manitoba and Saskatchewan[24] – and at least two of the Atlantic provinces comprising 50 percent of their combined population.[25] Under this arrangement, the consenting provinces would represent at least 92 percent of Canada's population.[26]

Defining and Removing Quebec

Foremost among the amendments that could be made pursuant to the '7/50' formula would certainly be defining the territory of Quebec and then removing it from the authority of the Constitution. Defining the territory of the new sovereign state of Quebec would, however, be among the most contentious issues to be negotiated following a sovereigntist referendum win.

Quebec's current boundaries are defined by a variety of legal sources. Section 6 of the *Constitution Act, 1867* defined the province of Quebec by reference to the pre-existing boundaries of Lower Canada, thus incorporating by reference the boundary between Lower and Upper Canada set out in a 1791 order-in-council and the boundary between New Brunswick and Lower Canada set out in 1851 British legislation.[27] The Ontario-Quebec boundary was clarified by British legislation passed in 1889.[28] The northern boundary of the province of Quebec was extended twice by federal legislation, in 1898 and 1912.29 Finally, the Quebec-Labrador boundary was established by a 1927 Privy Council decision.[30]

As long as Quebec remains a province of Canada, it can claim the protection of section 3 of the *Constitution Act, 1871*, which provides that its boundaries can be altered only with its consent. This does not mean, however, as some sovereigntists have asserted, that a sovereign Quebec would have a right to maintain its existing borders. The act refers to the alteration of the boundaries of provinces within Canada; it has nothing to say about the removal of a province from Confederation.

Following a sovereigntist referendum victory, the borders of a sovereign Quebec would be an issue for negotiation. Quebec's existing borders would be challenged on two fronts: by Aboriginal peoples, and by regions with federalist majorities in the referendum vote, especially those contiguous to the Ontario border.

At least some of Quebec's Aboriginal peoples would almost certainly insist on remaining part of Canada.[31] As we argued above, existing legal norms and moral principles dictate that new treaties among Quebec, Canada, and the Aboriginal nations of Quebec would have to be concluded. These treaties would include land-claim settlements and perhaps also self-government agreements following the pattern set by recently concluded agreements in British Columbia and the Yukon. They could thus have an impact on both the definition of Quebec's territory and the nature and scope of Quebec's jurisdiction over its territory.

It might take many years for Canada, a sovereign Quebec, and the Aboriginal nations to conclude such a round of treaty making; as a result, it is impossible to predict in advance the scope of the territory over which Quebec would be able to assert sovereignty. If treaty negotiations were still ongoing after all other matters relating to the transition to sovereignty had been negotiated and ratified, interim arrangements could be made; this issue is discussed in more detail in the next section.

In addition to Aboriginal peoples, other local federalist majorities unwilling to join the sovereigntist project would place a great deal of pressure on Canada not to cede territory they inhabit. Since the claims of non-Aboriginal federalist partitionists are not grounded in existing domestic and international law the way those of Aboriginal nations are, Canada would not be under the same legal and moral obligation to advance this issue in negotiations. However, federalist regional majorities' claims that they have the right to remain in Canada follow much the same logic as the sovereigntists' claim that they have the right to secede, so this issue should not be ruled out of the negotiating agenda. The suggestion of Monahan and Bryant that the issue be resolved by cascading referendums is worthy of consideration.[32] From a practical perspective, however, we have grave doubts as to whether the issue of federalist partition is capable of yielding compromises acceptable to both sovereigntists and federalists. If Canada were to insist on protecting the territorial claims of federalist minorities, it would very likely require the use of force and lead to communal violence. In our view, the Canadian negotiating team would be wise to respond to the concerns of Quebec's federalist regions by pressing for protection of language rights and dual citizenship rights in Quebec's constitution, rather than insisting on the partitionist approach.

Other '7/50' Amendments

Other constitutional changes that would likely be necessary for a legal secession could be enacted pursuant to the '7/50' rule, including:

- terminating the federal Parliament's authority to pass laws in relation to Quebec;
- terminating the application of the Charter of Rights and Freedoms in Quebec;
- terminating the authority of the Supreme Court of Canada and the Federal Court of Canada in relation to disputes arising in Quebec, as well as the jurisdiction of all courts in Quebec constituted pursuant to the Canadian Constitution;
- removing Quebec's seats from the Senate[33] (section 22 of the *Constitution Act, 1867* would have to be amended to reduce the number of regional divisions in the Senate from four to three, to delete the references to Quebec, and to remove the 24 Quebec senators; section 23(6), which deals with the qualifications of Quebec senators, would also need to be repealed);
- amending section 108 of the *Constitution Act, 1867*, which provides that certain kinds of federal property situated in the province (such as canals and post offices) belong to Canada, in order to transfer ownership of these properties to a sovereign Quebec in return for appropriate compensation; and
- establishing new links between Canada and Quebec of the kind discussed in category 3 of the previous section.

The 'Unanimity' Procedure

Following our interpretation of section 41, discussed above, unanimity would be required to authorize three kinds of changes that Quebec's accession to sovereignty would provoke.

The first of these changes are those required by the fact that a sovereign Quebec presumably would no longer be a monarchy.[34] In such circumstances, the office of the lieutenant governor would cease to exist, and unanimous consent would be required for the changes to the various provisions of the *Constitution Act, 1867* that set out the status and powers of that office.[35]

The second kind of changes are those required to remove Quebec's seats from the House of Commons. While changes to the makeup of the House can ordinarily be made by the federal government alone, pursuant to the unilateral formula in section 44 of the *Constitution Act, 1982*, an exception to this rule is made to protect guarantees of provincial representation from unilateral reduction. Pursuant to the 'Senate floor' provision of the *Constitution Act, 1867* (section 51(a)), Quebec is guaranteed at least 24 members in the House of Commons. Since the 'Senate floor' principle is a matter subject to the unanimity formula, it follows, in our view, that the removal of Quebec's seats from the House could be accomplished only by unanimous consent.[36]

Finally, unanimous consent would be necessary to sanction the fact that the following language rights would no longer apply in Quebec or to Quebecers:[37]

- the right to use English or French in Parliament and federal courts, as set out in section 133 of the *Constitution Act, 1867* and sections 16–19 of the Charter;
- the right to use English or French in federal government offices, as set out in section 20 of the Charter; and
- the right of Quebec anglophones to educate their children in English, as set out in section 23 of the Charter.

These are the only aspects of a sovereignty agreement that would require unanimous approval. It is true that the composition of the Supreme Court of Canada would have to be changed by removing the guarantee of three Quebec judges. But even though the Court's composition is a matter subject to the unanimity formula,[38] this change would not require a constitutional amendment because, oddly enough, that composition has never been set out anywhere in the Constitution.[39]

The 'Bilateral' Amending Procedure
The section 43 amending formula gives Parliament and the Quebec National Assembly the power to amend provisions of the Constitution that apply to some but not all of the provinces if the amendments have legal effect only in Quebec. In the event of Quebec sovereignty, only a few provisions of the Constitution could be altered or repealed pursuant to the section 43 bilateral procedure – namely:

- an amendment specifying that subsections 93(1) to (4) of the Constitution Act, 1867 in relation to denominational school rights no longer apply in Quebec;[40]
- the repeal of section 98 of the *Constitution Act, 1867*, which provides that Quebec judges will be appointed from the bar of Quebec;

- the repeal of the portions of section 133 of the *Constitution Act, 1867* relating to the use of English or French in the judicial and legislative branches of the Quebec government; and
- the repeal of section 59 of the *Constitution Act, 1982*, relating to minority language education rights in Quebec.

The 'Federal Unilateral' Procedure

Section 44 enables Parliament unilaterally to amend provisions of the Constitution relating to aspects of the legislative or executive branches of the federal government not of direct concern to the provinces. A few minor amendments of this type would relate to Quebec sovereignty:

- Consequential amendments to sections 26–28 of the *Constitution Act, 1867* would be required after the removal of Quebec senators to reflect the fact that there would be three, rather than four, regional divisions, and that the maximum number of senators would be reduced by 24; and
- the portions of section 40 of the *Constitution Act, 1867* that relate to Quebec's electoral districts would need to be repealed, along with related provisions in existing federal statutes, such as the *Electoral Boundaries Readjustment Act*.[41]

While it would not amount to an amendment to the Constitution, the federal government could pass legislation without the consent of the provinces to amend the *Supreme Court Act* to reflect Quebec's departure, deleting the guarantee in section 6 that three judges be appointed from Quebec.[42] Eventually, the composition of the Court would have to be redefined to better reflect the realities of Canada without Quebec. In the interim, a Court reduced by the loss of its Quebec members could nevertheless operate without further changes to the law: any five judges of the Supreme Court can 'constitute a quorum' and 'may lawfully hold the Court.'[43]

The 'Provincial Unilateral' Procedure

Section 45 enables a province unilaterally to alter provisions of the Canadian Constitution that form part of the 'constitution of the province' – that is, provisions that relate to matters internal to the province and its institutions and are not of concern to the federation as a whole. Thus, except for provisions relating to the office of the lieutenant governor, described above, Quebec could unilaterally repeal the provisions of the *Constitution Act, 1867* establishing the legislature of Quebec. It could, for example:

- repeal sections 72–79 of the act in relation to the legislative council of Quebec;
- repeal section 80 of the act constituting the legislature of Quebec; and
- amend sections 83–87 of the act to delete references to Quebec and its legislature.

Most of these provisions are of no practical significance in any case, as they have long been superseded by Quebec legislation. But to eliminate any possibility of confusion about the constitutional status of the Quebec legislature, it would be wise to repeal those provisions as part of the sovereignty agreement.

Summary

In order to comply with the legal requirements of the *Constitution Act, 1982*, the components of a sovereignty agreement would have to be ratified by the relevant legislatures to meet the requirements of the five amending formulas described above. This could be done by separating the components of the agreement and subjecting them to a multitrack process of legislative ratification, or by treating the agreement as a single package subject to the unanimity rule – as was attempted in the case of the failed Meech Lake Accord. The legal requirements of the 1982 act, however, are not the only elements of a legally sound and politically legitimate ratification process; in particular, both the emerging convention of a national referendum on substantial amendments and the federal government's legal obligations to Aboriginal peoples add further layers to the procedures that would have to be followed. In the next section, we expand our view beyond the legal requirements of the *Constitution Act, 1982* and the federal *Constitutional Amendments Act* to come up with a more complete description of the process for ratifying a sovereignty agreement.

The Ratification Process

Let us be clear that the ratification process discussed here would, in effect, be the third stage of the larger process through which Quebec sovereignty might be effected pursuant to the Canadian Constitution. Stage one would be a win for the 'yes' side in a sovereignty referendum. Stage two would be agreement on the terms of Quebec's accession to sovereignty reached through negotiations between Quebec and the rest of Canada. Accomplishing both these earlier stages would require agreement on a number of contentious procedural points, including the nature of the referendum question and the size of the majority needed for a sovereigntist win, and the participants, agenda, and organization of the negotiating process. This *Commentary* does not deal with these issues, but we have written it on the assumption that these matters could be dealt with successfully.[44]

The process for ratifying and giving legal effect to an agreement on the terms of Quebec's accession to sovereignty would have three distinct steps. The first would involve popular consultation through a Canada-wide referendum – a political imperative for a matter as important as the terms of Quebec's accession to sovereignty. In the second step, following a successful referendum, the various legislatures would take action to approve and give legal expression to the elements of the agreement. Both of these steps should be undertaken as quickly as possible following completion of the negotiation stage.

The third element of ratification would be the completion of treaty-like agreements with the Aboriginal peoples, which, though agreed to in principle in the negotiations, might take much longer to complete than the first two stages.

The Referendum Stage

The Case for a Referendum
A Canada-wide referendum is not a legally required part of the constitutional amendment process; at the moment, only Alberta and British Columbia legally require a referendum as a condition precedent to submitting a constitutional amendment to the legislature.[45] Nevertheless, to have political legitimacy, an agreement on Quebec sovereignty would need to be ratified by a referendum not only in Quebec but in all parts of Canada.

For a sovereign Quebec to have solid democratic foundations, its people would have to have the opportunity to pass judgment on the terms that their government has been able to negotiate with the rest of Canada for Quebec's accession to sovereignty. These terms might diverge on important points from what was hoped for – and perhaps even promised – by sovereigntist leaders in their successful referendum campaign. The 1980 Quebec referendum question, in which the government of Quebec asked for a mandate to negotiate a sovereignty-association agreement with Canada, contained a clear commitment to submit such an agreement for approval by the citizens of Quebec in a second referendum. The absence of such a commitment by the Quebec government in the 1995 referendum meant that Quebecers were being asked to vote for Quebec sovereignty on conditions set out in Bill 1 that were quite beyond the Quebec government's power to deliver (for example, continuation of Canadian citizenship and currency). To have established Quebec's sovereignty on the basis of a majority 'yes' vote in that referendum without securing the promised conditions would not have been in accord with democratic principle.[46] The terms of a negotiated agreement following a sovereigntist victory in a Quebec referendum are bound to be a compromise, falling short of the most optimistic expectations of sovereigntist leaders. If Quebec sovereignty is to be based on the will of Quebecers, its actual terms should be approved directly by them.

An equally compelling case can be made for consulting the Canadian people on the terms of a negotiated agreement on Quebec sovereignty. Here, we part company with Monahan and Bryant, who insist that, while Quebec would have to have a second referendum on the terms of sovereignty, no referendum on these terms would need be held in the rest of Canada other than in Alberta and British Columbia, where provincial statutes require them.[47] Not only would referendums in those provinces place political pressure on governments in other provinces to consult their own populations, but larger considerations of constitutional politics would also bear on the matter. At this stage in the democratization of Canada's constitutional politics, changes of the magnitude involved in the removal of Quebec from the federation and the terms on which that would be done would require the approval of Canadians in all parts of the country.

In his book on the use of referendums in Canada, Patrick Boyer writes:

Certainly major constitutional amendments should be submitted for ratification by a referendum, and it seems clear following the experience of October 26, 1992, they henceforth will be.[48]

We think most Canadians would agree with Boyer on this point. Submitting proposals for major constitutional amendments to the people is at least an emergent, if not yet crystallized, constitutional convention in Canada. Monahan and Bryant take the position that the democratic requirements of Canada's constitutional process would be satisfied for Canadians outside Quebec simply by their being well represented on the negotiating team. We argue, however, that the legitimacy of the negotiating process – Canadians' willingness to agree to terms that inevitably would be worked out by a small number of leaders and experts, sometimes operating in closed sessions – would be greatly enhanced if Canadians were assured that the product of the negotiation would be submitted to them for their approval.

To appreciate the need for a Canada-wide referendum, consider what would be at stake in an agreement on Quebec sovereignty. In all likelihood, Canadians would be asked to vote on the agreement in its entirety – that is, on both its non-constitutional components and its proposed constitutional amendments. We do not see how the agreement could be broken up for purposes of popular ratification. Its key terms would embody a set of interlocking agreements that would have to stand or fall as a whole. Some components – such as the apportioning of the public debt, citizenship issues, currency arrangements, trade relations, the issue of a land bridge to connect Atlantic Canada to the rest of the country, and a resolution of the Churchill Falls issue – even though they may not have been dealt with through formal amendments to the Constitution, would be of great importance to all Canadians. On the constitutional side, even if a strategy of minimal changes to existing constitutional structures were pursued, as we and Cairns advocate, major constitutional decisions would nonetheless be at issue. Indeed, it would be unwise to foist even this minimalist approach – whereby Canada minus Quebec would operate for some years under a federal system dominated by Ontario – on Canadians without a broad base of popular support. Moreover, the barest minimum of constitutional changes necessary to implement Quebec's sovereignty would, as we have discussed, include items of major significance such as the links, or the absence of them, between a sovereign Quebec and Canada, the principles and procedures that would apply to Aboriginal peoples, the treatment of linguistic minorities, and changes, if any, to Quebec's borders.

What Counts as a 'Yes'?
What level and distribution of popular approval for a negotiated agreement should be regarded as sufficient to go ahead with its formal legislative ratification? In the 1992 referendum on the Charlottetown Accord, the only precedent for a Canada-wide constitutional referendum, no official position was taken on this question – although there seems to have been a widespread expectation that a 'yes' win would have required majorities in every province. Of course, the question became academic when the accord failed to win even a national majority.[49]

There is an obvious logic to requiring majority approval in every province if some components of the agreement are subject to the unanimity constitutional amending rule. Still, we think a unanimity referendum rule creates too high a threshold for the federal government (at least) to commit itself to completing the formal ratification process and, in certain circumstances, which we discuss later, recognizing Quebec's sovereignty on the basis of the agreed-on terms. On the other hand, we are apprehensive about defining the threshold for such an undertaking simply as a majority 'yes' in both Quebec and Canada outside Quebec. Such a double majority rule would no doubt appeal to Quebec, but it would risk going ahead with an agreement that might have strong support in central Canada but that had been roundly rejected in other regions. Provincial governments, particularly in western and Atlantic Canada, would be unlikely to accept a process based on such a two-nations concept of the Canadian body politic.

The federal government, too, would find it difficult to endorse a rule so out of phase with its own 1996 *Constitutional Amendments Act* (which, it should be noted, implicitly allows provinces to give their consent either through their legislatures or in province-wide referendums).[50] In the event of Quebec sovereignty, we believe that a five-region referendum rule based on that act would have a good chance of being accepted by the rest of Canada.

The problem with a five-region referendum rule, of course, is that Quebec might regard it as a straitjacket. Indeed, sovereigntists likely would object to their project's having to garner the approval of a majority of Canadian voters outside Quebec in the first place. Nevertheless, if they are to avoid the risks associated with an unlawful and unconstitutional course of action, sovereigntists would be wise to respect the principles of democratic constitutionalism that Canadians now deem essential.

We doubt the requirements of Canadian constitutionalism could be made any lighter; indeed, some premiers might object even to a five-region rule, which, after all, would commit them to proceeding with legislative ratification of an agreement that might be rejected by a majority of voters in their province. Difficult as it might be for the sovereigntists to accept a five-region referendum rule, we still think they would find it prudent to do so

- if they are convinced that Canada would withhold recognition of a sovereign Quebec if Quebec were to refuse to effect sovereignty through a lawful process; and
- if Quebec were to retain the option of proceeding unilaterally should the constitutional process fail.

The Approval of Aboriginal Peoples

While a 'yes' under the five-region referendum rule would be a sufficient mandate for Ottawa and the provinces to proceed with formal ratification of a negotiated sovereignty agreement, those components of the agreement that pertained directly to Aboriginal peoples would, we argue, require their separate approval.[51] Aboriginal peoples constitute such a tiny fraction of the electorate that their consent to changes in their constitutional rights could possibly be said to have been given through approval of the agreement by majorities in five regions of Canada. Full implementation of the principles agreed to with respect to the position of Aboriginal peoples in a sovereign Quebec would require a trinational treaty process, but with proper safeguards this process need not be completed before recognition of Quebec's sovereignty. We discuss this more fully below.

The Legislative Ratification Stage

Once the requirements of the five-region referendum test had been met and the process of Aboriginal approval of provisions relevant to them was at least under way, the legislative ratification of a sovereignty agreement should not prove difficult. By that time, the agreement would have been approved by majorities in provinces representing at least 92 percent of Canada's population (at most, two Atlantic provinces and either Manitoba or Saskatchewan might have voted against the agreement). This means that legislative approval of the nonconstitutional components of the negotiated agreement, and most of its constitutional aspects, would be able to proceed smoothly. The nonconstitutional matters would require legislation simply by the federal Parliament and the Quebec National Assembly, while most of the important constitutional items would be subject to the '7/50' rule. Governments in the seven (or more) provinces whose electorates would have approved the agreement should have no difficulty moving ahead quickly with ratification in their legislatures.

The Unanimity Components

What about those few constitutional aspects of a secession agreement that would fall under section 41, the unanimity clause in the amending formula? If, in two or three provinces, majorities had voted against the agreement in a Canada-wide referendum, it is likely that the premiers of those provinces would still be committed to submitting to their legislative assemblies – and supporting – resolutions to adopt the constitutional components of the agreement. Except in Alberta and British Columbia, referendums are only consultative, not binding on governments.[52] And if majorities in all regions of the country were in favor of the agreement, it is doubtful that the majority opposed in any dissenting province would be very high. After the vast majority of Canadians both inside and outside Quebec had endorsed an agreement produced by a lengthy and stressful negotiating process, and with the knowledge that failure to ratify could plunge the country into chaos and confusion, it should not be difficult for premiers of dissenting provinces to summon up the political courage to steer the constitutional resolutions through their legislative assemblies.

A Multitrack Process

If this solution were to fail, it might be possible to break up the constitutional components of the agreement according to the different amending formulas that would apply to them, and then have each group of components voted on separately in the various legislatures. Some analysts have argued that such a multitrack ratification process should have been followed in the Meech Lake round, which failed when the Manitoba and Newfoundland legislatures did not pass the necessary resolutions – even though only one of the accord's five components, a change to constitutional amending formulas, required unanimous provincial support. To avoid a similar fate, the few constitutional elements of the sovereignty agreement that would be subject to the unanimity rule could be put before the legislatures in a separate resolution from the rest of the agreement.

This possibility would make it easier to rapidly ratify most of the negotiated agreement; indeed, our 'unpacking' of the various likely components of a sovereignty agreement was intended to facilitate discussion of this possibility. Yet we are not convinced that this would be the best way to deal with the potential straitjacket of unanimity.

To begin with, one could argue strongly that an agreement negotiated and voted on as a total package should be treated the same way by legislatures seeking to ratify it. The constitutional elements that required unanimous approval, though few in number, would not be insignificant parts of the agreement. To enact only a part of the agreement might well be to breach the understandings on which it was reached – unless, at the negotiating stage, there had been an agreement to do so – and some premiers might balk at participating in negotiations on that basis. We also note that amendments affecting the constitutional use of the English and French languages, a matter requiring unanimity, might well embody an agreement on the reciprocal treatment of linguistic minorities that was a critical part of the deal. Meanwhile, amendments to eliminate the monarchy in Quebec and to remove Quebec's members from the House of Commons, though less contentious, would still need to be put into legal effect to enable the new machinery of government to operate in Canada and a sovereign Quebec.

The Maastricht Approach

A more plausible and attractive approach would be to proceed as the European Union (EU) did when the Maastricht Treaty, approved by 11 of its 12 members, was rejected by a small majority of Danish voters in a referendum. Though subject legally to a unanimity rule, the EU agreed to go ahead with implementing the treaty while a special 'opt-out clause' to accommodate Denmark was negotiated. Danes subsequently approved the treaty, with this change incorporated, in another referendum.[53] A similar approach might work in Canada, too, if one of the smaller provinces refused to ratify a sovereignty agreement because of a discrete, negotiable provision dealing with, say, the continuing entrenchment of minority language rights in the Canadian Constitution as part of a reciprocal agreement with Quebec. In such a case, the dissenting province might be accommodated through an opting-out arrangement.

Bending the Rules: An Extreme Case

The possibility exists – though we think it is quite remote – that none of these approaches would work, and that the required legislative approval would not be forthcoming in one or more provinces whose electorates had rejected the agreement. Should this happen, we believe it would be reasonable for the federal government to press ahead with implementing the agreement and to recognize Quebec's sovereignty even though the constitutional requirements for amending the Constitution had not been fully met.

Bear in mind the setting in which this extralegal action would be taking place:

- after months of negotiations, an agreement covering all aspects of Quebec's accession to sovereignty would have been reached through a process representing all components of the federation;
- the agreement would have been approved in a referendum by an overall majority of Canadians and by majorities in provinces with 92 percent of the population;
- an effort would have been made to modify the agreement to satisfy dissenting provinces; and
- the consequences of not going ahead would almost certainly prolong and deepen a crisis that was already causing serious economic damage, paralyzing government, and traumatizing Canadians inside and outside Quebec.

At this point, under these conditions, to insist on full compliance with the constitutional amendment rules would be to turn the rule of law into a foolish fetish and the unanimity rule into a tyranny. In such circumstances, we hope that the governments of Canada, Quebec, and the other provinces that had supported the agreement would have the good sense to recognize Quebec's accession to sovereignty on the basis of the negotiated agreement. As Peter Hogg has argued, such a *de facto* secession:

is an important safeguard for Quebec against the possibility of Canada not fulfilling its obligation to provide constitutional force to a negotiated secession agreement. The possibility of a *de facto* secession would also act as a deterrent to any provincial government that might be inclined to withhold its assent to a negotiated secession agreement, making it less likely that the crisis would develop in the first place.[54]

The Aboriginal Treaty Stage

A crucial part of the negotiated sovereignty agreement would be the principles and procedures concerning Aboriginal peoples in Quebec. Aboriginal organizations would participate in these negotiations and, as we have discussed, their acceptance of this part of the agreement at the very least is required not only by the spirit of section 35.1 of the *Constitution Act, 1982*, but also by Canada's fiduciary obligation to Aboriginal peoples under Canadian law, and by emerging norms of international law.[55]

We think the approach most likely to be agreed to would involve a treaty process whereby the rights and status of each Aboriginal nation with some or all of its homeland in Quebec would be defined through three-way treaties among Canada, Quebec, and the relevant Aboriginal nation.[56] A nation-to-nation treaty approach is at the core of the structural relationship that Aboriginal peoples wish to have with Canadian and Quebec authorities.[57] This approach is also embodied in the comprehensive agreements signed by Canada, Quebec, and the Cree, Naskapi, and Inuit of Northern Quebec in the 1970s, and in the 'Comprehensive Offer' the Quebec government made to the Atikamekw and Montagnais nations in 1994.[58]

A genuine treaty-making process that has integrity and legitimacy cannot be carried out overnight. Working out and establishing treaty arrangements with Aboriginal nations in Quebec that have not yet negotiated land and self-government agreements and renovating the agreements of those that have done so would take years, not months, to complete. It would be unreasonable to expect a Quebec government that had won a referendum to postpone accession to sovereignty and recognition of its independence indefinitely until the treaty process had been completed with all of Quebec's Aboriginal peoples, if all other aspects of secession had been agreed to. Similarly, as a matter of principle, Aboriginal peoples could not reasonably be expected to accept Quebec sovereignty if it were attained in a form fundamentally inconsistent with their wishes, whether expressed in referendums or otherwise.

Instead, we suggest that Canada could recognize Quebec independence before the treaty-making phase was complete in a manner consistent with its fiduciary and constitutional obligations to Aboriginal peoples and without giving Quebecers' moral claim to self-determination priority over the similar claims of Aboriginal peoples. In such a situation, the fully sovereign powers of the new Quebec state would not extend over Aboriginal peoples and lands while the treaty-negotiating process was still under way. The existing situation, where sovereignty is shared among three orders of constitutional government, would remain in place. Canada, or some agreed-on international guarantor, could be granted responsibility for safeguarding Aboriginal rights during the treaty-making period. It is possible that one or more Aboriginal peoples might agree to a treaty with Quebec and Canada only on condition that a permanent condominium – a tripartite sharing of sovereignty – attach to their lands. In return, Quebec would likely insist that revenues from hydro-electric installations and other resource developments on treaty lands be guaranteed – without such a deal, the economic viability of an independent Quebec would be seriously compromised.

No doubt the qualified accession to sovereignty outlined above would not go down well with many Quebec sovereigntists. On the federal side, too, devotees of *realpolitik* likely would be willing to have Canada renege on its legal and moral obligations to Aboriginal peoples if that seemed the easiest way to conclude an agreement on Quebec sovereignty.[59] Nonetheless, we believe that Canada and Quebec should try to do better than this. Our approach holds out the possibility of securing the vital interests of the majority of both Quebecers and Canadians without sacrificing the rights of Aboriginal peoples or building a new relationship between Canada and Quebec by reimposing imperial control over native peoples.

Conclusion

We would prefer to see the aspirations of Quebecers accommodated within the Canadian federation. But after two failed attempts to achieve a post-1982 constitutional reconciliation with Quebec, the prospects of achieving formal constitutional change in the near future are not good.

Given the general rejection of the constitutional status quo in Quebec and the fact that, since fall 1995, polls have indicated that close to half of Quebec voters favor sovereignty, it would be foolhardy not to prepare to deal with the consequences of a possible 'yes' win in a future sovereignty referendum. Should that happen, we are convinced that an attempt ought to be made to resolve the issue of Quebec's accession to sovereignty through the Canadian Constitution. In this *Commentary*, we have suggested a strategy to make that process as flexible as possible while keeping it as just and as fair as possible for *all* Canadians. Granted, the process would be neither simple nor easy – although we do not think it would be as daunting as, say, the strictness of the unanimity formula initially might suggest.

The democratic imperative of a Canada-wide referendum is a prerequisite to invoking the amending formulas for constitutional changes as great as those that Quebec sovereignty would require. The results of that referendum would play a greater role in determining whether formal legislative ratification of a sovereignty agreement moved ahead than would the views of individual provincial governments. The major challenge posed by the ratification process we have outlined would thus be to fashion, and then to sell, a complicated sovereignty agreement to majorities of voters in the five regions of the country spelled out in the *Constitutional Amendments Act*. We are confident that an affirmative referendum vote on such an agreement would generate sufficient momentum to ensure Quebec's accession to sovereignty on the agreed-upon terms.

We do not claim that a constitutional process is the *only* way Quebec could effect sovereignty following a 'yes' win in a referendum. There are other paths by which Quebec could become sovereign and other ways of negotiating the terms of its sovereignty, and a point might be reached where the effort to comply with constitutional requirements no longer made sense. But the advantages to all sides in maintaining legal continuity and following constitutional processes – minimizing the risk of violence and economic dislocation, and maximizing the consensual nature of the sovereignty agreement – are such that it would be foolish not to try to make the transition to Quebec sovereignty through the disciplines of constitutionalism. Only if these disciplines failed would it make sense to step outside the process, and even then Canadians, including Quebecers, would be better off for having used the constitutional process to regulate their behavior to that point.

It is simplistic to argue that, because the Canadian Constitution has proven incapable of accommodating Quebec's aspirations in the recent past, the amending formulas would pose an insurmountable obstacle to the ratification of a sovereignty agreement. This argument fails to take into account the distinct political and economic conditions – and thus the unique bargaining dynamics – that would be created by a 'yes' win in a sovereignty referendum. We think the process would have a better chance of working *because* of the crisis environment in which it would take place; unlike Meech Lake and Charlottetown, this crisis would be real, not just a threat. The consequences of failure would be obvious to all, giving the proceedings a tighter discipline. Before rejecting the approach we have outlined, critics – Quebecers and non-Quebecers alike – should consider carefully the alternatives, and ask whether either side would really be better off if it did not even *try* to reach agreement through a constitutional process.

NOTES

We would like to thank Mark Oulton for his research assistance, and Ken Boessenkool, Alan Brousseau, Alan Cairns, David Cameron, Jamie Cameron, Peter Hogg, John Richards, Richard Simeon, and Brian Slattery for their helpful comments on an earlier draft of this *Commentary*.

1 We prefer the phrase 'accession to sovereignty' over 'secession' to describe the process of constitutional change likely to follow a 'yes' vote. 'Secession' suggests a

clean exit – the cutting of all political ties with Canada. But a 'yes' vote in a sovereignty referendum could lead to the creation of new federal or confederal arrangements ('sovereignty association') between Quebec and Canada. When we do use the term 'secession,' we are referring to the removal of Quebec from *existing* constitutional arrangements, understanding that *new* forms of political association between Quebec and Canada are possible.

2 See Patrick J. Monahan and Michael J. Bryant (with Nancy C. Coté), *Coming to Terms with Plan B: Ten Principles Governing Secession*, C.D. Howe Institute Commentary 83 (Toronto: C.D. Howe Institute, June 1996), pp. 3–4; and Alan C. Cairns, *Looking into the Abyss: The Need for a Plan C*, C.D. Howe Institute Commentary 96 (Toronto: C.D. Howe Institute, September 1997).

3 Canada, Parliament, House of Commons, *Debates*, September 26, 1996, p. 4707.

4 The arguments and literature are reviewed in Neil Finkelstein, George Vegh, and Camille Joly, 'Does Quebec Have a Right to Secede at International Law?' *Canadian Bar Review* 74 (1995): 225; Thomas Franck et al., 'L'intégrité territoriale du Québec dans l'hypothèse de l'accession à la souveraineté,' in Commission d'étude des questions afférentes à l'accession du Québec à la souveraineté, *Projet de Rapport (annexe)* (Quebec, 1992), pp. 382–383; Grand Council of the Crees, *Sovereign Injustice: Forcible Inclusion of the James Bay Crees and Cree Territory into a Sovereign Quebec* (Nemaska, Que., 1995), pp. 103–118; Sharon Williams, *International Legal Effects of Secession by Quebec* (North York, Ont.: York University, Centre for Public Law and Public Policy, 1992), pp. 13–22. See also James Crawford, 'State Practice and International Law in Relation to Unilateral Secession' (report filed with the factum of the Attorney General of Canada in the Supreme Court reference, February 19, 1997).

A contrary view can be found in Daniel Turp, 'Quebec's Democratic Right to Self-Determination: A Critical and Legal Reflection,' in Stanley H. Hartt et al., *Tangled Web: Legal Aspects of Deconfederation*, The Canada Round 15 (Toronto: C.D. Howe Institute, 1992), pp. 99–124.

5 Bill 1, *An Act Respecting the Future of Quebec*, 1st Session, 35th Leg., Quebec, 1995.

6 For example, in the *Bertrand* case, the Attorney General of Quebec's legal submissions stated:

[l]e processus d'accession du Québec à la souveraineté relève essentiellement d'une démarche démocratique fondamentale qui trouve sa sanction dans le droit international public.

Motion to dismiss (April 12, 1996), *Bertrand v. Bégin*, Quebec 200-05-002117-955 (Sup. Ct.).

7 See Grand Council of the Crees, *Sovereign Injustice*; S. James Anaya, Richard Falk,

and Donat Pharand, *Canada's Fiduciary Obligation to Aboriginal Peoples in the Context of Accession to Sovereignty by Quebec, Vol. 1: International Dimensions* (Ottawa: Canada Communications Group, 1995); Renée Dupuis and Kent McNeil, *Canada's Fiduciary Obligation to Aboriginal Peoples in the Context of Accession to Sovereignty by Quebec, Vol. 2: Domestic Dimensions* (Ottawa: Canada Communications Group, 1995); and Canada, Royal Commission on Aboriginal Peoples, *Report*, Volume 2(1) (Ottawa: Canada Communications Group, 1996), pp. 93–106.

8 See Mary Ellen Turpel, 'Does the Road to Quebec Sovereignty Run through Aboriginal Territory?' in Daniel Drache and Roberto Perin, eds., *Negotiating with a Sovereign Quebec* (Toronto: Lorimer, 1992), pp. 93–106; and Kent McNeil, 'Aboriginal Nations and Quebec's Boundaries: Canada Couldn't Give What It Didn't Have,' in Drache and Perin eds., *Negotiating with a Sovereign Quebec*, pp. 107–123.

For a discussion of the Aboriginal peoples of Quebec and their homelands, see Ovide Mercredi and Mary Ellen Turpel, *In the Rapids: Navigating the Future of First Nations* (Toronto: Viking, 1994), pp. 165–185.

9 See Guy Laforest, *Trudeau and the End of a Canadian Dream* (Montreal; Kingston, Ont.: McGill-Queen's University Press , 1995), for a thorough explication of the reasons the *Constitution Act, 1982* lacks legitimacy in Quebec.

10 *Re Objection by Quebec to a Resolution to Amend the Constitution*, [1982] 2 S.C.R. 793. After the federal government decided to proceed with patriation, the Quebec government asked the Supreme Court of Canada to rule on whether the conventional requirement of a substantial degree of provincial consent to amendments affecting provincial powers had to include Quebec. The Court, in this reference, answered no.

11 Cairns, *Looking into the Abyss.*

12 For an argument in favor of such an approach by a non-Quebec Canadian scholar, see Denis Stairs, *Canada and Quebec after Québécois Secession: 'Realist' Reflections on an International Relationship* (Halifax, NS: Dalhousie University, Centre for Foreign Policy Studies, 1996).

13 See also the arguments on this point in Monahan and Bryant, *Coming to Terms with Plan B*, pp. 21–25.

14 See s. 35.1, *Constitution Act, 1982.*

15 Monahan and Bryant, *Coming to Terms with Plan B*, pp. 31–33.

16 For example, Peter Hogg, *Constitutional Law of Canada*, 4th ed. (Toronto: Carswell, 1996), p. 125.

17 Monahan and Bryant, *Coming to Terms with Plan B*, pp. 651–652.

18 Cairns, *Looking into the Abyss.*

19 See Canada, Royal Commission on Aboriginal Peoples, *Report*, vol. 5, p. 130.

20 José Woehrling, 'Les aspects juridiques d'une éventuelle sécession du Québec,' *Canadian Bar Review* (74): 293. Woehrling's conclusion finds support in two influential textbooks: Hogg, *Constitutional Law of Canada*, p. 125; and Henri Brun and

G. Tremblay, *Droit constitutionnel*, 2d ed. (Cowansville, Que.: Yvon Blais, 1990), p. 236.

21 Patrick Monahan, 'The Law and Politics of Québec Secession,' *Osgoode Hall Law Journal* 33 (1, 1995): 9.

22 A similar test is proposed by James Ross Hurley, who states that, to determine whether section 41 applies to a proposed amendment, 'one would have to begin by asking whether [it] would materially alter or affect any matter subject to the unanimity procedure.' See *Amending Canada's Constitution: History, Processes, Problems and Prospects* (Ottawa: Canada Communications Group, 1996), p. 81.

23 S.C. 1996, c. 1.

24 Alberta has a *de facto* veto since it has more than half the population of the prairie provinces.

25 The Atlantic provinces' veto could be invoked by any two of the three most populous provinces (New Brunswick, Nova Scotia, and Newfoundland). In addition, pursuant to an executive agreement negotiated by the premiers of Prince Edward Island, Nova Scotia, and New Brunswick – an agreement with moral if not legal force – the Atlantic veto could be exercised by Prince Edward Island with the support of either New Brunswick or Nova Scotia. The premiers agreed that Prince Edward Island would receive the automatic veto support of both New Brunswick and Nova Scotia if it first obtains the agreement of either of those governments. See 'PEI wins share in veto plan for constitutional changes,' *Globe and Mail* (Toronto), January 4, 1996.

26 According to the 1991 census, the combined population of the relevant provinces would be at least 25.8 million (92 percent of the total national population of 28.1 million), as follows: Ontario, 10.47 million; Quebec, 7.08 million; British Columbia, 3.38 million; Alberta, 2.6 million; one of Manitoba or Saskatchewan, at least 1.00 million; and two of New Brunswick, Nova Scotia, or Newfoundland, at least 1.33 million.

27 See Norman L. Nicholson, *The Boundaries of the Canadian Confederation* (Toronto: Macmillan, 1979), pp. 33, 93, for a description of the 1791 and 1851 enactments, respectively.

28 *Canada (Ontario Boundary) Act, 1889*, 52 & 53 Vict., c. 28 (U.K.).

29 See *An Act respecting the North-Western, Northern and North-Eastern Boundaries of the Province of Quebec*, S.C. 1898 (61 Vict.), c. 3; *The Quebec Boundaries Extension Act, 1912*, S.C. 1912 (2 Geo. V), c. 45.

30 *Re Labrador Boundary*, [1927] 2 D.L.R. 401.

31 The Cree, Inuit, and Montagnais likely would reject Quebec sovereignty decisively in a future referendum, as they did in three separate ballots held immediately prior to the official 1995 referendum – by 96 percent, 95 percent, and 99 percent, respectively. See Alan C. Cairns, 'The Legacy of the Referendum: Who Are We Now?' *Constitutional Forum* 7 (winter/spring 1996, nos. 2 and 3): 36.

32 See the discussion of the process followed in determining the borders of the Swiss canton of Jura in Monahan and Bryant, *Coming to Terms with Plan B*, pp. 16-17, 36-37.

33 Section 42(1)(c) of the *Constitution Act, 1982* provides that the '7/50' formula applies to an amendment in relation to 'the number of members by which a province is entitled to be represented in the Senate.'

34 Section 41(a) of the *Constitution Act, 1982* requires unanimous approval of amendments in relation to 'the office of the Queen, the Governor General and the Lieutenant Governor of a province.'

35 See sections 63 (power to appoint Cabinet members), 65 (continuation of executive powers), 71 (definition of the Quebec legislature), 82 (the power to summon the Quebec legislature), and 90 (powers of reservation and disallowance) of the *Constitution Act, 1867*.

36 Section 41(b) of the *Constitution Act, 1982* requires unanimous approval of amendments in relation to:

the right of a province to a number of members in the House of Commons not less than the number of Senators by which the province is entitled to be represented at the time this Part comes into force.

37 Section 41(c) of the *Constitution Act, 1982* requires unanimous approval of amendments to provisions in relation to 'the use of the English or the French language' in all of the provinces. We agree with Monahan ('The Law and Politics of Quebec Secession,' pp. 11–13) that an amendment that has the effect of canceling the application of these provisions in Quebec qualifies for the purposes of section 41(c).

38 See section 41(d) of the *Constitution Act, 1982*.

39 Instead, an amendment to the *Supreme Court Act*, R.S.C. 1985, c. S-26, deleting the guarantee of three Quebec judges, could be passed through the ordinary legislative process. See Hogg, *Constitutional Law of Canada*, pp. 70–71, 80; Woehrling, 'Les aspect juridiques d'une éventuelle sécession du Québec,' p. 311, n. 38.

For arguments to the contrary, see Monahan, 'The Law and Politics of Quebec Secession,' pp. 14–15; and Robert A. Young, *The Secession of Quebec and the Future of Canada* (Kingston, Ont.; Montreal: McGill-Queen's University Press, 1995), p. 248.

40 An amendment to this effect will likely soon be passed in any case. A resolution introduced in the House of Commons by Stéphane Dion, Minister of Intergovernmental Affairs, on April 22, 1997, would, if ratified by Parliament and the National Assembly, end the application of subsections 93(1) to (4) in Quebec. See Canada, Parliament, House of Commons, Debates, April 22, 1997, p. 10029.

41 R.S.C. 1985, c. E-3.

42 R.S.C. 1985, c. S-26.

43 Section 25 of the *Supreme Court Act*, R.S.C. 1985, c. S-26.

44 One way of doing so has been put forward in Monahan and Bryant, *Coming to Terms with Plan B*.

45 In British Columbia, the relevant legislation is the *Constitutional Amendment Approval Act*, R.S.B.C. 1996, c. 67, s. 1 (obligation to hold referendum prior to intro-duction of motion to ratify constitutional amendment in the legislature) and the *Referendum Act*, R.S.B.C. 1996, c. 400, ss. 4 and 5 (preference of more than 50 percent of validly cast ballots is binding on the government that initiated the referendum). In Alberta, it is the *Constitutional Referendum Act*, S.A. 1992, c. 22.25, s. 2(1) (obliga-tion to hold referendum prior to holding ratification vote in legislature) and s. 4(1) (preference of majority of validly cast ballots binding on the government that initi-ated the referendum).

An Ontario legislative committee has recommended adopting requirements simi-lar to those in British Columbia and Alberta, and the government is considering introducing a bill to implement the committee's proposals in the fall of 1997. See Ontario, Legislative Assembly, Standing Committee on the Legislative Assembly, *Final Report on Referenda*, 1st Session, 36th Leg. (June 1997), pp. 6–9; and James Rusk, 'Tax referendums proposed in Ontario,' *Globe and Mail* (Toronto), July 4, 1997, p. A3.

At least four other jurisdictions have legislation that permits and facilitates, but does not require, the holding of a referendum on matters of public interest. See the *Referendum and Plebiscite Act*, S.S. 1990-91, c. R-8.01, s. 3(1); the *Election Act*, R.S.N., c. E-3; *Loi sur la consultation populaire*, R.S.Q., c. C-64.1; the *Referendum Act*, S.C. 1992, c. 30, s. 3(1).

46 For an elaboration of this argument, see Peter W. Hogg, 'The Effect of a Referendum on Quebec Sovereignty,' *Canada Watch* 4 (August 1996, nos. 5 & 6): 89.

47 Monahan and Bryant, *Coming to Terms with Plan B*, pp. 33–35.

48 Patrick Boyer, *Direct Democracy in Canada: The History and Future of Referen-dums* (Toronto: Dundurn Press, 1992), p. 254.

49 The accord garnered majority support in just four provinces. See Peter H. Russell, *Constitutional Odyssey: Can Canadians Become a Sovereign People?* 2nd ed. (Toronto: University of Toronto Press, 1993), ch. 11.

50 The act provides that federal ratification of an amendment to which the act applies will not proceed 'unless the amendment has first been consented to by a majority of the provinces' (*Constitutional Amendments Act*, S.C.1996, c.1, s.1(1)). In the absence of a definition of provincial consent, we submit that either legislative ratifi-cation or popular assent through a referendum would suffice.

51 Section 35.1 of the *Constitution Act, 1982* supports the participation of representa-tives of Aboriginal peoples in the negotiation of constitutional amendments related

directly to them. We do not rule out the possibility that these representatives might choose to be guided by the wishes of their peoples as expressed through referendums; how they seek to determine and express their position is their affair. Our point is that, in addition to a five-region 'yes' vote on a negotiated agreement as a whole, Aboriginal approval of the provisions affecting their rights would also be required.

52 The five-region referendum rule would require majority approval in these provinces in any case, since British Columbia is a region all its own and, as noted, Alberta has more than 50 percent of the population of the prairie provinces.

53 See J. Monar et al., *The Maastricht Treaty on European Union: Legal Complexity and Political Dynamic* (Brussels: European Interuniversity Press, 1993).

54 Peter W. Hogg, 'Principles Governing the Secession of Quebec' (paper presented at the conference on 'Law, Democracy and Self-Determination,' Canadian Bar Association, May 22–23, 1997), p. 10.

55 For a full elaboration of these points, see Grand Council of the Crees, *Sovereign Injustice*; Anaya, Falk, and Pharand, *Canada's Fiduciary Obligation*, vol. 1; and Dupuis and McNeil, *Canada's Fiduciary Obligation*, vol. 2.

56 These are the Abenaki, Algonquin, Atikamekw, Cree, Huron, Mikmaq, Mohawk, Montagnais, Naskapi, and Malicite, and the Inuit of Ungava.

57 See Grand Council of the Crees, *Sovereign Injustice*, ch. 8; and Canada, Royal Commission on Aboriginal Peoples, *Report*, vol. 2, ch. 2.

58 See Canada, Task Force to Review Comprehensive Claims Policy, *Living Treaties: Lasting Agreements* (Ottawa: Department of Indian Affairs and Northern Development, 1985), ch. 1; and Quebec, *Summary of the Comprehensive Offer of the Quebec Government to the Atikamekw and Montagnais Nations* (Quebec City: Government of Quebec, December 1994).

59 Robert Young suggests that there will be strong pressures in this direction; see *The Secession of Quebec and the Future of Canada*, pp. 226–227.

Walking the Tightrope: Canada's Financial System between a 'Yes' Vote and Quebec Secession

DAVID LAIDLER and WILLIAM B.P. ROBSON

The separatist program for an independent Quebec involves the use of the Canadian dollar by the prospective new country. The reasons are straightforward. Custom and experience are powerful forces in monetary affairs, and most Quebec residents seem to prefer conducting transactions and storing wealth in Canadian dollars. Furthermore, should Quebec secede, monetary continuity would help maintain financial stability in particular and promote economic efficiency in general, both in a newly independent Quebec and in the rest of Canada (ROC).

Obstacles to Maintaining the Currency Union

Yet no matter how sincere and emphatic the separatist commitment to continue using the Canadian dollar – or the ROC dollar, as it would be after secession – and no matter how desirable that outcome might now seem on all sides, there are reasons, by now well known,[1] for doubting that a currency union between the two new countries would survive.

A national currency issued by a national central bank is not merely a symbol of sovereignty; it is a tool of economic management. Governments can, depending on circumstances and policymakers' time horizons, use this tool to pursue inflation targets, influence short-term interest rates and the exchange rate, and support the banking system with potentially unlimited supplies of funds in the event of crisis. Numerous circumstances, both immediately after secession and in the more distant future, might prompt a future independent Quebec government to establish its own currency. Transitional pressure on its financial system, persistent balance of payments problems, major divergences in economic fortunes or policy between an independent Quebec and the ROC – one or more of these might make a new currency, which would be a currency of uncertain value, attractive to the Quebec government. This possibility would always exist, and households, businesses and policymakers on both sides of the new border would never forget it.

Furthermore, important parts of Canada's financial infrastructure would cease to exist on Quebec's independence unless negotiations launched well in advance of secession proved fruitful, a prospect made doubtful by serious political obstacles, and all but impossible if secession occurred through a unilateral act by Quebec. Independent Quebec financial institutions would very likely lose access to key elements of Canada's payments system and to the lender-of-last-resort facilities provided by the Bank of Canada, while their depositors would face an uncertain deposit insurance regime. These considerations would, in and of themselves, create nervousness in both an independent Quebec and the ROC.

If nervousness stemming from any of these considerations prompted a movement of funds out of an independent Quebec on any scale, or a deterioration of financial conditions in the Canadian monetary union as a whole, the attractiveness of maintaining the currency union in the eyes of an independent Quebec would decline. This decline would, in turn, provoke further reactions on the part of asset holders, and so on. The prospect of a breakdown of the monetary union might thus trigger the chain of events that would bring the breakdown about.

The Unique Challenge of the Postreferendum Period

Modern financial technology makes it easy for expectations about the future to influence current behaviour. There is, therefore, a strong possibility that a chain of events tending to undermine the currency union could begin before actual secession, when independence would appear inevitable to holders of money and other financial assets.

The uncertain and volatile period between a 'yes' victory and actual independence would present particular difficulties of this kind. During this interval, which might be quite protracted, existing federal laws and institutions would remain in place and existing regulatory relationships would remain in effect, but their ultimate durability would be in serious question. At the same time, efforts to prevent Canada's dissolution in some quarters and to negotiate it in others would add awkward political elements to the situation. The technical difficulties and policy dilemmas involved have not so far attracted the attention they merit in discussions of the economic consequences of Quebec secession – hence this *Commentary*.

Preview of Conclusions

Our first key conclusion is that federal politicians and institutions are ill placed to address these difficulties. There is not likely to be advance planning in Ottawa to preserve the monetary union after secession since, particularly if it involved potential co-management of financial infrastructure by the two successor states, such planning would appear to abet the separatist cause. In the absence of advance planning, the Bank of Canada and the Canada Deposit Insurance Corporation (CDIC) would find it difficult to act. Extending support to Quebec's financial system in the absence of enforceable agreements with the Quebec government about its own obligations could expose ROC taxpayers to sizable losses, so the guarantees the Bank and the CDIC currently offer to the financial system would acquire an expiry date once separation became imminent.

Our second key conclusion is that it therefore falls primarily to the Quebec government, whose jurisdiction would not be interrupted by independence, to work out and publicize plans for providing locally the transactions and insurance services to the financial sector that are currently available from federal insti tutions. If it is serious about preserving the Canadian monetary union while achieving political independence, the Quebec government must start to address these matters now, not leave them to be addressed in the charged environment of a referendum campaign and its aftermath.

Dimensions of the Problem

As recent events in Asia remind us, financial crises are multifaceted and tend to develop rapidly as changing expectations about future events influence present behavior. In preparation for detailed discussion of financial developments surrounding a Quebec secession, it helps therefore to start with an outline of political and economic possibilities.

Some Scenarios

On the political front, a number of events must happen before secession. Several are familiar and regularly attract attention: the separatists must first win the next Quebec election; they must then call a referendum; and then they must win it. The next stage in the process is murkier. Either negotiations between Quebec and the federal government (almost certainly involving, formally or informally, other provincial governments) would result in agreed terms of separation, or a period

Table 1
Possible Financial Consequences of Quebec Secession

Scenario	A+	A	A−	B+	B	B−	C	D	D−
Shift of deposits from Quebec	N	Y	Y	Y	Y	Y	Y	Y	Y
Weakness or failure of banks in Quebec	N	N	Y	Y	Y	Y	Y	Y	Y
Fiscal problems of the Quebec government	N	N	N	Y	Y	Y	Y	Y	Y
Currency crisis	N	N	N	N	Y	Y	Y	Y	Y
Weakness or failure of banks in the ROC	N	N	N	N	N	Y	Y	Y	Y
Fiscal problems of governments in the ROC	N	N	N	N	N	N	Y	Y	Y
Fiscal crisis in Quebec	N	N	N	N	N	N	N	Y	Y
Fiscal crisis in the ROC	N	N	N	N	N	N	N	N	Y

of no or fruitless negotiations would precede a unilateral declaration of Quebec independence. It is this last stage, with its profound uncertainties and unsettled political and legal environment, that is most challenging to think through.

On the economic front, various authors have devised secession-related scenarios, ranging from business as usual at one end to utter disaster at the other. In general, the former envision easy maintenance of the currency union; the latter, an immediate and damaging collapse. Given the uncertainties involved, it makes sense to consider a range of possibilities, as in Table 1, which identifies various possible events as either occurring (Y), or not occurring (N). Reading from the top left-hand corner, the table moves downwards through events of greater seriousness, which combine to produce, moving from left to right, scenarios of increasing unpleasantness.

Inspired by the 'B-movie scenario' label that some critics have applied to our earlier writing on this subject, we give letter grades to various points on this spectrum, ranging from an A+ situation in which the currency union's survival would scarcely be in question, to a D situation in which it would vanish in a matter of days or even hours. The progression from one to another situation is more continuous than a series of letter grades suggests, but Table 1 nevertheless highlights key events bearing on the union's chances of survival.

At the positive extreme, reflected in the first column of the table, Quebec's prospective and/or actual accession to independence might have negligible adverse financial or fiscal consequences: an A+ outcome, in which there was no appreciable movement of deposits out of Quebec. Less positively, as we move to the right (and start to factor in some of the more problematic developments listed vertically in the table), some capital flight might occur. If this flight were large enough, it might threaten the operations of one or more financial institutions in Quebec by draining them of liquidity.

If the disruption of credit markets in Quebec became serious enough, it could put the Quebec government under fiscal pressure as it faced demands for emergency loans or grants. Rating agencies might react to a deteriorating economic and financial environment by down- grading Quebec government debt, which would increase its borrowing costs and potentially restrict its access to credit.

The table shows a run on the (still common) currency as a further adverse event. In reality, downward pressure on the dollar would likely accompany the developments just described – indeed, moving from A+ to D would likely involve increasingly severe pressure – as both Canadian and foreign holders of Canadian-dollar assets sought the shelter of a more secure currency. There are two reasons, however, for thinking of a severe currency crisis as a quantum deterioration.

First, the Bank of Canada's usual response to weakness in the dollar's external value prompted by loss of confidence is to make dollars scarce, buying them in foreign exchange markets and choking their creation with high short-term interest rates. The adverse effect of higher interest rates on borrowers can put financial institutions under further pressure as prospects for loan repayment deteriorate.

Second, as the Asian crisis has recently reminded us, currency crises can be very damaging to financial institutions with large, un-hedged foreign-currency debts or a pronounced reliance on new foreign-currency deposits to fund their lending, adding the threat of insolvency to the illiquidity pressures just mentioned.

Moving further across and down Table 1, a more intense crisis could threaten the stability of financial institutions elsewhere in Canada and put fiscal pressure, including possible rating downgrades, on the federal government and perhaps provincial governments as well. And if the deterioration proceeded far enough, we would reach the right-hand side of the table – and encompass most or all of the negative developments listed: the Quebec government and conceivably the federal government could have trouble rolling over debts and have to approach creditors with rescheduling plans.[2]

Such outcomes are surely much worse than B scenarios, so we award them D ratings. Events a couple of years ago in Mexico and more recently in Asia hint at what the more difficult scenarios envisioned here might entail. As these examples also remind us, markets may overshoot in such cases, with currencies falling further, interest rates rising more, and economies suffering more in the short run than later on. Such temporary moves might warrant a grade of E or F, and they can leave long-lasting scars, as when a severely depressed currency bankrupts a basically sound business with heavy, unhedged short-term foreign-currency debts. The prospect of longer-term recovery for the economy overall, however, suggests stopping at D–.

Whatever the precise letter grade, the key point is that the currency union would likely not survive such events. In a financial crisis, the government of an independent Quebec would find the extra policy leverage of a separate currency – such as the ability to inject newly created money into staggering banks and the option of exchange-rate devaluation – extremely attractive.[3]

Political Twists

On quick examination, the unpleasant slide from A toward D makes seemingly clear the key challenge facing the two sides in the awkward interval between a 'yes' vote in a referendum and actual separation: do anything necessary to stay around A. There are, however, considerations that make this easier said than done.

For a start, in the period between a 'yes' vote and actual secession, some in the ROC would urge allowing the consequences of a capital flight to take their course in Quebec, expecting the movement toward secession to lose momentum even at that late date. We do not dwell on this line of argument here. It is not clear that such a tactic would succeed. Even if it did, it would hardly prepare the way for a lasting reconciliation between the two parties. It would, however, likely have advocates in the ROC, adding a highly awkward factor to the ROC's deliberations.

More generally, the earlier a drain of deposits began, the more scope there would be for the policy response to it to affect other developments. These would, in turn, tend to hasten or slow the flow of money. For example, the handling of any financial instability occurring during pre-independence negotiations could influence the remainder of the negotiations. During the possibly quite lengthy period between a referendum and independence, Ottawa's power over monetary arrangements would give its negotiators a bargaining lever with which to seek concessions from Quebec in other areas.

The Canadian Financial System

The possibility of monetary complications emerging in the runup to a Quebec secession and becoming intertwined with the politics of the process reflects the fact that there is more to the Canadian monetary union than a common currency. The monetary system is a means of effecting transactions of all sorts – for transferring funds between individuals as they trade with, and grant credit to, one another, both directly and through the mediation of financial institutions.

Many transfers of funds involve cash. Banknotes and coins have a couple of unique features that make them attractive to users. As liabilities of the Bank of Canada – rather than, say, of a private financial institution – cash is uniquely secure. And they are legal tender, which means that, in the absence of explicit agreements to do otherwise, individuals and businesses accept them within Canada.

Most transfers, however, involve moving funds between chartered banks, trust companies, *caisses populaires*, and other financial institutions – for example, when a customer uses a debit card and funds move from an account at the card-issuing bank to the retailer's account at a different bank, or when the retailer uses a cheque drawn on that account to pay a supplier. Such transfers between institutions occur through the Automated Clearing Settlement System (ACSS) operated by the Canadian Payments Association. A subset of 13 financial institutions, known as 'direct clearers,' plays a central role here. They use deposits held at the Bank of Canada to settle transactions both among themselves and on behalf of the other participants, known as 'indirect clearers.'[4] Deposits at the Bank of Canada are very like cash. They are uniquely secure because the institution at which they are held cannot fail and can provide funds in unlimited amounts, and participants in the clearing system have not the slightest doubt that they will be accepted in discharge of obligations.

In the current context, these details of clear- ing and settlement in Canada matter because such systems work smoothly only when each participant has assurance that all others will honor their obligations. Direct clearers pay close attention to the financial condition of other direct clearers, as well as that of the indirect clearers for whom they act. If the soundness of a direct clearer came into question, others would try to reduce their exposure to it, by ceasing to give immediate credit for cheques drawn on it, for example. If the financial condition of an indirect clearer came into question, the direct clearer that acted for it might start asking for collateral, or compensatory balances, in connection with any exposure the direct clearer assumed on its behalf. If the direct clearer's concerns became deep enough, it could, with 24 hours' notice, end its relationship with the indirect clearer.

Financial institutions involved in the ACSS not only know that their counterparties are financially sound: they also know that the Bank of Canada will provide temporary advances to cover potentially large end-of-day overdrafts in the settlement accounts of individual direct clearers that arise from normal day-to-day variations in the timing of transactions. These loans prevent sound institutions from getting into trouble because of temporary liquidity problems. The Bank's willingness to cover these overdrafts depends partly on the direct clearers' being subject to regulation and inspection by various supervisory agencies: the Office of the Superintendent of Financial Institutions (OSFI) in the case of federally chartered or incorporated institutions, and provincial agencies in the case of the Alberta Treasury Branches, credit unions, and *caisses populaires*. Furthermore, such overdrafts must be fully collateralized: the Bank knows that if, despite its vigilance, it makes loans to an institution that subsequently fails, it has first claim on the collateral pledged when it covered the overdraft, and it has recourse to the courts in recovering its funds. (Other clearing systems and inter-bank markets in Canada, and their relationship to the ACSS, are discussed in Box 1.)

The Impact of Secession on the Financial System

Although the extent of the disruption caused by a Quebec secession would depend on negotiations after a successful referendum, these arrangements would certainly change with secession. Once Quebec was independent, *all* financial institutions operating there would be regulated by its authorities and subject to its laws. These institutions and laws might initially be very similar to those of the ROC, and the formal regulatory environment affecting Quebec-based institutions already subject to provincial regulation might also change very little. It is nevertheless hard to see how – in the absence of a comprehensive agreement on matters such as the regulation of financial institutions and collateral arrangements – the Bank of Canada could have sufficient confidence in the actual application of the laws and regulations of an independent Quebec to treat its financial institutions in the ACSS in the same way the province's institutions are now treated. Without an explicit agreement negotiated in advance, financial institutions based in Quebec that currently have direct-clearer status would therefore lose it on independence.

Losing direct access to the ACSS and the services it provides would not, in the long run, be a crippling blow to residents of an independent Quebec. There are other avenues for carrying on Canadian dollar transactions among financial institutions. As long as a direct-clearer ACSS member remained confident in it, a financial institution in an independent Quebec might be able to access the ACSS as an indirect clearer through subsidiaries or through branches (if secession occurred after proposed reforms are implemented to allow foreign banking through branches in Canada). As well, depending on an independent Quebec's attitude toward branch banking, current branches of Canadian institutions located in Quebec could become branches either of ROC financial institutions or of their subsidiaries in an independent Quebec, with access to the ROC payments system through their ROC head offices or parents.

At the same time, the whole range of credit arrangements among financial institutions that support their exchanges of securities, foreign exchange, and Canadian dollar assets outside the payments system would be reorganized to function like those currently existing among institutions based in different countries. Ultimately, such a system would be less efficient than current arrangements within the Canadian monetary union, but there are countries (Liberia and Panama, for example) that use other countries' currencies; an independent Quebec using the ROC dollar would simply be a bigger and much more sophisticated example of such an arrangement.

In the runup to independence, however, disruptive forces might prevent such an arrangement coming into being in the longer run. In particular, an independent Quebec's financial institutions' prospective loss of access to the ACSS would create problems. As secession became imminent, financial institutions based in the ROC would become less willing to expose themselves to credit risks associated with institutions inside Quebec. As noted in Box 1, this reluctance would probably manifest itself first outside the payments system, where financial institutions would be able, often quietly, to draw back from riskier transactions by trimming the overall size of their exposures, cutting their links with smaller and weaker-looking partners, or changing the terms on which they would grant credit. Inside the payments system, participants would hestitate to take any defensive steps only so long as they were sure that the Bank of Canada was willing to continue in its backstopping role, making the Bank's reaction to the legal and financial uncertainties of secession critical.

How might the Bank of Canada act? It would have two related problems to ponder.

First, it would need to consider the financial stability of financial institutions exposed to developments in Quebec. It would be one thing for the Bank to cover normal liquidity shortfalls and quite another for it to provide extended support to institutions that seemed headed for insolvency. Second, it would need to make decisions about both the quality of collateral put up by exposed institutions and its ability to collect after secession. The more severe the problems of exposed institutions became, and the more doubtful the Bank was of its ability to realize collateral pledged against the loans it made, the less willing it would be to support them. And as the Bank's willingness diminished and it began, for example, to advance cash through purchase and resale agreements (of Government of Canada securities) rather than loans, the more nervous other ACSS members and depositors would become.

Anatomy of a Crisis

As Table 1 suggests, varying degrees of nervousness can have different effects. Let us begin with something closer to the A end.

**Box 1   Other Clearing and Settlement Systems and
Their Links to the ACSS**

The Automated Clearing Settlement System is the linchpin of Canada's infrastructure for financial transactions. The bulk of its activity, in terms of volume,
relates to retail transactions – cheques, bank drafts, and the like. Financial
institutions also transact with each other in many other ways. Some – such as
the Debt Clearing Service operated by the Canadian Depository for Securities
Limited, which handles transactions in federal government bonds and treasury
bills, and Multinet, which handles foreign exchange transactions – are centralized; others are decentralized. Currently, however, actual payments related to
dealings carried out in these other systems go through the ACSS.

The legal and financial uncertainties of secession probably would begin to
impede transactions outside the ACSS before they showed up in the ACSS
itself. When the Northland Bank and Canadian Commercial Bank got into
trouble in 1986, for example, they continued to participate in the ACSS even
after losing their ability to conduct many other kinds of interbank business.
The ACSS seems an apt focus for this investigation, however, because of the
Bank of Canada's intimate involvement in its operations and its key role in
daily reconciliation of outstanding obligations of Canada's principal financial
institutions (extenders of credit in the Debt Clearing Service, for example,
must be direct clearers). Simply put, the ACSS is the most robust element in
the Canadian financial system. An institution that loses access to it will
encounter, or will likely already have encountered, difficulties participating in
other systems.

The Canadian Payments Association will soon have a new Large Value
Transfer System (LVTS) in place that will provide finality of settlement for
the more sizable transactions that now pass through the ACSS. (LVTS participants will be required to have settlement accounts at the Bank of Canada.)
From the perspective of this *Commentary*, the LVTS matters because it will
put a large portion, by value, of the transactions now occuring through the
ACSS into a system where counterparty risk will become a more active concern of other participating financial institutions, and they will have greater lat-
itude in dealing with it. (The LVTS will have two streams of payments:
'tranche 1' payments fully collateralized by pledges from the sending institution to the system as a whole; and 'tranche 2' payments limited by the bilateral
lines of credit institutions extend to each other.) If legal and financial uncertainties prompt doubts about the soundness of institutions exposed to secession
or the quality of collateral such as Government of Quebec bonds, the LVTS is,
like other systems outside the ACSS, likely to become a more costly

and difficult environment for those institutions. The significance of the ACSS as the 'last, best' link in Canada's payments system grows when institutions are driven to funnel more of their business through it as they become less able to deal in the LVTS and other non-ACSS systems.

A final point of interest about non-ACSS systems is that the 1996 *Payment Clearing and Settlement Act* gave the Bank of Canada extensive powers to intervene in systems that appear to pose important risks for the financial system as a whole. In a 1997 guideline on the Bank's proposed uses of these powers, the first criterion listed under its minimum standards for a sound system was: 'Clearing and settlement systems should have a well-founded legal basis under all relevant jurisdictions.' Whether the Bank would react to secession-related concerns by intervening in non-ACSS systems under the act is unclear. Nonetheless, if it chose to do so, many of the same conundrums it would face in connection with the ACSS would also arise in those cases.

Shifts of Funds between Branches of the Same Institution

Initially, nervous depositors might only move funds out of branches of particular financial institutions in Quebec into branches of the same institutions in the ROC. Such a movement of funds within an institution would not affect its overall liquidity or the size of its assets and liabilities and would not, therefore, appear to present an immediate policy problem. It could, however, affect the riskiness of the institution's balance sheet. Canadian banks currently tolerate sizable mismatches between their assets and liabilities in various regions as a normal consequence of their role in matching saving and investment opportunities across the country. Although such mismatches are not alarming when a common legal framework and currency apply everywhere, the prospect of Quebec secession would change this situation in important ways.

Quebec-based assets would be threatened with a new legal framework and possible future redenomination in a new currency of unknown value. The total amount of exposed assets is uncertain, but as of mid-1997, Canada's chartered banks had $85 billion of Canadian-dollar assets (other than cash) booked in Quebec. Since the equivalent figure for liabilities was $71 billion, assets subject to secession-related impairment exceeded similarly exposed liabilities by $13 billion.[5] In an A environment, banks might view this gap without much alarm, but even in this rosy scenario, it seems unlikely they would let it grow. So a movement of funds out of Quebec, even if only to branches of the same institutions in the ROC, would likely produce downward pressure on the amount of credit extended in Quebec: a lending slowdown or even a credit crunch.

Drains of Deposits from Particular Institutions

Drains of funds that disproportionately affected the liabilities of specific institutions would present a more difficult problem. Depositors might move their funds out of institutions headquartered in Quebec only, or out of institutions headquartered elsewhere in Canada that seemed disproportionately exposed to secession-related risks or volatility in the financial system generally. Either way, the banks affected would have problems with both their liquidity and the overall size of their balance sheets.

If deposits began to move on any scale, even institutions with assets of unimpeachable quality might have trouble selling them fast enough to meet their depositors' demands for funds. If the quality of some of the assets themselves was impaired by the prospect of secession, sales over any reasonable time horizon could become impossible. Such developments would quickly manifest themselves in reduced access for the exposed institutions in interbank markets (as described in Box 1). These difficulties would begin to spill over into the payments system. Given the potential for problems in the financial system to propagate, affecting other financial institutions and credit markets more generally, it is easy to see why this A– scenario could lead to something worse in short order.

Coping in Principle

Until the moment of Quebec independence, there would continue to be an array of federal agencies with mandates to help financial institutions cope with the difficulties just described.

The Role of the Bank of Canada
The Bank of Canada, a Crown corporation, can trade in certain securities and lend to financial institutions on good collateral. These powers enable it to supply financial institutions with funds so that no solvent institution, faced with a temporary shortfall, need fail for want of an immediate buyer for otherwise sound assets. The very existence of these powers reduces the probability of such a drain, moreover, by eliminating the incentive for depositors to withdraw funds from institutions they think solvent, but whose liquidity they doubt.

The Role of the Superintendent of Financial Institutions
The Bank of Canada's mandate relates to liquidity problems. It is intended to prevent temporary shortfalls from triggering system-wide problems, not to support unsound institutions. The Bank does not, furthermore, itself make judg-

ments about solvency. This is mainly the task of the OSFI, a federal agency that, in turn, works closely with the CDIC in making such judgments about federally incorporated institutions. (The Bank has the power, if it wishes, to request the OSFI to undertake a special examination of an institution, a right it has never exercised.)

The Role of the CDIC

The CDIC, though privately funded through premiums paid by member institutions, is responsible to the federal government for its operations.[6] In pursuit of its fundamental goal of promoting the stability of the Canadian financial system, the CDIC has wide-ranging powers to deal with unsound and/or insolvent institutions. Its core function is to protect depositors, particularly small ones, from the consequences of an institution's closing its doors. It guarantees deposits at member institutions against losses up to $60,000. It also has discretion to compensate bigger losses in situations where doing so might reduce the cost of liquidating a failed institution. Equally important for this discussion, it can also arrange, or make, loans to institutions in difficulty and assist in the takeover of their business by a sound competitor.[7]

As with the Bank of Canada's lender-of-last-resort powers related to liquidity problems, the CDIC's safety net reduces depositors' incentive to withdraw funds from institutions whose soundness they doubt. It thus enhances the recovery prospects of institutions in difficulty and eases an orderly windup of those beyond recovery. It also reduces the chances of contagion in the rest of the system in the wake of one institution's difficulties.

Coping in Practice

Real-life financial crises – even ones arising from the functioning of markets, let alone from the dissolution of a country – present decisions less clear-cut than the foregoing account suggests. Liquidity and solvency problems are harder to distinguish in practice than in principle. To take the most obvious example: the difficulty of selling assets quickly may mean that an institution with positive value as a going concern will have negative value if wound up. Judgments about the worth of assets are also difficult to make when the environment affecting them is changing. Real estate, for instance, is obviously sensitive to the local economy and to political risks, of which secession is a particularly dramatic example.

It can also take some time for the true extent of an institution's problems to become evident. For example, the difficulties of the Northland Bank and Canadian Commercial Bank – both of which ultimately collapsed in 1985 – initially appeared to the Inspector General of Banks (the immediate predecessor of the

OSFI) merely to stem from lack of liquidity. Shutting down an institution, moreover, can inflict damage on its depositors, creditors, workers, and owners. Regulators and their political masters are naturally wary of taking such action.

Particular Problems of Quebec Secession

The Bank of Canada, the OSFI, and the CDIC were not designed to deal with financial instability arising from a political crisis of the magnitude Quebec secession would create. Consequently, it is not clear whether, and how, they would respond to its demands or how the key decisions would be made.

The Federal Government's Options

This lack of clarity about the roles and actions of federal agencies would be unlikely to change prior to the uncertainties following a 'yes' vote for Quebec independence.

Obstacles to Advance Preparation
One key impediment to advance planning for the financial events that might follow a 'yes' vote is uncertainty about how large and quick the reaction might be. The relatively calm financial environment immediately before the October 1995 referendum – a vote that polls had shown was going to be close – seems to support the argument that business would go on much as usual on the morning after the vote and that Ottawa could deal with anything that did happen on an *ad hoc* basis. Also weighing in favor of a do-nothing stance is fear that visible advance preparation would intensify any movement toward secession.

Yet one could also contend that the con-sequences of an actual 'yes' vote would be much more serious than those of the 'no' of the October 1995 referendum, however close it was. Moreover, the experience of that near miss likely would make depositors and financial institutions quicker to react next time. In the face of such conflicting tendencies, the do-nothing stance might prevail by default.

Even if knowledge of the likely market reaction to a 'yes' vote were more precise, however, neither the federal government nor any agency answerable to it would likely take prereferendum measures to guarantee the post-secession continuation of access by Quebec-based financial institutions to Canada's existing financial infrastructure. Particularly if such measures involved co-management of financial infrastructure by the two successor states, they would appear to encourage a 'yes' vote. For identical reasons, advance preparations for the interim period between a 'yes' vote and actual secession – discussions between Ottawa and Quebec City regarding collateral and judgments about financial institu-tion solvency, for example – are also highly unlikely.

It appears then that, in the awkward interval between a 'yes' vote in a referendum and actual secession, Canada would have substantially the same financial infrastructure and regulatory environment that it now has.

The Problematic 'Save-the-Monetary-Union-at-All-Costs' Strategy

Under those circumstances, federal politicians might try to stop a flow of money out of Quebec by short-circuiting normal procedures. They might, for example, lean on the OSFI to soften judgments about a Quebec-based institution's solvency by assuming that secession would not occur, and pressure the Bank of Canada to alleviate the institution's liquidity problems, despite possible doubts about the quality of its collateral.

As already noted, others might urge letting Quebecers 'twist in the wind,' hoping to weaken the secessionists' negotiating position. Even leaving this argument aside, however, there would be key reasons not to throw money at the problem. Suppose, for example, that secession went ahead and an institution that had received support failed while Bank of Canada loans made against Quebec government securities were still outstanding. The ROC's central bank could be left holding collateral of greatly impaired value. At worst, literally tens of billions of dollars in loans made to exposed financial institutions could turn to losses after secession if collateral pledged were to lose value or become inaccessible.[8]

The ROC electorate would not likely support such an operation long enough for the response to be effective in preventing a move- ment toward D, since its costs would be too uncertain and it would appear to appease separatists. Its principal beneficiaries, moreover, would be residents of Quebec – immediate authors of the crisis and soon-to-be residents of a foreign country.

The Reactions of Federal Institutions on Their Own

What if, on the other hand, elected politicians left it to the Bank of Canada, the OSFI, and the CDIC to cope with the crisis?

The Bank of Canada

The Bank of Canada's first reaction, as always in cases of liquidity problems, would be guided by two aims: to preserve the overall viability of the financial system; and to protect from losses its shareholder, the federal government (and through it Canadian taxpayers). Although last-resort loans presumably would be available to any institution suffering liquidity problems, the collateral requirements against such loans to exposed institutions could become more stringent, since not all securities would be equally attractive in the face of imminent secession.

The Superintendent of Financial Institutions
The position of the OSFI – the judge of the solvency of federally incorporated financial institutions and the agency whose judgment the Bank of Canada would formally seek if such an institution appeared to be in trouble – would be very difficult. The value of key parts of financial institutions' portfolios of assets in Quebec (such as the over $35 billion in mortgages held by chartered banks) would be sensitive to secession, making guesses about the likelihood of secession's actually occurring important in judging institutional solvency. Other assets, such as claims on other financial institutions, would be vulnerable to financial turbulence, giving an element of self-fulfilling prophecy to any assessment the OSFI made. Further complicating the OSFI's position would be the damage to public confidence – and possible consequences for the presecession negotiations – that acknowledgment of its difficulties in making judgments might create.

The CDIC
The CDIC, which presumably would continue covering new deposits at member institutions in Quebec until the moment of secession, would find itself in a position similar to that of both the Bank of Canada and the OSFI.[9] Any substantial flow of funds out of institutions in Quebec could result in calls on the CDIC for loans. It need not make such loans since it has the power to cancel the contracts of institutions it deems insolvent. But it would find those judgments difficult to make.

The CDIC would also find some of its usual tools hard to use. Once Quebec was firmly committed to independence, the CDIC could hardly, for example, arrange the takeover of a Quebec-headquartered institution in difficulty by one headquartered elsewhere in Canada. Even arranging a takeover by another headquartered in Quebec might encounter resistance from the Quebec government. The CDIC would also be unlikely to offer any *de facto* guarantees above the $60,000 deposit insurance limit, as it oriented itself more toward protecting its members and taxpayers in the ROC from losses. These considerations might also preclude the possibility of the CDIC's making last-resort loans on its own account to institutions in difficulty.

In short, the extent of the protection offered by the CDIC against losses encountered by institutions in Quebec and against financial instability more generally would be severely eroded by a 'yes' vote long before actual indecence shut down its operations in Quebec.

The Quebec Government's Role

To sum up, the search for ways in which existing federal institutions might cope effectively with a drain of deposits from Quebec financial institutions is frustrating. Key integration and backstopping functions that now underpin Canada's financial system would erode or disappear altogether if Quebec seceded. This fact would increase the stress on the payments system as other markets spanning the incipient border seized up. And it would inhibit Bank of Canada, OSFI, and CDIC actions during the period between a referendum and formal independence.

As depositors became aware of the constraints on these institutions, their nervousness would increase, making a drain out of Quebec – and a move from an A+ scenario toward less comfortable territory – more likely. On the federal side, the political obstacles to measures that would allow these institutions to act over the crisis period appear formidable. Even if the approach of secession lessened the constraint against appearing supportive of separatism, it would simultaneously increase fears of being left 'holding the bag.'

The search for a credible backup for Quebec institutions that is not time limited may, then, be more fruitful on the Quebec side of the border. The Quebec government would be better placed to provide such guarantees because its jurisdiction would continue to run in Quebec after independence. Moreover, at least one institution that could offer a measure of back-up in the event of separation already exists – the Quebec Deposit Insurance Board (QDIB).

Deposit Insurance

By law, the QDIB already insures retail deposits in Quebec, although overlap between its coverage and that of the CDIC has resulted in agreements between the two institutions as to which stands first in line in which cases. After secession, the QDIB would naturally expand its operations to the whole Quebec system. A secessionist Quebec government that intended to maintain the currency union could announce well before a referendum that, should a continuation of current Canadian monetary arrangements prove impossible, the QDIB would assume full responsibility for all deposit insurance in Quebec, with the backing of the financial resources of the Quebec government behind it.

As an important accompanying step, the Quebec government could prepare to provide the necessary support. The QDIB currently maintains a line of credit with the CDIC, which, in turn, has access to the federal treasury and thus ultimately to the money-creating power of the Bank of Canada. This arrangement, however, would not endure past secession and would therefore lose credibility before that event. Well before the uncertainties of the postreferendum period threatened difficulty in raising funds, the Quebec government would need to set aside a stock of Canadian dollars sufficiently large to provide a credible substitute backstop.

Backstopping Banks in an Independent Quebec
As for clearing and settlement arrangements, an independent Quebec could facilitate, perhaps through its existing credit-union structure, a system that would reduce its financial institutions need for access to the ACSS in dealing among themselves. A further stock of Canadian dollars held by the newly established clearing-house of an independent Quebec could deal with the end-of-day shortfalls that would occur in transactions internal to Quebec. A much larger stock – which, again, would be much easier and cheaper to raise in advance of the referendum – would be needed to deal with shortfalls that might occur in transactions with the ROC. Since the clearing house could not create new Canadian dollars, it could never provide as complete a backstop to the clearing system as that currently available from the Bank of Canada, so the amount would need to be large.

As with the war chest needed for credible deposit insurance, it is hard to put a figure on the exact amount of money needed. In qualitative terms, the sum would need to be big enough to engender confidence in its capacity to serve as the reserve base for an independent Quebec's financial system, not just in tranquil times but in the more difficult and possibly protracted circumstances that would surround secession. If it could not engender such confidence, there would always be the prospect that a credit crunch might induce Quebec to establish its own currency to inject funds into its banks. This prospect would make more likely the drain of funds out of Quebec that would create such a crunch in the first place.

Publicizing the New Arrangements
Since confidence in the durability of the monetary system is critical to its maintenance, a further key element in Quebec's advance planning is dissemination of information about the new arrangements. Stories of the Quebec government's financial preparations ('le plan O') around the October 1995 referendum began circulating only after the event and appear to have focused on supporting the government's finances rather than the financial system.[10] At the time of the referendum itself, there was no information at all of the kind that would give

households and businesses, inside Quebec as well as outside, confidence in the security of their assets.

Holders of deposits in Quebec-based financial institutions need to know that effective insurance coverage would be maintained after secession. Financial institutions in Quebec and in the ROC need to know, in advance, what resources would be available to ensure that cheques did not bounce after secession. One of the highest-profile ways the Quebec government could provide such assurance would be for it to report, as part of its regular fiscal policy pronouncements, its progress toward building up the necessary reserves of cash – although, as just noted, it is hard to be sure exactly how much would be needed.

Some Final Points

The unpleasant scenarios we have outlined in this Commentary may never, and need never, occur. Quebec secession is not a foregone conclusion, and even if it happened, both sides might muddle through and preserve the currency union. Still, scenarios deserving of a B or worse rating, as outlined in Table 1, are all too likely without concerted, visible action to prevent them.

It is hard to see how the federal government could do anything substantive in advance without appearing to give comfort to the separatist cause. Nor would the key federal institutions – the Bank of Canada, the OSFI, and the CDIC – be able to act decisively on their own accounts. Circumstances following a separatist referendum victory would force them into a defensive posture in which limiting losses to ROC taxpayers began to take priority over supporting exposed financial institutions.

The Quebec government is the only player to which one could look for decisive action in advance. The general outlines of that action are clear. Quebec should establish institutions that would allow its financial system to function smoothly during the volatile period surrounding a possible secession. It should amass sufficient reserves of Canadian dollars to underpin confidence in the system and publicize those arrangements widely.

The same feedback that makes fear of financial crisis a powerful cause of the very thing that is feared also works in reverse. Wide-spread public knowledge of a well-planned framework within which the Quebec authorities would respond to any financial crisis would do much to allay the fears that might otherwise set a crisis in motion. In the absence of such a framework for action, it is hard to see as credible any promises by a secessionist Quebec government to engineer a smooth transition to independence, with no disruptions to the operations of a financial system that would continue to be based on the Canadian dollar.

NOTES

We are grateful to Ken Boessenkool, David Cameron, Finn Poschmann, Daniel Schwanen, and many others for helpful comments and corrections. The responsibility for remaining errors, and for the conclusions of this Commentary, is ours alone.

1 David E.W. Laidler and William B.P. Robson, *Two Nations, One Money? Canada's Monetary System following a Quebec Secession*, The Canada Round 3 (Toronto: C.D. Howe Institute, 1991); William B.P. Robson, *Change for a Buck? The Canadian Dollar after Quebec Secession*, C.D. Howe Institute Commentary 68 (Toronto: C.D. Howe Institute, March 1995); and Michel Demers and Marcel Côté, 'Is a UDI Feasible? The Economic Impact of a Conflict of Legitimacy' (October 1997, mimeographed), especially section III, 'Capital Flight.'

2 Events such as those described under the C and D scenarios would have broader ramifications. Weaker fiscal positions on one or both sides would make negotiations about division of existing federal debt more difficult and, relatedly, would cause both domestic and foreign lenders to shun borrowers on both sides of the prospective new border, or to demand much higher interest rates for lending to them. By damaging the financial health of business in both an independent Quebec and the ROC, C and D events might also weaken support, at least in some sectors, for maintaining liberal trading arrangements within the old Canadian economic space or with outside trading partners.

3 Shoring up banks with injections of newly created currency would not end a crisis since financial institutions (and nonfinancial businesses as well) in an independent Quebec would be short of currencies, including the ROC dollar, that Quebec could not print. But the ability to devalue, thus gaining a competitive edge in trade and making Quebec's assets cheap enough to tempt capital back in, would be very useful. For more on this point, see Robson, Change for a Buck?

4 'Clearing' refers to a receiving institution's presentation of an instrument such as a cheque to the institution on which it is drawn for payment, and to the netting out and reconciliation of obligations among the institutions involved. 'Settlement' refers to the transfer of funds by a debtor institution from its own account at the Bank of Canada to that of a creditor institution. See Clyde Goodlet, 'Clearing and Settlement Systems and the Bank of Canada,' *Bank of Canada Review*, Autumn 1997, p. 51.

5 Caution is needed in drawing firm conclusions from such figures, for several reasons. Chartered banks are only a subset of Canadian financial institutions. Figures that break down chartered bank assets and liabilities by region show large unallocated amounts on both sides of the balance sheet, some of which might, if allocated according to the location of the owner/debtor, affect the apparent distribution among provinces (see *Bank of Canada Review*, Autumn 1997, tables C5, C6). It is nevertheless likely that several individual institutions have mismatches between their

exposed assets and liabilities in Quebec that would demand attention from their management if secession appeared imminent.

6 In addition to its private sector members, the board of directors of the CDIC includes the governor of the Bank of Canada, the deputy minister of finance, and the superintendent and deputy superintendent of financial institutions.

7 Such action can help eliminate fire sales, which also protects the interests of uninsured creditors.

8 The currency union originally envisioned between the successor Czech Republic and Slovakia when Czechoslovakia dissolved broke down under such circumstances. For a period, the Czech central bank provided massive support to Slovakia's banking system. When doubts about repayment multiplied, however, the bank ceased lending, and the currency union collapsed. See Robson, *Change for a Buck?*, notes 5, 24.

9 It is not clear what would happen to CDIC coverage after secession. Insurance on term instruments such as guaranteed investment certificates might continue until the end of their terms. Coverage on demand and saving accounts most likely would cease.

10 'Parizeau veut témoigner devant la CAI,' *La Presse* (Montreal), February 3, 1998.

Limits to Partnership: Canada-Quebec Relations in a Postsecession Era

RICHARD SIMEON

The idea of partnership is central to the proposals for independence that sovereignist provincial governments have put before the Quebec people. In 1980, the referendum question asked for a mandate to negotiate 'sovereignty-*association*'; in October 1995, it called for sovereignty with a 'new political and economic *partnership* between two new countries, Quebec and Canada' (italics added).

The critical fact, however, is that Quebec alone could not establish such a relationship. It takes two or more entities to form an association or partnership. So the focus inevitably shifts to the rest of the country.

Would the Canada that remained after a 'yes' vote on sovereignty have any interest in forming a partnership? Would it have the political capacity to do so? What, if any, kind of association would be either possible or desirable from the rest of Canada's (ROC's) perspective? What might possible models of partnership look like? How might they operate? Can we imagine circumstances in which the ROC would agree to negotiate a partnership agreement? Would it be possible in the tense environment that inevitably would follow a 'yes' vote in a referendum? These are the questions that underpin this *Commentary*.

I argue that partnership is not an idea to be dismissed out of hand. Thus, I begin by considering some reasons to take seriously and then set out a variety of possible models. Next I explore in some detail why the idea resonates so strongly in Quebec. I argue that, although the notion that a country can be at once independent and closely associated with another does have an important element of having one's cake and eating it too, such observations fail to take account of the real dynamic of the idea among Quebecers.

With the stage thus set, I examine in more detail the range of likely opinion about partnership both in Quebec and in different regions and sectors of the ROC. Then I explore some of the dynamics that would shape the politics of the Canada-Quebec relationship if sovereignty was accomplished.

My conclusion is that broad, expansive models of partnership would be extremely unlikely to succeed. Instead, assuming that the various actors display some level of stability and rationality, the more likely outcome would be a limited free trade arrangement combined with a number of *ad hoc*, temporary, incremental, and relatively informal linkages that could not be designed in advance but that would develop and evolve simply in accord with mutual needs – in effect, the kind of relationships one might expect between any two contiguous, interdependent states in the modern world.

Why Discuss Partnership?

Most non-Quebec commentators reject the prospect of any kind of partnership if Quebec decides to opt out of Canada. Their logic is indeed persuasive, on both substantive and strategic grounds.

Why, on the occasion of a divorce, would the parties simultaneously agree to a new form of cohabitation? If distinct society status and asymmetry in the division of powers are unacceptable within Confederation as it exists today, how could the ROC possibly be interested in supporting the much more radical option of a close association after separation?

Federalist politicians, for example, are un-equivocal in their view that a referendum question that linked sovereignty and partnership or association would be illegitimate. As former justice minister Allan Rock puts it: 'The question will be separation or not – nothing in between; not partnership or any such thing. Separation is the clear and honest question that must be asked.'[1] To Canadians who take this view, the position of the Parti Québécois' (PQ) is fundamentally dishonest and manipulative, seeking support for a model that it cannot deliver.

Strategy is another consideration. Even if Canadians in the ROC are prepared to contemplate some form of partnership – a Plan D – *after* a Quebec vote for sovereignty, how could they possibly signal their agreement in advance of that vote? Doing so would surely reassure Quebecers that the risks of voting for sovereignty were low, massively increasing the likelihood of a 'yes' in the next referendum. Thus, is not any discussion of partnership before the next referendum disloyal, if not mischievous? Should federalists not deny any possibility of partnership now, even if they know they might be forced to entertain the idea at some point in the future?

Persuasive as such substantive and strategic observations are, there are good reasons for greater public discussion of the possibility of partnership. Most important, if the 'yes' side succeeded, Quebec and Canada would continue to share the north of the North American continent and to be intermeshed economically and in a myriad other ways. Both sides would have to find some way to manage their mutual affairs. The two (or more) new entities would have a *relationship* (as do all countries or territories that abut each other). The question is what form it would take.

Undertaking this inquiry, however speculative it must be, is also useful to assist both Quebecers and non-Quebecers in this prereferendum period. To make their voting decision, the Québécois need a realistic assessment of what partnership possibilities might be feasible. The non-Québécois need to have thought through the possibilities and to have explored where their interests lie well before the shock and confusion that would inevitably accompany a 'yes' vote.

Whatever arrangements developed after a 'yes' vote, they would not take place in isolation from other events occurring more or less simultaneously. First would be the formalization of secession itself, which, as Monahan and Bryant and Russell and Rider demonstrate,[2] would be extremely difficult to achieve without a damaging constitutional rupture. Debates about partnership and events in other arenas would interact enormously. The bargaining dynamics would differ in a scenario that envisioned secession and partnership being accomplished at the same time and in one that assumed secession first, followed, perhaps only after some time, by the negotiation of future relationships. And the more acrimonious the secession itself, the more difficult partnership negotiations would be, however desirable that result might be.

Similarly, partnership discussions would interact very strongly with the processes through which the ROC rethought its own identity and redesigned its institutions to reflect the new makeup of the country. Any arrangements between Quebec and Canada would likely have major implications for the design of a new Canadian federation, and any such redesign would constrain the possibilities for partnership (as I discuss later).

Quebecers who wanted to achieve sovereignty and partnership simultaneously would probably be disappointed. The reality is that rest of Canadians would be most reluctant to enter partnership discussions before they had completed their own constitutional process for fear that the partnership tail would wag the Canadian dog. Alan Cairns persuasively argues that the reshaping of Canada without Quebec should await the completion of secession in order to avoid an impossible overload of difficult issues[3] (detailed later in the paper). But if the secession agreement were to include major elements of partnership, compartmentalizing the issues would probably be impossible.

How to Proceed

Despite these difficulties, I propose to explore the possibility of partnership in the most positive light. I want to reverse the burden of proof, placing it for the moment on those who believe partnership is impossible.

Thus, I start with the assumption that partnership is, in principle, possible. The idea deserves not to be rejected out of hand; rather, it needs a sympathetic hearing and then a careful testing of its desirability and feasibility.

The reason for this approach is twofold. I wish to test the possibilities for partnership under the most favorable possible circumstances. (If it is unlikely even under these conditions, it becomes even less likely under less favorable ones.) I also hope to provide a counterweight to the current tendency of Canadians outside Quebec to dismiss the idea out of hand and of sovereignist Quebecers to assume that partnership is a foregone conclusion.

Accordingly, I begin with a set of admittedly highly optimistic – indeed, perhaps unrealistic – assumptions about the situation after a 'yes' vote in a referendum held in the near future.

- Quebec would have voted for sovereignty in a clear, unequivocal manner with a strong majority on an unambiguous question. (A question that included an explicit or implied promise of partnership would not qualify because a Quebec government could not keep that promise unilaterally.)
- Political elites on both sides would respect the legitimacy and finality of the decision. Hence, the intention to pursue sovereignty would be uncontested by any major political actors. (The more contested the referendum process and its result, the less likely that any kind of successful, stable relationship could be quickly negotiated.)
- Non-Quebecers would not be in a mood to punish or exact retribution from Quebec. Any negotiations will be conducted in good faith.
- Good faith, however, does not necessarily mean goodwill or a sense of mutuality. For Canadians in the ROC, whatever sense of common interest, mutual regard, and the like they had associated with the relationship inside Confederation, would have vanished. Hence, the most optimistic view is that they would assess partnership options according to their own self-interest, uninfluenced either by recrimination or by lingering feelings of solidarity. Quebecers would do likewise.
- The negotiations that did take place would be more like international negotiations than negotiations within a country.

This paper is addressed to both sides of the Canadian divide; it is not a brief or set of debating points for either one. Much less am I trying to set up arguments whose purpose is to influence a referendum outcome. Clearly, any conclusions here have implications for that process, but as much as humanly possible, I seek to explore partnership possibilities on their merits, accepting Daniel Turp's invitation to look at the partnership proposal with 'an open mind and a critical eye.'[4]

For readers who are not sovereignists, I hope to provide a sympathetic reading of the Quebec case for partnership. I do not believe it is a cynical ploy to trick Quebecers into voting for independence by convincing them that nothing will have changed once they have done so; rather, it responds to deeply felt beliefs within Quebec – a point it is important for critics to recognize. And for sovereignists, I hope to give an equally sympathetic account of likely views in the ROC and the limits these would impose on the scope of partnership.

Whether either side will believe that I have succeeded in my aspiration to be even-handed remains to be seen.

Models of Partnership

What kind of a formal relationship might exist between a sovereign Quebec and the ROC? The words *association* and *partnership* imply some kind of permanent, ongoing, institutionalized relationship involving mechanisms of co-decision and harmonization on a fairly wide range of matters, one that is broader and deeper than that established by a simple treaty between countries on the model of the North American Free Trade Agreement (NAFTA). Indeed, the implication is the creation of a new political entity with its own structures, powers, and resources. Such a model, however, is only one of the ways in which a sovereign Quebec might interact with the ROC. The relationship could follow a number of different models, each suggesting a higher level of integration:

- *Splendid isolation*, governed only by the broad rules used to manage the international relations between any two independent states, and subject to the economic rules of the General Agreement on Tariffs and Trade, the World Trade Organization (WTO), and other multilateral institutional arrangements.
- A *treaty relationship*, related to essential, largely economic matters, with some limited, independent dispute-settlement mechanisms. The treaty would, subject to periodic amendments, be a once-and-for-all agreement, setting out rules governing the behavior of each of the parties; that is, there would be no provision for ongoing policymaking machinery or for co-decision or harmonization across a range of policy fields. This is the NAFTA model.
- A *'multiple-linkages' model*. The relationship would rest not on a single treaty or agreement covering all elements in it but on a large number of lim-

ited, incremental, issue-specific arrangements between the parties, subject to creation and elimination based on their continuing utility to both sides. Structures, powers, decision-rules, and participants would vary, depending on the matters covered in each agreement.

• *Full partnership.* A confederal relationship, in which the two new sovereign parties would create an ongoing and overarching set of institutions that were empowered to make collective decisions on a specified set of matters, which could go well beyond economic issues to include immigration and citizenship, mobility, environmental matters, and the like. This partnership model is the one sovereignist advocates frequently invoke. It is patterned broadly (but with some critical differences) after the European Union (EU).

Each of these possibilities, of course, has many variants. They could also be combined; for example, the multiple-linkages model could be blended with a free trade agreement.

I focus primarily on the confederal, partnership model, though I pay some attention to the other three since (to anticipate my conclusions) I think negotiating a formal partnership in a confederal form would prove impossible and that the most feasible arrangement would likely take the form of multiple linkages plus some kind of free trade agreement.

Before we go further, a note on how words are used. Some non-Quebecers try to cut through the ambiguities by asserting the need to speak of *separatists*, not *sovereignists*, of *independence* or *separation*, not *sovereignty*. I believe, however, that the softer terms do, in fact, capture Quebec opinion better than the harder ones.

Some History

What do the sovereignists themselves mean when they talk of *association* or *partnership*? The idea has a long history in the discourse of Quebec nationalists (see Box 1). It has gone through several permutations, and the PQ itself has not always been united as to whether partnership must accompany sovereignty or, if it is necessary, what form it should take. But it is important to note that association or partnership has been an integral element of the aspiration to sovereignty from the very beginning.

Indeed, it is interesting to note the striking similarities between René Lévesque's views (again, see Box 1) and those of a present-day sovereignist, Daniel Turp:

Sovereignists do not want to destroy and break up Canada. ... Their intention is to invent a new country with its own distinctiveness and ambitions to live their national aspira-

Box 1   From Lévesque and the MSA to Parizeau and *indépendance*

In 1967, René Lévesque and a band of followers left the Quebec Liberal Party to form the Mouvement souverainété-association, soon to evolve into the PQ. 'There are moments,' declared Lévesque, when 'courage and calm daring become the only form of prudence ... Quebec must become sovereign as soon as possible.'[a]

Significantly, the idea of association or partnership was central to the sovereignist program from its inception – indeed, it was built into the title of the new movement – though Lévesque was constantly in conflict with more radical elements seeking outright independence, a tension that has existed within the PQ ever since. Lévesque envisioned collaboration on the monetary system, tariffs, the postal system, treatment of minorities, defense, and foreign policy, constituting, in his words, 'The Canadian Union.'[b]

Lévesque's emphasis on association appears also to have been partly based on a genuine and strong attachment to Canada. 'We do not want to end but rather to radically transform our union with the rest of Canada, so that in the future, our relations will be built on full and complete equality.'[c] Canada and Quebec, he argued, must maintain a continuity 'which will be largely economic, but also political.' Sovereignty and association would be equal components of a single project. 'Association with Canada must be parallel with the independence of Quebec. It would be a crime to cripple with one blow two centuries of communal coexistence.' As for the possible breakup of the rest of Canada, 'To me the idea is catastrophic; I do not want to consider it.'[d]

The PQ, somewhat to its own surprise, came to provincial power in November 1976. The strategy it adopted toward sovereignty, crafted by Intergovernmental Affairs Minister Claude Morin, focused on a step-by-step process – *étapisme* – designed to allay popular fears of radical change by emphasizing a graduated approach. There would be a referendum, asking only for a mandate to negotiate sovereignty-association, followed by negotiations with the rest of Canada. Whatever the outcome, no final move toward independence would be taken without a second consultation with the people.[e]

The emphasis on association was fundamental to this strategy. Details of the proposed partnership were set out in two documents published in 1979. In June, the PQ ratified *Égal à égal*, and a few months later, the government issued a white paper, *Quebec-Canada: A New Deal*, subtitled *The Quebec Government's Proposal for a New Partnership between Equals: Sovereignty-Association*.

According to the white paper, the association would consist of a customs union with common external tariffs, free movement of capital and people, retention of the Canadian dollar, coordination of 'policies inspired by common trends,' and possible collaboration on transportation, including co-management of Air Canada and Canadian National Railways. The aim was to maintain the Canadian economic union with as little change and disruption as possible. The Canadian political union, however, would be radically changed. The association would be managed by a new set of institutions, created equally by the governments of Canada and Quebec: a ministerial community council; a court of justice for the association; a commission of experts, to act as adviser and general secretariat; and a common monetary authority. (There was no proposal for a common parliamentary assembly.)

These institutions would have no independent authority, revenue-raising capacity, or electoral base. All their members would be appointed delegates of the two governments. The general principle governing decisionmaking would be parity. Decisions of the council would require unanimity, while the court would have equal numbers of judges appointed by each government and a president approved by both.

The principle of parity would not, however, be absolute:

In an association between two partners, some fundamental subjects must naturally be subjected to parity; otherwise one of the parties would be at the mercy of the other. That does not mean, however, that in every day practice, everything will be subject to a double veto.[f]

Thus, representation on the monetary authority would be proportional to the relative sizes of the two economies. And in 'special cases,' the voting rule would reflect the 'predominant interest of one of the parties' (examples given are Canada with respect to wheat, Quebec with respect to asbestos). Thus, Quebec would acquire control over all its laws, taxes, territory, citizenship, courts, and external relations, but the extent to which these powers would equip the new country to pursue genuinely autonomous policies would be highly constrained by the commitment to full-scale continued economic integration and by political association. The dilemma for the sovereignists was – and remains – that, in order to win support for sovereignty, it must be accompanied by convincing assurances that continuity with Canada would be maintained.

This dilemma has continued to divide the PQ. Jacques Parizeau, who became party leader in 1987, was highly critical of the gradualist strategy and the proposal for association. Both, he argued, would make Quebec hostage to the goodwill of other Canadians. Hence, under his leadership, the party reoriented its strategy. Independence, not association, was the overall goal, to be achieved with or without the cooperation of the ROC. To the extent that a relationship would be worked out, it would be driven by the ROC's need to accommodate, however reluctantly, the reality of an independent Quebec, at least as much as by Quebec's needs.

The Parizeau strategy left Quebec much less hostage to the ROC's intentions, but at the cost of reducing public support for the project and of precipitating potentially far greater economic and social disruption in the subsequent transition processes.

[a]   Quoted in Peter Desbarats, *René: A Canadian in Search of a Country* (Toronto: McClelland and Stewart, 1976), p. 131.
[b]   Ibid.
[c]   Quoted in Graham Fraser, *PQ: René Lévesque and the Parti Québécois in Power* (Toronto: McClelland and Stewart, 1984), p. 171.
[d]   René Lévesque, *My Quebec* (Toronto: Methuen, 1979), pp. 58, 73, 84. The fullest exposition of Lévesque's views are found in his *An Option for Quebec* (Toronto: McClelland and Stewart, 1968).
[e]   For a good analysis, see Kenneth McRoberts and Dale Posgate, *Quebec: Social Change and Political Crisis*, rev. ed. (Toronto: McClelland and Stewart, 1980), p. 217.
[f]   Quebec, Executive Council, *Quebec-Canada: A New Deal: The Quebec Government's Proposal for a New Partnership between Equals: Sovereignty-Association* (Quebec: Éditeur officiel du Québec, 1979), p. 60.

tions. Yet, Quebecers are also committed to building new bridges with a neighbor, a country with which it would like to enter into a friendly, peaceful and novel form of Union, which could be labeled, for the sake of history and continuity, as a new Canadian Union.[5]

This sort of statement may reveal a breath-taking naiveté about how all this would be perceived and interpreted outside Quebec. But there is also a positive element, which needs to be understood by those who criticize association on the grounds that it is merely cynical opportunism.

The call for sovereignty with partnership can be seen as the reflection of a profound ambivalence about Canada and Quebec. Perhaps no one better illustrates this than the current premier of Quebec, Lucien Bouchard, who has over his career been a Pierre Trudeau federalist, an advocate of the Meech Lake Accord, the architect of Brian Mulroney's cooperative federalism, and a sovereignist. Sovereignty with partnership was one means of resolving the contradictions. As Lawrence Martin points out, many Quebecers do not see these changes as political opportunism. 'Bouchard,' they say, 'was simply following the tortuous route of the Quebec conscience on the unity issue.'[6]

One can see more of this ambivalence in the twists and turns of Quebec policy during the two or three years leading up to the October 1995 referendum. The PQ's plan for sovereignty published in 1993[7] included a discussion of 'economic association with Canada,' although the relevant institutions were given little emphasis and the word *partnership* did not appear. But as the referendum year of 1995 developed, the polls made it increasingly clear that outright independence, with no guarantee of a future association, had little chance of victory.

Bouchard, then leader of the Bloc Québécois (BQ) in Ottawa, first voiced concerns about this problem in April 1995. Regional commissions dispatched across the province to sound public opinion found much support for sovereignty but grave doubts about opting for it without the assurance of an association. Then a group of 'soft' sovereignists who had broken away from the Liberals to form a new party, Action démocratique du Québec (ADQ), led by Mario Dumont, made it clear that it would not support independence unless it was accompanied by some form of association.

Thus the stage was set for the great *virage*, an agreement among the PQ, BQ, and ADQ to propose a 'new Economic and Political Partnership' between a sovereign Quebec and the rest of Canada, signed on June 12, 1995.

The main elements of this proposed arrangement were spelled out in the agreement, and in Bill 1, which became *An Act Respecting the Future of Quebec*.[8] Quebec would indeed be sovereign, claiming the plenitude of state powers to make all laws, impose all taxes, sign all treaties, and write its own constitution. But, along with this goal, it wished 'in particular to invent with the people of Canada, our historic partners, new relations permitting us to maintain our economic links and to redefine our political relationships.' Hence, the accession to sovereignty would be preceded by an 'offer of partnership.'

Unlike earlier periods, when Quebec had called for offers from the ROC, this time it would be Quebec that would put the proposal on the table (see Box 2). And sovereignty itself would not depend on acceptance of the offer or on successful negotiation. The agreement stated that, after a 'yes' victory, 'The National Assembly will, on the one hand, be able to proclaim the sovereignty of Quebec,[9] and on the other hand, the government will have the duty of proposing to Canada a new treaty.'

If the negotiations were successful, the National Assembly would declare Quebec's sovereignty after the agreement is reached. But, 'in the event that

Box 2   Quebec's 1995 Proposal for Partnership

The arrangement Quebec proposed in 1995 was, as R.L. Watts describes it, a two-unit confederation.[a]

The partnership treaty, as set out in Bill 1, would maintain '*and improve*' (my italics) the existing Canadian economic space and establish rules for sharing the current federal debt and assets. The priority was the operation of a monetary and customs union, monetary policy, free circulation of goods, services, people, and capital, labor mobility, and citizenship.[b]

The partnership could be extended into other fields, which could include interprovincial and international trade, transportation, international representation, the possibility of the partnership's speaking 'with one voice' in international organizations, transportation, defense, the regulation of financial institutions, fiscal and budgetary policies, the environment, the fight against arms and drug smuggling, postal services, and 'all other matters that the parties could consider of common interest.'

Thus, the goals of the partnership would be primarily economic, 'to ensure continuity in the trade relations between Quebec and Canada,'[c] but they could expand well beyond. The political elements were much less clear, reflection the reluctance of many *péquistes* to consider rebuilding a political union that Quebec would just have decided to leave. As Daniel Turp, one of the architects of the *virage*, put it, 'The political partnership proposal deserves to be initially modest in its outlook.' Nevertheless, it could lead "progressively into more advanced forms of political union."[d]

The institutions described were much like those the PQ had proposed in 1979. A permanent secretariat would coordinate the partnership. Decisionmaking would rest with a 'partnership council' of ministers, with equal representation from Quebec and Canada, whose decisions would be based on unanimity.

The major change was the addition of a parliamentary assembly. Quebec would have 25 percent of the members, who would not be directly elected but appointed from the House of Commons and the National Assembly. The group would have no formal legislative powers, but it could review draft decisions of the council of ministers, make recommendations, and pass resolutions to discuss enlargement of common fields of action. (Thus, its powers would be fewer than those of the existing European Parliament.)

Finally, a tribunal would resolve disputes over the treaty's implementation and interpretation. It could be modeled after one or a combination of existing tribunals in the NAFTA, the WTO, and the Canadian Agreement on Internal Trade.

a R.L. Watts, 'The Limitations of Recent Proposals for Confederal Solutions for Canada' (Institute of Intergovernmental Relations, Queen's University, Kingston, Ont., 1994), mimeographed.

b Each of these issues is complex. For example, for the pitfalls facing the idea of a common currency, see David E.W. Laidler and William B.P. Robson, *Two Nations, One Money? Canada's Monetary System following a Quebec Secession*, The Canada Round 3 (Toronto: C.D. Howe Institute, 1991). For a powerful critique of common citizenship, see Stanley H. Hartt, *Divided Loyalties: Dual Citizenship and Reconstituting the Economic Union*, C.D. Howe Institute Commentary 67 (Toronto: C.D. Howe Institute, March 1995).

c Daniel Turp, 'From an Economic and Political Partnership between Quebec and Canada to a Canadian Union,' *Constitutional Forum* 7 (Winter/Spring 1996): 93.

d Ibid., 94.

negotiations prove to be fruitless, the National Assembly will be able to declare Quebec's sovereignty upon short notice.' Canada was to have a year to respond to the partnership offer and, as then-Premier Jacques Parizeau told a British audience, 'if Canada refuses, Quebec will become sovereign nonetheless.'[10]

Thus, sovereignty would not depend on prior agreement on partnership. Nor would there be a second referendum to seek citizens' further views before independence was declared. As Bouchard said, by virtue of being sovereign, Quebec would be able to discuss 'people to people, equal to equal with its neighbor of English Canada.'[11]

The Importance of Partnership to Sovereignists

Before assessing the plausibility and feasibility of the partnership proposal and reactions to it in the ROC, let us step back to ask how *association* and *partnership* resonate within Quebec.

Outside Quebec, the strong tendency is to dismiss the idea as a ploy designed to win support for a dubious proposition by making promises that are reassuring but that could not be redeemed without the cooperation of the ROC. Association and partnership, say many, are simply political responses to the blunt fact that outright sovereignty could never win in a Quebec referendum. The proposal of partnership is a scam, they suggest. Once separatist leaders have received their majority – once the lobsters are in the pot – the partnership idea will have served its purpose and be quickly abandoned.

Such assertions doubtless have a considerable measure of truth, but they fail to ask *why* the option of sovereignty-partnership or sovereignty-association has such a strong appeal among Quebecers. What looks like – and may indeed be – a political absurdity may refer to an important *psychological* reality, one to which observers outside Quebec should pay more attention.

The terms *sovereignty-association* and *sovereignty-partnership* encapsulate and combine two elements that appear to be deeply embedded in the political identities of a great many francophone Quebecers. The sovereignty side of the equation captures the deep sense that Quebec constitutes a distinct political community: that it is in this sense a *nation* or *people*, that this community is most fully represented and given political expression by the National Assembly and government of Quebec, and that it constitutes a minority within the larger federation of Canada.

If this were the whole story, however, then immediate, complete independence would be the option most likely to succeed in a referendum. But surveys repeatedly report that outright independence has always been a minority position, even among francophones, and that the numbers favoring it have been remarkably stable over many years.[12]

Association, then, captures the other side of the equation: that along with the primary Québécois identity, many Quebecers, even sovereignists, continue to maintain a strong identity with Canada. In a February 1996 Léger and Léger poll, 85.5 percent of Quebec respondents agreed 'somewhat or completely' with the statement that 'Canada is a good country where it is good to live.' And 78.1 percent agreed that 'we should be proud of what francophones and anglophones have accomplished together in Canada.'

Another survey of francophones in Quebec just before the 1995 referendum found that 29 percent identified themselves as 'Quebecers only,' 29.1 percent as 'Quebecers first, but also Canadian,' 28.1 per cent as Quebecers and Canadians equally, and 6.7 percent as Canadians only.[13]

This double set of attachments – which, I believe, goes well beyond a merely economic calculation of the benefits of association with Canada or the costs of breakup – explains the durability of Yvon Deschamps' observation that what Quebecers really want is an independent Quebec within a strong, united Canada. As Louis Balthazar puts it, ' 'We want to be with you, but we don't want to be part of you.'[14]

A host of surveys show that Deschamps was exactly right. His statement explains such apparent anomalies as the fact that large majorities of Quebecers, including many sovereignists, continue to agree with such statements as 'Canada is the best country in the world in which to live.' It may also explain the paradox that significant numbers of Quebecers believe that after sovereignty they would continue to carry Canadian passports and even to send members to the Canadian Parliament. In the 1996 Léger and Léger poll discussed above, a remarkable 58.4 percent of respondents agreed that 'No matter what the arrangement between Quebec and Canada, Quebec should be part of Canada.'

Such responses may indicate confusion, ignorance, and even perhaps manipulation by vote-seeking *péquiste* leaders. But they may also reflect the fact that the word sovereignty itself has an emotional or psychological meaning for many Québécois that is quite different from the formal, juridical sense of the term as used by constitutional lawyers and from the way it is interpreted by most anglophone Canadians. To the Québécois, it appears to be an affirmation of their identity and of their sense of a right to determine their future for themselves, an understanding not at all inconsistent with retaining attachments to Canada.

Indeed, the term *sovereignty-partnership* encapsulates the fundamental belief (shared by sovereignists and federalists alike) that from its inception Canada was seen as a partnership between the two great language groups. This language and this set of assumptions resonates through virtually all Quebec commentary on Canadian federalism.

In this sense, the ideas of sovereignty and partnership are deeply embedded in a Quebec political discourse that sees them as complementary, not contradictory. Quebecers have *always* thought of Canada as a partnership.[15] The term is familiar and comfortable. And it is the growing rejection of this conception of Canada, as reflected in the *Constitution Act of 1982* and the defeat of the Meech Lake and Charlottetown Accords that has tipped the balance for many people from trust in federalism to belief in the need for sovereignty.

'Partnership,' then, can be seen as an affirmation of 'openness to the rest of Canada, even if other Canadians would insist on a thorough separation.'[16] The central difficulty in finding a 'renewed federalism' (much less agreement on a partnership arrangement) is that the dominant conceptions of the ROC now argue for the equality of individuals and provinces and are deeply and increasingly hostile to dualism, partnership, or special treatment.

Thus, many Quebecers are only partial or reluctant sovereignists. Even if they feel driven to support sovereignty by their perception that the rest of the country is no longer prepared to accept a dualist vision of Canada, they retain the desire to maintain the historic partnership, albeit in a very different form.

The Implications

If my analysis is correct, it has a number of implications for thinking about institutional models of sovereignty and partnership. First, it suggests that the recent polarization of the alternatives – essentially between the status quo and outright independence – is, in terms of the attitudes of most Quebec citizens, artificial and distorted. Both are minority positions. Democrats must always worry when the alternatives that the political system is able to put before citizens are demonstrably both minority positions and when choices that do reflect the preponderance of opinion are simply not on the table.

Second, the broad range of Quebec opinion does indeed appear fall in the middle, around the alternatives of distinct society/special status in a renewed federalism, on one hand, and sovereignty with a strong partnership on the other. The numbers falling on either side of this balance vary according to changing political events (especially the perceived willingness or unwillingness of the ROC to recognize Quebec's distinctiveness in a reformed federalism.)

That point leads to a third important implication. For many Quebec voters, the two options are not sharply opposed; indeed, they flow into each other as parts of a continuum. In this sense, in the minds of many voters, renewed federalism (embracing recognition of Quebec's distinctiveness, with some associated powers) and sovereignty-partnership have more in common with each other than does either of the polar extremes: a federalism rigorously based on the equality of the provinces or outright independence. Rather, both options seek a balance between autonomy and sharing, with the emphasis wavering between one side and the other.

Former premier Jacques Parizeau argues that 'sovereignty is necessary and partnership desirable'[17] (although the public opinion data and the necessity of the *virage* of the 1995 referendum suggest he has it just the wrong way around; it really is: sovereignty is desirable and partnership necessary'). Many ROC opponents of distinct society believe secession is preferable to asymmetric federalism. The result is an odd alliance between the 'realists' on both sides. Both hard-line separatists and their hard-headed opponents say that a simple majority 'yes' vote would mean that Confederation was definitively ended and that independence straight up would be the inevitable outcome. But both groups, I believe, are out of step with the realities of public opinion in Quebec (and perhaps elsewhere), and both are likely to lead down a dangerous path.

The difficulty is that, at the political and juridical levels and in the reactions of most Canadians in the ROC, what to a Québécois voter might seem like a small shift – little more than another step in a long political evolution starting with the *Quebec Act* of 1774 – would, in fact, be the crossing of a great divide from which there would be no turning back.

The dominant assumption in anglophone Canada is that a 'yes' vote to sovereignty would change the country's politics forever in profound ways. Canada would exist no more; any sense of mutuality and solidarity within the larger Canadian community would disappear; Quebec would become the definitive 'other,' to be dealt with as a foreign power in terms of cold self-interest.

As Denis Stairs puts it:

The first reality that would play itself out in the post-secession environment would be the transformation of an important part of Canada's 'domestic' politics into a politics of a very different kind – namely, inter-national politics. ... The most obvious and immediate ... implication would be the absolute release of any Canadian government from the obligation to take into account the interests of the citizens of Quebec.[18]

Outside the ranks of PQ activists, few francophone Quebecers see it this way.

In brief, the very meaning of a 'yes' vote might well be different in the two linguistic communities. Thus, both sides could make a grievous error. Non-Quebecers would interpret a 'yes' as meaning that Quebec is gone, without realizing the vote might equally be a call for symbolic change and recognition. And Quebecers would believe that nothing fundamental had changed as a result of their vote, when in fact everything would have changed.

The consequences of such rival interpretations could be tragic, pushing everyone into choices and alternatives that very few actually preferred and creating a political crisis that might well become unmanageable (see Box 3).

The Cases For and Against Partnership

Once Quebec had successfully asserted its claim to sovereignty, what interest would either side have in exploring a subsequent partnership arrangement? The case is much clearer and stronger on the Quebec side.

Quebec Looks at Partnership

As already noted, a commitment to partnership would have obvious advantages for the success of the sovereignist cause in a referendum. A credible case that partnership is possible and could not be denied by the ROC would enormously strengthen sovereignists' electoral prospects. If partnership seemed possible, the fear of sovereignty's entailing large economic costs would recede dramatically. Moreover, as we have also already seen, a promise of sovereignty-partnership would accord closely with francophone Quebecers' sense of their own identity as Québécois and as Canadians.

The Case For Partnership

What about the case for actual association in the longer term?

Even unequivocal separatists such as Parizeau argue that an independent Quebec would remain in an economic union with Canada. No one wants to jeopardize the more than $60 billion in trade or the 500,000 jobs involved. But,

Box 3   Keeping Cool Heads after a 'Yes' Vote

The divergence of views discussed here suggests that, in the event of a 'yes' vote, leaders on both sides should be strongly urged not to rush to judgment. Rather, they should seek some means by which the meanings and nuances of the vote could be explored and in which the subsequent negotiations would not – at least not initially – be about the terms of separation, with or without partnership, but an occasion to explore a range of possibilities, some perhaps not yet articulated.

In the current atmosphere of polarization and tension, this hope is probably vain (especially among PQ militants, who would be unlikely to want to question a victory so recently achieved; economic or political events, however, could force their hand). But it is a hope that should be explored.

Another implication is that it is in both sides' interests to proceed step by step: to build into the process enough stages or decision-points that options and alternatives can be reconsidered, that conclusions can be revisited, that new paths can be explored, and that citizens' reactions to events can be monitored and expressed. In this sense, a 'yes' vote should be seen not as an end but a beginning, one in which a variety of different models for partnership – including even some form of renewed federalism – might be pursued.

In addition, as Marcel Côté observes, 'When the costs and disorder associated with the break-up of Canada emerge into the daylight, the Quebec people will turn against those who have fooled them.'[a] As the implications of their vote became clear, many Quebecers might wish to reconsider, and it would be tragic if they were not given some opportunity to do so.

Granted, Robert Young argues persuasively that, in the rush of events following a positive referendum vote, there would be no desire, no time, and no opportunity for such second thoughts.[b] PQ leaders would be triumphant, federalist leaders in disarray,[c] and financial markets exercising their own harsh discipline and calling for a rapid termination of the uncertainty, which could most quickly be achieved by completing the secession. He may be right, but, on the other hand, many of the factors he discusses could argue for an equally rapid reversal of the decision.

Thus, it could be important to ensure that the federalist ship had not sailed over the horizon. It might better stand by to lower the life lines.

[a]   Marcel Côté and David Johnston, *If Quebec Goes ... : The Real Costs of Separation* (Toronto: Stoddart, 1995), p.193.

b Robert Young, *The Secession of Quebec and the Future of Canada* (Montreal: McGill-Queen's University Press, 1995).

c This point is also argued by Keith Banting, 'If Quebec Separates: Restructuring Northern North America,' in R. Kent Weaver, ed., *The Collapse of Canada?* (Washington, DC: Brookings Institution, 1992).

goes one argument, these benefits could be maintained without the elaborate machinery of economic and political partnership – for example, through a nation-to-nation treaty modeled on the NAFTA.[19] Hard-liners also argue that nothing could stop an independent Quebec from unilaterally adopting the Canadian currency.[20] All it would take to maintain the economic union would be a few simple rules.

This approach ignores two fundamental facts. First, the NAFTA is far from a full economic union. Most obviously, it does not embody free movement of people. Moreover, the NAFTA and other such international arrangements are primarily about negative integration – the removal of barriers to trade. Unlike the European Union, they are not about positive integration or the strengthening of collective capacities to promote integration, growth, and competitiveness in transportation, communication, the environment, infrastructure, and the like. Nor do they embody any element of sharing or redistribution.

Second, the level of integration between Quebec and the ROC (especially Ontario and the Atlantic provinces) is many orders of magnitude greater than that between any region of Canada and the United States or Mexico.[21] This linkage is reflected not only in trade but also in a host of corporate structures and relationships. At the level of individuals and civil society, Canadians may have seen a progressive disengagement of their two societies, but the degree of integration is still much greater than that between any part of Canada and the United States, a direct result of the common standards, nondiscrimination, mutual recognition, and legal comity that come from living in the same country. It is highly unlikely that the interdependencies resulting from this economic and social integration could be managed by an arrangement such as the NAFTA.

Given the interdependencies and the differences in size between the Canadian and Quebec economies and populations, the lack of a partnership arrangement would force Quebec to become a 'policytaker.' It would be hugely influenced by Canadian policy decisions but have no formal voice in making them. It would be lobbying from the outside. If it unilaterally adopted the Canadian dollar, for example, it would have no say in the decisions of the Bank of Canada. Its fiscal policy would be profoundly influenced by Canadian fiscal policy, over which it would have little control. It would have to accommodate its taxation regimes to those in Canada. It would play second fiddle to Canada, Mexico, and the United States in the future development of the NAFTA. And so on.

Thus, without partnership or membership in the Canadian federation, Quebec might end up weaker, rather than stronger, than it is now. If the degree of integration that now exists between Quebec and Canada requires harmonization across many important policy areas, then without partnership, Quebec would be forced into accommodating its policies to those of the stronger player. Harmonization might well take place, but an independent Quebec would almost surely have to harmonize its policies with those of Canada more than the other way around. The more committed Quebec was to the maintenance of a full economic union, the greater these constraints would be.

Perhaps I am overstating this analysis of interdependence and the assumption that it would require considerable positive integration and harmonization. Federalism already permits, indeed encourages, much policy diversity, even in such fundamental areas as tax and fiscal policy. As William Robson suggests, it could probably survive more diversity.[22] Although I believe the pressures for harmonization would be strong, the model I propose later does not presume any particular desirable level of integration. Rather, it suggests that *ad hoc* measures would develop informally, as the parties came to feel them necessary.

In addition, some form of partnership might well be necessary if a sovereign Quebec was to be able to ensure order and stability and in its own society. Since the October 1995 referendum, it has become clear that the chief barrier to a successful drive for independence is not opposition outside Quebec but mobilization of minorities (anglophones, allophones, and aboriginal peoples) within the province against the sovereignty project. If secession is to be achieved without massive social conflict, then Quebec's minorities must be reconciled to the project.

As recent developments have shown, this task would not be easy. But a partnership that embodied mutually binding agreements on minority rights, aboriginal rights, citizenship, mobility, and even immigration might provide these minorities a measure of security that would ensure their acquiescence to sovereignty, however reluctantly.[23] A single, once-and-for-all, binding agreement might resolve all these issues. But that is not likely. They are all dynamic concerns in which policy needs to evolve and change. Dealing with them would take the question of partnership far beyond a narrowly defined economic union.

Thus, in the long run as well as the short run, a sovereign Quebec would have powerful reasons to seek a partnership. An arrangement in which Canada and Quebec dealt with each other as foreign powers would ignore the enormous interdependencies that currently exist. The NAFTA model might be more attractive to many Quebecers since it seems to preserve a single economic space while minimizing the need for complex institutions and continued shared decisionmaking. But this too would be insufficient if the goal was to maintain the existing Canadian economic union in its current essentials. A full economic union must be managed, and that is an ongoing process. A wide range of policies need to be harmonized, and if the outcome was to be more than Quebec's simply adjusting to the actions of its larger partner, ongoing institutions would be necessary.

Moreover, both non-francophones and federalists who are residents of Quebec would important bodies of opinion in any partnership discussions. Like other Canadians, their present position is focused on preventing secession. But if it became a reality, they might come to advocate partnership. In an independent Quebec, they would see ongoing protection of their rights and interests as paramount, and they might believe it could best be found in the provisions of a partnership with respect to mobility, citizenship, aboriginal governance, immigration, and the rights of linguistic minorities. (Exactly the same argument can be made for francophone minorities outside Quebec, whose language rights would be highly vulnerable if Quebec became independent.)

Thus, Quebec's interests would probably be served best by expansive, confederal or quasi-confederal models of partnership.

The Case Against Partnership
The primary Québécois case against partnership is Parizeau's tactical argument: to make secession dependent on partnership would be to make Quebec hostage to what the ROC was prepared to negotiate.

The longer-run argument is to ask why Quebec should exchange the constraints allegedly imposed by federalism for the constraints embodied in a partnership arrangement. (Indeed, the influence of Quebec on common policies might be no greater in such a partnership than it is today within the federation, where Quebec exercises influence both through its own government and through its role within the federal government.) The answer is that the constraints on an independent Quebec *without* partnership would be even greater.

Sovereignists would be wrong, however, to believe that the two-unit confederation embodied in their 1995 partnership proposal would serve their interests well. Having so few units limits the set of decision-rules. Essentially, the possibilities are just two: a mutual veto or unanimity rule, or a rule based on proportionality in terms of numbers and size.

From Quebec's perspective, both rules would be flawed. The unanimity rule would subject the National Assembly to a veto by the Canadian Parliament over all issues that were included in the agreement and, as we have seen, given Quebec's interests, that list is likelier to be long rather than short.

Proportionality, of course, would be even more dangerous, given the population difference. In all areas to which this rule applied, Canada would have the upper hand.

The dilemma for sovereignists is that, given the existing amount of interdependence, the commitment to maintain and strengthen the economic union, and the evident desire of citizens to maintain some form of union with Canada, the motivation would be to look for a broad, rather than narrow, partnership. But the decision-rule problem would immediately shift the incentives to make the agreement as narrow as possible and to operate it more as an enforceable treaty than as an ongoing set of policymaking procedures.

In addition, in a forum of two units, each must cast one vote and hence speak with a single voice – even though internal opinions may be diverse.

A confederation with more members can have much more flexible decision-rules: unanimity on some, a simple majority on others, and various forms of qualified majority (as practiced by the EU) on yet others. A greater number of units also opens up the possibility of shifting alliances and changing coalitions on different issues (as occur among the 15 members of the EU).

Such shifts are, of course, the case with federalism. Ontario and Quebec are natural allies on some questions; Quebec and the Atlantic provinces on others; Quebec and the West on still others. In a two-unit confederal model, none of these alliances would be possible, since Ontario, the Atlantic provinces, and the West would all be subsumed in the single partner 'Canada.' Moreover, Quebec's interests would have no part in shaping the position that this partner took.

Thus, even from the sovereignist perspective, Quebec might be better off in a ten-unit confederation or even in a decentralized federation. Even more desirable from a sovereignist standpoint might be a four- or five-member economic union, which could become a distinct possibility if the ROC was to break up in the aftermath of secession.

The ROC Looks at Partnership

Partnership would look very different from the perspective of the rest of Canada.

Recall one of my initial premises: that the ROC would examine the options without anger, vindictiveness, or a desire to punish Quebec. It would look at the pros and cons of partnership carefully and relatively objectively. That being said, however, sovereignists should realize that a considerable period of uncertainty would likely have to pass before the ROC was prepared to undertake discussions of its future relationship with Quebec. The reasons are several.

First, the ROC's greatest task following a 'yes' vote would be the need to come to terms with a fundamental, unprecedented challenge to the country's core values, identity, sense of self, and institutions – the most profound it has ever faced. Although many Canadians have now come to believe, at least intellectually, that reform of the federal system is probably impossible and that sovereignty or breakup is inevitable, I believe they are a small minority.

Moreover, intellectual acceptance of the proposition in the abstract is one thing; dealing with the emotions and conflicts that would be unleashed once a 'yes' vote had occurred would be quite another matter. The first preoccupation of most Canadians would be their own needs and their own future. Their long-term relations with a newly independent Quebec would be a distinctly second order of business.

Second, a vacuum of political leadership would be likely. Ottawa would have to bear responsibility for failing in the first duty of a government – to preserve the country. Its ability to command the loyalty and respect of Canadians and especially to motivate them sympathetically to embark on rebuilding relations with Quebec would be gravely undermined.

Even less legitimate than federal officials generally would be a prime minister and cabinet ministers based in Quebec. New leadership would have to come forward and grasp power before anyone could identify a clear set of interlocutors with whom negotiation about partnership could be held. There would be a strong demand for new elections without Quebec, and this call would carry the danger of increased chaos and heightened conflict. Alternatively, Quebec MPs might resign and a new government – perhaps a majority Reform Party government or a multiparty government of national unity – could be formed.

Third, most Canadians would be extremely reluctant to discuss the terms of partnership before it had become clear how the political system of the ROC was to be reordered. That, too, would inevitably be a drawn-out process. Much public discussion would be necessary before options and alternatives crystallized. Federal and a variety of provincial leaders would be contending for influence. Devising legitimate central institutions would be a major challenge. So would providing Westerners and Atlantic Canadians a sense of belonging since one province, Ontario, would be so dominant in population and economic strength.

Moreover, the possibilities for partnership would be greatly affected by the nature of the new regime that emerged. One possibility, not to be dismissed, is the breakup of the rest of the country. If that occurred, partnership would likely turn out to be a set of arrangements between Ontario, Quebec, the Atlantic provinces, and perhaps some portion of the West.

A perhaps more plausible alternative is that a reconstructed Canadian federation would be highly decentralized – indeed, a con- federal model itself. The most detailed Plan B enunciated so far is Gordon Gibson's, under which federal powers would be dramatically less than they are today. 'Indeed, the briefly famous "Allaire report" of the Quebec Liberal party might seem to be extravagant and generous to the central authority.'[24] Federalism would be seen to have failed. It would have little claim to revival, and burned by this failure, citizens would demand that power be brought close to home. Hence, Ottawa's political and policy significance would decline so that Parliament might as well be replaced by a council of ministers.

If this future were to occur, it would not include a central government that could negotiate and then manage a partnership with Quebec. More likely, Quebec would be invited to participate, as it wished, in the new, multimember confederation.

Yet another possible scenario envisions a stronger, reinvigorated federal government. Once Quebec was gone, proponents suggest, the single most powerful decentralizing force in Canadian federalism would have been removed. The ROC could then contemplate the federal regime its citizens want, rather than the one that has historically been acceptable to Quebec. And what its citizens want, it is suggested, is a regime in which Canadians generally look to Ottawa as the primary or most important level of government.

This view, of course, is the one PQ leaders have taken. It is consistent with their fundamental image of a two-partner, two-founding-nations Canada. Indeed, ever since the time of Lévesque, the PQ has argued that the federation frustrates both French and English, and that both would be better off by its demise.[25]

The perception of a ROC that would rally around a powerful Ottawa in the event of secession may have been plausible in the 1950s and 1960s. It is much less so today. Over the past two decades, Canada has experienced powerful provincializing and decentralizing forces. The fight against debts and deficits and the constraints of globalization have diminished the power and effectiveness of the federal government and hence its ability to compel loyalty and respect. A sense of regional imbalance, of an Ottawa preoccupied with central Canada, has driven regionalist movements in much of the West. Ontario, with its own position in the Canadian and North American political economy changing, has come to advocate a more province-centered position.[26] Provinces, self-confident, but stung by large cuts in federal transfer payments, are increasingly unwilling to accept federal leadership or a strong federal role in setting and enforcing national standards.

Indeed, most recent proposals for reform of the federal system envision increased transfers of power to the provinces and a quasi-confederal model in which national norms and standards are established though federal-provincial or interprovincial cooperation.[27] Although some analysts dissent from this view[28] and although support for further decentralization in the general public is by no means certain (recall that much of the public opposition to the relatively minor decentralizing steps and limits on the federal spending power in the Meech Lake and Charlottetown Accords was a major source of hostility), the pressures for decentralization appear strong.

If decentralization is the direction for the future, the implications for the possibility of partnership are important. Provinces would be highly unlikely to accord Ottawa much leeway as the 'Canadian' interlocutor with a sovereign Quebec at the partnership table. But Quebec sovereignists themselves might think about the possible virtues of a multi-unit, rather than two-member, confederal model – whether they were to participate fully as one of ten members or, in a more limited way, as a sovereign, associated state.

Finally, sovereignists need to realize, as they think through the pros and cons of partnership and its variants, that Canada without Quebec is not a monolith. Interest in partnership is likely to vary greatly across regions, provinces, and sectors.

Regional Interests
The most obvious differences would be regional. Incentives to engage in partnership would depend on each region's existing level of political integration with Quebec and hence on the costs of disrupting existing arrangements.

As sovereignists are fond of pointing out, Ontario and Quebec are tightly intermeshed in a myriad economic relationships, and their history of sharing the Empire of the St. Lawrence is a long one.

The complexity of these linkages makes it unlikely that they could be managed effectively through simple international relations or even through a NAFTA-like arrangement. If federalism fails, Ontario's economic interests would likely incline it to support a partnership model. But even this should not be taken for granted. Ontario's trading patterns have been changing, and its dependence on the Quebec market declining. The province would, therefore, have to weigh the advantages of partnership with Quebec against the implications that arrangement might have for its north-south and western trading relationships.

The Atlantic provinces would have even stronger economic interests in a partnership. Today they depend, only slightly less than Ontario, on the Quebec market for their exports. They would also have very strong incentives to ensure that surface transportation links between them and the ROC be maintained. Moreover, they would be very weak members of a reconstituted Canada dominated by Ontario. Since as poorer provinces they have much in common with Quebec, they would likely support any model that kept it closely tied to the Canadian economic union.

In the case of both Ontario and the Atlantic provinces, it is also conceivable that the legacy of historic ties and the desire not to sever them completely would play some role in building support for a partnership, once the initial shock had passed. Acadians in New Brunswick and francophones in other provinces would be particularly anxious not to sever all ties. Partnership might look like an acceptable second-best solution.

Recent surveys and the 1997 federal election results suggest that Ontarians tend to be more sympathetic than other Canadians to the idea of Canada as a partnership between two great language groups and to the idea of accommodating Quebec through recognizing it as a distinct society. It does not follow, however, that Ontarians would necessarily be sympathetic to partnership with a sovereign Quebec. Indeed, the very strength of current attachments might make the sense of anger and rejection following a 'yes' vote even stronger in Ontario than in other provinces, where emotional links to Quebec are weaker.

None of these factors would have much weight in the West. If partnership could be presented as a device essential to the preservation of the macro Canadian economy and to financial stability, in which Westerners do have an interest, it might draw some support. But the fact is that Western labor markets and trading relationships involve relatively few links with Quebec. Linkages through investment may be more important, but they are less vulnerable to disruption (especially if stronger international rules to ensure capital mobility come into force). Thus, there would be few issues on which interdependence was strong enough to justify partnership.

Moreover, a strong thread in Western politics has been that the Canadian political economy has been dominated by central Canada. There has also been much resentment against alleged special treatment for Quebec and the extent to which issues surrounding it dominate national politics. In the West, Ted Morton suggests, 'the strongest desire is for closure on the Quebec/national-unity question ... there is little place for Quebec in the West's New Canada.'[29] If this (deeply depressing) view is true, the implication is that Westerners would have little emotional resistance to Quebec's leaving, so they would look at the partnership proposal in purely cost-benefit terms.

In addition, partnership as envisioned by the PQ would have an enormous potential downside for the West. In any secession scenario, Westerners would be highly suspicious of the economic and political weight Ontario would exercise in a new federation, however reconstituted. Partnership would look even more threatening. Ontario would have the dominant weight within the federation and thus in shaping Canada's bargaining position. Ottawa would then sit with Quebec at the partnership table. Central Canadian domination would, in Westerners' eyes, be doubly reinforced. It is hard, therefore, to imagine their being interested in anything more than the most minimal future relationship. Thus, Westerners would strongly oppose broad partnership arrangements. The most they could be expected to support would be a very limited treaty-type model.

Indeed, the political structure of Western Canada after a Quebec secession remains very much in doubt. Many permutations are possible. Some commentators think the inevitable consequence would be the emergence of a sovereign West, or perhaps two or three such entities, opening up yet other models for partnership – one between Western Canada, Ontario, Quebec, and Atlantic Canada.

Others argue that the predominant feeling remains 'we want in,'[30] suggesting a decentralized federation with strong provincial representation at the center in order to counter-balance Ontario's numerical weight. In either case, the simple, two-unit partnership seems implausible.

Provincial Governments

If we think of provincial governments as distinct from the regions they represent, another set of interests comes into play. What impact might a Quebec-Canada partnership have on the powers and jurisdiction of the provinces? The division of powers in such a partnership could have major implications for the division of powers in the remaining federation.

The addition of a two-unit confederation on top of a nine-unit federation might be expected to undermine the provinces. Canada would need to speak with one voice at the partnership table, and some of the issues the new agreement would cover inevitably would encroach on provincial concerns and responsibilities. Provinces would strongly oppose any such development.

Moreover, the more any partnership came to look and act as a third level of government, [31] the more likely would be a sense of institutional overload, leading to demands for rationalization of the system, perhaps to the detriment of the provinces.

Overall, provincial governments, concerned with their own status, would likely be highly suspicious of partnership arrangements, especially since one of their number would have had its status elevated so dramatically. They would demand a voice both in negotiating the partnership and in its subsequent operation.

Business

Since so much of the PQ proposal for partnership is based on a desire to maintain the economic union, the attitudes of business toward partnership would be very important. Again, attitudes likely would vary by region and sector. The more dependent particular firms were on markets in both Quebec and the ROC and the more their office and manufacturing facilities were located across the country, the more concerned they would be that secession be achieved with as little disruption as possible and that future relationships accommodate their needs.

National and transnational firms would support models that maximized the chances of policy harmonization between Canada and Quebec; they would want to ensure that citizenship rules did not disrupt transfers of employees across borders. Similarly, industries and firms currently under federal jurisdiction – from airlines to banks to telecommunications companies – would have a particularly strong interest in consistency of regulatory regimes between the two new countries. Hence some important business interests would likely press for as close a relationship as possible.

Binding Quebec into a partnership with Canada might also alleviate fears that an independent state would, either out of ideology or necessity, pursue radically different policy directions, potentially hostile to business interests.

The attitudes of business people are particularly unclear and likely to shift rapidly with different economic circumstances. In a 1991 survey, taken after the failure of the Meech Lake Accord,[32] a slim majority (55.4 percent) of English-Canadian business people agreed that, if Quebec voted 'yes' in a referendum, it and the ROC should then negotiate economic ties. Support for free trade was highest (78.7 percent), followed by a common currency (46 percent), and a common central bank and army (both about 36 percent). Nevertheless, sovereignty-association as a preferred option was far behind both the status quo and new constitutional negotiations.

These responses contrast strongly with those of Quebec business people in the same survey. Seventy-two percent of them opted for sovereignty-association as their preferred option, and 95 percent supported economic ties in the event of a 'yes' vote. Large majorities favored a common currency, free trade, a common army, and a common central bank.

Coming to Terms with Partnership

After a 'yes' referendum victory, the evolution of ROC public opinion with respect to a future partnership arrangement with Quebec would clearly depend greatly on a number of broad considerations about what was possible and desirable.

First, people would need to believe that the decision to accomplish sovereignty was clear, decisive, and legitimate. There would have to be a broad realization that a sovereign Quebec was now an irreversible reality, that all avenues for exploring renewal within federalism had been exhausted, and that no reasonable chance of retreating from the decision existed. In other words, Canadians outside Quebec would need to come to terms fully with the idea of sovereignty itself – perhaps a long process – before they could give any serious consideration to anything but the narrowest and most frosty future relationship.

Second, thinking about relations with Quebec would take a distant second place to thinking about the reconstruction of the ROC. Again, the implication is that consideration of partnership would come later rather than sooner.

Third, the public would need to be convinced that a partnership arrangement would serve Canada's interest, not just Quebec's. Any idea that partnership was being done primarily 'for Quebec' would be fatal. Indeed, if the example of the Charlottetown referendum is any guide, any agreement would likely be weighed in terms of who got more out of it, and if the scales were seen to be unbalanced, the partnership project would certainly fail, even if it offered the ROC real benefits.

Fourth and closely related, it would be essential to allay fears that a partnership would result in a major shift of power between Ottawa and the provinces or give Quebec more weight in the making of decisions affecting the whole country than it has at present. Any plausible suggestion of these outcomes would doom the prospects for negotiation of a successful partnership. It would be one thing to accede to the desire for radically more autonomy for Quebec but quite another for that autonomy to be perceived as a device through which Quebec would have more, not less, influence over the rest of the country. As Roger Gibbins makes clear, partnership would have to mean not only that Quebec would gain greater autonomy from Canada, but also that Canada would have to gain greater autonomy from Quebec – as in having national political institutions in which Quebec did not play a part.[33]

Indeed, sovereignists have often tried to convince other Canadians that Quebec independence would benefit them too, providing them an opportunity to have the kind of federal system they wanted without continually being held hostage to what is acceptable to Quebec. As Lévesque put it 30 years ago, 'The present regime also frustrates the English-speaking majority from simplifying, rationalizing and centralizing certain institutions as it would like to do.'[34] The stronger the partnership, however, the less freedom the ROC would have. Similar fears could, of course, arise with a once-and-for-all treaty arrangement if its terms imposed strict constraints on the powers of either federal or provincial governments.

Negotiating Partnership

My survey of likely opinion in the ROC suggests that it would be little inclined to enter into partnership negotiations with enthusiasm or alacrity. But suppose our original assumptions hold and there is at least some willingness to explore the options of future association. Several sets of questions then arise. The key issue is the political dynamics that would attend secession and the subsequent economic and political events.

How would events unfold in the aftermath of a successful sovereignty referendum? There are two broad views.

The first, best exemplified by Robert Young,[35] is that, even with a small majority 'yes' vote, internal and external forces would push inexorably for a quick if messy completion of secession. Financial markets would panic, the dollar would go into free fall, capital flight would begin, social unrest would erupt. Something would have to be done – immediately – to restore calm. Sovereignist leaders would be triumphant, and francophone Quebecers would quickly rally around them. The ROC would be in disarray, and however discredited its federal leadership, the only alternative would be to have it bargain quickly with Quebec. International forces would push for an early settlement, which would likely be accomplished if only to avoid further drastic disruption of the two communities.

An alternative scenario suggests the process would be much more drawn out. Both sides would have to assess the meaning of the vote and the immediate political fallout. Financial panic might as easily provoke a move in Quebec to abort the secession, rather than expedite it. Even without partnership, the list of contentious issues to resolve would be long. Moreover, analysts such as Monahan and Bryant and Russell and Ryder[36] argue that a legitimate secession would have to be achieved through constitutional means, again opening up the possibility of a long process before the requisite consent was achieved.

Both models are plausible, and predicting which would be more likely to occur is difficult. There is also the possibility that they could be combined in the sense of the parties' coming to rapid agreement on a few basic issues immediately, in order to contain panic, and then following a more measured and lengthy process to formalize the secession and the subsequent relationship. The two stages, could not, of course, be neatly separated. Successful management of the first steps would facilitate later agreements; failure would poison the well for the future. And once in place, initial arrangements, even if conceived as temporary, would be hard to dislodge later. (See Box 3.)

Moments of Decision

Predicting the atmosphere in which postreferendum discussions would occur is indeed impossible. Sovereignist commentators appear remarkably confident that cool and rational heads would prevail and that mutual trust and goodwill would mark the discussions. They are confident negotiations could be managed successfully. Given recent events, this forecast seems hugely optimistic.

The debate does, however, suggest a number of moments at which possibilities for partnership might be addressed. It also suggests that the entire process is likely to involve a number of steps or stages, rather than be accomplished all at once.

Moment One. In some ways, the ideal time to sketch at least the broad outlines of a partnership would be *before* the next referendum.[37] The form could be a package linked to agreement – either explicit or implicitly accepted – on the referendum question, the acceptable majority, and the rules of the game for the referendum campaign.

The ROC would be saying, in effect, here are the tests that it believes any secession vote must pass in order to be considered decisive and legitimate. It would follow that such a set of tests would have to be accompanied by a commitment that, if they are passed, the ROC would be bound to give effect to secession with the least possible delay. To this could be added some broad principles to which the ROC would adhere in subsequent negotiations, including an indication of the principles that would govern Canada's approach to thinking about partnership.

The great advantage of this approach is that it would minimize uncertainty. Citizens on both sides of the divide would be reasonably sure of what consequences would flow from a 'yes' vote. Business and financial interests could be reassured. Quebecers would have a clear sense of just what they were getting – and losing – by virtue of supporting sovereignty. It would become clear that the PQ could not unilaterally allay fears by promising partnership and that the belief that nothing really would change after secession was wrong. Quebec voters would thus be in a better position to weigh the advantages and disadvantages of choosing independence over federalism. (Indeed, such a strategy could, in principle, be combined with a statement about what changes in federalism they might expect were they to vote 'no,' again enhancing the 'quality' of the vote.)

Desirable as such an approach might be, the chance of its happening is minute. Many politicians outside Quebec are quite prepared to state their conditions – Plan B – for a Quebec vote; they are much more reluctant to spell out subsequent steps in advance. If the proposed terms were at all reasonable or generous, they would be accused of selling the country out and predetermining a successful referendum vote.[38] If the conditions were tough and unyielding, they would be undermined by PQ arguments that they were just a bluff, not to be taken seriously. (Such arguments have already been remarkably successful

in counteracting apocalyptic predictions about the economic and social consequences of a decision to separate.)

In addition, no Canadian government now has a mandate to set out unilaterally the terms of a future partnership. Given the likely need for constitutional
amendment to give effect to any new relationship, no single government could
make a fully credible commitment to any particular postreferendum model.[39]

Nevertheless, virtually all advocates of Plan B say that Canada would not
stand in the way of a strongly and clearly expressed decision by Quebecers to
secede (even if it is difficult to imagine the constitutional process by which that
might be accomplished). Then there is indeed some obligation to indicate how
the ROC would proceed after a 'yes' vote.

Moment Two. A second moment for addressing a partnership arrangement
might occur in the immediate aftermath of a referendum 'yes.'

Let us assume for a moment that Young is correct in believing that confusion, panic in financial markets, and capital flight, not to mention social unrest,
would place powerful pressures on authorities to stabilize matters as quickly as
possible. Under these circumstances, an agreement, whether it mentioned or
implied partnership, would be cobbled together in great haste, with little opportunity to consider the longer term.

With a primary goal of restoring calm, any interim agreement would focus on
the critical immediate issues: the debt and management of Canada's financial
obligations, assurances about the continuity of laws, perhaps an interim
arrangement with respect to the currency, basic guarantees of minority rights
and borders, but little more.[40]

Once calm had been restored, the need for some elements of such an agreement might disappear. Others would appear, on reflection, to be undesirable,
unworkable, or inappropriate to one or both sides. Many important issues would
have been left aside. There would have been no opportunity to think about how
to design an institutional framework.

The legitimacy of those who negotiated such an agreement would be in question. It would probably have been made by the incumbent federal government,
which would have no authority to negotiate longer-term arrangements. And,
most important, citizens and governments would have had no opportunity to
think through their long-term interests or for new, more legitimate authorities to
have taken office.

Thus, although some elements of an interim agreement might turn out to be
permanent or to set a benchmark for any subsequent agreements, it is best seen
as a stopgap solution. The long-term relationship between the two entities
would remain to be settled.

Moment Three. The makeshift nature of any interim agreement would require a follow-up stage of negotiation, which might be coupled with final ratification of the terms of secession. But this stage might not – indeed, probably would not – come quickly. Much would need to be done.

Both parties would have to carefully assess the responses of economic and political actors to the initial vote and its aftermath. Public opinion in both Quebec and the ROC would no doubt be highly fluid and changeable. Would Quebecers be getting cold feet and thinking about ways to get back to federalism? Or would they display strong national solidarity, with even some federalists rallying around the great new project? As the implications became clear in the ROC, would anti-Quebec feelings harden, or would the dominant mood become acquiescence and a willingness to work things out? There can be no safe predictions about such matters.

Each side would also have to carefully think through its interests in light of the new circumstances. Quebec would be more likely than the ROC to act in a unified manner, partly because it has one government, rather than twelve, and partly because its government and civil society have so thoroughly considered the associated issues over a long period. (See, for example, report of the Bélanger-Campeau Commission,[41] though that report paid little attention to association or partnership.)

Yet even in Quebec, as already noted, views on the necessity and scope of a future partnership are by no means united, even among *péquistes*. Moreover, the province has become increasingly polarized on ethnic and linguistic lines. It would be impossible for its government to ignore internal dissent as it prepared to discuss the terms of secession and partnership with the ROC.

Nevertheless, formulating interests and objectives in the ROC would be a great deal harder for at least two reasons. First, the federal government, as presently constituted, would have no mandate to play a strong role, much less to claim to speak for a 'Canada' that had just been repudiated and in which Quebec representatives no longer played a part. No serious discussion of long-term relationships could occur before the formation of a new government. Until then, Quebec would have no authoritative interlocutor in the ROC.

Second, given the differing regional and governmental interests discussed earlier, the very notion of a ROC interest would remain unclear. An extended period of discussion and debate, both regional and intergovernmental, would be necessary before Canada could be prepared to come to the table.

Another delay might occur because Canada, even if it could agree within itself, might still be in no rush to start negotiations on a long-term relationship. Once the sovereignty vote had been successful, Quebec would need an agreement much more than most of the rest of the country. Even if an eventual agreement was in the interests of both sides, and even if no one had an interest in the collapse of the Quebec economy, this asymmetry would strengthen Canada's bargaining power.

Indeed, as time went on, the need for partnership would likely become more and more urgent to Quebecers but simultaneously be seen as less pressing in the ROC. If those shifts occurred, Quebec's bargaining power would decline further.

Remember that, in these negotiations, the default position would be no agreement. Although that situation would be costly for both sides, it would likely be costlier for Quebec, which, with no agreement, would find itself forced to adapt its own policies to those of Canada with no guarantee of continued access to the Canadian market.

Another important change from the dynamics of past constitutional discussions is that, in the past, Quebec awaited an offer from the rest of the country; this time, Quebec has asserted that it would make an offer of partnership to Canada. In doing so, it would risk rebuff. Thus, it is the ROC that potentially holds a 'knife to the throat.'

This analysis suggests that Young may be right in thinking that a quick agreement would emerge in the immediate aftermath of a successful referendum. But it would be a stopgap. An enormous number of tasks would need to be completed before the final terms of secession and the subsequent relationship were fully addressed.

Who Would Negotiate Partnership?

Perhaps the most persistent *péquiste* misunderstanding of the ROC is its sense that Canada is a single entity centered on the federal government. This view is less and less valid, as devolution and decentralization proceed apace. Who, then, would speak for Canada in a negotiation of future relationships?

Once the initial crisis was over, provincial deference to Ottawa would rapidly decline – unless the federal government proved exceptionally effective in managing the first stages of negotiation. Even if it did, the country would have to hold a federal election, without Quebec, in order to select a new national government with a mandate both to deal with Quebec and to help Canada redefine itself. If this election produced a government with strong support across the country, the initiative could remain with Ottawa. If not, provincial governments would emerge as the principal champions of each region's interests.

Whatever the result, the provinces would be important players in any final settlement, especially if it required constitutional amendment. They would have little patience with any federal claim that negotiation was now a matter of external affairs and hence of federal jurisdiction. They would also have a constitutional claim of their own: to the extent that any agreement involved matters under provincial jurisdiction, implementation would be a provincial responsibility.

In brief, the fact is that any Canadian position in the negotiations would first have to be negotiated between Ottawa and the provinces. And even given agreement on that position, the provinces would be unlikely to permit federal representatives alone to be at the bargaining table. Neither would the provinces agree to be merely consulted, as they were in the negotiations of the Canada-US Free Trade Agreement and the NAFTA. They would require direct membership on the negotiating team.

Greatly complicating federal-provincial coordination in negotiations with Quebec would be the fact that the reconstituting of the remaining federal partners would be going on simultaneously. The more extensive the partnership envisaged, the greater would be its implications for the new system. Hence, many provinces would be reluctant to commit themselves to a Quebec-Canada partnership before the shape of the new Canada had been decided.

Thus, any Quebec expectations that its representatives would be facing a single negotiating partner are likely to be wrong.

The Outcome

After a 'yes' referendum and subsequent negotiations, what might the new Canada-Quebec relationship look like?

At the outset, I suggested four forms that a future Canada-Quebec relationship could take: splendid isolation; a NAFTA-type treaty arrangement; a set of multiple, *ad hoc* linkages; and the full partnership proposed by the PQ. What does my analysis say about these alternatives?

Many in the ROC may desire isolation, but it would not be possible in its stark form. Canada and Quebec are linked in so many ways and at so many different levels that a surgical separation would be impossible. It would simply be too disruptive and costly to interests on all sides. So, although once separation occurred, the style of the relationship would include all the self-interest and wariness that normally characterizes international relations, the intensity of the relationship would necessarily be greater than usual.

Slightly more plausible would be a free trade agreement tied to the NAFTA. Negotiating even this would not be easy, since many of the issues that bedeviled the original NAFTA negotiations would once again be on the table. But assuming such an arrangement were completed, it would still be insufficient to maintain the Canadian economic union. A free trade agreement would be a necessary, but insufficient, part of future arrangements.

What about the alternatives: a comprehensive partnership or a much more flexible, unstructured set of linkages?

A Comprehensive Agreement

Most discussions of a Canada-Quebec partnership arrangement suggest (or imply) that it would be encompassed in a single document or treaty setting out in detail the areas of shared decisionmaking, along with the structure, membership, powers, and decision-rules of the institutional framework. There would be one comprehensive agreement (presumably subject to amendment by an agreed formula).

This *Commentary* has demonstrated, however, that such an arrangement would be virtually impossible to achieve. The more com-prehensive and definitive the agreement, the more difficulty Canada would have in arriving at its position, the more complex the bilateral discussions, and the less the probability of winning successful ratification in the ROC.

Given that Quebec would have recently said no to Canada, a global Canada-Quebec union likely would be unacceptable to most non-Quebecers. Debate about such a new union would have all the symbolic features that have made constitutional change within the federation so difficult.[42]

A new partnership would be constitutional in two senses. It would have implications for the existing Canadian Constitution and division of powers, and the agreement itself would have most of the characteristics of a constitution. Indeed, it could well be necessary to incorporate its terms into the constitutions of both new entities. If the agreement took this form, Canada would have to follow its existing rules of constitutional amendment (suitably modified to account for the absence of Quebec), with all the possibilities for rejection that the country has already experienced.

Multiple, Ad Hoc Agreements

All this suggests how difficult arriving at a comprehensive partnership would be. An alternative approach might be more successful. An incremental, *ad hoc*, and tentative route would use not one but many agreements, each covering different issues with different participants and different decision-rules.

This approach would still require a basic document of agreement on the terms of secession and on key issues, such as the debt, employees, assets, and the like. Such a document could also include the parties' general commitment to cooperate in any areas that were mutually beneficial and perhaps a limited agreement on free trade (or on Canada's backing Quebec's accession to the NAFTA). But that would be all.

What would follow would be a series of separate agreements. Some of them – such as those covering citizenship, minority rights. territory, and aboriginal peoples[43] – would need to come quickly. Others could be developed over time, as the need arose, in such areas as coordination of fiscal policies, harmonization of taxes and regulations, and environmental policy. The mechanisms for coordination could vary from area to area. Some might need formal joint decisionmakers or authoritative tribunals, but each would be separate, with a limited and specific mandate. In many other areas, there would be no need for formal decision-rules and voting procedures at all: consultation and information exchange would be sufficient, with each government responsible for its own policy formation and implementation.

Eventually, a large number of such *ad hoc* agreements might develop, weaving at the policy level a myriad linkages paralleling the economic interdependency and shared values and interests that now exist. Alternatively, the agreements could be restricted to a small number of critical areas.

This approach would have a number of major advantages over a single, global partnership. First, it would carry far less of the symbolic constitutional baggage; agreement and cooperation would clearly arise only out of mutual need. Most, if not all, the agreements could be achieved without constitutional change, and some could be accomplished administratively, without going to the legislatures.

Second, the fact that many agreements would require only consultation means that the decision-rule problem would be largely avoided. As noted at the outset, this problem is virtually insurmountable in a two-unit confederation. Each partner's having an equal vote is unacceptable to the larger one; anything less places the smaller in a permanent minority position. Varying the decision-rule to allow equality on some issues and proportionality on others is only a partial solution. Who decides which rules apply when? Multiple agreements would allow the rules to be tailored to the case at hand, not to abstract but irreconcilable principles.

A related advantage would be that a multiplicity of agreements also makes it possible to vary the number and character of the players from issue to issue. Where coordination was desirable on matters of provincial jurisdiction, there would be no reason the provinces would not become the 'Canadian' players at the table. Although this prospect offends the PQ's two-nations, equal-partners model, it opens for Quebec the possibility of coalition building, which is possible only with more than two players. It would also allay some of the provinces' fears that partnership would erode their powers. In many cases, the agreements would be bilateral or multilateral, involving Quebec and one or a few provinces, such as Ontario and New Brunswick.

Moreover, in some areas, such as management of the St. Lawrence Seaway, the participants might not be governments at all; there is no reason they could not be actors from the private sector exercising delegated powers.

Finally, a series of *ad hoc*, informal arrangements would alleviate two other problems potentially associated with the partnership model. One is the 'democratic deficit.' The PQ's partnership proposals include a council of ministers that would be the authoritative decisionmaker; its decrees in areas under the jurisdiction of the partnership would be binding on all other governments.

The resulting democratic deficit would pose a host of problems. The council's accountability to electorates and legislatures would be indirect at best. Any authority it exercised would be taken away from federal and provincial governments and, by extension, their citizens. This loss of accountability would be much more severe for Canada than for Quebec (because of the much greater diversity of interests the former would have to represent and because the responsibilities of the two levels of government would be involved).

Thus, a plenary council equipped with substantial powers would be a serious affront to democratic values, especially since the proposed parliamentary body would be even weaker than the European Parliament.[44] The *ad hoc* agreement approach would suffer from some of the same defects, but they would be limited because the agreements themselves would be limited and related directly to mutually agreed common tasks.

The same could be said of another potential deficit, the joint-decision trap. A unanimous decision-rule can lead to paralysis. With each side having a veto on key matters, there are few incentives to compromise and no deadlock-breaking mechanisms. The greater the range of issues covered in the partnership agreement and the broader the authority of the council, the greater this danger and the more constrained all governments would be in responding to their own needs and priorities. This powerful logic is what lies behind Parizeau's hostility to partnership: why gain independence only to subject oneself to constraints imposed by the polity one just left? The same logic would apply to the governments and citizens of the ROC.[45]

Again, this point strongly argues against the comprehensive model and in favor of the *ad hoc* approach.

Readers may ask if they have not seen this *ad hoc* approach somewhere before. Indeed they have. The Canada-US relationship is not defined completely by the NAFTA. It was preceded by and is still accompanied by a myriad other agreements, large and small. Some are between the governments of Canada and the United States, others are between contiguous provinces and states. Some, like the International Joint Commission, are long standing, others are temporary. Interdependence and integration breed a broad set of solutions, even without an overarching set of political institutions governing the relationship. This may be the most appropriate model for Canada and an independent Quebec.

Another useful analogy lies not in government but in civil society. Many Canadian associations and interest groups have divided on linguistic lines, establishing separate Quebec and Canadian organizations. For some, at least, this split has not precluded the development of *ad hoc* ways to cooperate and collaborate with respect to shared interests and common goals. This model too could prefigure a postsovereignty relationship.

Conclusion

The idea of partnership goes well beyond the question of whether and how the secession of Quebec might be achieved. Rather, it assumes secession would be accompanied by the building of a new relationship that, in effect, would be a two-unit confederation, in which two sovereign countries agreed to create a new, if limited, level of government, with authoritative decisionmaking institutions made up of representatives of each.

This *Commentary* began with the premise that such a model should not be rejected out of hand. Rather, it should be evaluated on its merits. Would such a model serve the interests of Canada-without-Quebec and of Quebec itself? Would it be preferable to the obvious alternatives, in which Canada and Quebec would simply treat each other as any two countries in the international arena or in which the two established a simple free trade area on the NAFTA model?

I identified several reasons why the broader relationship might be desirable. Between Quebec and the ROC, the degree of interdependence and the pervasiveness of linkages – in industry, labor, and financial markets and at the level of citizens and groups – is far greater than that between any two separate countries, even Canada and the United States. Maintaining and building these relationships would indeed be critical after a 'yes' referendum. And doing so would require more than the negative integration stipulated by a few rules on freedom of trade. Measures to sustain positive integration in infrastructure, communications, and financial institutions would also be needed.

Positive integration requires not a single, once-and-for-all set of rules but rather a set of ongoing adjustments to changing circumstances. Without it, the economic integration of Quebec and the rest of Canada would likely deteriorate rapidly.

A second reason to take partnership seriously relates to Quebec public opinion. Whether the province is inside or outside Confederation, any long-term solution to the Canadian question must involve ways of responding simultaneously to Quebec's sense of itself as a distinct national community and to its sense of identity and linkage with Canada. Both a model of federalism that insists on the undifferentiated equality of the provinces and one that seeks outright independence are at odds with the desires of the vast majority of Quebecers. The weight of their opinion wavers between recognition of Quebec's particularity within Canada and sovereignty combined with close association. If federalism cannot accommodate the first aspiration, then perhaps it should regard the second with more sympathy.

Thus the grounds for looking carefully at proposals for partnership are both practical and normative. Yet powerful objections exist. Some are expressed by Quebec sovereignists who do not wish to constrain the independence for which they would have struggled so hard. But most come from outside Quebec.

As I have argued, for most Quebecers, the move from reformed federalism to sovereignty- partnership would be just one step along a continuum. For most other Canadians, it would be the crossing of a Rubicon politically, legally, and emotionally. Reforming federalism and negotiating secession are totally different games. It would be an immense stretch for those outside Quebec to move from the anger, hostility, loss of confidence, and sense of betrayal that a decision to secede would produce to a calm, deliberate, cost-benefit analysis of partnership. It is even less likely that they would take pride in establishing a new partnership when the old one had just been broken. Supporters of partnership may applaud or deplore such sentiments, but on no account can they be ignored.

Opinion about sovereignty would also be divided in the ROC. Some business interests, anxious to avoid disruption, would probably support it, at least in some areas. Ontario, with its strong economic and historic ties to Quebec, might be sympathetic. So would the Atlantic provinces, anxious to minimize the costs of Pakistanization. The Western provinces, with fewer ties, would be far less likely to be sympathetic. Yet any partnership would require nationwide consent.

Moreover, negotiating a broad partnership agreement would also face numerous practical impediments. Who would be at the table? What role would the provinces play, in both the development of an agreement and its implementation? How would it be ratified and incorporated into the Canadian Constitution? How would the discussion of partnership relate to two other crucial processes going on at much the same time: the formal accession to sovereignty, and the necessary rearrangement and reconstitution of the ROC after secession?

Many of the issues to be resolved are both highly charged and highly complex. Even when negotiations did get under way, they would likely be drawn out – even as both sides had to grapple with the consequences of private actors and markets taking matters into their own hands.

More generally, it would be immensely difficult to operate a two-unit confederation. The decision-rule problem seems insurmountable. Any strong partnership model poses serious questions about democracy and accountability and about autonomous effective governance.

Hence, I conclude with a paradox: there are strong reasons to support the idea but powerful objections to its desirability and workability. The answer, in my view, is that there would and should be a relationship but not one in the form proposed by the PQ in its current legislation: a kind of master agreement setting out a list of shared functions and a set of institutions with specified powers and decision-rules. The PQ's promise to Quebecers – that with sovereignty and a partnership, life would be much as it was before – could not be met with or without such a partnership.

Rather, the regime that developed would be more *ad hoc* and incremental. It would comprise not a single agreement but a large number of limited, highly specific arrangements in particular policy areas where both sides felt harmonization and coordination would be useful. These agreements could form and dissolve with considerable frequency, the only test being their mutual utility.

The institutional arrangements, participants, and decision-rules could vary widely from agreement to agreement. Most, if not all, would have no constitutional status. Most would operate at the level of consultation, information exchange, and mutual influence (as federal intergovernmental relations do currently). Few, if any, would embody authoritative decisionmaking binding on all sides. Something akin to the PQ's proposed council (or the current first ministers' conference) might be desirable to oversee the relationship, but it would be a discussion forum, not a decisionmaker. Over time, the relationships might become deeper and more intense – or they might not. But they would evolve to the rhythm of practical needs on both sides, and the initial steps would be limited, rather than expansive.

Such an informal set of arrangements might be accompanied by some other agreements. These might include: (1) the essential agreement, made in the early days of secession, necessary to contain the initial economic and political fallout of a vote for sovereignty; (2) the terms of separation themselves; and (3) a limited free trade agreement, based on and perhaps eventually incorporated into the NAFTA.

In short, even in the most optimistic scenario, the relationships that developed after a 'yes' referendum would not constitute a partnership. There would be no Canada-Quebec union like the EU, if only because the EU reflects a building process, a coming together of previously independent countries, while the Canada-Quebec partnership would be the result of 'unbuilding' a previously existing federal structure. Whatever the superficial similarities of the result, the dynamics involved would be quite different.

The most likely relationship between an independent Quebec and the ROC would embody linkages appropriate to international relations between two states, albeit ones that share a continent and a wide range of common interests. Even getting to that point would require immense political skill.

Some sovereignists – Jacques Parizeau, for example – may be reassured by this analysis. Such an arrangement is all they really want anyway. But it is not the partnership that the PQ has presented to Quebecers, nor is it what Quebecers themselves want and expect if they were to opt for sovereignty. Moreover, although many of the common needs could be met by the *ad hoc* arrangements suggested here, the degree of joint decisionmaking that would be necessary to retain a full economic union or the economic integration that currently exists would require much more. Dealing in the future with such key issues as a customs union, common monetary policy, competition, and internal trade would require the broader political arrangements implied by partnership. And that, I believe, cannot be achieved.

NOTES

This paper has benefited greatly from the comments of many colleagues, notably Kenneth Boessenkool, Alan Cairns, David Cameron, Patrick Monahan, John Richards, William Robson, and Daniel Schwanen. Not all of them agree with the basic purpose and conclusions of the paper, but all helped me to clarify the argument and avoid at least some of the potholes in the road. Lee d'Anjou was a superlative editor.

1 *Globe and Mail* (Toronto), May 17, 1997, p. D6.
2 Patrick J. Monahan and Michael J. Bryant, with Nancy C. Coté, *Coming to Terms with Plan B: Ten Principles Governing Secession*, C.D. Howe Institute Commentary 83 (Toronto: C.D. Howe Institute, June 1996); and Peter Russell and Bruce Ryder, *Ratifying a Postreferendum Agreement on Quebec Sovereignty*, C.D. Howe Institute Commentary 97 (Toronto: C.D. Howe Institute, October 1997).
3 Alan C. Cairns, *Looking into the Abyss: The Need for a Plan C*, C.D. Howe Institute Commentary 96 (Toronto: C.D. Howe Institute, September 1997).
4 Daniel Turp, 'From an Economic and Political Partnership between Quebec and Canada to a Canadian Union,' *Constitutional Forum* 7 (Winter/Spring 1996): 95.
5 Ibid.
6 Lawrence Martin, *The Antagonist: Lucien Bouchard and the Politics of Delusion* (Toronto: Viking, 1997), p. 283.

7 Parti Québécois, National Executive Council, *Quebec in a New World*, trans. Robert Chodos (Toronto: James Lorimer, 1994).

8 The text of the tripartite agreement was attached as a schedule to the act. For a discussion, see Daniel Turp, 'Post-Referendum Reflections: Sovereignty Is Alive and Well, Partnership Remains the Roadmap to the Future,' *Canada Watch* 4 (November-December 1995): 17, 42–44.

9 Quebec's legal capacity to make such a unilateral declaration of independence is, of course, currently before the Supreme Court of Canada.

10 Jacques Parizeau, Speech to the Royal Institute of Inter-national Affairs, Chatham House, London, July 5, 1995.

11 Lucien Bouchard, speech, Lac St. Jean, Quebec, October 25, 1995.

12 For a very complete summary of Quebec opinion surveys, see Maurice Pinard et al., *Un combat inachevée* (Montréal: Presses de l'Université du Québec, 1997).

13 Quoted in Kenneth McRoberts, *Misconceiving Canada: The Search for National Unity* (Toronto: McClelland and Stewart, 1997), p. 247.

14 Louis Balthazar, 'Please, Let Us Breathe,' *Canada Watch* 4 (November-December 1995): 35.

15 This point is very well argued by Guy Laforest. See 'Standing in the Shoes of the Other Partners in the Canadian Union,' in Roger Gibbins and Guy Laforest, eds., *Beyond the Impasse: Toward Reconciliation* (Montreal: Institute for Research on Public Policy, 1998).

16 Ibid., p. 36.

17 Quoted in the *Globe and Mail* (Toronto), December 19, 1996, p. A21.

18 Denis Stairs, *Canada and Quebec after Québécois Secession: 'Realist' Reflections on an International Relationship* (Halifax: Dalhousie University, Centre for Foreign Policy Studies, 1996), pp. 11–12.

19 For this argument, see Kenneth Norrie and Michael Percy, 'A Canada-Quebec Partnership: The Economic Dimensions;' and François Rocher, 'Economic Partnership and Political Integration: Recasting Quebec-Canada's Economic Union,' both in Gibbins and Laforest, eds., *Beyond the Impasse*.

20 William Robson persuasively argues that this attempt would probably be doomed by the flight of capital and that, in any case, the retention of the Canadian currency would require much cooperation on arrange- ments for crossborder banking, backup for Quebec banks, agreement on the debt, and so on. See his *Change for a Buck? The Canadian Dollar after Quebec Secession*, C.D. Howe Institute Commentary 68 (Toronto: C.D. Howe Institute, March 1995).

21 See John McCallum, 'National Borders Matter: Canada-US Trade Patterns,' *American Economic Review* 85 (June 1995): 615–623; and John F. Helliwell, 'Do National Borders Matter for Quebec's Trade?' *Canadian Journal of Economics* 29 (August 1996): 507–522.

22 William B.P. Robson, *Dynamic Tensions: Markets, Federalism, and Canada's Economic Future*, Policy Review and Outlook, 1992 (Toronto: C.D. Howe Institute, 1992).

23 Roger Gibbins, 'Getting There from Here,' in Gibbins and Laforest, eds., *Beyond the Impasse*, p. 407.

24 Gordon Gibson, *Plan B: The Future of the Rest of Canada* (Vancouver: Fraser Institute, 1994), p. 165.

25 In his proposal for a Canada-Quebec Union, Philip Resnick argues that its great merit would be that English Canada would have a government of its own. 'Quebec can no longer stymie senate reform; we can give our federal government a more or less significant role over culture, higher education, or social affairs, as we see fit.' *Toward a Canada-Quebec Union* (Montreal: McGill-Queen's University Press, 1991), pp. 116–117.

26 See David Cameron and Richard Simeon, 'Ontario in Confederation: The Not So Friendly Giant,' in Graham White, ed., *The Government and Politics of Ontario*, 5th ed. (Toronto: University of Toronto Press, 1997).

27 See Thomas J. Courchene, 'ACCESS: A Convention on the Canadian Economic and Social Systems,' report prepared for the government of Ontario and reprinted, with commentary, in *Assessing ACCESS: Towards a New Social Union* (Kingston, Ont.: Queen's University, Institute of Intergovernmental Relations, 1997); André Burelle, *Le mal canadien.* (Montréal: Fides, 1995); and Richard Simeon, 'Rethinking Government, Rethinking Federalism,' in Mohamed Charih and Art Daniels, eds., *New Public Management and Public Administration in Canada* (Toronto: Institute of Public Administration of Canada, 1997). See also proposals put forward by the Group of 22, *Making Canada Work Better* ([Toronto], 1996); and the Business Council on National Issues, 'Memorandum for the Honourable Frank McKenna, Premier of New Brunswick and Chairman-Designate, Council of Premiers' and 'Building a Better Canada: A Declaration' (Toronto, July 15, 1997).

28 See Roger Gibbins, with Katherine Harmsworth, *Time Out: Assessing Incremental Strategies for Enhancing the Canadian Political Union*, C.D. Howe Institute Commentary 88 (Toronto: C.D. Howe Institute, 1997); and Resnick, *Toward a Canada-Quebec Union.*

29 F.L. Morton, 'The Quebec Referendum: A View from the West,' *Canada Watch* 4 (November-December 1995): 32–35.

30 See, for example, Resnick, *Toward a Canada-Quebec Union*, pp. 78–79.

31 For example, Philip Resnick proposes a complex condominium-type arrangement comprising the governments of the nine provinces and two territories, a government and parliament of English Canada with a parallel government of Quebec, and a government and parliament of the union. The parliament would be made up of elected senators on the English Canada side and of directly elected members on the Quebec

side. The union government would be responsible for foreign policy, defense, international trade, finance, the environment, and citizenship. See ibid.

32 Charles Macli, 'Dueling in the Dark,' *Globe and Mail* (Toronto), *Report on Business Magazine*, April 1991, pp. 29–39.

33 Gibbins, 'The Institutional Parameters of a Quebec-Canada Partnership,' in Gibbins and Laforest, eds., *Beyond the Impasse.*

34 René Lévesque, *An Option for Quebec* (Toronto: McClelland and Stewart, 1968), p. 25.

35 Robert Young, *The Secession of Quebec and the Future of Canada* (Montreal: McGill-Queen's University Press, 1995), passim.

36 Monahan and Bryant, Coming to Terms with Plan B; and Russell and Ryder, *Ratifying a Postreferendum Agreement on Quebec Sovereignty.*

37 This is the approach taken by Gibbins and Laforest. The commitment to partnership would emerge before a referendum; a constituent assembly would then be called, and the resulting partnership agreement them submitted to the people. See *Beyond the Impasse*, especially their 'Conclusion.'

38 Writing on the question of a common currency, Robson (*Change for a Buck?*, p. 17) captures this dilemma well:

> And from the point of view of those who seek to hold Canada together, it is imperative not to engage in discussions designed to make separation easier. ... [S]uch discussions are very unlikely to take place until the consequences of a 'yes' vote become known. And at that point, the agendas of both governments will fill rapidly with other issues, sharply lowering the chances of reaching agreement on measures to preserve the currency union before a collapse of confidence destroys it.

See also a similar analysis on negotiating commercial relations in Daniel Schwanen, *Break Up to Make Up: Trade Relations after a Quebec Declaration of Sovereignty*, C.D. Howe Institute Commentary 69 (Toronto: C.D. Howe Institute, March 1995).

39 Stairs, for one, argues that 'Ottawa should not, under any circumstances, agree to discuss the terms of Quebec's postsecession relationship with Canada in advance of secession having occurred' (*Canada and Quebec after Québécois Secession*, p. 36).

40 Even these are complex issues that would take time to work out, especially in the tense period following a vote for separation. See Robson, *Change for a Buck?*, pp. 17–18.

41 Quebec, Commission on the Political and Constitutional Future of Quebec, *Report*, chaired by Michel Bélanger and Jean Campeau (Quebec, 1991).

42 See Peter Russell, *Constitutional Odyssey: Can Canadians Be a Sovereign People?* 2nd ed. (Toronto: University of Toronto Press, 1994).

43 It is not too difficult to imagine reciprocal arrangements relating to linguistic minori-

ties or both parties' guaranteeing aboriginal self-government. Citizenship, however, would be a much more complex and tense issue. See Hartt, *Divided Loyalties*.

44 See R.L. Watts, 'The Limitations of Recent Proposals for Confederal Solutions for Canada' (Institute of Intergovernmental Relations, Queen's University, Kingston, Ont., 1994), mimeographed.

45 For such reasons, Patrick Monahan argues that creating common institutions would be in the interests of neither Canada nor Quebec. See 'La sécession du Québec: considerations juridiques et politiques,' *Choix: Série Québec-Canada* 1 (June 1995): 4–24.

Contributors

ALAN ALEXANDROFF is Director of the Program on Conflict Management and Negotiation, University of Toronto.

MICHAEL J. BRYANT is a lawyer in private practice and an Adjunct Professor at the University of Toronto.

ALAN C. CAIRNS is Law Foundation of Saskatchewan Professor, College of Law, University of Saskatchewan.

DAVID R. CAMERON is a Professor of Political Science at the University of Toronto.

NANCY C. COTE is an LL.M. candidate at Osgoode Hall Law School and a member of the Ontario Bar.

ROGER GIBBONS is a Professor of Political Science at the University of Calgary.

JANICE GROSS STEIN is Harrowston Professor of Conflict Management and Negotiation, University of Toronto.

ROBERT HOWSE is Associate Director, Centre for the Study of State and Market, University of Toronto.

DAVID LAIDLER is a Professor of Economics at the University of Western Ontario and an Adjunct Scholar of the C.D. Howe Institute.

PATRICK J. MONAHAN is a Professor of Law at Osgoode Hall Law School, York University.

JOHN RICHARDS is Associate Professor of Business Administration at Simon Fraser University and Adjunct Scholar of the C.D. Howe Institute.

WILLIAM B.P. ROBSON is a Senior Policy Analyst at the C.D. Howe Institute.

PETER RUSSELL is a Professor Emeritus at the University of Toronto.

BRUCE RYDER is a Professor of Law at Osgoode Hall Law School, York University.

DANIEL SCHWANEN is a Senior Policy Analyst at the C.D. Howe Institute.

RICHARD SIMEON is a Professor of Political Science at the University of Toronto and an Adjunct Scholar of the C.D. Howe Institute.

NOVELISTS
AND
NOVELS

NOVELISTS
AND
NOVELS

Harold Bloom
Sterling Professor of the Humanities
Yale University

Checkmark Books®
An imprint of Infobase Publishing

Novelists and Novels

Checkmark Books
An imprint of Infobase Publishing
132 West 31st Street
New York NY 10001

ISBN-10: 0-7910-9727-7
ISBN-13: 978-0-7910-9727-4

Library of Congress Cataloging-in-Publication Data
Bloom, Harold.
 Novelists and novels / Harold Bloom.
  p. cm. — (Bloom's literary criticism 20th anniversary collection)
 Includes bibliographical references.
 ISBN 0-7910-8227-X (hc: alk. paper)—ISBN 0-7910-9727-7 (pb: alk. paper)
 1. Fiction—History and criticism—Juvenile literature. I. Title.
 PN3365.B55 2005
 809.3—dc22   2005003269

Checkmark Books are available at special discounts when purchased in bulk quantities for businesses, associations, institutions, or sales promotions. Please call our Special Sales Department in New York at (212) 967-8800 or (800) 322-8755.

You can find Bloom's Literary Criticism on the World Wide Web at http://www.chelseahouse.com

Cover design by Ben Peterson

Printed in the United States of America

Bang EJB 10 9 8 7 6 5 4 3 2 1

This book is printed on acid-free paper.

Table of Contents

Preface to the 20th Anniversary Edition

Harold Bloom

I BEGAN EDITING ANTHOLOGIES OF LITERARY CRITICISM FOR CHELSEA House in early 1984, but the first volume, *Edgar Allan Poe: Modern Critical Views*, was published in January, 1985, so this is the twentieth anniversary of a somewhat Quixotic venture. If asked how many separate books have been issued in this project, I no longer have a precise answer, since in so long a span many volumes go out of print, and even whole series have been discontinued. A rough guess would be more than a thousand individual anthologies, a perhaps insane panoply to have been collected and introduced by a single critic.

Some of these books have surfaced in unlikely places: hotel rooms in Bologna and Valencia, Coimbra and Oslo; used-book stalls in Frankfurt and Nice; on the shelves of writers wherever I have gone. A batch were sent by me in answer to a request from a university library in Macedonia, and I have donated some of them, also by request, to a number of prisoners serving life sentences in American jails. A thousand books across a score of years can touch many shores and many lives, and at seventy-four I am a little bewildered at the strangeness of the endeavor, particularly now that it has leaped between centuries.

It cannot be said that I have endorsed every critical essay reprinted, as my editor's notes have made clear. Yet the books have to be reasonably reflective of current critical modes and educational fashions, not all of them provoking my own enthusiasm. But then I am a dinosaur, cheerfully naming myself as "Bloom Brontosaurus Bardolator." I accept only three criteria for greatness in imaginative literature: aesthetic splendor, cognitive power, wisdom. What is now called "relevance" will be in the dustbins in less than a generation, as our society (somewhat tardily) reforms prejudices and inequities. The fashionable in literature and criticism always ebbs away into Period Pieces. Old, well-made furniture survives as valuable antiques, which is not the destiny of badly constructed imaginings and ideological exhortings.

Time, which decays and then destroys us, is even more merciless in obliterating weak novels, poems, dramas, and stories, however virtuous these may be. Wander into a library and regard the masterpieces of thirty years ago: a handful of forgotten books have value, but the iniquity of oblivion has rendered most bestsellers instances of time's revenges. The other day a friend and former student told me that the first of the Poets Laureate of twentieth-century America had been Joseph Auslander, concerning whom even my still retentive memory is vacant. These days, Mrs. Felecia Hemans is studied and taught by a number of feminist Romantic scholars. Of the poems of that courageous wisdom, who wrote to support her brood, I remember only the opening line of "Casabianca" but only because Mark Twain added one of his very own to form a couplet:

The boy stood on the burning deck
Eating peanuts by the peck.

Nevertheless, I do not seek to affirm the social inutility of literature, though I admire Oscar Wilde's grand declaration: "All art is perfectly useless." Shakespeare may well stand here for the largest benign effect of the highest literature: properly appreciated, it can heal part of the violence that is built into every society whatsoever. In my own judgment, Walt Whitman is the central writer yet brought forth by the Americas—North, Central, South, Caribbean—whether in English, Spanish, Portuguese, French, Yiddish or other tongues. And Walt Whitman is a healer, a poet-prophet who discovered his pragmatic vocation by serving as a volunteer, unpaid wound-dresser and nurse in the Civil War hospitals of Washington, D.C. To read and properly understand Whitman can be an education in self-reliance and in the cure of your own consciousness.

The function of literary criticism, as I conceive it in my gathering old age, is primarily appreciation, in Walter Pater's sense, which fuses analysis and evaluation. When Pater spoke of "art for art's sake' he included in the undersong of his declaration what D.H. Lawrence meant by "art for life's sake," Lawrence, the most provocative of post-Whitmanian vitalists, has now suffered a total eclipse in the higher education of the English-speaking nations. Feminists have outlawed him with their accusations of misogyny, and they describe him as desiring women to renounce sexual pleasure. On this supposed basis, students lose the experience of reading one of the major authors of the twentieth century, at once an unique novelist, story-teller, poet, critic, and prophet.

An enterprise as vast as Chelsea House Literary Criticism doubtless reflects both the flaws and the virtues of its editor. Comprehensiveness has been a goal throughout, and I have (for the most part) attempted to set aside many of my own literary opinions. I sorrow when the market keeps an important volume out of print, though I am solaced by the example of my idol, Dr. Samuel Johnson, in his *Lives of the Poets*. The booksellers (who were both publishers and retailers) chose the poets, and Johnson was able to say exactly what he thought of each. Who remembers such worthies as Yalden, Sprat, Roscommon, and Stepney? It would be invidious for me to name the contemporary equivalents, but their name is legion.

I have been more fully educated by this quest for comprehensivness, which taught me how to write for a larger audience. Literary criticism is both an individual and communal mode. It has its titans: Johnson, Coleridge, Lessing, Goethe, Hazlitt, Sainte-Beuve, Pater, Curtius, Valèry, Frye, Empson, Kenneth Burke are among them. But most of those I reprint cannot be of that eminence: one makes a heap of all that can be found. Over a lifetime in reading and teaching one learns so much from so many that no one can be certain of her or his intellectual debts. Hundreds of those I have reprinted I never will meet, but they have helped enlighten me, insofar as I have been capable of learning from a host of other minds.

Introduction

Harold Bloom

1

THE NOVEL BEGAN AS THE UNGRATEFUL CHILD OF PROSE ROMANCE, BUT romance revenges itself these days with the apparent death of the novel, and a rebirth (in strange guises) of picaresque. Cervantes mocked and exorcized the romance form in *Don Quixote*, but from Mark Twain until now the influence of Cervantes has reversed direction, with parody and phantasmagoria, as embodied in the Knight of the Woeful Countenance, outdoing the realism and naturalism that dominate his career.

This large volume discourses upon some fifty-six novelists and one hundred (or so) novels, with some essays by James Baldwin and a play by Oliver Goldsmith inextricably mixed in. Certain huge structures, like Joyce's *Ulysses* and Proust's vast narrative have been excluded here, and located in the volume *The Epic* in this Anniversary Collection. Melville's *Moby-Dick* inevitably is also placed there.

In brooding upon my memories of these hundred novels, I find myself setting Samuel Richardson's *Clarissa* second only to *Don Quixote* in aesthetic eminence. I am aware that this judgment will seem eccentric to many, but I urge them to read the uncut *Clarissa*, knowing that Dr. Johnson, foremost among all literary critics ever, preceded me in such an estimate.

I have a few regrets about some novels missing from this volume, particularly Faulkner's *As I Lay Dying* and Pynchon's *The Crying of Lot 49*, which receive intense appreciations in my book, *How to Read and Why*.

2

The revival of romances from Twain on through Kipling and Kafka achieved a first apotheosis in D.H. Lawrence, now an absurdly neglected writer, because of a feminist crusade that has largely exiled him from the academies of the English-speaking world. In the United States, romance form dominated in the triad of Scott Fitzgerald, Faulkner, and Hemingway, all strongly influenced by Joseph Conrad.

The Brontës composed their own sub-genre of Northern romance, which has an echo in Ursula K. Le Guin's beautiful fantasy, *The Left Hand of Darkness*. Though Toni Morrison insists she is related only to black literary tradition, she fuses romance elements from Faulkner and from Virginia Woolf into her own highly individual art.

Faulkner's legacy is extensive and includes such varied figures as Robert Penn Warren, Ralph Ellison, Flannery O'Connor, Gabriel García Márquez, and Cormac McCarthy. There is a line of descent that moves from *Moby-Dick* through Faulkner to McCarthy's *Blood Meridian*, which for me stands with Philip Roth's *Sabbath's Theater*, Don DeLillo's *Underworld*, and Pynchon's *Mason & Dixon* as the four grand narratives composed by living Americans.

This volume, large as it is, cannot pretend to be a history-in-little of the birth, life, and death of the dominant literary form since Shakespeare ended his career as a dramatist. Shakespeare's own influence on the novel is reflected here from Jane Austen and Stendhal on through Balzac and Dickens until it culminates in Dostoevsky's nihilists, and in Hardy's pastoral tragedies, then to renew itself in Woolf and Joyce, Lawrence and Beckett, Iris Murdoch and the Philip Roth of *Sabbath's Theater*.

3

No one can prophesy the future of the novel, or even if it has a future, except in the mixed form of belated romances. There are, for me, several candidates for the great American book, and none of them is exactly a novel: *The Scarlet Letter*, *Moby-Dick*, *Leaves of Grass*, Emerson's *Essays*, and *Huckleberry Finn*. Doubtless Henry James's *The Portrait of a Lady* is the best-made American novel, but it cannot compete with the strongest works of the American Renaissance.

Though this is indeliberate on my part, almost a third of the novelists commented upon in this book are women. If there is a single thematic vision that links together the traditions of the Anglo-American novel, it is what I would name as the Protestant Will, whose prime novelistic instances are heroines, whether created by women or by men. From Richardson's Clarissa Harlowe through Austen's protagonists, and Hawthorne's Hester Prynne, the line continues unbroken through the Brontës, Hardy, James and Wharton to culminate in E.M. Forster, Woolf, and Lawrence. Toni Morrison may be the last exemplar of this tradition, which exalts the Protestant Will, however secularized, as the heroine's right of private judgment, particularly in exchanges of estimate and mutual esteem with male partners. It may be that the Protestant Will and the novel now are dying together, and that something beyond the revival of an eccentric romance form is yet to come.

Miguel de Cervantes

(1547–1616)

Don Quixote

DON QUIXOTE IS TO THE SPANISH LANGUAGE WHAT SHAKESPEARE IS TO English, Dante to Italian, and Goethe to German: the glory of that particular vernacular. There is no similar singular eminence in French: Rabelais, Montaigne, Molière, and Racine vie with Victor Hugo, Baudelaire, Stendhal, Balzac, Flaubert, and Proust. Perhaps Cervantes's masterwork is the central book of the last half-millennium, since all the greater novelists are as much *Don Quixote*'s children as they are Shakespeare's. As I have remarked elsewhere, Shakespeare pragmatically teaches us how to talk to ourselves, while Cervantes instructs us how to talk to one another. Hamlet scarcely listens to what anyone else says (except it be the Ghost), while Falstaff so delights himself that Prince Hal can seem merely the best of resentful students and half-voluntary audiences. But Don Quixote and Sancho Panza change and mature by listening to one another, and their friendship is the most persuasive in all of literature.

Don Quixote or Hamlet? Sancho Panza or Falstaff? The choice would be difficult. But Hamlet has only Horatio, and Falstaff ends in solitude, dying while playing with flowers and evidently dreaming of the table promised in Psalm 23, to be prepared for one by God in the midst of one's enemies. Don Quixote dies in Sancho's loving company, with the wise squire proposing fresh quests to the heroic knight. Perhaps Shakespeare did invent the ever-growing inner self, compelled to be its own adventure, as Emily Dickinson (an authentic heir of Shakespeare) proclaimed. Cervantes, whose life was arduous and darkly solitary, was able to achieve a miracle that Shakespeare evaded. Where in Shakespeare can we find two great natures in full communion with each other? Antony and Cleopatra are giant forms, but they never listen to what anyone else says, including one another. Lady Macbeth fades out, Lear is most himself addressing the heavens, while Prospero has no human peer. I fantasize sometimes that Shakespeare, in eternity, brings together his most vital characters upon one stage: Falstaff, Hamlet, Rosalind, Iago, Lear, Macbeth, Cleopatra. But in this life, he chose otherwise.

The reader needs no better company than Sancho and the Don: to make a third with them is to be blessed with happiness, yet also to be favored with self-insight. The Don and Sancho, between them, know all that there is to know. They know at last exactly who they are, which is what, finally, they will teach the rest of us.

Daniel Defoe

(1660-1731)

Of his prayers and the like we take no account, since they are a source of
pleasure to him, and he looks upon them as so much recreation.
 —KARL MARX on *Robinson Crusoe*

I got so tired of the very colors!
One day I dyed a baby goat bright red
with my red berries, just to see
something a little different.
And then his mother wouldn't recognize him.
 —ELIZABETH BISHOP, "Crusoe in England"

HAD KARL MARX WRITTEN *ROBINSON CRUSOE*, IT WOULD HAVE HAD EVEN
more moral vigor, but at the expense of the image of freedom it still provides for us. Had Elizabeth Bishop composed it, Defoe's narrative would
have been enhanced as image and as impulse, but at the expense of its
Puritan plainness, its persuasive search for some evidences of redemption.
Certainly one of Defoe's novelistic virtues is precisely what Ian Watt and
Martin Price have emphasized it to be: the puzzles of daily moral choice are
omnipresent. Robinson Crusoe and Moll Flanders are human—all-too-
human—and suffer what Calvin and Freud alike regarded as the economics of the spirit.

 Defoe comes so early in the development of the modern novel as a literary form that there is always a temptation to historicize rather than to
read him. But historicisms old and new are poor substitutes for reading,
and I do not find it useful to place *Robinson Crusoe* and *Moll Flanders* in their
contemporary context when I reread them, as I have just done. Ian Watt
usefully remarked that "Defoe's heroes ... keep us more fully informed of

their present stocks of money and commodities than any other characters in fiction." I suspect that this had more to do with Defoe than with his age, and that Defoe would have been no less obsessed with economic motives if he had written in the era of Queen Victoria. He was a hard man who had led a hard life: raised as a Dissenter in the London of the Great Plague and the Great Fire; enduring Newgate prison and the pillory in bankrupt middle age; working as a secret agent and a scandalous journalist until imprisoned again for debt and treason. Defoe died old and so may be accounted as a survivor, but he had endured a good share of reality, and his novels reflect that endurance.

Dr. Johnson once said that only three books ought to have been still longer than they were: *Don Quixote*, *The Pilgrim's Progress*, and *Robinson Crusoe*. Defoe has authentic affinities with Bunyan, but there is nothing quixotic about Robinson Crusoe or Moll Flanders. All of Defoe's protagonists are pragmatic and prudent, because they have to be; there is no play in the world as they know it.

Robinson Crusoe

I did not read *Robinson Crusoe* as a child, and so missed an experience that continues to be all but universal; it remains a book that cannot fail with children. Yet, as Dickens observed, it is also "the only instance of an universally popular book that could make no one laugh and could make no one cry." Crusoe's singular tone, his self-baffled affect, does not bother children, who appear to empathize with a near-perfect solipsist who nevertheless exhibits energy and inventiveness throughout a quarter-century of solitude. Perhaps Crusoe's survival argues implicitly against every child's fear of dependency and prophesies the longed-for individuality that is still to come. Or perhaps every child's loneliness is answered in Crusoe's remarkable strength at sustaining solitude.

Though the identification of Defoe with Crusoe is never wholly overt, the reader senses its prevalence throughout the narrative. Defoe seems to me the least ironic of writers, and yet Crusoe's story is informed by an overwhelming irony. A restless wanderer, driven to travel and adventure by forces that he (and the reader) cannot comprehend, Crusoe is confined to an isolation that ought to madden him by turning him towards an unbearable inwardness. Yet his sanity prevails, despite his apparent imprisonment. Defoe had borne much; Newgate and the pillory were nightmare experiences. Crusoe bears more, yet Defoe will not describe his hero's suffering as being psychic. As Virginia Woolf noted, Defoe "takes the opposite way from the psychologist's—he describes the effect of emotion on the body, not on the mind." Nowhere is this stronger than in Crusoe's agony as he views a shipwreck:

> Such certainly was the Case of these Men, of whom I could not so much as see room to suppose any of them were sav'd; nothing could make it rational, so much as to wish, or expect that they did not all perish there; except the Possibility only of their being taken up by another Ship in Company, and this was but meer Possibility indeed; for I saw not the least Signal or Appearance of any such Thing.
>
> I cannot explain by any possible Energy of Words what a strange longing or hankering of Desires I felt in my Soul upon this Sight; breaking out sometimes thus; O that there had been but one or two; nay, or but one Soul sav'd out of this Ship, to have escap'd to me, that I might but have had one Companion, one Fellow-Creature to have spoken to me, and to have convers'd with! In all the Time of my solitary Life, I never felt so earnest, so strong a Desire after the Society of my Fellow-Creatures, or so deep a Regret at the want of it.
>
> There are some secret moving Springs in the Affections, which when they are set a going by some Object in view; or be it some Object, though not in view, yet rendred present to the Mind by the Power of Imagination, that Motion carries out the Soul by its Impetuosity to such violent eager embracings of the Object, that the Absence of it is insupportable.
>
> Such were these earnest Wishings, That but one Man had been sav'd! *O that it had been but One!* I believe I repeated the Words, *O that it had been but One!* a thousand Times; and the Desires were so mov'd by it, that when I spoke the Words, my Hands would clinch together, and my Fingers press the Palms of my Hands, that if I had had any soft Thing in my Hand, it would have crusht it involuntarily; and my Teeth in my Head would strike together, and set against one another so strong, that for some time I could not part them again.

These are the reactions of a compulsive craftsman who has found his freedom but cannot bear its full sublimity. Crusoe, himself the least sublime of personages, is embedded throughout in a sublime situation best epitomized by the ghastly cannibal feasts he spies upon and from which he rescues his man Friday. Against his superior technology and Puritan resolve, the cannibals offer almost no resistance, so that the rapid conversion of the cannibal Friday to Protestant theology and diet is not unconvincing. What may baffle the average rereader is Crusoe's comparative dearth of Protestant inwardness. It is not that Marx was accurate and that Crusoe becomes Protestant only upon the Sabbath, but rather that Defoe's God is himself a technocrat and an individualist, not much given to the nicer emotions. Defoe's God can be visualized as a giant tradesman, coping with the universe as Crusoe makes do on his island, but with teeming millions of adoring Fridays where Crusoe enjoys the devotion of just one.

Moll Flanders

With *Robinson Crusoe*, aesthetic judgment seems redundant; the book's status as popular myth is too permanent, and so the critic must ground arms. *Moll Flanders* is another matter and provokes a remarkably wide range of critical response, from the late poet-critic Allen Tate, who once told me it was a great novel of Tolstoyan intensity, to equally qualified readers who deny that it is a novel at all. The overpraisers include James Joyce, who spoke of "the unforgettable harlot Moll Flanders," and William Faulkner, who coupled *Moby-Dick* and *Moll Flanders* as works he would like to have written (together with one of Milne's Pooh books!). Rereading *Moll Flanders* leaves me a touch baffled as I thought it had been better, it being one of those books that are much more vivid in parts than as a unit so that the memory holds on to episodes and to impressions, investing them with an aura that much of the narrative does not possess. The status of the narrative is curiously wavering; one is not always certain one is reading a novel rather than a colorful tract of the Puritan persuasion. Moll is a formidable person who sustains our interest and our good will. But the story she tells seems alternately formed and formless, and frequently confuses the rival authorities of fiction and supposed fact.

Martin Price notes how little thematic unity Defoe imposes upon the stuff of existence that constitutes *Moll Flanders*. As a man who had suffered Newgate, Defoe gives us only one key indication of his novel's vision; Moll was born in Newgate and will do anything to avoid ending there. The quest for cash is simply her equivalent of Crusoe's literal quest to survive physically upon his island, except that Moll is more imaginative than the strangely compulsive Crusoe. He does only what he must, she does more, and we begin to see that her obsession has in it an actual taste for adventures. This taste surprises her, but then, as Price observes, she is always "surprised by herself and with herself." She learns by what she does, and almost everything she does is marked by gusto. Her vehemence is her most winning quality, but most of her qualities are attractive. Male readers are charmed by her, particularly male readers who both exalt and debase women, among whom Joyce and Faulkner remain the most prominent.

Puritan force, the drive for the soul's exuberant self-recognition, is as much exemplified by Moll as by Bunyan's protagonist. I suspect that was why William Hazlitt, the greatest literary critic to emerge from the tradition of Protestant Dissent, had so violent a negative reaction to *Moll Flanders*, which otherwise I would have expected him to admire. But, on some level, he evidently felt that she was a great discredit to Puritan sensibility. Charles Lamb greatly esteemed her and understood how authentic the Puritan dialectic was in her, pointing to "the intervening flashes of religious visitation upon the rude and uninstructed soul" and judging this to "come near to the tenderness of Bunyan." Infuriated, Hazlitt responded, "Mr. Lamb admires *Moll Flanders*; would he marry Moll Flanders?" to which the only response a loyal Hazlittian could make is, "Would that Hazlitt had married a Moll Flanders, and been happy for once in a relationship with a woman." All proportion abandoned Hazlitt when he wrote about *Moll Flanders*:

> We ... may, nevertheless, add, for the satisfaction of the inquisitive reader, that *Moll Flanders* is utterly vile and detestable: Mrs. Flanders was evidently born in sin. The best parts are the account of her childhood, which is pretty and affecting; the fluctuation of her feelings between remorse and hardened impenitence in Newgate; and the incident of her leading off the horse from the inn-door, though she had no place to put it in after she had stolen it. This was carrying the love of thieving to an *ideal* pitch and making it perfectly disinterested and mechanical.

Hazlitt did not understand Moll because he could not bear to see the Puritan impulse displaced into "carrying the love of thieving to an *ideal* pitch." Brilliant as the horse-stealing is, it is surpassed by Moll's famous second theft, the episode of the child's necklace:

> I went out now by Day-light, and wandred about I knew not whither, and in search of I knew not what, when the Devil put a Snare in my way of a dreadful Nature indeed, and such a one as I have never had before or since; going thro' *Aldersgate-street* there was a pretty little Child had been at a Dancing School, and was going home, all alone, and my Prompter, like a true Devil, set me upon this innocent Creature; I talk'd to it, and it prattl'd to me again, and I took it by the Hand and led it a long till I came to a

pav'd Alley that goes into *Bartholomew Close*, and I led it in there; the Child said that was not its way home; I said, yes, my Dear it is, I'll show you the way home; the Child had a little Necklace on of Gold Beads, and I had my Eye upon that, and in the dark of the Alley I stoop'd, pretending to mend the Child's Clog that was loose, and took off her Necklace and the Child never felt it, and so led the Child on again: Here, I say, the Devil put me upon killing the child in the dark Alley, that it might not Cry; but the very thought frighted me so that I was ready to drop down, but I turn'd the Child about and bade it go back again, for that was not its way home; the Child said so she would, and I went thro' into *Bartholomew Close*, and then turn'd round to another Passage that goes into *Long-lane*, so away into *Charterhouse-Yard and* out into *St. John's-street*, then crossing into *Smithfield*, went down *Chick-lane* and into *Field-lane* to *Holbourn-bridge*, when mixing with the Crowd of People usually passing there, it was not possible to have been found out; and thus I enterpriz'd my second Sally into the World.

The thoughts of this Booty put out all the thoughts of the first, and the Reflections I had made wore quickly off; Poverty, as I have said, harden'd my Heart, and my own Necessities made me regardless of any thing: The last Affair left no great Concern upon me, for as I did the poor Child no harm, I only said to my self, I had given the Parents a just Reproof for their Negligence in leaving the poor little Lamb to come home by it self, and it would teach them to take more Care of it another time.

This String of Beads was worth about Twelve or Fourteen Pounds; I suppose it might have been formerly the Mother's, for it was too big for the Child's wear, but that, perhaps, the Vanity of the Mother to have her Child look Fine at the Dancing School, had made her let the Child wear it; and no doubt the Child had a Maid sent to take care of it, but she, like a careless jade, was taken up perhaps with some Fellow that had met her by the way, and so the poor Baby wandred till it fell into my Hands.

However, I did the Child no harm; I did not so much as fright it, for I had a great many tender Thoughts about me yet, and did nothing but what, as I may say, meer Necessity drove me to.

The remarkable moment, which horrifies us and must have scandalized Hazlitt, is when Moll says, "the Devil put me upon killing the Child in the dark Alley, that it might not Cry; but the very thought frighted me so that I was ready to drop down." We do not believe that Moll will slay the child, but she frightens us because of her capacity for surprising herself. We are reminded that we do not understand Moll, *because Defoe does not understand her*. That is his novel's most peculiar strength and its most peculiar weakness. Gide's Lafcadio, contemplating his own crime, murmurs that it is not about events that he is curious, but only about himself. That is in the spirit of Defoe's Moll. The Protestant sensibility stands back from itself, and watches the spirits of good and of evil contend for it, with the detachment of a certain estrangement, a certain wonder at the immense energies that God has placed in one's soul.

Jonathan Swift

(1667-1745)

TWICE A YEAR, FOR MANY YEARS NOW, I REREAD SWIFT'S *A TALE OF A TUB*, not because I judge it to be the most powerful prose work in the language (which it is) but because it is good for me, though I dislike this great book as much as I admire it. A literary critic who is speculative, Gnostic, still imbued with High Romantic enthusiasm even in his later middle age, needs to read *A Tale of a Tub* as often as he can bear to do so. Swift is the most savage and merciless satirist and ironist in the history of Western literature, and one of his particularly favorite victims is the critic given to Gnostic speculations and Romantic enthusiasms.

A Tale of a Tub is a queerly shaped work, by design a parody of the seventeenth-century "anatomy," as exemplified by Sir Thomas Browne's *Pseudodoxia Epidemica* or Robert Burton's magnificent *The Anatomy of Melancholy*. The most important section of the *Tale* outrageously is not even part of the book, but is the attached fragment, *A Discourse Concerning the Mechanical Operation of the Spirit*. The philosopher Descartes, one of the leaders of the Bowmen among the Moderns in their confrontation with the Ancients in Swift's *The Battle of the Books*, is the inventor of the dualism that always will haunt the West, a dualism called "the Ghost in the Machine" by the analytical philosopher, Gilbert Ryle, and more grimly named *The Mechanical Operation of the Spirit* by Jonathan Swift. In *The Battle of the Books*, Descartes expiates his radical dualism by dying of an Aristotelian arrow intended for Bacon:

> Then *Aristotle* observing Bacon advance with a furious Mien, drew his Bow to the Head, and let fly his Arrow, which mist the valiant *Modern*, and went hizzing over his Head; but *Des-Cartes* it hit; The Steel Point quickly found a *Defect* in his *Head-piece*; it pierced the

Leather and the Past-board, and went in at his Right Eye. The Torture of the Pain, whirled the valiant *Bow-man* round, till Death, like a Star of superior Influence, drew him into his own *Vortex*.

Not even the dignity of an heroic death is granted to poor Descartes, who pays for his cognitive defect and perishes via an anti-Baconian shaft, swallowed up into a vortex that parodies his own account of perception. Yet even this poor fate is better than the extraordinarily ferocious drubbing received by the Cartesian dualism in *The Mechanical Operation of the Spirit*:

But, if this Plant has found a Root in the Fields of *Empire*, and of *Knowledge*, it has fixt deeper, and spread yet farther upon *Holy Ground*. Wherein, though it hath pass'd under the general Name of *Enthusiasm*, and perhaps arisen from the same Original, yet hath it produced certain Branches of a very different Nature, however often mistaken for each other. The Word in its universal Acceptation, may be defined, *A lifting up of the Soul or its Faculties above Matter*. This Description will hold good in general; but I am only to understand it, as applied to *Religion*; wherein there are three general Ways of ejaculating the Soul, or transporting it beyond the Sphere of Matter. The first, is the immediate Act of God, and is called, *Prophecy* or *Inspiration*. The second, is the immediate Act of the Devil, and is termed *Possession*. The third, is the Product of natural Causes, the effect of strong imagination, Spleen, violent Anger, Fear, Grief, Pain, and the like. These three have been abundantly treated on by Authors, and therefore shall not employ my Enquiry. But, the fourth Method of *Religious Enthusiasm*, or launching out of the Soul, as it is purely an Effect of Artifice and *Mechanick Operation*, has been sparingly handled, or not at all, by any Writer; because tho' it is an Art of great Antiquity, yet having been confined to few Persons, it long wanted those Advancements and Refinements, which it afterwards met with, since it has grown so Epidemick, and fallen into so many cultivating Hands.

All four "methods" reduce the spirit or soul to a gaseous vapor, the only status possible for any transcendental entity in the cosmos of Hobbes and Descartes, where the soul must be ejaculated in sublime transport "beyond the Sphere of Matter." Within *A Tale of a Tub* proper, Swift keeps a very precarious balance indeed as he plays obsessively with the image of the spirit mechanically operated. So operated, the wretched soul is capable of only one mode of movement: digression. What Freud called the drive is to Swift merely digression. Digression is a turning aside, a kind of walking in which you never go straight. Digress enough, in discourse or in living, and you will go mad. *A Tale of a Tub* is nothing but digression, because Swift bitterly believes there is nothing else in a Cartesian universe. Spirit digressing is an oxymoronic operation, and so falls from spirit to gaseous vapor. Vapor properly moves only by turning aside, by digressing.

Swift's principal victims, all high priests of digression, he calls "the Learned *Aeolists*," acolytes of the god of the winds, among whom he counts: "All Pretenders to Inspiration whatsoever." His savage indignation, so constant in him as a writer, maintains a consistent fury whenever the *Aeolists* are his subject. They are introduced as apocalyptics for whom origin and end intermix:

> The Learned *Aeolists*, maintain the Original Cause of all Things to be *Wind*, from which Principle this whole Universe was at first produced, and into which it must at last be resolved; that the same Breath which had kindled, and blew up the Flame of Nature, should one Day blow it *out*.

As he is kindled by the Aeolists, Swift's Tale-teller mounts to an intensity worthy of his subject, and attains an irony that is itself a kind of hysteria:

> It is from this Custom of the Priests, that some Authors maintain these *Aeolists*, to have been very antient in the World. Because, the Delivery of their Mysteries, which I have just now mention'd, appears exactly the same with that of other antient Oracles, whose Inspirations were owing to certain subterraneous *Effluviums of Wind*, delivered with the same Pain to the Priest, and much about the *same* Influence on the People. It is true indeed, that these were frequently managed and directed by *Female* Officers, whose Organs were understood to be better disposed for the Admission of those Oracular *Gusts*, as entring and passing up thro' a Receptacle of greater Capacity, and causing also a Pruriency by the Way, such as with due Management; hath been refined from a Carnal, into a Spiritual Extasie. And to strengthen this profound Conjecture, it is farther insisted, that this Custom of *Female* Priests is kept up still in certain refined Colleges of our *Modern Aeolists*, who are agreed to receive their Inspiration, derived thro' the Receptacle aforesaid, like their Ancestors, the Sibyls.

This ends in a passing blow at the Quakers, but its power is dangerously close to its horror of becoming what it is working so hard to reject. Rather like King Lear, the Tale-teller fears the ascent of vapors from abdomen to head, fears that hysteria, the womb or mother, will unman him:

> O how this mother swells up toward my heart!
> *Hysterica passio*, down, thou climbing sorrow,
> Thy element's below.—

Swift cannot be, does not want to be, the Tale-teller, but the Tale-teller may be, in part, Swift's failed defense against the madness of digression, and the digressiveness that is madness. Compulsiveness of and in the Tale-teller becomes a terrifying counter-Sublime of counter-Enthusiasm, a digressiveness turned against digressiveness, a vapor against vapors:

> Besides, there is something Individual in human Minds, that easily kindles at the accidental Approach and Collision of certain Circumstances, which tho' of paltry and mean Appearance, do often flame out into the greatest Emergencies of Life. For great Turns are not always given by strong Hands, but by lucky Adaption, and at proper Seasons; and it is of no import, where the Fire was kindled, if the Vapor has once got up into the Brain. For the *upper Region* of Man, is furnished like the *middle Region* of the Air; The Materials are formed from Causes of the widest Difference, yet produce at last the same Substance and Effect. Mists arise from the Earth, Steams from Dunghils, Exhalations from the Sea, and Smoak from Fire; yet all Clouds are the same in Composition, as well as Consequences: and the Fumes issuing from a Jakes, will furnish as comely and useful a Vapor, as Incense from an Altar. Thus far, I suppose, will easily be granted me; and then it will follow, that as the Face of Nature never produces Rain, but when it is overcast and disturbed, so Human Understanding, seated in the Brain, must be troubled and overspread by Vapours, ascending from the lower Faculties, to water the Invention, and render it fruitful.

Are these the accents of satire? The passage itself is overcast and disturbed, not so much troubled and overspread by vapors ascending from below, as it is by the not wholly repressed anxiety that *anyone*, including the Tale-teller and Swift, is vulnerable to the Mechanical Operation of the

Spirit. King Henry IV of France (Henry of Navarre), rightly called "the Great," is the subject of the next paragraph, which tells of grand preparations for battle, perhaps to advance "a Scheme for Universal Monarchy," until the assassination of Henry IV released the spirit or mighty vapor from the royal body:

> Now, is the Reader exceeding curious to learn, from whence this *Vapour* took its Rise, which had so long set the Nations at a Gaze? What secret Wheel, what hidden Spring could put into Motion so wonderful an Engine? It was afterwards discovered, that the Movement of this whole Machine had been directed by an absent *Female*, whose Eyes had raised a Protuberancy, and before Emission, she was removed into an Enemy's Country. What should an unhappy Prince do in such ticklish Circumstances as these?

What indeed? This is genial, and quite relaxed, for Swift, but his subsequent analysis is darker, rhetorically and in moral substance:

> Having to no purpose used all peaceable Endeavours, the collected part of the *Semen*, raised and enflamed, became adust, converted to Choler, turned head upon the spinal Duct, and ascended to the Brain. The very same Principle that influences a *Bully* to break the Windows of a Whore, who has jilted him, naturally stirs up a Great Prince to raise mighty Armies, and dream of nothing but Sieges, Battles, and Victories.

As a reduction, this continues to have its exuberance, but the phrase, "raised and enflamed" is at the center, and is yet another Swiftian assault upon Enthusiasm, another classical irony set against a romantic Sublime. The Author or Tale-teller forsakes digressiveness to become Swift at his calmest and most deadly, a transformation itself digressive. Swift cannot be censured for wanting it every which way, since he is battling not for our right reason, but for our sanity, and ruggedly he fights for us, against us, and for himself, against himself.

Gulliver's Travels

The terrible greatness of *A Tale of a Tub* has much to do with our sense of its excess, with its force being so exuberantly beyond its form (or its calculated formlessness). *Gulliver's Travels*, the later and lesser work, has survived for the common reader, whereas Swift's early masterpiece has not. Like its descendant, Carlyle's Sartor Resartus, *A Tale of a Tub* demands too much of the reader, but it more than rewards those demands, and it now seems unclear whether Sartor Resartus does or not. Gulliver's first two voyages are loved by children (of all ages), while the third and fourth voyages, being more clearly by the Swift who wrote *A Tale of a Tub*, now make their appeal only to those who would benefit most from an immersion in the *Tub*.

Gulliver himself is both the strength and the weakness of the book, and his character is particularly ambiguous in the great fourth voyage, to the country of the rational Houyhnhnms and the bestial Yahoos, who are and are not, respectively, horses and humans. The inability to resist a societal perspectivism is at once Gulliver's true weakness, and his curious strength as an observer. Swift's barely concealed apprehension that the self is an abyss, that the ego is a fiction masking our fundamental nothingness, is exemplified by Gulliver, but on a level of commonplaceness far more bathetic than anything reductive in the Tale-teller. Poor Gulliver is a good enough man, but almost devoid of imagination. One way of describing him might be to name him the least Nietzschean character ever to appear in any narrative. Though a ceaseless traveler, Gulliver lacks any desire to be elsewhere, or to be different. His pride is blind, and all too easily magnifies to pomposity, or declines to a self-contempt that is more truly a contempt for all other humans. If the Tale-teller is a Swiftian parody of one side of Swift, the anti-Cartesian, anti-Hobbesian, then Gulliver is a Swiftian parody of the great ironist's own misanthropy.

The reader of "A Voyage to Lilliput" is unlikely to forget the fatuity of Gulliver at the close of chapter 6:

> I am here obliged to vindicate the Reputation of an excellent Lady, who was an innocent Sufferer upon my Account. The Treasurer took a Fancy to be jealous of his Wife, from the Malice of some evil Tongues, who informed him that her Grace had taken a violent Affection for my Person; and the Court-Scandal ran for some Time that she once came privately to my Lodging. This I solemnly declare to be a most infamous Falshood, without any Grounds, farther than that her Grace was pleased to treat me with all innocent Marks of Freedom and Friendship. I own she came often to my House, but always publickly ... I should not have dwelt so long upon this Particular, if it had been a Point wherein the Reputation of a great Lady is so nearly concerned, to say nothing of my own; although I had the Honour to be a *Nardac*, which the

Treasurer himself is not; for all the World knows he is only a
Clumglum, a Title inferior by one Degree, as that of a Marquess is
to a Duke in *England*; yet I allow he preceded me in right of his
Post.

The great *Nardac* has so fallen into the societal perspective of Lilliput,
that he sublimely forgets he is twelve times the size of the *Clumglum's* virtuous wife, who therefore would have been quite safe with him were they
naked and alone. Escaping back to England, Gulliver has learned nothing
and sets forth on "A Voyage to Brobdingnag," land of the giants, where he
learns less than nothing:

> The Learning of this People is very defective; consisting only in
> Morality, History, Poetry and Mathematicks; wherein they must
> be allowed to excel. But, the last of these is wholly applied to what
> may be useful in Life; to the Improvement of Agriculture and all
> mechanical Arts; so that among us it would be little esteemed. And
> as to Ideas, Entities, Abstractions and Transcendentals, I could
> never drive the least Conception into their Heads.
>
> No Law of that Country must exceed in Words the Number of
> Letters in their Alphabet; which consists only of two and twenty.
> But indeed, few of them extend even to that Length. They are
> expressed in the most plain and simple Terms, wherein those
> People are not Mercurial enough to discover above one
> Interpretation. And, to write a Comment upon any Law, is a cap-
> ital Crime. As to the Decision of civil Causes, or Proceedings
> against Criminals, their Precedents are so few, that they have lit-
> tle Reason to boast of any extraordinary Skill in either.

Effective as this is, it seems too weak an irony for Swift, and we are
pleased when the dull Gulliver abandons Brobdingnag behind him. The
Third Voyage, more properly Swiftian, takes us first to Laputa, the floating island, at once a parody of a Platonic academy yet also a kind of science
fiction punishment machine, always ready to crush earthlings who might
assert liberty:

> If any Town should engage in Rebellion or Mutiny, fall into vio-
> lent Factions, or refuse to pay the usual Tribute; the King hath
> two Methods of reducing them to Obedience. The first and the
> mildest Course is by keeping the Island hovering over such a
> Town, and the Lands about it; whereby he can deprive them of the

Benefit of the Sun and the Rain, and consequently afflict the Inhabitants with Dearth and Diseases. And if the Crime deserve it, they are at the same time pelted from above with great Stones, against which they have no Defence, but by creeping into Cellars or Caves, while the Roofs of their Houses are beaten to Pieces. But if they still continue obstinate, or offer to raise Insurrections; he proceeds to the last Remedy, by letting the Island drop directly upon their Heads, which makes a universal Destruction both of Houses and Men. However, this is an Extremity to which the Prince is seldom driven, neither indeed is he willing to put it in Execution; nor dare his Ministers advise him to an Action, which as it would render them odious to the People, so it would be a great Damage to their own Estates that lie all below; for the Island is the King's Demesn.

The maddening lack of affect on Gulliver's part begins to tell upon us here; the stolid narrator is absurdly inadequate to the grim force of his own recital, grimmer for us now even than it could have been for the prophetic Swift. Gulliver inexorably and blandly goes on to *Lagado*, where he observes the grand Academy of Projectors, Swift's famous spoof of the British Royal Society, but here the ironies go curiously flat, and I suspect we are left with the irony of irony, which wearies because by repetition it seems to become compulsive. Yet it may be that here, as subsequently with the immortal but senile and noxious *Struldbruggs*, the irony of irony is highly deliberate, in order to prepare Gulliver, and the battered reader, for the great shock of reversal that lies just ahead in the Country of the Houyhnhnms, which is also the land of the Yahoos, "a strange Sort of Animal."

Critical reactions to Gulliver's fourth voyage have an astonishing range, from Thackeray calling its moral "horrible, shameful unmanly, blasphemous" to T. S. Eliot regarding it as a grand triumph for the human spirit. Eliot's judgment seems to me as odd as Thackeray's, and presumably both writers believed that the Yahoos were intended as a just representation of the natural man, with Thackeray humanistically disagreeing, and the neo-Christian Eliot all too happy to concur. If that were the proper reading of Swift, we would have to conclude that the great satirist had drowned in his own misanthropy, and had suffered the terrible irony, after just evading the becoming one with his Tale-teller, of joining himself to the uneducable Gulliver. Fit retribution perhaps, but it is unwise to underestimate the deep cunning of Swift.

Martin Price accurately reminds us that Swift's attitudes do not depend solely upon Christian morals, but stem also from a traditional secular wisdom. Peace and decency are wholly compatible with Christian teaching, but are secular virtues as well. Whatever the Yahoos represent, they are *not* a vision of secular humanity devoid of divine grace, since they offend the classical view of man quite as profoundly as they seem to suit an ascetic horror of our supposedly natural condition.

Clearly, it is the virtues of the Houyhnhnms, and not the squalors of the Yahoos, that constitute a burden for critics and for common readers. I myself agree with Price, when he remarks of the Houyhnhnms: "They are rational horses, neither ideal men nor a satire upon others' ideals for man." Certainly they cannot represent a human rational ideal, since none of us would wish to lack all impulse, or any imagination whatsoever. Nor do they seem a plausible satire upon the Deistic vision, a satire worthier of Blake than of Swift, and in any case contradicted by everything that truly is admirable about these cognitively advanced horses. A rational horse is a kind of oxymoron, and Swift's irony is therefore more difficult than ever to interpret:

> My Master heard me with great Appearances of Uneasiness in his Countenance; because *Doubting* or *not believing*, are so little known in this Country, that the Inhabitants cannot tell how to behave themselves under such Circumstances. And I remember in frequent Discourses with my Master concerning the Nature of Manhood, in other Parts of the World; having Occasion to talk of *Lying*, and *false Representation*, it was with much Difficulty that he comprehended what I meant; although he had otherwise a most acute Judgment. For he argued thus; That the Use of Speech was to make us understand one another, and to receive Information of Facts; now if any one *said the Thing which was not*, these Ends were defeated; because I cannot properly be said to understand him; and I am so far from receiving information, that he leaves me worse than in Ignorance; for I am led to believe a Thing *Black* when it is *White*, and *Short* when it is *Long*. And these were all the Notions he had concerning the Faculty of *Lying*, so perfectly well understood, and so universally practised among human Creatures.

Are we altogether to admire Gulliver's Master here, when that noble Houyhnhnm not only does not know how to react to the human propensity to say *the thing which was not*, but lacks even the minimal imagination that might allow him to apprehend the human need for fictions, a "sickness not ignoble," as Keats observed in *The Fall of Hyperion*? Since the noble Houyhnhnm finds the notion "that the *Yahoos* were the only governing Animals" in Gulliver's country "altogether past his Conception," are we again to admire him for an inability that would make it impossible for us to read *Gulliver's Travels* (or *King Lear*, for that matter)? The virtues of Swift's rational horses would not take us very far, if we imported them into our condition, but can that really be one of Swift's meanings? And what are we to do with Swiftian ironies that are too overt already, and become aesthetically intolerable if we take up the stance of the sublimely rational Houyhnhnm?

> My Master likewise mentioned another Quality, which his Servants had discovered in several *Yahoos*, and to him was wholly unaccountable. He said, a Fancy would sometimes take a *Yahoo*, to retire into a Corner, to lie down and howl, and groan, and spurn away all that came near him, although he were young and fat, and wanted neither Food nor Water; nor did the Servants imagine what could possibly, ail him. And the only Remedy they found was to set him to hard Work, after which he would infallibly come to himself. To this I was silent out of Partiality to my own Kind; yet here I could plainly discover the true Seeds of *Spleen*, which only seizeth on the *Lazy*, the *Luxurious*, and the *Rich*; who, if they were forced to undergo the *same Regimen*, I would undertake for the Cure.
>
> His Honour had farther observed, that a Female-*Yahoo* would often stand behind a Bank or a Bush, to gaze on the young Males passing by, and then appear, and hide, using many antick Gestures and Grimaces; at which time it was observed, that she had a most *offensive Smell*; and when any of the Males advanced, would slowly retire, looking often back, and with a counterfeit Shew of Fear, run off into some convenient Place where she knew the Male would follow her.

Swift rather dubiously seems to want it every which way at once, so that the Yahoos both are and are not representations of ourselves, and the Houyhnhnms are and are not wholly admirable or ideal. Or is it the nature of irony itself, which must weary us, or finally make us long for a true sublime, even if it should turn out to be grotesque? Fearfully strong writer that he was, Swift as ironist resembles Kafka far more than say Orwell, among modern authors. We do not know precisely how to read "In the Penal Colony" or *The Trial*, and we certainly do not know exactly how to interpret Gulliver's fourth voyage. What most merits' interpretation in

Kafka is the extraordinary perversity of imagination with which he so deliberately makes himself uninterpretable. Is Swift a similar problem for the reader? What is the proper response to the dismaying conclusion of *Gulliver's Travels*?

> Having thus answered the *only* Objection that can be raised against me as a Traveller; I here take a final Leave of my Courteous Readers, and return to enjoy my own Speculations in my little Garden at *Redriff*; to apply those excellent Lessons of Virtue which I learned among the *Houyhnhnms*; to instruct the *Yahoos* of my own Family as far as I shall find them docible Animals; to behold my Figure often in a Glass, and thus if possible habituate my self by Time to tolerate the Sight of a human Creature: To lament the Brutality of *Houyhnhnms* in my own Country, but always treat their Persons with Respect, for the Sake of my noble Master, his Family, his Friends, and the whole *Houyhnhnm* Race, whom these of ours have the Honour to resemble in all their Lineaments, however their Intellectuals came to degenerate.
>
> I began last Week to permit my Wife to sit at Dinner with me, at the Farthest End of a long Table; and to answer (but with the utmost Brevity) the few Questions I ask her. Yet the Smell of a *Yahoo* continuing very offensive, I always keep my Nose well stopt with Rue, Lavender, or Tobacco-Leaves. And although it be hard for a Man late in Life to remove old Habits; I am not altogether out of Hopes in some Time to suffer a Neighbour *Yahoo* in my Company, without the Apprehensions I am yet under of his Teeth or his Claws.

Who are those "Courteous Readers" of whom Gulliver takes his final leave here? We pity the poor fellow, but we do not so much pity Mrs. Gulliver as wonder how she can tolerate the insufferable wretch. Yet the final paragraphs have a continued power that justifies their fame, even as we continue to see Gulliver as deranged:

> My Reconcilement to the *Yahoo*-kind in general might not be so difficult, if they would be content with those Vices and Follies only which Nature hath entitled them to. I am not in the least provoked at the Sight of a Lawyer, a Pick-pocket, a Colonel, a Fool, a Lord, a Gamster, a Politician, a Whoremunger, a Physician, an Evidence, a Suborner, an Attorney, a Traytor, or the

like: This is all according to the due Course of Things: But, when I behold a Lump of Deformity, and Diseases both in Body and Mind, smitten with *Pride*, it immediately breaks all the Measures of my Patience; neither shall I be ever able to comprehend how such an Animal and such a Vice could tally together. The wise and virtuous *Houyhnhnms*, who abound in all Excellencies that can adorn a rational Creature, have no Name for this Vice in their Language, whereby they describe the detestable Qualities of their *Yahoos*; among which they were not able to distinguish this of Pride, for want of thoroughly understanding Human Nature, as it sheweth it self in other Countries, where that Animal presides. But I, who had more Experience, could plainly observe some Rudiments of it among the wild *Yahoos*.

But the *Houyhnhnms*, who live under the Government of Reason, are no more proud of the good Qualities they possess, than I should be for not wanting a Leg or an Arm, which no Man in his Wits would boast of, although he must be miserable without them. I dwell the longer upon this Subject from the Desire I have to make the Society of an *English Yahoo* by any Means not insupportable; and therefore I here intreat those who have any Tincture of this absurd Vice, that they will not presume to appear in my Sight.

What takes precedence here, the palpable hit at the obscenity of false human pride, or the madness of Gulliver, who thinks he is a Yahoo, longs to be a Houyhnhnm, and could not bear to be convinced that he is neither? As in *A Tale of a Tub*, Swift audaciously plays at the farthest limits of irony, limits that make satire impossible, because no norm exists to which we might hope to return.

Samuel Richardson

(1689-1761)

Clarissa

I FIRST READ *CLARISSA* AS A CORNELL UNDERGRADUATE IN THE LATE 1940s, under the skilled direction of my teacher, William M. Sale, Jr., a fierce partisan of Richardson and a remarkable critic of fiction. Since I cannot read a novel other than the way that Sale taught me, it is not surprising that forty years later I hold on fast to his canonical judgment that *Clarissa* is the finest novel in the English language. Rereading it through the years, I find it the only novel that can rival even Proust, despite Proust's evident advantages. The long and astonishing sequence that ends the novel, Clarissa's protracted death and its aftermath, is clearly at one of the limits of the novel as an art. I find myself fighting not to weep just before the moment of Clarissa's death, but as a critic I submit that these would be *cognitive* tears, and would say little about me but much about Richardson's extraordinary powers of representation. It remains a mystery that Richardson, with no strong novelistic precursors, should have been able to make Clarissa Harlowe the most persuasive instance of a kind of secular saint, a strong heroine, in the entire subsequent history of the Western novel.

Ian Watt, still our best historian of the rise of the novel, emphasizes that one of Richardson's major advances upon Defoe was in solving the problem of plot by centering it upon a single action: courtship between the sexes. That action necessarily entails Richardson's other grand innovation: the novelistic representation of the protagonists' inwardness, a mode of mimesis in which Richardson had only the one inevitable precursor, Shakespeare. If Jan Hendrik van den Berg is right, then historical psychology is essentially the study of the growing inner self, from Luther's "inner man" (1520) through Shakespeare's almost fully secularized tragic heroes on to Rousseau's and Wordsworth's solitary egos confronting, with ecstasy, the estrangement of things in a "sense of nature." *Clarissa* (1747–48) preceded all of Rousseau's publications, so that while Rousseau could have had something to tell Richardson about the sentiments and sensibility of inwardness, he did not teach the first great English novelist about the fictional representation of the inner life.

Whether anyone since has surpassed Richardson in this mimetic mode seems to me at least doubtful. George Eliot's Dorothea Brooke, Henry James's Isabel Archer, D.H. Lawrence's Ursula Brangwen, and even Virginia Woolf's Clarissa Dalloway, do not take us farther into the portrayal of a single consciousness than the original Clarissa brings us, and perhaps they all of them retreat to some degree from her full inwardness. Price remarks that "Richardson has transformed highly particularized characters so that their dense and familiar social setting fades away in the course of the slow disclosure of consequences." That transformation, in Clarissa and to some extent in Lovelace, replaces the social and historical context with a not less than tragic inwardness. If Clarissa is a saint and a martyr, then what she bears heroic witness to is not so much supernatural faith in Christ as it is natural faith in the heroic integrity of her own perpetually growing inner self.

II

Richardson's power as a novelist centers in the wildly antithetical and fiercely ambivalent relationship between Clarissa and Lovelace, who destroy both themselves and one another in what may be the most equivocal instance of a mutual passion in all of Western literature. I do not venture that assertion lightly, but no single love affair in Shakespeare, Tolstoy, or Proust seems comparable in its strength and complexity to the terrible agon that consumes Clarissa and Lovelace. We can no more speculate upon what a marriage between Richardson's protagonists might have been than we can visualize a world harmoniously ruled by a perpetually united Antony and Cleopatra. Lovelace and Clarissa are mighty opposites yet uncannily complementary, and it is Richardson's consummate art to have so created them that they must undo one another.

I begin with Lovelace, if only because his power of being, immense as it is, finally is eclipsed by the transcendental transformation of the gorgeously dying Clarissa. But that indeed is a finality; until Clarissa begins to die, the sheer force of her resistance to Lovelace compels him to become even more himself. Conversely, Lovelace's aggression greatly strengthens Clarissa, though the cost of her confirmation is her life. In the novel's most

terrible irony, the slow dying of Clarissa directly causes a steady waning in
Lovelace, a dwindling down from a heroic Satanist to a self-ruined libertine, drowning in remorse and confusion.

A.D. McKillop usefully traced Lovelace's literary ancestry to the libertine man-of-fashion in Restoration comedy and to the Herculean hero
of Dryden's dramas, such as *Aureng-Zebe* and *The Conquest of Granada*. This
lineage accounts both for some of Lovelace's obvious faults and for his few
but authentic virtues: healthy disdain for societal appearances and for false
morality, a curiously wistful longing for true virtue, and a brutal honesty.
But a fusion of a Restoration witty rake and Herculean rhetorician is no
more a match for Clarissa Harlowe than a Jacobean hero-villain would
have been, and part of the novel's fascination is in watching Lovelace slowly realize that Clarissa is necessarily an apocalyptic defeat for him. The
turning point is not the rape, but a moment late in Letter 266, when
Lovelace suddenly apprehends the dialectical entrapment that he and
Clarissa constitute for one another:

> A horrid dear creature!—By my soul, she made me shudder! She
> had need, indeed, to talk of *her* unhappiness, in falling into the
> hands of the only *man* in the world who could have used her as I
> have used her! She is the only *woman* in the world who could have
> shocked and disturbed me as she has done—So we are upon a foot
> in that respect. And I think I have the *worst* of it by much. Since
> very little has been my joy; very much my trouble: and *her* pun-
> ishment, as she calls it, is *over*: but when *mine* will, or what it *may
> be*, who can tell?
>
> Here, only recapitulating (think, then, how I must be affected
> at the time), I was forced to leave off, and sing a song to myself. I
> aimed at a lively air; but I croaked rather than sung: and fell into
> the old dismal thirtieth of January strain. I hemmed up for a
> sprightlier note; but it would not do: and at last I ended, like a
> malefactor, in a dead psalm melody.
>
> High-ho!—I gape like an unfledged kite in its nest, wanting to
> swallow a chicken, bobbed at its mouth by its marauding dam!—
>
> What a devil ails me!—I can neither think nor write!—
>
> Lie down, pen, for a moment!—

The devil that ails him is the beginning of his own end, his falling outwards and downwards from his last shreds of a libertine ideology into the
dreadful inner space of his defeat by Clarissa, his enforced realization that
self-willing and self-assertion are permanently over for him. Clarissa, a

great Puritan withholder of esteem will not accept him at his own evaluation, and he begins to know that pragmatically they have destroyed one another. His actual death is a release from the death-in-life he has suffered since Clarissa's death:

> He was delirious, at times, in the two last hours; and then several times cried out, Take her away! Take her away! but named nobody. And sometimes praised some lady (that Clarissa, I suppose, whom he had called upon when he received his death's wound) calling her, Sweet Excellence! Divine Creature! Fair Sufferer!—And once he said, Look down, blessed Spirit, look down!—And there stopped—his lips however moving.
>
> At nine in the morning, he was seized with convulsions, and fainted away; and it was a quarter of an hour before he came out of them.
>
> His few last words I must not omit, as they show an ultimate composure; which may administer some consolation to his honourable friends.
>
> *Blessed*—said he, addressing himself no doubt to Heaven; for his dying eyes were lifted up—a strong convulsion prevented him for a few moments saying more—But recovering, he again with great fervour (lifting up his eyes, and his spread hands) pronounced the word *Blessed*—Then, in a seeming ejaculation, he spoke inwardly so as not to be understood: at last, he distinctly pronounced these three words,
>
> LET THIS EXPIATE!
>
> And then, his head sinking on his pillow, he expired; at about half an hour after ten.

Lovelace dies in his own acquired religion, which is the worship of the blessed Clarissa, whom he personally has converted into something considerably more than a saint or even an angel. Being himself pure will and having been conquered by an even purer one, he worships his conqueror as God. Dying as a Clarissian rather than a Christian, as it were; Lovelace sustains his final pride, a peculiar sense of glory that has gone beyond remorse and has little left in it of mere love. This is hardly expiation in any moral or spiritual sense whatsoever, as Richardson on some level must have known, but is certainly an aesthetic expiation, worthy of Baudelaire or of Proust.

III

Clarissa, as is radiantly appropriate, ends many trajectories beyond her lover's destination. I dissent from the entire critical tradition, from Watt and Price to my younger contemporaries, that has overemphasized Clarissa's sup posed self-deceptions. Dr. Samuel Johnson first noted that Clarissa could not confront the truth of having fallen in love with Lovelace, but that hardly seems to me a duplicity in her, however unknowing. We cannot choose whom we are free to love, but Clarissa wars more strongly against every mode of overdetermination than any comparable character in secular fiction. What matters to her, and this is her greatness, is that her will cannot be violated, even by her own affections. *She refuses to see herself as anyone's victim—* whether Lovelace's, her family's, or her own turning against the self.

Lovelace becomes a wounded narcissist, and so is aggressive down to the end. But Clarissa could honestly say, if she wanted to, that it is not her narcissism but her eros that has been crucified. If Lovelace indeed represented her desire for what she did not have, and was not in herself, then her desire died, not so paradoxically, with the violation of her body. Lovelace becomes still more naturalistic after the rape, but she is transformed into a dualist and begins the process of dying to the body of this life. The issue has nothing to do with society and little to do with conventional reality. It is an aesthetic issue, the ancient agon of the Sublime mode, which always seeks to answer the triple question: more? equal to? less than? She was never less than Lovelace, hoped vainly he could be reformed into her equal, and knows now that she is far more than he is, and more indeed than anyone else in her world. At that height of the Sublime, she can only commence dying.

If her will is to remain inviolate, then its independence and integrity must be manifested by a death that is anything but a revenge, whether it be against Lovelace, her family, herself, or even against time. Rather, *her* death is the true expiation, which can bring forgiveness upon everyone else involved, though I surmise that she is more interested in forgiving herself even as she forgives the bewildered Lovelace. A Puritan saint, as Shaw's St. Joan shows, is rather more interested in her own integrity than in anyone else's suffering. The cost for Clarissa or for Shaw's St. Joan is an absolute, inner isolation, but is that not the essence of Protestantism?

There is nothing like Clarissa's virtually endless death-scene in all of literature, and while no one would wish it longer I do not wish it any shorter. Extraordinary as the actual moment of death is, in Letter 481, the most characteristic revelation of Clarissa's apotheosis is in Letter 475:

Her breath being very short, she desired another pillow; and having two before, this made her in a manner sit up in her bed; and she spoke then with more distinctness; and seeing us greatly concerned, forgot her own sufferings to comfort us; and a charming lecture she gave us, though a brief one, upon the happiness of a timely preparation and upon the hazards of a late repentance, when the mind, as she observed, was so much weakened, as well as the body, as to render a poor soul unable to contend with its own infirmities.

I beseech ye, my good friends, proceeded she, mourn not for one who mourns not, nor has cause to mourn, for herself. On the contrary, rejoice with me that all my worldly troubles are so near their end. Believe me, sirs, that I would not, if I might, choose to live, although the pleasantest part of my life were to come over again: and yet eighteen years of it, out of nineteen, have been very pleasant. To be so much exposed to temptation, and to be so liable to fail in the trial, who would not rejoice that all her dangers are over!—All I wished was pardon and blessing from my dear parents. Easy as my departure seems to promise to be, it would have been still easier had I had that pleasure. BUT GOD ALMIGHTY WOULD NOT LET ME DEPEND FOR COMFORT UPON ANY BUT HIMSELF.

This is certainly the purest Protestantism, and we might still be tempted to call this pride, particularly since Clarissa reminds us that she is all of nineteen years old. But we do Clarissa violence to name her total knowledge as a form of pride. The Protestant will by now has been blamed for practically everything that has gone wrong in our spiritual, intellectual, economic, and political life, as well as our sexual life, and the United States is the evening land of Protestantism and so the final stage for the travails of its will. Clarissa, as she dies, shows us the other side, the glory of the Protestant will. If God would not let Clarissa depend for comfort upon any but himself, then he gave her the ultimate accolade of the Protestant will: to accept esteem only where it chose to bestow esteem, and only on its own terms.

Henry Fielding

(1707–1754)

MARTIN PRICE REMARKS THAT "FIELDING CAN REWARD HIS HEROES because they do not seek a reward." As a critical observation, this is in Fielding's own spirit and tells us again what kind of novel Fielding invented, a comic *Odyssey*, ancestor of Smollett and Dickens, and of Joyce's *Ulysses*. My teacher Frederick W. Hilles liked to compare *Tom Jones* to *Ulysses*, while acknowledging that Fielding the narrator was neither invisible nor indifferent. Certainly Fielding was a fabulous artificer, which must be why he provoked so formidable a critical enemy as Dr. Samuel Johnson, who loved Alexander Pope while despising the most Popean of all novelists. Johnson vastly preferred Samuel Richardson to Fielding, a preference I myself share, though without prejudice to Fielding, since Richardson's *Clarissa* seems to me still the strongest novel in the language, surpassing even Austen's *Emma*, Eliot's *Middlemarch*, and James's *Portrait of a Lady*, all of them its descendants. *Tom Jones* founds another line, the rival tradition that includes Dickens and Joyce, novelists as exuberant as Fielding, and metaphysically and psychologically more problematic.

Samuel Johnson evidently resented what he took to be Fielding's simplistic vision, a resentment understandable in a great moralist who believed that human life was everywhere a condition in which much was to be endured, and little to be enjoyed. No one can match Johnson as a compelling moralist, but he necessarily undervalued Fielding's moral shrewdness. The true issue between Richardson and Fielding was in modes of representation, in their different views of mimesis. It is as though Richardson and Fielding split Shakespeare between them, with Richardson absorbing the Shakespearean power to portray inwardness, and Fielding inheriting Shakespeare's uncanny ease in depicting a romance world that becomes more real than reality.

Johnson told the protesting Boswell that "there is more knowledge of the heart in one letter of Richardson's, than in all *Tom Jones*." To Johnson, the personages in Fielding were "characters of manners," but in Richardson they were "characters of nature." This distinction is at least critical; one feels that many modern scholars who prefer Fielding to Richardson do so upon Coleridge's affective premises: "and how charming, how wholesome, Fielding always is! To take him up after Richardson is like emerging from a sick-room heated by stoves into an open lawn on a breezy day in May." That has the same persuasiveness as Richardson's explanation of why he would not read *Tom Jones*: "I was told, that it was a rambling Collection of Waking Dreams, in which Probability was not observed."

The seven volumes of Clarissa were published throughout the year from December 1747 through December 1748; *Tom Jones* came out in February 1749. Rivalry between the two novels was inevitable, and both seem to have sold very well. Between them, they established the modern novel, still the dominant literary form now, after two and a half centuries. Ian Watt, the definitive chronicler of *The Rise of the Novel* (1957), probably achieved the most balanced judgment on Fielding's crucial strengths and limitations:

> In his effort to infuse the new genre with something of the Shakespearean virtues Fielding departed too far from formal realism to initiate a viable tradition, but his work serves as a perpetual reminder that if the new genre was to challenge older literary forms it had to find a way of conveying not only a convincing impression but a wise assessment of life, an assessment that could only come from taking a much wider view than Defoe or Richardson or the affairs of mankind.

Tom Jones

What is Shakespearean about *Tom Jones?* The violent, daemonic, mindless energy of Squire Western, or the bodily ego rampant, is certainly part of the answer. Martin Price calls Western the finest English comic character after Falstaff, and the judgment seems indisputable. Yet here also a shadow falls. Falstaff, like his precursor, the Wife of Bath, is a heroic vitalist, raising vitalism, as she does, to the sublime of wit. Like Falstaff, the Wife is a great parodist, and a dangerously sophisticated Bible interpreter, as Talbot Donaldson demonstrates. But Western is energy without mind, and so is himself a living parody of vitalism. Fielding's genius nevertheless is so incarnated in Western that he breaks the limits of representation, and leaps out of the novel into that supermimetic domain where Falstaff and the Wife of Bath join Don Quixote and Sancho Panza. Western's simplicity is so exuberant and physical that it achieves a new kind of complexity, as in this astonishing comic reversal:

> *Western* had been long impatient for the Event of this Conference, and was just now arrived at the Door to listen; when having heard the last Sentiments of his Daughter's Heart, he lost all Temper, and bursting open the Door in a Rage, cried out.—"It is a Lie. It is a d-n'd Lie. It is all owing to that d-d'd Rascal *Juones*; and if she could get at un, she'd ha un any Hour of the Day." Here *Allworthy* interposed, and addressing himself to the Squire with some Anger in his Look, he said, "Mr. *Western*, you have not kept your Word with me. You promised to abstain from all Violence."—"Why so I did," cries *Western*, "as long as it was possible; but to hear a Wench telling such confounded Lies.—Zounds! Doth she think if she can make Vools of other Volk, she can make one of me?—No, no, I know her better than thee dost." "I am sorry to tell you, Sir," answered *Allworthy*, "it doth not appear by your Behaviour to this young Lady, that you know her at all. I ask Pardon for what I say; but I think our Intimacy, your own Desires, and the Occasion justify me. She is your Daughter, Mr. *Western*, and I think she doth Honour to your Name. If I was capable of Envy, I should sooner envy you on this Account, than any other Man whatever."—"Odrabbit it," cries the Squire, "I wish she was thine with all my Heart—wouldst soon be glad to be rid of the Trouble o' her."—"Indeed, my good Friend," answered *Allworthy*, "you yourself are the Cause of all the Trouble you complain of. Place that Confidence in the young Lady which she so well deserves, and I am certain you will be the happiest Father on Earth."—"I Confidence in her!" cries the Squire.—"'Sblood! what Confidence can I place in her, when she won't do as I would ha her? Let her gi but Consent to marry as I would ha her, and I'll place as much Confidence in her as wouldst ha me."—"You have no Right, Neighbour," answered *Allworthy*, "to insist on any such Consent. A negative Voice your Daughter allows you, and God and Nature have thought proper to allow you no more." "A negative Voice?" cries the Squire—"Ay! ay! I'll shew you what a negative Voice I ha. Go along, go into your Chamber, go, you Stubborn."—"Indeed, Mr. *Western*," said *Allworthy*,—"Indeed, you use her cruelly—I cannot bear to see this—You shall, you must behave to her in a

kinder Manner. She deserves the best of Treatment." "Yes, yes," said the Squire, "I know what she deserves: Now she's gone, I'll shew you what she deserves—See here, Sir, here is a Letter from my Cousin, my Lady *Bellaston*, in which she is so kind to gi me to understand, that the Fellow is got out of Prison again; and here she advises me to take all the Care I can o' the Wench. Odzookers! Neighbour *Allworthy*, you don't know what it is to govern a Daughter."

The Squire ended his Speech with some Compliments to his own Sagacity; and then *Allworthy*, after a formal Preface, acquainted him with the whole Discovery which he had made concerning *Jones*, with his Anger to *Blifil*, and with every Particular which hath been disclosed to the Reader in the preceding Chapters.

Men over-violent in their Dispositions, are, for the most Part, as changeable in them. No sooner then was *Western* informed of Mr. *Allworthy*'s Intention to make *Jones* his Heir, then he joined heartily with the Uncle in every Commendation of the Nephew, and became as eager for her Marriage with *Jones*, as he had before been to couple her to *Blifil*.

Here Mr. *Allworthy* was again forced to interpose, and to relate what had passed between him and *Sophia*, at which he testified great Surprize.

The Squire was silent a Moment, and looked wild with Astonishment at this Account—At last he cried out, "Why what can be the Meaning of this, Neighbour *Allworthy*? Vond o un she was, that I'll be sworn to.—Odzookers! I have hit o't. As sure as a Gun I have hit o the very right o't. It's all along o Zister. The Girl hath got a Hankering after this son of a Whore of a Lord. I vound'em together at my Cousin, my Lady *Bellaston*'s. He hath turned the Head o' her that's certain—but d-n me if he shall ha her—I'll ha no Lords nor Courtiers in my Vamily."

Western is equally passionate, within moments, in swearing that Sophia shall *not* have Jones, and that she *shall*. We are delighted by his stance, either way, and most delighted at his childish ease in moving from one position to the other without pause, embarrassment, or reflection. A passionate infant, Squire Western is sublime on the page, or on the screen, where as played by Hugh Griffith he ran off with the Osborne-Richardson *Tom Jones*; but in mere reality he would be a monster. As a representation he is triumphant because like the much greater Falstaff he is free of the superego. We rejoice in Western because he is freedom gone wild, including freedom from nasty plotting; yet his mindlessness almost frightens us.

Price is as accurate as ever when he observes that "Fielding controls his characters by limiting them," but Western is the grand exception, being out of control and extravagant, beyond all limits. No other eighteenth-century novel could accommodate Western, which is another indication of the power of *Tom Jones*. Something primeval in the mode of romance survives in Western the wild man, who hardly seems to belong to a post-Swiftian novel that still exalts the Augustan vision. Fielding, like Pope and Swift, joins the Enlightenment consciousness and ideas of order to an ongoing sense of the demands of energy. Johnson, who shared with Fielding the heritage of Pope and Swift, may have felt, obscurely but accurately, that Fielding, like Swift, gave too much away to the daemonic force of vitalism. "This kind of writing may be termed not improperly the Comedy of Romance," Johnson said of Fielding, thus relegating Fielding to the dark and enchanted ground not yet purified by reason. Johnson meant to condemn, perhaps, but guides us instead to Fielding's most surprising strength.

Laurence Sterne

(1713-1768)

Tristram Shandy

STERNE REMARKED, IN A LETTER, THAT *TRISTRAM SHANDY* "WAS MADE AND formed to baffle all criticism," but he probably knew better. Dr. Johnson, greatest of critics, insisted that *Tristram Shandy* would not last, a hopelessly wrong prophecy. Sterne gives the critic and reader everything to do, and can anyone resist, one wonders, a novel in which the hero-narrator declares (volume 1, chapter 14) that "I have been at it these six weeks, making all the speed I possibly could,—and am not yet born"? Published in nine short volumes from 1760 to 1767, *Tristram Shandy* is the masterpiece of what Northrop Frye has taught us to call the Age of Sensibility, the era of Rousseau, and of a secularized, vernacular, "Orientalized" Bible, described by Bishop Lowth (*Lectures on the Sacred Poetry of the Hebrews*, 1753) as the true source of the "language of the passions." It is also the era of John Locke, much as we still live in the Age of Sigmund Freud. Johnson, who also opposed the poetry of Thomas Gray and of his own personal friend, William Collins, was quite consistent in setting himself against *Tristram Shandy*. Henry Fielding may have subverted novelistic forms, but Sterne subverts the entire Augustan mode of representation and truly ends the cultural enterprise in which Pope had triumphed.

It cannot be accidental that so many of the best contemporary Spanish-American novels are Shandean, whether or not the particular writer actually has read Sterne. One such distinguished novelist, when told by me how grand a fantasist he seemed, amiably assured me that his intentions were merely realistic. In the presence of extraordinary actuality, Wallace Stevens observed, consciousness could take the place of imagination. For Sterne, consciousness itself was the extraordinary actuality, so that sensibility

33

became one with imagination. Dualism, Cartesian and Lockean, comes to us now mostly in Freudian guise. "Shandean guise" would do as well, since Sterne is a thoroughgoing Freudian five generations before Freud. The fundamental Freudian frontier concepts—the drive, the bodily ego, the nonrepressive defenses of introjection and projection—are conceptually exemplified in *Tristram Shandy*, as is the central Freudian idea or trope of repression or defense. Most readers of Sterne see this at once, and many of his critics have reflected upon it. A Freudian exegesis of *Tristram Shandy* therefore becomes a redundancy. Far more vital is the question: What is Sterne trying to do for himself, as a novelist, by his dualistic, solipsistic, psychological emphasis?

That there is an aesthetic and moral program in the Shandean philosophy, most critics agree, but phrasing it has led to some unfortunate banalities. You can sum up Pope's or Fielding's designs upon the reader rather more easily than you can express Sterne's. This is not simply a rhetorical dilemma; Sterne is a great ironist and parodist, but so are Pope and Fielding, while Swift excels even Sterne in such modes. But if all three of the great Augustans are cognitively subtle, Sterne is preternaturally subtle, to the point of being daemonic. Swift is ferocious, yet Sterne is uncanny; his artistry is indeed diabolic as Martin Price comments, comparing it to the skill of Ionesco. The spirit of the comparison is right, but Ionesco hardly can work on Sterne's scale, which is both vast and minute. I prefer Richard Lanham's comparison of Sterne to Chaucer, who also is too wise to fall into an Arnoldian high seriousness. Like Chaucer and Cervantes, Sterne is very serious about play, but he is even more playful about form than they are.

II

What is love, to an almost perfect solipsist? Can it be more than sex? Is sex all, and does every trembling hand make us squeak, like dolls, the wished-for word? Sterne is reductive enough to muse on the question, and to intimate an affirmative answer:

> I had escaped, continued the corporal, all that time from falling in love, and had gone on to the end of the chapter, had it not been predestined otherwise—there is no resisting our fate.
> It was on a *Sunday*, in the afternoon, as I told your honour—
> The old man and his wife had walked out—
> Every thing was still and hush as midnight about the house—
> There was not so much as a duck or a duckling about the yard—

—When the fair *Beguine* came in to see me.

My wound was then in a fair way of doing well—the inflammation had been gone off for some time, but it was succeeded with an itching both above and below my knee, so insufferable, that I had not shut my eyes the whole night for it.

Let me see it, said she, kneeling down upon the ground parallel to my knee, and laying her hand upon the part below it—It only wants rubbing a little, said the *Beguine*; so covering it with the bed cloaths, she began with the fore-finger of her right-hand to rub under my knee, guiding her fore-finger backwards and forwards by the edge of the flannel which kept on the dressing.

In five or six minutes I felt slightly the end of the second finger—and presently it was laid flat with the other, and she continued rubbing in that way round and round for a good while; it then came into my head, that I should fall in love—I blush'd when I saw how white a hand she had—I shall never, an' please your honour, behold another hand so white whilst I live

—Not in that place: said my uncle *Toby*—

Though it was the most serious despair in nature to the corporal—he could not forbear smiling.

The young *Beguine*, continued the corporal, perceiving it was of great service to me—from rubbing, for some time, with two fingers—proceeded to rub at length, with three—till by little and little she brought down the fourth, and then rubb'd with her whole hand: I will never say another word, an' please your honour, upon hands again—but it was softer than satin—

—Prithee, *Trim*, commend it as much as thou wilt, said my uncle *Toby*, I shall hear thy story with the more delight—The corporal thank'd his master most unfeignedly; but having nothing to say upon the *Beguine*'s hand, but the same over again—he proceeded to the effects of it.

The fair *Beguine*, said the corporal, continued rubbing with her whole hand under my knee—till I fear'd her zeal would weary her—"I would do a thousand times more," said she, "for the love of Christ"—In saying which she pass'd her hand across the flannel, to the part above my knee, which I had equally complained of, and rubb'd it also.

I perceived, then, I was beginning to be in love—

As she continued rub-rub-rubbing—I felt it spread from under her hand, an' please your honour, to every part of my frame—The more she rubb'd, and the longer strokes she took—the more the fire kindled in my veins—till at length, by two or three strokes longer than the rest—my passion rose to the highest pitch—I seiz'd her hand—

—And then, thou clapped'st it to thy lips, *Trim*, said my uncle *Toby*—and madest a speech.

Whether the corporal's amour terminated precisely in the way my uncle Toby described it, is not material; it is enough that it contain'd in it the essence of all the love-romances which ever have been wrote since the beginning of the world. (8, 22)

To be in love is to be aroused; no more, no less. Sterne, something of an invalid, was abnormally sensitive, as W.B.C. Watkins remarked, "—partly because he was inevitably self-conscious physically to an abnormal degree. He was acutely aware of the very circulation of his blood and the beating of his heart." Much of Sterne's alleged prurience is actually his heightened vulnerability, cognitive and bodily, to sexual stimuli. The sense of "Sensibility" in Sterne is fully sexual, and aids us in seeing the true nature of the cultural term, both morally and aesthetically. A susceptibility to tender feelings, however fine, and whether one's own or those of others, becomes objectified as a quality or stance that turns away from the Stoic and Augustan ideal of reason in affective response. This is Sensibility or "the Sentimental" ideologically free from either right-wing celebration of bourgeois morality or left-wing idealization or proletarian or pastoral natural virtues. Its politics, though Whiggish in origin, diffuse into a universal and histrionic vision of the force and beauty of the habits of the heart. Martin Price terms it "a vehement, often defiant assertion of the value of man's feelings." Overtly self-conscious and dramatic, yet insisting upon its sincerity, the stance of Sensibility is a kind of sexualization of all the other effects, as Sterne most clearly knew, showed, and told. Richard Lanham sums this up when he writes that "For Sterne, we finally become not only insatiable pleasure-seekers but, by our nature, incurable poseurs."

All Shandeans have their favorite episodes, and I am tempted to cite all of volume 7, throughout which Tristram/Sterne flees from Death by taking a Sentimental journey through France. One could vote for the story of Amandus and Amanda, or for the concluding country-dance with Nanette, two superb moments in volume 7. But, if we are pleasure-seeking poseurs, we cannot do better than chapter 15 of volume 8, which precedes the Widow Wadman's direct attempt to light Uncle Toby at both ends at once, in the sentry-box:

It is a great pity—but 'tis certain from every day's observation of man, that he may be set on fire like a candle, at either end—provided there is a sufficient wick standing out; if there is not—there's an end of the affair; and if there is—by lighting it at the bottom, as the flame in that case has the misfortune generally to put out itself—there's an end of the affair again.

For my part, could I always have the ordering of it which way I would be burnt myself—for I cannot bear the thoughts of being burnt like a beast—I would oblige a housewife constantly to light me at the top; for then I should burn down decently to the socket; that is, from my head to my heart, from my heart to my liver, from my liver to my bowels, and so on by the meseraick veins and arteries, through all the turns and lateral insertions of the intestines and their tunicles to the blind gut—

—I beseech you, doctor *Slop*, quoth my uncle *Toby*, interrupting him as he mentioned the *blind gut*, in a discourse with my father the night my mother was brought to bed of me—I beseech you, quoth my uncle *Toby*, to tell me which is the blind gut; for, old as I am, I vow I do not know to this day where it lies.

The *blind gut*, answered doctor *Slop*, lies betwixt the *Illion* and *Colon*—

—In a man? said my father.

—'Tis precisely the same, cried doctor *Slop*, in a woman— That's more than I know; quoth my father. (8, 15)

We confront again Sterne's marvelous sense of the dualistic perplexities of human existence. Man is not exactly the Puritan candle of the Lord, burning with a preternatural will-to-holiness, but a sexual candle altogether, burning with the natural will-to-live. When Tristram/Sterne asks to be lit at the top, presumably with cognitive fire, then he asks also to "burn down decently to the socket." Sterne's fierce metaphor rejects the Cartesian ghost-in-the-machine (Gilbert Ryle's fine formulation) and desires instead a conflagration of the mind through the senses. Though he is perhaps the most satirical of all vitalists, Sterne's final affinities seem to be with Rabelais and Blake, visionaries who sought to redeem us through an improvement in sensual enjoyment.

Tobias Smollett

(1721-1771)

Humphry Clinker

DESPITE THE VIGOR AND HUMOR OF *HUMPHRY CLINKER*, SMOLLETT IS currently the most neglected of the major eighteenth-century British novelists. Since he is not of the aesthetic eminence of Richardson, Fielding, and Sterne, one would not expect him to provoke the intense critical interest that they perpetually sustain. But *Humphry Clinker*, in my judgment, is a stronger novel than Defoe's *Moll Flanders* or Goldsmith's *The Vicar of Wakefield*, and compares favorably also with Fanny Burney's *Evelina*. Since it is now less read and studied than any of those three, its eclipse perhaps indicates that something in Smollett is not available to what is dominant in our current sensibility. The era of Thomas Pynchon, apocalyptic and beyond the resources of any satiric vision, is not a time for accommodating Smollett's rough tumble of an expedition towards a yearned-for health.

Smollett, a surgeon, probably knew he had not long to live even as he composed *Humphry Clinker*. Resident in Italy from 1768 on, for his health, Smollett died there in 1771, just fifty, some three months after *Humphry Clinker* was published. The expedition that is the novel, winding from Wales up through the length of England well into Smollett's native Scotland, is the author's long farewell to life, rendering Britain with a peculiar vividness as he remembers it from abroad.

Why the novel is named for Humphry Clinker rather than its central figure, Matthew Bramble, who clearly is Smollett's surrogate, never has been clear to me, except that Clinker is a representative of the future and may be Smollett's wistful introjection of a life he would not survive to know. Clinker and Bramble rise together from the water, a natural son and the father he has saved from drowning, and both undergo a change of name into the same name: Matthew Loyd. This curious mutual baptism seems to have been a mythic transference for Smollett, since Matthew Loyd was Bramble's *former* name, and will be his son Humphry Clinker's *future* name. It is as though the slowly dying Smollett required a double vision of survival: as a Matthew Bramble largely purged of an irascibility close to madness, and as Humphry Clinker, a kindly and innocent youth restored to a lost heritage.

I have found that many of my friends and students, generally very good readers, shy away from *Humphry Clinker* and from Smollett in general, because they are repelled by his mode, which at its strongest tends toward grotesque farce. The mode by definition is not pleasant, but, like the much greater Swift, Smollett is a master in this peculiar subgenre. It is hardly accidental that Thomas Rowlandson illustrated Smollett in the early 1790s, because there is a profound affinity between the novelist and the caricaturist. Smollett's reality, at its most intense, is phantasmagoric, and there are moments early on in *Humphry Clinker* when the irritable (and well-named) Bramble seems close to madness. His speculations on the origins of the waters at Bath are not less than disgusting, and he is more than weary of mankind: "My curiosity is quite satisfied: I have done with the science of men, and must now endeavour to amuse myself with the novelty of things." Everywhere he finds only "food for spleen, and subject for ridicule."

Bramble satirizes everything he encounters, and is himself an instance of the mocker mocked or the satirist satirized. One can cultivate an amused affection for him, but he is not Don Quixote, and the vivid but unlikable Lismahago, my favorite character in the book, is no Sancho Panza. Smollett evidently identifies with Bramble, but we cannot do so, and surely Smollett intended it that way. We may enjoy farce, but we do not wish to find ourselves acting in one as we stumble on in our lives. I think of my favorite farce in the language, Marlowe's *The Jew of Malta*. I have acted on stage just once in my life, playing Falstaff in an emergency, an amateur pressed into service, and played the witty knight more or less in the style of the late, great Zero Mostel playing Leopold Bloom in *Ulysses in Nighttown*. The one part I would love to play on stage is Barabas, bloody Jew of Malta, but in life obviously I would prefer being Falstaff to being Barabas.

When a novel conducts itself as realistic farce, which is Smollett's mode, we are denied the pleasures of introjection and identification. But a novel is wiser to forsake realism when it moves into farce. Sometimes I wish, reading Smollett, that he had been able to read the Evelyn Waugh of *Decline and Fall*, *Vile Bodies*, *A Handful of Dust*, because I think that Waugh

would have been a good influence upon him. But that is to wish Smollett
other than Smollett; one of his strengths is that he drives realistic representation almost beyond its proper limits, in order to extend the empire of
farce. Perhaps his own fierce temperament required the extension, for he
was more than a little mad, in this resembling certain elements of temperament in Swift, Sterne, and Dr. Samuel Johnson.

Sterne, in *A Sentimental Journey*, robustly satirizes Smollett as "the
learned Smelfungus," who "set out with the spleen and jaundice, and every
object he passed by was discoloured or distorted." Coming out of the
Pantheon, Smelfungus comments, "'Tis nothing but a huge cock pit," and
all his travel adventures lead to similar judgments, provoking Sterne to a
good retort: "I'll tell it, cried Smelfungus, to the world. You had better tell
it, said I, to your physician." All of us would rather travel with Sterne than
with Smollett, but reading Smollett remains a uniquely valuable experience. Let us take him at his most ferociously grotesque, in the account of
the sufferings of Lismahago and the still more unfortunate Murphy at the
horrid hands of the Miami Indians:

> By dint of her interrogations, however, we learned, that he and
> ensign Murphy had made their escape from the French hospital at
> Montreal, and taken to the woods, in hope of reaching some
> English settlement; but mistaking their route, they fell in with a
> party of Miamis, who carried them away in captivity. The inten-
> tion of these Indians was to give one of them as an adopted son to
> a venerable sachem, who had lost his own in the course of the war,
> and to sacrifice the other according to the custom of the country.
> Murphy, as being the younger and handsomer of the two, was
> designed to fill the place of the deceased, not only as the son of the
> sachem, but as the spouse of a beautiful squaw, to whom his pred-
> ecessor had been betrothed; but in passing through the different
> whigwhams or villages of the Miamis, poor Murphy was so man-
> gled by the women and children, who have the privilege of tor-
> turing all prisoners in their passage, that, by the time they arrived
> at the place of the sachem's residence, he was rendered altogether
> unfit for the purposes of marriage: it was determined therefore, in
> the assembly of the warriors, that ensign Murphy should be
> brought to the stake, and that the lady should be given to lieu-
> tenant Lismahago, who had likewise received his share of tor-
> ments, though they had not produced emasculation.—A joint of
> one finger had been cut, or rather sawed off with a rusty knife; one
> of his great toes was crushed into a mash betwixt two stones; some

of his teeth were drawn, or dug out with a crooked nail; splintered reeds had been thrust up his nostrils and other tender parts; and the calves of his legs had been blown up with mines of gunpowder dug in the flesh with the sharp point of the tomahawk.

The Indians themselves allowed that Murphy died with great heroism, singing, as his death song, the *Drimmendoo*, in concert with Mr. Lismahago, who was present at the solemnity. After the warriors and the matrons had made a hearty meal upon the muscular flesh which they pared from the victim, and had applied a great variety of tortures, which he bore without flinching, an old lady, with a sharp knife, scooped out one of his eyes, and put a burning coal in the socket. The pain of this operation was so exquisite that he could not help bellowing, upon which the audience raised a shout of exultation, and one of the warriors stealing behind him, gave him the *coup de grace* with a hatchet.

Lismahago's bride, the squaw Squinkinacoosta, distinguished herself on this occasion.—She shewed a great superiority of genius in the tortures which she contrived and executed with her own hands.—She vied with the stoutest warrior in eating the flesh of the sacrifice; and after all the other females were fuddled with dram-drinking, she was not so intoxicated but that she was able to play the game of the platter with the conjuring sachem, and afterwards go through the ceremony of her own wedding, which was consummated that same evening. The captain had lived very happily with this accomplished squaw for two years, during which she bore him a son, who is now the representative of his mother's tribe; but, at length, to his unspeakable grief, she had died of a fever, occasioned by eating too much raw bear, which they had killed in a hunting excursion.

This is both dreadfully funny and funnily dreadful, and is quite marvelous writing, though evidently not to all tastes. If it were written by Mark Twain, we would know how to take it, but Smollett renders it with a dangerous relish, which makes us a little uncertain, since we do not wish to be quite as rancid as the learned Smelfungus, or even as the dreadful Lismahago for that matter. Reading Smollett is sometimes like eating too much raw bear, but that only acknowledges how authentic and strong his flavor is.

To have inspired Rowlandson and fostered Charles Dickens (who took his origins in a blend of Smollett and Ben Jonson) is enough merit for any one writer. Smollett is to Dickens what Marlowe was to Shakespeare, a forerunner so swallowed up by an enormous inheritor that the precursor sometimes seems a minnow devoured by a whale. But, considered in himself, Smollett has something of Marlowe's eminence. Each carried satirical farce and subversive melodrama to a new limit, and that too is merit enough.

Oliver Goldsmith

(1730–1774)

OLIVER GOLDSMITH, VERSATILE AND GRACEFUL IN EVERY GENRE, COMPELS a critic to speculate upon the disproportion between the writer-as-person and the writer-as-writer. Some (not all) of the most accomplished writers I have known have been the most colorless of personalities, or if more vivid and interesting as people, then they have been remarkably unpleasant or foolish or merely mawkish. Goldsmith appears to have been a luckless individual and even what Freud called a "moral masochist," a victim of his own death-drive at the age of forty-four. Indeed, Goldsmith is a fairly classic instance of many Freudian insights, and both *The Vicar of Wakefield* and *She Stoops to Conquer* sustain immediate illumination when Freudian categories are applied to them. What Freud termed "the most prevalent form of degradation in erotic life" is a clear guide to young Marlow's backwardness with well-born women, and exuberant aggressivity with inn barmaids, college bedmakers, and others of whom he remarks: "They are of us you know." And the lumpish Tony Lumpkin becomes an even more persuasive representation when his descent into the company of the alehouse is seen, again in Freudian guise, as a reaction-formation to his dreadful mother, Mrs. Hardcastle.

Goldsmith aped Johnson in most things, even to the copying of the critic's manner, according to Boswell. Johnson spoke the last word upon his friend and follower: "If nobody was suffered to abuse poor Goldy but those who could write as well, he would have few censors." Yet it is a curious sadness that the best lines in any poem by Goldsmith, the concluding passage of *The Deserted Village*, were written by Johnson himself:

That trade's proud empire hastes to swift decay,
As ocean sweeps the laboured mole away;

While self-dependent power can time defy,
As rocks resist the billows and the sky.

An ironical reading might interpret that humanly constructed break-water, "the laboured mole," as Goldsmith's ego, in contrast to Johnsonian self-dependence, the great critic's rock-like ego. Still, Goldsmith's laboured breakwater has defied time also, though not quite with the massive Johnsonian force. Goldsmith's writing survives on its curious grace, curious both because it resists strict definition and because it extends across the genres: from the Popean verse of *The Traveller*, through the Bunyanesque revision of the Book of Job in the sentimental novel *The Vicar of Wakefield*, on to the elegiac pastoralism of *The Deserted Village*, the permanently successful stage comedy *She Stoops to Conquer*, and the urbane good nature of the posthumously published poem *Retaliation*, a gentle satire upon the members of Dr. Johnson's Club.

The strongest case for Goldsmith was made by William Hazlitt, second only to Johnson in my estimate, among all critics in the language:

> Goldsmith, both in verse and prose, was one of the most delight-ful writers in the language.... His ease is quite unconscious. Everything in him is spontaneous, unstudied, yet elegant, harmo-nious, graceful, nearly faultless.

A kind of natural or unconscious artist, Goldsmith prevails by disarming his reader. He seems the least tendentious of all authors, writing as though he had no design upon us. Even now he has not lost his audience, although critics sometimes treat his works as period pieces. He is strangely close to popular literature, though he hardly can sustain comparison with the far more powerful Bunyan. Perhaps he moves us now primarily as an instance of our continuity with a past that we seem otherwise wholly to have abandoned.

The Vicar of Wakefield

The canonical status of *The Vicar of Wakefield* is beyond doubt, though I do not advise rereading it side by side with Bunyan's far stronger *The Pilgrim's Progress* as I have just done. But then, Bunyan is so powerful a visionary as to claim the company of Milton and Blake. Goldsmith gives us a gentle theodicy in the *Vicar*, and theodicy is hardly a gentle mode. Henry James, writing an introduction to the novel in 1900, called it "the spoiled child of our literature," a work so amiable that it seemed to him "happy in the manner in which a happy man is happy—a man, say, who has married an angel or been appointed to a sinecure."

Like the Book of Job, the *Vicar* brings a good man, here Dr. Primrose, into the power of Satan, here Squire Thornhill. Some recent revisionist readings of the *Vicar* have attempted to give us a Dr. Primrose who is more self-righteous than virtuous, more smugly egoistical than innocent. These seem to me weak misreadings because they overlook Goldsmith's most surprising revision of the Book of Job. With singular audacity, Goldsmith makes his Job the narrator. Whatever you have Job do, you ought not to make him the hero of a first-person narrative. Consider the aesthetic and spiritual effect that even the opening would then have upon us:

> I was a man in the land of Uz, and my name was Job; I was perfect and upright, and I feared God, and eschewed evil.

No one proclaims his own virtues without alienating us, and no one recites his own sufferings without embarrassing us. The opening of *The Vicar of Wakefield* is not quite like that of a first-person Book of Job, but it is problematic enough:

> I was ever of opinion, that the honest man who married and brought up a large family, did more service than he who continued single and only talked of population. From this motive, I had scarce taken orders a year, before I began to think seriously of matrimony, and chose my wife, as she did her wedding-gown, not for a fine glossy surface, but such qualities as would wear well.

At best, poor Primrose sounds a pompous fool; at worst, a bore rampant. Why did Goldsmith take the risk? Was Primrose intended to be a satiric butt and Burchell a reality instructor? Dickens evidently did not think so, and something of Primrose got into Mr. Pickwick. Unlike Goethe and Dickens, we do not find Primrose to be altogether comically lovable. However, we also ought not to fault him. Perhaps he does represent a secularization of the figure of Job or a Johnsonian allegory of an education in true humility, but I suspect that he is primarily Goldsmith's introjection of Job. This is not to suggest a composite figure, Job/Primrose-Goldsmith as it were, but to intimate that Primrose is a loving self-satire on Goldsmith's part, or an amiable Jobean parody directed against the feckless writer's own penchant for catastrophe.

Goldsmith takes the risk of first-person narration because he knows that the Vicar Primrose is his own somewhat ironic self-portrait and that his personal Jobean tribulations do not exactly achieve sublimity. Yet Goldsmith, in life, and the Vicar, in the novel, cannot refrain from self-praise, from a kind of snobbery of virtue, even as they are altogether the passive victims of fortune. Goldsmith, though an impossible personality, was a literary genius, but Dr. Primrose is simply not very clever. An unintelligent Job startles us, if only by reminding us what a formidable moral psychologist and reasoner the biblical Job was, so much so that he finally infuriated John Calvin, his greatest commentator. Calvin, in his sermons on the Book of Job, is finally provoked to cry out that God would have had to make new worlds to satisfy Job. No one would say that God would have had to make new worlds to satisfy Dr. Primrose. Goldsmith himself, I suspect, was about halfway between Job and the Vicar in this regard.

She Stoops to Conquer

The Citizen of the World, *The Vicar of Wakefield*, and the three major poems may be the best of Goldsmith, but I myself prefer *She Stoops to Conquer*. It has held the stage for more than two hundred years and may well be the authentic instance of a popular drama in English after Shakespeare. Though it was intended as a parody upon what Goldsmith called Sentimental as opposed to Laughing Comedy, we have lost the satire without losing the value of the work. It remains very funny and evidently always will be funny. Goldsmith did not intend farce, but that is what *She Stoops to Conquer* assuredly is: major farce. There is something Shakespearean about Kate Hardcastle, though to compare her to the Rosalind of *As You Like It* is an offence against literary tact, as is any comparison of Tony Lumpkin to Puck.

Goldsmith had the literary good sense to keep his farce simple, reductive, and almost primitive; the portrait of Mrs. Hardcastle has a kind of unrelenting savagery about it. And Tony Lumpkin's ordeal-by-fright for her is not less than sadistic, with a cruelty in which we are compelled to share:

> TONY. Never fear me. Here she comes. Vanish. She's got from the pond, and draggled up to the waist like a mermaid. *Enter Mrs Hardcastle.*
>
> MRS HARDCASTLE. Oh, Tony, I'm killed. Shook. Battered to death. I shall never survive it. That last jolt that laid us against the quickset hedge has done my business.
>
> TONY. Alack, mama, it was all your own fault. You would be for running away by night, without knowing one inch of the way.
>
> MRS HARDCASTLE. I wish we were at home again. I never met so

many accidents in so short a journey. Drenched in the mud, overturned in a ditch, stuck fast in a slough, jolted to a jelly, and at last to lose our way. Whereabouts do you think we are, Tony?

TONY. By my guess we should be upon Crack-skull Common, about forty miles from home.

MRS HARDCASTLE. O lud! O lud! the most notorious spot in all the country. We only want a robbery to make a complete night on't.

TONY. Don't be afraid, mama, don't be afraid. Two of the five that kept here are hanged, and the other three may not find us. Don't be afraid. Is that a man that's galloping behind us? No; it's only a tree. Don't be afraid.

MRS HARDCASTLE. The fright will certainly kill me.

TONY. Do you see anything like a black hat moving behind the thicket?

MRS HARDCASTLE. O death!

TONY. No, it's only a cow. Don't be afraid, mama; don't be afraid.

MRS HARDCASTLE. As I'm alive, Tony, I see a man coming towards us. Ah! I'm sure on't. If he perceives us we are undone.

TONY (*aside*). Father-in-law, by all that's unlucky, come to take one of his night walks. (*To her*) Ah, it's a highwayman, with pistols as long as my arm. A damned ill-looking fellow.

MRS HARDCASTLE. Good heaven defend us! He approaches.

TONY. Do you hide yourself in that thicket, and leave me to manage him. If there be any danger I'll cough and cry, Hem! When I cough be sure to keep close.

Mrs Hardcastle hides behind a tree in the Back Scene.

To find a comparable savagery, one would have to turn to W.S. Gilbert. There is a touch of Gilbert to *She Stoops to Conquer*, if only because we are already in that cosmos of nonsense that is shadowed by the Freudian reality principle. Freud, writing on "Humor" in 1928, heard in it the voice of the super-ego, speaking "kindly words of comfort to the intimidated ego." This does not take us far when we consider Shakespearean comedy at its most complex, *As You Like It* or *All's Well That Ends Well*. But it beautifully enlightens us as to Goldsmith's holiday from the superego in *She Stoops to Conquer*. Goldsmith was very uncomfortable as Job, even as that most amiable and silly of Jobs, Dr. Primrose. But he was supremely comfortable as Tony Lumpkin, his kindly word of comfort to his own intimidated ego.

Fanny Burney

(1752-1840)

Evelina

EVELINA OR THE HISTORY OF A YOUNG LADY'S ENTRANCE INTO THE WORLD (1778) earned the approbation of Dr. Samuel Johnson, who remains in my judgment, as in that of many others, the best critic in Western literary history. These days *Evelina* seems to attract mostly feminist critics, though it is hardly a precursor of their ideologies and sensibilities. A reader who knows the novels of Samuel Richardson will recognize immediately how indebted Fanny Burney was to him, and any reader of Jane Austen will be interested in *Evelina* in order to contrast the very different ways in which Richardson influenced the two women novelists. In itself, *Evelina* provides a rather mixed aesthetic experience upon rereading, at least to me. Its largest strength is in its humor and in Fanny Burney's quite extraordinary ear for modes of speech. What is rather disappointing is Evelina herself, who records the wit and spirits of others, while herself manifesting a steady goodness that is not ideally suited for fictional representation.

Entrance is indeed the novel's central metaphor, and Evelina enters the social world as a kind of lesser Sir Charles Grandison, rather than as a lesser Clarissa. This is not to say that Evelina's advent in the book does not please us. Fanny Burney shrewdly delays, and we do not have direct acquaintance with Evelina until the lively start of Letter 8:

> This house seems to be the house of joy; every face wears a smile, and a laugh is at every body's service. It is quite amusing to walk about and see the general confusion; a room leading to the garden is fitting up for Captain Mirvan's study. Lady Howard does not sit a moment in a place; Miss Mirvan is making caps; every body so

busy!—such flying from room to room!—so many orders given, and retracted, and given again! nothing but hurry and perturbation.

Ronald Paulson praises *Evelina* as a careful balance of the old and the new, of Smollettian satire and a pre-Austenian ironic sensibility. I am surprised always when Smollett's effect upon Fanny Burney is judiciously demonstrated, as it certainly is by Paulson, precisely because Evelina cannot be visualized as journeying in the superbly irascible company of Matthew Bramble, whereas one can imagine her in dignified converse with Sir Charles Grandison. That seems another indication of a trouble in *Evelina* as a novel, the trouble alas being Evelina herself. In a world of roughness and wit, she remains the perpetual anomaly, too good for her context and too undivided to fascinate her reader. One implicit defense of Evelina is the polemic of Susan Staves, who views the heroine's dominant affect as being one of acute anxiety, since she is frequently in danger of sexual (or quasi-sexual) assault. Staves has a telling and lovely sentence: "Evelina's progress through the public places of London is about as tranquil as the progress of a fair-haired girl through modern Naples." Surrounded by Smollettian characters, the non-Smollettian Evelina must struggle incessantly to maintain her delicacy. That is clearly the case, and yet again, this creates a problem for the reader. Delicacy under assault is very difficult to represent except in a comic mode, since more of our imaginative sympathy is given to rambunctiousness than to virtue.

This makes it highly problematic, at least for me, to read *Evelina* either as a study in the dynamics of fear or as a chronicle of assault. If I find Evelina herself a touch too bland in her benignity, nevertheless she seems to me commendably tough, and rather less traumatized than some feminist critics take her to be. Historical changes in psychology are very real, and eighteenth-century men and women (of the same social class) have more in common with one another than say eighteenth-century women intellectuals have in common with our contemporary feminist critics. Evelina (and Fanny Burney) are less obsessed by Electra complexes, and less dismayed by female difficulties, than many among us, and a curious kind of anachronism is too frequently indulged these days.

Like her creator, Fanny Burney, who knew so well how to live in the forceful literary world of her father's companions, Evelina is ultimately stronger and shrewder than any of the men, and nearly all of the women, in her own universe. They may assault her delicacy, but she outwits them, and subtly triumphs over them. Her goodness does not exclude the skills of a grand manipulator. She is an anomaly in her sensibility, but not in her admirably poised social sense, and her manifold virtues coexist with an enigmatic cunning, suitable to the social psychology of her era.

Jane Austen

(1775–1817)

THE ODDEST YET BY NO MEANS INAPT ANALOGY TO JANE AUSTEN'S ART OF representation is Shakespeare's—oddest, because she is so careful of limits, as classical as Ben Jonson in that regard, and Shakespeare transcends all limits. Austen's humor, her mode of rhetorical irony, is not particularly Shakespearean, and yet her precision and accuracy of representation is. Like Shakespeare, she gives us figures, major and minor, utterly consistent each in her or his own mode of speech and being, and utterly different from one another. Her heroines have firm selves, each molded with an individuality that continues to suggest Austen's reserve of power, her potential for creating an endless diversity. To recur to the metaphor of oddness, the highly deliberate limitation of social scale in Austen seems a paradoxical theater of mind in which so fecund a humanity could be fostered. Irony, the concern of most critics of Austen, seems more than a trope in her work, seems indeed to be the condition of her language, yet hardly accounts for the effect of moral and spiritual power that she so constantly conveys, however implicitly or obliquely.

Ian Watt, in his permanently useful *The Rise of the Novel*, portrays Austen as Fanny Burney's direct heir in the difficult art of combining the rival modes of Samuel Richardson and Henry Fielding. Like Burney, Austen is thus seen as following the Richardson of *Sir Charles Grandison*, in a "minute presentation of daily life," while emulating Fielding in "adopting a more detached attitude to her narrative material, and in evaluating it from a comic and objective point of view." Watt goes further when he points out that Austen tells her stories in a discreet variant of Fielding's manner "as a confessed author," though her ironical juxtapositions are made to appear not those of "an intrusive author but rather of some august and impersonal spirit of social and psychological understanding."

And yet, as Watt knows, Austen truly is the daughter of Richardson, and not of Fielding, just as she is the ancestor of George Eliot and Henry James, rather than of Dickens and Thackeray. Her inwardness is an ironic revision of Richardson's extraordinary conversion of English Protestant sensibility into the figure of Clarissa Harlowe, and her own moral and spiritual concerns fuse in the crucial need of her heroines to sustain their individual integrities, a need so intense that it compels them to fall into those errors about life that are necessary for life (to adopt a Nietzschean formulation). In this too they follow, though in a comic register, the pattern of their tragic precursor, the magnificent but sublimely flawed Clarissa Harlowe.

Richardson's *Clarissa*, perhaps still the longest novel in the language, seems to me also still the greatest, despite the achievements of Austen, Dickens, George Eliot, Henry James, and Joyce. Austen's Elizabeth Bennet and Emma Woodhouse, Eliot's Dorothea Brooke and Gwendolyn Harleth, James's Isabel Archer and Milly Theale—though all these are Clarissa Harlowe's direct descendants, they are not proportioned to her more sublime scale. David Copperfield and Leopold Bloom have her completeness; indeed Joyce's Bloom may be the most complete representation of a human being in all of literature. But they belong to the secular age; Clarissa Harlowe is poised upon the threshold that leads from the Protestant religion to a purely secular sainthood.

C.S. Lewis, who read Milton as though that fiercest of Protestant temperaments had been an orthodox Anglican, also seems to have read Jane Austen by listening for her echoings of the New Testament. Quite explicitly, Lewis named Austen as the daughter of Dr. Samuel Johnson, greatest of literary critics, and rigorous Christian moralist:

> I feel ... sure that she is the daughter of Dr. Johnson: she inherits his commonsense, his morality, even much of his style.

The Johnson of *Rasselas* and of *The Rambler*, surely the essential Johnson, is something of a classical ironist, but we do not read Johnson for his ironies, or for his dramatic representations of fictive selves. Rather, we read him as we read Koheleth; he writes wisdom literature. That Jane Austen is a wise writer is indisputable, but we do not read *Pride and Prejudice* as though it were Ecclesiastes. Doubtless, Austen's religious ideas were as profound as Samuel Richardson's were shallow, but *Emma* and *Clarissa* are Protestant novels without being in any way religious. What is most original about the representation of Clarissa Harlowe is the magnificent intensity of her slowly described dying, which goes on for about the last third of Richardson's vast novel, in a Puritan ritual that celebrates the preternatural strength of her will. For that is Richardson's sublime concern: the self-reliant apotheosis of the Protestant will. What is tragedy in *Clarissa* becomes serious or moral comedy in *Pride and Prejudice* and *Emma*, and something just the other side of comedy in *Mansfield Park* and *Persuasion*.

Pride and Prejudice

Rereading *Pride and Prejudice* gives one a sense of Proustian ballet beautifully working itself through in the novel's formal centerpiece, the deferred but progressive mutual enlightenment of Elizabeth and Darcy in regard to the other's true nature. "Proper pride" is what they learn to recognize in one another; propriety scarcely needs definition in that phrase, but precisely what is the pride that allows amiability to flourish? Whatever it is in Darcy, to what extent is it an art of the will in Elizabeth Bennet? Consider the superb scene of Darcy's first and failed marriage proposal:

> While settling this point, she was suddenly roused by the sound of the doorbell, and her spirits were a little fluttered by the idea of its being Colonel Fitzwilliam himself, who had once before called late in the evening, and might now come to inquire particularly after her. But this idea was soon banished, and her spirits were very differently affected, when, to her utter amazement, she saw Mr. Darcy walk into the room. In an hurried manner he immediately began an inquiry after her health, imputing his visit to a wish of hearing that she were better. She answered him with cold civility. He sat down for a few moments, and then getting up, walked about the room. Elizabeth was surprised, but said not a word. After a silence of several minutes, he came towards her in an agitated manner, and thus began:
> "In vain have I struggled. It will not do. My feelings will not be repressed. You must allow me to tell you how ardently I admire and love you."
> Elizabeth's astonishment was beyond expression. She stared, coloured, doubted, and was silent. This he considered sufficient encouragement; and the avowal of all that he felt, and had long felt for her, immediately followed. He spoke well; but there were feelings besides those of the heart to be detailed, and he was not more eloquent on the subject of tenderness than of pride. His sense of her inferiority—of its being a degradation—of the family

obstacles which judgment had always opposed to inclination, were dwelt on with a warmth which seemed due to the consequence he was wounding, but was very unlikely to recommend his suit.

In spite of her deeply-rooted dislike, she could not be insensible to the compliment of such a man's affection, and though her intentions did not vary for an instant, she was at first sorry for the pain he was to receive; till, roused to resentment by his subsequent language, she lost all compassion in anger. She tried, however, to compose herself to answer him with patience, when he should have done. He concluded with representing to her the strength of that attachment which, in spite of all his endeavours, he had found impossible to conquer; and with expressing his hope that it would now be rewarded by her acceptance of his hand. As he said this, she could easily see that he had no doubt of a favourable answer. He *spoke* of apprehension and anxiety, but his countenance expressed real security. Such a circumstance could only exasperate farther, and, when he ceased, the colour rose into her cheeks, and she said:

"In such cases as this, it is, I believe, the established mode to express a sense of obligation for the sentiments avowed, however unequally they may be returned. It is natural that obligation should be felt, and if I could *feel* gratitude, I would now thank you. But I cannot—I have never desired your good opinion, and you have certainly bestowed it most unwillingly. I am sorry to have occasioned pain to anyone. It has been most unconsciously done, however, and I hope will be of short duration. The feelings which, you tell me, have long prevented the acknowledgment of your regard, can have little difficulty in overcoming it after this explanation."

Mr. Darcy, who was leaning against the mantelpiece with his eyes fixed on her face, seemed to catch her words with no less resentment than surprise. His complexion became pale with anger, and the disturbance of his mind was visible in every feature. He was struggling for the appearance of composure, and would not open his lips till he believed himself to have attained it. The pause was to Elizabeth's feelings dreadful. At length, in a voice of forced calmness, he said:

"And this is all the reply which I am to have the honour of expecting) I might, perhaps, wish to be informed why, with so little *endeavour* at civility, I am thus rejected. But it is of small importance."

Stuart M. Tave believes that both Darcy and Elizabeth become so changed by one another that their "happiness is deserved by a process of mortification begun early and ended late," mortification here being the wounding of pride. Tave's learning and insight are impressive, but I favor the judgment that Elizabeth and Darcy scarcely change, and learn rather that they complement each other's not wholly illegitimate pride. They come to see that their wills are naturally allied, since they have no differences upon the will. The will to what? Their will, Austen's, is neither the will to live nor the will to power. They wish to be esteemed precisely where they estimate value to be high, and neither can afford to make a fundamental error, which is both the anxiety and the comedy of the first proposal scene. Why after all does Darcy allow himself to be eloquent on the subject of his pride, to the extraordinary extent of conveying "with a warmth" what Austen grimly names as "his sense of her inferiority"?

As readers, we have learned already that Elizabeth is inferior to no one, whoever he is. Indeed, I sense as the novel closes (though nearly all Austen critics, and doubtless Austen herself, would disagree with me) that Darcy is her inferior, amiable and properly prideful as he is. I do not mean by this that Elizabeth is a clearer representation of Austenian values than Darcy ever could be; that is made finely obvious by Austen, and her critics have developed her ironic apprehension, which is that Elizabeth incarnates the standard of measurement in her cosmos. There is also a transcendent strength to Elizabeth's will that raises her above that cosmos, in a mode that returns us to Clarissa Harlowe's transcendence of her society, of Lovelace, and even of everything in herself that is not the will to a self-esteem that has also made an accurate estimate of every other will to pride it ever has encountered.

I am suggesting that Ralph Waldo Emerson (who to me is sacred) was mistaken when he rejected Austen as a "sterile" upholder of social conformities and social ironies, as an author who could not celebrate the soul's freedom from societal conventions. Austen's ultimate irony is that Elizabeth Bennet is inwardly so free that convention performs for her the ideal function it cannot perform for us: it liberates her will without tending to stifle her high individuality. But we ought to be wary of even the most distinguished of Austen's moral celebrants, Lionel Trilling, who in effect defended her against Emerson by seeing *Pride and Prejudice* as a triumph "of morality as style." If Emerson wanted to see a touch more Margaret Fuller in Elizabeth Bennet (sublimely ghastly notion!), Trilling wanted to forget the Emersonian law of Compensation, which is that nothing is got for nothing:

The relation of Elizabeth Bennet to Darcy is real, is intense, but it expresses itself as a conflict and reconciliation of styles: a formal rhetoric, traditional and rigorous, must find a way to accomodate a female vivacity, which in turn must recognize the principled demands of the strict male syntax. The high moral import of the novel lies in the fact that the union of styles is accomplished without injury to either lover.

Yes and no, I would say. Yes, because the wills of both lovers work by similar dialectics, but also no, because Elizabeth's will is more intense and purer, and inevitably must be dimmed by her dwindling into a wife, even though Darcy may well be the best man that society could offer to her. Her pride has playfulness in it, a touch even of the Quixotic. Uncannily, she is both her father's daughter and Samuel Richardson's daughter as well. Her wit is Mr. Bennet's, refined and elaborated, but her will, and her pride in her will, returns us to Clarissa's Puritan passion to maintain the power of the self to confer esteem, and to accept esteem only in response to its bestowal.

Mansfield Park

John Locke argues against personifying the will: persons can be free, but not the will, since the will cannot be constrained, except externally. While one sleeps, if someone moved one into another room and locked the door, and there one found a friend one wished to see, still one could not say that one was free thus to see whom one wished. And yet Locke implies that the process of association does work as though the will were internally constrained. Association, in Locke's sense, is a blind substitution for reasoning, yet is within a reasoning process, though also imbued with affect. The mind, in association, is carried unwillingly from one thought to another, by accident as it were. Each thought appears, and carries along with it a crowd of unwanted guests, inhabitants of a room where the thought would rather be alone. Association, on this view, is what the will most needs to be defended against.

Fanny Price, in *Mansfield Park*, might be considered a co-descendant, together with Locke's association-menaced will, of the English Protestant emphasis upon the will's autonomy. Fanny, another precursor of the Virginia Woolf of *A Room of One's Own*, was shrewdly described by Lionel Trilling as "overtly virtuous and consciously virtuous," and therefore almost impossible to like, though Trilling (like Austen) liked Fanny very much. C.S. Lewis, though an orthodox moralist, thought Fanny insipid:

"But into Fanny, Jane Austen, to counterbalance her apparent insignificance, has put really nothing except rectitude of mind; neither passion, nor physical courage, nor wit, nor resource." Nothing, I would say, except the Protestant will, resisting the powers of association and asserting its very own persistence, its own sincere intensity, and its own isolate sanctions. Trilling secularized these as "the sanctions of principle" and saw *Mansfield Park* as a novel that "discovers in principle the path to the wholeness of the self which is peace." That is movingly said, but secularization, in literature, is always a failed trope, since the distinction between sacred and secular is not actually a literary but rather a societal or political distinction. *Mansfield Park* is not less Protestant than *Paradise Lost*, even though Austen, *as a writer*, was as much a sect of one as John Milton was.

Fanny Price, like the Lockean will, fights against accident, against the crowding out of life by associations that are pragmatically insincere not because they are random, but because they are irrelevant, since whatever is not the will's own is irrelevant to it. If Fanny herself is an irony it is as Austen's allegory of her own defense against influences, human and literary, whether in her family circle or in the literary family of Fanny Burney, Fielding, and Richardson. Stuart Tave shrewdly remarks that: "*Mansfield Park* is a novel in which many characters are engaged in trying to establish influence over the minds and lives of others, often in a contest or struggle for control." Fanny, as a will struggling only to be itself, becomes at last the spiritual center of Mansfield Park precisely because she has never sought power over any other will. It is the lesson of the Protestant will, whether in Locke or Austen, Richardson or George Eliot, that the refusal to seek power over other wills is what opens the inward eye of vision. Such a lesson, which, we seek in Wordsworth and in Ruskin, is offered more subtly (though less sublimely) by Austen. Fanny, Austen's truest surrogate, has a vision of what Mansfield Park is and ought to be, which means a vision also of what Sir Thomas Bertram is or ought to be. Her vision is necessarily moral, but could as truly be called spiritual, or even aesthetic.

Perhaps that is why Fanny is not only redeemed but can redeem others. The quietest and most mundane of visionaries, she remains also one of the firmest: her dedication is to the future of Mansfield Park as the idea of order it once seemed to her. Jane Austen may not be a Romantic in the high Shelleyan mode, but Fanny Price has profound affinities with Wordsworth, so that it is no accident that *Mansfield Park* is exactly contemporary with *The Excursion*. Wordsworthian continuity, the strength that carries the past alive into the present, is the program of renovation that Fanny's pure will brings to Mansfield Park, and it is a program more Romantic than Augustan, so that Fanny's will begins to shade into the

Wordsworthian account of the imagination. Fanny's exile to Portsmouth is so painful to her not for reasons turning upon social distinctions, but for causes related to the quiet that Wordsworth located in the bliss of solitude, or Virginia Woolf in a room of one's own:

> Such was the home which was to put Mansfield out of her head, and teach her to think of her cousin Edmund with moderated feelings. On the contrary, she could think of nothing but Mansfield, its beloved inmates, its happy ways. Everything where she now was was in full contrast to it. The elegance, propriety, regularity, harmony, and perhaps, above all, the peace and tranquillity of Mansfield, were brought to her remembrance every hour of the day, by the prevalence of everything opposite to them *here*.
>
> The living in incessant noise was, to a frame and temper delicate and nervous like Fanny's, an evil which no super-added elegance or harmony could have entirely atoned for. It was the greatest misery of all. At Mansfield, no sounds of contention, no raised voice, no abrupt bursts, no tread of violence, was ever heard; all proceeded in a regular course of cheerful orderliness; everybody had their due importance; everybody's feelings were consulted. If tenderness could be ever supposed wanting, good sense and good breeding supplied its place; and as to the little irritations, sometimes introduced by Aunt Norris, they were short, they were trifling, they were as a drop of water to the ocean, compared with the ceaseless tumult of her present abode. Here, everybody was noisy, every voice was loud (excepting, perhaps, her mother's, which resembled the soft monotony of Lady Bertram's, only worn into fretfulness). Whatever was wanted was halloo'd for, and the servants halloo'd out their excuses from the kitchen. The doors were in constant banging, the stairs were never at rest, nothing was done without a clatter, nobody sat still, and nobody could command attention when they spoke.
>
> In a review of the two houses, as they appeared to her before the end of a week, Fanny was tempted to apply to them Dr. Johnson's celebrated judgment as to matrimony and celibacy, and say, that though Mansfield Park might have some pains, Portsmouth could have no pleasures.

The citation of Dr. Johnson's aphorism, though placed here with superb wit, transcends irony. Austen rather seeks to confirm, however implicitly, Johnson's powerful warning, in *The Rambler*, number 4, against the overwhelming realism of Fielding and Smollett (though their popular prevalence is merely hinted):

> But if the power of example is so great, as to take possession of the memory by a kind of violence, and produce effects almost without the intervention of the will, care ought to be taken, that, when the choice is unrestrained, the best examples only should be exhibited; and that which is likely to operate so strongly, should not be mischievous or uncertain in its effects.

Fanny Price, rather more than Jane Austen perhaps, really does favor a Johnsonian aesthetic, in life as in literature. Portsmouth belongs to representation as practiced by Smollett, belongs to the cosmos of *Roderick Random*. Fanny, in willing to get back to Mansfield Park, and to get Mansfield Park back to itself, is willing herself also to renovate the world of her creator, the vision of Jane Austen that is *Mansfield Park*.

Emma

Sir Walter Scott, reviewing *Emma* in 1815, rather strangely compared Jane Austen to the masters of the Flemish school of painting, presumably because of her precision in representing her characters. The strangeness results from Scott's not seeing how English Austen was, though the Scots perspective may have entered into his estimate. To me, as an American critic, *Emma* seems the most English of English novels, and beyond question one of the very best. More than *Pride and Prejudice*, it is Austen's masterpiece, the largest triumph of her vigorous art. Her least accurate prophecy as to the fate of her fictions concerned *Emma*, whose heroine, she thought, "no one but myself will much like."

Aside from much else, Emma is immensely likable, because she is so extraordinarily imaginative, dangerous and misguided as her imagination frequently must appear to others and finally to herself. On the scale of being, Emma constitutes an answer to the immemorial questions of the Sublime: More? Equal to? Or less than? Like Clarissa Harlowe before her, and the strongest heroines of George Eliot and Henry James after her, Emma Woodhouse has a heroic will, and like them she risks identifying her will with her imagination. Socially considered, such identification is catastrophic, since the Protestant will has a tendency to bestow a ranking upon other selves, and such ranking may turn out to be a personal phantasmagoria. G. Armour Craig rather finely remarked that: "society in *Emma* is not a ladder. It is a web of imputations that link feelings and

conduct." Yet Emma herself, expansionist rather than reductionist in temperament, imputes more fiercely and freely than the web can sustain, and
she threatens always, until she is enlightened, to dissolve the societal links,
in and for others, that might allow some stability between feelings and
conduct.

Armour Craig usefully added that: "*Emma* does not justify its heroine
nor does it deride her." Rather it treats her with ironic love (not loving
irony). Emma Woodhouse is dear to Jane Austen, because her errors are
profoundly imaginative, and rise from the will's passion for autonomy of
vision. The splendid Jane Fairfax is easier to admire, but I cannot agree
with Wayne Booth's awarding the honors to her over Emma, though I
admire the subtle balance of his formulation:

> Jane is superior to Emma in most respects except the stroke of
> good fortune that made Emma the heroine of the book. In mat-
> ters of taste and ability, of head and of heart, she is Emma's supe-
> rior.

Taste, ability, head, and heart are a formidable fourfold; the imagination and the will, working together, are an even more formidable twofold,
and clearly may have their energies diverted to error and to mischief. Jane
Fairfax is certainly more *amiable* even than Emma Woodhouse, but she is
considerably less interesting. It is Emma who is meant to charm us, and
who does charm us. Austen is not writing a tragedy of the will, like *Paradise
Lost*, but a great comedy of the will, and her heroine must incarnate the full
potential of the will, however misused for a time. Having rather too much
her own way is certainly one of Emma's powers, and she does have a disposition to think a little too well of herself. When Austen says that these
were "the real evils indeed of Emma's situation," we read "evils" as lightly
as the author will let us, which is lightly enough.

Can we account for the qualities in Emma Woodhouse that make her
worthy of comparison with George Eliot's Gwendolen Harleth and Henry
James's Isabel Archer? The pure comedy of her context seems world
enough for her; she evidently is not the heiress of all the ages. We are persuaded, by Austen's superb craft, that marriage to Mr. Knightley will more
than suffice to fulfill totally the now perfectly amiable Emma. Or are we?
It is James's genius to suggest that while Osmond's "beautiful mind" was a
prison of the spirit for Isabel, no proper husband could exist anyway, since
neither Touchett nor Goodwood is exactly a true match for her. Do we,
presumably against Austen's promptings, not find Mr. Knightley something of a confinement also, benign and wise though he be?

I suspect that the heroine of the Protestant will, from Richardson's Clarissa Harlowe through to Virginia Woolf's Clarissa Dalloway, can never find fit match because wills do not marry. The allegory or tragic irony of this dilemma is written large in Clarissa, since Lovelace, in strength of will and splendor of being, actually would have been the true husband for Clarissa (as he well knows) had he not been a moral squalor. His death-cry ("Let this expiate!") expiates nothing, and helps establish the long tradition of the Anglo-American novel in which the heroines of the will are fated to suffer either overt calamities or else happy unions with such good if unexciting men as Mr. Knightley or Will Ladislaw in *Middlemarch*. When George Eliot is reduced to having the fascinating Gwendolen Harleth fall hopelessly in love with the prince of prigs, Daniel Deronda, we sigh and resign ourselves to the sorrows of fictive overdetermination. Lovelace or Daniel Deronda? I myself do not know a high-spirited woman who would not prefer the first, though not for a husband!

Emma is replete with grand comic epiphanies, of which my favorite comes in volume 3, chapter 11, when Emma receives the grave shock of Harriet's disclosure that Mr. Knightley is the object of Harriet's hopeful affections:

> When Harriet had closed her evidence, she appealed to her dear Miss Woodhouse, to say whether she had not good ground for hope.
>
> "I never should have presumed to think of it at first," said she, "but for you. You told me to observe him carefully, and let his behavior be the rule of mine—and so I have. But now I seem to feel that I may deserve him; and that if he does choose me, it will not be any thing so very wonderful."
>
> The bitter feelings occasioned by this speech, the many bitter feelings, made the utmost exertion necessary on Emma's side to enable her to say in reply,
>
> "Harriet, I will only venture to declare, that Mr. Knightley is the last man in the world, who would intentionally give any woman the idea of his feeling for her more than he really does."
>
> Harriet seemed ready to worship her friend for a sentence so satisfactory; and Emma was only saved from raptures and fondness, which at the moment would have been dreadful penance, by the sound of her father's footsteps. He was coming through the hall. Harriet was too much agitated to encounter him. "She could not compose herself—Mr. Woodhouse would be alarmed—she had better go;"—with most ready encouragement from her friend, therefore, she passed off through another door—and the moment

she was gone, this was the spontaneous burst of Emma's feelings: "Oh God! that I had never seen her!"

The rest of the day, the following night, were hardly enough for her thoughts.—She was bewildered amidst the confusion of all that had rushed on her within the last few hours. Every moment had brought a fresh surprise; and every surprise must be matter of humiliation to her.—How to understand it all! How to understand the deceptions she had been thus practising on herself, and living under!—The blunders, the blindness of her own head and heart!—she sat still, she walked about, she tried her own room, she tried the shrubbery—in every place, every posture, she perceived that she had acted most weakly; that she had been imposed on by others in a most mortifying degree; that she had been imposing on herself in a degree yet more mortifying; that she was wretched, and should probably find this day but the beginning of wretchedness.

The acute aesthetic pleasure of this turns on the counterpoint between Emma's spontaneous cry: "Oh God! that I had never seen her!" and the exquisite comic touch of: "She sat still, she walked about, she tried her own room, she tried the shrubbery—in every place, every posture, she perceived that she had acted most weakly." The acute humiliation of the will could not be better conveyed than by "she tried the shrubbery" and "every posture." Endlessly imaginative, Emma must now be compelled to endure the mortification of reducing herself to the postures and places of those driven into corners by the collapse of visions that have been exposed as delusions. Jane Austen, who seems to have identified herself with Emma, wisely chose to make this moment of ironic reversal a temporary purgatory, rather than an infernal discomfiture.

Persuasion

"Persuasion" is a word derived from the Latin for "advising" or "urging," for recommending that it is good to perform or not perform a particular action. The word goes back to a root meaning "sweet" or "pleasant," so that the good of performance or nonperformance has a tang of taste rather than of moral judgment about it. Jane Austen chose it as the title for her last completed novel. As a title, it recalls *Sense and Sensibility* or *Pride and Prejudice* rather than *Emma* or *Mansfield Park*. We are given not the name of a person or house and estate, but of an abstraction, a single one in this case. The title's primary reference is to the persuasion of its heroine, Anne

Elliot, at the age of nineteen, by her godmother, Lady Russell, not to marry Captain Frederick Wentworth, a young naval officer. This was, as it turns out, very bad advice, and, after eight years, it is mended by Anne and Captain Wentworth. As with all of Austen's ironic comedies, matters end happily for the heroine. And yet each time I finish a rereading of this perfect novel, I feel very sad.

This does not appear to be my personal vagary; when I ask my friends and students about their experience of the book, they frequently mention a sadness which they also associate with *Persuasion*, more even than with *Mansfield Park*. Anne Elliot, a quietly eloquent being, is a self-reliant character, in no way forlorn, and her sense of self never falters. It is not *her* sadness we feel as we conclude the book: it is the novel's somberness that impresses us. The sadness enriches what I would call the novel's canonical persuasiveness, its way of showing us its extraordinary aesthetic distinction.

Persuasion is among novels what Anne Elliot is among novelistic characters—a strong but subdued outrider. The book and the character are not colorful or vivacious; Elizabeth Bennett of *Pride and Prejudice* and Emma Woodhouse of *Emma* have a verve to them that initially seems lacking in Anne Elliot, which may be what Austen meant when she said that Anne was "almost too good for me." Anne is really almost too subtle for us, though not for Wentworth, who has something of an occult wavelength to her. Juliet McMaster notes "the kind of oblique communication that constantly goes on between Anne Elliot and Captain Wentworth, where, though they seldom speak to each other, each constantly understands the full import of the other's speech better than their interlocutors do."

That kind of communication in *Persuasion* depends upon deep "affection," a word that Austen values over "love." "Affection" between woman and man, in Austen, is the more profound and lasting emotion. I think it is not too much to say that Anne Elliot, though subdued, is the creation for whom Austen herself must have felt the most affection, because she lavished her own gifts upon Anne. Henry James insisted that the novelist must be a sensibility upon which absolutely nothing is lost; by that test (clearly a limited one) only Austen, George Eliot, and James himself, among all those writing in English, would join Stendhal, Flaubert, and Tolstoy in a rather restricted pantheon. Anne Elliot may well be the one character in all of prose fiction upon whom nothing is lost, though she is in no danger of turning into a novelist. The most accurate estimate of Anne Elliot that I have seen is by Stuart Tave:

> Nobody hears Anne, nobody sees her, but it is she who is ever at the center. It is through her ears, eyes, and mind that we are made

to care for what is happening. If nobody is much aware of her, she is very much aware of everyone else and she perceives what is happening to them when they are ignorant of themselves ... she reads Wentworth's mind, with the coming troubles he is causing for others and himself, before those consequences bring the information to him.

The aesthetic dangers attendant upon such a paragon are palpable: how does a novelist make such a character persuasive? Poldy, in Joyce's *Ulysses*, is overwhelmingly persuasive because he is so complete a person, which was the largest of Joyce's intentions. Austen's ironic mode does not sanction the representation of completeness: we do not accompany her characters to the bedroom, the kitchen, the privy. What Austen parodies in *Sense and Sensibility* she raises to an apotheosis in *Persuasion*: the sublimity of a particular, inwardly isolated sensibility. Anne Elliot is hardly the only figure in Austen who has an understanding heart. Her difference is in her almost preternatural acuteness of perception of others and of the self, which are surely the qualities that most distinguish Austen as a novelist. Anne Elliot is to Austen's work what Rosalind of *As You Like It* is to Shakespeare's: the character who almost reaches the mastery of perspective that can be available only to the novelist or playwright, lest all dramatic quality be lost from the novel or play. C.L. Barber memorably emphasized this limitation:

> The dramatist tends to show us one thing at a time, and to realize that one thing, in its moment, to the full; his characters go to extremes, comical as well as serious; and no character, not even a Rosalind, is in a position to see all around the play and so be completely poised, for if this were so the play would cease to be dramatic.

I like to turn Barber's point in the other direction: more even than Hamlet or Falstaff, or than Elizabeth Bennet, or than Fanny Price in *Mansfield Park*, Rosalind and Anne Elliot are almost completely poised, nearly able to see all around the play and the novel. Their poise cannot transcend perspectivizing completely, but Rosalind's wit and Anne's sensibility, both balanced and free of either excessive aggressivity or defensiveness, enable them to share more of their creators' poise than we ever come to do.

Austen never loses dramatic intensity; we share Anne's anxiety concerning Wentworth's renewed intentions until the novel's conclusion. But we rely upon Anne as we should rely upon Rosalind; critics would see the rancidity of Touchstone as clearly as they see the vanity of Jacques if they placed more confidence in Rosalind's reactions to everyone else in the play, as well as to herself. Anne Elliot's reactions have the same winning authority; we must try to give the weight to her words that is not extended by the other persons in the novel, except for Wentworth.

Stuart Tave's point, like Barber's, is accurate even when turned in the other direction; Austen's irony is very Shakespearean. Even the reader must fall into the initial error of undervaluing Anne Elliot. The wit of Elizabeth Bennet or of Rosalind is easier to appreciate than Anne Elliot's accurate sensibility. The secret of her character combines Austenian irony with a Wordsworthian sense of deferred hope. Austen has a good measure of Shakespeare's unmatched ability to give us persons, both major and minor, who are each utterly consistent in her or his separate mode of speech, and yet completely different from one another. Anne Elliot is the last of Austen's heroines of what I think we must call the Protestant will, but in her the will is modified, perhaps perfected, by its descendant, the Romantic sympathetic imagination, of which Wordsworth, as we have seen, was the prophet. That is perhaps what helps to make Anne so complex and sensitive a character.

Jane Austen's earlier heroines, of whom Elizabeth Bennet is the exemplar, manifested the Protestant will as direct descendants of Samuel Richardson's Clarissa Harlowe, with Dr. Samuel Johnson hovering nearby as moral authority. Marxist criticism inevitably views the Protestant will, even in its literary manifestations, as a mercantile matter, and it has become fashionable to talk about the socioeconomic realities that Jane Austen excludes, such as the West Indian slavery that is part of the ultimate basis for the financial security most of her characters enjoy. But all achieved literary works are founded upon exclusions, and no one has demonstrated that increased consciousness of the relation between culture and imperialism is of the slightest benefit whatsoever in learning to read *Mansfield Park*. *Persuasion* ends with a tribute to the British navy, in which Wentworth has an honored place. Doubtless Wentworth at sea, ordering the latest batch of disciplinary floggings, is not as pleasant as Wentworth on land, gently appreciating the joys of affection with Anne Elliot. But once again, Austen's is a great art founded upon exclusions, and the sordid realities of British sea power are no more relevant to *Persuasion* than West Indian bondage is to *Mansfield Park*. Austen was, however, immensely interested in the pragmatic and secular consequences of the Protestant will, and they seem to me a crucial element in helping us appreciate the heroines of her novels.

Austen's Shakespearean inwardness, culminating in Anne Elliot, revises the moral intensities of Clarissa Harlowe's secularized Protestant martyrdom, her slow dying after being raped by Lovelace. What removes Clarissa's will to live is her stronger will to maintain the integrity of her being. To yield to the repentant Lovelace by marrying him would compromise the essence of her being, the exaltation of her violated will. What is tragedy in Clarissa is converted by Austen into ironic comedy, but the will's drive to maintain itself scarcely alters in this conversion. In *Persuasion* the emphasis is on a willed exchange of esteems, where both the woman and the man estimate the value of the other to be high. Obviously outward considerations of wealth, property, and social standing are crucial elements here, but so are the inward considerations of common sense, amiability, culture, wit, and affection. In a way (it pains me to say this, as I am a fierce Emersonian) Ralph Waldo Emerson anticipated the current Marxist critique of Austen when he denounced her as a mere conformist who would not allow her heroines to achieve the soul's true freedom from societal conventions. But that was to mistake Jane Austen, who understood that the function of convention was to liberate the will, even if convention's tendency was to stifle individuality, without which the will was inconsequential.

Austen's major heroines—Elizabeth, Emma, Fanny, and Anne—possess such inward freedom that their individualities cannot be repressed. Austen's art as a novelist is not to worry much about the socioeconomic genesis of that inner freedom, though the anxiety level does rise in *Mansfield Park* and *Persuasion*. In Austen, irony becomes the instrument for invention, which Dr. Johnson defined as the essence of poetry. A conception of inward freedom that centers upon a refusal to accept esteem except from one upon whom one has conferred esteem, is a conception of the highest degree of irony. The supreme comic scene in all of Austen must be Elizabeth's rejection of Darcy's first marriage proposal, where the ironies of the dialectic of will and esteem become very nearly outrageous. That high comedy, which continued in *Emma*, is somewhat chastened in *Mansfield Park*, and then becomes something else, unmistakable but difficult to name, in *Persuasion*, where Austen has become so conscious a master that she seems to have changed the nature of willing, as though it, too, could be persuaded to become a rarer, more disinterested act of the self.

No one has suggested that Jane Austen becomes a High Romantic in *Persuasion*; her poet remained William Cowper, not Wordsworth, and her favorite prose writer was always Dr. Johnson. But her severe distrust of imagination and of "romantic love," so prevalent in the earlier novels, is not a factor in *Persuasion*. Anne and Wentworth maintain their affection for each other throughout eight years of hopeless separation, and each has the power of imagination to conceive of a triumphant reconciliation. This is the material for a romance, not for an ironical novel. The ironies of *Persuasion* are frequently pungent, but they are almost never directed at Anne Elliot and only rarely at Captain Wentworth. There is a difficult relation between Austen's repression of her characteristic irony about her protagonists and a certain previously unheard plangency that hovers throughout *Persuasion*. Despite Anne's faith in herself she is very vulnerable to the anxiety, which she never allows herself to express, of an unlived life, in which the potential loss transcends yet includes sexual unfulfillment. I can recall only one critic, the Australian Ann Molan, who emphasizes what Austen strongly implies, that "Anne ... is a passionate woman. And against her will, her heart keeps asserting its demand for fulfillment." Since Anne had refused Wentworth her esteem eight years before, she feels a necessity to withhold her will, and thus becomes the first Austen heroine whose will and imagination are antithetical.

Although Austen's overt affinities remained with the Aristocratic Age, her authenticity as a writer impelled her, in *Persuasion*, a long way toward the burgeoning Democratic Age, or Romanticism, as we used to call it. There is no civil war within Anne Elliot's psyche, or within Austen's; but there is the emergent sadness of a schism in the self, with memory taking the side of imagination in an alliance against the will. The almost Wordsworthian power of memory in both Anne and Wentworth has been noted by Gene Ruoff. Since Austen was anything but an accidental novelist, we might ask why she chose to found *Persuasion* upon a mutual nostalgia. After all, the rejected Wentworth is even less inclined to will a renewed affection than Anne is, and yet the fusion of memory and imagination triumphs over his will also. Was this a relaxation of the will in Jane Austen herself? Since she returns to her earlier mode in *Sanditon*, her unfinished novel begun after *Persuasion* was completed, it may be that the story of Anne Elliot was an excursion or indulgence for the novelist. The parallels between Wordsworth and *Persuasion* are limited but real. High Romantic novels in England, whether of the Byronic kind like *Jane Eyre* and *Wuthering Heights* or of a Wordsworthian sort like *Adam Bede*, are a distinctly later development. The ethos of the Austen heroine does not change in *Persuasion*, but she is certainly a more problematic being, tinged with a new sadness concerning life's limits. It may be that the elegant pathos *Persuasion* sometimes courts has a connection to Jane Austen's own ill health, her intimations of her early death.

Stuart Tave, comparing Wordsworth and Austen, shrewdly noted that both were "poets of marriage" and both also possessed "a sense of duty understood and deeply felt by those who see the integrity and peace of their own lives as essentially bound to the lives of others and see the lives of all in a more than merely social order." Expanding Tave's insight, Susan Morgan pointed to the particular affinity between Austen's *Emma* and Wordsworth's great "Ode: Intimations of Immortality from Recollections of Earliest Childhood." The growth of the individual consciousness, involving both gain and loss for Wordsworth but only gain for Austen, is the shared subject. Emma's consciousness certainly does develop, and she undergoes a quasi-Wordsworthian transformation from the pleasures of near solipsism to the more difficult pleasures of sympathy for others. Anne Elliot, far more mature from the beginning, scarcely needs to grow in consciousness. Her long-lamented rejection of Wentworth insulates her against the destructiveness of hope, which we have seen to be the frightening emphasis of the earlier Wordsworth, particularly in the story of poor Margaret. Instead of hope, there is a complex of emotions, expressed by Austen with her customary skill:

> How eloquent could Anne Elliot have been,—how eloquent, at least, were her wishes on the side of early warm attachment, and a cheerful confidence in futurity, against that over-anxious caution which seems to insult exertion and distrust Providence!—She had been forced into prudence in her youth, she learned romance as she grew older—the natural sequel of an unnatural beginning.

Here learning romance is wholly retrospective; Anne no longer regards it as being available to her. And indeed Wentworth returns, still resentful after eight years, and reflects that Anne's power with him is gone forever. The qualities of decision and confidence that make him a superb naval commander are precisely what he condemns her for lacking. With almost too meticulous a craft, Austen traces his gradual retreat from this position, as the power of memory increases its dominance over him and as he learns that his jilted sense of her as being unable to act is quite mistaken. It is a beautiful irony that he needs to undergo a process of self-persuasion while Anne waits, without even knowing that she is waiting or that there is anything that could rekindle her hope. The comedy of this is gently sad, as the reader waits also, reflecting upon how large a part contingency plays in the matter.

While the pre-Socratics and Freud agree that there are no accidents, Austen thinks differently. Character is fate for her also, but fate, once activated, tends to evade character in so overdetermined a social context as

Austen's world. In rereading *Persuasion*, though I remember the happy conclusion, I nevertheless feel anxiety as Wentworth and Anne circle away from each other in spite of themselves. The reader is not totally persuaded of a satisfactory interview until Anne reads Wentworth's quite agonized letter to her:

"I can listen no longer in silence. I must speak to you by such means as are within my reach. You pierce my soul. I am half agony, half hope. Tell me not that I am too late, that such precious feelings are gone for ever. I offer myself to you again with a heart more your own, than when you almost broke it eight years and a half ago. Dare not say that man forgets sooner than woman, that his love has an earlier death. I have loved none but you. Unjust I may have been, weak and resentful I have been, but never inconstant. You alone have brought me to Bath. For you alone I think and plan.—Have you not seen this? Can you fail to have understood my wishes?—I had not waited even these ten days, could I have read your feelings, as I think you must have penetrated mine. I can hardly write. I am every instant hearing something which overpowers me. You sink your voice, but I can distinguish the tones of that voice, when they would be lost on others.—Too good, too excellent creature! You do us justice indeed. You do believe that there is true attachment and constancy among men. Believe it to be most fervent, most undeviating in

"I must go, uncertain of my fate; but I shall return hither, or follow your party, as soon as possible. A word, a look will be enough to decide whether I enter your father's house this evening or never."

I cannot imagine such a letter in *Pride and Prejudice*, or even in *Emma* or *Mansfield Park*. The perceptive reader might have realized how passionate Anne was, almost from the start of the novel, but until this there was no indication of equal passion in Wentworth. His letter, as befits a naval commander, is badly written and not exactly Austenian, but it is all the more effective thereby. We come to realize that we have believed in him until now only because Anne's love for him provokes our interest. Austen wisely has declined to make him interesting enough on his own. Yet part of the book's effect is to persuade the reader of the reader's own powers of discernment and self-persuasion; Anne Elliot is almost too good for the reader, as she is for Austen herself, but the attentive reader gains the confidence to perceive Anne as she should be perceived. The subtlest element in this subtlest of novels is the call upon the reader's own power of memory to match the persistence and intensity of the yearning that Anne Elliot is too stoical to express directly.

The yearning hovers throughout the book, coloring Anne's perceptions and our own. Our sense of Anne's existence becomes identified with our own consciousness of lost love, however fictive or idealized that may be. There is an improbability in the successful renewal of a relationship devastated eight years before which ought to work against the texture of this most "realistic" of Austen's novels, but she is very careful to see that it does not. Like the author, the reader becomes persuaded to wish for Anne what she still wishes for herself. Ann Molan has the fine observation that Austen "is most satisfied with Anne when Anne is most dissatisfied with herself." The reader is carried along with Austen, and gradually Anne is also persuaded and catches up with the reader, allowing her yearning a fuller expression.

Dr. Johnson, in *The Rambler* 29, on "The folly of anticipating misfortunes," warned against anxious expectations of any kind, whether fearful or hopeful:

> because the objects both of fear and hope are yet uncertain, so we ought not to trust the representations of one more than the other, because they are both equally fallacious; as hope enlarges happiness, fear aggravates calamity. It is generally allowed, that no man ever found the happiness of possession proportionate to that expectation which incited his desire, and invigorated his pursuit; nor has any man found the evils of life so formidable in reality, as they were described to him by his own imagination.

This is one of a series of Johnsonian pronouncements against the dangerous prevalence of the imagination, some of which his disciple Austen had certainly read. If you excluded such representations, on the great critic's advice, then Wordsworth could not have written at all, and Austen could not have written *Persuasion*. Yet it was a very strange book for her to write, this master of the highest art of exclusion that we have known in the Western novel. Any novel by Jane Austen could be called an achieved ellipsis, with everything omitted that could disturb her ironic though happy conclusions. *Persuasion* remains the least popular of her four canonical novels because it is the strangest, but all her work is increasingly strange as we approach the end of the Democratic Age that her contemporary Wordsworth did so much to inaugurate in literature. Poised as she is at the final border of the Aristocratic Age, she shares with Wordsworth an art dependent upon a split between a waning Protestant will and a newly active sympathetic imagination, with memory assigned the labor of healing the divide. If the argument of my book has any validity, Austen will survive even the bad days ahead of us, because the strangeness of originality and of an individual vision are our lasting needs, which only literature can gratify in the Theocratic Age that slouches toward us.

Stendhal

(1783-1842)

The Red and the Black

NIETZSCHE SALUTED STENDHAL AS "THIS STRANGE EPICUREAN AND MAN of interrogation, the last great psychologist of France." Yet Stendhal is both less and more than a psychologist, even in the sense of moral psychologist intended by Nietzsche. If we are unhappy because we are vain, which seems true enough, then the insight seems related to the conviction that our sorrows come to us because we are restless, and cannot sit at our desks. To assimilate Stendhal to Pascal would be tasteless, yet to determine the pragmatic difference between them is a complex labor. Pascal, to me, is the authentic nihilist; Stendhal is something else. Call that Julien Sorel, who attracts us without compelling our liking. Or do we like him? Robert M. Adams coolly concludes that:

> Whether you like Julien Sorel, and for what parts of his behavior, depends, then, in some measure, on who you think you are and what conspiracies or complicities your imagination allows you to join, in the course of reading the book.

That may be giving Stendhal the best of it, since the reader's fundamental right, as critic, is to ask the writer "who do you think you are, anyway?" The reversal is shrewd, whether Stendhal's or Adams's, since we do not expect the author to be quite as aggressive as ourselves. Stendhal brazenly excels us, and Julien is more his surrogate than many have allowed. We admire Julien for the range of his imagination, and are a little estranged by his extraordinary (if intermittent) ability to switch his affections by acts of will. He is, of course, designedly a little Napoleon, and if one is not Hazlitt or Stendhal that may not move one to affection. But the Napoleonic is only one wave or movement in him, and Stendhal is one of that myriad of nineteenth-century writers of genius who fracture the self. A more crucial movement is the Byronic, and here Adams is very perceptive indeed, marvelously so:

> Most of what we think about Julien depends, of course, on our judgment of his behavior with the two ladies; and here we come up against the central paradox of the novel, that (like the ladies) we don't really think more highly of our hero the better he behaves. Quite the contrary. The worse he behaves, the more painful the sacrifices he requires of them, the more we are impressed by their determination to love him. Impervious to jealousy, untouched by his effort to murder her, Mme. de Rênal defies public scandal, leaves her husband and children, and comes to be with Julien in the hour of his anguish. Mathilde is in despair that he no longer loves her though she has sacrificed even more prodigally to her love of him. The revelation of Julien is not to be made directly, in the glare of open daylight, but only through the glow reflected on the faces of these devoted acolytes. As with Christ and Dionysus, the mystery of Julien is performed in the darkness of a prison-tomb, and his resurrection is celebrated in the presence of women. The cenacle of Julien allures its converts by withdrawing its mystery, etherealizing its cult: that is the work of the book's last important section.

One could argue that Julien, like Lord Byron, has that cool passivity which provokes his women into a return to themselves, so that his function is to spur these remarkable (and very dissimilar) ladies on to the epiphanies of their own modes of heroism. This could account for what I myself find most unsatisfactory about *The Red and the Black*, which is the obscurity (perhaps even obscuratism?) of Julien's final state of the soul:

> The bad air of the prison cell was becoming insupportable to Julien. Fortunately on the day set for his execution a bright sun was shining upon the earth, and Julien was in the vein of courage. To walk in the open air was for him a delicious experience, as treading the solid ground is for a sailor who has been long at sea. There now, things are going very well, he told himself, I shall have no lack of courage.
> Never had that head been so poetic as at the moment when it

was about to fall. The sweetest moments he had ever known in the woods at Vergy came crowding back into his mind, and with immense vividness.

Everything proceeded simply, decently, and without the slightest affectation on his part.

Two days before he had told Fouqué:

—As for emotion, I can't quite answer; this dungeon is so ugly and damp it gives me Feverish moments in which I don't recognize myself, but fear is another matter, I shall never be seen to grow pale.

He had made arrangements in advance that on the last day Fouqué should take away Mathilde and Mme. de Rênal.

—Put them in the same coach, he told him. Keep the post horses at a steady gallop. Either they will fall in one another's arms or they will fall into mortal hatred. In either case, the poor women will be somewhat distracted from their terrible grief. Julien had forced from Mme. de Rênal an oath that she would live to look after Mathilde's son.

—Who knows? Perhaps we retain some consciousness after death, he said one day to Fouqué. I should like to rest, since rest is the word, in that little cave atop the big mountain that overlooks Verrières. I've told how several times when I spent the night in that cave and looked out over the richest provinces of France, my heart was afire with ambition: that was my passion in those days.... Well, that cave is precious to me, and nobody can deny that it's located in a spot that a philosopher's heart might envy.... You know these good congregationists in Besançon can coin money out of anything; go about it the right way, and they'll sell you my mortal remains....

Julien's superb sense of humor, at the end, enchants us, but what precisely is Stendhal's final attitude towards his hero? I take this sentence as not being ironic: "Never had that head been so poetic as at the moment when it was about to fall." Julien is madly in love with Mme de Rênal; the sincerity of this madness cannot be doubted, but then the suicidal intensity or sustained drive beyond the pleasure principle of Julien's last days cannot be doubted either. Several critics have remarked upon the supposed similarity between Julien and Don Quixote, but I cannot see it. The Don lives in the order of play until he is battered out of it; then he dies. What others call madness is simply the Don's greatness. But Julien falls into pathology; it is an attractive craziness, because it makes him more likeable than before, yet it remains a kind of madness. Stendhal is poor at endings;

the conclusion of *The Charterhouse of Parma* is also weak and abrupt. But I feel a certain hesitancy in myself at these judgments. Perhaps I simply like both novels so much that I resent Stendhal's own apparent loss of interest when he nears an end. The best defense of Julien's demise was made by Stendhal's subtle disciple, the Prince of Lampedusa, author of *The Leopard*: "The author hastens to kill the character in order to be free of him. It is a dramatic and evocative conclusion unlike any other." One wants to protest to the Prince that it isn't dramatic enough, but he forestalls the complaint: "The impulsive, energetic handsome Julien spends his last words to tell his friend how he must go about buying back his body." Evidently, this is dramatic in the mode of *The Leopard*, where death takes place in the soul, and the body alone remains living. A Stendhalian pathos, the Prince implies, belongs only to the happy few; it is a pathos more of sensibility than of emotion.

Mathilde and Julien, on the occasion of their first night together, are comic triumphs of sensibility over emotion. "Their transports," Stendhal observes, "were a bit conscious," which is a delicious understatement:

> Mlle. de La Mole supposed she was fulfilling a duty to herself and to her lover. The poor boy, she thought to herself, he's shown perfect bravery, he ought to be happy or else the fault lies in my want of character. But she would have been glad to ransom herself, at the cost of eternal misery, from the cruel necessity imposed upon her.
>
> In spite of the frightful violence with which she repressed her feelings, she was in perfect command of her speech.
>
> No regret, no reproach came from her lips to spoil this night, which seemed strange to Julien, rather than happy. What a difference, good God! from his last stay of twenty-four hours at Verrières! These fancy Paris fashions have found a way to spoil everything, even love, he said to himself, in an excess of injustice.
>
> He was indulging in these reflections as he stood in one of the great mahogany wardrobes into which he had slipped at the first sounds coming from the next room, which was that of Mme. de La Mole. Mathilde went off with her mother to mass; the maids quickly left the room, and Julien easily escaped before they came back to finish their tasks.
>
> He took a horse and sought out the loneliest parts of the forest of Meudon near Paris. He was far more surprised than happy. The happiness that came from time to time like a gleam of light in his soul was like that of a young second lieutenant who after

some astounding action has just been promoted full colonel by the commanding general; he felt himself raised to an immense height. Everything that had been far above him yesterday was now at his level or even beneath him. Gradually Julien's happiness increased as it became more remote.

If there was nothing tender in his soul, the reason, however strange it may seem, was that Mathilde in all her dealings with him had been doing nothing but her duty. There was nothing unexpected for her in all the events of the night, except the misery and shame she had discovered instead of those divine raptures that novels talk about.

Was I mistaken, don't I love him at all? she asked herself.

This hilarity of mutual coldness is the prelude to the novel's most delightful pages, as Stendhal surpasses himself in depicting the agon that springs up between these two titanic vanities. What Hobbes was to the principles of civil society, Stendhal was to the principles of eros. Neither man should be called a cynic. Each is more than a psychologist, because both saw the truth of the state of nature. Hobbes is to Stendhal what Schopenhauer was to the Tolstoy of *Anna Karenina*, the philosopher who confirms the insights so central to the novelist that they scarcely require confirmation. I would prefer to put it more starkly; if you repeatedly read *The Red and the Black*, then *Leviathan* becomes a fascinating redundancy, just as a deep knowledge of *Anna Karenina* renders *The World as Will and Representation* almost superfluous. Stendhal, and Tolstoy, are in their antithetical ways the true philosophers of love between the sexes, the dark metaphysicians of the unconscious verities of desire.

Mary Wollstonecraft Shelley

(1797–1851)

Frankenstein

> *there is a fire*
> *And motion of the soul which will not dwell*
> *In its own narrow being, but aspire*
> *Beyond the fitting medium of desire.*
> BYRON. *Childe Harold's Pilgrimage*, canto 3

> *Ere Babylon was dust,*
> *The Magus Zoroaster, my dead child,*
> *Met his own image walking in the garden.*
> *That apparition, sole of men, he saw.*
> *For know there are two worlds of life and death:*
> *One that which thou beholdest; but the other*
> *Is underneath the grave, where do inhabit*
> *The shadows of all forms that think and live*
> *Till death unite them and they part no more*
> SHELLEY. *Prometheus Unbound*, act 1

THE MOTION-PICTURE viewer WHO CARRIES HIS OBSCURE BUT STILL
authentic taste for the sublime to the neighborhood theater, there to see
the latest in an unending series of *Frankensteins*, becomes a sharer in a
romantic terror now nearly one hundred and fifty years old. Mary Shelley,
barely nineteen years of age when she wrote the original Frankenstein, was
the daughter of two great intellectual rebels, William Godwin and Mary
Wollstonecraft, and the second wife of Percy Bysshe Shelley, another great
rebel and an unmatched lyrical poet. Had she written nothing, Mary

Shelley would be remembered today. She is remembered in her own right as the author of a novel valuable in itself but also prophetic of an intellectual world to come, a novel depicting a Prometheanism that is with us still.

"Frankenstein," to most of us, is the name of a monster rather than of a monster's creator, for the common reader and the common viewer have worked together, in their apparent confusion, to create a myth soundly based on a central duality in Mary Shelley's novel. A critical discussion of *Frankenstein* needs to begin from an insight first recorded by Richard Church and Muriel Spark: the monster and his creator are the antithetical halves of a single being. Spark states the antithesis too cleanly; for her Victor Frankenstein represents the feelings, and his nameless creature the intellect. In her view the monster has no emotion, and "what passes for emotion ... are really intellectual passions arrived at through rational channels." Spark carries this argument far enough to insist that the monster is asexual and that he demands a bride from Frankenstein only for companionship, a conclusion evidently at variance with the novel's text.

The antithesis between the scientist and his creature in *Frankenstein* is a very complex one and can be described more fully in the larger context of Romantic literature and its characteristic mythology. The shadow or double of the self is a constant conceptual image in Blake and Shelley and a frequent image, more random and descriptive, in the other major Romantics, especially in Byron. In *Frankenstein* it is the dominant and recurrent image and accounts for much of the latent power the novel possesses.

Mary Shelley's husband was a divided being, as man and as poet, just as his friend Byron was, though in Shelley the split was more radical. *Frankenstein; or, The Modern Prometheus* is the full title of Mary Shelley's novel, and while Victor Frankenstein is *not* Shelley (Clerval is rather more like the poet), the Modern Prometheus is a very apt term for Shelley or for Byron. Prometheus is the mythic figure who best suits the uses of Romantic poetry, for no other traditional being has in him the full range of Romantic moral sensibility and the full Romantic capacity for creation and destruction.

No Romantic writer employed the Prometheus archetype without a full awareness of its equivocal potentialities. The Prometheus of the ancients had been for the most part a spiritually reprehensible figure, though frequently a sympathetic one, in terms both of his dramatic situation and in his close alliance with mankind against the gods. But this alliance had been ruinous for man in most versions of the myth, and the Titan's benevolence toward humanity was hardly sufficient recompense for the alienation of man from heaven that he had brought about. Both sides of Titanism are evident in earlier Christian references to the story. The same Prometheus who is taken as an analogue of the crucified Christ is regarded also as a type of Lucifer, a son of light justly cast, out by an offended heaven.

In the Romantic readings of Milton's *Paradise Lost* (and Frankenstein is implicitly one such reading) this double identity of Prometheus is a vital element. Blake, whose mythic revolutionary named Orc is another version of Prometheus, saw Milton's Satan as a Prometheus gone wrong, as desire restrained until it became only the shadow of desire, a diminished double of creative energy. Shelley went further in judging Milton's Satan as an imperfect Prometheus, inadequate because his mixture of heroic and base qualities engendered in the reader's mind a "pernicious casuistry" inimical to the spirit of art.

Blake, more systematic a poet than Shelley, worked out an antithesis between symbolic figures he named Spectre and Emanation, the shadow of desire and the total form of desire, respectively. A reader of *Frankenstein*, recalling the novel's extraordinary conclusion, with its scenes of obsessional pursuit through the Arctic wastes, can recognize the same imagery applied to a similar symbolic situation in Blake's lyric on the strife of Spectre and Emanation:

My Spectre around me night and day
Like a Wild beast guards my way.
My Emanation far within
Weeps incessantly for my Sin.

A Fathomless and boundless deep,
There we wander, there we weep;
On the hungry craving wind
My Spectre follows thee behind.

He scents thy footsteps in the snow,
Wheresoever thou dost go
Thro' the wintry hail and rain.

Frankenstein's monster, tempting his revengeful creator on through a world of ice, is another Emanation pursued by a Spectre, with the enormous difference that he is an Emanation flawed, a nightmare of actuality, rather than dream of desire. Though abhorred rather than loved, the monster is the total form of Frankenstein's creative power and is more imaginative than his creator. The monster is at once more intellectual and more emotional than his maker; indeed he excels Frankenstein as much (and in the same ways) as Milton's Adam excels Milton's God in *Paradise Lost*. The greatest paradox and most astonishing achievement of Mary Shelley's novel is that the monster is *more human* than his creator. This nameless being, as much a Modern Adam as his creator is a Modern Prometheus, is more lovable than his creator and more hateful, more to be pitied and more to be feared, and above all more able to give the attentive reader that shock of added consciousness in which aesthetic recognition compels a heightened realization of the self. For like Blake's Spectre and Emanation or Shelley's Alastor and Epipsyche, Frankenstein and his monster are the solipsistic and generous halves of the one self. Frankenstein is the mind and emotions turned in upon themselves, and his creature is the mind and emotions turned imaginatively outward, seeking a greater humanization through a confrontation of other selves.

I am suggesting that what makes *Frankenstein* an important book, though it is only a strong, flawed novel with frequent clumsiness in its narrative and characterization, is that it contains one of the most vivid versions we have of the Romantic mythology of the self, one that resembles Blake's *Book of Urizen*, Shelley's *Prometheus Unbound*, and Byron's *Manfred*, among other works. Because it lacks the sophistication and imaginative complexity of such works, *Frankenstein* affords a unique introduction to the archetypal world of the Romantics.

William Godwin, though a tendentious novelist, was a powerful one, and the prehistory of his daughter's novel begins with his best work of fiction, *Caleb Williams* (1794). Godwin summarized the climactic (and harrowing) final third of his novel as a pattern of flight and pursuit, "the fugitive in perpetual apprehension of being overwhelmed with the worst calamities, and the pursuer, by his ingenuity and resources, keeping his victim in a state of the most fearful alarm." Mary Shelley brilliantly reverses this pattern in the final sequence of her novel, and she takes from *Caleb Williams* also her destructive theme of the monster's war against "the whole machinery of human society," to quote the words of Caleb Williams while in prison. Muriel Spark argues that *Frankenstein* can be read as a reaction "against the rational-humanism of Godwin and Shelley," and she points to the equivocal preface that Shelley wrote to his wife's novel, in order to support this view. Certainly Shelley was worried lest the novel be taken as a warning against the inevitable moral consequences of an unchecked experimental Prometheanism and scientific materialism. The preface insists that:

> The opinions which naturally spring from the character and situation of the hero are by no means to be conceived as existing

always in my own conviction; nor is any inference justly to be drawn from the following pages as prejudicing any philosophical doctrine of whatever kind.

Shelley had, throughout his own work, a constant reaction against Godwin's rational humanism, but his reaction was systematically and consciously one of heart against head. In the same summer in the Swiss Alps that saw the conception of *Frankenstein*, Shelley composed two poems that lift the thematic conflict of the novel to the level of the true sublime. In the "Hymn to Intellectual Beauty" the poet's heart interprets an inconstant grace and loveliness, always just beyond the range of the human senses, as being the only beneficent force in life, and he prays to this force to be more constant in its attendance upon him and all mankind. In a greater sister-hymn, "Mont Blanc," an awesome meditation upon a frightening natural scene, the poet's head issues an allied but essentially contrary report. The force, or power, is there, behind or within the mountain, but its external workings upon us are either indifferent or malevolent, and this power is not to be prayed to. It can teach us, but what it teaches us is our own dangerous freedom from nature, the necessity for our will to become a significant part of materialistic necessity. Though "Mont Blanc" works its way to an almost heroic conclusion, it is also a poem of horror and reminds us that Frankenstein first confronts his conscious monster in the brooding presence of Mont Blanc, and to the restless music of one of Shelley's lyrics of Mutability.

In *Prometheus Unbound* the split between head and heart is not healed, but the heart is allowed dominance. The hero, Prometheus, like Frankenstein, has made a monster, but this monster is Jupiter, the God of all institutional and historical religions, including organized Christianity. Salvation from this conceptual error comes through love alone; but love in this poem, as elsewhere in Shelley, is always closely shadowed by ruin. Indeed, what choice spirits in Shelley perpetually encounter is ruin masquerading as love, pain presenting itself as pleasure. The tentative way out of this situation in Shelley's poetry is through the quest for a feeling mind and an understanding heart, which is symbolized by the sexual reunion of Prometheus and his Emanation, Asia. Frederick A. Pottle sums up *Prometheus Unbound* by observing its meaning to be that "the head must sincerely forgive, must willingly eschew hatred on purely experimental grounds," while "the affections must exorcize the demons of infancy, whether personal or of the race." In the light cast by these profound and precise summations, the reader can better understand both Shelley's lyrical drama and his wife's narrative of the Modern Prometheus.

There are two paradoxes at the center of Mary Shelley's novel, and each illuminates a dilemma of the Promethean imagination. The first is that Frankenstein *was* successful, in that he did create Natural Man, not as he was, but as the meliorists saw such a man; indeed, Frankenstein did better than this, since his creature was, as we have seen, more imaginative than himself. Frankenstein's tragedy stems not from his Promethean excess but from his own moral error, his failure to love; he *abhorred his creature*, became terrified, and fled his responsibilities.

The second paradox is the more ironic. This either would not have happened or would not have mattered anyway, if Frankenstein had been an aesthetically successful maker; a beautiful "monster," or even a passable one, would not have been a monster. As the creature bitterly observes in chapter 17,

> Shall I respect man when he contemns me? Let him live with me in the interchange of kindness, and instead of injury I would bestow every benefit upon him with tears of gratitude at his acceptance. But that cannot be; the human senses are insurmountable barriers to our union.

As the hideousness of his creature was no part of Victor Frankenstein's intention, it is worth noticing how this disastrous matter came to be.

It would not be unjust to characterize Victor Frankenstein, in his act of creation, as being momentarily a moral idiot, like so many who have done his work after him. There is an indeliberate humor in the contrast between the enormity of the scientist's discovery and the mundane emotions of the discoverer. Finding that "the minuteness of the parts" slows him down, he resolves to make his creature "about eight feet in height and proportionably large." As he works on, he allows himself to dream that "a new species would bless me as its creator and source; many happy and excellent natures would owe their being to me." Yet he knows his is a "workshop of filthy creation," and he fails the fundamental test of his own creativity. When the "dull yellow eye" of his creature opens, this creator falls from the autonomy of a supreme artificer to the terror of a child of earth: "breathless horror and disgust filled my heart." He flees his responsibility and sets in motion the events that will lead to his own Arctic immolation, a fit end for a being who has never achieved a full sense of another's existence.

Haunting Mary Shelley's novel is the demonic figure of the Ancient Mariner, Coleridge's major venture into Romantic mythology of the purgatorial self trapped in the isolation of a heightened self-consciousness. Walton, in Letter 2 introducing the novel, compares himself "to that production of the most imaginative of modern poets." As a seeker-out of an unknown passage, Walton is himself a Promethean quester, like Frankenstein, toward whom he is so compellingly drawn. Coleridge's Mariner is of the line of Cain, and the irony of Frankenstein's fate is that he too is a Cain, involuntarily murdering all his loved ones through the agency of his creature. The Ancient Mariner is punished by living under the curse of his consciousness of guilt, while the excruciating torment of Frankenstein is never to be able to forget his guilt in creating a lonely consciousness driven to crime by the rage of unwilling solitude.

It is part of Mary Shelley's insight into her mythological theme that all the monster's victims are innocents. The monster not only refuses actively to slay his guilty creator, he mourns for him, though with the equivocal tribute of terming the scientist a "generous and self-devoted being." Frankenstein, the modern Prometheus who has violated nature, receives his epitaph from the ruined second nature he has made, the God-abandoned, who consciously echoes the ruined Satan of *Paradise Lost* and proclaims, "Evil thenceforth became my good." It is imaginatively fitting that the greater and more interesting consciousness of the creature should survive his creator, for he alone in Mary Shelley's novel possesses character. Frankenstein, like Coleridge's Mariner, has no character in his own right; both figures win a claim to our attention only by their primordial crimes against original nature.

The monster is of course Mary Shelley's finest invention, and his narrative (chaps. 11–16) forms the highest achievement of the novel, more absorbing even than the magnificent and almost surrealistic pursuit of the climax. In an age so given to remarkable depictions of the dignity of natural man, an age including the shepherds and beggars of Wordsworth and what W. J. Bate has termed Keats's "polar ideal of disinterestedness"—even in such a literary time Frankenstein's hapless creature stands out as a sublime embodiment of heroic pathos. Though Frankenstein lacks the moral imagination to understand him, the daemon's appeal is to what is most compassionate in us:

> Oh, Frankenstein, be not equitable to every other, and trample upon me alone, to whom thy justice, and even thy clemency and affection, is most due. Remember that I am thy creature; *I ought to be thy Adam, but I am rather the fallen angel, whom thou drivest from joy for no misdeed.* Everywhere I see bliss, from which I alone am irrevocably excluded. I was benevolent and good; misery made me a fiend. Make me happy, and I shall again be virtuous.

The passage I have italicized is the imaginative kernel of the novel and is meant to remind the reader of the novel's epigraph:

Did I request thee, Maker, from my clay
To mold me man? Did I solicit thee
From darkness to promote me?

That desperate plangency of the fallen Adam becomes the characteristic accent of the daemon's lamentations, with the influence of Milton cunningly built into the novel's narrative by the happy device of Frankenstein's creature receiving his education through reading *Paradise Lost* as "a true history." Already doomed because his standards are human, which makes him an outcast even to himself, his Miltonic education completes his fatal growth in self-consciousness. His story, as told to his maker, follows a familiar Romantic pattern "of the progress of my intellect," as he puts it. His first pleasure after the dawn of consciousness comes through his wonder at seeing the moon rise. Caliban-like, he responds wonderfully to music, both natural and human, and his sensitivity to the natural world has the responsiveness of an incipient poet. His awakening to a first love for other beings, the inmates of the cottage he haunts, awakens him also to the great desolation of love rejected when he attempts to reveal himself. His own duality of situation and character, caught between the states of Adam and Satan, Natural Man and his thwarted desire, is related by him directly to his reading of Milton's epic:

It moved every feeling of wonder and awe that the picture of an omnipotent God warring with his creatures was capable of exciting. I often referred the several situations, as their similarity struck me, to my own. Like Adam, I was apparently united by no link to any other being in existence, but his state was far different from mine in every other respect. He had come forth from the hands of God a perfect creature, happy and prosperous, guarded by the especial care of his Creator; he was allowed to converse with and acquire knowledge from beings of a superior nature; but I was wretched, helpless, and alone. Many times I considered Satan as the fitter emblem of my condition, for often, like him, when I viewed the bliss of my protectors, the bitter gall of envy rose within me.

From a despair this profound, no release is possible. Driven forth into an existence upon which "the cold stars shone in mockery," the daemon declares "everlasting war against the species" and enters upon a fallen existence more terrible than the expelled Adam's. Echoing Milton, he asks the ironic question "And now, with the world before me, whither should I bend my steps?" to which the only possible answer is, toward his wretched Promethean creator.

If we stand back from Mary Shelley's novel in order better to view its archetypal shape, we see it as the quest of a solitary and ravaged consciousness first for consolation, then for revenge, and finally for a self-destruction that will be apocalyptic, that will bring down the creator with his creature. Though Mary Shelley may not have intended it, her novel's prime theme is a necessary counterpoise to Prometheanism, for Prometheanism exalts the increase in consciousness despite all cost. Frankenstein breaks through the barrier that separates man from God and gives apparent life, but in doing so he gives only death-in-life. The profound dejection endemic in Mary Shelley's novel is fundamental to the Romantic mythology of the self, for all Romantic horrors are diseases of excessive consciousness, of the self unable to bear the self. Kierkegaard remarks that Satan's despair is absolute because Satan, as pure spirit, is pure consciousness, and for Satan (and all men in his predicament) every increase in consciousness is an increase in despair. Frankenstein's desperate creature attains the state of pure spirit through his extraordinary situation and is racked by a consciousness in which every thought is a fresh disease.

A Romantic poet fought against self-consciousness through the strength of what he called imagination, a more than rational energy by which thought could seek to heal itself. But Frankenstein's daemon, though he is in the archetypal situation of the Romantic Wanderer or Solitary, who sometimes was a poet, can win no release from his own story by telling it. His desperate desire for a mate is clearly an attempt to find a Shelleyan Epipsyche or Blakean Emanation for himself, a self within the self. But as he is the nightmare actualization of Frankenstein's desire, he is himself an emanation of Promethean yearnings, and his only double is his creator and denier.

When Coleridge's Ancient Mariner progressed from the purgatory of consciousness to his very minimal control of imagination, he failed to save himself, since he remained in a cycle of remorse, but he at least became a salutary warning to others and made of the Wedding Guest a wiser and a better man. Frankenstein's creature can help neither himself nor others, for he has no natural ground to which he can return. Romantic poets liked to return to the imagery of the ocean of life and immortality, for in the eddying to and fro of the healing waters they could picture a hoped-for process of restoration, of a survival of consciousness despite all its agonies. Mary Shelley, with marvelous appropriateness, brings her Romantic novel to a demonic conclusion in a world of ice. The frozen sea is the inevitable emblem for both the wretched daemon and his obsessed creator, but the daemon is allowed a final image of reversed Prometheanism. There is a heroism fully earned in the being who cries farewell in a claim of sad triumph: "I shall ascend my funeral pile triumphantly and exult in the agony of the torturing flames." Mary Shelley could not have known how dark a prophecy this consummation of consciousness would prove to be for the two great Promethean poets who were at her side during the summer of 1816, when her novel was conceived. Byron, writing his own epitaph at Missolonghi in 1824, and perhaps thinking back to having stood at Shelley's funeral pile two years before, found an image similar to the daemon's to sum up an exhausted existence:

> The fire that on my bosom preys
>   Is lone as some volcanic isle;
> No torch is kindled at its blaze—
>   A funeral pile.

The fire of increased consciousness stolen from heaven ends as an isolated volcano cut off from other selves by an estranging sea. "The light of that conflagration will fade away; my ashes will be swept into the sea by the winds" is the exultant cry of Frankenstein's. creature. A blaze at which no torch is kindled is Byron's self-image, but he ends his death poem on another note, the hope for a soldier's grave, which he found. There is no Promethean release, but release is perhaps not the burden of the literature of Romantic aspiration. There is something both Godwinian and Shelleyan about the final utterance of Victor Frankenstein, which is properly made to Walton, the failed Promethean whose ship has just turned back. Though chastened, the Modern Prometheus ends with a last word true, not to his accomplishment, but to his desire:

> Farewell, Walton! Seek happiness in tranquillity and avoid ambition, even if it be only the apparently innocent one of distinguishing yourself in science and discoveries. Yet why do I say this? I have myself been blasted in these hopes, yet another may succeed.

Shelley's Prometheus, crucified on his icy precipice, found his ultimate torment in a Fury's taunt: "And all best things are thus confused to ill." It seems a fitting summation for all the work done by modern Prometheanism and might have served as an alternate epigraph for Mary Shelley's disturbing novel.

Honoré de Balzac

(1799–1850)

Père Goriot

I LOVE BEST ABOUT BALZAC THAT HE RENEWS, FOR ME, THE ROMANCE OF reading, as even Henry James and Flaubert do not. Like every other young reader who first comes to Balzac in adolescence, I was swept away by the marvelous Vautrin, first encountered by me in *Père Goriot*:

> Vautrin, the forty-year-old with dyed side-whiskers, stood somewhere between these two and the rest of the lodgers. He was one of those about whom ordinary people say: "Now that's really *somebody*!" He was broad-shouldered with a well-developed chest and bulging muscles, and thick, square hands, the knuckles decorated with great tufts of flaming red hair. His face, scored by premature wrinkles, showed signs of a toughness that belied his good-natured, easy-going manners. His booming bass voice, which matched his loud cheerfulness, was emphatically pleasant. He was obliging and full of laughter. If a lock stopped working, he'd quickly take it apart, figure out what was wrong, file it down, oil it, then put it back together again, observing, "I know all about such things." There were a lot of other things he knew about—ships, the sea, France, foreign nations, business, psychology, current affairs, the law, hotels, and prisons. When anyone complained too much, he'd immediately offer his services. More than once, he'd lent money both to Madame Vauquer and to some of her lodgers, but his debtors would sooner have died than not repay him, because for all his friendliness he had a look about him, deep, determined, that made people afraid. The very way he spat showed

his unshakable composure; put in a difficult position, he'd obviously never hesitate to commit a crime, to get himself out of it. Like a stern judge, his glance seemed to pierce to the bottom of every issue, every conscience, every emotion.

Burton Raffel's translation splendidly conveys Balzac's fascination with Vautrin, the novelist's own daemon or genius. Graham Robb, Balzac's best biographer, tells us that the novelist's friends called him "Vautrin." Like Vautrin, Balzac divided the cosmos between deceivers and the deceived: the grand crimemaster exemplifies Balzac's own cynical egomania. Again like Balzac, Vautrin is a monster of energy: a force of nature who also happens to be a man.

Vautrin is overtly homoerotic; Balzac, sublime womanizer, projected his own barely repressed sexual duality, reminiscent of Byron's who, with Molière, Sir Walter Scott, Victor Hugo, Voltaire, and Rabelais, can be considered Balzac's literary forerunners. There is something of Byron's Manfred and Cain in Vautrin: the line of descent from Milton's Satan is clear, since Vautrin has read *Paradise Lost*. There is a Byronic-Satanic aura surrounding Vautrin, at once sinister, compelling, and strangely genial, intermixed with the savagery.

"Vautrin" is one of the pseudonyms of Jacques Collin, known to all as "Death-Dodger." The powerful scene of his arrest in Part Three of *Père Goriot* justifies his nickname:

> "In the name of the law, and the name of the King," announced one of the officers, though there was such a loud murmur of astonishment that no one could hear him.
>
> But silence quickly descended once again, as the lodgers moved aside, making room for three of the men, who came forward, their hands in their pockets, and loaded pistols in their hands. Two uniformed policemen stepped into the doorway they'd left, and two others appeared in the other doorway, near the stairs. Soldiers' footsteps, and the readying of their rifles, echoed from the pavement outside, in front of the house. Death-Dodger had no hope of escape; everyone stared at him, irresistibly drawn. Vidocq went directly to where he stood, and swiftly punched Collin in the head with such force that his wig flew off, revealing the stark horror of his skull. Brick-red, short-clipped hair gave him a look at once sly and powerful, and both head and face, blending perfectly, now, with his brutish chest, glowed with the fierce, burning light of a hellish mind. It was suddenly obvious to them all just who Vautrin

was, what he'd done, what he'd been doing, what he would go on
to do; they suddenly understood at a glance his implacable ideas,
his religion of self-indulgence, exactly the sort of royal sensibility
which tinted all his thoughts with cynicism, as well as all his
actions, and supported both by the strength of an organization
prepared for anything. The blood rose into his face, his eyes
gleamed like some savage cat's. He seemed to explode into a gesture of such wild energy, and he roared with such ferocity that,
one and all, the lodgers cried out in terror. His fierce, feral movement, and the general clamor he'd created, made the policemen
draw their weapons. But seeing the gleam of the cocked pistols,
Collin immediately understood his peril, and instantly proved
himself possessor of the highest of all human powers. It was a horrible, majestic spectacle! His face could only be compared to some
apparatus, full of billowing smoke capable of moving mountains,
but dissolved in the twinkling of an eye by a single drop of cold
water. The drop that doused his rage flickered as rapidly as a flash
of light. Then he slowly smiled, and turned to look down at his
wig.

"This isn't one of your polite days, is it, old boy?" he said to
Vidocq. And then he held out his hands to the policemen, beckoning them with a movement of his head. "Gentlemen, officers,
I'm ready for your handcuffs or your chains, as you please. I ask
those present to take due note of the fact that I offer no resistance."

That prenatural transition from absolute rage to cunning composure
is definitive of Vautrin. Is it not also definitive of the astonishing genius of
Balzac? The best critical remark yet made about Balzac is Baudelaire's:
"even the janitors have some sort of genius." The genius-of-geniuses, in
Balzac, is Vautrin, though the novelist himself might have voted for his
idealized visionary, Louis Lambert.

Zola, Balzac's disciple, dared to compare the author of *The Human
Comedy* to Shakespeare. Balzac cannot sustain the comparison: if somehow
you fused Dante and Cervantes, you would have Shakespeare's equal.
Proust, the culmination of the French novel, charmingly said of Balzac:
"He hides nothing, he says everything," and yet indicated the "silence" also
to be found amidst all that disclosure.

It seems odd to me that Henry James, who condemned the novels of
Tolstoy and Dostoevsky as "loose, baggy monsters," asserted that he had
learned "the lesson of Balzac." Though James does not say so explicitly, it

must have been the lesson of energy, of psychic force. Perhaps Balzac helped teach Henry James the fictive economy of energy, the transformation of instinctive vitality into art.

That returns me to Vautrin, the most vitalistic of all Balzac's creatures. Toward the close of *Lost Illusions*, the young poet Lucien Chardon, determined upon suicide, encounters a supposed Spanish priest, Carlos Herrera, Canon of Toledo, another disguise of Death-Dodger. Herrera-Vautrin restores Lucien to life with a torrent of money, at the expense of a clear enough homoerotic bond between the criminal-priest and the poet.

That bond is the center of the great novel, *A Harlot High and Low* (*Splendors and Miseries of the Courtesans*). Part Four of the novel is the extraordinary *The Last Incarnation of Vautrin*, in which Death Dodger becomes the head of the Sûreté, as titanic a police-chief as he had been King of the Underworld. It is as if Milton's Satan had entered again into God's favor and emerged as the Archangel Michael. Perhaps it is Balzac's ultimate thrust at societal power, and also the expression of the novelist's nostalgia for possession of and union with that power.

Nathaniel Hawthorne

(1804-1864)

The Scarlet Letter

THE LONELY ART OF NATHANIEL HAWTHORNE REMAINS ONE OF THE cultural monuments of our nation. It continues to provide for the deepest imaginative needs of the solitary reader, of whatever country. Hawthorne's vision of reality remains unsurpassed, short of Shakespeare and Dante. *The Scarlet Letter* and *The Marble Faun* trouble the heart and stimulate the intellect. As Herman Melville and Henry James testified, Hawthorne is a marvelously subtle storyteller and revealer of the soul. Only James himself and William Faulkner ultimately challenge Hawthorne as *the* American novelist (despite some remarkable tales, Melville remains the author of the one prose-epic, *Moby-Dick*, rather than a novelist as such, and Mark Twain abides primarily as the genial sage of *Huckleberry Finn*, most American of all narratives.)

Rereading *The Scarlet Letter* always constitutes a lesson in how to read and why. A procession of extraordinary representations of women has followed after Hester Prynne in American literature, yet even the strongest—Isabel Archer in James's *The Portrait of a Lady* and Ántonia in Willa Cather's *My Ántonia*—do not match Hester Prynne in her aesthetic and cultural reverberations. For Hester *is*, in many ways, the American Eve, the Emersonian vision that atones for our lack of any adequate representation of the American Adam. Like Milton's own Eve, Hester is far superior to her fate, and imaginatively preferable to Adam's (and Milton's) God. Hawthorne subtly conveys Hester's sexual power to us, with far less ambivalence than Milton manifests in celebrating Eve's sexual strength. Sensual and tragic, Hester is larger than her book and her world, because her greatness of spirit, like her heroic sexuality, is ill-served by the terrible alternatives of the Satanic Chillingworth (Iago's understudy) and the timid

Dimmesdale, an absurdly inadequate adulterous lover for the sublime Hester.

Hester's Self-Reliance is her authentic religion, and enables her to survive the outrages of societal ostracism and erotic repression. As critics rightly point out, Hester is herself an artist, whose work as embroiderer parallels Hawthorne's own art as romancer. Can we not call Hester Hawthorne's Muse or Interior Paramour (to employ a fine phrase of Wallace Stevens)? As such Hester exerts a fierce pressure upon Hawthorne himself, compelling him to abandon romance for the psychological novel, almost despite his own preferences.

Even *The Marble Faun*, so much prophecy of the novel of Americans abroad, from Henry James and Edith Wharton through Hemingway and Scott Fitzgerald, is not quite of the eminence of *The Scarlet Letter*. There are only a dozen or so of essential American literary classics, including *Moby-Dick* and *Huckleberry Finn*, Emerson's *Essays* and Thoreau's *Walden*, Whitman's *Leaves of Grass* and Emily Dickinson's poems, James's *The Portrait of a Lady* and Faulkner's *As I Lay Dying*, the poems of Wallace Stevens and Hart Crane, and Cormac McCarthy's *Blood Meridian*. That brief catalog would be achingly incomplete without *The Scarlet Letter*, a permanent center of our imaginative consciousness.

Charles Dickens

(1812-1870)

I

COURAGE WOULD BE THE CRITICAL VIRTUE MOST REQUIRED IF ANYONE were to attempt an essay that might be called "The Limitations of Shakespeare." Tolstoy, in his most outrageous critical performance, more or less tried just that, with dismal results, and even Ben Jonson might not have done much better, had he sought to extend his ambivalent *obiter dicta* on his great friend and rival. Nearly as much courage, or foolhardiness, is involved in discoursing on the limitations of Dickens, but the young Henry James had a critical gusto that could carry him through every literary challenge. Reviewing *Our Mutual Friend* in 1865, James exuberantly proclaimed that "*Bleak House* was forced; *Little Dorrit* was labored; the present work is dug out as with a spade and pickaxe." At about this time, reviewing *Drum-Taps*, James memorably dismissed Whitman as an essentially prosaic mind seeking to lift itself, by muscular exertion, into poetry. To reject some of the major works of the strongest English novelist and the greatest American poet, at about the same moment, is to set standards for critical audacity that no one since has been able to match, even as no novelist since has equalled Dickens, nor any poet, Walt Whitman.

James was at his rare worst in summing up Dickens's supposedly principal inadequacy:

> Such scenes as this are useful in fixing the limits of Mr. Dickens's insight. Insight is, perhaps, too strong a word; for we are convinced that it is one of the chief conditions of his genius not to see beneath the surface of things. If we might hazard a definition of his literary character, we should, accordingly, call him the greatest of

superficial novelists. We are aware that this definition confines him to an inferior rank in the department of letters which he adorns; but we accept this consequence of our proposition. It were, in our opinion, an offence against humanity to place Mr. Dickens among the greatest novelists. For, to repeat what we have already intimated, he has created nothing but figure. He has added nothing to our understanding of human character. He is master of but two alternatives: he reconciles us to what is commonplace, and he reconciles us to what is odd. The value of the former service is questionable; and the manner in which Mr. Dickens performs it sometimes conveys a certain impression of charlatanism. The value of the latter service is incontestable, and here Mr. Dickens is an honest, an admirable artist.

This can be taken literally, and then transvalued: to see truly the surface of things, to reconcile us at once to the commonplace and the odd—these are not minor gifts. In 1860, John Ruskin, the great seer of the surface of things, the charismatic illuminator of the commonplace and the odd together, had reached a rather different conclusion from that of the young Henry James, five years before James's brash rejection:

The essential value and truth of Dickens's writings have been unwisely lost sight of by many thoughtful persons merely because he presents his truth with some colour of caricature. Unwisely, because Dickens's caricature, though often gross, is never mistaken. Allowing for his manner of telling them, the things he tells us are always true. I wish that he could think it right to limit his brilliant exaggeration to works written only for public amusement; and when he takes up a subject of high national importance, such as that which he handled in *Hard Times*, that he would use severer and more accurate analysis. The usefulness of that work (to my mind, in several respects, the greatest he has written) is with many persons seriously diminished because Mr. Bounderby is a dramatic monster, instead of a characteristic example of a worldly master; and Stephen Blackpool a dramatic perfection, instead of a characteristic example of an honest workman. But let us not lose the use of Dickens's wit and insight, because he chooses to speak in a circle of stage fire. He is entirely right in his main drift and purpose in every book he has written; and all of them, but especially *Hard Times*, should be studied with close and earnest care by persons interested in social questions. They will find much that is partial, and, because partial, apparently unjust; but if they examine all the evidence on the other side, which Dickens seems to overlook, it will appear, after all their trouble, that his view was the finally right one, grossly and sharply told.

To say of Dickens that he chose "to speak in a circle of stage fire" is exactly right, since Dickens is the greatest actor among novelists, the finest master of dramatic projection. A superb stage performer, he never stops performing in his novels, which is not the least of his many Shakespearean characteristics. Martin Price usefully defines some of these as "his effortless invention, his brilliant play of language, the scope and density of his imagined world." I like also Price's general comparison of Dickens to the strongest satirist in the language, Swift, a comparison that Price shrewdly turns into a confrontation:

> But the confrontation helps us to define differences as well: Dickens is more explicit, more overtly compassionate, insisting always upon the perversions of feeling as well as of thought. His outrage is of the same consistency as his generous celebration, the satirical wit of the same copious extravagance as the comic elaborations. Dickens' world is alive with things that snatch, lurch, teeter, thrust, leer; it is the animate world of Netherlandish genre painting or of Hogarth's prints, where all space is a field of force, where objects vie or intrigue with each other, where every human event spills over into the things that surround it. This may become the typically crowded scene of satire, where persons are reduced to things and things to matter in motion; or it may pulsate with fierce energy and noisy feeling. It is different from Swift; it is the distinctive Dickensian plenitude, which we find again in his verbal play, in his great array of vivid characters, in his massed scenes of feasts or public declamations. It creates rituals as compelling as the resuscitation of Rogue Riderhood, where strangers participate solemnly in the recovery of a spark of life, oblivious for the moment of the unlovely human form it will soon inhabit.

That animate, Hogarthian world, "where all space is a field of force," indeed is a plenitude and it strikes me that Price's vivid description suggests Rabelais rather than Swift as a true analogue. Dickens, like Shakespeare in one of many aspects and like Rabelais, is as much carnival as stage fire, a kind of endless festival. The reader of Dickens stands in the midst of a festival, which is too varied, too multiform, to be taken in even by innumerable readings. Something always escapes our ken; Ben Jonson's sense of being "rammed with life" is exemplified more even by Dickens than by Rabelais, in that near-Shakespearean plenitude that is Dickens's peculiar glory.

Is it possible to define that plenitude narrowly enough so as to conceptualize it for critical use, though by "conceptualize" one meant only a critical metaphor? Shakespearean representation is no touchstone for Dickens or for anyone else, since above all modes of representation it turns upon an inward changing brought about by characters listening to themselves speak. Dickens cannot do that. His villains are gorgeous, but there are no Iagos or Edmunds among them. The severer, more relevant test, which Dickens must fail, though hardly to his detriment, is Falstaff, who generates not only his own meaning, but meaning in so many others besides, both on and off the page. Probably the severest test is Shylock, most Dickensian of Shakespeare's characters, since we cannot say of Dickens's Shylock, Fagin, that there is much Shakespearean about him at all. Fagin is a wonderful grotesque, but the winds of will are not stirred in him, while they burn on hellishly forever in Shylock.

Carlyle's injunction, to work in the will, seems to have little enough place in the cosmos of the Dickens characters. I do not say this to indicate a limitation, or even a limit, nor do I believe that the will to live or the will to power is ever relaxed in or by Dickens. But nothing is got for nothing, except perhaps in or by Shakespeare, and Dickens purchases his kind of plenitude at the expense of one aspect of the will. T.S. Eliot remarked that "Dickens's characters are real because there is no one like them." I would modify that to "They are real because they are not like one another, though sometimes they are a touch more like some of us than like each other." Perhaps the will, in whatever aspect, can differ only in degree rather than in kind among us. The aesthetic secret of Dickens appears to be that his villains, heroes, heroines, victims, eccentrics, ornamental beings, do differ from one another *in the kinds of will that they possess.* Since that is hardly possible for us, as humans, it does bring about an absence in reality in and for Dickens. That is a high price to pay, but it is a good deal less than everything and Dickens got more than he paid for. We also receive a great deal more than we ever are asked to surrender when we read Dickens. That may indeed be his most Shakespearean quality, and may provide the critical trope I quest for in him. James and Proust hurt you more than Dickens does, and the hurt is the meaning, or much of it. What hurts in Dickens never has much to do with meaning, because there cannot be a poetics of pain where the will has ceased to be common or sadly uniform. Dickens really does offer a poetics of pleasure, which is surely worth our secondary uneasiness at his refusal to offer us any accurately mimetic representations of the human will. He writes always the book of the drives, which is why supposedly Freudian readings of him always fail so tediously. The conceptual metaphor he suggests in his representations of character and personality is neither Shakespearean mirror nor Romantic lamp, neither Rabelaisian carnival nor Fieldingesque open country. "Stage fire" seems to me perfect, for "stage" removes something of the reality of the will, yet only as modifier. The substantive remains "fire." Dickens is the poet of the fire of the drives, the true celebrant of Freud's myth of frontier concepts, of that domain lying on the border between psyche and body, falling into matter, yet partaking of the reality of both.

A Tale of Two Cities

Except perhaps for *Pickwick Papers*, *A Tale of Two Cities* always has been the most popular of Dickens's books, if we set aside also the annual phenomenon of *A Christmas Carol* and the other Christmas books. No critic however would rank it with such other later novels as *Great Expectations* and *Our Mutual Friend* or the unfinished *Edwin Drood*, or with the many earlier and middle period masterpieces. The harshest single judgment remains that of the now forgotten but formidably pungent reviewer Sir James Fitzjames Stephen, who left Dickens nothing:

> The moral tone of the *Tale of Two Cities* is not more wholesome than that of its predecessors, nor does it display any nearer approach to a solid knowledge of the subject-matter to which it refers. Mr. Dickens observes in his preface—"It has been one of my hopes to add something to the popular and picturesque means of understanding that terrible time, though no one can hope to add anything to the philosophy of Mr. Carlyle's wonderful book." The allusion to Mr. Carlyle confirms the presumption which the book itself raises, that Mr. Dickens happened to have read the *History of the French Revolution*, and, being on the look-out for a subject, determined off-hand to write a novel about it. Whether he has any other knowledge of the subject than a single reading of Mr. Carlyle's work would supply does not appear, but certainly what he has written shows no more. It is exactly the sort of story which a man would write who had taken down Mr. Carlyle's theory without any sort of inquiry or examination, but with a comfortable conviction that "nothing could be added to its philosophy." The people, says Mr. Dickens, in effect, had been degraded

by long and gross misgovernment, and acted like wild beasts in consequence. There is, no doubt, a great deal of truth in this view of the matter, but it is such very elementary truth that, unless a man had something new to say about it, it is hardly worth mentioning; and Mr. Dickens supports it by specific assertions which, if not absolutely false, are at any rate so selected as to convey an entirely false impression. It is a shameful thing for a popular writer to exaggerate the faults of the French aristocracy in a book which will naturally find its way to readers who know very little of the subject except what he chooses to tell them; but it is impossible not to feel that the melodramatic story which Mr. Dickens tells about the wicked Marquis who violates one of his serfs and murders another, is a grossly unfair representation of the state of society in France in the middle of the eighteenth century. That the French *noblesse* had much to answer for in a thousand ways, is a lamentable truth; but it is by no means true that they could rob, murder, and ravish with impunity. When Count Horn thought proper to try the experiment under the Regency, he was broken on the wheel, notwithstanding his nobility; and the sort of atrocities which Mr. Dickens depicts as characteristic of the eighteenth century were neither safe nor common in the fourteenth.

The most palpable hit here is certainly Dickens's extraordinary reliance upon Carlyle's bizarre but effective *French Revolution*, which is not the history it purports to be but rather has the design, rhetoric, and vision of an apocalyptic fantasy. No one now would read either Carlyle or Dickens in order to learn anything about the French Revolution, and sadly enough no one now reads Carlyle anyway. Yet Stephen's dismay remains legitimate; countless thousands continue to receive the only impressions they ever will have of the French Revolution through the reading of *A Tale of Two Cities*. The book remains a great tale, a vivid instance of Dickens's preternatural gifts as a pure storyteller, though except for its depiction of the superbly ghastly Madame Defarge and her Jacobin associates it lacks the memorable grotesques and driven enthusiasts that we expect from Dickens.

The most palpable flaw in the novel is the weakness as representations of Lucie and Darnay, and the relative failure of the more crucial Carton, who simply lacks the aesthetic dignity that Dickens so desperately needed to give him. If Carton and Darnay, between them, really were meant to depict the spiritual form of Charles Dickens, then their mutual lack of gusto renders them even more inadequate. When Madame Defarge dies, slain by her own bullet, we are very moved, particularly by relief that such an unrelenting version of the death drive will cease to menace us. When Carton, looking "sublime and prophetic," goes to execution, Dickens attempts to move us: we receive the famous and unacceptable, "It is a far, far better thing that I do, than I have ever done; it is a far, far better rest that I go to than I have ever known." Dickens owes us a far, far better rhetoric than that, and generally he delivers it.

The life of *A Tale of Two Cities* is elsewhere, centered upon the negative sublimity of Madame Defarge and her knitting, which is one of Dickens's finest inventions, and is clearly a metaphor for the storytelling of the novel itself. Dickens hardly would have said: "I am Madame Defarge," but she, like the author, remorselessly controls the narrative, until she loses her struggle with the epitome of a loving Englishwoman, Miss Pross. The book's penultimate chapter, in which we are rid of Madame Defarge, is shrewdly called "The Knitting Done."

Even Dickens rarely surpasses the nightmare intensity of Madame Defarge, her absolute command of stage fire, and his finest accomplishment in the book is to increase her already stark aura as the narrative knits onwards. Here is a superb early epiphany of the lady, putting heart into her formidable husband, who seems weak only in comparison to his wife, less a force of nature than of history:

> The night was hot, and the shop, close shut and surrounded by so foul a neighbourhood, was ill-smelling. Monsieur Defarge's olfactory sense was by no means delicate, but the stock of wine smelt much stronger than it ever tasted, and so did the stock of rum and brandy and aniseed. He whiffed the compound of scents away, as he put down his smoked-out pipe.
>
> "You are fatigued," said madame, raising her glance as she knotted the money. "There are only the usual odours."
>
> "I am a little tired," her husband acknowledged.
>
> "You are a little depressed, too," said madame, whose quick eyes had never been so intent on the accounts, but they had had a ray or two for him. "Oh, the men, the men!"
>
> "But my dear!" began Defarge.
>
> "But my dear!" repeated madame, nodding firmly; "but my dear! You are faint of heart to-night, my dear!"
>
> "Well, then," said Defarge, as if a thought were wrung out of his breast, "it *is* a long time."
>
> "It is a long time," repeated his wife; "and when is it not a long time? Vengeance and retribution require a long time; it is the rule."

"It does not take a long time to strike a man with Lightning," said Defarge.

"How long," demanded madame, composely, "does it take to make and store the lightning? Tell me."

Defarge raised his head thoughtfully, as if there were something in that too.

"It does not take a long time," said madame, "for an earthquake to swallow a town. Eh well! Tell me how long it takes to prepare the earthquake?"

"A long time, I suppose," said Defarge.

"But when it is ready, it takes place, and grinds to pieces everything before it. In the meantime, it is always preparing, though it is not seen or heard. That is your consolation. Keep it."

She tied a knot with flashing eyes, as if it throttled a foe.

"I tell thee," said madame, extending her right hand, for emphasis, "that although it is a long time on the road, it is on the road and coming. I tell thee it never retreats, and never stops. I tell thee it is always advancing. Look around and consider the lives of all the world that we know, consider the faces of all the world that we know, consider the rage and discontent to which the Jacquerie addresses itself with more and more of certainty every hour. Can such things last? Bah! I mock you."

"My brave wife," returned Defarge, standing before her with his head a little bent, and his hands clasped at his back, like a docile and attentive pupil before his catechist, "I do not question all this. But it has lasted a long time, and it is possible—you know well, my wife, it is possible—that it may not come, during our lives."

"Eh well! How then?" demanded madame, tying another knot, as if there were another enemy strangled.

"Well!" said Defarge, with a half-complaining and half-apologetic shrug. "We shall not see the triumph."

"We shall have helped it," returned madame, with her extended hand in strong action. "Nothing that we do, is done in vain. I believe, with all my soul, that we shall see the triumph. But even if not, even if I knew certainly not, show me the neck of an aristocrat and tyrant, and still I would—"

Then madame, with her teeth set, tied a very terrible knot indeed.

"Hold!" cried Defarge, reddening a little as if he felt charged with cowardice; "I too, my dear, will stop at nothing."

"Yes! But it is your weakness that you sometimes need to see
your victim and your opportunity, to sustain you. Sustain yourself
without that. When the time comes, let loose a tiger and a devil;
but wait for the time with the tiger and the devil chained—not
shown—yet always ready."

To be always preparing, unseen and unheard, is Madame Defarge's one
consolation. Dickens has made her childless, somewhat in the mysterious
mode of Lady Macbeth, since somehow we believe that Madame Defarge
too must have nursed an infant. Her dialogue with Defarge has overtones
of Lady Macbeth heartening Macbeth, keying up his resolution to treason
and a kind of parricide. What Dickens has learned from Shakespeare is the
art of counterpointing degrees of terror, of excess, so as to suggest a dread
that otherwise would reside beyond representation. Macbeth, early doubting, seems weak in contrast to his wife's force, but we will see him at his
bloody work, until he becomes an astonishing manifestation of tyranny.
Similarly, Defarge seems little in juxtaposition to his implacable wife, but
we will see him as a demon of courage, skill, and apocalyptic drive, leading
the triumphant assault upon the Bastille.

In his final vision of Madame Defarge, Dickens brilliantly reveals his
masochistic passion for her:

Madame Defarge slightly waved her hand, to imply that she
heard, and might be relied upon to arrive in good time, and so
went through the mud, and round the corner of the prison wall.
The Vengeance and the Juryman, looking after her as she walked
away, were highly appreciative of her fine figure, and her superb
moral endowments.

There were many women at that time, upon whom the time
laid a dreadfully disfiguring hand; but, there was not one among
them more to be dreaded than this ruthless woman, now taking
her way along the streets. Of a strong and fearless character, of
shrewd sense and readiness, of great determination, of that kind of
beauty which not only seems to impart to its possessor firmness
and animosity, but to strike into others an instinctive recognition
of those qualities; the troubled time would have heaved her up,
under any circumstances. But, imbued from her childhood with a
brooding sense of wrong, and an inveterate hatred of a class,
opportunity had developed her into a tigress. She was absolutely
without pity. If she had ever had the virtue in her, it had quite
gone out of her.

It was nothing to her, that an innocent man was to die for the sins of his forefathers; she saw, not him, but them. It was nothing to her, that his wife was to be made a widow and his daughter an orphan; that was insufficient punishment, because they were her natural enemies and her prey, and as such had no right to live. To appeal to her, was made hopeless by her having no sense of pity, even for herself. If she had been laid low in the streets, in any of the many encounters in which she had been engaged, she would not have pitied herself; nor, if she had been ordered to the axe to-morrow, would she have gone to it with any softer feeling than a fierce desire to change places with the man who sent her there.

Such a heart Madame Defarge carried under her rough robe. Carelessly worn, it was a becoming robe enough, in a certain weird way, and her dark hair looked rich under her coarse red cap. Lying hidden in her bosom, was a loaded pistol. Lying hidden at her waist, was a sharpened dagger. Thus accoutred, and walking with the confident tread of such a character, and with the supple freedom of a woman who had habitually walked in her girlhood, bare-foot and bare-legged, on the brown sea-sand, Madame Defarge took her way along the streets.

We can discount Dickens's failed ironies here ("her superb moral endowments") and his obvious and rather tiresome moral judgments upon his own creation. What comes through overwhelmingly is Dickens's desire for this sadistic woman, which is the secret of our desire for her also, and so for her nightmare power over us. "Her fine figure," "that kind of beauty ... firmness and animosity," "a tigress ... absolutely without pity," "a becoming robe enough, in a certain weird way," "her dark hair looked rich," "confident tread ... supple freedom ... bare-foot and bare-legged"— these are the stigmata of a dominatrix. Loaded pistol in her bosom, sharpened dagger at her waist, Madame Defarge is the ultimate phallic woman, a monument to fetishism, to what Freud would have called the splitting of Dickens's ego in the defensive process.

That splitting attains a triumph in the grand wrestling match, where Miss Pross, a Jacob wrestling with the Angel of Death, holds off Madame Defarge in what is supposed to be an instance of Love stronger than Death, but which is all the more effective for its sexual overtones:

Madame Defarge made at the door. Miss Pross, on the instinct of the moment, seized her round the waist in both her arms, and held her tight. It was in vain for Madame Defarge to struggle and to strike; Miss Pross, with the vigorous tenacity of love, always so much stronger than hate, clasped her tight, and even lifted her from the floor in the struggle that they had. The two hands of Madame Defarge buffeted and tore her face; but, Miss Pross, with her head down, held her round the waist, and clung to her with more than the hold of a drowning woman.

Soon, Madame Defarge's hands ceased to strike, and felt at her encircled waist. "It is under my arm," said Miss Pross, in smothered tones, "you shall not draw it. I am stronger than you, I bless Heaven for it. I'll hold you till one or other of us faints or dies!"

Madame Defarge's hands were at her bosom. Miss Pross looked up, saw what it was, struck at it, struck out a flash and a crash, and stood alone—blinded with smoke.

The embrace of Miss Pross clearly has a repressed lesbian passion for Madame Defarge in it, so that more than a transcendent love for Lucie here endows the force of the good with its immovable tenacity. But for the pistol blast, Madame Defarge would have been held until one or the other lady fainted or died. Miss Pross had never struck a blow in her life, but then her father Jacob had been no warrior either. Dickens, master of stage fire, destroyed Madame Defarge in the grand manner, the only fate worthy of so vivid and so passionately desired a creation.

Great Expectations

Together with *David Copperfield*, *Great Expectations* is Dickens's most personal novel. He reread *Copperfield* "to be quite sure I had fallen into no unconscious repetitions" in composing *Great Expectations*, and his wariness helped make Pip his most complex protagonist. We hear Dickens's early traumas again in Pip's voice, and yet the author maintains considerable distance from Pip, as he scarcely does from David Copperfield, whose destiny is to become a Dickensian novelist.

Pip, like Copperfield, is a superb narrator, but he is frequently unkind to himself, and the reader is not expected to share in the severity of Pip's excessive self-condemnations, which partly ensue from his imaginative strength. Pip's imagination always mixes love and guilt, which is very much the mode of Charles Dickens.

George Bernard Shaw, introducing a reprint of *Great Expectations*, remarked that "Pip, like his creator, has no culture and no religion." We need to recall that Shaw told us also that he felt only pity for an even greater writer, whenever he compared the mind of Shakespeare with his own! Shaw's religion was a peculiar kind of Creative Evolution, and his culture compares poorly with his contemporary, Oscar Wilde's. Dickens indeed was a Dickensian in religion, and was deeply grounded in popular culture, as well as in literary culture.

Whether Pip's obsessive and unmerited guilt owes more to popular traditions of shame-culture, or emanates from literary guilt-culture, is very difficult to determine. One critic, Shuli Barzilai, wisely conjectures that Pip's guilt has a deep source in what Freud called "family romances," so that his relationship with Estella is quasi-incestuous, she being (unknowingly) Magwitch's daughter, while Pip becomes the escaped convict's adopted son. What is clear enough is that both Pip and Estella seem doomed to expiate a guilt not at all their own, the guilt of the fathers and the mothers.

Dickens notoriously weakened *Great Expectations* by revising its ending, so that Pip and Estella might be viewed as living together happily ever after. This revision is manifestly at variance with the imaginative spirit of the novel, and is best ignored. Pip, properly read, remains a permanent emblem of something that Dickens could not forgive in himself.

David Copperfield

If the strong writer be defined as one who confronts his own contingency, his own dependent relation on a precursor, then we can discover only a few writers after Homer and the Yahwist who are strong without that sense of contingency. These are the Great Originals, and they are not many; Shakespeare and Freud are among them and so is Dickens. Dickens, like Shakespeare and Freud, had no true precursors, or perhaps it might be more accurate to say he swallowed up Tobias Smollett rather as Shakespeare devoured Christopher Marlowe. Originality, or an authentic freedom from contingency, is Dickens's salient characteristic as an author. Since Dickens's influence has been so immense, even upon writers so unlikely as Dostoyevski and Kafka, we find it a little difficult now to see at first how overwhelmingly original he is.

Dickens now constitutes a facticity or contingency that no subsequent novelist can transcend or evade without the risk of self-maiming. Consider the difference between two masters of modern fiction, Henry James and James Joyce. Is not Dickens the difference? *Ulysses* comes to terms with Dickens, and earns the exuberance it manifests. Poldy is larger, I think, than any single figure in Dickens, but he has recognizably Dickensian qualities. Lambert Strether in *The Ambassadors* has none, and is the poorer for it. Part of the excitement of *The Princess Casamassima* for us must be that, for once, James achieves a Dickensian sense of the outward life, a sense that is lacking even in *The Portrait of a Lady*, and that we miss acutely (at least I do) amidst even the most inward splendors of *The Wings of the Dove* and *The Golden Bowl*.

The Personal History of David Copperfield, indeed the most personal and autobiographical of all Dickens's novels, has been so influential upon all subsequent portraits of the artist as a young man that we have to make a conscious effort to recover our appreciation of the book's fierce originality. It is the first therapeutic novel, in part written to heal the author's self, or at least to solace permanent anxieties incurred in childhood and youth. Freud's esteem for *David Copperfield* seems inevitable, even if it has led to a number of unfortunate readings within that unlikely compound oddly called "Freudian literary criticism."

Dickens's biographer Edgar Johnson has traced the evolution of *David Copperfield* from an abandoned fragment of autobiography, with its powerful but perhaps self-deceived declaration: "I do not write resentfully or angrily: for I know how all these things have worked together to make me what I am." Instead of representing his own parents as being David Copperfield's, Dickens displaced them into the Micawbers, a change that purchased astonishing pathos and charm at the expense of avoiding a personal pain that might have produced greater meaningfulness. But *David Copperfield* was, as Dickens said, his "favourite child," fulfilling his deep need to become his own father. Of no other book would he have said: "I seem to be sending some part of myself into the Shadowy World."

Kierkegaard advised us that "he who is willing to do the work gives birth to his own father," while Nietzsche even more ironically observed that "if one hasn't had a good father, then it is necessary to invent one." *David Copperfield* is more in the spirit of Kierkegaard's adage, as Dickens more or less makes himself David's father. David, an illustrious novelist, allows himself to narrate his story in the first person. A juxtaposition of the start and conclusion of the narrative may be instructive:

> Whether I shall turn out to be the hero of my own life, or whether that station will be held by anybody else, these pages must show. To begin my life with the beginning of my life, I record that I was born (as I have been informed and believe) on a Friday, at twelve o'clock at night. It was remarked that the clock began to strike, and I began to cry, simultaneously.
>
> In consideration of the day and hour of my birth, it was declared by the nurse, and by some sage women in the neighbourhood who had taken a lively interest in me several months

before there was any possibility of our becoming personally acquainted, first, that I was destined to be unlucky in life; and secondly, that I was privileged to see ghosts and spirits; both these gifts inevitably attaching, as they believed, to all unlucky infants of either gender, born towards the small hours on a Friday night.

I need say nothing here, on the first head, because nothing can show better than my history whether that prediction was verified or falsified by the result. On the second branch of the question, I will only remark, that unless I ran through that part of my inheritance while I was still a baby, I have not come into it yet. But I do not at all complain of having been kept out of this property; and if anybody else should be in the present enjoyment of it, he is heartily welcome to keep it.

And now, as I close my task, subduing my desire to linger yet, these faces fade away. But one face, shining on me like a Heavenly light by which I see all other objects, is above them and beyond them all. And that remains.

I turn my head, and see it, in its beautiful serenity, beside me.

My lamp burns low, and I have written far into the night; but the dear presence, without which I were nothing, bears me company.

O Agnes, O my soul, so may thy face be by me when I close my life indeed; so may I, when realities are melting from me, like the shadows which I now dismiss, still find thee near me, pointing upward!

No adroit reader could prefer the last four paragraphs of *David Copperfield* to the first three. The high humor of the beginning is fortunately more typical of the book than the sugary conclusion. Yet the juxtaposition does convey the single rhetorical flaw in Dickens that matters, by which I do not mean the wild pathos that marks the death of Steerforth, or the even more celebrated career of the endlessly unfortunate little Em'ly. If Dickens's image of voice or mode of representation is "stage fire," then his metaphors always will demand the possibility of being staged. Micawber, Uriah Heep, Steerforth in his life (not at the end) are all of them triumphs of stage fire, as are Peggotty, Murdstone, Betsey Trotwood, and even Dora Spenlow. But Agnes is a disaster, and that dreadful "pointing upward!" is not to be borne. You cannot stage Agnes, which would not matter except that she does represent the idealizing and self-mystifying side of David and so she raises the question, Can you, as a reader, stage David? How much stage fire got into him? Or, to be hopelessly reductive, has he a will, as Uriah Heep and Steerforth in their very different ways are wills incarnate?

If there is an aesthetic puzzle in the novel, it is why David has and conveys so overwhelming a sense of disordered suffering and early sorrow in his Murdstone phase, as it were, and before. Certainly the intensity of the pathos involved is out of all proportion to the fictive experience that comes through to the reader. Dickens both invested himself in and withdrew from David, so that something is always missing in the self-representation. Yet the will—to live, to interpret, to repeat, to write—survives and burgeons perpetually. Dickens's preternatural energy gets into David, and is at some considerable variance with the diffidence of David's apparent refusal to explore his own inwardness. What does mark Dickens's representation of David with stage fire is neither the excess of the early sufferings nor the tiresome idealization of the love for Agnes. It is rather the vocation of novelist, the drive to tell a story, particularly one's own story, that apparels David with the fire of what Freud called the drives.

Dickens's greatness in *David Copperfield* has little to do with the much more extraordinary strength that was to manifest itself in *Bleak House*, which can compete with *Clarissa*, *Emma*, *Middlemarch*, *The Portrait of a Lady*, *Women in Love*, and *Ulysses* for the eminence of being the inescapable novel in the language. *David Copperfield* is of another order, but it is the origin of that order, the novelist's account of how she or he burned through experience in order to achieve the Second Birth, into the will to narrate, the storyteller's destiny.

Hard Times

Hard Times is, for Dickens, a strikingly condensed novel, being about one-third of the length of *David Copperfield* and *Bleak House*, the two masterpieces that directly preceded it. Astonishing and aesthetically satisfying as it is, I believe it to be somewhat overpraised by modern criticism, or perhaps praised for some less than fully relevant reasons. Ruskin and Bernard Shaw after him admired the book as a testament to Dickens's conversion away from a commercialized and industrialized England and back towards a supposed juster and more humane society. But to like *Hard Times* because of its anti-Utilitarian ideology is to confuse the book with Carlyle and William Morris, as well as with Ruskin and Shaw. The most balanced judgment of the novel is that of Monroe Engel, who observes that "the greatest virtues of *Hard Times* are Dickens's characteristic virtues, but less richly present in the book than in many others." Gradgrind is poor stuff, and is not even an effective parody of Jeremy Bentham. The strength of the novel is indeed elsewhere, as we might expect in the theatrical Dickens.

And yet *Hard Times* is lacking in stage fire; compared to *Bleak House*, it possesses only a tiny component of the Sublime. Again, as an instance of the plain style, the mode of Esther Summerson's narrative, it is curiously weak, and has moreover such drab characterizations as Sissy Jupe and Stephen Blackpool. Indeed, the book's rhetoric is the most colorless in all of Dickens's work. Though, as Engel insisted, many of Dickens's authorial virtues are present, the book lacks the preternatural exuberance that makes Dickens unique among all novelists. Has it any qualities of its own to recommend our devotion?

I would suggest that the start of any critical wisdom about *Hard Times* is to dismiss every Marxist or other moral interpretation of the book. Yes, Dickens's heart was accurate, even if his notion of Benthamite social philosophy was not, and a great novelist's overt defense of imagination cannot fail to move us. Consider however the outrageous first chapter of *Hard Times*, "The One Thing Needful":

> "Now, what I want is, Facts. Teach these boys and girls nothing but Facts. Facts alone are wanted in life. Plant nothing else, and root out everything else. You can only form the minds of reasoning animals upon Facts; nothing else will ever be of any service to them. This is the principle on which I bring up my own children, and this is the principle on which I bring up these children. Stick to Facts, sir!"
>
> The scene was a plain, bare, monotonous vault of a schoolroom, and the speaker's square forefinger emphasized his observations by underscoring every sentence with a line on the schoolmaster's sleeve. The emphasis was helped by the speaker's square wall of a forehead, which had his eyebrows for its base, while his eyes found commodious cellarage in two dark caves, overshadowed by the wall. The emphasis was helped by the speaker's mouth, which was wide, thin, and hard set. The emphasis was helped by the speaker's voice, which was inflexible, dry, and dictatorial. The emphasis was helped by the speaker's hair, which bristled on the skirts of his bald head, a plantation of firs to keep the wind from its shining surface, all covered with knobs, like the crust of a plum pie, as if the head had scarcely warehouse-room for the hard facts stored inside. The speaker's obstinate carriage, square coat, square legs, square shoulders—nay, his very neckcloth, trained to take him by the throat with an unaccommodating grasp, like a stubborn fact, as it was—all helped the emphasis.

"In this life, we want nothing but Facts, sir; nothing but Facts!"

The speaker, and the schoolmaster, and the third grown person present, all backed a little, and swept with their eyes the inclined plane of little vessels then and there arranged in order, ready to have imperial gallons of facts poured into them until they were full to the brim.

Gradgrind is doubtless Dickens's ultimate revenge upon his own school sufferings; Gradgrind might be called Murdstone run wild, except that Murdstone stays within the circle of caricature, whereas Gradgrind's will is mad, is a drive towards death. And that is where, I now think, the peculiar aesthetic strength of *Hard Times* is to be located. The novel survives as phantasmagoria or nightmare, and hardly as a societal or conceptual bad dream. What goes wrong in it is what Freud called "family romances," which become family horrors. Critics always have noted how really dreadful family relations are in *Hard Times*, as they so frequently are elsewhere in Dickens. A particular power is manifest if we analyze a passage near the conclusion of the penultimate chapter of the first book of the novel, chapter 15, "Father and Daughter":

> "Louisa," returned her father, "it appears to me that nothing can be plainer. Confining yourself rigidly to Fact, the question of Fact you state to yourself is: Does Mr. Bounderby ask me to marry him? Yes, he does. The sole remaining question then is: Shall I marry him? I think nothing can be plainer than that?"
>
> "Shall I marry him?" repeated Louisa, with great deliberation. "Precisely. And it is satisfactory to me, as your father, my clear Louisa, to know that you do not come to the consideration of that question with the previous habits of mind, and habits of life, that belong to many young women."
>
> "No, father," she returned, "I do not."
>
> "I now leave you to judge for yourself," said Mr. Gradgrind. "I have stated the case, as such cases are usually stated among practical minds; I have stated it, as the case of your mother and myself was stated in its time. The rest, my dear Louisa, is for you to decide."
>
> From the beginning, she had sat looking at him fixedly. As he now leaned back in his chair, and bent his deep-set eyes upon her in his turn, perhaps he might have seen one wavering moment in her, when she was impelled to throw herself upon his breast, and give him the pent-up confidences of her heart. But, to see it, he must have overleaped at a bound the artificial barriers he had for

many years been erecting, between himself and all those subtle essences of humanity which will elude the utmost cunning of algebra until the last trumpet ever to be sounded shall blow even algebra to wreck. The barriers were too many and too high for such a leap. With his unbending, utilitarian, matter-of-fact face, he hardened her again; and the moment shot away into the plumbless depths of the past, to mingle with all the lost opportunities that are drowned there.

Removing her eyes from him, she sat so long looking silently towards the town, that he said, at length: "Are you consulting the chimneys of the Coketown works, Louisa?"

"There seems to be nothing there but languid and monotonous smoke. Yet when the night comes, Fire bursts out, father!" she answered, turning quickly.

"Of course I know that, Louisa. I do not see the application of the remark." To do him justice he did not, at all.

She passed it away with a slight motion of her hand, and concentrating her attention upon him again, said, "Father, I have often thought that life is very short."—This was so distinctly one of his subjects that he interposed.

"It is short, no doubt, my dear. Still, the average duration of human life is proved to have increased of late years. The calculations of various life assurance and annuity offices, among other figures which cannot go wrong, have established the fact."

"I speak of my own life, father."

"O indeed? Still," said Mr. Gradgrind, "I need not point out to you, Louisa, that it is governed by the laws which govern lives in the aggregate."

"While it lasts, I would wish to do the little I can, and the little I am fit for. What does it matter?"

Mr. Gradgrind seemed rather at a loss to understand the last four words; replying, "How, matter? What matter, my dear?"

"Mr. Bounderby," she went on in a steady, straight way, without regarding this, "asks me to marry him. The question I have to ask myself is, shall I marry him? That is so, father, is it not? You have told me so, father. Have you not?"

"Certainly, my dear."

"Let it be so. Since Mr. Bounderby likes to take me thus, I am satisfied to accept his proposal. Tell him, father, as soon as you please, that this was my answer. Repeat it, word for word, if you can, because I should wish him to know what I said."

"It is quite right, my dear," retorted her father approvingly, "to be exact. I will observe your very proper request. Have you any wish in reference to the period of your marriage, my child?"

"None, father. What does it matter?"

Mr. Gradgrind had drawn his chair a little nearer to her, and taken her hand. But, her repetition of these words seemed to strike with some little discord on his ear. He paused to look at her, and, still holding her hand, said:

"Louisa, I have not considered it essential to ask you one question, because the possibility implied in it appeared to me to be too remote. But perhaps I ought to do so. You have never entertained in secret any other proposal?"

"Father," she returned, almost scornfully, "what other proposal can have been made to me? Whom have I seen? Where have I been? What are my heart's experiences?"

"My dear Louisa," returned Mr. Gradgrind, reassured and satisfied. "You correct me justly. I merely wished to discharge my duty."

"What do *I* know, father," said Louisa in her quiet manner, "of tastes and fancies; of aspirations and affections; of all that part of my nature in which such light things might have been nourished? What escape have I had from problems that could be demonstrated, and realities that could be grasped?" As she said it, she unconsciously closed her hand, as if upon a solid object, and slowly opened it as though she were releasing dust or ash.

Caricature here has leaped into Ruskin's "stage fire." Gradgrind, quite mad, nevertheless achieves the wit of asking Louisa whether she is consulting the oracular vapors of the Coketown chimneys. Her magnificent, "Yet when the night comes, Fire bursts out, father!" is more than a prophecy of the return of the repressed. It prophesies also the exuberance of Dickens himself, which comes flooding forth in the obvious yet grand metaphor a page later, when poor Louisa closes her hand, as if upon a graspable reality, and slowly opens it to disclose that her heart, like that of Tennyson's protagonist in *Maud*, is a handful of dust.

That is the true, dark power of *Hard Times*. Transcending Dickens's social vision, or his polemic for imagination, is his naked return to the domain of the drives, Eros and Death. The novel ends with an address to the reader that necessarily is far more equivocal than Dickens can have intended:

Dear Reader! It rests with you and me, whether, in our two fields of action, similar things shall be or not. Let them be! We shall sit with lighter bosoms on the hearth, to see the ashes of our fires turn grey and cold.

Presumably, our imaginative escape from Gradgrindism into poetry will lighten our bosoms, even as we watch the reality principle overtake us. But the power of Dickens's rhetoric is in those gray and cold ashes, handfuls of dust that gather everywhere in the pages of *Hard Times*. Gradgrind, or the world without imagination, fails as a satire upon Utilitarianism, but triumphs frighteningly as a representation of the drive beyond the pleasure principle.

Bleak House

Bleak House may not be "the finest literary work the nineteenth century produced in England," as Geoffrey Tillotson called it in 1946. A century that gave us *The Prelude* and Wordsworth's major crisis lyrics, Blake's *Milton* and *Jerusalem*, Byron's *Don Juan*, the principal poems of Shelley, Keats, Tennyson, and Browning, and novels such as *Pride and Prejudice*, *Emma*, *Middlemarch*, and Dickens's own *Hard Times* and *Our Mutual Friend*, is an era of such literary plenitude that a single choice is necessarily highly problematic. Yet there is now something close to critical agreement that *Bleak House* is Dickens's most complex and memorable single achievement. W. J. Harvey usefully sketches just how formidably the novel is patterned:

> *Bleak House* is for Dickens a unique and elaborate experiment in narration and plot composition. It is divided into two intermingled and roughly concurrent stories; Esther Summerson's first-person narrative and an omniscient narrative told consistently in the historic present. The latter takes up thirty-four chapters; Esther has one less. Her story, however, occupies a good deal more than half the novel. The reader who checks the distribution of these two narratives against the original part issues will hardly discern any significant pattern or correlation. Most parts contain a mixture of the two stories; one part is narrated entirely by Esther and five parts entirely by the omniscient author. Such a check does, however, support the view that Dickens did not, as is sometimes supposed, use serial publication in the interest of crude suspense. A sensational novelist, for example, might well have ended a part issue with chapter 31; Dickens subdues the drama by adding

another chapter to the number. The obvious exception to this only proves the rule; in the final double number the suspense of Bucket's search for Lady Dedlock is heightened by cutting back to the omniscient narrative and the stricken Sir Leicester. In general, however, Dickens's control of the double narrative is far richer and subtler than this.

I would add to Harvey the critical observation that Dickens's own narrative will in "his" thirty-four chapters is a will again different in kind from the will to tell her story of the admirable Esther Summerson. Dickens's (or the omniscient, historical present narrator's) metaphor of representation is one of "stage fire": wild, free, unconditioned, incessant with the force of Freud's domain of those grandly indefinite frontier concepts, the drives. Esther's mode of representation is certainly not flat or insipid; for all of her monumental repressions, Esther finally seems to me the most mysteriously complex and profound personage in *Bleak House*. Her narrative is not so much plain style as it is indeed repressed in the precise Freudian sense of "repression," whose governing metaphor, in Esther's prose as in Freud's, is flight from, rather than a pushing down or pushing under. Esther frequently forgets, purposefully though "unconsciously," what she cannot bear to remember, and much of her narrative is her strong defense against the force of the past. Esther may not *appear* to change as she goes from little girl to adult, but that is because the rhythm of her psyche, unlike Dickens's own, is one of unfolding rather than development. She is Dickens's Muse, what Whitman would have called his "Fancy," as in the great death-lyric "Good-bye, my Fancy!" or what Stevens would have called Dickens's "Interior Paramour."

Contrast a passage of Esther's story with one of Dickens's own narrative, from the end of chapter 56, "Pursuit," and toward the close of the next chapter, "Esther's Narrative":

Mr. Jarndyce, the only person up in the house, is just going to bed; rises from his book, on hearing the rapid ringing at the bell; and comes down to the door in his dressing-gown.

"Don't be alarmed sir." In a moment his visitor is confidential with him in the hall, has shut the door, and stands with his hand upon the lock. "I've had the pleasure of seeing you before. Inspector Bucket. Look at that handkerchief, sir, Miss Esther Summerson's. Found it myself put away in a drawer of Lady Dedlock's, quarter of an hour ago. Not a moment to lose. Matter of life or death. You know. Lady Dedlock?"

"Yes."

"There has been a discovery there, to-day. Family affairs have come out. Sir Leicester Dedlock, Baronet, has had a fit—apoplexy or paralysis—and couldn't be brought to, and precious time has been lost. Lady Dedlock disappeared this afternoon, and left a letter for him that looks bad. Run your eye over it. Here it is!"

Mr. Jarndyce having read it, asks him what he thinks? "I don't know. It looks like suicide. Anyways, there's more and more danger, every minute, of its drawing to that. I'd give a hundred pound an hour to have got the start of the present time. Now, Mr. Jarndyce, I am employed by Sir Leicester Dedlock, Baronet, to follow her and find her—to save her, and take her his forgiveness. I have money and full power, but I want something else. I want Miss Summerson."

Mr. Jarndyce, in a troubled voice, repeats "Miss Summerson?"

"Now, Mr. Jarndyce"; Mr. Bucket has read his face with the greatest attention all along: "I speak to you as a gentleman of a humane heart, and under such pressing circumstances as don't often happen. If ever delay was dangerous, it's dangerous now; and if ever you couldn't afterwards forgive yourself for causing it, this is the time. Eight or ten hours, worth, as I tell you, a hundred pound apiece at least, have been lost since Lady Dedlock disappeared. I am charged to find her. I am Inspector Bucket. Besides all the rest that's heavy on her, she has upon her, as she believes, suspicion of murder. If I follow her alone, she, being in ignorance of what Sir Leicester Dedlock, Baronet, has communicated to me, may be driven to desperation. But if I follow her in company with a young lady, answering to the description of a young lady that she has a tenderness for—I ask no question, and I say no more than that—she will give me credit for being friendly. Let me come up with her, and be able to have the hold upon her of putting that young lady for'ard, and I'll save her and prevail with her if she is alive. Let me come up with her alone—a harder matter—and I'll do my best; but I don't answer for what the best may be. Time flies; it's getting on for one o'clock. When one strikes, there's another hour gone; and it's worth a thousand pound now, instead of a hundred."

This is all true, and the pressing nature of the case cannot be questioned. Mr. Jarndyce begs him to remain there, while he speaks to Miss Summerson. Mr. Bucket says he will; but acting on his usual principle, does no such thing—following up-stairs instead, and keeping his man in sight. So he remains, dodging and lurking about in the gloom of the staircase while they confer. In a very little time, Mr. Jarndyce comes down, and tells him that Miss Summerson will join him directly, and place herself under his protection, to accompany him where he pleases. Mr. Bucket, satisfied, expresses high approval; and awaits her coming, at the door.

There, he mounts a high tower in his mind, and looks out far and wide. Many solitary figures he perceives, creeping through the streets; many solitary figures out on heaths, and roads, and lying under haystacks. But the figure that he seeks is not among them. Other solitaries he perceives, in nooks of bridges, looking over; and in shadowed places down by the river's level; and a dark, dark, shapeless object drifting with the tide, more solitary than all, clings with a drowning hold on his attention.

Where is she? Living or dead, where is she? If, as he folds the handkerchief and carefully puts it up, it were able, with an enchanted power, to bring before him the place where she found it, and the night landscape near the cottage where it covered the little child, would he descry her there? On the waste, where the brick-kilns are burning with a pale blue flare; where the straw-roofs of the wretched huts in which the bricks are made, are being scattered by the wind; where the clay and water are hard frozen, and the mill in which the gaunt blind horse goes round all day, looks like an instrument of human torture; traversing this deserted blighted spot, there is a lonely figure with the sad world to itself, pelted by the snow and driven by the wind, and cast out, it would seem, from all companionship. It is the figure of a woman, too; but it is miserably dressed, and no such clothes ever came through the hall, and out at the great door, of the Dedlock mansion.

The transparent windows with the fire and light, looking so bright and warm from the cold darkness out of doors, were soon gone, and again we were crushing and churning the loose snow. We went on with toil enough; but the dismal roads were not much worse than they had been, and the stage was only nine miles. My companion smoking on the box—I had thought at the last inn of begging him to do so, when I saw him standing at a great fire in a comfortable cloud of tobacco—was as vigilant as ever; and as quickly down and up again, when we came to any human abode or any human creature. He had lighted his little dark lantern, which seemed to be a favourite with him, for we had lamps to the carriage; and every now and then he turned it upon me, to see that I was doing well. There was a folding-window to the carriage-head, but I never closed it, for it seemed like shutting out hope.

We came to the end of the stage, and still the lost trace was not recovered. I looked at him anxiously when we stopped to change; but I knew by his yet graver face, as he stood watching the ostlers, that he had heard nothing. Almost in an instant afterwards, as I leaned back in my seat, he looked in, with his lighted lantern in his hand, an excited and quite different man.

"What is it?" said I, starting. "Is she here?"

"No, no. Don't deceive yourself, my dear. Nobody's here. But I've got it!"

The crystallised snow was in his eyelashes, in his hair, lying in ridges on his dress. He had to shake it from his face, and get his breath before he spoke to me.

"Now, Miss Summerson," said he, beating his finger on the apron, "don't you be disappointed at what I'm a going to do. You know me. I'm Inspector Bucket, and you can trust me. We've come a long way; never mind. Four horses out there for the next stage up! Quick!"

There was a commotion in the yard, and a man carne running out of the stables to know "if he meant up or down?" "Up, I tell you! Up! Ain't it English? Up!"

"Up?" said I, astonished. "To London! Are we going back?"

"Miss Summerson," he answered, "back. Straight back as a die. You know me. Don't be afraid. I'll follow the other, by G—."

"The other?" I repeated. "Who?"

"You called her Jenny, didn't you? I'll follow her. Bring those two pair out here, for a crown a man. Wake up, some of you!"

"You will not desert this lady we are in search of; you will not abandon her on such a night, and in such a state of mind as I know her to be in!" said I, in an agony, and grasping his hand.

"You are right, my dear, I won't. But I'll follow the other. Look alive here with them horses. Send a man for'ard in the saddle to the next stage, and let him send another for'ard again, and order four on, up, right through. My darling, don't you be afraid!"

These orders, and the way in which he ran about the yard, urging them, caused a general excitement that was scarcely less bewildering to me than the sudden change. But in the height of the: confusion, a mounted man galloped away to order the relays, and our horses were put to with great speed.

"My dear," said Mr. Bucket, jumping up to his seat, and looking in again—"you'll excuse me if I'm too familiar—don't you fret
and worry yourself no more than you can help. I say nothing else
at present; but you know me, my dear; now, don't you?"

I endeavoured to say that I knew he was far more capable than
I of deciding what we ought to do; but was he sure that this was
right? Could I not go forward by myself in search of—I grasped
his hand again in my distress, and whispered it to him—of my own
mother.

"My dear," he answered, "I know, I know, and would I put you
wrong, do you think? Inspector Bucket. Now you know me, don't
you?"

What could I say but yes!

"Then you keep up as good a heart as you can, and you rely
upon me for standing by you, no less than by Sir Leicester
Dedlock, Baronet. Now, are you right there?"

"All right, sir!"

"Off she goes, then. And get on, my lads!"

We were again upon the melancholy road by which we had
come; tearing up the miry sleet and thawing snow, as if they were
torn up by a waterwheel.

Both passages are extraordinary, by any standards, and certainly
"Pursuit" has far more stage fire than "Esther's Narrative," but this time-
lier repressive shield, in part, is broken through, and a fire leaps forth out
of her. If we start with "Pursuit," however, we are likelier to see what it is
that returns from the repressed in Esther, returns under the sign of negation (as Freud prophesied), so that what comes back is primarily cognitive,
while the affective aspect of the repression persists. We can remember the
opening of *David Copperfield*, where Dickens in his *persona* as David dis-
avows the gift of second sight attributed to him by the wise women and
gossips. Inspector Bucket, at the conclusion of the "Pursuit" chapter, is
granted a great vision, a preternatural second sight of Esther's lost mother, Lady Dedlock. What Bucket *sees* is stage fire at its most intense, the
novelist's will to tell become an absolute vision of the will. Mounting a high
tower in his mind, Bucket (who thus becomes Dickens's authorial will)
looks out, far and wide, and sees the truth: "a dark, dark, shapeless object
drifting with the tide, more solitary than all," which "clings with a drowning hold on his attention." That "drowning hold" leads to the further
vision: "where the clay and water are hard frozen, and the mill in which the
gaunt blind horse goes round all day." I suspect that Dickens here has a

debt to Browning's great romance, "Childe Roland to the Dark Tower Came," where another apparent instrument of human torture in a deserted, blighted spot, is seen by a companionless figure as being in association with a starving blind horse, cast out from the Devil's stud, who provokes in Browning's narrator the terrible outcry that he never saw a beast he hated so, because: "He must be wicked to deserve such pain."

The ensuing chapter of "Esther's Narrative" brilliantly evokes the cognitive return of Esther's acknowledgment of her mother, under the sign of a negation of past affect. Here the narrative vision proceeds, not in the sublime mode of Bucket's extraordinary second sight, but in the grave, meditative lyricism that takes us first to a tentative return from unconscious flight through an image of pursuit of the fleeing, doomed mother: "The transparent windows with the fire and light, looking so bright and warm from the cold darkness out of doors, were soon gone, and again we were crushing and churning the loose snow." That "crushing and churning" images the breaking of the repressive shield, and Dickens shrewdly ends the chapter with Esther's counterpart to Bucket's concluding vision of a Browningesque demonic water mill, torturing consciousness into a return from flight. Esther whispers to Bucket that she desires to go forward by herself in search of her own mother, and the dark pursuit goes on in the sinister metaphor of the sleet and thawing snow, shield of repression, being torn up by a waterwheel that recirculates the meaning of memory's return, even as it buries part of the pains of abandonment by the mother once more: "We were again upon the melancholy road by which we had come; tearing up the miry sleet and thawing snow, as if they were torn up by a waterwheel."

It is a terrifying triumph of Dickens's art that, when "Esther's Narrative" resumes, in chapter 59, we know inevitably that we are headed straight for an apocalyptic image of what Shakespeare, in *King Lear*, calls "the promised end" or "image of that horror," here not the corpse of the daughter, but of the mother. Esther goes, as she must, to be the first to touch and to see, and with no affect whatsoever, unveils the truth:

> I passed on to the gate, and stooped down. I lifted the heavy head, put the long dank hair aside, and turned the face. And it was my mother, cold and dead.

Anthony Trollope

(1815–1882)

Barchester Towers and *The Warden*

THE WARDEN AND BARCHESTER TOWERS ARE VERY DIFFERENT NOVELS, BUT forever linked by continuities of composition, contest, and personages. Unlike *The Warden*, *Barchester Towers* essentially is a comic novel. Trollope is hardly a novelist whom we can characterize in simple terms, because there are wholly equivocal elements in his narrative art. He can be very funny indeed and I agree with Christopher Herbert's contention that Trollope subtly dissented from his era's overt deprecation of fleshly and worldly pleasures. But Trollope was scarcely a hedonist or a vitalist and his dissent was limited; not half-hearted, but rhetorically muted. You have to read him with an intense awareness of tone, as Herbert does, in order to hear his comic endorsement of desire and to apprehend that he is not a sentimentalist in the ostensible religion of married love that is generally imposed upon him. Herbert persuades me, as against the views of such critics as J. Hillis Miller and Walter M. Kendrick, who threaten unwittingly to drown Trollope in a bathos he himself had fought against. Yet there is a missing quality in Trollope, a zest or gusto that would recommend his more interesting immoralists to us unreservedly.

C.P. Snow remarked that Trollope was "both skeptical and secretive and it seems not unlikely that, alone with himself, he came to believe ratti-er little." That is convincing to me, since neither the theology nor the national church politics of *The Warden* and *Barchester Towers* greatly concern Trollope, whose interest is rather in the agon of personalities. Novels, as everyone agrees, trade in morals and manners, but the puzzle of Trollope is that we never quite can establish his stance as a moralist, if only because it is more evasive and more personal than it presents itself as being. Snow

119

usefully reminds us that, a decade after *Barchester Towers*, Trollope stood as a Liberal candidate for Parliament, a venture consonant with lifelong Whiggish sympathies on Trollope's part. In *Barchester Towers*, Trollope clearly favors the Tory, High Church group of the archdeacon and his friends over the Liberal Evangelicals: Bishop Proudie, the haughty Mrs. Proudie, the reprehensible chaplain Slope. Snow calls this a crossing of Trollope's vote, but I suppose instead we might call this Trollope's own version of comic realism, inherited by him from his master, Thackeray. More than Thackeray, Trollope seems to know implicitly that "comic realism" is a kind of oxymoron. Jacobean comedy, which Herbert demonstrates to be one of Trollope's prime sources, can be quite phantasmagoric, if not as wildly so as Jacobean tragedy. Fletcher, Massinger, and Middleton at once excited Trollope's overt moral disapproval and his deeper interest, since Fletcher in particular was a quarry for Trollope, as Herbert observes:

> It is easy to extract from Trollope's annotations a typical Victorian condemnation of the vein of sexual scandal that runs through comedy; Jeremy Collier himself was hardly more indignant than Trollope at the pervading immorality of the comic stage. Yet major qualifications must at once be made to such a comparison. For one thing, Trollope constantly declares that even the smuttiest and most "disgusting" comedies, such as Beaumont's and Fletcher's *The Knight of Malta* or Fletcher's *A Wife for a Month*, are in fact highly entertaining in spite of themselves. He condemns the bawdy-tongued heroines of Fletcher's *The Wild-Goose-Chase*, then praises this superlative comedy as "an excellent play, full of wit, with much language almost worthy of Shakespeare." The various characters, he says, "are kept up with such infinite life that the piece is charming to read, and must have charmed when acted"— an equation of "charm" with "life," incidentally, that goes to the heart of our theme. Divided judgments like these highlight the obvious paradox in the spectacle of a prudish Victorian moralist who endlessly describes himself as disgusted and repelled by Jacobean comedy, yet who reads it almost insatiably for decades, and shows, indeed, a special fascination for the very playwright he condemns most strongly for his lewdness (for Trollope read Fletcher's huge body of work twice, first in the early 1850s—this being the only reading project recorded for these dates—then again from 1869 to 1874). One need not be a Freudian analyst to draw the conclusion that Trollope was keenly attracted to the "indecency" of comedy and to the enfranchisement it offered

from the straitjacket of the Victorian cult of sexual purity, particularly with reference to women. His fulminations against it, we
may assume, are in direct proportion to his instinctive attraction
toward it.

The oddest aspect of Trollope in this matter is that he himself augments the repression, beyond even the call of his society, and then the
repressed returns in him, with necessarily greater force. I would revise
Herbert only to that degree; Trollope is far more prudish than his precursor Thackeray and subsequently he exceeds Thackeray in subverting societal expectations. Since Trollope, however, had internalized those expectations, he necessarily subverts himself. Such a narrative process is considerably more difficult to apprehend than is Thackeray's ambivalent stance,
which at once satirizes Vanity Fair yet also stays well within it. There is a
repressed Jacobean vitalist in Trollope, but mostly he maintained the
repression.

Barchester Towers is a social comedy whose realism is consistent if a little uneasy. Kafka partly derived from Dickens, monumental fantasist; we
could not envision Kafka reading, and being influenced by, Trollope. Yet
Trollope's most surprising talent is his inventiveness, which can be simul-
taneously outrageous and persuasive, like social reality itself. The glory of
Barchester Towers, and my own favorite moment in Victorian fiction, is the
superb apotheosis at Mrs. Proudie's reception, when the astonishing Bertie
Stanhope propels the sofa of his invalid sister, the grand vamp La Signora
Madeline Vesey Neroni, on its epic voyage into the proud torso of Mrs.
Proudie:

> "They've got this sofa into the worst possible part of the room;
> suppose we move it. Take care, Madeline."
>
> The sofa had certainly been so placed that those who were
> behind it found great difficulty in getting out; there was but a nar-
> row gangway, which one person could stop. This was a bad
> arrangement, and one which Bertie thought it might be well to
> improve.
>
> "Take care, Madeline," said he, and turning to the fat rector,
> added, "Just help me with a slight push."
>
> The rector's weight was resting on the sofa and unwittingly lent
> all its impetus to accelerate and increase the motion which Bertie
> intentionally originated. The sofa rushed from its moorings and
> ran half-way into the middle of the room. Mrs. Proudie was stand-
> ing with Mr. Slope in front of the signora, and had been trying to

be condescending and sociable; but she was not in the very best of tempers, for she found that, whenever she spoke to the lady, the lady replied by speaking to Mr. Slope. Mr. Slope was a favourite, no doubt, but Mrs. Proudie had no idea of being less thought of than the chaplain. She was beginning to be stately, stiff, and offended, when unfortunately the castor of the sofa caught itself in her lace train and carried away there is no saying how much of her garniture. Gathers were heard to go, stitches to crack, plaits to fly open, flounces were seen to fall, and breadths to expose themselves; a long ruin of rent lace disfigured the carpet and still clung to the vile wheel on which the sofa moved.

So, when a granite battery is raised, excellent to the eyes of warfaring men, is its strength and symmetry admired. It is the work of years. Its neat embrasures, its finished parapets, its casemated stories show all the skill of modern science. But, anon, a small spark is applied to the treacherous fusee—a cloud of dust arises to the heavens—and then nothing is to be seen but dirt and dust and ugly fragments.

We know what was the wrath of Juno when her beauty was despised. We know to what storms of passion even celestial minds can yield. As Juno may have looked at Paris on Mount Ida, so did Mrs. Proudie look on Ethelbert Stanhope when he pushed the leg of the sofa into her lace train.

"Oh, you idiot, Bertie!" said the signora, seeing what had been done and what were to be the consequences.

"Idiot!" re-echoed Mrs. Proudie, as though the word were not half strong enough to express the required meaning; "I'll let him know—" and then looking round to learn, at a glance, the worst, she saw that at present it behoved her to collect the scattered *débris* of her dress.

Bertie, when he saw what he had done, rushed over the sofa and threw himself on one knee before the offended lady. His object, doubtless, was to liberate the torn lace from the castor, but he looked as though he were imploring pardon from a goddess.

"Unhand it, sir!" said Mrs. Proudie. From what scrap of dramatic poetry she had extracted the word cannot be said, but it must have rested on her memory and now seemed opportunely dignified for the occasion.

"I'll fly to the looms of the fairies to repair the damage, if you'll only forgive me," said Ethelbert, still on his knees.

"Unhand it, sir!" said Mrs. Proudie with redoubled emphasis

and all but furious wrath. This allusion to the fairies was a direct mockery and intended to turn her into ridicule. So at least it seemed to her. "Unhand it, sir!" she almost screamed.

"It's not me; it's the cursed sofa," said Bertie, looking imploringly in her face and holding up both his hands to show that he was not touching her belongings, but still remaining on his knees.

Hereupon the signora laughed; not loud, indeed, but yet audibly. And as the tigress bereft of her young will turn with equal anger on any within reach, so did Mrs. Proudie turn upon her female guest.

"Madam!" she said—and it is beyond the power of prose to tell of the fire which flashed from her eyes.

The signora stared her full in the face for a moment, and then turning to her brother said playfully, "Bertie, you idiot, get up."

By this time the bishop, and Mr. Slope, and her three daughters were around her, and had collected together the wide ruins of her magnificence. The girls fell into circular rank behind their mother, and thus following her and carrying out the fragments, they left the reception-rooms in a manner not altogether devoid of dignity. Mrs. Proudie had to retire and re-array herself.

As soon as the constellation had swept by, Ethelbert rose from his knees and, turning with mock anger to the fat rector, said: "After all it was your doing, sir—not mine. But perhaps you are waiting for preferment, and so I bore it."

Were I the New Longinus, composing *Upon Strong Writing* or *On the Nov Sublime*, I would employ this as one of the greatest comic scenes in literature, when read within its full contest in *Barchester Towers*. Trollope somewhere declares that "the sublime may be mingled with the realistic, if the writer has the power." The creator of Bertie Stanhope—who cheerfully has failed at every possible and improbable career: the Anglican Church, the law, English and German universities, painter in Rome, the Jesuits, Jewish convert in Palestine, sculptor in Carrara, but who remains an absolute original—now gives that creation his finest moment, in the sofa debacle. The comparison of Mrs. Proudie's dress to the granite battery is merely perfect, since dress and granite contain the same entity, aggressive and hostile. The threefold "Unhand it, sir!" will not be matched for forty years, until Wilde's Lady Bracknell commands Jack: "Rise, sir, from this semi-recumbent posture," in one of the few literary works until the early Evelyn Waugh that might be worthy of accommodating Bertie Stanhope. But neither Wilde nor Waugh has anything like the military or naval maneuver in which the Proudie girls "fell into circular rank behind their mother, and thus following her and carrying out the fragments, they left the reception-rooms in a manner not altogether devoid of dignity." Trollope's triumph, more original than we now can realize, has had many imitators since, but this mode of comic disaster remains very much his own.

Charlotte Brontë

(1816-1855)

I

THE THREE BRONTË SISTERS—CHARLOTTE, EMILY JANE, AND ANNE—ARE
unique literary artists whose works resemble one another's far more than they
do the works of writers before or since. Charlotte's compelling novel *Jane
Eyre* and her three lesser yet strong narratives—*The Professor, Shirley,
Villette*—form the most extensive achievement of the sisters, but critics and
common readers alike set even higher the one novel of Emily Jane's,
Wuthering Heights, and a handful of her lyrical poems. Anne's two novels—
Agnes Grey and *The Tenant of Wildfell Hall*—remain highly readable, although
dwarfed by *Jane Eyre* and the authentically sublime *Wuthering Heights*.

Between them, the Brontës can be said to have invented a reltively new
genre, a kind of northern romance, deeply influenced both by Byron's poetry and by his myth and personality, but going back also, more remotely yet
as definitely, to the Gothic novel and to the Elizabethan drama. In a definite, if difficult to establish sense, the heirs of the Brontës include Thomas
Hardy and D.H. Lawrence. There is a harsh vitalism in the Brontës that
finds its match in the Lawrence of *The Rainbow* and *Women in Love*, though
the comparison is rendered problematic by Lawrence's moral zeal,
enchantingly absent from the Brontës' literary cosmos.

The aesthetic puzzle of the Brontës has less to do with the mature
transformations of their vision of Byron into Rochester and Heathcliff,
than with their earlier fantasy-life and its literature, and the relation of that
life and literature to its hero and precursor, George Gordon, Lord Byron.
At his rare worst and silliest, Byron has nothing like this scene from

Charlotte Brontë's "Caroline Vernon," where Caroline confronts the Byronic Duke of Zamorna:

> The Duke spoke again in a single blunt and almost coarse sentence, compressing what remained to be said, "If I were a bearded Turk, Caroline, I would take you to my harem." His deep voice as he uttered this, his high featured face, and dark, large eye burning bright with a spark from the depths of Gehenna, struck Caroline Vernon with a thrill of nameless dread. Here he was, the man Montmorency had described to her. All at once she knew him. Her guardian was gone, something terrible sat in his place.

Byron died his more-or-less heroic death at Missolonghi in Greece on April 19, 1824, aged thirty-six years and three months, after having set an impossible paradigm for authors that has become what the late Nelson Algren called "Hemingway all the way," in a mode still being exploited by Norman Mailer, Gore Vidal, and some of their younger peers. Charlotte was eight, Emily Jane six, and Anne four when the Noble Lord died and when his cult gorgeously flowered, dominating their girlhood and their young womanhood. Byron's passive-aggressive sexuality—at once sadomasochistic, homoerotic, incestuous, and ambivalently narcissistic—clearly sets the pattern for the ambiguously erotic universes of *Jane Eyre* and *Wuthering Heights*. What Schopenhauer named (and deplored) as the Will to Live, and Freud subsequently posited as the domain of the drives, is the cosmos of the Brontës, as it would come to be of Hardy and Lawrence. Byron rather than Schopenhauer is the source of the Brontës' vision of the Will to Live, but the Brontës add to Byron what his inverted Calvinism only partly accepted, the Protestant will proper, a heroic zest to assert one's own election, one's place in the hierarchy of souls.

Jane Eyre and Catherine Earnshaw do not fit into the grand array of heroines of the Protestant will that commences with Richardson's Clarissa Harlowe and goes through Austen's Emma Woodhouse and Fanny Price to triumph in George Eliot's Dorothea Brooke and Henry James's Isabel Archer. They are simply too wild and Byronic, too High Romantic, to keep such company. But we can see them with Hardy's Tess and, even more, his Eustacia Vye, and with Lawrence's Gudrun and Ursula. Their version of the Protestant will stems from the Romantic reading of Milton, but largely in its Byronic dramatization, rather than its more dialectical and subtle analyses in Blake and Shelley, and its more normative condemnation in Coleridge and in the Wordsworth of *The Borderers*.

Jane Eyre

II

The Byronism of Rochester in *Jane Eyre* is enhanced because the narrative is related in the first person by Jane Eyre herself, who is very much an overt surrogate for Charlotte Brontë. As Rochester remarks, Jane is indomitable; as Jane says, she is altogether "a free human being with an independent will." That will is fiercest in its passion for Rochester, undoubtedly because the passion for her crucial precursor is doubly ambivalent; Byron is both the literary father to a strong daughter, and the idealized object of her erotic drive. To Jane, Rochester's first appearance is associated not only with the animal intensities of his horse and dog, but with the first of his maimings. When Jane reclaims him at the novel's conclusion, he is left partly blinded and partly crippled. I do not think that we are to apply the Freudian reduction that Rochester has been somehow castrated, even symbolically, nor need we think of him as a sacrificed Samson figure, despite the author's allusions to Milton's *Samson Agonistes*. But certainly he has been rendered dependent upon Jane, and he has been tamed into domestic virtue and pious sentiment, in what I am afraid must be regarded as Charlotte Brontë's vengeance upon Byron. Even as Jane Eyre cannot countenance a sense of being in any way inferior to anyone whatsoever, Charlotte Brontë could not allow Byron to be forever beyond her. She could acknowledge, with fine generosity, "that I regard Mr. Thackeray as the first of modern masters, and as the legitimate high priest of Truth; I study him accordingly with reverence." But *Vanity Fair* is hardly the seedbed of *Jane Eyre*, and the amiable and urbane Thackeray was not exactly a prototype for Rochester.

Charlotte Brontë, having properly disciplined Rochester, forgave him his Byronic past, as in some comments upon him in one of her letters (to W.S. Williams, August 14, 1848):

> Mr. Rochester has a thoughtful nature and a very feeling heart; he is neither selfish nor self-indulgent; he is ill-educated, misguided; errs, when he does err, through rashness and inexperience: he lives for a time as too many other men live, but being radically better than most men, he does not like that degraded life, and is never happy in it. He is taught the severe lessons of experience and has sense to learn wisdom from them. Years improve him; the effervescence of youth foamed away, what is really good in him still remains. His nature is

like wine of a good vintage, time cannot sour, but only mellows him.
Such at least was the character I meant to portray.

Poor Rochester! If that constituted an accurate critical summary, then
who would want to read the novel? It will hardly endear me to feminist
critics if I observe that much of the literary power of *Jane Eyre* results from
its authentic sadism in representing the very masculine Rochester as a victim of Charlotte Brontë's will-to-power over the beautiful Lord Byron. I
partly dissent, with respect, from the judgment in this regard of our best
feminist critics, Sandra M. Gilbert and Susan Gubar:

> It seems not to have been primarily the coarseness and sexuality of
> *Jane Eyre* which shocked Victorian reviewers ... but ... its "anti-
> Christian" refusal to accept the forms, customs, and standards of
> society—in short, its rebellious feminism. They were disturbed
> not so much by the proud Byronic sexual energy of Rochester as
> by the Byronic pride and passion of Jane herself.

Byronic passion, being an ambiguous entity, is legitimately present
in Jane herself as a psychosexual aggressivity turned both against the self
and against others. Charlotte Brontë, in a mode between those of
Schopenhauer and Freud, knows implicitly that Jane Eyre's drive to
acknowledge no superior to herself is precisely on the frontier between
the psychical and the physical. Rochester is the outward realm that must
be internalized, and Jane's introjection of him does not leave him wholly
intact. Gilbert and Gubar shrewdly observe that Rochester's extensive
sexual experience is almost the final respect in which Jane is not his
equal, but they doubtless would agree that Jane's sexual imagination
overmatches his, at least implicitly. After all, she has every advantage,
because she tells the story, and very aggressively indeed. Few novels
match this one in the author's will-to-power over her reader. "Reader!"
Jane keeps crying out, and then she exuberantly cudgels that reader into
the way things are, as far as she is concerned. Is that battered reader a
man or a woman?
   I tend to agree with Sylvère Monod's judgment that "Charlotte Brontë
is thus led to bully her reader because she distrusts him ... he is a vapid,
conventional creature, clearly deserving no more than he is given."
Certainly he is less deserving than the charmingly wicked and Byronic
Rochester, who is given a lot more punishment than he deserves. I verge
upon saying that Charlotte Brontë exploits the masochism of her male
readers, and I may as well say it, because much of *Jane Eyre*'s rather nasty

power as a novel depends upon its author's attitude towards men, which is nobly sadistic as befits a disciple of Byron.

"But what about female readers?" someone might object, and they might add: "What about Rochester's own rather nasty power? Surely he could not have gotten away with his behavior had he not been a man and well-financed to boot?" But is Rochester a man? Does he not share in the full ambiguity of Byron's multivalent sexual identities? And is Jane Eyre a woman? Is Byron's Don Juan a man? The nuances of gender, *within literary representation*, are more bewildering even than they are in the bedroom. If Freud was right when he reminded us that there are never two in a bed, but a motley crowd of forebears as well, how much truer this becomes in literary romance than in family romance.

Jane Eyre, like *Wuthering Heights*, is after all a romance, however northern, and not a novel, properly speaking. Its standards of representation have more to do with Jacobean melodrama and Gothic fiction than with George Eliot and Thackeray, and more even with Byron's *Lara* and *Manfred* than with any other works. Rochester is no Heathcliff; he lives in a social reality in which Heathcliff would be an intruder even if Heathcliff cared for social realities except as fields in which to take revenge. Yet there is a daemon in Rochester. Heathcliff is almost nothing but daemonic, and Rochester has enough of the daemonic to call into question any current feminist reading of *Jane Eyre*. Consider the pragmatic close of the book, which is Jane's extraordinary account of her wedded bliss:

> I have now been married ten years. I know what it is to live entirely for and with what I love best on earth. I hold myself supremely blest—blest beyond what language can express; because I am my husband's life as fully as he is mine. No woman was ever nearer to her mate than I am; ever more absolutely bone of his bone and flesh of his flesh.
>
> I know no weariness of my Edward's society: he knows none of mine, any more than we each do of the pulsation of the heart that beats in our separate bosoms; consequently, we are ever together. To be together is for us to be at once as free as in solitude, as gay as in company. We talk, I believe, all day long: to talk to each other is but a more animated and an audible thinking. All my confidence is bestowed on him, all his confidence is devoted to me; we are precisely suited in character—perfect concord is the result.
>
> Mr. Rochester continued blind the first two years of our union: perhaps it was that circumstance that drew us so very near—that knit us so very close! for I was then his vision, as I am still his right

hand. Literally, I was (what he often called me) the apple of his eye. He saw nature—he saw books through me; and never did I weary of gazing for his behalf, and of putting into words the effect of field, tree, town, river, cloud, sunbeam—of the landscape before us; of the weather round us—and impressing by sound on his ear what light could no longer stamp on his eye. Never did I weary of reading to him: never did I weary of conducting him where he wished to go: of doing for him what he wished to be done. And there was a pleasure in my services, most full, most exquisite, even though sad—because he claimed these services without painful shame or damping humiliation. He loved me so truly that he knew no reluctance in profiting by my attendance: he felt I loved him so fondly that to yield that attendance was to indulge my sweetest wishes.

What are we to make of Charlotte Brontë's strenuous literalization of Gen. 2:23, her astonishing "ever more absolutely bone of his bone and flesh of his flesh"? Is *that* feminism? And what precisely is that "pleasure in my services, most full, most exquisite, even though sad"? In her "Farewell to Angria" (the world of her early fantasies), Charlotte Brontë asserted that "the mind would cease from excitement and turn now to a cooler region." Perhaps that cooler region was found in *Shirley* or in *Villette*, but fortunately it was not discovered in *Jane Eyre*. In the romance of Jane and Rochester, or of Charlotte Brontë and George Gordon, Lord Byron, we are still in Angria, "that burning clime where we have sojourned too long—its skies flame—the glow of sunset is always upon it—."

Emily Brontë

(1818-1848)

Wuthering Heights

WUTHERING HEIGHTS IS AS UNIQUE AND IDIOSYNCRATIC A NARRATIVE AS *Moby-Dick*, and like Melville's masterwork breaks all the confines of genre. Its sources, like the writings of the other Brontës, are in the fantasy literature of a very young woman, in the poems that made up Emily Brontë's Gondal saga or cycle. Many of those poems, while deeply felt, simply string together Byronic commonplaces. A few of them are extraordinarily strong and match *Wuthering Heights* in sublimity, as in the famous lyric dated January 2, 1846:

No coward soul is mine
No trembler in the world's storm-troubled sphere
I see Heaven's glories shine
And Faith shines equal arming me from Fear

O God within my breast
Almighty ever-present Deity
Life, that in me hast rest
As I Undying Life, have power in Thee

Vain are the thousand creeds
That move men's hearts, unutterably vain,
Worthless as withered weeds
Or idlest froth amid the boundless main

To waken doubt in one
Holding so fast by thy infinity

So surely anchored on
The steadfast rock of Immortality

With wide-embracing love
Thy spirit animates eternal years
Pervades and broods above,
Changes, sustains, dissolves, creates and rears

Though Earth and moon were gone
And suns and universes ceased to be
And thou wert left alone
Every Existence would exist in thee

There is not room for Death
Nor atom that his might could render void
Since thou art Being and Breath
And what thou art may never be destroyed.

We could hardly envision Catherine Earnshaw, let alone Heathcliff, chanting these stanzas. The voice is that of Emily Jane Brontë addressing the God within her own breast, a God who certainly has nothing in common with the one worshipped by the Reverend Patrick Brontë. I do not hear in this poem, despite all its Protestant resonances, any nuance of Byron's inverted Miltonisms. *Wuthering Heights* seems to me a triumphant revision of Byron's *Manfred*, with the revisionary swerve taking Emily Brontë into what I would call an original gnosis, a kind of poetic faith, like Blake's or Emerson's, that resembles some aspects (but not others) of ancient Gnosticism without in any way actually deriving from Gnostic texts. "No coward soul is mine" also emerges from an original gnosis, from the poet's knowing that her *pneuma* or breath-soul, as compared to her less ontological psyche, is no part of the created world, since that world fell even as it was created. Indeed the creation, whether heights or valley, appears in *Wuthering Heights* as what the ancient Gnostics called the *kenoma*, a cosmological emptiness into which *we have been thrown*, a trope that Catherine Earnshaw originates for herself. A more overt Victorian Gnostic, Dante Gabriel Rossetti, made the best (if anti-feminist) observation on the setting of *Wuthering Heights*, a book whose "power and sound style" he greatly admired:

It is a fiend of a book, an incredible monster, combining all the stronger female tendencies from Mrs. Browning to Mrs.

Brownrigg. The action is laid in Hell,—only it seems places and people have English names there.

Mrs. Brownrigg was a notorious eighteenth-century sadistic and murderous midwife, and Rossetti rather nastily imputed to *Wuthering Heights* a considerable female sadism. The book's violence is astonishing but appropriate, and appealed darkly both to Rossetti and to his close friend, the even more sadomasochistic Swinburne. Certainly the psychodynamics of the relationship between Heathcliff and Catherine go well beyond the domain of the pleasure principle. Gilbert and Gubar may stress too much that Heathcliff is Catherine's whip, the answer to her most profound fantasies, but the suggestion was Emily Brontë's before it became so fully developed by her best feminist critics.

Walter Pater remarked that the precise use of the term *romantic* did not apply to Sir Walter Scott, but rather:

> Much later, in a Yorkshire village, the spirit of romanticism bore a more really characteristic fruit in the work of a young girl, Emily Brontë, the romance of *Wuthering Heights*; the figures of Hareton Earnshaw, of Catherine Linton, and of Heathcliff—tearing open Catherine's grave, removing one side of her coffin, that he may really lie beside her in death—figures so passionate, yet woven on a background of delicately beautiful, moorland scenery, being typical examples of that spirit.

I always have wondered why Pater found the Romantic spirit more in Hareton and the younger Catherine than in Catherine Earnshaw, but I think now that Pater's implicit judgment was characteristically shrewd. The elder Catherine is the problematical figure in the book; she alone belongs to both orders of representation, that of social reality and that of otherness, of the Romantic Sublime. After she and the Lintons, Edgar and Isabella, are dead, then we are wholly in Heathcliff's world for the last half-year of his life, and it is in that world that Hareton and the younger Catherine are portrayed for us. They are—as Heathcliff obscurely senses—the true heirs to whatever societally possible relationship Heathcliff and the first Catherine could have had.

Emily Brontë died less than half a year after her thirtieth birthday, having finished *Wuthering Heights* when she was twenty-eight. Even Charlotte, the family survivor, died before she turned thirty-nine, and the world of *Wuthering Heights* reflects the Brontë reality: the first Catherine dies at eighteen, Hindley at twenty-seven, Heathcliff's son Linton at seventeen, Isabella at thirty-one, Edgar at thirty-nine, and Heathcliff at thirty-seven or thirty-eight. It is a world where you marry early, because you will not live long. Hindley is twenty when he marries Frances, while Catherine Earnshaw is seventeen when she marries the twenty-one-year-old Edgar Linton. Heathcliff is nineteen when he makes his hellish marriage to poor Isabella, who is eighteen at the time. The only happy lovers, Hareton and the second Catherine, are twenty-four and eighteen, respectively, when they marry. Both patterns—early marriage and early death—are thoroughly High Romantic, and emerge from the legacy of Shelley, dead at twenty-nine, and of Byron, martyred to the cause of Greek independence at thirty-six.

The passions of Gondal are scarcely moderated in *Wuthering Heights*, nor could they be; Emily Brontë's religion is essentially erotic, and her vision of triumphant sexuality is so mingled with death that we can imagine no consummation for the love of Heathcliff and Catherine Earnshaw except death. I find it difficult therefore to accept Gilbert and Gubar's reading in which *Wuthering Heights* becomes a Romantic feminist critique of *Paradise Lost*, akin to Mary Shelley's *Frankenstein*. Emily Brontë is no more interested in refuting Milton than in sustaining him. What Gilbert and Gubar uncover in *Wuthering Heights* that is antithetical to *Paradise Lost* comes directly from Byron's *Manfred*, which certainly is a Romantic critique of *Paradise Lost*. *Wuthering Heights* is *Manfred* converted to prose romance, and Heathcliff is more like Manfred, Lara, and Byron himself than is Charlotte Brontë's Rochester.

Byronic incest—the crime of Manfred and Astarte—is no crime for Emily Brontë, since Heathcliff and Catherine Earnshaw are more truly brother and sister than are Hindley and Catherine. Whatever inverted morality—a curious blend of Catholicism and Calvinism—Byron enjoyed, Emily Brontë herself repudiates, so that *Wuthering Heights* becomes a critique of *Manfred*, though hardly from a conventional feminist perspective. The furious energy that is loosed in *Wuthering Heights* is precisely Gnostic; its aim is to get back to the original Abyss, before the creation-fall. Like Blake, Emily Brontë identifies her imagination with the Abyss, and her *pneuma* or breath-soul with the Alien God, who is antithetical to the God of the creeds. The heroic rhetoric of Catherine Earnshaw is beyond every ideology, every merely social formulation, beyond even the dream of justice or of a better life, because it is beyond this cosmos, "this shattered prison":

"Oh, you see, Nelly! he would not relent a moment, to keep me out of the grave! *That* is how I'm loved! Well, never mind! That is

not my Heathcliff. I shall love mine yet; and take him with me—
he's in my soul. And," added she, musingly, "the thing that irks me
most is this shattered prison, after all. I'm tired, tired of being
enclosed here. I'm wearying to escape into that glorious world,
and to be always there; not seeing it dimly through tears, and
yearning for it through the walls of an aching heart; but really
with it, and in it. Nelly, you think you are better and more fortunate than I; in full health and strength. You are sorry for me—very
soon that will be altered. I shall be sorry for *you*. I shall be incom-
parably beyond and above you all. I *wonder* he won't be near me!"
She went on to herself. "I thought he wished it. Heathcliff, dear!
you should not be sullen now. Do come to me, Heathcliff."

Whatever we are to call the mutual passion of Catherine and
Heathcliff, it has no societal aspect and neither seeks nor needs societal
sanction. Romantic love has no fiercer representation in all of literature.
But "love" seems an inadequate term for the connection between Catherine
and Heathcliff. There are no elements of transference in that relation, nor
can we call the attachment involved either narcissistic or anaclitic. If Freud
is not applicable, then neither is Plato. These extraordinary vitalists,
Catherine and Heathcliff, do not desire in one another that which each does
not possess, do not lean themselves against one another, and do not even
find and thus augment their own selves. They *are* one another, which is neither sane nor possible, and which does not support any doctrine of liberation whatsoever. Only that most extreme of visions, Gnosticism, could
accommodate them, for, like the Gnostic adepts, Catherine and Heathcliff
can only enter the *pleroma* or fullness together, as presumably they have
done after Heathcliff's self-induced death by starvation.

Blake may have promised us the Bible of Hell; Emily Brontë seems to
have disdained Heaven and Hell alike. Her finest poem (for which we have
no manuscript, but it is inconceivable that it could have been written by
Charlotte) rejects every feeling save her own inborn "first feelings" and every
world except a vision of earth consonant with those inaugural emotions:

Often rebuked, yet always back returning
    To those first feelings that were born with me,
And leaving busy chase of wealth and learning
    For idle dreams of things which cannot be:

To-day, I will seek not the shadowy region;
    Its unsustaining vastness waxes drear;

And visions rising, legion after legion,
　　Bring the unreal world too strangely near.

I'll walk, but not in old heroic traces,
　　And not in paths of high morality,
And not among the half-distinguished faces,
　　The clouded forms of long-past history.

I'll walk where any own nature would be leading:
　　It vexes me to choose another guide:
Where the gray flocks in ferny glens are feeding;
　　Where the wild wind blows on the mountain side.

What have those lonely mountains worth revealing?
　　More glory and more grief than I can tell:
The earth that wakes *one* human heart to feeling
　　Can centre both the worlds of Heaven and Hell.

Whatever that centering is, it is purely individual, and as beyond gender as it is beyond creed or "high morality." It is the voice of Catherine Earnshaw, celebrating her awakening from the dream of heaven:

"I was only going to say that heaven did not seem to be my home; and I broke my heart with weeping to come back to earth; and the angels were so angry that they flung me out, into the middle of the heath on the top of Wuthering Heights; where I woke sobbing for joy."

George Eliot

(1819-1880)

Even taken in its derivative meaning of outline, what is form but the limit of that deference by which we discriminate one object from another?—a limit determined partly by the intrinsic relations or composition of the object, & partly by the extrinsic action of other bodies upon it. This is true whether the object is a rock or a man ...
—GEORGE ELIOT, "Notes on Forms in Art"

I

IT WAS FREUD, IN OUR TIME, WHO TAUGHT US AGAIN WHAT THE PRE-Socratics taught: *ethos* is the *daimon*, character is fate. A generation before Freud, George Eliot taught the same unhappy truth to her contemporaries. If character is fate, then in a harsh sense there can be no accidents. Character presumably is less volatile than personality, and we tend to disdain anyone who would say: personality is fate. Personalities suffer accidents; characters endure fate. If we seek major personalities among the great novelists, we find many competitors: Balzac, Tolstoi, Dickens, Henry James, even the enigmatic Conrad. By general agreement, the grand instance of a moral character would be George Eliot. She has a nearly unique spiritual authority, best characterized by the English critic Walter Allen about twenty years ago:

> George Eliot is the first novelist in the world in some things, and they are the things that come within the scope of her moral interpretation of life. Circumscribed though it was, it was certainly not narrow; nor did she ever forget the difficulty attendant upon the moral life and the complexity that goes to its making.

Her peculiar gift, almost unique despite her place in a tradition of displaced Protestantism that includes Samuel Richardson's *Clarissa* and Wordsworth's poetry, is to dramatize her interpretations in such a way as to abolish the demarcations between aesthetic pleasure and moral renunciation. Richardson's heroine, Clarissa Harlowe, and Wordsworth in his best poems share in a compensatory formula: experiential loss can be transformed into imaginative gain. Eliot's imagination, despite its Wordsworthian antecedents, and despite the ways in which Clarissa Harlowe is the authentic precursor of Dorothea Brooke in *Middlemarch*, is too severe to accept the formula of compensation. The beauty of renunciation in Eliot's fiction does not result from a transformation of loss, but rather from a strength that is in no way dependent upon exchange or gain. Eliot presents us with the puzzle of what might be called the Moral Sublime. To her contemporaries, this was no puzzle. F.W.H. Myers, remembered now as a "psychic researcher" (a marvelous metaphor that we oddly use as a title for those who quest after spooks) and as the father of L.H. Myers, author of the novel *The Near and the Far*, wrote a famous description of Eliot's 1873 visit to Cambridge:

> I remember how at Cambridge I walked with her once in the Fellows' Garden of Trinity, on an evening of rainy May; and she, stirred somewhat beyond her wont, and taking as her text the three words which had been used so often as the inspiring trumpet-call of men—the words God, Immortality, Duty—pronounced with terrible earnestness how inconceivable was the first, how unbelievable was the second, and yet how peremptory and absolute the third. Never, perhaps, have sterner accents confirmed the sovereignty of impersonal and unrecompensing Law. I listened, and night fell; her grave, majestic countenance turned towards me like a sybil's in the gloom; it was as though she withdrew from my grasp, one by one, the two scrolls of promise and left me the third scroll only, awful with inevitable fates. And when we stood at length and parted, amid that columnar circuit of forest trees, beneath the last twilight of starless skies, I seemed to be gazing, like Titus at Jerusalem, on vacant seats and empty halls—on a sanctuary with no Presence to hallow it, and heaven left empty of God.

However this may sound now, Myers intended no ironies. As the sybil of "unrecompensing Law," Eliot joined the austere company of nineteenth-century prose prophets: Carlyle, Ruskin, Newman and Arnold in England; Emerson in America; Schopenhauer, Nietzsche, Kierkegaard and finally Freud on the Continent. But this ninefold, though storytellers of a sort, wrote no novels. Eliot's deepest affinities were scarcely with Dickens, Thackeray, and Trollope, and yet her formal achievement requires us to read her as we read them. This causes difficulties, since Eliot was not a great stylist, and was far more immersed in philosophical than in narrative tradition. Yet her frequent clumsiness in authorial asides and her hesitations in storytelling matter not at all. We do not even regret her absolute lack of any sense of the comic, which never dares take revenge upon her anyway. Wordsworth at his strongest, as in "Resolution and Independence," still can be unintentionally funny (which inspired the splendid parodies of the poem's leech-gatherer and its solipsistic bard in Lewis Carroll's "White Knight's Ballad," and Edward Lear's "Incidents in the Life of my uncle Arly"). But I have seen no effective parodies of George Eliot, and doubt their possibility. It is usually unwise to be witty concerning our desperate need, not only to decide upon right action, but also to will such action, against pleasure and against what we take to be self-interest. Like Freud, Eliot ultimately is an inescapable moralist, precisely delineating our discomfort with culture, and remorselessly weighing the economics of the psyche's civil wars.

II

George Eliot is not one of the great letter writers. Her letters matter because they are hers, and in some sense do tell part of her own story, but they do not yield to a continuous reading. On a scale of nineteenth-century letter-writing by important literary figures, in which Keats would rank first, and Walter Pater last (the Paterian prose style is never present in his letters), Eliot would find a place about dead center. She is always herself in her letters, too much herself perhaps, but that self is rugged, honest, and formidably inspiring. Our contemporary feminist critics seem to me a touch uncomfortable with Eliot. Here she is on extending the franchise to women, in a letter to John Morley (May 14, 1867):

Thank you for your kind remembrance. Your attitude in relation to Female Enfranchisement seems to be very nearly mine. If I were called on to act in the matter, I would certainly not oppose any plan which held out a reasonable promise of tending to establish as far as possible an equivalence of advantages for the two sexes, as to education and the possibilities of free development. I fear you may have misunderstood something I said the other evening about nature. I never meant to urge the "intention of Nature" argument, which is to me a pitiable fallacy. I mean that as a fact of mere zoological evolution, woman seems to me to have the worst share in existence. But for that very reason I would the more contend that in the moral evolution we have "an art which does mend nature"—an art which "itself is nature." It is the function of love in the largest sense, to mitigate the harshness of all fatalities. And in the thorough recognition of that worse share, I think there is a basis for a sublimer resignation in woman and a more regenerating tenderness in man.

However, I repeat that I do not trust very confidently to my own impressions on this subject. The peculiarities of my own lot may have caused me to have idiosyncrasies rather than an average judgment. The one conviction on the matter which I hold with some tenacity is, that through all transitions the goal towards which we are proceeding is a more clearly discerned distinctness of function (allowing always for exceptional cases of individual organization) with as near an approach to equivalence of good for woman and for man as can be secured by the effort of growing moral force to lighten the pressure of hard non-moral outward conditions. It is rather superfluous, perhaps injudicious, to plunge into such deeps as these in a hasty note, but it is difficult to resist the desire to botch imperfect talk with a little imperfect writing.

This is a strong insistence upon form in life as in art, upon the limit of that difference by which we discriminate one object from another. I have heard feminist critics decry it as defeatism, though Eliot speaks of "mere zoological evolution" as bringing about every woman's "worse share in existence." "A sublimer resignation in woman" is not exactly a popular goal these days, but Eliot never speaks of the sublime without profundity and an awareness of human loss. When she praises Ruskin as a teacher "with the inspiration of a Hebrew prophet," she also judges him to be "strongly akin to the sublimest part of Wordsworth," a judgment clearly based upon the Wordsworthian source of Ruskin's tropes for the sense of loss that dominates the sublime experience. The harshness of being a woman, however mitigated by societal reform, will remain, Eliot reminds us, since we cannot mend nature and its unfairness. Her allusion to the Shakespearean "art which does mend nature," and which "itself is nature" (*Winter's Tale*, IV.iv.88–96) subtly emends Shakespeare in the deliberately wistful hope for a moral evolution of love between the sexes. What dominates this letter to Morley is a harsh plangency, yet it is anything but defeatism. Perhaps Eliot should have spoken of a "resigned sublimity" rather than a "sublime resignation," but her art, and life, give the lie to any contemporary feminist demeaning of the author of *Middlemarch*, who shares with Jane Austen and Emily Dickinson the eminence of being the strongest women writers in the English language.

Daniel Deronda

All seven novels by Eliot were immensely popular in her own lifetime. Today there is common consent that *The Mill on the Floss* (1860) and *Middlemarch* (1871–72) are as vital as they were more than a century ago. *Adam Bede* (1859) is respected but not widely read or studied, while *Romola* (1862–63) is rightly forgotten. *Felix Holt, the Radical* (1866) retains some current interest, but less perhaps than *Adam Bede*. *Silas Marner* (1861) remains an extraordinary reading experience, and probably is undervalued by most critics. Rereading it after decades away from it, I find astonishing mythological power throughout its apparently serene pastoralism. The problematic novel by Eliot is of course *Daniel Deronda* (1876), which has divided its readers and will go on confusing them. Dr. Leavis and others proposed the radical solution of quarrying a new novel, *Gwendolyn Harleth*, out of the book, thus creating an achievement for Eliot not unlike the *Emma* or *Persuasion* of Jane Austen. In this drastic operation, the hero, Daniel Deronda himself, was to be all but discarded, primarily on the grounds that his endless nobility was wearisome. Deronda is an incipient Zionist leader who is nine-tenths a prig and only one-tenth a passionate idealist. He simply is not a male Dorothea Brooke, as his scenes with Gwendolyn Harleth invariably show. She vaults off the page; he lacks personality, or else possesses so much character that he sinks with it, into a veritable bathos in a few places.

And yet, as many critics keep remarking, Deronda is not quite so easily discarded, because the remarkable Gwendolyn is convincingly in love with him and also because the even more remarkable George Eliot is in love with him also. Her portrait of George Henry Lewes, her common-law husband, as Will Ladislaw in *Middlemarch* does not persuade us that he is a wholly fit partner, whether for George Eliot or for Dorothea Brooke. Deronda sometimes makes me think him a Jewish Caspar Goodwood, just as Gwendolyn seems half-way between Elizabeth Bennet and Isabel Archer. Henry James, in his equivocal "Daniel Deronda: A Conversation," neatly gives his "Theodora" a positive judgment of Deronda, "Pulcheria" a rather more pungent negative one, and the judicious "Constantius" an ambiguous balance between the two:

Theodora. And the advice he gives Gwendolyn, the things he says to her, they are the very essence of wisdom, of warm human wisdom, knowing life and feeling it. "Keep you fear as a safeguard, it may make consequences passionately present to you." What can be better than that?

Pulcheria. Nothing, perhaps. But what can be drearier than a novel in which the function of the hero—young, handsome, and brilliant—is to give didactic advice, in a proverbial form, to the young, beautiful, and brilliant heroine?

Constantius. That is not putting it quite fairly. The function of Deronda is to have Gwendolyn fall in love with him ...

Constantius adds, rather mordantly: "Poor Gwendolyn's falling in love with Deronda is part of her own luckless history, not of his." The implied view of Deronda here is not too far from that of Robert Louis Stevenson, for whom the visionary Zionist was "the Prince of Prigs." Against all this must be set the reaction of George Eliot herself, dismissing "the laudation of readers who cut the book into scraps and talk of nothing in it but Gwendolyn. I meant everything in the book to be related to everything else there." We can test this relatedness in one of the novel's great moments, when Gwendolyn is compelled to recognize a rejection that she legitimately cannot be expected to understand:

> That was the sort of crisis which was at this moment beginning in Gwendolyn's small life: she was for the first time feeling the pressure of a vast mysterious movement, for the first time being dislodged from her supremacy in her own world, and getting a sense that her horizon was but a dipping onward of an existence with which her own was revolving. All the troubles of her wifehood and widowhood had still left her with the implicit impression which had accompanied her from childhood, that whatever surrounded her was somehow specially for her, and it was because of this that no personal jealousy had been roused in her in relation to Deronda: she could not spontaneously think of him as rightfully belonging to others more than to her. But here had come a shock which went deeper than personal jealousy—something spiritual and vaguely tremendous that thrust her away, and yet quelled all anger into self-humiliation.

Perhaps this is Eliot's greatest power: to represent the falling away of a solipsism, not ignoble as an involuntary movement, into the terror of a sublime solitude. Gwendolyn after all is losing not only her potential lover, but her virtual superego, though a superego very different from the Freudian model. The Freudian superego demands that the hapless ego surrender its aggressivities, and then continues to torment the ego for being too aggressive still. But Deronda is the gravest and most gentlemanly of consciences, perhaps because he mysteriously associates his own shrouded origins with Gwendolyn's undeveloped self. This is the subtle surmise of Martin Price in his *Forms of Life,* a study of "Character and Moral Imagination in the Novel." Price reads Gwendolyn as a character terrorized by her own empty strength of will, oppressed by the potential solitude to which her own will may convey her. Ironically, that fear of the sublime attracts its own doom in the sadistic Grandcourt, who marries Gwendolyn in certainly the most dreadful of all mismatches, even in Eliot. Her strength blocked, her will thwarted, Gwendolyn seems condemned to perpetual death-in-life, until George Eliot rescues her heroine by one of her characteristic drownings, thus relieving Gwendolyn of her error but depriving the reader of a splendidly hateful object in Grandcourt, who is one of Eliot's negative triumphs.

Eliot is masterly in never quiet explaining precisely what draws Deronda to Gwendolyn. Absurd high-mindedness aside, it does seem that Deronda needs the lady's well-developed sense of self, as Price suggests. Himself a kind of changeling, Deronda needs to enact rescue-fantasies, with Gwendolyn taking the place of the absent mother. If that seems too close to Freud's essay "Family Romances," and too far from Eliot's fiction, then we ought to recall the yearnings of Dorothea Brooke and of Lydgate in *Middlemarch*, and Eliot's own lifelong yearnings to "rescue" distinguished male intellectuals. Instilling a moral conscience in the charming Gwendolyn may seem a curious training for a future Zionist uplifter, but in Eliot's universe it is perhaps an inevitable induction for someone determined to be a prophet of his people's moral regeneration.

Price sums up Gwendolyn by associating her with Estella in *Great Expectations* and with Marianne Dashwood in *Sense and Sensibility.* Like them, the even more charming and forceful Gwendolyn must be reduced in scope and intensity in order to become a better person, or perhaps only an imperfect solipsist. Price is very much in Eliot's mode when he counts and accepts the cost of assigning sublimity to *moral* energy: "There is a loss of scale as one dwindles to a moral being; yet it is also the emergence of a self from the welter of assertion and impulse that has often provided an impressive substitute." Something in the reader, something not necessarily daemonic, wants to protest, wants to ask Eliot: "Must there always be a loss in scope? Must one *dwindle* to a moral being?"

* * *

Eliot herself, in her letters, gives one answer theoretically (and it is consistent with the burden of *Daniel Deronda*, and a very different one pragmatically), since she palpably gains scale even as she gorgeously augments her self as a moral being. Whatever her letters may lack as narrative, or in Ruskinian madness, they continuously teach us the necessity of confronting our own moral evasions and self-disenchantments. Here she is in full strength, writing to Mrs. Harriet Beecher Stowe on October 29, 1876:

> As to the Jewish element in "Deronda," I expected from first to last in writing it, that it would create much stronger resistance and even repulsion than it has actually met with. But precisely because I felt that the usual attitude of Christians towards Jews is—I hardly know whether to say more impious or more stupid when viewed in the light of their professed principles, I therefore felt urged to treat Jews with such sympathy and understanding as my nature and knowledge could attain to. Moreover, not only towards the Jews, but towards all oriental peoples with whom we English come in contact, a spirit of arrogance and contemptuous dictatorialness is observable which has become a national disgrace to us. There is nothing I should care more to do, if it were possible, than to rouse the imagination of men and women to a vision of human claims in those races of their fellow-men who most differ from them in customs and beliefs. But towards the Hebrews we western people who have been reared in Christianity, have a peculiar debt and, whether we acknowledge it or not, a peculiar thoroughness of fellowship in religious and moral sentiment. Can anything be more disgusting than to hear people called "educated" making small jokes about eating ham, and showing themselves empty of any real knowledge as to the relation of their own social and religious life to the history of the people they think themselves witty in insulting? They hardly know that Christ was a Jew. And I find men educated at Rugby supposing that Christ spoke Greek. To my feeling, this deadness to the history which has prepared half our world for us, this inability to find interest in any form of life that is not clad in the same coat-tails and flounces as our own lies very close to the worst kind of irreligion. The best that can be said of it is, that it is a sign of the intellectual narrowness—in plain English, the stupidity, which is still the average mark of our culture.

Yes, I expected more aversion than I have found ... I sum up with the writer of the Book of Maccabees "if I have done well, and as befits the subject, it is what I desired, but if I have done ill, it is what I could attain unto" ...

Confronted by that power of moral earnestness, the critic is properly disarmed. It hardly suffices to murmur that Deronda is the Prince of Prigs, or to lament that Gwendolyn's imaginative force and human charm deserved something better than a dwindling down into moral coherence. Eliot is too modest in summing up with the barely inspired writer of the Book of the Maccabees. She sums up with the author of Job, and with Tolstoi. *Daniel Deronda* may be a more vexed creation than *The Mill on the Floss* or *Middlemarch*, but it carries their moral authority, Biblical and Tolstoyan. No one after Eliot has achieved her peculiar and invaluable synthesis between the moral and aesthetic, and perhaps it never will be achieved again.

The Mill on the Floss

The Mill on the Floss (1860) is George Eliot's strongest achievement before *Middlemarch* (1871–72) and remains a vital novel by any standards. Rereading it confirms my earlier annoyance at its inadequate conclusion, the drowning of the heroine Maggie Tulliver, and her beloved brother Tom, by the Floss river in full flood. But this seems the only substantial blemish in one of the major autobiographical novels in the language, comparable to Dickens's *David Copperfield* and prophetic of Lawrence's *Sons and Lovers*. The splendor of *The Mill on the Floss* is almost entirely in Eliot's portrayal of her own earlier phases in the intensely sympathetic: Maggie, whose death most readers fiercely resent. There is no tragic necessity in Maggie's drowning, and I do not believe that literary criticism is capable of explaining why Eliot made so serious a blunder, though recently feminist critics have ventured upon correcting some of Eliot's perspectives. Moral criticism of George Eliot, in my judgment, does not work very well, since the critic, of whatever gender or ideological persuasion, presumes to enter upon a contest with the most formidable and imaginative moralist in the history of the British novel.

I myself can only speculate upon why Eliot decided to destroy her earlier self by drowning the humane and luminous Maggie. Certainly it was not because the novelist could not imagine a form of life for her surrogate self. Maggie moves us most because her yearning demand is for more life, for a sublime relationship to herself, to other selves and to the world. Dr.

F.R. Leavis, who made of an ill-defined "maturity" a critical shibboleth, decided that Maggie was immature and lacked self-knowledge, and so must have reflected a phase in Eliot's development when she was not yet worthy of Leavisite endorsement. Rereading *The Mill on the Floss* is likelier to show the reader that Maggie has a healthy sexual nature and does the best she can for herself in a harsh society, while ultimately restrained by the considerable moral perplexities of her own passionately divided psyche. The center of Maggie's dilemma is her erotic attachment to Stephen Guest, a whipping-boy for critics from Eliot's contemporaries on to ours. Readers of *The Mill on the Floss* need to ask why George Eliot has Maggie renounce Stephen, before they can ask why the author concludes by Maggie's gratuitous death.

"Renunciation," as Emily Dickinson wrote with wit grand and grim, "is a piercing virtue," and perhaps it killed Maggie Tulliver, which is a curious paradox at best, since George Eliot consciously cannot have intended some causal connection between her heroine's abandonment of sexual happiness and subsequent drowning in her brother's embrace. Yet there is an authentic link between the almost unmotivated renunciation and the arbitrarily imposed conclusion. We sense that if Maggie had married Stephen, the Floss would not have flooded. That is an outrageous sentence, I suppose, but not nearly so outrageous as the renunciation, which is a self-violation rather than a self-sacrifice on Maggie's part. And the renunciation, though senseless, is far short of the sentimental outrageousness of the conclusion, with its veiled metaphor of incestuous passion:

> Nothing else was said; a new danger was being carried towards them by the river. Some wooden machinery had just given way on one of the wharves, and huge fragments were being floated along. The sun was rising now, and the wide area of watery desolation was spread out in dreadful clearness around them—in dreadful clearness floated onwards the hurrying, threatening masses. A large company in a boat that was working its way along under the Tofton houses, observed their danger, and shouted, "Get out of the current!"
>
> But that could not be done at once, and Tom, looking before him, saw Death rushing on them. Huge fragments, clinging together in fatal fellowship, made one wide mass across the stream.
>
> "It is coming, Maggie!" Tom said, in a deep hoarse voice, loosing the oars, and clasping her.
>
> The next instant the boat was no longer seen upon the water— and the huge mass was hurrying on in hideous triumph.

> But soon the keel of the boat reappeared, a black speck on the golden water.
>
> The boat reappeared—but brother and sister had gone down in an embrace never to be parted—living through again in one supreme moment, the days when they had clasped their little hands in love, and roamed the daisied fields together.

"Clinging together in fatal fellowship" is the darkly revelatory emphasis of this ending, which compels the reader to surmise that the repressed motive for the renunciation of Stephen was the attachment between sister and brother.

"One supreme moment," since sexual union is barred, has to be mutual immolation. This may seem more like the Shelley of *The Revolt of Islam* than the Wordsworth of *The Excursion*, and certainly would have been rejected as an interpretation by George Eliot herself. But it may help explain so wayward and inadequate a culmination to a novel otherwise worthy of the intense and varied existence, tragically brief, of Maggie Tulliver.

Silas Marner

Silas Marner: The Weaver of Raveloe remains a beautiful and highly readable book, still immensely popular 130 years after its initial publication. It is not quite of the aesthetic eminence of George Eliot's masterwork, *Middlemarch*, but only because it is much the less ambitious novel, far shorter and confined as it is to a small village in the Midlands. Its protagonists are simple people, seen against a background in which the common folk of the countryside and the natural world itself are so interpenetrated that we feel we might be reading a narrative poem by William Wordsworth, whose spirit hovers everywhere. Henry James, writing about *Silas Marner*, and the early *Adam Bede*, George Eliot's first full-length novel, said "her perception was a perception of nature much more than of art," by which he meant that both books thus displayed an artistic weakness. James was not much interested in country folk, and *Silas Marner* is very much a pastoral novel, prophesying Thomas Hardy. We learn to read *Silas Marner* as we read the Book of Ruth in the Bible, or as we mull over Wordsworth's *The Ruined Cottage* or Hardy's *The Return of the Native*. A vision of nature and its processes is as much a part of such pastoral stories as the leading characters are, and Henry James's distinction between a perception of nature and a perception of art fades away in great writings of this kind.

F.R. Leavis sensibly compares *Silas Marner* to Charles Dickens's *Hard Times*, pointing out that both were "moral fables." A moral fable presumably allows for somewhat different standards of probability than a wholly naturalistic fiction could sustain. Silas is truly a rather unlikely prospect, being a half-mad solitary, to have a deserted child deposited upon his hearth, but within the aesthetic borders of what is almost a fairy story (as Leavis observed) the substitution of the little Eppie for Silas's stolen gold and dead sister is wonderfully persuasive:

> When Marner's sensibility returned, he continued the action Which had been arrested, and closed his door, unaware of the Chasm in his consciousness, unaware of any intermediate Change, except that the light had grown dim, and that he was Chilled and faint. He thought he had been too long standing at the door and looking out. Turning towards the hearth where the two logs had fallen apart, and sent forth only a red uncertain glimmer, he seated himself on his fireside chair, and was stooping to push his logs together, when, to his blurred vision, it seemed as if there were on the floor in front of the hearth. Gold!—his own gold!—brought back to him as mysteriously as it had been taken away! He felt his heart beginning to beat violently, and for a few moments he was unable to stretch out his hand and grasp the restored treasure. The heap of gold seemed to glow and get larger beneath his agitated gaze. He leaned forward at last, and stretched forth his hand; but instead of the hard coin with the familiar resisting outline, his fingers encountered oft warm curls. In utter amazement, Silas fell on his knees and bent his head low to examine the marvel: it was a sleeping child—a round, fair thing, with soft yellow rings all over its head. Could this be his little sister come back to him in a dream—his little sister whom he carried about in his arms for a year before she died, when he was a small boy without shoes or stockings? That was the first thought that darted across Silas's blank wonderment. *Was* it a dream? He rose to his feet again, pushed his logs together, and, throwing on some dried leaves and sticks, raised a flame; but the flame did not disperse the vision—it only lit up more distinctly the little round form of the child and its shabby clothing. It was very much like his little sister.

In a fable of regeneration, like Silas Marner, this epiphany has extraordinary plangency and force. George Eliot's art, throughout the book, is almost flawless in its patience. The narrator's stance is one of

Wordsworthian "wise passivity"; it is nature and community working slowly and silently together that regenerate Silas and that punish both the Cass brothers, each in proportion to his hardness of heart. It is the same spirit, of what might be called the natural, simple heart, that is manifested by Eppie when she chooses to stay with Silas rather than return to the wealthy father who abandoned her:

> 'Thank you, ma'am—thank you, sir, for your offers—they're very great, and far above my wish. For I should have no delight in my life any more if I was forced to go away from my father, and knew he was sitting at home, a-thinking of me and feeling lone. We've been used to be happy together every day, and I can't Think o' no happiness without him. And he says he'd nobody i' The world till I was sent to him, and he'd have nothing when I Was gone. And he's took care of me and loved me from the First, and I'll cleave to him as long as he lives, and nobody shall Ever come between him and me.'

"Cleaving" is the Biblical metaphor there and throughout *Silas Marner*. Most moral fables in literature fall away into an Abstract harshness, and become rather bad books. George Eliot's genius vitalizes he fairy story or fabulistic aspect of *Silas Marner*, because of her uncanny power of humanizing all concerns of morality. In a letter to her publisher, she remarked upon "the remedial influence of pure, natural human relations," as she had sought to portray them, and then added a fine, afterthought: "The Nemesis is a very mild one."

Middlemarch

What can we mean when we speak of the "moral authority" of a great novelist? To invoke the phrase, in English, is to intimate George Eliot, rather than Charles Dickens, Henry James, or Joseph Conrad. This is hardly to deny *Bleak House*, *The Bostonians*, or *The Secret Agent* their wealth of moral insight, but rather recognizes an uniqueness in George Eliot.

That there is something grave and majestic that informs *Middlemarch*, we scarcely can evade sensing. The protagonist, Dorothea Brooke, is more than a secular St. Theresa; she is a preternaturally strong soul capable of fighting through her own errors. The strong figures who go under— Bulstrode, the peculiar Casaubon, the self-ruined Lydgate (precursor of Dick Diver in Scott Fitzgerald's *Tender is the Night*)—yield to flaws in their natures. Dorothea, like George Eliot, is a Wordsworthian. Projected sublimity, traditional heroism, is set aside, and a new sublimity shared by the self and nature takes its place.

Dorothea, in her moral intensity, is the ancestress of figures in Thomas Hardy and D.H. Lawrence, but her curious, inward strength has few analogues in other heroines. Henry James, subtly unnerved by *Middlemarch*, indulged in defensive fault-finding, much as he had done with *The Scarlet Letter*. What made James uncomfortable was a sublimity that his great characters, Isabel Archer in particular, were too evasive to sustain.

It has been too easy to confuse George Eliot's moral vision, as even Nietzsche showed, when he scorned her for supposedly believing that you could retain Christian morality while discarding the Christian God. George Eliot's advocacy of renunciation is not Christian, any more than Goethe's was. The moral sublime in Eliot is allied to Goethe's view that our virtues become our errors as we seek to expand life. Goethe, keenly ironical, is very different from George Eliot, who rarely allows herself irony. But then, no critic gets anywhere by bringing an ironic perspective to George Eliot.

Wisdom literature, in modern times, is very rare: who except George Eliot could write it? She surprises us by her affinities to the greatest poets—Shakespeare and Dante—affinities that are manifest in the dark individuality with which she endows the tragic Lydgate and the undefeated quester, Dorothea.

Moral authority in imaginative literature cannot be distinguished from clarity and power of intellect, and from the faculty of inventiveness. I cannot think of any novelist except for George Eliot who can be compared to Shakespeare and to Dante in these matters.

Gustave Flaubert

(1821–1880)

Madame Bovary

At six o'clock this evening, as I was writing the word "hysterics," I was so swept away, was bellowing so loudly and feeling so deeply what my little Bovary was going through, that I was afraid of having hysterics myself. I got up from my table and opened the window to calm myself. My head was spinning. Now I have great pains in my knees, in my back, and in my head. I feel like a man who has ———ed too much (forgive me for the expression)—a kind of rapturous lassitude.

(Flaubert to Louise Colet, letter of 23 December 1853)

I will not echo the Lycanthrope [Petrus Borel], remembered for a subversiveness which no longer prevails, when he said: "Confronted with all that is vulgar and inept in the present time, can we not take refuge in cigarettes and adultery?" But I assert that our world, even when it is weighed on precision scales, turns out to be exceedingly harsh considering it was engendered by Christ; it could hardly be entitled to throw the first stone at adultery. A few cuckolds more or less are not likely to increase the rotating speed of the spheres and to hasten by a second the final destruction of the universe.

(Baudelaire on *Madame Bovary*)

THE SOCIETAL SCANDAL OF *MADAME BOVARY* IS AS REMOTE NOW AS THE asceticism of the spirit practised by Flaubert and Baudelaire, who seem almost self-indulgent in the era of Samuel Beckett. Rereading *Madame*

Bovary side-by-side with say *Malone Dies* is a sadly instructive experience. Emma seems as boisterous as Hogarth or Rabelais in the company of Malone and Macmann. And yet she is their grandmother, even as the personages of Proust, Joyce, and Kafka are among her children. With her the novel enters the realm of inactivity, where the protagonists are bored, but the reader is not. Poor Emma, destroyed by usury rather than love, is so vital that her stupidities do not matter. A much more than average sensual woman, her capacity for life and love is what moves us to admire her, and even to love her, since like Flaubert himself we find ourselves in her.

Why is Emma so unlucky? If it can go wrong, it will go wrong for her. Freud, like some of the ancients, believed there were no accidents. Ethos is the daimon, your character is your fate, and everything that happens to you starts by being you. Rereading, we suffer the anguish of beholding the phases that lead to Emma's self-destruction. That anguish multiplies despite Flaubert's celebrated detachment, partly because of his uncanny skill at suggesting how many different consciousnesses invade and impinge upon any single consciousness, even one as commonplace as Emma's. Emma's I is an other, and so much the worse for the sensual apprehensiveness that finds it has become Emma.

"Hysterics suffer mainly from reminiscences" is a famous and eloquent formula that Freud outgrew. Like Flaubert before him, he came to see that the Emmas—meaning nearly all among us—were suffering from repressed drives. Still later, in his final phase, Freud arrived at a vision that achieves an ultimate clarity in the last section of *Inhibitions, Symptoms, and Anxiety*, which reads to me as a crucial commentary on Emma Bovary. It is not repressed desire that ensues in anxiety, but a primal anxiety that issues in repression. As for the variety of neurosis involved, Freud speculated that hysteria results from fear of the loss of love. Emma kills herself in a hysteria brought on by a fairly trivial financial mess, but underlying the hysteria is the terrible fear that there will be no more lovers for her.

The most troubling critique of *Madame Bovary* that I know is by Henry James, who worried whether we could sustain our interest in a consciousness as narrow as Emma's:

> The book is a picture of the middling as much as they like, but does Emma attain even to *that*? Hers is a narrow middling even for a little imaginative person whose "social" significance is small. It is greater on the whole than her capacity of consciousness, taking this all round; and so in a word, we feel her less illustrational than she might have been not only if the world had offered her more points of contact, but if she had had more of these to give it.

That *sounds* right enough, yet rereading the novel does not make us desire a larger or brighter Emma. Until she yields to total hysteria, she incarnates the universal wish for sensual life, for a more sensual life. Keats would have liked her, and so do we, though she is not exactly an Isabel Archer or Millie Theale. A remarkable Emma might have developed the hardness and resourcefulness that would have made her a French Becky Sharp, and fitted her for survival even in mid-nineteenth century Paris. But James sublimely chose to miss the point, which Albert Thibaudet got permanently right:

> She is more ardent than passionate. She loves life, pleasure, love itself much more than she loves a man; she is made to have lovers rather than a lover. It is true that she loves Rodolphe with all the fervor of her body, and with him she experiences the moment of her complete, perfect and brief fulfillment; her illness, however, after Rodolphe's desertion, is sufficient to cure her of this love. She does not die from love, but from weakness and a total inability to look ahead, a naivete which makes her an easy prey to deceit in love as well as in business. She lives in the present and is unable to resist the slightest impulse.

I like best Thibaudet's comparison between Flaubert's attitude towards Emma and Milton's towards his Eve: "Whenever Emma is seen in purely sensuous terms, he speaks of her with a delicate, almost religious feeling, the way Milton speaks of Eve." One feels that Milton desires Eve; Flaubert indeed is so at one with Emma that his love for her is necessarily narcissistic. Cervantes, not Milton, was in some sense Flaubert's truest precursor, and Emma (as many critics have remarked) has elements of a female Quixote in her. Like the Don, she is murdered by reality. Milton's Eve, tough despite her yielding beauty, transcends both the order of reality and the order of play. Emma, lacking a Sancho, finds her enchanted Dulcinea in the paltry Rodolphe. Flaubert punished himself harshly, in and through Emma, by grimly mixing in a poisonous order of provincial social reality, and an equally poisonous order of hallucinated play, Emma's fantasies of an ideal passion. The mixing in is cruel, formidable, and of unmatched aesthetic dignity. Emma has no Sublime, but the inverted Romantic vision of Flaubert persuades us that the strongest writing can represent ennui with a life-enhancing power.

Sartre, very early in his endless meditations upon Flaubert, sensibly observed that: "Flaubert despised realism and said so over and over throughout his life; he loved only the absolute purity of art." *Madame*

Bovary has little to do with realism, and something to do with a prophecy of impressionism, but in a most refracted fashion. All of poor Emma's moments are at once drab and privileged; one remembers Browning's Andrea del Sarto intoning: "A common grayness silvers everything." The critical impressionism of Walter Pater is implicit in *Madame Bovary*; imagery of hallucinatory intensity is always a step away from suddenly bursting forth as secularized epiphanies. The Impressionist painters and Proust lurk in the ironies of Flaubert's style, but the uncanny moral energy remains unique:

> The priest rose to take the crucifix; then she stretched forward her neck like one suffering from thirst, and glueing her lips to the body of the Man-God, she pressed upon it with all her expiring strength the fullest kiss of love that she had ever given. Then he recited the *Misereatur* and the *Indulgentiam*, dipped his right thumb in the oil, and began to give extreme unction. First, upon the eyes, that had so coveted all worldly goods; then upon the nostrils, that had been so greedy of the warm breeze and the scents of love; then upon the mouth, that had spoken lies, moaned in pride and cried out in lust; then upon the hands that had taken delight in the texture of sensuality; and finally upon the soles of the feet, so swift when she had hastened to satisfy her desires, and that would now walk no more.

This is Flaubert's elegy for Emma, and ultimately transcends its apparent ironies, if only because we hear in it the novelist's deeper elegy for himself. He refuses to mourn for himself, as befits the high priest of a purer art than the novel knew before him, yet his lament for Emma's sensual splendor is an authentic song of loss, a loss in which he participates.

Fyodor Dostoevsky

(1821-1881)

Crime and Punishment

REREADING *CRIME AND PUNISHMENT*, I AM HAUNTED SUDDENLY BY A REC-
ollection of my worst experience as a teacher. Back in 1955, an outcast
instructor in the then New Critical, Neo-Christian Yale English department
dominated by acolytes of the churchwardenly T.S. Eliot, I was compelled to
teach *Crime and Punishment* in a freshman course to a motley collection of
Yale legacies masquerading as students. Wearied of their response to
Dostoevsky as so much more Eliotic Original Sin, I endeavored to cheer
myself up (if not them) by reading aloud in class S.J. Perelman's sublime parody "A Farewell to Omsk," fragments of which are always with me, such as
the highly Dostoevskian portrayal of the tobacconist Pyotr Pyotrvitch:

> "Good afternoon, Afya Afyakievitch!" replied the shopkeeper
> warmly. He was the son of a former notary public attached to the
> household of Prince Grashkin and gave himself no few airs in con-
> sequence. Whilst speaking it was his habit to extract a greasy
> barometer from his waistcoat and consult it importantly, a trick he
> had learned from the Prince's barber. On seeing Afya Afyakievitch
> he skipped about nimbly, dusted off the counter, gave one of his
> numerous offspring a box on the ear, drank a cup of tea, and on the
> whole behaved like a man of the world who has affairs of moment
> occupying him.

Unfortunately, my class did not think this funny and did not even enjoy
the marvelous close of Perelman's sketch:

"Don't take any flannel kopecks," said Afya gloomily. He dislodged a piece of horse-radish from his tie, shied it at a passing Nihilist, and slid forward into the fresh loam.

Dostoevsky had his own mode of humor, but he might not have appreciated Perelman either. *Crime and Punishment* is less apocalyptic than *The Brothers Karamazov*, but it is apocalyptic enough. It is also tendentious in the extreme, which is the point of Perelman's parody, but Dostoevsky is so great a tragedian that this does not matter. Raskolnikov is a powerful representation of the will demonized by its own strength, while Svidrigailov is beyond that, and stands on the border of a convincing phantasmagoria. Until the unfortunate epilogue, no other narrative fiction drives itself onwards with the remorseless strength of *Crime and Punishment*, truly a shot out of hell and into hell again. To have written a naturalistic novel that reads like a continuous nightmare is Dostoevsky's unique achievement.

Raskolnikov never does repent and change, unless we believe the epilogue, in which Dostoevsky himself scarcely believed. Despair causes his surrender to Porfiry, but even his despair never matches the fierce ecstasy he has achieved in violating all limits. He breaks what can be broken and yet does not break himself. He cannot be broken, not because he has found any truth, objective or psychological, but because he has known, however momentarily, the nihilistic abyss, a Gnostic freedom of what is beyond our sense of being creatures in God's creation. Konstantin Mochulsky is surely right to emphasize that Raskolnikov never comes to believe in redemption, never rejects his theory of strength and power. His surrender, as Mochulsky says, "is not a sign of penitence but of pusillanimity." We end up with a pre-Christian tragic hero ruined by blind fate, at least in his own vision. But this is about as unattractive as a tragic hero can be, because Raskolnikov comes too late in cultural history to seem a Prometheus rather than a bookish intellectual. In a Christian context, Prometheus assimilates to Satan, and Raskolnikov's pride begins to seem too satanic for tragedy.

Raskolnikov hardly persuades us on the level of Dostoevsky's Christian polemic, but psychologically he is fearsomely persuasive. Power for Raskolnikov can be defined as the ability to kill someone else, anyone at all, rather than oneself. I meet Raskolnikov daily, though generally not in so extreme a form, in many young contemporaries who constitute what I would call the School of Resentment. Their wounded narcissism, turned against the self, might make them poets or critics; turned outward, against others, it makes them eminent unrest-inducers. Raskolnikov does not move our sympathy *for him*, but he impresses us with his uncompromising intensity.

Svidrigailov may have been intended as Raskolnikov's foil, but he got away from Dostoevsky, and runs off with the book, even as old Karamazov nearly steals the greater work away from the extraordinary Dmitri. Raskolnikov is too pure a Promethean or devil to be interested in desire, unless the object of desire be metaphysical freedom and power. He is a kind of ascetic Gnostic, while Svidrigailov is a libertine Gnostic, attempting to liberate the sparks upward. If Raskolnikov portrays the madness of the Promethean will, then Svidrigailov is beyond the will, as he is beyond the still-religious affirmations of atheism. He lives (if that can be the right word) a negativity that Raskolnikov is too much himself to attain. Raskolnikov killed for his own sake, he tells Sonia, to test his own strength. Svidrigailov is light years beyond that, on the way downwards and outwards into the abyss, his foremother and forefather.

The best of all murder stories, *Crime and Punishment* seems to me beyond praise and beyond affection. Dostoevsky doubtless would impress me even more than he does already if I could read Russian, but I would not like him any better. A vicious obscurantism inheres in the four great narratives, including *The Idiot* and *The Possessed*, and it darkens *Crime and Punishment*. Only *The Brothers Karamazov* transcends Dostoevsky's hateful ideology because the Karamazovs sweep past the truths that the novelist continues to shout at us. Tolstoy did not think that Dostoevsky's final and apocalyptic novel was one of the summits of the genre, but then he liked to think of Dostoevsky as the Russian Harriet Beecher Stowe and would have wanted old Karamazov to have resembled Simon Legree.

What seems to me strongest in Dostoevsky is the control of visionary horror he shares with Blake, an imaginative prophet with whom he has absolutely nothing else in common. No one who has read *Crime and Punishment* ever can forget Raskolnikov's murder of poor Lizaveta:

> There in the middle of the floor, with a big bundle in her arms, stood Lizaveta, as white as a sheet, gazing in frozen horror at her murdered sister and apparently without the strength to cry out. When she saw him run in, she trembled like a leaf and her face twitched spasmodically; she raised her hand as if to cover her mouth, but no scream came and she backed slowly away from him towards the corner, with her eyes on him in a fixed stare, but still without a sound, as though she had no breath left to cry out. He flung himself forward with the axe; her lips writhed pitifully, like those of a young child when it is just beginning to be frightened and stands ready to scream, with its eyes fixed on the object of its fear. The wretched Lizaveta was so simple, brow-beaten, and

utterly terrified that she did not even put up her arms to protect her face, natural and almost inevitable as the gesture would have been at this moment when the axe was brandished immediately above it. She only raised her free left hand a little and slowly stretched it out towards him as though she were trying to push him away. The blow fell on her skull, splitting it open from the top of the forehead almost to the crown of the head, and felling her instantly. Raskolnikov, completely beside himself, snatched up her bundle, threw it down again, and ran to the entrance.

Nothing could be more painfully effective than: "She only raised her free left hand a little and slowly stretched it out towards him as though she were trying to push him away." We think of the horrible dream in which Raskolnikov sees a poor, lean, old mare beaten to death with a crowbar, and we may reflect upon Nietzsche's darkest insights: that pain creates memory, so that the pain is the meaning, and meaning is therefore painful. Dostoevsky was a great visionary and an exuberant storyteller, but there is something paradoxically nihilistic in his narrative visions. The sublime mode asks us to give up easier pleasures for more difficult pleasures, which is altogether an aesthetic request. Dostoevsky belongs not to the sublime genre but to the harsher perspectives of the apocalyptic. He insists that we accept pains that transcend aesthetic limits. His authority at apocalypse is beyond question, but such authority also has its own aesthetic limits.

Brothers Karamazov

For a critic who cannot read Russian, *The Brothers Karamazov* needs considerable mediation, more perhaps than *War and Peace* or *Fathers and Sons*. Much of this mediation is provided by Victor Terras, in his admirable commentary *A Karamazov Companion*, to which I am indebted here.

Dostoevsky's final novel, completed only two months before his death, when he was nine months short of sixty, *The Brothers Karamazov* was intended as Dostoevsky's apocalypse. Its genre might best be called Scripture rather than novel or tragedy, saga or chronicle. Dostoevsky's scope is from Genesis to Revelation, with the Book of Job and the Gospel of John as the centers. Old Karamazov is a kind of Adam, dreadfully vital and vitalistically dreadful. His four sons resist allegorical reduction, but William Blake would have interpreted them as being his Four Zoas or living principles of fallen man, with Ivan as Urizen, Dmitri as Luvah, Alyosha as Los, and the bastard Smerdyakov as a very debased Tharmas. On the model of this rather Hermetic mythology, Ivan is excessively dominated by the anxieties of the skeptical and analytic intellect, while Dmitri is culpable for "reasoning from the loins in the unreal forms of Beulah's night" and so is a victim of his own overly sensual affective nature. The image of imaginative and spiritual salvation, Alyosha, is thus seen as the true Christian visionary, while the natural—all too natural—Smerdyakov represents the drives or instincts turned murderously against the father and against the self.

That there may be affinities between English Blake and Great Russian Dostoevsky is itself surprising and ought not to be magnified, since the differences between the two seers are far more serious than any parallels in mythic projection. Despite his extraordinary powers of characterization and representation, the Dostoevsky of Karamazov is essentially an obscurantist, and Blake would have judged him to have been a greatly exalted version of his own Smerdyakov. Tolstoy entertained outrageous moralizations about the proper modes and uses for literature, but, compared to the author of *The Brothers Karamazov*, Tolstoy will seem an Enlightened rationalist to a Western reader at the present time. Perhaps that is only to say that Dostoevsky is less universal than Tolstoy in spirit, less the Russian Homer and more the Russian Dante.

The Brothers Karamazov is frequently an outrageous narrative and evidently has strong parodistic elements. Its narrator is faceless; John Jones calls him "a crowd in trousers." His story is told with a sly artlessness, which suits a novel whose burden is that we are all sinful, for even holy Russia swarms with sin, with the universal desire, conscious and unconscious, to murder the father. Old Karamazov is a monster, but a heroic vitalist, fierce in his drive for women and for drink. Dostoevsky evidently did not much care for Ivan either, and no one could care for Smerdyakov. Yet all the Karamazovs burn with psychic energy, all are true sons of that terrible but exuberant father. Freud's essay *"Dostoyevski and Parricide"* (1928) should be supplemented by his *Totem and Taboo*, because the violent tyrant-father murdered by his sons in the Primal History Scene is akin to old Karamazov, who also wishes to appropriate all the women for himself.

Old Karamazov is actually just fifty-five, though ancient in debauchery. He could be judged a Falstaffian figure, not as Shakespeare wrote Falstaff, but as moralizing critics too frequently view the fat knight, forgetting his supreme wit, his joy in play, and his masterful insights into reality. If Falstaff had continued the decline we observe in *Henry IV, Part 2*, then he might have achieved the rancid vitality of the father of the Karamazovs. Fyodor Pavlovich's peculiar vice however is non-Falstaffian. Falstaff after all is not a father, despite his longing to make Hal his son. Old Karamazov is primarily a father, the parody indeed of a bad father, almost the Freudian primitive father of *Totem and Taboo*. Still, this buffoon and insane sensualist is a fool in a complex way, almost a Shakespearean fool, seeing through all impostures, his own included. Fyodor Pavlovich lies to keep in practice, but his lies generally work to expose more truth. He lives to considerable purpose, doubtless despite himself. The largest purpose, in one of Dostoevsky's terrible ironies, is to be the inevitable victim of patricide, of his four sons' revenge for their abused mothers.

The image of the father, for the reactionary Dostoevsky, is ultimately also the image of the Czar and of God. Why then did Dostoevsky risk the ghastly Fyodor Pavlovich as his testament's vision of the father? I can only surmise that Dostoevsky's motivation was Jobean. If Old Karamazov is to be our universal father, then by identifying with Dmitri, or Ivan, or Alyosha (no one identifies with Smerdyakov!), we assume their Jobean situation. If your faith can survive the torment of seeing the image of paternal authority in Karamazov, then you are as justified as Job. Reversing Kierkegaard and Nietzsche, Dostoevsky persuades us that if we haven't had a bad enough father, then it is necessary to invent one. Old Karamazov is an ancestor-demon rather than an ancestor-god, a darkness visible rather than a luminous shadow. You do not mourn his murder, but as a reader you certainly miss him when he is gone. Nor can you hate him the way you despise the hideous Rakitin. Again, I admire John Jones's emphasis:

> The old man's complicity in his own murder gets carried by the book's master metaphor. His house stinks. His life stinks. Yet his mystic complicity never quite hardens into the judgment that he deserves to die. His nature is too broad to allow that.

By "broad" Jones means simply just too alive to deserve to die, which is what I myself would judge. So rammed with life is old Karamazov that his murder is a sin against life, life depraved and corrupt, yet fierce life, life refusing death. Even Dmitri falls short of his father's force of desire. Strangely like Blake again, Dostoevsky proclaims that everything that lives is holy, though he does not share Blake's conviction that nothing or no one is holier than anything or anyone else.

In his *Notebooks*, Dostoevsky insisted that "we are all, to the last man, Fyodor Pavloviches," because in a new, original form "we are all nihilists." A reader, but for the intercessions of his superego, might like to find himself in Falstaff, but hardly in Fyodor Pavlovich. Yet the honest reader should, and does, and no one wants to be murdered. As an apocalypse, *The Brothers Karamazov* forces identification upon one. The father in each male among us is compelled to some uncomfortable recognition in Old

Karamazov; the son in each can choose among the three attractive brothers (Zosima is hardly a possibility). It cannot be said that Dostoevsky does as well with women; Grushenka and Katerina Ivanovna may divide male fantasy between them, but that is all. Dostoevsky does not match Tolstoy as a portrayer of women, let alone Shakespeare.

Much of the permanent fascination of *The Brothers Karamazov* invests itself in the extraordinary differences between Dmitri and Ivan, and in Ivan's two phantasmagorias, his "poem" of the Grand Inquisitor and his mad confrontation with the Devil. Dmitri, though he yields us no phantasmagorias, is more endless to meditation than his half-brother, Ivan. Dostoevsky evidently saw Dmitri as the archetypal Great Russian: undisciplined, human—all too human, lustful, capable of all extremes, but a man of deep feeling and compassion, and an intuitive genius, a poet of action, an authentic comedian of the spirit, and potentially a Christian. Ivan is his father's son in a darker sense; turned inward, his ravening intellect destroys a sense of other selves, and his perpetually augmenting inner self threatens every value that Dostoevsky seeks to rescue. If Dmitri is the exemplary Russian, then Ivan is the Western intellectual consciousness uneasily inhabiting the Russian soul, with murderous consequences that work themselves through in his parody, Smerdyakov.

The legend of the Grand Inquisitor has achieved a fame that transcends *The Brothers Karamazov* as a whole, hardly a result Dostoevsky could have endured, partly because Ivan's parable tells us nothing about Dmitri, who is the authentic center of the novel, and partly because, out of context, Ivan's prose poem can be mistaken for Dostoevsky's, which is *The Brothers Karamazov*. Ivan's legend is one that Dostoevsky rejects, and yet Ivan also, like Old Karamazov, is Dostoevsky, even if Dmitri is more of Dostoevsky. The Grand Inquisitor stamps out human freedom because humans are too weak to endure their own freedom. If Dostoevsky really intended Zosima to be his answer to the Inquisitor, then he erred badly. Zosima, to an American ear anyway, is a muddle, and his interpretation of the Book of Job is the weakest failure in the history of theodicy. What is least acceptable about the Book of Job, its tacked-on conclusion in which God gives Job a perfect new set of sons and daughters, every bit as good as the old, is saluted by Zosima as the height of holy wisdom. It is difficult to answer the Grand Inquisitor with such sublime idiocy.

But then the Grand Inquisitor speaks a sublime idiocy, despite the grand reputation that the Legend has garnered as an excerpt. Dostoevsky is careful to distance himself and us, with the highest irony, from Ivan's dubious rhetoric. The Inquisitor rants on for too long, and just does not frighten us enough; he is more Gothic than we can accept, just as Ivan's

Devil is too much a confused projection of Ivan. To be effective, the legend of the Inquisitor should have been composed and told by Dmitri, but then *The Brothers Karamazov* would have been a different and even stronger novel.

Freud, for polemical and tendentious reasons, overrated *The Brothers Karamazov*, ranking it first among all novels ever written, close to Shakespeare in eminence, and finding the rather lurid legend of the Grand Inquisitor to be a peak of world literature. That latter judgment is clearly mistaken; the status of the novel among all novels whatsoever is perhaps a touch problematic. The book's enormous gusto is unquestionable; the Karamazov family, father and sons, sometimes seems less an image of life, a mimesis, and more a super-mimesis, an evocation of a more abundant life than representation ought to be able to portray. There cannot be a more intense consciousness than that of Dmitri in a novel; only a few figures elsewhere can match him. Doubtless he speaks for what Dostoevsky could not repress in himself: "If they drive God from the earth, we shall shelter Him underground." If you wish to read "God" there as the God of Abraham, Isaac, and Jacob, the God of Moses and Jesus, you are justified; you follow Dostoevsky's intention. I am willing to read "God," here and elsewhere, as the desire for the transcendental and extraordinary, or Dmitri's and Dostoevsky's desire for the completion of what was already transcendental and extraordinary in themselves.

Leo Tolstoy

(1828-1910)

Anna Karenina

SCHOPENHAUER'S FIERCE VISION OF THE RAVENING WILL TO LIVE FOUND a receptive sharer in Tolstoy, whose ferocious drives hardly needed guidance from Schopenhauer. *Anna Karenina* can be called the novel of the drives, since no other narrative that I have read centers so fully upon its protagonist's being so swept away by her will to live that almost nothing else matters to her. Anna's love for Vronsky may have its few rivals in Western literature, but I can recall no similar representation of erotic passion quite so intense. Tolstoy, with enormous shrewdness, explains nothing about Anna's object-choice to us, whether in idealizing or in reductive terms. What he does show us, with overwhelming persuasiveness, is that there is no choice involved. Anna, vital and attractive in every way, is someone with whom most male readers of the novel fall in love, and Tolstoy clearly loves her almost obsessively. He would not have said that he *was* Anna, but she resembles him rather more than Levin does, let alone Vronsky or Kitty.

Why does Anna kill herself? Would we find it as plausible if a contemporary Anna emulated her? Could there be a contemporary Anna? The questions may reduce to: Why did Tolstoy kill her? Did he mean to punish her? I think not. Anna's suicide saddens us, but it also relieves us from shared suffering. Doubtless it relieved Tolstoy also, who was suffering with her. Other legitimate questions would be: How would Schopenhauer have received Anna's death? Is it an heroic release, or a failure in endurance?

Tolstoy read Schopenhauer in the interval between *War and Peace* and *Anna Karenina*, an uneasy interregnum in which he was defeated by his attempt to write a novel about the era of Peter the Great. His enthusiasm for Schopenhauer was essentially a reaffirmation of his own darkest convictions, since he had always been both an apocalyptic vitalist and a dark moralist appalled by some of the consequences of his own vitalism. Schopenhauer's Will to Live, with its metaphysical status as the true thing-in-itself, is simply the Tolstoyan natural ethos turned into prose. The Will to Live is unitary, active, rapacious, indifferent, universal desire; one of the most extraordinary of nineteenth-century hyperboles:

> Let us now add the consideration of the human race. The matter indeed becomes more complicated, and assumes a certain serious-ness of aspect; but the fundamental character remains unaltered. Here also life presents itself by no means as a gift for enjoyment, but as a task, a drudgery to be performed; and in accordance with this we see, in great and small, universal need, ceaseless cares, con-stant pressure, endless strife, compulsory activity, with extreme exertion of all the powers of body and mind. Many millions, unit-ed into nations, strive for the common good, each individual on account of his own; but many thousands fall as a sacrifice for it. Now senseless delusions, now intriguing politics, incite them to wars with each other; then the sweat and the blood of the great multitude must flow, to carry out the ideas of individuals, or to expiate their faults. In peace industry and trade are active, inven-tions work miracles, seas are navigated, delicacies are collected from all ends of the world, the waves engulf thousands. All strive, some planning, others acting; the tumult is indescribable. But the ultimate aim of it all, what is it? To sustain ephemeral and tor-mented individuals through a short span of time in the most for-tunate case with endurable want and comparative freedom from pain, which, however, is at once attended with ennui; then the reproduction of this race and its striving. In this evident dispro-portion between the trouble and the reward, the will to live appears to us from this point of view, if taken objectively, as a fool, or subjectively, as a delusion, seized by which everything living works with the utmost exertion of its strength for something that is of no value. But when we consider it more closely, we shall find here also that it is rather a blind pressure, a tendency entirely without ground or motive.

If this is the characterization of the Will to Live, then the metaphysics of the love of the sexes will reduce to a kind of treason:

> In between, however, in the midst of the tumult, we see the

glances of two lovers meet longingly: yet why so secretly, fearfully, and stealthily? Because these lovers are the traitors who seek to perpetuate the whole want and drudgery, which would otherwise speedily reach an end; this they wish to frustrate, as others like them have frustrated it before.

Schopenhauer presumably would have found this exemplified as much by Levin and Kitty as by Vronsky and Anna, but there he and Tolstoy part, as even Tolstoy is a touch saner upon the metaphysics of sexual love. What matters most about Anna, at least to the reader, is her intensity, her will to live (I deliberately remove the Schopenhauerian capitalization). Anna's aura renders her first meeting with Vronsky unforgettable for us:

> Vronsky followed the guard to the Carriage, and had to stop at the entrance of the compartment to let a lady pass out.
>
> The trained insight of a Society man enabled Vronsky with a single glance to decide that she belonged to the best Society. He apologized for being in her way and was about to enter the carriage, but felt compelled to have another look at her, not because she was very beautiful nor because of the elegance and modest grace of her whole figure, but because he saw in her sweet face as she passed him something specially tender and kind. When he looked round she too turned her head. Her bright grey eyes which seemed dark because of their black lashes rested for a moment on his face as if recognizing him, and then turned to the passing crowd evidently in search of some one. In that short look Vronsky had time to notice the subdued animation that enlivened her face and seemed to flutter between her bright eyes and a scarcely perceptible smile which curved her rosy lips. It was as if an excess of vitality so filled her whole being that it betrayed itself against her will, now in her smile, now in the light of her eyes. She deliberately tried to extinguish that light in her eyes, but it shone despite of her in her faint smile.

A benign vitality, however excessive, is what Tolstoy recognized in himself. What he teaches himself in this novel is that a vitality so exuberant transcends benignity as it does every other quality. The brief but overwhelming chapter 11 of part 2 is not only the novel in embryo, and the essence of Anna, but it is also, to me, the most revelatory scene that Tolstoy ever wrote:

That which for nearly a year had been Vronsky's sole and exclusive desire, supplanting all his former desires: that which for Anna had been an impossible, dreadful, but all the more bewitching dream of happiness, had come to pass. Pale, with trembling lower jaw, he stood over her, entreating her to be calm, himself not knowing why or how.

"Anna, Anna," he said in a trembling voice, "Anna, for God's sake! ..."

But the louder he spoke the lower she drooped her once proud, bright, but now shame-stricken head, and she writhed, slipping down from the sofa on which she sat to the floor at his feet. She would have fallen on the carpet if he had not held her.

"My God! Forgive me!" she said, sobbing and pressing Vronsky's hand to her breast.

She felt so guilty, so much to blame, that it only remained for her to humble herself and ask to be forgiven; but she had no one in the world now except him, so that even her prayer for forgiveness was addressed to him. Looking at him, she felt her humiliation physically, and could say nothing more. He felt what a murderer must feel when looking at the body he has deprived of life. The body he had deprived of life was their love, the first period of their love. There was something frightful and revolting in the recollection of what had been paid for with this terrible price of shame. The shame she felt at her spiritual nakedness communicated itself to him. But in spite of the murderer's horror of the body of his victim, that body must be cut in pieces and hidden away, and he must make use of what he has obtained by the murder.

Then, as the murderer desperately throws himself on the body, as though with passion, and drags it and hacks it, so Vronsky covered her face and shoulders with kisses.

She held his hand and did not move. Yes! These kisses were what had been bought by that shame! "Yes, and this hand, which will always be mine, is the hand of my accomplice." She lifted his hand and kissed it. He knelt down and tried to see her face, but she hid it and did not speak. At last, as though mastering herself, she sat up and pushed him away. Her face was as beautiful as ever, but all the more piteous.

"It's all over," she said. "I have nothing but you left. Remember that."

"I cannot help remembering what is life itself to me! For one moment of that bliss ..."

"What bliss?" she said with disgust and horror, and the horror was involuntarily communicated to him. "For heaven's sake, not another word."

She rose quickly and moved away from him.

"Not another word!" she repeated, and with a look of cold despair, strange to him, she left him. She felt that at that moment she could not express in words her feeling of shame, joy, and horror at this entrance on a new life, and she did not wish to vulgarize that feeling by inadequate words. Later on, the next day and the next, she still could not even find words to describe all the complexity of those feelings, and could not even find thoughts with which to reflect on all that was in her soul.

She said to herself: "No, I can't think about it now; later, when I am calmer." But that calm, necessary for reflection, never came. Every time the thought of what she had done, and of what was to become of her and of what she should do, came to her mind, she was seized with horror and drove these thoughts away.

"Not now; later, when I am calmer!" she said to herself.

But in her dreams, when she had no control over her thoughts, her position appeared to her in all its shocking nakedness. One dream she had almost every night. She dreamt that both at once were her husbands, and lavished their caresses on her. Alexey Alexandrovich wept, kissing her hands, saying: "How beautiful it is now!" and Alexey Vronsky was there too, and he also was her husband. And she was surprised that formerly this had seemed impossible to her, and laughingly explained to them how much simpler it really was, and that they were both now contented and happy. But this dream weighed on her like a nightmare, and she woke from it filled with horror.

Abruptly, without even an overt hint of the nature of the consummation, Tolstoy places us after the event. Anna's tragedy, and in some sense Tolstoy's own, is implicit in this majestic scene. Poor Vronsky, at once victim and executioner, is hopelessly inadequate to Anna's intensity. There is of course nothing he can say and nothing he can do, because he is the wrong man, and always will be. But who could have been the right man? Levin? Perhaps, but Tolstoy and life (the two are one) would not have it so. The calm, necessary for reflection, might have come to Anna with Levin, yet that is highly doubtful. Tolstoy himself, her double and brother, her psychic twin, would have been inadequate to Anna, and she to him. Anna's dream, with both Alexeys happy as her joint husbands, is a peculiar horror to her, because it so horrified Tolstoy. The outrage expressed by D.H. Lawrence at what he judged to be Tolstoy's murder of Anna might have been mitigated had Lawrence allowed himself to remember that Tolstoy, nearly thirty-five years after Anna, also died in a railroad station.

"Characters like Anna are tragic figures because, for reasons that are admirable, they cannot live divided lives or survive through repression." That sentence of Martin Price's is the best I have read about Anna, but I wonder if Anna can be called a tragic figure, any more than she can be what Schopenhauer grimly would have called her, a traitor. Tragedy depends upon division and repression, and Anna is betrayed by nature itself, which does not create men as vital as herself, or, if it does, creates them as savage moralists, like Tolstoy. Anna is too integral for tragedy, and too imbued with reality to survive in any social malforming of reality whatsoever. She dies because Tolstoy could not sustain the suffering it would have cost him to imagine a life she could have borne to go on living.

Mark Twain

(1835-1910)

Huckleberry Finn

MARK TWAIN'S GREATNESS IS CENTERED IN *THE ADVENTURES OF HUCKLEBERRY Finn*, and in the best of his shorter tales. By common consent, *Huckleberry Finn* belongs to a very select group of American novels: Hawthorne's *The Scarlet Letter*, Melville's *Moby-Dick*, Henry James's *The Portrait of a Lady*, Willa Cather's *My Ántonia*, Theodore Dreiser's *An American Tragedy*, F. Scott Fitzgerald's *The Great Gatsby*, Ernest Hemingway's *The Sun Also Rises*, and William Faulkner's *As I Lay Dying* and *Light in August*. Later additions to that tenfold might well include Nathanael West's *Miss Lonelyhearts*, Ralph Ellison's *Invisible Man*, Flannery O'Connor's *The Violent Bear It Away*, Nabokov's *Pale Fire*, Don DeLillo's *Underworld*, Philip Roth's *Sabbath's Theater*, Thomas Pynchon's *The Crying of Lot 49*, and Cormac McCarthy's *Blood Meridian*. Taking the eighteen books together, if I could have just one on the proverbial desert island, it would have to be *The Adventures of Huckleberry Finn*. Its only true rival as the one, essential American book would be Whitman's *Leaves of Grass*. Twain and Whitman between them best define what is uniquely American about American literature.

Huck Finn, like the "Walt Whitman" of *Song of Myself*, is an authentic American Original. As with Walt, Huck is Adam early in the morning, a fresh start in the Evening Land that is the United States. European man is fallen; Huck and Walt, each free of Original Sin, light out for the territory and stop somewhere up ahead of us, perhaps still waiting to see if we can catch up to them. We never will, but that only augments their value. They represent freedom (and loneliness), which according to Emerson is a kind of wildness. And they are undying; Huck in particular need never dwindle into the compromises of old age.

Walt Whitman (the poet, not so much the character) hymned the ultimate unity of night, death, the mother, and the sea. Huck is motherless, and rightly fears any return visits of his dreadful father. Twain hymns for him instead a unity of night, freedom, and the river, all as emblems of vitality. What we care for most in Huck is his comic decency and his vision of reality, in which fear yields to the pragmatic courage of always going on. Hemingway's protagonists, cultivating their style of grace under pressure, seem to me only parodies of Huck Finn, whose inwardness transcends any question of style.

Mark Twain, like most great comic writers, is never far away from representing a fundamental savagery in human nature and human society. Huck, a grand survivor, is the representation of the opposite of savagery. Cruelty and hatred form no part of his vision. His self-reliance and self-esteem are Twain's closest approach to transcendence. No other figure in our novelistic tradition is as likable or as influential as Huckleberry Finn.

Émile Zola

(1840-1902)

Thérèse Raquin

TIME HALLOWS ZOLA'S GREATNESS, AS NOVELIST AND AS PERSON, THOUGH increasingly we see that he transcended his naturalistic aesthetic. Frederick Brown, his crucial scholar-critic, surmises that the novelist's death at sixty-two, by asphyxiation, may have been murder, a final revenge by the proto-Fascist anti-Dreyfusards against the leader of those who had exonerated Dreyfus.

Zola, far more even than Balzac, needs to be read in bulk: no single novel carries his full greatness, not even the sequence of *L'Assommoir* (1877), *Nana* (1880), *Pot-Bouille* (1882), *Germinal* (1885), *La Terre* (1887), *Le Rêve* (1888), *La Bête humaine* (1890), *Le Débâcle* (1892), and *Le Docteur Pascal* (1893). Those nine carry through his "Master Plan", as set forth by Frederick Brown in a chapter of his *Zola: A Life* (1995), which I have reprinted in this volume.

Here I wish to consider only *Thérèse Raquin*, the starting-point of his art, published in 1867, and written when he was just twenty-six, strongly influenced by Balzac, and perhaps also by Stendhal and by Victor Hugo. Defending his novel in a preface to the second edition (1868), Zola fiercely absolves himself of all charges of immorality and pornography:

> In *Thérèse Raquin* my aim has been to study temperaments and not characters. That is the whole point of the book. I have chosen people completely dominated by their nerves and blood, without free will, drawn into each action of their lives by the inexorable laws of their physical nature. Thérèse and Laurent are human animals, nothing more. I have endeavoured to follow these animals through

the devious working of their passions, the compulsion of their instincts, and the mental unbalance resulting from a nervous crisis. The sexual adventures of my hero and heroine are the satisfaction of a need, the murder they commit a consequence of their adultery, a consequence they accept just as wolves accept the slaughter of sheep. And finally, what I have had to call their remorse really amounts to a simple organic disorder, a revolt of the nervous system when strained to breaking-point. There is a complete absence of soul, I freely admit, since that is how I meant it to be.

A disciple of Taine, Zola calls his enterprise "scientific", or "sociological" in our current language. Hippolyte Taine himself, though he admired the novel, urged Zola to work on a more panoramic scale. It is true *Thérèse Raquin* is a closed-in nightmare; Brown usefully stresses that Zola's own recurrent nightmare was to be buried alive, as in Poe's dreadful fantasy.

The novel is the story of the half Algerian Thérèse, her sickly husband whom she does not love, and of Laurent, her lover, who murders the weak husband, Camille, by pushing him into the Seine. The result is the victim's triumph over his murderers, who eventually share the same glass of poison.

The novel remains grimly memorable, and far more of a phantasmagoric than a realistic work. Though it failed to gain Zola a public, it is a presage of a greatness to come. Like so much of Nineteenth Century "realism" and "naturalism", Zola seems now a visionary fantasist, akin to the sublime Balzac.

Thomas Hardy

(1840-1928)

The Mayor of Casterbridge

I

FOR ARTHUR SCHOPENHAUER, THE WILL TO LIVE WAS THE TRUE THING-in-itself, not an interpretation but a rapacious, active, universal, and ultimately indifferent drive or desire. Schopenhauer's great work, *The World as Will and Representation*, had the same relation to and influence upon many of the principal nineteenth- and early twentieth-century novelists that Freud's writings have in regard to many of this century's later, crucial masters of prose fiction. Zola, Maupassant, Turgenev, and Tolstoy join Thomas Hardy as Schopenhauer's nineteenth-century heirs, in a tradition that goes on through Proust, Conrad, and Thomas Mann to culminate in aspects of Borges and of Beckett, the most eminent living writer of narrative. Since Schopenhauer (despite Freud's denials) was one of Freud's prime precursors, one could argue that aspects of Freud's influence upon writers simply carry on from Schopenhauer's previous effect. Manifestly, the relation of Schopenhauer to Hardy is different in both kind and degree from the larger sense in which Schopenhauer was Freud's forerunner or Wittgenstein's. A poet-novelist like Hardy turns to a rhetorical speculator like Schopenhauer only because he finds something in his own temperament and sensibility confirmed and strengthened, and not at all as Lucretius turned to Epicurus, or as Whitman was inspired by Emerson.

The true precursor for Hardy was Shelley, whose visionary skepticism permeates the novels as well as the poems and *The Dynasts*. There is some technical debt to George Eliot in the early novels, but Hardy in his depths was little more moved by her than by Wilkie Collins, from whom he also learned elements of craft. Shelley's tragic sense of eros is pervasive throughout Hardy, and ultimately determines Hardy's understanding of his strongest heroines: Bathsheba Everdene, Eustacia Vye, Marty South, Tess Durbeyfield, Sue Bridehead. Between desire and fulfillment in Shelley falls the shadow of the selfhood, a shadow that makes love and what might be called the means of love quite irreconcilable. What M.D. Zabel named as "the aesthetic of incongruity" in Hardy and ascribed to temperamental causes is in a profound way the result of attempting to transmute the procedures of *The Revolt of Islam* and *Epipsychidion* into the supposedly naturalistic novel.

J. Hillis Miller, when he worked more in the mode of a critic of consciousness like Georges Poulet than in the deconstruction of Paul de Man and Jacques Derrida, saw the fate of love in Hardy as being darkened always by a shadow cast by the lover's consciousness itself. Hugh Kenner, with a distaste for Hardy akin to (and perhaps derived from) T.S. Eliot's in *After Strange Gods*, suggested that Miller had created a kind of Proustian Hardy, who turns out to be a case rather than an artist. Hardy was certainly not an artist comparable to Henry James (who dismissed him as a mere imitator of George Eliot) or James Joyce, but the High Modernist shibboleths for testing the novel have now waned considerably, except for a few surviving high priests of Modernism like Kenner. A better guide to Hardy's permanent strength as a novelist was his heir D.H. Lawrence, whose *The Rainbow* and *Women in Love* marvelously brought Hardy's legacy to an apotheosis. Lawrence, praising Hardy with a rebel son's ambivalence, associated him with Tolstoy as a tragic writer:

> And this is the quality Hardy shares with the great writers, Shakespeare or Sophocles or Tolstoi, this setting behind the small action of his protagonists the terrific action of unfathomed nature; setting a smaller system of morality, the one grasped and formulated by the human consciousness within the vast, uncomprehended and incomprehensible morality of nature or of life itself, surpassing human consciousness. The difference is, that whereas in Shakespeare or Sophocles the greater, uncomprehended morality, or fate, is actively transgressed and gives active punishment, in Hardy and Tolstoi the lesser, human morality, the mechanical system is actively transgressed, and holds, and punishes the protagonist, whilst the greater morality is only passively, negatively transgressed, it is represented merely as being present in background, in scenery, not taking any active part, having no direct connexion with the protagonist. Oedipus, Hamlet, Macbeth set themselves

up against, or find themselves set up against, the unfathomed moral forces of nature, and out of this unfathomed force comes their death. Whereas Anna Karenina, Eustacia, Tess, Sue, and Jude find themselves up against the established system of human government and morality, they cannot detach themselves, and are brought down. Their real tragedy is that they are unfaithful to the greater unwritten morality, which would have bidden Anna Karenina be patient and wait until she, by virtue of greater right, could take what she needed from society; would have bidden Vronsky detach himself from the system, become an individual, creating a new colony of morality with Anna; would have bidden Eustacia fight Clym for his own soul, and Tess take and claim her Angel, since she had the greater light; would have bidden Jude and Sue endure for very honour's sake, since one must bide by the best that one has known, and not succumb to the lesser good.

("Study of Thomas Hardy")

This seems to me powerful and just, because it catches what is most surprising and enduring in Hardy's novels—the sublime stature and aesthetic dignity of his crucial protagonists—while exposing also his great limitation, his denial of freedom to his best personages. Lawrence's prescription for what would have saved Eustacia and Clym, Tess and Angel, Sue and Jude, is perhaps not as persuasive. He speaks of them as though they were Gudrun and Gerald, and thus have failed to be Ursula and Birkin. It is Hardy's genius that they are what they had to be: as imperfect as their creator and his vision, as impure as his language and his plotting, and finally painful and memorable to us:

Note that, in this bitterness, delight,
Since the imperfect is so hot in us,
Lies in flawed words and stubborn sounds.

II

Of Hardy's major novels, *The Mayor of Casterbridge* is the least flawed and clearly the closest to tragic convention in Western literary tradition. If one hesitates to prefer it to *The Return of the Native*, *Tess*, or *Jude*, that may be because it is the least original and eccentric work of the four. Henchard is certainly the best articulated and most consistent of Hardy's male personages, but Lucetta is no Eustacia, and the amiable Elizabeth Jane does not compel much of the reader's interest. The book's glory, Henchard, is

so massive a self-punisher that he can be said to leap over the psychic cosmos of Schopenhauer directly into that of Freud's great essay on the economics of masochism, with its grim new category of "moral masochism."
In a surprising way, Hardy reverses, through Henchard, one of the principal *topoi* of Western tragedy, as set forth acutely by Northrop Frye:

> A strong element of demonic ritual in public punishments and
> similar mob amusements is exploited by tragic and ironic myth.
> Breaking on the wheel becomes Lear's wheel of fire; bear-baiting
> is an image for Gloucester and Macbeth, and for the crucified
> Prometheus the humiliation of exposure, the horror of being
> watched, is a greater misery than the pain. *Derkou theama* (behold
> the spectacle; get your staring over with) is his bitterest cry. The
> inability of Milton's blind Samson to stare back is his greatest tor-
> ment, and one which forces him to scream at Delilah, in one of the
> most terrible passages of all tragic drama, that he will tear her to
> pieces if she touches him.

For Henchard "the humiliation of exposure" becomes a terrible passion, until at last he makes an exhibition of himself during a royal visit.
Perhaps he can revert to what Frye calls "the horror of being watched"
only when he knows that the gesture involved will be his last. Hence his
Will, which may be the most powerful prose passage that Hardy ever
wrote:

> They stood in silence while he ran into the cottage; returning in a
> moment with a crumpled scrap of paper. On it there was pencilled
> as follows:—
> "MICHAEL HENCHARD'S WILL
> "That Elizabeth-Jane Farfrae be not told of my death, or made
> to grieve on account of me.
> "& that I be not bury'd in consecrated ground.
> "& that no sexton be asked to toll the bell.
> "& that nobody is wished to see my dead body.
> "& that no murners walk behind me at my funeral.
> "& that no flours be planted on my grave.
> "& that no man remember me.
> "To this I put my name.
> "Michael Henchard."

That dark testament is the essence of Henchard. It is notorious that "tragedy" becomes a very problematical form in the European Enlightenment and afterwards. Romanticism, which has been our continuous Modernism from the mid-1740s to the present moment, did not return the tragic hero to us, though from Richardson's Clarissa Harlowe until now we have received many resurgences of the tragic heroine. Hardy and Ibsen can be judged to have come closest to reviving the tragic hero, in contradistinction to the hero-villain who, throughout Romantic tradition, limns his night-piece and judges it to have been his best. Henchard, despite his blind strength and his terrible errors, is no villain, and as readers we suffer with him, unrelievedly, because our sympathy for him is unimpeded.

Unfortunately, the suffering becomes altogether *too* unrelieved, as it does again with Jude Fawley. Rereading *The Mayor of Casterbridge* is less painful than rereading *Jude the Obscure*, since at least we do not have to contemplate little Father Time hanging the other urchins and himself, but it is still very painful indeed. Whether or not tragedy should possess some catharsis, we resent the imposition of too much pathos upon us, and we need some gesture of purification if only to keep us away from our own defensive ironies. Henchard, alas, *accomplishes nothing*, for himself or for others. Ahab, a great hero-villain, goes down fighting his implacable fate, the whiteness of the whale, but Henchard is a self-destroyer to no purpose. And yet we are vastly moved by him and know that we should be. Why?

The novel's full title is *The Life and Death of the Mayor of Casterbridge: A Story of a Man of Character*. As Robert Louis Stevenson said in a note to Hardy, "Henchard is a great fellow," which implies that he is a great personality rather than a man of character. This is, in fact, how Hardy represents Henchard, and the critic R.H. Hutton was right to be puzzled by Hardy's title, in a review published in *The Spectator* on June 5, 1886:

> Mr. Hardy has not given us any more powerful study than that of Michael Henchard. Why he should especially term his hero in his title-page a "man of character," we do not clearly understand. Properly speaking, character is the stamp graven on a man, and character therefore, like anything which can be graven, and which, when graven, remains, is a word much more applicable to that which has fixity and permanence, than to that which is fitful and changeful, and which impresses a totally different image of itself on the wax of plastic circumstance at one time, from that which it impresses on a similarly plastic surface at another time. To keep strictly to the associations from which the word "character" is derived, a man of character ought to suggest a man of steady and

unvarying character, a man who conveys very much the same conception of his own qualities under one set of circumstances, which
he conveys under another. This is true of many men, and they
might be called men of character *par excellence*. But the essence of
Michael Henchard is that he is a man of large nature and depth of
passion, who is yet subject to the most fitful influences, who can
do in one mood acts of which he will never cease to repent in
almost all his other moods, whose temper of heart changes many
times even during the execution of the same purpose, though the
same ardour, the same pride, the same wrathful magnanimity, the
same inability to carry out in cool blood the angry resolve of the
mood of revenge or scorn, the same hasty unreasonableness, and
the same disposition to swing back to an equally hasty reasonable-
ness, distinguish him throughout. In one very good sense, the
great deficiency of Michael Henchard might be said to be in
"character." It might well be said that with a little more character,
with a little more fixity of mind, with a little more power of recovering *himself* when he was losing his balance, his would have been
a nature of gigantic mould; whereas, as Mr. Hardy's novel is meant
to show, it was a nature which ran mostly to waste. But, of course,
in the larger and wider sense of the word "character," that sense
which has less reference to the permanent definition of the stamp,
and more reference to the confidence with which the varying
moods may be anticipated, it is not inadmissible to call Michael
Henchard a "man of character." Still, the words on the title-page
rather mislead. One looks for the picture of a man of much more
constancy of purpose, and much less tragic mobility of mood, than
Michael Henchard. None the less, the picture is a very vivid one,
and almost magnificent in its fullness of expression. The largeness
of his nature, the unreasonable generosity and suddenness of his
friendships, the depth of his self-humiliation for what was evil in
him, the eagerness of his craving for sympathy, the vehemence of
his impulses both for good and evil, the curious dash of stoicism
in a nature so eager for sympathy, and of fortitude in one so
moody and restless,—all these are lineaments which, mingled
together as Mr. Hardy has mingled them, produce a curiously
strong impression of reality, as well as of homely grandeur.

One can summarize Hutton's point by saying that Henchard is
stronger in pathos than in ethos, and yet ethos is the daimon, character is
fate, and Hardy specifically sets out to show that Henchard's character is

his fate. The strength of Hardy's irony is that it is also life's irony, and will become Sigmund Freud's irony: Henchard's destiny demonstrates that there are no accidents, meaning that nothing happens to one that is not already oneself. Henchard stares out at the night as though he were staring at an adversary, but there is nothing out there. There is only the self turned against the self, only the drive, beyond the pleasure principle, to death.

The pre-Socratic aphorism that character is fate seems to have been picked up by Hardy from George Eliot's *The Mill on the Floss*, where it is attributed to Novalis. But Hardy need not have gleaned it from anywhere in particular. Everyone in Hardy's novels is overdetermined by his or her past, because for Hardy, as for Freud, everything that is dreadful has already happened and there never can be anything absolutely new. Such a speculation belies the very word "novel," and certainly was no aid to Hardy's inventiveness. Nothing that happens to Henchard surprises us. His fate is redeemed from dreariness only by its aesthetic dignity, which returns us to the problematical question of Hardy's relation to tragedy as a literary form.

Henchard is burdened neither with wisdom nor with knowledge; he is a man of will and of action, with little capacity for reflection, but with a spirit perpetually open and generous towards others. J. Hillis Miller sees him as being governed erotically by mediated desire, but since Miller sees this as the iron law in Hardy's erotic universe, it loses any particular force as an observation upon Henchard. I would prefer to say that Henchard, more even than most men and like all women in Hardy, is hungry for love, desperate for some company in the void of existence. D.H. Lawrence read the tragedy of Hardy's figures not as the consequence of mediated desire, but as the fate of any desire that will not be bounded by convention and community.

> This is the tragedy of Hardy, always the same: the tragedy of those who, more or less pioneers, have died in the wilderness, whither they had escaped for free action, after having left the walled security, and the comparative imprisonment, of the established convention. This is the theme of novel after novel: remain quite within the convention, and you are good, safe, and happy in the long run, though you never have the vivid pang of sympathy on your side: or, on the other hand, be passionate, individual, wilful, you will find the security of the convention a walled prison, you will escape, and you will die, either of your own lack of strength to bear the isolation and the exposure, or by direct revenge from the

community, or from both. This is the tragedy, and only this: it is nothing more metaphysical than the division of a man against himself in such a way: first, that he is a member of the community, and must, upon his honour, in no way move to disintegrate the community, either in its moral or its practical form; second, that the convention of the community is a prison to his natural, individual desire, a desire that compels him, whether he feel justified or not, to break the bounds of the community, lands him outside the pale, there to stand alone, and say: "I was right, my desire was real and inevitable; if I was to be myself I must fulfil it, convention or no convention," or else, there to stand alone, doubting, and saying: "Was I right, was I wrong? If I was wrong, oh, let me die!"—in which case he courts death.

The growth and the development of this tragedy, the deeper and deeper realisation of this division and this problem, the coming towards some conclusion, is the one theme of the Wessex novels.

("Study of Thomas Hardy")

This is general enough to be just, but not quite specific enough for the self-destructive Henchard. Also not sufficiently specific is the sympathetic judgment of Irving Howe, who speaks of "Henchard's personal struggle—the struggle of a splendid animal trying to escape a trap and thereby entangling itself all the more." I find more precise the dark musings of Sigmund Freud, Hardy's contemporary, who might be thinking of Michael Henchard when he meditates upon "The Economic Problem in Masochism":

The third form of masochism, the moral type, is chiefly remarkable for having loosened its connection with what we recognize to be sexuality. To all other masochistic sufferings there still clings the condition that it should be administered by the loved person; it is endured at his command; in the moral type of masochism this limitation has been dropped. It is the suffering itself that matters; whether the sentence is cast by a loved or by an indifferent person is of no importance; it may even be caused by impersonal forces or circumstances, but the true masochist always holds out his cheek wherever he sees a chance of receiving a blow.

The origins of "moral masochism" are in an unconscious sense of guilt, a need for punishment that transcends actual culpability. Even

Henchard's original and grotesque "crime," his drunken exploit in wife-selling, does not so much engender in him remorse at the consciousness of wrongdoing, but rather helps engulf him in the "guilt" of the moral masochist. That means Henchard knows his guilt not as affect or emotion but as a negation, as the nullification of his desires and his ambitions. In a more than Freudian sense, Henchard's primal ambivalence is directed against himself, against the authority principle in his own self.

If *The Mayor of Casterbridge* is a less original book than *Tess* or *Jude*, it is also a more persuasive and universal vision than Hardy achieved else-where. Miguel de Unamuno, defining the tragic sense of life, remarked that: "The chiefest sanctity of a temple is that it is a place to which men go to weep in common. A *miserere* sung in common by a multitude torment-ed by destiny has as much value as a philosophy." That is not tragedy as Aristotle defined it, but it is tragedy as Thomas Hardy wrote it.

The Return of the Native

I first read *The Return of the Native* when I was about fifteen, forty years ago, and had reread it in whole or in part several times through the years before rereading it now. What I had remembered most vividly then I am likely to remember again: Eustacia, Venn the red man, the Heath. I had almost forgotten Clym, and his mother, and Thomasin, and Wildeve, and probably will forget them again. Clym, in particular, is a weak failure in characterization, and nearly sinks the novel; indeed ought to capsize any novel whatsoever. Yet *The Return of the Native* survives him, even though its chief glory, the sexually enchanting Eustacia Vye, does not. Her suicide is so much the waste of a marvelous woman (or representation of a woman, if you insist upon being a formalist) that the reader finds Clym even more intolerable than he is, and is likely not to forgive Hardy, except that Hardy clearly suffers the loss quite as much as any reader does.

Eustacia underwent a singular transformation during the novel's com-position, from a daemonic sort of female Byron, or Byronic witch-like creature, to the grandly beautiful, discontented, and human—all too human but hardly blameworthy—heroine, who may be the most desirable woman in all of nineteenth-century British fiction. "A powerful personali-ty uncurbed by any institutional attachment or by submission to any objec-tive beliefs; unhampered by any ideas"—it would be a good description of Eustacia, but is actually Hardy himself through the eyes of T.S. Eliot in *After Strange Gods*, where Hardy is chastised for not believing in Original Sin and deplored also because "at times his style touches sublimity without ever having passed through the stage of being good."

Here is Eustacia in the early "Queen of Night" chapter:

She was in person full-limbed and somewhat heavy; without rud-
diness, as without pallor; and soft to the touch as a cloud. To see
her hair was to fancy that a whole winter did not contain darkness
enough to form its shadow: it closed over her forehead like night-
fall extinguishing the western glow.

   Her nerves extended into those tresses, and her temper could
always be softened by stroking them down. When her hair was
brushed she would instantly sink into stillness and look like the
Sphinx. If, in passing under one of the Egdon banks, any of its
thick skeins were caught, as they sometimes were, by a prickly tuft
of the large *Ulex Europaeus*—which will act as a sort of hair-
brush—she would go back a few steps, and pass against it a second
time.

   She had Pagan eyes, full of nocturnal mysteries, and their light,
as it came and went, and came again, was partially hampered by
their oppressive lids and lashes; and of these the under lid was
much fuller than it usually is with English women. This enabled
her to indulge in reverie without seeming to do so: she might have
been believed capable of sleeping without closing them up.
Assuming that the souls of men and women were visible essences,
you could fancy the colour of Eustacia's soul to be flame-like. The
sparks from it that rose into her dark pupils gave the same impression.

Hardy's Eustacia may owe something to Walter Pater's *The
Renaissance*, published five years before *The Return of the Native*, since in
some ways she makes a third with Pater's evocations of the Botticelli Venus
and Leonardo's Mona Lisa, visions of antithetical female sexuality.
Eustacia's flame-like quality precisely recalls Pater's ecstasy of passion in
the "Conclusion" to *The Renaissance*, and the epigraph to *The Return of the
Native* could well have been:

This at least of flame-like our life has, that it is but the concurrence, renewed from moment to moment, of forces parting sooner or later on their ways.

This at least of flame-like Eustacia's life has, that the concurrence of
forces parts sooner rather than later. But then this most beautiful of
Hardy's women is also the most doom-eager, the color of her soul being

flame-like. The Heath brings her only Wildeve and Clym, but Paris doubtless would have brought her scarce better, since as Queen of Night she attracts the constancy and the kindness of sorrow.

If Clym and Wildeve are bad actors, and they are, what about Egdon Heath? On this, critics are perpetually divided, some finding the landscape sublime, while others protest that its representation is bathetic. I myself am divided, since clearly it is both, and sometimes simultaneously so! Though Eustacia hates it fiercely, it is nearly as Shelleyan as she is, and rather less natural than presumably it ought to be. That it is more overwritten than overgrown is palpable:

> To recline on a stump of thorn in the central valley of Egdon, between afternoon and night, as now, where the eye could reach nothing of the world outside the summits and shoulders of heath-land which filled the whole circumference of its glance, and to know that everything around and underneath had been from pre-historic times as unaltered as the stars overhead, gave ballast to the mind adrift on change, and harassed by the irrepressible New. The great inviolate place had an ancient permanence which the sea cannot claim. Who can say of a particular sea that it is old? Distilled by the sun, kneaded by the moon, it is renewed in a year, in a day, or in an hour. The sea changed, the fields changed, the rivers, the villages, and the people changed, yet Egdon remained. Those surfaces were neither so steep as to be destructible by weather, nor so flat as to be the victims of floods and deposits. With the exception of an aged highway, and a still more aged bar-row presently to be referred to—themselves almost crystallized to natural products by long continuance—even the trifling irregular-ities were not caused by pickaxe, plough, or spade, but remained as the very finger-touches of the last geological change.

Even Melville cannot always handle this heightened mode; Hardy rarely can, although he attempts it often. And yet we do remember Egdon Heath, years after reading the novel, possibly because something about it wounds us even as it wounds Eustacia. We remember also Diggory Venn, not as the prosperous burgher he becomes, but as we first encounter him, permeated by the red ochre of his picturesque trade:

> The decayed officer, by degrees, came up alongside his fellow-wayfarer, and wished him good evening. The reddleman turned his head and replied in sad and occupied tones. He was young, and

his face, if not exactly handsome, approached so near to handsome
that nobody would have contradicted an assertion that it really
was so in its natural colour. His eye, which glared so strangely
through his stain, was in itself attractive—keen as that of a bird of
prey, and blue as autumn mist. He had neither whisker nor mous-
tache, which allowed the soft curves of the lower part of his face
to be apparent. His lips were thin, and though, as it seemed, com-
pressed by thought, there was a pleasant twitch at their corners
now and then. He was clothed throughout in a tight-fitting suit of
corduroy, excellent in quality, not much worn, and well-chosen for
its purpose; but deprived of its original colour by his trade. It
showed to advantage the good shape of his figure. A certain well-
to-do air about the man suggested that he was not poor for his
degree. The natural query of an observer would have been, Why
should such a promising being as this have hidden his prepossess-
ing exterior by adopting that singular occupation?

Hardy had intended Venn to disappear mysteriously forever from
Egdon Heath, instead of marrying Thomasin, but yielded to the anxiety of
giving the contemporary reader something cheerful and normative at the
end of his austere and dark novel. He ought to have kept to his intent, but
perhaps it does not matter. The Heath endures, the red man either vanishes or is transmogrified into a husband and a burgher. Though we see
Clym rather uselessly preaching to all comers as the book closes, our spirits are elsewhere, with the wild image of longing that no longer haunts the
Heath, Hardy's lost Queen of Night.

Tess of the D'Urbervilles

Of all the novels of Hardy, *Tess of the D'Urbervilles* now appeals to the widest
audience. The book's popularity with the common reader has displaced the
earlier ascendancy of *The Return of the Native*. It can even be asserted that
Hardy's novel has proved to be prophetic of a sensibility by no means fully
emergent in 1891. Nearly a century later, the book sometimes seems to
have moments of vision that are contemporary with us. These tend to come
from Hardy's intimate sympathy with his heroine, a sympathy that verges
upon paternal love. It is curious that Hardy is more involved with Tess than
with Jude Fawley in *Jude the Obscure*, even though Jude is closer to being
Hardy's surrogate than any other male figure in the novels.

J. Hillis Miller, in the most advanced critical study yet attempted of
less, reads it as "a story about repetition," but by "repetition" Miller

appears to mean a linked chain of interpretations. A compulsion to interpret may be the reader's share, and may be Hardy's own stance towards his own novel (and perhaps even extends to Angel Clare's role in the book), but seems to me fairly irrelevant to Tess herself. Since the novel is a story about Tess, I cannot regard it as being "about" repetition, or even one that concerns a difference in repetitions. Hardy's more profound ironies are neither classical nor Romantic, but Biblical, as Miller himself discerns. Classical irony turns upon contrasts between what is said and what is meant, while Romantic irony inhabits the gap between expectation and fulfillment. But Biblical irony appears whenever giant incongruities clash, which happens when Yahweh, who is incommensurate, is closely juxtaposed to men and women and their vain imaginings. When Yahweh devours roast calf under the terebinths at Mamre, or when Jacob wrestles with a nameless one among the Elohim at Penuel, then we are confronted by an irony neither classical nor Romantic.

Hardy, like his master Shelley, is an unbeliever who remains within the literary context of the Bible, and again like Shelley he derives his mode of prophetic irony from the Bible. A striking instance (noted by Hillis Miller) comes in chapter 11:

> In the meantime Alec d'Urberville had pushed on up the slope to clear his genuine doubt as to the quarter of The Chase they were in. He had, in fact, ridden quite at random for over an hour, taking any turning that came to hand in order to prolong companionship with her, and giving far more attention to Tess's moonlit person than to any wayside object. A little rest for the jaded animal being desirable, he did not hasten his search for landmarks. A clamber over the hill into the adjoining vale brought him to the fence of a highway whose contours he recognized, which settled the question of their whereabouts. D'Urberville thereupon turned back; but by this time the moon had quite gone down, and partly on account of the fog The Chase was wrapped in thick darkness, although morning was not far off. He was obliged to advance with outstretched hands to avoid contact with the boughs, and discovered that to hit the exact spot from which he had started was at first entirely beyond him. Roaming up and down, round and round, he at length heard a slight movement of the horse close at hand; and the sleeve of his overcoat unexpectedly caught his foot.
>
> "Tess!" said d'Urberville.
>
> There was no answer. The obscurity was now so great that he could see absolutely nothing but a pale nebulousness at his feet,

which represented the white muslin figure he had left upon the
dead leaves. Everything else was blackness alike. D'Urberville
stooped; and heard a gentle regular breathing. He knelt and bent
lower, till her breath warmed his face, and in a moment his cheek
was in contact with hers. She was sleeping soundly, and upon her
eyelashes there lingered tears.

Darkness and silence ruled everywhere around. Above them
rose the primeval yews and oaks of The Chase, in which were
poised gentle roosting birds in their last nap; and about them stole
the hopping rabbits and hares. But, might some say, where was
Tess's guardian angel? where was the providence of her simple
faith? Perhaps, like that other god of whom the ironical Tishbite
spoke, he was talking, or he was pursuing, or he was in a journey,
or he was sleeping and not to be awaked.

Why it was that upon this beautiful feminine tissue, sensitive as
gossamer, and practically blank as snow as yet, there should have
been traced such a coarse pattern as it was doomed to receive; why
so often the coarse appropriates the finer thus, the wrong man the
woman, the wrong woman the man, many thousand years of analytical philosophy have failed to explain to our sense of order. One
may, indeed, admit the possibility of a retribution lurking in the
present catastrophe. Doubtless some of Tess d'Urberville's mailed
ancestors rollicking home from a fray had dealt the same measure
even more ruthlessly towards peasant girls of their time. But
though to visit the sins of the fathers upon the children may be a
morality good enough for divinities, it is scorned by average
human nature; and it therefore does not mend the matter.

As Tess's own people down in those retreats are never tired of
saying among each other in their fatalistic way: "It was to be."
There lay the pity of it. An immeasurable social chasm was to
divide our heroine's personality thereafter from that previous self
of hers who stepped from her mother's door to try her fortune at
Trantridge poultry-farm.

The ironical Tishbite is the savage Elijah the prophet, who mocks the
priests of Baal, urging them: "Cry aloud: for he is a god; either he is talking, or he is pursuing, or he is in a journey, or peradventure he sleepeth,
and must be awaked." Elijah's irony depends upon the incommensurate-
ness of Yahweh and the human—all too human—Baal. Hardy's irony cannot be what Hillis Miller deconstructively wishes it to be when he rather
remarkably suggests that Tess herself is "like the prophets of Baal," nor

does it seem right to call Yahweh's declaration that He is a jealous (or zealous) God "the divine lust for vengeance," as Miller does. Yahweh, after all, has just given the Second Commandment against making graven images or idols, such as the Baal whom Elijah mocks. Hardy associates Alec's "violation" of Tess with a destruction of pastoral innocence, which he scarcely sees as Baal-worship or idolatry. His emphasis is precisely that no mode of religion, revealed or natural, could defend Tess from an overdetermined system in which the only thing-in-itself is the rapacious Will to Live, a Will that itself is, as it were, the curse of Yahweh upon the hungry generations.

Repetition in *Tess* is repetition as Schopenhauer saw it, which is little different from how Hardy and Freud subsequently saw it. What is repeated, compulsively, is a unitary desire that is rapacious, indifferent, and universal. The pleasures of repetition in Hardy's Tess are not interpretive and perspectival, and so engendered by difference, but are actually masochistic, in the erotogenic sense, and so ensue from the necessity of similarity. Hardy's pragmatic version of the aesthetic vision in this novel is essentially sado-masochistic, and the sufferings of poor Tess give an equivocal pleasure of repetition to the reader. The book's extraordinary popularity partly results from its exquisitely subtle and deeply sympathetic unfolding of the torments of Tess, a pure woman because a pure nature, and doomed to suffer merely because she is so much a natural woman. The poet Lionel Johnson, whose early book (1895) on Hardy still seems to me unsurpassed, brought to the reading of *Tess* a spirit that was antithetically both Shelleyan and Roman Catholic:

> as a girl of generous thought and sentiment, rich in beauty, rich in the natural joys of life, she is brought into collision with the harshness of life.... The world was very strong; her conscience was blinded and bewildered; she did some things nobly, and some despairingly: but there is nothing, not even in studies of criminal anthropology or of morbid pathology, to suggest that she was wholly an irresponsible victim of her own temperament, and of adverse circumstances.... She went through fire and water, and made no true use of them: she is pitiable, but not admirable.

Johnson is very clear-sighted, but perhaps too much the Catholic moralist. To the common reader, Tess is both pitiable and admirable, as Hardy wanted her to be. Is it admirable, though, that, by identifying with her, the reader takes a masochistic pleasure in her suffering? Aesthetically, I would reply yes, but the question remains a disturbing one. When the black flag goes slowly up the staff and we know that the beautiful Tess has been executed, do we reside in Hardy's final ironies, or do we experience a pleasure of repetition that leaves us void of interpretive zeal, yet replete with the gratification of a drive beyond the pleasure principle?

Jude the Obscure

Thomas Hardy lived to be eighty-seven and a half years old, and his long life (1840–1928) comprised two separate literary careers, as a late Victorian novelist (1871–1897), and as a poet who defies temporal placement (1898–1928). The critical reaction to his final novels, *The Well-Beloved* and *Jude the Obscure*, ostensibly motivated Hardy's abandonment of prose fiction, but he always had thought of himself as a poet, and by 1897 was financially secure enough to center himself upon his poetry. He is—with Housman, Yeats, D.H. Lawrence, Wilfred Owen, and Geoffrey Hill—one of the half-dozen or so major poets of the British Isles in the century just past. But this little volume concerns itself with several of his best novels, where again he can be judged to be one of the crucial novelists of the final three decades of the nineteenth century, the bridge connecting George Eliot and the Brontës to Lawrence's novels in the earlier twentieth-century.

T.S. Eliot, who continues to enjoy a high critical reputation despite being almost always wrong, attacked Hardy in a dreadful polemic, *After Strange Gods*, where the novelist-poet is stigmatized as not believing in Original Sin, which turns out to be an aesthetic criterion, since Hardy's style "touches sublimity without ever having passed through the stage of being good." This inaccurate wisecrack is prompted by Eliot's severe summary of the post-Protestant Hardy: "A powerful personality uncurbed by any institutional attachment or by submission to any objective beliefs; unhampered by any ideas." Eliot's institutional attachment was to the Anglo-Catholic Church: his "objective beliefs" were Christianity, royalism, and what he called "classicism" and his "ideas" excluded Freud and Marx.

Hardy, as High Romantic as Shelley and the Brontës, or as Lawrence and Yeats, cannot be judged by Neo-Christian ideology. The best books upon him remain, in my judgment, Lionel Johnson's early *The Art of Thomas Hardy*, and D.H. Lawrence's outrageous *A Study of Thomas Hardy*—which is mostly about Hardy's impact on Lawrence. Michael Millgate's remains the best biography, but since Hardy burned letters and concealed relationships, we still do not know enough to fully integrate the work and the life. Both of Hardy's marriages evidently did not fulfill him, and his lifelong attraction to women much younger than himself has an Ibsenite and Yeatsian aura to it. There is a dark intensity, in the novels and poems alike, that has marked sado-masochistic overtones.

Hardy's personal greatness as a novelist is enhanced (and enabled) by his freedom from T.S. Eliot's attachments and submissions. The agnostic Hardy was Schopenhauerian before he read Schopenhauer, and found a name for the Will to Live that destroys the protagonists of his novels. Hardy's women and men are driven by the tragic forces that are incarnated in Sophocles's Electra, Shakespeare's Lear and Macbeth, and Tolstoy's Anna Karenina. Henry James, who regarded Hardy as a poor imitator of George Eliot, was as mistaken as T.S. Eliot was after him. D.H. Lawrence, in his *Study of Thomas Hardy*, was much more accurate:

> And this is the quality Hardy shares with the great writers, Shakespeare or Sophocles or Tolstoi, this setting behind the small action of his protagonists the terrific action of unfathomed nature; setting a smaller system of morality, the one grasped and formulated by the human consciousness. The difference is, that whereas in Shakespeare or Sophocles the greater, uncomprehended morality, or fate, is actively transgressed, and holds, and punishes the protagonist, whilst the greater morality is only passively, negatively transgressed, it is represented merely as being present in background, in scenery, not taking any active part, having no direct connexion with the protagonist. Oedipus, Hamlet, Macbeth set themselves up against, or find themselves set up against, the unfathomed moral forces of nature, and out of this unfathomed force comes their death. Whereas Anna Karenina, Eustacia, Tess, Sue, and Jude find themselves up against the established system of human government and morality, they cannot detach themselves, and are brought down. Their real tragedy is that they are unfaithful to the greater unwritten morality, which would have bidden Anna Karenina be patient and wait until she, by virtue of greater right, could take what she needed from society; would have bidden Vronsky detach himself from the system, become an individual, creating a new colony of morality with Anna; would have bidden Eustacia fight Clym for his own soul, and Tess take and claim her Angel, since she had the greater light; would have bidden Jude and Sue endure for very honour's sake, since one must bide by the best that one has known, and not succumb to the lesser good.

What matters most, in Hardy's women and men, is their tragic dignity, though their author denies them the ultimate freedom of choice. Hardy's chief limitation, as a novelist, is his sense that the will is over-determined, as it is in Schopenhauer. What saves Hardy's novels is that pragmatically he cannot maintain the detachment he seeks in regard to his central personages. I recall, at fifteen, first reading *The Return of the Native*, and falling-in-love with a second Hardy heroine, thus becoming unfaithful to my love, Marty South in *The Woodlanders*. Hardy himself was ambivalent towards Eustacia Vye, and yet he invokes her as a goddess, Queen of Night, in a rhapsody not less than astonishing:

> Eustacia Vye was the raw material of a divinity. On Olympus she would have done well with a little preparation. She had the passions and instincts which make a model goddess, that is, those which make not quite a model woman. Had it been possible for the earth and mankind to be entirely in her grasp for a while, had she handled the distaff, the spindle, and the shears at her own free will, few in the world would have noticed the change of government. There would have been the same inequality of lot, the same heaping up of favours here, of contumely there, the same generosity before justice, the same perpetual dilemmas, the same captious alternation of caresses and blows that we endure now.
>
>   She was in person full-limbed and somewhat heavy; without ruddiness, as without pallor; and soft to the touch as a cloud. To see her hair was to fancy that a whole winter did not contain darkness enough to form its shadow: it closed over her forehead like nightfall extinguishing the western glow.
>
>   Her nerves extended into those tresses, and her temper could always be softened by stroking them down. When her hair was brushed she would instantly sink into stillness and look like the Sphinx. If, in passing under one of the Egdon banks, any of its thick skeins were caught, as they sometimes were, by a prickly tuft of the large *Ulex Europoeus*—which will act as a sort of hairbrush— she would go back a few steps, and pass against it a second time.
>
>   She had Pagan eyes, full of nocturnal mysteries, and their light, as it came and went, and came again, was partially hampered by their oppressive lids and lashes; and of these the under lid was much fuller than it usually is with English women. This enabled her to indulge in reverie without seeming to do so: she might have been believed capable of sleeping without closing them up. Assuming that the souls of men and women were visible essences, you could

fancy the colour of Eustacia's soul to be flame-like. The sparks from it that rose into her dark pupils gave the same impression.

The Return of the Native was published in 1878, five years after Pater's *Renaissance*, and Walter Pater's visions of Botticelli's Venus and of Leonardo's Mona Lisa clearly influence Hardy's description of his magnetic Eustacia, another fatal woman of the High Decadence, portrayed with a sado-masochistic flavoring. Hardy, perhaps involuntarily, alludes to a memorable sentence of the "Conclusion" to *The Renaissance*:

> This at least of flame-like our life has, that it is but the concurrence, renewed from moment to moment, of forces parting sooner or later on their ways.

A heroine with a flame-like soul is bound to destroy herself, and Hardy's ambivalence seems to me purely defensive. Hardy rather liked the inscrutable Pater when they met, and their affinities—aside from temperament—were considerable. We do not ordinarily think of Hardy's Wessex as an aesthetic realm, but what else is it? Pater's conception of tragedy is close to Hardy's: both indirectly descend from Hegel's idea that the genre must feature a conflict between right and right. But Hegel was not an impressionist, and both Pater and Hardy tend to be, as is their common descendent Virginia Woolf.

Yeats, very much in Pater's tradition, said that: "We begin to live when we conceive of life as tragedy." Hardy would not have remarked that, but he believed it, and exemplifies it in his novels. *The Mayor of Casterbridge*, *Tess of the d'Urbervilles*, and *Jude the Obscure* are novelistic tragedies, closer to Shakespeare than to George Eliot. *Tess* in particular has something of the universal appeal of Shakespearean tragedy, though the sado-masochistic gratification of the audience/readership is again an equivocal element in Hardy's aesthetic power. And yet who would have it otherwise? *Tess* is the most beautiful of Hardy's pastoral visions, and the tragic Tess is the most disturbing of all his heroines, because the most desirable.

Henry James

(1843-1916)

I

THE INTENSE CRITICAL ADMIRERS OF HENRY JAMES GO SO FAR AS TO CALL him the major American writer, or even the most accomplished novelist in the English language. The first assertion neglects only Walt Whitman, while the second partly evades the marvelous sequence that moves from Samuel Richardson's *Clarissa* through Jane Austen on to George Eliot, and the alternative tradition that goes from Fielding through Dickens to Joyce. James is certainly the crucial American novelist, and in his best works the true peer of Austen and George Eliot. His precursor, Hawthorne, is more than fulfilled in the splendors of *The Portrait of a Lady* and *The Wings of the Dove*, giant descendants of *The Marble Faun*, while the rival American novelists—Melville, Mark Twain, Dreiser, Faulkner—survive comparison with James only by being so totally unlike him. Unlikeness makes Faulkner— particularly in his great phase—a true if momentary rival, and perhaps if you are to find a non-Jamesian sense of sustained power in the American novel, you need to seek out our curious antithetical tradition that moves between *Moby-Dick* and its darker descendants: *As I Lay Dying, Miss Lonelyhearts, The Crying of Lot 49*. The normative consciousness of our prose fiction, first prophesied by *The Scarlet Letter*, was forged by Henry James, whose spirit lingers not only in palpable disciples like Edith Wharton in *The Age of Innocence* and Willa Cather in her superb *A Lost Lady*, but more subtly (because merged with Joseph Conrad's aura) in novelists as various as Fitzgerald, Hemingway, and Warren. It seems clear that the relation of James to American prose fiction is precisely analogous to Whitman's relation to our poetry; each is, in his own sphere, what Emerson prophesied as the Central Man who would come and change all things for-ever, in a celebration of the American Newness.

The irony of James's central position among our novelists is palpable, since, like the much smaller figure of T.S. Eliot later on, James abandoned his nation and eventually became a British subject, after having been born a citizen in Emerson's America. But it is a useful commonplace of criticism that James remained the most American of novelists, not less peculiarly nationalistic in *The Ambassadors* than he had been in "Daisy Miller" and *The American*. James, a subtle if at times perverse literary critic, understood very well what we continue to learn and relearn; an American writer can be Emersonian or anti-Emersonian, but even a negative stance towards Emerson always leads back again to his formulation of the post-Christian American religion of Self-Reliance. Overt Emersonians like Thoreau, Whitman, and Frost are no more pervaded by the Sage of Concord than are anti-Emersonians like Hawthorne, Melville, and Eliot. Perhaps the most haunted are those writers who evade Emerson, yet never leave his dialectical ambiance, a group that includes Emily Dickinson, Henry James, and Wallace Stevens.

Emerson was for Henry James something of a family tradition, though that in itself hardly accounts for the plain failure of very nearly everything that the novelist wrote about the essayist. James invariably resorts to a tone of ironic indulgence on the subject of Emerson, which is hardly appropriate to the American prophet of Power, Fate, Illusion, and Wealth. I suggest that James unknowingly mixed Emerson up with the sage's good friend Henry James Sr., whom we dismiss as a Swedenborgian, but who might better be characterized as an American Gnostic speculator, in Emerson's mode, though closer in eminence to, say, Bronson Alcott than to the author of *The Conduct of Life*.

The sane and sacred Emerson was a master of evasions, particularly when disciples became too pressing, whether upon personal or spiritual matters. The senior Henry James is remembered now for having fathered Henry, William, and Alice, and also for his famous outburst against Emerson, whom he admired on the other side of idolatry: "O you man without a handle!" The junior Henry James, overtly celebrating Emerson, nevertheless remarked: "It is hardly too much, or too little, to say of Emerson's writings in general that they were not composed at all." "Composed" is the crucial word there, and makes me remember a beautiful moment in Stevens's "The Poems of Our Climate":

There would still remain the never-resting mind,
So that one would want to escape, come back
To what had been so long composed.

Emerson's mind, never merely restless, indeed was never-resting, as was the mind of every member of the James family. The writings of Emerson, not composed at all, constantly come back to what had been so long composed, to what his admirer Nietzsche called the primordial poem of mankind, the fiction that we have knocked together and called our cosmos. James was far too subtle not to have known this. He chose not to know it, because he needed a provincial Emerson even as he needed a provincial Hawthorne, just as he needed a New England that never was: simple, gentle, and isolated, even a little childlike.

The days when T.S. Eliot could wonder why Henry James had not carved up R.W. Emerson seem safely past, but we ought to remember Eliot's odd complaint about James as critic: "Even in handling men whom he could, one supposes, have carved joint from joint—Emerson or Norton—his touch is uncertain; there is a desire to be generous, a political motive, an admission (in dealing with American writers) that under the circumstances this was the best possible, or that it has fine qualities." Aside from appearing to rank Emerson with Charles Eliot Norton (which is comparable to ranking Freud with Bernard Berenson), this unamiable judgment reduces Emerson, who was and is merely the mind of America, to the stature of a figure who might, at most, warrant the condescension of James (and of Eliot). The cultural polemic involved is obvious, and indeed obsessive, in Eliot, but though pleasanter in James is really no more acceptable:

> Of the three periods into which his life divides itself, the first was (as in the case of most men) that of movement, experiment and selection—that of effort too and painful probation. Emerson had his message, but he was a good while looking for his form—the form which, as he himself would have said, he never completely found and of which it was rather characteristic of him that his later years (with their growing refusal to give him the word), wishing to attack him in his most vulnerable point, where his tenure was least complete, had in some degree the effect of despoiling him. It all sounds rather bare and stern, Mr. Cabot's account of his youth and early manhood, and we get an impression of a terrible paucity of alternatives. If he would be neither a farmer nor a trader he could "teach school"; that was the main resource and a part of the general educative process of the young New Englander who proposed to devote himself to the things of the mind. There was an advantage in the nudity, however, which was that, in Emerson's case at least, the things of the mind did get themselves admirably well

considered. If it be his great distinction and his special sign that he had a more vivid conception of the moral life than any one else, it is probably not fanciful to say that he owed it in part to the limited way in which he saw our capacity for living illustrated. The plain, God-fearing, practical society which surrounded him was not fertile in variations: it had great intelligence and energy, but it moved altogether in the straightforward direction. On three occasions later—three journeys to Europe—he was introduced to a more complicated world; but his spirit, his moral taste, as it were, abode always within the undecorated walls of his youth. There he could dwell with that ripe unconsciousness of evil which is one of the most beautiful signs by which we know him. His early writings are full of quaint animadversion upon the vices of the place and time, but there is something charmingly vague, light and general in the arraignment. Almost the worst he can say is that these vices are negative and that his fellow-townsmen are not heroic. We feel that his first impressions were gathered in a community from which misery and extravagance, and either extreme, of any sort, were equally absent. What the life of New England fifty years ago offered to the observer was the common lot, in a kind of achromatic picture, without particular intensifications. It was from this table of the usual, the merely typical joys and sorrows that he proceeded to generalise—a fact that accounts in some degree for a certain inadequacy and thinness in his enumerations. But it helps to account also for his direct, intimate vision of the soul itself—not in its emotions, its contortions and perversions, but in its passive, exposed, yet healthy form. He knows the nature of man and the long tradition of its dangers; but we feel that whereas he can put his finger on the remedies, lying for the most part, as they do, in the deep recesses of virtue, of the spirit, he has only a kind of hearsay, uninformed acquaintance with the disorders. It would require some ingenuity, the reader may say too much, to trace closely this correspondence between his genius and the frugal, dutiful, happy but decidedly lean Boston of the past, where there was a great deal of will but very little fulcrum—like a ministry without an opposition.

The genius itself it seems to me impossible to contest—I mean the genius for seeing character as a real and supreme thing. Other writers have arrived at a more complete expression: Wordsworth and Goethe, for instance, give one a sense of having found their form, whereas with Emerson we never lose the sense that he is still seeking it. But no one has had so steady and constant, and above all so natural, a vision of what we require and what we are capable of in the way of aspiration and independence. With Emerson it is ever the special capacity for moral experience—always that and only that. We have the impression, somehow, that life had never bribed him to look at anything but the soul; and indeed in the world in which he grew up and lived the bribes and lures, the beguilements and prizes, were few. He was in an admirable position for showing, what he constantly endeavoured to show, that the prize was within. Any one who in New England at that time could do that was sure of success, of listeners and sympathy: most of all, of course, when it was a question of doing it with such a divine persuasiveness. Moreover, the way in which Emerson did it added to the charm—by word of mouth, face to face, with a rare, irresistible voice and a beautiful mild, modest authority. If Mr. Arnold is struck with the limited degree in which he was a man of letters I suppose it is because he is more struck with his having been, as it were, a man of lectures. But the lecture surely was never more purged of its grossness—the quality in it that suggests a strong light and a big brush—than as it issued from Emerson's lips; so far from being a vulgarisation, it was simply the esoteric made audible, and instead of treating the few as the many, after the usual fashion of gentlemen on platforms, he treated the many as the few. There was probably no other society at that time in which he would have got so many persons to understand that; for we think the better of his audience as we read him, and wonder where else people would have had so much moral attention to give. It is to be remembered however that during the winter of 1847–48, on the occasion of his second visit to England, he found many listeners in London and in provincial cities. Mr. Cabot's volumes are full of evidence of the satisfactions he offered, the delights and revelations he may be said to have promised, to a race which had to seek its entertainment, its rewards and consolations, almost exclusively in the moral world. But his own writings are fuller still; we find an instance almost wherever we open them.

It is astonishing to me that James judged Emerson's "great distinction" and "special sign" to be "that he had a more vivid conception of the moral life than any one else," unless "the moral life" has an altogether Jamesian meaning. I would rather say that the great distinction and special sign of James's fiction is that it represents a more vivid conception of the moral life than even Jane Austen or George Eliot could convey to us. Emerson is not much more concerned with morals than he is with manners; his subjects are power, freedom, and fate. As for "that ripe unconsciousness of evil" that James found in Emerson, I have not been able to find it myself, after reading Emerson almost daily for the last twenty years, and I am reminded of Yeats's late essay on Shelley's *Prometheus Unbound*, in which Yeats declares that his skeptical and passionate precursor, great poet that he certainly was, necessarily lacked the Vision of Evil. The necessity in both strong misreadings, James's and Yeats's, was to clear more space for themselves.

Jealous as I am for Emerson, I can recognize that no critic has matched James in seeing and saying what Emerson's strongest virtue is: "But no one has had so steady and constant, and above all so natural, a vision of what we require and what we are capable of in the way of aspiration and independence." No one, that is, except Henry James, for that surely is the quest of Isabel Archer towards her own quite Emersonian vision of aspiration and independence. "The moral world" is James's phrase and James's emphasis. Emerson's own emphasis, I suspect, was considerably more pragmatic than that of James. When James returned to America in 1904 on a visit, after twenty years of self-exile, he went back to Concord and recorded his impressions in *The American Scene*:

> It is odd, and it is also exquisite, that these witnessing ways should be the last ground on which we feel moved to ponderation of the "Concord school"—to use, I admit, a futile expression; or rather, I should doubtless say, it would be odd if there were not inevitably something absolute in the fact of Emerson's all but lifelong connection with them. We may smile a little as we "drag in" Weimar, but I confess myself, for my part, much more satisfied than not by our happy equivalent, "in American money," for Goethe and Schiller. The money is a potful in the second case as in the first, and if Goethe, in the one, represents the gold and Schiller the silver, I find (and quite putting aside any bimetallic prejudice) the same good relation in the other between Emerson and Thoreau. I open Emerson for the same benefit for which I open Goethe, the sense of moving in large intellectual space, and that of the gush, here and there, out of the rock, of the crystalline cupful, in wisdom and poetry, in Wahrheit and Dichtung; and whatever I open Thoreau for (I needn't take space here for the good reasons) I open him oftener than I open Schiller. Which comes back to our feeling that the rarity of Emerson's genius, which has made him

so, for the attentive peoples, the first, and the one really rare, American spirit in letters, couldn't have spent his career in a charming woody, watery place, for so long socially and typically and, above all, interestingly homogeneous, without an effect as of the communication to it of something ineffaceable. It was during his long span his immediate concrete, sufficient world; it gave him his nearest vision of life, and he drew half his images, we recognize, from the revolution of its seasons and the play of its manners. I don't speak of the other half, which he drew from elsewhere. It is admirably, to-day, as if we were still seeing these things *in* those images, which stir the air like birds, dim in the eventide, coming home to nest. If one had reached a "time of life" one had thereby at least heard him lecture; and not a russet leaf fell for me, while I was there, but fell with an Emersonian drop.

That is a beautiful study of the nostalgias and tells us, *contra* T.S. Eliot, what James's relation to Emerson actually was. We know how much that is essential in William James was quarried out of Emerson, particularly from the essay "Experience," which gave birth to Pragmatism. Henry James was not less indebted to Emerson than William James was. *The Portrait of a Lady* is hardly an Emersonian novel; perhaps *The Scarlet Letter* actually is closer to that. Yet Isabel Archer is Emerson's daughter, just as Lambert Strether is Emerson's heir. The Emersonian aura also lingers on even in the ghostly tales of Henry James.

The Ambassadors

James thought *The Ambassadors* was the best of all his novels. I myself prefer not only *The Portrait of A Lady* and *The Wings of the Dove*, but even *The Bostonians*, upon the simple test of rereading. All of the novelistic virtues that critics have found in *The Ambassadors* are certainly there, but they are rather too overtly there. The novel is a beautiful pattern and a model of artistic control, but is Strether of the company of Isabel Archer and Milly Theale? He is intended to be, in the best sense, James's *Portrait of a Gentleman*. Every good reader admires him and finds him sympathetic, yet across the years he comes to seem less and less memorable. I suspect that is because he does not give us enough grief; his story is not painful to us, whereas Isabel's is. Isabel, Emersonian and Paterian, nevertheless has in her the force of the Protestant will in its earlier intensity, almost the force of Dorothea Brooke, though not of their common ancestress, Clarissa Harlowe. But Lewis Lambert Strether is denied any field in which the will might be exercised heroically, since James will not even let him fall in love, except perhaps with the rather too symbolic or idealized Madame de Vionnet.

Everything in the art of Henry James is sublimely deliberate, which means that the imbalance between the matter and the manner of *The Ambassadors* is James's peculiar mode of taking those ultimate risks that alone allow him to make distinctions and achieve distinction. Strether's mission is to rescue Chad from Madame de Vionnet, but is Chad worth rescuing? The best thing about Chad is that he becomes Horatio to Strether's Hamlet, and so serves as the reader's surrogate for appreciating Strether. However, Horatio floats about the court of Elsinore as a kind of privileged outsider, and his splendid destiny is to survive as the teller of Hamlet's story. Chad will go back to Woollett and enthusiastically pioneer in the art of advertising so as to raise the Newsome domestic device to undreamed-of heights of use and profit. The irony of irony is all very well in high romance or in High Romanticism, but not even the comic sense of Henry James quite saves *The Ambassadors* from a certain readerly listlessness that follows Strether's terminal "Then there we are!" to the endlessly receptive Maria Gostrey.

James is perfectly ruthless in his application of what has come to be the Formalist principle that subject matter in literary art is precisely what does not matter. The *Iliad* after all, from any ironic perspective, like that of Shakespeare's more than mordant *Troilus and Cressida*, has as its matter the quarrels between brawny and vainglorious chieftains over the possession of the whore Helen, or of this or that despoiled captive woman. That is not Homer's *Iliad*, nor is *The Ambassadors* the story of the education of Lambert Strether, until at last he can warn little Bilham (one wearies of the "little"!) that life's meaning is that we must *live*. *Seeing* is living, for Strether, as for James, as for Carlyle, for Ruskin, for Emerson, for Pater.

"Impressionism," as a literary term, is not very useful, since even Pater is not an Impressionist in a painterly sense. What Strether *sees* is simply what is there, and what is there would appear to be loss, very much in Pater's sense of loss. James's aesthetic has its differences from Pater's, but I am not so certain that Strether's vision and Pater's are easily to be distinguished from one another. When Strether experiences his crisis (or epiphany) in Gloriani's garden, we are in the cosmos of Pater and of Nietzsche, in which life can be justified only as an aesthetic phenomenon. Strether has just met Madame de Vionnet for the first time: "She was dressed in black, but in black that struck him as light and transparent; she was exceedingly fair, and, though she was as markedly slim, her face had a roundness, with eyes far apart and a little strange." Perhaps that is love at first sight, and certainly Madame de Vionnet is herself the epiphany. "In black that struck him as light and transparent" would have alerted any Emersonian or Paterian, and this is the prelude to the central paragraph of *The Ambassadors*, Strether's famous address to little Bilham:

"It's not too late for you, on any side, and you don't strike me as in danger of missing the train; besides which people can be in general pretty well trusted, of course—with the clock of their freedom ticking as loud as it seems to do here—to keep an eye on the fleeting hour. All the same don't forget that you're young—blessedly young; be glad of it on the contrary and live up to it. Live all you can; it's a mistake not to. It doesn't so much matter what you do in particular, so long as you have your life. If you haven't had that what *have* you had? This place and these impressions—mild as you may find them to wind a man up so; all my impressions of Chad and of people I've seen at *his* place—well, have had their abundant message for me, have just dropped *that* into my mind. I see it now. I haven't done so enough before—and now I'm old; too old at any rate for what I see. Oh I *do* see, at least; and more than you'd believe or I can express. It's too late. And it's as if the train had fairly waited at the station for me without my having had the gumption to know it was there. Now I hear its faint receding whistle miles and miles down the line. What one loses one loses; make no mistake about that. The affair—I mean the affair of life— couldn't, no doubt, have been different for me; for it's at the best a tin mould, either fluted and embossed, with ornamental excrescences, or else smooth and dreadfully plain, into which, a helpless jelly, one's consciousness is poured—so that one 'takes' the form, as the great cook says, and is more or less compactly held by it: one lives in fine as one can. Still, one has the illusion of freedom; therefore don't be, like me, without the memory of that illusion. I was either, at the right time, too stupid or too intelligent to have it; I don't quite know which. Of course at present I'm a case of reaction against the mistake; and the voice of reaction should, no doubt, always be taken with an allowance. But that doesn't affect the point that the right time is now yours. The right time is any time that one is still so lucky as to have. You've plenty; that's the great thing; you're, as I say, damn you, so happily and hatefully young. Don't at any rate miss things out of stupidity. Of course I don't take you for a fool, or I shouldn't be addressing you thus awfully. Do what you like so long as you don't make *my* mistake.

For it was a mistake. Live!" ... Slowly and sociably, with full paus-
es and straight dashes, Strether had so delivered himself; holding
little Bilham from step to step deeply and gravely attentive. The
end of all was that the young man had turned quite solemn, and
that this was a contradiction of the innocent gaiety the speaker
had wished to promote. He watched for a moment the consequence of his words, and then, laying a hand on his listener's knee
and as if to end with the proper joke: "And now for the eye I shall
keep on you!"

The loud ticking of the clock of freedom is Strether's version of Pater's
"We have an interval, and then our place knows us no more," itself a
Paterian commentary upon Victor Hugo's "We are all condemned men,
with a kind of indefinite reprieve." Pater's question is how are we to spend
that interval, and his answer is in perception and sensation as memorial-
ized by art. Strether is not a questioner because Pater is a theoretician of
seeing, but Strether *does* see, indeed always has seen, but was too morally
intelligent to have had the illusion of freedom at the right time. And yet:
"The right time is *any* time that one is still so lucky as to have." James calls
Strether elderly, at fifty-five, but even in 1903 that was not necessarily elderly. Strether, like Pater's Mona Lisa, is older than the rocks among which
he sits, or he is like Nietzsche's Emerson: "He does not know how old he
is already, or how young he is still going to be." James's way of expressing
that Nietzschean paradox has less wit but more American pragmatism.
Strether, like Emerson, is a man of imagination who achieves "an amount
of experience out of any proportion to his adventures." There truly is no
past for Strether; he is an intuitive Emersonian who knows that there is no
history, only biography. Strether has seen in Madame de Vionnet what
Pater saw in Leonardo's Lady Lisa (I owe this insight to F.O. Matthiessen):
a goddess, a nymph, a woman-of-women, infinitely nuanced, endlessly varied.

But if Strether has fallen in love with his vision, his love is like the love
of Pater or of Henry James himself, a wholly aesthetic phenomenon. We
do not expect to see Strether replace Chad as the lady's lover any more
than we could expect him to settle down with the accommodating Maria
Gostrey, let alone attempt to marry Mrs. Newsome upon his return to
Woollett. The sad truth is that none of these ladies, not even the superbly
unreal Madame de Vionnet, would be adequate to Lewis Lambert
Strether, anymore than Touchett, Warburton, Goodwood would be adequate to Isabel Archer. Strether at least does not suffer a female version
of Osmond, but then Strether is hardly the heir of all the ages. He is the

surrogate for Henry James, novelist, who inevitably preferred his own spiritual self-portrait to all his other novels.

The Portrait of a Lady

Hester Prynne in Hawthorne's *The Scarlet Letter* permanently usurped the role of the American Eve. Henry James, in his little book on Hawthorne, allowed himself to be both condescending and evasive towards his authentic American predecessor, a pattern he repeated in writing about George Eliot. Both were too close for comfort, so much so that I risk that cliché with high deliberation. James's deprecation of *The Scarlet Letter* is notorious, and has not prevented several critics from noting the parallel between Hester's ultimate return to Boston, and Isabel's decision to go back to Osmond, her horrible choice of a husband.

Hester and Isabel are fascinating to compare, because they remain the major representations of an American woman anywhere in our imaginative literature, and yet their divergences ultimately transcend their resemblances. Hester necessarily is the grander figure, because she is the more audacious and heroic, but also her situation is more extreme and dramatic. By refusing to identify Dimmesdale as her partner in "sin," she defies Puritan Boston and its theocracy. More important, she never yields to them inwardly, and her self-affirmation is majestic. Aesthetically, she has other advantages over Isabel Archer. Though Isabel is beautiful, and inspires love, she experiences it only in a sisterly mode for Ralph Touchett and as a foster-mother for Pansy, Osmond's daughter by Madame Merle. Inadequate as Dimmesdale be, he has aroused a superb passion in Hester, whose every appearance in the novel radiates sexual power, whereas Isabel flees from Goodwood's fierce desire. And the wretched Osmond—hypocrite, pseudo-aesthete, fortune-hunter—dwindles away next to Hester's husband, the Satanic Chillingworth. If you add Hester's indubitable status as an artist in her embroidery, contrasted to Isabel's lack of all vocation or occupation, then Hawthorne's Eve far outshines James's.

And yet Isabel Archer more than sustains a comparison with her forerunner. Hawthorne, like many readers, is in love with Hester: one might even speak of his desiring her, since he has created her as the image of desire. But Hawthorne maintains a distance from her, whereas James could have said (though he would not) of his heroine what Flaubert had said of Emma Bovary: "I am Isabel Archer." Flaubert lovingly murders Emma, even as Tolstoy amorously murdered his Anna Karenina. James, preserving Isabel as he would himself, merely ruins her life, which is not his judgment, and which Isabel herself reversed as a possible judgment. She goes back to

Osmond in order to proclaim her self-reliance, indeed to establish a continuity in her self-identity. It intrigues me that I do not resist Hester's return to Boston and her scarlet letter, whereas I both aesthetically approve yet humanly resent and am saddened by Isabel's return to Osmond. James has implied clearly enough that, by mutual consent, sexual relations have long since ceased for Osmond and Isabel, so that one does not regard Isabel as a sexual sacrifice. Nor does one regard either Goodwood or Warburton as worthy of Isabel: James has provided no alternative to Osmond, Ralph Touchett being frail and soon to die. The great enigma remains: however well we understand the aesthetic and spiritual inevitability of Isabel's decision, how can we accept it emotionally? Her initial choice of Osmond is appalling enough; her return violates our sense of fairness and increases our distance from her, despite our intense caring.

The Scarlet Letter is a romance, a genre it shares with Sir Walter Scott's *Ivanhoe. The Portrait of a Lady* is a Balzacian novel, in which Osmond and Madame Merle are motivated by financial considerations, which would be absurd in the realm of Hester, Dimmesdale and Chillingworth. Freedom in a novel is very different from independence in a romance. Both Hester and Isabel are Ralph Waldo Emerson's daughters, as it were, but Isabel is by far the more socialized figure. James certainly would have argued that Isabel, particularly at the book's conclusion, represents a significant advance in consciousness over Hester. Isabel has to be more advanced in worldly sophistication, but one wonders if her emphasis upon her own identity, and her insistence upon accepting the contract with life she has made, is not achieved at the cost of otherness, since the wretched Osmond scarcely is her concern, and Ralph Touchett is dead. Hester, befriending outcast women and brooding deeply upon the nature of human love, is at least as rich a consciousness.

Perhaps Isabel is closer to us not just because of history, but because Hester has a tragic grandeur. Isabel is vastly superior to most of us, in fineness of sensibility and of aspiration, and yet she is one of us, poor in judgment and unlucky where she had seemed luckiest. That may be why *The Portrait of a Lady* seems more relevant each passing day, in a society where American women of education and beauty are more free than ever before to choose, and to fall.

Kate Chopin

(1851-1904)

I

THE COMPLETE WORKS OF KATE CHOPIN (1969) COMPRISE ONLY TWO VOLUMES. In her own lifetime (1851–1904), she published two novels, *At Fault* (1890), which I have not read, and the now celebrated *The Awakening* (1899), as well as two volumes of short stories, *Bayou Folk* (1894) and *A Night in Acadie* (1897). The short stories—out of Maupassant—are very mixed in quality, but even the best are fairly slight. *The Awakening*, a flawed but strong novel, now enjoys an eminent status among feminist critics, but I believe that many of them weakly misread the book, which is anything but feminist in its stance. It is a Whitmanian book, profoundly so, not only in its echoes of his poetry, which are manifold, but more crucially in its erotic perspective, which is narcissistic and even autoerotic, very much in Whitman's true mode. The sexual awakening that centers the novel involves a narcissistic self-investment that constitutes a new ego for the heroine. Unfortunately, she fails to see that her passion is for herself, and this error perhaps destroys her.

Lest I seem ironic, here at the start, I protest that irony is hardly my trope; that Walt Whitman, in my judgment, remains the greatest American writer; and that I continue to admire *The Awakening*, though a bit less at the second reading than at the first. Its faults are mostly in its diction; Chopin had no mastery of style. As narrative, it is simplistic rather than simple, and its characters have nothing memorable about them. Chopin's exuberance as a writer was expended where we would expect a daughter of Whitman to locate her concern: the ecstatic rebirth of the self. Since Chopin was not writing either American epic or American elegy, but rather an everyday domestic novel, more naturalistic than Romantic, fissures were bound to appear in her work. The form of Flaubert does not accommodate what

Emerson—who may be called Chopin's literary grandfather—named as the great and crescive self. Nevertheless, as a belated American Transcendentalist, Chopin risked the experiment, and what Emerson called the Newness breaks the vessels of Chopin's chosen form. I would call this the novel's largest strength, though it is also its formal weakness.

The Awakening

Walt Whitman the man doubtless lusted after what he termed the love of comrades, but Walt Whitman the poet persuades us rhetorically only when he lusts after himself. To state this more precisely, Walt Whitman, one of the roughs, an American, the self of *Song of Myself*, lusts after "the real me" or "me myself" of Walt Whitman. Chopin's heroine, Edna, becomes, as it were, one of the roughs, an American, when she allows herself to lust after her real me, her me myself. That is why Chopin's *The Awakening* gave offense to reviewers in 1899, precisely as *Leaves of Grass* gave offense from its first appearance in 1855, onwards to Whitman's death, and would still give offense, if we read it as the Pindaric celebration of masturbation that it truly constitutes. Edna, like Walt, falls in love with her own body, and her infatuation with the inadequate Robert is merely a screen for her over-whelming obsession, which is to nurse and mother herself. Chopin, on some level, must have known how sublimely outrageous she was being, but the level was not overt, and part of her novel's power is in its negation of its own deepest knowledge. Her reviewers were not stupid, and it is shallow to condemn them, as some feminist critics now tend to do. Here is the crucial paragraph in a review by one Frances Porcher (in *The Mirror* 9, May 4, 1899), who senses obscurely but accurately that Edna's desire is for herself:

> It is not a pleasant picture of soul-dissection, take it anyway you like; and so, though she finally kills herself, or rather lets herself drown to death, one feels that it is not in the desperation born of an over-burdened heart, torn by complicating duties but rather because she realizes that something is due to her children, that she cannot get away from, and she is too weak to face the issue. Besides which, and this is the stronger feeling, she has offered herself wholly to the man, who loves her too well to take her at her word; "she realizes that the day would come when he, too, and the thought of him, would melt out of her existence," she has awakened to know the shifting, treacherous, fickle deeps of her own soul in which lies, alert and strong and cruel, the fiend called

Passion that is all animal and all of the earth, earthy. It is better to lie down in green waves and sink down in close embraces of old ocean, and so she does.

The metaphor of "shifting, treacherous, fickle deeps" here, however unoriginal, clearly pertains more to Edna's body than to her soul, and what is most "alert and strong and cruel" in Edna is manifestly a passion for herself. The love-death that Edna dies has its Wagnerian element, but again is more Whitmanian, suggesting the song of death sung by the hermit thrush or solitary singer in "When Lilacs Last in the Dooryard Bloom'd." Edna moves in the heavy, sensual and sensuous atmosphere of Whitman's "The Sleepers," and she dies only perhaps as Whitman's real me or me myself dies, awash in a body indistinguishable from her own, the body of the mother, death, the ocean, and the night of a narcissistic dream of love that perfectly restitutes the self for all its losses, that heals fully the original, narcissistic scar.

Sandra M. Gilbert, who seems to me our most accomplished feminist critic, reads the novel as a female revision of the male aesthetic reveries of Aphrodite's rebirth. I would revise Gilbert only by suggesting that the major instances of such reverie—in Dante Gabriel Rossetti, Swinburne, Pater, and Wilde—are not less female than Chopin's vision is, and paradoxically are more feminist than her version of the myth. The autoerotic seems to be a realm where, metaphorically anyway, there are no major differences between male and female seers, so that Chopin's representation of Edna's psychic self-gratification is not essentially altered from Whitman's solitary bliss:

Edna, left alone in the little side room, loosened her clothes, removing the greater part of them. She bathed her face, her neck and arms in the basin that stood between the windows. She took off her shoes and stockings and stretched herself in the very center of the high, white bed. How luxurious it felt to rest thus in a strange, quaint bed, with its sweet country odor of laurel lingering about the sheets and mattress! She stretched her strong limbs that ached a little. She ran her fingers through her loosened hair for a while. She looked at her round arms as she held them straight up and rubbed them one after the other, observing closely, as if it were something she saw for the first time, the fine, firm quality and texture of her flesh. She clasped her hands easily above her head, and it was thus she fell asleep.

Edna observing, as a discovery, "the fine, firm quality and texture of her flesh," is the heir of Whitman proclaiming: "If I worship one thing more than another it shall be the spread of my own body, or any part of it." Chopin seems to have understood, better than most readers in 1899, what Whitman meant by his crucial image of the tally: "My knowledge my live parts, it keeping tally with the meaning of all things." As the erotic image of the poet's voice, the tally obeys Emerson's dark law of Compensation: "Nothing is got for nothing." If Edna awakens to her own passion for her own body and its erotic potential, then she must come also to the tally's measurement of her own death.

II

Some aspects of Whitman's influence upon *The Awakening* have been traced by Lewis Leary and others, but since the influence is not always overt but frequently repressed, there is more to be noticed about it. Edna first responds to "the everlasting voice of the sea" in chapter 4, where its maternal contrast to her husband's not unkind inadequacy causes her to weep copiously. At the close of chapter 6, the voice of the Whitmanian ocean is directly associated with Edna's awakening to self:

> The voice of the sea is seductive; never ceasing, whispering, clamoring, murmuring, inviting the soul to wander for a spell in abysses of solitude; to lose itself in mazes of inward contemplation.
>
> The voice of the sea speaks to the soul. The touch of the sea is sensuous, enfolding the body in its soft, close embrace.

This is a palpable and overt influence; far subtler, because repressed, is the Whitmanian aura with which Kate Chopin associates the ambivalence of motherhood. Whitman himself both fathered and mothered all of his mostly tormented siblings, as soon as he was able, but his own ambivalences toward both fatherhood and motherhood inform much of his best poetry. Something of the ambiguous strength of *The Awakening*'s conclusion hovers in its repressed relation to Whitman. Edna leaves Robert, after their mutual declaration of love, in order to attend her close friend Adèle in her labor pains:

> Edna began to feel uneasy. She was seized with a vague dread. Her own like experiences seemed far away, unreal, and only half remembered. She recalled faintly an ecstasy of pain, the heavy odor of

chloroform, a stupor which had deadened sensation, and an awakening to find a little new life to which she had given being, added to the great unnumbered multitude of souls that come and go.

She began to wish she had not come; her presence was not necessary. She might have invented a pretext for staying away; she might even invent a pretext now for going. But Edna did not go. With an inward agony, with a flaming, outspoken revolt against the ways of Nature, she witnessed the scene [of] torture.

She was still stunned and speechless with emotion when later she leaned over her friend to kiss her and softly say good-by. Adèle, pressing her cheek, whispered in an exhausted voice: "Think of the children, Edna. Oh think of the children! Remember them!"

The protest against nature here is hardly equivocal, yet it has the peculiar numbness of "the great unnumbered multitude of souls that come and go." Schopenhauer's influence joins Whitman's as Chopin shows us Edna awakening to the realization of lost individuality, of not wanting "anything but my own way," while knowing that the will to live insists always upon its own way, at the individual's expense:

Despondency had come upon her there in the wakeful night, and had never lifted. There was no one thing in the world that she desired. There was no human being whom she wanted near her except Robert; and she even realized that the day would come when he, too, and the thought of him would melt out of her existence, leaving her alone. The children appeared before her like antagonists who had overcome her; who had overpowered and sought to drag her into the soul's slavery for the rest of her days. But she knew a way to elude them. She was not thinking of these things when she walked down to the beach.

The water of the Gulf stretched out before her, gleaming with the million lights of the sun. The voice of the sea is seductive, never ceasing, whispering, clamoring, murmuring, inviting the soul to wander in abysses of solitude. All along the white beach, up and down, there was no living thing in sight. A bird with a broken wing was beating the air above, reeling, fluttering, circling disabled down, down to the water.

The soul's slavery, in Schopenhauer, is to be eluded through philosophical contemplation of a very particular kind, but in Whitman only through a dangerous liaison with night, death, the mother, and the sea. Chopin is closer again to Whitman, and the image of the disabled bird circling downward to darkness stations itself between Whitman and Wallace Stevens, as it were, and constitutes another American approach to the Emersonian abyss of the self. Edna, stripped naked, enters the mothering sea with another recall of Whitman: "The foamy wavelets curled up to her white feet, and coiled like serpents about her ankles." In the hermit thrush's great song of death that is the apotheosis of "When Lilacs Last in the Dooryard Bloom'd," death arrives coiled and curled like a serpent, undulating round the world. Whitman's "dark mother always gliding near with soft feet" has come to deliver Edna from the burden of being a mother, and indeed from all burden of otherness, forever.

Joseph Conrad

(1857–1924)

In Conrad's "Youth" (1898), Marlow gives us a brilliant description of the sinking of the *Judea*:

"Between the darkness of earth and heaven she was burning fiercely upon a disc of purple sea shot by the blood-red play of gleams; upon a disc of water glittering and sinister. A high, clear flame, an immense and lonely flame, ascended from the ocean, and from its summit the black smoke poured continuously at the sky. She burned furiously; mournful and imposing like a funeral pile kindled in the night, surrounded by the sea, watched over by the stars. A magnificent death had come like a grace, like a gift, like a reward to that old ship at the end of her laborious day. The surrender of her weary ghost to the keeper of the stars and sea was stirring like the sight of a glorious triumph. The masts fell just before daybreak, and for a moment there was a burst and turmoil of sparks that seemed to fill with flying fire the night patient and watchful, the vast night lying silent upon the sea. At daylight she was only a charred shell, floating still under a cloud of smoke and bearing a glowing mass of coal within.

"Then the oars were got out, and the boats forming in a line moved around her remains as if in procession—the longboat leading. As we pulled across her stern a slim dart of fire shot out viciously at us, and suddenly she went down, head first, in a great hiss of steam. The unconsumed stern was the last to sink; but the paint had gone, had cracked, had peeled off, and there were no letters, there was no word, no stubborn device that was like her soul, to flash at the rising sun her creed and her name.

The apocalyptic vividness is enhanced by the visual namelessness of the "unconsumed stern," as though the creed of Christ's people maintained both its traditional refusal to violate the Second Commandment, and its traditional affirmation of its not-to-be-named God. With the *Judea*, Conrad sinks the romance of youth's illusions, but like all losses in Conrad this submersion in the destructive element is curiously dialectical, since only experiential loss allows for the compensation of an imaginative gain in the representation of artistic truth. Originally the ephebe of Flaubert and of Flaubert's "son," Maupassant, Conrad was reborn as the narrative disciple of Henry James, the James of *The Spoils of Poynton* and *What Maisie Knew*, rather than the James of the final phase.

Ian Watt convincingly traces the genesis of Marlow to the way that "James developed the indirect narrative approach through the sensitive central intelligence of one of the characters." Marlow, whom James derided as "that preposterous magic mariner," actually represents Conrad's swerve away from the excessive strength of James's influence upon him. By always "mixing himself up with the narrative," in James's words, Marlow guarantees an enigmatic reserve that increases the distance between the impressionistic techniques of Conrad and James. Though there is little valid comparison that can be made between Conrad's greatest achievements and the hesitant, barely fictional status of Pater's *Marius the Epicurean*, Conrad's impressionism is as extreme and solipsistic as Pater's. There is a definite parallel between the fates of Sebastian Van Storck (in Pater's *Imaginary Portraits*) and Decoud in *Nostromo*.

In his 1897 "Preface" to *The Nigger of the "Narcissus,"* Conrad famously insisted that his creative task was "before all to make you *see*." He presumably was aware that he thus joined himself to a line of prose seers whose latest representatives were Carlyle, Ruskin, and Pater. There is a movement in that group from Carlyle's exuberant "Natural Supernaturalism" through Ruskin's paganization of Evangelical fervor to Pater's evasive and skeptical Epicurean materialism, with its eloquent suggestion that all we can see is the flux of sensations. Conrad exceeds Pater in the reduction of impressionism to a state of consciousness where the seeing narrator is hopelessly mixed up with the seen narrative. James may seem an impressionist when compared to Flaubert, but alongside of Conrad he is clearly shown to be a kind of Platonist, imposing forms and resolutions upon the flux of human relations by an exquisite formal geometry altogether his own.

To observe that Conrad is metaphysically less of an Idealist is hardly to argue that he is necessarily a stronger novelist than his master, James. It may suggest though that Conrad's originality is more disturbing than that of James, and may help explain why Conrad, rather than James, became the dominant influence upon the generation of American novelists that included Hemingway, Fitzgerald, and Faulkner. The cosmos of *The Sun Also Rises*, *The Great Gatsby*, and *As I Lay Dying* derives from *Heart of Darkness* and *Nostromo* rather than from *The Ambassadors* and *The Golden Bowl*. Darl Bundren is the extreme inheritor of Conrad's quest to carry impressionism into its heart of darkness in the human awareness that we are only a flux of sensations gazing outwards upon a flux of impressions.

Heart of Darkness

Heart of Darkness may always be a critical battleground between readers who regard it as an aesthetic triumph, and those like myself who doubt its ability to rescue us from its own hopeless obscurantism. That Marlow seems, at moments, not to know what he is talking about, is almost certainly one of the narrative's deliberate strengths, but if Conrad also seems finally not to know, then he necessarily loses some of his authority as a storyteller. Perhaps he loses it to death our death, or our anxiety that he will not sustain the illusion of his fiction's duration long enough for us to sublimate the frustrations it brings us.

These frustrations need not be deprecated. Conrad's diction, normally flawless, is notoriously vague throughout *Heart of Darkness*. E.M. Forster's wicked comment on Conrad's entire work is justified perhaps only when applied to *Heart of Darkness*:

> Misty in the middle as well as at the edges, the secret cask of his genius contains a vapour rather than a jewel.... No creed, in fact.

Forster's misty vapor seems to inhabit such Conradian recurrent modifiers as "monstrous," "unspeakable," "atrocious," and many more, but these are minor defects compared to the involuntary self-parody that Conrad inflicts upon himself. There are moments that sound more like James Thurber lovingly satirizing Conrad than like Conrad:

> "We had carried Kurtz into the pilot house: there was more air there. Lying on the couch, he stared through the open shutter. There was an eddy in the mass of human bodies, and the woman with helmeted head and tawny cheeks rushed out to the very brink of the stream. She put out her hands, shouted something, and all that wild mob took up the shout in a roaring chorus of articulated, rapid, breathless utterance.
>   "'Do you understand this?' I asked.

"He kept on looking out past me with fiery, longing eyes, with a mingled expression of wistfulness and hate. He made no answer, but I saw a smile, a smile of indefinable meaning, appear on his colorless lips that a moment after twitched convulsively. 'Do I not?' he said slowly, gasping, as if the words had been torn out of him by a supernatural power.

This cannot be defended as an instance of what Frank Kermode calls a language "needed when Marlow is not equal to the experience described." Has the experience been described here? Smiles of "indefinable meaning" are smiled once too often in a literary text if they are smiled even once. *Heart of Darkness* has taken on some of the power of myth, even if the book is limited by its involuntary obscurantism. It has haunted American literature from T.S. Eliot's poetry through our major novelists of the era 1920 to 1940, on to a line of movies that go from the *Citizen Kane* of Orson Welles (a substitute for an abandoned Welles project to film *Heart of Darkness*) on to Coppola's *Apocalypse Now*. In this instance, Conrad's formlessness seems to have worked as an aid, so diffusing his conception as to have made it available to an almost universal audience.

Nostromo

An admirer of Conrad is happiest with his five great novels: *Lord Jim* (1900), *Nostromo* (1904), *The Secret Agent* (1906), *Under Western Eyes* (1910), and *Victory* (1914). Subtle and tormented narratives, they form an extraordinarily varied achievement, and despite their common features they can make a reader wonder that they all should have been composed by the same artist. Endlessly enigmatic as a personality and as a formidable moral character, Conrad pervades his own books, a presence not to be put by, an elusive storyteller who yet seems to write a continuous spiritual autobiography. By the general consent of advanced critics and of common readers, Conrad's masterwork is *Nostromo*, where his perspectives are largest, and where his essential originality in the representation of human blindnesses and consequent human affections is at its strongest. Like all overwhelming originalities, Conrad's ensues in an authentic difficulty, which can be assimilated only very slowly, if at all. Repeated rereadings gradually convince me that *Nostromo* is anything but a Conradian litany to the virtue he liked to call "fidelity." The book is tragedy, of a post-Nietzschean sort, despite Conrad's strong contempt for Nietzsche. Decoud, void of all illusions, is self-destroyed because he cannot sustain solitude. Nostromo, perhaps the only persuasive instance of the natural sublime in a twentieth-century hero of fiction, dies "betrayed he hardly knows by what or by whom," as Conrad says. But this is Conrad at his most knowing, and the novel shows us precisely how Nostromo is betrayed, by himself, and by what in himself.

It is a mystery of an overwhelming fiction why it can sustain virtually endless rereadings. *Nostromo*, to me, rewards frequent rereadings in something of the way that *Othello* does; there is always surprise waiting for me. Brilliant as every aspect of the novel is, Nostromo himself is the imaginative center of the book, and yet Nostromo is unique among Conrad's personae, and not a Conradian man whom we could have expected. His creator's description of this central figure as "the Magnificent Capataz, the Man of the People," breathes a writer's love for his most surprising act of the imagination. So does a crucial paragraph from the same source, the "Author's Note" that Conrad added as a preface thirteen years after the initial publication:

> In his firm grip on the earth he inherits, in his improvidence and generosity, in his lavishness with his gifts, in his manly vanity, in the obscure sense of his greatness and in his faithful devotion with something despairing as well as desperate in its impulses, he is a Man of the People, their very own unenvious force, disdaining to lead but ruling from within. Years afterwards, grown older as the famous Captain Fidanza, with a stake in the country, going about his many affairs followed by respectful glances in the modernized streets of Sulaco, calling on the widow of the cargador, attending the Lodge, listening in unmoved silence to anarchist speeches at the meeting, the enigmatical patron of the new revolutionary agitation, the trusted, the wealthy comrade Fidanza with the knowledge of his moral ruin locked up in his breast, he remains essentially a man of the People. In his mingled love and scorn of life and in the bewildered conviction of having been betrayed, of dying betrayed he hardly knows by what or by whom, he is still of the People, their undoubted Great Man—with a private history of his own.

Despite this "moral ruin," and not because of it, Conrad and his readers share the conviction of Nostromo's greatness, share in his sublime self-recognition. How many persuasive images of greatness, of a natural sublimity, exist in modern fiction? Conrad's may be the last enhanced vision of Natural Man, of the Man of the People, in which anyone has found it possible to believe. Yet Conrad himself characteristically qualifies his own belief in Nostromo, and critics too easily seduced by ironies have weakly misread the only apparent irony of Conrad's repeated references to Nostromo as "the magnificent Capataz de Cargadores." Magnificent, beyond the reach of all irony, Nostromo manifestly is. It is the magnificence of the natural leader who disdains leadership, yet who loves reputation. Though he is of the People, Nostromo serves no ideal, unlike old Viola the Garibaldino. With the natural genius for command, the charismatic endowment that could make him another Garibaldi, Nostromo nevertheless scorns any such role, in the name of any cause whatsoever. He is a pure Homeric throwback, not wholly unlike Tolstoi's Hadji Murad, except that he acknowledges neither enemies nor friends, except for his displaced father, Viola. And he enchants us even as he enchants the populace of Sulaco, though most of all he enchants the skeptical and enigmatic Conrad, who barely defends himself against the enchantment with some merely rhetorical ironies.

Ethos is the daimon, character is fate, in Conrad as in Heracleitus, and Nostromo's tragic fate is the inevitable fulfillment of his desperate grandeur, which Conrad cannot dismiss as mere vanity, despite all his own skepticism. Only Nostromo saves the novel, and Conrad, from nihilism, the nihilism of Decoud's waste in suicide. Nostromo is betrayed partly by Decoud's act of self-destruction, with its use of four ingots of silver to send his body down, but largely by his own refusal to maintain the careless preference for glory over gain which is more than a gesture or a style, which indeed is the authentic mode of being that marks the hero. Nostromo is only himself when he can say, with perfect truth: "My name is known from one end of Sulaco to the other. What more can you do for me?"

II

Towards the end of Chapter Ten of Part Third, "The Lighthouse," Conrad renders his own supposed verdict upon both Decoud and Nostromo, in a single page, in two parallel sentences a paragraph apart:

A victim of the disillusioned weariness which is the retribution meted out to intellectual audacity, the brilliant Don Martin Decoud, weighted by the bars of San Tomé silver, disappeared without a trace, swallowed up in the immense indifference of things.

The magnificent Capataz de Cargadores, victim of the disenchanted vanity which is the reward of audacious action, sat in the weary pose of a hunted outcast through a night of sleeplessness as tormenting as any known to Decoud, his companion in the most desperate affair of his life. And he wondered how Decoud had died.

Decoud's last thought, after shooting himself was: "I wonder how that Capataz died." Conrad seems to leave little to choose between being "a victim of the disillusioned weariness which is the retribution meted out to intellectual audacity" or a "victim of the disenchanted vanity which is the reward of audacious action." The brilliant intellectual and the magnificent man of action are victimized alike for their audacity, and it is a fine irony that "retribution" and "reward" become assimilated to one another. Yet the book is Nostromo's and not Decoud's, and a "disenchanted vanity" is a higher fate than a "disillusioned weariness," if only because an initial enchantment is a nobler state than an initial illusion. True that Nostromo's enchantment was only of and with himself, but that is proper for an Achilles or a Hadji Murad. Decoud dies because he cannot bear solitude, and so cannot bear himself. Nostromo finds death-in-life and then death because he has lost the truth of his vanity, its enchanted insouciance, the *sprezzatura* which he, a plebian, nevertheless had made his authentic self.

Nostromo's triumph, though he cannot know it, is that an image of this authenticity survives him, an image so powerful as to persuade both Conrad and the perceptive reader that even the self-betrayed hero retains an aesthetic dignity that renders his death tragic rather than sordid. Poor Decoud, for all his brilliance, dies a nihilistic death, disappearing "without a trace, swallowed up in the immense indifference of things." Nostromo, after his death, receives an aesthetic tribute beyond all irony, in the superb closing paragraph of the novel:

> Dr. Monygham, pulling round in the police-galley, heard the name pass over his head. It was another of Nostromo's triumphs, the greatest, the most enviable, the most sinister of all. In that true cry of undying passion that seemed to ring aloud from Punta Mala to Azuera and away to the bright line of the horizon, overhung by a big white cloud shining like a mass of solid silver, the genius of the magnificent Capataz de Cargadores dominated the dark gulf containing his conquests of treasure and love.

Lord Jim

Lord Jim (1900) is the first of Conrad's five great novels, followed by what seems to me the finest, *Nostromo* (1904), and then by the marvelous sequence of *The Secret Agent* (1906), *Under Western Eyes* (1910), and finally

Victory (1914). Of these, it seems clear that *Lord Jim* has the closest to universal appeal; I have rarely met a reader who was not fascinated by it. Martin Price, the subtlest of Conrad's moral critics, prefers *Lord Jim* to *Nostromo* because he finds that both the author's skepticism and the author's romanticism are given their full scope in *Lord Jim* rather than in *Nostromo*. Doubtless this is true, but Jim himself lacks the high romantic appeal of the magnificent *Nostromo*, and I prefer also the corrosive skepticism of Decoud to the skeptical wisdom of Marlow and Stein. Not that I would deprecate *Lord Jim*; had Conrad written nothing else, this single novel would have guaranteed his literary survival.

Aaron Fogel, writing on *Nostromo*, sees it as marking Conrad's transition from an Oedipal emphasis (as in *Lord Jim*) to a representation of the self's struggle against more outward influences. Certainly Jim's struggle does suit Fogel's formulation of the earlier mode in Conrad: "the denial, by internalization, of the Oedipal order of forced dialogue in the outside world—the translation of inquisition into an inner feeling of compulsion to quarrel with a forebear or with oneself." Though there is much of Conrad in Marlow, and a little of him in Stein, his true surrogate is surely Jim, whose dialectics of defeat are in some sense a late version of Polish romanticism, of the perpetual defeat of Polish heroism. This is only to intimate that Jim's Byronism is rather more Polish than British. Jim rarely demands anything, and he never demands victory. One way of understanding the novel is to see how incomprehensible it would be if Conrad had chosen to make his hero an American.

Marlow, our narrator, becomes something like a father to Jim, in an implicit movement that has been shrewdly traced by Ian Watt. There is an impressive irony in the clear contrast between the eloquent father, Marlow, and the painfully inarticulate son, Jim. The relation between the two poignantly enhances our sense of just how vulnerable Jim is and cannot cease to be. Marlow is a survivor, capable of withstanding nearly the full range of human experience, while Jim is doom-eager, as much a victim of the romantic imagination as he is a belated instance of its intense appeal to us.

Albert J. Guerard associated *Lord Jim* with *Absalom, Absalom!* (a not un-Conradian work) as novels that become different with each attentive reading. Jim's "simplicity" takes the place of the charismatic quality we expect of the romantic protagonist, and Guerard sees Jim as marked by a conflict between personality and will. But Jim's personality remains a mystery to us, almost despite Marlow, and Jim's will is rarely operative, so far as I can see. What we can know about Jim is the enormous strength and prevalence of his fantasy-making powers, which we need not confuse with a romantic imagination, since *that* hardly excludes self-knowledge. Indeed, the deepest puzzle of Jim is why should he fascinate anyone at all, let alone Marlow, Stein, Conrad, and ourselves? Why is he endless to meditation?

Everyone who has read *Lord Jim* (and many who have not) remember its most famous statement, which is Stein's:

> A man that is born falls into a dream like a man who falls into the sea. If he tries to climb out into the air as inexperienced people endeavour to do, he drowns—*nicht wahr?* ... No! I tell you! The way is to the destructive element submit yourself, and with the exertions of your hands and feet in the water make the deep, deep sea keep you up.

That describes Stein's romanticism, but hardly Jim's, since Jim cannot swim in the dream-world. When he seems to make the destructive element keep him up, as in Patusan, there would always have to be a Gentleman Brown waiting for him. An imagination like Jim's, which has little sense of otherness, falls into identification as the truly destructive element, and the error of identifying with the outrageous Brown is what kills Jim. Tony Tanner deftly compares Brown to Iago, if only because Brown's hatred for Jim approximates Iago's hatred for Othello, but Brown has a kind of rough justice in denying Jim's moral superiority. That returns us to the enigma of Jim: why does he make such a difference for Marlow—and for us?

We know the difference between Jim and Brown, even if Jim cannot, even as we know that Jim never will mature into Stein. Is Jim merely the spirit of illusion, or does there linger in him something of the legitimate spirit of romance? Marlow cannot answer the question, and we cannot either, no matter how often we read *Lord Jim*. Is that a strength or a weakness in this novel? That Conrad falls into obscurantism, particularly in *Heart of Darkness*, is beyond denial. Is *Lord Jim* simply an instance of such obscurantism on a larger scale?

Impressionist fiction necessarily forsakes the Idealist metaphysics of the earlier romantic novel, a metaphysics that culminated in George Eliot. Marlow beholding Jim is a concourse of sensations recording a flood of impressions; how can a sensation distinguish whether an impression is authentic or not? Yet Marlow is haunted by the image of heroism, and finds an authentic realization of the image in Stein. The famous close of Marlow's narrative invokes Jim as an overwhelming force of real existence, and also as a disembodied spirit among the shades:

> "And that's the end. He passes away under a cloud, inscrutable at heart, forgotten, unforgiven, and excessively romantic. Not in the

wildest days of his boyish visions could he have seen the alluring shape of such an extraordinary success! For it may very well be that in the short moment of his last proud and unflinching glance, he had beheld the face of that opportunity which, like an Eastern bride, had come veiled to his side.

"But we can see him, an obscure conqueror of fame, tearing himself out of the arms of a jealous love at the sign, at the call of his exalted egoism. He goes away from a living woman to cele-brate his pitiless wedding with a shadowy ideal of conduct. Is he satisfied—quite, now, I wonder? We ought to know. He is one of us—and have I not stood up once, like an evoked ghost, to answer for his eternal constancy? Was I so very wrong after all? Now he is no more, there are days when the reality of his existence comes to me with an immense, with an overwhelming force; and yet upon my honour there are moments, too, when he passes from my eyes like a disembodied spirit astray amongst the passions of his earth, ready to surrender himself faithfully to the claim of his own world of shades.

"Who knows? He is gone, inscrutable at heart, and the poor girl is leading a sort of soundless, inert life in Stein's house. Stein has aged greatly of late. He feels it himself, and says often that he is 'preparing to leave all this; preparing to leave …' while he waves his hand sadly at his butterflies."

Stein's sadness is that he had hoped to find a successor in Jim and now wanes into the sense that he is at the end of a tradition. Enigmatic as always, Marlow cannot resolve his own attitude towards Jim. I do not sup-pose that we can either and I wonder if that is necessarily an aesthetic strength in Conrad's novel. Perhaps it is enough that we are left pondering our own inability to reconcile the authentic and the heroic.

Edith Wharton

(1862-1937)

Age of Innocence

A PROFOUND STUDY OF EDITH WHARTON'S OWN NOSTALGIAS, *THE AGE OF Innocence* (1920) achieved a large discerning audience immediately and has retained it since. For Wharton herself, the novel was a prelude to her auto-biography, *A Backward Glance*, published 14 years later and three years before her death. Wharton, who was 57 in 1919 when *The Age of Innocence* was in most part composed, associated herself with both her protagonists, Newland Archer and Ellen Olenska. *The Age of Innocence* is a historical novel set in socially prominent Old New York of the early 1870s, a vanished world indeed when seen from a post–World War I perspective. Wrongly regarded by many critics as a novel derived from Henry James, *The Age of Innocence* is rather a deliberate complement to *The Portrait of a Lady*, seek-ing and finding a perspective that James was conscious of having excluded from his masterpiece. Wharton might well have called her novel *The Portrait of a Gentleman*, since Newland Archer's very name is an allusion to Isabel Archer, a far more attractive and fascinating character than Wharton's unheroic gentleman of Old New York.

Not that Newland is anything but a very decent and good man who will become a useful philanthropist and civic figure. Unfortunately, howev-er, he has no insight whatsoever as to the differences between men and women, and his passion is of poor quality compared to Ellen's. R.W.B. Lewis, Wharton's biographer, regards *The Age of Innocence* as a minor mas-terpiece. Time so far has confirmed Lewis's judgment, but we now suffer through an age of ideology, and I am uncertain as to whether *The Age of Innocence* will be strong enough to endure. I have no doubts about Wharton's *The House of Mirth* and *The Custom of the Country*, but I wonder whether Newland Archer may yet sink his own book. The best historical novel of Old New York, *The Age of Innocence* retains great interest both as social history and as social anthropology. One is always startled by the farewell dinner of Ellen Olenska, where Newland realizes that he is attending "the tribal rally around a kinswoman about to be eliminated from the tribe." Wharton's own judgment, as narrator, sums up this tribal expulsion.

> It was the Old New York way of taking life "without effusion of blood": the way of people who dreaded scandal more than disease, who placed decency above courage, and who considered that nothing was more ill-bred than "scenes," except the behavior of those who gave rise to them.

That seems a condemnation of Old New York, and yet it is not. Throughout the novel, Wharton acknowledges that Newland's world centers upon an idea of order, a convention that stifles passion and yet liberates from chaos. The old order at least was an order; Wharton was horrified at the post–World War I United States. Newland Archer is flawed in perception: of his world, of his wife, most of all of Ellen. And yet Wharton subtly makes it clear that even a more courageous and perceptive Newland would not have made a successful match with Ellen. Their relationship in time must have dissolved, with Newland returning to the only tribe that could sustain him. Henry James's Isabel Archer, returning to her dreadful husband Osmond, also accepts an idea of order, but one in which her renunciation has a transcendental element. Wharton, shrewder if less sublime than her friend James, gives us a more realistic yet a less consequential Archer.

The Custom of the Country

Edith Wharton's three principal women characters—Lily Bart, Undine Spragg, Ellen Olenska—are remarkably varied, though Lily and Ellen both are motherless members of Old New York society, and Undine is an outsider who conquers and destroys that society, on her own egregious terms. Lily, though she struggles tenaciously, is finally too weak to survive the contradictions between her upbringing and her situation. It is Ellen, superbly self-reliant, who reconciles her heritage and her dilemmas, and who evokes our admiration. Lily dies of a sleeping-drug overdose; Undine, the American answer to Thackeray's Becky Sharp, holds on unpleasantly in our memory; while Ellen, who has affinities to Henry James's Isabel Archer, in *The Portrait of a Lady*, declines Isabel's example, and flourishes (so far as we know) apart from the dying society of Old New York, in which Edith Wharton had been raised.

I once was outrageous enough to ask a group of students whom they would choose—either to love or to be—among Lily, Undine, and Ellen, and was startled by their consensus, which was Undine, since sensibly I had expected Ellen to be their answer. Since I knew that they also had read *Vanity Fair*, I protested that Becky Sharp was charming if unsettling, but that Undine frightened me. She did not dismay them, whereas Lily's ill luck depressed them, and Ellen they felt was rather too good to be true. Perhaps Wharton, a powerful ironist, would have appreciated their choice, but to an archaic Romantic like myself, it came as a considerable surprise, or as another instance of what my mentor, Frederick A. Pottle, had called shifts of sensibility.

Undine, I protested lamely, was bad news, but they forgave her vulgarity (as Wharton could not) and one of them accurately indicated that the novel's famous conclusion was now seriously outdated:

> "Oh, that reminds me—" instead of obeying her he unfolded the paper. "I brought it in to show you something. Jim Driscoll's been appointed Ambassador to England."
>
> "Jim Driscoll— !" She caught up the paper and stared at the paragraph he pointed to. Jim Driscoll—that pitiful nonentity, with his stout mistrustful commonplace wife! It seemed extraordinary that the government should have hunted up such insignificant people. And immediately she had a great vague vision of the splendours they were going to—all the banquets and ceremonies and precedences...
>
> "I shouldn't say she'd want to, with so few jewels—" She dropped the paper and turned to her husband. "If you had a spark of ambition, that's the kind of thing you'd try for. You could have got it just as easily as not!"
>
> He laughed and thrust his thumbs in his waistcoat armholes with the gesture she disliked. "As it happens, it's about the one thing I couldn't."
>
> "You couldn't? Why not?"
>
> "Because you're divorced. They won't have divorced Ambassadresses."
>
> "They won't? Why not, I'd like to know?"
>
> "Well, I guess the court ladies are afraid there'd be too many pretty women in the Embassies," he answered jocularly.
>
> She burst into an angry laugh, and the blood flamed up into

her face. "I never heard of anything so insulting!" she cried, as if the rule had been invented to humiliate her.

There was a noise of motors backing and advancing in the court, and she heard the first voices on the stairs. She turned to give herself a last look in the glass, saw the blaze of rubies, the glitter of her hair, and remembered the brilliant names on her list.

But under all the dazzle a tiny black cloud remained. She had learned that there was something she could never get, something that neither beauty nor influence nor millions could ever buy for her. She could never be an Ambassador's wife; and as she advanced to welcome her first guests she said to herself that it was the one part she was really made for.

In our current political climate, Undine could well be appointed an ambassador, and thus transcend being an Ambassador's wife. It is eighty-eight years since the publication of *The Custom of the Country*, and I have met Undine many times, here and abroad, in the universities, the media, and among diplomats. Wharton may have rendered Undine Spragg with a vividness beyond authorial intention. One remembers Lily Bart for her brave pathos, and Ellen Olenska for her decency and vitality. But Undine Spragg is one of the great white sharks of literature: dangerous, distasteful, and yet permanently valid as a representation of reality.

Ethan Frome

In 1911, two years before *The Custom of the Country* was published, Wharton brought out the short novel that seems her most American story, the New England tragedy *Ethan Frome*. I would guess that it is now her most widely read book, and is likely to remain so. Certainly *Ethan Frome* is Wharton's only fiction to have become part of the American mythology, though it is hardly an early-twentieth-century *Scarlet Letter*. Relentless and stripped, *Ethan Frome* is tragedy not as Hawthorne wrote it, but in the mode of pain and of a reductive moral sadism, akin perhaps to Robert Penn Warren's harshness toward his protagonists, particularly in *World Enough and Time*. The book's aesthetic fascination, for me, centers in Wharton's audacity in touching the limits of a reader's capacity at absorbing really extreme suffering, when that suffering is bleak, intolerable, and in a clear sense unnecessary. Wharton's astonishing authority here is to render such pain with purity and economy, while making it seem inevitable, as much in the nature of things and of psyches as in the social customs of its place and time.

R.W.B. Lewis praises *Ethan Frome* as "a classic of the realistic genre"; doubtless it is, and yet literary "realism" is itself intensely metaphorical, as Lewis keenly knows. *Ethan Frome* is so charged in its representation of reality as to be frequently phantasmagoric in effect. Its terrible vividness estranges it subtly from mere naturalism, and makes its pain just bearable. Presumably Edith Wharton would not have said: "Ethan Frome—that is myself," and yet he is more his author than Undine Spragg was to be. Like Wharton, Ethan has an immense capacity for suffering, and an overwhelming sense of reality; indeed like Edith Wharton, he has too strong a sense of what was to be the Freudian reality principle.

Though an exact contemporary of Freud, Edith Wharton showed no interest in him, but she became an emphatic Nietzschean, and *Ethan Frome* manifests both a Nietzschean perspectivism, and an ascetic intensity that I suspect goes back to a reading of Schopenhauer, Nietzsche's precursor. What fails in Ethan, and in his beloved Mattie, is precisely what Schopenhauer urged us to overcome: the Will to Live, though suicide was hardly a Schopenhauerian solution. In her introduction to *Ethan Frome*, Wharton states a narrative principle that sounds more like Balzac, Browning, or James, but that actually reflects the Nietzsche of *The Genealogy of Morals*:

> Each of my chroniclers contributes to the narrative *just so much as he or she is capable of understanding* of what, to them, is a complicated and mysterious case; and only the narrator of the tale has scope enough to see it all, to resolve it back into simplicity, and to put it in its rightful place among his larger categories.

But does Wharton's narrator have scope enough to see all of the tale that is *Ethan Frome*? Why is the narrator's view more than only another view, and a simplifying one at that? Wharton's introduction memorably calls her protagonists "these figures, my *granite outcroppings*; but half-emerged from the soil, and scarcely more articulate." Yet her narrator (whatever her intentions) lacks the imagination to empathize with granite outcroppings who are also men and women:

> Though Harmon Gow developed the tale as far as his mental and moral reach permitted there were perceptible gaps between his facts, and I had the sense that the deeper meaning of the story was in the gaps. But one phrase stuck in my memory and served as the nucleus about which I grouped my subsequent inferences: "Guess he's been in Starkfield too many winters."

Before my own time there was up I had learned to know what that meant. Yet I had come in the degenerate day of trolley, bicycle and rural delivery, when communication was easy between the scattered mountain villages, and the bigger towns in the valleys, such as Bettsbridge and Shadd's Falls, had libraries, theatres and Y.M.C.A. halls to which the youth of the hills could descend for recreation. But when winter shut down on Starkfield, and the village lay under a sheet of snow perpetually renewed from the pale skies, I began to see what life there—or rather its negation—must have been in Ethan Frome's young manhood.

I had been sent up by my employers on a job connected with the big power-house at Corbury Junction, and a long-drawn carpenters' strike had so delayed the work that I found myself anchored at Starkfield—the nearest habitable spot—for the best part of the winter. I chafed at first, and then, under the hypnotising effect of routine, gradually began to find a grim satisfaction in the life. During the early part of my stay I had been struck by the contrast between the vitality of the climate and the deadness of the community. Day by day, after the December snows were over, a blazing blue sky poured down torrents of light and air on the white landscape, which gave them back in an intenser glitter. One would have supposed that such an atmosphere must quicken the emotions as well as the blood; but it seemed to produce no change except that of retarding still more the sluggish pulse of Starkfield. When I had been there a little longer, and had seen this phase of crystal clearness followed by long stretches of sunless cold; when the storms of February had pitched their white tents about the devoted village and the wild cavalry of March winds had charged down to their support; I began to understand why Starkfield emerged from its six months' siege like a starved garrison capitulating without quarter. Twenty years earlier the means of resistance must have been far fewer, and the enemy in command of almost all the lines of access between the beleaguered villages; and, considering these things, I felt the sinister force of Harmon's phrase: "Most of the smart ones get away." But if that were the case, how could any combination of obstacles have hindered the flight of a man like Ethan Frome?

The narrator's "mental and moral reach" is not in question, but his vision has acute limitations. Winter indeed is the cultural issue, but *Ethan Frome* is not exactly Ursula K. Le Guin's *The Left Hand of Darkness*. It is not a "combination of obstacles" that hindered the flight of Ethan Frome, but a terrible fatalism which is a crucial part of Edith Wharton's Emersonian heritage. Certainly the narrator is right to express the contrast between the winter sublimity of: "a blazing blue sky poured down torrents of light and air on the white landscape, which gave them back in an intenser glitter," and the inability of the local population to give back more than sunken apathy. But Frome, as the narrator says on the novel's first page, is himself a ruined version of the American Sublime: "the most striking figure in Starkfield ... his great height ... the careless powerful look he had ... something bleak and unapproachable in his face." Ethan Frome is an Ahab who lacks Moby-Dick, self-lamed rather than wounded by the white whale, and by the whiteness of the whale. Not the whiteness of Starkfield but an inner whiteness or blankness has crippled Ethan Frome, perhaps the whiteness that goes through American tradition "from Edwards to Emerson" and on through Wharton to Wallace Stevens contemplating the beach world lit by the glare of the Northern Lights in "The Auroras of Autumn":

> Here, being visible is being white,
> Is being of the solid of white, the accomplishment
> Of an extremist in an exercise ...
>
> The season changes. A cold wind chills the beach.
> The long lines of it grow longer, emptier,
> A darkness gathers though it does not fall
>
> And the whiteness grows less vivid on the wall.
> The man who is walking turns blankly on the sand.
> He observes how the north is always enlarging the change,
>
> With its frigid brilliances, its blue-red sweeps
> And gusts of great enkindlings, its polar green,
> The color of ice and fire and solitude.

That, though with a more sublime eloquence, is the visionary world of *Ethan Frome*, a world where the will is impotent, and tragedy is always circumstantial. The experiential puzzle of *Ethan Frome* is ultimately also its aesthetic strength: we do not question the joint decision of Ethan and Mattie to immolate themselves, even though it is pragmatically outrageous and psychologically quite impossible. But the novel's apparent realism is a mask for its actual fatalistic mode, and truly it is a northern romance, akin even to *Wuthering Heights*. A visionary ethos dominates Ethan and Mattie, and would have dominated Edith Wharton herself, had she not battled against it with her powerful gift for social reductiveness. We can wonder whether even *The Age of Innocence*, with its Jamesian renunciations in the mode of *The Portrait of a Lady*, compensates us for what Wharton might have written, had she gone on with her own version of the American romance tradition of Hawthorne and Melville.

Rudyard Kipling

(1865-1936)

I

TWENTY YEARS AFTER WRITING HIS ESSAY OF 1943 ON KIPLING (REPRINTED in *The Liberal Imagination*, 1951), Lionel Trilling remarked that if he could write the critique again, he would do it "less censoriously and with more affectionate admiration." Trilling, always the representative critic of his era, reflected a movement in the evaluation of Kipling that still continues in 1987. I suspect that this movement will coexist with its dialectical counter-movement, of recoil against Kipling, as long as our literary tradition lasts. Kipling is an authentically *popular* writer, in every sense of the word. Stories like "The Man Who Would Be King"; children's tales from *The Jungle Books* and the *Just So Stories*; the novel *Kim*, which is clearly Kipling's masterwork; certain late stories and dozens of ballads—these survive both as high literature and as perpetual entertainment. It is as though Kipling had set out to refute the Sublime function of literature, which is to make us forsake easier pleasures for more difficult pleasures.

In his speech on "Literature," given in 1906, Kipling sketched a dark tale of the storyteller's destiny:

There is an ancient legend which tells us that when a man first achieved a most notable deed he wished to explain to his Tribe what he had done. As soon as he began to speak, however, he was smitten with dumbness, he lacked words, and sat down. Then there arose—according to the story—a masterless man, one who had taken no part in the action of his fellow, who had no special virtues, but who was afflicted—that is the phrase—with the magic of the necessary word. He saw; he told; he described the merits of the notable deed in such a fashion, we are assured, that the words "became alive and walked up and down in the hearts of all his hearers." Thereupon, the Tribe seeing that the words were certainly alive, and fearing lest the man with the words would hand down untrue tales about them to their children, took and killed him. But, later, they saw that the magic was in the words, not in the man.

Seven years later, in the ghastly Primal History Scene of *Totem and Taboo's* fourth chapter, Freud depicted a curiously parallel scene, where a violent primal father is murdered and devoured by his sons, who thus bring to an end the patriarchal horde. Kipling's Primal Storytelling Scene features "a masterless man" whose only virtue is "the necessary word." But he too is slain by the Tribe or primal horde, lest he transmit fictions about the Tribe to its children. Only later, in Freud, do the sons of the primal father experience remorse, and so "the dead father became stronger than the living one had been." Only later, in Kipling, does the Tribe see "that the magic was in the words, not in the man."

Freud's true subject, in his Primal History Scene, was the transference, the carrying-over from earlier to later attachments of an over-determined affect. The true subject of Kipling's Primal Storytelling Scene is not so much the Tale of the Tribe, or the magic that was in the words, but the storyteller's freedom, the masterless man's vocation that no longer leads to death, but that can lead to a death-in-life. What Kipling denies is his great fear, which is that the magic indeed is just as much in the masterless man as it is in the words.

Kipling, with his burly imperialism and his indulgences in anti-intellectualism, would seem at first out of place in the company of Walter Pater, Oscar Wilde, and William Butler Yeats. Nevertheless, Kipling writes in the rhetorical stance of an aesthete, and is very much a Paterian in the metaphysical sense. The "Conclusion" to Pater's *Renaissance* is precisely the credo of Kipling's protagonists:

> Not to discriminate every moment some passionate attitude in those about us, and in the brilliancy of their gifts some tragic dividing of forces on their ways, is, on this short day of frost and sun, to sleep before evening. With this sense of the splendour of our experience and of its awful brevity, gathering all we are into one desperate effort to see and touch, we shall hardly have time to make theories about the things we see and touch. What we have to do is to be for ever curiously testing new opinions and courting new impressions.

Frank Kermode observed that Kipling was a writer "who steadfastly preferred action and machinery to the prevalent Art for Art's Sake," but that is to misread weakly what Pater meant by ending the "Conclusion" to *The Renaissance* with what soon became a notorious formula:

> We have an interval, and then our place knows us no more. Some spend this interval in listlessness, some in high passions, the wisest, at least among "the children of this world," in art and song. For our one chance lies in expanding that interval, in getting as many pulsations as possible into the given time. Great passions may give us this quickened sense of life, ecstasy and sorrow of love, the various forms of enthusiastic activity, disinterested or otherwise, which come naturally to many of us. Only be sure it is passion—that it does yield you this fruit of a quickened, multiplied consciousness. Of this wisdom, the poetic passion, the desire of beauty, the love of art for art's sake, has most; for art comes to you professing frankly to give nothing but the highest quality to your moments as they pass, and simply for those moments' sake.

Like Pater, like Nietzsche, Kipling sensed that we possess and cherish fictions because the reductive truth would destroy us. "The love of art for art's sake" simply means that we choose to believe in a fiction, while knowing that it is not true, to adopt Wallace Stevens's version of the Paterian credo. And fiction, according to Kipling, was written by daemonic forces within us, by "some tragic dividing of forces on their ways." Those forces are no more meaningful than the tales and ballads they produce. What Kipling shares finally with Pater is a deep conviction that we are caught always in a vortex of sensations, a solipsistic concourse of impressions piling upon one another, with great vividness but little consequence.

Kim

Kipling's authentic precursor and literary hero was Mark Twain, whose *Huckleberry Finn* and *Tom Sawyer* are reflected inescapably in *Kim*, certainly Kipling's finest achievement. "An Interview with Mark Twain" records Kipling's vision of the two hours of genial audience granted him, starting with Twain's:

> "Well, you think you owe me something, and you've come to tell me so. That's what I call squaring a debt handsomely."

Kim, permanent work as it is, does not square the debt, partly because Kim is, as David Bromwich notes, both Huck Finn and Tom Sawyer, which is to confuse essentially opposed personalities. Since Kim is founded upon *Huckleberry Finn*, and not on *Don Quixote*, the mixing of Huck and Tom in Kim's nature brings about a softening of focus that malforms the novel. We cannot find Sancho Panza in Kim, though there is a touch of the Don, as well as of Nigger Jim, in the lama. Insofar as he is free but lonely, Kim is Huck; insofar as he serves the worldly powers, he is Tom. It is striking that in his "Interview with Mark Twain," Kipling expresses interest only in Tom Sawyer, asking Twain "whether we were ever going to hear of Tom Sawyer as a man." I suspect that some anxiety of influence was involved, since Kim is the son of the *Adventures of Huckleberry Finn* and not of the lesser novel.

Kim is one of the great instances in the language of a popular adventure story that is also exalted literature. *Huckleberry Finn* is too astonishing a book, too nearly the epic of the American consciousness, together with *Leaves of Grass* and *Moby-Dick*, to be regarded as what it only pretends to be: a good yarn. *Kim* stations itself partly in that mode which ranges from Rider Haggard, at its nadir, to Robert Louis Stevenson, at its zenith: the boy's romance crossing over into the ancient form of romance proper.

There are many splendors in *Kim*, but the greatest is surely the relation between Kim and his master, the lovable, half-mad Tibetan lama, who proves to be Kim's true father, and to whom Kim becomes the best of sons. It is a triumph of the exact representation of profound human affection, rather than a sentimentality of any kind, that can move us to tears as the book ends:

> "Hear me! I bring news! The Search is finished. Comes now the Reward: ... Thus. When we were among the Hills, I lived on thy strength till the young branch bowed and nigh broke. When we came out of the Hills, I was troubled for thee and for other matters which I held in my heart. The boat of my soul lacked direction; I could not see into the Cause of Things. So I gave thee over to the virtuous woman altogether. I took no food. I drank no water. Still I saw not the Way. They pressed food upon me and cried at my shut door. So I removed myself to a hollow under a tree. I took no food. I took no water. I sat in meditation two days and two nights, abstracting my mind; inbreathing and outbreathing in the required manner.... Upon the second night—so great was my reward—the wise Soul loosed itself from the silly Body and went free. This I have never before attained, though I have stood on the threshold of it. Consider, for it is a marvel!"

"A marvel indeed. Two days and two nights without food! Where was the Sahiba?" said Kim under his breath.

"Yea, my Soul went free, and, wheeling like an eagle, saw indeed that there was no Teshoo Lama nor any other soul. As a drop draws to water, so my soul drew near to the Great Soul which is beyond all things. At that point, exalted in contemplation, I saw all Hind, from Ceylon in the sea to the Hills, and my own Painted Rocks at Such-zen; I saw every camp and village, to the least, where we have ever rested. I saw them at one time and in one place; for they were within the Soul. By this I knew the Soul had passed beyond the illusion of Time and Space and of Things. By this I knew that I was free. I saw thee lying in thy cot, and I saw thee falling down hill under the idolater—at one time, in one place, in my Soul, which, as I say, had touched the Great Soul. Also I saw the stupid body of Teshoo Lama lying down, and the *bakim* from Dacca kneeled beside, shouting in its ear. Then my Soul was all alone, and I saw nothing, for I was all things, having reached the Great Soul. And I meditated a thousand years, passionless, well aware of the Causes of all Things. Then a voice cried: 'What shall come to the boy if thou art dead?' and I was shaken back and forth in myself with pity for thee; and I said: 'I will return to my *chela*, lest he miss the Way.' Upon this my Soul, which is the soul of Teshoo Lama, withdrew itself from the Great Soul with strivings and yearnings and retchings and agonies not to be told. As the egg from the fish, as the fish from the water, as the water from the cloud, as the cloud from the thick air, so put forth, so leaped out, so drew away, so fumed up the soul of Teshoo Lama from the Great Soul. Then a voice cried: 'The River! Take heed to the River!' and I looked down upon all the world, which was as I had seen it before—one in time, one in place—and I saw plainly the River of the Arrow at my feet. At that hour my Soul was hampered by some evil or other whereof I was not wholly cleansed, and it lay upon my arms and coiled round my waist; but I put it aside, and I cast forth as an eagle in my flight for the very place of the River. I pushed aside world upon world for thy sake. I saw the River below me—the River of the Arrow—and, descending, the waters of it closed over me; and behold I was again in the body of Teshoo Lama, but free from sin, and the *bakim* from Dacca bore up my head in the waters of the River. It is here! It is behind the mango-tope here—even here!"

"Allah Kerim! Oh, well that the Babu was by! Wast thou very wet?"

"Why should I regard? I remember the *hakim* was concerned for the body of Teshoo Lama. He haled it out of the holy water in his hands, and there came afterwards thy horse-seller from the North with a cot and men, and they put the body on the cot and bore it up to the Sahiba's house."

"What said the Sahiba?"

"I was meditating in that body, and did not hear. So thus the Search is ended. For the merit that I have acquired, the River of the Arrow is here. It broke forth at our feet, as I have said. I have found it. Son of my Soul, I have wrenched my Soul back from the Threshold of Freedom to free thee from all sin—as I am free, and sinless. Just is the Wheel! Certain is our deliverance. Come!"

He crossed his hands on his lap and smiled, as a man may who has won Salvation for himself and his beloved.

This long passage builds, through radiant apprehensions, to an extraordinarily controlled and calm epiphany of parental love. The vision of the lama, though it presents itself as the wise soul's freedom from the silly body, is clearly not dualistic, but is caused by the lama's honest declaration: "I was troubled for thee." Caught up in the freedom from illusion, and free therefore supposedly of any concern for other souls, since, like one's own, they are not, the lama is close to the final freedom: "for I was all things." The voice that cries him back to life is the voice of his fatherly love for Kim, and the reward for his return to existence, negating mystical transport, is his true vision of the River, goal of his quest. It breaks forth at his feet, and is better than freedom, because it is not merely solitary, but is Salvation for his beloved adopted son, as well as for himself.

Certainly this is Kipling's most humane and hopeful moment, normative and positive. *Kim* is, like its more masterly precursor work, *Huckleberry Finn*, a book that returns us to the central values, avoiding those shadows of the abyss that hover uneasily elsewhere in Kipling. Yet even here the darker and truer Kipling lingers, in the sudden vision of nothingness that Kim experiences, only a few pages before his final reunion with the lama:

At first his legs bent like bad pipe-stems, and the flood and rush of the sunlit air dazzled him. He squatted by the white wall, the mind rummaging among the incidents of the long *dooli* journey, the lama's weaknesses, and, now that the stimulus of talk was removed, his own self-pity, of which, like the sick, he had great store. The unnerved brain edged away from all the outside, as a raw horse, once rowelled, sidles from the spur. It was enough,

amply enough, that the spoil of the *kilta* was away—off his
hands—out of his possession. He tried to think of the lama,—to
wonder why he had tumbled into a brook,—but the bigness of the
world, seen between the forecourt gates, swept linked thought
aside. Then he looked upon the trees and the broad fields, with
the thatched huts hidden among crops—looked with strange eyes
unable to take up the size and proportion and use of things—
stared for a still half-hour. All that while he felt, though he could
not put it into words, that his soul was out of gear with its sur-
roundings—a cog-wheel unconnected with any machinery, just
like the idle cog-wheel of a cheap Beheea sugar-crusher laid by in
a corner. The breezes fanned over him, the parrots shrieked at
him, the noises of the populated house behind—squabbles, orders,
and reproofs—hit on dead ears.

"I am Kim. I am Kim. And what is Kim?" His soul repeated it
again and again.

Despite the Indian imagery and the characteristic obsession of Kipling
with machinery, the mark of Walter Pater's aesthetic impressionism, with
its sensations beckoning us to the abyss, is clearly set upon this passage.
Identity flees with the flux of impressions, and the dazzlement of "the flood
and rush of the sunlit air" returns us to the cosmos of the "Conclusion" to
The Renaissance. Kipling's art, in *Kim*, is after all art for art's sake, in the
dark predicate that there is nothing else. The extravagant fiction of the
great love between an Irish boy gone native in India, half a Huck Finn
enthralled with freedom and half a Tom Sawyer playing games with
authority, and a quixotic, aged Tibetan lama is Kipling's finest invention,
and moves us endlessly. But how extravagant a fiction it is, and had to be!
Kipling refused to profess the faith of those who live and die for and by art,
yet in the end he had no other faith.

Willa Cather

(1873–1947)

WILLA CATHER, THOUGH NOW SOMEWHAT NEGLECTED, HAS FEW RIVALS among the American novelists of this century. Critics and readers frequently regard her as belonging to an earlier time, though she died in 1947. Her best novels were published in the years 1918–31, so that truly she was a novelist of the 1920's, an older contemporary and peer of Hemingway and of Scott Fitzgerald. Unlike them, she did not excel at the short story, though there are some memorable exceptions scattered through her four volumes of tales. Her strength is her novels and particularly, in my judgment, *My Ántonia* (1918), *A Lost Lady* (1923) and *The Professor's House* (1925); fictions worthy of a disciple of Flaubert and Henry James. Equally beautiful and achieved, but rather less central, are the subsequent historical novels, the very popular *Death Comes for the Archbishop* (1927) and *Shadows on the Rock* (1931). Her second novel, *O Pioneers!* (1913), is only just short of the eminence of this grand sequence. Six permanent novels is a remarkable number for a modern American writer; I can think only of Faulkner as Cather's match in this respect, since he wrote six truly enduring novels, all published during his great decade, 1929–39.

Cather's remoteness from the fictive universe of Fitzgerald, Hemingway and Faulkner is palpable, though all of them shared her nostalgia for an older America. She appears, at first, to have no aesthetic affinities with her younger contemporaries. We associate her instead with Sarah Orne Jewett, about whom she wrote a loving essay, or even with Edith Wharton, whom she scarcely resembles. Cather's mode of engaging with the psychic realities of post–World War I America is more oblique than Fitzgerald's or Hemingway's, but it is just as apposite a representation of the era's malaise. The short novel *A Lost Lady* (1923) is not out of its aesthetic context when we read it in the company of *The Waste Land, The*

Comedian as the Letter C, *The Sun Also Rises*, *The Great Gatsby* and *An American Tragedy*. Subtler and gentler than any of these, *A Lost Lady* elegizes just as profoundly a lost radiance or harmony, a defeat of a peculiarly American dream of innocence, grace, hope.

My Ántonia and *A Lost Lady*

Henry James, Cather's guide both as critic and novelist, died in England early in 1916. The year before, replying to H.G. Wells after being satirized by him, James wrote a famous credo: "Art *makes* life, makes interest, makes importance." This is Cather's faith also. One hears the voice of James when, in her essay "On the Art of Fiction," she writes: "Any first-rate novel or story must have in it the strength of a dozen fairly good stories that have been sacrificed to it." Those sacrifices of possibility upon the altar of form were the ritual acts of Cather's quite Paterian religion of art, too easily misread as a growing religiosity by many critics commenting upon *Death Comes for the Archbishop*. Herself a belated Aesthete, Cather emulated a familiar pattern of being attracted by the aura and not the substance of Roman Catholicism. New Mexico, and not Rome, is her place of the spirit, a spirit of the archaic and not of the supernatural.

Cather's social attitudes were altogether archaic. She shared a kind of Populist anti-Semitism with many American writers of her own generation and the next: Sherwood Anderson, Theodore Dreiser, Ezra Pound, Thomas Wolfe, even Hemingway and Fitzgerald. Her own version of anti-Semitism is curiously marked by her related aversion to heterosexuality. She had lost her first companion, Isabelle McClung, to a Jewish violinist, Jan Hambourg, and the Jewish figures in her fiction clearly represent the aggressivity of male sexuality. *The Professor's House* is marred by the gratuitous identification of the commercial exploitation of Cather's beloved West with Marcellus, the Professor's Jewish son-in-law. Doubtless, Cather's most unfortunate piece of writing was her notorious essay in 1914, "Potash and Perlmutter," in which she lamented, mock-heroically, that New York City was becoming too Jewish. Perhaps she was learning the lesson of the master again, since she is repeating, in a lighter tone, the complaint of Henry James in *The American Scene* (1907). She repeated her own distaste for "Jewish critics," tainted as they were by Freud, in the essay on Sarah Orne Jewett written quite late in her career, provoking Lionel Trilling to the just accusation that she had become a mere defender of gentility, mystically concerned with pots and pans.

This dark side of Cather, though hardly a value in itself, would not much matter except that it seeped into her fiction as a systemic resentment of her own era. Nietzsche, analyzing resentment, might be writing of Cather. Freud, analyzing the relation between paranoia and homosexuality, might be writing of her also. I am wary of being reductive in such observations, and someone perpetually mugged by Feminist critics as "the Patriarchal critic" is too battered to desire any further polemic. Cather, in my judgment, is aesthetically strongest and most persuasive in her loving depiction of her heroines and of Ántonia and the lost lady Mrs. Forrester in particular. She resembles Thomas Hardy in absolutely nothing, except in the remarkable ability to seduce the reader into joining the novelist at falling in love with the heroine. I am haunted by memories of having fallen in love with Marty South in *The Woodlanders*, and with Ántonia and Mrs. Forrester when I was a boy of fifteen. Rereading *My Ántonia* and *A Lost Lady* now at fifty-four, I find that the love renews itself. I doubt that I am falling again into what my late and honored teacher William K. Wimsatt named as the Affective Fallacy, since love for a woman made up out of words is necessarily a cognitive affair.

Cather's strength at representation gives us Jim Burden and Niel Herbert as her clear surrogates, unrealized perhaps as figures of sexual life, but forcefully conveyed as figures of capable imagination, capable above all of apprehending and transmitting the extraordinary actuality and visionary intensity of Ántonia and Mrs. Forrester. Like her masters, James and Pater, Cather had made her supposed deficiency into her strength, fulfilling the overt program of Emersonian self-reliance. But nothing is got for nothing, Emerson also indicated, and Cather, again like James and Pater, suffered the reverse side of the law of Compensation. The flaws, aesthetic and human, are there, even in *My Ántonia*, *A Lost Lady* and *The Professor's House*, but they scarcely diminish the beauty and dignity of three profound studies of American nostalgias.

II

Cather is hardly the only vital American novelist to have misread creatively the spirit of his or her own work. Her essential imaginative knowledge was of loss, which she interpreted temporally, though her loss was aboriginal, in the Romantic mode of Wordsworth, Emerson and all their varied descendants. The glory that had passed away belonged not to the pioneers but to her own transparent eyeball, her own original relation to the universe. Rhetorically, she manifests this knowledge, which frequently is at odds with her overt thematicism. Here is Jim Burden's first shared moment with Ántonia, when they both were little children:

We sat down and made a nest in the long red grass. Yulka curled up like a baby rabbit and played with a grasshopper. Ántonia pointed up to the sky and questioned me with her glance. I gave her the word, but she was not satisfied and pointed to my eyes. I told her, and she repeated the word, making it sound like "ice." She pointed up to the sky, then to my eyes, then back to the sky, with movements so quick and impulsive that she distracted me, and I had no idea what she wanted. She got up on her knees and wrung her hands. She pointed to her own eyes and shook her head, then to mine and to the sky, nodding violently.

"Oh," I exclaimed, "blue; blue sky."

She clapped her hands and murmured, "Blue sky, blue eyes," as if it amused her. While we snuggled down there out of the wind, she learned a score of words. She was quick, and very eager. We were so deep in the grass that we could see nothing but the blue sky over us and the gold tree in front of us. It was wonderfully pleasant. After Ántonia had said the new words over and over, she wanted to give me a little chased silver ring she wore on her middle finger. When she coaxed and insisted, I repulsed her quite sternly. I didn't want her ring, and I felt there was something reckless and extravagant about her wishing to give it away to a boy she had never seen before. No wonder Krajiek got the better of these people, if this was how they behaved.

One imagines that Turgenev would have admired this, and it would not be out of place inserted in his *A Sportman's Sketchbook*. Its naturalistic simplicity is deceptive. Wallace Stevens, in a letter of 1940, observed of Cather: "you may think she is more or less formless. Nevertheless, we have nothing better than she is. She takes so much pains to conceal her sophistication that it is easy to miss her quality." The quality here is partly manifested by an exuberance of trope and a precision of diction, both in the service of a fresh American myth of origin. Nesting and curling up in an embowered world of baby rabbits and grasshoppers, the children are at home in a universe of "blue sky, blue eyes." Heaven and earth come together, where vision confronts only the gold of trees. Ántonia, offering the fullness of a symbolic union to him, is rebuffed partly by the boy's shyness, and partly by Cather's own proleptic fear that the reckless generosity of the pioneer is doomed to exploitation. Yet the passage's deepest intimation is that Jim, though falling in love with Ántonia, is constrained by an inner recalcitrance, which the reader is free to interpret in several ways, none of which need exclude the others.

This is Cather in the springtide of her imagination. In her vision's early fall, we find ourselves regarding her lost lady Mrs. Forrester and we are comforted, as the boy Niel Herbert is, "in the quick recognition of her eyes, in the living quality of her voice itself." The book's splendor is that, like Mrs. Forrester's laughter, "it often told you a great deal that was both too direct and too elusive for words." As John Hollander shrewdly notes, Mrs. Forrester does not become a lost lady in any social or moral sense, but imaginatively she is transformed into Niel's "long-lost lady." Lost or refound, she is "his" always, even as Ántonia always remains Jim Burden's "my Ántonia." In her ability to suggest a love that is permanent, life-enhancing, and in no way possessive, Cather touches the farthest limit of her own strength as a novelist. If one could choose a single passage from all her work, it would be the Paterian epiphany or privileged moment in which Mrs. Forrester's image returned to Niel as "a bright, impersonal memory." Pater ought to have lived to have read this marvelous instance of the art he had celebrated and helped to stimulate in Cather:

> Her eyes; when they laughed for a moment into one's own, seemed to provide a wild delight that he had not found in life. "I know where it is," they seemed to say, "I could show you!" He would like to call up the shade of the young Mrs. Forrester, as the witch of Endor called up Samuel's, and challenge it, demand the secret of that ardour; ask her whether she had really found some ever-blooming, ever-burning, ever-piercing joy, or whether it was all fine play-acting. Probably she had found no more than another; but she had always the power of suggesting things much lovelier than herself, as the perfume of a single flower may call up the whole sweetness of spring.

It is the perfection of Cather's difficult art, when that art was most balanced and paced, and Mrs. Forrester here is the emblem of that perfection. Cather's fiction, at its frequent best, also suggests things much lovelier than itself. The reader, demanding the secret of Cather's ardour, learns not to challenge what may be remarkably fine play-acting, since Cather's feigning sometimes does persuade him that really she had found some perpetual joy.

Herman Hesse

(1877-1962)

Magister Ludi (*The Glass Bead Game*) and *Steppenwolf*

WHEN I WAS YOUNG, BOTH THOMAS MANN'S *DOCTOR FAUSTUS* (1947) AND Hermann Hesse's *The Glass Bead Game* (1943) were accepted as the two indubitable post–World War II German classics. Hesse, on the strength of *The Glass Bead Game*, his final novel, joined Mann as a Nobel laureate. The two novels seemed the last words of an older, Liberal Germany upon the dreadful debasement of the German spirit under the Nazis.

Mann's *The Magic Mountain* and Hesse's *Steppenwolf* each attracts more readers today than *Doctor Faustus* and *The Glass Bead Game*, at least in the United States, if not also in Germany. The ironies of both Mann and Hesse have obscured their comedic aspects: Thomas von der Trave in *The Glass Bead Game* is a parodistic portrait of Thomas Mann, while Hesse's Fritz Tegularius plainly parodies Friedrich Nietzsche, and his Father Jacobus is an ironical version of Jakob Burckhardt.

Hesse had a posthumous revival in the Counter-Cultural American Seventies, when *Demian, Siddhartha*, and *Steppenwolf* suited the *Zeitgeist*. The complex allegory of *The Glass Bead Game* attracted far fewer readers, though for a time *Doctor Faustus* had a substantial audience. Today both books, though admirably composed, are rather neglected, and rereading demonstrates that each remains considerably more than a Period Piece. The dumbing-down of high culture makes the survival of either book somewhat problematical, alas.

In some ways the Glass Bead Game, the game rather than the book, can now be regarded as a synthesis of Western literary and musical culture akin to the Western Canons of literature and of "classical" music. The imaginary province of Castalia (the fountain of the Muses) is a science-fiction projection into a nonexistent cultural future. Joseph Knecht (whose name means "servant") is both the fulfillment and the reduction of the Castalian aesthetic ideal.

I find myself, in 2002, regarding Hesse's Castalia with a certain nostalgia, for its equivalents in literary criticism—such as the work of E.R. Curtius, Northrop Frye, Kenneth Burke—largely have been replaced by the curious entity now called Cultural Studies in most Anglo-American universities. As a strenuous opponent of Cultural Studies, I myself have just published a vast book that is a kind of Kabbalistic Glass Bead Game, *Genius: A Mosaic of One Hundred Exemplary Creative Minds*. Hesse is not among those minds (though Mann is) but I find myself ironically wondering if my book is not, after all, another vision of Castalia, another metaphor for a waning, soon perhaps to be lost high culture.

Aestheticism, in the face of the Nazi horror, seemed not a pragmatic possibility for Hesse and for Mann. Without necessarily regarding both *The Glass Bead Game* and *Doctor Faustus* as more than great but flawed fictions, Aestheticism in 2002 hardly seems a useless alternative to the Age of Information, Corporate corruption, and Bushian bellicose sanctimoniousness. Bach, Mozart, Shakespeare and Dante seem absolute goods in themselves, even when cut off from our dwindling cultural possibilities.

Castalia, rejected by Knecht, looks very different to me in 2002 than it did in the 1940s. The American equivalent of the musical aspect of the Glass Bead Game is the jazz of Louis Armstrong and Duke Ellington, Charlie Parker and Bud Powell, Charles Mingus, and Thelonious Monk. An American Castalia might counterpoint classic jazz with the superb American poetical tradition: Walt Whitman and Emily Dickinson, Robert Frost and T.S. Eliot, Hart Crane and Elizabeth Bishop, James Merrill and John Ashbery and A.R. Ammons. Our Glass Bead Game might fuse Charlie Parker and Wallace Stevens, thus synthesizing an art of nuance that transcends the concerns and the capacities of Cultural Criticism.

In 2002, the sacrifice of Joseph Knecht seems to me a spiritual mistake. The cultural commissars of Resentment regard Knecht's demise as another proof of their polemic that all art must be political. Hesse, a sensitive lyric novelist, was not an adequate prophet of the cultural malaise we all need to combine to defeat.

Upton Sinclair

(1878–1968)

The Jungle

MY INTRODUCTION RELUCTANTLY ADMITS THAT *THE JUNGLE* (1906) IS A period piece: to read it, one puts one's uphill shoulder to the wheel, and feels proper gratitude to Upton Sinclair's book, which helped give us the Pure Food and Drug Act of 1906.

Jon A. Yoder sadly comments that the public received *The Jungle* as muckraking, rather than as an indictment of capitalism, while Michael Brewster Folsom accurately indicts Upton Sinclair for racism, and for spoiling his novel's conclusion.

A poignant defense of the book is offered by the scholarly and brilliant Morris Dickstein, who tries to save *The Jungle* by citing our New Age of the nonfiction novel and the New Journalism.

Timothy Cook usefully traces the influence of Upton Sinclair's novel upon George Orwell's *Animal Farm*, after which Carl S. Smith recounts Sinclair's description of the stockyards as a "combination of Babel, bedlam, and hell."

In R.N. Mookerjee's reading, the novel comes apart when Sinclair moves from a vision of human suffering to a sermon for socialism, while Emory Elliott, though acknowledging Sinclair's racism, praised him for showing the destructive effect upon poor people when they live without hope for the future.

The analogue between Jack London's *The Call of the Wild* and *The Jungle* is worked through by Jacqueline Tavernier-Courbin, after which Scott Derrick meditates upon Sinclair's bondage to masculine myths of gender-rules.

In this volume's final essay, Matthew J. Morris interestingly analyzes

Sinclair's unsuccessful struggle to find a narrative mode that could show the killing power of capitalism without adding just one more representation of that power that involuntarily helps to prolong it.

In his ninety years Upton Sinclair wrote ninety books, almost got elected Governor of California (1934), and died knowing that he had helped pass the Pure Food and Drug Act of 1906, and had lived to be Lyndon Johnson's guest observer of the signing of the Wholesome Meat Act (1967). That is hardly a wasted life, though *The Jungle* is now only a rather drab period piece, and the other books are totally unreadable.

Morris Dickstein and Emory Elliott between them have done as much as can be done for *The Jungle*, which I have just reread, with curiosity and revulsion, more than half a century after my first encounter with the book. I dimly recall having found it both somber and harrowing, but I was very young, and both experiential and literary sorrows have made me more impatient with it now. American naturalistic writing can survive a certain crudity in style and procedure; Dreiser in particular transcends such limitations in *Sister Carrie* and *An American Tragedy*. But Sinclair has nothing of Dreiser's preternatural powers of empathy. What Sinclair tries to do is simply beyond his gifts: his people are names on the page, and his inability to represent social reality makes me long for Balzac and Zola, or even Tom Wolfe.

Time is cruel to inadequate literature, though it can be slow in its remorselessness. The young have a remarkable taste for period pieces; I note that my paperback copy of *The Jungle*, published in 1981, is in its thirty-third printing, and I suspect that most of it has been sold to younger people, in or out of class. I meditate incessantly on the phenomenon of period pieces, surrounded as I am by so many bad books proclaimed as instant classics, while John Crowley's *Little, Big* (1981), a fantasy novel I have read through scores of times, is usually out-of-print, as it is at the moment. Patience, patience. The Harry Potter books will be on the rubbish piles, though after I myself are gone, and *Little, Big* will join the *Alice* books of Lewis Carroll and Kenneth Grahame's *The Wind in the Willows*.

As a literary critic who has covered the waterfront, for a while now, I find the mountain of mail that comes to me instructive, even though I cannot answer it, or even acknowledge it, if I myself am to go on reading, writing, teaching, and living. The two constant piles of vituperative missives come from Oxfordians, poor souls desperate to prove that Edward De Vere wrote all of Shakespeare, and Harry Potterites, of all ages and nationalities. The rage of the partisans of the Earl of Oxford, though crazy and unpleasant, baffles me less than the outrage of the legions of Potterites. Why are they so vulnerable to having their taste and judgment questioned?

No matter how fiercely we dumb down, led in this by *The New York Times Book Review* and the once-elite universities, period pieces seem to induce uneasy sensations in their contemporary enthusiasts. On tour in Turin, a year ago, I found myself talking about my *How to Read and Why* (Italian version) at an academy for writers called the Holden School, in honor of Salinger's hero. When the school's head, my host, a novelist, asked me why my book said nothing about *The Catcher in the Rye*, I gently intimated that I considered it a period piece, that would go on, perhaps for quite a while, but then would perish. Honest judgment has its costs, and I was shown out rather coldly when I departed. All critics, I know, are subject to error: my hero, Dr. Samuel Johnson, nodded in the terrible sentence: "*Tristram Shandy* did not last." And yet I wonder, as I age onwards, what it is in us that makes us so bitter when period pieces expire, if we are one of the survivors of a dead vogue?

Stephen Crane

(1879-1900)

STEPHEN CRANE'S CONTRIBUTION TO THE CANON OF AMERICAN LITERATURE is fairly slight in bulk: one classic short novel, three vivid stories, and two or three ironic lyrics. *The Red Badge of Courage*; "The Open Boat," "The Blue Hotel," and "The Bride Comes to Yellow Sky"; "War is Kind" and "A Man Adrift on a Slim Spar"—a single small volume can hold them all. Crane was dead at twenty-eight, after a frantic life, but a longer existence probably would not have enhanced his achievement. He was an exemplary American writer, flaring in the forehead of the morning sky and vanishing in the high noon of our evening land. An original, if not quite a Great Original, he prophesied Hemingway and our other journalist-novelists and still seems a forerunner of much to come.

The Red Badge of Courage

Rereading *The Red Badge of Courage*, it is difficult to believe that it was written by a young man not yet twenty-four, who had never seen battle. Dead of tuberculosis at twenty-eight, Stephen Crane nevertheless had written a canonical novel, three remarkable stories, and a handful of permanent poems. He was a singular phenomenon: his father, grandfather and great-uncle all were evangelical Methodists, intensely puritanical. Crane, precocious both as man-of-letters and as journalist, kept living out what Freud called "rescue of fantasies," frequently with prostitutes. His common-law marriage, which sustained him until his early death, was with Cora Taylor, whom he first met when she was madame of a Florida bordello. Incongruously, Crane—who was *persona non-grata* to the New York City police—lived a brief, exalted final phase in England, where he became close to the great novelists Joseph Conrad and Henry James, both of whom greatly admired Crane's writing.

Had Crane lived, he doubtless would have continued his epic impressions of war, and confirmed his status as a crucial forerunner of Ernest Hemingway. And yet his actual observations of battle, of Americans against Spaniards in Cuba, and of Greeks against Turks, led to war-writing greatly inferior to his imaginings in *The Red Badge of Courage*. Perhaps Crane would have developed in other directions, had he survived. It is difficult to envision Crane improving upon *The Red Badge of Courage*, which is better battle-writing than Hemingway and Norman Mailer could accomplish. The great visionaries of warfare—Homer, Virgil, Shakespeare, Tolstoy— necessarily are beyond Crane's art, but in American literature he is surpassed in this mode only by the Cormac McCarthy of *Blood Meridian*. McCarthy writes in the baroque, high rhetorical manner of Melville and Faulkner. Crane, a very original impressionist, was a Conradian before he read Conrad. I sometimes hear Kipling's prose style in Crane, but the echoes are indistinct and fleeting, almost as though the battlefield visionary had just read *The Jungle Book*. Kipling, though also a great journalist, could not provide Crane with a paradigm to assist in the recreation of the bloody battle of Chancellorsville (May 2–4, 1863). Harold Beaver suggests that Stendhal and Tolstoy did that labor for Crane, which is highly feasible, and Beaver is also interesting in suggesting that Crane invented a kind of expressionism in his hallucinatory, camera-eye visions, as here in Chapter 7 of the *Red Badge*:

Once he found himself almost into a swamp. He was obliged to walk upon bog tufts and watch his feet to keep from the oily mire. Pausing at one time to look about him he saw, out at some black water, a small animal pounce in and emerge directly with a gleaming fish.

The youth went again into the deep thickets. The brushed branches made a noise that drowned the sound of cannon. He walked on, going from obscurity into promises of a greater obscurity.

At length he reached a place where the high, arching boughs made a chapel. He softly pushed the green doors aside and entered. Pine needles were a gentle brown carpet. There was a religious half light.

Near the threshold he stopped, horror-stricken at the sight of a thing.

He was being looked at by a dead man who was seated with his back against a columnlike tree. The corpse was dressed in a uniform that once had been blue, but was now faded to a melancholy shade of green. The eyes, staring at the youth, had changed to the dull hue to be seen on the side of a dead fish. The mouth was open. Its red had changed to an appalling yellow. Over the gray skin of the face ran little ants. One was trundling some sort of a bundle along the upper lip.

This is a kind of pure, visual irony, nihilistic and parodistic, beyond meaning, or with meanings beyond control. On a grander scale, here is the famous account of the color sergeant's death in Chapter 19:

Over the field went the scurrying mass. It was a handful of men splattered into the faces of the enemy. Toward it instantly sprang the yellow tongues. A vast quantity of blue smoke hung before them. A mighty banging made ears valueless.

The youth ran like a madman to reach the woods before a bullet could discover him. He ducked his head low, like a football player. In his haste his eyes almost closed, and the scene was a wild blur. Pulsating saliva stood at the corners of his mouth.

Within him, as he hurled himself forward, was born a love, a despairing fondness for this flag which was near him. It was a creation of beauty and invulnerability. It was a goddess, radiant, that bended its form with an imperious gesture to him. It was a woman, red and white, hating and loving, that called him with the voice of his hopes. Because no harm could come to it he endowed it with power. He kept near, as if it could be a saver of lives, and an imploring cry went from his mind.

In the mad scramble he was aware that the color sergeant flinched suddenly, as if struck by a bludgeon. He faltered, and then became motionless, save for his quivery knees.

He made a spring and a clutch at the pole. At the same instant his friend grabbed it from the other side. They jerked at it, stout and furious, but the color sergeant was dead, and the corpse would not relinquish its trust. For a moment there was a grim encounter. The dead man, swinging with bended back, seemed to be obstinately tugging, in ludicrous and awful ways, for the possession of the flag.

It was past in an instant of time. They wrenched the flag furiously from the dead man, and, as they turned again, the corpse swayed forward with bowed head. One arm swung high, and the curved hand fell with heavy protest on the friend's unheeding shoulder.

The flag and the color sergeant's corpse become assimilated to one another, and the phantasmagoria of the flag-as-woman is highly ambivalent, being both an object of desire, and potentially destructive: "hating and loving." Crane's vision again is nihilistic, and reminds us that even his title is an irony, since the ultimate red badge of courage would be a death-wound.

Maggie

As in his masterpiece, *The Red Badge of Courage* (1895), Stephen Crane relies upon pure imagination in composing his first narrative fiction, *Maggie: A Girl of the Streets* (1893). Crane had never seen a battle when he wrote *The Red Badge of Courage*, and he scarcely had encountered the low life of the Bowery before he produced *Maggie*. Ironically, he was to have all too much of slum life after *Maggie* was printed, and to see more than enough bloodshed as a war correspondent, after *The Red Badge of Courage* had made him famous.

Maggie is a curious book to reread, partly because of its corrosive irony, but also it hurts to encounter again the over-determined ruin of poor Maggie. Her ghastly family, dreadful lover, and incessant poverty all drive her into prostitution and the ambiguous death by drowning, which may be suicide or victimage by murder.

The minimal but authentic aesthetic dignity of *Maggie* results from the strangeness so frequently characteristic of nineteenth-century realism and naturalism. Zola, whose influence seems strong in *Maggie*, actually created a visionary naturalism, more phantasmagoric than realistic. Crane, impressionist and ironist, goes even further in *Maggie*, a laconic experiment in word-painting. Crane's imagery is Hogarthian yet modified by an original perspectivism, irrealistic and verging upon surrealism. Maggie herself is an uncanny prophecy of what was to be the central relationship of Crane's brief life, his affair with Cora Taylor, who ran a bordello in Jacksonville, Florida. She accompanied him to England, where their friends included Joseph Conrad and Henry James, and she sustained him through the agony of his early death.

E.M. Forster

(1879–1970)

Howards End and *A Passage to India*

E.M. FORSTER'S CANONICAL CRITIC WAS LIONEL TRILLING, WHO MIGHT
have written Forster's novels had Forster not written them and had Trilling
been English. Trilling ended his book on Forster (1924) with the tribute that
forever exalts the author of *Howards End* and *A Passage to India* as one of those
storytellers whose efforts "work without man's consciousness of them, and even
against his conscious will." In Trilling's sympathetic interpretation (or identification), Forster was the true antithesis to the world of telegrams and anger:

> A world at war is necessarily a world of will; in a world at war
> Forster reminds us of a world where the will is not everything, of
> a world of true order, of the necessary connection of passion and
> prose, and of the strange paradoxes of being human. He is one of
> those who raise the shield of Achilles, which is the moral intelli-
> gence of art, against the panic and emptiness which make their
> onset when the will is tired from its own excess.

Trilling subtly echoed Forster's own response to World War I, a response
which Forster recalled as an immersion in Blake, William Morris, the early
T.S. Eliot, J.K. Huysmans, Yeats: "They took me into a country where the
will was not everything." Yet one can wonder whether Forster and Trilling,
prophets of the liberal imagination, did not yield to a vision where there
was not quite enough conscious will. *A Passage to India*, Forster's most
famous work, can sustain many rereadings, so intricate is its orchestration.
It is one of only a few novels of this century that is *written-through*, in the
musical sense of thorough composition. But reading it yet again, after

twenty years away from it, I find it to be a narrative all of whose principal figures—Aziz, Fielding, Adela Quested, Mrs. Moore, Godbole—lack conscious will. Doubtless, this is Forster's deliberate art, but the consequence is curious; the characters do not sustain rereading so well as the novel does, because none is larger than the book. Poldy holds my imagination quite apart from Joyce's *Ulysses*, as Isabel Archer does in James's *The Portrait of a Lady*, or indeed as Mrs. Wilcox does in Forster's *Howards End*, at least while she is represented as being alive. The aesthetic puzzle of *A Passage to India* is why Aziz and Fielding could not have been stronger and more vivid beings than they are.

What matters most in *A Passage to India* is India, and not any Indians nor any English. But this assertion requires amendment, since Forster's India is not so much a social or cultural reality as it is an enigmatic vision of the Hindu religion, or rather of the Hindu religion as it is reimagined by the English liberal mind at its most sensitive and scrupulous. The largest surprise of a careful rereading of *A Passage to India* after so many years is that, in some aspects, it now seems a strikingly *religious* book. Forster shows us what we never ought to have forgotten, which is that any distinction between religious and secular literature is finally a mere political or societal polemic, but is neither a spiritual nor an aesthetic judgment. There is no sacred literature and no post-sacred literature, great or good. *A Passage to India* falls perhaps just short of greatness, in a strict aesthetic judgment, but spiritually it is an extraordinary achievement.

T.S. Eliot consciously strove to be a devotional poet, and certainly did become a Christian polemicist as a cultural and literary critic. Forster, an amiable freethinker and secular humanist, in his *Commonplace Book* admirably compared himself to Eliot:

> With Eliot? I feel now to be as far ahead of him as I was once behind. Always a distance—and a respectful one. How I dislike his homage to pain! What a mind except the human could have excogitated it? Of course there's pain on and off through each individual's life, and pain at the end of most lives. You can't shirk it and so on. But why should it be endorsed by the schoolmaster and sanctified by the priest
>
> until the fire and the rose are
>
> one when so much of it is caused by disease or by bullies? It is here that Eliot becomes unsatisfactory as a seer.

One could add: it is here that Forster becomes most satisfactory as a seer, for that is the peculiar excellence of *A Passage to India*. We are reminded that Forster is another of John Ruskin's heirs, together with Proust, whom Forster rightly admired above all other modern novelists. Forster too wishes *to make us see*, in the hope that by seeing we will learn to connect, with ourselves and with others, and like Ruskin, Forster knows that seeing in this strong sense is religious, but in a mode beyond dogmatism.

II

A Passage to India, published in 1924, reflects Forster's service as private secretary to the Maharajah of Dewas State Senior in 1921–22, which in turn issued from his Indian visit of 1912–13 with G. Lowes Dickinson. It was not until 1953 that Forster published *The Hill of Devi*, utilizing letters he had written home from India, both forty and thirty years before. *The Hill of Devi* celebrates Forster's Maharajah as a kind of saint, indeed as a religious genius, though Forster is anything but persuasive when he attempts to sustain his judgment of his friend and employer. What does come through is Forster's appreciation of certain elements in Hinduism, an appreciation that achieves its apotheosis in *A Passage to India*, and particularly in "Temple," the novel's foreshortened final part. Forster's ultimate tribute to his Maharajah, a muddler in practical matters and so one who died in disgrace, is a singular testimony for a freethinker. *The Hill of Devi* concludes with what must be called a mystical apprehension:

> His religion was the deepest thing in him. It ought to be studied— neither by the psychologist nor by the mythologist but by the individual who has experienced similar promptings. He penetrated in to rare regions and he was always hoping that others would follow him there.

What are those promptings? Where are those regions? Are these the questions fleshed out by *A Passage to India*? After observing the mystical Maharajah dance before the altar of the God Krishna, Forster quotes from a letter by the Maharajah describing the festival, and then attempts what replies seem possible:

> Such was his account. But what did he feel when he danced like King David before the altar? What were his religious opinions?
>   The first question is easier to answer than the second. He felt as King David and other mystics have felt when they are in the

mystic state. He presented well-known characteristics. He was convinced that he was in touch with the reality he called Krishna. And he was unconscious of the world around him. "You can come in during my observances tomorrow and see me if you like, but I shall not know that you are there," he once told Malcolm. And he didn't know. He was in an abnormal but recognisable state; psychologists have studied it.

More interesting, and more elusive, are his religious opinions. The unseen was always close to him, even when he was joking or intriguing. Red paint on a stone could evoke it. Like most people, he implied beliefs and formulated rules for behaviour, and since he had a lively mind, he was often inconsistent. It was difficult to be sure what he did believe (outside the great mystic moments) or what he thought right or wrong. Indians are even more puzzling than Westerners here. Mr. Shastri, a spiritual and subtle Brahmin, once uttered a puzzler: "If the Gods do a thing, it is a reason for men not to do it." No doubt he was in a particular religious mood. In another mood he would have urged us to imitate the Gods. And the Maharajah was all moods. They played over his face, they agitated his delicate feet and hands. To get any pronouncement from so mercurial a creature on the subject, say, of asceticism, was impossible. As a boy, he had thought of retiring from the world, and it was an ideal which he cherished throughout his life, and which, at the end, he would have done well to practise. Yet he would condemn asceticism, declare that salvation could not be reached through it, that it might be Vedantic but it was not Vedic, and matter and spirit must both be given their due. Nothing too much! In such a mood he seemed Greek.

He believed in the heart, and here we reach firmer ground. "I stand for the heart. To the dogs with the head," cries Herman Melville, and he would have agreed. Affection, or the possibility of it, quivered through everything, from Gokul Ashtami down to daily human relationships. When I returned to England and he heard that I was worried because the post-war world of the '20's would not add up into sense, he sent me a message. "Tell him," it ran, "tell him from me to follow his heart, and his mind will see everything clear." The message as phrased is too facile: doors open into silliness at once. But to remember and respect and prefer the heart, to have the instinct which follows it wherever possible—what surer help than that could one have through life? What better hope of clarification? Melville goes on: "The reason that the mass of men fear God and at bottom dislike Him, is because they rather distrust His heart." With that too he would have agreed.

With all respect for Forster, neither he nor his prince is coherent here, and I suspect that Forster is weakly misreading Melville, who is both more ironic and more Gnostic than Forster chooses to realize. Melville, too, distrusts the heart of Jehovah, and consigns the head to the dogs precisely because he associates the head with Jehovah and identifies Jehovah with the Demiurge, the god of this world. More vital would be the question: what does Professor Godbole in *A Passage to India* believe? Is he more coherent than the Maharajah, and does Forster himself achieve a more unified vision there than he does in *The Hill of Devi?*

Criticism from Lionel Trilling on has evaded these questions, but such evasion is inevitable because Forster may be vulnerable to the indictment that he himself made against Joseph Conrad, to the effect that

> he is misty in the middle as well as at the edges, that the secret casket of his genius contains a vapour rather than a jewel; and that we need not try to write him down philosophically, because there is, in this particular direction, nothing to write. No creed, in fact. Only opinions, and the right to throw them overboard when facts make them look absurd. Opinions held under the semblance of eternity, girt with the sea, crowned with the stars, and therefore easily mistaken for a creed.

Heart of Darkness sustains Forster's gentle wit, but *Nostromo* does not. Is there a vapor rather than a jewel in Forster's consciousness of Hinduism, at least as represented in *A Passage to India*? "Hinduism" may be the wrong word in that question; "religion" would be better, and "spirituality" better yet. For I do not read Forster as being either hungry for belief or skeptical of it. Rather, he seems to me an Alexandrian, of the third century before the common era, an age celebrated in his *Alexandria: A History and a Guide* (1922), a book that goes back to his happy years in Alexandria (1915–19). In some curious sense, Forster's India is Alexandrian, and his vision of Hinduism is Plotinean. *A Passage to India* is a narrative of Neo-Platonic spirituality, and the true heroine of that narrative, Mrs. Moore, is the Alexandrian figure of Wisdom, the Sophia, as set forth in the Hellenistic Jewish Wisdom of Solomon. Of Wisdom, or Sophia, Forster says: "She is a messenger who bridges the gulf and makes us friends of God," which is a useful description of the narrative function of Mrs. Moore. And after quoting Plotinus (in a passage that includes one of his book's epigraphs): "To any vision must be brought an eye adapted to what is to be seen," Forster comments:

> This sublime passage suggests three comments, with which our glance at Plotinus must close. In the first place its tone is religious, and in this it is typical of all Alexandrian philosophy. In the second place it lays stress on behaviour and training; the Supreme Vision cannot be acquired by magic tricks—only those will see it who are fit to see. And in the third place the vision of oneself and the vision of God are really the same, because each individual *is* God, if only he knew it. And here is the great difference between Plotinus and Christianity. The Christian promise is that a man shall see God, the Neo-Platonic—like the Indian—that he shall be God. Perhaps, on the quays of Alexandria, Plotinus talked with Hindu merchants who came to the town. At all events his system can be paralleled in the religious writings of India. He comes nearer than any other Greek philosopher to the thought of the East.

Forster's Alexandria is in the first place personal; he associated the city always with his sexual maturation as a homosexual. But, as the book *Alexandria* shrewdly shows, Forster finds his precursor culture in ancient Alexandria; indeed he helps to teach us that we are all Alexandrians, insofar as we now live in a literary culture. Forster's insight is massively supported by the historian F.E. Peters in the great study *The Harvest of Hellenism*, when he catalogs our debts to the Eastern Hellenism of Alexandria:

> Its monuments are gnosticism, the university, the catechetical school, pastoral poetry, monasticism, the romance, grammar, lexicography, city planning, theology, canon law, heresy, and scholasticism.

Forster would have added, thinking of the Ptolemaic Alexandria of 331–30 B.C.E., that the most relevant legacy was an eclectic and tolerant liberal humanism, scientific and scholarly, exalting the values of affection over those of belief. That is already the vision of *A Passage to India*, and it opens to the novel's central spiritual question: how are the divine and the human linked? In *Alexandria*, Forster presents us with a clue by his account of the Arian heresy:

Christ is the Son of God. Then is he not younger than God? Arius held that he was and that there was a period before time began when the First Person of the Trinity existed and the Second did not. A typical Alexandrian theologian, occupied with the favourite problem of linking human and divine, Arius thought to solve the problem by making the link predominately human. He did not deny the Godhead of Christ, but he did make him inferior to the Father—of *like* substance, not of the *same* substance, which was the view held by Athanasius, and stamped as orthodox by the Council of Nicaea. Moreover the Arian Christ, like the Gnostic Demiurge, made the world;—creation, an inferior activity, being entrusted to him by the Father, who had Himself created nothing but Christ.

It is easy to see why Arianism became popular. By making Christ younger and lower than God it brought him nearer to us— indeed it tended to level him into a mere good man and to forestall Unitarianism. It appealed to the untheologically minded, to emperors and even more to empresses. But St. Athanasius, who viewed the innovation with an expert eye, saw that while it popularised Christ it isolated God, and he fought it with vigour and venom. His success has been described. It was condemned as heretical in 325, and by the end of the century had been expelled from orthodox Christendom. Of the theatre of this ancient strife no trace remains at Alexandria; the church of St. Mark where Arius was presbyter has vanished: so have the churches where Athanasius thundered—St. Theonas and the Caesareum. Nor do we know in which street Arius died of epilepsy. But the strife still continues in the hearts of men, who always tend to magnify the human in the divine, and it is probable that many an individual Christian to-day is an Arian without knowing it.

To magnify the human in the divine is certainly Forster's quest, and appears to be his interpretation of Hinduism in *A Passage to India*:

Down in the sacred corridors, joy had seethed to jollity. It was their duty to play various games to amuse the newly born God, and to simulate his sports with the wanton dairymaids of Brindaban. Butter played a prominent part in these. When the cradle had been removed, the principal nobles of the state gathered together for an innocent frolic. They removed their turbans, and one put a lump of butter on his forehead, and waited for it to slide down his nose into his mouth. Before it could arrive, another stole up behind him, snatched the melting morsel, and swallowed it himself. All laughed exultantly at discovering that the divine sense of humour coincided with their own. "God is love!" There is fun in heaven. God can play practical jokes upon Himself, draw chairs away from beneath His own posteriors, set His own turbans on fire, and steal His own petticoats when He bathes. By sacrificing good taste, this worship achieved what Christianity has shirked: the inclusion of merriment. All spirit as well as all matter must participate in salvation, and if practical jokes are banned, the circle is incomplete. Having swallowed the butter, they played another game which chanced to be graceful: the fondling of Shri Krishna under the similitude of a child. A pretty red and gold ball is thrown, and he who catches it chooses a child from the crowd, raises it in his arms, and carries it round to be caressed. All stroke the darling creature for the Creator's sake, and murmur happy words. The child is restored to his parents, the ball thrown on, and another child becomes for a moment the World's desire. And the Lord bounds hither and thither through the aisles, chance, and the sport of chance, irradiating little mortals with His immortality.... When they had played this long enough—and being exempt from boredom, they played it again and again, they played it again and again—they took many sticks and hit them together, whack smack, as though they fought the Pandava wars, and threshed and churned with them, and later on they hung from the roof of the temple, in a net, a great black earthenware jar, which was painted here and there with red, and wreathed with dried figs. Now came a rousing sport. Springing up, they struck at the jar with their sticks. It cracked, broke, and a mass of greasy rice and milk poured on to their faces. They ate and smeared one another's mouths and dived between each other's legs for what had been pashed upon the carpet. This way and that spread the divine mess, until the line of schoolboys, who had somewhat fended off the crowd, broke for their share. The corridors, the courtyard, were filled with benign confusion. Also the flies awoke and claimed their share of God's bounty. There was no quarrelling, owing to the nature of the gift, for blessed is the man who confers it on another, he imitates God. And those "imitations," those "substitutions," continued to flicker through the assembly for many hours, awaking in each man, according to his capacity, an emotion that he would not have had otherwise. No definite image survived; at the Birth it was questionable whether a silver doll or a mud village, or a silk napkin, or an intangible spirit, or a pious resolution, had been born. Perhaps all these things! Perhaps none! Perhaps all birth is an allegory! Still, it was the main event of the religious year. It caused strange thoughts. Covered with grease and dust, Professor Godbole had once more developed the life of his spirit. He had, with increasing vividness, again seen Mrs. Moore, and round her faintly clinging forms of trouble. He was a Brahman, she Christian, but it made no difference, it made no difference whether she was a trick of his memory or a telepathic appeal. It was his duty, as it was his desire, to place himself in the position of the God and to love her, and to place himself in her position and to say to the God, "Come, come, come, come." This was all he could do. How inadequate! But each according to his own capacities, and he knew that his own were small. "One old Englishwoman and one little, little wasp," he thought, as he stepped out of the temple into the grey of a pouring wet morning. "It does not seem much, still it is more than I am myself."

Professor Godbole's epiphany, his linkage of Mrs. Moore's receptivity toward the wasp with his own receptivity toward Mrs. Moore, has been much admired by critics, deservedly so. In this moment-of-moments, Godbole receives Mrs. Moore into Forster's own faithless faith: a religion of love between equals, as opposed to Christianity, a religion of love between the incommensurate Jehovah and his creatures. But though beautifully executed, Forster's vision of Godbole and Mrs. Moore is spiritually a little too easy. Forster knew that, and the finest moment in *A Passage to India* encompasses this knowing. It comes in a sublime juxtaposition, in the crossing between the conclusion of part 2, "Caves," and the beginning of part 3, "Temple," where Godbole is seen standing in the presence of God. The brief and beautiful chapter 32 that concludes "Caves" returns Fielding to a Western and Ruskinian vision of form in Venice:

Egypt was charming—a green strip of carpet and walking up and down it four sorts of animals and one sort of man. Fielding's business took him there for a few days. He re-embarked at Alexandria—bright blue sky, constant wind, clean low coastline, as against the intricacies of Bombay. Crete welcomed him next with the long snowy ridge of its mountains, and then came Venice. As he landed on the piazzetta a cup of beauty was lifted to his lips, and he drank with a sense of disloyalty. The buildings of Venice, like the mountains of Crete and the fields of Egypt, stood in the right place, whereas in poor India everything was placed wrong. He had forgotten the beauty of form among idol temples and lumpy hills; indeed, without form, how can there be beauty? Form stammered here and there in a mosque, became rigid through nervousness even, but oh these Italian churches! San Giorgio standing on the island which could scarcely have risen from the waves without it, the Salute holding the entrance of a canal which, but for it, would not be the Grand Canal! In the old undergraduate days he had wrapped himself up in the many-coloured blanket of St. Mark's, but something more precious than mosaics and marbles was offered to him now: the harmony between the works of man and the earth that upholds them, the civilization that has escaped muddle, the spirit in a reasonable form, with flesh and blood subsisting. Writing picture post-cards to his Indian friends, he felt that all of them would miss the joys he experienced now, the joys of form, and that this constituted a serious barrier. They would see the sumptuousness of Venice, not its shape, and though Venice was not Europe, it was part of the Mediterranean harmony. The Mediterranean is the human norm. When men leave that exquisite lake, whether through the Bosphorus or the Pillars of Hercules, they approach the monstrous and extraordinary; and the southern exit leads to the strangest experience of all. Turning his back on it yet again, he took the train northward, and tender romantic fancies that he thought were dead for ever, flowered when he saw the buttercups and daisies of June.

After the muddle of India, where "everything was placed wrong," Fielding learns again "the beauty of form." Alexandria, like Venice, is part of the Mediterranean harmony, the human norm, but India is the cosmos of "the monstrous and extraordinary." Fielding confronting the Venetian churches has absolutely nothing in common with Professor Godbole confronting the God Krishna at the opposite end of the same strip of carpet upon which Godbole stands. Forster is too wise not to know that the passage to India is only a passage. A passage is a journey, or an occurrence between two persons. Fielding and Aziz do not quite make the passage together, do not exchange vows that bind. Perhaps that recognition of limits is the ultimate beauty of form in *A Passage to India*.

Robert Musil

(1880–1942)

The Man Without Qualities

ROBERT MUSIL'S LITERARY EMINENCE IS BEYOND DOUBT. BECAUSE OF THE unfinished (and unfinishable) nature of his masterwork, *The Man Without Qualities*, he cannot quite be placed in the company of Joyce and Proust and Kafka, or even of Thomas Mann and William Faulkner, among the High Modernists. His aesthetic splendor rivals that of Broch and Hofmannsthal, hardly a second order except in comparison to Joyce and Proust, Kafka and Beckett.

Proust and Kafka each loses by translation, rather more than Mann and Broch do, but Musil loses most, despite the distinguished and devoted efforts of Sophie Wilkins and Burton Pike. Musil's language is as unique as Paul Celan's, and Musil's styles (there are several, beautifully modulated) never stay fixed. Burton Pike contributes an eloquent "Translator's Afterword" (pp. 1771–1774) to the 1995 American edition, in which he aptly remarks that there is no author in English who could provide a model for Musil's fusion of sound and sense. It is unnerving that Musil is both essayistic and a curious blend of Taoist-Sufi in his procedures. He also combines an inward voicing with an outward panoply that verges upon prose-poetry.

Musil's actual precursor was the Shakespeare of *Hamlet*, where the representation of thinking-in-language touches a limit in the Prince of Denmark's seven soliloquies that even Musil cannot attain. Ulrich is a descendant of Hamlet, who haunts German literature as pervasively as he does the Anglo-American tradition. Incest, termed by Shelley the most poetical of circumstances, is deferred throughout Part III of the novel, and evidently continues to be deferred in the sixty hundred and fifty pages from the Posthumous Papers that Pike translates. The consummation of Ulrich's and Agathe's mutual passion would have been a kind of suicide, probably followed by a literal double-suicide, the only way in which this unfinishable novel could have been finished. Musil's own death became the circumstance that concluded what could not reach conclusion, the full union of Agathe and Ulrich, a cosmological metaphor for the end of Musil's cultural would.

And yet the word "incest" is grossly imprecise for the love between these extraordinary siblings. What after all *is* incest in a fictive work? In Musil, the long-impending but unrealizable total relationship between Agathe and Ulrich is the ultimate trope for the new kind of secular transcendence that is the endless quest of *The Man Without Qualities*. Perhaps it might have been an atonement or sacrifice to avert the death of European culture, had the actual intercourse between brother and sister taken place. Throughout Part III of the novel, and in the Posthumous Papers, Musil manifests an uncanny precision in the dangerous conversations between brother and sister:

> "And it's not at all against nature for a child to be the object of such feelings?" Agathe asked.
>
> "What would be against nature would be a straight-out lustful desire," Ulrich replied. "But a person like that also drags the innocent or, in any event, unready and helpless creature into actions for which it is not destined. He must ignore the immaturity of the developing mind and body, and play the game of his passion with a mute and veiled opponent; no, he not only ignores whatever would get in his way, but brutally sweeps it aside! That's something quite different, with different consequences!"
>
> "But perhaps a touch of the perniciousness of this 'sweeping aside' is already contained in the 'ignoring'?" Agathe objected. She might have been jealous of her brother's tissue of thoughts; at any rate, she resisted. "I don't see any great distinction in whether one pays no attention to what might restrain one, or doesn't feel it!"
>
> Ulrich countered: "You're right and you're not right. I really just told the story because it's a preliminary state of the love between brother and sister."
>
> "Love between brother and sister?" Agathe asked, and pretended to be astonished, as if she were hearing the term for the first time; but she was digging her nails into Ulrich's arm again, and perhaps she did so too strongly, and her fingers trembled.

Ulrich, feeling as if five small warm wounds had opened side by side in his arm, suddenly said: "The person whose strongest stimulation is associated with experiences each of which is, in some way or other, impossible, isn't interested in possible experiences. It may be that imagination is a way of fleeing from life, a refuge and a den of iniquity, as many maintain; I think that the story of the little girl, as well as all the other examples we've talked about, point not to an abnormality or a weakness but to a revulsion against the world and a strong recalcitrance, an excessive and overpassionate desire for love!" He forgot that Agathe could know nothing of the other examples and equivocal comparisons with which his thoughts had previously associated this kind of love; for he now felt himself in the clear again and had overcome, for the time being, the anesthetizing taste, the transformation into the will-less and lifeless, that was part of his experience, so that the automatic reference slipped inadvertently through a gap in his thoughts.

> From the *Posthumous Papers*, pp. 1399–1400,
> translated by Burton Pike

As an instance of what is most original in Musil, this is both altogether typical yet also totally unique, the paradox that makes for what is greatest but sometimes maddening about *The Man Without Qualities*. Some of the details in this passage I myself find unforgettable: Ulrich's brilliant evasion of "against nature," Agathe's "digging her nails into Ulrich's arm" so as to intimate "five small warm wounds," and Ulrich's subtle equation of revulsion against "the world" and a totalizing "desires for love." Is that world nature, history, society or immemorial morality? Musil insists that his reader decide that for herself.

Virginia Woolf

(1882-1941)

IN MAY 1940, LESS THAN A YEAR BEFORE SHE DROWNED HERSELF, VIRGINIA Woolf read a paper to the Worker's Educational Association in Brighton. We know it as the essay entitled "The Leaning Tower," in which the Shelleyan emblem of the lonely tower takes on more of a social than an imaginative meaning. It is no longer the point of survey from which the poet Athanase gazes down in pity at the dark estate of mankind, and so is not an image of contemplative wisdom isolated from the mundane. Instead, it is "the tower of middle-class birth and expensive education," from which the poetic generation of W.H. Auden and Louis MacNeice stare sidelong at society. Woolf does not say so, but we can surmise that she preferred Shelley to Auden, while realizing that she herself dwelt in the leaning tower, unlike Yeats, to whom the lonely tower remained an inevitable metaphor for poetic stance.

It is proper that "The Leaning Tower," as a speculation upon the decline of a Romantic image into belatedness, should concern itself also with the peculiarities of poetic influence:

> Theories then are dangerous things. All the same we must risk making one this afternoon since we are going to discuss modern tendencies. Directly we speak of tendencies or movements we commit ourselves to the belief that there is some force, influence, outer pressure which is strong enough to stamp itself upon a whole group of different writers so that all their writing has a certain common likeness. We must then have a theory as to what this influence is. But let us always remember—influences are infinitely numerous; writers are infinitely sensitive; each writer has a differ-ent sensibility. That is why literature is always changing, like the

weather, like clouds in the sky. Read a page of Scott; then of
Henry James; try to work out the influences that have transformed
the one page into the other. It is beyond our skill. We can only
hope therefore to single out the most obvious influences that have
formed writers into groups. Yet there are groups. Books descend
from books as families descend from families. Some descend from
Jane Austen; others from Dickens. They resemble their parents, as
human children resemble their parents; yet they differ as children
differ, and revolt as children revolt. Perhaps it will be easier to
understand living writers as we take a quick look at some of their
forbears.

A critic of literary influence learns to be both enchanted and wary
when such a passage is encountered. Sensibility is indeed the issue, since
without "a different sensibility" no writer truly is a writer. Woolf's sensibility essentially is Paterian, as Perry Meisel accurately demonstrated. She
is hardly unique among the great Modernist writers in owing much to
Pater. That group includes Wilde, Yeats, Wallace Stevens, Hart Crane, as
well as Pound and Eliot. Among the novelists, the Paterians, however
involuntary, include Scott Fitzgerald, the early Joyce, and in strange ways
both Conrad and Lawrence, as well as Woolf. Of all these, Woolf is most
authentically Pater's child. Her central tropes, like his, are personality and
death, and her ways of representing consciousness are very close to his.
The literary ancestor of those curious twin sensibilities—Septimus Smith
and Clarissa Dalloway—is Pater's Sebastian Van Storck, except that Woolf
relents, and they do not go into Sebastian's "formless and nameless infinite
world, quite evenly grey."

Mrs. Dalloway

Mrs. Dalloway (1925), the fourth of Woolf's nine novels, is her first
extraordinary achievement. Perhaps she should have called it *The Hours*, its
original working title. To speak of measuring one's time by days or months,
rather than years, has urgency, and this urgency increases when the fiction
of duration embraces only hours, as *Mrs. Dalloway* does. The novel's peculiar virtue is the enigmatic doubling between Clarissa Dalloway and
Septimus Smith, who do not know one another. We are persuaded that the
book is not disjointed because Clarissa and Septimus uncannily share what
seem a single consciousness, intense and vulnerable, each fearing to be
consumed by a fire perpetually about to break forth. Woolf seems to cause
Septimus to die instead of Clarissa, almost as though the novel is a single

apotropaic gesture on its author's part. One thinks of the death died for Marius by Cornelius in Pater's *Marius the Epicurean*, but that is one friend atoning for another. However unified, does *Mrs. Dalloway* cogently link Clarissa and Septimus?

Clearly the book does, but only through its manipulation of Parer's evasions of the figure or trope of the self as the center of a flux of sensations. In a book review written when she was only twenty-five, Woolf made a rough statement of the stance towards the self she would take throughout her work-to-come, in the form of a Paterian rhetorical question: "Are we not each in truth the centre of innumerable rays which so strike upon one figure only, and is it not our business to flash them straight and completely back again, and never suffer a single shaft to blunt itself on the far side of us?" Here is Clarissa Dalloway, at the novel's crucial epiphany, not suffering the rays to blunt themselves on the far side of her:

> What business had the Bradshaws to talk of death at her party? A young man had killed himself. And they talked of it at her party— the Bradshaws talked of death. He had killed himself—but how? Always her body went through it first, when she was told, suddenly, of an accident; her dress flamed, her body burnt. He had thrown himself from a window. Up had flashed the ground; through him, blundering, bruising, went the rusty spikes. There he lay with a thud, thud, thud in his brain, and then a suffocation of blackness. So she saw it. But why had he done it? And the Bradshaws talked of it at her party!
>
> She had once thrown a shilling into the Serpentine, never anything more. But he had flung it away. They went on living (she would have to go back; the rooms were still crowded; people kept on coming). They (all day she had been thinking of Bourton, of Peter, of Sally), they would grow old. A thing there was that mattered; a thing, wreathed about with chatter, defaced, obscured in her own life, let drop every day in corruption, lies, chatter. This he had preserved. Death was defiance. Death was an attempt to communicate; people feeling the impossibility of reaching the centre which, mystically, evaded them; closeness drew apart; rapture faded, one was alone. There was an embrace in death.

The evasiveness of the center is defied by the act of suicide, which in Woolf is a communication and not, as it is in Freud, a murder. Earlier, Septimus had been terrified by a "gradual drawing together of everything to one centre before his eyes." The doubling of Clarissa and Septimus implies that there is only a difference in degree, not in kind, between Clarissa's sensibility and the naked consciousness or "madness" of Septimus. Neither needs the encouragement of "Fear no more the heat o' the sun," because each knows that consciousness is isolation and so untruth, and that the right worship of life is to defy that isolation by dying. J. Hillis Miller remarks that: "A novel, for Woolf, is the place of death made visible." It seems to me difficult to defend *Mrs. Dalloway* from moral judgments that call Woolf's stance wholly nihilistic. But then, *Mrs. Dalloway*, remarkable as it is, is truly Woolf's starting-point as a strong writer, and not her conclusion.

To the Lighthouse

Critics tend to agree that Woolf's finest novel is *To the Lighthouse* (1927), which is certainly one of the central works of the modern imagination, comparable to Lawrence's *The Rainbow* or Conrad's *Victory*, if not quite of the range of *Women in Love* or *Nostromo*. Perhaps it is the only novel in which Woolf displays all of her gifts at once. Erich Auerbach, in his *Mimesis*, lucidly summing up Woolf's achievement in her book, could be expounding Pater's trope of the privileged moment:

> What takes place here in Virginia Woolf's novel is ... to put the emphasis on the random occurrence, to exploit it not in the service of a planned continuity of action but in itself. And in the process something new and elemental appeared: nothing less than the wealth of reality and depth of life in every moment to which we surrender ourselves without prejudice. To be sure, what happens in that moment—be it outer or inner processes—concerns in a very personal way the individuals who live in it, but it also (and for that very reason) concerns the elementary things which men in general have in common. It is precisely the random moment which is comparatively independent of the controversial and unstable orders over which men fight and despair; it passes unaffected by them, as daily life. The more it is exploited, the more the elementary things which our lives have in common come to light. The more numerous, varied, and simple the people are who appear as subjects of such random moments, the more effectively must what they have in common shine forth.

The shining forth is precisely Pater's secularization of the epiphany, in which random moments are transformed: "A sudden light transfigures a trivial thing, a weathervane, a windmill, a winnowing flail, the dust in the barn door; a moment—and the thing has vanished, because it was pure effect." Woolf, like Pater sets herself "to realize this situation, to define, in a chill and empty atmosphere, the focus where rays, in themselves pale and impotent, unite and begin to burn ..." To realize such a situation is to set oneself against the vision of Mr. Ramsay (Woolf's father, the philosopher Leslie Stephen), which expresses itself in the grimly empiricist maxim that: "The very stone one kicks with one's boot will outlast Shakespeare." Against this can be set Lily Briscoe's vision, which concludes the novel:

> Quickly, as if she were recalled by something over there, she turned to her canvas. There it was—her picture. Yes, with all its greens and blues, its lines running up and across, its attempt at something. It would be hung in the attics, she thought; it would be destroyed. But what did that matter? she asked herself, taking up her brush again. She looked at the steps; they were empty; she looked at her canvas; it was blurred. With a sudden intensity, as if she saw it clear for a second, she drew a line there, in the centre. It was done; it was finished. Yes, she thought, laying down her brush in extreme fatigue, I have had my vision.

"An attempt at something" postulates, for Woolf, a center, however evasive. The apotheosis of aesthetic or perceptive principle here is Woolf's beautifully poised and precarious approach to an affirmation of the difficult possibility of meaning. *The Waves* (1931) is a large-scale equivalent of Lily Briscoe's painting. Bernard, the most comprehensive of the novel's six first-person narrators, ends the book with a restrained exultation, profoundly representative of Woolf's feminization of the Paterian aesthetic stance:

> "Again I see before me the usual street. The canopy of civilisation is burnt out. The sky is dark as polished whale-bone. But there is a kindling in the sky whether of lamplight or of dawn. There is a stir of some sort—sparrows on plain trees somewhere chirping. There is a sense of the break of day. I will not call it dawn. What is dawn in the city to an elderly man standing in the street looking up rather dizzily at the sky? Dawn is some sort of whitening of the sky; some sort of renewal. Another day; another Friday; another twentieth of March, January, or September. Another general awakening. The stars draw back and are extinguished. The bars deepen themselves between the waves. The film of mist

thickens on the field. A redness gathers on the roses, even on the pale rose that hangs by the bedroom window. A bird chirps. Cottagers light their early candles. Yes, this is the eternal renewal, the incessant rise and fall and fall and rise again.

"And in me too the wave rises. It swells; it arches its back. I am aware once more of a new desire, something rising beneath me like the proud horse whose rider first spurs and then pulls him back. What enemy do we now perceive advancing against us, you whom I ride now, as we stand pawing this stretch of pavement? It is death. Death is the enemy. It is death against whom I ride with my spear couched and my hair flying back like a young man's, like Percival's, when he galloped in India. I strike spurs into my horse. Against you I will fling myself, unvanquished and unyielding, O Death!"

The waves broke on the shore.

"Incessant rise and fall and fall and rise again," though ascribed to Bernard, has in it the fine pathos of a recognition of natural harshness that does not come often to a male consciousness. And for all the warlike imagery, the ride against death transcends aggressivity, whether against the self or against others. Pater had insisted that our one choice lies in packing as many pulsations of the artery, or Blakean visions of the poet's work, into our interval as possible. Woolf subtly hints that even Pater succumbs to a male illusion of experiential quantity, rather than to a female recognition of gradations in the quality of possible experience. A male critic might want to murmur, in defense of Pater, that male blindness of the void within experience is very difficult to overcome, and that Pater's exquisite sensibility is hardly male, whatever the accident of his gender.

Between the Acts (1941), Woolf's final novel, can be read as a covert and witty subversion of late Shakespeare, whose romances Woolf attempts to expose as being perhaps more male than universal in some of their implications. Parodying Shakespeare is a dangerous mode; the flat-out farce of Max Beerbohm and Nigel Dennis works more easily than Woolf's allusive deftness, but Woolf is not interested in the crudities of farce. *Between the Acts* is her deferred fulfillment of the polemical program set forth in her marvelous polemic *A Room of One's Own* (1929), which is still the most persuasive of all feminist literary manifestos. To me the most powerful and unnerving stroke in that book is in its trope for the enclosure that men have forced upon women:

For women have sat indoors all these millions of years, so that by this time the very walls are permeated by their creative force, which has, indeed, so overcharged the capacity of bricks and mortar that it must needs harness itself to pens and brushes and business and politics. But this creative power differs greatly from the creative power of man ....

That last assertion is becoming a kind of shibboleth in contemporary feminist literary criticism. Whether George Eliot and Henry James ought to be read as instances of a gender-based difference in creative power is not beyond all critical dispute. Is Dorothea Brooke more clearly the product of a woman's creative power than Isabel Archer would be? Could we necessarily know that Clarissa Harlowe ensues from a male imagination? Woolf, at the least, lent her authority to provoking such questions. That authority, earned by novels of the splendour of *To the Lighthouse* and *Between the Acts*, becomes more formidable as the years pass.

James Joyce

(1882–1941)

A Portrait of the Artist as a Young Man

THE LATE SIR WILLIAM EMPSON, IN AN ESSAY ON "JOYCE'S INTENTIONS," sought to rescue *Ulysses* and *A Portrait of the Artist as a Young Man* from the school of Christianizing critics, called for short by Empson "the Kenner Smear." Though the Kenner Smear essentially baptizes Joyce's writings (following the lead of T.S. Eliot, who found Joyce eminently orthodox), it also deprecates the representation of Stephen, particularly in the *Portrait*, as Empson protested:

> One or two minor points need fitting in here. It is part of Kenner's argument, to prove that Stephen is already damned, that he is made to expound the wrong aesthetic philosophy. Joyce was letting him get the theory right in *Stephen Hero*, but when he rewrote and concentrated the material as the *Portrait* Stephen was turned into a sentimental neo-Platonist; that is, he considered the artist superior to earthly details, instead of letting the artist deduce realism from Aquinas. If we actually did find this alteration, I agree that the argument would carry some weight, though the evidence would need to he very strong. But, so far as I can see, there is only one definite bit of evidence offered, that Joyce in rewriting left out the technical term 'epiphany', invented by himself to describe the moment of insight which sums up a whole situation. I can tell you why he left it out; because he was not always too egotistical to write well. Even he, during revision, could observe that it was tiresome to have Stephen spouting to his young friends about this invented term. But I find no change in doctrine; he still firmly

rejects "Idealism, the supreme quality of beauty being a light from some other world, the idea of which the matter was but the shadow," and explains that the 'claritas' of Aquinas comes when the image "is apprehended luminously by the mind which has been arrested by its wholeness and fascinated by its harmony." This is surely the doctrine which Kenner approves, and we next have as clear a pointer from the novelist as he ever allows us: "Stephen paused and, though his companion did not speak, felt that his words had called up around them a thought enchanted silence." A critic who can believe that Joyce wrote this whole passage in order to jeer at it has, I submit, himself taken some fatal turning, or slipped unawares over the edge of some vast drop.

I am happy to agree with Empson against Hugh Kenner on this, but I myself find Aquinas a surrogate here for Joyce's ghostly aesthetic father, Walter Pater, actual inventor of *Stephen Hero*'s "epiphanies" and so of a mode of intellectual vision that dominates the *Portrait*, remains crucial in *Ulysses*, but largely subsides in *Finnegans Wake*.

Pater founded his criticism upon perception and sensation, the perception of privileged moments of vision, and the sensation of the intensity and brevity of those epiphanies, sudden manifestations or shinings forth of power, order, beauty or of a transcendental or sublime experience fading into the continuum of the commonplace. Like Joyce after him, Pater asked very little of these epiphanies, far less than Wordsworth or Ruskin had asked, let alone the eminently orthodox, from Gerard Manley Hopkins (Pater's student at Oxford) through T.S. Eliot and his New Critical followers, against whom Empson fought his anticlerical campaigns. The essential formula for Stephen's epiphanies in the *Portrait* is set forth in Pater's study of the Renaissance:

> A sudden light transfigures a trivial thing, a weathervane, a windmill, a winnowing flail, the dust in the barn door; a moment—and the thing has vanished, because it was pure effect; but it leaves a relish behind it, a longing that the accident may happen again.

Himself an Epicurean and so a metaphysical materialist, Pater's achievement was to remove from the epiphany its theological and idealistic colorings. Joyce, certainly not a Catholic believer, accepts the epiphany from Pater as a secular and naturalistic phenomenon, purged of its Wordsworthian and Ruskinian moralizings. The Joycean epiphany is still "a sudden spiritual manifestation" in which an object's "whatness" or "soul" can be seen as leaping "to us from the vestment of its appearance." But that is spiritual only in the Epicurean sense, in which the "what" is unknowable anyway, and Joyce is no more Christian than Whitman is in *Song of Myself* when the child asks him what the grass is, or than Stevens is in his apprehension of sudden radiances.

Just before the close of the *Portrait*, Stephen records a vision that is an epitome of epiphanies in a passage both Ovidian and Paterian:

> The spell of arms and voices: the white arms of roads, their promise of close embraces and the black arms of tall ships that stand against the moon, their tale of distant nations. They are held out to say: We are alone. Come. And the voices say with them: We are your kinsmen. And the air is thick with their company as they call to me, their kinsman, making ready to go, shaking the wings of their exultant and terrible youth.

The flight of Icarus and his fall are assimilated to the Paterian sense of belatedness, of coming at the end of a long and high tradition of Romantic vision. Joyce, like Pater, longs for a renaissance, for a rebirth into the company of exiles to worldliness who found another country in the strongest imaginative literature. Ovid, who knew the bitterness of exile, prefigured Dante in at least that regard, and there is a Dantesque quality to Stephen's epiphany here. That hovering company of visionaries is pervaded with the auras of solitude and of departure, and their exultant youth may yield to the terrible fate of Icarus. If this epiphany's eroticism is palpable and plangent, its darker reverberations intimate deathliness as the price of the freedom of art. Echoes of Ibsen and Blake combine in Stephen's famous penultimate declaration:

> Welcome, O life! I go to encounter for the millionth time the reality of experience and to forge in the smithy of my soul the untreated conscience of my race.

"Forge" is a blacksmith's term in this context, and not a penman's. The very name of Ibsen's *Brand* suggests the heat that can forge what Ibsen's protagonist calls "the untreated soul of man," and we can remember also Blake's Los at the smithy, hammering out the engraved plates of his vision. Again one votes for Empson, against Kenner, as to the high seriousness of Stephen's aspirations and the aesthetic dignity with which Joyce chose to invest them.

Franz Kafka

(1883-1924)

I

IN HER OBITUARY FOR HER LOVER, FRANZ KAFKA, MILENA JESENSKÁ sketched a modern Gnostic, a writer whose vision was of the *kenoma*, the cosmic emptiness into which we have been thrown:

> He was a hermit, a man of insight who was frightened by life.... He saw the world as being full of invisible demons which assail and destroy defenseless man.... All his works describe the terror of mysterious misconceptions and guiltless guilt in human beings.

Milena—brilliant, fearless, and loving—may have subtly distorted Kafka's beautifully evasive slidings between normative Jewish and Jewish Gnostic stances. Max Brod, responding to Kafka's now-famous remark— "We are nihilistic thoughts that came into God's head"—explained to his friend the Gnostic notion that the Demiurge had made this world both sinful and evil. "No," Kafka replied, "I believe we are not such a radical relapse of God's, only one of His bad moods. He had a bad day." Playing straight man, the faithful Brod asked if this meant there was hope outside our cosmos. Kafka smiled, and charmingly said: "Plenty of hope—for God—no end of hope—only not for us."

Kafka, despite Gershom Scholem's authoritative attempts to claim him for Jewish Gnosticism, is both more and less than a Gnostic, as we might expect. Yahweh can be saved, and the divine degradation that is fundamental to Gnosticism is not an element in Kafka's world. But we were fashioned out of the clay during one of Yahweh's bad moods; perhaps there was divine dyspepsia, or sultry weather in the garden that Yahweh had planted in the

East. Yahweh is hope, and we are hopeless. We are the jackdaws or crows, the kafkas (since that is what the name means, in Czech) whose impossibility is what the heavens signify: "The crows maintain that a single crow could destroy the heavens. Doubtless that is so, but it proves nothing against the heavens, for the heavens signify simply: the impossibility of crows."

In Gnosticism, there is an alien, wholly transcendent God, and the adept, after considerable difficulties, can find the way back to presence and fullness. Gnosticism therefore is a religion of salvation, though the most negative of all such saving visions. Kafkan spirituality offers no hope of salvation, and so is not Gnostic. But Milena Jesenská certainly was right to emphasize the Kafkan terror that is akin to Gnosticism's dread of the *kenoma*, which is the world governed by the Archons. Kafka takes the impossible step beyond Gnosticism, by denying that there is hope for us anywhere at all.

In the aphorisms that Brod rather misleadingly entitled "Reflections on Sin, Pain, Hope and The True Way," Kafka wrote: "What is laid upon us is to accomplish the negative; the positive is already given." How much Kabbalah Kafka knew is not clear. Since he wrote a new Kabbalah, the question of Jewish Gnostic sources can be set aside. Indeed, by what seems a charming oddity (but I would call it yet another instance of Blake's insistence that forms of worship are chosen from poetic tales), our understanding of Kabbalah is Kafkan anyway, since Kafka profoundly influenced Gershom Scholem, and no one will be able to get beyond Scholem's creative or strong misreading of Kabbalah for decades to come. I repeat this point to emphasize its shock value: we read Kabbalah, via Scholem, from a Kafkan perspective, even as we read human personality and its mimetic possibilities by way of Shakespeare's perspectives, since essentially Freud mediates Shakespeare for us, yet relies upon him nevertheless. A Kafkan facticity or contingency now governs our awareness of whatever in Jewish cultural tradition is other than normative.

In his diaries for 1922, Kafka meditated, on January 16, upon "something very like a breakdown," in which it was "impossible to sleep, impossible to stay awake, impossible to endure life, or, more exactly, the course of life." The vessels were breaking for him as his demoniac, writerly inner world and the outer life "split apart, and they do split apart, or at least clash in a fearful manner." Late in the evening, K. arrives at the village, which is deep in snow. The Castle is in front of him, but even the hill upon which it stands is veiled in mist and darkness, and there is not a single light visible to show that the Castle was there. K. stands a long time on a wooden bridge that leads from the main road to the village, while gazing, not at the village, but "into the illusory emptiness above him," where the Castle should be. He does not know what he will always refuse to learn, which is that the emptiness is "illusory" in every possible sense, since he does gaze at the *kenoma*, which resulted initially from the breaking of the vessels, the splitting apart of every world, inner and outer.

Writing the vision of K., Kafka counts the costs of his confirmation, in a passage prophetic of Scholem, but with a difference that Scholem sought to negate by combining Zionism and Kabbalah for himself. Kafka knew better, perhaps only for himself, but perhaps for others as well:

Second: This pursuit, originating in the midst of men, carries one in a direction away from them. The solitude that for the most part has been forced on me, in part voluntarily sought by me—but what was this if not compulsion too?—is now losing all its ambiguity and approaches its denouement. Where is it leading? The strongest likelihood is that it may lead to madness; there is nothing more to say, the pursuit goes right through me and rends me asunder. Or I can—can I?—manage to keep my feet somewhat and be carried along in the wild pursuit. Where, then, shall I be brought? "Pursuit," indeed, is only a metaphor. I can also say, "assault on the last earthly frontier," an assault, moreover, launched from below, from mankind, and since this too is a metaphor, I can replace it by the metaphor of an assault from above, aimed at me from above.

All such writing is an assault on the frontiers; if Zionism had not intervened, it might easily have developed into a new secret doctrine, a Kabbalah. There are intimations of this. Though of course it would require genius of an unimaginable kind to strike root again in the old centuries, or create the old centuries anew and not spend itself withal, but only then begin to flower forth.

Consider Kafka's three metaphors, which he so knowingly substitutes for one another. The pursuit is of ideas, in that mode of introspection which is Kafka's writing. Yet this metaphor of pursuit is also a piercing "right through me" and a breaking apart of the self. For "pursuit," Kafka then substitutes mankind's assault, from below, on the last earthly frontier. What is that frontier? It must lie between us and the heavens. Kafka, the crow or jackdaw, by writing, transgresses the frontier and implicitly maintains that he could destroy the heavens. By another substitution, the metaphor changes to "an assault from above, aimed at me from above," the aim simply being the signifying function of the heavens, which is to mean the impossibility of Kafkas or crows. The heavens assault Kafka *through his writing*; "all such writing is an assault on the frontiers," and these must now be Kafka's own frontiers. One thinks of Freud's most complex "frontier concept," more complex even than the drive: the bodily ego. The heavens assault Kafka's bodily ego, *but only through his own writing*. Certainly such an assault is not un-Jewish, and has as much to do with normative as with esoteric Jewish tradition.

Yet, according to Kafka, his own writing, were it not for the intervention of Zionism, might easily have developed into a new Kabbalah. How are we to understand that curious statement about Zionism as the blocking agent that prevents Franz Kafka from becoming another Isaac Luria? Kafka darkly and immodestly writes: "There are intimations of this." Our teacher Gershom Scholem governs our interpretation here, of necessity. Those intimations belong to Kafka alone, or perhaps to a select few in his immediate circle. They cannot be conveyed to Jewry, even to its elite, because Zionism has taken the place of messianic Kabbalah, including presumably the heretical Kabbalah of Nathan of Gaza, prophet of Sabbatai Zvi and of all his followers down to the blasphemous Jacob Frank. Kafka's influence upon Scholem is decisive here, for Kafka already has arrived at Scholem's central thesis of the link between the Kabbalah of Isaac Luria, the messianism of the Sabbatarians and Frankists, and the political Zionism that gave rebirth to Israel.

Kafka goes on, most remarkably, to disown the idea that he possesses "genius of an unimaginable kind," one that either would strike root again in archaic Judaism, presumably of the esoteric sort, or more astonishingly "create the old centuries anew," which Scholem insisted Kafka had done. But can we speak, as Scholem tried to speak, of the Kabbalah of Franz Kafka? Is there a new secret doctrine in the superb stories and the extraordinary parables and paradoxes, or did not Kafka spend his genius in the act of new creation of the old Jewish centuries? Kafka certainly would have judged himself harshly as one spent withal, rather than as a writer who "only then began to flower forth." Kafka died only two and a half years after this meditative moment, died, alas, just before his forty-first birthday. Yet as the propounder of a new Kabbalah, he had gone very probably as far as he (or anyone else) could go. No Kabbalah, be it that of Moses de Leon, Isaac Luria, Moses Cordovero, Nathan of Gaza or Gershom Scholem, is exactly easy to interpret, but Kafka's secret doctrine, if it exists at all, is designedly uninterpretable. My working principle in reading Kafka is to observe that he did everything possible to evade interpretation, which only means that what most needs and demands interpretation in Kafka's writing is its perversely deliberate evasion of interpretation. Erich Heller's formula for getting at this evasion is: "Ambiguity has never been considered an elemental force; it is precisely this in the stories of Franz Kafka." Perhaps, but evasiveness is not the same literary quality as ambiguity.

Evasiveness is purposive; it writes between the lines, to borrow a fine trope from Leo Strauss. What does it mean when a quester for a new Negative, or perhaps rather a revisionist of an old Negative, resorts to the evasion of every possible interpretation as his central topic or theme? Kafka does not doubt guilt, but wishes to make it "possible for men to enjoy sin without guilt, almost without guilt," by reading Kafka. To enjoy sin almost without guilt is to evade interpretation, in exactly the dominant Jewish sense of interpretation. Jewish tradition, whether normative or esoteric, never teaches you to ask Nietzsche's question: "Who is the interpreter, and what power does he seek to gain over the text?" Instead, Jewish tradition asks: "Is the interpreter in the line of those who seek to build a hedge about the Torah in every age?" Kafka's power of evasiveness is not a power over his own text, and it does build a hedge about the Torah in our age. Yet no one before Kafka built up that hedge wholly out of evasiveness, not even Maimonides or Judah Halevi or even Spinoza. Subtlest and most evasive of all writers, Kafka remains the severest and most harassing of the belated sages of what will yet become the Jewish cultural tradition of the future.

II

The jackdaw or crow or Kafka is also the weird figure of the great hunter Gracchus (whose Latin name also means a crow), who is not alive but dead, yet who floats, like one living, on his death-bark forever. When the fussy Burgomaster of Riva knits his brow, asking: "And you have no part in the other world (*das Jenseits*)?", the Hunter replies, with grand defensive irony:

> I am forever on the great stair that leads up to it. On that infinitely wide and spacious stair I clamber about, sometimes up, sometimes down, sometimes on the right, sometimes on the left, always in motion. The Hunter has been turned into a butterfly. Do not laugh.

Like the Burgomaster, we do not laugh. Being a single crow, Gracchus would be enough to destroy the heavens, but he will never get there. Instead, the heavens signify his impossibility, the absence of crows or hunters, and so he has been turned into another butterfly, which is all we can be, from the perspective of the heavens. And we bear no blame for that:

"I had been glad to live and I was glad to die. Before I stepped aboard, I joyfully flung away my wretched load of ammunition, my knapsack, my hunting rifle that I had always been proud to carry, and I slipped into my winding sheet like a girl into her marriage dress. I lay and waited. Then came the mishap."

"A terrible fate," said the Burgomaster, raising his hand defensively. "And you bear no blame for it?"

"None," said the hunter. "I was a hunter; was there any sin in that? I followed my calling as a hunter in the Black Forest, where there were still wolves in those days. I lay in ambush, shot, hit my mark, flayed the skin from my victims: was there any sin in that? My labors were blessed. 'The Great Hunter of Black Forest' was the name I was given. Was there any sin in that?"

"I am not called upon to decide that," said the Burgomaster, "but to me also there seems to be no sin in such things. But then, whose is the guilt?"

"The boatman's," said the Hunter. "Nobody will read what I say here, no one will come to help me; even if all the people were commanded to help me, every door and window would remain shut, everybody would take to bed and draw the bedclothes over his head, the whole earth would become an inn for the night. And there is sense in that, for nobody knows of me, and if anyone knew he would not know where I could be found, and if he knew where I could be found, he would not know how to deal with me, he would not know how to help me. The thought of helping me is an illness that has to be cured by taking to one's bed."

How admirable Gracchus is, even when compared to the Homeric heroes! They know, or think they know, that to be alive, however miserable, is preferable to being the foremost among the dead. But Gracchus wished only to be himself, happy to be a hunter when alive, joyful to be a corpse when dead: "I slipped into my winding sheet like a girl into her marriage dress." So long as everything happened in good order, Gracchus was more than content. The guilt must be the boatman's, and may not exceed mere incompetence. Being dead and yet still articulate, Gracchus is beyond help: "The thought of helping me is an illness that has to be cured by taking to one's bed."

When he gives the striking trope of the whole earth closing down like an inn for the night, with the bedclothes drawn over everybody's head, Gracchus renders the judgment: "And there is sense in that." There is sense in that only because in Kafka's world as in Freud's, or in Scholem's, or in any world deeply informed by Jewish memory, there is necessarily sense in everything, total sense, even though Kafka refuses to aid you in getting at or close to it.

But what kind of a world is that, where there is sense in everything, where everything seems to demand interpretation? There can be sense in everything, as J.H. Van den Berg once wrote against Freud's theory of repression, only if everything is already in the past and there never again can be anything wholly new. That is certainly the world of the great normative rabbis of the second century of the Common Era, and consequently it has been the world of most Jews ever since. Torah has been given, Talmud has risen to complement and interpret it, other interpretations in the chain of tradition are freshly forged in each generation, but the limits of Creation and of Revelation are fixed in Jewish memory. There is sense in everything because all sense is present already in the Hebrew Bible, which by definition must be totally intelligible, even if its fullest intelligibility will not shine forth until the Messiah comes.

Gracchus, hunter and jackdaw, is Kafka, pursuer of ideas and jackdaw, and the endless, hopeless voyage of Gracchus is Kafka's passage, only partly through a language not his own, and largely through a life not much his own. Kafka was studying Hebrew intensively while he wrote "The Hunter Gracchus," early in 1917, and I think we may call the voyages of the dead but never-buried Gracchus a trope for Kafka's belated study of his ancestral language. He was still studying Hebrew in the spring of 1923, with his tuberculosis well advanced, and down to nearly the end he longed for Zion, dreaming of recovering his health and firmly grounding his identity by journeying to Palestine. Like Gracchus, he experienced life-in-death, though unlike Gracchus he achieved the release of total death.

"The Hunter Gracchus" as a story or extended parable is not the narrative of a Wandering Jew or Flying Dutchman, because Kafka's trope for his writing activity is not so much a wandering or even a wavering, but rather a repetition, labyrinthine and burrow-building. His writing repeats, not itself, but a Jewish esoteric interpretation of Torah that Kafka himself scarcely knows, or even needs to know. What this interpretation tells Kafka is that there is no written Torah but only an oral one. However, Kafka has no one to tell him what this Oral Torah is. He substitutes his own writing therefore for the Oral Torah not made available to him. He is precisely in the stance of the Hunter Gracchus, who concludes by saying, "'I am here, more than that I do not know, further than that I cannot go. My ship has no rudder, and it is driven by the wind that blows in the undermost regions of death.'"

III

"What is the Talmud if not a message from the distance?", Kafka wrote to Robert Klopstock, on December 19, 1932. What was all of Jewish tradition, to Kafka, except a message from an endless distance? That is surely part of the burden of the famous parable, "An Imperial Message," which concludes with you, the reader, sitting at your window when evening falls and dreaming to yourself the parable—that God, in his act of dying, has sent you an individual message. Heinz Politzer read this as a Nietzschean parable, and so fell into the trap set by the Kafkan evasiveness:

Describing the fate of the parable in a time depleted of metaphysical truths, the imperial message has turned into the subjective fantasy of a dreamer who sits at a window with a view on a darkening world. The only real information imported by this story is the news of the Emperor's death. This news Kafka took over from Nietzsche.

No, for even though you dream the parable, the parable conveys truth. The Talmud does exist; it really is an Imperial message from the distance. The distance is too great; it cannot reach you; there is hope, but not for you. Nor is it so clear that God is dead. He is always dying, yet always whispers a message into the angel's ear. It is said to you that: "Nobody could fight his way through here even with a message from a dead man," but the Emperor actually does not die in the text of the parable.

Distance is part of Kafka's crucial notion of the Negative, which is not a Hegelian nor a Heideggerian Negative, but is very close to Freud's Negation and also to the Negative imaging carried out by Scholem's Kabbalists. But I want to postpone Kafka's Jewish version of the Negative until later. "The Hunter Gracchus" is an extraordinary text, but it is not wholly characteristic of Kafka at his strongest, at his uncanniest or most sublime.

When he is most himself, Kafka gives us a continuous inventiveness and originality that rivals Dante, and truly challenges Proust and Joyce as that of the dominant Western author of our century, setting Freud aside, since Freud ostensibly is science and not narrative or mythmaking, though if you believe that, then you can be persuaded of anything. Kafka's beast fables are rightly celebrated, but his most remarkable fabulistic being is neither animal nor human, but is little Odradek, in the curious sketch, less than a page and a half long, "The Cares of a Family Man," where the title might have been translated: "The Sorrows of a Paterfamilias." The family man narrates these five paragraphs, each a dialectical lyric in itself, beginning with one that worries the meaning of the name:

> Some say the word Odradek is of Slavonic origin, and try to account for it on that basis. Others again believe it to be of German origin, only influenced by Slavonic. The uncertainty of both interpretations allows one to assume with justice that neither is accurate, especially as neither of them provides an intelligent meaning of the word.

This evasiveness was overcome by the scholar Wilhelm Emrich, who traced the name Odradek to the Czech word *odraditi*, meaning to dissuade anyone from doing anything. Like Edward Gorey's Doubtful Guest, Odradek is uninvited yet will not leave, since implicitly he dissuades you from doing anything about his presence, or rather something about his very uncanniness advises you to let him alone:

> No one, of course, would occupy himself with such studies if there were not a creature called Odradek. At first glance it looks like a flat star-shaped spool for thread, and indeed it does seem to have thread wound upon it; to be sure, they are only old, broken-off bits of thread, knotted and tangled together, of the most varied sorts and colors. But it is not only a spool, for a small wooden crossbar sticks out of the middle of the star, and another small rod is joined to that at a right angle. By means of this latter rod on one side and one of the points of the star on the other, the whole thing can stand upright as if on two legs.

Is Odradek a "thing," as the bemused family man begins by calling him, or is he not a childlike creature, a daemon at home in the world of children? Odradek clearly was made by an inventive and humorous child, rather in the spirit of the making of Adam out of the moistened red clay by the J writer's Yahweh. It is difficult not to read Odradek's creation as a deliberate parody when we are told that "the whole thing can stand upright as if on two legs," and again when the suggestion is ventured that Odradek, like Adam, "once had some sort of intelligible shape and is now only a broken-down remnant." If Odradek is fallen, he is still quite jaunty, and cannot be closely scrutinized, since he "is extraordinarily nimble and can never be laid hold of," like the story in which he appears. Odradek not only advises you not to do anything about him, but in some clear sense he is yet another figure by means of whom Kafka advises you against interpreting Kafka.

One of the loveliest moments in all of Kafka comes when you, the *paterfamilias*, encounter Odradek leaning directly beneath you against the banisters. Being inclined to speak to him, as you would to a child, you receive a surprise: "'Well, what's your name?' you ask him. 'Odradek,' he says. 'And where do you live?' 'No fixed abode,' he says and laughs; but it is only the kind of laughter that has no lungs behind it. It sounds rather like the rustling of fallen leaves."

"The 'I' is another," Rimbaud once wrote, adding: "So much the worse for the wood that finds it is a violin." So much the worse for the wood that finds it is Odradek. He laughs at being a vagrant, if only by the bourgeois definition of having "no fixed abode," but the laughter, not being human, is uncanny. And so he provokes the family man to an uncanny reflection, which may be a Kafkan parody of Freud's death drive beyond the pleasure principle:

> I ask myself, to no purpose, what is likely to happen to him? Can he possibly die? Anything that dies has had some kind of aim in life, some kind of activity, which has worn out; but that does not apply to Odradek. Am I to suppose, then, that he will always be rolling down the stairs, with ends of thread trailing after him, right before the feet of my children? He does no harm to anyone that I can see, but the idea that he is likely to survive me I find almost painful.

The aim of life, Freud says, is death, is the return of the organic to the inorganic, supposedly our earlier state of being. Our activity wears out, and so we die because, in an uncanny sense, we wish to die. But Odradek, harmless and charming, is a child's creation, aimless, and so not subject to the death drive. Odradek is immortal, being daemonic, and he represents also a Freudian return of the repressed, of something repressed in the *paterfamilias*, something from which the family man is in perpetual flight. Little Odradek is precisely what Freud calls a cognitive return of the repressed, while (even as) a complete affective repression is maintained. The family man introjects Odradek intellectually, but totally projects him affectively. Odradek, I now suggest, is best understood as Kafka's synecdoche for *Verneinung*; Kafka's version (not altogether un-Freudian) of Jewish Negation, a version I hope to adumbrate in what follows.

IV

Why does Kafka have so unique a spiritual authority? Perhaps the question should be rephrased. What kind of spiritual authority does Kafka have for us or why are we moved or compelled to read him as one who has such authority? Why invoke the question of authority at all? Literary authority, however we define it, has no necessary relation to spiritual authority, and to speak of a spiritual authority in Jewish writing anyway always has been to speak rather dubiously. Authority is not a Jewish concept but a Roman one, and so makes perfect contemporary sense in the context of the Roman Catholic Church, but little sense in Jewish matters, despite the squalors of Israeli politics and the flaccid pieties of American Jewish nostalgias. There is no authority without hierarchy, and hierarchy is not a very Jewish concept either. We do not want the rabbis, or anyone else, to tell us what or who is or is not Jewish. The masks of the normative conceal not only the eclecticism of Judaism and of Jewish culture, but also the nature of the J writer's Yahweh himself. It is absurd to think of Yahweh as having mere authority. He is no Roman godling who augments human activities, nor a Homeric god helping to constitute an audience for human heroism.

Yahweh is neither a founder nor an onlooker, though sometimes he can be mistaken for either or both. His essential trope is fatherhood rather than foundation, and his interventions are those of a covenanter rather than of a spectator. You cannot found an authority upon him, because his benignity is manifested not through augmentation but through creation. He does not write; he speaks, and he is heard, in time, and what he continues to create by his speaking is *olam*, time without boundaries, which is more than just an augmentation. More of anything else can come through authority, but more life is the blessing itself, and comes, beyond authority, to Abraham, to Jacob, and to David. No more than Yahweh, do any of them have mere authority. Yet Kafka certainly does have literary authority, and in a troubled way his literary authority is now spiritual also, particularly in Jewish contexts. I do not think that this is a post-Holocaust phenomenon, though Jewish Gnosticism, oxymoronic as it may or may not be, certainly seems appropriate to our time, to many among us. Literary Gnosticism does not seem to me a time-bound phenomenon, anyway. Kafka's *The Castle*, as Erich Heller has argued, is clearly more Gnostic than normative in is spiritual temper, but then so is Shakespeare's *Macbeth*, and Blake's *The Four Zoas*, and Carlyle's *Sartor Resartus*. We sense a Jewish element in Kafka's apparent Gnosticism, even if we are less prepared than Scholem was to name it as a new Kabbalah. In his 1922 Diaries, Kafka subtly insinuated that even his espousal of the Negative was dialectical:

> The Negative alone, however strong it may be, cannot suffice, as in my unhappiest moments I believe it can. For if I have gone the tiniest step upward, won any, be it the most dubious kind of security for

myself, I then stretch out on my step and wait for the Negative, not to climb up to me, indeed, but to drag me down from it. Hence it is a defensive instinct in me that won't tolerate my having the slightest degree of lasting ease and smashes the marriage bed, for example, even before it has been set up.

What is the Kafkan Negative, whether in this passage or elsewhere? Let us begin by dismissing the Gallic notion that there is anything Hegelian about it, any more than there is anything Hegelian about the Freudian *Verneinung*. Kafka's Negative, unlike Freud's, is uneasily and remotely descended from the ancient tradition of negative theology, and perhaps even from that most negative of ancient theologies, Gnosticism, and yet Kafka, despite his yearnings for transcendence, joins Freud in accepting the ultimate authority of the fact. The given suffers no destruction in Kafka or in Freud, and this given essentially is the way things are, for everyone, and for the Jews in particular. If fact is supreme, then the mediation of the Hegelian Negative becomes an absurdity, and no destructive use of such a Negative is possible, which is to say that Heidegger becomes impossible, and Derrida, who is a strong misreading of Heidegger, becomes quite unnecessary.

The Kafkan Negative most simply is his Judaism, which is to say the spiritual form of Kafka's self-conscious Jewishness, as exemplified in that extraordinary aphorism: "What is laid upon us is to accomplish the negative; the positive is already given." The positive here is the Law or normative Judaism; the negative is not so much Kafka's new Kabbalah, as it is that which is still laid upon us: the Judaism of the Negative, of the future as it is always rushing towards us.

His best biographer to date, Ernst Pawel, emphasizes Kafka's consciousness "of his identity as a Jew, not in the religious, but in the national sense." Still, Kafka was not a Zionist, and perhaps he longed not so much for Zion as for a Jewish language, be it Yiddish or Hebrew. He could not see that his astonishing stylistic purity in German was precisely his way of *not* betraying his self-identity as a Jew. In his final phase, Kafka thought of going to Jerusalem, and again intensified his study of Hebrew. Had he lived, he would probably have gone to Zion, perfected a vernacular Hebrew, and given us the bewilderment of Kafkan parables and stories in the language of the J writer and of Judah Halevi.

V

What calls out for interpretation in Kafka is his refusal to be interpreted, his evasiveness even in the realm of his own Negative. Two of his most beautifully enigmatical performances, both late, are the parable, "The Problem of Our Laws," and the story or testament "Josephine the Singer and the Mouse Folk." Each allows a cognitive return of Jewish cultural memory, while refusing the affective identification that would make either parable or tale specifically Jewish in either historical or contemporary identification. "The Problem of Our Laws" is set as a problem in the parable's first paragraph:

> Our laws are not generally known; they are kept secret by the small group of nobles who rule us. We are convinced that these ancient laws are scrupulously administered; nevertheless it is an extremely painful thing to be ruled by laws that one does not know. I am not thinking of possible discrepancies that may arise in the interpretation of the laws, or of the disadvantages involved when only a few and not the whole people are allowed to have a say in their interpretation. These disadvantages are perhaps of no great importance. For the laws are very ancient; their interpretation has been the work of centuries, and has itself doubtless acquired the status of law; and though there is still a possible freedom of interpretation left, it has now become very restricted. Moreover the nobles have obviously no cause to be influenced in their interpretation by personal interests inimical to us, for the laws were made to the advantage of the nobles from the very beginning, they themselves stand above the laws, and that seems to be why the laws were entrusted exclusively into their hands. Of course, there is wisdom in that—who doubts the wisdom of the ancient laws?—but also hardship for us; probably that is unavoidable.

In Judaism, the Law is precisely what is generally known, proclaimed, and taught by the normative sages. The Kabbalah was secret doctrine, but increasingly was guarded not by the normative rabbis, but by Gnostic sectaries, Sabbatarians, and Frankists, all of them ideologically descended from Nathan of Gaza, Sabbatai Zvi's prophet. Kafka twists askew the relations between normative and esoteric Judaism, again making a synecdochal representation impossible. It is not the rabbis or normative sages who stand above the Torah but the *minim*, the heretics from Elisha ben Abuyah through to Jacob Frank, and in some sense, Gershom Scholem as well. To these Jewish Gnostics, as the parable goes on to insinuate: "The Law is whatever the nobles do." So radical a definition tells us "that the tradition is far from complete," and that a kind of messianic expectation is therefore necessary. This view, so comfortless as far as the present is concerned, is lightened only by the belief that a time will eventually come when the tradition and our research into it will jointly reach their conclusion, and as it were gain a breathing space, when everything will have become clear, the law will belong to the people, and the nobility will vanish.

If the parable at this point were to be translated into early Christian terms, then "the nobility" would be the Pharisees, and "the people" would be the Christian believers. But Kafka moves rapidly to stop such a translation: "This is not maintained in any spirit of hatred against the nobility; not at all, and by no one. We are more inclined to hate ourselves, because we have not yet shown ourselves worthy of being entrusted with the laws."

"We" here cannot be either Christians or Jews. Who then are those who "have not yet shown ourselves worthy of being entrusted with the laws"? They would appear to be the crows or jackdaws again, a Kafka or a Hunter Gracchus, wandering about in a state perhaps vulnerable to self-hatred or self-distrust, waiting for a Torah that will not be revealed. Audaciously, Kafka then concludes with overt paradox:

> Actually one can express the problem only in a sort of paradox: Any party that would repudiate not only all belief in the laws, but the nobility as well, would have the whole people behind it; yet no such party can come into existence, for nobody would dare to repudiate the nobility. We live on this razor's edge. A writer once summed the matter up in this way: The sole visible and indubitable law that is imposed upon us is the nobility, and must we ourselves deprive ourselves of that one law?

Why would no one dare to repudiate the nobility, whether we read them as normative Pharisees, Jewish Gnostic heresiarchs, or whatever? Though imposed upon us, the sages or the *minim* are the only visible evidence of law that we have. Who are we then? How is the parable's final question, whether open or rhetorical, to be answered? "Must we ourselves deprive ourselves of that one law?" Blake's answer, in *The Marriage of Heaven and Hell*, was: "One Law for the Lion and the Ox is Oppression." But what is one law for the crows? Kafka will not tell us whether it is oppression or not.

Josephine the singer also is a crow or Kafka, rather than a mouse, and the folk may be interpreted as an entire nation of jackdaws. The spirit of the Negative, dominant if uneasy in "The Problem of Our Laws," is loosed into a terrible freedom in Kafka's testamentary story. That is to say: in the parable, the laws could not be Torah, though that analogue flickered near. But in Josephine's story, the mouse folk simultaneously are *and* are not the Jewish people, and Franz Kafka both is *and* is not their curious singer.

Cognitively the identifications are possible, as though returned from forgetfulness, but affectively they certainly are not, unless we can assume that crucial aspects making up the identifications have been purposefully, if other than consciously, forgotten. Josephine's piping is Kafka's story, and yet Kafka's story is hardly Josephine's piping.

Can there be a mode of negation neither conscious nor unconscious, neither Hegelian nor Freudian? Kafka's genius provides one, exposing many shades between consciousness and the work of repression, many demarcations far ghostlier than we could have imagined without him. Perhaps the ghostliest come at the end of the story:

> Josephine's road, however, must go downhill. The time will soon come when her last notes sound and die into silence. She is a small episode in the eternal history of our people, and the people will get over the loss of her. Not that it will be easy for us; how can our gatherings take place in utter silence? Still, were they not silent even when Josephine was present? Was her actual piping notably louder and more alive than the memory of it will be? Was it even in her lifetime more than a simply memory? Was it not rather because Josephine's singing was already past losing in this way that our people in their wisdom prized it so highly?
>
> So perhaps we shall not miss so very much after all, while Josephine, redeemed from the earthly sorrows which to her thinking lay in wait for all chosen spirits, will happily lose herself in the numberless throng of the heroes of our people, and soon, since we are no historians, will rise to the heights of redemption and be forgotten like all her brothers.

"I am a Memory come alive," Kafka wrote in the Diaries. Whether or not he intended it, he was Jewish memory come alive. "Was it even in her lifetime more than a simple memory?" Kafka asks, knowing that he too was past losing. The Jews are no historians, in some sense, because Jewish memory, as Yosef Yerushalmi has demonstrated, is a normative mode and not a historical one. Kafka, if he could have prayed, might have prayed to rise to the heights of redemption and be forgotten like most of his brothers and sisters. But his prayer would not have been answered. When we think of *the* Catholic writer, we think of Dante, who nevertheless had the audacity to enshrine his Beatrice in the hierarchy of Paradise. If we think of *the* Protestant writer, we think of Milton, a party or sect of one, who believed that the soul was mortal, and would be resurrected only in conjunction with the body. Think of *the* Jewish writer, and you must think of

Kafka, who evaded his own audacity, and believed nothing, and trusted only in the Covenant of being a writer.

The Castle

The full-scale instance of Kafka's new Negative or new Kabbalah is *The Castle*, an unfinished and unfinishable autobiographical novel which is the story of K., the land-surveyor. What is written between its lines? Assaulting the last earthly frontier, K. is necessarily audacious, but if what lies beyond the frontier is represented ultimately by Klamm, an imprisoning silence, lord of the *kenoma* or cosmic emptiness, then no audacity can suffice. You cannot redraw the frontiers, even if the authorities desired this, when you arrive at the administrative center of a catastrophe creation, where the demarcations hold fast against a supposed chaos or abyss, which is actually the negative emblem of the truth that the false or marred creation refuses. *The Castle* is the tale of how Kafka cannot write his way back to the abyss, of how K. cannot do his work as land-surveyor.

Part of K.'s burden is that he is not audacious enough, even though audacity could not be enough anyway. Here is the interpretive audacity of Erich Heller, rightly rejecting all those who identify the Castle with spirituality and authentic grace, but himself missing the ineluctable evasiveness of Kafka's new Kabbalah:

> The Castle of Kafka's novel is, as it were, the heavily fortified garrison of a company of Gnostic demons, successfully holding an advanced position against the maneuvers of an impatient soul. There is no conceivable idea of divinity which could justify those interpreters who see in the Castle the residence of "divine law and divine grace." Its officers are totally indifferent to good if they are not positively wicked. Neither in their decrees nor in their activities is there any trace of love, mercy, charity, or majesty. In their icy detachment they inspire certainly no awe, but fear and revulsion. Their servants are a plague to the village, "a wild, unmanageable lot, ruled by their insatiable impulses ... their scandalous behavior knows no limits," an anticipation of the blackguards who were to become the footmen of European dictators rather than the office boys of a divine ministry. Compared to the petty and apparently calculated torture of this tyranny, the gods of Shakespeare's indignation who "kill us for their sport" are at least majestic in their wantonness.

On such a reading, Klamm would be the Demiurge, leader of a company of Archons, gods of this world. Kafka is too evasive and too negative to give us so positive and simplistic an account of triumphant evil, or at least of reigning indifference to the good. Such Gnostic symbolism would make Klamm and his cohorts representatives of ignorance, and K. in contrast a knower, but K. knows almost nothing, particularly about his own self, and from the start overestimates his own strength even as he deceives himself into the belief that the Castle underestimates him. The Castle is there primarily because K. is ignorant, though K.'s deepest drive is for knowledge. K.'s largest error throughout is his desire for a personal confrontation with Klamm, which necessarily is impossible. K., the single crow or jackdaw, would be sufficient to destroy the authority of Klamm, but Klamm and the Castle of Westwest signify simply the absence of crows, the inability of K. to achieve knowledge and therefore the impossibility of K. himself, the failure of land-surveying or of assaulting the frontiers, of writing a new Kabbalah.

Klamm is named by Wilhelm Emrich as the interpersonal element in the erotic, which seems to me just as subtle an error as judging Klamm to be the Demiurge, leader of a company of Gnostic demons. It might be more accurate to call Klamm the impersonal element in the erotic, the drive, as Martin Greenberg does, yet even that identification is evaded by Kafka's text. Closer to Klamm, as should be expected, is the negative aspect of the drive, its entropy, whose effect upon consciousness is nihilistic. Freud, in his posthumous *An Outline of Psychoanalysis* (1940) says of the drives that "they represent the somatic demands upon mental life." That approximates Klamm, but only if you give priority to Thanatos over Eros, to the death drive over sexuality. Emrich, a touch humorlessly, even identifies Klamm with Eros, which would give us a weird Eros indeed:

> Accordingly, then, Klamm is the "power" that brings the lovers together as well as the power which, bestowing happiness and bliss, is present within love itself. K. seeks contact with this power, sensing its proximity in love, a proximity great enough for communicating in whispers; but he must "manifest" such communication and contact with this power itself through a spiritual-intellectual expression of his own; this means that, as an independent spiritual-intellectual being, he must confront this power eye to eye, as it were; he must "manifest" to this superpersonal power his own understanding, his own relation with it, a relation "known" only to him at the present time; that means, he must make this relation known to the power as well.

Emrich seems to found this equation on the love affair between K. and Frieda, which begins, in famous squalor, on the floor of a bar:

Fortunately Frieda soon came back; she did not mention K., she only complained about the peasants, and in the course of looking round for K. went behind the counter, so that he was able to touch her foot. From that moment he felt safe. Since Frieda made no reference to K., however, the landlord was compelled to do it. "And where is the Land-Surveyor?" he asked. He was probably courteous by nature, refined by constant and relatively free intercourse with men who were much his superior, but there was remarkable consideration in his tone to Frieda, which was all the more striking because in his conversation he did not cease to be an employer addressing a servant, and a saucy servant at that. "The Land-Surveyor—I forgot all about him," said Frieda, setting her small foot on K.'s chest. "He must have gone out long ago." "But I haven't seen him," said the landlord, "and I was in the hall nearly the whole time." "Well, he isn't in here," said Frieda coolly. "Perhaps he's hidden somewhere," said the landlord. "From the impression I had of him, he's capable of a good deal." "He would hardly dare to do that," said Frieda, pressing her foot down on K. There was a certain mirth and freedom about her which K. had not previously noticed, and quite unexpectedly it took the upper hand, for suddenly laughing she bent down to K. with the words: "Perhaps he's hidden underneath here," kissed him lightly, and sprang up again saying with a troubled air: "No, he's not there." Then the landlord, too, surprised K. when he said: "It bothers me not to know for certain that he's gone. Not only because of Herr Klamm, but because of the rule of the house. And the rule applies to you, Fräulein Frieda, just as much as to me. Well, if you answer for the bar, I'll go through the rest of the rooms. Good night! Sleep well!" He could hardly have left the room before Frieda had turned out the electric light and was under the counter beside K. "My darling! My darling!" she whispered, but she did not touch him. As if swooning with love, she lay on her back and stretched out her arms; time must have seemed endless to her in the prospect of her happiness, and she sighed rather than sang some little song or other. Then as K. still lay absorbed in thought, she started up and began to tug at him like a child. "Come on, it's too close down here," and they embraced each other, her little body burned in K.'s hands, in a state of unconsciousness which K. tried

again and again but in vain to master they rolled a little way, landing with a thud on Klamm's door, where they lay among the small
puddles of beer and other refuse scattered on the floor.

"Landing with a thud on Klamm's door" is Kafka's outrageously rancid trope for a successful completion to copulation, but that hardly makes
Klamm into a benign Eros, with his devotees lying "among the small puddles of beer and other refuse scattered on the floor." One could recall the
libertines among the Gnostics, ancient and modern, who seek to redeem
the sparks upwards by a redemption *through* sin. Frieda, faithful disciple
and former mistress of Klamm, tells K. that she believes it is Klamm's,
"doing that we came together there under the counter; blessed, not cursed,
be the hour." Emrich gives full credence to Frieda, a rather dangerous act
for an exegete, and certainly K. desperately believes Frieda, but then, as
Heller remarks, "K. loves Frieda—if he loves her at all—entirely for
Klamm's sake." That K., despite his drive for freedom, may be deceived as
to Klamm's nature is understandable, but I do not think that Kafka was
deceived or wished to be deceived. If Klamm is to be identified, it ought to
be with what is silent, imprisoned, and unavailable in copulation, something that partakes of the final Negative, the drive towards death.

Whether *The Castle* is of the aesthetic eminence of Kafka's finest stories, parables, and fragments is open to considerable doubt, but *The Castle*
is certainly the best text for studying Kafka's Negative, his hidden and subversive New Kabbalah. It abides as the most enigmatic major novel of our
century, and one sees why Kafka himself thought it a failure. But all
Kabbalah—old and new—has to fail when it offers itself openly to more
than a handful. Perhaps *The Castle* fails as the *Zohar* fails, but like the
Zohar, Kafka's *Castle* will go on failing from one era to another.

The Trial

"Guilt" generally seems more a Christian than a Jewish category, even if
the guilt of Joseph K. is primarily ignorance of the Law. Certainly Kafka
could be judged closer to Freud in *The Trial* than he usually is, since
Freudian "guilt" is also hardly distinct from ignorance, not of the Law but
of the Reality Principle. Freud insisted that all authority, communal or
personal, induced guilt in us, since we share in the murder of the totemic
father. Guilt therefore is never to be doubted, but only because we are all
of us more or less ill, all plagued by our discomfort with culture. Freudian
and Kafkan guilt alike is known only under the sign of negation, rather
than as emotion. Joseph K. has no consciousness of having done wrong,

but just as Freudian man nurtures the desire to destroy authority or the father, so even Joseph K. has his own unfulfilled wishes against the image of the Law.

The process that Joseph K. undergoes is hopeless, since the Law is essentially a closed Kabbalah; its books are not available to the accused. If traditional questers suffered an ordeal by landscape, Joseph K.'s ordeal is by nearly everything and everyone he encounters. The representatives of the Law, and their camp followers, are so unsavory that Joseph K. seems sympathetic by contrast, yet he is actually a poor fellow in himself, and would be as nasty as the keepers of the Law, if only he could. *The Trial* is a very unpleasant book, and Kafka's own judgment of it may have been spiritually wiser than anything its critics have enunciated. Would there be any process for us to undergo if we were not both lazy and frightened? Nietzsche's motive for metaphor was the desire to be different, the desire to be elsewhere, but Kafka's sense of our motive is that we want to rest, even if just for a moment. The world is our Gnostic catastrophe creation, being broken into existence by the guilt of our repose. Yet this is creation, and can be visibly beautiful, even as the accused are beautiful in the gaze of the camp followers of the Law.

I do not think that the process Joseph K. undergoes can be called "interpretation," which is the judgment of Ernst Pawel, who follows Jewish tradition in supposing that the Law is language. *The Trial*, like the rest of Kafka's writings, is a parable not of interpretation, but of the necessary failure of interpretation. I would surmise that the Law is not all of language, since the language of *The Trial* is ironic enough to suggest that it is not altogether bound to the Law. If *The Trial* has a center, it is in what Kafka thought worthy of publishing: the famous parable "Before the Law." The dialogue concerning the parable between Joseph K. and the prison chaplain who tells it is remarkable, but less crucial than the parable itself:

> Before the Law stands a doorkeeper on guard. To this doorkeeper there comes a man from the country who begs for admittance to the Law. But the doorkeeper says that he cannot admit the man at the moment. The man, on reflection, asks if he will be allowed, then, to enter later. "It is possible," answers the doorkeeper, "but not at this moment." Since the door leading into the Law stands open as usual and the doorkeeper steps to one side, the man bends down to peer through the entrance. When the doorkeeper sees that; he laughs and says: "If you are so strongly tempted, try to get in without my permission. But note that I am powerful. And I am only the lowest doorkeeper. From hall to hall keepers stand at

every door, one more powerful than the other. Even the third of
these has an aspect that even I cannot bear to look at." These are
difficulties which the man from the country has not expected to
meet; the Law, he thinks, should be accessible to every man and at
all times, but when he looks more closely at the doorkeeper in his
furred robe, with his huge pointed nose and long, thin, Tartar
beard, he decides that he had better wait until he gets permission
to enter. The doorkeeper gives him a stool and lets him sit down
at the side of the door. There he sits waiting for days and years.
He makes many attempts to be allowed in and wearies the doorkeeper with his importunity. The doorkeeper often engages him
in brief conversation, asking him about his home and about other
matters, but the questions are put quite impersonally, as great men
put questions, and always conclude with the statement that the
man cannot be allowed to enter yet. The man, who has equipped
himself with many things for his journey, parts with all he has,
however valuable, in the hope of bribing the doorkeeper. The
doorkeeper accepts it all, saying, however, as he takes each gift: "I
take this only to keep you from feeling that you have left something undone." During all these long years the man watches the
doorkeeper almost incessantly. He forgets about the other door-
keepers, and this one seems to him the only barrier between himself and the Law. In the first years he curses his evil fate aloud;
later, as he grows old, he only mutters to himself. He grows childish, and since in his prolonged watch he has learned to know even
the fleas in the doorkeeper's fur collar, he begs the very fleas to
help him and to persuade the doorkeeper to change his mind.
Finally his eyes grow dim and he does not know whether the
world is really darkening around him or whether his eyes are only
deceiving him. But in the darkness he can now perceive a radiance
that streams immortally from the door of the Law. Now his life is
drawing to a close. Before he dies, all that he has experienced during the whole time of his sojourn condenses in his mind into one
question, which he has never yet put to the doorkeeper. He beck-
ons the doorkeeper, since he can no longer raise his stiffening
body. The doorkeeper has to bend far down to hear him, for the
difference in size between them has increased very much to the
man's disadvantage. "What do you want to know now?" asks the
doorkeeper, "you are insatiable." "Everyone strives to attain the
Law," answers the man, "how does it come about, then, that in all
these years no one has come seeking admittance but me?" The

doorkeeper perceives that the man is at the end of his strength and that his hearing is failing, so he bellows in his ear: "No one but you could gain admittance through this door, since this door was intended only for you. I am now going to shut it."

Does he actually perceive a radiance, or are his eyes perhaps still deceiving him? What would admittance to the radiance mean? The Law, I take it, has the same status it has in the later parable "The Problem of Our Laws," where it cannot be Torah, or the Jewish Law, yet Torah flickers uneasily near as a positive analogue to the negation that is playing itself out. Joseph K. then is another jackdaw, another Kafkan crow in a cosmos of crows, waiting for that new Torah that will not be revealed. Does such a waiting allow itself to be represented in or by a novel? No one could judge *The Trial* to be grander as a whole than in its parts, and "Before the Law" bursts out of its narrative shell in the novel. The terrible greatness of Kafka is absolute in the parable but wavering in the novel, too impure a casing for such a fire.

That there should be nothing but a spiritual world, Kafka once wrote, denies us hope but gives us certainty. The certainty would seem to be not so much that a radiance exists, but that all access to it will be barred by petty officials at least countenanced, if not encouraged, by what passes for the radiance itself. This is not paradox, any more than is the Kafkan principle propounded by the priest who narrates "Before the Law": accurate interpretation and misreading cannot altogether exclude one another. Kafka's aesthetic compulsion (can there be such?) in *The Trial* as elsewhere is to write so as to create a necessity, yet also so as to make interpretation impossible, rather than merely difficult.

Kafka's permanent centrality to the post-normative Jewish dilemma achieves one of its monuments in *The Trial*. Gershom Scholem found in Kafka not only the true continuator of the Gnostic Kabbalah of Moses Cordovero, but also the central representative for our time of an even more archaic splendor, the broken radiance of Hebraic revelation. Perhaps Scholem was right, for no other modern Jewish author troubles us with so strong an impression that we are in the presence of what Scholem called "the strong light of the canonical, of the perfection that destroys."

D.H. Lawrence

(1885-1930)

LAWRENCE, HARDLY A LIBERTINE, HAD THE RADICALLY PROTESTANT sensibility of Milton, Shelley, Browning, Hardy—none of them Eliotic favorites. To say that Lawrence was more a Puritan than Milton is only to state what is now finely obvious. What Lawrence shares with Milton is an intense exaltation of unfallen human sexuality. With Blake, Lawrence shares the conviction that touch, the sexual sense proper, is the least fallen of the senses, which implies that redemption is most readily a sexual process. Freud and Lawrence, according to Lawrence, share little or nothing, which accounts for Lawrence's ill-informed but wonderfully vigorous polemic against Freud:

> This is the moral dilemma of psychoanalysis. The analyst sets out to core neurotic humanity by removing the cause of the neurosis. He finds that the cause of neurosis lies in some unadmitted sex desire. After all he has said about inhibition of normal sex, he is brought at last to realize that at the root of almost every neurosis lies some incest-craving, and that this incest-craving is *not the result of inhibition and normal sex-craving*. Now see the dilemma—it is a fearful one. If the incest-craving is not the outcome of any inhibition of normal desire, if it actually exists and refuses to give way before any criticism, what then? What remains but to accept it as part of the normal sex-manifestation?
>
> Here is an issue which analysis is perfectly willing to face. Among themselves the analysts are bound to accept the incest-craving as part of the normal sexuality of man, normal, but suppressed, because of moral and perhaps biological fear. Once, however, you accept the incest-craving as part of the normal sexuality

of man, you must remove all repression of incest itself. In fact, you must admit incest as you now admit sexual marriage, as a duty even. Since at last it works out that neurosis is not the result of inhibition of so-called *normal sex*, but of inhibition of incest-craving. Any inhibition must be wrong, since inevitably in the end it causes neurosis and insanity. Therefore the inhibition of incest-craving is wrong, and this wrong is the cause of practically all modern neurosis and insanity.

To believe that Freud thought that "any inhibition must be wrong" is merely outrageous. Philip Rieff subtly defends Lawrence's weird accusation by remarking that: "As a concept, the incest taboo, like any other Freudian hypothesis, represents a scientific projection of the false standards governing erotic relations within the family." Lawrence surely sensed this, but chose to misunderstand Freud for some of the same reasons he chose to misunderstand Walt Whitman. Whitman provoked in Lawrence an anxiety of influence in regard to stance and form. Freud, also too authentic a precursor, threatened Lawrence's therapeutic originality. Like Freud's, Lawrence's ideas of drive or will stem from Schopenhauer and Nietzsche. Again like Freud, Lawrence derived considerable stimulus from later nineteenth-century materialistic thought. It is difficult to remember that so flamboyant a mythmaker as Lawrence was also a deidealizer with a reductionist aspect, but then we do not see that Freud was a great mythmaker only because we tend to believe in Freud's myths. When I was young, I knew many young women and young men who believed in Lawrence's myths, but they all have weathered the belief, and I do not encounter any Lawrentian believers among the young today.

Sons and Lovers

Lawrence's *Sons and Lovers* (1913), his third novel, was begun in 1910 as *Paul Morel*, and in some sense was finished by Edward Garnett, who made severe cuts in the final manuscript. The change of title from *Paul Morel* to *Sons and Lovers* may have been Lawrence's gesture towards Freud, as mediated by Frieda Weekley, with whom Lawrence eloped in the spring of 1912 and under whose early influence the novel was completed. Lawrence attempted to fight off Freud later on, in two very odd books on the unconscious, but *Sons and Lovers* is so available to Freudian reduction as to make a Freudian reading of the novel quite uninteresting.

Though *Sons and Lovers* is clearly the work of the author of *The Rainbow* and *Women in Love*, it retains many of the characteristics of the fiction of

Thomas Hardy and has little of the visionary intensity that the mature Lawrence shares with *Moby-Dick*, *Wuthering Heights*, and only a few other novels. Rereading *Sons and Lovers* is a somber and impressive experience, if a rather mixed one aesthetically. It is difficult to know if we are reading an autobiographical novel rather than a novelistic autobiography. The aesthetic puzzle is in deciding how to receive Lawrence's self-portrait as Paul Morel. If the reader simply decides that the identification of the writer and his hero is complete, then the experience of reading necessarily is vexed by the identification of Gertrude Morel with Lydia Lawrence, the novelist's mother, and so also by the parody of Arthur Lawrence in the novel's Walter Morel. Even more troublesome is the identification of Jessie Chambers, the novelist's first love, with Miriam. By the time one has read *D.H. Lawrence: A Personal Record* by Jessie Chambers and studied such standard biographies of Lawrence as those by Nehls, Moore, and Sagar, it becomes very difficult to know whether the novel is the appropriate genre for Lawrence's story. Miriam and Walter Morel seem abused in *Sons and Lovers*, and Paul Morel seems quite blind to his mother's real culpability in malforming his psychosexual development.

A curious reader or student of D.H. Lawrence will search out the appropriate material in the composite biography of Nehls, but I am dubious as to whether *Sons and Lovers* gains aesthetically by such an enrichment of personal context. Louis L. Martz has argued that a close reading will show that the novel depicts Miriam as life-enhancing and Gertrude Morel as an agent of repression, but the book's actual narrative voice tends to give an impression much closer to that of Paul, who ends by leaving Miriam and then confronting a motherless Sublime that has no place for him:

> He shook hands and left her at the door of her cousin's house. When he turned away he felt the last hold for him had gone. The town, as he sat upon the car, stretched away over the bay of railway, a level fume of lights. Beyond the town the country, little smouldering spots for more towns—the sea—the night—on and on! And he had no place in it! Whatever spot he stood on, there he stood alone. From his breast, from his mouth, sprang the endless space, and it was there behind him, everywhere. The people hurrying along the streets offered no obstruction to the void in which he found himself. They were small shadows whose footsteps and voices could be heard, but in each of them the same night, the same silence. He got off the car. In the country all was dead still. Little stars shone high up; little stars spread far away in the flood-waters, a firmament below. Everywhere the vastness and

terror of the immense night which is roused and stirred for a brief while by the day, but which returns, and will remain at last eternal, holding everything in its silence and its living gloom. There was no Time, only Space. Who could say his mother had lived and did not live? She had been in one place, and was in another; that was all. And his soul could not leave her, wherever she was. Now she was gone abroad into the night, and he was with her still. They were together. But yet there was his body, his chest, that leaned against the stile, his hands on the wooden bar. They seemed something. Where was he?—one tiny upright speck of flesh, less than an ear of wheat lost in the field. He could not bear it. On every side the immense dark silence seemed pressing him, so tiny a spark, into extinction, and yet, almost nothing, he could not be extinct. Night, in which everything was lost, went reaching out, beyond stars and sun. Stars and sun, a few bright grains, went spinning round for terror, and holding each other in embrace, there in a darkness that outpassed them all, and left than tiny and daunted. So much, and himself, infinitesimal, at the core a nothingness, and yet not nothing.

"Mother!" he whimpered—"mother!"

She was the only thing that held him up, himself, amid all this. And she was gone, intermingled herself. He wanted her to touch him, have him alongside with her.

But no, he would not give in. Turning sharply, he walked towards the city's gold phosphorescence. His fists were shut, his mouth set fast. He would not take that direction, to the darkness, to follow her. He walked towards the faintly humming, glowing town, quickly.

We understand, after reading this conclusion to *Sons and Lovers*, why Walt Whitman came to have so powerful an influence upon Lawrence's later poetry, since the elegiac Whitman identified night, death, the mother, and the sea, and only the sea is absent from the fusion here. Nothing else in *Sons and Lovers* is quite as strong as this closing vision, which does prophesy the greater harmonies and discords of *The Rainbow* and *Women in Love*.

Aside from the troublesome strains of unassimilated autobiography, the principal defect of *Sons and Lovers* is that Paul Morel does not always seem energetic or sympathetic enough to sustain our interest. At moments we might be reading *A Portrait of the Artist as a Young Prig*, and we then want to congratulate Miriam for not ending up with the hero.

The novel has force of narrative despite lack of plot, and deserves all the praise it has received as an unmatched account of English working-class life. But the sincerity or veracity of Lawrence's story of his own origins is more of a social than an aesthetic virtue in *Sons and Lovers*. What redeems the book aesthetically is a series of passages and incidents that presage the massive excursions into the Sublime made in *The Rainbow* and *Women in Love*. The concluding passage is one of these; others include such fatuous moments as Paul and Miriam taking turns on the swing, and the fight between Paul and Baxter Dawes (who is oddly the most convincing character in the novel). These are early forms of what might be called Lawrence's epiphanies, times when elemental forces break through the surfaces of existence. Lawrence hardly knows what to do with them in *Sons and Lovers*; they do not reverberate with enormous possibilities as do such moments in *Women in Love* as Birkin stoning the moon's reflection in the water, or Birkin and Gerald caught up in their wrestling match. Yet the shadowy epiphanies of *Sons and Lovers* have the value of preparatory exercises for those fragments of a giant art that Lawrence later scattered so generously in his work.

The Rainbow and Women in Love

Lawrence's greatest achievement is his double-novel, *The Rainbow* (1915) and *Women in Love* (1920). Together with his short stories and the best of his poems, these represent his absolute literary permanence, obscured as that currently may be by the virulence of much Feminist criticism.

I recall, many years ago, writing that, "In the endless war between men and women, Lawrence fights on both sides." The twenty-third chapter of *Women in Love*, "Excurse," is an eminent instance:

> "I jealous! *I*—jealous! You *are* mistaken if you think that. I'm not jealous in the least of Hermione, she is nothing to me, not *that*!" And Ursula snapped her fingers. "No, it's you who are a liar. It's you who must return, like a dog to his vomit. It is what Hermione *stands* for that I *hate*. I *hate* it. It is lies, it is false, it is death. But you want to, you can't help it, you can't help yourself. You belong to that old, deathly way of living—then go back to it. But don't come to me, for I've nothing to do with it."
>
> And in the stress of her violent emotion, she got down from the car and went to the hedgerow, picking unconsciously some flesh-pink spindleberries, some of which were burst, showing their orange seeds.

"Ah, you are a fool," he cried bitterly, with some contempt.

"Yes, I am. I *am* a fool. And thank God for it. I'm too big a fool to swallow your cleverness. God be praised. You go to your women—go to them—they are your sort—you've always had a string of them trailing after you—and you always will. Go to your spiritual brides—but don't come to me as well, because I'm not having any, thank you. You're not satisfied, are you? Your spiritual brides can't give you what you want, they aren't common and fleshy enough for you, aren't they? So you come to me, and keep them in the background! You will marry me for daily use. But you'll keep yourself well provided with spiritual brides in the background. I know your dirty little game." Suddenly a flame ran over her, and she stamped her foot madly on the road, and he winced, afraid she would strike him. "And *I, I'm* not spiritual enough. *I'm* not as spiritual as that Hermione—!" Her brows knitted, her eyes blazed like a tiger's. "Then *go* to her, that's all I say, *go* to her, go. Ha, she spiritual—*spiritual*, she! A dirty materialist as she is. *She* spiritual? What does she care for, what is her spirituality? What *is* it?" Her fury seemed to blaze out and burn his face. He shrank a little. "I tell you, it's *dirt*, *dirt*, and nothing *but* dirt. And it's dirt you want, you crave for it. Spiritual! Is *that* spiritual, her bullying, her conceit, her sordid materialism? She's a fishwife, a fishwife, she is such a materialist. And all so sordid. What does she work out to, in the end, with all her social passion, as you call it. Social passion—what social passion has she?—show it me!— where is it? She wants petty, immediate *power*, she wants the illusion that she is a great woman, that is all. In her soul she's a devilish unbeliever, common as dirt. That's what she is, at the bottom. And all the rest is pretence—but you love it. You love the sham spiritually, it's your food. And why? Because of the dirt underneath. Do you think I don't know the foulness of your sex life— and hers?—I do. And it's that foulness you want, you liar. Then have it, have it. You're such a liar."

She turned away, spasmodically tearing the twigs of spindleberry from the hedge, and fastening them, with vibrating fingers, in the bosom of her coat.

He stood watching in silence. A wonderful tenderness burned in him at the sight of her quivering, so sensitive fingers: and at the same time he was full of rage and callousness.

The ambivalence of the lovers, so memorably rendered, reflects not only Lawrence's stormy marriage with Frieda, but his own repressed bisexuality as well. And yet the passage matters aesthetically because of the marvelous detail, at once literal and metaphoric, or Ursula's tearing of the spindleberries, flesh-like and bursting with life. Lawrence had the rare gift, inherited from Charlotte Brontë and Thomas Hardy, of portraying a woman's anger with total sympathy and virtual identification. Since Birkin is a deliberate parody of the prophetic Lawrence, fiercely exalting yet also recoiling from sexual love, Ursula's fury is accurate and precise.

After Shakespeare and Tolstoy, no writer expresses more vividly than Lawrence the perpetually prevalent male ambivalence towards female superiority in natural sexuality. A powerful example in Lawrence is the farewell love-making between Ursula and Skrebensky near the close of *The Rainbow*:

> Then there in the great flare of light, she clinched hold of him, hard, as if suddenly she had the strength of destruction, she fastened her arms round him and tightened him in her grip, whilst her mouth sought his in a hard, rending, ever-increasing kiss, till his body was powerless in her grip, his heart melted in fear from the fierce, beaked, harpy's kiss. The water washed again over their feet, but she took no notice. She seemed unaware, she seemed to be pressing in her beaked mouth till she had the heart of him. Then, at last, she drew away and looked at him—looked at him. He knew what she wanted. He took her by the hand and led her across the foreshore, back to the sandhills. She went silently. He felt as if the ordeal of proof was upon him, for life or death. He led her to a dark hollow.
>
> "No, here," she said, going out to the slope full under the moonshine. She lay motionless, with wide-open eyes looking at the moon. He came direct to her, without preliminaries. She held him pinned down at the chest, awful. The fight, the struggle for consummation was terrible. It lasted till it was agony to his soul, till he succumbed, till he gave way as if dead, lay with his face buried, partly in her hair, partly in the sand, motionless now for ever, hidden away in the dark, buried, only buried, he only wanted to be buried in the goodly darkness, only that, and no more.
>
> He seemed to swoon. It was a long time before he came to himself. He was unaware of an unusual motion of her breast. He looked up. Her face lay like an image in the moonlight, the eyes wide open, rigid. But out of her eyes, slowly, there rolled a tear, that glittered in the moonlight as it ran down her cheek.

He felt as if the knife were being pushed into his already dead body. With head strained back, he watched, drawn tense, for some minutes, watched the unaltering, rigid face like metal in the moonlight, the fixed, unseeing eye, in which slowly the water gathered, shook with glittering moonlight, then surcharged, brimmed over and ran trickling, a tear with its burden of moonlight, into the darkness, to fall in the sand.

In his great poem, "Tortoise Shout," Lawrence epitomized the *gnosis* of Skrebensky's "bitterness of ecstasy":

Why were we crucified into sex?
Why were we not left rounded off, and finished in ourselves,
As we began,
As he certainly began, so perfectly alone?

Lawrence's unique power, as a prophetic novelist, tends now to make even his admirers a touch uneasy. In his later novels, such as *Kangaroo* (1923) and *The Plumed Serpent* (1926), as well as *Lady Chatterley's Lover* (1928), the literary artist is overcome by the prophet, and Lawrence bruises the limits of narrative, making it difficult to reread him with sustained attention. But in *The Rainbow* and *Women in Love* we trust the tales, and not their teller.

Sinclair Lewis

(1885-1951)

Arrowsmith and *Babbitt*

I

IT CANNOT BE SAID, THIRTY-FIVE YEARS AFTER HIS DEATH, THAT SINCLAIR Lewis is forgotten or ignored, yet clearly his reputation has declined considerably. *Arrowsmith* (1925) is still a widely read novel, particularly, among the young, but *Main Street* (1920) and *Babbitt* (1922) seem to be best known for their titles, while *Elmer Gantry* (1927) and *Dodsworth* (1929) are remembered in their movie versions. Rereading *Main Street* and *Elmer Gantry* has disappointed me, but *Babbitt* and *Dodsworth*, both good novels, deserve more readers than they now seem to have. Lewis is of very nearly no interest whatsoever to American literary critics of my own generation and younger, so that it seems likely his decline in renown will continue.

A Nobel prizewinner, like John Steinbeck, Lewis resembles Steinbeck only in that regard, and is now being eclipsed by Faulkner, Hemingway, Fitzgerald, and such older contemporaries as Cather and Dreiser. Lewis venerated Dickens, but the critical age when Lewis's achievement could be compared to that of Dickens or of Balzac is long ago over. Hamlin Garland, an actual precursor, is necessarily far more comparable to Lewis than Dickens or Balzac are. If, as Baudelaire may have remarked, every janitor in Balzac is a genius, then every genius in Lewis is something of a janitor. Essentially a satirist with a camera-eye, Lewis was a master neither of narrative nor of characterization. And his satire, curiously affectionate at its base (quite loving towards Babbitt), has no edge in the contemporary United States, where reality is frequently too outrageous for any literary satire to be possible.

Lewis has considerable historical interest, aside from the winning qualities of *Babbitt* and the surprising *Dodsworth*, but he is likely to survive because of his least characteristic, most idealistic novel, *Arrowsmith*. A morality tale, with a medical research scientist as hero, *Arrowsmith* has enough mythic force to compel a young reader to an idealism of her or his own. Critics have found in *Arrowsmith* Lewis's version of the idealism of Emerson and Thoreau, pitched lower in Lewis, who had no transcendental yearnings. The native strain in our literature that emanated out from Emerson into Whitman and Thoreau appears also in *Arrowsmith*, and helps account for the novel's continued relevance as American myth.

II

H.L. Mencken, who greatly admired *Arrowsmith*, upon expectedly ideological grounds, still caught the flaw in the hero, and the aesthetic virtue in the splendid villain, Pickerbaugh:

> Pickerbaugh exists everywhere, in almost every American town. He is the quack who flings himself melodramatically upon measles, chicken pox, whooping cough—the organizer of Health Weeks and author of prophylactic, Kiwanian slogans—the hero of clean-up campaigns—the scientific beau ideal of newspaper reporters, Y.M.C.A. secretaries, and the pastors of suburban churches. He has been leering at the novelists of America for years, and yet Lewis and De Kruif were the first to see and hail him. They have made an almost epic figure of him. He is the Babbitt of this book—far more charming than Arrowsmith himself, and far more real. Arrowsmith fails in one important particular: he is not typical, he is not a good American. I daresay that many a reader, following his struggles with the seekers for "practical" results, will sympathize frankly with the latter. After all, it is not American to prefer honor to honors; no man, pursuing that folly, could ever hope to be president of the United States. Pickerbaugh will cause no such lifting of eyebrows. Like Babbitt, he will be recognized instantly and enjoyed innocently. Within six weeks, I suspect, every health officer in America will be receiving letters denouncing him as a Pickerbaugh. Thus nature imitates art.

Mencken's irony has been denuded by time; Arrowsmith is indeed not typical, not a good American, not a persuasive representation of a person.

Neither is anyone else in the novel a convincing mimesis of actuality; that was hardly Lewis's strength, which resided in satiric caricature. *Arrowsmith* ought to be more a satire than a novel, but unfortunately its hero is an idealized self-portrait of Sinclair Lewis. Idealization of science, and of the pure scientist—Arrowsmith and his mentor, Gottlieb—is what most dates the novel. I myself first read it in 1945, when I was a student at the Bronx High School of Science, then an abominable institution of the highest and most narrow academic standards. As a nonscientist, I found myself surrounded by a swarm of hostile and aggressive fellow-students, most of whom have become successful Babbitts of medicine, physics, and related disciplines. *Arrowsmith*, with its naive exaltation of science as a pure quest for truth, had a kind of biblical status in that high school, and so I read it with subdued loathing. Rereading it now, I find a puzzled affection to be my principal reaction, but I doubt the aesthetic basis for my current attitude.

Though sadly dated, *Arrowsmith* is too eccentric a work to be judged a period piece. It is a romance, with allegorical overtones, but a romance in which everything is literalized, a romance of science, as it were, rather than a science fiction. Its hero, much battered, does not learn much; he simply becomes increasingly more abrupt and stubborn, and votes with his feet whenever marriages, institutions, and other societal forms begin to menace his pure quest for scientific research. In the romance's pastoral conclusion, Arrowsmith retreats to the woods, a Thoreau pursuing the exact mechanism of the action of quinine derivatives. Romance depends upon a curious blend of wholeheartedness and sophistication in its author, and Sinclair Lewis was not Edmund Spenser:

> His mathematics and physical chemistry were now as sound as Terry's, his indifference to publicity and to flowery hangings as great, his industry as fanatical, his ingenuity in devising new apparatus at least comparable, and his imagination far more swift. He had less ease but more passion. He hurled out hypotheses like sparks. He began, incredulously, to comprehend his freedom. He would yet determine the essential nature of phage; and as he became stronger and surer—and no doubt less human—he saw ahead of him innumerable inquiries into chemotherapy and immunity; enough adventures to keep him busy for decades.
>
> It seemed to him that this was the first spring he had ever seen and tasted. He learned to dive into the lake, though the first plunge was an agony of fiery cold. They fished before breakfast, they supped at a table under the oaks, they tramped twenty miles

on end, they had bluejays and squirrels for interested neighbors; and when they had worked all night, they came out to find serene dawn lifting across the sleeping lake.

Martin felt sun-soaked and deep of chest, and always he hummed.

I do not believe that this could sustain commentary, of any kind. It is competent romance writing, of the Boy's Own Book variety, but cries out for the corrected American version, as carried through by Nathanael West in *A Cool Million*, and in *Miss Lonelyhearts*. West's Shrike would be capable of annihilating salvation through back to nature and pure research, by promising: "You feel sun-soaked, and deep of chest, and always you hum."

Arrowsmith was published in the same year as *The Great Gatsby* and *An American Tragedy*, which was hardly Lewis's fault, but now seems his lasting misfortune. *Babbitt* came out the same year as *Ulysses*, while *Dodsworth* confronted *The Sound and the Fury*. None of this is fair, but the agonistic element in literature is immemorial. *Arrowsmith* is memorable now because it is a monument to another American lost illusion, the idealism of pure science, or the search for a truth that could transcend the pragmatics of American existence. It is a fitting irony that the satirist Sinclair Lewis should be remembered now for this idealizing romance.

Zora Neale Hurston

(1891–1960)

Their Eyes Were Watching God

I

EXTRA-LITERARY FACTORS HAVE ENTERED INTO THE PROCESS OF EVEN secular canonization from Hellenistic Alexandria into the High Modernist Era of Eliot and Pound, so that it need not much dismay us if contemporary work by women and by minority writers becomes esteemed on grounds other than aesthetic. When the High Modernist critic Hugh Kenner assures us of the permanent eminence of the novelist and polemicist Wyndham Lewis, we can be persuaded, unless of course we actually read books like *Tarr* and *Hitler*. Reading Lewis is a rather painful experience, and makes me skeptical of Kenner's canonical assertions. In the matter of Zora Neale Hurston, I have had a contrary experience, starting with skepticism when I first encountered essays by her admirers, let alone by her idolators. Reading *Their Eyes Were Watching God* dispels all skepticism. *Moses: Man of the Mountain* is an impressive book in its mode and ambitions, but a mixed achievement, unable to resolve problems of diction and of rhetorical stance. Essentially, Hurston is the author of one superb and moving novel, unique not in its kind but in its isolated excellence among other stories of the kind.

The wistful opening of *Their Eyes Were Watching God* pragmatically affirms greater repression in women as opposed to men, by which I mean "repression" only in Freud's sense: unconscious yet purposeful forgetting:

> Now, women forget all those things they don't want to remember, and remember everything they don't want to forget. The dream is the truth. Then they act and do things accordingly.

Hurston's Janie is now necessarily a paradigm for women, of whatever race, heroically attempting to assert their own individuality in contexts that continue to resent and fear any consciousness that is not male. In a larger perspective, should the contexts modify, the representation of Janie will take its significant place in a long tradition of such representations in English and American fiction. This tradition extends from Samuel Richardson to Doris Lessing and other contemporaries, but only rarely has been able to visualize authentically strong women who begin with all the deprivations that circumstance assigns to Janie. It is a crucial aspect of Hurston's subtle sense of limits that the largest limitation is that imposed upon Janie by her grandmother, who loves her best, yet fears for her the most.

As a former slave, the grandmother, Nanny, is haunted by the compensatory dream of making first her daughter, and then her granddaughter, something other than "the mule of the world," customary fate of the black woman. The dream is both powerful enough, and sufficiently unitary, to have driven Janie's mother away, and to condemn Janie herself to a double disaster of marriages, before the tragic happiness of her third match completes as much of her story as Hurston desires to give us. As readers, we carry away with us what Janie never quite loses, the vivid pathos of her grandmother's superb and desperate displacement of hope:

> "And, Janie, maybe it wasn't much, but Ah done de best Ah kin by you. Ah raked and scraped and bought dis lil piece uh land so you wouldn't have to stay in de white folks' yard and tuck yo' head befo' other chillun at school. Dat was all right when you was little. But when you got big enough to understand things, Ah wanted you to look upon yo'self. Ah don't want yo' feathers always crumpled by folks throwin' up things in yo' face. And Ah can't die easy thinkin' maybe de menfolks white or black is makin' a spit cup outa you: Have some sympathy fuh me. Put me down easy, Janie, Ah'm a cracked plate."

II

Hurston's rhetorical strength, even in *Their Eyes Were Watching God*, is frequently too overt, and threatens an excess, when contrasted with the painful simplicity of her narrative line and the reductive tendency at work in all her characters except for Janie and Nanny. Yet the excess works, partly because Hurston is so considerable and knowing a mythologist. Hovering in *Their Eyes Were Watching God* is the Mosaic myth of deliverance, the pattern of revolution and exodus that Hurston reimagines as her prime trope of power:

> But there are other concepts of Moses abroad in the world. Asia and all the Near East are sown with legends of this character. They are so numerous and so varied that some students have come to doubt if the Moses of the Christian concept is real. Then Africa has her mouth on Moses. All across the continent there are the legends of the greatness of Moses, but not because of his beard nor because he brought the laws down from Sinai. No, he is revered because he had the power to go up the mountain and to bring them down. Many men could climb mountains. Anyone could bring down laws that had been handed to them. But who can talk with God face to face? Who has the power to command God to go to a peak of a mountain and there demand of Him laws with which to govern a nation? What other man has ever commanded the wind and the hail? The light and darkness? That calls for power, and that is what Africa sees in Moses to worship. For he is worshipped as a god.

Power in Hurston is always *potentia*, the demand for life, for more life. Despite the differences in temperament, Hurston has affinities both with Dreiser and with Lawrence, heroic vitalists. Her art, like theirs, exalts an exuberance that is beauty, a difficult beauty because it participates in reality-testing. What is strongest in Janie is a persistence akin to Dreiser's Carrie and Lawrence's Ursula and Gudrun, a drive to survive in one's own fashion. Nietzsche's vitalistic injunction, that we must try to live as though it were morning, is the implicit basis of Hurston's true religion, which in its American formulation (Thoreau's), reminds us that only that day dawns to which we are alive. Something of Lawrence's incessant sense of the sun is paralleled by Hurston's trope of the solar trajectory, in a cosmos where: "They sat on the boarding house porch and saw the sun plunge into the same crack in the earth from which the night emerged" and where: "Every morning the world flung itself over and exposed the town to the sun."

Janie's perpetual sense of the possibilities of another day propels her from Nanny's vision of safety first to the catastrophe of Joe Starks and then to the love of Tea Cake, her true husband. But to live in a way that starts with the sun is to become pragmatically doom-eager, since mere life is deprecated in contrast to the possibility of glory, of life more abundant, rather than Nanny's dream of a refuge from exploitation. Hurston's most effective irony is that Janie's drive toward her own erotic potential should transcend her grandmother's categories, since the marriage with Tea Cake is also Janie's pragmatic liberation from bondage toward men. When he tells her, in all truth, that she has the keys to the kingdom, he frees her from living in her grandmother's way.

A more pungent irony drove Hurston to end Janie's idyll with Tea Cake's illness and the ferocity of his subsequent madness. The impulse of her own vitalism compels Janie to kill him in self-defense, thus ending necessarily life and love in the name of the possibility of more life again. The novel's conclusion is at once an elegy and a vision of achieved peace, an intense realization that indeed we are all asleep in the outer life:

> The day of the gun, and the bloody body, and the courthouse came and commenced to sing a sobbing sigh out of every corner in the room; out of each and every chair and thing. Commenced to sing, commenced to sob and sigh, singing and sobbing. Then Tea Cake came prancing around her where she was and the song of the sigh flew out of the window and lit in the top of the pine trees. Tea Cake, with the sun for a shawl. Of course he wasn't dead. He could never be dead until she herself had finished feeling and thinking. The kiss of his memory made pictures of love and light against the wall. Here was peace. She pulled in her horizon like a great fish-net. Pulled it from around the waist of the world and draped it over her shoulder. So much of life in its meshes! She called in her soul to come and see.

III

Hurston herself was refreshingly free of all the ideologies that currently obscure the reception of her best book. Her sense of power has nothing in common with politics of any persuasion, with contemporary modes of feminism, or even with those questers who search for a black aesthetic. As a vitalist, she was of the line of the Wife of Bath and Sir John Falstaff and Mynheer Peeperkorn. Like them, she was outrageous, heroically larger than life, witty in herself and the cause of wit in others. She belongs now to literary legend, which is as it should be. Her famous remark in response to Carl Van Vechten's photographs is truly the epigraph to her life and work: "I love myself when I am laughing. And then again when I am looking mean and impressive." Walt Whitman would have delighted in that as in her assertion: "When I set my hat at a certain angle and saunter down Seventh Avenue ... the cosmic Zora emerges.... How can any deny themselves the pleasure of my company? It's beyond me." With Whitman, Hurston herself is now an image of American literary vitality, and a part also of the American mythology of exodus, of the power to choose the party of Eros, of more life.

F. Scott Fitzgerald

(1896–1940)

The Great Gatsby

THE GREAT GATSBY, AFTER THREE-QUARTERS OF A CENTURY, REMAINS A fresh and vibrant short novel, an acknowledged American masterpiece. Its fable has become part of the American mythology, or perhaps the American Dream so pervades *The Great Gatsby* that Fitzgerald's true achievement was to appropriate American legend. Either way, Fitzgerald gave us both the romance of love-and-money, and the anti-romance of its collapse into tragedy, if "tragedy" does not seem too exalted a term for Jay Gatsby. The book is profoundly Conradian, since Nick Carraway mediates Gatsby for us rather in the way that Joseph Conrad's Marlow mediates Kurtz or Lord Jim. We do not see, hear, or know Gatsby except through Carraway's eyes, ears, and heart, and for Nick his friend Jay is the Romantic hero of the American Dream.

For Carraway, Gatsby is an idealist, with a "Platonic conception of himself." Time, other selves, history: all these are set aside by Gatsby's vision of himself and the perfectly insipid Daisy Buchanan as the American Adam and Eve. Gatsby himself is an improbable but persuasive amalgam of an American gangster and the poet John Keats, dreaming an impossible dream of love with *his* Daisy, Fanny Brawne. Gatsby is great, not just in Carraway's vision, but in ours, because Fitzgerald brilliantly represents in Gatsby both the failure of the American Dream, and its perpetual refusal to die.

Tender Is the Night, with its Keatsian title, was intended by Fitzgerald to be his masterwork. Though the novel is at least partly a failure, it is a fascinating debacle, intensely readable though somewhat diffuse. Dick Diver is a pale figure when compared to Gatsby; the reader cannot help like

Diver, but he lacks Gatsby's obsessive force. Is Diver defeated by the rich, who fascinate him, or by his own inner weakness? Rather clearly, Diver is Fitzgerald's own surrogate, as Gatsby never was. Diver fails and dwindles away because of a weakness in the will, in profound contrast to Gatsby. Perhaps all that could have saved *Tender Is the Night* would have been Jay Gatsby's resurrection from the dead, since the gangster-poet's vitality never possesses Dick Diver.

William Faulkner

(1897–1962)

I

No critic need invent William Faulkner's obsessions with what Nietzsche might have called the genealogy of the imagination. Recent critics of Faulkner, including David Minter, John T. Irwin, David M. Wyatt and Richard H. King, have emphasized the novelist's profound need to believe himself to have been his own father, in order to escape not only the Freudian family romance and literary anxieties of influence, but also the cultural dilemmas of what King terms "the Southern family romance." From *The Sound and the Fury* through the debacle of *A Fable*, Faulkner centers upon the sorrows of fathers and sons, to the disadvantage of mothers and daughters. No feminist critic ever will be happy with Faulkner. His brooding conviction that female sexuality is closely allied with death seems essential to all of his strongest fictions. It may even be that Faulkner's rhetorical economy, his wounded need to get his cosmos into a single sentence, is related to his fear that origin and end might prove to be one. Nietzsche prophetically had warned that origin and end were separate entities, and for the sake of life had to be kept apart, but Faulkner (strangely like Freud) seems to have known that the only Western trope participating neither in origin nor end is the image of the father.

By universal consent of critics and common readers, Faulkner now is recognized as the strongest American novelist of this century, clearly surpassing Hemingway and Fitzgerald, and standing as an equal in the sequence that includes Hawthorne, Melville, Mark Twain and Henry James. Some critics might add Dreiser to this group; Faulkner himself curiously would have insisted upon Thomas Wolfe, a generous though dubious judgment. The American precursor for Faulkner was Sherwood Anderson,

but perhaps only as an impetus; the true American forerunner is the poetry of T.S. Eliot, as Judith L. Sensibar demonstrates. But the truer precursor for Faulkner's fiction is Conrad, inescapable for the American novelists
of Faulkner's generation, including Hemingway and Fitzgerald.
Comparison to Conrad is dangerous for any novelist, and clearly Faulkner
did not achieve a *Nostromo*. But his work of the decade 1929–39 does
include four permanent books: *The Sound and the Fury*, *As I Lay Dying*,
Light in August, and *Absalom, Absalom!* If one adds *Sanctuary* and *The Wild
Palms*, and *The Hamlet* and *Go Down, Moses* in the early forties, then the
combined effect is extraordinary.

From Malcolm Cowley on, critics have explained this effect as the
consequence of the force of mythmaking, at once personal and local.
Cleanth Brooks, the rugged final champion of the New Criticism, essentially reads Faulkner as he does Eliot's *The Waste Land*, finding the hidden
God of the normative Christian tradition to be the basis for Faulkner's attitude towards nature. Since Brooks calls Faulkner's stance Wordsworthian,
and finds Wordsworthian nature a Christian vision also, the judgment
involved necessarily has its problematical elements. Walter Pater, a critic
in a very different tradition, portrayed a very different Wordsworth in
terms that seem to me not inapplicable to Faulkner:

> Religious sentiment, consecrating the affections and natural
> regrets of the human heart, above all, that pitiful awe and care for
> the perishing human clay, of which relic-worship is but the cor-
> ruption, has always had much to do with localities, with the
> thoughts which attach themselves to actual scenes and places.
> Now what is true of it everywhere, is truest of it in those seclud-
> ed valleys where one generation after another maintains the same
> abiding place; and it was on this side, that Wordsworth appre-
> hended religion most strongly. Consisting, as it did so much, in
> the recognition of local sanctities, in the habit of connecting the
> stones and trees of a particular spot of earth with the great events
> of life, till the low walls, the green mounds, the half-obliterated
> epitaphs seemed full of voices, and a sort of natural oracle, the
> very religion of those people of the dales, appeared but as anoth-
> er link between them and the earth, and was literally a religion of
> nature.

A kind of stoic natural religion pervades this description, something
close to the implicit faith of old Isaac McCaslin in *Go Down, Moses*. It seems
unhelpful to speak of "residual Christianity" in Faulkner, as Cleanth

Brooks does. Hemingway and Fitzgerald, in their nostalgias, perhaps were closer to a Christian ethos than Faulkner was in his great phase. Against current critical judgment, I prefer *As I Lay Dying* and *Light in August* to *The Sound and the Fury* and *Absalom, Absalom!* partly because the first two are more primordial in their vision, closer to the stoic intensities of their author's kind of natural piety. There is an *otherness* in Lena Grove and the Bundrens that would have moved Wordsworth, that is, the Wordsworth of *The Tale of Margaret, Michael,* and *The Old Cumberland Beggar.* A curious movement that is also a stasis becomes Faulkner's pervasive trope for Lena. Though he invokes the imagery of Keats's urn, Faulkner seems to have had the harvest-girl of Keats's *To Autumn* more in mind, or even the stately figures of the *Ode to Indolence.* We remember Lena Grove as stately, calm, a person yet a process, a serene and patient consciousness, full of wonder, too much a unitary being to need even her author's variety of stoic courage.

The uncanniness of this representation is exceeded by the Bundrens, whose plangency testifies to Faulkner's finest rhetorical achievement. *As I Lay Dying* may be the most original novel ever written by an American. Obviously it is not free of the deepest influence Faulkner knew as a novelist. The language is never Conradian, and yet the sense of the reality principle is. But there is nothing in Conrad like Darl Bundren, not even in *The Secret Agent. As I Lay Dying* is Faulkner's strongest protest against the facticity of literary convention, against the force of the familial past, which tropes itself in fiction as the repetitive form of narrative imitating prior narrative. The book is a sustained nightmare, insofar as it is Darl's book, which is to say, Faulkner's book, or the book of his daemon.

II

Canonization is a process of enshrining creative misinterpretations, and no one need lament this. Still, one element that ensues from this process all too frequently is the not very creative misinterpretation in which the idiosyncratic is distorted into the normative. Churchwardenly critics who assimilate the Faulkner of the Thirties to spiritual, social, and moral orthodoxy can and do assert Faulkner himself as their preceptor. But this is the Faulkner of the Fifties, Nobel laureate, State Department envoy and author of *A Fable*, a book of badness simply astonishing for Faulkner. The best of the normative critics, Cleanth Brooks, reads even *As I Lay Dying* as a quest for community, an exaltation of the family, an affirmation of Christian values. The Bundrens manifestly constitute one of the most terrifying visions of the family romance in the history of literature. But their extremism is not eccentric in the 1929–39 world of Faulkner's fiction.

That world is founded upon a horror of families, a limbo of outcasts, an evasion of all values other than stoic endurance. It is a world in which what is silent in the other Bundrens speaks in Darl, what is veiled in the Compsons is uncovered in Quentin. So tangled are these returns of the repressed with what continues to be estranged that phrases like "the violation of the natural" and "the denial of the human" become quite meaningless when applied to Faulkner's greater fictions. In that world, the natural is itself a violation and the human already a denial. Is the weird quest of the Bundrens a violation of the natural, or is it what Blake would have called a terrible triumph for the selfish virtues of the natural heart? Darl judges it to be the latter, but Darl luminously denies the sufficiency of the human, at the cost of what seems schizophrenia.

Marxist criticism of imaginative literature, if it had not regressed abominably in our country, so that now it is a travesty of the dialectical suppleness of Adorno and Benjamin, would find a proper subject in the difficult relationship between the 1929 business panic and *As I Lay Dying*. Perhaps the self-destruction of our delusive political economy helped free Faulkner from whatever inhibitions, communal and personal, had kept him earlier from a saga like that of the Bundrens. Only an authentic seer can give permanent form to a prophecy like *As I Lay Dying*, which puts severely into question every received notion we have of the natural and the human. Darl asserts he has no mother, while taunting his enemy brother, Jewel, with the insistence that Jewel's mother was a horse. Their little brother, Vardaman, says: "My mother is a fish." The mother, dead and undead, is uncannier even than these children, when she confesses the truth of her existence, her rejecting vision of her children:

> I could just remember how my father used to say that the reason for living was to get ready to stay dead a long time. And when I would have to look at them day after day, each with his and her single and selfish thought, and blood strange to each other blood and strange to mine, and think that this seemed to be the only way I could get ready to stay dead, I would hate my father for having ever planted me. I would look forward to the times when they faulted, so I could whip them. When the switch fell I could feel it upon my flesh; when it welted and ridged it was my blood that ran, and I would think with each blow of the switch: Now you are aware of me! Now I am something in your secret and selfish life, who have marked your blood with my own for ever and ever.

This veritable apocalypse of any sense of otherness is no mere "denial of community." Nor are the Bundrens any "mimesis of essential nature." They are a super-mimesis, an over-representation mocking nature while shadowing it. What matters in major Faulkner is that the people have gone back, not to nature but to some abyss before the Creation-Fall. Eliot insisted that Joyce's imagination was eminently orthodox. This can be doubted, but in Faulkner's case there is little sense in baptizing his imagination. One sees why he preferred reading the Old Testament to the New, remarking that the former was stories and the latter, ideas. The remark is inadequate except insofar as it opposes Hebraic to Hellenistic representation of character. There is little that is Homeric about the Bundrens, or Sophoclean about the Compsons. Faulkner's irony is neither classical nor romantic, neither Greek nor German. It does not say one thing while meaning another, nor trade in contrasts between expectation and fulfillment. Instead, it juxtaposes incommensurable realities: of self and other, of parent and child, of past and future. When Gide maintained that Faulkner's people lacked souls, he simply failed to observe that Faulkner's ironies were Biblical. To which an amendment must be added. In Faulkner, only the ironies are Biblical. What Faulkner's people lack is the blessing; they cannot contend for a time without boundaries. Yahweh will make no covenant with them. Their agon therefore is neither the Greek one for the foremost place nor the Hebrew one for the blessing, which honors the father and the mother. Their agon is the hopeless one of waiting for their doom to lift.

The Sound and the Fury

The Sound and the Fury always moved Faulkner to tenderness, far more than his other novels. It was for him a kind of Keatsian artifact, vase or urn invested with a permanent aesthetic dignity. His judgment has prevailed with his critics, though some doubts and reservations have been voiced. Like *Absalom, Absalom!*, *The Sound and the Fury* seems to me a lesser work than *Light in August*, or than *As I Lay Dying*, which is Faulkner's masterwork. The mark of Joyce's *Ulysses* is a little too immediate on *The Sound and the Fury*, which does not always sustain its intense rhetoricity, its anguished word-consciousness. There is something repressed almost throughout *The Sound and the Fury*, some autobiographical link between Quentin's passion for his sister Caddy and a nameless passion of Faulkner's, perhaps (as David Minter surmises) for the sister he never had, perhaps his desire for Estelle Oldham, later to be his wife, but only after being married to another. Jealousy, intimately allied to the fear of mortality, is a central element in *The Sound and the Fury*.

Hugh Kenner, comparing Faulkner's novel to its precursors by Conrad and Joyce, dismisses the Compson family saga as excessively arty. The judgment is cruel, yet cogent if Joyce and Conrad are brought too close, and Faulkner does not distance himself enough from them. This makes for an unhappy paradox; *The Sound and the Fury* is a little too elaborately wrought to sustain its rather homely substance, its plot of family disasters. But that substance, those familial disorders, are entirely too available to Freudian and allied reductions; such repetitions and doublings are prevalent patterns, vicissitudes of drives too dismally universal truly to serve novelistic ends. Only Jason, of all the Compsons, is individual enough to abide as an image in the reader's memory. His Dickensian nastiness makes Jason an admirable caricature, while Quentin, Caddy, and Benjy blend into the continuum, figures of thought for whom Faulkner has failed to find the inevitable figures of speech.

Faulkner's Appendix for *The Sound and the Fury*, written for Malcolm Cowley's *The Portable Faulkner*, not only has become part of the novel, but famously constitutes the definitive interpretation of the novel, or Faulkner's will-to-power over his own text. The Appendix is very much Faulkner the yarn-spinner of 1946, soon to write such feebler works as *Intruder in the Dust*, *Knight's Gambit*, and *Requiem for a Nun*, before collapsing into the disaster of *A Fable*. It is not the Faulkner of 1928, commencing his major phase, and yet the Appendix does have a curious rhetorical authority, culminating in Faulkner's tribute to the blacks (after simply listing Dilsey's name, since she is beyond praise): "They endured." Sadly, this is an authority mostly lacking in the actual text of *The Sound and the Fury*. Quentin's voice makes me start when it is too clearly the voice of Stephen Daedalus, and Joyce's medley of narrative voices fades in and out of Faulkner's story with no clear relation to Faulkner's purposes. Only Poldy, fortunately, is kept away, for his sublime presence would be sublimely irrelevant and so would sink the book.

I emphasize the limitations of *The Sound and the Fury* only because we are in danger of overlooking them, now that Faulkner has become, rightly, our canonical novelist in this century, clearly our strongest author of prose fiction since the death of Henry James. *As I Lay Dying* was a radical experiment that worked magnificently; its forms and voices are apposite metaphors for the fierce and terrifying individualities of the Bundrens. *The Sound and the Fury* was also a remarkable experiment, but too derivative from Joyce's *Ulysses*, and perhaps too dark for Faulkner's own comfort.

What saves the Compson saga is that it is a saga; and finds a redeeming context in the reader's sense of larger significances that always seem to pervade Faulkner's major writings. We read *The Sound and the Fury* and we hear a tale signifying a great deal, because Faulkner constitutes for us a literary cosmos of continual reverberations. Like Dilsey, we too are per-suaded that we have seen the first and the last, the beginning and the end-ing of a story that transcends the four Compson children, and the squalors of their family romance.

Sanctuary

In *Sanctuary*, no one even bothers to wait for doom to lift; the novel is as nihilistic as John Webster's *The White Devil* or Cyril Tourneur's *The Atheist's Tragedy*. Malraux asserted that Greek tragedy entered the detective story in *Sanctuary*. Had Malraux spoken of Jacobean tragedy, his remarks would have been to some purpose. Though directly influenced by Conrad and Dostoevsky, *Sanctuary* comes closer to Webster and Tourneur than T.S. Eliot does, even when he explicitly imitates them. Robert Penn Warren, much under Faulkner's influence (and Eliot's), is the other modern writer who unmistakably reminds us of the Jacobeans. Tragic farce is the true Jacobean mode, and the mixed genre of *Sanctuary*—Gothic thriller, detective and gangster story, shocker, entertainment—quite accurately can be termed tragic farce.

Sanctuary is the enigma among Faulkner's novels; intended as a pot-boiler and moneymaker, it very nearly achieves major status and can sustain many rereadings. Its protagonists, like Webster's, designedly resist psychologizing. *Sanctuary's* extraordinary humor and what might be called a grotesque assortment of eloquences in Faulkner's rhetoric, high and low, combine to keep the book alive in the memory of the reader. Famous passages at its start and its conclusion remain remarkable as epiphanies—Paterian, Conradian, Joycean—in which spiritual realities flare forth against mundane backgrounds. Here is the novel's opening:

> From beyond the screen of bushes which surrounded the spring, Popeye watched the man drinking. A faint path led from the road to the spring. Popeye watched the man—a tall, thin man, hatless, in worn gray flannel trousers and carrying a tweed coat over his arm—emerge from the path and kneel to drink from the spring.
>
> The spring welled up at the root of a beech tree and flowed away upon a bottom of whorled and waved sand. It was surround-ed by a thick growth of cane and brier, of cypress and gum in which broken sunlight lay sourceless. Somewhere, hidden and secret yet nearby, a bird sang three notes and ceased.
>
> In the spring the drinking man leaned his face to the broken and myriad reflection of his own drinking. When he rose up he

saw among them the shattered reflection of Popeye's straw hat, though he had heard no sound.

He saw, facing him across the spring, a man of under size, his hands in his coat pockets, a cigarette slanted from his chin. His suit was black, with a tight, high-waisted coat. His trousers were rolled once and caked with mud above mud-caked shoes. His face had a queer, bloodless color, as though seen by electric light; against the sunny silence, in his slanted straw hat and his slightly akimbo arms, he had that vicious depthless quality of stamped tin.

Behind him the bird sang again, three bars in monotonous repetition: a sound meaningless and profound out of a suspirant and peaceful following silence which seemed to isolate the spot, and out of which a moment later came the sound of an automobile passing along a road and dying away.

No reader is going to become at ease with Popeye (Faulkner thought him a monster, but sympathized with him anyway) and no reader forgets him either. I recall Faulkner's observation somewhere that his Popeye, in the movies, ought to be played by Mickey Mouse, a rather more amiable cartoon than Popeye constitutes. Popeye is nightmare, as this opening passage conveys; he is a phantasmagoria of flesh illuminated by electric light, a two-dimensional figure stamped out of tin. We are not surprised that his sexual organ pragmatically should be a corncob, or that he passively allows himself to be executed at the book's close. He represents not a dualism, whether Platonic or Freudian, but a monistic nihilism, a machine uninhabited by a ghost. The bird, singing from its hidden and secret recess nearby, is part of that nihilism, "in monotonous repetition: a sound meaningless and profound." Perhaps by way of Eliot's *The Waste Land*, Faulkner returns us to the great American trope of a hidden bird singing from a dark and secret place in a swamp, Whitman's hermit thrush in *When Lilacs Last in the Dooryard Bloom'd*. Whitman's bird sang a song of sane and sacred death; the bird of Popeye's epiphany might as well be a clock, sounding the repetitions for death in *Sanctuary*, insane and obscene death.

The impressionism of *Sanctuary* derives from Conrad, almost as though *Sanctuary* is Conrad's *Chance* gone mad. *Sanctuary* will not sustain aesthetic comparison with Conrad's *The Secret Agent*, but there are spiritual and structural affinities between the two novels. Faulkner's detachment in *Sanctuary* is astonishing and empties out the book with high deliberateness. Against Cleanth Brooks, I must assert that there is no Vision of Evil in *Sanctuary*. A narrative whose central protagonists are Popeye and Temple Drake, not Horace Benbow and Ruby Lamar, knows itself too well to desire any pandering to moral judgments. Popeye is a mechanical jack-in-the-box; Temple ends as a mechanical figurine in *Sanctuary*'s concluding passage:

> It had been a gray day, a gray summer, a gray year. On the street old men wore overcoats, and in the Luxembourg Gardens as Temple and her father passed the women sat knitting in shawls and even the men playing croquet played in coats and capes, and in the sad gloom of the chestnut trees the dry click of balls, the random shouts of children, had that quality of autumn, gallant and evanescent and forlorn. From beyond the circle with its spurious Greek balustrade, clotted with movement, filled with a gray light of the same color and texture as the water which the fountain played into the pool, came a steady crash of music. They went on, passed the pool where the children and an old man in a shabby brown overcoat sailed toy boats, and entered the trees again and found seats. Immediately an old woman came with decrepit promptitude and collected four sous.
>
> In the pavilion a band in the horizon blue of the army played Massenet and Scriabine, and Berlioz like a thin coating of tortured Tschaikovsky on a slice of stale bread, while the twilight dissolved in wet gleams from the branches, onto the pavilion and the sombre toadstools of umbrellas. Rich and resonant the brasses crashed and died in the thick green twilight, rolling over them in rich sad waves. Temple yawned behind her hand, then she took out a compact and opened it upon a face in miniature sullen and discontented and sad. Beside her her father sat, his hands crossed on the head of his stick, the rigid bar of his moustache beaded with moisture like frosted silver. She closed the compact and from beneath her smart new hat she seemed to follow with her eyes the waves of music, to dissolve into the dying brasses, across the pool and the opposite semicircle of trees where at sombre intervals the dead tranquil queens in stained marble mused, and on into the sky lying prone and vanquished in the embrace of the season of rain and death.

This high rhetoric is as much a failure as the book's opening passage was a success. Faulkner, self-consciously invading the ambiance of Hemingway and Fitzgerald, is anxious and over-writes. He ought to have ended *Sanctuary* with the hanging of Popeye, affectless and economical. We are embarrassed by that "sky lying prone and vanquished in the embrace of the season of rain and death," partly because the sky there is a trope substituting for the violated sanctuary of Temple's body. *Sanctuary* does not share the strength of Faulkner's best work, *As I Lay Dying* and *Light in August*, but I perversely prefer it to *The Sound and the Fury* and *Absalom, Absalom!* It lacks their aspirations and their pretensions, and may in time seem a more original work than either. Its uneven and conflicting rhetorics wound it, but it survives as narrative and as fearsome image, still representative of American realities after more than a half-century.

Light in August

There are exceptions to the ironic laws of tragic farce even in Faulkner, by which I mean major Faulkner, 1928–1942. The Faulkner of the later forties and the fifties, author of *A Fable* and other inadequate narratives, had been abandoned by the vision of the abyss that had given him *As I Lay Dying* and *Sanctuary*. But even in his fourteen years of nihilistic splendor, he had invented a few beings whose mythic sense of persistence conveys a sense of the biblical blessing. I have already remarked on Lena Grove's stately role as a version of the harvest-girl in Keats's *To Autumn*. Rather than discuss Joe Christmas or Joanna Burden or Hightower, I will center only upon Lena, a vision Wordsworthian and Keatsian, and more satisfying as such than anything akin to her since George Eliot and Thomas Hardy.

One way of seeing the particular strength of *Light in August* as against Faulkner's other major novels is to speculate as to which could contain Lena. Her massively persuasive innocence hardly could be introduced into *The Sound and the Fury* or *Absalom, Absalom!*, and would destroy utterly *As I Lay Dying* or *Sanctuary*. Natural sublimity, Wordsworthian and almost Tolstoyan, requires a large cosmos if it is to be sustained. *As I Lay Dying* is Faulkner's most original fiction and my own favorite among all modern American narratives, yet *Light in August* must be Faulkner's grandest achievement. The book's ability to hold Lena as well as Joe, Joanna, and Hightower, makes it the American novel of this century, fit heir of Melville, Hawthorne, Mark Twain. Difficult as it is to imagine Henry James getting through *Light in August* (after all, he had trouble with Dickens!), the book might have shown James again some possibilities that he had excluded.

Albert J. Guerard, perhaps too absorbed in tracing Faulkner's indubitable misogyny, assimilated Lena to "the softer menace of the fecund and the bovine," but offered as evidence only that "she is, at her best, a serenely comic creation." Fecund certainly, bovine certainly not, and to "serenely" add the further modifier "loving." Judith Bryant Wittenberg, in her feminist consideration of Faulkner, startles me by linking Lena Grove to Joe Christmas, because they "are both products of an exploited childhood now restlessly on the move and aggressive in different ways." Rather, Lena is never-resting, Joe is restless; Joe is aggressive, but Lena moves on, a natural force, innocent and direct but free of the death drive, which is incarnated in Joe, Joanna, and so many others in the novel.

John T. Irwin, keen seer of repetition and revenge in Faulkner, intimates that the association of Lena with Keats's Grecian Urn necessarily links her also to Faulkner's consciousness of his own mortality and to his acceptance of his own writing as a form of dying. Nevertheless, Lena is certainly one of the most benign visions of a reality principle imaginable, and I return to my own Paterian conviction that she resembles the creations of Pater's Wordsworth more than the figures of Keats's tragic naturalism. Lena may be a projection of comic pastoral, but she seems to me more pastoral than comic, and an image of natural goodness invested by Faulkner's genius with considerable aesthetic dignity.

What would *Light in August* be like without her? The story of Joe Christmas and Joanna is almost unrelievedly bitter, though redeemed by its extraordinary social poignance. Hightower is a superb representation of Southern Romanticism destroying itself, while generating a great music from the destruction. What was strongest and clearest in Faulkner's narrative imagination prompted him to place Lena, who gives us a sense of time without boundaries, at the visionary center of the novel. She hardly unifies the book, but *Light in August* has an exuberant abundance that can dispense with an overt unity. Lena will be "light in August," when her child is born, but she is most of the light that the novel possesses throughout. Perhaps she is the answer, in Faulkner, to the poet's old prayer: "make my dark poem light."

Absalom, Absalom!

In a cosmos where only the ironies are biblical, the self, like the father and the past, becomes what Nietzsche called a "numinous shadow," an ancestor rather than a personal possession. Where the self is so estranged, we are not on Shakespeare's stage but on John Webster's, so that the Thomas Sutpen of *Absalom, Absalom!* is in some respects another Jacobean hero-villain who would end by saying (if he could), "I limned this night-piece, and it was my best." *Absalom, Absalom!* is a tragic farce, like *The White Devil*, and shares in some of the formal difficulties that are endemic in tragic farce. Rather than add to the distinguished discourse on the narrative perplexities that figure so richly in *Absalom, Absalom!*, I wish to address the question of comparative value. Does the novel have the aesthetic dignity that justifies its problematic form, or have we canonized it prematurely?

For reasons that I do not altogether comprehend, *Absalom, Absalom!* seems to me a less original book than the three great novels by Faulkner that preceded it: *The Sound and the Fury, As I Lay Dying, Light in August.* The precursors—Conrad profoundly, Joyce, Eliot, and even Tennyson more superficially—manifest themselves in Faulkner's text more overtly than they do in the three earlier works. One misses also the intensely sympathetic figures—Dilsey, Darl Bundren, Lena Grove—and their dreadful obverses Jason Compson, Addie Bundren, Percy Grimm—who help make the three earlier masterpieces so memorable. A shadow falls upon Faulkner's originality, both of style and of representation, in *Absalom, Absalom!* Can that shadow be named?

There seems to be an element of obscurantism in *Absalom, Absalom!*, even as there is in Conrad's *Heart of Darkness*. I do not find any obscurantism in *As I Lay Dying* or *Light in August*, even as *Nostromo* and *Victory* seem to be free of it. It hovers uneasily in *The Sound and the Fury* as it does in *Lord Jim*, yet it scarcely mars those books. Sometimes in *Absalom*, as in *Heart of Darkness*, I lose confidence that the author knows precisely what he is talking about. The consequence is a certain bathos which necessarily diminishes the aesthetic dignity of the work:

> "'You see, I had a design in my mind. Whether it was a good or a bad design is beside the point; the question is, Where did I make the mistake in it, what did I do or misdo in it, whom or what injure by it to the extent which this would indicate. I had a design. To accomplish it I should require money, a house, a plantation, slaves, a family—incidentally of course, a wife. I set out to acquire these, asking no favor of any man. I even risked my life at one time, as I told you, though as I also told you I did not undertake this risk purely and simply to gain a wife, though it did have that result. But that is beside the point also: suffice that I had the wife, accepted her in good faith, with no reservations about myself, and I expected as much from them. I did not even demand, mind, as one of my obscure origin might have been expected to do (or at least be condoned in the doing) out of ignorance of gentility in dealing with gentleborn people. I did not demand; I accepted them at their own valuation while insisting on my own part upon explaining fully about myself and my progenitors: yet they deliberately withheld from me the one fact which I have reason to know they

were aware would have caused me to decline the entire matter, otherwise they would not have withheld it from me—a fact which I did not learn until after my son was born. And even then I did not act hastily. I could have reminded them of these wasted years, these years which would now leave me behind with my schedule not only the amount of elapsed time which their number represented, but that compensatory amount of time represented by their number which I should now have to spend to advance myself once more to the point I had reached and lost. But I did not. I merely explained how this new fact rendered it impossible that this woman and child be incorporated in my design, and following which, as I told you, I made no attempt to keep not only that which I might consider myself to have earned at the risk of my life but which had been given to me by signed testimonials, but on the contrary I declined and resigned all right and claim to this in order that I might repair whatever injustice I might be considered to have done by so providing for the two persons whom I might be considered to have deprived of anything I might later possess: and this was agreed to, mind; agreed to between the two parties. And yet, and after more than thirty years, more than thirty years after my conscience had finally assured me that if I had done an injustice, I had done what I could to rectify it—' and Grandfather not saying 'Wait' now but saying, hollering maybe even: 'Conscience? Conscience? Good God, man, what else did you expect? Didn't the very affinity and instinct for misfortune of a man who had spent that much time in a monastery even, let alone one who had lived that many years as you lived them, tell you better than that? didn't the dread and fear of females which you must have drawn in with the primary mammalian milk teach you better? What kind of abysmal and purblind innocence could that have been which someone told you to call virginity? what conscience to trade with which would have warranted you in the belief that you could have bought immunity from her for no other coin but justice?'—"

This is Sutpen, as reported by Quentin's Grandfather, and ends with the latter admonishing Sutpen. For the rhetoric here of both men not to seem excessive, Sutpen must be of some eminence and his "design" of some consequence. But nothing in the novel persuades one of Sutpen's stature or of his design's meaningfulness. Like Kurtz in *Heart of Darkness*, Sutpen is a blind will in a cognitive vacuum; both figures seem to represent nothing more than a Nietzschean spirit of mere resentment, rather than the will's deep revenge against time, and time's "It was." Faulkner evident-ly was persuaded of Sutpen's importance, if only as a vital synecdoche for southern history. More a process than a man, Sutpen has drive without personality. One can remember a few of his acts, but none of his words, let alone his thoughts—if he has thoughts. He is simply too abrupt a mythic representation, rather than a man who becomes a myth. Only the scope of his failure interests Faulkner, rather than anything he is or means as a person.

Good critics confronting *Absalom, Absalom!* are fascinated by its intri-cate and enormous narrative procedures and by its genealogical patterns: doubling, incest, repetition, revenge—as John Irwin catalogs them. But narrative complications and structures of human desire, however titanic, are not necessarily aesthetic achievements. The Johnsonian questions, decisive for the common reader, always remain: how significant is the action that is represented, and how persuasive is the representation of the actors? Abstractly, the founding of a house and clan ought to outweigh the lunatic quest to bury a bad mother in the face of appalling obstacles, and yet Faulkner fails to make the former project as vital as the latter. Sutpen's design does not in itself move me, while the Bundrens' journey never loses its capacity to shock me into a negative Sublime. As a minority of one (so far as I can tell), I would yield to other critics on the greatness of *Absalom, Absalom!*, except that the best of them simply assume the eminence and mythic splendor of the book.

Time may reveal such assumptions to be accurate and thus justify readings that take delight in aspects of the book that make it more prob-lematic than nearly any other comparable novel. Still, Faulkner's *A Fable*, surely his worst book by any critical standards, will sustain post-Structuralist readings almost as well as *Absalom, Absalom!* does. Perhaps Faulkner's most comprehensive and ambitious novel justifies its vast inclu-siveness that is so uneasily allied to its deliberately unfinished quality. But Sutpen is indeed more like Conrad's Kurtz than like Melville's Ahab, in that his obsessions are not sufficiently metaphysical. Sutpen's Hundred is too much Kurtz's Africa, and too little the whiteness of the whale.

Ernest Hemingway

(1899-1961)

I

HEMINGWAY FREELY PROCLAIMED HIS RELATIONSHIP TO *HUCKLEBERRY Finn*, and there is some basis for the assertion, except that there is little in common between the rhetorical stances of Twain and Hemingway. Kipling's *Kim*, in style and mode, is far closer to *Huckleberry Finn* than anything Hemingway wrote. The true accent of Hemingway's admirable style is to be found in an even greater and more surprising precursor:

> This grass is very dark to be from the white heads of old mothers,
> Darker than the colorless beards of old men,
> Dark to come from under the faint red roofs of mouths.

Or again:

> I clutch the rails of the fence, my gore drips, thinn'd with the ooze
>   of my skin,
> I fall on the weeds and stones,
> The riders spur their unwilling horses, haul close,
> Taunt my dizzy ears and beat me violently over the head with
>   whip-stocks.
> Agonies are one of my changes of garments,
> I do not ask the wounded person how he feels, I myself become the
>   wounded person,
> My hurts turn livid upon me as I lean on a cane and observe.

Hemingway is scarcely unique in not acknowledging the paternity of

Walt Whitman; T.S. Eliot and Wallace Stevens are far closer to Whitman than William Carlos Williams and Hart Crane were, but literary influence is a paradoxical and antithetical process, about which we continue to know all too little. The profound affinities between Hemingway, Eliot, and Stevens are not accidental, but are family resemblances due to the repressed but crucial relation each had to Whitman's work. Hemingway characteristically boasted (in a letter to Sara Murphy, February 72, 1936) that he had knocked Stevens down quite handily: "... for statistics sake Mr. Stevens is 6 feet 2 weighs 522 lbs. and ... when he hits the ground it is highly spectaculous." Since this match between the two writers took place in Key West on February 19, 1936, I am moved, as a loyal Stevensian, for statistics' sake to point out that the victorious Hemingway was born in 1899, and the defeated Stevens in 1879, so that the novelist was then going on thirty-seven, and the poet verging on fifty-seven. The two men doubtless despised one another, but in the letter celebrating his victory Hemingway calls Stevens "a damned fine poet" and Stevens always affirmed that Hemingway was essentially a poet, a judgment concurred in by Robert Penn Warren when he wrote that Hemingway "is essentially a lyric rather than a dramatic writer." Warren compared Hemingway to Wordsworth, which is feasible, but the resemblance to Whitman is far closer. Wordsworth would not have written, "I am the man, I suffer'd, I was there," but Hemingway almost persuades us he would have achieved that line had not Whitman set it down first.

II

It is now more than twenty years since Hemingway's suicide, and some aspects of his permanent canonical status seem beyond doubt. Only a few modern American novels seem certain to endure: *The Sun Also Rises*, *The Great Gatsby*, *Miss Lonelyhearts*, *The Crying of Lot 49*, and at least several by Faulkner, including *As I Lay Dying*, *Sanctuary*, *Light in August*, *The Sound and the Fury*, *Absalom, Absalom!* Two dozen stories by Hemingway could be added to the group, indeed perhaps all of *The First Forty-Nine Stories*. Faulkner is an eminence apart, but critics agree that Hemingway and Fitzgerald are his nearest rivals, largely on the strength of their shorter fiction. What seems unique is that Hemingway is the only American writer of prose fiction in this century who, as a stylist, rivals the principal poets: Stevens, Eliot, Frost, Hart Crane, aspects of Pound, W.C. Williams, Robert Penn Warren, and Elizabeth Bishop. This is hardly to say that Hemingway, at his best, fails at narrative or the representation of character. Rather, his peculiar excellence is closer to Whitman than to Twain, closer to Stevens than to Faulkner, and even closer to Eliot than to Fitzgerald, who was his friend and rival. He is an elegiac poet who mourns the self, who celebrates the self (rather less effectively) and who suffers divisions in the self. In the broadest tradition of American literature, he stems ultimately from the Emersonian reliance on the god within, which is the line of Whitman, Thoreau, and Dickinson. He arrives late and dark in this tradition, and is one of its negative theologians, as it were, but as in Stevens the negations, the cancellings, are never final. Even the most ferocious of his stories, say "God Rest You Merry, Gentlemen" or "A Natural History of the Dead," can be said to celebrate what we might call the Real Absence. Doc Fischer, in "God Rest You Merry, Gentlemen," is a precursor of Nathanael West's Shrike in *Miss Lonelyhearts*, and his savage, implicit religiosity prophesies not only Shrike's Satanic stance but the entire demonic world of Pynchon's explicitly paranoid or Luddite visions. Perhaps there was a nostalgia for a Catholic order always abiding in Hemingway's consciousness, but the cosmos of his fiction, early and late, is American Gnostic, as it was in Melville, who first developed so strongly the negative side of the Emersonian religion of self-reliance.

III

Hemingway notoriously and splendidly was given to overtly agonistic images whenever he described his relationship to canonical writers, including Melville, a habit of description in which he has been followed by his true ephebe, Norman Mailer. In a grand letter (September 6–7, 1949) to his publisher, Charles Scribner, he charmingly confessed, "Am a man without any ambition, except to be champion of the world, I wouldn't fight Dr. Tolstoi in a 20 round bout because I know he would knock my ears off." This modesty passed quickly, to be followed by, "If I can live to 60 I can beat him. (MAYBE)." Since the rest of the letter counts Turgenev, de Maupassant, Henry James, even Cervantes, as well as Melville and Dostoyevski, among the defeated, we can join Hemingway, himself, in admiring his extraordinary self-confidence. How justified was it, in terms of his ambitions?

It could be argued persuasively that Hemingway is the best short-story writer in the English language from Joyce's *Dubliners* until the present. The aesthetic dignity of the short story need not be questioned, and yet we seem to ask more of a canonical writer. Hemingway wrote *The Sun Also Rises* and not *Ulysses*, which is only to say that his true genius was for very short stories, and hardly at all for extended narrative. Had he been primarily a poet, his lyrical gifts would have sufficed: we do not hold it against

Yeats that his poems, not his plays, are his principal glory. Alas, neither Turgenev nor Henry James, neither Melville nor Mark Twain provide true agonists for Hemingway. Instead, de Maupassant is the apter rival. Of Hemingway's intensity of style in the briefer compass, there is no question, but even *The Sun Also Rises* reads now as a series of epiphanies, of brilliant and memorable vignettes.

Much that has been harshly criticized in Hemingway, particularly in *For Whom the Bell Tolls*, results from his difficulty in adjusting his gifts to the demands of the novel. Robert Penn Warren suggests that Hemingway is successful when his "system of ironies and understatements is coherent." When incoherent, then, Hemingway's rhetoric fails as persuasion, which is to say, we read *To Have and Have Not or For Whom the Bell Tolls* and we are all too aware that the system of tropes is primarily what we are offered. Warren believes this not to be true of *A Farewell to Arms*, yet even the celebrated close of the novel seems now a worn understatement:

> But after I had got them out and shut the door and turned off the light it wasn't any good. It was like saying good-by to a statue. After a while I went out and left the hospital and walked back to the hotel in the rain.

Contrast this to the close of "Old Man at the Bridge," a story only two and a half pages long:

> There was nothing to do about him. It was Easter Sunday and the Fascists were advancing toward the Ebro. It was a gray overcast day with a low ceiling so their planes were not up. That and the fact that cats know how to look after themselves was all the good luck that old man would ever have.

The understatement continues to persuade here because the stoicism remains coherent, and is admirably fitted by the rhetoric. A very short story concludes itself by permanently troping the mood of a particular moment in history. Vignette is Hemingway's natural mode, or call it hard-edged vignette: a literary sketch that somehow seems to be the beginning or end of something longer, yet truly is complete in itself. Hemingway's style encloses what ought to be unenclosed, so that the genre remains subtle yet trades its charm for punch. But a novel of three hundred and forty pages (*A Farewell to Arms*) which I have just finished reading again (after twenty years away from it) cannot sustain itself upon the rhetoric of vignette. After many understatements, too many, the reader begins to believe that he is reading a Hemingway imitator, like the accomplished John O'Hara, rather than the master himself. Hemingway's notorious fault is the monotony of repetition, which becomes a dulling litany in a somewhat less accomplished imitator like Nelson Algren, and sometimes seems self-parody when we must confront it in Hemingway.

Nothing is got for nothing, and a great style generates defenses in us, particularly when it sets the style of an age, as the Byronic Hemingway did. As with Byron, the color and variety of the artist's life becomes something of a veil between the work and our aesthetic apprehension of it. Hemingway's career included four marriages (and three divorces); service as an ambulance driver for the Italians in World War I (with an honorable wound); activity as a war correspondent in the Greek-Turkish War (1922), the Spanish Civil War (1937–39), the Chinese-Japanese War (1941) and the War against Hitler in Europe (1944–45). Add big-game hunting and fishing, safaris, expatriation in France and Cuba, bullfighting, the Nobel prize, and ultimate suicide in Idaho, and you have an absurdly implausible life, apparently lived in imitation of Hemingway's own fiction. The final effect of the work and the life together is not less than mythological, as it was with Byron and with Whitman and with Oscar Wilde. Hemingway now is myth, and so is permanent as an image of American heroism, or perhaps more ruefully the American illusion of heroism. The best of Hemingway's work, the stories and *The Sun Also Rises*, are also a permanent part of the American mythology. Faulkner, Stevens, Frost, perhaps Eliot, and Hart Crane were stronger writers than Hemingway, but he alone in this American century has achieved the enduring status of myth.

The Sun Also Rises

Rereading *The Sun Also Rises* provides a few annoyances, particularly if one is a Jewish literary critic and somewhat skeptical of Hemingway's vision of the matador as messiah. Romero seems to me about as convincing a representation as Robert Cohn; they are archetypes for Hemingway in 1926, but hardly for us sixty years after. Brett and Mike are period pieces also; Scott Fitzgerald did them better. But these are annoyances only; the novel is as fresh now as when I first read it in 1946 when I was sixteen. Like *The Great Gatsby*, *The Sun Also Rises* ages beautifully. Why? What are the qualities that save this novel from its own *mystique*, its self-intoxication with its own rhetorical stance? What does it share with Hemingway's best stories, like those in the fine collection *Winner Take Nothing*?

A great style is itself necessarily a trope, a metaphor for a particular attitude towards reality. Hemingway's is an art of evocation, hardly a singular or original mode, except that Hemingway evokes by parataxis, in the manner of Whitman, or of much in the English Bible. This is parataxis with a difference, a way of utterance that plays at a withdrawal from all affect, while actually investing affect in the constancy of the withdrawal, a willing choice of the void as object, rather than be void of object, in Nietzschean terms. Not that Hemingway is spurred by Nietzsche, since Conrad is clearly the largest precursor of the author of *The Sun Also Rises*. The stance of Marlow in *Lord Jim* and *Heart of Darkness* is the closest analogue to Hemingway's own rhetorical stance in *The Sun Also Rises* and *A Farewell to Arms*.

Erich Auerbach and Angus Fletcher are among the notable modern critics who have illuminated the literary uses of parataxis. Fletcher lucidly summarizes parataxis as a syntactic parallel to the symbolic action of literature:

> This term implies a structuring of sentences such that they do not convey any distinctions of higher or lower order. "Order" here means intensity of interest, since what is more important usually gets the greater share of attention.

Fletcher, without implying childlike or primitive behavior, indicates the psychological meaning of parataxis as being related to "the piecemeal behavior of young children or primitive peoples." As Fletcher notes, this need not involve the defense Freud named as regression, because a paratactic syntax "displays ambiguity, suggesting that there is a rhythmic order even deeper in its organizing force than the syntactic order."

Hemingway's parataxis is worthy of the full-length studies it has not yet received. Clearly it is akin to certain moments in Huck Finn's narration, Walt Whitman's reveries, and even Wallace Stevens's most sustained late meditations, such as *The Auroras of Autumn*. John Hollander usefully compares it also to "an Antonioni shooting script in the relation of dialogue and shots of landscape cut away to as a move in the dialogue itself, rather than as mere punctuation, and ultimately in the way in which dialogue and uninterpreted glimpse of scene interpret each other." I take it that the refusal of emphasis, the maintaining of an even tonality of apparent understatement, is the crucial manifestation of parataxis in Hemingway's prose style. Consider the celebrated conclusion of *The Sun Also Rises*:

> Down-stairs we came out through the first-floor dining-room to the street. A waiter went for a taxi. It was hot and bright. Up the

street was a little square with trees and grass where there were taxis parked. A taxi came up the street, the waiter hanging out at the side. I tipped him and told the driver where to drive, and got in beside Brett. The driver started up the street. I settled back. Brett moved close to me. We sat close against each other. I put my arm around her and she rested against me comfortably. It was very hot and bright, and the houses looked sharply white. We turned out onto the Gran Via.

"Oh, Jake," Brett said, "we could have had such a damned good time together."

Ahead was a mounted policeman in khaki directing traffic. He raised his baton. The car slowed suddenly pressing Brett against me.

"Yes," I said. "Isn't it pretty to think so?"

The question of Jakes' impotence is more than relevant here. It is well to remember Hemingway's description of authorial intention, given in the interview with George Plimpton:

Actually he had been wounded in quite a different way and his testicles were intact and not damaged. Thus he was capable of all normal feelings as a man but incapable of consummating them. The important distinction is that his wound was physical and not psychological and that he was not emasculated.

The even, understated tone at the end of *The Sun Also Rises* depends upon a syntax that carries parataxis to what might have been parodistic excess, if Hemingway's art were less deliberate. Sentences such as "It was hot and bright" and the sly "He raised his baton" are psychic images of lost consummation, but they testify also to Jake's estrangement from the earlier intensities of his love for Brett. Reduced by his betrayal of the matador-messiah to Brett's rapacity, Jake is last heard in transition towards a less childlike, less primitive mode of reality-testing: "'Yes.' I said. 'Isn't it pretty to think so?'" One remembers Nietzsche's reflection that what we find words for is something we already despise in our hearts, so that there is always a sort of contempt in the act of speaking. Kenneth Burke, in *Counter-Statement*, rejoined that the contempt might be in the act, but not contempt for speaking. Jake, as the novel ends, is in transition towards Burke's position.

Hemingway possessed both a great style and an important sensibility. He was not an original moralist, a major speculative intellect, a master of narrative, or superbly gifted in the representation of persons. That is to say, he was not Tolstoy, whom he hoped to defeat he said, if only he could live long enough. But style and sensibility can be more than enough, as *The Sun Also Rises* demonstrates. Style alone will not do it; consider Updike or Cheever. We go back to *The Sun Also Rises* to learn a sensibility and to modify our own in the process of learning.

A Farewell to Arms

If *A Farewell to Arms* fails to sustain itself as a unified novel, it does remain Hemingway's strongest work after the frequent best of the short stories and *The Sun Also Rises*. It also participates in the aura of Hemingway's mode of myth, embodying as it does not only Hemingway's own romance with Europe but the permanent vestiges of our national romance with the Old World. The death of Catherine represents not the end of that affair, but its perpetual recurrence. I assign classic status in the interpretation of that death to Leslie Fiedler, with his precise knowledge of the limits of literary myth: "Only the dead woman becomes neither a bore nor a mother; and before Catherine can quite become either she must die, killed not by Hemingway, of course, but by childbirth!" Fiedler finds a touch of Poe in this, but Hemingway seems to me far healthier. Death, to Poe, is after all less a metaphor for sexual fulfillment than it is an improvement over mere coition, since Poe longs for a union in essence and not just in act.

Any feminist critic who resents that too-lovely Hemingwayesque ending, in which Frederic Henry gets to walk away in the rain while poor Catherine takes the death for both of them, has my sympathy, if only because this sentimentality that mars the aesthetic effect is certainly the mask for a male resentment and fear of women. Hemingway's symbolic rain is read by Louis L. Martz as the inevitable trope for pity, and by Malcolm Cowley as a conscious symbol for disaster. A darker interpretation might associate it with Whitman's very American confounding of night, death, the mother, and the sea, a fourfold mingling that Whitman bequeathed to Wallace Stevens, T.S. Eliot, and Hart Crane, among many others. The death of the beloved woman in Hemingway is part of that tropological cosmos, in which the moist element dominates because death the mother is the true image of desire. For Hemingway, the rain replaces the sea, and is as much the image of longing as the sea is in Whitman or Hart Crane.

Robert Penn Warren, defending a higher estimate of *A Farewell to Arms* than I can achieve, interprets the death of Catherine as the discovery that "the attempt to find a substitute for universal meaning in the limited meaning of the personal relationship is doomed to failure." Such a reading, though distinguished, seems to me to belong more to the literary cosmos of T.S. Eliot than to that of Hemingway. Whatever nostalgia for transcendental verities Hemingway may have possessed, his best fiction invests its energies in the representation of personal relationships, and hardly with the tendentious design of exposing their inevitable inadequacies. If your personal religion quests for the matador as messiah, then you are likely to seek in personal relationships something of the same values enshrined in the ritual of bull and bullfighter: courage, dignity, the aesthetic exaltation of the moment, and an all but suicidal intensity of being—the sense of life gathered to a crowded perception and graciously open to the suddenness of extinction. That is a vivid but an unlikely scenario for an erotic association, at least for any that might endure beyond a few weeks.

Wyndham Lewis categorized Hemingway by citing Walter Pater on Prosper Merimée: "There is the formula ... the enthusiastic amateur of rude, crude, naked force in men and women.... Painfully distinct in outline, inevitable to sight, unrelieved, there they stand." Around them, Pater added, what Merimée gave you was "neither more nor less than empty space." I believe that Pater would have found more than that in Hemingway's formula, more in the men and women, and something other than empty space in their ambiance. Perhaps by way of Joseph Conrad's influence upon him, Hemingway had absorbed part at least of what is most meaningful in Pater's aesthetic impressionism. Hemingway's women and men know, with Pater, that we have an interval, and then our place knows us no more. Our one chance is to pack that interval with the multiplied fruit of consciousness, with the solipsistic truths of perception and sensation. What survives time's ravages in *A Farewell to Arms* is precisely Hemingway's textually embodied knowledge that art alone apprehends the moments of perception and sensation, and so bestows upon them their privileged status. Consider the opening paragraph of chapter 16:

> That night a bat flew into the room through the open door that led onto the balcony and through which we watched the night over the roofs of the town. It was dark in our room except for the small light of the night over the town and the bat was not frightened but hunted in the room as though he had been outside. We lay and watched him and I do not think he saw us because we lay so still. After he went out we saw a searchlight come on and watched the beam

move across the sky and then go off and it was dark again. A breeze came in the night and we heard the men of the anti-aircraft gun on the next roof talking. It was cool and they were putting on their capes. I worried in the night about some one coming up but Catherine said they were all asleep. Once in the night we went to sleep and when I woke she was not there but I heard her coming along the hall and the door opened and she came back to the bed and said it was all right she had been downstairs and they were all asleep. She had been outside Miss Van Campen's door and heard her breathing in her sleep. She brought crackers and we ate them and drank some vermouth. We were very hungry but she said that would all have to be gotten out of me in the morning. I went to sleep again in the morning when it was light and when I was awake I found she was gone again. She came in looking fresh and lovely and sat on the bed and the sun rose while I had the thermometer in my mouth and we smelled the dew on the roofs and then the coffee of the men at the gun on the next roof.

The flight of the bat, the movement of the searchlight's beam and of the breeze, the overtones of the antiaircraft gunners blend into the light of the morning, to form a composite epiphany of what it is that Frederic Henry has lost when he finally walks back to the hotel in the rain. Can we define that loss? As befits the aesthetic impressionism of Pater, Conrad, Stephen Crane, and Hemingway, it is in the first place a loss of vividness and intensity in the world as experienced by the senses. In the aura of his love for Catherine, Frederic Henry knows the fullness of "It was dark" and "It was cool," and the smell of the dew on the roofs, and the aroma of the coffee being enjoyed by the anti-aircraft gunners. We are reminded that Pater's crucial literary ancestors were the unacknowledged Ruskin and the hedonistic visionary Keats, the Keats of the "Ode on Melancholy." Hemingway too, particularly in *A Farewell to Arms*, is an heir of Keats, with the poet's passion for sensuous immediacy, in all of its ultimate implications. Is not Catherine Barkley a belated and beautiful version of the goddess Melancholy, incarnating Keats's "Beauty that must die"? Hemingway too exalts that quester after the Melancholy,

>   whose strenuous tongue
> Can burst Joy's grape against his palate fine;
>   His soul shall taste the sadness of her might,
>   And be among her cloudy trophies hung.

The Old Man and the Sea

Hemingway's greatness is in his short stories, which rival any other master of the form, be it Joyce or Chekhov or Isaak Babel. Of his novels, one is constrained to suggest reservations, even of the very best: *The Sun Also Rises*. *The Old Man and the Sea* is the most popular of Hemingway's later works, but this short novel alas is an indeliberate self-parody, though less distressingly so than *Across the River and Into the Trees*, composed just before it. There is a gentleness, a nuanced tenderness, that saves *The Old Man and the Sea* from the self-indulgences of *Across the River and Into the Trees*. In an interview with George Plimpton, Hemingway stated his pride in what he considered to be the aesthetic economy of *The Old Man and the Sea*:

> *The Old Man and the Sea* could have been over a thousand pages long and had every character in the village in it and all the processes of the way they made their living, were born, educated, bore children, etc. That is done excellently and well by other writers. In writing you are limited by what has already been done satisfactorily. So I have tried to learn to do something else. First I have tried to eliminate everything unnecessary to conveying experience to the reader so that after he or she has read something it will become part of his or her experience and seem actually to have happened. This is very hard to do and I've worked at it very hard.
>
> Anyway, to skip how it is done, I had unbelievable luck this time and could convey the experience completely and have it be one that no one had ever conveyed. The luck was that I had a good man and a good boy and lately writers have forgotten there still are such things. Then the ocean is worth writing about just as a man is. So I was lucky there. I've seen the marlin mate and known about that. So I leave that out. I've seen a school (or pod) of more than fifty sperm whales in that same stretch of water and once harpooned one nearly sixty feet in length and lost him. So I left that out. But the knowledge is what makes the underwater part of the iceberg.

The Old Man and the Sea unfortunately is too long, rather than exquisitely curtailed, as Hemingway believed. The art of ellipsis, or leaving things out, indeed is the great virtue of Hemingway's best short stories. But *The Old Man and the Sea* is tiresomely repetitive, and Santiago the old fisherman is too clearly an idealization of Hemingway himself, who thinks in the style of the novelist attempting to land a great work:

> Only I have no luck anymore. But who knows? Maybe today. Every day is a new day. It is better to be lucky. But I would rather be exact. Then when luck comes you are ready.

Contemplating the big fish, Santiago is even closer to Hemingway the literary artist, alone with his writerly quest:

> His choice had been to stay in the deep dark water far out beyond all snares and traps and treacheries. My choice was to go there to find him beyond all people. Beyond all people in the world. Now we are joined together and have been since noon. And no one to help either one of us.

Santiago's ordeal, first in his struggle with the big fish, and then in fighting against the sharks, is associated by Hemingway with Christ's agony and triumph. Since it is so difficult to disentangle Santiago and Hemingway, this additional identification is rather unfortunate in its aesthetic consequences, because it can render a reader rather uncomfortable. There is a longing or nostalgia for faith in Hemingway, at least from *The Sun Also Rises* until the end of his career. But if *The Old Man and the Sea* is a Christian allegory, then the book carries more intended significance than it can bear. The big fish is no Moby-Dick or Jobean adversary; Santiago loves the fish and sees it as his double. What can we do with Santiago-as-Christ when we attempt to interpret the huge marlin?

William Faulkner praised *The Old Man and the Sea* as being Hemingway's best work, but then Faulkner also considered Thomas Wolfe to be the greatest American novelist of the century. The story, far from Hemingway's best, cannot be both a parable of Christian redemption and of a novelist's triumph, not so much because these are incompatible, but because so repetitive and self-indulgent a narrative cannot bear that double burden. Sentimentality, or emotion in excess of the object, floods *The Old Man and the Sea*. Hemingway himself is so moved by Hemingway that his famous, laconic style yields to uncharacteristic overwriting. We are not shown "grace under pressure," but something closer to Narcissus observing himself in the mirror of the sea.

Vladimir Nabokov

(1899-1977)

Lolita

I

LOLITA, BAROQUE AND SUBTLE, IS A BOOK WRITTEN TO BE REREAD, BUT whether its continued force matches the intricacy of its design seems to me problematic. Little is gained for Nabokov by comparing him to Sterne or to Joyce. Borges, who was essentially a parodist, is an apter parallel to Nabokov. Perhaps parodists are fated to resent Sigmund Freud; certainly Borges and Nabokov are the modern writers who most consistently and ignorantly abuse Freud.

Where Nabokov hardly can be overpraised is in his achievement as a stylist. This is one of the endlessly dazzling paragraphs of *Lolita*:

> So Humbert the Cubus schemed and dreamed—and the red sun of desire and decision (the two things that create a live world) rose higher and higher, while upon a succession of balconies a succession of libertines, sparkling glass in hand, toasted the bliss of past and future nights. Then, figuratively speaking, I shattered the glass, and boldly imagined (for I was drunk on those visions by then and underrated the gentleness of my nature) how eventually I might blackmail—no, that is too strong a word—mauvemail big Haze into letting me consort with little Haze by gently threatening the poor doting Big Dove with desertion if she tried to bar me from playing with my legal stepdaughter. In a word, before such an Amazing Offer, before such a vastness and variety of vistas, I was as helpless as Adam at the preview of early oriental history, miraged in his apple orchard.

It is a grand prose-poem, and the entire book in little. Reading it aloud is a shocking pleasure, and analyzing it yet another pleasure, more inward and enduring. Humbert, more "cubus" than "incubus," casts the red sun of his lustful will over the aptly named Haze females, yet avoids incurring our moral resentment by the exuberance of his language, with its zest for excess. What could be more captivating and memorable than: "while upon a succession of balconies a succession of libertines, sparkling glass in hand, toasted the bliss of past and future nights?" That delicious double "succession" achieves a kind of higher innocence, insouciant and stylized, delighting more in the language than in the actual possibility of sensual bliss. Shattering the sparkling glass, Humbert breaks the vessels of reverie in order to achieve a totally drunken vision of sexual exploitation, indeed like a new Adam overcome by the fumes of the fruit.

What Nabokov offers, in *Ada* as well as *Lolita*, is an almost pure revel in language, by no means necessarily allied with insight. His loathing of Freud reduces, I think, to a fear of meaning, to a need to defend against overdetermined sense, a sense that would extend to everything. Memory, in Nabokov, fears not so much Oedipal intensities as it does more-than-Oedipal genealogies. Here, Nabokov compares weakly to Proust, his most daunting precursor. *Lolita* gives us Marcel as Humbert and Albertine as Lolita, which is to replace a sublime temporal pathos by a parodistic cunning that unfortunately keeps reminding us how much we have lost when we turn from Proust to Nabokov.

II

Early defenses of *Lolita* by John Hollander and Lionel Trilling centered upon the insistence that it was an authentic love story. Rereading *Lolita* now, when no one would accuse the book of being pornography, I marvel that acute readers could take it as a portrayal of human love, since Humbert and Lolita are hardly representations of human beings. They are deliberate caricatures, as fabulistic as Charlotte Haze and Clare Quilty. Solipsistic nightmares, they wander in the America of highways and motels, but would be more at home in *Through the Looking-Glass* or *The Hunting of the Snark*. Poor Lolita indeed is a Snark, who precisely does not turn out to be a Boojum.

Nabokov, like Borges, is the most literary of fantasists, and takes from reality only what is already Nabokovian. Jane Austen, a powerful Protestant will, was as interested in social reality as the compulsive Dreiser was, but Nabokov's social reality died forever with the Bolshevik Revolution. Admirers who defend Nabokov's writing as mimesis do him violence. His genius was for distorted self-representation. Whether the Proustian intensities of sexual jealousy lend themselves to the phantasmagoric mode of Gogol is a considerable question, but Nabokov intrepidly did not wait for an answer.

"So what is that queer world, glimpses of which we keep catching through the gaps of the harmless looking sentences. It is in a way the *real* one but it looks wildly absurd to us, accustomed as we are to the stage setting that screens it." That is Nabokov on Gogol, or Nabokov on Nabokov. It is not Humbert on Humbert. Nabokov's uncanny art refuses identification with his protagonist, yet lends the author's voice to the comically desperate pursuer of nymphets. "The science of nympholepsy is a precise science," says Humbert and we reflect that Nabokov is the scientist, rather than poor Humbert, a reflection that is proved by an even more famous declaration:

> I am not concerned with so-called "sex" at all. Anybody can imagine those elements of animality. A greater endeavor lures me on: to fix once for all the perilous magic of nymphets.

Humbert perhaps knows that "the perilous magic" of eroticism crosses animality with death; Nabokov certainly knows, though he rejects so crassly the greatest of modern knowers, Freud. Rejecting Freud however is not a possible option in our time, and the whole of Part Two of *Lolita* is an involuntary repetition of *Beyond the Pleasure Principle*. The death drive, fueled by that negative libido Freud once toyed with calling "destrudo," takes over poor Humbert completely, through the agency of his dark double and despoiler, Clare Quilty. Refusing to compound with Freud, who is the greatest and most pervasive of modern imaginations, Nabokov is doomed merely to repeat the Freudian mythology of the dual drives, Eros-Humbert and Thanatos-Quilty. All of Part Two of *Lolita* becomes, not a parody, but a Freudian allegory, considerably less splendid than the joyous Part One.

Humbert's murder of Quilty is at once the most curious and the least persuasive episode in *Lolita*. Each figure is the "familiar and innocuous hallucination" of the other, and Humbert's bungling execution of his double lifts the book momentarily into the category of nightmare. It is no accident that Humbert returns to the slain Quilty (C.Q.) in the novel's closing sentences:

> And do not pity C.Q. One had to choose between him and H.H., and one wanted H.H. to exist at least a couple of months longer,

so as to have him make you live in the minds of later generations.
I am thinking of aurochs and angels, the secret of durable pig-
ments, prophetic sonnets, the refuge of art. And this is the only
immortality you and I may share, my Lolita.

That doesn't *sound* to me like Humbert, and rather clearly Nabokov
has usurped these closing tonalities, explaining why he did not have Quilty
murder Humbert, which I suspect would have made a better end. I don't
hear remoteness in this final tone, but rather an attempt to recover something of the aura of Part One, so sadly lost in the frenzies of Humbert's
later sorrows.

André Malraux

(1901–1976)

Man's Fate

LA CONDITION HUMAINE (1933, KNOWN IN ENGLISH AS *MAN'S FATE*) IS judged universally to have been André Malraux's major novel. Rereading it in 1987, sixty years after the Shanghai insurrection of 1927, which it commemorates, is a rather ambiguous experience. One need not have feared that it would seem a mere period piece; it is an achieved tragedy, with the aesthetic dignity that the genre demands. What renders it a little disappointing is its excessive abstractness. Malraux may have known a touch too clearly exactly what he was doing. Rereading Faulkner always surprises; there is frequently a grace beyond the reach of art. Malraux's fictive economy is admirable, but the results are somewhat schematic. Clarity can be a novelistic virtue; transparency grieves us with the impression of a certain thin quality.

The idealistic revolutionaries are persuasive enough in *Man's Fate*; they are even exemplary. But, like all of Malraux's protagonists, they are diminished by their sense of coming after their inspirers; they are not forerunners, but belated imitators of the Revolution. Malraux's protagonists designedly quest for strength by confronting death, thus achieving different degrees either of communion or of solitude. Their models in fiction are the obsessed beings of Dostoevsky or of Conrad. *Man's Fate* cannot sustain comparison with *Nostromo*, let alone with the anguished narratives of Dostoevsky. There are no originals in Malraux, no strong revolutionaries who are the equivalents of strong poets, rather than of philosophers. Geoffrey Hartman, defending Malraux's stature as tragedian, sees the heroes of *Man's Fate* as understanding and humanizing the Nietzschean Eternal Recurrence:

The tragic sentiment is evoked most purely not by multiplying lives ... but by repeating the chances of death, of unique, fatal acts. A hero like Tchen, or his fellow conspirators Kyo and Katov, dies more than once.

But is that the Nietzschean issue, the Nietzschean test for strength? Do Malraux's heroes take on what Richard Rorty, following Nietzsche, has called "the contingency of selfhood"? Do they fully appreciate their own contingency? Here is Rorty's summary of this crucial aspect of Nietzsche's perspectivism:

His perspectivism amounted to the claim that the universe had no lading-list to be known, of determinate length. He hoped that, once we realized that Plato's "true world" was just a fable, we would seek consolation, at the moment of death, not in having transcended the animal condition but in being that peculiar sort of dying animal who, by describing himself in his own terms, had created himself.

Nietzsche understood that political revolutionaries are more like philosophers than like poets, since revolutionaries also insist that the human condition bears only one true analysis. Malraux's heroes attempt to escape from contingency rather than, like the strong poets, accepting and then appropriating contingency. Though the heroes of *Man's Fate*, and of Malraux's other novels, meditate endlessly upon death, if only in order to achieve a sense of being, they never succeed in describing themselves entirely in their own terms. This is a clue to Malraux's ultimate inadequacy as a novelist, his failure to join himself to the great masters of French fiction: Stendhal, Balzac, Flaubert, Proust, or to the international novelists he most admired: Dostoevsky, Conrad, Faulkner. Would we say of the protagonists of Stendhal and Balzac that the death which overcomes them "is no more than the symbol of an ultimate self-estrangement"? Hartman's remark is valid for Malraux's heroes, but not for Stendhal's or Balzac's.

Malraux, a superb and wary critic, defended himself against Gaëtan Picon's shrewd observation that: "Malraux, unlike Balzac or Proust, in no way seeks to give each character a personal voice, to free each character from its creator." His response was: "The autonomy of characters, the particular vocabulary given to each of them are powerful techniques of fictional action; they are not necessities ... I do not believe that the novelist must create *characters*; he must create a particular and coherent world." *Man's Fate* certainly does create such a world; is it a liability or not that

Kyo, Katov, Gisors and the others fall short as characters, since they do not stride out of the novel, breaking loose from Malraux, and they all of them do sound rather alike. I finish rereading *Nostromo*, and I brood on the flamboyant Capataz, or I put down *As I Lay Dying*, and Darl Bundren's very individual voice haunts me. But Kyo and Katov give me nothing to meditate upon, and Gisors and Ferral speak with the same inflection and vocabulary. Fate or contingency resists appropriation by Malraux's heroes, none of whom defies, or breaks free of, his creator.

Despite Malraux's defense, the sameness of his protagonists constitutes a definite aesthetic limitation. It would be one thing to create varied individuals with unique voices and then to show that they cannot communicate with one another. It is quite another thing to represent so many aspects of the author as so many characters, all speaking with his voice, and then demonstrate the deathliness of their inability to speak truly to another. Malraux confused death with contingency, which is a philosopher's error, rather than a strong novelist's.

This may be why the women throughout Malraux's novels are so dismal a failure in representation. Unamuno ironically jested that "all women are one woman," which is just the way things are in Malraux's fictions. A novelist so intent upon Man rather than men is unlikely to give us an infinite variety of women.

What redeems *Man's Fate* from a reader's frustration with the sameness of its characters is the novel's indubitable capture of a tragic sense of life. Tragedy is not individual in Malraux, but societal and cultural, particularly the latter. Malraux's Marxism was always superficial, and his aestheticism fortunately profound. The tragedy of the heroes in *Man's Fate* is necessarily belated tragedy, which is fitting for idealists whose place in revolutionary history is so late. That is why Gisors is shown teaching his students that: "Marxism is not a doctrine, it is a *will* ... it is the will to know themselves ... to conquer without betraying yourselves." Just as the imagination cannot be distinguished from the will as an artistic tradition grows older and longer, so ideology blends into the will as revolutionary tradition enters a very late phase. Tragedy is an affair of the will, and not of doctrine. Kyo and Katov die in the will, and so achieve tragic dignity. Gisors, the best mind in the novel, sums up for Malraux, just a few pages from the end:

> She was silent for a moment:
> "They are dead, now," she said finally.
> "I still think so, May. It's something else.... Kyo's death is not only grief, not only change—it is ... a metamorphosis. I have never loved the world over-much: it was Kyo who attached me to men,

it was through him that they existed for me.... I don't want to go to Moscow. I would teach wretchedly there. Marxism has ceased to live in me. In Kyo's eyes it was a will, wasn't it? But in mine, it is a fatality, and I found myself in harmony with it because my fear of death was in harmony with fatality. There is hardly any fear left in me, May; since Kyo died, I am indifferent to death. I am freed (freed! ...) both from death and from life. What would I do over there?"

"Change anew, perhaps."

"I have no other son to lose."

The distinction between a will and a fatality is the difference between son and father, activist and theoretician, latecomer and forerunner. For Malraux, it is an aesthetic distinction, rather than a psychological or spiritual difference. As novelist, Malraux takes no side in this dichotomy, an impartiality at once his narrative strength and his representational weakness. He gives us forces and events, where we hope for more, for access to consciousnesses other than our own, or even his. As a theorist of art, Malraux brilliantly grasped contingency, but as a novelist he suffered it. He saw that the creator had to create his own language out of the language of precursors, but he could not enact what he saw. *Man's Fate* is a memorable tragedy without memorable persons. Perhaps it survives as a testament of Malraux's own tragedy, as a creator.

John Steinbeck

(1902–1968)

IT IS EIGHTEEN YEARS SINCE JOHN STEINBECK DIED, AND WHILE HIS popularity as a novelist still endures, his critical reputation has suffered a considerable decline. His honors were many and varied, and included the Nobel Prize and the United States Medal of Freedom. His best novels came early in his career: *In Dubious Battle* (1936); *Of Mice and Men* (1937); *The Grapes of Wrath* (1939). Nothing after that, including *East of Eden* (1952), bears rereading. It would be good to record that rereading his three major novels is a valuable experience, from an aesthetic as well as an historical perspective.

Of Mice and Men, an economical work, really a novella, retains considerable power, marred by an intense sentimentality. But *In Dubious Battle* is now quite certainly a period piece, and is of more interest to social historians than to literary critics. *The Grapes of Wrath*, still Steinbeck's most famous and popular novel, is a very problematical work, and very difficult to judge. As story, or rather, chronicle, it lacks invention, and its characters are not persuasive representations of human inwardness. The book's wavering strength is located elsewhere, in a curious American transformation of biblical substance and style that worked splendidly in Whitman and Hemingway, but seems to work only fitfully in Steinbeck.

The Grapes of Wrath

Steinbeck suffers from too close a comparison with Hemingway, his authentic precursor though born only three years before his follower. I think that Steinbeck's aesthetic problem *was* Hemingway, whose shadow always hovered too near. Consider the opening of *The Grapes of Wrath*:

To the red country and part of the gray country of Oklahoma, the last rains came gently, and they did not cut the scarred earth. The plows crossed and recrossed the rivulet marks. The last rains lifted the corn quickly and scattered weed colonies and grass along the sides of the roads so that the gray country and the dark red country began to disappear under a green cover. In the last part of May the sky grew pale and the clouds that had hung in high puffs for so long in the spring were dissipated. The sun flared down on the growing corn day after day until a line of brown spread along the edge of each green bayonet. The clouds appeared, and went away, and in a while they did not try any more. The weeds grew darker green to protect themselves, and they did not spread any more. The surface of the earth crusted, a thin hard crust, and as the sky became pale, so the earth became pale, pink in the red country and white in the gray country.

In the water-cut gullies the earth dusted down in dry little streams. Gophers and ant lions started small avalanches. And as the sharp sun struck day after day, the leaves of the young corn became less stiff and erect; they bent in a curve at first, and then, as the central ribs of strength grew weak, each leaf tilted downward. Then it was June, and the sun shone more fiercely. The brown lines on the corn leaves widened and moved in on the central ribs. The weeds frayed and edged back toward their roots. The air was thin and the sky more pale; and every day the earth paled.

This is not so much biblical style as mediated by Ernest Hemingway, as it is Hemingway assimilated to Steinbeck's sense of biblical style. The monosyllabic diction is hardly the mode of the King James Version, but certainly is Hemingway's. I give, very nearly at random, passages from *The Sun Also Rises*:

We passed through a town and stopped in front of the posada, and the driver took on several packages. Then we started on again, and outside the town the road commenced to mount. We were going through farming country with rocky hills that sloped down into the fields. The grain-fields went up the hillsides. Now as we went higher there was a wind blowing the grain. The road was white and dusty, and the dust rose under the wheels and hung in the air behind us. The road climbed up into the hills and left the rich grain-fields below. Now there were only patches of grain on the bare hillsides and on each side of the water-courses. We turned sharply out to the side of the road to give room to pass to a long string of six mules, following one after the other, hauling a high-hooded wagon loaded with freight. The wagon and the mules were covered with dust. Close behind was another string of mules and another wagon. This was loaded with lumber, and the arriero driving the mules leaned back and put on the thick wooden brakes as we passed. Up here the country was quite barren and the hills were rocky and hard-baked clay furrowed by the rain.

The bus climbed steadily up the road. The country was barren and rocks stuck up through the clay. There was no grass beside the road. Looking back we could see the country spread out below. Far back the fields were squares of green and brown on the hillsides. Making the horizon were the brown mountains. They were strangely shaped. As we climbed higher the horizon kept changing. As the bus ground slowly up the road we could see other mountains coming up in the south. Then the road came over the crest, flattened out, and went into a forest. It was a forest of cork oaks, and the sun came through the trees in patches, and there were cattle grazing back in the trees. We went through the forest and the road came out and turned along a rise of land, and out ahead of us was a rolling green plain, with dark mountains beyond it. These were not like the brown, heat-baked mountains we had left behind. These were wooded and there were clouds coming down from them. The green plain stretched off. It was cut by fences and the white of the road showed through the trunks of a double line of trees that crossed the plain toward the north. As we came to the edge of the rise we saw the red roofs and white houses of Burguete ahead strung out on the plain, and away off on the shoulder of the first dark mountain was the gray metal-sheathed roof of the monastery of Roncevalles.

Hemingway's Basque landscapes are described with an apparent literalness and in what seems at first a curiously dry tone, almost flat in its evident lack of significant emotion. But a closer reading suggests that the style here is itself a metaphor for a passion and a nostalgia that is both defensive and meticulous. The contrast between rich soil and barren ground, between wooded hills and heat-baked mountains, is a figure for the lost potency of Jake Barnes, but also for a larger sense of the lost possibilities of life. Steinbeck, following after Hemingway, cannot learn the lesson. He gives us a vision of the Oklahoma Dust Bowl, and it is effective enough, but it is merely a landscape where a process of entropy has been enacted. It has a social and economic meaning, but as a vision of loss lacks spiritual and personal intensity. Steinbeck is more overtly biblical than Hemingway, but too obviously so. We feel that the Bible's sense of meaning in landscape has returned from the dead in Hemingway's own colors, but hardly in Steinbeck's.

If Steinbeck is not an original or even an adequate stylist, if he lacks skill in plot, and power in the mimesis of character, what then remains in his work, except its fairly constant popularity with an immense number of liberal middlebrows, both in his own country and abroad? Certainly, he aspired beyond his aesthetic means. If the literary Sublime, or contest for the highest place, involves persuading the reader to yield up easier pleasures for more difficult pleasures, and it does, then Steinbeck modestly should have avoided Emerson's American Sublime, but he did not. Desiring it both ways, he fell into bathos in everything he wrote, even in *Of Mice and Men* and *The Grapes of Wrath*.

Yet Steinbeck had many of the legitimate impulses of the Sublime writer, and of his precursors Whitman and Hemingway in particular. Like them, he studied the nostalgias, the aboriginal sources that were never available for Americans, and like them he retained a profound hope for the American as natural man and natural woman. Unlike Whitman and Hemingway and the origin of this American tradition, Emerson, Steinbeck had no capacity for the nuances of literary irony. He had read Emerson's essay "The Over-Soul" as his precursors had, but Steinbeck literalized it. Emerson, canniest where he is most the Idealist, barbs his doctrine of "that Unity, that Over-soul, within which every man's particular being is contained and made one with all other." In Emerson, that does not involve the sacrifice of particular being, and is hardly a program for social action:

> We live in succession, in division, in parts, in particles. Meantime within man is the soul of the whole....
> The soul knows only the soul; all else is idle weeds for her wearing.

There always have been Emersonians of the Left, like Whitman and Steinbeck, and Emersonians of the Right, like Henry James and Wallace Stevens. Emerson himself, rather gingerly planted on the moderate Left, evaded all positions. Social action is also an affair of succession, division, parts, particles; if "the soul knows only the soul," then the soul cannot know doctrines, or even human suffering. Steinbeck, socially generous, a writer on the left, structured the doctrine of *The Grapes of Wrath* on Jim Casy's literalization of Emerson's vision: "Maybe all men got one big soul and everybody's a part of it." Casy, invested by Steinbeck with a rough eloquence that would have moved Emerson, speaks his orator's epitaph just before he is martyred: "They figger I'm a leader 'cause I talk so much." He is a leader, an Okie Moses, and he dies a fitting death for the visionary of an Exodus.

I remain uneasy about my own experience of rereading *The Grapes of Wrath*. Steinbeck is not one of the inescapable American novelists of our century; he cannot be judged in close relation to Cather, Dreiser, and Faulkner, Hemingway and Fitzgerald, Nathanael West, Ralph Ellison, and Thomas Pynchon. Yet there are no canonical standards worthy of human respect that could exclude *The Grapes of Wrath* from a serious reader's esteem. Compassionate narrative that addresses itself so directly to the great social questions of its era is simply too substantial a human achievement to be dismissed. Whether a human strength, however generously worked through, is also an aesthetic value, in a literary narrative, is one of those larger issues that literary criticism scarcely knows how to decide. One might desire *The Grapes of Wrath* to be composed differently, whether as plot or as characterization, but wisdom compels one to he grateful for the novel's continued existence.

Of Mice and Men

The late Anthony Burgess, in a touching salute from one professional writer to another, commended *Of Mice and Men* as "a fine novella (or play with extended stage directions) which succeeds because it dares sentimentality." Rereading *Of Mice and Men*, I remain impressed by its economical intensity, which has authentic literary power, though the sentimentality sometimes seems to me excessive. The book has been called Darwinian and naturalistic; it does share in the kind of dramatic pathos featured also in the plays of Eugene O'Neill and the novels of Theodore Dreiser. Reality is harsh and ultimately scarcely to be borne; dreams and delusions alone allow men to keep going. George and Lennie share the hopeless dream of a little ranch of their own, where George could keep the well-meaning but disaster-prone Lennie out of trouble and sorrow. As several critics have noted, this is one of Steinbeck's recurrent dreams of a lost Eden, sadly illusory yet forever beckoning.

As in the works of O'Neill and of Dreiser, the anxiety that afflicts all of Steinbeck's male protagonists is a desperate solitude. Despite his frequent use of Biblical style, more marked in *The Grapes of Wrath* than in *Of*

Mice and Men, Steinbeck was anything but a religious writer, by temperament and by belief. His heavy naturalism is very close to fatalism: Lennie is doomed by his nature, which craves affection, softness, the childlike, yet which is overwhelmingly violent and pragmatically brutal because of childish bafflement and defensiveness. What could anyone have done to save Lennie? Since George is truly responsible and caring and still fails to keep Lennie safe, it seems clear that even institutionalization could not have saved Steinbeck's most pathetic version of natural man. That returns the burden of Steinbeck's sad fable to Steinbeck himself: What has the author done for himself as a novelist by telling us this overdetermined story, and what do we gain as readers by attending to it? Though there are dramatic values in *Of Mice and Men*, they are inadequate compared to O'Neill at his best. There is an authentic dignity in the brotherhood of George and Lennie, but it too seems stunted compared to the massive humanity of the major figures in Dreiser's strongest narratives, *Sister Carrie* and *An American Tragedy*. Clearly there is something that endures in *Of Mice and Men* as in *The Grapes of Wrath*, though the novella lacks the social force of Steinbeck's major novel. Is it the stoic minimalism of George and Lennie and their fellow wandering ranch hands that somehow achieves a memorable image of human value?

Steinbeck resented Hemingway because he owed Hemingway too much, both in style and in the perception of the aesthetic dignity of natural men, at once unable to bear either society or solitude. The counterinfluence in *Of Mice and Men* seems to be the Faulkner of *The Sound and the Fury*, particularly in the representation of poor Lennie, who may have in him a trace of the benign idiot, Benjy. Any comparison of Faulkner and Steinbeck will tend to lessen Steinbeck, who is overmatched by Faulkner's mythic inventiveness and consistent strength of characterization. Yet there is a mythic quality to *Of Mice and Men*, a clear sense that Lennie and George ultimately represent something larger than either their selves or their relationship. They touch a permanence because their mutual care enhances both of them. That care cannot save Lennie, and it forces George to execute his friend to save him from the hideous violence of a mob. But the care survives Lennie's death; Slim's recognition of the dignity and the value of the care is the novel's final gesture, and is richly shared by the reader.

Nathanael West

(1903-1940)

Miss Lonelyhearts

NATHANAEL WEST, WHO DIED IN AN AUTOMOBILE ACCIDENT IN 1940 AT the age of thirty-seven, wrote one remorseless masterpiece, *Miss Lonelyhearts* (1933). Despite some astonishing sequences, *The Day of the Locust* (1939) is an overpraised work, a waste of West's genius. Of the two lesser fictions, *The Dream Life of Balso Snell* (1931) is squalid and dreadful, with occasional passages of a rancid power, while *A Cool Million* (1934), though an outrageous parody of American picaresque, is a permanent work of American satire and seems to me underpraised. To call West uneven is therefore a litotes; he is a wild medley of magnificent writing and inadequate writing, except in *Miss Lonelyhearts* which excels *The Sun Also Rises*, *The Great Gatsby*, and even *Sanctuary* as the perfected instance of a negative vision in modern American fiction. The greatest Faulkner, of *The Sound and the Fury, As I Lay Dying, Absalom, Absalom!* and *Light in August,* is the only American writer of prose fiction in this century who can be said to have surpassed *Miss Lonelyhearts*. West's spirit lives again in *The Crying of Lot 49* and some sequences in *Gravity's Rainbow*, but the negative sublimity of *Miss Lonelyhearts* proves to be beyond Pynchon's reach, or perhaps his ambition.

West, born Nathan Weinstein, is a significant episode in the long and tormented history of Jewish Gnosticism. The late Gershom Scholem's superb essay, "Redemption Through Sin," in his *The Messianic Idea in Judaism,* is the best commentary I know upon *Miss Lonelyhearts*. I once attempted to convey this to Scholem, who shrugged West off, quite properly from Scholem's viewpoint, when I remarked to him that West was manifestly a Jewish anti-Semite, and admitted that there were no allusions to Jewish esotericism or Kabbalah in his works. Nevertheless, for the stance of literary criticism, Jewish Gnosticism, as defined by Scholem, is the most illuminating context in which to study West's novels. It is a melancholy paradox that West, who did not wish to be Jewish in any way at all, remains the most indisputably Jewish writer yet to appear in America, a judgment at once aesthetic and moral. Nothing by Bellow, Malamud, Philip Roth, Mailer, or Ozick can compare to *Miss Lonelyhearts* as an achievement. West's Jewish heir, if he has one, may be Harold Brodkey, whose recent *Women and Angels*, excerpted from his immense novel-in-progress, can be regarded as another powerful instance of Jewish Gnosis, free of West's hatred of his own Jewishness.

Stanley Edgar Hyman, in his pamphlet on West (1962), concluded that, "His strength lay in his vulgarity and bad taste, his pessimism, his nastiness." Hyman remains West's most useful critic, but I would amend this by observing that these qualities in West's writing emanate from a negative theology, spiritually authentic, and given aesthetic dignity by the force of West's eloquent negations. West, like his grandest creation, Shrike, is a rhetorician of the abyss, in the tradition of Sabbatian nihilism that Scholem has expounded so masterfully. One thinks of ideas such as "the violation of the Torah has become its fulfillment, just as a grain of wheat must rot in the earth" or such as Jacob Frank's: "We are all now under the obligation to enter the abyss." The messianic intensity of the Sabbatians and Frankists results in a desperately hysterical and savage tonality which prophesies West's authentically religious book, *Miss Lonelyhearts*, a work profoundly Jewish but only in its negations, particularly the negation of the normative Judaic assumption of total sense in everything, life and text alike. *Miss Lonelyhearts* takes place in the world of Freud, where the fundamental assumption is that everything already has happened, and that nothing can be made new because total sense has been achieved, but then repressed or negated. Negatively Jewish, the book is also negatively American. Miss Lonelyhearts is a failed Walt Whitman (hence the naming of the cripple as Peter Doyle, Whitman's pathetic friend) and a fallen American Adam to Shrike's very American Satan. Despite the opinions of later critics, I continue to find Hyman's argument persuasive, and agree with him that the book's psychosexuality is marked by a repressed homosexual relation between Shrike and Miss Lonelyhearts. Hyman's Freudian observation that all the suffering in the book is essentially female seems valid, reminding us that Freud's "feminine masochism" is mostly encountered among men, according to Freud himself. Shrike, the butcherbird impaling his victim, Miss Lonelyhearts, upon the thorns of Christ, is himself as much an instance of "feminine masochism" as his victim. If Miss Lonelyhearts is close to pathological frenzy, Shrike is also consumed by religious hysteria, by a terrible nostalgia for God.

The book's bitter stylistic negation results in a spectacular verbal economy, in which literally every sentence is made to count, in more than one sense of "count." Freud's "negation" involves a cognitive return of the repressed, here through West's self-projection as Shrike, spit out but not disavowed. The same Freudian process depends upon an affective continuance of repression, here by West's self-introjection as Miss Lonelyhearts, at once West's inability to believe and his disavowed failure to love. Poor Miss Lonelyhearts, who receives no other name throughout the book, has been destroyed by Shrike's power of Satanic rhetoric before the book even opens. But then Shrike has destroyed himself first, for no one could withstand the sustained horror of Shrike's impaling rhetoric, which truly can be called West's horror:

> "I am a great saint," Shrike cried, "I can walk on my own water. Haven't you ever heard of Shrike's Passion in the Luncheonette, or the Agony in the Soda Fountain? Then I compared the wounds in Christ's body to the mouths of a miraculous purse in which we deposit the small change of our sins. It is indeed an excellent conceit. But now let us consider the holes in our own bodies and into what these congenital wounds open. Under the skin of man is a wondrous jungle where veins like lush tropical growths hang along overripe organs and weed-like entrails writhe in squirming tangles of red and yellow. In this jungle, flitting from rock-gray lungs to golden intestines, from liver to lights and back to liver again, lives a bird called the soul. The Catholic hunts this bird with bread and wine, the Hebrew with a golden ruler, the Protestant on leaden feet with leaden words, the Buddhist with gestures, the Negro with blood. I spit on them all. Phooh! And I call upon you to spit. Phooh! Do you stuff birds? No, my dears, taxidermy is not religion. No! A thousand times no. Better, I say unto you, better a live bird in the jungle of the body than two stuffed birds on the library table."

I have always associated this great passage with what is central to West: the messianic longing for redemption, through sin if necessary. West's humor is almost always apocalyptic, in a mode quite original with him, though so influential since his death that we have difficulty seeing how strong the originality was. Originality, even in comic writing, becomes a difficulty. How are we to read the most outrageous of the letters sent to Miss Lonelyhearts, the one written by the sixteen-year-old girl without a nose?

I sit and look at myself all day and cry. I have a big hole in the middle of my face that scares people even myself so I cant blame the boys for not wanting to take me out. My mother loves me, but she crys terrible when she looks at me.

What did I do to deserve such a terrible bad fate? Even if I did do some bad things I didnt do any before I was a year old and I was born this way. I asked Papa and he says he doesnt know, but that maybe I did something in the other world before I was born or that maybe I was being punished for his sins. I dont believe that because he is a very nice man. Ought I commit suicide?
Sincerely yours,
Desperate

Defensive laughter is a complex reaction to grotesque suffering. In his 1928 essay on humor, Freud concluded that the above-the-I, the superego, speaks kindly words of comfort to the intimidated ego, and this speaking is humor, which Freud calls "the triumph of narcissism, the ego's victorious assertion of its own invulnerability." Clearly, Freud's "humor" does not include the Westian mode. Reading Desperate's "What did I do to deserve such a terrible bad fate?," our ego knows that it is defeated all the time, or at least is vulnerable to undeserved horror. West's humor has *no* liberating element whatsoever, but is the humor of a vertigo ill-balanced on the edge of what ancient Gnosticism called the *kenoma*, the cosmological emptiness.

II

Shrike, West's superb Satanic tempter, achieves his apotheosis at the novel's midpoint, the eighth of its fifteen tableaux, accurately titled "Miss Lonelyhearts in the Dismal Swamp." As Miss Lonelyhearts, sick with despair, lies in bed, the drunken Shrike bursts in, shouting his greatest rhetorical set piece, certainly the finest tirade in modern American fiction. Cataloging the methods that Miss Lonelyhearts might employ to escape out of the Dismal Swamp, Shrike begins with a grand parody of the later D.H. Lawrence, in which the vitalism of *The Plumed Serpent* and *The Man Who Died* is carried into a gorgeous absurdity, a heavy sexuality that masks Shrike's Satanic fears of impotence:

"You are fed up with the city and its teeming millions. The ways and means of men, as getting and lending and spending, you lay waste your inner world, are too much with you. The bus takes too long, while the subway is always crowded. So what do you do? So you buy a farm and walk behind your horse's moist behind, no collar or tie, plowing your broad swift acres. As you turn up the rich black soil, the wind carries the smell of pine and dung across the fields and the rhythm of an old, old work enters your soul. To this rhythm, you sow and weep and chivy your kine, not kin or kind, between the pregnant rows of corn and taters. Your step becomes the heavy sexual step of a dance-drunk Indian and you tread the seed down into the female earth. You plant, not dragon's teeth, but beans and greens."

Confronting only silence, Shrike proceeds to parody the Melville of *Typee* and *Omoo*, and also Somerset Maugham's version of Gauguin in *The Moon and Sixpence*:

"You live in a thatch but with the daughter of a king, a slim young maiden in whose eyes is an ancient wisdom. Her breasts are golden speckled pears, her belly a melon, and her odor is like nothing so much as a jungle fern. In the evening, on the blue lagoon, under the silvery moon, to your love you croon in the soft sylabelew and vocabelew of her langorour tongorour. Your body is golden brown like hers, and tourists have need of the indignant finger of the missionary to point you out. They envy you your breech clout and carefree laugh and little brown bride and fingers instead of forks. But you don't return their envy, and when a beautiful society girl comes to your but in the night, seeking to learn the secret of your happiness, you send her back to her yacht that hangs on the horizon like a nervous racehorse. And so you dream away the days, fishing, hunting, dancing, kissing, and picking flowers to twine in your hair."

As Shrike says, this is a played-out mode, but his savage gusto in rendering it betrays his hatred of the religion of art, of the vision that sought a salvation in imaginative literature. What Shrike goes on to chant is an even more effective parody of the literary stances West rejected. Though Shrike calls it "Hedonism," the curious amalgam here of Hemingway and Ronald Firbank, with touches of Fitzgerald and the earlier Aldous Huxley, might better be named an aesthetic stoicism:

"You dedicate your life to the pursuit of pleasure. No overindulgence, mind you, but knowing that your body is a pleasure machine, you treat it carefully in order to get the most out of it.

Golf as well as booze, Philadelphia Jack O'Brien and his chest-weights as well as Spanish dancers. Nor do you neglect the pleasures of the mind. You fornicate under pictures by Matisse and Picasso, you drink from Renaissance glassware, and often you spend an evening beside the fireplace with Proust and an apple. Alas, after much good fun, the day comes when you realize that soon you must die. You keep a stiff upper lip and decide to give a last party. You invite all your old mistresses, trainers, artists and boon companions. The guests are dressed in black, the waiters are coons, the table is a coffin carved for you by Eric Gill. You serve caviar and blackberries and licorice candy and coffee without cream. After the dancing girls have finished, you get to your feet and call for silence in order to explain your philosophy of life. 'Life,' you say, 'is a club where they won't stand for squawks, where they deal you only one hand and you must sit in. So even if the cards are cold and marked by the hand of fate, play up, play up like a gentleman and a sport. Get tanked, grab what's on the buffet, use the girls upstairs, but remember, when you throw box cars, take the curtain like a dead game sport, don't squawk.'"

Even this is only preparatory to Shrike's bitterest phase in his tirade, an extraordinary send-up of High Aestheticism proper, of Pater, George Moore, Wilde and the earlier W.B. Yeats:

"Art! Be an artist or a writer. When you are cold, warm yourself before the flaming tints of Titian, when you are hungry, nourish yourself with great spiritual foods by listening to the noble periods of Bach, the harmonies of Brahms and the thunder of Beethoven. Do you think there is anything in the fact that their names all begin with a B? But don't take a chance, smoke a 3 B pipe, and remember these immortal lines: *When to the suddenness of melody the echo parting falls the failing day.* What a rhythm! Tell them to keep their society whores and pressed duck with oranges. For you *l'art vivant*, the living art, as you call it. Tell them that you know that your shoes are broken and that there are pimples on your face, yes, and that you have buck teeth and a club foot, but that you don't care, for to-morrow they are playing Beethoven's last quartets in Carnegie Hall and at home you have Shakespeare's plays in one volume."

That last sentence, truly and deliciously Satanic, is one of West's greatest triumphs, but he surpasses it in the ultimate Shrikean rhapsody, after Shrike's candid avowal: "God alone is our escape." With marvelous appropriateness, West makes this at once the ultimate Miss Lonelyhearts letter, and also Shrike's most Satanic self-identification, in the form of a letter to Christ dictated for Miss Lonelyhearts by Shrike, who speaks absolutely for both of them:

> *Dear Miss Lonelyhearts of Miss Lonelyhearts—*
> *I am twenty-six years old and in the newspaper game. Life for me is a desert empty of comfort. I cannot find pleasure in food, drink, or women—nor do the arts give me joy any longer. The Leopard of Discontent walks the streets of my city; the Lion of Discouragement crouches outside the walls of my citadel. All is desolation and a vexation of spirit. I feel like hell. How can I believe, how can I have faith in this day and age? Is it true that the greatest scientists believe again in you?*
> *I read your column and like it very much. There you once wrote: 'When the salt has lost its savour, who shall savour it again?' Is the answer: 'None but the Saviour?'*
> *Thanking you very much for a quick reply, I remain yours truly,*
> *A Regular Subscriber*

"I feel like hell," the Miltonic "Myself am Hell," is Shrike's credo, and West's.

III

What is the relation of Shrike to West's rejected Jewishness? The question may seem illegitimate to many admirers of West, but it acquires considerable force in the context of the novel's sophisticated yet unhistorical Gnosticism. The way of nihilism means, according to Scholem, "to free oneself of all laws, conventions, and religions, to adopt every conceivable attitude and to reject it, and to follow one's leader step for step into the abyss." Scholem is paraphrasing the demonic Jacob Frank, an eighteenth-century Jewish Shrike who brought the Sabbatian messianic movement to its final degradation. Frank would have recognized something of his own negations and nihilistic fervor in the closing passages that form a pattern in West's four novels:

His body screamed and shouted as it marched and uncoiled; then, with one heaving shout of triumph, it fell back quiet.

The army that a moment before had been thundering in his body retreated slowly—victorious, relieved.
(*The Dream Life of Balso Snell*)

While they were struggling, Betty came in through the street door. She called to them to stop and started up the stairs. The cripple saw her cutting off his escape and tried to get rid of the package. He pulled his hand out. The gun inside the package exploded and Miss Lonelyhearts fell, dragging the cripple with him. They both rolled part of the way down the stairs.
(*Miss Lonelyhearts*)

"Alas, Lemuel Pitkin himself did not have this chance, but instead was dismantled by the enemy. His teeth were pulled out. His eye was gouged from his head. His thumb was removed. His scalp was torn away. His leg was cut off. And, finally, he was shot through the heart.

"But he did not live or die in vain. Through his martyrdom the National Revolutionary Party triumphed, and by that triumph this country was delivered from sophistication, Marxism and International Capitalism. Through the National Revolution its people were purged of alien diseases and America became again American."

"Hail the martyrdom in the Bijou Theater!" roar Shagpoke's youthful hearers when he is finished.

"Hail, Lemuel Pitkin!"

"All hail, the American Boy!"
(*A Cool Million*)

He was carried through the exit to the back street and lifted into a police car. The siren began to scream and at first he thought he was making the noise himself. He felt his lips with his hands. They were clamped tight. He knew then it was the siren. For some reason this made him laugh and he began to imitate the siren as loud as he could.
(*The Day of the Locust*)

All four passages mutilate the human image, the image of God that normative Jewish tradition associates with our origins. "Our forefathers were always talking, only what good did it do them and what did they accomplish? But we are under the burden of silence," Jacob Frank said.

What Frank's and West's forefathers always talked about was the ultimate forefather, Adam, who would have enjoyed the era of the Messiah, had he not sinned. West retains of tradition only the emptiness of the fallen image, the scattered spark of creation. The screaming and falling body, torn apart and maddened into a siren-like laughter, belongs at once to the American Surrealist poet, Balso Snell; the American Horst Wessel, poor Lemuel Pitkin; to Miss Lonelyhearts, the Whitmanian American Christ; and to Tod Hackett, painter of the American apocalypse. All are nihilistic versions of the mutilated image of God, or of what the Jewish Gnostic visionary, Nathan of Gaza, called the "thought-less" or nihilizing light.

IV

West was a prophet of American violence, which he saw as augmenting progressively throughout our history. His satirical genius, for all its authentic and desperate range, has been defeated by American reality. Shagpoke Whipple, the Calvin Coolidge-like ex-President who becomes the American Hitler in *A Cool Million*, talks in terms that West intended as extravagant, but that now can be read all but daily in our newspapers. Here is Shagpoke at his best, urging us to hear what the dead Lemuel Pitkin has to tell us:

> "Of what is it that he speaks? Of the right of every American boy to go into the world and there receive fair play and a chance to make his fortune by industry and probity without being laughed at or conspired against by sophisticated aliens."

I turn to today's *New York Times* (March 29, 1985) and find there the text of a speech given by our President:

> But may I just pause here for a second and tell you about a couple of fellows who came to see me the other day, young men. In 1981, just four years ago, they started a business with only a thousand dollars between them and everyone told them they were crazy. Last year their business did a million and a half dollars and they expect to do two and a half million this year. And part of it was because they had the wit to use their names productively. Their business is using their names, the Cain and Abell electric business.

Reality may have triumphed over poor West, but only because he, doubtless as a ghost, inspired or wrote these Presidential remarks. The

Times reports, sounding as deadpan as Shrike, on the same page (B4), that the young entrepreneurs brought a present to Mr. Reagan. " 'We gave him a company jacket with Cain and Abell, Inc. on it,' Mr. Cain said." Perhaps West's ghost now writes not only Shagpokian speeches, but the very text of reality in our America.

George Orwell

(1903–1950)

1984

THERE IS AN EQUIVOCAL IRONY TO READING, AND WRITING, ABOUT George Orwell in 1986. I have just reread *1984*, *Animal Farm*, and many of the essays for the first time in some years, and I find myself lost in an interplay of many contending reactions, moral and aesthetic. Orwell, aesthetically considered, is a far better essayist than a novelist. Lionel Trilling, reviewing *1984*, in 1949, praised the book, with a singular moral authority:

> The whole effort of the culture of the last hundred years has been directed toward teaching us to understand the economic motive as the irrational road to death, and to seek salvation in the rational and the planned. Orwell marks a turn in thought; he asks us to consider whether the triumph of certain forces of the mind, in their naked pride and excess, may not produce a state of things far worse than any we have ever known. He is not the first to raise the question, but he is the first to raise it on truly liberal or radical grounds, with no intention of abating the demand for a just society, and with an overwhelming intensity and passion. This priority makes his book a momentous one.

The book remains momentous; perhaps it always will be so. But there is nothing intrinsic to the book that will determine its future importance. Its very genre will be established by political, social, economic events. Is it satire or science fiction or dystopia or countermanifesto? Last week I read newspaper accounts of two recent speeches, perorations delivered by President Reagan and by Norman Podhoretz, each favorably citing Orwell.

The President, awarding medals to Senator Barry Goldwater and Helen Hayes, among others, saw them as exemplars of Orwell's belief in freedom and individual dignity, while the sage Podhoretz allowed himself to observe that Orwell would have become a neoconservative had he but survived until this moment. Perhaps irony, however equivocal, is inadequate to represent so curious a posthumous fate as has come to the author of *Homage to Catalonia*, a man who went to Barcelona to fight for the Party of Marxist Unity and the Anarcho-Syndicalists.

V.S. Pritchett and others were correct in describing Orwell as the best of modern pamphleteers. A pamphlet certainly can achieve aesthetic eminence; "tracts and pamphlets" is a major genre, particularly in Great Britain, where its masters include Milton, Defoe, Swift, Dr. Johnson, Burke, Blake, Shelley, Carlyle, Ruskin, and Newman. Despite his celebrated mastery of the plain style, it is rather uncertain that Orwell has joined himself to that company. I suspect that he is closer to the category that he once described as "good bad books," giving Harriet Beecher Stowe's *Uncle Tom's Cabin* as a supreme instance. Aesthetically considered, 1984 is very much the *Uncle Tom's Cabin* of our time, with poor Winston Smith as Uncle Tom, the unhappy Julia as little Eva, and the more-than-sadistic O'Brien as Simon Legree. I do not find O'Brien to be as memorable as Simon Legree, but then that is part of Orwell's point. We have moved into a world in which our torturers also have suffered a significant loss of personality.

II

Orwell's success as a prophet is necessarily a mixed one, since his relative crudity as a creator of character obliges us to read *1984* rather literally. What works best in the novel is its contextualization of all the phrases it has bequeathed to our contemporary language, though whether to *the* language is not yet certain. Newspeak and doublethink, "War Is Peace," "Freedom Is Slavery," "Ignorance Is Strength," "Big Brother Is Watching You," the Thought Police, the Two Minutes Hate, the Ministry of Truth, and all the other Orwellian inventions that are now wearisome clichés, are restored to some force, though little freshness, when we encounter them where they first arose.

Unfortunately, in itself that does not suffice. Even a prophetic pamphlet requires eloquence if we are to return to it and find ourselves affected at least as much as we were before. *1984* can hurt you a single time, and most likely when you are young. After that, defensive laughter becomes the aesthetic problem. Rereading *1984* can be too much like watching a really persuasive horror movie; humor acquires the validity of health. Contemporary reviewers, even Trilling, were too overwhelmed by the book's relevance to apprehend its plain badness as narrative or Orwell's total inability to represent even a curtailed human personality or moral character. Mark Schorer's response in the *New York Times Book Review* may have seemed appropriate on June 12, 1949, but its hyperboles now provoke polite puzzlement:

> No real reader can neglect this experience with impunity. He will be moved by Smith's wistful attempts to remember a different kind of life from his. He will make a whole new discovery of the beauty of love between man and woman, and of the strange beauty of landscape in a totally mechanized world. He will be asked to read through pages of sustained physical and psychological pain that have seldom been equaled and never in such quiet, sober prose. And he will return to his own life from Smith's escape into living death with a resolution to resist power wherever it means to deny him his individuality, and to resist for himself the poisonous lures of power.

Would it make a difference now if Orwell had given his book the title "1994"? Our edge of foreboding has vanished when we contemplate the book, if indeed we ought to regard it as a failed apocalypse. Yet all apocalypses, in the literary sense, are failed apocalypses, so that if they fade, the phenomenon of literary survival or demise clearly takes precedence over whatever status social prophecy affords. The limits of Orwell's achievement are clarified if we juxtapose it directly to the authentic American apocalypses of our time: Faulkner's *As I Lay Dying*, Nathanael West's *Miss Lonelyhearts*, Thomas Pynchon's *Gravity's Rainbow*. Why do they go on wounding us, reading after reading, while *1984* threatens to become a period piece, however nightmarish? It would be absurdly unfair to look at *1984* side by side with Kafka and Beckett; Orwell was in no way an aspirant after the sublime, however demonic or diminished. But he was a satirist, and in *1984* a kind of phantasmagoric realist. If his O'Brien is not of the stature of the unamiable Simon Legree, he is altogether nonexistent as a Satanic rhetorician if we attempt to bring him into the company of West's Shrike.

Can a novel survive praise that endlessly centers upon its author's humane disposition, his indubitable idealism, his personal honesty, his political courage, his moral nature? Orwell may well have been the exemplary and representative Socialist intellectual of our time (though Raymond Williams, the crucial Marxist literary critic in Great Britain, definitely does not think so). But very bad men and women have written superb novels, and great moralists have written unreadable ones. *1984* is neither superb nor unreadable. If it resembles the work of a precursor figure, that figure is surely H.G. Wells, as Wyndham Lewis shrewdly realized. Wells surpasses Orwell in storytelling vigor, in pungency of characterization, and in imaginative invention, yet Wells now seems remote and Orwell remains very close. We are driven back to what makes *1984* a good bad book: relevance. The book substitutes for a real and universal fear: that in the political and economic area, the dreadful is still about to happen. Yet the book again lacks a defense against its own blunderings into the ridiculous. As social prophecy, it is closer to Sinclair Lewis's now forgotten *It Can't Happen Here* than to Nathanael West's still hilarious *A Cool Million*, where Big Brother, under the name of Shagpoke Whipple, speaks uncannily in the accents shared by Calvin Coolidge and Ronald Reagan. Why could not Orwell have rescued his book by some last touch of irony or by a valid invocation of the satiric Muse?

III

What Max Horkheimer and T.W. Adorno grimly called the Culture Industry has absorbed Orwell, and his *1984* in particular. Is this because Orwell retains such sentimentalities or soft idealisms as the poignance of true love? After all, Winston and Julia are terrorized out of love by brute pain and unendurable fear; no one could regard them as having been culpable in their forced abandonment of one another. This is akin to Orwell's fantastic and wholly unconvincing hope that the proles might yet offer salvation, a hope presumably founded upon the odd notion that Oceania lets eighty-five percent of its population go back to nature in the slums of London and other cities. Love and the working class are therefore pretty much undamaged in Orwell's vision. Contrast Pynchon's imaginative "paranoia" in *Gravity's Rainbow*, where all of us, of whatever social class, live in the Zone which is dominated by the truly paranoid System, and where authentic love can be represented only as sado-masochism. There is a Counterforce in *Gravity's Rainbow* that fights the System, but it is ineffectual, farcical, and can be animated only by the peculiar ideology that Pynchon calls sado-anarchism, an ideology that the Culture Industry cannot absorb, and that I suspect Adorno gladly would have embraced.

I don't intend this introduction as a drubbing or trashing of Orwell and *1984*, and *Gravity's Rainbow*, being an encyclopedic prose epic, is hardly a fair agonist against which *1984* should be matched. But the aesthetic badness of *1984* is palpable enough, and I am a good enough disciple of the divine Oscar Wilde to wonder if an aesthetic inadequacy really can be a moral splendor? Simon Legree beats poor old Uncle Tom to death, and O'Brien pretty well wrecks Winston Smith's body and then reduces him to supposed ruin by threatening him with some particularly nasty and hungry rats. Is Uncle Tom's Cabin actually a moral achievement, even if Harriet Beecher Stowe hastened both the Civil War and the Emancipation Proclamation? Is *1984* a moral triumph, even if it hastens a multiplication of neoconservatives?

The defense of a literary period piece cannot differ much from a defense of period pieces in clothes, household objects, popular music, movies, and the lower reaches of the visual arts. A period piece that is a political and social polemic, like *Uncle Tom's Cabin* and *1984*, acquires a curious charm of its own. What partly saves *1984* from Orwell's overliteralness and failures in irony is the strange archaism of its psychology and rhetoric:

> He paused for a few moments, as though to allow what he had been saying to sink in.
>
> "Do you remember," he went on, "writing in your diary, 'Freedom is the freedom to say that two plus two make four'?"
>
> "Yes," said Winston.
>
> O'Brien held up his left hand, its back toward Winston, with the thumb hidden and the four fingers extended.
>
> "How many fingers am I holding up, Winston?"
>
> "Four."
>
> "And if the Party says that it is not four but five—then how many?"
>
> "Four."
>
> The word ended in a gasp of pain. The needle of the dial had shot up to fifty-five. The sweat had sprung out all over Winston's body. The air tore into his lungs and issued again in deep groans which even by clenching his teeth he could not stop. O'Brien watched him, the four fingers still extended. He drew back the lever. This time the pain was only slightly eased.
>
> "How many fingers, Winston?"
>
> "Four."
>
> The needle went up to sixty.
>
> "How many fingers, Winston?"
>
> "Four! Four! What else can I say? Four!"
>
> The needle must have risen again, but he did not look at it. The heavy, stern face and the four fingers filled his vision. The fingers

stood up before his eyes like pillars, enormous, blurry, and seeming to vibrate, but unmistakably four.

"How many fingers, Winston?"

"Four! Stop it, stop it! How can you go on? Four! Four!"

"How many fingers, Winston?"

"Five! Five! Five!"

"No, Winston, that is no use. You are lying. You still think there are four. How many fingers, please?"

"Four! Five! Four! Anything you like. Only stop it, stop the pain!"

Abruptly he was sitting up with O'Brien's arm round his shoulders. He had perhaps lost consciousness for a few seconds. The bonds that had held his body down were loosened. He felt very cold, he was shaking uncontrollably. His teeth were chattering, the tears were rolling down his cheeks. For a moment he clung to O'Brien like a baby, curiously comforted by the heavy arm round his shoulders. He had the feeling that O'Brien was his protector, that the pain was something that came from outside, from some other source, and that it was O'Brien who would save him from it.

"You are a slow learner, Winston," said O'Brien gently.

"How can I help it?" he blubbered. "How can I help seeing what is in front of my eyes? Two and two are four."

"Sometimes. Winston. Sometimes they are five. Sometimes they are three. Sometimes they are all of them at once. You must try harder. It is not easy to become sane."

He laid Winston down on the bed. The grip on his limbs tightened again, but the pain had ebbed away and the trembling had stopped, leaving him merely weak and cold. O'Brien motioned with his head to the man in the white coat, who had stood immobile throughout the proceedings. The man in the white coat bent down and looked closely into Winston's eyes, felt his pulse, laid an ear against his chest, tapped here and there; then he nodded to O'Brien.

"Again," said O'Brien.

The pain flowed into Winston's body. The needle must be at seventy, seventy-five. He had shut his eyes this time. He knew that the fingers were still there, and still four. All that mattered was somehow to stay alive until the spasm was over. He had ceased to notice whether he was crying out or not. The pain lessened again. He opened his eyes. O'Brien had drawn back the lever.

"How many fingers, Winston?"

"Four. I suppose there are four. I would see five if I could. I am trying to see five."

"Which do you wish: to persuade me that you see five, or really to see them?"

"Really to see them."

"Again," said O'Brien.

If we took this with high seriousness, then its offense against any persuasive mode of representation would make us uneasy. But it *is* a grand period piece, parodying not only Stalin's famous trials, but many theologically inspired ordeals before the advent of the belated Christian heresy that Russian Marxism actually constitutes. Orwell was a passionate moralist, and an accomplished essayist. The age drove him to the composition of political romance, though he lacked nearly all of the gifts necessary for the writer of narrative fiction. *1984* is an honorable aesthetic failure, and perhaps time will render its crudities into so many odd period graces, remnants of a vanished era. Yet the imagination, as Wallace Stevens once wrote, is always at the end of an era. Lionel Trilling thought that O'Brien's torture of Winston Smith was "a hideous parody on psychotherapy and the Platonic dialogues." Thirty-seven years after Trilling's review, the scene I have quoted above seems more like self-parody, as though Orwell's narrative desperately sought its own reduction, its own outrageous descent into the fallacy of believing that only the worst truth about us can be the truth.

Orwell was a dying man as he wrote the book, suffering the wasting away of his body in consumption. D.H. Lawrence, dying the same way, remained a heroic vitalist, as his last poems and stories demonstrate. But Lawrence belonged to literary culture, to the old, high line of transcendental seers. What wanes and dies in *1984* is not the best of George Orwell, not the pamphleteer of *The Lion and the Unicorn* nor the autobiographer of *Homage to Catalonia* nor the essayist of *Shooting an Elephant*. That Orwell lived and died an independent Socialist, hardly Marxist but really a Spanish Anarchist, or an English dissenter and rebel of the line of Cromwell and of Cromwell's celebrators, Milton and Carlyle. *1984* has the singular power, not aesthetic but social, of being the product of an age, and not just of the man who set it down.

Animal Farm

Animal Farm is a beast fable, more in the mode of Jonathan Swift's savage indignation than in Chaucer's gentler irony. George Orwell was startled when the book became children's literature, rather like *Gulliver's Travels* before it. And yet that is what saves the book aesthetically; *Nineteen*

Eighty-Four is very thin when compared to *Animal Farm*. Boxer the cart-horse, Clover the mare, and Benjamin the donkey all have considerably more personality than does Winston Smith, the protagonist of *Nineteen Eighty-Four*. Fable necessarily suited Orwell better than the novel, because he was essentially an essayist and a satirist, and not a storyteller. *Animal Farm* is best regarded as a fusion of satirical political pamphlet and beast fable, but since the collapse of the Soviet Union, the historical aspect of the book necessarily has faded. The end of Stalinism removed the immediacy of *Animal Farm*, which now survives only by its pathos. Children are the book's best audience because of its simplicity and directness. Something in Orwell entertained a great nostalgia for an older, rural England, one that preceded industrial blight. The vision of Old Major, the boar who prophesies the transformation of Manor Farm into *Animal Farm*, is essentially Orwell's own ideal, and has a childlike quality that is very poignant.

It is very difficult to understand the psychology of any of the animals in Orwell's fantasy. How does Snowball (Trotsky) differ from Napoleon (Stalin) in his motivations? We cannot say; either Orwell does not know or he does not care. We are moved by poor Boxer, who works himself to death for the supposed common good, but we could not describe Boxer's personality. Even as a fabulist, Orwell has acute limitations; he could not create distincts. He was a considerable moralist, who passionately championed individuality, but he had no ability to translate that passion into imagining separate individuals. The creatures of *Animal Farm* compare poorly to those of Kenneth Grahame's *The Wind in the Willows*. Toad of Toad Hall and Badger are sustained literary characters; Boxer and Benjamin are not. Whether *Animal Farm* truly can survive as children's literature seems to me rather doubtful, in the longest perspective.

Still, the narrative of *Animal Farm* is ingenious, and its twists retain a certain charm. The plain decency of Orwell's outlook still comes through clearly, and his fable's force is benign. Like his hero, the sublime Charles Dickens, Orwell was a "free intelligence," and his liberal passion against ideology is now his best legacy. Our era is again ideological, and *Animal Farm* now would make most sense if it satirized not the Soviet tyranny but the political correctness that blights our universities. Those resenters of individuality, for whom "social energies" are everything and personal genius is nothing, are now our Napoleons and Snowballs. Orwell's liberalism finds no home in Departments of Resentment. He should have lived to revise *Animal Farm* into a satire upon the way we teach now; and upon the way most fail to learn Orwell's longing for "free intelligence," which would find little to encourage it in English-speaking higher education as we approach the Millennium. Liberal humanism and individualist anarchism are condemned by our current gender-and-power dogmatists in the name of a new conformism. Its motto might well be: "All animals are resentful but some are more resentful than others."

Graham Greene

(1904–1991)

THOUGH HE IS MUCH HONORED AS AN EMINENT CONTEMPORARY NOVELIST, it is not yet clear that Graham Greene will survive among the greater masters of fiction, rather than among the masterful writers of adventure stories. Henry James and Joseph Conrad seem less relevant to their disciple's achievement than do Rider Haggard, John Buchan, and even perhaps Edgar Wallace. The true comparison may he to Robert Louis Stevenson, since neither author is demeaned by such an association, though I myself prefer Stevenson. Greene, always generous and candid, paid tribute to what he called "Rider Haggard's Secret."

> How seldom in the literary life do we pause to pay a debt of gratitude except to the great or the fashionable, who are like those friends that we feel do us credit. Conrad, Dostoevsky, James, yes, but we are too ready to forget such figures as A.E.W. Mason, Stanley Weyman, and Rider Haggard, perhaps the greatest of all who enchanted us when we were young. Enchantment is just what this writer exercised; he fixed pictures in our minds that thirty years have been unable to wear away: the witch Gagool screaming as the rock-door closed and crushed her; Eric Bright-eyes fighting his doomed battle; the death of the tyrant Chaka; Umslopagaas holding the queen's stairway in Milosis. It is odd how many violent images remain like a prophecy of the future; the love passages were quickly read and discarded from the mind, though now they seem oddly moving (as when Queen Nyleptha declares her love to Sir Henry Curtis in the midnight hall), a little awkward and stilted perhaps, but free from ambiguities and doubts, and with the worn rhetoric of honesty.

To be "free from ambiguities and doubts and, with the worn rhetoric of honesty," to express love—that is the hopeless nostalgia of Greene's protagonists, and of Greene himself. Greene tells us that he had a happy childhood, and a sad adolescence, and what he finds in Rider Haggard is a childhood vision, rather than an adolescent fantasy. Of Haggard's life, Greene observed that it "does not belong to the unhappy world of letters; there are no rivalries, jealousies, nerve storms, no toiling miserably against the grain, no ignoble ambivalent vision which finds a kind of copy even in personal grief." I would observe, rather sadly, that what Greene describes so negatively here is indeed an inescapable aspect of the creative lives of strong writers. Inescapable because they have chosen to overcome mortality through, in, and by their work, and such an overcoming requires rivalries—with figures of the past, the present, the future.

"Rider Haggard's Secret" turns out to be, according to Greene, what Greene least led us to expect: an obsessive fear of mortality, expressed in an anecdote concerning Haggard and the much stronger Kipling:

> There are some revealing passages in his friendship with Rudyard Kipling. Fishing together for trout at Bateman's, these two elderly men—in some ways the most successful writers of their time, linked together to their honour even by their enemies ("the prose that knows no reason, and the unmelodious verse," "When the Rudyards cease from Kipling, and the Haggards ride no more"), suddenly let out the secret. "I happened to remark," Haggard wrote, "that I thought this world was one of the hells. He replied he did not think—he was certain of it. He went on to show that it had every attribute of hell; doubt, fear, pain, struggle, bereavement, almost irresistible temptations springing from the nature with which we are clothed, physical and mental suffering, etc., ending in the worst fate man can devise for man, Execution."

Kipling's nihilism, akin to Walter Pater's, was partly assuaged by Kipling's surprisingly Paterian devotion to stories for stories' sake, poems for poems' sake. Greene's novels and entertainments have one pervasive fault: tendentiousness. We are never given a narrative for the narrative's sake, or the representation of a person for that person's sake. I have read no stranger criticism of Henry James than that ventured by Graham Greene, who has contrived to persuade himself that James was essentially a religious novelist. *The Portrait of a Lady* is scarcely *The Heart of the Matter*, or *The Wings of the Dove* a version of *The End of the Affair*, yet Greene seems not to know the difference. His Henry James is hardly the son of

Henry James, Senior, disciple of Emerson and of Swedenborg, but rather someone "near in spirit ... to the Roman Catholic Church." This is too high-handed to be funny, and too inaccurate to be excusable. As a critic, Greene remains a minor ephebe of T.S. Eliot, the "Are you worthy to be damned?" man, author of such tractates as *After Strange Gods* and *The Idea of a Christian Society*. In his egregious essay, "Henry James: The Religious Aspect," Greene approvingly quotes Eliot on our glorious capacity for damnation, in order to suggest that James shared Eliot's enthusiasm for so sublime a human possibility:

> human nature is not despicable in Osmond or Densher, for they are both capable of damnation. "It is true to say," Mr. Eliot has written in an essay on Baudelaire, "that the glory of man is his capacity for salvation; it is also true to say that his glory is his capacity for damnation. The worst that can be said of most male-factors, from statesmen to thieves, is that they are not men enough to be damned." This worst cannot be said of James's characters: both Densher and the prince have on their faces the flush of the flames.

That is rather severe, and leads me to an apprehension that in Greene's hell there are many mansions. It leads Greene to the exuberant conclusion that Henry James "is only just prevented from being as explic-itly religious as Dostoevsky by the fact that neither a philosophy nor a creed ever emerged from his religious sense." James and Dostoyevski? Why not James and G.K. Chesterton? Or James and Evelyn Waugh? My questions are extravagant, but not so extravagant as Greene's, since he real-ly means to ask the question: James and Graham Greene? There is a ready answer which is the critical truth about Greene, despite his journalistic idolators. *The Heart of the Matter*, *The Power and the Glory*, *The Quiet American*, and Greene's other ambitious novels cannot sustain a close rereading, and are destroyed by being compared to the major novels of Henry James and Joseph Conrad. Greens is most himself only in the com-pany of Anthony Hope's *The Prisoner of Zenda*, Rider Haggard's *She* and *King Solomon's Mines*, John Buchan's *The Thirty-Nine Steps*, Edgar Wallace's *The Four Just Men*, and more lastingly, Stevenson's *Weir of Hermiston*, *Treasure Island*, *Kidnapped*. Of Greene's "entertainments," the most famous are *The Third Man* and *Our Man in Havana*, but the best seem to me the early group that includes *This Gun for Hire*, *The Confidential Agent*, and *The Ministry of Fear*. These are finer achievements than anything by John Le Carré, Greene's haunted disciple, and they have retained a curious freshness that might turn out to be as permanent as the quality of Stevenson's romances.

Greene's most vital "entertainments" have a Jacobean quality, reminding us of his intense admiration for the tragedies of John Webster, the thrillers of their age, together with the plays of Marston, Ford, and Tourneur. The motto for Greene's thrillers could be Webster's: "I hunted this night-piece, and it was my best." This could also he the epigraph to what seems to me Greene's most enduring novel, *Brighton Rock* (1938), which is on the border between an entertainment like *This Gun for Hire* and his "Catholic novels," such as *The Power and the Glory* and its companions. Crudely worked out as the book is, *Brighton Rock* has a Websterian intensity that is displaced by piety and moralizing, however inverted, in Greene's most ambitious attempts to be the Catholic Henry James or Joseph Conrad of his own time.

Brighton Rock

Brighton Rock's protagonist, the seventeen-year-old thug Pinkie, is at once the most memorable and the most vicious representation of a person in Greene's fiction. He may be regarded, ironically, as a considerable advance in malevolence over his immediate forerunner, the killer Raven in *This Gun for Hire*. Contrast the deaths of Raven and Pinkie, and you see that the essential Graham Greene came into full existence during 1936–38:

> Raven watched him with bemused eyes, trying to take aim. It wasn't a difficult shot, but it was almost as if he had lost interest in killing. He was only aware of a pain and despair which was more like a complete weariness than anything else. He couldn't work up any sourness, any bitterness, at his betrayal. The dark Weevil under the storm of frozen rain flowed between him and any human enemy. "Ah, Christ that it were possible," but he had been marked from his birth for this end, to be betrayed in turn by everyone until every avenue into life was safely closed: by his mother bleeding in the basement, by the chaplain at the home, by the soft kids who had left it with him, by the shady doctor off Charlotte Street. How could he have expected to escape the commonest betrayal of all, to go soft on a skirt? Even Kite would have been alive now if it hadn't been for a skirt. They all went soft at some time or another: Penrith and Carter, Jossy and Ballard, Barker and the Great Dane. He took aim slowly, absentmindedly, with a curious humility, with almost a sense of companionship in

his loneliness: the trooper and Mayhew. They had all thought at one time or another that their skirt was better than other men's skirts, that there was something exalted in *their* relation. The only problem when you were once born was to get out of life more neatly and expeditiously than you had entered it. For the first time the idea of his mother's suicide came to him without bitterness, as he fixed his aim at the long reluctant last and Saunders shot him in the back through the opening door. Death came to him in the form of unbearable pain. It was as if he had to deliver this pain as a woman delivers a child, and he sobbed and moaned in the effort. At last it came out of him, and he followed his only child into a vast desolation.

A voice called sharply "Pinkie" and she heard somebody splashing in the puddles. Footsteps ran ... she couldn't tell where. It seemed to her that this must be news, that this must make a difference. She couldn't kill herself when this might mean good news. It was as if somewhere in the darkness the will which had governed her hand relaxed, and all the hideous forces of self-preservation came flooding back. It didn't seem real that she had really intended to sit there and press the trigger. "Pinkie," the voice called again, and the splashing steps came nearer. She pulled the car door open and flung the revolver far away from her towards the damp scrub.

In the light from the stained glass she saw Dallow and the woman—and a policeman who looked confused as if he didn't quite know what was happening. Somebody came softly round the car behind her and said, "Where's that gun? Why don't you shoot? Give it me."

She said, "I threw it away."

The others approached cautiously like a deputation. Pinkie called out suddenly in a breaking childish voice, "You bloody squealer, Dallow."

"Pinkie," Dallow said, "it's no use. They got Prewitt." The policeman looked ill-at-ease like a stranger at a party.

"Where's that gun?" Pinkie said again. He screamed with hate and fear, "My God, have I got to have a massacre?"

She said, "I threw it away."

She could see his face indistinctly as it leant in over the little dashboard light. It was like a child's, badgered, confused, betrayed: fake years slipped away—he was whisked back towards the unhappy playground. He said, "You little ..." he didn't finish—the deputation approached, he left her, diving into his pocket for something. "Come on, Dallow," he said, "you bloody squealer," and put his hand up. Then she couldn't tell what happened: glass—some-where—broke, he screamed and she saw his face—steam. He screamed and screamed, with his hands up to his eyes; he turned and ran; she saw a police baton at his feet and broken glass. He looked half his size, doubled up in appalling agony: it was as if the flames had literally got him and he shrank—shrank into a school-boy flying in panic and pain, scrambling over a fence, running on.

"Stop him," Dallow cried: it wasn't any good: he was at the edge, he was over: they couldn't even hear a splash. It was as if he'd been withdrawn suddenly by a hand out of any existence—past or present, whipped away into zero—nothing.

Both scenes are Jacobean, and very much in the mode of Webster, but the second, from *Brighton Rock*, has learned better the aesthetic lesson that the poet of *The White Devil* and *The Duchess of Malfi* teaches so superbly. Webster's hero-villains—Bosola, Flamineo, Ludovico—flare out sublimely as they die. They are indeed the best night-pieces that they have limned, *and they know it*, which is a peculiarly negative glory, to them and to us, but a glory nevertheless. Raven dies badly; the Jacobean groundlings would have shrugged him off as a weak wastrel. If your only issue is your death, if your only mark is "to get out of life more neatly and expeditiously than you had entered it," why then you have no greatness, no bad eminence that might be called the stuff of tragedy in which someone high, however hol-low, falls downward and outward into the dark backward and abyss of time.

But Pinkie, unlike Raven, dies in the mode of Webster's sublime Bosola. Pinkie has the true Jacobean hero-villain's inverted Puritanism: disgust for human sexuality, hatred of mere life, "his virginity straightened in him like sex." Born a Catholic, Pinkie is somewhere between a repressed Jansenist and a crazed Manichaean, always ready for one death after anoth-er, a more than Eliotic believer in the glory of his own damnation. Quite literally, Pinkie dies a flaming death as he falls into nothingness, his face on fire as he goes off the cliff, memorably consumed by his own hatred of every existence, his own most of all.

The strength of *Brighton Rock*, which is likely to assure its perma-nence, is that it is all one thing, Greene's shot out of hell, as it were. Pinkie persuades us as I believe that the nameless whiskey priest in *The Power and the Glory* and Scobie the colonial policeman in *The Heart of the Matter* cannot. The problem is hardly what several critics have asserted it to be:

the difficulty of representing vexed goodness or flawed sainthood as contrasted with the absolute moral depravity of the young devil Pinkie.
Rather, it is the aesthetic question of just what Greene's creative exuberance is, and just how such gusto contrives to manifest itself in the representation of human qualities. Scobie and the whiskey priest move Greene,
but they do not enchant him. His imagination is moved by Pinkie, because
only Pinkie sustains the vision of evil that kindled Greene into narrative art
in his most vital years as a story-teller.

However out of sympathy one is with the Eliotic mode of neo-
Christianity, and I cannot imagine a critic who cares less for its aesthetic
embodiment than my sad self, *Brighton Rock* has the strength of pathos that
overcomes the critic's resentment of theological tendentiousness. I think
always, in this regard, of the end of part six of *Brighton Rock*, where Pinkie
has "such a vision of the street / as the street hardly understands," a vision
deeply indebted to Eliot's superb "preludes," with their "notion of some
infinitely gentle / Infinitely suffering thing," and their phantasmagoria in
which "the worlds revolve like ancient women / Gathering fuel in vacant
lots." Pinkie sees what can be seen, and experiences the "horrified fascination" of the damned, as they contemplate the saved:

> He was taken by a craving for air, walked softly to the door. In the
> passage he could see nothing: it was full of the low sound of
> breathing—from the room he had left, from Dallow's room. He
> felt like a blind man watched by people he couldn't see. He felt his
> way to the stair-head and on down to the hall, step by step, creak-
> ingly. He put out his hand and touched the telephone, then with
> his arm outstretched made for the door. In the street the lamps
> were out, but the darkness no longer enclosed between four walls
> seemed to thin out across the vast expanse of a city. He could see
> basement railings, a cat moving, and, reflected on the dark sky, the
> phosphorescent glow of the sea. It was a strange world: he had
> never been alone in it before. He had a deceptive sense of freedom
> as he walked softly down towards the Channel.
>   The lights were on in Montpellier Road. Nobody was about, and
> an empty milk bottle stood outside a gramophone shop; far down
> were the illuminated clock tower and the public lavatories. The air
> was fresh like country air. He could imagine he had escaped. He
> put his hands for warmth into his trouser-pockets and felt a scrap
> of paper which should not have been there. He drew it out—a
> scrap torn from a notebook—big, unformed, stranger's writing. He
> held it up into the grey light and read—with difficulty. "I love you,

Pinkie. I don't care what you do. I love you for ever. You've been good to me. Wherever you go, I'll go too." She must have written it while he talked to Cubitt and slipped it into his pocket while he slept. He crumpled it in his fist: a dustbin stood outside a fishmonger's—then he held his hand. An obscure sense told him you never knew—it might prove useful one day.

He heard a whisper, looked sharply round, and thrust the paper back. In an alley between two shops, an old woman sat upon the ground; he could just see the rotting and discoloured face: it was like the sight of damnation. Then he heard the whisper, "Blessed art thou among women," saw the grey fingers fumbling at the beads. This was not one of the damned: he watched with horrified fascination: this was one of the saved.

This was Greene's true sense of the heart of the matter, and his abiding vision of what could touch him, with full authenticity, as the power and the glory. His more celebrated novels fade already into the continuum of literary tradition. *Brighton Rock*, a terrible crystal of a book, may well be *The White Devil* of our era.

Robert Penn Warren

(1905-1989)

I

ROBERT PENN WARREN, BORN APRIL 24, 1905, IN GUTHRIE, KENTUCKY, AT the age of eighty our most eminent man of letters. That truism is vitalized by his extraordinary persistence of development into a great poet. A reader thinks of the handful of poets triumphant in their later or last phases: Browning, Hardy, Yeats, Stevens, Warren. Indeed, "Myth of Mountain Sunrise," the final poem among the new work in this fifth Warren *Selected Poems*, will remind some readers of Browning's marvelous "Prologue" to *Asolando*, written when the poet was seventy-seven. Thinking back fifty years to the first time he saw Asolo, a village near Venice, Browning burns through every sense of loss to a final transcendence:

How many a year, my Asolo,
Since—one step just from sea to land—
I found you, loved yet feared you so—
For natural objects seemed to stand
Palpably fire-clothed! No—

"God is it who transcends," Browning ends by asserting. Warren, older even than Browning was, also ruggedly remains a poet of immanence, of something indwelling and pervasive, though not necessarily sustaining, that can be sensed in, for example, a mountain sunrise:

The curdling agony of interred dark strives dayward, in stone
                                        strives though
No light here enters, has ever entered but

In ageless age of primal flame. But look! All mountains want
slowly to bulge outward extremely. The leaf, whetted on light,
will cut
Air like butter. Leaf cries: "I feel my deepest filament in dark
rejoice.
I know the density of basalt has a voice."

Two primal flames, Browning's and Warren's, but at the close of
"Myth of Mountain Sunrise" we read not "God is it who transcends" but
"The sun blazes over the peak. That will be the old tale told." The epigraph to the new section of this *Selected Poems* is from Warren's favorite
theologian, St. Augustine: "Will ye not now after that life is descended
down to you, will not you ascend up to it and live?" One remembers another epigraph Warren took from the *Confessions*, for the book of poems *Being
Here* (1980): "I thirst to know the power and nature of time." Warren now
has that knowledge, and his recent poems show him ascending up to living
in the present, in the presence of time's cumulative power. Perhaps no single new poem here quite matches the extraordinary group of visions and
meditations in his previous work that includes "Red-Tail Hawk and Pyre
of Youth," "Heart of Autumn," "Evening Hawk," "Birth of Love," "The
Leaf," "Mortmain," "To a Little Girl, One Year Old, in a Ruined Fortress,"
and so many more. But the combined strength of the eighty-five pages of
new poems that Warren aptly calls *Altitudes and Extensions* is remarkable,
and extends the altitudes at which our last poet of the Sublime continues
to live, move and have his being.

II

Warren's first book was *John Brown: The Making of a Martyr* (1929). I
have just read it, for the first time, and discovered, without surprise, that it
made me very unhappy. The book purports to be history, but is Southern fiction of Allen Tate's ideology, and portrays Brown as a murderous nihilist, fit
hero for the equally repellent Ralph Waldo Emerson. Indeed I find it difficult to decide, after suffering the book, whether the young Warren loathed
Brown or Emerson more. Evidently both Brown and his intellectual sup-
porter seemed to represent for Warren an emptiness making ruthless and
passionate attempts to prove itself fullness. But *John Brown*, if read as a first
work of fiction, does presage the Warren of *Night Rider* (1939), his first published novel, which I have just re-read with great pleasure.

Night Rider is an exciting and remorseless narrative, wholly characteristic of what were to be Warren's prime virtues as a novelist: good story-

telling and intensely dramatic unfolding of the moral character of his doom-eager men and women. Mr. Munn, upon whom *Night Rider* centers, is as splendidly unsympathetic as the true Warren heroes continued to be: Jerry Calhoun and Slim Sarrett in *At Heaven's Gate* (1943), Jack Burden and Willie Stark in *All the King's Men* (1946), Jeremiah Beaumont and Cassius Fort in *World Enough and Time* (1950). When Warren's central personages turned more amiable, starting with poor Amantha Starr in *Band of Angels* (1955), the books alas turned much less interesting. This unfortunate phenomenon culminated in Warren's last novel (so far), *A Place to Come To* (1977), which Warren himself ranks with *All the King's Men* and *World Enough and Time*. I wish I could agree, but re-reading *A Place to Come To* confirms an earlier impression that Warren likes his hero, Jed Tewksbury, rather too much. Without some real moral distaste to goad him, Warren tends to lose his narrative drive. I find myself wishing that Tewksbury had in him a touch of what might be called Original John Brown.

Warren's true precursor, as a novelist, is not Faulkner but Conrad, the dominant influence upon so many American novelists of Warren's generation. In one of his best critical essays, written in 1951 on Conrad's *Nostromo*, Warren gave an unwitting clue to why all his own best work, as a novelist, already was over:

> There is another discrepancy, or apparent discrepancy, that we must confront in any serious consideration of Conrad—that between his professions of skepticism and his professions of faith....
>
> Cold unconcern, an "attitude of perfect indifference" is, as he says in the letter to Galsworthy, "the part of creative power." But this is the same Conrad who speaks of Fidelity and the human communion, and who makes Kurtz cry out in the last horror and Heyst come to his vision of meaning in life. And this is the same Conrad who makes Marlow of "Heart of Darkness" say that what redeems is the "idea only" ....
>
> It is not some, but all, men who must serve the "idea." The lowest and the most vile creature must, in some way, idealize his existence in order to exist, and must find sanctions outside himself ....

Warren calls this a reading of Conrad's dual temperament, skepticism struggling with a last-ditch idealism, and remarks, much in T.S. Eliot's spirit:

We must sometimes force ourselves to remember that the act of creation is not simply a projection of temperament, but a criticism and a purging of temperament.

This New Critical shibboleth becomes wholly Eliotic if we substitute the word "personality" for the word "temperament." As an analysis of the moral drama in Conrad's best novels, and in *Nostromo* in particular, this is valuable, but Warren is not Conrad, and like his poetic and critical precursor, Eliot, Warren creates by projecting temperament, not by purging it. There is no "cold unconcern," no "attitude of perfect indifference," no escape from personality in Eliot, and even more nakedly Warren's novels and poems continually reveal his passions, prejudices, convictions. Conrad is majestically enigmatic, beyond ideology; Warren, like Eliot, is an ideologue, and his temperament is far more ferocious than Eliot's.

What Warren rightly praises in Conrad is not to be found in Warren's own novels, with the single exception of *All the King's Men*, which does balance skepticism against belief just adroitly enough to ward off Warren's moralism. *World Enough and Time*, Warren's last stand as a major novelist, is an exuberant work marred finally by the author's singular fury at his own creatures. As a person who forgives himself nothing, Warren abandons Conradian skepticism and proceeds to forgive his hero and heroine nothing. Re-reading *World Enough and Time*, I wince repeatedly at what the novelist inflicts upon Jeremiah Beaumont and Rachel Jordan. Warren, rather like the Gnostics' parody of Jehovah, punishes *his* Adam and Eve by denying them honorable or romantic deaths. Their joint suicide drug turns into an emetic, and every kind of degradation subsequently is heaped upon them. Warren, who can be a superb ironist in his novels as well as in his poetry, nevertheless so loves the world that he will forgive it nothing; and a poet can make more of such a position than a novelist.

All the King's Men

I first read *All the King's Men* as a Cornell undergraduate in the late 1940s, under the tutelage of a great teacher, William M. Sale, who remarked of the book that it had nearly every possible flaw, but that it was also unmistakably part of the permanent tradition or canon of the American novel. Sale's canonical judgment, uttered only two or three years after the novel's first publication (1946) has been confirmed. Rereading the book now, nearly forty years after first studying it, I marvel at its triumph over the author's restless temperament. Too passionate a moralist, perhaps too great a visionary, to cultivate the patience of a novelist, Warren instead became a major poet, probably our finest since the death of Wallace Stevens. *All the King's Men* is likely to be his principal legacy after the extraordinary poetry he has written in the two decades since 1966.

Remembering *All the King's Men*, I had thought of it as Willie Stark's story; rereading it, I see that it is far more Jack Burden's than it is Stark's. Warren is ambivalent enough towards Stark; in regard to Burden, "ambivalence" seems almost too weak a term for Warren's stance. The author nearly identifies himself with his narrator, yet that identification is dialectical in the mode of what Freud called "negation." Burden is Warren's burden: a cognitive return of the repressed while the affective aspect of repression continues. The mind of Robert Penn Warren at meridian is introjected as Jack Burden, while the passional life of Warren, domain of the drives, is projected and so spit out as Burden, morally rejected by his creator, in a way that Willie Stark is not, if only because Stark is stark—strong and active—where Burden is weak and passive, a burden to himself and to others.

Yet he remains, to me, Warren's most interesting fictive person, perhaps because he is and is not Warren, the portrait of the artist as a failed (momentarily) youngish man. One of the hidden splendors, tawdry yet fascinating, of the novel is Burden's failed first marriage (as it will prove to be, since at the end, he does marry Anne Stanton). The truth of the first marriage emerges with a fine clarity in the famous sentence that ends Burden's account of it: "Good-bye, Lois, and I forgive you for everything I did to you." The bitterness is only towards the self, for only the self existed. When he cannot bring the past alive into the present, then Burden becomes a pure solipsist, aware neither of neighbors nor of the sun.

It is the peculiar strength of Willie Stark that he breaks through Burden's defenses sufficiently so that the novel's narrator becomes at most an imperfect solipsist, brilliantly capable of telling an intensely dramatic story. *All the King's Men*'s prime literary virtue is the wonderfully old-fashioned one of being compulsively readable. That this is wholly due to Willie Stark is unquestionable. He is one of the last authentic hero-villains of the high Jacobean mode, worthy of a twentieth-century John Webster, or of Faulkner, or even of Conrad. Burden's relation to Stark is not that of Conrad's Marlow to Kurtz in *Heart of Darkness*, or of Faulkner's Quentin to Sutpen in *Absalom, Absalom!*, but rather is that of Warren himself to the historical figure of the Kingfish, Huey Long of Louisiana. This necessarily has caused some confusions in the critical apprehension of *All the King's Men*. Burden's barely repressed love for Stark, essentially filial in nature, does not represent Warren's hidden fondness for the most persuasive of our country's native Fascists, our Franco or Mussolini, as it were. Rather,

Stark's fascination for Warren is dramatic, and aesthetic, even as it is for us as Warren's readers.

The movement from the factual, historical Huey Long to the fictive Willie Stark is epitomized by the difference between Long's "I know the hearts of the people because I have not colored my own" and Stark's "My study is the heart of the people." Willie is pithier than Huey, and even more persuasive. He is the answer to a universal Oedipus complex, an answer conveyed most poignantly in the novel's central moment, the final meeting between Jack Burden and his crucial father-substitute, Willie Stark, dying but still the Boss:

> He lifted the forefinger and the next finger of his right hand, which lay prone on the sheet, in an incipient salute, then let them drop. The strength of the muscles which held his mouth twisted gave out, too, and the grin slid off his face and the weight of flesh sagged back.
>
> I stood up close to the bed and looked down at him, and tried to think of something to say. But my brain felt as juiceless as an old sponge left out in the sun a long time.
>
> Then he said, in something a little better than a whisper, "I wanted to see you, Jack."
>
> "I wanted to see you, too, Boss."
>
> For a minute he didn't speak, but his eyes looked up at me, with the light still flickering in them. Then he spoke: "Why did he do it to me?"
>
> "Oh, God damn it," I burst out, very loud, "I don't know. "
>
> The nurse looked warningly at me.
>
> "I never did anything to him," he said.
>
> "No, you never did."
>
> He was silent again, and the flicker went down in his eyes. Then, "He was all right. The Doc."
>
> I nodded.
>
> I waited, but it began to seem that he wasn't going to say any more. His eyes were on the ceiling and I could scarcely tell that he was breathing. Finally, the eyes turned toward me again, very slowly, and I almost thought that I could hear the tiny painful creak of the balls in their sockets. But the light flickered up again. He said, "It might have been all different, Jack."
>
> I nodded again.
>
> He roused himself more. He even seemed to be straining to lift his head from the pillow. "You got to believe that," he said hoarsely.

The nurse stepped forward and looked significantly at me.

"Yes," I said to the man on the bed.

"You got to," he said again. "You got to believe that."

"All right."

He looked at me, and for a moment it was the old strong, probing, demanding glance. But when the words came this time, they were very weak. "And it might even been different yet," he whispered. "If it hadn't happened, it might—have been different—even yet."

He barely got the last words out, he was so weak.

The nurse was making signals to me.

I reached down and took the hand on the sheet. It felt like a piece of jelly.

"So long, Boss," I said. "I'll be seeing you."

He didn't answer, and I wasn't even sure that there was recognition in the eyes now. I turned away and went out.

It is the father as man-of-action saying farewell to his true son as intellectual or spiritual discerner, and trying, somewhat heroically, to give a final blessing by way of expiation. For Willie Stark has been a castrating father, and in ways that transcended his taking Anne Stanton away from Jack Burden. "It might have—been different—even yet" is more than a political reference or ruined social prophecy. As a reference to the buried relationship between Stark and Burden, it implies a belated recognition of the burden of a better fatherhood, and better filial vision, than either figure has known before. That seems the profoundest meaning of Burden's final rumination that concludes the novel:

We shall come back, no doubt, to walk down the Row and watch young people on the tennis courts by the clump of mimosas and walk down the beach by the bay, where the diving floats lift gently in the sun, and on out to the pine grove, where the needles thick on the ground will deaden the footfall so that we shall move among trees as soundlessly as smoke. But that will be a long time from now, and soon now we shall go out of the house and go into the convulsion of the world, out of history into history and the awful responsibility of Time. To go out of history into history is to take up Time's awful responsibility of the agon between fathers and sons, never confronted by Stark and Burden, who evaded their mutual recognition until it was too late.

Samuel Beckett

(1906-1989)

Molloy, Malone Dies, The Unnamable

JONATHAN SWIFT, SO MUCH THE STRONGEST IRONIST IN THE LANGUAGE AS to have no rivals, wrote the prose masterpiece of the language in *A Tale of a Tub*. Samuel Beckett, as much the legitimate descendant of Swift as he is of his friend, James Joyce, has written the prose masterpieces of the language in this century, sometimes as translations from his own French originals. Such an assertion does not discount the baroque splendors of *Ulysses* and *Finnegans Wake*, but prefers to them the purity of *Murphy* and *Watt*, and of Beckett's renderings into English of *Malone Dies*, *The Unnamable* and *How It Is*. Unlike Swift and Joyce, Beckett is only secondarily an ironist and, despite his brilliance at tragicomedy, is something other than a comic writer. His Cartesian dualism seems to me less fundamental than his profoundly Schopenhauerian vision. Perhaps Swift, had he read and tolerated Schopenhauer, might have turned into Beckett.

A remarkable number of the greatest novelists have found Schopenhauer more than congenial: one thinks of Turgenev, Tolstoy, Zola, Hardy, Conrad, Thomas Mann, even of Proust. As those seven novelists have in common only the activity of writing novels, we may suspect that Schopenhauer's really horrifying system helps a novelist to do his work. This is not to discount the intellectual and spiritual persuasiveness of Schopenhauer. A philosopher who so deeply affected Wagner, Nietzsche, Wittgenstein and (despite his denials) Freud, hardly can be regarded only as a convenient aid to story-tellers and story-telling. Nevertheless, Schopenhauer evidently stimulated the arts of fiction, but why? Certain it is that we cannot read *The World As Will and Representation* as a work of fiction. Who could bear it as fiction? Supplementing his book, Schopenhauer characterizes the Will to live:

> Here also life presents itself by no means as a gift for enjoyment, but as a task, a drudgery to be performed; and in accordance with this we see, in great and small, universal need, ceaseless cares, constant pressure, endless strife, compulsory activity, with extreme exertion of all the powers of body and mind ... All strive, some planning, others acting; the tumult is indescribable. But the ultimate aim of it all, what is it? To sustain ephemeral and tormented individuals through a short span of time in the most fortunate case with endurable want and comparative freedom from pain, which, however, is at once attended with ennui; then the reproduction of this race and its striving. In this evident disproportion between the trouble and the reward, the will to live appears to us from this point of view, if taken objectively, as a fool, or subjectively, as a delusion, seized by which everything living works with the utmost exertion of its strength for something that is of no value. But when we consider it more closely, we shall find here also that it is rather a blind pressure, a tendency entirely without ground or motive.

Hugh Kenner suggests that Beckett reads Descartes as fiction. Beckett's fiction suggests that Beckett reads Schopenhauer as truth. Descartes as a precursor is safely distant; Joyce was much too close, and *Murphy* and even *Watt* are Joycean books. Doubtless, Beckett turned to French in *Molloy* so as to exorcise Joyce, and certainly, from *Malone Dies* on, the prose when translated back into English has ceased to be Joycean. Joyce is to Beckett as Milton was to Wordsworth. *Finnegans Wake*, like *Paradise Lost*, is a triumph demanding study; Beckett's trilogy, like *The Prelude*, internalizes the triumph by way of the compensatory imagination, in which experience and loss become one. Study does little to unriddle Beckett or Wordsworth. The Old Cumberland Beggar, Michael, Margaret of *The Ruined Cottage*; these resist analysis as do Molloy, Malone, and the Unnamable. Place my namesake, the sublime Poldy, in *Murphy* and he might fit, though he would explode the book. Place him in *Watt*? It cannot be done, and Poldy (or even Earwicker) in the trilogy would be like Milton (or Satan) perambulating about in *The Prelude*.

The fashion (largely derived from French misreaders of German thought) of denying a fixed, stable ego is a shibboleth of current criticism. But such a denial is precisely like each literary generation's assertion that it truly writes the common language rather than a poetic diction. Both stances define modernism, and modernism is as old as Hellenistic Alexandria. Callimachus is as modernist as Joyce, and Aristarchus, like Hugh Kenner, is an antiquarian modernist or modernist antiquarian. Schopenhauer dismissed the ego as an illusion, life as torment, and the universe as nothing, and he rightly credited these insights to that great modernist, the Buddha. Beckett too is as modernist as the Buddha, or as Schopenhauer, who disputes with Hume the position of the best writer among philosophers since Plato. I laugh sometimes in reading Schopenhauer, but the laughter is defensive. Beckett provokes laughter, as Falstaff does, or in the mode of Shakespeare's clowns.

II

In his early monograph, *Proust*, Beckett cites Schopenhauer's definition of the artistic procedure as "the contemplation of the world independently of the principle of reason." Such more-than-rational contemplation gives Proust those Ruskinian or Paterian privileged moments that are "epiphanies" in Joyce but which Beckett mordantly calls "fetishes" in Proust. Transcendental bursts of radiance necessarily are no part of Beckett's cosmos, which resembles, if anything at all, the Demiurge's creation in ancient Gnosticism. Basilides or Valentinus, Alexandrian heresiarchs, would have recognized instantly the world of the trilogy and of the major plays: *Waiting for Godot, Endgame, Krapp's Last Tape*. It is the world ruled by the Archons, the *kenoma*, non-place of emptiness. Beckett's enigmatic spirituality quests, though sporadically, for a void that is a fulness, the Abyss or *pleroma* that the Gnostics called both forefather and foremother. Call this a natural rather than a revealed Gnosticism in Beckett's case, but Gnosticism it is nevertheless. Schopenhauer's quietism is at last not Beckett's, which is to say that for Beckett, as for Blake and for the Gnostics, the Creation and the Fall were the same event.

The young Beckett, bitterly reviewing a translation of Rilke into English, memorably rejected Rilke's transcendental self-deceptions, where the poet mistook his own tropes as spiritual evidences:

> Such a turmoil of self-deception and naif discontent gains nothing in dignity from that prime article of the Rilkean faith, which provides for the interchangeability of Rilke and God ... He has the fidgets, a disorder which may very well give rise, as it did with Rilke on occasion, to poetry of a high order. But why call the fidgets God, Ego, Orpheus and the rest?

In 1938, the year that *Murphy* was belatedly published, Beckett declared his double impatience with the language of transcendence and with the transcendence of language, while intimating also the imminence of the swerve away from Joyce in the composition of *Watt* (1942–44):

> At first it can only be a matter of somehow finding a method by which we can represent this mocking attitude towards the word, through words. In this dissonance between the means and their use it will perhaps become possible to feel a whisper of that final music or that silence that underlies All.
>
> With such a program, in my opinion, the latest work of Joyce has nothing whatever to do. There it seems rather to be a matter of an apotheosis of the word. Unless perhaps Ascension to Heaven and Descent to Hell are somehow one and the same.

As a Gnostic imagination, Beckett's way is Descent, in what cannot be called a hope to liberate the sparks imprisoned in words. Hope is alien to Beckett's mature fiction, so that we can say its images are Gnostic but not its program, since it lacks all program. A Gnosticism without potential transcendence is the most negative of all possible negative stances, and doubtless accounts for the sympathetic reader's sense that every crucial work by Beckett necessarily must be his last. Yet the grand paradox is that lessness never ends in Beckett.

III

"Nothing is got for nothing." That is the later version of Emerson's law of Compensation, in the essay "Power" of *The Conduct of Life*. Nothing is got for nothing even in Beckett, this greatest master of nothing. In the progression from *Murphy* through *Watt* and the trilogy on to *How It Is* and the briefer fictions of recent years, there is loss for the reader as well as gain. The same is true of the movement from *Godot*, *Endgame* and *Krapp's Last Tape* down to the short plays of Beckett's current and perhaps final phase. A wild humor abandons Beckett, or is transformed into a comedy for which we seem not to be ready. Even an uncommon reader can long for those marvelous Pythagoreans, Wylie and Neary, who are the delight of *Murphy*, or for the sense of the picturesque that makes a last stand in *Molloy*. Though the mode was Joyce's, the music of Wylie and Neary is Beckett's alone:

> "These are dark sayings," said Wylie.
> Neary turned his cup upside down.

"Needle," he said, "as it is with the love of the body, so with the friendship of the mind, the full is only reached by admittance to the most retired places. Here are the pudenda of my psyche."

"Cathleen," cried Wylie.

"But betray me," said Neary; "and you go the way of Hippasos."

"The Adkousmatic, I presume," said Wylie. "His retribution slips my mind."

"Drowned in a puddle," said Neary, "for having divulged the incommensurability of side and diagonal."

"So perish all babblers," said Wylie....

"Do not quibble," said Neary harshly. "You saved my life. Now palliate it."

"I greatly fear," said Wylie, "that the syndrome known as life is too diffuse to admit of palliation. For every symptom that is eased, another is made worse. The horse leech's daughter is a closed system. Her quantum of wantum cannot vary."

"Very prettily put," said Neary.

One can be forgiven for missing this, even as one surrenders these easier pleasures for the more difficult pleasures of *How It Is*:

> my life above what I did in my life above a little of everything tried everything then gave up no worse always a hole a ruin always a crust never any good at anything not made for that farrago too complicated crawl about in comers and sleep all I wanted I got it nothing left but go to heaven

The Sublime mode, according to a great theorist, Angus Fletcher, has "the direct and serious function of destroying the slavery of pleasure." Beckett is certainly the strongest Western author living in the year 1985, the last survivor of the sequence that includes Proust, Kafka and Joyce. It seems odd to name Beckett, most astonishing of minimalists, as a representative of the Sublime mode, but the isolation and terror of the High Sublime return in the catastrophe creations of Beckett, in that vision Fletcher calls "catastrophe as a gradual grinding down and slowing to a dead stop." A Sublime that moves towards silence necessarily relies upon a rhetoric of waning lyricism, in which the entire scale of effects is transformed, as John Hollander notes:

> Sentences, phrases, images even, are the veritable arias in the plays and the later fiction. The magnificent rising of the kite at the end

of *Murphy* occurs in a guarded but positive surge of ceremonial song, to which he will never return.

Kafka's Hunter Gracchus, who had been glad to live and was glad to die, tells us that: "I slipped into my winding sheet like a girl into her marriage dress. I lay and waited. Then came the mishap." The mishap, a moment's error on the part of the death-ship's pilot, moves Gracchus from the heroic world of romance to the world of Kafka and of Beckett, where one is neither alive nor dead. It is Beckett's peculiar triumph that he disputes with Kafka the dark eminence of being the Dante of that world. Only Kafka, or Beckett, could have written the sentence in which Gracchus sums up the dreadfulness of his condition: "The thought of helping me is an illness that has to be cured by taking to one's bed." Murphy might have said that; Malone is beyond saying anything so merely expressionistic. The "beyond" is where Beckett's later fictions and plays reside. Call it the silence, or the abyss, or the reality beyond the pleasure principle, or the metaphysical or spiritual reality of our existence at last exposed, beyond further illusion. Beckett cannot or will not name it, but he has worked through to the art of representing it more persuasively than anyone else.

Richard Wright

(1908-1960)

Native Son

WHAT REMAINS OF RICHARD WRIGHT'S WORK IF WE APPLY TO IT ONLY aesthetic standards of judgment? This is to assume that strictly aesthetic standards exist, and that we know what they are. Wright, in *Native Son*, essentially the son of Theodore Dreiser, could not rise always even to Dreiser's customarily bad level of writing. Here is Bigger Thomas, condemned to execution, at the start of his death vigil:

> In self-defense he shut out the night and day from his mind, for if he had thought of the sun's rising and setting, of the moon or the stars, of clouds or rain, he would have died a thousand deaths before they took him to the chair. To accustom his mind to death as much as possible, he made all the world beyond his cell a vast gray land where neither night nor day was, peopled by strange men and women whom he could not understand, but with those lives he longed to mingle once before he went.
>
> He did not eat now; he simply forced food down his throat without tasting it, to keep the gnawing pain of hunger away, to keep from feeling dizzy. And he did not sleep; at intervals he closed his eyes for a while, no matter what the hour, then opened them at some later time to resume his brooding. He wanted to be free of everything that stood between him and his end, him and the full and terrible realization that life was over without meaning, without anything being settled, without conflicting impulses being resolved.

If we isolate these paragraphs, then we do not know the color or background of the man awaiting execution. The intense sociological pathos of Wright's narrative vanishes, and we are left in the first paragraph with an inadequate rhetoric: "shut out the night and day," "died a thousand deaths," "a vast gray land," "strange men and women," "with those lives he longed to mingle." Yet the second paragraph is even more unsatisfactory, as the exact word is nowhere: "gnawing pain of hunger," "resume his brooding," "full and terrible realization," "conflicting impulses being resolved." Wright's narrative requires from him at this point some mode of language that would individuate Bigger's dread, that would catch and fix the ordeal of a particular black man condemned by a white society. Unfortunately, Wright's diction does not allow us even to distinguish Bigger's horror from any other person's apprehension of judicial murder. Nor does Bigger's own perspective enter into Wright's rhetorical stance. The problem is not so much Wright's heritage from Dreiser's reductive naturalism as it is, plainly stated, a bad authorial ear.

It is rather too late to make so apparently irrelevant an observation, since Wright has become a canonical author, for wholesome societal purposes, with which I am happy to concur. Rereading *Native Son* or *Black Boy* cannot be other than an overdetermined activity, since Wright is a universally acknowledged starting point for black literature in contemporary America. Canonical critics of Wright speak of him as a pioneer, a man of rare courage, as a teacher and forerunner. None of this can or should be denied. I myself would praise him for will, force, and drive, human attributes that he carried just over the border of aesthetic achievement, without alas getting very far once he had crossed over. His importance transcends the concerns of a strictly literary criticism, and reminds the critic of the claims of history, society, political economy, and the longer records of oppression and injustice that history continues to scant.

II

Bigger Thomas can be said to have become a myth without first having been a convincing representation of human character and personality. Wright listed five "Biggers" he had encountered in actuality, five violent youths called "bad Niggers" by the whites. The most impressive, Bigger No. 5, was a knife-wielding, prideful figure "who always rode the Jim Crow streetcars without paying and sat wherever he pleased." For this group of precursors of his own protagonist in *Native Son*, Wright gave us a moving valediction:

The Bigger Thomases were the only Negroes I know of who consistently violated the Jim Crow laws of the South and got away with it, at least for a sweet brief spell. Eventually, the whites who restricted their lives made them pay a terrible price. They were shot, hanged, maimed, lynched, and generally hounded until they were either dead or their spirits broken.

Wright concluded this same "Introduction" to *Native Son* with his own vision of the United States as of March 7, 1940:

I feel that I'm lucky to be alive to write novels today, when the whole world is caught in the pangs of war and change. Early American writers, Henry James and Nathaniel Hawthorne, complained bitterly about the bleakness and flatness of the American scene. But I think that if they were alive, they'd feel at home in modern America. True, we have no great church in America; our national traditions are still of such a sort that we are not wont to brag of them; and we have no army that's above the level of mercenary fighters; we have no group acceptable to the whole of our country upholding certain humane values; we have no rich symbols, no colorful rituals. We have only a money-grubbing, industrial civilization. But we do have in the Negro the embodiment of a past tragic enough to appease the spiritual hunger of even a James; and we have in the oppression of the Negro a shadow athwart our national life dense and heavy enough to satisfy even the gloomy broodings of a Hawthorne. And if Poe were alive, he would not have to invent horror; horror would invent him.

The citation of James, Hawthorne, and Poe is gratuitous, and the perspective upon the United States in the months preceding the fall of France lacks authority and precision, even in its diction. But the dense and heavy shadow athwart our national life indubitably was there, always had been there, and for many is there still. That shadow is Richard Wright's mythology, and his embryonic strength. He was not found by Henry James, or by Hawthorne, or by Poe, and scarcely would have benefitted by such a finding. A legitimate son of Theodore Dreiser, he nevertheless failed to write in *Native Son* a *Sister Carrie* or a new version of *An American Tragedy*. The reality of being a gifted young black in the United States of the thirties and forties proved too oppressive for the limited purposes of a narrative fiction. Rereading *Native Son* is an experience of renewing the dialectical awareness of history and society, but is not in itself an aesthetic experience.

And yet, I do not think that *Native Son*, and its reception, present us with a merely aesthetic dilemma. In the "afterword" to the current paperback reprint of *Native Son*, one of Wright's followers, John Reilly, defends Bigger Thomas by asserting that: "The description of Mary's murder makes clear that the white world is the cause of the violent desires and reactions" that led Bigger to smother poor Mary. I would think that what the description makes clear enough is that Bigger is indeed somewhat overdetermined, but to ascribe the violence of his desires and reactions to any context whatsoever is to reduce him to the status of a replicant or of a psychopathic child. The critical defenders of *Native Son* must choose. Either Bigger Thomas is a responsible consciousness, and so profoundly culpable, or else only the white world is responsible and culpable, which means however that Bigger ceases to be of fictive interest and becomes an ideogram, rather than a persuasive representation of a possible human being. Wright, coming tragically early in what was only later to become his own tradition, was not able to choose, and so left us with something between an ideological image, and the mimesis of an actuality.

III

I remember reading *Black Boy: A Record of Childhood and Youth* when Wright's autobiographical book first appeared, in 1945. A boy of fifteen, I was frightened and impressed by the book. Reading it again after more than forty years, the old reactions do not return. Instead, I am compelled to ask the Nietzschean question: who is the interpreter, and what power does he seek to gain over the text, whether it be his own text or the text of his life? Wright, an anguished and angry interpreter, wrote a far more political work in *Black Boy* than in *Native Son*. What passes for a Marxist analysis of the relation between society and Bigger Thomas seems to me always a kind of authorial afterthought in *Native Son*. In *Black Boy*, this pseudo-Marxism usurps the narrator's function, and the will-to-power over interpretation becomes the incessant undersong of the entire book. Contrast the opening and closing paragraphs of *Black Boy*:

> One winter morning in the long-ago, four-year-old days of my life
> I found myself standing before a fireplace, warming my hands
> over a mound of glowing coals, listening to the wind whistle past
> the house outside. All morning my mother had been scolding me,
> telling me to keep still, warning me that I must make no noise.
> And I was angry, fretful, and impatient. In the next room Granny
> lay ill and under the day and night care of a doctor and I knew that

I would be punished if I did not obey. I crossed restlessly to the window and pushed back the long fluffy white curtains—which I had been forbidden to touch—and looked yearningly out into the empty street. I was dreaming of running and playing and shouting, but the vivid image of Granny's old, white, wrinkled, grim face, framed by a halo of tumbling black hair, lying upon a huge feather pillow, made me afraid.

With ever watchful eyes and bearing scars, visible and invisible, I headed North, full of a hazy notion that life could be lived with dignity, that the personalities of others should not be violated, that men should be able to confront other men without fear or shame, and that if men were lucky in their living on earth they might win some redeeming meaning for their having struggled and suffered here beneath the stars.

The young man going North, scarred and watchful, in search of redemption by meaning, has remarkably little connection with the four-year-old boy, impatient for the dream of running, playing, and shouting. Wright's purpose is to explain his fall from impulse into care, and his inevitable explanation will be social and historical. Yet much that he loses is to his version of the family romance, as he himself describes it, and some of what vanishes from him can be ascribed, retrospectively, to a purely personal failure; in him the child was not the father of the man.

What survives best in *Black Boy*, for me, is Wright's gentle account of his human rebirth, as a writer. At eighteen, reading Mencken, he learns audacity, the agonistic use of language, and an aggressive passion for study comes upon him. After reading the *Main Street* of Sinclair Lewis, he is found by the inevitable precursor in Theodore Dreiser:

> "That's deep stuff you're reading, boy."
> "I'm just killing time, sir."
> "You'll addle your brains if you don't watch out."
>
> I read Dreiser's *Jennie Gerhardt* and *Sister Carrie* and they revived in me a vivid sense of my mother's suffering; I was overwhelmed. I grew silent, wondering about the life around me. It would have been impossible for me to have told anyone what I derived from these novels, for it was nothing less than a sense of life itself. All my life had shaped me for the realism, the naturalism of the modern novel, and I could not read enough of them.
>
> Steeped in new moods and ideas, I bought a ream of paper and

tried to write; but nothing would come, or what did come was flat beyond telling. I discovered that more than desire and feeling were necessary to write and I dropped the idea. Yet I still wondered how it was possible to know people sufficiently to write about them? Could I ever learn about life and people? To me, with my vast ignorance, my Jim Crow station in life, it seemed a task impossible of achievement. I now knew what being a Negro meant. I could endure the hunger. I had learned to live with hate. But to feel that there were feelings denied me, that the very breath of life itself was beyond my reach, that more than anything else hurt, wounded me. I had a new hunger.

Dreiser's taut visions of suffering women renew in Wright his own memories of his mother's travails, and make him one of those authors for whom the purpose of the poem (to cite Wallace Stevens) is the mother's face. There is an Oedipal violence in Wright that sorts strangely with his attempt to persuade us, and himself, that all violence is socially overdetermined. *Black Boy*, even now, performs an ethical function for us by serving as a social testament, as Wright intended it to do. We can hope that, some day, the book will be available to us as a purely individual testament, and then, may read very differently.

William Golding

(1911-1993)

Lord of the Flies

POPULAR AS IT CONTINUES TO BE, *LORD OF THE FLIES* ESSENTIALLY IS A period piece. Published in 1954, it is haunted by William Golding's service in the Royal Navy (1940–45), during the Second World War. The hazards of the endless battles of the North Atlantic against German submarines culminated in Golding's participation in D-Day, the Normandy invasion of June 6, 1944. Though *Lord of the Flies* is a moral parable in the form of a boys' adventure story, in a deeper sense it is a war story. The book's central emblem is the dead parachutist, mistaken by the boys for the Beast Beelzebub, diabolic Lord of the Flies. For Golding, the true shape of Beelzebub is a pig's head on a stick, and the horror of war is transmuted into the moral brutality implicit (in his view) in most of us. The dead parachutist, in Golding's own interpretation, represents History, one war after another, the dreadful gift adults keep presenting to children. Golding's overt intention has some authority, but not perhaps enough to warrant our acceptance of so simplistic a symbol.

Judging *Lord of the Flies* a period piece means that one doubts its long-range survival, if only because it is scarcely a profound vision of evil. Golding's first novel, *Lord of the Flies* does not sustain a critical comparison with his best narratives: *The Inheritors, Pincher Martin* (his masterpiece), *Free Fall*, and the much later *Darkness Visible*. All these books rely upon nuance, irony, intelligence, and do not reduce to a trite moral allegory. Golding acknowledged the triteness, yet insisted upon his fable's truth:

> Man is a fallen being. He is gripped by original sin. His nature is sinful and his state perilous. I accept the theology and admit the

triteness; but what is trite is true; and a truism can become more than a truism when it is a belief passionately held.

Passion is hardly a standard of measurement in regard to truth. *Lord of the Flies* aspires to be a universal fable, but its appeal to American school-children partly inheres in its curious exoticism. Its characters are implausible because they are humorless; even one ironist among them would explode the book. The Christ-like Simon is particularly unconvincing; Golding does not know how to portray the psychology of a saint. Whether indeed, in his first novel, he knew how to render anyone's psychology is disputable. His boys are indeed British private school boys: regimented, subjected to vicious discipline, and indoctrinated with narrow, restrictive views of human nature. Golding's long career as a teacher at Bishop Wordsworth's School in Salisbury was a kind of extension of his Naval service: a passage from one mode of indoctrination and strict discipline to another. The regression to savagery that marks *Lord of the Flies* is a peculiarly British scholastic phenomenon, and not a universal allegory of moral depravity.

By indicating the severe limitations of Golding's first novel, I do not intend to deny its continued cultural value. Any well-told tale of a reversion to barbarism is a warning against tendencies in many groups that may become violent, and such a warning remains sadly relevant as we approach Millennium. Though in itself a non-event, the year 2000 will arouse some odd expectations among extremists, particularly in the United States, most millennial of nations. Golding's allegorical fable is no *Gulliver's Travels*; the formidable Swiftian irony and savage intellectualism are well beyond Golding's powers. *Literary* value has little sway in *Lord of the Flies*. Ralph, Piggy, Simon, and Jack are ideograms, rather than achieved fictive characters. Compare them to Kipling's Kim, and they are sadly diminished; invoke Huck Finn, and they are reduced to names on a page. *Lord of the Flies* matters, not in or for itself, but because of its popularity in an era that continues to find it a useful admonition.

Albert Camus

(1913-1960)

The Stranger

SARTRE REMAINS THE CLASSIC COMMENTATOR UPON CAMUS, WHOM HE assimilated to Pascal, to Rousseau, and to other French moralists, "the precursors of Nietzsche." To Sartre, Camus was "very much at peace within disorder," and so *The Stranger* was "a classical work, an orderly work, composed about the absurd and against the absurd." Shrewdly, Sartre finally assigned *The Stranger* not to the company of Heidegger or Hemingway, but to that of *Zadig* and *Candide*, the tales of Voltaire. Rereading Camus's short novel after forty years, I marvel at Sartre's keen judgment, and find it very difficult to connect my present impression of the book with my memory of how it seemed then. What Germaine Brée termed its heroic and humanistic hedonism seems, with the years, to have dwindled into an evasive hedonism, uncertain of its own gestures. The bleak narrative retains its Hemingwayesque aura, but the narrator, Meursault, seems even smaller now than he did four decades ago, when his dry disengagement had a certain novelty. Time, merciless critic, has worn *The Stranger* rather smooth, without however quite obliterating the tale.

René Girard, the most Jansenist of contemporary critics, "retried" *The Stranger*, and dissented from the verdict of "innocent" pronounced by Camus upon Meursault:

> If supernatural necessity is present in *L'Étranger*, why should Meursault alone come under its power? Why should the various characters in the same novel be judged by different yardsticks? If the murderer is not held responsible for his actions, why should the judges be held responsible for theirs?

Girard is reacting to an unfortunate comment by Camus himself: "A man who does not cry at the funeral of his mother is likely to be sentenced to death." In Girard's judgment, the quest of Camus was to convince us that judgment of guilt is always wrong. Girard calls this an "egotistical Manichaeism" and convicts Camus of "literary solipsism," particularly in one devastating sentence: "Camus betrays solipsism when he writes *L'Étranger* just as Meursault betrays it when he murders the Arab." On this reading, the "innocent murder" is a metaphor for the creative process. Meursault is a bad child and Camus becomes as a child again when he writes Meursault's novel. Girard considers the novel an aesthetic success, but a morally immature work, since Meursault himself is guilty of judgment, though Camus wishes his protagonist not to be judged. "The world in which we live is one of perpetual judgment," Girard reminds us, in Pascalian vein. For Girard, the figures comparable to Meursault are Dostoevsky's Raskolnikov and Dimitri Karamazov. For Camus, those figures presumably were Kafka's Joseph K, and K the land surveyor. Either comparison destroys *The Stranger*, which has trouble enough competing with Malraux and Hemingway. Against Girard, I enter my own dissent. *The Stranger* is barely able to sustain an aesthetic dignity and certainly is much slighter than we thought it to be. But it is not morally flawed or inconsistent. In its cosmos, guilt and innocence are indistinguishable, and Jewish or Christian judgments are hopelessly irrelevant. Meursault is not, as Girard says, a juvenile delinquent, but an inadequate consciousness dazed by the sun, overwhelmed by a context that is too strong for him:

> On seeing me, the Arab raised himself a little, and his hand went to his pocket. Naturally, I gripped Raymond's revolver in the pocket of my coat. Then the Arab let himself sink back again, but without taking his hand from his pocket. I was some distance off, at least ten yards, and most of the time I saw him as a blurred dark form wobbling in the heat haze. Sometimes, however, I had glimpses of his eyes glowing between the half-closed lids. The sound of the waves was even lazier, feebler, than at noon. But the light hadn't changed; it was pounding as fiercely as ever on the long stretch of sand that ended at the rock. For two hours the sun seemed to have made no progress; becalmed in a sea of molten steel. Far out on the horizon a steamer was passing; I could just make out from the corner of an eye the small black moving patch, while I kept my gaze fixed on the Arab.
>
> It struck me that all I had to do was to turn, walk away, and think no more about it. But the whole beach, pulsing with heat,

was pressing on my back. I took some steps toward the stream. The Arab didn't move. After all, there was still some distance between us. Perhaps because of the shadow on his face, he seemed to be grinning at me.

I waited. The heat was beginning to scorch my cheeks; beads of sweat were gathering in my eyebrows. It was just the same sort of heat as at my mother's funeral, and I had the same disagreeable sensations—especially in my forehead, where all the veins seemed to be bursting through the skin. I couldn't stand it any longer, and took another step forward. I knew it was a fool thing to do; I wouldn't get out of the sun by moving on a yard or so. But I took that step, just one step, forward. And then the Arab drew his knife and held it up toward me, athwart the sunlight.

A shaft of light shot upward from the steel, and I felt as if a long, thin blade transfixed my forehead. At the same moment all the sweat that had accumulated in my eyebrows splashed down on my eyelids, covering them with a warm film of moisture. Beneath a veil of brine and tears my eyes were blinded; I was conscious only of the cymbals of the sun clashing on my skull, and, less distinctly, of the keen blade of light flashing up from the knife, scarring my eyelashes, and gouging into my eyeballs.

Then everything began to reel before my eyes, a fiery gust came from the sea, while the sky cracked in two, from end to end, and a great sheet of flame poured down through the rift. Every nerve in my body was a steel spring, and my grip closed on the revolver. The trigger gave, and the smooth underbelly of the butt jogged my palm. And so, with that crisp, whipcrack sound, it all began. I shook off my sweat and the clinging veil of light. I knew I'd shattered the balance of the day, the spacious calm of this beach on which I had been happy. But I fired four shots more into the inert body, on which they left no visible trace. And each successive shot was another loud, fateful rap on the door of my undoing.

The "absurd" and the "gratuitous" seem wrong categories to apply here. We have a vision of possession by the sun, an inferno that fuses consciousness and will into a single negation, and burns through it to purposes that may exist, but are not human. Gide's Lafcadio, a true absurdist, said he was not curious about events but about himself, while Meursault is not curious about either. What Meursault at the end calls "the benign indifference of the universe" is belied by the pragmatic malevolence of the sun.

The true influence upon *The Stranger* seems to me Melville's *Moby-Dick*, and for the whiteness of the whale Camus substitutes the whiteness of the sun. Meursault is no quester, no Ahab, and Ahab would not have allowed him aboard the *Pequod*. But the cosmos of *The Stranger* is essentially the cosmos of *Moby-Dick*; though in many of its visible aspects Meursault's world might seem to have been formed in love, its invisible spheres were formed in fright. The Jansenist Girard is accurate in finding Gnostic hints in the world of Camus, but not so accurate in judging Camus to possess only a bad child's sense of innocence. Judging Meursault is as wasteful as judging his judges; that blinding light of the sun bums away all judgment.

The Plague

Forty years after its initial publication, Camus's *The Plague* (1947) has taken on a peculiar poignance in the era of our new plague, the ambiguously named AIDS. *The Plague* is a tendentious novel, more so even than *The Stranger*. A novelist requires enormous exuberance to sustain tendentiousness; Dostoevsky had such exuberance, Camus did not. Or a master of evasions, like Kafka, can evade his own compulsions, but Camus is all too interpretable. The darkest comparison would be to Beckett, whose trilogy of *Molloy*, *Malone Dies*, and *The Unnamable* conveys a sense of menace and anguish, metaphysical and psychological, that dwarfs *The Plague*.

Oran, spiritually rejecting the healthy air of the Mediterranean, in some sense brings the Plague upon itself; indeed Oran is the Plague, before the actual infection arrives. That may sound impressive, but constitutes a novelistic blunder, because Camus wants it both ways and cannot make it work either way. Either the relatively innocent suffer an affliction from outside, or the at least somewhat culpable are compelled to suffer the outward sign of their inward lack of grace. Truth doubtless lies in between, in our lives, but to *represent* so mixed a truth in your novel you must be an accomplished novelist, and not an essayist, or writer of quasi-philosophical tales. Dostoevsky dramatized the inwound textures of transcendence and material decay in nearly every event and every personage, while *The Plague* is curiously bland whenever it confronts the necessity of dramatizing anything.

I am unfair in comparing Camus to Beckett, Kafka, Dostoevsky, titanic authors, and it is even more unfair to contrast *The Plague* with Dickens's *A Tale of Two Cities*, since Dickens is very nearly the Shakespeare of novelists. Yet the two books are surprisingly close in vision, structure, theme, and in the relation of language to a reality of overwhelming menace. Camus's Plague is a version of Dickens's Terror, and Dr. Rieux, Rambert,

Father Paneloux, Tarrou, and the volunteer sanitary workers all follow in the path of the noble Carton, since all could proclaim: "It is a far, far better thing that I do, than I have ever done." One can think of the Plague as AIDS, Revolutionary Terror, the Nazi occupation, or what one will, but one still requires persuasive representations of persons, whether in the aggregate or in single individuals.

"Indifference," properly cultivated, can be a stoic virtue, even a mode of heroism, but it is very difficult to represent. Here also Camus fails the contest with Melville or Dostoevsky. Consider a crucial dialogue between Tarrou and Dr. Rieux, both of them authentic heroes, by the standards of measurement of any morality, religion, or societal culture:

> "My question's this," said Tarrou. "Why do you yourself show such devotion, considering you don't believe in God? I suspect your answer may help me to mine."
>
> His face still in shadow, Rieux said that he'd already answered: that if he believed in an all-powerful God he would cease curing the sick and leave that to Him. But no one in the world believed in a God of that sort; no, not even Paneloux, who believed that he believed in such a God. And this was proved by the fact that no one ever threw himself on Providence completely. Anyhow, in this respect Rieux believed himself to be on the right road—in fighting against creation as he found it.
>
> "Ah," Tarrou remarked. "So that's the idea you have of your profession?"
>
> "More or less." The doctor came back into the light.
>
> Tarrou made a faint whistling noise with his lips, and the doctor gazed at him.
>
> "Yes, you're thinking it calls for pride to feel that way. But I assure you I've no more than the pride that's needed to keep me going. I have no idea what's awaiting me, or what will happen when all this ends. For the moment I know this; there are sick people and they need curing. Later on, perhaps, they'll think things over; and so shall I. But what's wanted now is to make them well. I defend them as best I can, that's all."
>
> "Against whom?"
>
> Rieux turned to the window. A shadow-line on the horizon told of the presence of the sea. He was conscious only of his exhaustion, and at the same time was struggling against a sudden, irrational impulse to unburden himself a little more to his companion; an eccentric, perhaps, but who, he guessed, was one of his own kind.

"I haven't a notion, Tarrou; I assure you I haven't a notion. When I entered this profession, I did it 'abstractedly,' so to speak; because I had a desire for it, because it meant a career like another, one that young men often aspire to. Perhaps, too, because it was particularly difficult for a workman's son, like myself. And then I had to see people die. Do you know that there are some who *refuse* to die? Have you ever heard a woman scream 'Never!' with her last gasp? Well, I have. And then I saw that I could never get hardened to it. I was young then, and I was outraged by the whole scheme of things, or so I thought. Subsequently I grew more modest. Only, I've never managed to get used to seeing people die. That's all I know. Yet after all—"

Rieux fell silent and sat down. He felt his mouth dry.

"After all—?" Tarrou prompted softly.

"After all," the doctor repeated, then hesitated again, fixing his eyes on Tarrou, "it's something that a man of your sort can understand most likely, but, since the order of the world is shaped by death, mightn't it be better for God if we refuse to believe in Him and struggle with all our might against death, without raising our eyes toward the heaven where He sits in silence?"

Tarrou nodded.

"Yes. But your victories will never be lasting; that's all." Rieux's face darkened.

"Yes, I know that. But it's no reason for giving up the struggle."

"No reason, I agree. Only, I now can picture what this plague must mean for you."

"Yes. A never ending defeat"

Tarrou stared at the doctor for a moment, then turned and tramped heavily toward the door. Rieux followed him and was almost at his side when Tarrou, who was staring at the floor, suddenly said:

"Who taught you all this, Doctor?"

The reply came promptly:

"Suffering"

"Indifference" to transcendence here is a humanistic protest "in fighting against creation as he found it," a defense of the dying against death. It is a stoicism because Rieux is no longer "outraged by the whole scheme of things," even though he continues to know that "the order of the world is shaped by death." The best aesthetic touch here is the moment when Tarrou and Rieux come to understand one another, each finding the meaning of the Plague to be "a never ending defeat." But this is wasted when, at the conclusion of the passage I have quoted, Rieux utters the banality that "suffering" has taught him his pragmatic wisdom. Repeated rereadings will dim the passage further. "A shadow-line on the horizon told of the presence of the sea." Conrad would have known how to integrate that into his complex Impressionism, but in Camus it constitutes another mechanical manifestation of symbolism, reminding us that Oran opened itself to the Plague by turning its back upon the sea.

Camus was an admirable if confused moralist and the legitimate heir of a long tradition of rational lucidity. He did not write a *Candide* or even a *Zadig*; I cannot recall one humorous moment anywhere in his fiction. *The Stranger* and *The Plague*, like his other fictions, are grand period pieces, crucial reflectors of the morale and concerns of France and the Western world in the 1940s, both before and after the Liberation from the Nazis. Powerful representations of an era have their own use and justification and offer values not in themselves aesthetic.

Bernard Malamud

(1914–1986)

The Fixer and *The Tenants*

MALAMUD IS PERHAPS THE PUREST STORY TELLER SINCE LESKOV. I READ ON always to team what will come next, and usually in at least faint dread of what may happen. The dreadful in Malamud is not what already has happened, not at least until the horrible final page of *The Tenants*. Perhaps the sense of impending dread, even in the comic mode, is one of the genuinely negative Jewish qualities that Malamud's work possesses. "Every Jew is a meteorologist" says the Israeli humorist Kishon, and certainly Malamud's creatures live in their sense that lightning bolts will need to be dodged.

The Jewishness of Malamud's fiction has been a puzzle from the start, as his better critics always indicated. Malamud's vision is personal, original, and almost wholly unrelated to the most characteristic or normative Jewish thought and tradition. As for Malamud's style, it too is a peculiar (and dazzling) invention. It may give off the aura of Yiddish to readers who do not know the language, but to anyone who spoke and studied Yiddish as a child, the accents of memory emerge from the pages of *Herzog* but not of *The Fixer*. Malamud's idiom, like his stance, is a beautiful and usurping achievement of the imagination. His triumph is to have given us Malamud, and somehow then compelled us to think, as we read, how Jewish it all seems. I can summon up no contemporary writer who suffers less from the anxiety-of-influence, whose books are less concerned to answer the self-crippling question: "Is there anything left to be done?" Like his own first hero, he is a Natural.

Yet having said this, I become uneasy, for the truth here must be more complex. When I think back over Malamud, I remember first stories like "The Jewbird" and "The Magic Barrel," and it seems ridiculous to call such stories anything but Jewish. Malamud's most impressive novel remains *The Fixer*, which is essentially a premonitory vision of a time that the Russian Jews might all too easily enter again. Perhaps in reading Malamud as an extravagantly vivid expressionist whose art seduces us into a redefinition of Jewishness, we in fact are misreading him. A pure enough storyteller, in Jewish tradition, ultimately tells not a story but the truth, and the burden of *The Fixer* and *The Tenants* may yet prove to be the burden of the valley of vision. It may be time to read Malamud as a modest but genuine version of prophecy.

Critical accounts of Malamud tend to diverge widely. Thus Harold Fisch, in his *The Dual Image*, a brief but packed survey on the figure of the Jew as both noble and ignoble in English and American literature, sees the theme of *The Fixer* as "the experience of victimization in general." But to Allen Guttmann the theme is the very different one of "the responsibilities of peoplehood." Robert Alter finds the probable balance: "Though to be a Jew in this novel does involve a general moral stance, it also means being involved in the fate of a particular people, actively identifying with its history." The most hopeful view is that of Ruth R. Wisse, in a fine monograph on *The Schlemiel As Modern Hero*, which sees Bok's acceptance of his imprisonment as "the crucial moment of initiation" and can even speak of "the liberating effects of imprisonment."

But Yakov Bok is recalcitrant to all these views, which might be summed up best in Alter's notion that in Malamud the fundamental metaphor for Jewishness is imprisonment, imprisonment being "a general image for the moral life with all its imponderable obstacles to spontaneous self-fulfillment." If I understand Alter, imprisonment in this wide sense equals civilization and its discontents, and all sublimation thus becomes a kind of incarceration. This is ingenious, but threatens a diffusion of meaning that few storytellers could survive.

Malamud-on-Malamud has been more than a touch misleading, and his critics have suffered by following him. If being Jewish were simply the right combination of suffering and moralism, and nothing more, then all people indeed would be Jews, when their lives were considered under those aspects alone. *The Assistant* encourages such a reading, but is a very unformed book compared to *The Fixer* and *The Tenants*. Though Yakov Bok's covenant is ostensibly only with himself, it is with himself as representative of all other Jews, and so might as well be with God. And where there is covenant, and trust in covenant, which is what sustains Bok at the end, there is the Jewish as opposed to any Christian idea of faith. Bok is, as all the critics have seen, a terribly ordinary man, yet his endurance becomes extraordinary in his refusal to implicate all Jews in the "crime" of ritual murder. Though the process of hardening his will is what makes Bok a Jew, and only *initially* despite himself, I cannot agree with Alter that Bok becomes a Jew in Malamud's special sense, rather than in the traditional sense. Alter may be right in discerning Malamud's intentions, but the storyteller's power breaks through those intentions and joins Bok to a strength greater than his own simplicity could hope to give him. If part of Bok's birthright as a Jew is being vulnerable to history's worst errors, there is another part, a tempering of the will that turns Bok against time's injustices, and makes of this simple man a rebel against history, like so many of his people:

> As for history, Yakov thought, there are ways to reverse it. What the Tsar deserves is a bullet in the gut. Better him than us.... Death to the anti-Semites! Long live revolution! Long live liberty!

In context, as the end of Bok's evolution from a solitary fixer, scarcely Jewish, wholly without a sense of community, this has considerable force, of a kind previously unsuspected in Malamud. With the grim strength of *The Tenants* now known to us, it is possible to see retrospectively that Malamud underwent a change in *The Fixer*. His private vision of Jewishness was absorbed by a more historical understanding of a phenomenon too large to be affected by individual invention. Added to this, I suspect, came a more historicized dread than had been operative in the earlier Malamud.

Coming together in *The Tenants* are elements from the story "Black is My Favorite Color" and a number of themes from the Fidelman saga, including the destroyed manuscript. Lesser, the obsessed Jewish writer, desperate to finish his book, which is about love, is swept up into a dance of death with the black writer Willie Spearmint. The dance takes place in a tenement ready for demolition, from which Lesser declines to move. For Lesser writes only by rewriting, a revisionary constantly swerving away from himself, and he cannot bear to leave the scene of his book's birth until he is willing to call it complete. But an end is more than he can stand. It will be, if ever done, his third novel, but Lesser has worked on it for nine and a half years, and is now thirty-six and still unmarried. Lesser's deepest obsession is that he has never really told the truth, but in fact he is addicted to truth-telling.

Spearmint, archetypal Black Writer, wishing to be "the best Soul Writer," but balked in creation, persuades Lesser to read his manuscript. The rest is disaster, or as Lesser says towards the end: "Who's hiring Willie Spearmint to be my dybbuk?" But each becomes the other's dybbuk.

Intending only the truth of art, Lesser destroys Spearmint's self-confidence in his writing, and compounds the destruction by falling in love with Spearmint's Jewish girl friend, and taking her away from her black lover. Spearmint retaliates by destroying the manuscript of Lesser's nearly complete novel. Tied to one another by a hatred transcending everything else, the two writers stalk one another in the ruined tenement, Spearmint with a saber, Lesser with an ax, like the hideous death-duel in the Hall of Spiders between Swelter and Flay in Mervyn Peake's *Titus Groan*. The title of Lesser's destroyed novel about love was *The Promised End*, with the epigraph, also from *King Lear*: "Who is it that can tell me who I am?" The Fool's reply to Lear's bitter question is: "Lear's shadow," and Spearmint is Lesser's shadow, his cabalistic Other Side. When Lear, at the close, enters with the dead Cordelia in his arms, Kent says: "Is this the promised end?" and Edgar adds: "Or image of that horror?" I suppose Malamud wants us to ask the same as his novel ends:

> Neither of them could see the other but sensed where he stood. Each heard himself scarcely breathing.
> "Bloodsuckin Jew Niggerhater."
> "Anti-Semitic Ape."
> Their metal glinted in hidden light.... They aimed at each other accurate blows. Lesser felt his jagged ax sink through bone and brain as the groaning black's razor-sharp saber, in a single boiling stabbing slash, cut the white's balls from the rest of him.
> Each, thought the writer, feels the anguish of the other.

Whether as parable or as prophecy, *The Tenants* holds together, all one thing, a unity dependent upon Lesser's love of the truth (which for him is the novelist's art) over love itself. Ultimately, Lesser loves only the Book, and when Levenspiel, the landlord who wants him out, sarcastically asks, "... what are you writing, the Holy Bible?" Lesser comes back with, "Who can say? Who really knows?" In the parallel obsession of Spearmint, which the black writer is at last unable to sustain, a troubling reflection of Lesser's zeal is meant to haunt us. *The Tenants*, like Bellow's *Mr. Sammler's Planet*, is Jewish wisdom literature, and perhaps both books lose as fictions what they gain as parables.

Ralph Waldo Ellison

(1914-1994)

The Invisible Man

MORE THAN A THIRD OF A CENTURY AFTER ITS ORIGINAL PUBLICATION (1952), Ralph Ellison's *Invisible Man* is fully confirmed as an American Classic. I remember reading *Invisible Man* when it first appeared, and joining in the enthusiastic reception of the book. A number of readings since have caused the novel to seem richer, and rereading it now brings no temptation to dissent from the general verdict. One can prophesy that *Invisible Man* will be judged, some day, as the principal work of American fiction between Faulkner's major phase and *Gravity's Rainbow* by Pynchon. Only West's *Miss Lonelyhearts*, of all the novels between Faulkner and Pynchon, rivals *Invisible Man* as an eminent instance of the American imagination in narrative, and West's scope is specialized and narrow, however intense in its superbly negative exuberance.

Rereading *Invisible Man*, the exuberance of the tale and the strength of its nameless narrator seem to me far less negative than they did back in 1952. I agree with Douglas Robinson that Ellison gave us a Book of Jonah in descent from *Moby-Dick*, and so I agree also with Robinson's argument against R.W.B. Lewis's distinguished and influential contention that *Invisible Man* is an apocalyptic work. Ellison's novel is the narrator's book, and not the book of Rinehart or of Ras the Exhorter, and the narrator goes underground only as Jonah does, to come up again, in order to live as a narrator. Like Jonah, like the Ancient Mariner of Coleridge, like Melville's Ishmael, and even like Job, the narrator escapes apocalypse and returns to tell us his story.

When we first meet the narrator, he is living an underground existence that seems to have suggested to Pynchon the grand invention of the story of Byron the Light Bulb in *Gravity's Rainbow* (I owe this allusive link to Pamela Schirmeister). Byron the Bulb's war against the System which insists that he burn out is a precisely apocalyptic transumption of the Invisible Man's struggle against Monopolated Light & Power:

> That is why I fight my battle with Monopolated Light & Power. The deeper reason, I mean: It allows me to feel my vital aliveness. I also fight them for taking so much of my money before I learned to protect myself. In my hole in the basement there are exactly 1,369 lights. I've wired the entire ceiling, every inch of it. And not with fluorescent bulbs, but with the older, more-expensive-to-operate kind, the filament type. An act of sabotage, you know. I've already begun to wire the wall. A junk man I know, a man of vision, has supplied me with wire and sockets. Nothing, storm or flood, must get in the way of our need for light and ever more and brighter light. The truth is the light and light is the truth. When I finish all four walls, then I'll start on the floor. Just how that will go, I don't know. Yet when you have lived invisible as long as I have you develop a certain ingenuity. I'll solve the problem. And maybe I'll invent a gadget to place my coffee pot on the fire while I lie in bed, and even invent a gadget to warm my bed—like the fellow I saw in one of the picture magazines who made himself a gadget to warm his shoes! Though invisible, I am in the great American tradition of tinkers. That makes me kin to Ford, Edison and Franklin. Call me, since I have a theory and a concept, a "thinker-tinker." Yes, I'll warm my shoes; they need it, they're usually full of holes. I'll do that and more.

Even Pynchon must have envied those 1,369 lights, all of them old-fashioned filaments if none of them an immortal Byron the Bulb. Ellison's Invisible Man is another ancestor of all those heroic schlemiels who constitute Pynchon's hopeless preterites, the Counterforce of Tyrone Slothrop, Roger Mexico, poor Byron the Bulb, and the other Gnostic sparks of light who flash on amidst the broken vessels of the Zone. As befits his great namesake Emerson, Ellison is both pragmatist and transcendentalist, a combination that in Pynchon falls downwards and outwards into entropy and paranoia. It is a perplexing irony that Ellison's narrator ends with a prophecy that Ellison himself has been unable to fulfill (*Invisible Man* being his first and last novel) but that Pynchon has inherited:

> Yes, but what *is* the next phase? How often have I tried to find it!

Over and over again I've gone up above to seek it out. For, like almost everyone else in our country, I started out with my share of optimism. I believed in hard work and progress and action, but now, after first being "for" society and then "against" it, I assign myself no rank or any limit, and such an attitude is very much against the trend of the times. But my world has become one of infinite possibilities. What a phrase—still it's a good phrase and a good view of life, and a man shouldn't accept any other; that much I've learned underground. Until some gang succeeds in putting the world in a strait-jacket, its definition is possibility. Step outside the narrow borders of what men call reality and you step into chaos—ask Rinehart, he's a master of it—or imagination. That too I've learned in the cellar, and not by deadening my sense of perception; I'm invisible, not blind.

Pynchon has stepped, of course, into both chaos and imagination, but his chaos is the apocalyptic Zone where we may yet live again (if we live), and his imagination is his Kabbalistic vision that he calls "sado-anarchism." The step beyond *Invisible Man* is one that Ellison is too humane and too humanistic to have taken. Pynchon, chronicler of the Counterforce but hardly its prophet, gives us the Invisible Man a generation later in the image of Rocketman, the sublimely inane Slothrop, who is literally scattered into more than invisibility in the Zone, and who may have been sighted for a final time as a fleeting photograph on the record jacket of a rock band.

II

The antinomies between which Ellison's narrator moves are Rinehart (more an image than a man) and the poignant figure of Ras the Exhorter, very much a man, indeed the most sympathetic personality in the novel, more so even than the martyred Tod Clifton. Driven mad by white oppression and brutality, Ras becomes Ras the Destroyer, at once Ahab and Moby-Dick, and is silenced by his own spear, slung back at him by the narrator, an Ishmael turned avenger in self-defense. But Ras, though he suffers Ahab's fate, is no Ahab, and his remains an uncanny prophecy to blacks and whites alike. Clifton speaks the truth when he observes: "But it's on the inside that Ras is strong. On the inside he's dangerous." Ras speaks the dangerous eloquence of justified indignation and despair:

Ras struck his thighs with his fists. "*Me* crazy, mahn? You call *me* crazy? Look at you two and look at me—is this sanity? Standing here in three shades of blackness! Three black men fighting in the street because of the white enslaver? Is that sanity? Is that consciousness, scientific understahnding? Is that the modern black mahn of the twentieth century? Hell, mahn! Is it self-respect—black against black? What they give you to betray—their women? You fall for that?"

"Let's go," I said, listening and remembering and suddenly alive in the dark with the horror of the battle royal, but Clifton looked at Ras with a tight, fascinated expression, pulling away from me.

"Let's go," I repeated. He stood there, looking.

"Sure, you go," Ras said, "but not him. You contahminated but he the real black mahn. In Africa this mahn be a chief, a black king! Here they say he rape them godahm women with no blood in their veins. I bet this mahn can't beat them off with baseball bat-shit! What kind of foolishness is it? Kick him ass from cradle to grave then call him *brother*? Does it make mahthematics? Is it logic? Look at him, mahn; open your eyes," he said to me. "I look like that I rock the blahsted world! They know about me in Japan, India—all the colored countries. Youth! Intelligence! The mahn's a natural prince! Where is your eyes? Where your self-respect? Working for them dahm people? Their days is numbered, the time is almost here and you fooling 'round like this was the nineteenth century. I don't understand you. Am I ignorant? Answer me, mahn!"

If Ras is the imagination ruined by apocalyptic expansiveness, verging upon Pynchonean paranoia, then the image of Rinehart is chaos come again, but chaos verging upon an entropy that negates any new origin out of which a fresh creation might come. Rinehart is visibility personified, a moving shadow identified by and identical with what he wears: dark glasses, in particular, interpreted by the narrator as the Pauline "through a glass, darkly," and a white hat. If Ras is both Exhorter and Destroyer, Rinehart is both numbers runner and the Reverend B.P. Rinehart, Spiritual Technologist, who makes the Seen Unseen and tells us to Behold the Invisible. The narrator, gazing into Rinehart's church, experiences a true defeat, subtler than any Ras could hope to inflict:

Then the door opened and I looked past their heads into a small crowded room of men and women sitting in folding chairs, to the front where a slender woman in a rusty black robe played passionate boogie-woogie on an upright piano along with a young man wearing a skull cap who struck righteous riffs from an electric guitar which was connected to an amplifier that hung from the ceiling above a gleaming white and gold pulpit. A man in an elegant red cardinal's robe and a high lace collar stood resting against an enormous Bible and now began to lead a hard-driving hymn which the congregation shouted in the unknown tongue. And back and high on the wall above him there arched the words in letters of gold:

LET THERE BE LIGHT!

The whole scene quivered vague and mysterious in the green light, then the door closed and the sound muted down.

It was too much for me. I removed my glasses and tucked the white hat carefully beneath my arm and walked away. Can it be, I thought, can it actually be? And I knew that it was. I had heard of it before but I'd never come so close. Still, could he be all of them: Rine the runner and Rine the gambler and Rine the briber and Rine the lover and Rinehart the Reverend? Could he himself be both rind and heart? What is real anyway? But how could I doubt it? He was a broad man, a man of parts who got around. Rinehart the rounder. It was true as I was true. His world was possibility and he knew it. He was years ahead of me and I was a fool. I must have been crazy and blind. The world in which we lived was without boundaries. A vast seething, hot world of fluidity, and Rine the rascal was at home. Perhaps only Rine the rascal was at home in it. It was unbelievable, but perhaps only the unbelievable could be believed. Perhaps the truth was always a lie.

In some sense, Rinehart's truth which was always a lie becomes the dominant influence upon the narrator. It not only drives him underground, but it confirms his obsession with illumination, his parodistic reliance upon 1,369 lights. Rinehart is the authentic dweller in possibility, which Emily Dickinson called a fairer house than prose, being as it is superior of windows, more numerous of doors. Harlem or black existence is again either chaos or imagination, the possibility of Rinehart or the increasingly furious possibility of Ras the Destroyer.

The narrator, though, is finally the only authentic American, black or white, because he follows *the* American Religion, which is Emersonian Self-Reliance. He insists upon himself, refuses to go on imitating his false fathers, and evades both Rinehart and Ras. True, he is the Emersonian driven underground, but he will emerge more Emersonian than ever, insisting that he has become Representative Man:

Who knows but that, on the lower frequencies, I speak for you?

The Invisible Man says that he is frightened by this truth, and so are we. What is more frightening, for us and for him, is truer now than it was a third of a century ago, and is even more Emersonian. We have learned that, on the higher frequencies, Ellison speaks for us.

Saul Bellow

(1915–)

Herzog

I

BY GENERAL CRITICAL AGREEMENT, SAUL BELLOW IS THE STRONGEST American novelist of his generation, presumably with Norman Mailer as his nearest rival. What makes this canonical judgment a touch problematic is that the indisputable achievement does not appear to reside in any single book. Bellow's principal works are: *The Adventures of Augie March*, *Herzog*, *Humboldt's Gift*, and in a briefer compass, *Seize the Day*. The earlier novels, *Dangling Man* and *The Victim*, seem now to be period pieces, while *Henderson the Rain King* and *Mr. Sammler's Planet* share the curious quality of not being quite worthy of two figures so memorable as Henderson and Mr. Sammler. *The Dean's December* is a drab book, its dreariness unredeemed by Bellow's nearly absent comic genius.

Herzog, still possessing the exuberance of *Augie March*, while anticipating the tragicomic sophistication of *Humboldt's Gift*, as of now seems to be Bellow's best and most representative novel. And yet its central figure remains a wavering representation, compared to some of the subsidiary male characters, and its women seem the wish-fulfillments, negative as well as positive, of Herzog and his creator. This seems true of almost all of Bellow's fiction: a Dickensian gusto animates a fabulous array of secondary and minor personalities, while at the center a colorful but shadowy consciousness is hedged in by women who do not persuade us, though evidently once they persuaded him.

In some sense, the canonical status of Bellow is already assured, even if the indubitable book is still to come. Bellow's strengths may not have come together to form a masterwork, but he is hardly the first novelist of real eminence whose books may be weaker as aggregates than in their component parts or aspects. His stylistic achievement is beyond dispute, as are his humor, his narrative inventiveness, and his astonishing inner car, whether for monologue or dialogue. Perhaps his greatest gift is for creating subsidiary and minor characters of grotesque splendor, sublime in their vivacity, intensity, and capacity to surprise. They may be caricatures, yet their vitality seems permanent: Einhorn, Clem Tembow, Bateshaw, Valentine Gersbach, Sandor Himmelstein, Von Humboldt Fleisher, Cantabile, Alec Szathmar. Alas, compared to them, the narrator-heroes, Augie, Herzog, and Citrine, are diffuse beings, possibly because Bellow cannot disengage from them, despite heroic efforts and revisions. I remember *Augie March* for Einhorn, *Herzog* for Gersbach, *Humboldt's Gift* for Humboldt, and even that last preference tends to throw off-center an apprehension of the novel. Augie March and Herzog narrate and speak with tang and eloquence, yet they themselves are less memorable than what they say. Citrine, more subdued in his language, fades yet more quickly into the continuum of Bellow's urban cosmos. This helps compound the aesthetic mystery of Bellow's achievement. His heroes are superb observers, worthy of their Whitmanian heritage. What they lack is Whitman's Real Me or Me Myself, or else they are blocked from expressing it.

II

Few novelists have ever surpassed Bellow at openings and closings:

I am an American, Chicago born—Chicago, that somber city—and go at things' as I have taught myself, free-style, and will make the record in my own way: first to knock, first admitted; sometimes an innocent knock, sometimes a not so innocent. But a man's character is his fate, says Heraclitus, and in the end there isn't any way to disguise the nature of the knocks by acoustical work on the door or gloving the knuckles.

Look at me, going everywhere! Why, I am a sort of Columbus of those near-at-hand and believe you come to them in this immediate *terra incognita* that spreads out in every gaze. I may well be a flop at this line of endeavor. Columbus too thought he was a flop, probably, when they sent him back in chains. Which didn't prove there was no America.

The end and the start cunningly interlace, very much in the mode of *Song of Myself*, or of the first and last chapters of Emerson's *Nature*. Augie too is an American Transcendentalist, a picaresque quester for the god within the self. *Ethos* is the *Daimon*, both passages say, with Augie as ethos and Columbus as the daimon. One remembers the aged Whitman's self-identification in his "Prayer of Columbus," and it seems right to rejoice, as Whitman would have rejoiced, when Augie comes full circle from going at things, self-taught and free-style, to discovering those near-at-hand, upon the shores of America. That is Bellow at his most exuberant. When weathered, the exuberance remains, but lies in shadow:

> If I am out of my mind, it's all right with me, thought Moses Herzog.
>
> Some people thought he was cracked and for a time he himself had doubted that he was all there. But now, though he still behaved oddly, he felt confident, cheerful, clairvoyant, and strong. He had fallen under a spell and was writing letters to everyone under the sun.... Hidden in the country, he wrote endlessly, fanatically, to the newspapers, to people in public life, to friends and relatives and at last to the dead, his own obscure dead, and finally the famous dead.
>
> Perhaps he'd stop writing letters. Yes, that was what was coming, in fact. The knowledge that he was done with these letters. Whatever had come over him during these last months, the spell, really seemed to be passing, really going. He set down his hat, with the roses and day lilies, off the half-painted piano, and went into his study, carrying the wine bottles in one hand like a pair of Indian clubs. Walking over notes and papers, he lay down on his Récamier couch. As he stretched out, he took a long breath, and then he lay, looking at the mesh of the screen, pulled loose by vines, and listening to the steady scratching of Mrs. Tuttle's broom. He wanted to tell her to sprinkle the floor. She was raising too much dust. In a few minutes he would call down to her, "Damp it down, Mrs. Tuttle. There's water in the sink." But not just yet. At this time he had no messages for anyone. Nothing. Not a single word.

Another *ritorno*, but this time the cycle has been broken. Augie March, like Emerson and Whitman, knows that there is no history, only biography. Moses Herzog has been a long time discovering this truth, which ends his profession, and Charlie Citrine also goes full-circle:

The book of ballads published by Von Humboldt Fleisher in the Thirties was an immediate hit. Humboldt was just what everyone had been waiting for. Out in the Midwest I had certainly been waiting eagerly, I can tell you that. An avant-garde writer, the first of a new generation, he was handsome, fair, large, serious, witty, he was learned. The guy had it all. All the papers reviewed his book. His picture appeared in *Time* without insult and in *Newsweek* with praise. I read *Harlequin Ballads* enthusiastically. I was a student at the University of Wisconsin and thought about nothing but literature day and night. Humboldt revealed to me new ways of doing things. I was ecstatic. I envied his luck, his talent, and his fame, and I went cast in May to have a look at him— perhaps to get next to him. The Greyhound bus, taking the Scranton route, made the trip in about fifty hours. That didn't matter. The bus windows were open. I had never seen real mountains before. Trees were budding. It was like Beethoven's *Pastorale*. I felt showered by the green, within ... Humboldt was very kind. He introduced me to people in the Village and got me books to review. I always loved him.

Within the grave was an open concrete case. The coffins went down and then the yellow machine moved forward and the little crane, making a throaty whir, picked up a concrete slab and laid it atop the concrete case. So the coffin was enclosed and the soil did not cone directly upon it. But then, how did one get out? One didn't, didn't, didn't! You stayed, you stayed! There was a dry light grating as of crockery when contact was made, a sort of sugarbowl sound. Thus, the condensation of collective intelligences and combined ingenuities, its cables silently spinning, dealt with the individual poet....

Menasha and I went toward the limousine. The side of his foot brushed away some of last autumn's leaves and he said, looking through his goggles, "What this, Charlie, a spring flower?"

"It is. I guess it's going to happen after all. On a warm day like this everything looks ten times deader."

"So it's a little flower," Menasha said. "They used to tell one about a kid asking his grumpy old man when they were walking in the park, 'What's the name of this flower, Papa?' and the old guy is peevish and he yells, 'How should I know? Am I in the millinery business?' Here's another, but what do you suppose they're called, Charlie?"

"Search me," I said. "I'm a city boy myself. They must be crocuses."

The cycle is from Citrine's early: "I felt showered by the green, within" to his late, toneless, "They must be crocuses," removed from all affect
not because he has stopped loving Humboldt, but because he is chilled
preternaturally by the effective if unfair trope Bellow has found for the
workings of canonical criticism: "Thus, the condensation of collective
intelligences and combined ingenuities, its cables silently spinning, dealt
with the individual poet." There is no history, and now there is also no
biography, but only the terrible dehumanizing machine of a technocratic
intelligentsia, destroying individuality and poetry, and stealing from the
spring of the year the green that no longer is to be internalized.

III

Bellow's endless war against each fresh wave of literary and intellectual modernism is both an aesthetic resource and all aesthetic liability in his
fiction. As resource, it becomes a drive for an older freedom, all energy of
humane protest against over-determination. As liability, it threatens to
become repetition, or a merely personal bitterness, even blending into
Bellow's acerbic judgments upon the psychology of women. When it is
most adroitly balanced, in *Herzog*, the polemic against modernism
embraces the subtle infiltrations of dubious ideologies into the protesting
Moses Herzog himself. When it is least balanced, we receive the narrative
rant that intrudes into Mr. Sammler's cosmos, or the dankness that pervades both Chicago and Bucharest in *The Dean's December*. Like Ruskin
lamenting that the water in Lake Como was no longer blue, Bellow's
Alexander Corde tells us that "Chicago wasn't Chicago anymore." What
The Dean's December truly tells us is that "Bellow wasn't Bellow anymore,"
in this book anyway. The creator of Einhorn and Gersbach and Von
Humboldt Fleisher gives us no such figure this time around, almost as
though momentarily he resents his own genius for the high comedy of the
grotesque.

Yet Bellow's lifelong polemic against the aestheticism of Flaubert and
his followers is itself the exuberant myth that made *Augie March*, *Herzog*,
and *Humboldt's Gift* possible. In an act of critical shrewdness, Bellow once
associated his mode of anti-modernist comedy with Svevo's *Confessions of
Zeno* and Nabokov's *Lolita*, two masterpieces of ironic parody that actually
surpass Bellow's *Henderson the Rain King* in portraying the modernist consciousness as stand-up comic. Parody tends to negate outrage, and Bellow

is too vigorous to be comfortable at masking his own outrage. When restrained, Bellow is too visibly restrained, unlike the mordant Svevo or the Nabokov who excels at deadpan mockery. Henderson may be more of a self-portrait, but Herzog, scholar of High Romanticism, better conveys Bellow's vitalistic version of an anti-modernistic comic stance. Bellow is closest to Svevo and to Nabokov in the grand parody of Herzog-Hamlet declining to shoot Gersbach-Claudius when he finds the outrageous adulterer scouring the bathtub after bathing Herzog's little daughter. Daniel Fuchs, certainly Bellow's most careful and informed scholar, reads this scene rather too idealistically by evading the parodic implications of "Moses might have killed him now." Bathing a child is our sentimental version of prayer, and poor Herzog, unlike Hamlet, *is* a sentimentalist, rather than a triumphant rejecter of nihilism, as Fuchs insists.

Bellow, though carefully distanced from Herzog, is himself something of a sentimentalist, which in itself need not be an aesthetic disability for a novelist. Witness Samuel Richardson and Dickens, but their sentimentalism is so titanic as to become something different in kind, a sensibility of excess larger than even Bellow can hope to display. In seeking to oppose an earlier Romanticism (Blake, Wordsworth, Whitman) to the belated Romanticism of literary modernism (Gide, Eliot, Hemingway), Bellow had the peculiar difficulty of needing to avoid the heroic vitalism that he regards as an involuntary parody of High Romanticism (Rimbaud, D. H. Lawrence, and, in a lesser register, Norman Mailer). Henderson, Bellow's Gentile surrogate, is representative of just how that difficulty constricts Bellow's imagination. The Blakean dialectic of Innocence and Experience, clearly overt in the scheme of the novel, is at odds with Henderson's characteristically Bellovian need for punishment or unconscious sense of guilt, which prevails in spite of Bellow's attempts to evade Freudian overdetermination. Though he wants and indeed needs a psychology of the will, Bellow is much more Freudian than he can bear to know. Henderson is a superbly regressive personality, very much at one with the orphan child he holds at the end of the novel. Dahfu, of whom Norman Mailer strongly approved, is about as persuasive a representation as are his opposites in Bellow, all of those sadistic and compelling fatal ladies, pipe dreams of a male vision of otherness as a castrating force. Bellow disdains apocalypse as a mode, but perhaps the Bellovian apocalypse would be one in which all of the darkly attractive women of these novels converged upon poor Dahfu, Blakean vitalist, and divested him of the emblem of his therapeutic vitalism.

Without his polemic, Bellow never seems able to get started, even in *Humboldt's Gift*, where the comedy is purest. Unfortunately, Bellow cannot match the modernist masters of the novel. In American fiction, his chronological location between, say, Faulkner and Pynchon exposes him to comparisons he does not seek yet also cannot sustain. Literary polemic within a novel is dangerous because it directs the critical reader into the areas where canonical judgments must be made, as part of the legitimate activity of reading. Bellow's polemic is normative, almost Judaic in its moral emphases, its passions for justice and for more life. The polemic sometimes becomes more attractive than its aesthetic embodiments. Would we be so charmed by Herzog if he did not speak for so many of us? I become wary when someone tells me that she or he "loves" *Gravity's Rainbow*. The grand Pynchonian doctrine of sado-anarchism scarcely should evoke *affection* in anyone, as opposed to the shudder of recognition that the book's extraordinary aesthetic dignity demands from us. It is the aesthetic failure of Bellow's polemic, oddly combined with its moral success, that increasingly drives Bellow's central figures into dubious mysticisms. Citrine's devotion to Rudolf Steiner is rather less impressive, intellectually and aesthetically, than the obsessive Kabbalism of *Gravity's Rainbow*. If Steiner is the ultimate answer to literary modernism, then Flaubert may rest easy in his tomb.

IV

And yet Bellow remains a humane comic novelist of superb gifts, almost unique in American fiction since Mark Twain. I give the last words here to what moves me as the most beautiful sequence in Bellow, Herzog's final week of letters, starting with his triumphant overcoming of his obsession with Madeleine and Gersbach. On his betraying wife, Herzog is content to end with a celebration now at last beyond masochism: "To put on lipstick, after dinner in a restaurant, she would look at her reflection in a knife blade. He recalled this with delight." On Gersbach, with his indubitable, latently homosexual need to cuckold his best friend, Herzog is just and definitive: "*Enjoy her—rejoice in her. You will not reach me through her, however, I know you sought me in her flesh. But I am no longer there.*" The unmailed messages go on, generously assuring Nietzsche of Herzog's admiration while telling the philosopher: "*Your immoralists also eat meat. They ride the bus. They are only the most bus-sick travelers.*" The sequence magnificently includes an epistle to Dr. Morgenfruh, doubtless a Yiddish version of the Nietzschean Dawn of Day, of whom Herzog wisely remarks: "He was a splendid old man, only partly fraudulent, and what more can you ask of anyone?" Addressing Dr. Morgenfruh, Herzog speculates darkly "that the territorial instinct is stronger than the sexual." But then, with exquisite grace, Herzog signs off. *"Abide in light, Morgenfruh. I will keep you posted from time to time."* This benign farewell is made not by an overdetermined bundle of territorial and sexual instincts, but by a persuasive representative of the oldest ongoing Western tradition of moral wisdom and familial compassion.

Walker Percy

(1916-1990)

The Moviegoer

I

WITH MANY OTHER READERS, I DISCOVERED *THE MOVIEGOER* IN 1961, AND was delighted. Rereading it a quarter-century later, the delight returns, but perhaps somewhat darkened by intimations in the novel of the moral and religious obsessions that have made each subsequent fiction by Walker Percy rather more problematic than the one before. As a storyteller, Percy chooses to follow the downward path to wisdom, perhaps at the expense of his stories. *The Last Gentleman* (1966) had not abandoned all the narrative concerns of *The Moviegoer*, but *Love in the Ruins* (1971) resorts to apocalyptic yearnings, and *Lancelot* (1977) seems to address a saving remnant. *The Second Coming* (1980) is a wholly tendentious narrative and hardly seems to be by the author of *The Moviegoer*. Acclaimed as a Southern prophet, Percy may have become precisely that. There is a curious progression in his novels' closing passages that is revelatory of a metamorphosis from the language of story to the urgencies that transcend art:

> I watch her walk toward St. Charles, cape jasmine held against her cheek, until my brothers and sisters call out behind me.
>
> (*The Moviegoer*)

> "Wait," he shouted in a dead run. The Edsel paused, sighed, and stopped. Strength flowed like oil into his muscles and he ran with great joyous ten-foot antelope bounds. The Edsel waited for him.
>
> (*The Last Gentleman*)

To bed we go for a long winter's nap, twined about each other as the ivy twineth not under a bush or in a car or on the floor or any such humbug as marked the past peculiar years of Christendom, but at home in bed where all good folk belong.

(*Love in the Ruins*)

Do you know her well?
Yes.
Will she join me in Virginia and will she and I and Siobhan begin a new life there?
Yes.
Very well. I've finished. Is there anything you wish to tell me before Heave?
Yes.

(*Lancelot*)

His heart leapt with a secret joy. What is it I want from her and him, he wondered, not only want but must have? Is she a gift and therefore a sign of a giver? Could it be that the Lord is here, masquerading behind this simple silly holy face? Am I crazy to want both, her and Him? No, not want, must have. And will have.

(*The Second Coming*)

Even out of context, Percy's conclusions move him and his readers from a narrative poignance to a theocentric anxiety. It cannot be gratuitous that both *Lancelot* and *The Second Coming* end with the hero conversing with a kindly priest. "The past peculiar years of Christendom" craze Percy's protagonists, and by implication Percy thinks the worse of us for not being so crazed. Despite the manifest humor of his *Lost in the Cosmos: The Last Self-Help Book* (1983), Percy intends its conclusion as what can only be called a low seriousness:

Repeat. Do you read? Do you read? Are you in trouble? How did you get in trouble? If you are in trouble, have you sought help? If you did, did help come? If it did, did you accept it? Are you out of trouble? What is the character of your consciousness? Are you conscious? Do you have a self? Do you know who you are? Do you know what you are doing? Do you love? Do you know how to love? Are you loved? Do you hate? Do you read me? Come back. Repeat. Come back. Come back. Come back.

(CHECK ONE)

II

A rereading of *The Moviegoer* after a first reading of *Lancelot* and *The Second Coming* must confront a critic with a bemused sense of loss. Binx Bolling is more than the most amiable of Percy's surrogates; his freedom from the drive to moralize has about it now the aura of his author's lost freedom. Aunt Emily, the book's moralizer, is a presage of many a Percyan denunciation to come, and yet her highly individual style allows us to absorb her condemnations as we cannot quite sustain the scoldings that come in Percy's later novels:

> Our civilization has achieved a distinction of sorts. It will be remembered not for its technology nor even its wars but for its novel ethos. Ours is the only civilization in history which has enshrined mediocrity as its national ideal. Others have been corrupt, but leave it to us to invent the most undistinguished of corruptions. No orgies, no blood running in the street, no babies thrown off cliffs. No, we're sentimental people and we horrify easily. True, our moral fiber is rotten. Our national character stinks to high heaven. But we are kinder than ever. No prostitute ever responded with a quicker spasm of sentiment when our hearts are touched. Nor is there anything new about thievery, lewdness, lying, adultery. What is new is that in our time liars and thieves and whores and adulterers wish also to be congratulated and are congratulated by the great public, if their confession is sufficiently psychological or strikes a sufficiently heartfelt and authentic note of sincerity.

However much we admire the formidable Aunt Emily and rightly find this rhetoric to be suitable to her, none among us could regard this as what is best or most enduring in *The Moviegoer*. Binx is just that; he is a kind of grown-up, ruefully respectable New Orleans version of Twain's Huckleberry Finn. Like Huck, Binx longs for freedom while fearing solitude. But an Existentialist Huck Finn is a sublime joke, and this joke still seems to me Percy's authentic and very considerable achievement. *The Moviegoer* alone of Percy's fictions, to date, is a permanent American book. If that judgment is right, then the waste of Percy's authentic talents is a lamentable instance of art yielding to moralism, of storytelling subverted by religious nostalgias.

I remember how much I initially liked *The Moviegoer's* first paragraph, and am very fond of it still:

This morning I got a note from my aunt asking me to come for lunch. I know what this means. Since I go there every Sunday for dinner and today is Wednesday, it can mean only one thing: she wants to have one of her serious talks. It will be extremely grave, either a piece of bad news about her stepdaughter Kate or else a serious talk about me, about the future and what I ought to do. It is enough to scare the wits out of anyone, yet I confess I do not find the prospect altogether unpleasant.

The whole of the book is subtly present in this beginning, since Kate's suicidal despairs are the dark center of the moviegoer's life as a man, to borrow Philip Roth's foreboding phrase. Present also is the antithetical strain in Binx Bolling, who finds reality in his aunt's moral stance, without however being able to erase the distance that divides him from it, and from every other conceivable position. Yet Binx, as he reveals to us very early, is nothing but a quester, who seeks what everyone else asserts they have found:

> What do you seek—God? you ask with a smile.
> I hesitate to answer, since all other Americans have settled the matter for themselves and to give such an answer would amount to setting myself a goal which everyone else has reached—and therefore raising a question in which no one has the slightest interest. Who wants to be dead last among one hundred and eighty million Americans? For, as everyone knows, the polls report that 98% of Americans believe in God and the remaining 2% are atheists and agnostics—which leaves not a single percentage point for a seeker. For myself, I enjoy answering polls as much as anyone and take pleasure in giving intelligent replies to all questions.
> Truthfully, it is the fear of exposing my own ignorance which constrains me from mentioning the object of my search. For, to begin with, I cannot even answer this, the simplest and most basic of all questions: Am I, in my search, a hundred miles ahead of my fellow Americans or a hundred miles behind them? That is to say: Have 98% of Americans already found what I seek or are they so sunk in everydayness that not even the possibility of a search has occurred to them?
> On my honor, I do not know the answer.

Binx clearly would not have written *Lancelot*, *The Second Coming*, and

Lost in the Cosmos, but then neither would Kate, nor even Aunt Emily, whose realistic sense of cultural and societal crisis eschews violence, even rhetorical violence, as a response. When she impressively observes that "it should be quite a sight, the going under of the evening land," Binx thinks, "For her too the fabric is dissolving, but for her even the dissolving makes sense." That may be the difference between Aunt Emily and the later Percy; if for you even the dissolving makes sense, then your response will be wholly coherent, and you will be saved from responding to violence with violence.

Binx, as the moviegoer, has become a quietist, who neither judges nor can be judged. His bond with Kate is that both seek "certification" in his special sense:

> Afterwards in the street, she looks around the neighborhood. "Yes, it is certified now."
>
> She refers to a phenomenon of moviegoing which I have called certification. Nowadays when a person lives somewhere, in a neighborhood, the place is not certified for him. More than likely he will live there sadly and the emptiness which is inside him will expand until it evacuates the entire neighborhood. But if he sees a movie which shows his very neighborhood, it becomes possible for him to live, for a time at least, as a person who is Somewhere and not Anywhere.

This, in a touchingly minimal way, is somehow to be provisionally redeemed by representation, which no longer augments the self, as it did for Walt Whitman, but at least keeps one's context from becoming totally emptied out. Binx and Kate win our affection, as no one subsequently in Percy can. Doubtless, Percy did not care to give us such charming protagonists in his later novels, precisely because they subvert his prophetic concerns. Still, it seems not wrong to hope that the novelist might yet return to his gentler and more qualified visions.

III

Walker Percy is scarcely alone in attempting to employ the novel as a spiritual weapon against the malaise of the age. He is not even unique in combining an apocalyptic temperament with Roman Catholicism, though *Lancelot* does not match Flannery O'Connor in that odd blend. Yet he does have a singular predilection for moral theology, and at times achieves a curious authority in his uncanny mode. With a stance very different from that of Protestant Fundamentalists, he regards the Jews as the eternal evidence for the reality of Yahweh, and the historical authenticity of the Roman Catholic Church. Like most of the Jewish people, I am normally rather wary of such a search for evidences, but Percy handles it with tact and humane wit, benign if a little unnerving. In *The Moviegoer*, Binx identifies his own, internal exile with that of the Jews:

> An odd thing. Ever since Wednesday I have become acutely aware of Jews. There is a clue here, but of what I cannot say. How do I know? Because whenever I approach a Jew, the Geiger counter in my head starts rattling away like a machine gun; and as I go past with the utmost circumspection and with every sense alert—the Geiger counter subsides.
>
> There is nothing new in my Jewish vibrations. During the years when I had friends my Aunt Edna, who is a theosophist, noticed that all my friends were Jews. She knew why moreover: I had been a Jew in a previous incarnation. Perhaps that is it. Anyhow it is true that I am Jewish by instinct. We share the same exile. The fact is, however, I am more Jewish than the Jews I know. They are more at home than I am. I accept my exile.
>
> Another evidence of my Jewishness: the other day a sociologist reported that a significantly large percentage of solitary moviegoers are Jews.
>
> Jews are my first real clue.
>
> When a man is in despair and does not in his heart of hearts allow that a search is possible and when such a man passes a Jew in the street, he notices nothing.
>
> When a man becomes a scientist or an artist, he is open to a different kind of despair. When such a man passes a Jew in the street, he may notice something but it is not a remarkable encounter. To him the Jew can only appear as a scientist or artist like himself or as a specimen to be studied.
>
> But when a man awakes to the possibility of a search and when such a man passes a Jew in the street for the first time, he is like Robinson Crusoe seeing the footprint on the beach.

The wit of assimilating the Jewish Sabbath, which begins at sundown on Friday, to the trace of Defoe's Friday, conceals the moral intensity of the passage. Miraculously surviving, the Jews are the searcher's prime mark or sign of the promise of God that cannot be voided. The culmination of this sign in Percy is Will Barrett's humorous but obsessive concern with the supposed absence or flight of Jews from North Carolina in *The Second Coming*. Barrett's equivocal madness keeps returning him to the Jews as a sign, particularly in an extraordinary letter that he writes:

> To be specific: I wish you to monitor the demographic move-
> ment of Jews not only from North Carolina but from other states
> and other countries as well, to take note of any extraordinary
> changes which go contrary to established demographic patterns—
> such as the emigration of blacks from the South (and their present
> return). If, for example, there has occurred or should occur a mas-
> sive exodus of Jews from the U.S. to Israel, I request that you
> establish an observation post in the village of Megiddo in the nar-
> row waist of Israel (the site, as you may know, of ancient
> Armageddon), where a foe from the east would logically attempt
> to cut Israel in two. From this point you can monitor any unusu-
> al events in the Arab countries to the east, particularly the emer-
> gence of a leader of extraordinary abilities—another putative sign
> of the last days.

The saving difference between this madness, and the somber stuff I hear from television evangelists every night, is that Barrett is only mad north-northwest, and Percy's apocalyptic wind is blowing at us from the south. Still in midcareer, the author of *The Moviegoer* may yet cease search-ing for signs, and instead return to his gift for ruefully comic narrative. As a critic, I want to approach Walker Percy while waving a banner before me: "Bring back Binx Bolling!"

Carson McCullers

(1917–1967)

The Heart Is a Lonely Hunter and *The Ballad of the Sad Café*

I

"I BECOME THE CHARACTERS I WRITE ABOUT AND I BLESS THE LATIN POET Terence who said 'Nothing human is alien to me.'" That was the aesthetic credo of Carson McCullers, and was her program for a limited yet astonishingly intense art of fiction. Rereading her after nearly twenty years away from her novels and stories, I discover that time has enhanced *The Heart Is a Lonely Hunter* and *The Ballad of the Sad Café*, and perhaps rendered less problematic *Reflections in a Golden Eye*. What time cannot do is alter the burden for critics that McCullers represents. Her fiction, like her person, risked that perpetual crisis of Eros of which D.H. Lawrence was the poet and Freud the theoretician. Call it the tendency to make false connections, as set forth by Freud with mordant accuracy in the second paragraph of his crucial paper of 1912, "The Dynamics of the Transference":

> Let us bear clearly in mind that every human being has acquired, by the combined operation of inherent disposition and of external influences in childhood, a special individuality in the exercise of his capacity to love—that is, in the conditions which he sets up for loving, in the impulses he gratifies by it, and in the aims he sets out to achieve in it. This forms a *cliché* or stereotype in him, so to speak (or even several), which perpetually repeats and reproduces itself as life goes on, in so far as external circumstances and the nature of the accessible love-objects permit, and is indeed itself to some extent modifiable by later impressions. Now our experience has

shown that of these feelings which determine the capacity to love only a part has undergone full psychical development; this part is directed towards reality, and can be made use of by the conscious personality, of which it forms part. The other part of these libidinal impulses has been held up in development, withheld from the conscious personality and from reality, and may either expend itself only in phantasy, or may remain completely buried in the unconscious so that the conscious personality is unaware of its existence. Expectant libidinal impulses will inevitably be roused, in anyone whose need for love is not being satisfactorily gratified in reality, by each new person coming upon the scene, and it is more than probable that both parts of the libido, the conscious and the unconscious, will participate in this attitude.

All of McCullers's characters share a particular quirk in the exercise of their capacity to love—they exist, and eventually expire, by falling in love with a hopeless hope. Their authentic literary ancestor is Wordsworth's poignant Margaret, in *The Ruined Cottage*, and like his Margaret they are destroyed, not by despair, but by the extravagance of erotic hope. It is no accident that McCullers's first and best book should bear, as title, her most impressive, indeed unforgettable metaphor: *The Heart Is a Lonely Hunter*.

McCullers's few ventures into literary criticism, whether of Gogol, Faulkner, or herself, were not very illuminating, except in their obsession with loneliness. Her notes on writing, "The Flowering Dream," record her violent, physical response to reading Anne Frank's diary, which caused a rash to break out on her hands and feet. The fear of insulation clearly was the enabling power of McCullers's imagination. When she cited Faulkner and Eugene O'Neill as her major influences, she surprisingly added the Flaubert of *Madame Bovary*, where we might have expected the Lawrence of *The Rainbow* and "The Prussian Officer." But it was Emma's *situation* rather than Flaubert's stance or style that engrossed her.

Mick Kelly, McCullers's surrogate in *The Heart Is a Lonely Hunter*, remains her absolute achievement at representing a personality, presumably a vision of her own personality at the age of twelve. Vivid as the other lonely hunters are—the deaf mute John Singer; Biff Brannon, the café proprietor; Jake Blount, alcoholic revolutionary; Dr. Benedict Mady Copeland, black liberal and reformer—the book still lives in the tormented intensity of Mick Kelly, who knows early to be "grieved to think how power and will / In opposition rule our mortal day, / And why God made irreconcilable / Good and the means of Good." That is the dark wisdom of Shelley in *The Triumph of Life*, but it is also a wisdom realized perfectly and independently by Mick Kelly, who rightly fears the triumph of life over her own integrity, her own hope, her own sense of potential for achievement or for love. The Shelleyan passage becomes pure McCullers if we transpose it to: "And why God made irreconcilable / Love and the means of Love."

II

The Heart Is a Lonely Hunter would not maintain its force if its only final vision were to be the triumph of life, in Shelley's ironic sense. McCullers gives us a tough-grained, last sense of Mick Kelly, bereaved, thrown back into an absolute loneliness, but ongoing nevertheless:

> But now no music was in her mind. That was a funny thing. It was like she was shut out from the inside room. Sometimes a quick little tune would come and go—but she never went into the inside room with music like she used to do. It was like she was too tense. Or maybe because it was like the store took all her energy and time. Woolworth's wasn't the same as school. When she used to come home from school she felt good and was ready to start working on the music. But now she was always tired. At home she just ate supper and slept and then ate breakfast and went off to the store again. A song she had started in her private notebook two months before was still not finished. And she wanted to stay in the inside room but she didn't know how. It was like the inside room was locked somewhere away from her. A very hard thing to understand.
>
> Mick pushed her broken front tooth with her thumb. But she did have Mister Singer's radio. All the installments hadn't been paid and she took on the responsibility. It was good to have something that had belonged to him. And maybe one of these days she might be able to set aside a little for a second-hand piano. Say two bucks a week. And she wouldn't let anybody touch this private piano but her—only she might teach George little pieces. She would keep it in the back room and play on it every night. And all day Sunday. But then suppose some week she couldn't make a payment. So then would they come to take it away like the little red bicycle? And suppose like she wouldn't let them. Suppose she hid the piano under the house. Or else she would meet them at the front door. And fight. She would knock down both the two men so they would have shiners and broke noses and would be passed out on the hall floor.

Mick frowned and rubbed her fist hard across her forehead. That was the way things were. It was like she was mad all the time. Not how a kid gets mad quick so that soon it is all over—but in another way. Only there was nothing to be mad at. Unless the store. But the store hadn't asked her to take the job. So there was nothing to be mad at. It was like she was cheated. Only nobody had cheated her. So there was nobody to take it out on. However, just the same she had that feeling. Cheated.

But maybe it would be true about the piano and turn out O.K. Maybe she would get a chance soon. Else what the hell good had it all been—the way she felt about music and the plans she had made in the inside room? It had to be some good if anything made sense. And it was too and it was too and it was too and it was too. It was some good.

All right!

O.K.!

Some good.

One can call this "Portrait of the Artist as a Young Girl," and see Mick as a visionary of "the way things were." She has the strength of McCullers's endings that are not wholly negations:

Biff wet his handkerchief beneath the water tap and patted his drawn, tense face. Somehow he remembered that the awning had not yet been raised. As he went to the door his walk gained steadiness. And when at last he was inside again he composed himself soberly to await the morning sun.
(*The Heart Is a Lonely Hunter*)

Even in death the body of the soldier still had the look of warm, animal comfort. His grave face was unchanged, and his sun-browned hands lay palm upwards on the carpet as though in sleep.
(*Reflections in a Golden Eye*)

The most remarkable of these conclusions is the vignette called "The Twelve Mortal Men" that serves as epilogue or coda to *The Ballad of the Sad Café*:

THE TWELVE MORTAL MEN

The Forks Falls highway is three miles from the town, and it is here the chain gang has been working. The road is of macadam, and the county decided to patch up the rough places and widen it at a certain dangerous place. The gang is made up of twelve men, all wearing black and white striped prison suits, and chained at the ankles. There is a guard, with a gun, his eyes drawn to red slits by the glare. The gang works all the day long, arriving huddled in the prison cart soon after daybreak, and being driven off again in the gray August twilight. All day there is the sound of the picks striking into the clay earth, hard sunlight, the smell of sweat. And every day there is music. One dark voice will start a phrase, half-sung, and like a question. And after a moment another voice will join in, soon the whole gang will be singing. The voices are dark in the golden glare, the music intricately blended, both somber and joyful. The music will swell until at last it seems that the sound does not come from the twelve men on the gang, but from the earth itself, or the wide sky. It is music that causes the heart to broaden and the listener to grow cold with ecstasy and fright. Then slowly the music will sink down until at last there remains one lonely voice, then a great hoarse breath, the sun, the sound of the picks in the silence.

And what kind of gang is this that can make such music? Just twelve mortal men, seven of them black and five of them white boys from this county. Just twelve mortal men who are together.

The rhetorical stance or tone of this is wholly McCullers's, and is rather difficult to characterize. In context, its reverberation is extraordinary, working as it does against our incapacity to judge or even comprehend the grotesque tragedy of the doomed love between Miss Amelia Evans and Cousin Lymon, with its consequence in the curious flowering and subsequent demise of the sad café. We, as readers, also would rather love than be loved, a preference that, in the aesthetic register, becomes the defense of reading more intensely lest we ourselves be read, whether by ourselves or by others. The emotion released by the juxtaposition between the music and its origin in the chain gang is precisely akin to the affect arising from McCullers's vision of the tragic dignity of the death of love arising so incongruously from the story of Miss Amelia, Cousin Lymon, and the hideous Marvin Macy.

Anthony Burgess

(1917-1993)

The Enderby Cycle and *Nothing Like the Sun*

I

ANTHONY BURGESS HAS THE SAME RELATIONSHIP TO JAMES JOYCE THAT Samuel Beckett has; dangerous as this comparison is (and Burgess has too much sense to welcome it), we can utilize it to define the nature and limits of Burgess's considerable achievement as a novelist and man-of-letters. Though Burgess has no *Murphy* (Beckett's genial, early comic masterpiece) he has the marvelous Enderby saga (*Inside Mr. Enderby*; *Enderby Outside*; *The Clockwork Testament; or, Enderby's End*; *Enderby's Dark Lady; or, No End to Enderby*) and the even grander *Nothing Like the Sun: A Story of Shakespeare's Love-life*. Whether writing about Enderby (a vision of Burgess himself as uncompromising poet) or Shakespeare, Burgess truly writes about Joyce's Poldy Bloom, and so about Joyce himself.

Murphy is as much an interpretation of *Ulysses* as the Enderby cycle or *Nothing Like the Sun* is, but *Murphy* already manifests a revisionary swerve away from the master, "a *clinamen* to the ideal," as Coleridge once called it. Beckett revised Joyce more cunningly still in *Watt* and the great trilogy of *Molloy*, *Malone Dies*, and *The Unnamable*, and that sly misprision of the only twentieth-century novelist to rival Proust is the foundation of Beckett's eminence as the strongest living writer in English or French today. Burgess has a more limited ambition, and enters into no *agon* with Joyce, however loving. Towards Joyce, he is the thankful receiver or good son, a humanly heartening stance but perhaps also one that balks the full freedom of creation.

Reviewing a biography of Beckett, Burgess shrewdly caught the subtle

438

relationship between Joyce and Beckett, strong father and strong, so necessarily cast-out, son:

> Beckett's books and plays posit a Cartesian division between mind
> and body. (His fast published work, the poem *Whoroscope*, is a kind
> of gorblimied life of Descartes.) Those heroes and heroines on their
> last, or nonexistent, legs, assert a powerful identity in spite of the
> wreck of the flesh. It is the kind of work one might expect from a
> lifelong invalid. His biography shows that Beckett was always an
> athlete, a well-coordinated car driver and motorbike rider who
> could smash the machine but emerge whole, an excellent swimmer
> and fine cricketer—the only Nobel Prizeman to be mentioned in
> *Wisden*. His body has always been spare and tough, able to take any
> amount of punishment from drink and cigarettes. But one notes a
> kind of self-flagellancy. A worshipper of Joyce, he took to pretend-
> ing he had Joyce's feet, which were small and dainty and pleased
> their owner: he crippled himself with unsuitable shoes. But the
> body's main pains, and its Oblomov lethargy, seem to have most to
> do with Beckett's complicated relationship with his mother....
>
> It is somewhat eery to find that the ancient *faible* of Lucia Joyce
> continued, long after her father's death and the end of Ellmann's
> record. Time stopped for her, and Beckett remained the young
> hawklike man who shared the masters silences and, after his rejec-
> tion of the demented girl's advances, was icily told not to call
> again. Beckett's devotion to Joyce continues, and his own artistic
> perfectionism, in the study and theatre alike, is its best expression.
> He works himself and his actors to the limit. The account of Billie
> Whitelaw's creative ordeal with him is one of the most remarkable
> chapters of this book.

The Muse his mother reclaims Beckett from Joyce here in the first
paragraph, moving us from the cheerful, curious, active Poldy to the sublimely lethargic Murphy, and all the nearly inanimate Beckett protagonists
who came after him. Icily rejected after refusing Lucia's schizophrenic
advances, Beckett is seen by Burgess as carrying the father's aesthetic per-
fectionism to new limits. This is legitimate enough, but chooses to evade
the dwindling of Joyce's idiom in Beckett, from its palpable presence in
Murphy to its total absence in the later, astonishingly laconic narratives, if
narratives they be.

Contrast Burgess on his "favorite novel," Ulysses:

And yet it is not quite a novel. I have lived long enough with *Ulysses* to be fully aware of its faults, and its major fault is that it evades the excruciating problem that most novelists set themselves: how, without blatant contrivance, to show character in the process of change, so that the reader, saying goodbye to Mr X or Miss Y, realizes that these are not quite the people he met at the beginning. There is, in every non-Joycean novel, a psychological watershed hardly discernible to the reader; without the imposition of a journey to this watershed fictional character can hardly be said to exist. In *Ulysses*, whose action covers less than twenty-four hours, there is no time for change. Indeed, nothing happens of sufficient gravity to induce change. The ordinary man Bloom meets the extraordinary youth Stephen and then says a goodnight which is probably a goodbye. Molly Bloom dreams of Stephen as a kind of messianic son-lover. Whatever happens in the novel, it does not happen today. It ends on the brink of tomorrow, when something may possibly happen, but tomorrow never comes. That is the novel's major fault.

It is a fault so massive that it can only be compensated for by exceptional virtues, and these virtues I have already hinted at—the epic vitality of the scheme, the candour of the presentation of human life as it really is, the awe-inspiring virtuosity of the language. Add to these the comprehensiveness of the urban vision it provides. When we visit Dublin we carry that vision with us; it is more real than the flesh-and-blood or stone-and-mortar reality. We cannot, I suppose, finally judge *Ulysses* as a work of fiction at all. It is a kind of magical codex, of the carne order as Dante's *Divine Comedy* (in which hell, heaven and purgatory go on forever and nothing changes). But, in the practical terms in which writers are forced to think, it is a terrible literary challenge. To call it my favourite novel is, I see, shame-fully inept. It is the work I have to measure myself hopelessly against each time I sit down to write fiction.

Has Burgess found, in the manner of the strong novelist, the fault that is not there in his precursor's masterwork? I suspect that he is asking Joyce to be Shakespeare, whose greatest originality came in representing how his characters changed through the process of listening to what they themselves had said. Burgess's Shakespeare is overtly Joyce's Shakespeare, so that *Nothing Like the Sun* is not less overtly Joycean than is the Enderby cycle. Joyce's own originality, even as a parodist, is rightly celebrated as being extraordinary. Even as Proust was found by his true precursor in the not-very-novelistic Ruskin (who nevertheless fused with Flaubert in the influence process), so Joyce owed less to Flaubert than he did to Shakespeare. *Ulysses* is not so much an interpretation of Homer, or even of Dante, as it is of *Hamlet*.

Joyce's *Hamlet* is an act of strong misreading, in which the poetic father, Shakespeare, is diminished so that the vital son, Joyce, can mature. This creation by interpretation, marked by zest, verve, saturnine wit, must be the most striking account of *Hamlet* ever given to us. Shakespeare is not Hamlet, but the ghost of Hamlet's father, a role that he actually played on stage (doubling as the Player King), according to tradition. Hamlet is Stephen, or the portrait of the artist as a young man. Poor Shakespeare has been cuckolded not just by one brother, as Hamlet senior was by Claudius, but by two, both of whom have had their way with Anne Hathaway. If this were not sexual defeat enough, Shakespeare in addition has lost the dark lady of the sonnets, presumably to an honorary third brother, or best friend. Stephen's theory proposes that Shakespeare's dead son, Hamnet, enters the play as Hamlet, to recover his fathers honor through an act of revenge. This resurrected son of Shakespeare does not lust after Anne Hathaway, or Gertrude, and can be regarded as a proleptic representation of Anthony Burgess, who did not refuse the gift.

In the Circe episode of *Ulysses*, Poldy and Stephen, each a representative of Shakespeare/Joyce, stare into a mirror and confront a transmogrified Shakespeare, beardless and "rigid in facial paralysis." Joyce is a beardless Shakespeare, lacking the Bard's virility, and frozen-faced where the precursor is mobile and expressive. Again, Burgess took the hint, even if he did not quite join in Joyce's ironic self-judgment. Stephen cites the Sabellian heresy, which holds that the Father was Himself His Own Son, a view that makes Shakespeare into Joyce, and Joyce into Burgess. Burgess, a good Freudian (Joyce evaded Freud, properly), believes rather that the Son was Himself His Own Father, a faith that makes Joyce into Shakespeare, and Burgess, rather wistfully, almost into Joyce.

II

Burgess, by need and conviction, exuberantly exemplifies the Johnsonian apothegm that only a blockhead would write for anything except money. The consequence is an immense output, not much of which bears rereading. His most famous novel, *A Clockwork Orange* (1962), owes its notoriety more to Stanley Kubrick's film version than to its own text, and his overtly religious narratives (the book-length poem *Moses* and such excursions as *Man of Nazareth*) are interesting primarily as instances of the writer's Manichean dualism, which has replaced Burgess's lapsed Catholicism. But two of the novels I reread annually: *Inside Mr. Enderby* (1963) and *Nothing Like the* Sun (1964). Enderby triumphantly returned in *Enderby Outside* (1968), only to be killed off by his ungrateful creator in *The Clockwork Testament; or, Enderby's End* (1975), which provoked a fierce out-cry by devoted Enderbyans, among whom I number myself. In response to our laments and protests, Burgess gave us *Enderby's Dark Lady; or, No End to Enderby*, a superb amalgam of *Inside Mr. Enderby* and *Nothing Like the Sun*. It is now to be hoped that Enderby, and "William Shakespeare," will last as long as Burgess does, may it be forever.

Inside Mr. Enderby is one of my own candidates for the most underval-ued English novel of our era, since the raffish narrative clearly has immor-tality in it. Enderby himself is at once Leopold Bloom, James Joyce, William Shakespeare, and Anthony Burgess, which is merely outrageous, and totally successful. As a true poet, Enderby is also Samuel Johnson, Jonathan Swift, John Keats, Walt Whitman, and perhaps such modern roisterers as Dylan Thomas and Brendan Behan, which only means that Enderby is a universal representation of the fate of the poet in a world nec-essarily and simultaneously too good for him and not quite good enough for anyone of imagination.

Everything that is conceivable happens to Enderby, or perhaps rather Enderby is what happens to everyone else in his world. Like Poldy, Enderby is the complete man or the compassionate man, except that Poldy is a Jewish respecter of learning and art and a bit of an artist himself, but no poet, which is Stephen's vocation—and Enderby's. Enderby is also obsessed by guilt, quite unmerited, whereas Poldy is beyond guilt, being a kind of Messiah, a text that is an answer, though obscure. The Enderby books, never obscure, refuse all answers. Amidst so much tawdry splendor, which never ceases to proliferate, I cite as a favorite passage the sublime moment when Enderby graciously declines the Goodby gold medal for poetry at a luncheon in London, a paradigm of all the literary luncheons where, like Enderby, the critic Bloom has gotten quite drunk:

> "And it is for this reason that it gives me pleasure to bestow on our fellow singing-bird here, er er Enderby, the Goodby gold medal." Enderby rose to applause loud enough to drown three cracking intestinal reports. "And a cheque," said Sir George, with nostalgia of poet's poverty, "that is very very small but, one trusts, will stave off pangs for a month or two." Enderby took his trophies, shook hands, simpered, then sat down again. "Speech," said somebody.

Enderby rose again, with a more subdued report, then realised that he was unsure of the exordial protocol. Did he say, "Mr. Chairman"? Was there a chairman? If Sir George was the chairman should he say something other than "Mr. Chairman"? Should he just say, "Sir George, ladies and gentlemen"? But, he noticed, there seemed to be somebody with a chain of office gleaming on his chest, hovering in the dusk, a mayor or lord mayor. What should he say—"Your Worship"? In time he saw that this was some sort of menial in charge of wine. Holding in wind, a nervously smiling Aeolus, Enderby said, loud and clear:

"St George." There was a new stir of tittering. "And the dragon," Enderby now had to add. "A British cymbal," he continued, seeing with horror that orthographical howler in a sort of neon lights before him. "A cymbal that tinkles in unsound brass if we are without clarity." There were appreciative easings of buttocks and shoulders: Enderby was going to make it brief and humorous. Desperately Enderby said, "As most of us are or are not, as the case may be. Myself included." Sir George, he saw, was throwing up wide face-holes at him, as though he, Enderby, were on a girder above the street. "Clarity," said Enderby, almost in tears, "is red wine for yodellers. And so," he gaped aghast at himself, "I am overjoyed to hand back this cheque to St George for charitable disposal. The gold medal he knows what he can do with." He could have died with shock and embarrassment at what he was saying; he was hurled on to the end in killing momentum, however. "Dross of the workaday world," he said "as our fellow-singer Goodby so adequately disproves. And so," he said, back in the Army giving a talk on the British Way and Purpose, "we look forward to a time when the world shall be free of the shadow of oppression, the iron heel with its swastika spur no longer grinding into the face of supine freedom, democracy a reality, a fair day's pay for a fair day's work, adequate health services and a bit of peace hovering dovelike in the declining days of the aged. And in that belief and aspiration we move forward." He found that he could not stop. "Forward," he insisted, "to a time when the world shall be free of the shadow of oppression." Sir George had risen and was tottering out. "A fair day's work," said Enderby feebly, "for a fair day's pay. Fair play for all," he mumbled doubtfully. Sit George had gone. "And thereto," ended Enderby wretchedly,

"I plight thee my truth."

The model for Enderby's peroration is Poldy's proclamations of the New Bloomusalem in the Nova Hibernia of the future, in the Nighttown episode of *Ulysses*, except that Poldy, as always, is sober, while Enderby, as always, is drunk. In some ways Enderby combines the traits of a Buck Mulligan emptied out of all malice, with the lovable amiability of Poldy, gentlest of all representations in fiction. This may be too much of a problem in depiction for Burgess and may account for the gradual evolution of Enderby away from Poldy and Joyce and towards Burgess's "William Shakespeare," as the cycle takes its labyrinthine pratfalls on to *Enderby's Dark Lady*. What is certain is that no single Enderby book is quite as effective as *Nothing Like the Sun*, not even *Inside Mr. Enderby*, though finally I might set that highest in the Burgess canon. For sustained command of language, Shakespearean and Joycean, *Nothing Like the Sun* is Burgess's most accomplished performance, as here in a vision of Elizabethan London as the demonic context of the great love affair between Shakespeare and the dark lady of the *Sonnets*:

> London, the defiled city, became a sweet bower for their lover's wandering, even in the August heat. The kites that hovered or, perched, picked at the flesh of traitors' skulls became good cleansing birds, bright of eye and feather, part of the bestiary of myth that enthralled them as they made it. The torn and screaming bears and dogs and apes in the pits of Paris Garden were martyrs who rose at once into gold heraldic zoomorphs to support the scutcheon of their static and sempiternal love. The wretches that lolled in chains on the lapping edges of the Thames, third tide washed over, noseless, lipless, eye-eaten, joined the swinging hanged at Tyburn and the rotting in the jails to be made heroes of a classical hell that, turned into music by Vergil, was sweet and pretty schoolday innocence. But it was she who shook her head often in sadness, smiling beneath her diaphanous veil as they took the evening air in passion's convalescence, saying that autumn would soon be on them, that love's fire burned flesh and then itself—out, gone for ever.

This is the only apocalypse acceptable to Burgess, heroic vitalist and celebrator of the things of this world: "Love's fire burned flesh and then itself—out, gone for ever." That is a burden hardly unique to Burgess, and the accent remains Joycean, yet the music of this mortality verges upon being Burgess's alone.

Iris Murdoch

(1919-1999)

The Good Apprentice

AT THE END OF HER FIRST BOOK, AN ENDURING STUDY OF SARTRE PUBLISHED in 1953, Iris Murdoch prophetically lamented that Sartre's "inability to write a great novel is a tragic symptom of a situation which afflicts us all." Her own inability has extended now through twenty-two novels, of which the best seem to me *Bruno's Dream* (1969), *The Black Prince* (1973), *A Word Child* (1975), and her latest, *The Good Apprentice*. So fecund and exuberant is Murdoch's talent that many more novels may be expected from her. If *The Good Apprentice* marks the start of her strongest phase, and it may, then a great novel could yet come, rather surprisingly in the incongruous form of the nineteenth-century realistic novel. The age of Samuel Beckett and Thomas Pynchon, post-Joycean and post-Faulknerian, is set aside by Murdoch's novelistic procedures, almost as though she thus chose to assert her own direct continuity with the major nineteenth-century Russian and British masters of fiction.

Murdoch's anachronistic style and outmoded narrative devices are not, in my experience of reading her, the principal flaws in her work. Like Gabriel García Márquez, she favors a realism that can be more phantasmagoric than naturalistic, but she tends not to be able to sustain this mixed mode, whereas he can. Consistency of stance is one of Murdoch's problems. She is both fantasist and realist, each on principle, but her abrupt modulations between the two visions sometimes seem less than fully controlled. Her novels rush by us, each a successful entertainment, but none perhaps filly distinct from the others in our memories.

Yet her fictions fuse into a social cosmos, one that is reasonably recognizable as contemporary British upper-middle-class. Of all her talents,

445

the gift of plotting is the most formidable, including a near-Shakespearean faculty for intricate double plots. Again her strength seems sometimes uncontrolled, and even the most responsive reader can feel harried and at last indifferent as labyrinthine developments work themselves through. Yet that is how Murdoch tends to manifest her considerable exuberance as a writer, rather than in the creation of endless otherness in her characters, which nevertheless (and rather sadly) seems to constitute her largest ambition. She does not excel at fresh invention of personalities. We learn to expect certain basic types to repeat themselves in her novels: fierce, very young women, compulsive and cunning, violent in their pursuit of much older men, are omnipresent. Their quarry, those older men, are narcissistic charmers but weak, self-indulgent, hesitant skeptics, fearful of reality. Then there are the power figures whom Murdoch once called "alien gods." These are frequently male, Middle European, Jewish charismatics, who may be presumed to have some allegorical or ironic link to the writer Elias Canetti, a friend of Murdoch in her youth. Unfulfilled older women abound also; they are marked by resentment, identity anxieties, and by a tendency to fall in love drastically, absurdly, and abruptly.

Murdoch's particular mastery is in representing the maelstrom of falling in love, which is the characteristic activity of nearly all her men and women, who somehow have time for busy professional careers in London while obsessively suffering convulsive love relationships. Somewhere in one of her early novels, Murdoch cannily observes that falling out of love is one of the great human experiences, a kind of rebirth in which we see the world with freshly awakened eyes. Though an academic philosopher earlier in her career, Murdoch's actual philosophical achievement is located where she clearly wishes it to be, in her novels, which demonstrate her to be a major student of Eros, not of the stature of Freud or Proust, but still an original and endlessly provocative theorist of the tragicomedy of sexual love, with its peculiar hell of jealousy and self-hatred. Her nearest American equivalent in this dark area is Saul Bellow, a novelist whom otherwise she does not much resemble.

Indeed, she resembles no other contemporary novelist, in part because she is essentially a religious fabulist, of an original and unorthodox sort, and therefore very unlike Graham Greene or John Updike or Walker Percy or Cynthia Ozick, whose varied religious outlooks are located in more definite normative traditions. Murdoch thinks for herself theologically as well as philosophically, and her conceptual originality is difficult for readers to apprehend, particularly when it is veiled by her conventional forms of storytelling and her rather mixed success in the representation of original characters. There is a perpetual incongruity between Murdoch's formulaic procedures and her spiritual insights, an incongruity that continues in *The Good Apprentice*.

The good apprentice is twenty-year-old Edward Baltram, a university student who begins the novel by slyly feeding a drug-laden sandwich to his best friend and fellow-student Mark Wilsden. While Edward goes off to make love to a girl in the neighborhood, Mark wakes up and falls or jumps out of the window to his death. Edward's grief and guilt dominate the book, which is his quest for a secular absolution at the hands of his actual father, Jesse Bahrain, an insane vitalist and reclusive painter who begat Edward upon one of his models and subsequently has not seen his son apart from a childhood meeting or two. Murdoch's ironic opening sentence is the novels spiritual signature:

> I will arise and go to my father, and will say unto him, Father I
> have sinned against heaven and before thee, and am no more wor-
> thy to be called thy son.

In a narrative that chronicles Edward's journey from hell to purgatory, we might expect that Edward would encounter at least one figure who unequivocally embodies love, wisdom, or at least power. But that underestimates Murdoch's authentic spiritual originality which has now matured to the point that all such figures are negated. Though Edward regards himself as a dead soul, he is nevertheless the book's only legitimate representative of the good, in however apprentice a guise. His elders all fail him, and themselves are exposed as souls deader than he is. Jesse Baltram, his mad father, is a magician but a perpetually dying one until his mysterious death by water. Mother May, Jesse's wife, seems at first as charming and innocent as her daughters, Bettina and Ilona, Edward's half-sisters, and the long middle section of the book set at Seegard, Jesse's estate, begins as the most beautiful of all Murdoch's pastoral idylls. But May is revealed to he scheming, resentful, and jealous, Bettina scarcely less so, and the ineffable Ilona is transmogrified into a Soho stripper. The book's wisdom figure, Thomas McCaskerville, Edward's uncle by marriage, is at once a subtle Scottish-Jewish psychoanalyst, uttering a parodistic version of R.D. Laing's madness-as-spiritual-journey ideology, and also a bemused cuckold, preaching about the reality principle of death while understanding very little of life as it touches him most closely.

With her alien gods and charismatics so discredited, Murdoch boldly steps into their place herself, editorializing directly about her characters' psychological and spiritual miseries. Here she analyzes the meditative stance of Stuart, Edward's step-brother and foil, who also has rejected life in favor of a death that might precede a more abundant life:

> A disinterested observer might have wondered why Stuart so ardently rejected God, since he did not simply sit and meditate, he also knelt down, sometimes even prostrated himself. Once again, Stuart, recognising no problem, instinctively resolved apparent contradictions. Meditation was refuge, quietness, purification, replenishing, return to whiteness. Prayer was struggle, reflection, self-examination, it was more particular, involving concern about other people and naming of names. Harry had said that Stuart wanted to be like Job, always guilty before God, an exalted form of sadomasochism. Stuart's rejection of God was, in effect, his rejection of that "old story," to use Ursula's words, as alien to his being. His mind refused it, spewed it out, not as a dangerous temptation, but as alien tissue. Of course he wanted to be "good"; and so he wanted to avoid guilt and remorse, but those states did not *interest* him. Towards his sins and failures he felt cold, no warmth was generated there. So little did he feel himself menaced from that quarter that in prayer he would even say (for he used words) *dominus et deus*, without attaching the old meaning to those dread sounds. (Perhaps it was important that the words were Latin, not English.) He knew there was no supernatural being and did not design to try to attach the concept in any way to his absolutes. If something, "good" or something, was his "master," it was in no personal or reciprocal relation. His language was thus indeed odd as when he sometimes said "forgive me," or "help me," or when he commended others, Edward for instance, to the possibility of being helped. Stuart understood the phrase "love is only of God"; his love went out into the cosmos as a lonely signal, but also miraculously could return to earth. His belief that his supplication for Edward, his concern for Edward, could help Edward was not a hypothesis about actions which he might, as a result of well-intentioned thoughts, later perform for his brother (though this aspect of the matter was not excluded); nor of course was he resorting to some paranormal telepathic form of healing. He simply felt sure that the purer his love the more efficacious it would be in some "immediate" sense which put in question the ordinary pit-pat of time.

Admirers of Murdoch are fond of defending such authorial

interpolations by citing their prevalence in the nineteenth-century novel. It is certainly true that George Eliot is never more impressive than in such interventions, and Murdoch indeed is recognizably in Eliot's explicitly moral tradition. Unfortunately, what worked sublimely for Eliot cannot work so well for Murdoch, despite her engaging refusal to be self-conscious about her belatedness. As speculation, this paragraph is impressive, but as fiction it makes us wonder why Murdoch *tells us* what we expect her to *show us*. Her gifts for dramatic action are considerable, but her own narrative voice lacks George Eliot's authority, being too qualified and fussy when a rugged simplicity is required. She is no less acute a moral analyst than Eliot, but she does not persuade us that her judgments are a necessary part of the story she has made for us.

Yet I do not wish to slight her conceptual strength as a religious writer, which is her particular excellence, since she has taught herself how subtly story and tragic, narrative art and the questing spirit, can fuse in a novel, even if the fusion is incomplete so far in her work. Starting as an existentialist writer in *Under the Net*, she has evolved into that curious oxymoron, a Platonist novelist, perpetually in pursuit of the Good, a quest that she herself parodies in the hilarious and painful couplings of her erotomaniac protagonists. Her obsessive symbol for this sadomasochistic pattern is the myth of Apollo and Marsyas, which was exploited in *The Black Prince* and several other novels, and which is repeated in *The Good Apprentice*. Marsyas the musician, having challenged Apollo to a music contest, loses and suffers the penalty of being flayed to death. Murdoch reads the myth so that the agony of Marsyas is our agony now in seeking to know God in an age when God is dead. So, in *The Good Apprentice*:

> Thomas recalled Edward's weird exalted stare, his uncanny smile. A (lemon who had nothing to do with the well-being of the ordinary "real" Edward had for a moment looked out. How ambiguous such conditions were. The entranced face of the tortured Marsyas, as Apollo kneels lovingly to tear his skin off, prefigures the death and resurrection of the soul.

Our shudder here is not shared by Murdoch, whose version of a post-Christian religion is marked by violence and deathliness. Whatever Socrates meant by saying we should study dying, Murdoch harshly means that death is the truth, since it destroys every image and every story. Her savage Platonism in the novels is consistent with her stance in *The Fire and the Sun: Why Plato Banished the Artists* (1977):

Escape from the Cave and approach to the Good is a progressive discarding of relative false goods, of hypotheses, images, and shadows, eventually seen as such.

These are the accents not just of a Platonic exegesis, but of Murdoch's firmest beliefs, expressed overtly in the closing paragraph of *The Fire and the Sun*:

> Plato feared the consolations of art. He did not offer a consoling theology. His psychological realism depicted God as subjecting mankind to a judgment as relentless as that of the old Zeus, although more just. A finely meshed moral causality determines the fate of the soul. That the movement of the saving of Eros is toward an impersonal pictureless void is one of the paradoxes of a complete religion. To present the idea of God at all, even as myth, is a consolation, since it is impossible to defend this image against the prettifying attentions of art. Art will mediate and adorn, and develop magical structures to conceal the absence of God or his distance. We live now amid the collapse of many such structures, and as religion and metaphysics in the West withdraw from the embraces of art, we are it might seem being forced to become mystics through the lack of any imagery which could satisfy the mind. Sophistry and magic break down at intervals, but they never go away and there is no end to their collusion with art and to the consolations which, perhaps fortunately for the human race, they can provide; and art, like writing and like Eros, goes on existing for better and for worse.

This bitter Platonism resembles that of Simone Weil, a powerful early influence upon Murdoch. Whatever one thinks of the spiritual stance of Weil and Murdoch (I personally find it repellant), it seems at once antithetical to the interests of art yet also a powerful goad to Murdoch's development as a novelist who exploits magic while endlessly disowning it.

The Good Apprentice seems to me an advance upon all of Murdoch's previous novels, even *The Black Prince*, because the morally ferocious Platonist finally has allowed herself a wholly sympathetic protagonist in the self purging Edward. His progress out of an inner hell has no false consolations or illusory images haunting it. In some sense, Edward's achievement and torment is wholly Freudian in its spirit, resembling as it does the later Freud of *Beyond the Pleasure Principle* through *Civilization and Its Discontents*. Freud's last vestige of Platonism, his only transcendentalism, was his worship of reality testing or the reality principle, which was his way of naming the conditions imposed by the outwardness of the world, whose final form is death. Murdoch's only consistent transcendentalism is grimly parallel to Freud's, since her novels insist that religious consciousness, in our post-religious era, must begin with the conviction that only death centers life, that death is the only valid representation of a life better than the life-in-death we all suffer daily.

This is the impressive if rather stark structure that Murdoch imposes upon *The Good Apprentice*, where the first section is called "The Prodigal Son," and depicts Edward's descent into a private hell, and the second, "Seegard," recounts his purgatorial search for his enigmatic magician of a father. The third and last part Murdoch names "Life After Death," implying that the still anguished Edward has begun an ascent into the upper reaches of his personal purgatory.

Like nearly all of her twenty-two novels, Murdoch's *The Good Apprentice* has a surface that constitutes a brilliant entertainment, a social comedy of and for the highly literate. Beneath that surface an astringent post-Christian Platonism has evolved into a negative theology that pragmatically offers only the Gnostic alternatives of either total libertinism or total puritanism in the moral life. The aesthetic puzzle is whether the comic story and the Platonic kernel can be held together by Murdoch's archaic stance as an authorial will. And yet no other contemporary British novelist seems to me of Murdoch's eminence. Her formidable combination of intellectual drive and storytelling exuberance may never fuse into a great novel, but she has earned now the tribute she made to Jean Paul Sartre more than thirty years ago. She too has the style of the age.

William Gaddis

(1922-1998)

The Recognitions

MY ONE PERSONAL MEMORY OF WILLIAM GADDIS GOES BACK TO A MEETING of the American Academy of Arts and Letters, sometime in the later 1990s. We had been introduced perhaps a year before, and he approached me, expressing gratification that I had included *The Recognitions* in a canonical catalog published in 1994. Not knowing him, yet apprehending that his grave and courteous manner did not seem ironic, I stammered that I had admired the novel since 1955, when it was first published, and had reread it several times since, always with a sense of gratitude. Gaddis graciously nodded his head, and walked away. Returning to New Haven that night, I rather weirdly found a copy of the Penguin paperback of *The Recognitions* in my briefcase, where I had not placed it.

This oddity (and I still do not know how the book got there) reflects for me the uncanniness of *The Recognitions*, where the inexplicable is marvelously omnipresent, in an almost Dickensian way. Jonathan Raban sensibly notes that Gaddis, the first so-called Post-Modernist of the American novel, actually is Victorian in sensibility, and might well have pleased Trollope. I wish I could share Raban's admiration for *A Frolic of His Own*, or my close friend the novelist Walter Abish's high regard for *JR*, but alas I don't. *Carpenter's Gothic* also continues to evade me, though it has a legitimate place in a tradition that moves from Brockden Brown through Hawthorne on to Faulkner, Flannery O'Connor, and Cormac McCarthy.

The Recognitions is so rich a work that Gaddis could have rested on his oars forever. It has an authentic literary lineage that begins with the Third Century *Clementine Recognitions*, an early Christian romance. Simon Magus, supposed by some to be the inventor of Gnosticism, is the villain of this curious tale, and this Simon of Samaria, known as the Magus, is the first manifestation of Faustus, the Favored one. Gaddis also draws upon St. Augustine and St. John of the Cross, but is closer in spirit to Melville's *Moby-Dick*, to Goethe's *Faust*, and very overtly to T.S. Eliot, whose "The Love Song of J. Alfred Prufrock," *The Waste Land* and *Four Quartets* are echoed throughout. In a rather disturbing way, *The Recognitions* parodies Joyce's *Ulysses*, which Gaddis insisted he never had read.

The influence of *The Recognitions* upon novelists from Thomas Pynchon to Jonathan Franzen's *The Corrections* is palpable, and not always fortunate, but Gaddis's outrageous first fiction bridges the long morass in the American novel from Faulkner's major phase to the full maturing of Philip Roth, Don DeLillo, and Cormac McCarthy, and to Pynchon's triumphant resurrection in *Mason and Dixon*. Doubtless the death of Nathanael West, in a car crash, removed an extraordinary imagination far too early, and yet it cleared a visionary space for Gaddis, who was thirty-three, the Chistological age, when *The Recognitions* appeared.

Like Joyce's *Ulysses*, Gaddis's masterwork is less a narrative fiction than it is an epic of consciousness. But *whose* consciousness? Hamlet has his own consciousness, different from what we may infer was Shakespeare's, yet we are not persuaded that Wyatt Gwyon has a mind all his own. Willie the writer (see pp. 272–3 and 478 of *The Recognitions*) is the endless consciousness of his book, and the implicit protagonist of its quest for transcendence.

The Recognitions goes on for fifty-six pages after we behold the last of Wyatt on page 900:

> He had left his windows opened, and the bird was sitting on one of the framed pictures when he came in, and closed the door behind him.
>
> But he had already paused to make his notation, "What mean?" before he saw it, when it fluttered across the room to the other picture, and though he tried frantically to chase it toward the front, toward the windows and out, it fluttered the more frantically from one picture to the other, and back across the room and back, as he passed the mirror himself in both directions, where he might have glimpsed the face of a man having, or about to have, or at the very least valiantly fighting off, a religious experience.

The religious experience, conveyed by gentle irony, is the descent of the dove, the Pentecost of the Paraclete, Christ-as-comforter. Here Gaddis affects the ambiguous undulations of the end of Pynchon's *The*

Crying of Lot 49, and the more overt intimations of a possible transcendence that culminate Don DeLillo's major works, from *White Noise* through *Underworld*. The sequence of Gaddis, Pynchon, and DeLillo constitutes an ambivalent opening to glory in ongoing American fiction.

José Saramago

(1922-)

REREADING SARAMAGO, I ALWAYS FEEL LIKE ULYSSES TRYING TO KEEP MY hold on Proteus, the metamorphic god of ocean; he keeps slipping away. From *Baltasar and Blimunda* on through *The Cave*, Saramago is in constant change, not merely from fiction to fiction, but within each work. I don't know the genre of any of his books, except his masterpiece (in my view), *The Gospel According to Jesus Christ*, as that I suppose has to be called a gospel, though it brings very bad news indeed: a Jesus betrayed by God the Father; a Satan who is a mild bystander, really a good shepherd, and so named Pastor; a God so self-indulgent that he sacrifices Jesus solely in order to extend his worshippers from the small elite of the Jews, to a myriad of Christians. There is also this God's evident, sadistic relish in sacrificing not only Jesus but a vast array of subsequent martyrs, all tortured to death or executed by an exuberant panoply of ingenious devices.

But I have considered Saramago's *Gospel* elsewhere, and shall revisit it later only in passing. Here I begin with the outrageous and delicious *Baltasar and Blimunda* (1987), though to characterize any single narrative by Saramago as being more deliciously outrageous than the others is a disputable judgment.

T.S. Eliot was fond of describing himself as Anglo-Catholic, Royalist, and classicist. He could have added anti-Semite, and I have always wondered how he would have reacted had Great Britain been successfully invaded and occupied by the Nazis? I don't know that Saramago needs to describe himself at all: he is certainly neither Catholic nor Royalist, and he is too diverse and inventive for any stance like classicist to subsume him. Like Jorge Luis Borges, Saramago is a free man, and his books exalt freedom, generally by depicting its dreadful alternatives. *Baltasar and Blimunda* is Saramago's historical romance, set in the frightening Portugal of the early eighteenth century, a country where the Enlightenment had not yet arrived. Public entertainment still was constituted by acts of faith, in which heretics, Jews, and everyone else who offended either Church or King were burned alive, to the edification of the true believers.

These fires burn throughout the book, but most dreadfully at the close, when Baltasar is consumed. He is an admirable soul, as is his beloved seeress Blimunda, but I defer consideration of them until further on, when I can compare their tragic love to other erotic splendors in Saramago. The other visionary center of this turbulent book is the inventive and heretical Padre Bartholomew Lorenzo, an actual personage, who arrived in Portugal from Brazil in 1708. Known to his enemies as "the Flying Man," he invented a bird-like flying machine, called "La passarola," which figures crucially in Saramago's story. I assume Saramago invented the magnificent notion that Domenico Scarlatti himself serenades Baltasar as the one-handed former soldier builds the "Passarola" designed by Padre Lourenço.

It is pure Saramago that the fuel for the flying bird should be provided by Blimunda, who has the unique power to bottle human wills. No surprise here; we are in a romance where the seagulls are "anxious to know if God has aged much." It is however a romance that crosses over into scabrous realism:

> People are saying that the realm is badly governed, and that there is no justice. They fail to understand that this is how the realm ought to be, with its eyes blindfolded and bearing its scales and sword. What more could we wish for, when that is all that has been required: that we should be the weavers of bandages, the inspectors of the weights, the armorers of the sword, constantly mending the holes, adjusting the balance, sharpening the edge of the blade, and then asking the defendant if he is satisfied with the sentence passed on him once he has won or lost his case. We are not referring here to sentences passed by the Holy Office of the Inquisition, which is very astute and prefers an olive branch to scales and a keen blade to one that is jagged and blunt. Some mistake the olive branch as a gesture of peace when it is all too clear that it is kindling wood for the funeral pyre. Either I stab you or I burn you. Therefore, in the absence of any law, it is preferable to stab a woman suspected of infidelity than to honor the faithful who have passed on. It is a question of having protectors who are likely to forgive homicide, and a thousand cruzados to put on the scales, which explains why justice holds the latter in her hand. Let blacks and hoodlums be punished so that the importance of good

example may be upheld. Let people of rank and wealth be honored, without demanding that they pay their debts, that they renounce vengeance or mitigate their hatred. And while the lawsuits are being fought, since certain little irregularities cannot be totally avoided, let there be chicanery, swindling, appeals, formalities, and evasions, so that those likely to gain a just decision will not gain it too readily, and those likely to lose their appeal will not lose it too soon. In the meantime teats are milked for that delicious milk, money, those rich curds, prime cheese, and a tasty morsel for the bailiff and the solicitor, for the witness and the judge;

Saramago's Swiftian irony will become subtler in later books, but one is dazzled by its pungency here, with that marvelous, pragmatic motto for the Inquisition: "Either I stab you or I burn you." We are not quite in the United States of the second George Bush or in contemporary Portugal, but the implications are there. A great moment comes when the lovers and Padre Lourenço take off together in the Passarolo. As they descend, Saramago invokes the image of Camões, the heroic one-eyed national warrior-epic poet:

> Who knows what dangers await them, what Adamastor they will encounter, what Saint Elmo's fires they will see rise from the sea, what columns of water will suck in the air only to expel it once it has been settled? Then Blimunda asks where are we going. And the priest replies: where the arm of the Inquisition cannot reach us if such a place exists.

They come down in the mountains, and Lourenço disappears. Baltasar and Blimunda make their way to his parents' home, where eventually Scarlatti will come to tell them that Padre Bartholomew, pursued by the Inquisition, escaped to Spain and then died in Toledo. Poor Baltasar is impressed into a work crew to build a great Franciscan convent. When he gets free again, he finds and flies in the Passarolo. Meanwhile, poor Blimunda, who is being raped by a properly pious friar, kills him with the detachable spike that Baltasar usually wears. For nine long years, Blimunda searches for her Baltasar, and finds him already burning in a glorious act-of-faith involving the usual collection of Jews, playwrights, and similar riffraff.

Then Blimunda said: Come. The will of Baltasar Sete-Sóis broke free from his body, but did not ascend to the stars, for it belonged to the earth and to Blimunda. Though this is a marvelous aesthetic conclusion, it leaves us a little sad. What can happen next? Perhaps Blimunda will find the Passarola and use Baltasar's will for a final flight, but she will be alone in a melancholy freedom, wherever she lands, if ever she lands. Portugal in the early 18th century has yielded us the following. The country is Hell, governed by a viciously stupid royal family, and tortured incessantly by a Church indistinguishable from the Inquisition. What saves it from hellishness? Only four beings: the partly Jewish witch Blimunda; the heroic, Cervantes-like one-armed soldier, Baltasar; the inventor of the Passarolo, Padre Lourenço, who converts to the unitive God of Judaism, and then goes off to die in Spain; and the survivor, Domenico Scarlatti, who will go on playing his ethereal melodies that alone redeem such a world. Saramago prophetically consigns Portugal, the Catholic Church and the monarchy to the hell of history. The Passarola, image of illusory freedom, saves no one, and its great inventor exiles himself to die in Toledo. Our lovers never totally lose one another and what redeems the book is Saramago's real love for them, which transcends all his ironies. I pass to the wonderful irreality of *The Year of the Death of Ricardo Reis* (1984). We are in Hell again, that is to say historical Portugal in December 1935, with Salazar come to power, and Spain about to endure the Fascist usurpation. Acts of faith will be performed by machine guns and rifles, less pleasant to God than the aroma of burning flesh. Our hero is the amiable poet, Dr. Ricardo Reis, one of Pessoa's heteronyms: a mild, Horatian Epicurean, who has returned from Brazil to Lisbon. He checks into his hotel, and then goes out to read a newspaper that reports the death of Fernando Pessoa, and naturally pays a visit of respect to his creator's tomb. Already we have had allusions to Eça and to Borges: we are in the reality of the fabulists and poets.

Ricardo Reis pursues two erotic quests, an idealized one for Marcenda, paralyzed in her left hand, and a fleshly one with Lydia, the hotel chambermaid. But first he returns from dinner, to find the ghostly Pessoa waiting for him in his hotel room, and they converse like the old friends they are. They will go on meeting, since ghosts have eight months of freedom, and in the meantime Lydia enters the bed of Ricardo Reis.

Though Salazar's Portugal is always in the background, we essentially are in a pleasant realm: literary, erotic, nostalgic. I pause to note that I know no other novelistic atmosphere at all like the ambiance of *The Year of the Death of Ricardo Reis*. It is an utterly new mode of aestheticism: both visionary and realistic, the cosmos of the great poet Pessoa and of the Fascist dictator Salazar and yet it presents us also with an original literary enigma: how long can Ricardo Reis survive the death of Fernando Pessoa? For three hundred and fifty pages we have experienced the life and loves of a heteronym. What a triumph for Pessoa, and for Saramago. The novel's beautifully modulated closing passage has an utterly unprecedented tonality:

> As they left the apartment, Fernando Pessoa told him, you forgot your hat. You know better than I do that hats aren't worn where we're going. On the sidewalk opposite the park, they watched the pale lights flicker on the river, the ominous shadows of the mountains. Let's go then, said Fernando Pessoa. Let's go, agreed Ricardo Reis. Adamastor did not turn around to look, perhaps afraid that if he did, he might let out finally his mighty howl. Here, where the sea ends and the earth awaits.

The will of Baltasar belonged to Blimunda and the earth, and the earth awaits both poets, Pessoa and Reis. The earth is always waiting for us in Saramago; at the close of his magnificent fantasy, *The Stone Raft* (1986), we are gently assured: "The elm branch is green. Perhaps it will flower again next year." The book's epigraph quotes the great Cuban fabulist, Alejo Carpentier, who is of Saramago's school: "Every future is fabulous." In Carpentier, yes, but in Saramago, these things are ordered differently. That elm branch starts all the trouble anyway, and converts Iberia into a stone raft, after Joana Carda scratches the ground with it, having no idea it was a magic wand. The genius of Saramago is off and running, fulfilling its destiny of disturbing us into a fuller realization of what it means to read and to write.

It would madden me, and all of us, if I attempted to summarize this sublimely zany narrative. Its given is summary enough; the entire slab of Spain and Portugal has spun loose from Europe, and heads out into the Atlantic. Saramago's aesthetic burden therefore is immense; if you start your story with *that*, how are you to catch up to yourself? I retract; there is no aesthetic burden for the cunning Saramago. We never get at all far from that original outrage. It is almost halfway through the novel, on page 127, that Joanna Carda explains why and how the catastrophe happened? She required a symbolic act to indicate that she was separating from her husband: They are standing on the edge of the clearing, Joana Carda detains the men a bit longer, these are her final words, I picked up the stick from the ground, the wood seemed to be living as if it were the whole tree from which it had been cut, or rather this is what I now feel as it comes back to me, and at that moment, with a gesture more like a child's than an adult's, I drew a line that separated me forever from Coimbra and the man with whom I lived, a line that divided the world into two halves, as you can see from here.

They advanced to the middle of the clearing, drew close, there was the line, as clear as if it had just been drawn, the earth piled up on either side, the bottom layer still damp despite the warmth of the sun. They remain silent, the men are at a loss for words, Joana Carda has nothing more to say, this is the moment for a daring gesture that could make a mockery of her wonderful tale. She drags one foot over the ground, smooths the soil as if she were using a level, stamps on it and presses down, as if committing an act of sacrilege. The next moment, before the astonished gaze of all the onlookers, the line reappears, it looks exactly as it was before, the tiny particles of soil, the grains of sand resume their previous shape and form, return to where they were before, and the line is back. Between the part that was obliterated and the rest, between one side and the other, there is no visible difference. Her nerves on edge, Joana Carda says in a shrill voice, I've already swept away the entire line, I've covered it with water, yet it keeps reappearing, try for yourselves if you wish, I even put stones on top, and when I removed them the line was still there, why don't you try if you still need convincing.

Nothing works; she is accurate. When then is to be done? Saramago, who is the Devil, is not so much making fun of Europe, or even of Nato or the European Community, but of the ultimate ideas of the geopolitical, the geological, and of all related fantasies that pass as realities. By page 139. he is in a hilarious ecstasy:

> Let us wage that we will ultimately be reduced to a single nation, the quintessence of the European spirit, a single and perfect sublimation, Europe, namely, Switzerland.

The joke, once started cannot be stopped. The late J.F.K. is permanently repaid for his "Ich bin ein Berliner" when all Europe is swept by the slogan: *We also are Iberians*. Anarchist outrages follow, as millions of youths repeat the Great Awakening of the late 1960's, smashing TV stations and shop-fronts, turning Europe into Seattle: For the catalogs of memoirs and reminiscences there remained those dying words of the handsome young Dutchman hit by a rubber bullet ... At last, I'm Iberian, and with these words he expired ...

Except for Joana Carda, I have not mentioned the three other early protagonists, and don't really want to, because they are mere males and they do not seem as important as the curious dog who tags along throughout. Or rather, they tag along, as only the dog seems to know where they are going. One of them, José Anaiço, is taken, by Joana Carda. Another, Joaquim Sassa, will be selected by Maire Guavaira, to whose house the dog leads them. That leaves Pedro Orce, who is closest to the wise dog, whose name sometimes in Pilot. Now that everyone has a home, the peninsula's dilemma remains: Portugal is rushing towards the Azores. In a general time of anxiety and exodus, we now see that Saramago has constructed an oasis, where two women, three men, a dog, and now also a horse, live in perfect harmony. Fortunately, Iberia alters course, and there is no disaster, and the little group (the dog now named Constant) waits to see whether they will surge on to join Canada or the United States.

Sadly, our little community falls out, for a time, even as Portugal and Spain drift towards North America. But the peninsula begins to move away, and rotate, and Pedro Orce dies, and everyone weeps, the dog included. He is buried, the dog Ardent departs, the peninsula has stopped, and the two couples will continue on their wanderings, carrying the elm branch with them.

This rugged narrative does not want to be interpreted, nor should we be tactless, but I will hover round it, as Werner Herzog keeps our eyes circling his raft in *Aguirre the Wrath of God* (my favorite movie, with Klaus Kinski as Aguirre as Kinski). We don't ever see why Joana should want José Anaiço, whose only salient quality is that he activates starlings, or again why Maria takes Sassa, whose role as stone-thrower into oceans hardly seems enough to individuate him. Pedro Orce has the Hemingwayesque ability to kick up earth-tremblings, but all it gets him is the dog. The book-long hegira of the group cannot sustain interpretation or rather interprets itself as a sustained irony. At least these men and women are not going to become the unctuous Portuguese prime-minister, who drones on exhorting the noble Portuguese to be steadfast while he secretly entreats Galicia to come over to Portugal. The Church, after being obliterated in *Baltasar and Blimunda* and *The Year of the Death of Ricardo Reis*, is largely ignored in *The Stone Raft*, presumably because Saramago was preserving his firepower for the Christian God in *The Gospel According to Jesus Christ* (1991).

The Gospel, as I've said already, seems to me Saramago upon his heights, but as I've written about it elsewhere at some length I want here only to admire its sexual love affair between Jesus Christ and Mary Magdalene, which is the most poignant and persuasive of all Saramago's High Romantic couplings. It breathes authentic ardour; read it side-by-side with the roughly similar matter in D.H. Lawrence's *The Man Who Died*, and Saramago will win the palm.

I have passed over my personal favorite in Saramago, *The History of the Siege of Lisbon* (1989), because I want to dwell awhile in this magnificent demonstration that there is no history, only biography, as Emerson polemically assured us. Saramago, more pugnaciously, tells us that there is no history, only fiction, but Emerson hardly would have been bothered, since for him fiction was only another mask for biography. I add the assertion of the divine Oscar Wilde, which is that the highest criticism is the only form of autobiography that avoids vulgarity. Fusing Emerson, Saramago, and Wilde I joyously join in *The History of the Siege of Lisbon*.

In 1147 the King of Portugal took Lisbon back from the Moors with significant aid from Crusaders, European knights battling at the Church's summons. Raimundo Silva, a proofreader, audaciously revises this history, so that only the Portuguese King retakes his own capital. Though I regard *The Gospel According to Jesus Christ* as Saramago's masterwork to date, I love *The History of the Siege of Lisbon* best among his books because it is the most light-hearted. *The Stone Raft* is crossed by the irony of Europe's hypocrisies, and *The Year of the Death of Ricardo Reis* is a parable of the triumph of Iberian Fascism. *Baltasar and Blimunda* is properly full of scorn of Church and Kingdom, but that also curbs exuberance. The later books—*Blindness* and *All the Names*—are dark works, though to very different degrees. For me the heart of Saramago is *The History of the Siege of Lisbon*, possibly because it communicates so freely Saramago's own pleasure in his work. But, going on seventy-one, I am willing to be sentimental. The love-story of Raimundo Silva and Maria Sara is sweet, not bittersweet. It breathes wholeheartedness, and is gentler, easier to linger with than the sublime embrace of Mary Magdalene and God's victimized son, Jesus Christ. Both Raimundo and Maria Sara are weather-beaten, and the mutual love that comes to them is an enchantment for the reader, whoever she or he is.

But I digress to Saramago's *Journey to Portugal* (1990), which arrived in the midst of this meditation, and gives me a more personal insight into someone whom I regard as our planet's strongest living novelist, beyond any contemporary European or any of the Americans, whether they write in English, Spanish, or Portuguese. *Journey to Portugal* pursues the nation's culture and history, but as only the living eminence of that culture could seek it. The traveller is like William Blake's Mental Traveller, who makes the observations of a visionary. An American reviewer, long resident in Portugal, deprecated Saramago's *Journey*, saying it was not useful, but it does not take a great imaginer to compose a guide-book. Like Blake, Saramago sees *through* the eye, not with it. The traveler gives us the spiritual form of Portugal: a compound of culture and history with what only the inner eye can behold. Sometimes, in reading *Journey to Portugal*, I am haunted by subtly complex intimations of the dark novel of 1995, the disturbing fantasy called *Blindness*. Only so comprehensive and searching a seer would turn, years later, to such a fantasy. To see so much, and so well, is to anticipate the terrors and yet also the dignity of loss.

The concept of dignity returns me to the love of Maria Sara and Raimundo, and to the humane comedy of *The History of the Siege of Lisbon*. This is the most charming of Saramago's books; the novelist himself is so moved by the love of Raimundo and Maria Sara that he all but abdicates social satire, though his genius for irony manifests itself incessantly. Whenever I seek to introduce friends or students to Saramago, I suggest they begin with *The Siege of Lisbon*, surely a fiction that every sensitive reader of good will would embrace.

The Gospel According to Jesus Christ (1991) changed these notes to that of cosmological tragedy. Saramago's Jesus, his God, his devil: all are open to interpretation, including Saramago's own, with which I do not always agree. Myself a Jewish Gnostic by persuasion, I am delighted by the hangman God of Saramago's *Gospel*, but I suspect that Saramago may agree with his own Christ's benign farewell to the heavenly father: "Men, forgive Him, for He knows not what He has done." If that is not irony, what is it?

The *Gospel*, in my reading, stands apart among Saramago's fictions, partly because of its aesthetic eminence, yet also because I cannot locate Saramago in it. He has always, as narrator, been his own best character: both in and out of his work, and watching and wondering at it. But where he stands in his *Gospel* seems disputable. "He stands with his Jesus Christ" might be the answer, but only extends the question. The *Gospel*'s God is certainly worthy of denial: he is the unpleasantest person in all of Saramago. But here I am perhaps at odds with Saramago and would prefer that anyone interested consult my extended essay on the *Gospel*.

Blindness (1995) reminds us again of Saramago's uncanny power as a fabulist, but also as an imaginative moralist. Nothing in contemporary fiction reveals so clearly the contingent nature of our social realities. Saramago's deepest insight is that our mundane existence is profoundly fragile, dependent upon givens that may be withdrawn any instant. If I compare *Blindness* with *The Plague* by Camus, I find I favor Saramago. Whether or not intentional, the open nature of the allegory in *Blindness* allows the reader to wonder if this is not another parable of the perpetual possibility of the return of Fascism, or of its first advent. As with the *Gospel*, this austere masterpiece is too complex for simple summary, and I hope to write of it elsewhere.

Saramago's Portuguese is still too difficult for me, and so I eagerly await the English translation of his *Caverno*. I close here with a brief coda on *All the Names* (1997), his closest approach to Kafka, though light years from Kafka's "Plenty of hope, for God, but not for us." Senhor José, clerkiest of clerks, quests for an unknown woman, who alas is dead. And that is all. And that is far from all, for since you only can love what you cannot ever know, completely, Senhor José cannot abandon the quest. Perhaps not Kafka, but a curious blend of Robert Louis Stevenson and Melville, might be the paradigm, but the vision of Saramago has Borgesian elements in it, and these precursors are folded in a single flame.

The Registrar, for whom Senhor José works, seems to me less God than he is Saramago himself, teaching men and women of letters that: "we who write and manipulate the papers of life and death should reunite the dead and living in one single archive." As a literary critic, I take heart from the wisdom of Saramago. For what am I but one of the last Defenders of the Old Aesthetic Faith, the trust in the Covenant between the writers of genius and the discerning reader?

The Gospel According to Jesus Christ

José Saramago published *The Gospel According to Jesus Christ* in 1991, when he approached his seventieth year. As Saramago's fierce critical admirer, I am reluctant to choose it over all his other novels, but it is an awesome work, imaginatively superior to any other life of Jesus, including the four canonical Gospels. It loses some aspects of irony in Giovanni Pontiero's fine translation, but more than enough survives to overcome the aware reader.

Saramago's audacity is triumphant in his *Gospel* (the short title that I will employ). God, in Saramago's *Gospel*, has some affinities to the J Writer's Yahweh and some to Blake's Nobodaddy, but it is important to see that Saramago resists giving us the Gnostics' Ialdaboth. Kierkegaard in his *Concluding Unscientific Postscript* ironically observed that "to give thinking supremacy over everything else is gnosticism" (341). Yet Saramago's God scandalizes us in ways that transcend the intellect, since a God who is both truth and time is the worst possible bad news. Saramago's devil, delightfully named Pastor, is mildness itself compared to Saramago's God, who refuses Pastor's attempt to be reconciled, and who manifests neither love nor compassion for Jesus or for any other human being.

That must make the book seem sublimely outrageous, yet it is not, and I think that only a bigot or a fool would judge Saramago's *Gospel* to be blasphemous. Saramago's God can be both wily and bland, and he has a capacity for savage humor. No one is going to love this god, but then he doesn't ask or expect love. Worship and obedience are his requirements, and sacred violence is his endless resource. Baruch Spinoza insisted that it was necessary for us to love God without ever expecting that God would love us in return. No one could love Saramago's God, unless the lover were so deep in sado-masochism as to be helpless before its drive.

God tells us in the Gospel that he is dissatisfied with the small con-
stituency provided him by his chosen people, the Jews:

> For the last four thousand and four years I have been the God of
> the Jews, a quarrelsome and difficult race by nature, but on the
> whole I have got along fairly well with them, they now take Me
> seriously and are likely to go on doing so for the foreseeable
> future. So, You are satisfied, said Jesus. I am and I am not, or
> rather, I would be were it not for this restless heart of Mine, which
> is forever telling Me, Well now, a fine destiny you've arranged
> after four thousand years of trial and tribulation that no amount
> of sacrifice on altars will ever be able to repay, for You continue to
> be the god of a tiny population that occupies a minute part of this
> world You created with everything that's on it, so tell Me, My son,
> if I should be satisfied with this depressing situation. Never hav-
> ing created a world, I'm in no position to judge, replied Jesus.
> True, you cannot judge, but you could help. Help in what way. To
> spread My word, to help Me become the god of more people. I
> don't understand. If you play your part, that is to say, the part I
> have reserved for you in My plan, I have every confidence that
> within the next six centuries or so, despite all the struggles and
> obstacles ahead of us, I will pass from being God of the Jews to
> being God of those whom we will call Catholics, from the Greek.
> And what is this part You have reserved for me in Your plan. That
> of martyr, My son, that of victim, which is the best role of all for
> propagating any faith and stirring up fervor. God made the words
> martyr and victim seem like milk and honey on his tongue, but
> Jesus felt a sudden chill in his limbs, as if the mist had closed over
> him, while the devil regarded him with an enigmatic expression
> which combined scientific curiosity with grudging compassion.
> (311–12)

God is restless and does not wish to be depressed; those are his
motives for victimizing Jesus, and subsequently for torturing to death the
millions who will die as sacrifices to Jesus, whether they affirm him or deny
him. That God is the greatest of comedians we learn from his chant of the
martyrs: "a litany, in alphabetical order so as not to hurt any feelings about
precedence and importance" (321). The litany is quite marvelous, from
Adalbert of Prague, executed with a seven-pronged pikestaff, on to
"Wolgefortis or Livrade or Eutropia the bearded virgin crucified" (325).
Four long pages in length, the catalogue of sacred violence has such

delights as Blandina of Lyons, gored by a savage bull, and the unfortunate Januaris of Naples, first thrown to wild beasts, then into a furnace, and finally decapitated. The gusto of Saramago's God recalls Edward Gibbon's in Chapter XVI of *The History of the Decline and Fall of the Roman Empire*, except that Gibbon, maintaining decorum, avoids detailing the many varieties of martyrdom by torture. But Gibbon again anticipates Saramago by observing that Christians "have inflicted far greater severities on each other than they had experienced from the zeal of infidels" (452–53). Saramago's God, his voice a little tired, speaks of the Inquisition as a necessary evil, and defends the burning of thousands because the cause of Jesus demands it. One blinks at the dustjacket of the American edition of Saramago's *Gospel*, where we are assured that defying the authority of God the Father "is still not denial of Him."

Though necessarily a secondary character in comparison to Saramago's Jesus, God demands scrutiny beyond his menacingly comic aspects. Primarily, the *Gospel*'s God is time, and not truth, the other attribute he asserts. Saramago, a Marxist (an eccentric one), and not a Christian, subverts St. Augustine on the theodicy of time. If time is God, then God can be forgiven nothing, and who would desire to forgive him anyway? But then, the Gospel's God is not the least interested in forgiveness: he forgives no one, not even Jesus, and he declines to forgive Pastor, when the devil makes an honest offer of obedience. Power is God's only interest, and the sacrifice of Jesus employs the prospect of forgiveness of our sins only as an advertisement. God makes clear that all of us are guilty, and that he prefers to keep it that way. Jesus is no atonement: his crucifixion is merely a device by which God ceases to be Jewish, and becomes Catholic, a *converso* rather than a *marrano*. That is superb irony, and Saramago makes it high art, though to thus reduce it critically to invite a Catholic onslaught. Of all fictive representations of God since the Yahwist's, I vote for Saramago's: he is at once the funniest and the most chilling, in the mode of the Shakespearean hero-villains: Richard III, Iago, Edmund in *King Lear*.

II

Pastor, or the devil, has his own charm, as befits a very original representation of Satan. A giant of a man, with a huge head, Pastor allows Jesus to become his assistant shepherd for a large flock of sheep and goats. In response to Jesus' Pious exclamation—"The Lord alone is God"—the non-Jewish Pastor replies with grand pungency:

Certainly if God exists, He must be only one, but it would be better if He were two, then there would be a god for the wolf and one
for the sheep, a god for the victim and one for the assassin, a god
for the condemned man and one for the executioner. (192–93)

This sensible dualism is not exactly Satanic, and Pastor remains considerably more likeable than God throughout the novel. In the dialogues
between the devil and the younger Jesus, the devil's part clearly prevails,
though honorably, unlike God's dominance of Jesus when father and son
first meet in the desert. God demands a sheep dear to Jesus as a sacrifice,
and Jesus reluctantly assents. Pastor, on hearing of this, gives up on Jesus:
"You've learned nothing, begone with you" (222). And Pastor, so far, is
right: Jesus' education as to God's nature will be completed only upon the
cross.

What then are we to make of Pastor? Saramago's devil is humane yet
scarcely a skeptic: he knows too much about God. If Saramago's God is a
Portuguese *converso*, then Saramago's devil was never Jewish, and seems
curiously unrelated both to God and to Jesus Christ. Why is Pastor in the
book? Evidently, only as a witness, I think one has to conclude. Saramago
seems to take us back to the unfallen Satan of the Book of Job, who goes
to-and-fro on the earth, and walks up and down on it. And yet Job's Satan
was an Accuser; Pastor is not. Why does Jesus sojourn four years with
Pastor, as an apprentice shepherd? The angel, who comes belatedly to tell
Mary that Jesus is God's son tells us that "the devil only denies himself"
(263), which is extravagantly ambiguous, and could mean that Pastor
resists playing the role that God hag assigned him. Mary's angel, after
telling us that Pastor was his schoolfellow, says that Pastor prospers
because "the harmony of the universe requires it" (264). There is then a
secret relationship between Pastor and God, a truth that dismays Jesus'
disciples (302).

When God, dressed like a wealthy Jew, appears to Jesus in the boat,
Saramago imagines a magnificent re-entry for Pastor:

The boat swayed, the swimmer's head emerged from the water,
then his torso, splashing water everywhere, then his legs, a
leviathan rising from the depths, and it turned out to be Pastor,
reappearing after all these years. I've come to join you, he said,
settling himself on the side of the boat, equidistant between Jesus
and God, and yet oddly enough this time the boat did not tip to
his side, as if Pastor had no weight or he was levitating and not
really sitting, I've come to join you, he repeated, and hope I'm in

time to take part in the conversation. We've been talking but still haven't got to the heart of the matter, replied God, and turning to Jesus, He told him, This is the devil whom we have just been discussing. Jesus looked from one to the other, and saw that without God's beard they could have passed for twins, although the devil was younger and less wrinkled. Jesus said, I know very well who he is, I lived with him for four years when he was known as pastor, and God replied, You had to live with someone, it couldn't be with Me, and you didn't wish to be with your family, so that left only the devil. Did he come looking for me or did You send him. Neither one nor the other, let's say we agreed that this was the best solution. So that's why, when he spoke through the possessed man from Gadara, he called me Your son. Precisely. Which means that both of you kept me in the dark. As happens to all humans. But You said I was not human. And that is true, but you have been what might technically be called incarnated. And now what do you two want of me. I'm the one who wants something, not he. But both of you are here, I noticed that Pastor's appearance came as no surprise, You must have been expecting him. Not exactly, although in principle one should always expect the devil. But if the matter You and I have to resolve affects only us, what is he doing here and why don't You send him away. One can dismiss the rabble in the devil's service if they become troublesome in word or deed, but not Satan himself. Then he's here because this conversation concerns him too. My son, never forget what I'm about to tell you, everything that concerns God also concerns the devil. (309–10)

As God and the devil are twins (we have suspected this), it is a delight to be told that we cannot live with God, and so must choose between our families and the devil. God speaks of his desire to be God of the Catholics, but this ambition I have glanced at already, and wish here only to ask: why is Pastor in the boat? His expression combines "scientific curiosity with grudging compassion" (312), but he is there because, as Jesus accurately surmises, extending God's domain also extends the devil's. And yet poor Pastor has his perplexities:

I'm staying, said Pastor, and these were the first words he spoke since revealing his identity. I'm staying, he said a second time, and added, I myself can see things in the future, but I'm not always certain if what I see there is true or false, in other words, I can see my lies for what they are, that is, my truths, but I don't know to what extent the truths of others are their lies. (318)

Saramago dryly calls this a "torturous statement," but he means that it clearly indicts God, whose truths indeed are his lies. God's account of the Catholic Church that will be founded upon Jesus is true only insofar as it is historically horrible, and the zest God manifests as he itemizes martyrs and sums up the Inquisition has unmistakable sadistic overtones. Most alarmingly, God (a good Augustinian, before Augustine) deprecates all human joys as being false, since all of them emanate from original sin: "lust and fear are weapons the demon uses to torment wretched mankind" (325). When Jesus asks Pastor whether this is true, the devil's reply is eloquently illuminating:

More or less, I simply took what God didn't want, the flesh with all its joys and sorrows, youth and senility, bloom and decay, but it isn't true that fear is one of my weapons, I don't recall having invented sin and punishment or the terror they inspire. (325–26)

We tend to believe this when God snaps in response: "Be quiet ... sin and the devil are one and the same thing." Does it need God to say that? Wouldn't the Cardinal-Archbishop of Lisbon do as well? Saramago's reply is uncanny. God describes the Crusades, to be waged against the unnamed Allah, whom Pastor disowns creating:

Who, then, will create this hostile god, asked Pastor. Jesus was at a loss for an answer, and God, who had been silent, remained silent, but a voice came down from the mist and said, Perhaps this god and the one to come are the same god. Jesus, God, and the devil pretended not to hear but could not help looking at one another in alarm, mutual fear is like that, it readily unites enemies. (328–29)

Only here, in Saramago's *Gospel*, do we hear a voice beyond God's. Whose is it? Who could proclaim what God does not wish to say, which is that he and Allah are one? With a God as sly and unlovable as Saramago's, both we and Saramago long for a God beyond God, perhaps the Alien or Stranger God of the Gnostics. But whoever that God is, he does not speak again in this novel. Very deftly, Saramago has just told us explicitly what he tells us implicitly throughout: God and Jesus pragmatically are enemies, even as Pastor is the unwilling enemy of both. Yet in what does that enmity consist? Reacting to God's account of the Inquisition, Pastor remarks: "One has to be God to countenance so much blood" (330).

Pastor's great moment—and it is one of the handful of key passages in the book—comes in his vain attempt at reconciliation with God:

> Pastor searched for the right words before explaining, I've been listening to all that has been said here in this boat, and although I myself have caught glimpses of the light and darkness ahead, I never realized the light came from the burning stakes and the darkness from great piles of bodies. Does this trouble you. It shouldn't trouble me, for I am the devil, and the devil profits from death even more than You do, it goes without saying that hell is more crowded than heaven. Then why do you complain. I'm not complaining, I'm making a proposal. Go ahead, but be quick, I cannot loiter here for all eternity. No one knows better than You that the devil too has a heart. Yes, but you make poor use of it. Today I use it by acknowledging Your power and wishing that it spread to the ends of the earth without the need of so much death, and since You insist that whatever thwarts and denies You comes from the evil I represent and govern in this world, I propose that You receive me into Your heavenly kingdom, my past offenses redeemed by those I will not commit in future, that You accept my obedience as in those happy days when I was one of Your chosen angels, Lucifer You called me, bearer of light, before my ambition to become Your equal consumed my soul and made me rebel against You. And would you care to tell Me why I should pardon you and receive you into My Kingdom. Because if You grant me that same pardon You will one day promise left and right, then evil will cease, Your son will not have to die, and Your kingdom will extend beyond the land of the Hebrews to embrace the whole globe, good will prevail everywhere, and I shall stand among the lowliest of the angels who have remained faithful, more faithful than all of them now that I have repented, and I shall sing Your praises, everything will end as if it had never been, everything will become what it should always have been. (330–31)

The irony of the humane Pastor and the inhumane God could not be better juxtaposed. God makes clear that he would prefer an even worse devil, if that were possible, and that without the devil, God cannot be God. Pastor, who has been persuasively sincere, shrugs and goes off, after collecting from Jesus the old black bowl from Nazareth into which the blood of Jesus will drip in the novel's closing words.

It is not sufficient to praise Saramago's originality in limning his wholly undiabolic devil. One must go further. The enigmatic Pastor is the only devil who could be aesthetically and intellectually appropriate as we conclude the Second Millennium. Except that he cannot be crucified, this fallen angel has far more in common with Saramago's Jesus than with Saramago's God. They both are God's victims, suffering the tyranny of time, which God calls truth. Pastor is resigned, and less rebellious than Jesus, yet that is because Pastor knows all there is to know. As readers, we remain more akin to Saramago's uncanny devil than we are to his malevolent ironist of a God.

III

The glory of Saramago's *Gospel* is Saramago's Jesus, who seems to me humanly and aesthetically more admirable than any other version of Jesus in the literature of the century now ending. Perhaps D.H. Lawrence's *The Man Who Died* is a near-rival, but Lawrence's Jesus is a grand Lawrencian vitalist, rather than a possible human being. Saramago's Jesus paradoxically is the novelist's warmest and most memorable character of any of his books. W.H. Auden, Christian poet-critic, oddly found in Shakespeare's Falstaff a type of Christ. I cite a paragraph of Auden to emphasize how far both Saramago's God and Saramago's Jesus are from even a generous, undogmatic Christian view:

> The Christian God is not a self-sufficient being like Aristotle's First Cause, but a God who creates a world which he continues to love although it refuses to love him in return. He appears in this world, not as Apollo or Aphrodite might appear, disguised as man so that no mortal should recognize his divinity, but as a real man who openly claims to be God. And the consequence is inevitable. The highest religious and temporal authorities condemn Him as a blasphemer and a Lord of Misrule, as a bad Companion for mankind. Inevitable because, as Richelieu said, "The salvation of State is in this world," and history has not as yet provided us with any evidence that the Prince of this world has changed his character. (207–08)

Saramago's God, as I have said, neither loves the world nor does he expect it to love him in return. He wishes power, as widely extended as possible. And Saramago's Jesus is anything but an appearance of God "disguised as man"; rather his Jesus has been shanghaied by God, for God's own purposes of power. As for Satan, "the Prince of this world," we know that Saramago *has* changed his character.

The title of the novel is *The Gospel According to Jesus* Christ, where "according" matters most. Saramago's Jesus is an ironist, an amazingly mild one considering his victimization by God. Before meeting John the Baptist, Jesus is told that John is taller, heavier, more bearded, is hardly clothed, and subsists on locust and wild honey. "He sounds more like the Messiah than I do, Jesus said, rising from the circle" (354).

Saramago's novel begins and ends with the Crucifixion, *presented* at the start with considerable irony, but at the close with a terrible pathos:

> Jesus is dying slowly, life ebbing from him, ebbing, when suddenly the heavens overhead open wide and God appears in the same attire He wore in the boat, and His words resound throughout the earth, This is My beloved son, in whom I am well pleased. Jesus realized then that he had been tricked, as the lamb led to sacrifice is tricked, and that his life had been planned for death from the very beginning. Remembering the river of blood and suffering that would flow from his side and flood the globe, he called out to the open sky, where God could be seen smiling, Men, forgive Him, for He knows nor what He has done. Then he began expiring in the midst of a dream. He found himself back in Nazareth and saw his father shrugging his shoulders and smiling as he told him, just as I cannot ask you all the questions, neither can you give me all the answers. There was still some life in him when he felt a sponge soaked in water and vinegar moisten his lips, and looking down, he saw a man walking away with a bucket, a staff over his shoulder. But what Jesus did not see, on the ground, was the black bowl into which his blood was dripping. (376–77)

"Men, forgive Him, for He knows not what He has done" testifies both to Jesus' *sweetness* and to Saramago's aesthetically controlled fury. No disinterested reader, free of ideology and of creed, is going to forgive Saramago's God for the murder of Jesus and the subsequent torrents of human blood that will result. Joyce's Stephen speaks of the "hangman God," as some Italians still call him, and that precisely is Saramago's God. This would be appalling enough in itself but is augmented by the long and loving portrait that Saramago gives of his Jesus.

The story of this Jesus begins and ends with an earthenware bowl, first presented to Mary the mother of Jesus by a beggar, an apparent angel. That bowl overflows with luminous earth, presumably unfallen; at the close it catches the blood of the dying Jesus. The beggar is God, rather than Pastor, and appears again to Mary in a dream-vision that is also a tryst. When Jesus is born, God manifests again as the third of three passing shepherds, bringing bread of an occult kind. One supposes that this is subtly akin to God's seed resulting in the flesh of Jesus, but so nuanced is Saramago that supposition sometimes needs to be evaded, in this mysterious book.

The thirteen-year-old Jesus leaves home because the Romans have crucified his father Joseph, an invention entirely Saramago's own, just as Joseph's partial complicity in Herod's massacre of the innocents is also Saramago's rather startling suggestion, and is another trouble for Jesus that sends him forth on his road. But why does Saramago so alter the story? Perhaps this most humane of all versions of Jesus has to suffer the darkness of two fathers, the loving, unlucky, and guilty Joseph, and the unloving, fortunate, and even guiltier God.

When the boy Jesus disputes with the doctors of the Law in the Temple, I am reminded again of how Augustinian Saramago has made both God and the Law. One doesn't quarrel with this anachronism, because Saramago's God is himself so anxious to forsake Judahism (to call it that) for Catholicism. And besides, one grants Saramago his anachronisms in this marvelous book just as one grants them endlessly to Shakespeare. Still, guilt is not a concern of the only traditional Jesus who moves me, the Gnostic Jesus of the Gospel of Thomas. Yet I am a Jewish Gnostic explicating a beautiful book by a Portuguese who is no Catholic, anymore than Fernando Pessoa was. At just this point in his narrative, Saramago brings Jesus and Pastor together, and that curious sojourn I have examined already.

And yet Jesus' principal relationship in his life, as Saramago sees it and tells it, is to neither of his fathers, nor to the devil, nor to Mary his mother, but to the whore Mary Magdalene. Of all the splendors of Saramago's Gospel, the love between Jesus and the Magdalene is the grandest, and their meeting and union (231–43) is for me the summit of Saramago's achievement, up to the present time. Echoing the Song of Songs, Saramago is most the artist when he intertwines a reply to Pastor with Jesus' awakening to sexual life:

> Jesus breathed so fast, for one moment he thought he would faint when her hands, the left hand on his forehead, the right hand on his ankles, began caressing him, slowly coming together, meeting

in the middle, then starting all over again. You've learned nothing, begone with you, Pastor had told him, and who knows, perhaps he meant to say that Jesus had not learned to cherish life. Now Mary Magdalene instructed him.... (236)

We can void the "perhaps," and Mary Magdalene is Jesus' best teacher, eclipsing Joseph, God, Pastor, and Mary the mother. In what may be the book's greatest irony she teaches him freedom, which God will not permit any man, but in particular not to God's only son.

I myself have just turned seventy, and ask more urgently than before: where shall wisdom be found? The wisdom of Saramago's *Gospel* is very harsh: we can emulate Jesus only by forgiving God, but we do not believe, with Jesus, that God does not know what God has done.

I find the epilogue to Saramago's *Gospel* not in *Blindness*, a parable as dark as any could be, but in the charming *The Tale of the Unknown Island*, a brief fable composed in 1998, the year of his Nobel Prize, and translated a year later by Margaret Jull Costa. In the wonderful comic vein of *The Siege of Lisbon*, Saramago's tale begins with a man asking a king for a boat which can sail in quest of the unknown island. The boat granted, the man goes off to the harbor, followed by the king's cleaning woman, who will constitute the rest of the crew.

The cleaning woman, with superb resolution, vows that she and the man will be sufficient to sail the caravel to the unknown island, thus heartening the man, whose will cannot match hers. They go to bed in separate bunks, port and starboard, and he dreams bad dreams, until he finds her shadow beside his shadow:

> He woke up with his arms about the cleaning woman, and her arms about him, their bodies and their bunks fused into one, so that no one can tell any more if this is port or starboard. Then, as soon as the sun had risen, the man and the woman went to paint in white letters on both sides of the prow the name that the caravel still lacked. Around midday, with the tide, The Unknown Island finally set to sea, in search of itself. (51)

Saramago names no one: I am critically outrageous enough to venture upon some experimental namings, as an antithesis to Saramago's *Gospel*. Let us call the man Jesus Christ, try the cleaning woman as Mary Magdalene, and the king, who exists to receive favors, will do for God. Doubtless, Saramago would shake his head, but so audacious a narrative genius inspires audacity in his critic. No one will be crucified upon the masts of the Unknown Island, and the bad dreams of *this* Jesus will not be realized. Saramago's happy tale is a momentary antidote to the most tragic of his works. Beware a God who is at once truth and time, Saramago warns us, and abandon such a God to sail out in search of yourself.

Works Cited

Auden, W.H. "The Prince's Dog." *The Dyer's Hand and Other Essays*. New York: Random House, 1962. 182–208.

Gibbon, Edward. *The History of the Decline and fall of the Roman Empire*. Vol. 1. New York Heritage Press, 1946.

Kierkegaard, Søren. *Concluding Unscientific Postscript to Philosophical Fragments*. Vol. l. Ed. and trans. Howard V. Hong and Edna H. Hong. Princeton: Princeton UP, 1992.

Saramago, José. *The Gospel According to Jesus Christ*, Trans. Giovanni Pontiero. New York: Harcourt Brace, 1994.

———. *The Tale of the Unknown Island*. Trans. Margaret Jull Costa. New York: Harcourt Brace, 1999.

Norman Mailer

(1923–)

Ancient Evenings

MAILER IS THE MOST VISIBLE OF CONTEMPORARY NOVELISTS, JUST AS Thomas Pynchon is surely the most invisible. As the inheritor of the not exactly unfulfilled journalistic renown of Hemingway, Mailer courts danger, disaster, even scandal. Thinking of Mailer, Pynchon, and Doctorow among others, Geoffrey Hartman remarks that:

> The prose of our best novelists is as fast, embracing, and abrasive as John Donne's *Sermons*. It is polyphonic despite or within its monologue, its confessional stream of words....
>
> Think of Mailer, who always puts himself on the line, sparring, taunting, as macho as Hemingway but deliberately renouncing taciturnity. Mailer places himself too near events, as science fiction or other forms of romance place themselves too far....

Elizabeth Hardwick, a touch less generous than the theoretical Hartman, turns Gertrude Stein against Mailer's oral polyphony:

> We have here a "literature" of remarks, a fast-moving confounding of Gertrude Stein's confident assertion that "remarks are not literature." Sometimes remarks are called a novel, sometimes a biography, sometimes history.

Hardwick's Mailer is "a spectacular mound of images" or "anecdotal pile." He lacks only an achieved work, in her view, and therefore is a delight to biographers, who resent finished work as a "sharp intrusion," beyond their ken. Her observations have their justice, yet the phenomenon is older than Mailer, or even Hemingway. The truly spectacular mound of images and anecdotal pile was George Gordon, Lord Byron, but he wrote *Don Juan*, considered by Shelley to be the great poem of the age. Yet even *Don Juan* is curiously less than Byron was, or seemed, or still seems. Mailer hardly purports to be the Byron of our day (the Hemingway will do), but he might fall back upon Byron as an earlier instance of the literary use of celebrity, or of the mastery of polyphonic remarks.

Is Mailer a novelist? His best book almost certainly is *The Executioner's Song*, which Ms. Hardwick calls "the apotheosis of our flowering 'oral literature'—thus far," a triumph of the tape recorder. My judgment of its strength may be much too fast, as Ms. Hardwick warms, and yet I would not call *The Executioner's Song* a novel. *Ancient Evenings* rather crazily is a novel, Mailer's *Salammbô* as it were, but clearly more engrossing as visionary speculation than as narrative or as the representation of moral character. Richard Poirier, Mailer's best critic, prefers *An American Dream* and *Why Are We In Vietnam?*, neither of which I can reread with aesthetic pleasure. Clearly, Mailer is a problematical writer; he has written no indisputable book, nothing on the order of *The Sun Also Rises*, *The Great Gatsby*, *Miss Lonelyhearts*, *The Crying of Lot 49*, let alone *As I Lay Dying*, *The Sound and the Fury*, *Light in August*, *Absalom, Absalom!* His formidable literary energies have not found their inevitable mode. When I think of him, *Advertisements for Myself* comes into my memory more readily than any other work, perhaps because truly he is his own supreme fiction. He is the author of "Norman Mailer," a lengthy, discontinuous, and perhaps canonical fiction.

II

Advertisements for Myself (1960) sums up Mailer's ambitions and accomplishments through the age of thirty-six. After a quarter-century, I have just reread it, with an inevitable mixture of pleasure and a little sadness. Unquestionably, Mailer has not fulfilled its many complex promises, and yet the book is much more than a miscellany. If not exactly a "Song of Myself," nevertheless *Advertisements* remains Mailer at his most Whitmanian, as when he celebrates his novel-in-progress:

> If it is to have any effect, and I can hardly look forward to exhausting the next ten years without hope of a deep explosion of effect, the book will be fired to its fuse by the rumor that once I pointed to the farthest fence and said that within ten years I would try to

hit the longest ball ever to go up into the accelerated hurricane air of our American letters. For if I have one ambition above all others, it is to write a novel which Dostoyevsky and Marx; Joyce and Freud; Stendhal, Tolstoy, Proust and Spengler; Faulkner, and even old moldering Hemingway might have come to read, for it would carry what they had to tell another part of the way.

Hemingway in 1959 reached the age of sixty, but was neither old nor moldering. He was to kill himself on July 2, 1961, but Mailer could hardly have anticipated that tragic release. In a letter to George Plimpton (January 17, 1961) Hemingway characterized *Advertisements for Myself* as the sort of ragtag assembly of his rewrites, second thoughts and ramblings shot through with occasional brilliance." As precursor, Hemingway would have recognized Mailer's vision of himself as Babe Ruth, hitting out farther than Stendhal, Tolstoy, *et al.*, except that the agonistic trope in the master is more agile than in the disciple, because ironized:

> Am a man without any ambition, except to be champion of the world, I wouldn't fight Dr. Tolstoy in a 20 round bout because I know he would knock my ears off. The Dr. had terrific wind and could go on forever and then some....
>   But these Brooklyn jerks are so ignorant that they start off fighting Mr. Tolstoy. And they announce they have beaten him before the fight starts.

That is from a letter to Charles Scribner (September 6–7, 1949), and "these Brooklyn jerks" indubitably refers to the highly singular author of *The Naked and the Dead* (1948), who had proclaimed his victory over Hemingway as a tune-up for the Tolstoy match. Hemingway's irony, directed as much towards himself as against Mailer, shrewdly indicates Mailer's prime aesthetic flaw: a virtually total absence of irony. Irony may or may not be what the late Paul de Man called it, "the condition of literary language itself," but Mailer certainly could use a healthy injection of it. If Thomas Mann is at one extreme—the modern too abounding in irony—then Mailer clearly hugs the opposite pole. The point against Mailer is made best by Max Apple in his splendid boxing tale, "Inside Norman Mailer" (*The Oranging of America*, 1976), where Mailer is handled with loving irony, and Hemingway's trope touches its ultimate limits as Apple challenges Mailer in the ring:

> "Concentrate," says Mailer, "so the experience will not be wasted on you.

"It's hard," I say, "amid the color and distraction."

"I know," says my gentle master, "but think about one big thing."

I concentrate on the new edition of the *Encyclopedia Britannica*. It works. My mind is less a palimpsest, more a blank page.

"You may be too young to remember," he says, "James Jones and James T. Farrell and James Gould Cozzens and dozens like them. I took them all on, absorbed all they had and went on my way, just like Shakespeare ate up Tottel's *Miscellany*."

There are no such passages in Mailer himself. One cannot require a novelist to cultivate irony, but its absolute absence causes difficulties, particularly when the writer is a passionate and heterodox moralist. Mailer's speculations upon time, sex, death, cancer, digestion, courage, and God are all properly notorious, and probably will not earn him a place as one of the major sages. The strongest aesthetic defense of Mailer as speculator belongs to Richard Poirier, in his book of 1972:

> Mailer insists on living *at* the divide, living *on* the divide, between the world of recorded reality and a world of omens, spirits, and powers, only that his presence there may blur the distinction. He seals and obliterates the gap he finds, like a sacrificial warrior or, as he would probably prefer, like a Christ who brings not peace but a sword, not forgiveness for past sins but an example of the pains necessary to secure a future.

This has force and some persuasiveness, but Poirier is too good a critic not to add the shadow side of Mailer's "willingness not to foreclose on his material in the interests of merely formal resolutions." Can there be any resolutions then for his books? Poirier goes on to say that: "There is no satisfactory form for his imagination when it is most alive. There are only exercises for it." But this appears to imply that Mailer cannot shape his fictions, since without a sacrifice of possibility upon the altar of form, narrative becomes incoherent, frequently through redundance (as in *Ancient Evenings*). Mailer's alternative has been to forsake Hemingway for Dreiser, as in the exhaustive narrative of *The Executioner's Song*. In either mode, finally, we are confronted by the paradox that Mailer's importance seems to transcend any of his individual works. The power of *The Executioner's Song* finally is that of "reality in America," to appropriate Lionel Trilling's phrase for Dreiser's appropriation of the material of *An American Tragedy*. Are we also justified in saying that *An American Dream* essentially is Mailer's comic-strip appropriation of what might be called "irreality in America"? Evidently there will never be a mature book by Mailer that is not problematical in its form. To Poirier, this is Mailer's strength. Poirier's generous overpraise of *An American Dream* and *Why Are We In Vietnam?* perhaps can be justified by Mailer's peculiarly American aesthetic, which has its Emersonian affinities. Mailer's too is an aesthetic of use, a pragmatic application of the American difference from the European past. *The Armies of the Night* (1968), rightly praised by Poirier, may seem someday Mailer's best and most permanent book. It is certainly not only a very American book, but today is one of the handful of works that vividly represent an already lost and legendary time, the era of the so-called Counterculture that surged up in the later 1960's, largely in protest against our war in Vietnam. Mailer, more than any other figure, has broken down the distinction between fiction and journalism. This sometimes is praised in itself. I judge it an aesthetic misfortune, in everyone else, but on Mailer himself I tend to reserve judgment, since the mode now seems his own.

III

Mailer's validity as a cultural critic is always qualified by his own immersion in what he censures. Well known for being well known, he is himself inevitably part of what he deplores. As a representation, he at least rivals all of his fictive creations. *Ancient Evenings*, his most inventive and exuberant work, is essentially a self-portrait of the author as ancient Egyptian magician, courtier, lover and anachronistic speculator. Despite Poirier's eloquent insistences, the book leaves Mailer as he was judged to be by Poirier in 1972, "like Melville without *Moby Dick*, George Eliot without *Middlemarch*, Mark Twain without *Huckleberry Finn*." Indeed, the book is Mailer's *Pierre*, his *Romola*, his *Connecticut Yankee in King Arthur's Court*. At sixty-two, Mailer remains the author of *Advertisements for Myself*, *The Armies of the Night* and *The Executioner's Song*.

Is he then a superb accident of personality, wholly adequate to the spirit of the age? Though a rather bad critic of novelists, he is one of the better critics of Norman Mailer. His one critical blindness, in regard to himself, involves the destructive nature of Hemingway's influence upon him. Hemingway was a superb storyteller and an uncanny prose poet; Mailer is neither. Essentially, Mailer is a phantasmagoric visionary who was found by the wrong literary father, Hemingway. Hemingway's verbal economy is not possible for Mailer. There are profound affinities between Hemingway and Wallace Stevens, but none between Mailer and the best poetry of his age. This is the curious sadness with which the "First Advertisements for Myself" reverberates after twenty-five years:

> So, mark you. Every American writer who takes himself to be both major and macho must sooner or later give a *faena* which borrows from the self-love of a Hemingway style ...
>
> For you see I have come to have a great sympathy for the Master's irrepressible tantrum that he is the champion writer of this time, and of all time, and that if anyone can pin Tolstoy, it is Ernest H.

By taking on Hemingway, Mailer condemned himself to a similar agon, which harmed Hemingway, except in *The Sun Also Rises* and in *The First Forty-Nine Stories*. It has more than harmed Mailer's work. *The Deer Park* defies rereading, and *An American Dream* and *Why Are We In Vietnam?* have now lost the immediacy of their occasions, and are scarcely less unreadable. In what now is the Age of Pynchon, Mailer has been eclipsed as a writer of fictions, though hardly at all as a performing self. He may be remembered more as a prose prophet than as a novelist, more as Carlyle than as Hemingway. There are worse literary fates. Carlyle, long neglected, doubtless will return. Mailer, now celebrated, doubtless will vanish into neglect, and yet always will return, as a historian of the moral consciousness of his era, and as the representative writer of his generation.

James Baldwin

(1924–1987)

I

WHATEVER THE ULTIMATE CANONICAL JUDGMENT UPON JAMES BALDWIN'S fiction may prove to be, his nonfictional work clearly has permanent status in American literature. Baldwin seems to me the most considerable moral essayist now writing in the United States, and is comparable to George Orwell as a prose Protestant in stance. The evangelical heritage never has abandoned the author of *Go Tell It on the Mountain*, and Baldwin, like so many American essayists since Emerson, possesses the fervor of a preacher. Unlike Emerson, Baldwin lacks the luxury of detachment, since he speaks, not for a displaced Yankee majority, but for a sexual minority within a racial minority, indeed for an aesthetic minority among black homosexuals.

Ultimately, Baldwin's dilemma as a writer compelled to address social torments and injustices is that he is a minority of one, a solitary voice breaking forth against himself (and all others) from within himself. Like Carlyle (and a single aspect of the perspectivizing Nietzsche), Baldwin is of the authentic lineage of Jeremiah, most inward of prophets. What Baldwin opposes is what might be called, in Jeremiah's language, the injustice of outwardness, which means that Baldwin always must protest, even in the rather unlikely event that his country ever were to turn from selfishness and cruelty to justice and compassion in confronting its underclass of the exploited poor, whether blacks, Hispanics, or others cast out by the Reagan Revolution.

It seems accurate to observe that we remember Jeremiah, unlike Amos or Micah, for his individuation of his own suffering, rather than for his social vision, such as it was. Baldwin might prefer to have been an Amos or a Micah, forerunners of Isaiah, rather than a Jeremiah, but like Jeremiah he is vivid as a rhetorician of his own psychic anguish and perplexities, and most memorable as a visionary of a certain involuntary isolation, an election that requires a dreadful cost of confirmation. As Baldwin puts it, the price of the ticket is to accept the real reasons for the human journey:

> The price the white American paid for his ticket was to become white—: and, in the main, nothing more than that, or, as he was to insist, nothing less. This incredibly limited not to say dimwitted ambition has choked many a human being to death here: and this, I contend, is because the white American has never accepted the real reasons for his journey. I know very well that my ancestors had no desire to come to this place: but neither did the ancestors of the people who became white and who require of my captivity a song. They require of me a song less to celebrate my captivity than to justify their own.

The Biblical text that Baldwin alludes to here, Psalm 137, does begin with the song of the exiles from Zion ("and they that wasted us required of us mirth") but ends with a ferocious prophecy against the wasters, ourselves. No writer—black or white—warns us so urgently of "the fire next time" as Baldwin and Jeremiah do, but I hear always in both prophets the terrible pathos of origins:

> Then the word of the Lord came unto me, saying,
> Before I formed thee in the belly I knew thee; and before thou camest forth out of the womb I sanctified thee, and I ordained thee a prophet unto the nations.
> Then said I, Ah, Lord God! behold, I cannot speak: for I am a child.
> *We*: my family, the living and the dead, and the children coming along behind us. This was a complex matter, for I was not living with my family in Harlem, after all, but "down-town," in the "white world," in alien and mainly hostile territory. On the other hand, for me, then, Harlem was almost as alien and in a yet more intimidating way and risked being equally hostile, although for very different reasons. This truth cost me something in guilt and confusion, but it was the truth. It had something to do with my being the son of an evangelist and having been a child evangelist, but this is not all there was to it—that is, guilt is not all there was to it.
> The fact that this particular child had been born when and

where he was born had dictated certain expectations. The child does not really know what these expectations are—does not know how real they are—until he begins to fail, challenge, or defeat them. When it was clear, for example, that the pulpit, where I had made so promising a beginning, would not be my career, it was hoped that I would go on to college. This was never a very realistic hope and—perhaps because I knew this—I don't seem to have felt very strongly about it. In any case, this hope was dashed by the death of my father.

Once I had left the pulpit, I had abandoned or betrayed my role in the community—indeed, my departure from the pulpit and my leaving home were almost simultaneous. (I had abandoned the ministry in order not to betray myself by betraying the ministry.)

Reluctant prophets are in the position of Jonah; they provide texts for the Day of Atonement. Baldwin is always at work reexamining everything, doing his first works over; as he says: "Sing or shout or testify or keep it to yourself: but *know whence you came.*" We came crying hither because we came to this great stage of fools, but Baldwin, like Jeremiah and unlike Shakespeare, demands a theology of origins. He finds it in self-hatred, which he rightly insists is universal, though he seems to reject or just not be interested in the Freudian account of our moral masochism, our need for punishment. The evangelical sense of conscious sin remains strong in Baldwin. Yet, as a moral essayist, he is post-Christian, and persuades us that his prophetic stance is not so much religious as aesthetic. A kind of aesthetic of the moral life governs his vision, even in the turbulence of *The Fire Next Time* and *No Name in the Street*, and helps make them his finest achievements so far.

The Fire Next Time

The center of Baldwin's prophecy can be located in one long, powerful paragraph of *The Fire Next Time*:

"The white man's Heaven," sings a Black Muslim minister, "is the black man's Hell." One may object—possibly—that this puts the matter somewhat too simply, but the song is true, and it has been true for as long as white men have ruled the world. The Africans put it another way: When the white man came to Africa, the white man had the Bible and the African had the land, but now it is the white man who is being, reluctantly and bloodily, separated from the land,

and the African who is still attempting to digest or to vomit up the Bible. The struggle, therefore, that now begins in the world is extremely complex, involving the historical role of Christianity in the realm of power—that is, politics—and in the realm of morals. In the realm of power, Christianity has operated with an unmitigated arrogance and cruelty—necessarily, since a religion ordinarily imposes on those who have discovered the true faith, the spiritual duty of liberating the infidels. This particular true faith, moreover, is more deeply concerned about the soul than it is about the body, to which fact the flesh (and the corpses) of countless infidels bears witness. It goes without saying, then, that whoever questions the authority of the true faith also contests the right of the nations that hold this faith to rule over him—contests, in short, their title to his land. The spreading of the Gospel, regardless of the motives or the integrity or the heroism of some of the missionaries, was an absolutely indispensable justification for the planting of the flag. Priests and nuns and schoolteachers helped to protect and sanctify the power that was so ruthlessly being used by people who were indeed seeking a city, but not one in the heavens, and one to be made, very definitely, by captive hands. The Christian church itself—again, as distinguished from some of its ministers—sanctified and rejoiced in the conquests of the flag, and encouraged, if it did not formulate, the belief that conquest, with the resulting relative well-being of the Western populations, was proof of the favor of God. God had come a long way from the desert—but then so had Allah, though in a very different direction. God, going north, and rising on the wings of power, had become white, and Allah, out of power, and on the dark side of Heaven, had become—for all practical purposes, anyway—black. Thus, in the realm of morals the role of Christianity has been, at best, ambivalent. Even leaving out of account the remarkable arrogance that assumed that the ways and morals of others were inferior to those of Christians, and that they therefore had every right, and could use any means, to change them, the collision between cultures—and the schizophrenia in the mind of Christendom—had rendered the domain of morals as chartless as the sea once was, and as treacherous as the sea still is. It is not too much to say that whoever wishes to become a truly moral human being (and let us not ask whether or not this is possible; I think we must *believe* that it is possible) must first divorce himself from all the prohibitions, crimes, and hypocrisies of the Christian church. If the concept of God has any validity or any use, it can only be to make us larger, freer, and more loving. If God cannot do this, then it is time we got rid of Him.

This superb instance of Baldwin's stance and style as a moral essayist depends for its rhetorical power upon a judicious blend of excess and restraint. Its crucial sentence achieves prophetic authority:

> It is not too much to say that whoever wishes to become a truly moral human being (and let us not ask whether or not this is possible; I think we must *believe* that it is possible) must first divorce himself from all the prohibitions, crimes, and hypocrisies of the Christian church.

The parenthesis, nobly skeptical, is the trope of a master rhetorician, and placing "believe" in italics nicely puts into question the problematics of faith. "Divorce," denounced by St. Paul as having been introduced because of our hardness of hearts, acquires the antithetical aura of the Church itself, while Christian prohibitions are assimilated (rather wickedly) to Christian crimes and hypocrisies. This is, rhetorically considered, good, unclean fun, but the burden is savage, and steeped in moral high seriousness. The strength of The *Fire Next Time* comes to rest in its final paragraph, with the interplay between two italicized rhetorical questions, an interplay kindled when "*then*" is added to the second question:

> When I was very young, and was dealing with my buddies in those wine- and urine-stained hallways, something in me wondered, *What will happen to all that beauty?* For black people, though I am aware that some of us, black and white, do not know it yet, are very beautiful. And when I sat at Elijah's table and watched the baby, the women, and the men, and we talked about God's—or Allah's—vengeance, I wondered, when that vengeance was achieved, *What will happen to all that beauty then?* I could also see that the intransigence and ignorance of the white world might make that vengeance inevitable—a vengeance that does not really depend on, and cannot really be executed by, any person or organization, and that cannot be prevented by any police force or army: historical vengeance, a cosmic vengeance, based on the law that we recognize when we say, "Whatever goes up must come down." And here we are, at the center of the arc, trapped in the gaudiest, most valuable, and most improbable water wheel the world has

ever seen. Everything now, we must assume, is in our hands; we have no right to assume otherwise. If we—and now I mean the relatively conscious whites and the relatively conscious blacks, who must, like lovers, insist on, or create, the consciousness of the others—do not falter in our duty now, we may be able, handful that we are, to end the racial nightmare, and achieve our country, and change the history of the world. If we do not now dare everything, the fulfillment of that prophecy, recreated from the Bible in song by a slave, is upon us: "God gave Noah the rainbow sign, No more water, the fire next time!"

The shrewd rhetorical movement here is from the waterwheel to the ambivalent divine promise of no second flood, the promise of covenant with its dialectical countersong of the conflagration ensuing from our violation of covenant. That vision of impending fire re-illuminates the poignant question: *"What will happen to all that beauty then?"* All that beauty that is in jeopardy transcends even the beauty of black people, and extends to everything human, and to bird, beast, and flower.

No Name in the Street takes its fierce title from Job 18:16–19, where it is spoken to Job by Bildad the Shuhite, concerning the fate of the wicked:

His roots shall be dried up beneath, and above shall his branch be cut off.

His remembrance shall perish from the earth, and he shall have no name in the street.

He shall be driven from light into darkness, and chased out of the world.

He shall neither have son nor nephew among his people, nor any remaining in his dwellings.

They that come after him shall be astonished at his day, as they that went before were affrighted.

I have to admit, having just read (and re-read) my way through the 690 pages of *The Price of the Ticket*, that frequently I am tempted to reply to Baldwin with Job's response to Bildad:

How long will ye vex my soul, and break me in pieces with words?

These ten times have ye reproached me: ye are not ashamed that ye make yourselves strange to me. And be it indeed that I have erred, mine error remaineth with myself.

If indeed ye will magnify yourselves against me, and plead
against me my reproach.

Baldwin's rhetorical authority as prophet would be seriously impaired
if he were merely a job's comforter, Bildad rather than Jeremiah. *No Name
in the Street* cunningly evades the risk that Baldwin will magnify himself
against the reader, partly by the book's adroitness at stationing the author
himself in the vulnerable contexts of his own existence, both in New York
and in Paris. By not allowing himself (or his readers) to forget how perpetually a black homosexual aesthete and moralist, writer and preacher,
must fight for his life, Baldwin earns the pathos of the prophetic predicament:

> I made such motions as I could to understand what was happen-
> ing, and to keep myself afloat. But I had been away too long. It
> was not only that I could not readjust myself to life in New
> York—it was also that I would not: I was never going to be any-
> body's nigger again. But I was now to discover that the world has
> more than one way of keeping you a nigger, has evolved more
> than one way of skinning the cat; if the hand slips here, it tight-
> ens there, and now I was offered, gracefully indeed: membership
> in the club. I had lunch at some elegant bistros, dinner at some
> exclusive clubs. I tried to be understanding about my country-
> men's concern for difficult me, and unruly mine—and I really was
> trying to be understanding, though not without some bewilder-
> ment, and, eventually, some malice. I began to be profoundly
> uncomfortable. It was a strange kind of discomfort, a terrified
> apprehension that I had lost my bearings. I did not altogether
> understand what I was hearing. I did not trust what I heard
> myself saying. In very little that I heard did I hear anything that
> reflected anything which I knew, or had endured, of life. My
> mother and my father, my brothers and my sisters were not pres-
> ent at the tables at which I sat down, and no one in the company
> had ever heard of them. My own beginnings, or instincts, began
> to shift as nervously as the cigarette smoke that wavered around
> my head. I was not trying to hold on to my wretchedness. On the
> contrary, if my poverty was coming, at last, to an end, so much
> the better, and it wasn't happening a moment too soon—and yet,
> I felt an increasing chill, as though the rest of my life would have
> to be lived in silence.

The discomfort of having lost bearings is itself a prophetic trope, and comes to its fruition in the book's searing final paragraph:

> To be an Afro-American, or an American black, is to be in the situation, intolerably exaggerated, of all those who have ever found themselves part of a civilization which they could in no wise honorably defend—which they were compelled, indeed, endlessly to attack and condemn—and who yet spoke out of the most passionate love, hoping to make the kingdom new, to make it honorable and worthy of life. Whoever is part of whatever civilization helplessly loves some aspects of it, and some of the people in it. A person does not lightly elect to oppose his society. One would much rather be at home among one's compatriots than be mocked and detested by them. And there is a level on which the mockery of the people, even their hatred, is moving because it is so blind: it is terrible to watch people cling to their captivity and insist on their own destruction. I think black people have always felt this about America, and Americans, and have always seen, spinning above the thoughtless American head, the shape of the wrath to come.

Not to be at home among one's compatriots is to avoid the catastrophe of being at ease in the new Zion that is America. A reader, however moved by Baldwin's rhetorical authority, can be disturbed here by the implication that all blacks are prophets, at least in our society. Would to God indeed that all the Lord's people were prophets, but they are not, and cannot be. Fourteen years after the original publication of *No Name in the Street*, I am confronted by polls indicating that the President of the United States, currently enjoying a sixty-eight percent approval rating among all his constituents, also possesses a rather surprising fifty percent endorsement from my black fellow citizens. Whatever the President's place in history may prove to be, time has darkened Baldwin's temporal prophecy that his own people could remain an undivided witness against our civilization.

The Price of the Ticket

Like every true prophet, Baldwin passionately would prefer the fate of Jonah to that of Jeremiah, but I do not doubt that his authentic descent from Jeremiah will continue to be valid until the end of his life (and mine). The final utterance in *The Price of the Ticket* seems to me Baldwin's most poignant, ever:

Freaks are called freaks and are treated as they are treated—in the main, abominably—because they are human beings who cause to echo, deep within us, our most profound terrors and desires.

Most of us, however, do not appear to be freaks—though we are rarely what we appear to be. We are, for the most part, visibly male or female, our social roles defined by our sexual equipment.

But we are all androgynous, not only because we are all born of a woman impregnated by the seed of a man but because each of us, helplessly and forever, contains the other—male in female, female in male, white in black and black in white. We are a part of each other. Many of my countrymen appear to find this fact exceedingly inconvenient and even unfair, and so, very often, do I. But none of us can do anything about it.

Baldwin is most prophetic, and most persuasive, when his voice is as subdued as it is here. What gives the rhetorical effect of self-subdual is the precise use of plural pronouns throughout. Moving from his own predicament to the universal, the prophet achieves an effect directly counter to Jeremiah's pervasive trope of individualizing the prophetic alternative. The ultimate tribute that Baldwin has earned is his authentic share in Jeremiah's most terrible utterance:

O Lord, thou has deceived me, and I was deceived: thou art stronger than I, and hast prevailed: I am in derision daily, every one mocketh me.

For since I spake, I cried out, I cried violence and spoil; because the word of the Lord was made a reproach unto me, and a derision, daily.

Then I said, I will not make mention of him, nor speak any more in his name. But his word was in mine heart as a burning fire shut up in my bones, and I was weary with forbearing, and I could not stay,

Flannery O'Connor

(1925-1964)

The Violent Bear It Away

I

A PROFESSEDLY ROMAN CATHOLIC PROSE ROMANCE BEGINS WITH THE death of an eighty-four-year-old Southern American Protestant, self-called prophet, and professional moonshiner, as set forth in this splendidly comprehensive sentence:

> Francis Marion Tarwater's uncle had been dead for only half a day when the boy got too drunk to finish digging his grave and a Negro named Buford Munson, who had come to get a jug filled, had to finish it and drag the body from the breakfast table where it was still sitting and bury it in a decent and Christian way, with the sign of its Saviour at the head of the grave and enough dirt on top to keep the dogs from digging it up.

Flannery O'Connor's masterwork, *The Violent Bear It Away*, ends with the fourteen-year-old Tarwater marching towards the city of destruction, where his own career as prophet is to be suffered:

> Intermittently the boy's jagged shadow slanted across the road ahead of him as if it cleared a rough path toward his goal. His singed eyes, black in their deep sockets, seemed already to envision the fate that awaited him but he moved steadily on, his face set toward the dark city, where the children of God lay sleeping.

In Flannery O'Connor's fierce vision, the children of God, all of us, always are asleep in the outward life. Young Tarwater, clearly O'Connor's surrogate, is in clinical terms a borderline schizophrenic, subject to auditory hallucinations in which he hears the advice of an imaginary friend who is overtly the Christian Devil. But clinical terms are utterly alien to O'Connor, who accepts only theological namings and unnamings. This is necessarily a spiritual strength in O'Connor, yet it can be an aesthetic distraction also, since *The Violent Bear It Away* is a fiction of preternatural power, and not a religious tract. Rayber, the antagonist of both prophets, old and young Tarwater, is an aesthetic disaster, whose defects in representation alone keep the book from making a strong third with Faulkner's *As I Lay Dying* and Nathanael West's *Miss Lonelyhearts*. O'Connor despises Rayber, and cannot bother to make him even minimally persuasive. We wince at his unlikely verbal mixture of popular sociology and confused psychology, as even Sally Fitzgerald, O'Connor's partisan, is compelled to admit:

> Her weaknesses—a lack of perfect familiarity with the terminology of the secular sociologists, psychologists, and rationalists she often casts as adversary figures, and an evident weighting of the scales against them all—are present in the character of Rayber (who combines all three categories).

One hardly believes that a perfect familiarity with the writings say of David Riesman, Erik Erikson, and Karl Popper would have enabled O'Connor to make poor Rayber a more plausible caricature of what she despised. We remember *The Violent Bear It Away* for its two prophets, and particularly young Tarwater, who might be called a Gnostic version of Huckleberry Finn. What makes us free is the Gnosis, according to the most ancient of heresies. O'Connor, who insisted upon her Catholic orthodoxy, necessarily believed that what makes us free is baptism in Christ, and for her the title of her novel was its most important aspect, since the words are spoken by Jesus himself:

> But what went ye out for to see? A prophet? yea, I say unto you, and more than a prophet.
>
> For this is *he*, of whom it is written, Behold, I send my messenger before thy face, which shall prepare thy way before thee.
>
> Verily I say unto you, Among them that are born of women there hath not risen a greater than John the Baptist: notwithstanding he that is least in the kingdom of heaven is greater than he.

And from the days of John the Baptist until now the kingdom
of heaven suffereth violence, and the violent take it by force.

I have quoted the King James Version of Matt. 11:9–12, where "and
the violent take it by force" is a touch more revealing than O'Connor's
Catholic version, "and the violent bear it away." For O'Connor, we are
back in or rather never have left Christ's time of urgency, and her heart is
with those like the Tarwaters who know that the kingdom of heaven will
suffer them to take it by force:

> The lack of realism would be crucial if this were a realistic novel
> or if the novel demanded the kind of realism you demand. I don't
> believe it does. The old man is very obviously not a Southern
> Baptist, but an independent, a prophet in the true sense. The true
> prophet is inspired by the Holy Ghost, not necessarily by the
> dominant religion of his region. Further, the traditional
> Protestant bodies of the South are evaporating into secularism
> and respectability and are being replaced on the grass roots level
> by all sorts of strange sects that bear not much resemblance to tra-
> ditional Protestantism—Jehovah's Witnesses, snake-handlers,
> Free Thinking Christians, Independent Prophets, the swindlers,
> the mad, and sometimes the genuinely inspired. A character has to
> be true to his own nature and I think the old man is that. He was
> a prophet, not a church-member. As a prophet, he has to be a nat-
> ural Catholic. Hawthorne said he didn't write novels, he wrote
> romances; I am one of his descendants.

O'Connor's only disputable remark in this splendid defense of her
book is the naming of old Tarwater as "a natural Catholic." Hawthorne's
descendant she certainly was, by way of Faulkner, T.S. Eliot, and
Nathanael West, but though Hawthorne would have approved her mode,
he would have been shocked by her matter. To ignore what is authentically shocking about O'Connor is to misread her weakly. It is not her incessant violence that is troublesome but rather her passionate endorsement of
that violence as the only way to startle her secular readers into a spiritual
awareness. As a visionary writer, she is determined to take us by force, to
bear us away so that we may be open to the possibility of grace. Her unbe-
lieving reader is represented by the grandmother in the famous story "A
Good Man Is Hard to Find":

She saw the man's face twisted close to her own as if he were going to cry and she murmured, "Why you're one of my babies. You're one of my own children!" She reached out and touched him on the shoulder. The Misfit sprang back as if a snake had bitten him and shot her three times through the chest. Then he put his gun down on the ground and took off his glasses and began to clean them.

That murmur of recognition is what matters for O'Connor. The Misfit speaks for her in his mordant observation: "She would of been a good woman, if it had been somebody there to shoot her every minute of her life." Secular critic as I am, I need to murmur: "Surely that does make goodness a touch too strenuous?" But O'Connor anticipates our wounded outcries of nature against grace, since we understandably prefer a vision that corrects nature without abolishing it. Young Tarwater himself, as finely recalcitrant a youth as Huckleberry Finn, resists not only Rayber but the tuition of old Tarwater. A kind of swamp fox, like the Revolutionary hero for whom he was named, the boy Tarwater waits for his own call, and accepts his own prophetic election only after he has baptized his idiot cousin Bishop by drowning him, and even then only in consequence of having suffered a homosexual rape by the Devil himself. O'Connor's audacity reminds us of the Faulkner of *Sanctuary* and the West of *A Cool Million*. Her theology purports to be Roman Catholicism, but her sensibility is Southern Gothic, Jacobean in the mode of the early T. S. Eliot, and even Gnostic, in the rough manner of Carlyle, a writer she is likely never to have read.

I myself find it a critical puzzle to read her two novels, *Wise Blood* and *The Violent Bear It Away*, and her two books of stories, *A Good Man Is Hard to Find* and *Everything That Rises Must Converge*, and then to turn from her fiction to her occasional prose in *Mystery and Manners*, and her letters in *The Habit of Being*. The essayist and letter-writer denounces Manichaeism, Jansenism, and all other deviations from normative Roman Catholicism, while the storyteller seems a curious blend of the ideologies of Simone Weil reading the New Testament into the *Iliad*'s "poem of force" and of René Girard assuring us that there can be no return of the sacred without violence. Yet the actual O'Connor, in her letters, found Weil "comic and terrible," portraying the perpetual waiter for grace as an "angular intellectual proud woman approaching God inch by inch with ground teeth," and I suspect she would have been as funny about the violent thematicism of Girard.

To find something of a gap between O'Connor as lay theologue and O'Connor as a storyteller verging upon greatness may or may not be accurate but in any case intends to undervalue neither the belief nor the fiction. I suspect though that the fiction's implicit theology is very different from what O'Connor thought it to be, a difference that actually enhances the power of the novels and stories. It is not accidental that *As I Lay Dying* and *Miss Lonelyhearts* were the only works of fiction that O'Connor urged upon Robert Fitzgerald, or that her own prose cadences were haunted always by the earlier rather than the later Eliot. *The Waste Land*, *As I Lay Dying*, and *Miss Lonelyhearts* are not works of the Catholic imagination but rather of that Gnostic pattern Gershom Scholem termed "redemption through sin." *Wise Blood*, *The Violent Bear It Away*, and stories like "A Good Man Is Hard to Find" and the merciless "Parker's Back," take place in the same cosmos as *The Waste Land*, *As I Lay Dying*, and *Miss Lonelyhearts*. This world is the American version of the cosmological emptiness that the ancient Gnostics called the *kenoma*, a sphere ruled by a demiurge who has usurped the alien God, and who has exiled God out of history and beyond the reach of our prayers.

II

In recognizing O'Connor's fictive universe as being essentially Gnostic, I dissent not only from her own repudiation of heresy but from the sensitive reading of Jefferson Humphries, who links O'Connor to Proust in an "aesthetic of violence":

> For O'Connor, man has been his own demiurge, the author of his own fall, the keeper of his own cell....
>
> The chief consequence of this partly willful, partly inherited alienation from the sacred is that the sacred can only intrude upon human perception as a violence, a rending of the fabric of daily life.

On this account, which remains normative, whether Hebraic or Catholic, we are fallen into the *kenoma* through our own culpability. In the Gnostic formulation, creation and fall were one and the same event, and all that can save us is a certain spark within us, a spark that is no part of the creation but rather goes back to the original abyss. The grandeur or sublimity that shines through the ruined creation is a kind of abyss-radiance, whether in Blake or Carlyle or the early Eliot or in such novelistic masters of the grotesque as Faulkner, West, and O'Connor.

The ugliest of O'Connor's stories, yet one of the strongest, is "A View of the Woods" in *Everything That Rises Must Converge*. Its central characters are the seventy-nine-year-old Mr. Fortune, and his nine-year-old grand-daughter, Mary Fortune Pitts. I am uncertain which of the two is the more abominable moral character or hideous human personality, partly because they resemble one another so closely in selfishness, obduracy, false pride, sullenness, and just plain meanness. At the story's close, a physical battle between the two leaves the little girl a corpse, throttled and with her head smashed upon a rock, while her grandfather suffers a heart attack, during which he has his final "view of the woods," in one of O'Connor's typically devastating final paragraphs:

> Then he fell on his back and looked up helplessly along the bare trunks into the tops of the pines and his heart expanded once more with a convulsive motion. It expanded so fast that the old man felt as if he were being pulled after it through the woods, felt as if he were running as fast as he could with the ugly pines toward the lake. He perceived that there would be a little opening there, a little place where he could escape and leave the woods behind him. He could see it in the distance already, a little opening where the white sky was reflected in the water. It grew as he tan toward it until suddenly the whole lake opened up before him, riding majestically in little corrugated folds toward his feet. He realized suddenly that he could not swim and that he had not bought the boat. On both sides of him he saw that the gaunt trees had thickened into mysterious dark files that were marching across the water and away into the distance. He looked around desperately for someone to help him but the place was deserted except for one huge yellow monster which sat to the side, as stationary as he was, gorging itself on clay.

The huge yellow monster is a bulldozer, and so is the dying Mr. Fortune, and so was the dead Mary Fortune Pitts. What sustains our interest in such antipathetic figures in so grossly unsympathetic a world? O'Connor's own commentary does not help answer the question, and introduces a bafflement quite its own:

> The woods, if anything, are the Christ symbol. They walk across the water, they are bathed in a red light, and they in the end escape the old man's vision and march off over the hills. The name of the story is a view of the woods and the woods alone are pure enough to be a Christ symbol if anything is. Part of the tension of the story is created by Mary Fortune and the old man being images of

each other but opposite in the end. One is saved and the other is dammed [*sic*] and there is no way out of it, it must be pointed out and underlined. Their fates are different. One has to die first because one kills the other, but you have read it wrong if you think they die in different places. The old man dies by her side; he only thinks he runs to the edge of the lake, that is his vision.

What divine morality it can be that saves Mary Fortune and damns her wretched grandfather is beyond my ken, but the peculiarities of O'Connor's sense of the four last things transcend me at all times, anyway. What is more interesting is O'Connor's own final view of the woods. Her sacramental vision enables her to see Christ in "the gaunt trees [that] had thickened into mysterious dark files that were marching across the water and away into the distance." Presumably their marching away is emblematic of Mr. Fortune's damnation, so far as O'Connor is concerned. As a reader of herself, I cannot rank O'Connor very high here. Surely Mary Fortune is as damnable and damned as her grandfather, and the woods are damnable and damned also. They resemble not the normative Christ but the Jesus of the Gnostic texts, whose phantom only suffers upon the cross while the true Christ laughs far off in the alien heavens, in the ultimate abyss.

O'Connor's final visions are more equivocal than she evidently intended. Here is the conclusion of "Revelation":

Until the sun slipped finally behind the tree line, Mrs. Turpin remained there with her gaze bent to them as if she were absorbing some abysmal life-giving knowledge. At last she lifted her head. There was only a purple streak in the sky, cutting through a field of crimson and leading, like an extension of the highway, into the descending dusk. She raised her hands from the side of the pen in a gesture hieratic and profound. A visionary light settled in her eyes. She saw the streak as a vast swinging bridge extending upward from the earth through a field of living fire. Upon it a vast horde of souls were rumbling toward heaven. There were whole companies of white-trash, clean for the first time in their lives, and bands of black niggers in white robes, and battalions of freaks and lunatics shouting and clapping and leaping like frogs. And bringing up the end of the procession was a tribe of people whom she recognized at once as those who, like herself and Claud, had always had a little of everything and the God-given wit to use it right. She leaned forward to observe them closer. They were marching behind the others with great dignity, accountable as they had always been for good order and common sense and respectable behavior. They alone were on key. Yet she could see by their shocked and altered faces that even their virtues were being burned away. She lowered her hands and gripped the rail of the hog pen, her eyes small but fixed unblinkingly on what lay ahead. In a moment the vision faded but she remained where she was, immobile.

At length she got down and turned off the faucet and made her slow way on the darkening path to the house. In the woods around her the invisible cricket choruses had struck up, but what she heard were the voices of the souls climbing upward into the starry field and shouting hallelujah.

This is meant to burn away false or apparent virtues, and yet consumes not less than everything. In O'Connor's mixed realm, which is neither nature nor grace, Southern reality nor private phantasmagoria, all are necessarily damned, not by an aesthetic of violence but by a Gnostic aesthetic in which there is no knowing unless the knower becomes one with the known. Her Catholic moralism masked from O'Connor something of her own aesthetic of the grotesque. Certainly her essay on "Some Aspects of the Grotesque in Southern Fiction" evades what is central in her own praxis:

> Whenever I'm asked why Southern writers particularly have a penchant for writing about freaks, I say it is because we are still able to recognize one. To be able to recognize a freak, you have to have some conception of the whole man, and in the South the general conception of man is still, in the main, theological. That is a large statement, and it is dangerous to make it, for almost anything you say about Southern belief can be denied in the next breath with equal propriety. But approaching the subject from the standpoint of the writer, I think it is safe to say that while the South is hardly Christ-centered, it is most certainly Christ-haunted. The Southerner, who isn't convinced of it, is very much afraid that he may have been formed in the image and likeness of God. Ghosts can be very fierce and instructive. They cast strange shadows, particularly in our literature. In any case, it is when the freak can be sensed as a figure for our essential displacement that he attains some depth in literature.

The freakish displacement here is from "wholeness," which is then described as the state of having been made in the image or likeness of God. But that mode, displacement, is not what is operative in O'Connor's fiction. Her own favorite, among her people, is young Tarwater, who is not a freak, and who is so likeable because he values his own freedom above everything and anyone, even his call as a prophet. We are moved by Tarwater because of his recalcitrance, because he is the Huck Finn of visionaries. But he moves O'Connor, even to identification, because of his inescapable prophetic vocation. It is the interplay between Tarwater fighting to be humanly free, and Tarwater besieged by his great-uncle's training, by the internalized Devil, and most of all by O'Connor's own ferocious religious zeal, that constitutes O'Connor's extraordinary artistry. Her pious admirers to the contrary, O'Connor would have bequeathed us even stronger novels and stories, of the eminence of Faulkner's, if she had been able to restrain her spiritual tendentiousness.

Gabriel García Márquez

(1928–)

One Hundred Years of Solitude

MACONDO, ACCORDING TO CARLOS FUENTES, "BEGINS TO PROLIFERATE with the richness of a Columbian Yoknapatawpha." Faulkner, crossed by Kafka, is the literary origins of Gabriel García Márquez. So pervasive is the Faulknerian influence that at times one hears Joyce and Conrad, Faulkner's masters, echoed in García Márquez, yet almost always as mediated by Faulkner. The *Autumn of the Patriarch* may be too pervaded by Faulkner, but *One Hundred Years of Solitude* absorbs Faulkner, as it does all other influences, into a phantasmagoria so powerful and self-consistent that the reader never questions the authority of García Márquez. Perhaps, as Reinard Argas suggested, Faulkner is replaced by Carpentier and Kafka by Borges in *One Hundred Years of Solitude*, so that the imagination of García Márquez domesticates itself within its own language. Macondo, visionary realm, is an Indian and Hispanic act of consciousness, very remote from Oxford, Mississippi, and from the Jewish cemetery in Prague. In his subsequent work, García Márquez went back to Faulkner and Kafka, but then *One Hundred Years of Solitude* is a miracle and could only happen once, if only because it is less a novel than it is a Scripture, the Bible of Macondo; Melquíades the Magus, who writes in Sanskrit, may be more a mask for Borges than for the author himself, and yet the Gypsy storyteller also connects García Márquez to the archaic Hebrew storyteller, the Yahwist, at once the greatest of realists and the greatest of fantasists but above all the only true rival of Homer and Tolstoy as a storyteller.

My primary impression, in the act of rereading *One Hundred Years of Solitude*, is a kind of aesthetic battle fatigue, since every page is rammed full of life beyond the capacity of any single reader to absorb. Whether the impacted quality of this novel's texture is finally a virtue I am not sure, since sometimes I feel like a man invited to dinner who has been served nothing but an enormous platter of Turkish Delight. Yet it is all story, where everything conceivable and inconceivable is happening at once, from creation to apocalypse, birth to death. Roberto González Echevarría has gone so far as to surmise that in some sense it is the reader who must die at the end of the story, and perhaps it is the sheer richness of the text that serves to destroy us. Joyce half-seriously envisioned an ideal reader cursed with insomnia who would spend her life in unpacking *Finnegans Wake*. The reader need not translate *One Hundred Years of Solitude*, a novel that deserves its popularity as it has no surface difficulties whatsoever. And yet, a new dimension is added to reading by this book. Its ideal reader has to be like its most memorable personage, the sublimely outrageous Colonel Aureliano Buendía, who "had wept in his mother's womb and been born with his eyes open." There are no wasted sentences, no mere transitions, in this novel, and you must notice everything at the moment you read it. It will all cohere, at least as myth and metaphor if not always as literary meaning.

In the presence of an extraordinary actuality, consciousness takes the place of imagination. That Emersonian maxim is Wallace Stevens's and is worthy of the visionary of *Notes toward a Supreme Fiction* and *An Ordinary Evening in New Haven*. Macondo is a supreme fiction, and there are no ordinary evenings within its boundaries. Satire, even parody, and most fantasy—these are now scarcely possible in the United States. How can you satirize Ronald Reagan or Jerry Falwell? Pynchon's *The Crying of Lot 49* ceases to seem fantasy whenever I visit Southern California, and a ride on the New York City subway tends to reduce all literary realism to an idealizing projection. Some aspects of Latin American existence transcend even the inventions of García Márquez. I am informed, on good authority, that the older of the Duvalier dictators of Haiti, the illustrious Papa Doc, commanded that all black dogs in his nation be destroyed when he came to believe that a principal enemy had transformed himself into a black dog. Much that is fantastic in *One Hundred Years of Solitude* would be fantastic anywhere, but much that seems unlikely to a North American critic may well be a representation of reality.

Emir Monegal emphasized that García Márquez's masterwork was unique among Latin American novels, being radically different from the diverse achievements of Julio Cortázar, Carlos Fuentes, Lezama Lima, Mario Vargas Llosa, Miguel Angel Asturias, Manuel Puig, Guillermo Cabrera Infante, and so many more. The affinities to Borges and to Carpentier were noted by Monegal as by Arenas, but Monegal's dialectical

point seemed to be that García Márquez was representative only by joining all his colleagues in not being representative. Yet it is now true that, for
most North American readers, *One Hundred Years of Solitude* comes first to
mind when they think of the Hispanic novel in America. Alejo Carpentier's
Explosion in a Cathedral may be an even stronger book, but only Borges has
dominated the North American literary imagination as García Márquez
has with his grand fantasy. It is inevitable that we are fated to identify *One
Hundred Years of Solitude* with an entire culture, almost as though it were a
new *Don Quixote*, which it most definitely is not. Comparisons to Balzac
and even to Faulkner are also not very fair to García Márquez. The titanic inventiveness of Balzac dwarfs the later visionary, and nothing even in
Macondo is as much a negative Sublime as the fearsome quest of the
Bundrens in *As I Lay Dying*. *One Hundred Years of Solitude* is more of the
stature of Nabokov's *Pale Fire* and Pynchon's *Gravity's Rainbow*, latecom-
ers' fantasies, strong inheritors of waning traditions.

Whatever its limitations may or may not be, García Márquez's major
narrative now enjoys canonical status as well as a representative function.
Its cultural status continues to be enhanced, and it would be foolish to
quarrel with so large a phenomenon. I wish to address myself only to the
question of how seriously, as readers, we need to receive the book's scrip-
tural aspect. The novel's third sentence is: "The world was so recent that
things lacked names, and in order to indicate them it was necessary to
point," and the third sentence from the end is long and beautiful:

> Macondo was already a fearful whirlwind of dust and rubble being
> spun about by the wrath of the biblical hurricane when Aureliano
> skipped eleven pages so as not to lose time with facts he knew only
> too well, and he began to decipher the instant that he was living,
> deciphering it as he lived it, prophesying himself in the act of deci-
> phering the last page of the parchment, as if he were looking into
> a speaking mirror.

The time span between this Genesis and this Apocalypse is six generations, so that José Arcadio Buendía, the line's founder, is the grandfather
of the last Aureliano's grandfather. The grandfather of Dante's grandfather,
the crusader Cassaguida, tells his descendant Dante that the poet perceives
the truth because he gazes into that mirror in which the great and small of
this life, before they think, behold their thought. Aureliano, at the end,
reads the Sanskrit parchment of the gypsy, Borges-like Magus, and looks
into a speaking mirror, beholding his thought before he thinks it. But does
he, like Dante, behold the truth? Was Florence, like Macondo, a city of

mirrors (or mirages) in contrast to the realities of the Inferno, the Purgatorio, the Paradiso? Is *One Hundred Years of Solitude* only a speaking mirror? Or does it contain, somehow within it, an Inferno, a Purgatorio, a Paradiso?

Only the experience and disciplined reflections of a great many more strong readers will serve to answer those questions with any conclusiveness. The final eminence of *One Hundred Years of Solitude* for now remains undecided. What is clear to the book's contemporaries is that García Márquez has given contemporary culture, in North America and Europe, as much as in Latin America, one of its double handful of necessary narratives, without which we will understand neither one another nor our own selves.

Love in the Time of Cholera

The aesthetic principle of *Love in the Time of Cholera* is only a slightly chastened version of what might be the motto of *One Hundred Years of Solitude*: "Anything goes", or even "Everything goes". Anything and everything goes into the mix: Faulkner, Kafka Borges, Carpentier, Conrad, Joyce. Both novels are Scriptures: *Solitude* is an Old Testament, and *Cholera* a New Testament, at least for García Márquez and the most devoted of his readers and critics. I myself have come to value *Cholera* over *Solitude*, but that is a choice of riches.

What Faulkner—who most valued the Bible (as literature only), Shakespeare, Melville, Conrad, and Joyce—would have made of these New World Hispanic masterpieces, I cannot surmise. The verbal cascades he would have recognized as akin to his own, and the heroic individualism surely would have moved him. Yet he went about while waiting for his doom to lift, and his greatest figures—Darl Bundren, Quentin Compson, Sutpen, Joe Christmas, Popeye—are damned beyond damnation. Though Faulkner could be as grandly comic as Dickens, as is witnessed by the Snopes family, who now constitute the Texan Republican party, led by Tom De Lay Snopes, while our nation has chosen Benito Bush as Il Duce. Oscar Wilde was always right: life has no choice but to imitate art.

The antic joy of García Márquez might have been shrugged away by Faulkner, at least in his tragic mode, but he would have approved the last-ditch humanism affirmed both by precursor and latecomer. Decadence, the obsessive fear of incest, the drowning out of creative solitude by an ocean of information: these are common themes and apprehensions. What then is the saving difference, besides amazing high spirits in García Márquez, that distinguishes the two?

Faulkner's hopes rarely are persuasive: his greatest characters are as nihilistic as Shakespeare's. The immense popularity of García Márquez was earned by his exuberance, which veils his own apocalyptic forebodings. What Shakespeare was to Faulkner, Cervantes necessarily is to García Márquez: the truest ancestor. Cervantes, in his dark wisdom, is not less nihilistic than Shakespeare, and I do not believe that either ultimately was a Christian believer, any more than Faulkner or García Márquez can be said to be.

García Márquez's difference from all three is more evident in *Cholera* than in *Solitude*: he really does have a High Romantic faith in Eros, though he knows the Freudian truth that love too frequently is a mask for the Death Drive. Yet I prefer *Cholera* to *Solitude* finally because Florentine Ariza is dauntless, as here in the novel's closing passage:

> "Let us keep going, going, going, back to La Dorada."
>
> Fermina Daza shuddered because she recognized his former voice, illuminated by the grace of the Holy Spirit, and she looked at the Captain: he was their destiny. But the Captain did not see her because he was stupefied by Florentino Ariza's tremendous powers of inspiration.
>
> "Do you mean what you say?" he asked.
>
> "From the moment I was born," said Florentino Ariza, "I have never said anything I did not mean."
>
> The Captain looked at Fermina Daza and saw on her eyelashes the first glimmer of wintry frost. Then he looked at Florentino Ariza, his invincible power, his intrepid love, and he was overwhelmed by the belated suspicion that it is life, more than death, that has no limit.
>
> "And how long do you think we can keep up this goddamn coming and going?" he asked.
>
> Florentino Ariza had kept his answer ready for fifty-three years, seven months, and eleven days and nights.
>
> "Forever," he said.

Ursula K. Le Guin

(1929-)

The Left Hand of Darkness

I

IN A RECENT PARABLE, "SHE UNNAMES THEM" (*THE NEW YORKER*, JANUARY 21, 1985), the best contemporary author of literary fantasy sums up the consequences of Eve's unnaming of the animals that Adam had named:

> None were left now to unname, and yet how close I felt to them when I saw one of them swim or fly or trot or crawl across my way or over my skin, or stalk me in the night, or go along beside me for a while in the day. They seemed far closer than when their names had stood between myself and them like a clear barrier: so close that my fear of them and their fear of me became one same fear. And the attraction that many of us felt, the desire to smell one another's scales or skin or feathers or fur, taste one another's blood or flesh, keep one another warm—that attraction was now all one with the fear, and the hunter could not be told from the hunted, nor the eater from the food.

This might serve as a coda for all Ursula Kroeber Le Guin's varied works to date. She is essentially a mythological fantasist; the true genre for her characteristic tale is romance, and she has a high place in the long American tradition of the romance, a dominant mode among us from Hawthorne down to Pynchon's *The Crying of Lot Forty-Nine*. Because science fiction is a popular mode, she is named as a science-fiction writer, and a certain defiance in her proudly asserts that the naming is accurate. But no one reading, say Philip K. Dick, as I have been doing after reading Le Guin's discussion of his work in *The Language of the Night*, is likely to associate the prose achievement of Le Guin with that of her acknowledged precursor. She is a fierce defender of the possibilities for science fiction, to the extent of calling Philip K. Dick "our own homegrown Borges" and even of implying that Dick ought not to be compared to Kafka only because Dick is "not an absurdist" and his work "is not (as Kafka's was) autistic."

After reading Dick, one can only murmur that a literary critic is in slight danger of judging Dick to be "our Borges" or of finding Dick in the cosmos of Kafka, the Dante of our century. But Le Guin as critic, loyal to her colleagues who publish in such periodicals as *Fantastic, Galaxy, Amazing, Orbit* and the rest, seems to me not the same writer as the visionary of *The Earthsea Trilogy, The Left Hand of Darkness, The Dispossessed* and *The Beginning Place.* Better than Tolkien, far better than Doris Lessing, Le Guin is the overwhelming contemporary instance of a superbly imaginative creator and major stylist who chose (or was chosen by) "fantasy and science fiction." At her most remarkable, as in what still seems to me her masterpiece, *The Left Hand of Darkness*, she offers a sexual vision that strangely complements Pynchon's *Gravity's Rainbow* and James Merrill's *Changing Light at Sandover.* I can think of only one modern fantasy I prefer to *The Left Hand of Darkness*, and that is David Lindsay's *Voyage to Arcturus* (1920), but Lindsay's uncanny nightmare of a book survives its dreadful writing, while Le Guin seems never to have written a wrong or bad sentence. One has only to quote some of her final sentences to know again her absolute rhetorical authority:

> But he had not brought anything. His hands were empty, as they had always been.
> (*The Dispossessed*)

> Gravely she walked beside him up the white streets of Havnor, holding his hand, like a child coming home.
> (*The Tombs of Atuan*)

> There is more than one road to the city.
> (*The Beginning Place*)

> But the boy, Therem's son, said stammering, "Will you tell us how he died?—Will you tell us about the other worlds out among the stars—the other kinds of men, the other lives?"
> (*The Left Hand of Darkness*)

When her precise, dialectical style—always evocative, sometimes sublime in its restrained pathos—is exquisitely fitted to her powers of invention, as in *The Left Hand of Darkness*, Le Guin achieves a kind of sensibility very nearly unique in contemporary fiction. It is the pure storyteller's sensibility that induces in the reader a state of uncertainty, of *not knowing what comes next*. What Walter Benjamin praised in Leskov is exactly relevant to Le Guin:

> Death is the sanction of everything that the storyteller can tell. He has borrowed his authority from death....
>
> The first true storyteller is, and will continue to be, the teller of fairy tales. Whenever good counsel was at a premium, the fairy tale had it, and where the need was greatest, its aid was nearest. This need was the need created by the myth. The fairy tale tells us of the earliest arrangements that mankind made to shake off the nightmare which the myth had placed upon its chest....

Elsewhere in his essay on Leskov, Benjamin asserts that: "The art of storytelling is reaching its end because the epic side of truth, wisdom, is dying out." One can be skeptical of Benjamin's Marxist judgment that such a waning, if waning it be, is "only a concomitant symptom of the secular productive forces of history." Far more impressively, Benjamin once remarked of Kafka's stories that in them, "narrative art regains the significance it had in the mouth of Scheherazade: to postpone the future." Le Guin's narrative art, though so frequently set in the future, not only borrows its authority from death but also works to postpone the future, works to protect us against myth and its nightmares.

I am aware that this is hardly consonant with the accounts of her narrative purposes that Le Guin gives in the essays of *The Language of the Night*. But Lawrence's adage is perfectly applicable to Le Guin: trust the tale, not the teller, and there is no purer storyteller writing now in English than Le Guin. Her true credo is spoken by one of her uncanniest creations, Faxe the Weaver, master of the Foretelling, to conclude the beautiful chapter, "The Domestication of Hunch," in *The Left Hand of Darkness*:

> "The unknown," said Faxe's soft voice in the forest, "the unforetold, the unproven, that is what life is based on. Ignorance is the ground of thought. Unproof is the ground of action. If it were proven that there is no God there would be no religion. No Handdara, no Yomesh, no hearth gods, nothing. But also if it were proven that there is a God, there would be no religion..... Tell me,

Genry, what is known? What is sure, predictable, inevitable—the one certain thing you know concerning your future, and mine?"

"That we shall die."

"Yes. There's really only one question that can be answered, Genry, and we already know the answer ... the only thing that makes life possible is permanent, intolerable uncertainty: not knowing what comes next."

The fine irony, that this is the master Foreteller speaking, is almost irrelevant to Le Guin's profound narrative purpose. She herself is the master of a dialectical narrative mode in which nothing happens without involving its opposite. The shrewdly elliptical title, *The Left Hand of Darkness*, leaves out the crucial substantive in Le Guin's Taoist verse:

Light is the left hand of darkness
and darkness the right hand of light.
Two are one, life and death, lying
together like lovers in kemmer,
like hands joined together,
like the end and the way.

The way is the Tao, exquisitely fused by Le Guin into her essentially Northern mythology. "Kemmer" is the active phase of the cycle of human sexuality on the planet Gethen or Winter, the site of *The Left Hand of Darkness*. Winter vision, even in the books widely separated in substance and tone from her masterpiece, best suits Le Guin's kind of storytelling. Mythology, from her childhood on, seems to have meant Norse rather than Classical stories. Like Blake's and Emily Brontë's, her imagination is at home with Odin and Yggdrasil. Yet she alters the cosmos of the Eddas so that it loses some, not all, of its masculine aggressiveness and stoic harshness. Her Taoism, rather than her equivocal Jungianism, has the quiet force that tempers the ferocity of the Northern vision.

II

"Visibility without discrimination, solitude without privacy," is Le Guin's judgment upon the capital of the Shing, who in 4370 A.D. rule what had been the United States, in her novel, *City of Illusions*. In an introduction to *The Left Hand of Darkness*, belatedly added to the book seven years after its publication, Le Guin sharply reminds us that: "I write science fiction, and science fiction isn't about the future. I don't know any more about the future than you do, and very likely less." Like Faxe the Weaver, she prefers ignorance of the future, and yet, again like Faxe, she is a master of Foretelling, which both is and is not a mode of moral prophecy. It is, in that it offers a moral vision of the present; it is not, precisely because it refuses to say that "If you go on so, the result is so." The United States in 1985 still offers "visibility without discrimination, solitude without privacy." As for the United States in 4370, one can quote "Self," a lyric meditation from Le Guin's rather neglected *Hard Words and Other Poems* (1981):

> You cannot measure the circumference
> but there are centerpoints:
> stones, and a woman washing at a ford,
> the water runs red-brown from what she washes.
> The mouths of caves. The mouths of bells.
> The sky in winter under snowclouds
> to northward, green of jade.
> No star is farther from it than the glint
> of mica in a pebble in the hand,
> or nearer. Distance is my god.

Distance, circumference, the unmeasurable, goal, the actual future which can only be our dying; Le Guin evades these, and her narratives instead treasure wisdom or the centerpoints. Yet the poem just before "Self" in *Hard Words*, cunningly titled "Amazed," tells us where wisdom is to be found, in the disavowal of "I" by "eye," a not un-Emersonian epiphany:

> The center is not where the center is
> but where I will be when I follow
> the lines of stones that wind about a center
> that is not there
>   but there.
> The lines of stones lead inward, bringing
> the follower to the beginning
> where all I knew
>   is flew.
> Stone is stone and more than stone;
> the center opens like an eyelid opening.
> Each rose a maze: the hollow hills:
> I am not I
>   but eye.

One thinks of the shifting centers in every Le Guin narrative, and of her naming the mole as her totem in another poem. She is a maze maker or "shaper of darkness / into ways and hollows," who always likes the country on the other side. Or she is "beginning's daughter" who "sings of stones." Her Taoism celebrates the strength of water over stone, and yet stone is her characteristic trope. As her words are hard, so are most of her women and men, fit after all for Northern or winter myth. One can say off her that she writes a hard-edged phantasmagoria, or that it is the Promethean rather than the Narcissistic element in her literary fantasy that provides her with her motive for metaphor.

In some sense, all of her writings call us forth to quest into stony places, where the object of the quest can never quite he located. Her most mature quester, the scientist Shevek in *The Dispossessed*, comes to apprehend that truly he is both subject and object in the quest, always already gone on, always already there. A Promethean anarchist, Shevek has surmounted self-consciousness and self-defense, but at the cost of a considerable loss in significance. He represents Le Guin's ideal Odonian society, where the isolated idealist like Shelley or Kropotkin has become the norm, yet normative anarchism cannot be represented except as permanent revolution, and permanent revolution defies aesthetic as well as political representation. Shevek is beyond these limits of representation and more than that, "his hands were empty, as they had always been." Deprived of the wounded self-regard that our primary narcissism converts into aggression, Shevek becomes nearly as colorless as the actual personality upon whom he is based, the physicist Robert Oppenheimer. Even Le Guin cannot have it both ways; the ideological anarchism of *The Dispossessed* divests her hero of his narcissistic ego, and so of much of his fictive interest. Jung is a better psychological guide in purely mythic realms, like Le Guin's Earthsea, then he is in psychic realms closer to our own, as in *The Dispossessed*.

III

Le Guin's greatest accomplishment, certainly reflecting the finest balance of her powers, is *The Left Hand of Darkness*, though I hasten to name this her finest work *to date*. At fifty-five, she remains beginning's daughter, and there are imaginative felicities in *The Beginning Place* (1980) that are subtler and bolder than anything in *The Left Hand of Darkness* (1969). But conceptually and stylistically, *Left Hand* is the strongest of her dozen or so major narratives. It is a book that sustains many rereadings, partly because its enigmas are unresolvable, and partly because it has the crucial quality of a great representation, which is that it yields up new perspectives upon what we call reality. Though immensely popular (some thirty paperback printings), it seems to me critically undervalued, with rather too much emphasis upon its supposed flaws. The best known negative critique is by Stanislaw Lem, who judged the sexual element in the book irrelevant to its story, and improbably treated in any case. This is clearly a weak misreading on Lem's part. What the protagonist, Genly Ai, continuously fails to understand about the inhabitants of the planet Winter is precisely that their sexuality gives them a mode of consciousness profoundly alien to his (and ours). Le Guin, with admirable irony, replied to feminist and other critics that indeed she had "left out too much" and could "only be very grateful to those readers, men and women, whose willingness to participate in the experiment led them to fill in that omission with the work of their own imagination." Too courteous to say, with Blake, that her care was not to make matters explicit to the idiot, Le Guin wisely has relied upon her extraordinary book to do its work of self-clarification across the fifteen years of its reception.

The book's principal aesthetic strength is its representation of the character and personality of Estraven, the Prime Minister who sacrifices position, honor, freedom and finally his life in order to hasten the future, by aiding Genly Ai's difficult mission. As the ambassador of the Ekumen, a benign federation of planets, Ai needs to surmount his own perspective as a disinterested cultural anthropologist if he is to understand the androgynes who make up the entire population of the isolated planet alternatively called Gethen or Winter. Without understanding, there is no hope of persuading them, even for their own obvious good, to join with the rest of the cosmos. What is most interesting about Ai (the name suggesting at once the ego, the eye, and an outcry of pain) is his reluctance to go beyond the limits of his own rationality, which would require seeing the causal link between his sexuality and mode of consciousness.

The sexuality of the dwellers upon the planet Winter remains Le Guin's subtlest and most surprising invention:

> A Gethenian in first-phase kemmer, if kept alone or with others not in kemmer, remains incapable of coitus. Yet the sexual impulse is tremendously strong in this phase, controlling the entire personality, subjecting all other drives to its imperative. When the individual finds a partner in kemmer, hormonal secretion is further stimulated (most importantly by touch—secretion? scent?) until in one partner either a male or female hormonal dominance is established. The genitals engorge or shrink accordingly, foreplay intensifies, and the partner, triggered by the chance, takes on

the other sexual role (? without exception? If there are exceptions, resulting in kemmer—partners of the same sex, they are so rare as to be ignored).

The narrator here is neither Ai nor Le Guin but a field investigator of the Ekumen, wryly cataloging a weird matter. Her field notes add a number of sharper observations: these androgynes have no sexual drive at all for about 21 or 22 out of every 26 days. Anyone can and usually does bear children, "and the mother of several children may he the father of several more," descent being reckoned from the mother, known as "the parent in the flesh." There is no Oedipal ambivalence of children toward parents, no rape or unwilling sex, no dualistic division of humankind into active and passive. All Gethenians are natural monists, with no need to sublimate anything, and little inclination towards warfare.

Neither Le Guin nor any of her narrators give us a clear sense of any casual relation between a world of nearly perpetual winter and the ambisexual nature of its inhabitants, yet an uncanny association between the context of coldness and the unforeseeable sexuality of each individual persists throughout. Though Lem insisted anxiety must attend the unpredictability of one's gender, Le Guin's book persuasively refuses any such anxiety. There is an imaginative intimation that entering upon any sexual identity for about one-fifth of the time is more than welcome to anyone who must battle perpetually just to stay warm! Le Guin's humor, here as elsewhere, filters in slyly, surprising us in a writer who is essentially both somber and serene.

The one Gethenian we get to know well is Estraven, certainly a more sympathetic figure than the slow-to-learn Ai. Estraven is Le Guin's greatest triumph in characterization, and yet remains enigmatic, as he must. How are we to understand the psychology of a manwoman, utterly free of emotional ambivalence, of which the masterpiece after all is the Oedipal conflict? And how are we to understand a fiercely competitive person, since the Gethenians are superbly agonistic, who yet lacks any component of sexual aggressiveness, let alone its cause in a sexually wounded narcissism? Most fundamentally we are dualists, and perhaps our involuntary and Universal Freudianism (present even in a professed Jungian, like Le Guin) is the result of that being the conceptualized dualism most easily available to us. But the people of Winter are Le Guin's shrewd way of showing us that all our dualisms—Platonic, Pauline, Cartesian, Freudian—not only have a sexual root but are permanent because we are bisexual rather than ambisexual beings. Freud obviously would not have disagreed, and evidently Le Guin is more Freudian than she acknowledges herself to be.

Winter, aside from its properly ghastly weather, is no Utopia. Karhide,

Estraven's country, is ruled by a clinically mad king, and the rival power, Orgoreyn, is founded upon a barely hidden system of concentration camps. Androgyny is clearly neither a political nor a sexual ideal in *The Left Hand of Darkness*. And yet, mysteriously and beautifully, the book suggests that Winter's ambisexuality is a more imaginative condition than our bisexuality. Like the unfallen Miltonic angels, the Gethenians know more than either men or women can know. As with the angels, this does not make them better or wiser, but evidently they see more than we do, since each one of them is Tiresias, as it were. This, at last, is the difference between Estraven and Genly Ai. Knowing and seeing more, Estraven is better able to love, and freer therefore to sacrifice than his friend can be.

Yet that, though imaginative, is merely a generic difference. Le Guin's art is to give us also a more individual difference between Ai and Estraven. Ai is a kind of skeptical Horatio who arrives almost too late at a love for Estraven as a kind of ambisexual Hamlet, but who survives, like Horatio, to tell his friend's story:

> For it seemed to me, and I think to him, that it was from that sexual tension between us, admitted now and understood, but not assuaged, that the great and sudden assurance of friendship between us rose: a friendship so much needed by us both in our exile, and already so well proved in the days and nights of our bitter journey, that it might as well be called, now as later, love. But it was from the difference between us, not from the affinities and likenesses, but from the difference, that that love came....

The difference is more than sexual, and so cannot be bridged by sexual love, which Ai and Estraven avoid. It is the difference between Horatio and Hamlet, between the audience's surrogate and the tragic hero, who is beyond both surrogate and audience. Estraven dies in Ai's arms, but uttering his own dead brother's name, that brother having peen his incestuous lover, and father of Estraven's son. In a transference both curious and moving, Estraven has associated Ai with his lost brother-lover, to whom he had vowed faithfulness. It is another of Le Guin's strengths that, in context, this has intense pathos and nothing of the grotesque whatsoever. More than disbelief becomes suspended by the narrative art of *The Left Hand of Darkness*.

IV

That Le Guin, more than Tolkien, has raised fantasy into high literature, for our time, seems evident to me because her questers never abandon the world where we have to live, the world of Freud's reality principle. Her praise of Tolkien does not convince me that *The Lord of the Rings* is not tendentious and moralizing, but her generosity does provide an authentic self-description:

> For like all great artists he escapes ideology by being too quick for its nets, too complex for its grand simplicities, too fantastic for its rationality, too real for its generalizations.

This introduction could end there, but I would rather allow Le Guin to speak of herself directly:

> Words are my matter. I have chipped one stone
> for thirty years and still it is not done,
> that image of the thing I cannot see.
> I cannot finish it and set it free,
>
> > transformed to energy.

There is a touch of Yeats here, Le Guin's voice being most her own in narrative prose, but the burden is authentic Le Guin: the sense of limit, the limits of the senses, the granite labor at hard words, and the ongoing image that is her characteristic trope, an unfinished stone. Like her Genly Ai, she is a far-fetcher, to use her own term for visionary metaphor. It was also the Elizabethan rhetorician Puttenham's term for transumption or metalepsis, the trope that reverses time, and makes lateness into an earliness. Le Guin is a grand far-fetcher or transumer of the true tradition of romance we call literary fantasy. No one else now among us matches her at rendering freely "that image of the thing I cannot see."

Toni Morrison

(1931–)

Sula

POLITICAL INTERPRETATION HAS BEEN ALL THE RAGE, ACADEMIC AND journalistic, during the last thirty years. No contemporary novelist of anything like Toni Morrison's eminence is so insistent that she desires political interpretation by her exegetes. She certainly has received what she calls for: an entire sect of cheerleaders crowd in her wake. Very little can be done against such a fashion at this time. If the United States achieves a larger measure of social justice in a generation or so, then Morrison yet may be esteemed more for her narrative art, invention, and style than for her exemplary political correctness. Myself an archaic survival, a dinosaur still lurching about the halls of Yale and New York University, I go on reading for aesthetic experience only. This introduction therefore will consider *Sula* only as an artistic achievement, and not as a weapon wielded against indubitable societal oppression by a celebrated African-American feminist Marxist.

Sula herself is a total rebel against all society, all conventions and nearly all moralities. A "demon" in the eyes of the black community, Sula is a kind of Lilith, taking sexual satisfaction where she will. No evil but doomeager, Sula quests desperately for freedom, but she necessarily is self-victimized, as Morrison make clear:

> In a way, her strangeness, her naiveté, her craving for the other half of her equation was the consequence of an idle imagination. Had she paints, or clay, or knew the discipline of the dance, or strings; had she anything to engage her tremendous curiosity and her gift for metaphor, she might have exchanged the restlessness and preoccupation with whim for an activity that provided her

with all she longed for. And like any artist with no art form, she became dangerous.

Trust the tale and not the teller: is Sula an artist without an art form, or is she a Zora Neale Hurston-like vitalist who has wandered into the wrong novel? Morrison brooks no rivals: Ralph Ellison is a hidden target in *The Bluest Eye* and *Song of Solomon*, while Hurston's heroic egoism is parodied in *Sula*. Aesthetically, this is all to the good; Morrison is at her best when she is most agonistic. Sula Peace bears a name itself ironic, since her mode of individualism can achieve no peace whatsoever. Her mother Hannah, the freest of all erotic beings, dies in an accidental fire that can be interpreted as a punishment only if you are morally diseased. Sula, like Hannah, is a natural seductress, a witch if again you have it so. But ideological readings of her pathos seem to me as irrelevant as moral judgments; Sula floats free of interpretative designs, including Morrison's own. She remains Morrison's most memorable character, largely because she resists categorization. Her challenge to the community is both ancient and original; doom-eagerness cannot be confined. Her intensity and fatedness are alike Faulknerian; she would give another dimension to *Sanctuary*, without disturbing the violent cosmos of that now underrated novel. As a vivid figure, she is curiously unique in Morrison's fiction, and we allegorize or moralize Sula to our own loss. No program of Liberation would have saved her from herself, or from the individuality of her familial past.

The Bluest Eye

The Bluest Eye, Morrison's first novel, was published when she was thirty-nine and is anything but novice work. Michael Wood, an authentic literary critic, made the best comment on this "lucid and eloquent" narrative that I have ever seen:

> Each member of the family interprets and acts out of his or her ugliness, but none of then understands that the all-knowing master is not God but only history and habit; the projection of their own numbed collusion with the mythology of beauty and ugliness that oppresses them beyond their already grim social oppression.

Morrison herself, in an Afterword of 1994, looked back across a quarter-century and emphasized her "reliance for full comprehension in codes embedded in black culture." A reader who is not black or female must do the best he can; like Michael Wood, I have found *The Bluest Eye* to be completely lucid since I first read it, back in 1970. Like *Sula* and *The Song of Solomon* after it, the book seems to me successful in universal terms, even if one shares neither Morrison's origins nor her ideologies. *Beloved*, Morrison's most famous romance narrative, seems to be to be problematic, though it has reached a vast audience. A generation or two will have to pass before a balanced judgment could be rendered upon *Beloved* or Morrison's later novels, *Jazz* and *Paradise*. But her early phase has many of the canonical qualifications of the traditional Western literary kind that she fiercely rejects as being irrelevant to her.

The essays reprinted in this volume are, almost all of them, ideological, and follow Morrison's lead in being the kind of appreciation that she wants. I add a brief appreciation here, in the full awareness that I am necessarily incorrect, since I am an outworn aesthete, and not a "cultural critic." What I never forget about *The Bluest Eye* is its terrifying penultimate paragraph, where the narrator censures herself and her friends for turning away from Pecola because the child's madness, engendered by the trauma of being raped by her father, Cholly, "bored us in the end":

> Oh, some of us "loved" her. The Maginot Line. And Cholly loved her. I'm sure he did. He, at any rate, was the one who loved her enough to touch her, envelope her, give something of her filled the matrix of her agony with death. Love is never any better than the lover. Wicked people love wickedly, violent people love violently, weak people love weakly, stupid people love stupidly, but the love of a free man is never safe. There is no gift for the beloved. The lover alone possesses his gift of love. The loved one is shorn, neutralized, frozen in the glare of the lover's inward eye.

The unhappy wisdom of this is happily free of any cultural narcissism whatsoever. Class, race, even gender do not over-determine *this* bleakness. Morrison's heroic survivors in *Beloved* are intended to stand up both in and against their history. Perhaps they do, but the torments they have endured also are tendentiously elaborated, because the author has an ideological design upon us, her guilty readers, white and black, male and female. The narrator of *The Bluest Eye* persuades me, where the narration of *Beloved* does not. In D.H. Lawrence's terms, I trust both the tale and the teller in *The Bluest Eye*. In *Beloved*, I do not trust the tale.

Song of Solomon

Toni Morrison's third novel, *Song of Solomon* (1977), seems to me her masterwork to date, though *Beloved* (1987) has even more readers. A superb, highly conscious artist from her beginning, Morrison is also a committed social activist. Exemplary as it is, her African-American feminist stance is the prime concern of nearly all her critics, which makes for a certain monotony in their cheerleading. Morrison is scarcely responsible for them, though I detect an intensification of ideological fervor when I pass from rereading *Song of Solomon* to rereading *Beloved* and then go on to *Jazz* and *Paradise*, her most recent novels. A novelist's politics are part of her panoply, her arms and armor. Time stales our coverings; fictions that endure do so despite the passionate commitments of their authors, while claques, however sincere, do not assure literary survival. The very titles of many of the essays in this volume testify to political obsessions: "black cultural nationalism," "myth, ideology, and gender," "race and class consciousness," "political identity," "competing discourses." Morrison, far cannier than her enthusiasts, at her most persuasive transcends her own indubitable concerns. Her art, grounded in African-American realities and concerns, is nevertheless not primarily naturalistic in its aims and modes.

Morrison has been vehement in asserting that African-American literature is her aesthetic context: she has invoked slave narratives, folklore, spirituals, and jazz songs. So advanced a stylist and storyteller is not likely to celebrate Zora Neale Hurston as a forerunner, or to imagine a relation between herself and Richard Wright, or James Baldwin. Her authentic rival is the late Ralph Waldo Ellison, whose *Invisible Man* remains the most extraordinary achievement in African-American fiction. Morrison subtly wards off *Invisible Man* (1952), from *The Bluest Eye* (1970) on to *Paradise*. Though she has deprecated the "complex series of evasions" of Modernist literature and its criticism, no one is more brilliant at her own complex series of evasions, particularly of Ralph Ellison, unwanted strong precursor. This is not to suggest that Ellison is her prime precursor: William Faulkner shadows Morrison's work always, and inspires even more creative evasions in her best writing.

I am aware that I am at variance with nearly all of Morrison's critics, who take their lead from her *Playing in the Dark: Whiteness and the Literary Imagination*, one of her most adroit evasions of the central Western literary tradition that, in mere fact, has fostered her. But then, as a professional literary critic, I must declare an interest, since my argument for the inescapability of what I have termed "the anxiety of influence" is contested by the culturally correct. There is no anguish of contamination or guilt of inheritance for black women writers in particular, I frequently am admonished. Patriarchal, capitalistic, phallocentric notions must be swept aside: they are racist, sexist, exclusionary, exploitative. If even Shakespeare can become Alternative Shakespeare, then Toni Morrison can spring full-grown from the head of Black Athena.

Every strong writer welcomes the opportunity to be an original, and Morrison's literary achievement more than justifies her sly embrace of African-American cultural narcissism. Her critics seem to me quite another matter, but my Editor's Note is an appropriate context for commenting upon them. Here I desire only to discuss, rather briefly, the genesis of *Song of Solomon*'s authentic aesthetic strength from the creative agony with Faulkner and with Ellison. Morrison deftly uses Faulkner while parrying Ellison: out of the strong comes forth sweetness. *Song of Solomon* exuberantly is informed by the creative gusto of Morrison's sense of victory in the contest that is inevitable for the art of literature. Jacob Burckhardt and Friedrich Nietzsche both pioneered in reminding us that the Athenians conceived of literature as an agony. Nietzsche admirably condensed this insight in his grand fragment, "Homer's Contest":

> Every talent must unfold itself in fighting ... And just as the youths were educated through contests, their educators were also engaged in contests with each other. The great musical masters, Pindar and Simonides, stood side by side, mistrustful and jealous; in the spirit of contest. The sophist, the advanced teacher of antiquity, meets another sophist; even the most universal type of instruction, through the drama, was meted out to the people only in the form of a tremendous wrestling among the great musical and dramatic artists. How wonderful! "Even the artist hates the artist." Whereas modern man fears nothing in an artist more than the emotion of any personal fight, the Greek knows the artist *only as engaged in a personal fight*. Precisely where modern man senses the weakness of a work of art, the Hellene seeks the source of its greatest strength.

Probably Morrison would dissent from Nietzsche, but that would be Morrison the critic, not Morrison the novelist, who is engaged in a personal fight with *Invisible Man* and with Faulkner's *Light in August*. Morrison's career is still in progress; it is too soon to prophesy whether she will yet surpass *The Song of Solomon*. Again, I am aware that admirers of *Beloved*, a highly deliberate work of art, believe that Morrison has transcended her earlier work. Since I find *Beloved* ideologically over-determined, and therefore in places somewhat tendentious, I prefer *Song of Solomon*. Highly conscious as she is of the American romance tradition, from Hawthorne and Melville through Faulkner and Ellison, Morrison wonderfully subverts that tradition in *Song of Solomon*. This subversion is not primarily ideological, but properly imaginative and revisionary. Great solitaries—Hester Prynne, Captain Ahab, Joe Christmas, Invisible Man— are joined by a different kind of solitary, Milkman Dead. Milkman, like his precursors, quests for the restoration of his true self, lest he remain a Jonah, but Morrison shapes her protagonist's quest so that it is communitarian despite itself. She does the same in *Beloved*, yet with an inverted sentimentalism that may be the consequence of too overt a reliance upon the political myth of a social energy inherent in the souls of Southern blacks. In *Song of Solomon*, a work of more individual mythopoeia, the refining of community is aesthetically persuasive.

Ellison's nameless Invisible Man is massively persuasive in his final judgment that there is *no* community for him, black or white:

> Step outside the narrow borders of what men call reality and you step into chaos ... or imagination. That too I've learned in the cellar, and not by deadening my sense of perception; I'm invisible, not blind.

Morrison's Milkman Dead reaches a conclusion radically revisionary of Ellison's nameless man:

> How many dead lives and fading memories were buried in and beneath the names of the places in this country. Under the recorded names were other names, just as "Macon Dead," recorded for all time in some dusty file, hid from view the real names of people, places, and things. Names that had meaning ... When you know your name, you should hang to it, for unless it is noted down and remembered, it will die when you do.

The Invisible Man, who will accept no name whatsoever, has stepped into chaos *or* imagination, two words for the same entity, or are they antithesis? Ellison, as an Emersonian, allows for both readings. Morrison, born Chloe Anthony Wofford, has held on to her original middle name as the "real" one. Milkman loses the false name, "Dead," to acquire the ancestral real name, Solomon or Shalimar. Ellison perhaps would have judged that Morrison had kept within narrower borders than she required; I never discussed her work with him, so I do not know, but African-American nationalism, or any sort, was what he had rejected in his poignant and deluded Ras the Exhorter. Milkman's superb poignance is that he is anything but an Exhorter.

Faulkner I find everywhere in Morrison, generally transmuted, yet never finally transcended. In our century, Wallace Stevens wrote the poems of our climate, and Faulkner wrote the best of our novels, particularly in *As I Lay Dying* and *Light in August*. Returning to a fictive South, Milkman also returns to Faulkner, primarily to *The Bear* and its rituals of initiation. I dislike going against Morrison's own passionate critical pronouncements, yet I hardly am attempting "to *place* value only where that influence is located." Joseph Conrad does not crowd out Faulkner, nor does Faulkner render Morrison less gifted, less black, less female, less Marxist. Even the strongest of novelists cannot choose their own precursors. Hemingway wanted to assert *Huckleberry Finn* as his origin, but the ethos and mode of *The Sun Also Rises* are distinctly Conradian. "Africanism is inextricable from the definition of Americanness," Morrison insists. She ought to be right, and as a nation we would be better if she were right. One learns the truth about American Religion, I am convinced, if we trace its origin to the early black Baptists in America, who carried an African *gnosis* with them, in which "the little me within the big me" was the ultimate, unfallen reality. Morrison, like Faulkner, has a great deal to teach us about both "white" American and African-American identity. In a long enough perspective, Faulkner and Morrison may be teaching the same troubled truths.

Beloved

The cultural importance of Toni Morrison's most popular novel, *Beloved* (1987), hardly can be overstressed. I have just reread it, after a decade, in a paperback printing numbered 41; in time doubtless there will be hundreds of reprintings. Of all Morrison's novels, it puzzles me most: the style is remarkably adroit, baroque in its splendor, and the authority of the narrative is firmly established. The characters are problematic, for me; unlike the protagonists of Morrison's earlier novels, they suggest ideograms. I think that is because *Beloved* is a powerfully tendentious romance; it has too clear a design upon its readers, of whatever race and gender. The storyteller of *Sula* (1975) and of *Song of Solomon* (1977) has been replaced by a formidable ideologue, who perhaps knows too well what she wishes her book to accomplish.

Morrison strongly insists that her literary context is essentially African American, and *Beloved* overtly invokes slave narratives as its precursors. I hardly doubt that the novel's stance is African-American feminist Marxist, as most of the exegetes reprinted in this volume proclaim. And yet the style and narrative procedures have more of a literary relationship to William

Faulkner and Virginia Woolf than to any African-American writers. I am
aware that such an assertion risks going against Morrison's own warning
"that finding or imposing Western influences in/on Afro-American literature had value, provided the valued process does not become self-anoint-
ing." I mildly observe (since both my personal and critical esteem for
Morrison is enormous) that "finding *or* imposing" (italics mine, of course)
is a very shrewd equivocation. Morrison, both in prose style and in narrative mode, has a complex and permanent relationship to Faulkner and to
Woolf. *Beloved*, in a long perspective, is a child of Faulkner's masterpiece,
As I Lay Dying, while the heroine, Sethe, has more in common with Lena
Grove of *Light in August* than with any female character of African-
American fiction. This is anything but a limitation, aesthetically considered, but is rejected by Morrison and her critical disciples alike. Ideology
aside, Morrison's fierce assertion of independence is the norm for any
strong writer, but I do not think that this denial of a swerve from indubitable literary origins can be a critical value in itself.

None of this would matter if the ideologies of political correctness
were not so deeply embedded in *Beloved* as to make Sethe a less persuasive
representation of an possible human being than she might have been.
Trauma has much less to do with Sethe's more-than-Faulknerian sense of
guilt than the novel's exegetes have argued. The guilt of being a survivor is
not unique to any oppressed people; programs in guilt are an almost universal temptation. Beloved is a calculated series of shocks; whether the
memory of shock is aesthetically persuasive has to seem secondary in a
novel dedicated to the innumerable victims of American slavery. One steps
very warily in raising the aesthetic issue in regard to a book whose moral
and social value is beyond dissent. Still, Sethe is a character in a visionary
romance that also insists upon its realistic and historical veracity. A literary
character has to be judged finally upon the basis of literary criteria, which
simply are not "patriarchal" or "capitalistic" or "Western imperialist."
Morrison, whose earlier novels were not as over-determined by ideological considerations as *Beloved* is, may have sacrificed much of her art upon
the altar of a politics perhaps admirable in itself, but not necessarily in the
service of high literature (if one is willing to grant that such an entity still
exists.)

The terrors depicted in *Beloved* may be beyond the capacity of literary
representation itself, which is an enigma that has crippled every attempt to
portray the Nazi slaughter of European Jewry. The African-American critic Stanley Crouch has been much condemned for expressing his disdain in
regard to *Beloved*. Crouch, I think, underestimated the book's stylistic
achievement, but his healthy distrust of ideologies is, alas, germane to

aspects of *Beloved*. Sentimentalism is not in one sense relevant to *Beloved*: how can any emotion be in excess of its object when slavery is the object? And yet the novel's final passage about Sethe could prove, someday, to be a kind of period piece:

> He is staring at the quilt but he is thinking about her wrought-iron back; the delicious mouth still puffy at the corner from Ella's fist. The mean black eyes. The wet dress steaming before the fire. Her tenderness about his neck jewelry—its three wands, like attentive baby rattlers, curving two feet into the air. How she never mentioned or looked at it, so he did not have to feel the shame of being collared like a beast. Only this woman Sethe could have left him his manhood like that. He wants to put his story next to hers.
>
> "Sethe," he says, "me and you, we got more yesterday than anybody. We need some kind of tomorrow."
>
> He leans over and takes her hand. With the other he touches her face. "You your best thing, Sethe. You are." His holding fingers are holding hers.
>
> "Me? Me?"

The pathos is admirable, rather too much so. Sethe is given the explicit tribute that the entire book as sought to constitute. She is the heroic African-American mother, who has survived terrors both natural and supernatural, and has maintained her integrity and her humanity. Morrison's design has been fulfilled, but is Sethe a person or an abstraction? Time will sift this matter out; cultural politics do not answer such a question. Morrison must be judged finally, in *Beloved*, against *As I Lay Dying* and *Mrs. Dalloway*, rather than against Harriet Jacobs's *Incidents in the Life of a Slave Girl* (1861). The canonical novelist of *Song of Solomon* deserves no less.

Philip Roth

(1933-)

The *Zuckerman* Tetralogy

PHILIP ROTH'S *ZUCKERMAN BOUND* BINDS TOGETHER *THE GHOST WRITER*, *Zuckerman Unbound* and *The Anatomy Lesson*, adding to them as epilogue a wild short novel, *The Prague Orgy*, which is at once the bleakest and funniest writing Roth has done. The totality is certainly the novelist's finest achievement to date, eclipsing even his best single fictions, the exuberantly notorious *Portnoy's Complaint*, and the undervalued and ferocious *My Life As a Man*. *Zuckerman Bound* is a classic apologia, an aggressive defense of Roth's moral stance as an author. Its cosmos derives candidly from the Freudian interpretation as being unbearable. Roth knows that Freud and Kafka mark the origins and limits of still-emerging literary culture, American and Jewish, which has an uneasy relationship to normative Judaism and its waning culture. I suspect that Roth knows and accepts also what his surrogate, Zuckerman, is sometimes too outraged to recognize: breaking a new road both causes outrage in others, and demands payment in which the outrageous provoker punishes himself. Perhaps that is the Jewish version of Emerson's American Law and Compensation: nothing is got for nothing.

    Zuckerman Bound merits something reasonably close to the highest level of aesthetic praise for tragicomedy, partly because as a formal totality it becomes much more than the sum of its parts. Those parts are surprisingly diverse: *The Ghost Writer* is a Jamesonian parable of fictional influence, economical and shapely, beautifully modulated, while *Zuckerman Unbound* is more characteristically Rothian, being freer in form and more joyously expressionalistic in its diction. *The Anatomy Lesson* is a farce bordering on fantasy, closer in mode and spirit to Nathanael West than is anything else by Roth. With *The Prague Orgy*, Roth has transcended himself, or perhaps shown himself and others that, being just past fifty, he has scarcely begun to display his powers. I have read nothing else in recent American fiction that rivals Thomas Pynchon's *The Crying Lot of 49* and episodes like the story of Byron the light bulb in the same author's *Gravity's Rainbow. The Prague Orgy* is of that disturbing eminence: obscenely outrageous and yet brilliantly reflective of a paranoid reality that has become universal. But the Rothian difference from Nathanael West and Pynchon should also be emphasized. Roth paradoxically is still engaged in moral prophecy; he continues to be outraged by the outrageous—in societies, others and himself. There is in him nothing of West's Gnostic preference for the posture of the Satanic editor, Shrike, in *Miss Lonelyhearts,* or of Pynchon's Kabbalistic doctrine of sado-anarchism. Roth's negative exuberance is not in the service of negative theology, but intimates instead a nostalgia for the morality once engendered by the Jewish normative tradition.

This is the harsh irony, obsessively exploited throughout *Zuckerman Bound*, of the attack made upon Zuckerman's *Carnovsky* (Roth's *Portnoy's Complaint*) by the literary critic Milton Appel (Irving Howe). Zuckerman has received a mortal wound from Appel, and Roth endeavors to commemorate the wound and the wounder, in the spirit of James Joyce permanently impaling the Irish poet, physician and general roustabout, Oliver St. John Gogarty, as the immortally egregious Malachi (Buck) Mulligan of *Ulysses*. There is plenty of literary precedent for settling scores in this way; it is as old as Hellenistic Alexandria, and ass recent as Saul Bellow's portrait of Jack Ludwig as Valentine Gersbach in *Herzog*. Roth, characteristically scrupulous, presents Appel as dignified, serious and sincere, and Zuckerman as dangerously lunatic in this matter, but since the results are endlessly hilarious, the revenge is sharp nevertheless.

Zuckerman Unbound makes clear, at least to me, that Roth indeed is a Jewish writer in the sense that Saul Bellow and Bernard Malamud are not, and do not care to be. Bellow and Malamud, in their fiction, strive to be North American Jewish only as Tolstoy was Russian, or Faulkner was American Southern. Roth is certainly Jewish in his fiction, because his absolute concern never ceases to be the pain of the relations between children and parents, and between husband and wife, and in him this pain invariably results from the incommensurability between rigorously moral normative tradition whose expectations rarely can be satisfied, and the reality of the way we live now. Zuckerman's insane resentment of the moralizing Milton Appel, and of even fiercer critics, is a deliberate self-parody of Roth's more-than-ironic reaction to how badly he has been read. Against both Appel and the covens of maenads, Roth defends Zuckerman (and so himself) as a kind of Talmudic Orpheus, by defining any man as "clay with aspirations."

What wins over the reader is that both defense and definition are conveyed by the highest humor now being written. *The Anatomy Lesson* and *The Prague Orgy*, in particular, provoke a cleansing and continuous laughter, sometimes so intense that in itself it becomes astonishingly painful. One of the many aesthetic gains of binding together the entire Zuckerman ordeal (it cannot be called a saga) is to let the reader experience the gradual acceleration of wit from the gentle Chekhovian wistfulness of *The Ghost Writer*, on to the Gogolian sense of the ridiculous in *Zuckerman Unbound*, and then the boisterous Westian farce of *The Anatomy Lesson*, only to end in the merciless Kafkan irrealism of *The Prague Orgy*.

I will center most of what follows on *The Prague Orgy*, both because it is the only part of *Zuckerman Unbound* that is new, and because it is the best of Roth, a kind of coda to all his fiction so far. Haunting it necessarily is the spirit of Kafka, a dangerous influence upon any writer, and particularly dangerous, until now, for Roth. Witness his short novel, *The Breast*, his major aesthetic disaster so far, surpassing such livelier failures as *Our Gang* and *The Great American Novel*. Against the error of *The Breast*, can be set the funniest pages in *The Professor of Desire*, where the great dream concerning "Kafka's whore" is clearly the imaginative prelude to *The Prague Orgy*. David Kepesh, Roth's Professor of Desire, falls asleep in Prague and confronts "everything I ever hoped for," a guided visit with an official interpreter to an old woman, possibly once Kafka's whore. The heart of her revelation is Rothian rather than Kafkan, as she integrates the greatest modern Jewish writers with all the other ghosts of her Jewish clientele:

> "They were clean and they were gentlemen. As God is my witness, they never beat on my backside. Even in bed they had manners."
>
> "But is there anything about Kafka in particular that she remembers? I didn't come here, to her, to Prague, to talk about nice Jewish boys."
>
> She gives some thought to the question; or, more likely, no thought. Just sits there trying out being dead.
>
> "You see, he wasn't so special," she finally says. "I don't mean he wasn't a gentleman. They were all gentlemen."

This could be the quintessential Roth passage: the Jewish joke turned, not against itself, nor against the Jews, and certainly not against Kafka, but against history, against the way things were, and are, and yet will be. Unlike the humor of Nathanael West (particularly in his *The Dream Life of*

Balso Snell) and of Woody Allen, there is no trace of Jewish anti-Semitism in Roth's pained laughter. Roth's wit uncannily follows the psychic pattern set out by Freud in his late paper on "Humor" (1928), which speculates that the superego allows jesting so as to speak some "kindly words of comfort to the intimidated ego." The ego of poor Zuckerman is certainly intimidated enough, and the reader rejoices at being allowed to share some hilarious words of comfort with him.

When last we saw the afflicted Zuckerman, at the close of *The Anatomy Lesson*, he had progressed (or regressed) from painfully lying back on his play-mat, *Roger's Thesaurus* propped beneath his head and four women serving his many needs, to wandering the corridors of a university hospital, a patient playing at being an intern. A few years later, a physically recovered Zuckerman is in Prague, as visiting literary lion, encountering so paranoid a social reality that New York seems, by contrast, the forest of Arden. Zuckerman, "the American authority on Jewish demons," quests for the unpublished Yiddish stories of the elder Sinovsky, perhaps murdered by the Nazis. The exiled younger Sinovsky's abandoned wife, Olga, guards the manuscripts in Prague. In a deliberate parody of James's "The Aspern Papers," Zuckerman needs somehow to seduce the alcoholic and insatiable Olga into releasing stories supposedly worthy of Sholom Aleichem of Isaac Babel, written in "the Yiddish of Flaubert."

Being Zuckerman, he seduces no one and secures the Yiddish manuscripts anyway, only to have them confiscated by the Czech Minister of Culture and his thugs, who proceed to expel "Zuckerman the Zionist agent" back to "the little world around the corner" in New York City. In a final scene subtler, sadder, and funnier than all previous Roth, the frustrated Zuckerman endures the moralizing of the Minister of Culture, who attacks America for having forgotten that "masterpiece," Betty MacDonald's *The Egg and I*. Associating himself with K., the hero of Kafka's *The Castle*, Zuckerman is furious at his expulsion, and utters a lament for the more overt paranoia he must abandon:

> ... here where there's no nonsense about purity and goodness, where the division is not that easy to discern between the heroic and the perverse, where every sort of repression foments a parody of freedom and the suffering of their historical misfortune engenders in its imaginative victims these clownish forms of human despair.

That farewell-to-Prague has as its undersong: here where Zuckerman is not an anomaly, but indeed a model of decorum and restraint compared to anyone else who is at all interesting. Perhaps there is another undertone: a farewell-to-Zuckerman on Roth's part. The author of *Zuckerman Bound* at last my have exorcised the afterglow of *Portnoy's Complaint*. There is an eloquent plea for release in *The Anatomy Lesson*, where Zuckerman tries to renounce his fate as a writer:

> It may look to outsiders like the life of freedom—not on a schedule, in command of yourself, singled out for glory, the choice apparently to write about anything. But once one's writing, it's *all* limits. Bound to a subject. Bound to make a book of it...

Zuckerman bound, indeed, but bound in particular to the most ancient of Covenants—that is Roth's particular election, or self-election. In his critical book, *Reading Myself and Others* (1975), the last and best essay, "Looking at Kafka," comments on the change that is manifested in Kafka's later fiction, observing that it is:

> ... touched by a spirit of personal reconciliation and sardonic self acceptance, by a tolerance of one's own brand of madness ... the piercing masochistic irony ... has given way here to a critique of the self and its preoccupations that, though bordering on mockery, no longer seeks to resolve itself in images of the uttermost humiliation and defeat.... Yet there is more here than a metaphor for the insanely defended ego, whose striving for invulnerability produces a defensive system that must in its turn become the object of perpetual concern—there is also a very unromantic and hardheaded fable about how and why art is made, a portrait of the artist in all his ingenuity, anxiety, isolation, dissatisfaction, relentlessness, obsessiveness, secretiveness, paranoia, and self-addiction, a portrait of the magical thinker at the end of his tether...

Roth intended this as commentary on Kafka's "The Burrow." Eloquent and poignant, it is far more accurate as a descriptive prophecy of *Zuckerman Bound*. Kafka resists nearly all interpretation, so that what most *needs* interpretation in him is his evasion of interpretation. That Roth reads himself into his precursor is a normal and healthy procedure in the literary struggle for self-identification. Unlike Kafka, Roth tries to evade, not interpretation, but guilt, partly because he lives the truth of Kafka's motto of the penal colony: "Guilt is never to be doubted." Roth has earned a permanent place in American literature by a comic genius that need never be doubted again, wherever it chooses to take him next.

Portnoy's Complaint

After a full generation since it first appeared, *Portnoy's Complaint* superbly sustains rereading. Nothing of Roth's has dwindled to a Period Piece, even if *Letting Go* and *When She Was Good* now seem uncharacteristic for the author of *Sabbath's Theater, American Pastoral*, and *The Human Stain*. There are fictions by Roth that never found me: *Our Gang, The Breast, The Great American Novel*. From *My Life as a Man* (1974) to the present, Roth has been an Old Master, but *Portnoy's Complaint* remains the most vital of his earlier works.

Vitality, in the Shakespearean or Falstaffian sense, and its representation in personality and character, is Roth's greatest gift, which is why I would nominate *Sabbath's Theater* as his sublime achievement. It matters that we see how astonishing a creation *Sabbath's Theater* is. What are the authentic eminences of American fiction in the second half of the Twentieth century? My experience as an obsessive reader would center first upon Thomas Pynchon's *The Crying of Lot 49, Gravity's Rainbow*, and *Mason & Dixon*, to which one adds Cormac McCarthy's *Blood Meridian* and Don DeLillo's *Underworld*. When I turn to Roth, I happily am deluged: the tetralogy *Zuckerman Bound; The Counterlife, Operation Shylock*, and then the American historical sequence that includes *Sabbath's Theater, American Pastoral, I Married a Communist*, and *The Human Stain*. The sheer drive and fecundity of this later Roth makes me think of Faulkner at his earlier splendor: *As I Lay Dying, The Sound and the Fury, Light in August, Absalom, Absalom*! Faulkner upon his heights is a frightening comparison to venture, but *Sabbath's Theater* and *American Pastoral* will sustain the contrast. Nothing even by Roth has the uncanny originality of *As I Lay Dying*, yet *Sabbath's Theater* and the terrible pathos of *American Pastoral* have their own uncanniness. The wildness and freedom of *Portnoy's Complaint* now seem very different when taken as a prelude to the advent of *Sabbath's Theater*, just over a quarter-century later.

Though the confrontation between the late Irving Howe and Roth over Roth's supposed self-hatred is pragmatically prehistoric (in 2003), it has left some scars upon what ought to be called the novelist's aesthetic consciousness. In Shakespearean terms, Roth writes comedy or tragi-comedy, in the mode of the Problem Plays: *Troilus and Cressida, All's Well That Ends Well, Measure for Measure*. The exquisite rancidities of this Shakespearean mode do not appear to be Roth's object. He seems to prefer Falstaff and Lear among Shakespeare's characters, and both of them get into Mickey Sabbath, who necessarily lacks the Falstaffian wit and Learian grandeur. Sabbath is an heroic vitalist, but in retrospect what else is Alex

Portnoy? The comedy, painful to start with, hurts unbearably when you reread *Sabbath's Theater*. How hurtful is the hilarity of *Portnoy's Complaint*?

My favorite Yiddish apothegm, since my childhood, I translate as: "Sleep faster, we need the pillows." Roth's inescapability is that he has usurped this mode, perhaps not forever, but certainly for the early twenty-first century. Sleeping faster is a cure for the anguish of contamination: by Jewish history; by Kafka; by one's audience after achieving celebrity with *Portnoy's Complaint*.

Alex Portnoy is not going to age into Mickey Sabbath: Roth's protagonists are neither Roth nor one another. But viewing Portnoy retrospectively, through Sabbath's outrageousness, allows readers to see what otherwise we may be too dazzled or too overcome by laughter to realize. Alex Portnoy, however mother-ridden, has an extraordinary potential for more life that he is unlikely to fulfill. Not that fulfillment would be glorious or redemptive; Sabbath's grinding vitalism carries him past the edge of madness. Portnoy, liberal and humane (except, of course, in regard to women he desires), calls himself "rich with rage", but his fiercest anger is light years away from Sabbath's erotic fury.

Aside from Roth's complex aesthetic maturation, the differences between Portnoy and Sabbath is the shadow of Shakespeare, of King Lear's madness and Falstaff's refusal of embitterment and estrangement. Sabbath is fighting for his life, within the limits of what he understands life to be: the erotic, in all its ramifications. So intense is Sabbath that the denunciations directed at him are at once accurate and totally irrelevant, as here from his friend, Norman:

> "The walking panegyric for obscenity," Norman said. "The inverted saint whose message is desecration. Isn't it tiresome in 1994, this role of rebel-hero? What an odd time to be thinking of sex as rebellion. Are we back to Lawrence's gamekeeper? At this late hour? To be out with that beard of yours, upholding the virtues of fetishism and voyeurism. To be out with that belly of yours, championing pornography and flying the flag of your prick. What a pathetic, outmoded old crank you are, Mickey Sabbath. The discredited male polemic's last gasp. Even as the bloodiest of all centuries comes to an end, you're out working day and night to create an erotic scandal. You fucking relic, Mickey! You fifties antique! Linda Lovelace is already light-years behind us, but you persist in quarreling with society as though Eisenhower is president!" But then, almost apologetically, he added, "The immensity of your isolation is horrifying. That's all I really mean to say."

"And there you'd be surprised," Sabbath replied. "I don't think you ever gave isolation a real shot. It's the best preparation I know of for death."

Roth has placed Sabbath near the outer limit of organized society: a beggar, vagrant, and courter of death. It does not matter: Sabbath is redeemed through sheer vitalism. Alex Portnoy now seems more a parody of that frenetic drive. *Portnoy's Complaint* is a marvelous comedy; *Sabbath's Theater* is a tragi-comedy, and its Shakespearean reverberations are legitimate and persuasive.

Cormac McCarthy

(1933-)

Blood Meridian

BLOOD MERIDIAN (1985) SEEMS TO ME THE AUTHENTIC AMERICAN APOCALYPTIC novel, more relevant even in 2000 than it was fifteen years ago. The fulfilled renown of *Moby-Dick* and of *As I Lay Dying* is augmented by *Blood Meridian*, since Cormac McCarthy is the worthy disciple both of Melville and of Faulkner. I venture that no other living American novelist, not even Pynchon, has given us a book as strong and memorable as *Blood Meridian*, much as I appreciate Don DeLillo's *Underworld*, Philip Roth's *Zuckerman Bound, Sabbath's Theater*, and *American Pastoral*, and Pynchon's *Gravity's Rainbow* and *Mason & Dixon*. McCarthy himself, in his recent Border trilogy, commencing with the superb *All the Pretty Horses*, has not matched *Blood Meridian*, but it is the ultimate Western, not to be surpassed.

My concern being the reader, I will begin by confessing that my first two attempts to read through *Blood Meridian* failed, because I flinched from the overwhelming carnage that McCarthy portrays. The violence begins on the novel's second page, when the fifteen-year-old Kid is shot in the back and just below the heart, and continues almost with no respite until the end, thirty years later, when Judge Holden, the most frightening figure in all of American literature, murders the Kid in an outhouse. So appalling are the continuous massacres and mutilations of *Blood Meridian* that one could be reading a United Nations report on the horrors of Kosovo in 1999.

Nevertheless, I urge the reader to persevere, because *Blood Meridian* is a canonical imaginative achievement, both an American and a universal tragedy of blood. Judge Holden is a villain worthy of Shakespeare, Iago-like and demoniac, a theoretician of war everlasting. And the book's magnificence—its language, landscape, persons, conceptions—at last transcends the violence, and convert goriness into terrifying art, an art comparable to Melville's and to Faulkner's. When I teach the book, many of my students resist it initially (as I did, and as some of my friends continue to do). Television saturates us with actual as well as imagined violence, and I turn away, either in shock or in disgust. But I cannot turn away from *Blood Meridian*, now that I know how to read it, and why it has to be read. None of its carnage is gratuitous or redundant; it belonged to the Mexico–Texas borderlands in 1849–50, which is where and when most of the novel is set. I suppose one could call *Blood Meridian* a "historical novel," since it chronicles the actual expedition of the Glanton gang, a murderous paramilitary force sent out both by Mexican and Texan authorities to murder and scalp as many Indians as possible. Yet it does not have the aura of historical fiction, since what it depicts seethes on, in the United States, and nearly everywhere else, as we enter the third millennium. Judge Holden, the prophet of war, is unlikely to be without honor in our years to come.

Even as you learn to endure the slaughter McCarthy describes, you become accustomed to the book's high style, again as overtly Shakespearean as it is Faulknerian. There are passages of Melvillean-Faulknerian baroque richness and intensity in *The Crying of Lot 49*, and elsewhere in Pynchon, but we can never be sure that they are not parodistic. The prose of *Blood Meridian* soars, yet with its own economy, and its dialogue is always persuasive, particularly when the uncanny Judge Holden speaks (chapter 14, p. 199):

> The judge placed his hands on the ground. He looked at his inquisitor. This is my claim, he said. And yet everywhere upon it are pockets of autonomous life. Autonomous. In order for it to be mine nothing must be permitted to occur upon it save by my dispensation.
>
> Toadvine sat with his boots crossed before the fire. No man can acquaint himself with everything on this earth, he said.
>
> The judge tilted his great head. The man who believes that the secrets of this world are forever hidden lives in mystery and fear. Superstition will drag him down. The rain will erode the deeds of his life. But that man who sets himself the task of singling out the thread of order from the tapestry will by the decision alone have taken charge of the world and it is only by such taking charge that he will effect a way to dictate the terms of his own fate.

Judge Holden is the spiritual leader of Glanton's filibusters, and McCarthy persuasively gives the self-styled judge a mythic status, appropriate for a deep Machiavelli whose "thread of order" recalls Iago's magic web, in which Othello, Desdemona, and Cassio are caught. Though all of the more colorful and murderous raiders are vividly characterized for us, the killing-machine Glanton with the others, the novel turns always upon its two central figures, Judge Holden and the Kid. We first meet the Judge on page 6: an enormous man, bald as a stone, no trace of a beard, and eyes without either brows or lashes. A seven-foot-tall albino, he almost seems to have come from some other world, and we learn to wonder about the Judge, who never sleeps, dances and fiddles with extraordinary art and energy, rapes and murders little children of both sexes, and who says that he will never die. By the book's close, I have come to believe that the Judge is immortal. And yet the Judge, while both more and less than human, is as individuated as Iago or Macbeth, and is quite at home in the Texan–Mexican borderlands where we watch him operate in 1849–50, and then find him again in 1878, not a day older after twenty-eight years, though the Kid, a sixteen-year-old at the start of Glanton's foray, is forty-five when murdered by the Judge at the end.

McCarthy subtly shows us the long, slow development of the Kid from another mindless scalper of Indians to the courageous confronter of the Judge in their final debate in a saloon. But though the Kid's moral maturation is heartening, his personality remains largely a cipher, as anonymous as his lack of a name. The three glories of the book are the Judge, the landscape, and (dreadful to say this) the slaughters, which are aesthetically distanced by McCarthy in a number of complex ways.

What is the reader to make of the Judge? He is immortal as principle, as War Everlasting, but is he a person, or something other? McCarthy will not tell us, which is all the better, since the ambiguity is most stimulating. Melville's Captain Ahab, though a Promethean demigod, is necessarily mortal, and perishes with the *Pequod* and all its crew, except for Ishmael. After he has killed the Kid, *Blood Meridian*'s Ishmael, Judge Holden is the last survivor of Glanton's scalping crusade. Destroying the Native-American nations of the Southwest is hardly analogous to the hunt to slay Moby-Dick, and yet McCarthy gives us some curious parallels between the two quests. The most striking is between Melville's chapter 19, where a ragged prophet, who calls himself Elijah, warns Ishmael and Queequeg against sailing on the *Pequod*, and McCarthy's chapter 4, where "an old disordered Mennonite" warns the Kid and his comrades not to join Captain Worth's filibuster, a disaster that preludes the greater catastrophe of Glanton's campaign.

McCarthy's invocation of *Moby-Dick*, while impressive and suggestive, in itself does not do much to illuminate Judge Holden for us. Ahab has his preternatural aspects, including his harpooner Fedellah and Parsee whale-boat crew, and the captain's conversion to their Zoroastrian faith. Elijah tells Ishmael touches of other Ahabian mysteries: a three-day trance off Cape Horn, slaying a Spaniard in front of a presumably Catholic altar in Santa Ysabel, and a wholly enigmatic spitting into a "silver calabash." Yet all these are transparencies compared to the enigmas of Judge Holden, who seems to judge the entire earth, and whose name suggests a holding, presumably of sway over all he encounters. And yet, the Judge, unlike Ahab, is not wholly fictive; like Glanton, he is a historic filibuster or free-booter. McCarthy tells us most in the Kid's dream visions of Judge Holden, towards the close of the novel (chapter 22, pp. 309–10):

> In that sleep and in sleep to follow the judge did visit. Who would come other? A great shambling mutant, silent and serene. Whatever his antecedents, he was something wholly other than their sum, nor was there system by which to divide him back into his origins for he would not go. Whoever would seek out his history through what unraveling of loins and ledgerbooks must stand at last darkened and dumb at the shore of a void without terminus or origin and whatever science he might bring to bear upon the dusty primal matter blowing down out of the millennia will discover no trace of ultimate atavistic egg by which to reckon his commencing.

I think that McCarthy is warning his reader that the Judge is Moby-Dick rather than Ahab. As another white enigma, the albino Judge, like the albino whale, cannot be slain. Melville, a professed Gnostic, who believed that some "anarch hand or cosmic blunder" had divided us into two fallen sexes, gives us a Manichean quester in Ahab. McCarthy gives Judge Holden the powers and purposes of the bad angels or demiurges that the Gnostics called archons, but he tells us not to make such an identification (as the critic Leo Daugherty eloquently has). Any "system," including the Gnostic one, will not divide the Judge back into his origins. The "ultimate atavistic egg" will not be found. What can the reader do with the haunting and terrifying Judge?

Let us begin by saying that Judge Holden, though his gladsome prophecy of eternal war is authentically universal, is first and foremost a Western American, no matter how cosmopolitan his background (he speaks all languages, knows all arts and sciences, and can perform magical, shamanistic metamorphoses). The Texan–Mexican border is a superb place for a war-god like the Judge to be. He carries a rifle, mounted in silver, with its name inscribed under the checkpiece: *Et In Arcadia Ego.* In the American Arcadia, death is also always there, incarnated in the Judge's weapon, which never misses. If the American pastoral tradition essentially is the Western film, then the Judge incarnates that tradition, though he would require a director light-years beyond the late Sam Peckinpah, whose *The Wild Bunch* portrays mildness itself when compared to Glanton's para-militaries. I resort though, as before, to Iago, who transfers war from the camp and the field to every other locale, and is a pyromaniac setting everything and everyone ablaze with the flame of battle. The Judge might be Iago before *Othello* begins, when the war-god Othello was still worshipped by his "honest" color officer, his ancient or ensign. The Judge speaks with an authority that chills me even as Iago leaves me terrified:

> This is the nature of war, whose stake is at once the game and the authority and the justification. Seen so, war is the truest form of divination. It is the testing of one's will and the will of another within that larger will which because it binds them is therefore forced to select. War is the ultimate game because war is at last a forcing of the unity of existence.

If McCarthy does not want us to regard the Judge as a Gnostic archon or supernatural being, the reader may still feel that it hardly seems sufficient to designate Holden as a nineteenth-century Western American Iago. Since *Blood Meridian*, like the much longer *Moby-Dick*, is more prose epic than novel, the Glanton foray can seem a post-Homeric quest, where the various heroes (or thugs) have a disguised god among them, which appears to be the Judge's Herculean role. The Glanton gang passes into a sinister aesthetic glory at the close of chapter 13, when they progress from murdering and scalping Indians to butchering the Mexicans who have hired them:

> They entered the city haggard and filthy and reeking with the blood of the citizenry for whose protection they had contracted. The scalps of the slain villagers were strung from the windows of the governor's house and the partisans were paid out of the all but exhausted coffers and the Sociedad was disbanded and the bounty rescinded. Within a week of their quitting the city there would be a price of eight thousand pesos posted for Glanton's head.

I break into this passage, partly to observe that from this point on the filibusters pursue the way down and out to an apocalyptic conclusion, but also to urge the reader to hear, and admire, the sublime sentence that follows directly, because we are at the visionary center of *Blood Meridian*.

> They rode out on the north road as would parties bound for El Paso but before they were even quite out of sight of the city they had turned their tragic mounts to the west and they rode infatuate and half fond toward the red demise of that day, toward the evening lands and the distant pandemonium of the sun.

Since Cormac McCarthy's language, like Melville's and Faulkner's, frequently is deliberately archaic, the *meridian* of the title probably means the zenith or noon position of the sun in the sky. Glanton, the Judge, the Kid, and their fellows are not described as "tragic"—their long-suffering horses are—and they are "infatuate" and half-mad ("fond") because they have broken away from any semblance of order. McCarthy knows, as does the reader, that an "order" urging the destruction of the entire Native American population of the Southwest is an obscene idea of order, but he wants the reader to know also that the Glanton gang is now aware that they are unsponsored and free to run totally amok. The sentence I have just quoted has a morally ambiguous greatness to it, but that is the greatness of *Blood Meridian*, and indeed of Homer and of Shakespeare. McCarthy so contextualizes the sentence that the amazing contrast between its high gestures and the murderous thugs who evoke the splendor is not ironic but tragic. The tragedy is ours, as readers, and not the Glanton gang's, since we are not going to mourn their demise except for the Kid's, and even there our reaction will be equivocal.

My passion for *Blood Meridian* is so fierce that I want to go on expounding it, but the courageous reader should now be (I hope) pretty well into the main movement of the book. I will confine myself here to the final encounter between the preternatural Judge Holden and the Kid, who had broken with the insane crusade twenty-eight years before, and now at middle age must confront the ageless Judge. Their dialogue is the finest achievement in this book of augmenting wonders, and may move the reader as nothing else in *Blood Meridian* does. I reread it perpetually and cannot persuade myself that I have come to the end of it.

The Judge and the Kid drink together, after the avenging Judge tells the Kid that this night his soul will be demanded of him. Knowing he is no match for the Judge, the Kid nevertheless defies Holden, with laconic replies playing against the Judge's rolling grandiloquence. After demanding to know where their slain comrades are, the Judge asks: "And where is the fiddler and where the dance?"

I guess you can tell me.

I tell you this. As war becomes dishonored and its nobility called into question those honorable men who recognize the sanctity of blood will become excluded from the dance, which is the warrior's right, and thereby will the dance become a false dance and the dancers false dancers. And yet there will be one there always who is a true dancer and can you guess who that might be?

You aint nothin.

To have known Judge Holden, to have seen him in full operation, and to tell him that he is nothing, is heroic. "You speak truer than you know," the Judge replies, and two pages later murders the Kid, most horribly. *Blood Meridian*, except for a one-paragraph epilogue, ends with the Judge triumphantly dancing and fiddling at once, and proclaiming that he never sleeps and he will never die. But McCarthy does not let Judge Holden have the last word.

The strangest passage in *Blood Meridian*, the epilogue is set at dawn, where a nameless man progresses over a plain by means of holes that he makes in the rocky ground. Employing a two-handled implement, the man strikes "the fire out of the rock which God has put there." Around the man are wanderers searching for bones, and he continues to strike fire in the holes, and then they move on. And that is all.

The subtitle of *Blood Meridian* is *The Evening Redness in the West*, which belongs to the Judge, last survivor of the Glanton gang. Perhaps all that the reader can surmise with some certainty is that the man striking fire in the rock at dawn is an opposing figure in regard to the evening redness in the West. The Judge never sleeps, and perhaps will never die, but a new Prometheus may be rising to go up against him.

All the Pretty Horses

If there is a pragmatic tradition of the American Sublime, then Cormac McCarthy's fictions are its culmination. *Moby-Dick* and Faulkner's major, early novels are McCarthy's prime precursors. Melville's Ahab fuses together Shakespeare's tragic protagonists—Hamlet, Lear, Macbeth—and crosses them with a quest both Promethean and American. Even as Montaigne's Plato became Emerson's, so Melville's Shakespeare becomes Cormac McCarthy's. Though critics will go on associating McCarthy with Faulkner, who certainly affected McCarthy's style in *Suttree* (1979), the visionary of *Blood Meridian* (1985) and *The Border Trilogy* (1992, 1994, 1998) has much less in common with Faulkner, and shares more profoundly in Melville's debt to Shakespeare.

Melville, by giving us Ahab and Ishmael, took care to distance the reader from Ahab, if not from his quest. McCarthy's protagonists tend to be apostles of the will-to-identity, except for the Iago-like Judge Holden of *Blood Meridian*, who is the Will Incarnate. John Grady Cole, who survives in *All the Pretty Horses* only to be destroyed in *Cities of the Plain*, is replaced in *The Crossing* by Billy Parham, who is capable of learning what the heroic Grady Cole evades, the knowledge that Jehovah (Yahweh) holds in his very name: "Where that is I am not." God will be present where and when he chooses to be present, and absent more often than present.

The aesthetic achievement of *All the Pretty Horses* surpasses that of *Cities of the Plain*, if only because McCarthy is too deeply invested in John Grady Cole to let the young man (really still a boy) die with the proper distancing of authorial concern. No one will compose a rival to *Blood Meridian*, not even McCarthy, but *All the Pretty Horses* and *The Crossing* are of the eminence of *Suttree*. If I had to choose a narrative by McCarthy that could stand on its own in relation to *Blood Meridian*, it probably would be *All the Pretty Horses*. John Grady Cole quests for freedom, and discovers what neither Suttree nor Billy Parham needs to discover, which is that freedom in an American context is another name for solitude. The self's freedom, for Cormac McCarthy, has no social aspect whatsoever.

I speak of McCarthy as visionary novelist, and not necessarily as a citizen of El Paso, Texas. Emerson identified freedom with power, only available at the crossing, in the shooting of a gulf, a darting to an aim. Since we care for Hamlet, even though he cares for none, we have to assume that Shakespeare also had a considerable investment in Hamlet. The richest aspect of *All the Pretty Horses* is that we learn to care strongly about the development of John Grady Cole, and perhaps we can surmise that Cormac McCarthy is also moved by this most sympathetic of his protagonists.

All the Pretty Horses was published seven years after *Blood Meridian*, and is set almost a full century later in history. John Grady Cole is about the same age as McCarthy would have been in 1948. There is no more an identification between McCarthy and the young Cole, who evidently will not live to see twenty, than there is between Shakespeare and Prince Hamlet. And yet the reverberation of an heroic poignance is clearly heard throughout *All the Pretty Horses*. It may be that McCarthy's hard-won authorial detachment toward the Kid in *Blood Meridian* had cost the novelist too much, in the emotional register. Whether my surmise is accurate or not, the reader shares with McCarthy an affectionate stance toward the heroic youth at the center of *All the Pretty Horses*.

Don DeLillo

(1936-)

IN DIFFERENT WAYS, I PREFER *WHITE NOISE*, *LIBRA*, AND *UNDERWORLD* TO *Mao II*, but a crucial element of Don DeLillo's achievement is his uncanny, proleptic sense of the triumph of the Age of Terror, which is the peculiar strength of *Mao II*. In 2002, *Mao II* is the way we live now, in the Age of George W. Bush, John Ashcroft, and Osama bin Laden. One can venture that character is irrelevant to DeLillo because he has a good claim to have invented those clearly fictive personages: Dubya, Ashcroft, Osama. As for plot, what relevance can it have in a cosmos where *everything* can turn out to be part of a terror scheme. That may seem the anarcho-sadism of Thomas Pynchon, whose earlier, paranoid visions were the prime precursors of DeLillo. And yet Pynchonian paranoia was systematic; DeLillon paranoia retains a random element, which probably has something to do with the Romantic Transcendentalism that somehow lingers in DeLillo.

DeLillo is soft-spoken, without pretence, a man of good will. You could not insert him into one of his novels, not even as Nick Shay in *Underworld*. He is the antitype of *Mao II*'s Bill Gray, despite some superficial resemblances. Gray, like Pynchon, hides himself in order to write, but dies as a witness to a new reality, in which the terrorist has usurped the novelist. East Beirut, where the novel closes, is the New Everywhere.

A novel that begins in Yankee Stadium (sacred ground for DeLillo and myself), with 6,500 couples simultaneously being married by the Reverend Moon, ends with an East Beirut wedding escorted by a tank and jeep mounted with a recoilless rifle. And all this would be routine, were it not for the intimations of a pathos, almost a transcendence, that DeLillo imparts to that final vision of marriage:

Civilians talking and laughing and well dressed, twenty adults and half as many children, mostly girls in pretty dresses and white knee-stockings and patent-leather shoes. And here is the stunning thing that takes her a moment to understand, that this is a wedding party going by. The bride and groom carry champagne glasses and some of the girls hold sparklers that send off showers of excited light. A guest in a pastel tuxedo smokes a long cigar and does a dance around a shell hole, delighting the kids. The bride's gown is beautiful, with lacy appliqué at the bodice, and she looks surprisingly alive, they all look transcendent, free of limits and unsurprised to be here. They make it seem only natural that a wedding might advance in resplendence with a free-lance tank as escort. Sparklers going. Other children holding roses tissued in fern. Brita is gripping the rail. She wants to dance or laugh or jump off the balcony. It seems completely possible that she will land softly among them and walk along in her pajama shirt and panties all the way to heaven.

If there is a DeLillon counter-force to the Age of Terror, it must be there: "they all look transcendent, free of limits." We learn to recognize a DeLillo scene from such near-epiphanies. Unlike most of his critics, DeLillo has an Emersonian longing for the transcendental and extraordinary, for privileged moments.

How permanent an achievement is *Mao II*, compared to *Underworld?* Let it be affirmed at once that DeLillo does *not* write Period Pieces, as Updike and Bellow go on doing. Bill Gray is a sad creation, and yet his aesthetic dignity is considerable. He is an authentic writer deeply fearful that the new Time of Terror renders his art irrelevant. Samuel Beckett could alter consciousness; Bill Gray knows that he cannot. Any bomb-thrower is far more competent to modify our consciousness of reality.

It is disconcerting to reread *Mao II* just eleven years after its publication, and one year after the destruction of the World Trade Center. What shocked us must have confirmed DeLillo in his anguished apprehension of reality. *Mao II* in time may seem like secondary DeLillo, but it will lose its wisdom only if someday we pass out of our unhappy time.

White Noise

Don DeLillo's masterwork is *Underworld* (1997), which is long, uneven, and wonderful. *White Noise* (1985) would appear to be his most popular novel: the paperback in which I have just reread it is the thirty-first printing. I doubt that it will prove as permanent as *Underworld*, but revisiting clearly demonstrates that it is much more than a period piece. Critics frequently associate DeLillo with William Gaddis and Robert Coover, as with the formidable Thomas Pynchon. *Underworld* is something different, and may have more affinities with Philip Roth than with Pynchon. DeLillo, in *White Noise*, is a High Romantic in the age of virtual reality and related irrealisms. Frank Lentricchia, who has become DeLillo's canonical critic, is accurate in suggesting that Jack Gladney descends from Joyce's Poldy Bloom, and like Poldy, DeLillo's protagonist has a touch of the poet about him. One large difference is that Gladney is a first-person narrator; another is that Poldy has a benign immensity that Gladney cannot match. Though another cuckold, Poldy is a Romantic individualist, like Joyce himself. A century later, the amiable Gladney is trapped in a network of systems, another unit in the Age of Information.

DeLillo is a comedian of the spirit, haunted by omens of the end of our time. *White Noise* is very funny, and very disturbing: it is another of the American comic apocalypses that include Mark Twain's *The Mysterious Stranger*, Herman Melville's *The Confidence Man*, Nathaniel West's *Miss Lonelyhearts* and Pynchon's *The Crying of Lot 49*. That is a high order of company, and *White Noise* almost sustains it.

DeLillo is a master of deadpan outrageousness: Jack Gladney is chairman and professor of Hitler Studies at the College-on-the-Hill. Though he is the American inventor of his discipline, Gladney has no affective reaction to Hitler: it appears to be a subject like any other these days, be it Eskimo Lesbian Studies or Post-Colonialism.

But all of *White Noise* is comic outrage; everything becomes funny, be it the fear of death, adultery, airborne toxic events, the struggles of the family romance, advanced supermarkets, or what you will. Simultaneously, everything becomes anxious, in a world where even the nuns only pretend to believe, and where the first three of Gladney's four wives each had some connection to the world of espionage.

Until *Underworld*, DeLillo's characters are curious blends of personalities and ideograms. Gladney is such a blend: we are persuaded by his love for Babette, his adulterous but well-meaning wife, and by his warm relations with his rather varied children. And yet he is as just as much Fear-of-Death as he is a husband and a father.

Where is DeLillo in *White Noise*? Close to the end of the book, he gives us a long paragraph of astonishing power and distinction, one of the most memorable passages in American writing of the later twentieth century:

> We go to the overpass all the time. Babette, Wilder and I. We take
> a thermos of iced tea, park the car, watch the setting sun. Clouds

are no deterrent. Clouds intensify the drama, trap the shape of light. Heavy overcasts have little effect. Light bursts through, tracers and smoky arcs. Overcasts enhance the mood. We find little to say to each other. More cars arrive, parking in a line that extends down to the residential zone. People walk up the incline and onto the overpass, carrying fruit and nuts, cool drinks, mainly the middle-aged, the elderly, some with webbed beach chairs which they set out on the sidewalk, but younger couples also, arm in arm at the rail, looking west. The sky takes on content, feeling, an exalted narrative life. The bands of color reach so high, seem at times to separate into their constituent parts. There are turreted skies, light storms, softly falling streamers. It is hard to know how we should feel about this. Some people are scared by the sunsets, some determined to be elated, but most of us don't know how to feel, are ready to go either way. Rain is no deterrent. Rain brings on graded displays, wonderful running hues. More cars arrive, people come trudging up the incline. The spirit of these warm evenings is hard to describe. There is anticipation in the air but it is not the expectant midsummer hum of a shirtsleeve crowd, a sandlot game, with coherent precedents, a history of secure response. The waiting is introverted, uneven, almost backward and shy, tending toward silence. What else do we feel? Certainly there is awe, it is all awe, it transcends previous categories of awe, but we don't know whether we are watching in wonder or dread, we don't know what we are watching or what it means, we don't know whether it is permanent, a level of experience to which we will gradually adjust, into which our uncertainty will eventually be absorbed, or just some atmospheric weirdness, soon to pass. The collapsible chairs are yanked open, the old people sit. What is there to say? The sunsets linger and so do we. The sky is under a spell, powerful and storied. Now and then a car actually crosses the overpass, moving slowly, deferentially. People keep coming up the incline, some in wheelchairs, twisted by disease, those who attend them bending low to push against the grade. I didn't know how many handicapped and helpless people there were in town until the warm nights brought crowds to the overpass. Cars speed beneath us, coming from the west, from out of the towering light, and we watch them as if for a sign, as if they carry on their painted surfaces some residue of the sunset, a barely detectable luster or film of telltale dust. No one plays a radio or speaks in a voice that is much above a whisper. Something golden falls, a softness delivered to the air. There are people walking dogs, there are kids on bikes, a man with a camera and long lens, waiting for his moment. It is not until some time after dark has fallen, the insects screaming in the heat, that we slowly begin to disperse, shyly, politely, car after car, restored to our separate and defensible selves.

It is a major American prose-poem, marked by the aura of the airborne toxic event, and yet balanced upon the edge of a transcendental revelation. DeLillo, who is so easily mistaken for a Post-Modernist End-Gamer, is rather clearly a visionary, a late Emersonian American Romantic, like the Wallace Stevens who turns blankly on the sand in *The Auroras of Autumn*. Light bursts through, and the sky, as in Stevens, takes on an exalted narrative life. Awe transcends fear, transcends the past of awe. Is it wonder or dread, an epiphany or mere, reductive pollution? What matters is that brightness falls from the air, before all the viewers return to their separate selves.

This is more than Transcendentalism in the last ditch, or Romanticism on the wane. Nothing is affirmed, not even illusion. We turn to DeLillo for woe and wonder alike, accurately persuaded of his high artistry, of something well beyond a study of the nostalgias.

Underworld

One can venture that the major American novelists now at work are Thomas Pynchon, Don DeLillo, Philip Roth, and Cormac McCarthy. They write the Style of our Age, and each has composed canonical works. For DeLillo, I would name these as *White Noise, Libra*, and *Underworld*, certainly his principal book up to this time. Roth, immensely prolific, wrote his masterpiece in the scabrous *Sabbath's Theater*, while his tetralogy, *Zuckerman Bound*, and *American Pastoral* are equally likely to survive our era. McCarthy's *Blood Meridian* continues to overwhelm me: *Suttree* before it, *All the Pretty Horses* more recently, also should be permanent. Pynchon, named by Tony Tanner as DeLillo's precursor, is an central to our narrative fiction now as John Ashbery is to our poetry. *The Crying of Lot 49* and *Gravity's Rainbow* have defined our culture—to call it that—and *Mason & Dixon* is even more remarkable, a work of amazing geniality and a kind of hopeless hope.

If just four recent fictions are to be selected for the United States in the early years of the twenty-first century, then name them as *Blood Meridian, Sabbath's Theater, Mason & Dixon*, and *Underworld*. All of DeLillo is in *Underworld*, and so is New York City 1951–96. He has not written the epic of the city; perhaps Hart Crane did that forever, with *The Bridge* (1930). But DeLillo's sense of America, in the second half of the twentieth century, is achieved perfectly in *Underworld*.

DeLillo, a wisdom writer, makes no Hemingwayesque attempt to challenge Shakespeare and Tolstoy. Nor does he desire any contest with Pynchon, though Tony Tanner shrewdly implies that this was unavoidable. Pynchon's cosmos of paranoia, indispensable waste, plastic consumerism is the literary context of *Underworld*. DeLillo is highly aware of his own belatedness, yet his resources are extraordinary, and he so subsumes Pynchon so as to achieve a distinguished triumph over any anguish of contamination that might have impeded *Underworld*. By the time the vast book concludes, DeLillo's relation to Pynchon is like Pynchon's own relation to *The Recognitions* of William Gaddis and to Borges. The Pynchon–DeLillo implicit contest becomes akin to *Blood Meridian*'s struggle with Melville and Faulkner or Roth's permanent status as Franz Kafka's grandnephew (as it were).

Tanner, disappointed with *Underworld*, argued otherwise, and sometimes cannot be refuted. I wince when Tanner observes: "And, crucially, *Underworld* has no Tristero." Tristero remains the greatest of Pynchonian inventions: *The Crying of Lot 49*'s sublimely mad, subversive alternative to the United States Postal Service is not matched by *Gravity's Rainbow*'s interplay between the System and the Zone. Nor, as Tanner insists, does *Underworld* have so persuasive a universal connection to justify its declarations that everything is linked and connected. But again, DeLillo knows this and makes of his supposed weakness a radical strength.

Tanner is again accurate when he observes that Nick Shay, DeLillo's surrogate, as a character is just not there at all, nor does Shay want to be. The only character with a consciousness before Mason and Dixon, anywhere in Pynchon, is Oedipa Maas, and she is there only in the closing moments of the novella. The only consciousness in DeLillo is DeLillo; despite his supposed Post-Modernism, he is a High Romantic Transcendentalist determined not to be out of his time. If there is religiosity in *Underworld*, it is not DeLillo's and is portrayed as part of the waste. And yet there is something more profound than mere nostalgia in DeLillo's Romanticism. His authentic masters are Emerson, Thoreau, Whitman, and his visions, flashing out against the noise and the waste, are enduring illuminations.

At the opening of "Self-Reliance," Emerson gave us a superb irony:

In every work of genius we recognize our own rejected thoughts: they come back to us with a certain alienated majesty.

DeLillo lovingly parodies this in Nick Shay's final meditation:

> Maybe we feel a reverence for waste, for the redemptive qualities
> of the things we use and discard. Look how they come back to us,
> alight with a kind of brave aging.

Tanner was anxious about the epiphanies of DeLillo's urban transcendentalism, and wondered if they were only evidences of a decayed
Catholicism. And yet, DeLillo's vibrant Emersonianism seems to me clear
enough. *Underworld*, which Tanner says is totally reliant on history, actually is self-reliant and like Emerson is adversarial to history. Old Bronx boy
and baseball fan that I am (like DeLillo, addicted to the Yankees), I thrill
to the Prologue of *Underworld*, which I wish had kept its title of "Pafko at
the Wall." Though you *could* say that DeLillo is following baseball history
in his vision of Bobby Thomson's Shot Heard Round the World in
October 1951, I myself have strong memories of that moment at the old
Polo Grounds, and what I recall is mere history, and "it is all falling indeli-
bly into the past." Romantic vision of the high mode, whether in *Song of
Myself* or *Underworld*, is precisely what does not fall.

Thomas Pynchon

(1937–)

I SUPPOSE THAT PYNCHON'S MASTERWORK, TO DATE, IS *MASON & DIXON*, but my personal passion for *The Crying of Lot 49* is too strong to yield to any other book. Visionary romance is the genre of *The Crying of Lot 49*. The book seems like a lot of other things: detective story turned inside out, social satire, American apocalypse, but essentially it is romance, a narrative that so meshes fantasy and American reality that they cannot be disengaged. Its protagonist, Oedipa, is amiable but persuasive neither as personality nor as character. She doesn't have to be. After thirty-six years, *The Crying of Lot 49* is perfectly revelatory of current American paranoia in the Age of George W. Bush.

Since the United States, at this time, looks to me like a disorganized paranoia (though such mighty archons as Ashcroft and Poindexter labor to organize it), one feels that it ought to engender an opposing force like the Tristero, an underground postal system that is something of an alternative culture. There cannot, in our America, be any alternative cultures because Dubya, the entertainment industry, the universities, the media, all have subsumed one another. The Tristero, sublimely paranoid, is too different to be absorbed. It will not go to war with Iraq, it will not vote, it will not pay taxes or postal fees. It is what Pynchon elsewhere terms sado-anarchism.

As such, it is a parody of Pentecostalism; *The Crying of Lot 49* is neither political nor religious in its stance. But it is very concerned with the United States of America: is the Tristero system an anarchist alternative to America? Pynchon answers no questions, but something in Oedipa's final meditation may constitute an implicit answer:

> Another mode of meaning behind the obvious, or none. Either Oedipa in the orbiting ecstasy of a true paranoia, or a real Tristero.

For there either was some Tristero beyond the appearance of the legacy America, or there was just America and if there was just America then it seemed the only way she could continue, and manage to be at all relevant to it, was as an alien, unfurrowed, assumed full circle into some paranoia.

This marvelously intricate passage comes down to a grim choice of realities: paranoia or sado-anarchism. I wake up these mornings, drink tea, and stare at (I cannot quite read it) *The New York Times*, which clearly is paranoid. The first page (Monday, November 25, 2002) tells me about a young female evangelist murdered in Lebanon, and imparts the news (which is no news) that the middle class in Dubya's paranoia are losing their health benefits. Further down, there is a story about whether or not women will join a golf club. And so it goes. There had better be a Tristero, at least in our imaginations.

Gravity's Rainbow

We all carry about with us our personal catalog of the experiences that matter most—our own versions of what they used to call the Sublime. So far as aesthetic experience in twentieth-century America is concerned, I myself have a short list for the American Sublime: the war that concludes the Marx Brothers' *Duck Soup*; Faulkner's *As I Lay Dying*; Wallace Stevens's "The Auroras of Autumn"; nearly all of Hart Crane; Charlie Parker playing "Parker's Mood" and "I Remember You"; Bud Powell performing "Un Poco Loco"; Nathanael West's *Miss Lonelyhearts*; and most recently, the story of Byron the light bulb in Pynchon's *Gravity's Rainbow*.

I am not suggesting that there is not much more of the Sublime in *Gravity's Rainbow* than the not quite eight pages that make up the story of Byron the Bulb. Pynchon is the greatest master of the negative Sublime at least since Faulkner and West, and if nothing besides Byron the Bulb in *Gravity's Rainbow* seems to me quite as perfect as all of *The Crying of Lot 49*, that may be because no one could hope to write the first authentic post-Holocaust novel and achieve a total vision without fearful cost. Yet the story of Byron the Bulb, for me, touches one of the limits of art, and I want to read it very closely here, so as to suggest what is most vital and least problematic about Pynchon's achievement as a writer, indeed as the crucial American writer of prose fiction at the present time. We are now, in my judgment, in the Age of John Ashbery and of Thomas Pynchon, which is not to suggest any inadequacy in such marvelous works as James Merrill's *The Changing Light at Sandover* or Philip Roth's *Zuckerman Bound* but only to indicate one critic's conviction as to what now constitutes the Spirit of the Age.

For Pynchon, ours is the age of plastics and paranoia, dominated by the System. No one is going to dispute such a conviction; reading the *New York Times* first thing every morning is sufficient to convince one that not even Pynchon's imagination can match journalistic irreality. What is more startling about Pynchon is that he has found ways of representing the impulse to defy the System, even though both the impulse and its representations always are defeated. In the Zone (which is our cosmos as the Gnostics saw it, the *kenoma* or Great Emptiness) the force of the System, of They (whom the Gnostics called the Archons) is in some sense irresistible, as all overdetermination must be irresistible. Yet there is a Counterforce, hardly distinguished in its efficacy, but it never does (or can) give up. Unfortunately, its hero is the extraordinarily ordinary Tyrone Slothrop, who is a perpetual disaster, and whose ultimate fate, being "scattered" (rather in the biblical sense), is accomplished by Pynchon with dismaying literalness. And yet—Slothrop, who has not inspired much affection even in Pynchon's best critics, remains more hero than antihero, despite the critics, and despite Pynchon himself.

There are more than four hundred named characters in *Gravity's Rainbow*, and perhaps twenty of these have something we might want to call personality, but only Tyrone Slothrop (however negatively) could be judged a self-representation (however involuntary) on the author's part. Slothrop is a Kabbalistic version of Pynchon himself, rather in the way that Scythrop the poet in Thomas Love Peacock's *Nightmare Abbey* is intentionally a loving satire upon Peacock's friend the poet Shelley, but Kabbalistically is a representation of Peacock himself. I am not interested in adding *Nightmare Abbey* to the maddening catalog of "sources" for *Gravity's Rainbow* (though Slothrop's very name probably alludes to Scythrop's, with the image of a giant sloth replacing the acuity of the Shelleyan scythe). What does concern me is the Kabbalistic winding path that is Pynchon's authentic and Gnostic image for the route through the *kelippot* or evil husks that the light must take if it is to survive in the ultimate breaking of the vessels, the Holocaust brought about by the System at its most evil, yet hardly at its most prevalent.

The not unimpressive polemic of Norman Mailer—that Fascism always lurks where plastic dominates—is in Pynchon not a polemic but a total vision. Mailer, for all his legitimate status as Representative Man, lacks invention except in *Ancient Evenings*, and there he cannot discipline his inventiveness. Pynchon surpasses every American writer since Faulkner at invention, which Dr. Samuel Johnson, greatest of Western literary critics, rightly considered to be the essence of poetry or fiction. What can be judged Pynchon's greatest talent is his vast control, a preternatural ability to order so immense an exuberance at invention. Pynchon's supreme aesthetic quality is what Hazlitt called *gusto*, or what Blake intended in his Infernal proverb: "Exuberance is Beauty."

Sadly, that is precisely what the Counterforce lacks: gusto. Slothrop never gives up; always defeated, he goes on, bloody and bowed, but has to yield to entropy, to a dread scattering. Yet he lacks all exuberance; he is the American as conditioned reflex, colorless and hapless.

Nothing holds or could hold *Gravity's Rainbow* together—except Slothrop. When he is finally scattered, the book stops, and the apocalyptic rocket blasts off. Still, Slothrop is more than a Derridean dissemination, if only because he does enable Pynchon to gather together seven hundred and sixty pages. Nor is *Gravity's Rainbow* what is now called "a text." It is a novel, with a beginning, an end, and a monstrous conglomerate of middles. This could not be if the *schlemiel* Slothrop were wholly antipathetic. Instead, he does enlist something crucial in the elitest reader, a something that is scattered when the hero, poor Plasticman or Rocketman, is apocalyptically scattered.

Pynchon, as Richard Poirier has best seen and said, is a weird blend of the esoteric and insanely learned with the popular or the supposedly popular. Or, to follow Pynchon's own lead, he is a Kabbalistic writer, esoteric not only in his theosophical allusiveness (like Yeats) but actually in his deeper patterns (like Malcolm Lowry in *Under the Volcano*). A Kabbalistic novel is something beyond an oxymoron not because the Kabbalah does not tell stories (it does) but because its stories are all exegetical, however wild and mythical. That does give a useful clue for reading Pynchon, who always seems not so much to be telling his bewildering, labyrinthine story as writing a wistful commentary upon it as a story already twice-told, though it hasn't been, and truly can't be told at all.

II

That returns us to Byron the Bulb, whose story can't be told because poor Byron the indomitable really is immortal. He can never burn out, which at least is an annoyance for the whole paranoid System, and at most is an embarrassment for them. They cannot compel Byron to submit to the law of entropy, or the death drive, and yet they can deny him any context in which his immortality will at last be anything but a provocation to his own madness. A living reminder that the System can never quite win, poor Byron the Bulb becomes a death-in-life reminder that the System also can never quite lose. Byron, unlike Slothrop, cannot be scattered, but his high consciousness represents the dark fate of the Gnosis in Pynchon's vision. For all its negativity, Gnosticism remains a mode of transcendental belief. Pynchon's is a Gnosis without transcendence. There is a Counterforce, but there is no fathering and mothering abyss to which it can return.

And yet the light bulb is named Byron, and is a source of light and cannot burn out. Why Byron? Well, he could hardly be Goethe the Bulb or Wordsworth the Bulb or even Joyce the Bulb. There must be the insouciance of personal myth in his name. Probably he could have been Oscar the Bulb, after the author of *The Importance of Being Earnest* or of that marvelous fairy tale "The Remarkable Rocket." Or perhaps he might have been Groucho the Bulb. But Byron the Bulb is best, and not merely for ironic purposes. Humiliated but immortal, this Byron, too, might proclaim:

> But there is that within me which shall tire
> Torture and Time, and breathe when I expire;
> Something unearthly, which they deem not of,
> Like the remembered tone of a mute lyre.

Byron the Bulb is essentially Childe Harold in the Zone:

> He would not yield dominion of his mind
> To spirits against whom his own rebell'd.

Like Childe Harold, Byron the Bulb is condemned to the fate of all High-Romantic Prometheans:

>   there is a fire
> And motion of the soul which will not dwell
> In its own narrow being, but aspire
> Beyond the fitting medium of desire;
> And, but once kindled, quenchless evermore,
> Preys upon high adventure, nor can tire
> Of aught but rest; a fever at the core,
> Fatal to him who bears, to all who ever bore.

There are, alas, no high adventures for Byron the Bulb. We see him first in the Bulb Baby Heaven, maintained by the System or Company as part of its business of fostering demiurgic illusions:

One way or another, these Bulb folks are in the business of providing the appearance of power, power against the night, without
the reality.

From the start, Byron is an anomaly, attempting to recruit the other
Baby Bulbs in his great crusade against the Company. His is already a voice
in the Zone, since he is as old as time.

Trouble with Byron's he's an old, old soul, trapped inside the glass
prison of a Baby Bulb.

Like the noble Lord Byron plotting to lead the Greeks in their
Revolution against the Turks, Byron the Bulb has his High-Romantic
vision:

> When M-Day finally does roll around, you can bet Byron's elated.
> He has passed the time hatching some really insane grandiose
> plans—he's gonna organize all the Bulbs, see, get him a power
> base in Berlin, he's already hep to the Strobing Tactic, all you do
> is develop the knack (Yogic, almost) of shutting off and on at a rate
> close to the human brain's alpha rhythm, and you can actually
> trigger an *epileptic fit*! True. Byron has had a vision against the
> rafters of his ward, of 20 million Bulbs, all over Europe, at a given
> synchronizing pulse arranged by one of his many agents in the
> Grid, all these Bulbs beginning to strobe *together*, humans thrash-
> ing around the 20 million rooms like fish on the beaches of
> Perfect Energy—Attention, humans, this has been a warning to
> you. Next time, a few of us will *explode*. Ha-ha. Yes we'll unleash
> our *Kamikaze squads*! You've heard of the Kirghiz Light? well
> that's the ass end of a firefly compared to what we're gonna—oh,
> you haven't heard of the—oh, well, too bad. Cause a few Bulbs,
> say a million, a mere 5% of our number, are more than willing to
> flame out in one grand burst instead of patiently waiting out their
> design hours.... So Byron dreams of his Guerrilla Strike Force,
> gonna get Herbert Hoover, Stanley Baldwin, all of them, right in
> the face with one coordinated blast.

The rhetoric of bravado here is tempered and defeated by a rhetoric
of desperation. A rude awakening awaits Byron, because the System has in
place already its branch, "Phoebus," the international light-bulb cartel,
headquartered of course in Switzerland. Phoebus, god of light and of

pestilence "determines the operational lives of all the bulbs in the world," and yet does not as yet know that Byron, rebel against the cartel's repression, is immortal. As an immortal, bearer of the Gnostic Spark or *pneuma*, Byron must acquire knowledge, initially the sadness of the knowledge of love:

> One by one, over the months, the other bulbs burn out, and are gone. The first few of these hit Byron hard. He's still a new arrival, still hasn't accepted his immortality. But on through the burning hours he starts to learn about the transience of others: learns that loving them while they're here becomes easier, and also more intense—to love as if each design-hour will be the last. Byron soon enough becomes a Permanent Old-Timer. Others can recognize his immortality on sight, but it's never discussed except in a general way, when folklore comes flickering in from other parts of the Grid, tales of the Immortals, one in a kabbalist's study in Lyons who's supposed to know magic, another in Norway outside a warehouse facing arctic whiteness with a stoicism more southerly bulbs begin strobing faintly just at the thought of. If other Immortals *are* out there, they remain silent. But it is a silence with much, perhaps, everything, in it.

A silence that may have everything in it is a Gnostic concept but falls away into the silence of impotence, on the part of the other bulbs, when the System eventually sends its agent to unscrew Byron:

> At 800 hours—another routine precaution—a Berlin agent is sent out to the opium den to transfer Byron. She is wearing asbestos-lined kid gloves and seven-inch spike heels, no not so she can fit in with the crowd, but so that she can reach that sconce to unscrew Byron. The other bulbs watch, in barely subdued terror. The word goes out along the Grid. At something close to the speed of light, every bulb, Azos looking down the empty black Bakelite streets, Nitralampen and Wotan Gs at night soccer matches, Just-Wolframs, Monowatts and Siriuses, every bulb in Europe knows what's happened. They are silent with impotence, with surrender in the face of struggles they thought were all myth. *We can't help*, this common thought humming through pastures of sleeping sheep, down Autobahns and to the bitter ends of coaling piers in the North, *there's never been anything we could do....* Anyone shows us the meanest hope of transcending and the Committee on Incandescent Anomalies comes in and takes him away. Some do

protest, maybe, here and there, but it's only information, glow-modulated, harmless, nothing close to the explosions in the faces of the powerful that Byron once envisioned, back there in his Baby ward, in his innocence.

Romantics are Incandescent Anomalies, a phrase wholly appropriate to John Ashbery's belated self-illuminations also, defeated epiphanies that always ask the question: Was it information? The information that Pynchon gives us has Byron taken to a "control point," where he burns on until the committee on Incandescent Anomalies sends a hit man after him. Like the noble Lord Byron, who was more than half in love with easeful death before he went off to die in Greece, Byron the Bulb is now content to be recycled also, but he is bound upon his own wheel of fire, and so must continue as a now involuntary prophet and hero:

> But here something odd happens. Yes, damned odd. The plan is to smash up Byron and send him back right there in the shop to cullet and batch—salvage the tungsten, of course—and let him be reincarnated in the glassblower's next project (a balloon setting out on a journey from the top of a white skyscraper). This would-n't be too bad a deal for Byron—he knows as well as Phoebus does how many hours he has on him. Here in the shop he's watched enough glass being melted back into the structureless pool from which all glass forms spring and re-spring, and wouldn't mind going through it himself. But he is trapped on the Karmic wheel. The glowing orange batch is a taunt, a cruelty. There's no escape for Byron, he's doomed to an infinite regress of sockets and bulb-snatchers. In zips young Hansel Geschwindig, a Weimar street urchin—twirls Byron out of the ceiling into a careful pocket and Gessssschhhh*win*dig! out the door again. Darkness invades the dreams of the glassblower. Of all the unpleasantries his dreams grab in out of the night air, an extinguished light is the worst. Light, in his dreams, was always hope: the basic, mortal hope. As the contacts break helically away, hope turns to darkness, and the glassblower wakes sharply tonight crying, "Who? *Who?*"

Byron the Bulb's Promethean fire is now a taunt and a cruelty. A mad comedy, "an infinite regress of sockets and bulbsnatchers," will be the poor Bulb's destiny, a repetition-compulsion akin to the entropic flight and scattering of the heroic *schlemiel* Slothrop. The stone-faced search parties of the Phoebus combine move out into the streets of Berlin. But Byron is off upon his unwilling travels: Berlin to Hamburg to Helgoland to Nürnberg, until (after many narrow escapes):

> He is scavenged next day (the field now deathempty, columned, pale, streaked with long mudpuddles, morning clouds lengthening behind the gilded swastika and wreath) by a poor Jewish ragpicker, and taken on, on into another 15 years of preservation against chance and against Phoebus. He will be screwed into mother (*Mutter*) after mother, as the female threads of German light-bulb sockets are known, for some reason that escapes everybody.

Can we surmise the reason? The cartel gives up, and decides to declare Byron legally burned out, a declaration that deceives nobody.

> Through his years of survival, all these various rescues of Byron happen as if by accident. Whenever he can, he tries to instruct any bulbs nearby in the evil nature of Phoebus, and in the need for solidarity against the cartel. He has come to see how Bulb must move beyond its role as conveyor of light-energy alone. Phoebus has restricted Bulb to this one identity. "But there are other frequencies, above and below the visible band. Bulb can give heat. Bulb can provide energy for plants to grow, illegal plants, inside closets, for example. Bulb can penetrate the sleeping eye, and operate among the dreams of men." Some bulbs listened attentively—others thought of ways to fink to Phoebus. Some of the older anti-Byronists were able to fool with their parameters in systematic ways that would show up on the ebonite meters under the Swiss mountain: there were even a few self-immolations, hoping to draw the hit men down.

This darkness of vain treachery helps to flesh out the reason for Byron's survival. Call it the necessity of myth, or of gossip aging productively into myth. Not that Phoebus loses any part of its profit; rather, it establishes a subtler and more intricate international cartel pattern:

> Byron, as he burns on, sees more and more of this pattern. He learns how to make contact with other kinds of electric appliances, in homes, in factories and out in the streets. Each has something to tell him. The pattern gathers in his soul (*Seele*, as the core of the earlier carbon filament was known in Germany), and the grander and clearer it grows, the more desperate Byron gets. Someday he

will know everything, and still be as impotent as before. His youthful dreams of organizing all the bulbs in the world seem impossible now—the Grid is wide open, all messages can be overheard, and there are more than enough traitors out on the line. Prophets traditionally don't last long—they are either killed outright, or given an accident serious enough to make them stop and think, and most often they do pull back. But on Byron has been visited an even better fate. He is condemned to go on forever, knowing the truth and powerless to change anything. No longer will he seek to get off the wheel. His anger and frustration will grow without limit, and he will find himself, poor perverse bulb, enjoying it.

This seems to me the saddest paragraph in all of Pynchon; at least, it hurts me the most. In it is Pynchon's despair of his own Gnostic Kabbalah, since Byron the Bulb does achieve the Gnosis, complete knowledge, but purchases that knowledge by impotence, the loss of power. Byron can neither be martyred, nor betray his own prophetic vocation. What remains is madness: limitless rage and frustration, which at last he learns to enjoy.

That ends the story of Byron the Bulb, and ends something in Pynchon also. What is left—whether in *Gravity's Rainbow* or in the immense work-in-progress, a historical novel depicting the coming-on of the American Civil War and reported to have the title *The Mason-Dixon Line*—is the studying of new modalities of post-Apocalyptic silence. Pynchon seems now to be where his precursor Emerson prophesied the American visionary must be:

There may be two or three or four steps, according to the genius of each, but for every seeing soul there are two absorbing facts,— *I and the Abyss.*

If at best, the I is an immortal but hapless light bulb and the *Abyss*, our Gnostic foremother and forefather, is the socket into which that poor I of a bulb is screwed, then the two absorbing facts themselves have ceased to absorb.

Paul Auster

(1947–)

The New York Trilogy

REREADING AUSTER'S *NEW YORK TRILOGY* IS FOR ME, AN ODD EXPERIENCE, if only because I never can decide how to regard these three spare, refined narratives. Auster can seem a French novelist who writes in American English, but his American literary culture is extensive and finally decisive. He acknowledges Kafka and Beckett as his masters, while finding Cervantes to be his imaginative ideal. The curious version of "detective stories" that determines the shape of the *Trilogy* is more in the mode of Borges (itself Kafkan) than in that of the hard-boiled genre of Raymond Chandler and his followers. If there is an American counter-tradition that turns the detective stories of Poe inside out, its chief practitioners are Hawthorne and Melville, the principal narrative writers of the Age of Emerson and Walt Whitman.

Auster can be said to cross Hawthorne with Kafka, as Borges did. The Argentine fabulist remarked that his favorite story was Hawthorne's "Wakefield", an altogether Austerian tale. Wakefield vanishes from home and marriage, but only to establish residence a few streets away. After a considerable interval, he returns to his life, in a reunion as inexplicable as his withdrawal. Auster, a more considerable poet in prose than in verse, is perhaps less a novelist than he is a romancer, really a pre-Cervantine kind of exposition.

Aesthetic dignity is the keynote of everything I have read by Auster. If there is a missing element in Auster's achievement, it is comedy, even of a grotesque variety. It seems fair to contrast Auster with Philip Roth, half a generation older, yet another lifelong disciple of Franz Kafka. Painful as Roth's humor tends to be, it is uproarious and heartening. Perhaps it carries the Blessing, the "more life" of Jewish tradition, though in singular form. Weirdly enough, by implication, Kafka's "The Hunger Artist" (a favorite of both Roth and Auster) also bears the Blessing. Kafka is comprehensive enough, in his extreme way, to sustain both Roth and Auster. But Kafka's somber comedy remains comic: in Auster no one seems to laugh. The Jewish joke, which links Freud, Kafka, and Roth, has no presence in Auster.

What—I think—takes its place are Auster's own appearances in his fictions. In *City of Glass* the protagonist, Quinn, who writes mystery novels under the name of Poe's William Wilson, enjoys an omelette prepared for him by "Paul Auster". Quinn and Auster have an unsurprising conversation about Cervantes, and then Quinn meets Auster's wife, Siri, and son, Daniel. Again, this is unsurprising, and is charming, yet puzzling, at least to me. What does it do for *City of Glass*? Now that "French Theory" is only still hot in Peoria, the disruption of representation is hardly worth a shrug, since in no way does Auster practice an art that seeks to imitate social reality. His *Art of Hunger* celebrates Beckett, Kafka, Kanut Hamsun and Paul Celan as seers of absence. I want to murmur: "Yes, but," and then enlarge the "but." These elliptical literary artists also manifest a richness that makes me care about *what happens next*. Auster seems to have no such concern.

Auster's creative minimalism has moved many good readers, both here and abroad. If Auster evades me, I therefore blame myself. And even so, I go back to my master, Dr. Samuel Johnson, who rightly commended Shakespeare for his just representations of general nature.

Amy Tan

(1952-)

The Joy Luck Club

IN AN ACCOMPLISHED ESSAY, MYRA JEHLEN SEES AMY TAN, AGAINST ALL odds, returning to Whitman's stance and singing a latter-day *Song of Myself*. That implicitly is high praise, and if justified might give *The Joy Luck Club* an aesthetic dignity beyond the popular success it continues to enjoy. Will it be a permanent part of the revised canon of an American literature "opened up" by consideration of gender and ethnicity, or will it prove only another period piece, in which we currently abound?

Amy Tan is a skilled storyteller, and a remarkable personality. Jehlen charmingly says: "Amy Tan has read her Emerson, and she doesn't believe him. This is not surprising, as he probably would have doubted her." I would murmur that it all depends upon *which* Emerson Tan has read, as there are so many. Having met and admired Tan, I would recommend *The Conduct of Life*, which is consonant with her rugged but amiable stance towards reality.

Jehlen eloquently concludes by stating both Tan's relation to Whitman and the significant differences:

> Jing-Mei becomes herself finally when, like Whitman, she can be the writer of the Body and the writer of the Soul, can sing both others and herself. If she is Whitman's critic as well as his descendant, it is because America has lost its innocence in the matter of individualism. Moreover, the duplicities of the notion of the universal self have been revealed in our time especially by the protestations of people of Amy Tan's kind: women and non-whites. It is not surprising that Jing-Mei's claim be not as universal as

Whitman's, nor that its costs be apparent. It is surprising to find
her claiming the old transcendent, appropriating self at all, and, in
the name of culture, singing a latter-day "Song of Myself."

Jehlen is aware, as I am, that Whitman attempted to speak for women
as for men, and for all ethnic strains. What she doubts is the Whitmanian
possibility of universal representation, since we are in a time of group identities: gendered, diversely oriented sexual preferences, ethnicities. And yet
Whitman, at his best, permanently has reached and held a universal audience. *Song of Myself* is not a period piece.

Further Reading

Armstrong, Nancy. *Desire and Domestic Fiction: A Political History of the Novel*. New York: Oxford University Press, 1995.

Bartram, Graham, ed. *The Cambridge Companion to the Modern German Novel*. Cambridge: Cambridge University Press, 2004.

Bloom, Harold. *The Western Canon: The Books and School of the Ages*. New York: Harcourt Brace & Company, 1994.

Bradbury, Malcom, ed. *The Atlas of Literature*. London : De Agostini Editions, 1996.

Chase, Richard Volney. *The American Novel and Its Tradition*. Baltimore: Johns Hopkins University Press, 1980.

Davis, Lennard. *Factual Fictions: the Origins of the English Novel*. New York: Columbia University Press, 1983.

Denby, David. *Great Books*. New York: Simon and Schuster, 1996.

Doody, Margaret Anne. *The True Story of the Novel*. New Brunswick: Rutgers University Press, 1996.

Fiedler, Leslie. *Love and Death in the American Novel*. New York: Anchor Books, 1992 (reprint edition).

Forster, E.M. *Aspects of the Novel*. New York: Harcourt Brace, 1956.

Fowler, Alister. *A History of English Literature*. Cambridge: Harvard University Press, 1987

Hunter, J.P. *Before Novels: The Cultural Contexts of Eighteenth-Century English Fiction*. New York: Norton and Co., 1990.

James, Henry. *The Future of the Novel: Essays on the Art of Fiction*. New York: Vintage Books, 1956.

Lukacs, Georg. *The Theory of the Novel*. Cambridge: MIT Press, 1974.

McKeon, Michael. *The Origins of the English Novel, 1600–1740*. Baltimore: Johns Hopkins University Press, 1987.

McKeon, Michael, ed. *Theory of the Novel: A Historical Approach*. Baltimore: Johns Hopkins University Press, 2000.

Mirsky, D.S., and Francis J. Whitfield. *A History of Russian Literature: From Its Beginnings to 1900*. Evanston: Northwestern University Press, 1999.

Muir, Edwin. *The Structure of the Novel*. London: Hogarth Press, 1957.

Pascal, Roy. *The German Novel*. Toronto: University of Toronto Press, 1956.

Rascoe, Burton. *Titans of Literature: From Homer to the Present*. London: Routledge, 1933.

Ruland, Richard and Malcom Bradbury. *From Puritanism to Postmodernism: A History of American Literature*. New York: Penguin Books, 1992.

Turnell, Martin. *The Novel in France: Mme. De La Fayette, Laclos, Constant, Stendhal, Balzac, Flaubert, Proust*. New York: New Directions, 1951.

Turner, Harriet, and Adelaida López de Martínez ed. *The Cambridge Companion to the Spanish Novel*. Cambridge: Cambridge University Press, 2003.

Unwin, Timothy, ed. *The Cambridge Companion to the French Novel*. Cambridge: Cambridge University Press, 1997.

Watt, Ian. *The Rise of the Novel: Studies in Defoe, Richardson, and Fielding*. Berkley: University of California Press, 1957.

Index

About the Author

HAROLD BLOOM is Sterling Professor of the Humanities at Yale University. He is the author of over 20 books, including *Shelley's Mythmaking* (1959), *The Visionary Company* (1961), *Blake's Apocalypse* (1963), *Yeats* (1970), *A Map of Misreading* (1975), *Kabbalah and Criticism* (1975), *Agon: Toward a Theory of Revisionism* (1982), *The American Religion* (1992), *The Western Canon* (1994), and *Omens of Millennium: The Gnosis of Angels, Dreams, and Resurrection* (1996). *The Anxiety of Influence* (1973) sets forth Professor Bloom's provocative theory of the literary relationships between the great writers and their predecessors. His most recent books include *Shakespeare: The Invention of the Human* (1998), a 1998 National Book Award finalist, *How to Read and Why* (2000), *Genius: A Mosaic of One Hundred Exemplary Creative Minds* (2002), *Hamlet: Poem Unlimited* (2003), and *Where Shall Wisdom be Found* (2004). In 1999, Professor Bloom received the prestigious American Academy of Arts and Letters Gold Medal for Criticism, and in 2002 he received the Catalonia International Prize.